IRB International Rugby Yearbook 2002-03

John Griffiths
Mick Cleary

CollinsWillow
An Imprint of HarperCollins*Publishers*

First published in Great Britain in 2002 by
CollinsWillow an imprint of
HarperCollins*Publishers* London

© International Rugby Board 2002

1 3 5 7 9 8 6 4 2

The views expressed in this book are not necessarily
the views of the IRB

A CIP catalogue record for this book is available
from the British Library

The HarperCollins website address is:
www.fireandwater.com

ISBN 0 00 714046 0

Typeset by Letterpart Ltd, Reigate, Surrey

Printed and bound Clays Ltd, St Ives plc.

Picture acknowledgements

All photographs courtesy of Allsport

CONTENTS

ABBREVIATIONS USED IN THIS YEARBOOK

International Teams

A – Australia; Arg – Argentina; AU – Australian Universities; AW – Anglo-Welsh; B – British Forces and Home Unions teams; Bb – Barbarians; Be – Belgium; BI – British/Irish teams; Bu – Bulgaria; C – Canada; Ch – Chile; Cr – Croatia; Cv – New Zealand Cavaliers; CT – Chinese Taipei; Cz – Czechoslovakia; E – England; F – France; Fj – Fiji; Gg – Georgia; H – Netherlands; HK – Hong Kong; I – Ireland; It – Italy; Iv – Ivory Coast; J – Japan; K – New Zealand Services; M – Maoris; Mo – Morocco; NAm – North America; Nm – Namibia; NZ – New Zealand; NZA – New Zealand Army; P – President's XV; Pg – Paraguay; Po – Poland; Pt – Portugal; R – Romania; Ru – Russia; S – Scotland; SA – South Africa; SAm – South America; SK – South Korea; Sm – Samoa; Sp – Spain; Tg – Tonga; U – Uruguay; US – United States; W – Wales; Wld – World Invitation XV; WS – Western Samoa; Y – Yugoslavia; Z – Zimbabwe.

Other Abbreviations used in the International Listings

(R) – Replacement or substitute; (t) – temporary replacement; [ ] – Rugby World Cup appearances.

NB: When a series has taken place, figures are used to denote the particular matches in which players have featured. Thus NZ 1,3, would indicate that a player has appeared in the First and Third Tests of the relevant series against New Zealand.

Irish Clubs

CIYMS – Church of Ireland Young Men's Society; KCH – King's College Hospital; NIFC – North of Ireland Football Club.

French Clubs

ASF – Association Sportive Française; BEC – Bordeaux Etudiants Club; CASG – Club Athlétique des Sports Generaux; PUC – Paris Université Club; RCF – Racing Club de France; SB – Stade Bordelais; SBUC – Stade Bordelais Université; SCUF – Sporting Club Universitaire de France; SF – Stade Français; SOE – Stade Olympien des Etudiants; TOEC – Toulouse Olympique Employés Club.

South African Provinces

BB – Blue Bulls; Bol – Boland; Bor – Border; EP – Eastern Province; FSC– Free State Cheetahs; GL – Gauteng Lions; GW – Griqualand West; Mp – Mpumulanga N – Natal; NT – Northern Transvaal; OFS – Free State; R – Rhodesia; SET – South-East Transvaal; SWA – South-West Africa; SWD – South-West Districts; Tvl – Transvaal; WP – Western Province; WT – Western Transvaal; Z–R – Zimbabwe–Rhodesia.

Australian States

ACT – Australian Capital Territory; NSW – New South Wales; Q – Queensland; V – Victoria; WA – Western Australia.

PREFACE

The content of this, the second edition of the *IRB International Rugby Yearbook*, has been enlarged to provide coverage of the game not only world-wide but across the senior competitive age range.

We have expanded our records sections to include, for the first time in print as far as we are aware, full Test statistics for Samoa and Japan, two nations with distinguished international playing records dating back to the period between the world wars. There is also a new section covering the Test seasons in Japan, Samoa, Fiji and Tonga, and full coverage of the Women's World Cup played in Spain, the inaugural IRB Rugby World Cup for Under 21s and the new Celtic Leagues.

Few, we expect, will quarrel with the choice of the five players of the year for 2002. From these nominations, the player of the year will be selected. Keith Wood was the popular winner last season. Perhaps this time the balance will tilt in favour of one of the three backs named among the contenders?

Still, forwards feature prominently in our other main articles this season. Jason Leonard's achievement of 100-plus Test appearances, we felt, deserved recognition, and who better than Terry Cooper, who hasn't missed one of Jason's international matches, to pen an appreciation? Wynne Gray assesses the task ahead of John Mitchell, the New Zealand coach charged with bringing the Webb Ellis Trophy back from Australia next November, and Frank Keating brings his unique style to an appreciation of Bill McLaren, a forward when he appeared in the final Scottish trial of December 1947 before going on for 50 years to charm countless millions of television viewers and radio listeners with his expert rugby commentaries.

Our thanks go to our team of correspondents and statisticians who have contributed from all the major rugby-playing nations. Geoff Miller, Chris Rhys, Matthew Alvarez, Brian Newth, Michel Breton, Walter Pigatto, Matteo Silini, Doug Sturrock and Frankie Deges patiently updated and checked the smallprint, while the IRB's Michelle Treacy and Chris Thau provided copy from several of the important international competitions that the Board supports.

Finally, special tributes are due to the in-house team. Michael Doggart, Tarda Davison-Aitkins and Tom Whiting at HarperCollinsWillow put an immense amount of time into the publication of this year's edition, while Chris Leggatt at Letterpart once again skilfully prepared our copy for printing.

London, 7th September 2002

Mick Cleary & John Griffiths

*The international match statistics in this edition are complete up to **31st August 2002**.*

EDITORIAL

Flames are fanned over Burn-out Issue
Mick Cleary

No wonder Martin Johnson bridled. 'Look,' he said, in that blunt, exasperated way of his. 'It wasn't a summer's rest. It was a summer away from touring. In fact, I've trained harder than ever.'

For Johnson read George Gregan in Australia or Andrew Mehrtens in New Zealand or Ireland's Keith Wood. The clock is ticking – faster for some than others in the remorseless world of the professional rugby player where new kids storm the block each season – and every international player has one eye firmly fixed on the 2003 World Cup that will be in full swing just 12 months from now. Everything is geared to that end.

Johnson and many of his England mates did have a summer's respite from the grind of travel as coach Clive Woodward left behind about 20 of his leading lights for the tour to Argentina in June 2002. No Jonny Wilkinson, no Richard Hill, no Kyran Bracken or Matt Dawson, likewise Mike Catt, Will Greenwood, Jason Robinson – you name them, they weren't there. Either injured, or recuperating from the effects of the Lions tour to Australia the previous year. Woodward took a stance. He took a gamble, too, one that paid off handsomely as his tyro England beat a Pumas side that had seen off France only seven days earlier. Woodward's horizon was also the 2003 World Cup. He knew that if England were to have any chance at all of lifting the Webb Ellis trophy for the first time then his men needed a break.

How will Woodward's southern hemisphere counterparts – John Mitchell in New Zealand, Eddie Jones across the Tasman and Rudi Straeuli in South Africa – react to that? Will they come to Europe in autumn 2002 with a full contingent? If Woodward thinks his men will benefit, then ought not the same apply to their guys? Cat and mouse – it's one of the riveting side-shows in the run-up to the fifth Rugby World Cup.

But Woodward's action raises a serious issue. Burn-out is one of the most pressing concerns for the game. Players are being flogged from pillar to rugby post all round the globe as unions and clubs chase the golden ace for all it is worth. A professional game needs cash. Bums on seats, either in stadiums or on TV couches, pay the wages.

The more games there are, the more money there is? Thank goodness the fallacy of that last statement has been exposed, a recent realisation that is beginning – and no more than beginning – to be appreciated in some quarters. The players cannot be used as mere fodder to fill the coffers. It's a short-term route to riches and a long-term route to ruin. The public want quality not quantity. There is every indication too that they are seduced by the less is more theory of consumerism. The overwhelming success of the recent Lions tour is proof of that. The less often we see the Lions – and every four years is the regular cycle – the more we cherish them.

Praise the day when that philosophy applies to the global calendar. It needs overhauling. The International Board are sensitive to the problem and will be reviewing the tours schedule. And not before time. England are down to play Japan and Romania next summer along with Australia and New Zealand. Such an itinerary suits no-one. It would be marvellous too if some semblance of an old tour could be re-instigated. Wouldn't it be something to cherish if New Zealand were about to arrive in England for a three match series and not a one-off Test? With all due respect to Australia and South Africa, who have both played England at least once a year since 1997, the All Blacks are eagerly-awaited visitors. Their last tour to England was five years ago. The equation has become terribly lop-sided in favour of the supposedly money-spinning one-off international match.

Back to burn-out. A two day conference in September 2002 debated the very question and resolved to tackle the issue. The tackle needs to be firm and decisive. There has been too much talk and not enough action for too long.

Someone has to take a stand. Woodward did it, but only for his own purposes. If it had suited him to tour with a full contingent he would have done. England have 14 Tests in the lead-up to the World Cup. Hard labour all round. No country, no union, no club, no player has yet to opt out of the merry-go-round. Everybody wants a slice of the pie.

The issue is the biggest challenge facing the IRB at this time. It's not just that the product becomes over-exposed and so diminished. There are many other negative side-effects. And the most damaging of all these is the spectre of drugs.

The harder the slog, the faster the treadmill, the more the player is open to temptation. The case of Wallaby wing Ben Tune, who was found to have traces of a banned substance in his system following treatment for a knee injury, should set alarm bells ringing. Tune was backed by the Australian union who prescribed the treatment. The IRB, meanwhile, is eager to clarify procedures. And damn right too.

So much for the warning shots. The game as a whole is in good shape. A year away from the World Cup there is a growing sense of excitement about the tournament as well as about the sport itself. The 2002 Tri Nations, won by the All Blacks under new coach John Mitchell, set pulses racing. The game's popularity in the northern hemisphere continues to grow. Or least as far as its spectator base is concerned. There is still a disturbing tail-off in numbers playing the game, particularly at a social Third XV or so level.

However, those clicking their way through turnstiles up and down England in particular seem to have few doubts about the game. For the third year in succession attendances rose in the English Zurich Premiership with overall figures up by 21% to an average gate of 7,490, a total just in excess of rugby league's Super League. Leicester, champions for the fourth year in a row, topped the billing with an average gate of 15,384, with Gloucester (9,397) and Northampton (9,300) tucked in just behind. 11 of the 12 clubs showed an increase. Inevitably some of those Third XVers might well now be sitting in the stands.

The RFU announced a 30% increase in profits, up from £5.6million to £7.3million, not a bad return considering that they were reporting £10million losses in 1998.

It's not just England that has seen growth. The 72,500 sell-out crowd at the Millennium Stadium for the Heineken Cup final between Leicester and Munster was no more than the inevitable conclusion of yet another prodigious season's competition. TV audiences grew across all territories while the two semi-finals at neutral venues – Leicester against Llanelli at the City Ground in Nottingham and Munster against Castres in Béziers – drew substantial crowds.

The public like what they see. Or most of them do. One moron by the name of Pieter van Zyl, ugly in appearance and in manner, ran on to the field at King's Park, Durban and assaulted Irish referee David McHugh during the Tri Nations match between South Africa and New Zealand, dislocating the Irishman's shoulder.

Of course the man should be locked up and has no place in a rugby crowd. Yet to view the matter as an isolated incident would be to bury one's head in the sand. There is a price to pay for rugby's burgeoning profile. The more spectators there are, the greater the risk of a potential nutter being among them. The more the stakes are raised, the more matches are talked up through the media and the more charged the atmosphere becomes, then the greater the risks of crowd trouble become.

Newcastle director of rugby, Rob Andrew, sounded very alarmist last year when he spoke of possible crowd trouble in the wake of his side's explosive match against Gloucester, the game that saw Newcastle's Epi Taione and Gloucester's Olivier Azam sent off for fighting. The real story of that December day was the allegations of racial abuse made against Azam by Andrew on behalf of Taione. The former England fly-half also alleged that sections of the Kingsholm crowd had made racist comments. There was a huge furore over the incident and after an exhaustive RFU investigation no evidence could be found on either front. Andrew, belatedly and curtly, apologised.

If his allegations were made in haste and proved unfounded, then remarks about the need for vigilance on crowd control should be heeded. Those who dismiss his comments as alarmist should take a good look at the beer-bellied prat that ran on to the field in Durban. It only takes one . . .

There is little doubt that the Australian Rugby Union will take the necessary security precautions for next year's World Cup. They are all the more intent on giving the rugby world a show to remember after being granted sole host status in March 2002. The losers were the New Zealand Rugby Union, not to mention the sport itself, as it suffered an embarrassing few weeks in the eye of the sporting world. The New Zealanders had failed to comply with RWC criteria that all stadiums should be commercially clean. They were given repeated warnings through the autumn of 2001 that RWC directors were viewing this matter seriously. Finally their patience ran out. On March 8th 2002 came the news that sub-host status had been withdrawn. The news did not go down well in New Zealand. 'RWC are being bloody-minded and arrogant,' said NZRFU chief executive, David Rutherford.

The NZRFU stuck to their forlorn case that they had obligations to domestic sponsors and could not insist on them removing their branding from stadiums. 'We're not prepared to commit to what we can't deliver,' said NZRFU chairman, Murray McCaw. 'That is, 100% clean. The NZRFU is not prepared to mortgage New Zealand's future to the whim of the RWC. We are not prepared to sell New Zealand's soul.'

It was emotive stuff. It got bitter and personal with IB chairman, Vernon Pugh, the target of some pretty nasty invective. Former All Black Zinzan Brooke was none too impressed. 'This is a kick in the teeth for New Zealand rugby,' said Brooke. 'I would like to see the All Blacks respond by threatening to pull out of the tournament.'

They did nothing of the sort, if only because the best thing they could now do would be to go out to win the tournament. Once the sub-host status was withdrawn Australia had 21 days within which to produce a bid on its own.

It did so. And in impressive style. They will stage 48 games in 44 days across the country with all 20 teams rotating through the ten cities. The evening and weekend kick-off slots for many games mean that the northern hemisphere TV audience will be able to tune in. 'Rugby World Cup 2003 promises to be the most exciting and vital yet,' said Vernon Pugh.

The IRB itself was mindful of how harmful the whole episode had been. 'There is little doubt that relationships have been damaged as a result of these unhappy events,' read their official statement at the time. 'The IRB was sensitive to the impact of their decision upon the game in New Zealand but it was left with no alternative. Generous accommodations made by Rugby World Cup Ltd to meet the needs and problems of the NZRFU were repaid with consistent failures and wholly inappropriate behaviour. Despite this, the Council determined to give full and fair hearing to New Zealand's position. However, the outstanding proposal held an attraction, a professionalism and a logic which were irresistible. The IRB now holds out the hope that all parties will accept the outcome with dignity and that the truly international spirit which cements the sport will quickly heal any wounds.'

New Zealand's triumph in the Tri Nations, their continued dominance of the Sevens international circuit – they secured the IRB World Sevens Series title for the third successive season and retained the Commonwealth title at the Manchester Games – and the continued success of the U19 side in the IRB's annual World Junior Championships will have brought some solace to the New Zealand public.

John Mitchell took over the All Black reins from Wayne Smith in autumn 2001 and immediately found himself back in Europe where he had played and coached with distinction at Sale, Wasps and, of course, England. He has had 11 Tests in charge and lost only once. Already he is leaving his stamp – mean defence and attention to basics. His first tour selection showed his intent – no Jeff Wilson, Christian Cullen or Taine Randell. There were 11 new All Blacks. Open-side Richie McCaw was one of his most enterprising selections. Wilson announced his retirement in order to concentrate on his second sporting love – cricket. Wilson scored 44 tries in 60 Tests.

There were new men in office across the southern hemisphere with Eddie Jones getting to grips with the Wallabies and Rudi Straeuli with the Springboks. To judge by the quality of the 2002 Tri Nations, their influence is just beginning to be felt. It was the most engaging Tri Nations in recent times.

The IRB's commitment to the worldwide development of the game across the age range continues apace. The Board announced a package of measures aimed at developing the game in the South Seas Islands, New Zealand won the IRB Women's World Cup staged so successfully in Spain, and South Africa won the inaugural IRB U21 World Cup. Elsewhere, there was the first meeting at international level of Japan and Russia, while Romania won the burgeoning European Nations Cup competition. All told, 31 European countries will underpin the main Six Nations this season in six divisions of European competition.

The 2002 Six Nations championship was non-vintage. France won the Grand Slam for the seventh time, their 20-15 victory over England at Stade de France seeing off their closest rival. Wales lost a coach, Graham Henry, but managed to salvage some self-respect on their summer tour to South Africa under new coach, Steve Hansen. Ireland too parted company with their coach, Warren Gatland, who was moved aside for Eddie O'Sullivan. It wasn't the smoothest of transitions, Ireland's 45-11 thumping at Twickenham giving off too acute a sense of *déjà vu* for Irish supporters. Mind you, England played what many regarded as the best 50 minutes of rugby ever seen at Twickenham as they cut Ireland to shreds.

Italy, too, were to finish the season with a new man at the helm, former All Black wing John Kirwan stepping up to replace Brad Johnstone. Italy finished bottom of the Six Nations pile for the third year in succession, their only victory in 15 starts coming in their first ever championship match against Scotland. To those who suggest their position ought to be reviewed, then consider that rugby's competitive base is already tiny by comparison with football. To shrink it still further makes no sense. Italy deserve our support and our patience, although we needn't be too patronisingly indulgent here given that Italy A beat England last season.

Henry's departure was inevitable after the shambles of Wales's humiliating 54-10 defeat in Dublin on the opening weekend of the championship. Henry did the decent thing and resigned three days later, still with 18 months of his five-year £1.25 million contract to run. Under Henry, the 13th national coach in Wales, the team initially showed great heart and racked up an impressive 10-match winning streak, including a first ever win over South Africa. There was also the first win in Paris for 24 years to savour. His final ledger is no mean achievement with 20 wins, 13 defeats and one draw. 'It is no knee jerk reaction to the result in Ireland,' said Henry of his resignation. 'I feel that the time has come for the team to hear a new voice.'

The game in Wales is still at war with itself. A players' strike prior to the game against England was only narrowly averted. However, pledges made have still not been nailed down and there is still an acute sense of a power-struggle between club and country.

Wales lost some faithful servants through the course of the year – prop Dai Young, centre Scott Gibbs and scrum-half Robert Howley all retired. You can't help but feel that Howley and Gibbs might have played through to the World Cup if they did not have the weight of the in-fighting bearing down on their shoulders.

Not that everything was sweetness and light across the border either. Several of the English Premiership clubs saw a change of face – Jon Callard was dismissed at Bath, with former Wallaby hooker Michael Foley taking over. One-time Bath Midas man Jack Rowell returned from Bristol in the summer in a bid to turn around the plummeting Bath fortunes that saw them finish 11th in the Premiership without a league win away from home all season. François Pienaar stepped aside at Saracens, who also had a disappointing season. Former All Black captain Buck Shelford stepped in. A change at Bristol saw Peter Thorburn move up to overall control, with Dean Ryan moving to Gloucester where Nigel Melville had come in a couple of months before the season's end to replace Philippe Saint-André.

Northampton went through their upheaval in mid-season, former All Black coach Wayne Smith arriving in December to succeed John Steele as chief coach. Wasps recruited Warren Gatland to replace Melville. Harlequins chief executive Mark Evans was once more obliged to trade suit for track-suit as he took overall responsibility for coaching. John Kingston moved aside to look after the forwards.

Was it mere coincidence that the top two teams in the Premiership, Leicester and Sale, had settled managements? The Manchester club, along with London Irish, were the surprise packages in the league, Sale finishing as runners-up 14 points behind champions Leicester. Sale also won the Parker Pen Shield. London Irish, galvanised by former Springbok centre Brendan Venter, came fourth in the league and won the Powergen Cup by demolishing Northampton. Gloucester beat Bristol in the unloved Zurich Championship, the end-of-season play-off competition that has undergone a change in format for 2002-03 when only the top three teams will play-off. The side finishing first in the Premiership will go straight through to the final but will no longer be known as England's champion club. That accolade will go to the winner of the Championship play-off.

Leeds did a fine job in their first season in the Premiership, winning six games, but still finishing bottom. They were saved from relegation on a technicality, the RFU controversially ruling that Rotherham had failed to meet the entry criteria for promotion from national Division One. Rotherham could not produce the necessary legal contracts to prove that they were going to play at Millmoor, the home of Rotherham United FC, their own Clifton Lane ground being inadequate for Premiership rugby. It was a sorry affair. Rotherham's paperwork was self-evidently not in order but there was little sense of sportsmanship about the whole matter. 'It was disgusting,' said Rotherham player-coach, Mike Schmid.

There was controversy too over the decision to ban Leicester captain Martin Johnson for a punch thrown at Saracens hooker Robbie Russell. Johnson was sin-binned at the time for a scuffle but TV replays showed the England captain catching Russell with an uppercut that caused Russell to have several stitches. The affair ignited when the RFU decided to arraign Johnson for effectively bringing the game into disrepute. Leicester appealed, thereby freeing Johnson to lead England against France in the crucial Six Nations match. When Johnson's case was eventually heard he was banned for three weeks.

Discipline is a sensitive and fraught issue. Two players, Sale's Pete Anglesea and Castres' Ismaella Lassissi, had 12-month bans overturned on appeal. Anglesea was adjudged to have gouged a Newcastle player while Lassissi was found guilty of biting. Both cases were then thrown out.

A bizarre case saw Agen excluded from European competition for 12 months after being found guilty of bringing the game into disrepute by deliberately losing by a margin of eight tries against Ebbw Vale in a Parker Pen Shield match. They thereby saved themselves from qualifying for the knockout stages so enabling them to concentrate on the French championship. Their arrogance and naïvety cost them a place in the Heineken Cup.

Leinster beat Munster to win the Celtic League as the Irish provinces continue to prosper in the various cross-border competitions. Once again a Scottish side failed to make it through to the knockout stages of the Heineken Cup. The debut this season of the Borders team as Scotland's third professional outfit is eagerly awaited.

Pontypridd came through the season strongly to win the Principality Cup by beating Llanelli 20-17. They also won through to the final of the Parker Pen Shield. Llanelli, beaten so cruelly in the Heineken Cup semi-final by Leicester, won the Welsh-Scottish League.

There are new faces to be seen this season – former All Black backs Bruce Reihana at Northampton and Daryl Gibson at Bristol, Springboks Percy Montgomery at Newport, Thinus Delport at Gloucester and Pieter

Rossouw at London Irish, and Wallaby centre Graeme Bond at Sale. They are much younger than the first generation of overseas stars that headed north from the southern hemisphere.

So much for new faces. Rugby mourned the passing of a sagacious administrator in Hermas Evans, who was an IRB member for a dozen years. There was sorrow, too, at the announcement of the death of David Brooks, a popular former captain of Harlequins in the early 1950s who later managed the 1968 Lions in South Africa and became president of the Rugby Football Union in 1981-82.

South Africans stood in silence to remember Gawie Carelse, Pat Lyster and Stephen Fry, the Springboks' captain in the exciting series with the 1955 Lions. New Zealand lost Jack Griffiths and Mike Gilbert of the 1935-36 Third All Blacks and as this book went to press, sad news came through from Australia of the death aged 52 of their former coach Greg Smith.

In the Home Unions, those who relied on radio commentaries or black-and-white television for their early fixes of international rugby remembered the names of Peter Wright and Peter Young (England), Hamish Kemp (Scotland), Jimmy Corcoran, Con Murphy and Kevin Quinn (1947-53 Ireland) and, from an earlier vintage in Wales, Bill Hopkin, W A (Billy) Williams and W T H (Willie) Davies whose deaths were announced.

And what about a much-cherished old voice? Bill McLaren's distinctive tones will no longer be heard on BBC television. And they'll no' be dancing in the streets of Hawick about that.

Enough said.

IRB FIVE PLAYERS OF THE YEAR

Mick Cleary

Fabien Galthié (France)

If any player knows every contour of rugby's switchback it's Fabien Galthié. He's a veteran of three World Cups, veteran also of several career-threatening injuries and veteran too of the occasional spat with officialdom. At the start of the 1999 World Cup he was sitting at home drinking beer with a mate after being left out of the squad. By the end of the tournament he was in the team to face Australia in the final. In true Tina Turner fashion, he has survived. And this season, perhaps more than any other in his long career, he has thrived.

As he has done so, so too have France. There are a few telling reasons why France managed to win their seventh Grand Slam. They discovered the strange art of self-discipline, as alien to a Frenchman's natural inclination as fish 'n' chips with mushy peas might be. They found patience and structure and composure – elements that don't sit too easily in the French temperament either. And the man who epitomises all these virtues is 33-year-old Fabien Galthié.

Professional rugby likes to think that it has every base covered in these days of high-tech preparation. Diet – OK, covered. Conditioning – that covered too. Video analysis, individual CD-Roms, deep-freeze post-match recuperation – all covered. And yet so much can still come down to one man's influence, one man's ability to bring all those strands together and make each and every player believe in each and in the cause. Galthié managed that with France.

Without him – and he again missed a chunk of the season with a troublesome knee – France lacked both shape and sharpness. With him at the helm, they were a different item. His first match of the 2002 Six Nations championship was against England. Galthié pinpointed the inconsistencies on the eve of the game: 'France has the capacity to beat any team in the world,' he said. 'We can soar with the birds but sometimes we are just complete crap.'

Galthié had already faced the old foe six times in his career. He'll cherish the memory of the seventh encounter. It was his sharp-eyed break that led to a try for wing Aurélien Rougerie. It was Galthié's constant chivvying and chasing that kept England on the back foot. It was Galthié's calm in the midst of such sustained pressure that kept French goal-posts largely intact from the damage that Jonny Wilkinson might have inflicted upon them.

Fabien Galthié gets his line moving with a textbook pass against Ireland as France head for the Grand Slam.

France won the day, more handsomely than the 20-15 scoreline might indicate. Galthié's lasting appeal is that he defies so many modern conventions. His service is not the quickest, nor his physique the most intimidating. He has pace – or certainly had – but at such an age the gap is not so easily breached. That said, he did score a cracking individual try against Scotland when has raced in from 45 metres outstripping anything that the Scottish defence could muster, admittedly not too much on the day.

He should win his 50th cap for France this autumn. The milestone is richly deserved.

Richard McCaw (New Zealand)

That beer-bellied madman made a very rash decision when he launched himself at referee David McHugh during the Tri Nations match between South Africa and New Zealand in Durban. There was instant retribution on hand in the form of All Black flanker Richard McCaw, who made sure that Piet van Zyl had a few bruises to show for his crazed antics the next morning.

McCaw has made a proper name for himself during the season in far more wholesome circumstances. The 21-year-old from Oamaru in New Zealand's South Island has been first-choice on the All Black open-side flank right through the front-line season. He was rested for the Tests against Italy and Fiji only to be recalled when the hard yards were needed in the Tri Nations.

McCaw was one of John Mitchell's inspired choices for his first touring party as All Black coach in autumn 2001. The youngster had been a regular in the Canterbury team that won the 2001 NPC. He had made his mark that summer when captaining the New Zealand U21 side that won the SANZAR/UAR International Championship, a tournament that is now under the auspices of the IRB. If the season had begun quietly with McCaw getting only two appearances as a sub for the Crusaders in the Super Twelve, it was to finish in some style.

McCaw was voted man-of-the-match on his debut against Ireland. He had stepped into the lineage of the cherished No 7 All Black shirt, worn with distinction by the likes of Michael Jones and Josh Kronfeld to mention just those of recent vintage, with real aplomb.

McCaw comes from farming stock and has a decent pedigree with a couple of uncles who played representative rugby. He was talent-spotted by Canterbury's Steve Hansen, now Wales coach, who fixed a move to Christchurch after coming across the Otago High School player. Also at Otago HS at the same time was Leeds and one-cap England lock, Tom Palmer. Palmer, who struck up a friendship with McCaw, staying with him on the family farm, returned to England while McCaw headed north from Dunedin to study agriculture at Lincoln University.

In 1999, McCaw was part of the New Zealand U19 side that won the IRB/FIRA-AER World Junior Championship in Wales. It was the start of

Richard McCaw on his Test debut for New Zealand against Ireland in Dublin.

the rise to real prominence. He was voted U21 and NPC First Division Player of the Year. McCaw is a modest, down-to-earth lad by inclination. The sudden fame has certainly not gone to his head even if he looks set to grace the All Black side for many a year to come. He shares a birthday, New Year's Eve, with Jean-Pierre Rives, who was not a bad flanker in his time. McCaw may lack the blond locks of the Frenchman. All the other attributes look to be in place . . .

Brian O'Driscoll (Ireland)

It was a quieter year. Except that is for the hat-trick against Scotland. Oh, and the constant terrorising of defences for province and country. The prospect of a drop of the shoulders and a sharp side-step, magic and mayhem in equal measure, is never far away in the world of Brian O'Driscoll, nominated for the second year running as one of the five IRB Players of the Year.

O'Driscoll, 23, came of age over the last 12 months. By the start of this season he had already won 27 caps and scored 13 tries. O'Driscoll was the toast of the Lions tour to Australia in summer 2001, fulfilling the promise that had been so gloriously announced to the wider world when he scored a hat-trick against France in 2000 to help his side to their first win in Paris in 28 years.

The sublime gifts on show that day are still very much there. And flourishing. They are keenly-marshalled by opposition defences but their vigilance will only take them so far. His hat-trick in the 43-22 defeat of Scotland demonstrated as much. His first try came from some crass ill-discipline from Scotland, who yapped and argued when a decision went against them. O'Driscoll was not distracted and was on hand to snap up a pass from his fly-half David Humphreys to skip over. Alert and poised – simple hallmarks. It helps too to have a dab of pace. O'Driscoll hit the afterburner just before half-time, latching on to a loose pass from Scotland's Gregor Townsend to blast 80 metres downfield with vapour trails of glory his only companion. His third try in the second-half showed all the trademark traits. Never mind that Scotland were poor that day. International hat-tricks are not a thing of mere chance.

O'Driscoll is now a mature presence in the Ireland midfield. And a selfless one too. 'It's hard to imagine that he could come on in leaps and bounds,' said his Leinster and Ireland colleague, full-back Girvan Dempsey. 'But he has. His general touch and how he gets himself out of a tight corner with his footwork are awesome. But the thing Brian doesn't get credit for is his defensive tackling. It's fantastic. He reads a back-line attack really well. He is always in the right position. As a full-back you appreciate that.'

O'Driscoll's great challenge is to retain his enthusiasm and composure in the face of so much expectation. Irish rugby has flourished in recent years but, even so, O'Driscoll stands out as the team's trump card. Supporters will

Brian O'Driscoll weighs up his options as he is tackled by Gérald Merceron during the Six Nations match in Paris last season.

want to see him scoop the pot every time he takes the field. It's an understandable reaction. And a wholly unreasonable one. But O'Driscoll has to live with that. So far he has shown every sign of dealing with that pressure.

Joe van Niekerk (South Africa)

Clichés only tend to have a certain life-span. The dull old Bokke stereotype – big set-piece forwards, big-banging, one-dimensional attack – looks to be past its sell-by date. Just take a look at the impact made by 22-year-old loose-forward, Joe van Niekerk. He's not a classic, nose-to-dirt flanker. Nor even a thumping monster in the tackle, although he can handle both those aspects of the flanking game. No, what van Niekerk has is pace. Lots of it. And it shows.

The Springboks may well have finished bottom of the pile in the Tri Nations. But they won many hearts and minds with their fast-footed rugby. Van Niekerk was central to that style with his ability to get wide in support as well as make inroads himself. He was the perfect foil to Bobby Skinstad alongside him in the back-row or any one of a host of newcomers across the back-line – Johannes Conradie, André Pretorius and Werner Greeff among them. Van Niekerk flourished in their company and they in his.

Van Niekerk was born in Port Elizabeth on 14th May, 1980. He was a prominent schoolboy player and went on to captain South Africa Schools in 1998. The following year he graduated to the U19 side and it was little surprise when he led the Springbok U21 side in the SANZAR champion-ship. He was voted Player of the tournament in a poll among referees.

His talent was evident enough for him to be called into the senior Springbok squad following that tournament in 2001, an exceptional achieve-ment for a forward, given that he had yet to make his debut in either Currie Cup or Super 12. That was quickly remedied. He has been a central figure for the Lions and the Cats over the last 18 months.

Van Niekerk was part of the 2001 Tri Nations squad and made a couple of appearances as a substitute. He toured Europe and North America in autumn 2001, but missed out on the England Test. His stock has rocketed in the last six months. He scored an eye-catching final try in the 60-18 demolition of Samoa, a try that triggered some wild and unfortunate celebrations with Van Niekerk clattering into some opponents. Youthful exuberance. He'd hoped to put that to rights. 'Not the tries,' said van Niekerk. 'Just the behaviour afterwards.'

Van Niekerk already has 14 caps to his name and is sure to add to that tally on the November tour to Europe.

Joe Van Niekerk sets off on a characteristic charge during the Tri Nations match between South Africa and New Zealand in Durban.

Jason Robinson (England)

It was a good line and one worth repeating. Paul Hayward captured the essence of Jason Robinson when summing-up his impact on England's opening match in the 2002 Six Nations championship. Scotland were in opposition. Or they were until Robinson got the ball. 'In darker days Jason Robinson found God,' wrote the *Daily Telegraph* chief sports writer. 'But that was after God found Jason Robinson and endowed him with the talent that cut Scotland to bits.'

Robinson scored two tries that afternoon but there was danger, and no little panic, in the air every time he touched the ball. He brings menace and unpredictability to the England attack and a delicious sense of anticipation to England followers. Or perhaps that should be rugby followers. For the measure of Robinson's achievement in rugby union is that he has fired the imagination of everyone. There are not many sportsmen on the world stage – Seve in his pomp, so too George Best, or Viv Richards walking to the crease – who send a ripple round the watching gallery. Robinson has that effect. And all in such a short space of time.

He switched codes from Wigan for good and proper in November 2000, having had a brief stint with Bath in 1996. Only seven months later he was donning the British/Irish Lions shirt. He immediately gave us one of those special moments, fixing Wallaby full-back Chris Latham before skinning him through the narrowest of corridors *en route* to the try-line. The Gabba gasped.

There has been much intake of breath since. He didn't win his first start for England until the following October in the held-over Six Nations game against Ireland in Dublin. Clive Woodward went for broke that day and chose Robinson at full-back ahead of Austin Healey. English hopes may have nose-dived that afternoon. Robinson's career has not.

He now has 11 caps to his name and has scored eight tries, a strike-rate that stands the test against the very best. He was the top try scorer for the Lions with ten tries. But if he doesn't get on the score-sheet then others around him surely will. His trademark mid-air side-step has flummoxed many a defence in either code. The 28-year-old is a modest, self-contained man, very aware that he has so much still to learn.

'I am still a novice,' said Robinson early in the year. 'I still have to think about what I do in union, whereas in league there was always the comfort of knowing that you could go to ground.'

There will be many a coach plotting on how to restrict Robinson, how to box him into his corner at the rear of the field. Looking at the video they may think that they have found the answer. Looking at the field of play there is no evidence whatsoever to suggest that is the case.

Jason Robinson breaks through the Italian defence to score a try for England in the final Six Nations Championship match of 2002.

NO MORE DANCING IN THE STREETS

Frank Keating

For a mighty fortunate generation of Brits, many now past their allotted three-score-and-10, a lifetime's affection for all matters sporting has happily coincided with the resplendent miracle of live broadcasting in sound and vision. Those voices which have logged the lustrous matches, men, and moments of their particular games with an instructive clarity and sometimes obsessive devotion have become part of the cultural fabric, significant figures not only in the activity they are describing but in the broader national consciousness itself. They are rightly esteemed as household names. Cricket's contentment of its place in society, for instance, could be said to have been richly enhanced when the differently distinctive voices of John Arlott and Brian Johnston were recording its progress, same for tennis and Dan Maskell, horse-racing and Peter O'Sullevan . . . and what about Murray Walker in motor sport, Kenneth Wolstenholme and John Motson in football, Henry Longhurst and Peter Alliss in golf?

Not many in that litany has been cherished with more fondness by his sport and beyond, nor possessed a voice as resonantly recognisable, than rugby's mellifluous tartan sage Bill McLaren, who has retired from BBC television's microphone just a single birthday away from his 80th.

The first international rugby match to be televised by the experimental and fledgling BBC service was the Calcutta Cup match and historic Scottish victory at Twickenham in 1938. From up beyond Hadrian's Wall, Bill McLaren's father had taken his lank of a boy down on the night-sleeper to watch it. Omens, omens, for – with a world war in between – that was only seven international rugby seasons before the young fellow himself was perched high in the BBC's rickety eyrie above Murrayfield tremulously attempting his first live commentary (for radio then) when Wales came up in February of the 1952-53 season. He was wracked with nerves, hadn't dared eat for a day. 'Somehow I muddled through. Wales won by 12 points to nothing, inspired by Cliff Morgan, crafty as a bag of weasels and with that scuttling pace like a kind of flying Charlie Chaplin.'

A broadcasting style was born. Half a century on, Wales v Scotland again in 2002 and, admitting to 'those same petrified butterflies clamping around my tummy in their hobnail boots', the now craggy old hunk from Hawick laid down his microphone for the final time – and acclaim for him from the throng enveloped the great crucible of Cardiff's Millennium Stadium in a farewell and all-hail, not only as clamorous testament to an inimitable broadcaster whom length of service had made a national treasure, but for his being as well a genuine four-square talisman and touchstone for the

Cue Bill. The voice that launched more than a thousand TV and radio commentaries announced his retirement in 2002 after 50 seasons of service.

innate and bonny goodness of a worldwide game in spite of all its recent turbulence and upheaval, its 'wee bit of argy-bargy in the committee-room' as he might have put it himself.

McLaren had switched from radio to television in 1960. Thirty years later he was 'utterly astonished' at the money ITV offered him to transfer. 'Sorry, I'm BBC through and through,' he apologised when he took the call. That first match at Murrayfield in 1953 had come about after his venerable editor on the *Hawick Express* had suggested BBC Scotland gave a trial to his temporary cub reporter. After a seriously active war with the Royal Artillery in Africa and Italy, McLaren had enrolled for teacher-training, but in 1948 he was stricken with tuberculosis and spent two desperate years in hospital. Discharged in his mid-20s, he worked on his local rag while waiting for a vacancy as a PE teacher. He was to combine his broadcasting with full-time teaching till he retired from the blackboard in 1987.

During that brief spell as a journalist, he had covered the visit to Hawick of BBC eminence Richard Dimbleby for his *Down Your Way* radio series. Bill noticed how Dimbleby had his mike in one hand and, with the other, clung desperately to reams of research notes. 'I doubt I'll use five per cent, but the other 95 per cent is insurance just in case I'm stumped', Dimbleby told him. When his turn came, McLaren determined on obsessive home-work 'just in case' – he has seldom missed each team's training session the day before an international match, latterly carrying his touchline 'identity recce' to cantankerously fusspot levels – and for five decades famed in rugby around the world has been 'old Bill's big sheet', a double-foolscap lined page with the home team tabulated down the left, the away side on the right and, in between, a dense maze of hieroglyphics in various coloured pens, starred or squiggled, arrowed or underlined, of past matches, milestones, and immensely unmemorable trivia. He has filed each one and I daresay they'll be worth thousands to some anorak when he's dead. 'Och, yes,' he laughs at himself, 'I do love my research . . . when you hear me announce someone's 20th cap or, praise be, his 50th, it gives me a right old buzz I can tell you . . . or how many points a place-kicker will have logged up if this one goes over . . . and if, by golly, just seemingly off-the-cuff and in passing I can toss in the club or locality he comes from, then can't you almost hear me purr with pleasure as I do so?' Whether the bulk of his audience at home remotely cared less about such pedant's swotting is a moot point – but, whatever, they'd just grin, and sigh fondly, 'Ah, dear ol' Bill.'

Which is probably one reason he nominates as the most stirring match of the zillion he has described Scotland's epic Grand Slammer against England in Edinburgh in 1990. 'Will Carling's English lads looked invincible' – but the winger who scored the decisive try for Bill's bravehearts in blue was Tony Stanger, not only of the Hawick club but also a former pupil of teacher Bill himself. So when Tony tumultuously tumbled over the try-line as he followed up Gavin Hastings's legendary chip-and-chase, hoots-man, it was not only a matter of 'they'll be dancing on the tables in the Mansfield Park clubhouse tonight' but also 'on the desks at Wilton primary school on Monday morning'!

Only joking – for in fact, and in spite of the timelessly textured Caledonian cadence, McLaren possessed an unimpeachable reporter's neutrality in never letting his heart rule his hurrahs by even the teeniest inflection when Scotland mounted a charge for the line (not even when his son-in-law scored a try). So much so that some 30 years ago, after a too-long lunch, I doodled in homage an equally too-long drunken doggerel to that effect on the eve of a Scotland-Wales match, and not only did the *Guardian* ruddy well print it, but some long-haired fellow later paid me to recite it at a poetry concert in London's Festival Hall, no less. A couple of the verses went, as they say, something like this:

> 'Stagg palms . . . wee Hastie gathers . . .
> Chisholm . . . big Frame upon the burrrst . . .'
> A crescendo that ever, too, was flattened
> So we only sensed McCurses being currrsed . . .
>
> How many times has expectation leapt
> Into his throat when Andy's on the ball,
> But then is strangled (like Bill's cry!)
> By hordes of red, in ruck, set-piece or maul?

From such a diverting 'fun among friends' agenda of those dear and dopey days, McLaren leaves his game fearing it might be heading for too cold-eyed a reliance on power and muscle. 'Once you were fairly keen on winning all right, but now it's an utter necessity. I worry, too, in this new rugby of weight-training and bulk if any inheritors of those magical wee 10-stone darters and dodgers, your Barrys and Phils and Ollies, will even be offered a trial game in the not-too-distant future.'

Before TB put paid to any loftier ambition, McLaren played one Scotland trial match, a flanker at Murrayfield in 1947. It was 'power and muscle' which did for him. He had to mark Dougie Elliot, raw-boned rough-edged all-time great. 'First lineout I was enmeshed in a vice-like grip,' remembers Bill, 'and those two great iron bars manacled me for most of the match. Of all the grand back-row fellows we've had up here I'd still put Elliot at the top – well, him David Leslie and Iain Paxton . . .'

None of that trio, however, made McLaren's all-time World XV which *The Times* printed with pride, player by player for 15 Saturdays through Bill's 2001-02 valedictory season. No Hastings nudged the selector, neither a Brown nor a Calder, no Renwick, no Arthur Smith, no shark-like Jeffrey, not even the wondrous Rutherford nor Scotland's eponymous Ken. Impartial rectitude to the end, Bill found room for only one Scot, the utterly energising sprite Andy Irvine at full-back, followed by wingers Gerald Davies and Campese, Gerber and Gibson at centre, Andrew at fly-half, Edwards inside him, and an eightsome reel of Cotton, Fitzpatrick, Price;

Meads and Du Preez; Brooke, Slattery, and Mervyn Davies. After the No 10 Saturday and Bill's barmily eccentric choice there was an outcry particularly, as you can imagine, from Wales. McLaren's Hawick telephone was besieged: 'Hey, Bill, Rob Andrew at fly? Have you taken leave of your bloody senses, man?' Replied Bill cheerfully, typically: 'I'm sticking to my guns. The deed is done.'

And so it is. The whole deed done and dusted. The End. The Final Whistle. No-Side, as he would say. And now Back to the Studio . . . The baggy has eeled back to his Borders' burn, not that this one's ever really been away. The octogenarian-to-be still has his daily golf with his beloved and still bonny Bette – he daringly asked her for a tango when Oscar Rabin and his band came to the Hawick Town Hall in March 1947 and they have been passionately tripping the light fantastic ever since. He will pretend not to, but he'll miss his research and the spotlight and the autograph signing, even, I daresay, those butterflies stomping around his tummy before the two words 'Cue Bill' would dispatch them. A very nice man, an enthusiast and dalliant amateur who somehow turned himself into a pro, just as his care-free and appealingly amateur pastime turned itself into a marketable, deadly serious, global professional sport. Certainly, it was time to go. He knew it, and we knew it. Half a century on, McLaren's antique and folksy 'argy-bargy' old rugby is a totally different game now. Mind you, what is also for sure is that it is going to be an altogether more different game without him.

A CHIPPY OFF THE OLD BLOCK

Terry Cooper

Englishmen in Buenos Aires for the first Test against Argentina in July 1990 watched an exceptionally young, new prop called Jason Leonard. With conspiratorial winks, we concluded: 'This one's here to stay,' and it is pleasant for Press Box inhabitants to break the habits of a lifetime and get something right.

When Leonard went to Buckingham Palace 12 Julys later to collect his OBE awarded by The Queen in her Golden Jubilee Honours, Her Majesty was knowledgeably recognising that he had trodden the turf in 102 international fixtures – 97 for England and five for the Lions – with power to add.

Brian Moore, propped by Leonard on that debut, had a closer view than spectators. He was emphatic that the pair would stand literally shoulder to shoulder in numerous Tests. 'It was patently obvious that he was going to be an outstanding player.' During the following winter Dick Best predicted: 'England have found a prop for ten years.'

Within 15 months of his debut we began to think the unthinkable of 100 England caps for Jason (in September 1991, the world's most-capped player was the sublime Serge Blanco with 87). By the end of the 1991 World Cup, he had scooped in 15 caps, including playing in the first of his three Grand Slams, after England had monumentally flopped in 1990. The stats were revealing – and favourable if he proved durable and good enough. He was 21 in Argentina. Both Jeff Probyn, who was on the other side of the scrum in BA, and Paul Rendall, Leonard's predecessor at loose-head, were uncapped until they were past 30. And the schedule showed that internationals were due to increase sharply.

Well, he has clearly endured, outlasting a couple of generations who arrived, starred and retired while he props on. Indeed, the same Probyn believes that he should return as first-choice instead of benching, as he did for much of season 2001-2. 'He still retains the ability to be in the starting team. The circle will come round to needing huge-strength scrummagers like Jason – a true piano-shifter, always high in the tackle-rankings. He also remains the outstanding character he was when he began. He was the first of the new breed to bring real fitness and diets to the squad, when me and Judge Rendall were ducking and diving between beer and bleep-tests.'

One of Probyn's successors on the right-hand side of England's front-row, Phil Vickery, would also have no hang-ups if he trotted out again with Leonard. 'Jason is, and would be, irreplaceable. He is a special guy. He is very awkward to pack against. I have the utmost respect for him, and in front-rows that respect's earned, not inherited. There's a belief that Jason isn't as hard as some scrummagers. Do people think that realists like Geoff

Jason Leonard leads England out against Romania to win his 93ʳᵈ England cap and pass Sean Fitzpatrick's world record for most caps by a forward for his country.

Cooke, Jack Rowell, Clive Woodward, Ian McGeechan on Lions tours would have chosen him year in year out if he had any defects in that department?'

Leonard admits that he is not a snarling, shouting, provocative in-yer-face prop, who goes about whacking and stamping, though Scotland Rugby Director, Jim Telfer, was volcanic when videos failed to support his citing that Leonard had concussed Rob Wainwright with a blow during a game at Murrayfield.

Jason-followers have wondered if he would have amassed those caps if he had stayed with Saracens. He recalls: 'I came back from Argentina fully intending to remain. Despite rumours of being tapped-up by Will Carling and Peter Winterbottom, I went to pre-season training. We were asked to scrum on a concrete-hard pitch by the second-team coach. It was a farce. Wearing boots we went down in a heap and in trainers we collapsed like sacks of spuds. I told him it was dangerous, but he blamed the shambles on my binding, which had been good enough to match the Pumas. I gave him two most familiar short words of dismissal and contacted Dick Best and Winterbottom round at Quins.'

As transfers go, that's fairly unusual at high level. 'I joined an amazing pack at Quins and learned more in one season than in the previous three. I packed down with Moore, Paul Ackford, Winterbottom and Mick Skinner, who were in that World Cup scrum, plus Andy Mullins and Chris Butcher, both internationals, and Troy Coker, the tough Wallaby.'

Even then Leonard was not the drinker of popular myth. 'I liked socialising on Saturday night and Sunday lunchtime, but I couldn't have coped with alcohol sloshing inside me when confronted with a day that started at 7am for my job as a joiner followed by club training three nights a week.'

'Now, drink is only for big celebrations, but for all sorts of extra reasons you cannot compare fitness today to the pre-professional era. My fit state has enabled me to play into my mid-30s and my physical shape has changed hugely. When I left Saracens I was 16½ stones. Now I'm two stones heavier.'

Mind you, part of that body has been shifted around. There was the serious operation in 1992 when he needed a bone-graft from his pelvis to reinforce a damaged disc in his neck. His attitude to the injury and recovery illustrate the steel and dedication of the outwardly amiable Leonard. 'Against Wales it got bad. I couldn't lift my arm. Probyn had to help me bind. I got through, had the operation and then spent the summer working to re-develop my body, obeying the medics' advice.' Those close to him were awed by his single-mindedness. It worked. There was no tour in summer 1992 and there he was in October running out at Wembley to face Canada, maintaining an unbroken run in England's front-row that lasted from 1990 to 1997, bar a one-match rest during the 1995 World Cup.

We have to say front-row, because Rowell had replicated a selection first used by McGeechan in New Zealand in 1993, when the tight-heads were inadequate. 'Nick Popplewell and me were the loose-heads. Poppy was not going anywhere, so across I went.' The Lions won that Test in Wellington, with one supreme turning-point. Scrum on the Lions line. New Zealand put-in. 'We actually pushed them back,' reflects Leonard proudly, and the look on Craig Dowd's face at being seen off by a loose-head novice was worth the 12,000-mile trip. Poppy and Leonard were loose-heads on the loose that tour. They gamely volunteered for the demanding task of seeking out the Irish pubs in each New Zealand town and grading their quality for their colleagues' use – on match nights only, of course.

Leonard concedes that his most testing opponent has been the other All Blacks prop that day, Olo Brown, though their contests have been at least even, and probably the balance lies with the white shirt.

Rowell watched Leonard perform that switch, and for expedience gave him two years in the No 3 shirt to accommodate Graham Rowntree. But Clive Woodward put him back in his best position for a bucket-load more caps until he dropped to the bench last season. 'They are such different jobs. I hope to dominate on the left, but hope to get away with it on the right.'

He would go into the jungle with pretty much all his colleagues during such a long career, but, off the top of his head, names players he has spent years with on the factory floor – 'Moore, Winters and Martin Johnson are right up there.'

It was Johnson, however, who caused him the potential embarrassment of losing his only match as England captain in 1996. Johnson assaulted an Argentinian just as Jerry Guscott was loping nonchalantly over for a try. Penalty to the Pumas. England faced the final minutes trailing. They managed to maul over for the winner. 'That 'Ronnie' Regan wanted the try. When I said it was mine, he had the cheek to say, "Call it a pack try." I wasn't having that and, because I was in the Press conference as captain, I managed to bring the subject up. It's still my only try.'

Above all, Probyn looms large in the Leonard memory – no this is not a back-scratching *Hello!* feature. They have tangled ruthlessly in the bitter Quins v Wasps bashes. 'Jeff was phenomenal – perfect technique and incredible strength. He could turn a Test pack inside out single-handed.'

Career highlights are obvious. 'Three Grand Slams and caps on three Lions tours. The first Grand Slam was a delight for me, but ecstasy for those who suffered Murrayfield, 1990. In 1992 we played great rugby, scored plenty of tries and had the satisfaction of knowing that we could do it twice. And in 1995 there was the knowledge that, at least in Europe, some major careers had a late highlight. We've enjoyed beating the southern hemisphere sides regularly. The next step is to take them in World Cups and maybe we can nail down another Grand Slam, because we can't say we are as good as we think we are if we can't prove it away from Twickenham.'

Jason, the lad from Cockney outskirts in Barking – the local club still has his devotion – is imbued with the team ethic and might appreciate Will Carling's summing-up: 'Jase made my job easier.'

BACK TO BASICS

Wynne Gray

When New Zealand rugby hit another of the snags which seem to have troubled their rugby passage in recent years, the nation's administrators turned to former assistant England coach John Mitchell for help.

It was a strange time late last year when incumbent coach Wayne Smith indicated his hesitation about taking the All Blacks through to the 2003 World Cup. His side had beaten the Springboks twice but also fallen on the back of repeat mistakes to twin defeats against the Wallabies.

Smith was hugely affected by the final loss and questioned whether he was the appropriate coach to continue with the job. With that background the New Zealand Rugby Union chose to change leaders. It was an unparalleled decision for the NZRFU since the 1987 introduction of World Cup tournaments. While other coaches were under strenuous challenge at various times in their careers, Sir Brian Lochore, Alex Wyllie, Laurie Mains and John Hart all saw out their full terms.

As the NZRFU cast about for potential replacements, they believed there had to be a greater emphasis on forward coaching. Smith and his predecessor Hart were back coaches who co-opted forward assistance. This time the NZRFU was keen to reverse the trend.

That brief helped Mitchell. His deeds with England's pack were noted while he was also helped by the exit of Steve Hansen to Wales and uncertainty about other forward coaches.

Mitchell himself thought it was too early. He had only been back in New Zealand long enough to coach the Waikato B side in the NPC and to take the Chiefs into a mid-table position in his first stint as a Super Twelve boss. But as he told himself and the NZRFU, there was never a perfect time and he was sure of his ability. His persuasion, planning and organisation won the ballot.

The coaching crossover was messy. Mitchell and his assistant Robbie Deans had just a few weeks to pick their side and take them to Ireland, Scotland and Argentina. They made some changes, rewarding players for a strong NPC and punting on youngsters like Richard McCaw and Aaron Mauger in the Tests. There was controversy with Mitchell ignoring experienced men like Jeff Wilson, Christian Cullen and Taine Randell. Their form had wavered in the NPC but Mitchell later accepted he had been too blunt in not talking to them about their non-selection.

He also knew the end-of-year tour was not the time to be making significant coaching changes, it was a matter of getting through undefeated. The All Blacks did – just – after strong scares from Ireland and finally Argentina in Buenos Aires.

New Zealand coach John Mitchell makes a point to the media. The All Blacks have lost only one of the eleven Tests played since he took over last year.

New Zealand accepted Mitchell's predicament and waited for him to show his real style this year. His first move was to install former All Blacks Mark Shaw and Kieran Crowley as his selectors, before they went through six months of planning, watching the Super 12 and making their decisions. There were hiccups. Injuries eliminated captain Anton Oliver, Troy Flavell and Ron Cribb, but there was a massive encouragement from the Crusaders who went through the Super 12 undefeated. Their standards were a level above others, their style, cohesion and teamwork inspiring. It was a great framework on which Mitchell could attach his ideas and other star performers from the rest of the country.

Crucially, during negotiations to have Deans as his assistant, there had been a concession that Deans could hold twin posts with the All Blacks and Crusaders. While other franchises may have bridled, the information overlap was going to benefit the All Blacks. He picked a form squad and two extras: superstars Christian Cullen and Jonah Lomu who had been in erratic form. But that showed Mitchell's strength. He backed his coaching to get the pair back into shape.

'My aim is to develop a pool of players to be ready for October 2003,' he said, 'players who will challenge themselves and each other. This is the start of the journey.'

Performances, he said, would draw rewards. The reverse would mean the door for others and New Zealand believed him. He had demanded much from himself as a provincial player and captain of Waikato, a hard-nosed No 8 who captained the midweek All Blacks in their 1993 tour to the UK. His aims were clear.

'The All Blacks need to have a far more physical approach this year, skills have to improve and we need to continue with our strong defence.' Mitchell also wanted to advance the back play used by Deans and his Crusaders where they used the width of the park and counter-attacked from depth in numbers.

The coach broke the year into three phases. Section one was against Italy, Ireland and Fiji when there would be some experiments, section two the Tri Nations when he would reassess his selections and the last stage when he would mix form, experience and his increased knowledge to tangle with England, France and Wales in November.

It was a programme of 11 Tests with internationals against the All Blacks' four toughest opponents, a schedule which Mitchell saw as the opening part in the 18 Test schedule before the All Blacks had to be ready for the 2003 World Cup.

The Wallabies appeared to be the most difficult mid-season hurdle. They had beaten the All Blacks in seven of their last nine Tests although they did not look quite so stable without the influence of John Eales. Under new coach Rudolf Straeuli, the Springboks had to regroup after finishing bottom in the previous three Tri Nations series.

Mitchell's return to the northern hemisphere at the end of the year coincides with a massive task. The All Blacks will not be short of match-play after the NPC, but many will be tired or troubled by injury at the end of a long season. They then have to combine to meet England at Twickenham without the advantage of a warm-up match.

Those difficulties were evident when the All Blacks played Ireland last season at Lansdowne Road. There is no respite after England with a trip to Paris to play the rejuvenated French and a final Test against Wales. In those final three weeks, the challenge of coping with massive pressure will tell the world and New Zealand a lot about Mitchell and his All Blacks.

New Zealand's Test Record under John Mitchell: Played 11, won 10, lost 1

Opponents	Date	Venue	Result
Ireland	17th November 2001	A	Won 40-29
Scotland	24th November 2001	A	Won 37-6
Argentina	1st December 2001	A	Won 24-20
Italy	8th June 2002	H	Won 64-10
Ireland	15th June 2002	H	Won 15-6
Ireland	22nd June 2002	H	Won 40-8
Fiji	29th June 2002	H	Won 68-18
Australia	13th July 2002	H	Won 12-6
South Africa	20th July 2002	H	Won 41-20
Australia	3rd August 2002	A	Lost 14-16
South Africa	10th August 2002	A	Won 30-23

RUGBY WORLD CUP 2003

Battle Hots up for Final Placings

Brendan Gallagher

Though no country appears to have made dramatic strides
forward among the smaller European nations, there has been an entertaining jostling for position with the general level of competitiveness on the up as the scramble for a place in the fifth RWC tournament Finals, in 2003, intensifies.

In Round Two Pool A the Czech Republic waged a strong campaign, their key win coming away to Croatia, when they squeezed home 13-5. In Pool B Poland hinted at a return to former glories by qualifying comfortably for Round Three where they acquitted themselves very well, storming to a famous 27-15 home win over Spain, although alas it wasn't quite enough to see the Poles through to the next stage. The Czech Republic didn't disgrace themselves in Round Three either with an impressive 54-12 win over Holland, though Russia proved too strong up front in the decisive game, their forwards paving the way to a 37-18 win.

The final batting order in Europe will be decided this autumn with Ireland favourite to top Pool A in Round Four from Georgia and Russia. With two to qualify from the Pool, either Georgia or Russia are set to make their debut in the World Cup Finals while even the third-placed side could conceivably qualify via the repechage system. In Pool B, Italy will be clear favourites to qualify ahead of Romania and Spain.

In the Oceania qualifying group everything went much as expected with Fiji and Samoa booking their places in Australia and Tonga advancing to the repechage. Making time to fit the fixtures in was the main problem, but once the mini tournament got underway the old rivalries took over and during the course of a month the three Pacific nations served up some fine rugby. Both Fiji and Samoa lost once – to each other – but Fiji topped the group on points difference after scoring three late tries to win their final pool match against Tonga, 47-20.

As usual it was the Fijian backs who caught the eye – Nicky Little growing in stature at fly-half, Vili Satala and Seru Rabeni back to their best at centre and Norman Ligairi looking an exciting prospect at full-back. For Samoa, there was a notable first in their 22-12 win over Fiji at Nadi when three brothers uniquely represented the country – Freddie, Henry and Alesana Tuilagi.

As the dust settles, Fiji can reflect on their qualification for Pool B in Australia alongside France and Scotland, while Samoa find themselves in

Group C, where they will have to get to grips with South Africa and England. All is by no means lost for Tonga who one day will harness all their great potential and cause a major upset. Their route to the final is now through the repechage, starting with a game against the winner of Papua New Guinea's double header against the Cook Islands.

There were no real surprises in the Africa group with Namibia, calling on the experience of regular Vodacom Cup rugby in South Africa, making their untroubled way to their play-off games against Tunisia this autumn. In the early rounds the Madagascar squad, benefiting from a significant ex-pat French contingent, were the surprise package with wins over Botswana and Swaziland in Round One before scoring sensational wins in Round Two over favourites Kenya and Cameroon. The fairy-tale, however, came to an end when they moved up another level and found life very hard against Zimbabwe and Namibia, losing 52-3 and 116-0 respectively. Still, rugby has established a niche for itself in Madagascar and plans are already afoot for an even stronger qualification campaign for the 2007 tournament.

In the North of the continent Morocco, Ivory Coast and Tunisia fought out their perennial battle, the key match on this occasion being Tunisia's 13-8 win against the Ivory Coast in Abidjan.

Japan have always been capable of playing pleasing rugby with their ball skills and incredible fitness but in recent years appear to have grown weary of the unequal struggle against bigger opponents. Last summer, however, they rediscovered their zest for the game and Japan absolutely blitzed the Asian qualifying competition recording a massive 90-24 home win over bitter rivals Korea and then dishing out another hammering in the rain of Seoul, where they triumphed 55-17. Against Chinese Taipei, who normally provide meaningful opposition, they amassed an astonishing 275 points in two matches.

A quartet of naturalised New Zealanders and Tongans – Andy Miller, Adam Parker, Dean Anglesey and Luantagi Vatuvei – contributed significantly, but Korea's coach An Deog Gyun stressed after his side's two heavy defeats that it was the native-born Japanese players who had impressed him most. Increasingly Japan's top players are playing overseas to gain experience – the likes of Kensuke Iwabucki (Saracens), Wataru Murata (Bayonne), Ryohei Mike (Stirling County), Daisuke Ohata (Northern Suburbs, Sydney), Soshi Fuchigami and Takuro Miuchi (both Oxford Univeristy) – and their travels seem to be paying dividends.

It wouldn't be a World Cup without Canada and the Canuks experienced little difficulty in securing their qualification after claiming doubles over the United States and Chile. They broke even against Uruguay, who move through as runners-up. In the earlier rounds Brazil emerged strongly, performing the double over Trinidad and Tobago in Round Two before finding life much tougher against Chile and Paraguay.

Rugby World Cup 2003 qualifying results (up to 7 September, 2002)

EUROPE

Round One Pool One: Monaco 15, Moldova 17 (Menton); Belgium 24, Slovenia 10 (Brussels); Slovenia 19, Lithuania 19 (Ljubljana); Moldova 58, Malta 8 (Chisinau); Malta 0, Belgium 26 (Marsa); Monaco 8, Slovenija 13 (Monte Carlo); Malta 3, Monaco 9 (Marsa); Monaco 12, Belgium 18 (St Laurent du Var); Belgium 26, Moldova 10 (Brussels); Slovenia 30, Moldova 15 (Ljubljana); Malta 11, Lithuania 39 (Marsa); Belgium 29, Lithuania 20 (Laakdal); Slovenia 45, Malta 5 (Ljubljana); Lithuania 33, Monaco 10 (Vilnius); Moldova 20, Lithuania 16 (Chisinau)

Belgium qualify for Round Two

Round One Pool Two: Bosnia 13, Hungary 12 (Zenica); Switzerland 43, Bosnia 6 (Geneva); Andorra 12, Yugoslavia 9 (Andorra); Bulgaria 9, Switzerland 90 (Pernik); Hungary 27, Andorra 21 (Szazhalombatta); Yugoslavia 46, Bulgaria 6 (Dimitrovgrad); Yugoslavia 25, Hungary 10 (Dimitrovgrad); Switzerland 38, Andorra 25 (Lausanne); Bulgaria 30, Bosnia 8 (Pernik); Switzerland 61, Hungary 23 (Basle); Bosnia 23, Yugoslavia 13 (Zenica); Andorra 59, Bulgaria 10 (Andorra); Hungary 46, Bulgaria 7 (Szazhalombatta); Yugoslavia 13, Switzerland 10 (Gornji); Andorra 23, Bosnia 13 (Andorra)

Switzerland qualify for Round Two

Round One Pool Three: Norway 9, Luxembourg 41 (Stavanger); Austria 10, Sweden 42 (Vienna); Latvia 24, Luxembourg 19 (Riga); Sweden 44, Norway 3 (Enköping); Latvia 38, Austria 12 (Riga); Luxembourg 3, Israel 62 (Cessange); Israel 3, Latvia 21 (Herzliyya); Israel 43, Norway 3 (Tel Aviv); Luxembourg 3, Sweden 116 (Cessange); Austria 77, Luxembourg 0 (Vienna); Sweden 35, Israel 20 (Växjö); Latvia 37, Norway 0 (Riga); Austria 21, Israel 6 (Vienna); Norway 7, Austria 51 (Horten); Sweden 17, Latvia 10 (Enköping)

Sweden and Latvia (Best runners-up) qualify for Round Two

Round Two Pool A: Czech Republic 46, Belgium 3; Switzerland 6, Czech Republic 32; Ukraine 21, Belgium 10; Croatia 5, Czech Republic 13; Uukraine 41, Croatia 7; Belgium 15, Switzerland 22; Czech Republic 26, Ukraine 8; Croatia 18, Switzerland 16; Belgium 0, Croatia 26; Switzerland 11, Ukraine 30

Czech Republic advance to Round Three

Round Two Pool B: Latvia 18, Poland 60; Poland 10, Sweden 3; Sweden 37, Latvia 12; Sweden 32, Germany 10; Denmark 33, Sweden 21; Denmark 19, Poland 26; Germany 34, Denmark 24; Germany 44, Latvia 0; Latvia 8, Denmark 32; Poland 20, Germany 12

Poland win and advance to Round Three

Round Three Pool A: Czech Republic 18, Russia 37; Holland 12, Czech Republic 54; Russia 65, Holland 3

Russia win and advance to Round Four

Round Three Pool B: Poland 27, Spain 15; Portugal 39, Poland 26; Spain 34, Portugal 21

Spain win and advance to Round Four

Round Four: (Autumn 2002):

Pool A: Russia, Georgia, Ireland.

Pool B: Italy, Romania, Spain

First two in each pool to qualify. Losers into repechage

OCEANIA

Eastern Zone Pool: Cook Islands 86, Tahiti 0; (Rarotonga); Tahiti 6, Niue Island 41 (Papeete); Niue Island 8, Cook Islands 28 (Paliati)

Cook Islands qualify for repechage

Round One Western Zone Pool: Papua New Guinea 32, Solomon Islands 10 (Port Moresby); Vanuatu 10, Papua New Guinea 32 (Port Vila); Solomon Islands 11, Vanuatu 3 (Honiara)

Papua New Guinea qualify for repechage.

Round Two: Samoa 16, Fiji 17 (Apia); Tonga 22, Fiji 47 (Nuku'alofa); Tonga 16, Samoa 25 (Nuku'alofa); Fiji 12, Samoa 22 (Nadi); Samoa 31, Tonga 13 (Apia); Fiji 47, Tonga 20 (Nadi)

Fiji and Samoa qualify; Tonga qualify for repechage

AFRICA

Round One Pool A: Zambia 25, Cameroon 24; Uganda 21, Zambia 12; Cameroon 17, Uganda 0

Round One Pool B: Botswana 13, Swaziland 3; Madagascar 33, Botswana 11; Swaziland 21, Madagascar 26

Round Two: Madagascar 27, Kenya 20; Cameroon 24, Madagascar 30; Kenya 40, Cameroon 15

Round Three North: Tunisia 27, Morocco 26; Ivory Coast 8, Tunisia 13; Morocco 23, Ivory Coast 21

Round Three South: Madagascar 3, Zimbabwe 52; Namibia 116, Madagascar 0; Zimbabwe 30, Namibia 42

Round Four: Winner North plays Winner South over two legs.

Winner qualifies. Loser qualifies for repechage

AMERICAS

Round One: Venezuela 55, Colombia 0; Venezuela 46, Peru 19; Brazil 51, Peru 9; Colombia 12, Brazil 47; Brazil 14, Venezuela 3; Peru 31, Colombia 10

Round Two: Trinidad & Tobago 51, Jamaica 5; Cayman Islands 32, Guyana 13; Barbados 25, Bahamas 18; Barbados 5, Bermuda 13; Trinidad & Tobago 12, Cayman Islands 8; Bermuda 12, Trinidad & Tobago 23; Trinidad & Tobago 10, Brazil 11; Brazil 9, Trinidad & Tobago 0

Round Three: Brazil 6, Chile 46; Paraguay 14, Brazil 3; Chile 57, Paraguay 5

Round Four: Canada 26, United States 9; United States 13, Canada 36; Chile 10, Uruguay 6; United States 28, Uruguay 24; United States 35, Chile 22; Canada 51, Uruguay 16; Canada 27, Chile 6; Uruguay 25, Canada 23; Chile 21, United States 13; Uruguay 10, United States 9; Chile 11, Canada 29; Uruguay 34, Chile 23

Canada and Uruguay qualify. United States qualifies for repechage.

ASIA

Round One: Malaysia 3, Chinese Taipei 57; Singapore 34, Malaysia 5; Chinese Taipei w/o Singapore; Arabian Gulf 40, Thailand 20; Thailand 8, Hong Kong 15; Hong Kong 17, Arabian Gulf 7; Sri Lanka 9, China 7; China 24, Kazakstan 10; Kazakstan 20, Sri Lanka 14

China, Chinese Taipei and Hong Kong qualify for Round Two

Round Two: Chinese Taipei 20, Hong Kong 15; China 21, Chinese Taipei 29; Hong Kong 34, China 7

Chinese Taipei and Hong Kong qualify for Round Three

Round Three: Japan 90, Korea 24; Chinese Taipei 31, Hong Kong 54; Korea 119, Chinese Taipei 7; Japan 155, Chinese Taipei 3; Korea 17, Japan 55; Chinese Taipei 3, Japan 120

Japan qualify. Korea into repechage.

Rugby World Cup Update: October 2002

While this Yearbook was being prepared for the printers, five more teams guaranteed their passages to the 2003 finals.

In Europe, Ireland undertook a marathon journey across seven time zones to play their qualifying fixture with Russia in Krasnoyarsk. The temperatures in Siberia reached an unseasonal 80F during a match that Keith Wood's side comfortably won by 35-3. Then, a week later, but this time without their injured skipper, Ireland regrouped to see off the Georgians by 63-14 at Lansdowne Road. They qualify for Australia's pool in RWC 2003 and Georgia, who defeated Russia 17-13 in front of nearly 40,000 spectators in Tbilisi, go into England's group with South Africa in the finals. Georgia have never previously reached the finals of the Rugby World Cup.

Elsewhere in Europe, Italy and Romania overcame Spain while Italy's 25-17 win against Romania guaranteed them a place in the group that will feature New Zealand and Wales. The Romanians, who had warmed up for the qualifiers with a 39-8 defeat in early September against Ireland in Limerick, outscored Italy by two tries to one. They will play in the same group as Australia and Ireland next year.

Russia and Spain's chances of qualifying now depend on their progress through the repechages. Namibia have secured their place alongside Romania in Australia by winning the African qualifying tournament. They tied 43-all on aggregate with Tunisia over a two-leg North-South play-off, but go through on superior try-count.

Recent Results:

Russia 3, Ireland 35 (Krasnoyarsk); Ireland 63, Georgia 14 (Dublin); Georgia 17, Russia 13 (Tbilisi). *Ireland and Georgia qualify; Russia qualify for repechage*

Spain 3, Italy 50 (Valladolid); Italy 25, Romania 17 (Parma); Romania 67, Spain 6 (Iasi). *Italy and Romania qualify; Spain qualify for repechage*

Namibia 26, Tunisia 19 (Windhoek); Tunisia 24, Namibia 17 (Tunis). *Namibia qualify; Tunisia qualify for repechage*

RUGBY WORLD CUP RECORDS

(Final stages only)

Overall Records

Most overall points in final stages

227	A G Hastings	Scotland	1987-95
195	M P Lynagh	Australia	1987-95
170	G J Fox	New Zealand	1987-91

Most overall tries in final stages

15	J T Lomu	New Zealand	1995-99
11	R Underwood	England	1987-95
10	D I Campese	Australia	1987-95

Leading Scorers

Most points in one competition

126	G J Fox	New Zealand	1987
112	T Lacroix	France	1995
104	A G Hastings	Scotland	1995
102	G Quesada	Argentina	1999
101	M Burke	Australia	1999

Most tries in one competition

8	J T Lomu	New Zealand	1999
7	M C G Ellis	New Zealand	1995
7	J T Lomu	New Zealand	1995

Most conversions in one competition

30	G J Fox	New Zealand	1987
20	S D Culhane	New Zealand	1995
20	M P Lynagh	Australia	1987

Most penalty goals in one competition

31	G Quesada	Argentina	1999
26	T Lacroix	France	1995
21	G J Fox	New Zealand	1987
20	C R Andrew	England	1995

Most dropped goals in one competition

6	J H de Beer	South Africa	1999
3	G P J Townsend	Scotland	1999
3	A P Mehrtens	New Zealand	1995
3	J T Stransky	South Africa	1995
3	C R Andrew	England	1995
3	J Davies	Wales	1987

Match Records

Most Points in a Match
by a team

145	New Zealand v Japan	1995
101	New Zealand v Italy	1999
101	England v Tonga	1999
89	Scotland v Ivory Coast	1995
74	New Zealand v Fiji	1987
72	Canada v Namibia	1999

by a player

45	S D Culhane	New Zealand v Japan	1995
44	A G Hastings	Scotland v Ivory Coast	1995
36	T E Brown	New Zealand v Italy	1999
36	P J Grayson	England v Tonga	1999
34	J H de Beer	South Africa v England	1999
32	J P Wilkinson	England v Italy	1999

Most Tries in a Match
by a team

21	New Zealand v Japan	1995
14	New Zealand v Italy	1999
13	England v Tonga	1999
13	Scotland v Ivory Coast	1995
13	France v Zimbabwe	1987

by a player

6	M C G Ellis	New Zealand v Japan	1995
4	K G M Wood	Ireland v United States	1999
4	A G Hastings	Scotland v Ivory Coast	1995
4	C M Williams	South Africa v Western Samoa	1995
4	J T Lomu	New Zealand v England	1995
4	B F Robinson	Ireland v Zimbabwe	1991
4	I C Evans	Wales v Canada	1987
4	C I Green	New Zealand v Fiji	1987
4	J A Gallagher	New Zealand v Fiji	1987

Most Conversions in a Match
by a team

20	New Zealand v Japan	1995
12	England v Tonga	1999
11	New Zealand v Italy	1999
10	New Zealand v Fiji	1987
9	Canada v Namibia	1999
9	Scotland v Ivory Coast	1995
9	France v Zimbabwe	1987

by a player

20	S D Culhane	New Zealand v Japan	1995
12	P J Grayson	England v Tonga	1999
11	T E Brown	New Zealand v Italy	1999
10	G J Fox	New Zealand v Fiji	1987
9	G L Rees	Canada v Namibia	1999
9	A G Hastings	Scotland v Ivory Coast	1995
9	D Camberabero	France v Zimbabwe	1987

Most Penalty Goals in a Match
by a team

8	Australia v South Africa	1999
8	Argentina v Samoa	1999
8	Scotland v Tonga	1995
8	France v Ireland	1995

by a player

8	M Burke	Australia v South Africa	1999
8	G Quesada	Argentina v Samoa	1999
8	A G Hastings	Scotland v Tonga	1995
8	T Lacroix	France v Ireland	1995

Most Dropped Goals in a Match
by a team

5	South Africa v England	1999
3	Fiji v Romania	1991

by a player

5	J H de Beer	South Africa v England	1999
2	P C Montgomery	South Africa v New Zealand	1999
2	C Lamaison	France v New Zealand	1999
2	J T Stransky	South Africa v New Zealand	1995
2	C R Andrew	England v Argentina	1995
2	T Rabaka	Fiji v Romania	1991
2	L Arbizu	Argentina v Australia	1991
2	J Davies	Wales v Ireland	1987

Rugby World Cup Tournaments: 1987 To 1999

First Tournament: 1987 In Australia & New Zealand

Pool 1

Australia	19	England	6
USA	21	Japan	18
England	60	Japan	7
Australia	47	USA	12
England	34	USA	6
Australia	42	Japan	23

	P	W	D	L	F	A	Pts
Australia	3	3	0	0	108	41	6
England	3	2	0	1	100	32	4
USA	3	1	0	2	39	99	2
Japan	3	0	0	3	48	123	0

Pool 2

Canada	37	Tonga	4
Wales	13	Ireland	6
Wales	29	Tonga	16
Ireland	46	Canada	19
Wales	40	Canada	9
Ireland	32	Tonga	9

	P	W	D	L	F	A	Pts
Wales	3	3	0	0	82	31	6
Ireland	3	2	0	1	84	41	4
Canada	3	1	0	2	65	90	2
Tonga	3	0	0	3	29	98	0

Pool 3

New Zealand	70	Italy	6
Fiji	28	Argentina	9
New Zealand	74	Fiji	13
Argentina	25	Italy	16
Italy	18	Fiji	15
New Zealand	46	Argentina	15

	P	W	D	L	F	A	Pts
New Zealand	3	3	0	0	190	34	6
Fiji	3	1	0	2	56	101	2
Argentina	3	1	0	2	49	90	2
Italy	3	1	0	2	40	110	2

Pool 4

Romania	21	Zimbabwe	20
France	20	Scotland	20
France	55	Romania	12
Scotland	60	Zimbabwe	21
France	70	Zimbabwe	12
Scotland	55	Romania	28

	P	W	D	L	F	A	Pts
France	3	2	1	0	145	44	5
Scotland	3	2	1	0	135	69	5
Romania	3	1	0	2	61	130	2
Zimbabwe	3	0	0	3	53	151	0

Quarter-finals

New Zealand	30	Scotland	3
France	31	Fiji	16
Australia	33	Ireland	15
Wales	16	England	3

Semi-finals

France	30	Australia	24
New Zealand	49	Wales	6

Third Place match

Wales	22	Australia	21

First World Cup Final, Eden Park, Auckland, 20 June 1987

New Zealand 29 *Tries:* Jones, Kirk, Kirwan *Conversion:* Fox *Penalty Goals:* Fox (4) *Drop Goal:* Fox

France 9 *Try:* Berbizier *Conversion:* Camberabero *Penalty Goal:* Camberabero
Attendance: 48,350

Second Tournament: 1991 In Britain, Ireland & France

Pool 1

New Zealand	18	England	12
Italy	30	USA	9
New Zealand	46	USA	6
England	36	Italy	6
England	37	USA	9
New Zealand	31	Italy	21

	P	W	D	L	F	A	Pts
New Zealand	3	3	0	0	95	39	9
England	3	2	0	1	85	33	7
Italy	3	1	0	2	57	76	5
USA	3	0	0	3	24	113	3

Pool 2

Scotland	47	Japan	9
Ireland	55	Zimbabwe	11
Ireland	32	Japan	16
Scotland	51	Zimbabwe	12
Scotland	24	Ireland	15
Japan	52	Zimbabwe	8

	P	W	D	L	F	A	Pts
Scotland	3	3	0	0	122	36	9
Ireland	3	2	0	1	102	51	7
Japan	3	1	0	2	77	87	5
Zimbabwe	3	0	0	3	31	158	3

Pool 3

Australia	32	Argentina	19
Western Samoa	16	Wales	13
Australia	9	Western Samoa	3
Wales	16	Argentina	7
Australia	38	Wales	3
Western Samoa	35	Argentina	12

	P	W	D	L	F	A	Pts
Australia	3	3	0	0	79	25	9
Western Samoa	3	2	0	1	54	34	7
Wales	3	1	0	2	32	61	5
Argentina	3	0	0	3	38	83	3

Pool 4

France	30	Romania	3
Canada	13	Fiji	3
France	33	Fiji	9
Canada	19	Romania	11
Romania	17	Fiji	15
France	19	Canada	13

	P	W	D	L	F	A	Pts
France	3	3	0	0	82	25	9
Canada	3	2	0	1	45	33	7
Romania	3	1	0	2	31	64	5
Fiji	3	0	0	3	27	63	3

Quarter-finals

England	19	France	10
Scotland	28	Western Samoa	6
Australia	19	Ireland	18
New Zealand	29	Canada	13

Semi-finals

| England | 9 | Scotland | 6 |
| Australia | 16 | New Zealand | 6 |

Third Place match

| New Zealand | 13 | Scotland | 6 |

Second World Cup Final, Twickenham, 2 November 1991

Australia 12 *Try:* Daly *Conversion:* Lynagh *Penalty Goals:* Lynagh (2)
England 6 *Penalty Goals:* Webb (2)
Attendance: 56,208

Third Tournament: 1995 In South Africa

Pool A

South Africa	27	Australia	18
Canada	34	Romania	3
South Africa	21	Romania	8
Australia	27	Canada	11
Australia	42	Romania	3
South Africa	20	Canada	0

	P	W	D	L	F	A	Pts
South Africa	3	3	0	0	68	26	9
Australia	3	2	0	1	87	41	7
Canada	3	1	0	2	45	50	5
Romania	3	0	0	3	14	97	3

Pool B

Western Samoa	42	Italy	18
England	24	Argentina	18
Western Samoa	32	Argentina	26
England	27	Italy	20
Italy	31	Argentina	25
England	44	Western Samoa	22

	P	W	D	L	F	A	Pts
England	3	3	0	0	95	60	9
Western Samoa	3	2	0	1	96	88	7
Italy	3	1	0	2	69	94	5
Argentina	3	0	0	3	69	87	3

Pool C

Wales	57	Japan	10
New Zealand	43	Ireland	19
Ireland	50	Japan	28
New Zealand	34	Wales	9
New Zealand	145	Japan	17
Ireland	24	Wales	23

	P	W	D	L	F	A	Pts
New Zealand	3	3	0	0	222	45	9
Ireland	3	2	0	1	93	94	7
Wales	3	1	0	2	89	68	5
Japan	3	0	0	3	55	252	3

Pool D

Scotland	89	Ivory Coast	0
France	38	Tonga	10
France	54	Ivory Coast	18
Scotland	41	Tonga	5
Tonga	29	Ivory Coast	11
France	22	Scotland	19

	P	W	D	L	F	A	Pts
France	3	3	0	0	114	47	9
Scotland	3	2	0	1	149	27	7
Tonga	3	1	0	2	44	90	5
Ivory Coast	3	0	0	3	29	172	3

Quarter-finals

France	36	Ireland	12
South Africa	42	Western Samoa	14
England	25	Australia	22
New Zealand	48	Scotland	30

Semi-finals

South Africa	19	France	15
New Zealand	45	England	29

Third Place match

France	19	England	9

Third World Cup Final, Ellis Park, Johannesburg, 24 June 1995

South Africa 15 * *Penalty Goals:* Stransky (3) *Drop Goals:* Stransky (2)
New Zealand 12 *Penalty Goals:* Mehrtens (3) *Drop Goal:* Mehrtens
Attendance: 63,000
* *after extra time: 9-9 after normal time*

Fourth Tournament: 1999 In Britain, Ireland & France

Pool A

Spain	15	Uruguay	27
South Africa	46	Scotland	29
Scotland	43	Uruguay	12
South Africa	47	Spain	3
South Africa	39	Uruguay	3
Scotland	48	Spain	0

	P	W	D	L	F	A	Pts
South Africa	3	3	0	0	132	35	9
Scotland	3	2	0	1	120	58	7
Uruguay	3	1	0	2	42	97	5
Spain	3	0	0	3	18	122	3

Pool B

England	67	Italy	7
New Zealand	45	Tonga	9
England	16	New Zealand	30
Italy	25	Tonga	28
New Zealand	101	Italy	3
England	101	Tonga	10

	P	W	D	L	F	A	Pts
New Zealand	3	3	0	0	176	28	9
England	3	2	0	1	184	47	7
Tonga	3	1	0	2	47	171	5
Italy	3	0	0	3	35	196	3

Pool C

Fiji	67	Namibia	18
France	33	Canada	20
France	47	Namibia	13
Fiji	38	Canada	22
Canada	72	Namibia	11
France	28	Fiji	19

	P	W	D	L	F	A	Pts
France	3	3	0	0	108	52	9
Fiji	3	2	0	1	124	68	7
Canada	3	1	0	2	114	82	5
Namibia	3	0	0	3	42	186	3

Pool D

Wales	23	Argentina	18
Samoa	43	Japan	9
Wales	64	Japan	15
Argentina	32	Samoa	16
Wales	31	Samoa	38
Argentina	33	Japan	12

	P	W	D	L	F	A	Pts
Wales	3	2	0	1	118	71	7
Samoa	3	2	0	1	97	72	7
Argentina	3	2	0	1	83	51	7
Japan	3	0	0	3	36	140	3

Pool E

Ireland	53	United States	8
Australia	57	Romania	9
United States	25	Romania	27
Ireland	3	Australia	23
Australia	55	United States	19
Ireland	44	Romania	14

	P	W	D	L	F	A	Pts
Australia	3	3	0	0	135	31	9
Ireland	3	2	0	1	100	45	7
Romania	3	1	0	2	50	126	5
United States	3	0	0	3	52	135	3

Play-offs for quarter-final places

England	45	Fiji	24
Scotland	35	Samoa	20
Ireland	24	Argentina	28

Quarter-finals

Wales	9	Australia	24
South Africa	44	England	21
France	47	Argentina	26
Scotland	18	New Zealand	30

Semi-finals

| South Africa | 21 | Australia | 27 |
| New Zealand | 31 | France | 43 |

Third Place match

| South Africa | 22 | New Zealand | 18 |

Fourth World Cup Final, Millennium Stadium, Cardiff Arms Park, 6 November 1999

Australia 35 *Tries:* Tune, Finegan *Conversions:* Burke (2) *Penalty Goals:* Burke (7)
France 12 *Penalty Goals:* Lamaison (4)
Attendance: 72,500

THE 2002 SIX NATIONS

France and England a class apart

Mick Cleary

The talk can get fanciful late at night, particularly during the Six Nations festival of fun when, so it's said, drink is taken. One particular flight of fancy, soon dismissed, was that there should be relegation and promotion for the Six Nations Championship, the bottom side trading places with the likes of Georgia, Russia, Spain and Romania who have their own parallel tournament.

Never mind those two divisions. What about the split that is opening up between the two tiers of the Six Nations Championship itself? Once again France and England were a class apart, comfortably the better sides in a disturbingly uneven tournament. The overall quality was low and it was left to the big two countries to show us some style and substance. The final honours went to France, who won the Paris showdown, 20-15, to tee themselves up for their seventh Grand Slam. Good luck to them. It was a well-deserved victory on the day. It would, though, be perfectly reasonable to argue that England played rugby of a consistently higher standard through the championship, scoring more tries and points, but having to settle for the runners-up slot. And quite right too. Rugby has yet to go down the ice-skating route and award marks for artistic merit. The final table did not lie.

Even though France were fitful at times, they also gave us two towering performances to beat England and then to claim the Slam itself in demolishing Ireland on the final weekend. They gave us much more besides – the outstanding newcomer of the tournament, No 8 Imanol Harinordoquy; the most influential leader in scrum-half Fabien Galthié; the most potent prop in Stade Français tight-head, Pieter de Villiers; and the best back-row combo with the young Pau No 8 bedding down alongside Serge Betsen and Olivier Magne.

There was a great sense too of a squad taking shape, of a great rugby nation finally getting on the straight and narrow. Although let's hope there are a few kinks and detours in that route to success for nobody kinks or detours quite like the French. Nonetheless coach Bernard Laporte does seem to have got his message through, that self-discipline and control are the essentials of modern rugby. The frills can come later. That France should only concede six penalties in two of their championship games suggests that they are all on-message.

England hit the straps against Ireland and Wales and shone sporadically against Scotland and Italy. 'We were mentally stale this championship,' was the verdict of manager Clive Woodward.

For the others, the tale of comparative woe continues. Ireland promised much in the autumn but delivered little in the championship, their hammering of Wales on the opening weekend apart. Even so, they were ahead of Wales and Scotland, both of whom are floundering. Wales lost their coach, Graham Henry, after that Dublin debacle and, although they ran France close in Cardiff, finished lamely against Scotland.

The Scots, too, have fault lines to tend to, albeit not as many as Wales. Once again their lineout prospered through Scott Murray. They need to offer more than that.

Italy, without a win for the second year in succession, are hanging in there. They have commendable spirit and resilience, although they do need to curb their flagrant infringing which cost them a heap of points and several yellow cards. Their coach, Brad Johnstone, was also out of office by the end of the championship.

Six Nations 2002: Final Table

	P	W	D	L	F	A	Pts
France	5	5	0	0	156	75	10
England	5	4	0	1	184	53	8
Ireland	5	3	0	2	145	138	6
Scotland	5	2	0	3	91	128	4
Wales	5	1	0	4	119	188	2
Italy	5	0	0	5	70	183	0

Points: win 2; draw 1; defeat 0.

There were 765 points scored at an average of 51 a match. The Championship record (803 points at an average of 53.5 a match) was set in 2000. Gérald Merceron was the leading individual points scorer with 80, nine shy of the Championship record set in 2001. For the second Championship running, Will Greenwood scored most tries (five – three short of the all time record).

2 February, Stade de France, Paris
France 33 (1G 7PG 1T)   Italy 12 (4PG)

It was not a landmark that anyone either playing or among the 60,000 watching at the Stade de France will recall with relish. Irish referee Alan Lewis dished out five yellow cards, the most ten minute sin-bin punishments ever recorded in an international between the leading countries. It was not an even distribution: four Italians did time on the sidelines along with one Frenchmen. Carlo Checcinato, Marco Bortolami, Matt Phillips and Diego Dominguez were the guilty quartet with French lock David Auradou also in the dock.

It was an offence by French captain Olivier Magne, however, that was to excite post-match controversy after video footage showed the Montferrand flanker stamping on Italian wing, Denis Dallan. Match commissioner Matt

Bayliss eventually called Magne to book and he subsequently received a three-week ban that forced him out of the side for the visit to Cardiff.

It was an unsavoury incident in a very undistinguished match. Hopes that France would kick-start their Six Nations campaign with a flourish came to naught, their ambitions mired in their own inadequacies and the cloying grip of the Italian defence.

Italy led 12-3 by the 35th minute but were unable to score thereafter as France gathered themselves. By the interval France had taken a seven-point lead through four penalty goals from Gérald Merceron and his conversion of a try by Pau centre Damien Traille.

Merceron reaped the return from some cynical play by the Italians to score three more penalty goals in the second-half and create a new French record for the Championship by kicking seven penalties in the match. His overall kicking record in his Six Nations career at this stage was 84 goal points with a staggering 91% success-rate (29 out of 32).

Béziers flanker, Serge Betsen, scored a late try to seal the first victory on the road to the Grand Slam.

France: N Jeanjean; A Rougerie, T Marsh, D Traille, D Bory; G Merceron, F Michalak; J-J Crenca, Y Bru, P de Villiers, D Auradou, T Privat, S Betsen, S Hall, O Magne (*captain*) *Substitutions:* X Garbajosa for Jeanjean (52 mins); R Ibañez for Bru (58 mins); F Pelous for Auradou (58 mins); A Albouy for Michalak (81 mins)

Scorers *Tries:* Traille, Betsen *Conversion:* Merceron *Penalty Goals:* Merceron (7)

Italy: P Vaccari; R Pedrazzi, L Martin, C Stoica, D Dallan; D Dominguez, A Troncon; A Lo Cicero, A Moscardi (*captain*), A Muraro, C Checchinato, S Dellape, M Bortolami, M Phillips, Mauro Bergamasco *Substitutions:* G de Carli for Lo Cicero (temp 26 to 29 mins and 57 mins); Mirco Bergamaso for Pedrazzi (temp 47 to 49 mins) and for Vaccari (72 mins); A Moreno for Muraro (58 mins); M Giacheri for Dellape (77 mins); A Persico for Mauro Bergamasco (80 mins)

Scorers *Penalty Goals:* Dominguez (4)

Referee A Lewis (Ireland)

2 February, Murrayfield
Scotland 3 (1PG) England 29 (3G 1PG 1T)

If the portents had been encouraging, with forecasts for the sort of storm-lashed weather that had accompanied Scotland's unlikely victory two years earlier, then the reality was very much a damp squib. England won with ease and without playing particularly well in recording their biggest ever margin of victory at Murrayfield. They ran in four tries and with more controlled build-up work would surely have had more. It was a dark day for Scotsmen. Even the promised storms failed to materialise. Rather like the team itself, lightning did not strike twice.

England shuffled their team, even though they had enjoyed a successful autumn. Out went centre Mike Catt and lock Danny Grewcock, with Mike Tindall resuming his place at outside-centre and Leicester duo Ben Kay and Martin Johnson bedding down in the second-row. There was a first cap for

Northampton hooker, Steve Thompson, who was reacquainted with the man who instigated his switch of positions from back to front-row, Scotland and former Saints coach, Ian McGeechan.

The die was cast within the first quarter of an hour by which time Jason Robinson had brazenly breezed in for two tries. There was no way back. The first came from a midfield tap penalty and involved a deft flip-on pass from man-of-the-match Will Greenwood. The Harlequin centre also did his impressive stuff in helping tee up the second try.

England stuttered through the rest of the half. 11 minutes after the break a chip kick from Tindall broke luckily his way. The fourth try was triggered by a charge down on Hodge and rounded off by Ben Cohen. 20-year-old Harlequin scrum-half Nick Duncombe made his debut after just three and a half matches of senior rugby as a second-half replacement for Kyran Bracken. Jonny Wilkinson's seven points saw him past the 500 point mark in major Tests. Attendance: 67,500.

Scotland: G H Metcalfe; B J Laney, J G McLaren, G P J Townsend,
C D Paterson; D W Hodge, B W Redpath; T J Smith, G C Bulloch, M J Stewart,
S Murray, S B Grimes, J P R White, S M Taylor, A C Pountney (*captain*)
Substitution: G Graham for Smith (63 mins)

Scorer *Penalty Goal:* Hodge

England: J Robinson; A S Healey, W J H Greenwood, M J Tindall, B C Cohen;
J P Wilkinson, K P P Bracken; G C Rowntree, S Thompson, J White,
M O Johnson (*captain*), B J Kay, R A Hill, J P R Worsley, N A Back *Substitutions:*
N Duncombe for Bracken (40 mins); D J Grewcock for Kay (69 mins);
I R Balshaw for Tindall (72 mins); J Leonard for White (75 mins); C Hodgson for
Wilkinson (82 mins)

Scorers *Tries:* Robinson (2), Tindall, Cohen *Conversions:* Wilkinson (2), Hodgson
Penalty Goals: Wilkinson

Referee S R Walsh (New Zealand)

3 February, Lansdowne Road, Dublin
Ireland 54 (3G 6PG 3T) Wales 10 (1G 1PG)

It was a match that raised hopes and ended careers. While Irish fans danced jigs of delight round Dublin after this record-breaking victory and nursed outlandish dreams of storming Twickenham in a fortnight's time, the Welsh supporters could only but wonder how long it would be before coach Graham Henry bowed to the inevitable and resigned. Four days was the answer, no surprise given the calamitous nature of Welsh play in this game.

Ireland were bright and inventive, it's true, but the most vivid image of the match is the look of bewilderment and despair on the faces of several Welsh players as their defence time and again ran up the white flag. This was their second worst defeat ever in the championship and only a lapse of concentration by their opponents spared them the ultimate indignity.

Wales showed nine changes from the team also humbled by Ireland a few months earlier in the held-over championship match in Cardiff. Cardiff wing Craig Morgan won his first cap, Craig Quinnell and Chris Wyatt formed the second-row partnership, while flankers Martyn Williams and Nathan Budgett were restored to the back-row. Juggling with selection made no difference.

Ireland, for whom Peter Clohessy won his 50th cap, were without injured hooker and captain, Keith Wood, as well as lock Malcolm O'Kelly and wing Shane Horgan. They were also without coach Warren Gatland, who had been sacked in the autumn and replaced by Eddie O'Sullivan. Some start for the new man.

Leicester wing Geordan Murphy scored a brace of tries and was quickly on the score sheet, finishing off good approach work by David Humphreys and David Wallace. Four Humphreys penalties followed before debutant lock Paul O'Connell was driven over. Murphy's second try after the break was the pick of the bunch, forwards and backs combining splendidly. Wales stirred themselves slightly with Stephen Jones scoring a try.

Ireland finished in style with wing Denis Hickie, flanker Keith Gleeson, the former Australia under-21 captain who came on as a substitute to win his first cap, and fly-half Ronan O'Gara – another substitute – scoring tries.

Many Welsh fans among the 48,898 present had endured troublesome journeys to Dublin owing to adverse weather. They must have wished that they hadn't bothered.

Ireland: G T Dempsey; G E A Murphy, B G O'Driscoll, K M Maggs, D A Hickie; D G Humphreys, P A Stringer; P M Clohessy, F J Sheahan, J J Hayes, M J Galwey (*captain*), P J O'Connell, S H Easterby, A G Foley, D P Wallace *Substitutions:* G W Longwell for O'Connell (31 mins); J S Byrne for Sheahan (71 mins); P S Wallace for Clohessy 71 mins); K D Gleeson for Galwey (71 mins); R J R O'Gara for Humphreys (74 mins); R A J Henderson for Hickie (74 mins); G Easterby for Stringer (76 mins)

Scorers *Tries:* Murphy (2), O'Connell, O'Gara, Hickie, Gleeson *Conversions:* Humphreys (2), O'Gara *Penalty Goals:* Humphreys (6)

Wales: K A Morgan; D R James, J P Robinson, I R Harris, C S Morgan; S M Jones, R Howley; S C John, R C McBryde, C T Anthony, J C Quinnell, C P Wyatt, N J Budgett, L S Quinnell (*captain*), M E Williams *Substitutions:* I M Gough for Wyatt (6 mins); A W N Marinos for Robinson (9 mins); D Jones for John (56 mins); D Peel for Howley (56 mins); B Williams for McBryde (70 mins)

Scorer *Try:* S Jones *Conversion:* S Jones *Penalty Goal:* S Jones

Referee P C Deluca (Argentina)

16 February, Millennium Stadium, Cardiff Arms Park
Wales 33 (3G 4PG)   France 37 (2G 5PG 1DG 1T)

The armchair referee had a decisive influence on this scrappy yet entertaining match. Italian Claudio Giacomel was called upon to make several key rulings from his TV booth up in the stand, two of them in stoppage time as Wales mounted a furious late assault. First Scott Quinnell made a trademark thrust for the line only to come up just short when he failed to ground the

Gérald Merceron prepares to kick a goal against Wales. The Frenchman finished with 80 points for the Championship season, a new French record.

ball correctly. Then, in the seventh minute of added time, wing Dafydd James made a despairing lunge for the corner. He did manage to ground the ball correctly, but had been nudged into touch by a flying tackle from Aurélien Rougerie. Giacomel made the correct call on both incidents but was amiss in awarding a touchdown early in the second half to Rougerie, the France wing chasing a kick ahead from Damien Traille but appearing to be beaten to the touchdown by Kevin Morgan. The Welsh wing had some consolation when Giacomel gave him the benefit for his own try midway through the second half. There was some doubt too over Nathan Budgett's score, although this ruling was made by match referee, David McHugh.

The delayed and disputed decisions added to the drama of the game, one that had been awaited with some trepidation in Wales after the fuss surrounding Graham Henry's resignation. This was Steve Hansen's first game in charge and at least he saw a resurgence of spirit and devil in the Welsh side after the abject flatness of the display in Dublin. Hansen made his own mark by demoting Iestyn Harris to the bench and bringing in Tom Shanklin for his Championship debut. The Saracens centre thus followed in the footsteps of his Pembrokeshire-born father, Jim, who had won his Welsh spurs some 32 years earlier on the same ground against the same opponents.

The mix was a modified success. France, who had made a stand on discipline by leaving out David Auradou and demoting Fabien Pelous to the bench, built up a 15-point lead early in the second-half after Scott Quinnell had spent ten minutes in the sin-bin. Wales, though, roused themselves and ensured some comfort for their fans and a busy time for the video referee.

Wales: K A Morgan; D R James, T Shanklin, A W N Marinos, C S Morgan; S M Jones, R Howley; S C John, R C McBryde, C T Anthony, J C Quinnell, A P Moore, N J Budgett, L S Quinnell (*captain*), M E Williams *Substitutions:* D Jones for John (48 mins); B Williams for McBryde (62 mins); I M Gough for C Quinnell (67 mins); G R Williams for Marinos (70 mins)
Scorers *Tries:* C Quinnell, Budgett, K Morgan *Conversions:* S Jones (3) *Penalty Goals:* S Jones (4)

France: N Brusque; A Rougerie, T Marsh, D Traille, X Garbajosa; G Merceron, P Mignoni; J-J Crenca, R Ibañez (*captain*), P de Villiers, T Privat, O Brouzet, S Betsen, S Hall, I Harinordoquy *Substitutions:* F Pelous for Privat (59 mins); S Bruno for Ibañez (65 mins); A Audebert for Hall (69 mins); O Milloud for Crenca (83 mins)
Scorers *Tries:* Marsh (2), Rougerie *Conversions:* Merceron (2) *Penalty Goals:* Merceron (4), Traille *Drop Goal:* Merceron

Referee D T M McHugh (Ireland)

16 February, Twickenham
England 45 (6G 1PG)   Ireland 11 (2PG 1T)

High hopes – they came with such high hopes. All the emerald hype and expectation came crashing to earth on a sobering Twickenham afternoon. If Irish supporters really did think that their team was on track to consistently compete with the best in Europe then this crushing defeat rapidly disabused them of such a fanciful notion.

Jonny Wilkinson on his way to a 20-point haul against Ireland at Twickenham.

England scored six tries, all converted, and for 50 minutes played some of the best rugby – an intricate mix of purpose and precision – ever witnessed at HQ. Clive Woodward hailed that opening spell as the best of his four-and-a-half-year tenure. Even though there was a sense of all-round excellence, one individual stood out. Jonny Wilkinson gave a master-class in fly-half play. He scored 20 points with a try, six conversions and a penalty goal. The figures tell you little of the total assurance with which he ran the show, mixing his options with short and long passes, deft grubbers and booming cross-kicks.

There were mature performances to admire too from lock Ben Kay and tyro hooker Steve Thompson. Tight-head prop, Phil Vickery, the only change from the side that beat Scotland, also shone.

England tailed off after that devastating burst, trying to force the pace rather than attend to the basics. Ireland were hampered by an early injury to wing Geordan Murphy and later to substitute Rob Henderson.

Wilkinson opened the try-scoring with a well-worked effort in the 23rd minute. Two minutes later Ben Cohen rounded off a terrific sequence, the ball travelling 70 metres and passing through numerous pairs of hands with Austin Healey, Richard Hill and Joe Worsley most prominent. Ireland were reeling. Will Greenwood crossed for a try in the 32nd minute, Worsley for another ten minutes later.

If Ireland thought that the half-time break might enable them to regroup, then Ben Kay's try just four minutes after the interval showed the folly of such thinking. Will Greenwood wrapped up England's try-scoring in the 55th minute. Ronan O'Gara scored Ireland's try on the hour. It was no consolation whatsoever.

This was England's 14th Test victory in succession at Twickenham, overtaking the previous unbeaten run at the ground set between 1913 and 1924.

England: J Robinson; A S Healey, W J H Greenwood, M J Tindall, B C Cohen; J P Wilkinson, K P P Bracken; G C Rowntree, S Thompson, P J Vickery, M O Johnson (*captain*), B J Kay, R A Hill, J P R Worsley, N A Back *Substitutions:* J Leonard for Rowntree (16 mins); D J Grewcock for Johnson (60 mins); L W Moody for Hill (60 mins); I R Balshaw for Healey (60 mins); N Duncombe for Bracken (77 mins); C Hodgson for Wilkinson (77 mins)

Scorers *Tries:* Greenwood (2), Wilkinson, Cohen, Worsley, Kay *Conversions:* Wilkinson (6) *Penalty Goal:* Wilkinson

Ireland: G T Dempsey; G E A Murphy, B G O'Driscoll, K M Maggs, D A Hickie; D G Humphreys, P A Stringer; P M Clohessy, F J Sheahan, J J Hayes, M J Galwey (*captain*), M E O'Kelly, E R P Miller, A G Foley, D P Wallace *Substitutions:* R A J Henderson for Murphy (8 mins); R J R O'Gara for Henderson (40 mins); J S Byrne for Sheahan (52 mins); S H Easterby for Miller (57 mins); G W Longwell for Galwey (57 mins); P S Wallace for Clohessy (78 mins)

Scorers Try: O'Gara *Penalty Goals:* Humphreys (2)

Referee P R Marshall (Australia)

16 February, Stadio Flaminio, Rome
Italy 12 (4PG)   Scotland 29 (2G 5PG)

On their last visit here Scotland managed to add another ruin to the tourist itinerary with their totally unexpected 34-20 defeat in Italy's first ever match in the championship. They were on their mettle for this second visit and even though they rarely looked like being headed by their opponents it was another unconvincing display.

They came through on the back of a 24-point haul – a new Scottish championship record – by full-back Brendan Laney. The New Zealander's arrival in Scotland had aroused a storm of protest in the autumn when he was rushed into the side to face his native countrymen, the All Blacks, barely a week after arriving in Scotland.

Perhaps this was pay-back time, a chance to win the hearts of disaffected Scotsmen, although it is ironic, some might say insulting, that Laney should knock such a renowned Scot as Gavin Hastings out of the record books with this return. Laney took over goal-kicking duties after Chris Paterson made a complete hash of his first effort. He landed seven from ten attempts, his only fallibility coming from long range. Laney also scored a fine try in the closing moments, selling an outrageous dummy to cross in the corner after being teed-up by a pass from centre Andrew Henderson, who was making his first international start.

Gregor Townsend, switched back to his favoured position of fly-half in place of Duncan Hodge, scored Scotland's other try in the 73rd minute, intercepting a pass from Luca Martin and racing 40 metres to score.

Scotland, captained by Bryan Redpath in the absence of the injured Budge Pountney, had other chances to score but could not execute the final pass properly. Italy, spirited as ever, once again had to rely on the boot of Diego Dominguez, the fly-half landing four penalty goals.

Italy: P Vaccari; R Pedrazzi, Mirco Bergamasco, C Stoica, D Dallan; D Dominguez, A Troncon; G De Carli, A Moscardi (*captain*), F Pucciariello, S Dellape, C Checchinato, M Bortolami, M Phillips, Mauro Bergamasco *Substitutions:* A Moreno for Pucciariello (52 mins); A Lo Cicero for De Carli (60 mins); M Giacheri for Delappe (62 mins); L Martin for Vaccari (68 mins); R Pez for Dominguez (80 mins); A Persico for Phillips 80 mins)

Scorers *Penalty Goals:* Dominguez (4)

Scotland: B J Laney; G H Metcalfe, J G McLaren, A R Henderson, C D Paterson; G P J Townsend, B W Redpath (*captain*); T J Smith, G C Bulloch, M J Stewart, S Murray, S B Grimes, J P R White, S M Taylor, A L Mower *Substitutions:* G Graham for Stewart (60 mins); M D Leslie for Mower (70 mins)

Scorers *Tries:* Townsend, Laney *Conversions:* Laney (2) *Penalty Goals:* Laney (5)

Referee K M Deaker (New Zealand)

2 March, Stade de France, Paris
France 20 (2G 2PG)   England 15 (1G 1PG 1T)

The Grand Slam chariot slewed off its allotted path in shuddering fashion at the Stade de France. For once the vast stands of the stadium, filled to capacity with a record crowd of 79,502, shook with noise as the French supporters roared their side to victory. This was no fancy, frilly triumph, built on instinctive flair and individual brilliance. It was a hard-nosed collective effort, forged in a spirit of new-age thinking. Discipline, pragmatism and patience were the order of the French day, the touchstones of France coach, Bernard Laporte, who had been hell-bent on ridding the French game of its maverick tendencies.

France did play with wonderful zip too, but only on the back of solid approach work. They led 14-0 after just 18 minutes with tries from Gérald Merceron and Imanol Harinordoquy, an advantage extended by Merceron's 36th minute penalty goal. England were not at the races as France exploited weaknesses in their blind-side defence.

France finished with ruthless conviction. It took a classic moment of impish brilliance for England to get back into the match, Jason Robinson fixing the defence with one of his hallmark in-and-out shimmies to score just on the stroke of half-time.

There was a time when doubt and anxiety might have eaten away at French resolve and belief. Not on this occasion. Even though England hammered at them through the second-half, there was never a sense that they would give way. Only a late try by Ben Cohen, who latched on to a high, floated pass from Austin Healey, got England to within touching distance on the scoreboard.

The French back-row laid bare their substantial credentials. Serge Betsen hounded Jonny Wilkinson all afternoon, accompanied by his more illustrious partner-in-arms, Olivier Magne. Harinordoquy, the new No 8, was agile and perceptive, laying claim to the title of newcomer to the tournament. It was his well-timed support run that helped send Merceron to the posts in the ninth minute. Nine minutes later he took up position on the wide flank to be on hand to score in the corner after a sustained French attack that began when Jason Robinson was caught in possession.

Henry Paul won his first cap when coming on to replace Mike Tindall in the 39th minute. It was no day for English celebrations.

France: N Brusque; A Rougerie, T Marsh, D Traille, D Bory; G Merceron, F Galthié (*captain*); J-J Crenca, R Ibañez, P de Villiers, D Auradou, O Brouzet, S Betsen, I Harinordoquy, O Magne *Substitutions:* F Pelous for Auradou (60 mins); O Milloud for Crenca (60 mins); P Mignoni for Galthié (67 mins); O Azam for Ibañez (74 mins); R Martin for Betsen (57 to 63 mins) and for Harinordoquy (78 mins)

Scorers *Tries:* Merceron, Harinordoquy *Conversions:* Merceron (2) *Penalty Goals:* Merceron (2)

England: J Robinson; A S Healey, W J H Greenwood, M J Tindall, B C Cohen; J P Wilkinson, K P P Bracken; G C Rowntree, S Thompson, P J Vickery,

Imanol Harinordoquy, one of France's try scorers against England, is held up in a double tackle by Steve Thompson (left) and Jason Robinson (right)

M O Johnson (*captain*), B J Kay, R A Hill, J P R Worsley, N A Back *Substitutions:* H Paul for Tindall (39 mins); M E Corry for Back (temp 47 to 54 mins) and for Worsley (60 mins); J Leonard for Rowntree (74 mins); D D Luger for Wilkinson (74 mins); D E West for Thompson (74 mins); D J Grewcock for Kay (74 mins)

Scorers *Tries:* Robinson, Cohen *Conversion:* Wilkinson *Penalty Goal:* Wilkinson
Referee A Watson (South Africa)

2 March, Millennium Stadium, Cardiff Arms Park
Wales 44 (5G 3PG)   Italy 20 (2G 2PG)

A picture of deposed coach, Graham Henry, was captured on the giant screen during this game, the New Zealander clad in a red and white scarf. There was a loud, appreciative burst of applause for him. If only the mutual show of support had been evident earlier in Wales's Six Nations campaign. At least Steve Hansen, Henry's successor and a fellow Kiwi, enjoyed his first success here.

He could take some satisfaction too from the sharpness out wide of wings Craig Morgan and Dafydd James, both of whom scored first-half tries. Morgan finished a 60-metre counter-attack by touching down his own kick ahead for the opening try. There was still too much muddle on show though for Hansen's peace of mind. Scott Quinnell had an uncharacteristically slipshod game and was eventually replaced by Brett Sinkinson just after the hour mark.

Italy had their own difficulties coming into the game. They were without injured fly-half Diego Dominguez. Ramiro Pez, who spearheaded Rotherham's push for promotion, took over from Dominguez while there was a call-up too for Gert Peens, a goal-kicking full-back from South Africa. There were six changes in all.

Italy, as usual, competed well and were still in contention at 23-13 at the interval. Wales had been forced to adjust their midfield midway through the first half after centre Tom Shanklin went off injured following a thumping tackle. Rhys Williams came on and brought some snap and sparkle to the Welsh attack. Five minutes into the second half, an arcing 35-metre run saw him touchdown for a try that ended any flickering Italian hopes of an upset. It was the brightest moment of a dark season for the Welsh.

Scott Quinnell and Andy Marinos scored further tries, taking advantage of Italy being reduced to 14 men when Aaron Persico was sent to the sin-bin. Persico was the 16th Italian to be yellow-carded in 13 championship games.

Wales: K A Morgan; D R James, T Shanklin, A W N Marinos, C S Morgan; S M Jones, R Howley; I D Thomas, R C McBryde, C T Anthony, I M Gough, A P Moore, N J Budgett, L S Quinnell (*captain*), M E Williams *Substitutions:* G R Williams for Shanklin (20 mins); D Peel for Howley (52 mins); C P Wyatt for Gough (52 mins); B Williams for McBryde (59 mins); I R Harris for K Morgan (59 mins); B D Sinkinson for Quinnell (63 mins); S C John for Anthony (77 mins)

Scorers *Tries:* C Morgan, James, G R Williams, Quinnell, Marinos *Conversions:* Jones (5) *Penalty Goals:* Jones (3)

Italy: G Peens; R Pedrazzi, Mirco Bergamasco, C Stoica, N Mazzucato; R Pez, A Troncon; G de Carli, A Moscardi (*captain*), S Perugini, M Giacheri, M Bortolami, A Persico, C Checchinato, Mauro Bergamasco *Substitutions:* A Lo Cicero for de Carli (48 mins); M Phillips for Giacheri (62 mins); G Raineri for Mirco Bergamasco (65 mins); F Mazzariol for Pez (65 mins); A Benatti for Pedrazzi (67 mins); F Pucciariello for Perugini (69 mins)

Scorers *Tries:* Checchinato, Mazzariol *Conversions:* Pez, Peens *Penalty Goals:* Pez, Peens

Referee C White (England)

2 March, Lansdowne Road, Dublin
Ireland 43 (3G 4PG 2T)   Scotland 22 (1G 5PG)

The high-scoring detail of the game masks a low-quality display by both teams. Ireland once again had cause to be thankful for the keen-eyed, sharp-heeled talent of centre Brian O'Driscoll. His hat-trick of tries – the second time he has achieved such a feat in the Six Nations – was a blend of opportunism and blistering pace. Scotland more than played into his hands with some jittery handling and madcap rugby, turning the ball over or throwing sloppy passes. O'Driscoll and his mates were only too happy to make hay.

Even though Ireland were to outscore Scotland by five tries to one, they were actually trailing midway through the first half, Brendan Laney having kicked three penalty goals to one from David Humphreys. Then the mood of the match changed significantly. Scotland were penalised at a line-out and then proceeded to dispute the decision. As they were marched back 10 metres, Ireland scrum-half Peter Stringer tapped the ball and fed Humphreys who sent O'Driscoll over for a simple score.

Ten minutes later Scotland blundered again. They were turned over, Eric Miller flung a long pass out to O'Driscoll who dummied before sending Shane Horgan in for the touchdown. On the stroke of half-time, Scotland gifted another try to Ireland as Gregor Townsend's pass fell at the feet of Laney. O'Driscoll swooped and hared off towards the try-line 80 metres away.

Laney somehow kept Scotland in the game after the interval, his two penalties closing the gap to just seven points. Even though Ireland were misfiring themselves, they were still much sharper than their opponents. Three penalties from Humphreys settled their own anxieties.

Scotland added to their own downfall as a mistake by James McLaren allowed Horgan to snaffle possession, Simon Easterby eventually scoring. Martin Leslie got a try back for Scotland, but any satisfaction was wiped out by O'Driscoll's third.

Ireland: G T Dempsey; S P Horgan, B G O'Driscoll, K M Maggs, D A Hickie; D G Humphreys, P A Stringer; P M Clohessy, F J Sheahan, J J Hayes, M J Galwey (*captain*), M E O'Kelly, E R P Miller, A G Foley, D P Wallace *Substitutions:* J S Byrne for Sheahan (34 mins); S H Easterby for Miller (47 mins); G W Longwell for Galwey (70 mins); P S Wallace for Clohessy (78 mins); R J R

O'Gara for Humphreys (78 mins); G Easterby for Stringer (80 mins)

Scorers *Tries:* O'Driscoll (3), Horgan, S Easterby *Conversions:* Humphreys (2), O'Gara *Penalty Goals:* Humphreys (4)

Scotland: B J Laney; G H Metcalfe, J G McLaren, A R Henderson, C D Paterson; G P J Townsend, B W Redpath (*captain*); T J Smith, G C Bulloch, M J Stewart, S Murray, S B Grimes, J P R White, S M Taylor, A C Pountney *Substitutions:* M D Leslie for White (56 mins); G Graham for Stewart (62 mins); K M Logan for Metcalfe (71 mins)

Scorers *Try:* Leslie *Conversion:* Laney *Penalty Goals:* Laney (5)

Referee N Whitehouse (Wales)

23 March, Lansdowne Road, Dublin
Ireland 32 (1G 5PG 2T)   Italy 17 (2G 1DG)

Italy have grown used to feeding off crumbs at the Six Nations feast. Their rations of consolation were sparse, but enough to give them sustenance. Their forward pack did some damage, particularly after Gloucester prop Federico Pucciariello entered the fray. The back-line, however, was one-dimensional when it came to creativity, but superbly cussed and emphatic in its defence. Brian O'Driscoll was kept in check by the firm double-act of Cristian Stoica and Giovanni Raineri.

Italy, however, were in familiar territory when it came to falling foul of the referee. They had two players sin-binned, props Salvatore Perugini and Giampiero de Carli, both in the first-half. Perugini was fortunate to escape with only a yellow card for his head-butt on Peter Stringer, a view that was also taken by a subsequent disciplinary tribunal which suspended the L'Aquila prop for five months.

Italy only conceded three penalties despite being down to 14 men following Perugini's transgression. Their resolve slipped, however, wing Denis Dallan letting new cap John Kelly through for the first of his two tries. The Munster wing scored his second when De Carli was in the bin for punching Peter Clohessy.

Clohessy took an emotional bow as he trotted off the field four minutes from time in what was to be his last international appearance at Lansdowne Road. It had been a typical afternoon for one of Ireland's favoured sons and everyone else's favoured villains. He too was lucky to escape censure for a swinging punch as well as reckless use of the boot.

Italy rallied well to score second-half tries through De Carli and Mauro Bergamasco. Gert Peens also landed a 50-metre angled drop-goal.

Ireland: G T Dempsey; J P Kelly, B G O'Driscoll, S P Horgan, D A Hickie; D G Humphreys (*captain*), P A Stringer; P M Clohessy, J S Byrne, J J Hayes, G W Longwell, M E O'Kelly, S H Easterby, A G Foley, D P Wallace *Substitutions:* R J R O'Gara for Humphreys (temp 32 to 40 mins); P J O'Connell for O'Kelly (69 mins); P S Wallace for Clohessy (75 mins); E R P Miller for D Wallace (79 mins); T G Howe for Hickie (79 mins)

Scorers *Tries:* Kelly (2), Hickie *Conversion:* O'Gara *Penalty Goals:* Humphreys (4), O'Gara

Italy: G Peens; N Mazzucato, C Stoica, G Raineri, D Dallan; D Dominguez, A Troncon; G De Carli, A Moscardi (*captain*), S Perugini, M Bortolami, M Giacheri, A Persico, M Phillips, M Bergamasco *Substitutions:* F Pucciariello for Persico (temp 26 to 36 mins) and for Perugini (36 mins); S Dellape for Bortolami (59 mins); A De Rossi for Phillips (68 mins); S Perugini for Persico (temp 43 to 50 mins)

Scorers *Tries:* Bergamasco, De Carli *Conversions:* Dominguez (2) *Drop Goal:* Peens

Referee R Dickson (Scotland)

23 March, Twickenham
England 50 (5G 4PG 1DG)   **Wales 10** (1G 1PG)

England landed the Triple Crown for the 22nd time with this emphatic victory, a record margin for the fixture. The old bauble does not have the same romantic appeal as once it did and thumping wins of this nature do not carry the shock value that once they did either. England were so comfortably the better side, so sure of themselves and their strategy, that there was not the slightest chance of a Welsh victory once the first three minutes of play had elapsed. That was the only brief period in the match when they troubled England, only to waste the early pressure which finally ran out of steam when Andy Marinos fluffed an overlap.

It was not that Wales threw in the towel as they had in done in Dublin. They tackled stoutly for the most part and even managed a flicker of resistance when Iestyn Harris skipped through for a try in the final stages. However, they were always on the back foot and an air of almost dreary inevitability hung over proceedings as England ran in five converted tries.

They had been forced to make changes for the game, through injuries and suspension. Martin Johnson was serving his 21-day ban for punching Saracens hooker Robbie Russell, while injury had forced both Phil Vickery and Jason Robinson to withdraw. Reserve fly-half Charlie Hodgson was a late withdrawal the day before the game, as was Wales fly-half Stephen Jones. Iestyn Harris stepped back into the firing line.

Neil Back captained England and did a good job in readying his men. England led 19-3 at the break. Jonny Wilkinson started the ball rolling with a dropped goal and then put in a clever chip to open the way for Will Greenwood to score. Wilkinson converted, kicked three more penalties before half-time and finished a splendid performance with 30 points.

Wales didn't help their cause with their mistakes. Early in the second-half the ball was coughed up enabling Wilkinson to touchdown. Another turnover was punished shortly afterwards by Dan Luger, the first of his two tries around the hour mark. Tim Stimpson rounded matters off just before the final whistle, popping up outside Danny Grewcock to score. Emphatic yet strangely unfulfilling.

Austin Healey, by appearing at full-back in place of the injured Jason Robinson, matched Mike Catt's rare distinction of starting for England in four different positions.

England: A S Healey; D D Luger, W J H Greenwood, M J Tindall, B C Cohen; J P Wilkinson, K P P Bracken; G C Rowntree, S Thompson, J White, D J Grewcock, B J Kay, L W Moody, R A Hill, N A Back (*captain*) *Substitutions:* M E Corry for Kay (temp 19 to 27 mins); M J S Dawson for Bracken (59 mins); T R G Stimpson for Tindall (63 mins); D E West for Thompson (69 mins); J P R Worsley for Moody (temp 42 to 53 mins) and for Hill (80 mins)

Scorers *Tries:* Luger (2), Greenwood, Wilkinson, Stimpson *Conversions:* Wilkinson (5) *Penalty Goals:* Wilkinson (4) *Drop Goal:* Wilkinson

Wales: K A Morgan; D R James, G Thomas, A W N Marinos, C S Morgan; I R Harris, R Howley; I D Thomas, R C McBryde, C T Anthony, A P Moore, C P Wyatt, N J Budgett, L S Quinnell (*captain*), M E Williams *Substitutions:* G R Williams for G Thomas (48 mins); C L Charvis for M Williams (50 mins); G O Llewellyn for Wyatt (54 mins); D Peel for Howley (59 mins); B Williams for McBryde (69 mins)

Scorers *Try:* Harris *Conversion:* Harris *Penalty Goal:* Harris

Referee A J Cole (Australia)

23 March, Murrayfield
Scotland 10 (1G 1PG)   France 22 (2G 1PG 1T)

France sent for the cotton-wool after a win that set them up for a Grand Slam party on home soil. No sooner had the final whistle sounded than the protective wrapping was applied to their captain Fabien Galthié. The veteran scrum-half, who had made his debut 11 years earlier in 1991, was once again the pivotal figure in the new-look French side. He brought both composure and self-belief to the party as France revealed that the rigour and discipline they had shown in beating England was no fluke. They conceded only six penalties in this match, an incredible return for a team once renowned for their loose morals.

They never hit the top notes, but had enough in the locker to see off a lively but ultimately limited Scotland side who were also well-served by their own captain and scrum-half Bryan Redpath. He kept his men honest and ensured that Scotland, roared on by 65,562 spectators, finished strongly after trailing 22-3 in the 50th minute.

That lead was established on the back of two tries within four minutes of the second-half restart. An up-and-under caused no little panic in the defence from where Gérald Merceron combined with his pack to send Tony Marsh, the man-of-the-match, over in the corner. The New Zealand-born Montferrand centre had been on hand in the first half to support a fine break from fellow centre Damien Traille and finish off a move that had begun back in their own half.

France's third try in the 44th minute was a smart piece of opportunism from Galthié, the scrum-half spotting a gap near a ruck and bolting through to score from 40 metres.

Scotland had their moments too but lacked the killer instinct. Four half-chances went begging in the opening exchanges. Chris Paterson looked sharp on the wing and Brendan Laney was again solid in his kicking. He

Fabien Galthié, the French captain, launches another attack in the 44-5 defeat of Ireland in Paris.

looked vulnerable, however, in defence, but did well to take the game back to France in the last quarter, his jinking run almost resulting in a try for Redpath.

Scotland: B J Laney; G H Metcalfe, J G McLaren, J A Leslie, C D Paterson; G P J Townsend, B W Redpath (*captain*); T J Smith, G C Bulloch, M J Stewart, S Murray, J P R White, M D Leslie, S M Taylor, A C Pountney *Substitutions:* J M Petrie for M Leslie (temp 28 to 40 mins); G Graham for Stewart (60 mins); S B Grimes for Murray (62 mins); R R Russell for Bulloch (76 mins); K M Logan for McLaren (78 mins)

Scorers *Try:* Redpath *Conversion:* Laney *Penalty Goal:* Laney

France: N Brusque; A Rougerie, T Marsh, D Traille, D Bory; G Merceron, F Galthié (*captain*); J-J Crenca, R Ibañez, J-B Poux, F Pelous, O Brouzet, S Betsen, I Harinordoquy, O Magne *Substitutions:* J Marlu for Brusque (49 mins); S Marconnet for Poux (62 mins); T Privat for Pelous (74 mins); R Martin for Betsen (77 mins)

Scorers *Tries:* Marsh (2), Galthié *Conversions:* Merceron (2) *Penalty Goals:* Merceron

Referee A C Rolland (Ireland)

6 April, Stade de France, Paris
France 44 (2G 5PG 3T)   Ireland 5 (1T)

The talking started only when the final whistle had blown. Only then were the words Grand Slam allowed to be used. France had taken nothing for granted all through the championship, one that was claimed with a regal sweep in their final match. If they had faltered in the early stages of the tournament, then France were intent on leaving a good and lasting impression.

They might well have scored at least three more tries, heroic tackling from Brian O'Driscoll denying them at the death on several occasions. There was real punch and purpose in their play, composure too. Once again the most significant statistic of the day was the one that showed that France had conceded only six penalties, a sign of self-discipline and maturity.

There was another splendid showing from the middle five – half-backs Fabien Galthié and Gérald Merceron who formed a perfect link with their back-row confrères Serge Betsen, Olivier Magne and Imanol Harinordoquy. So often all five were involved in the build-up to tries, Betsen netting two himself. For Magne, this was his third Grand Slam.

Ireland were chasing shadows for much of the game. Their scrum was under terrible strain throughout, a sobering thought for Peter Clohessy on his last international appearance. Keith Wood, restored to the side after a calf injury, won the occasional troublesome clatter and even scored with one typical short-range burst in the 10th minute. But that was the sum of Ireland's attacking defiance.

It was one-way, all-blue traffic. A deft chip and gather by Merceron caused enough panic in the Irish defence for Betsen to eventually score in the second minute. Wood's try caused few ripples. Merceron knocked over a couple of goals before Damien Traille and Tony Marsh combined well to

Tony Marsh, the New Zealand-born French centre, breaks through the tackle of Keith Gleeson in the Grand Slam win against Ireland.

send Nicolas Brusque to the line. A searing blast of pace from Aurélien Rougeris took him to the try-line. Further kicks by Merceron gave France a deserved 28-5 half-time lead.

It was the same story after the break. Betsen scored his second after powerful work by the forwards. Wonderful handling by Marsh in particular cleared the way for Brusque's try. Glorious stuff.

France: N Brusque; A Rougerie, T Marsh, D Traille, D Bory; G Merceron, F Galthié (*captain*); J-J Crenca, R Ibañez, P de Villiers, F Pelous, O Brouzet, S Betsen, I Harinordoquy, O Magne *Substitutions:* J-B Poux for Crenca (64 mins); F Gelez for Merceron (64 mins); D Auradou for Brouzet (72 mins); J Marlu for Bory (76 mins); O Azam for Ibañez (76 mins); R Martin for Magne (76 mins); P Mignoni for Galthié (76 mins)

Scorers *Tries:* Betsen (2), Brusque (2), Rougerie *Conversions:* Merceron (2) *Penalty Goals:* Merceron (4), Gelez

Ireland: G T Dempsey; S P Horgan, B G O'Driscoll, R A J Henderson, D A Hickie; D G Humphreys, P A Stringer; P M Clohessy, K G M Wood (*captain*), J J Hayes, G W Longwell, M E O'Kelly, S H Easterby, A G Foley, D P Wallace *Substitutions:* K D Gleeson for D Wallace (48 mins); R J R O'Gara for Humphreys (48 mins); P S Wallace for Clohessy (62 mins); P J O'Connell for Longwell (64 mins)

Scorer *Try:* Wood

Referee P D O'Brien (New Zealand)

6 April, Millennium Stadium, Cardiff Arms Park
Wales 22 (1G 5PG) Scotland 27 (1G 5PG 1T)

This was Bill McLaren's sign-off to championship rugby. Even the resonant tones of the great man could do little to enhance the poor quality of the game down below. There was a false air of excitement about proceedings with the lead changing hands four times in the final quarter before Scotland edged clear through injury time kicks from Brendan Laney and Duncan Hodge. Those kicks didn't even manage to get people to the edge of their seats. Many had already vacated them long before that.

There was another farewell to record, to one of Wales's finest, scrum-half Robert Howley. He, alongside captain for the day, the oft-discarded Colin Charvis, did manage to bring a few touches of class to the event. Howley was substituted after 65 minutes. He was well out of it.

Wales's forward-defence cost them the game. Twice they were done by one of the most obvious ploys in the book, Scotland hooker Gordon Bulloch burrowing over from line-out drives for two tries within the space of ten minutes, the first of them coming at the end of the first quarter.

At that point Wales led 9-0 through three smartly taken penalty goals from Stephen Jones. The Wales fly-half was also instrumental in setting up his side's only try, stealing away with the ball from a ruck in the 45th minute. From there crisp handling among Howley, Charvis, Iestyn Harris and Martyn Williams put Rhys Williams clear. It was a rare moment of illumination on another dark day for Welsh rugby. Stephen Jones popped over another two penalties to see his side in front 22-21 with ten minutes remaining. That was as good as it got.

Wales: K A Morgan; G R Williams, M Taylor, A W N Marinos, C S Morgan; S M Jones, R Howley; I D Thomas, B Williams, C T Anthony, I M Gough, A P Moore, N J Budgett, C L Charvis (*captain*), M E Williams *Substitutions:* C P Wyatt for Moore (12 mins); Gavin Thomas for Budgett (40 mins); R C McBryde for B Williams (43 mins); I R Harris for Marinos (43 mins); S C John for I Thomas (57 mins); D Peel for Howley (66 mins); D R James for C Morgan (72 mins)

Scorers *Try*: R Williams *Conversion:* Jones *Penalty Goals:* Jones (5)

Scotland: B J Laney; K M Logan, J G McLaren, J A Leslie, C D Paterson; G P J Townsend, B W Redpath (*captain*); T J Smith, G C Bulloch, M J Stewart, S Murray, J P R White, M D Leslie, S M Taylor, A C Pountney *Substitutions:* G Graham for Stewart (40 mins); S B Grimes for White (57 mins); G H Metcalfe for Logan (60 mins); J M Petrie for M Leslie (71 mins); R R Russell for Bulloch (75 mins); D W Hodge for Laney (84 mins)

Scorers *Tries:* Bulloch (2) *Conversion:* Laney *Penalty Goals:* Laney (4), Hodge

Referee J Jutge (France)

7 April, Stadio Flaminio, Rome
Italy 9 (3PG)   England 45 (6G 1PG)

The party was happening elsewhere and the players seemed to know it. France's victory the previous day had settled the championship. There was only pride at stake here and England did just enough to settle that account. Italy, too, in their own way. They defended hard and long but offered little creative intent. They tackled through to the final whistle apart from their now routine, occasional lapses of concentration. Three times in the first half they fell off the tackle or lost their alignment and three times England took full advantage with tries from Will Greenwood, Ben Cohen and Jason Robinson.

England were comfortably in control of the game by half-time. They were well enough set to bring on a heavyweight platoon of four former England captains, Martin Johnson, Lawrence Dallaglio, Matt Dawson and Jason Leonard all taking to the field at the same time in the 56th minute. Johnson, returning from a 21-day suspension, had been overlooked for a starting place in favour of Danny Grewcock at lock. Neil Back again captained the side.

The quartet soon made their mark, Dallaglio scoring a try within four minutes after good pressurising work by Johnson. There was a collector's item among England's six tries with Dawson bamboozling the Italian defence by chipping over their heads from a short-range penalty for an alert Greenwood to run on to and touchdown. Greenwood had another fine game, his two tries giving him five for the championship and seeing him finish as the tournament's top try scorer for the second year in succession. England's sixth try was scored by Austin Healey in injury time after a fine angled run by Greenwood.

This was Italy's 14th successive defeat in the championship and was to be Brad Johnstone's last match in charge.

Italy: G Peens; N Mazzucato, C Stoica, G Raineri, D Dallan; D Dominguez, A Troncon; G de Carli, A Moscardi (*captain*), F Pucciariello, M Bortolami, M Giacheri, A Persico, M Phillips, Mauro Bergamasco *Substitutions:* C Zanoletti for Raineri (48 mins); A de Rossi for Phillips (48 mins); C Nieto for Pucciariello (59 mins); S Dellape for Giacheri (59 mins); R Pez for Peens (73 mins); A Moretti for Moscardi (76 mins); F Pucciariello for De Carli (80 mins); M Mazzantini for Stoica (82 mins)

Scorer *Penalty Goals:* Dominguez (3)

England: J Robinson; D D Luger, W J H Greenwood, M J Tindall, B C Cohen; J P Wilkinson, K P P Bracken; G C Rowntree, S Thompson, J White, D J Grewcock, B J Kay, L W Moody, R A Hill, N A Back (*captain*) *Substitutions:* M O Johnson for Grewcock (temp 19 to 23 mins and 55 mins); M J S Dawson for Bracken (55 mins); J Leonard for Rowntree (55 mins); L B N Dallaglio for Back (55 mins); A S Healey for Cohen (69 mins); D E West for Thompson 72 mins); C Hodgson for Tindall (76 mins)

Scorers *Tries:* Greenwood (2), Cohen, Robinson, Dallaglio, Healey *Conversions:* Wilkinson (5), Dawson *Penalty Goal:* Wilkinson

Referee M Lawrence (South Africa)

INTERNATIONAL CHAMPIONSHIP RECORDS 1883-2002

Previous winners:

1883 England; 1884 England; 1885 Not completed; 1886 England & Scotland; 1887 Scotland; 1888 Not completed; 1889 Not completed; 1890 England & Scotland; 1891 Scotland; 1892 England; 1893 Wales; 1894 Ireland; 1895 Scotland; 1896 Ireland; 1897 Not completed; 1898 Not completed; 1899 Ireland; 1900 Wales; 1901 Scotland; 1902 Wales; 1903 Scotland; 1904 Scotland; 1905 Wales; 1906 Ireland & Wales; 1907 Scotland; 1908 Wales; 1909 Wales; 1910 England; 1911 Wales; 1912 England & Ireland; 1913 England; 1914 England; 1920 England & Scotland & Wales; 1921 England; 1922 Wales; 1923 England; 1924 England; 1925 Scotland; 1926 Scotland & Ireland; 1927 Scotland & Ireland; 1928 England; 1929 Scotland; 1930 England; 1931 Wales; 1932 England & Ireland & Wales; 1933 Scotland; 1934 England; 1935 Ireland; 1936 Wales; 1937 England; 1938 Scotland; 1939 England & Ireland & Wales; 1947 England & Wales; 1948 Ireland; 1949 Ireland; 1950 Wales; 1951 Ireland; 1952 Wales; 1953 England; 1954 England & Wales & France; 1955 Wales & France; 1956 Wales; 1957 England; 1958 England; 1959 France; 1960 England & France; 1961 France; 1962 France; 1963 England; 1964 Scotland & Wales; 1965 Wales; 1966 Wales; 1967 France; 1968 France; 1969 Wales; 1970 Wales & France; 1971 Wales; 1972 Not completed; 1973 Five Nations tie; 1974 Ireland; 1975 Wales; 1976 Wales; 1977 France; 1978 Wales; 1979 Wales; 1980 England; 1981 France; 1982 Ireland; 1983 Ireland & France; 1984 Scotland; 1985 Ireland; 1986 Scotland & France; 1987 France; 1988 Wales & France; 1989 France; 1990 Scotland; 1991 England; 1992 England; 1993 France; 1994 Wales; 1995 England; 1996 England; 1997 France; 1998 France; 1999 Scotland; 2000 England; 2001 England; 2002 France.

England have won the title outright 24 times; Wales 22; Scotland 14; France 13; Ireland 10; Italy 0.

Triple Crown winners:

England (22 times) 1883, 1884, 1892, 1913, 1914, 1921, 1923, 1924, 1928, 1934, 1937, 1954, 1957, 1960, 1980, 1991, 1992, 1995, 1996, 1997, 1998, 2002

Wales (17 times) 1893, 1900, 1902, 1905, 1908, 1909, 1911, 1950, 1952, 1965, 1969, 1971, 1976, 1977, 1978, 1979, 1988.

Scotland (10 times) 1891, 1895, 1901, 1903, 1907, 1925, 1933, 1938, 1984, 1990.

Ireland (Six times) 1894, 1899, 1948, 1949, 1982, 1985.

Grand Slam winners:

England (11 times) 1913, 1914, 1921, 1923, 1924, 1928, 1957, 1980, 1991, 1992, 1995.

Wales (Eight times) 1908, 1909, 1911, 1950, 1952, 1971, 1976, 1978.

France (Seven times) 1968, 1977, 1981, 1987, 1997, 1998, 2002

Scotland (Three times) 1925, 1984, 1990.

Ireland (Once) 1948.

Chief Records

Record	Detail		Set
Most team points in season	229 by England	in five matches	2001
Most team tries in season	29 by England	in five matches	2001
Highest team score	80 by England	80-23 v Italy	2001
Biggest team win	57 by England	80-23 v Italy	2001
Most team tries in match	12 by Scotland	v Wales	1887
Most appearances	56 for Ireland	C M H Gibson	1964 – 1979
Most points in matches	406 for Wales	N R Jenkins	1991 – 2001
Most points in season	89 for England	J P Wilkinson	2001
Most points in match	35 for England	J P Wilkinson	v Italy, 2001
Most tries in matches	24 for Scotland	I S Smith	1924 – 1933
Most tries in season	8 for England	C N Lowe	1914
	8 for Scotland	I S Smith	1925
Most tries in match	5 for Scotland	G C Lindsay	v Wales, 1887
Most cons in matches	61 for England	J P Wilkinson	1998 – 2002
Most cons in season	24 for England	J P Wilkinson	2001
Most cons in match	9 for England	J P Wilkinson	v Italy, 2001
Most pens in matches	93 for Wales	N R Jenkins	1991 – 2001
Most pens in season	18 for England	S D Hodgkinson	1991
	18 for England	J P Wilkinson	2000
	18 for France	G Merceron	2002
Most pens in match	7 for England	S D Hodgkinson	v Wales, 1991
	7 for England	C R Andrew	v Scotland,
	7 for England	J P Wilkinson	1995v France, 1999
	7 for Wales	N R Jenkins	v Italy, 2000
	7 for France	G Merceron	v Italy, 2002
Most drops in matches	9 for France	J-P Lescarboura	1982 – 1988
	9 for England	C R Andrew	1985 – 1997
Most drops in season	5 for France	G Camberabero	1967
	5 for Italy	D Dominguez	2000
	5 for Wales	N R Jenkins	2001
Most drops in match	3 for France	P Albaladejo	v Ireland, 1960
	3 for France	J-P Lescarboura	v England, 1985
	3 for Italy	D Dominguez	v Scotland 2000
	3 for Wales	N R Jenkins	v Scotland 2001

THE SIX NATIONS CHAMPIONSHIP 2000–2002: COMPOSITE THREE-SEASON TABLE

	P	W	D	L	Pts
England	15	12	0	3	24
France	15	10	0	5	20
Ireland	15	10	0	5	20
Wales	15	6	1	8	13
Scotland	15	5	1	9	11
Italy	15	1	0	14	2

THE 2002 TRI NATIONS

A Tale of Three Nations
Paul Dobson

It was the best of Tri Nations. It was the worst of Tri Nations. It was the most dramatic of Tri Nations. It was the most controversial of Tri Nations, as Dickens may have recorded it. There were times when it shot up to the stars, and times when it plunged into foetid mud. It was never dull.

There were thrilling matches – as in Australia's last-minute win over New Zealand, New Zealand's last-minute win over South Africa and South Africa's last-minute win over Australia. Where in 2001 only 13 tries were scored in the Tri Nations, this year there were 32. South Africa showed the greatest improvement in this regard, going from two tries in 2001 to 13 in 2002.

It was a Tri Nations which any of the three sides could have won, but in the end victory went to the steadiest – the All Blacks, who continued, in personnel and style, where the all-conquering Crusaders had left off at the end of their successful Super Twelve campaign.

All teams were in with a chance up to the penultimate match. Then New Zealand beat and eliminated South Africa. Australia had an outside chance of winning the title at the last match, but fell well short. To overtake New Zealand they needed to beat South Africa by at least 26 points and score at least four tries. They lost and scored three tries.

The surprise package turned out to be the Springboks, a young team that began with a hiding from the All Blacks before steadily improving. South Africans have always prided themselves on their defence. This team scored tries but leaked them at a greater rate. They scored the most tries in the competition and had the most scored against them. Astonishingly they scored nine tries against Australia's adamantine defence, where New Zealand scored only one. New Zealand conceded fewest tries (six) and conceded fewest penalties.

Thrilling matches, exciting tries and the emergence of great new talents – these were the highlights of the Tri Nations. The lowlights were the squabbling on and off the field. The players let their emotions flow over at Wellington and then at Brisbane when it seemed that the age of the flare-up and the mob fight were back. In the midst of it all there was an inquiry into the Ben Tune affair. Tune had tested positive for the ingestion of a banned substance early in 2001, but it all came suddenly to light in 2002 with much embarrassment for the player and his unions.

The centre of the controversy that overflowed from on-field to off-field was the refereeing. It started after the Wellington Test when the South

African management criticised Stuart Dickinson's refereeing. Then Andrew Mehrtens told André Watson in public that he should be ashamed of himself. But the nadir came in Durban when refereeing, a patriotic paranoia in South Africa, was struck a physical blow. For the first time in a rugby international a spectator ran onto the field and assaulted the referee.

Before and after matches teams – coaches and players – cast verbal slings and arrows at each other with much immature posturing, challenging and threatening, thus fuelling feuds in the manner of professional wrestling. SANZAR looked a rocky ship, kept afloat by the sheer brilliance of its players.

Tri Nations is a great breeding ground for new talent. Some of those who emerged in 2002 are Aaron Mauger, Richie McCaw and Simon Maling of New Zealand, Nathan Sharpe and Mat Rogers of Australia for whom George Smith showed his commitment and value. Brent Russell, Werner Greeff, André Pretorius, Lawrence Sephaka and Jannes Labuschagne stood out for South Africa while their loose forward Joe van Niekerk may just have been the brightest of the whole tournament.

Some of the more seasoned players remained golden – Andrew Mehrtens, Justin Marshall, Chris Jack, Scott Robertson, Greg Somerville, Ben Tune, Matthew Burke, Bill Young, George Gregan, Stephen Larkham, Corné Krige and, rejuvenated, Bob Skinstad.

It was a brilliant but flawed Tri Nations.

Tri Nations 2002: Final Table

	P	W	D	L	F	A	Bonus Points	Pts
New Zealand	4	3	0	1	97	65	3	15
Australia	4	2	0	2	91	86	3	11
South Africa	4	1	0	3	103	140	3	7

Points: win 4; draw 2; four or more tries, or defeat by seven or fewer points 1

13 July, Jade Stadium, Christchurch
New Zealand 12 (4PG)   **Australia 6** (2PG)

Tri Nations 2002 kicked off in pouring rain and agonising cold at Jade Stadium in Christchurch. Despite the weather it was a great clash – thoroughly absorbing as two great teams battled the elements, themselves and their opponents. It was a match of great competence from both sides.

In the end victory went to the dominant pack and the superior boot. The All Black pack – really the Crusaders in different jerseys – beat the Wallaby pack, save only at the line-outs, and two boots capitalised on the forwards' domination – those of Andrew Mehrtens and Aaron Mauger. Their tactical kicking was better than that of their opponents, and Mehrtens's goal-kicking was more accurate than Matthew Burke's.

Burke missed two kicks at goal, Mehrtens none. But it went beyond that as Mehrtens and Mauger found awkward places to boot the ball behind the Wallabies. But for a lesser full-back than Chris Latham, the Wallabies would have been severely beaten.

Mehrtens put his side ahead in only the third minute of the match when he goaled a penalty at a tackle and then added another to make it 6-0. Burke, who had missed one, then managed a penalty just before half-time to make the score 6-3 at the break. Mehrtens made it 9-3 and Burke made it 9-6 with a second penalty against Richard McCaw, the young, ball-greedy New Zealand flanker. Mehrtens scored again and Burke missed again.

Then, with only eight minutes to go there was drama. Stephen Larkham charged down a left-footed kick by Mauger. Daniel Herbert picked up the skidding ball with great skill and played inside to Jeremy Paul, who was steaming up in support. Before the ball reached Paul, Mark Robinson, the New Zealand outside-centre, enveloped Paul who was then some 18 metres from the goal-line. The Wallabies wanted a penalty try. The referee agreed that the situation had try-scoring potential, but without sufficiently high probability. He penalised Robinson and sent him to the sin bin.

For the last eight minutes the Wallabies attacked and the All Blacks defended frantically. It was a drama-filled time when the cold and the rain were forgotten in the heroics of two great teams. At length, the All Blacks nudged the Wallabies back into their own half and forced a turnover. Gratefully Justin Marshall gathered the ball and hoofed it into touch.

For the first time since 1991 a match between New Zealand and Australia failed to produce a single try and yet it was an absorbing encounter. The concentration of the two teams seemed unblinking in its absolute determination. In the ghastly weather the All Blacks conceded only eight scrums, won the turn-over count substantially and were penalised less often. They were more controlled where it counted. On the other hand they lost seven of their own line-outs.

The win gave New Zealand hope of wresting the Bledisloe Cup from the tight grip of the Wallabies, who took a bonus point for losing by fewer than seven points. It also suggested that New Zealand were on track to win the Tri Nations which the Wallabies had won for the previous two years.

New Zealand: C M Cullen; D C Howlett, M P Robinson, A J D Mauger, C S Ralph; A P Mehrtens, J W Marshall; D N Hewett, M G Hammett, G M Somerville, C R Jack, T S Maling R D Thorne (*captain*), S M Robertson, R H McCaw

Scorer *Penalty Goals:* Mehrtens (4)

Australia: C E Latham; B N Tune, M C Burke, D J Herbert, S A Mortlock; S J Larkham, G M Gregan (*captain*); W K Young, J A Paul, E P Noriega, N C Sharpe, J B G Harrison, O D A Finegan, R S T Kefu, G B Smith
Substitutions: M S Rogers for Mortlock (40 mins); E J Flatley for Herbert (temp 59 to 69 mins) and for Larkham (79 mins); M J Cockbain for Finegan (61 mins); D J Lyons for Smith (65 mins); B J Darwin for Noriega (69 mins)

Scorer *Penalty Goals:* Burke (2)

Referee J I Kaplan (South Africa)

20 July, WestpacTrust Stadium, Wellington
New Zealand 41 (2G 3PG 1DG 3T) South Africa 20 (2G 1PG 1DG)

After the try-drought in the Christchurch wet, this match produced seven tries in the Wellington wind. It was a match of much drama with plenty to evoke excitement, argument, cheers, annoyance and groans. It even had three scuffles – not the flare-ups of yesteryear, but still moments of heated argument and much shoving.

The young Springbok side started in thrilling fashion, dominating the first twenty minutes and scoring a try of rare refinement when full-back Werner Greeff tiptoed and accelerated through the New Zealand defence to score at the posts. At one stage South Africa led 13-3, but back came the unmoved New Zealand machine, efficient, clever and making telling use of every opportunity until the score was 21-13 at half-time.

In that period New Zealand scored two tries, one by Doug Howlett after a sustained attack and one by Mark Hammett after a clever ploy at the front of the line-out which sent the legal boffins into debate for several days afterwards, for there may well have been irregularities with Hammett's throw.

There were two happy bounces in the second half, to give each side a try. Reuben Thorne scored the first when several fortuitous bounces were turned into gold by the alchemy of quick phases. Marius Joubert claimed the second when an attempt to kick a penalty into touch failed hopelessly and the big centre followed up, took a sympathetic bounce and scored. He was soon afterwards sent to the sin bin for a high tackle, which also led to an unedifying outbreak of emotions. While he was away the All Blacks attacked sharply and Justin Marshall raced over for the try which gave his side a bonus point.

After Joubert's return the Springboks attacked with force and were over the line when Richard McCaw took the ball from their hands and started a promising counterattack. From a line-out five metres from the Springbok line big Scott Robertson, the colossus of the match, scored a try to make it 41-20.

The defeat in Wellington was the second highest the Springboks had ever suffered at the hands of the All Blacks, surpassed only by the 28-0 loss in 1999. The match was more even than the score suggests. It was just that the All Blacks had their priorities right and grabbed every opportunity to score.

New Zealand: C M Cullen; D C Howlett, M P Robinson, A J D Mauger, C S Ralph; A P Mehrtens, J W Marshall; D N Hewett, M G Hammett, G M Somerville, C R Jack, T S Maling, R D Thorne (*captain*), S M Robertson, R H McCaw *Substitutions:* J F Umaga for Robinson (30 mins); T E Willis for Hammett (48 mins); J T Lomu for Howlett (60 mins); R K Willis for Maling (70 mins); B T Kelleher for Marshall (74 mins); S R Broomhall for McCaw (74 mins); J M McDonnell for Somerville (78 mins)

Scorers *Tries:* Howlett, Hammett, Thorne, Marshall, Robertson *Conversions:* Mehrtens (2) *Penalty Goals:* Mehrtens (3) *Dropped Goal:* Mehrtens

South Africa: W W Greeff; C S Terblanche, M C Joubert, D W Barry, D B Hall; A S Pretorius, J H Conradie; L D Sephaka, J Dalton, W Meyer, J J Labuschagne, V Matfield, C P J Krige (*captain*), R B Skinstad, J C van Niekerk *Substitutions:* A-H le Roux for Sephaka (29 mins); A A Jacobs for Barry (temp 34 to 40 mins and 71 mins); A J Venter for Matfield (63 mins); S J Rautenbach for Meyer (63 mins); N A de Kock for Conradie (70 mins)

Scorers *Tries:* Greeff, Joubert *Conversions:* Pretorius (2) *Penalty Goal:* Pretorius *Dropped Goal:* Greeff

Referee S J Dickinson (Australia)

27 July, The Gabba, Brisbane
Australia 38 (3G 4PG 1T)   South Africa 27 (2G 1PG 2T)

Set against the ugliness of an unseemly week in SANZAR rugby the match was a glittering jewel, though a flawed one. During the week all three nations produced unhappiness for rugby as the South Africans complained about Stuart Dickinson's refereeing of their New Zealand match and then slung challenges at the Wallabies. The Australians were rocked by the news of Ben Tune's ingestion of a banned substance during last year's Super Twelve and his Union's subsequent concealment of the results of the testing. There was bloodletting in New Zealand when the report of Sir Thomas Eichelbaum accused the NZRFU's council for the country's loss of co-host status for the final round of the 2003 Rugby World Cup, followed by the resignations and continued dissatisfaction amongst the provincial unions.

The match at the Gabba could have made up for all of that as it produced moments of sublime rugby, flawed by a mad outbreak of uncontrolled emotion that ended with yellow cards for Werner Greeff of South Africa and Justin Harrison and Jeremy Paul of Australia followed by a retrospective 'yellow card' for Faan Rautenbach of South Africa after a post-match citing and hearing.

Australia started the match as if it were a one-horse race. They dominated possession and from a scrum some clever positioning sent Ben Tune powering over for the first try after four minutes. Stirling Mortlock carved his way over for the second ten minutes later and then Chris Latham came in from full-back to weigh in with a third. After 26 minutes Australia led 28-3. But they did not score another try for the next 60 minutes.

Most of the intervening hour belonged to South Africa who raced in three of the most thrilling tries from far out to lead Australia four-three on the try stakes. But still they were six points behind as the penalty count flowed 20-8 against them.

The first Springbok try started near their own goal line and Marius Joubert was inside his own ten-metre line before he broke through the midfield, skated past Latham and scored under the posts. Joubert's second try was more orthodox as the Springboks attacked and he swept over in Latham's tackle. Next, full-back Greeff caught an up-and-under and the Springboks started a counter-attack from well inside their own half. De Wet

Barry kicked ahead, Breyton Paulse gathered as Tune fumbled and fed Bob Skinstad who stretched over for a try in the tackle.

Once more the Springboks attacked wide from out of defence and Joubert sent replacement Brent Russell scurrying down the touch-line. As he out-sprinted the cover, he stumbled in Larkham's despairing ankle tap before recovering smartly to cross for another thrilling try. The Springboks had now secured a bonus point and at 33-27 with seven minutes left were within sight of a second bonus point and possible victory.

Australia did not yield. The Springboks, seeking to attack from inside their own half, fluffed a pass and the Wallabies took advantage. They eschewed a penalty kick at goal after the siren had wailed, opted for a scrum and eventually Latham powered through two tackles to score, underscoring yet again his match-winning worth.

Australia: C E Latham; B N Tune, M C Burke, D J Herbert, S A Mortlock; S J Larkham, G M Gregan (*captain*); W K Young, J A Paul, E P Noriega, N C Sharpe, J B G Harrison, O D A Finegan, R S T Kefu, G B Smith
Substitutions: B J Cannon for Smith (temp 34 to 42 mins); D J Lyons for Finegan (61 mins); M S Rogers for Burke (68 mins); M J Cockbain for Sharpe (70 mins); B J Darwin for Noriega (70 mins); E J Flatley for Larkham (78 mins)

Scorers *Tries:* Latham (2), Tune, Mortlock *Conversions:* Burke (3) *Penalty Goals:* Burke (3), Mortlock

South Africa: W W Greeff, C S Terblanche, M C Joubert, D W Barry, B J Paulse; A S Pretorius, J H Conradie; L D Sephaka, J Dalton, S J Rautenbach, J J Labuschagne, V Matfield, C P J Krige *(captain)*, R B Skinstad, J C van Niekerk
Substitutions: H Scholtz for Krige (31 mins); A-H le Roux for Sephaka (61 mins); G J D du Preez for Dalton (71 mins); R B Russell for Terblanche (71 mins); A A Jacobs for Greeff (74 mins)

Scorers *Tries:* Joubert (2), Skinstad, Russell *Conversions:* Pretorius (2) *Penalty Goal:* Pretorius

Referee S J Lander (England)

3 August, Telstra Stadium Australia, Sydney
Australia 16 (2PG 2T)   New Zealand 14 (3PG 1T)

The Bledisloe Cup beckoned New Zealand to victory and the opportunity to clinch the Tri Nations before setting off for South Africa. It looked to be happening till, after the no-side siren, the touch judges' flags signalled a successful penalty goal and a thrilling Australian victory. Matthew Burke's boot scored the winning penalty goal on a day of poor kicking in the swirling wind at Telstra Stadium, its name recently changed from Stadium Australia.

Two streakers arrived on the field and sought to put Andrew Mehrtens off as he prepared to kick at goal with New Zealand 11-8 up. Mehrtens missed. The streakers were advertising Vodafone, Telstra's opposition, and apparently did so with some sort of collusion from the CEO of Vodafone.

The day was dry but the wind made great goal-kickers mediocre. Mehrtens missed three penalty kicks at goal and a conversion, Burke a penalty goal and two conversions – all kicks well within their range.

The Wallabies dominated the first half. After 17 minutes they attacked with several fast phases after a poor clearance to touch by Christian Cullen and a sharp run by Ben Tune. Young lock Nathan Sharpe powered over for a try in a good position. The Wallabies came close to scoring again when they attacked from a five-metre lineout and Jeremy Paul was actually sent over in the corner, but Patricio Noriega was penalised.

A late tackle by Chris Jack on Tune gave Burke the opportunity to put the Wallabies 8-0 ahead, though two minutes later Mehrtens pulled the score back to 8-3 after George Smith was penalised at a tackle.

The All Blacks took the lead in the second half after Chris Latham had been penalised for holding on, and then Richard McCaw crossed for a try that came from a horrible Wallaby error. The throw-in to a five-metre lineout was too high, too long and skew. McCaw surged onto it and dived over the line unchallenged for the try which made the score 11-8 to New Zealand.

It became 14-8 with 17 minutes to go when Toutai Kefu was penalised for coming in at the side. The Wallabies then brought on fresh legs and attacked relentlessly and quickly but calmly. The New Zealanders defended with efficient calm, but under it all there was a storm of excitement brewing as the Wallabies carried the ball to victory. Stephen Larkham found a way through a maze of defenders but was brought down. The ball went to the Wallaby left where Rogers weaved out and in and dotted down for the try that made it 14-13. Burke's conversion attempt hit the upright and bounced out.

In the end the match was decided by a penalty kick. Leon MacDonald used his hand to try to haul the ball back in a ruck and was penalised. It was roughly the same kick as the missed conversion attempt. This time Burke steadied and kicked with conviction the goal that kept the Bledisloe Cup in Australia. They had scored two tries to one, which suggests that the better side won. In addition their tries had been well-constructed.

Australia: C E Latham; B N Tune, M C Burke, D J Herbert, S A Mortlock; S J Larkham, G M Gregan (*captain*); W K Young, J A Paul, E P Noriega, N C Sharpe, J B G Harrison, O D A Finegan, R S T Kefu, G B Smith
Substitutions: E J Flatley for Larkham (temp 56 to 61 mins); D J Lyons for Finegan (58 mins); M S Rogers for Latham (61 mins); B J Darwin for Noriega (63 mins); M J Cockbain for Sharpe (63 mins)

Scorers *Tries:* Sharpe, Rogers *Penalty Goals:* Burke (2)

New Zealand: C M Cullen; D C Howlett, J F Umaga, A J D Mauger, C S Ralph; A P Mehrtens, J W Marshall; D N Hewett, T E Willis, G M Somerville, C R Jack, T S Maling, R D Thorne (*captain*), S M Robertson, R H McCaw
Substitutions: M R Holah for McCaw (temp 50 to 58 mins); J M McDonnell for Somerville (73 mins); D P E Gibson for Mehrtens (79 mins); L R MacDonald for Cullen (79 mins)

Scorers *Try:* McCaw *Penalty Goals:* Mehrtens (3)
Referee A Watson (South Africa)

10 August, ABSA Stadium, King's Park, Durban
South Africa 23 (2G 2PG 1DG)   New Zealand 30 (2G 2PG 2T)

Like a wrong note in a beautiful piece of music the bizarre intrusion of a spectator in the action in Durban was all the uglier for the thrilling quality of the rugby played. Pieter van Zyl of Potchefstroom gained historic notoriety when he invaded the pitch and tackled Ireland's David McHugh early in the second half. The referee dislocated his shoulder and was replaced by a touch judge. Van Zyl was charged with assault intent to cause grievous bodily harm and banned for life from watching rugby in South Africa. For most South Africans it was a cause of acute embarrassment.

The rugby was of high quality on a warm wind-free day in Durban in front of a sell-out crowd. New Zealand attacked first, but lost the ball and South Africa raced almost the length of the field. Dean Hall made most of the running and in the end Neil de Kock scored. South Africa led 7-0 after only three minutes, but it was not long before New Zealand replied when Andrew Mehrtens broke sharply and Tana Umaga sent Leon MacDonald in for an unconverted try.

The first controversy of the afternoon was the award of a penalty try to New Zealand after De Wet Barry had tackled Umaga high. That put New Zealand 12-7 in the lead. It was the fourth penalty try against South Africa in Tests and the second in 2002. The next controversy came when James Dalton was penalised for obstructive running when the Springboks looked certain to score.

They did eventually score again through André Pretorius, who first goaled a penalty and then chased his own kick to score a try which he converted. South Africa led 17-12, but New Zealand drew level five minutes before half-time when Umaga ran well to take out two defenders and sent Doug Howlett over far out.

There was a long break early in the second half after Van Zyl had attacked Dave McHugh. Eventually Chris White of England took over the refereeing. Pretorius and then Mehrtens goaled penalties, before Pretorius again put the Springboks ahead with a dropped goal. He thus became the second South African, after Joel Stransky against Australia in the 1995 Rugby World Cup opening match, to score a full house in a Test match – try, conversion, dropped goal and penalty goal.

At this stage the Springboks were well on top and could well have put the game beyond doubt, but the All Blacks finished more strongly. First Mehrtens tied the scores with a penalty goal. Then they surged over the line in a group. The matter was referred to Jim Fleming, the television match official, who was unable to determine if a try had been scored. Soon afterwards Aaron Mauger cut through from close in to score a try after a sustained attack, giving the All Blacks a bonus point.

There were still six minutes to play but the score remained unchanged.

South Africa: W W Greeff; B J Paulse, M C Joubert, D W Barry, D B Hall; A S Pretorius, N A de Kock; L D Sephaka, J Dalton, W Meyer, J J Labuschagne, A J Venter, C P J Krige *(captain)*, R B Skinstad, J C van Niekerk *Substitutions:* R B Russell for Barry (50 mins); J H Conradie for De Kock (50 mins); A-H le Roux for Sephaka (58 mins); S J Rautenbach for Meyer (58 mins); H Scholtz for Krige (74 mins); V Matfield for Venter (74 mins)

Scorers *Tries:* De Kock, Pretorius *Conversions:* Pretorius (2) *Penalty Goals:* Pretorius (2) *Dropped Goal:* Pretorius

New Zealand: L R MacDonald; D C Howlett, J F Umaga, A J D Mauger, C S Ralph; A P Mehrtens, J W Marshall; D N Hewett, T E Willis, G M Somerville, C R Jack, T S Maling, R D Thorne *(captain)*, S M Robertson, R H McCaw *Substitutions:* S R Broomhall for Maling (57 mins); M G Hammett for Willis (57 mins); D P E Gibson for MacDonald (62 mins); B T Kelleher for Marshall (62 mins)

Scorers *Tries:* MacDonald, pen try (Umaga), Howlett, Mauger *Conversions:* Mehrtens (2) *Penalty Goals:* Mehrtens (2)

Referee D T M McHugh (Ireland) replaced by C White (England) (43 mins)

17 August, Ellis Park, Johannesburg
South Africa 33 (4G 1T)   **Australia 31** (2G 3PG 1DG 1T)

Like the Brisbane battle, this match had its ugly moments as Marius Joubert was given a red card and his centre partner De Wet Barry a yellow one. Then when the Wallabies scored what they expected to be the winning try, exaggerated celebrations by George Gregan saw objects pelted down onto the field, resulting in seven arrests.

It was a match South Africa should never have been in danger of losing as they built up a 26-9 lead after 61 minutes, a lead that could have been greater had they had a reliable goal-kicker. Early in the match the Springboks had missed two penalties from straight in front of the posts, before Matthew Burke kicked three that were more difficult to give the Wallabies a 9-0 lead. After a long period of pressure and good running by Joubert, Breyton Paulse skipped over for a try and, minutes later, Jannes Labuschagne led a drive, Joubert carried the ball on and eventually Brent Russell swerved past Chris Latham to score near the posts seconds before the interval. The second half was barely on the go when Jannes Labuschagne charged straight ahead again, before Joubert made a quick pass to Paulse who scored easily to make it 21-9.

Barry was sent to the sin bin for punching Chris Latham when the two were on the ground. Down to 14 men, the Springboks scored again when Bob Skinstad led a sweeping movement down field before getting a clever pass behind Ben Tune to Van Niekerk on his left. The young loose forward sped down the wing and scored to give South Africa a 17-point cushion.

Then the Springbok tackling lost contact with reality. From the restart the Wallabies were awarded a free kick at a scrum. Kefu tapped and surged for Mat Rogers to weave, spin over and score. Next, Australia attacked this way

Tana Umaga prepares to hand off Bolla Conradie during the Tri Nations match between South Africa and New Zealand in Durban.

and that while the referee played advantage and eventually Kefu stepped past two defenders to score close in. Burke converted. 26-23.

With ten minutes to go, Joubert was sent off for a high tackle. The penalty became a line-out from which the Wallabies drove. The referee was again playing advantage when Gregan stepped back and dropped a goal to level the scores. Then, with five minutes to go, George Smith caught the ball and raced away from a line-out to work Brendan Cannon over in the corner.

The Springboks attacked from a scrum as the siren went to signal the end of the match. Play continued and Conradie fired a pass to Werner Greeff who had come running in at full tilt from wide out. He burst through Nathan Sharpe and Matt Cockbain to score. Greeff's kick was true and South Africa had won 33-31.

South Africa: W W Greeff; B J Paulse, M C Joubert, D W Barry, D B Hall; R B Russell, N A de Kock; L D Sephaka, J Dalton, W Meyer, J J Labuschagne, A J Venter, C P J Krige *(captain)*, R B Skinstad, J C van Niekerk *Substitutions:* H Scholtz for Krige (51 mins); S J Rautenbach for Meyer (53 mins); J H Conradie for De Kock (61 mins); A-H le Roux for Dalton (61 mins); C S Terblanche for Hall (78 mins)

Scorers Tries: Paulse (2), Russell, Van Niekerk, Greeff *Conversions:* Greeff (4)

Australia: C E Latham; B N Tune, M C Burke, D J Herbert, S A Mortlock; S J Larkham, G M Gregan *(captain)*; W K Young, J A Paul, B J Darwin, N C Sharpe, J B G Harrison, O D A Finegan, R S T Kefu, G B Smith *Substitutions:* D J Lyons for Smith (temp 23 to 24 mins) and for Finegan (49 mins); M S Rogers for Tune (temp 49 to 58 mins) and for Latham (58 mins); M J Cockbain for Harrison (49 mins); B J Cannon for Paul (55 mins); R C Moore for Darwin (62 mins)

Scorers Tries: Rogers, Kefu, Cannon *Conversions:* Burke (2) *Penalty Goals:* Burke (3) *Dropped Goal:* Gregan

Referee P D O'Brien (New Zealand)

TRI NATIONS RECORDS 1996-2002

Previous winners: 1996 New Zealand; 1997 New Zealand; 1998 South Africa; 1999 New Zealand; 2000 Australia; 2001 Australia; 2002 New Zealand
Grand Slam winners: New Zealand (Twice) 1996, 1997; South Africa (Once) 1998

Team Record	Detail		Set
Most team points in season	159 by N Zealand	in four matches	1997
Most team tries in season	18 by S Africa	in four matches	1997
Highest team score	61 by S Africa	61-22 v Australia (h)	1997
Biggest team win	39 by S Africa	61-22 v Australia (h)	1997
Most team tries in match	8 by S Africa	v Australia	1997

Individual Record	Detail		Set
Most appearances	27 for N Zealand	J W Marshall	1996 to 2002
	27 for Australia	G M Gregan	1996 to 2002
Most points in matches	309 for N Zealand	A P Mehrtens	1996 to 2002
Most points in season	84 for N Zealand	C J Spencer	1997
Most points in match	29 for N Zealand	A P Mehrtens	v Australia (h) 1999
Most tries in matches	16 for N Zealand	C M Cullen	1996 to 2002
Most tries in season	7 for N Zealand	C M Cullen	2000
Most tries in match	2 on many occasions		
Most cons in matches	32 for N Zealand	A P Mehrtens	1996 to 2002
Most cons in season	13 for N Zealand	C J Spencer	1997
Most cons in match	6 for S Africa	J H de Beer	v Australia (h),1997
Most pens in matches	77 for N Zealand	A P Mehrtens	1996 to 2002
Most pens in season	19 for N Zealand	A P Mehrtens	1996
	19 for N Zealand	A P Mehrtens	1999
Most pens in match	9 for N Zealand	A P Mehrtens	v Australia (h) 1999

WOMEN'S RUGBY WORLD CUP 2002

Black Ferns Sweep Clean

Nicola Goodwin

Barcelona in May staged the second women's tournament supported and funded by the IRB. Tournament Director Gethin Jenkins had made some controversial but necessary changes to the structure of the tournament and the funding process, with the focus being to ensure all countries were given an equal chance to improve their rugby status. Funding was given for flights to Barcelona with countries then financing their own accommodation in the city. Matches were arranged so that teams were re-seeded after the group rounds thus giving every country the chance to improve upon their seeding.

Every nation was therefore ensured four games in Barcelona and, perhaps more importantly in an age of funding targets and close monitoring of development, every nation had the chance to come away with an official mark of either gain or loss in performance.

Spain, who gave England a run for their money in an intensely-fought second round tie before finishing in eighth place, proved themselves to be a more than able host. Certainly their decision to stage pool games in suburbs of the city that promoted the adoption of locally-based countries was an inspired move. The IRB chairman, Vernon Pugh, has referred to women's rugby as 'one of the world's fastest-growing sports.' Events in Barcelona bore rich testimony to his assertion. The largest crowds seen at a Women's World Cup flocked to the 32-match tournament spread over twelve days.

The group rounds passed mainly according to seed, with New Zealand's 117-0 thrashing of Germany highlighting the massive gulf in standards at the competition. The Black Ferns' wing, Vanessa Cootes, crossed for five of the 19 tries, while replacement Hannah Myers landed seven of their 11 conversions.

The second round would prove crucial as teams fought for semi-final places and the match between New Zealand and Australia, watched by 3,000 people, was an outstanding example of the improving standards in the women's game. Forceful forward play and inventive work behind the scrum were the features of New Zealand's 36-3 win. Their scrum took three tight-heads off the Wallaroos and prop Helen Vaaga bumped off four would-be tacklers on a memorable 30-metre charge to the try-line for a score in the closing quarter. The only try scored by the backs came from recycled ball at a ruck. A quick transfer wide culminated in wing Dianne Kahura outflanking a tight Australian defence for a score in the opening ten minutes.

France provided the biggest upset of the tournament by beating number two seeds, the United States, by 21-9 for a place in the last four. The Americans have a long history in this version of the game and brought with them a proud record of past achievement at international level. They were winners of the inaugural Women's World Cup in 1991 and finished as runners-up in each of the last two tournaments, in 1994 and 1998. But they were unable to break the French defence in a quarter-final match that was one of the most entertaining of the entire competition.

Canada deservedly progressed to the last four, beating Ireland by 57-0 in the first round and Scotland by 11-0 before losing to a well-drilled England side in the semi-finals of the principal competition. The English had under performed in their two opening matches, but now hit the right notes to outclass the Canadians in a match played in searing heat. They pitched their game perfectly, played expansive rugby and moved the ball with stunning speed. Gill Burns, the experienced No 8 who has appeared in every Women's World Cup to date, had an immense game. She launched countless attacks off the base of the scrum and was a deadly attacking weapon in broken play, often popping up in midfield to threaten the Canadian defence.

England were in the saddle at 31-5 by the break and finished winners by 53-10. Sue Day was the pick of their threequarters, running in two tries in each half and running out of defence to create the try of the match for right-wing Nicola Crawford. Shelley Rae supplied 13 goal points. Colette McAuley scored Canada's points with two tries.

New Zealand, as expected, won the second semi-final of the main Cup competition. The Ferns were disappointing despite a convincing 30-0 scoreline. Two of their players spent time in the sin-bin and the performance was so littered with elementary errors that the side was barely able to develop any fluency. Their best moments came in the last ten minutes of a scrappy match after Dianne Kahura had replaced Vanessa Cootes. She scored with her first touch of the ball after New Zealand had won a scrum against the head on the French 22. Then, near the end, she made the run of the match to cut the Six Nations champions to ribbons with a 50-metre break which led to a ruck on the French line from which prop Rebecca Luia'ana scored.

The final two days of the tournament brought the players to the impressive Olympic Stadium in Barcelona where all of the nations played in a final match to determine a tournament ranking between first and sixteenth. The ever-improving France gained a much-deserved third-place finish to add to their European Six Nations title by defeating Canada by 41-7, while Australia and Samoa both climbed three places up the rankings as the Southern Hemisphere continued to show their passion for the sport. The Australians were the winners of the Plate, finishing in fifth place overall, while World Cup newcomers Samoa beat Wales in the Bowl final to decide the ninth-placed nation.

Women's World Cup Final

25 May 2002, Olympic Stadium, Barcelona
New Zealand 19 (2PG 2T)   England 9 (2PG 1DG)

The final between England and New Zealand was everything that had been predicted and the two sides gave an outstanding display of women's rugby at its finest. The 1998 World Champions eventually proved to be too strong for the 1994 World Champions as the Black Ferns ran in two sharply-taken tries beyond England's reach.

Coach Darryl Suasua, in his last match in charge of the Black Ferns, put the success down to the think tank that helped him to prepare for the World Cup in the wake of New Zealand's shock defeat by England barely twelve months earlier. Among the big names drafted in to help in the preparations were legendary All Black skipper Sean Fitzpatrick, Crusaders coach Robbie Deans, former rugby league coach Mark Graham and two All Black managers in John Sturgeon and Andrew Martin.

The effect was to give the Ferns a competitive edge, a mental toughness that was to see them through a final of absorbing interest. It is said that their move book is based on the tried-and-tested All Black manual and there was more than a passing resemblance to the familiar All Black professionalism in the Ferns' approach. They were too strong for England up front and the tactical kicking of their half-backs placed enormous pressure on the English defence.

New Zealand's path to the Olympic Stadium had generated so much support at home that this final was screened live in the middle of the night in New Zealand. Those who stayed up to watch and the 8,000 present in the stadium saw England take a 9-6 lead in the first half-hour. Tammi Wilson kicked penalties in the fourth and 14th minutes for New Zealand, Shelley Rae replying for England with similar scores in the 5th and 30th minutes to add to her dropped goal midway through the half.

But England's lead was short-lived, New Zealand delivering telling blows either side of the break. Minutes before half-time, Monique Hirovanaa, their courageous scrum-half, exploited an opening to run 22 metres along the touchline for a try. Then, seven minutes into the second half she was off again. This time the England back-row came off a defensive lineout too early, leaving a gap for Hirovanaa to race through and send flanker Cheryl Waaka in for the try that put New Zealand seven points clear.

England brought Gill Burns off the bench for the final stages, but the Waterloo stalwart could not inspire a last-ditch recovery. New Zealand replacement Hannah Myers added a penalty at the death leaving the Black Ferns to cherish a ten-point victory in a competition in which they had scored 202 points and conceded no tries.

New Zealand: T Wilson; D Kahura, A Rush, S Shortland, A Marsh; A Richards, M Hirovanaa; R Sheck, F Palmer (*captain*), R Luia'ana, M Codling, V Heighway, C Waaka, R Martin, A Lili'i *Substitutions:* H Vaaga for Sheck (52 mins); H Myers for Shortland (66 mins); M Robinson for Lili'i (75 mins)

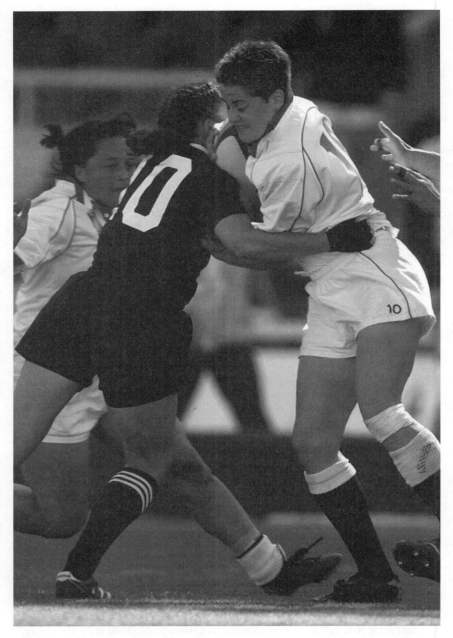

Battle of the fly-halves. England's Shelley Rae is tackled by her opposite number Anna Richards in the Final at the Olympic Stadium, Barcelona.

Scorers *Tries:* Hirovanaa, Waaka *Penalty Goals:* Wilson (2), Myers

England: P George (*captain*); N Crawford, N Jupp, S Rudge, S Day; S Rae, J Yapp; M Edwards, A Garnett, V Huxford, K Henderson, T Andrews, J Phillips, C Frost, G Stevens *Substitutions:* T O'Reilly for Edwards (53 mins); S Appleby (temp 56 to 61 mins) for Rae; H Clayton for Phillips (63 mins); A de Baise for Rudge (73 mins); G Burns for Andrews (75 mins)

Scorer *Penalty Goals:* Rae (2) *Dropped Goal:* Rae

Referee G de Santis (Italy)

Tournament Seedings and Pool Groupings (*seedings in brackets*)

GROUP A: New Zealand (1), Australia (8), Wales (9), Germany (16)
GROUP B: United States (2), France (7), Kazakhstan (10), Netherlands (15)
GROUP C: England (3), Spain (6), Japan (11), Italy (14)
GROUP D: Canada (4), Scotland (5), Samoa (12), Ireland (13)
Results

Round One: New Zealand 117, Germany 0; Australia 30, Wales 0; United States 87, Netherlands 0; France 31, Kazakhstan 12; England 63, Italy 9; Spain 62, Japan 0; Canada 57, Ireland 0; Scotland 13, Samoa 3.

Round Two: Germany 0, Wales 77; Netherlands 10, Kazakhstan 37; Italy 30, Japan 3; Ireland 9, Samoa 22; New Zealand 36, Australia 3; United States 9, France 21; England 13, Spain 5; Canada 11, Scotland 0

Round Three: Germany 0, Ireland 18; Japan 37, Netherlands 3; Wales 35, Italy 3; Samoa 9, Kazakhstan 5; Australia 17, United States 5; Scotland 23, Spain 16

Semi Finals: New Zealand 30, France 0; Canada 10, England 53

Place Play-Offs: Germany 19, Netherlands 20; Ireland 23, Japan 3; Italy 3, Kazakhstan 20; Wales 14, Samoa 17; United States 23, Spain 5; Australia 30, Scotland 0; France 41, Canada 7

Final:

New Zealand 19, England 9

Final Places: (*previous ranking in brackets*)
1 New Zealand (1); **2** England (3); **3** France (7); **4** Canada (4); **5** Australia (8); **6** Scotland (5); **7** United States (2); **8** Spain (6); **9** Samoa (12); **10** Wales (9); **11** Kazakhstan (10); **12** Italy (14); **13** Ireland (13); **14** Japan (11); **15** Netherlands (15); **16** Germany (16)

Previous Women's World Cup Finals : 1991 United States 19, England 6 (Cardiff); 1994 England 38, United States 23 (Edinburgh); 1998 New Zealand 44, United States 12 (Amsterdam); 2002 New Zealand 19, England 9 (Barcelona)

New Zealand's Black Ferns celebrate their triumph.

MAJOR TEST TOURS 2001-02

Australia to Europe 2001

Tour party

Full-backs: M C Burke (Eastwood & NSW), C E Latham (Wests & Queensland)

Threequarters: B N Tune (GPS & Queensland), S N G Staniforth (Eastwood & NSW), G S G Bond (Northern Suburbs & ACT), S Kefu (Souths & Queensland), D J Herbert (GPS & Queensland), N P Grey (Manly & NSW), J W C Roff (Biarritz & ACT)

Half-backs: E J Flatley (Brothers & Queensland), M H M Edmonds (Warringah & NSW), S J Larkham (Canberra & ACT), G M Gregan (Randwick & ACT) (*captain*), C J Whitaker (Randwick & NSW)

Forwards: M A Foley (Wests & Queensland), B J Cannon (Sydney University & NSW), N B Stiles (University & Queensland), W K Young (Eastwood & ACT), B J Darwin (Northern Suburbs & ACT), R C Moore (Eastwood & NSW), D T Giffin (Canberra & ACT), J B G Harrison (Canberra & ACT), M R Connors (Souths & Queensland), T M Bowman (Eastern Suburbs & NSW), O D A Finegan (Randwick & ACT), M J Cockbain (GPS & Queensland), G B Smith (Manly & ACT), P R Waugh (Sydney University & NSW), R S T Kefu (Souths & Queensland), D J Lyons (Sydney University & NSW)

Manager: P Thomson **National Coach:** E Jones Assistant **Coach:** Glen Ella
Tour record P 7 W 5 L 2 For 276 Against 142
28 October Won 34-22 v English National Divisions (Leicester)
1 November Won 92-10 v SPAIN (Madrid)
4 November Won 52-27 v Oxford University (Oxford)
10 November Lost 15-21 v ENGLAND (Twickenham)
17 November Lost 13-14 v FRANCE (Marseilles)
24 November Won 21-13 v WALES (Cardiff)
28 November Won 49-35 v Barbarians (Cardiff)

Details

28 October, Welford Road, Leicester
English National Divisions XV 22 (1G 4PG 1DG)   **Australia XV 34** (4G 2PG)

English National Divisions XV scorers: *Try:* Greaves *Conversion:* Burns *Penalty Goals:* Burns (4) *Dropped Goal:* Burns

Australian XV scorers *Tries:* Herbert, Latham, Tune, Lyons *Conversions:* Flatley (4) *Penalty Goals:* Flatley (2)

Test Match 1 November, Cuidad University Ground, Madrid
Spain 10 (1G 1PG)   Australia 92 (12G 1PG 1T)

Spain: F Velazco; M-A Frechilla, Alberto Socias, F Diez, N Macias; M Ventura, J Alonso-Lasheras; J Salazar, R Ripol, J-I Zapatero, J-M Villaú, S Souto, C Souto, A Mata, A Leon (*captain*) *Substitutions:* M Garcia for Leon (45 mins); A Martinez for Ventura (46 mins); S Tuineau for S Souto (50 mins); F de la Calle for Ripol (52 mins); Antonio Socias for Macias (56 mins); J de Urquiza for Alonso-Lasheras (75 mins); A Fortet for Zapatero (78 mins)

Scorers *Try:* Villaú *Conversion:* Martinez *Penalty Goal:* Alonso-Lasheras

Australia: M C Burke; C E Latham, D J Herbert, N P Grey, J W C Roff; S J Larkham, G M Gregan (*captain*); N B Stiles, M A Foley, B J Darwin, J B G Harrison, D T Giffin, O D A Finegan, R S T Kefu, G B Smith *Substitutions:* M J Cockbain & B J Cannon for Harrison & Foley (57 mins); P R Waugh for Smith (61 mins); C J Whitaker & E J Flatley for Gregan & Larkham (65 mins); G S G Bond for Latham (66 mins); R C Moore for Finegan (temp 70 to 73 mins) and for Stiles (75 mins)

Scorers *Tries:* Latham (3), Roff (2), Herbert, Grey, Stiles, Foley, Smith, Kefu, Cockbain, Bond *Conversions:* Burke (10), Flatley (2) *Penalty Goal:* Burke

Referee J Jutge (France)

4 November, University Ground, Iffley Road, Oxford
Oxford University 27 (3G 1PG 1DG)   Australian XV 52 (6G 2T)

Oxford University scorers: *Tries:* Rubie, Tkachuk, Taberner *Conversions:* Fitzgerald (3) *Penalty Goal:* Fitzgerald *Dropped Goal:* Fitzgerald

Australian XV scorers: *Tries:* Latham (2), Staniforth (2), Bond, Whitaker, Waugh, Grey *Conversions:* Edmunds (6)

Test Match 10 November, Twickenham
England 21 (5PG 2DG)   Australia 15 (1G 1PG 1T)

England: J Robinson; A S Healey, W J H Greenwood, M J Catt, D D Luger; J P Wilkinson, K P P Bracken; G C Rowntree, D E West, P J Vickery, B J Kay, D J Grewcock, R A Hill, J P R Worsley, N A Back (*captain*)

Scorers *Penalty Goals:* Wilkinson (5) *Dropped Goals:* Wilkinson (2)

Australia: M C Burke; C E Latham, D J Herbert, N P Grey, J W C Roff; S J Larkham, G M Gregan (*captain*); N B Stiles, M A Foley, B J Darwin, J B G Harrison, D T Giffin, O D A Finegan, R S T Kefu, G B Smith *Substitutions:* M J Cockbain for Harrison (50 mins); G S G Bond for Herbert (68 mins); P R Waugh for Smith (68 mins); R C Moore for Darwin (80 mins)

Scorers *Tries:* Burke, Waugh *Conversion:* Burke *Penalty Goal:* Burke

Referee P D O'Brien (New Zealand)

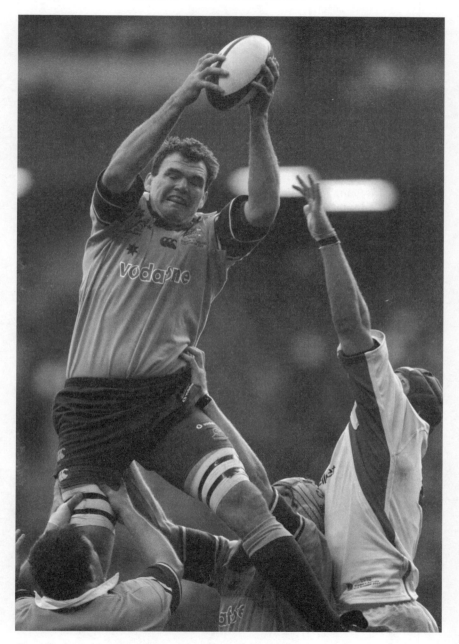

Owen Finegan wins a lineout during the 2001 Cook Cup Test between England and Australia at Twickenham.

Test Match 17 November, Stade Vélodrome, Marseilles
France 14 (3PG 1T) Australia 13 (1G 2PG)

France: C Poitrenaud; A Rougerie, T Marsh, D Traille, D Bory; F Michalak, F Galthié (*captain*); J-J Crenca, R Ibañez, P de Villiers, D Auradou, T Privat, S Betsen, P Tabacco, O Magne *Substitutions:* N Jeanjean for Poitrenaud (58 mins); L Nallet for Privat (73 mins); Y Bru for Ibañez (76 mins)

Scorers *Try:* Marsh *Penalty Goals:* Traille (2), Michalak

Australia: M C Burke; C E Latham, N P Grey, G S G Bond, J W C Roff; S J Larkham, G M Gregan (*captain*); N B Stiles, M A Foley, B J Darwin, J B G Harrison, D T Giffin, O D A Finegan, R S T Kefu, P R Waugh *Substitutions:* M J Cockbain for Finegan (temp 34 to 40 mins) and for Harrison (54 mins); G B Smith for Waugh (50 mins); B N Tune for Burke (57 mins); R C Moore, B J Cannon & E J Flatley for Darwin, Foley & Grey (76 mins)

Scorers *Try:* Tune *Conversion:* Flatley *Penalty Goals:* Burke (2)

Referee C J Hawke (New Zealand)

Test Match 25 November, Millennium Stadium, Cardiff
Wales 13 (1G 2PG) Australia 21 (7PG)

Wales: K A Morgan; W T Proctor, J P Robinson, I R Harris, Gareth Thomas; S M Jones, R Howley; S C John, R C McBryde, D R Morris, I M Gough, A P Moore, C L Charvis, L S Quinnell (*captain*), B D Sinkinson *Substitutions:* G R Williams for Robinson (46 mins); C P Wyatt for Gough (50 mins); Duncan Jones for John (57 mins); Gavin Thomas for Sinkinson (63 mins); B H Williams for McBryde (72 mins); John for Morris (74 mins)

Scorers *Try:* Gavin Thomas *Conversion:* Harris *Penalty Goals:* Harris (2)

Australia: M C Burke; B N Tune, E J Flatley, G S G Bond, J W C Roff; S J Larkham, G M Gregan (*captain*); N B Stiles, M A Foley, B J Darwin, M J Cockbain, D T Giffin, O D A Finegan, R S T Kefu, P R Waugh *Substitutions:* G B Smith for Wauigh (55 mins); S Kefu for Flatley (63 mins); J B G Harrison for Cockbain (68 mins); B J Cannon for Foley (74 mins); R C Moore & C E Latham for Darwin & Roff (75 mins); C J Whitaker for Gregan (80 mins)

Scorer *Penalty Goals:* Burke (7)

Referee S J Lander (England)

1 December, Millennium Stadium, Cardiff
Barbarians 35 (5G) Australian XV 49 (7G)

Barbarians scorers *Tries:* Paulse (3), Glas, Lam *Conversions:* Van Straaten (5)

Australian XV scorers *Tries:* Staniforth (3), Latham, Flatley, T Kefu, Tune *Conversions:* Flatley (5), Edmunds (2)

New Zealand to Britain, Ireland and Argentina 2001

Tour party

Full-backs: B A Blair (Canterbury), L R MacDonald (Canterbury)

Threequarters: D C Howlett (Auckland), J T Lomu (Wellington), N K Mauger (Canterbury), C S Ralph (Canterbury), R Q Randle (Waikato), J F Umaga (Wellington), P F Alatini (Otago), A J D Mauger (Canterbury)

Half-backs: D W Hill (Waikato), A P Mehrtens (Canterbury), B T Kelleher (Otago), M D Robinson (North Harbour), J E Spice (Wellington)

Forwards: A D Oliver (Otago) (*captain*), T E Willis (Otago), G M Somerville (Canterbury), K J Meeuws (Otago), D N Hewett (Canterbury), G E Feek (Canterbury), D A G Waller (Wellington), N M C Maxwell (Canterbury), T S Maling (Otago), C R Jack (Canterbury), R D Thorne (Canterbury), S M Robertson (Canterbury), P C Miller (Otago), R H McCaw (Canterbury), M R Holah (Waikato), J Collins (Wellington)

Manager: A J Martin **Assistant manager:** G Enoka **Coach:** J E P Mitchell **Coaching co-ordinator:** R M Deans

Tour record P 5 W 5 For 179 Against 98

13 November Won 43-30 v Ireland A (Belfast)

17 November Won 40-29 v IRELAND (Dublin)

20 November Won 35-13 v Scotland A (Perth)

24 November Won 37-6 v SCOTLAND (Murrayfield)

1 December Won 24-20 v ARGENTINA (Buenos Aires)

Details

13 November, Ravenhill, Belfast
Ireland A 30 (1G 6PG 1T)   New Zealand XV 43 (4G 5PG)

Ireland A scorers *Tries:* A Horgan (2) *Conversion:* P Wallace *Penalty Goals:* P Wallace (6)

New Zealand XV scorers *Tries:* Blair (3), Miller *Conversions:* Blair (4) *Penalty Goals:* Blair (5)

Test Match 17 November, Lansdowne Road, Dublin
Ireland 29 (1G 2PG 2DG 2T)   New Zealand 40 (5G 1T)

Ireland: G T Dempsey; S P Horgan, B G O'Driscoll, K M Maggs, D A Hickie; D G Humphreys, P A Stringer; P M Clohessy, K G M Wood (*captain*), J J Hayes, M J Galwey, M E O'Kelly, E R P Miller, A G Foley, D P Wallace *Substitutions:* E Byrne for Hayes (53 mins); M J Mullins & G W Longwell for Horgan & Galwey (57 mins)

Scorers *Tries:* Maggs, Hickie, Miller *Conversion:* Humphreys *Penalty Goals:* Humphreys (2) *Dropped Goals:* Humphreys (2)

New Zealand: L R MacDonald; D C Howlett, J F Umaga, A J D Mauger, J T Lomu; A P Mehrtens, B T Kelleher; G E Feek, A D Oliver (*captain*), G M Somerville, C R Jack, N M C Maxwell, R D Thorne, S M Robertson,

Brian O'Driscoll draws Andrew Mehrtens before delivering his pass during the Test in Dublin last November.

R H McCaw *Substitution:* D N Hewett for Feek (62 mins)

Scorers *Tries:* Jack, Thorne, Howlett, Mauger, Lomu, Hewett *Conversions:* Mehrtens (5)

Referee A Watson (South Africa)

20 November, McDiarmid Park, Perth
Scotland A 13 (1G 2PG)   New Zealand XV 35 (3G 3PG 1T)

Scotland A scorers *Try:* Hodge *Conversion:* Hodge *Penalty Goals:* Hodge (2)

New Zealand XV scorers *Tries:* Ralph, Robinson, Blair, Alatini *Conversions:* Blair (3) *Penalty Goals:* Blair (3)

Test Match 24 November, Murrayfield, Edinburgh
Scotland 6 (2PG)   New Zealand 37 (2G 6PG 1T)

Scotland: B J Laney; J F Steel, J G McLaren, J A Leslie, C D Paterson; G P J Townsend, A D Nicol; T J Smith (*captain*), G C Bulloch, M J Stewart, S Murray, S B Grimes, J P R White, G L Simpson, A L Mower *Substitutions:* S M Taylor & G Graham for Simpson & Stewart (48 mins); G G Burns for Nicol (62 mins); A R Henderson for J Leslie (69 mins); S Scott for Bulloch (72 mins); I A Fullarton for Murray (79 mins)

Scorer *Penalty Goals:* Paterson (2)

New Zealand: L R MacDonald; D C Howlett, J F Umaga, A J D Mauger, J T Lomu; A P Mehrtens, B T Kelleher; G E Feek, A D Oliver (*captain*), G M Somerville, C R Jack, N M C Maxwell, R D Thorne, S M Robertson, R H McCaw *Substitutions:* M D Robinson for Kelleher (33 mins); D N Hewett for Feek (61 mins); B A Blair for MacDonald (61 mins)

Scorers *Tries:* Umaga, Robinson, Lomu *Conversions:* Mehrtens (2) *Penalty Goals:* Mehrtens (6)

Referee P C Deluca (Argentina)

Test Match 1 December, Estadio Monumental Antonio V Liberti, River Plate, Buenos Aires
Argentina 20 (2G 2PG)   New Zealand 24 (1G 4PG 1T)

Argentina: I Corleto; G F Camardon, J Orengo, L Arbizu (*captain*), D L Albanese; F Contepomi, A Pichot; M Reggiardo, F E Mendez, O J Hasan, C I Fernandez Lobbe, R Alvarez, S Phelan, G Longo, R A Martin *Substitutions:* G Quesada for Arbizu (temp 49 to 53 mins); R D Grau for Reggiardo (61 mins); M Durand for Phelan (64 mins); M E Ledesma for Hasan (72 mins); B Stortoni for Camardon (78 mins)

Scorers *Tries:* Arbizu (2) *Conversions:* Contepomi (2) *Penalty Goals:* Contepomi (2)

New Zealand: B A Blair; D C Howlett, J F Umaga, A J D Mauger, J T Lomu; A P Mehrtens, M D Robinson; D N Hewett, A D Oliver (*captain*), K J Meeuws, C R Jack, N M C Maxwell, R D Thorne, S M Robertson, R H McCaw *Substitutions:* G M Somerville for Meeuws (temp 34 to 40 mins and from 55 mins); D A G Waller for Maxwell (temp 41 to 47 mins)

Scorers *Tries:* Lomu, Robertson *Conversion:* Mehrtens *Penalty Goals:* Mehrtens (4)

Referee S M Young (Australia)

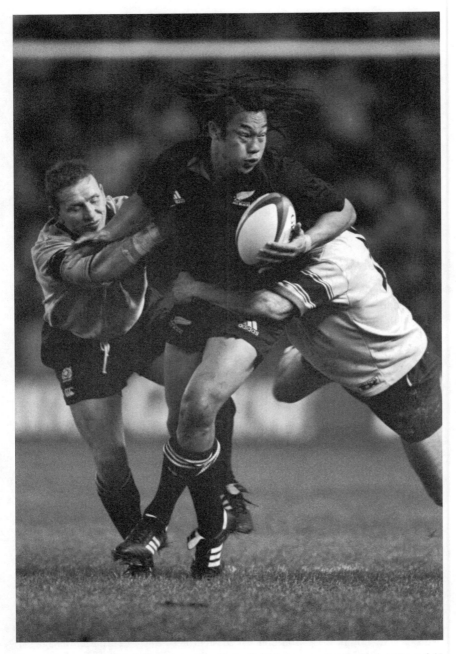

Tana Umaga is temporarily held up during New Zealand's 37-6 victory against Scotland at Murrayfield.

South Africa to Europe and United States 2001

Tour party

Full-backs: C A Jantjes (Lions), P C Montgomery (Western Province)

Threequarters: D B Hall (Lions), B J Paulse (Western Province), P W G Rossouw (Western Province), T M Halstead (Natal), A A Jacobs (Mpumalanga Falcons), A H Snyman (Natal), D W Barry (Western Province)

Half-backs: L J Koen (Lions), A J J van Straaten (Western Province), J H van der Westhuizen (Blue Bulls), D de Kock (Mpumalanga Falcons)

Forwards: W J Smit (Natal), L van Biljon (Natal), I J Visagie (Western Province), A van der Linde (Western Province), L D Sephaka (Lions), W Meyer (Lions), A-H le Roux (Natal), M G Andrews (Natal), V Matfield (Blue Bulls), P A van den Berg (Natal), A J Venter (Natal), A N Vos (Lions), A G Venter (Free State), J C van Niekerk (Lions), R B Skinstad (Western Province) *(captain)*, C P J Krige (Western Province)

Manager: M Hendricks **Coach:** H Viljoen **Assistant Coaches:** T Lane, H Meyer

Tour record P 4 W 2 L 2 For 116 Against 95

10 November Lost 10-20 v FRANCE (Paris)

17 November Won 54-26 v ITALY (Genoa)

24 November Lost 9-29 v ENGLAND (Twickenham)

1 December Won 43-20 v UNITED STATES (Houston)

Details

Test Match 10 November, Stade de France, Paris
France 20 (5PG 1T)   South Africa 10 (1G 1PG)

France: C Poitrenaud; A Rougerie, T Marsh, D Traille, D Bory; F Gelez, F Galthié *(captain)*; J-J Crenca, R Ibañez, P de Villiers, D Auradou, T Privat, P Tabacco, F Ntamack, O Magne *Substitutions:* L Nallet for Privat (68 mins); F Michalak & N Jeanjean for Gelez & Poitrenaud (80 mins); S Betsen for Ntamack (81 mins)

Scorers *Try:* Ibañez *Penalty Goals:* Gelez (4), Traille

South Africa: C A Jantjes; B J Paulse, A H Snyman, T M Halstead, P W G Rossouw; A J J van Straaten, J H van der Westhuizen; A-H le Roux, L van Biljon, I J Visagie, V Matfield, M G Andrews; A N Vos, R B Skinstad *(captain)*, A J Venter *Substitutions:* A van der Linde for Le Roux (60 mins); W J Smit & W Meyer for Van Biljon & Visagie (68 mins); P C Montgomery for Snyman (72 mins); J C van Niekerk for A J Venter (76 mins); A G Venter for Andrews (79 mins)

Scorers *Try:* Rossouw *Conversion:* Van Straaten *Penalty Goal:* Van Straaten

Referee A Lewis (Ireland)

Test Match 17 November, Stadio Luigi Ferraris, Genoa
Italy 26 (2G 3PG 1DG)   South Africa 54 (7G 1T)

Italy: L Martin; M Perziano, W Pozzebon, C Stoica, D Dallan; D Dominguez, A Troncon; A Lo Cicero, A Moscardi (*captain*), A Muraro, W Visser, M Giacheri, A Persico, C Checchinato, M Bergamasco *Substitutions:* C Paoletti & M Bortolami for Muraro & Giacheri (40 mins); S Pace for Perziano (53 mins); G de Carli for Lo Cicero (temp 7 to 9 mins and 58 mins); F Mazzariol & A Benatti for Dominguez & Checchinato (77 mins)

Scorers *Tries:* Dominguez, Benatti *Conversions:* Dominguez, Mazzariol *Penalty Goals:* Dominguez (3) *Dropped Goal:* Dominguez

South Africa: C A Jantjes; B J Paulse, T M Halstead, A J J van Straaten, D B Hall; L J Koen, J H van der Westhuizen; A-H le Roux, W J Smit, W Meyer, V Matfield, A J Venter, A N Vos, R B Skinstad (*captain*), J C van Niekerk *Substitutions:* D de Kock & C P J Krige for Van der Westhuizen & Vos (40 mins); A G Venter for Van Niekerk (56 mins); L van Biljon for Le Roux (62 mins); A A Jacobs for Van Straaten (65 mins); P C Montgomery for Paulse (73 mins); I J Visagie for Meyer (77 mins)

Scorers *Tries:* Halstead (2), Van der Westhuizen, Hall, Smit, Matfield, Meyer, Skinstad *Conversions:* Van Straaten (5), Koen (2)

Referee W J Erickson (Australia)

Test Match 24 November, Twickenham
England 29 (7PG 1DG 1T)   South Africa 9 (3PG)

England: J Robinson; A S Healey, W J H Greenwood, M J Catt, D D Luger; J P Wilkinson, K P P Bracken; G C Rowntree, D E West, PJ Vickery, M O Johnson (*captain*), D J Grewcock, R A Hill, J P R Worsley, N A Back *Substitutions:* L W Moody for Hill (57 mins); B J Kay for Back (temp 76 to 78 mins) and for Johnson (79 mins); M J Tindall for Catt (78 mins)

Scorers *Try:* Luger *Penalty Goals:* Wilkinson (7) *Dropped Goal:* Catt

South Africa: C A Jantjes; B J Paulse, T M Halstead, A J J van Straaten, D B Hall; L J Koen, J H van der Westhuizen; A-H le Roux, W J Smit, W Meyer, V Matfield, M G Andrews, A N Vos, R B Skinstad (*captain*), A J Venter *Substitutions:* I J Visagie for Meyer (temp 24 to 31 mins and 40 mins); A G Venter for Andrews (temp 44 to 49 mins and 66 mins); L van Biljon & C P J Krige for Smit & Vos (66 mins)

Scorer *Penalty Goals:* Van Straaten (3)

Referee S J Dickinson (Australia) *replaced* by D T M McHugh (Ireland) (12 mins)

Test Match 1 December, Robertson Stadium, Houston
United States 20 (4PG 1DG 1T)   South Africa 43 (5G 1PG 1T)

United States: K Shuman; J Naqica, P Eloff, J Grobler, J Keyter; L Wilfley, K Dalzell; M MacDonald, K Khasigian, P Still, L Gross, E Reed, K Schubert, D J Lyle, D W Hodges (*captain*) *Substitutions:* O Fifita for Lyle (48 mins); M Timoteo for Eloff (temp 58 to 62 mins) and for Naqica (62 mins); D Dorsey for Still (62 mins); B Surgener for Reed (72 mins); K Kjar for Dalzell (79 mins)

Scorers *Try:* MacDonald *Penalty Goals:* Wilfley (4) *Dropped Goal:* Keyter

England's Will Greenwood is stopped by Louis Koen in the Springboks' Twickenham Test last November.

South Africa: C A Jantjes; P W G Rossouw, A H Snyman, A A Jacobs, D B Hall; L J Koen, D de Kock; L D Sephaka, L van Biljon, I J Visagie, V Matfield, P A van den Berg, A N Vos, J C van Niekerk, A J Venter *Substitutions:* A G Venter for Van Niekerk (21 mins); W Meyer for A G Venter (temp 27-36 mins) and for Visagie (46 mins); A-H le Roux for Sephaka (46 mins); J H van der Westhuizen for De Kock (52 mins); D W Barry for Snyman (53 mins); W J Smit & T M Halstead for Van Biljon & Jacobs (69 mins)

Scorers *Tries:* Jantjes (2), Van Biljon, Vos, Rossouw, Hall *Conversions:* Koen (5) *Penalty Goal:* Koen

Referee D Mené (France)

103

Argentina to Wales and Scotland 2001

Tour party

Full-backs: I Corleto (Narbonne, Fra), B Stortoni (CASI)

Threequarters: D L Albanese (Gloucester, Eng), F Soler (Tala, Cordoba), G F Camardon (Roma, Italy), L Arbizu (Begles-Bordeaux, Fra) (*captain*), J de la C Fernandez Miranda (Hindu), D Giannantonio (La Rochelle, Fra), J Orengo (Perpignan, Fra)

Half-backs: F Contepomi (Bristol, Eng), G Quesada (Narbonne, Fra), N Fernandez Miranda (Hindu), A Pichot (Bristol, Eng)

Forwards: J Garcia (Perpignan, Fra), R D Grau (Liceo, Mendoza), O J Hasan (Agen, Fra), M Scelzo (Narbonne, Fra), M Reggiardo (Castres, Fra), M E Ledesma (Narbonne, Fra), F E Mendez (Mendoza RC), R Alverez (Perpignan, Fra), C I Fernandez Lobbe (Castres, Fra), M Sambucetti (Buenos Aires Cricket & Rugby Club), P L Sporleder (Curupayti), M Durand (Chamapgnat), R A Martin (SIC), S Phelan (CASI), G Longo (Narbonne, Fra), L Ostiglia (Hindu)

Manager: E Perasso **Head Coach:** M Loffreda **Assistant Coach:** D Baetti

Tour record P 4 W 3 L 1 For 120 Against 86

6 November Won 30-14 v Wales A (Pontypridd)
10 November Won 30-16 v WALES (Cardiff)
14 November Lost 35-40 v Scotland A (Selkirk)
18 November Won 25-16 v SCOTLAND (Murrayfield)

Details

6 November, Sardis Road, Pontypridd
Wales A 14 (3PG 1T)   Argentinian XV 30 (1G 6PG 1T)

Wales A scorers *Try:* A Powell *Penalty Goals:* Robinson (2), Jarvis

Argentinian XV scorers *Tries:* Corleto, Durand *Conversion:* Quesada *Penalty Goals:* Quesada (6)

Test Match 10 November, Millennium Stadium, Cardiff
Wales 16 (1G 3PG)   Argentina 30 (1G 5PG 1DG 1T)

Wales: K A Morgan; G R Williams, Gareth Thomas, S M Jones, A C Sullivan; I R Harris, R Howley; D R Morris, R C McBryde, D Young (*captain*), J C Quinnell, A P Moore, C L Charvis, L S Quinnell, Gavin Thomas *Substitutions:* I D Thomas for Morris (40 mins); A G Bateman & C P Wyatt for G R Williams & J C Quinnell (62 mins); B D Sinkinson for Gavin Thomas (69 mins); J P Robinson for Gareth Thomas (80 mins)

Scorers *Try:* Morris *Conversion:* Harris *Penalty Goals:* Harris (3)

Argentina: I Corleto; G F Camardon, J Orengo, L Arbizu (*captain*), D L Albanese; F Contepomi, A Pichot; M Reggiardo, F E Mendez, O J Hasan, C I Fernandez Lobbe, R Alvarez, S Phelan, G Longo, R A Martin *Substitutions:* L Ostiglia for Alvarez (temp 18 to 32 mins) and for Phelan (70 mins); R D Grau for Hasan (64 mins); M E Ledesma for Reggiardo (79 mins)

League convert Iestyn Harris makes his Union debut for Wales against Argentina in Cardiff, where the Pumas won 30-16.

Scorers *Tries:* Contepomi. Camardon *Conversion:* Contepomi *Penalty Goals:* Contepomi (5) *Dropped Goal:* Contepomi

Referee J Dumé (France)

14 November, Philiphaugh, Selkirk
Scotland A 40 (4G 3PG 1DG)   Argentinian XV 35 (5G)

Scotland A scorers *Tries:* Jacobsen (2), A Bulloch, Kerr *Conversions:* Hodge (4) *Penalty Goals:* Hodge (3) *Dropped Goal:* Hodge

Argentinian XV scorers *Tries:* pen tries (2), Corleto, Grau, Martin *Conversions:* Quesada (5)

Test Match 18 November, Murrayfield, Edinburgh
Scotland 16 (2PG 2T)   Argentina 25 (1G 6PG)

Scotland: D J Lee; C A Murray, J G McLaren, J A Leslie, R E Reid; G P J Townsend, A D Nicol; T J Smith *(captain)*, G C Bulloch, M J Stewart, S Murray, S B Grimes, J P R White, J M Petrie, A L Mower *Substitutions:* G L Simpson for Petrie (55 mins); G Graham for Stewart (61 mins)

Scorers *Tries:* Townsend, Lee *Penalty Goals:* Townsend (2)

Argentina: I Corleto; G F Camardon, J Orengo, L Arbizu *(captain)*, D L Albanese; F Contepomi, A Pichot; M Reggiardo, F E Mendez, O J Hasan, C I Fernandez Lobbe, R Alvarez, S Phelan, G Longo, R A Martin *Substitutions:* R D Grau for Reggiardo (64 mins); L Ostiglia for Phelan (65 mins)

Scorers *Try:* Corleto *Conversion:* Contepomi *Penalty Goals:* Contepomi (6)

Referee J Jutge (France)

Tonga to Scotland and Wales 2001

Tour party

Full-backs: S Tui'pulotu (Worcester, Eng & Wellington, NZ), P Hola (West Harbour, NZ)

Threequarters: S Matangi (Fasi Ma'ufanga), E Taione (Newcastle, Eng), T Taufahema (Caerphilly, Wal), S Kiole (South Canterbury, NZ), S Taumalolo (Bridgend, Wal), S Moimoi (Manakau, NZ), T Tiueti (Neath, Wal), G Leger (Counties, NZ), S Finau (Llanelli, Wal), A Mailei (North Harbour, NZ), A Havili (Vavengamavie)

Half-backs: V Afeaki (Fasi Ma'ufanga), E Vunipola (Coventry, Eng), T Alatini (North Harbour, NZ), S Martens (Swansea, Wal)

Forwards: A Lutui (Bay of Plenty, NZ), V Ma'asi (Fasi Ma'ufanga), F Ula (Fasi Ma'ufanga), T Taumoepeau (Auckland,NZ), T Fainga'anuku (Marlborough, NZ), T Filise (Bay of Plenty, NZ), J Pale (Wellington, NZ), I Afeaki (Wellington, NZ) *(captain)*, V Vaki (Lavengamalie), F Molitika (Whitland, Wal), F Faka'ongo (North Harbour, NZ), M Molitika (Bridgend, Wal), T Fifita (Lavengamalie), C Hala'ufia (Police Blues), L Lokotui (Suburbs, NZ), N Naufahu (Hawkes Bay, NZ), M Te Pou (Limerick, Ire)

Manager: B Manson **Assistant manager:** C John **Coach:** J Love **Assistant Coach:** T Tonga

Tour record P 4 L 4 For 70 Against 160
6 November Lost 20-40 v Scotland Development XV (Jedburgh)
10 November Lost 20-43 v SCOTLAND (Murrayfield)
13 November Lost 23-26 v Wales A (Llanelli)
17 November Lost 7-51 v WALES (Cardiff)

Details

6 November, Riverside Park, Jedburgh
Scottish Development XV 40 (2G 7PG 1T)　Tongan XV 20 (2G 2PG)

Scottish Development XV scorers *Tries:* Moffat, Kerr, Hines *Conversions:* Hodge (2) *Penalty Goals:* Hodge (7)

Tongan XV scorers *Tries:* Taione, Moimoi *Conversions:* Tu'ipulotu, Hola *Penalty Goals:* Hola (2)

Test Match 10 November, Murrayfield, Edinburgh
Scotland 43 (4G 5PG)　Tonga 20 (5PG 1T)

Scotland: G H Metcalfe; J F Steel, J G McLaren, J A Leslie, C A Murray; G Ross, A D Nicol; T J Smith (*captain*), G C Bulloch, M J Stewart, S Murray, S B Grimes, J P R White, J M Petrie, A L Mower *Substitutions:* G L Simpson for Mower (51 mins); G Graham for Stewart (53 mins); R E Reid for C Murray (66 mins); A R Henderson for McLaren (78 mins); G G Burns & S Scott for Nicol & Bulloch (78 mins)

Scorers *Tries:* McLaren, Metcalfe, Reid, Simpson *Conversions:* Ross (4) *Penalty Goals:* Ross (5)

Tonga: S Tu'ipulotu; T Tiueti, S Taumalolo, G Leger, E Taione; E Vunipola, S Martens; J Pale, A Lutui, T Taumoepeau, F Fakaongo, V Vaki, M Molitika, M Te Pou, I Afeaki (*captain*) *Substitutions:* V Ma'asi for M Molitika (temp 35 to 40 mins); F Molitika for Vaki (57 mins); T Alatini & T Taufahema for Martens & Tu'ipulotu (70 mins); S Finau & T Filise for Leger & Pale (75 mins)

Scorers *Try:* Vaki *Penalty Goals:* Tu'ipulotu (4), Taumalolo

Referee N Whitehouse (Wales)

13 November, Stradey Park, Llanelli
Wales A 26 (2G 3PG 1DG)　Tongan XV 23 (2G 3PG)

Wales A scorers *Tries:* G Wyatt, penalty try *Conversions:* Jarvis (2) *Penalty Goals:* Jarvis (3) *Dropped Goal:* Jarvis

Tongan XV scorers *Tries:* Lutui, Fainga'anuku *Conversions:* Hola (2) *Penalty Goals:* Hola (3)

Test Match 17 November, Millennium Stadium, Cardiff
Wales 51 (3G 5PG 3T)　Tonga 7 (1G)

Wales: K A Morgan; Gareth Thomas, A G Bateman, I R Harris, A C Sullivan; S M Jones, R Howley; I D Thomas, R C McBryde, D R Morris, I M Gough, A P Moore, C L Charvis, L S Quinnell (*captain*), B D Sinkinson *Substitutions:*

S C John for I Thomas (5 mins); G R Williams for Sullivan (10 mins);
J P Robinson for Bateman (59 mins); B H Williams & C P Wyatt for McBryde &
Moore (67 mins); D Peel for Howley (73 mins); Gavin Thomas for Sinkinson (75 mins)

Scorers *Tries:* Gareth Thomas, Howley, Quinnell, Robinson, G R Williams,
B H Williams *Conversions:* Harris (3) *Penalty Goals:* Harris (5)

Tonga: T Taufahema; E Taione, S Taumalolo, G Leger T Tiueti; P Hola,
S Martens; J Pale, V Ma'asi, T Taumoepeau, F Fakaongo, V Vaki, N Naufahu,
M Te Pou, I Afeaki *(captain) Substitutions:* C Hala'ufia for Fakaongo (40 mins);
A Lutui for Ma'asi (63 mins); T Filise for Taumoepeau (68 mins); S Moimoi for
Tiueti (73 mins); L Lokotui for Vaki (76 mins)

Scorers *Try:* Afeaki *Conversion:* Hola

Referee R Dickson (Scotland)

Romania to England 2001

Tour party

Full-backs: M Piciou (Farul Constanta), G Brezoianu (Begles-Bordeaux, Fra)

Threequarters: I Teodorescu (Universitatea Cluj), V Ghioc (Dinamo Bucharest),
F Dobre (Dinamo Bucharest), N Oprea (Dinamo Bucharest), C Lupu (Dinamo
Bucharest)

Half-backs: B Munteanu (Dinamo Bucharest), I Tofan (Steaua Bucharest),
M Codea (Farul Constanta), M Ciolacu (Albertville, Fra), L Sirbu (Steaua
Bucharest)

Forwards: D Dima (Castres, Fra), M Socaciu (Rovigo, Ita), P Teoderasc (Farul
Constanta), S Florea (Grivita Bucharest), P Balan (Grenoble, Fra), L Dumitrescu
(Steaua Bucharest), Marian Constantin (Stiinta Petrosani), V Nedelcu (Dinamo
Bucharest), Marius Dragomir (Dinamo Bucharest), S Rusu (CSM Eldoforest),
C Petre (Universitatea Cluj), Mihaita Dragomir (Steaua Bucharest), C Cirtiu
(Universitatea Remin Baia Mare), A Petrache (Dinamo Bucharest) *(captain)*,
F Corodeanu (Aurillac, Fra), M Bejan (Steaua Bucharest), R Samuil (Universitatea
Cluj), G Pasache (Dinamo Bucharest)

Manager: E Stoica **Head Coach:** M Paraschiv **Assistant Coaches:** C P Fugici,
D Alexandru

Tour record P 3 W 2 L 1 For 49 Against 160

8 November Won 21-11 v England Students (Cambridge)

13 November Won 28-15 v Combined Services (Portsmouth)

17 November Lost 0-134 v ENGLAND (Twickenham)

Details

8 November, University Ground, Grange Road, Cambridge
England Students 11 (2PG 1T)   Romanian XV 21 (3G)

England Students scorers *Try:* Hunt *Penalty Goals:* Niarchos (2)

Romanian XV scorers *Tries:* Petrache (2), Tofan *Conversions:* Tofan (3)

13 November, United Services Ground, Portsmouth
Combined Services 15 (4PG 1DG)   Romanian XV 28 (4G)

Combined Services scorer *Penalty Goals:* Morgan (4) *Dropped Goal:* Morgan

Romanian XV scorers *Tries:* Teodorescu (2), Petrache, Brezioanu *Conversions:* Ciolacu (4)

Test Match 17 November, Twickenham
England 134 (14G 2PG 6T)   Romania 0

England: J Robinson; B C Cohen, W J H Greenwood, M J Tindall, D D Luger; C Hodgson, A S Healey; G C Rowntree, M P Regan, J Leonard, B J Kay, S W Borthwick, L W Moody, J P R Worsley, N A Back (*captain*) *Substitutions:* K P P Bracken, J White & A Sanderson for Healey, Rowntree & Back (40 mins); D J Grewcock for Kay (62 mins); M J Catt for Greenwood (63 mins)

Scorers *Tries:* Robinson (4), Cohen (3), Luger (3), Hodgson (2), Moody (2), Tindall (2), Healey, Sanderson, Regan, Worsley *Conversions:* Hodgson (14) *Penalty Goals:* Hodgson (2)

Romania: G Brezoianu; I Teodorescu, F Dobre, N Oprea, V Ghioc; I Tofan, L Sirbu; D Dima, P Balan, M Sociacu, C Petre, V Nedelcu, F Corodeanu, A Petrache (*captain*), R Samuil *Substitutions:* Mihaita Dragomir for Petre (39 mins); M Ciolacu for Oprea (40 mins); G Pasache & S Florea for Samuil & Sociacu (57 mins); P Toderasc for Dima (65 mins); M Codea for Sirbu (76 mins)

Referee P C Deluca (Argentina)

Samoa to Europe 2001

Tour party

Full-back: S Leaega (Bologna, Ita)

Threequarters: L Fa'atau (Wellington, NZ), G Harder (Auckland, NZ), B Lima (Swansea, Wal), A So'oalo (Canterbury, NZ), E Seveali'i (Wellington, NZ), V L Tuigamala (Newcastle, Eng), T Vaega (Exeter, Eng), T Vili (Wellington, NZ)

Half-backs: E Va'a (Southland, NZ), S So'oialo (Wellington, NZ), D Tyrell (Taranaki, NZ)

Forwards: J Meredith (Auckland, NZ), M Schwalger (Hawkes Bay, NZ), F Lalomilo (Marist St Joseph's), T Leupolu (Auckland), J Tomuli (Colomiers, Fra), T Curtis (Auckland, NZ), O Palepoi (Wellington, NZ), K Viliamu (Waikato, NZ), P Segi (Auckland, NZ), S Sititi (Cardiff, Wal) (*captain*), G Stowers (Counties, NZ), A P Sufia (Vaimoso), A Toala (Rotherham, Eng), S Vaili (Auckland, NZ)

Manager: K Tuuau **Coach:** J Boe **Assistant Coach:** M N Jones
Tour record P 3 W 1 L 2 For 43 Against 67
4 November Lost 18-23 v Irish Development XV (Dublin)
11 November Lost 8-35 v IRELAND (Dublin)
24 November Won 17-9 v ITALY (L'Aquila)

Details

4 November, Donnybrook, Dublin
Irish Development XV 23 (1G 2PG 2T)   Samoan XV 18 (1G 2PG 1T)

Irish Development XV scorers *Tries:* Dunne, D Clohessy, Coulter *Conversion:* Keane *Penalty Goals:* Dunne, Keane

Samoan XV scorers *Tries:* Leupolu, Leaega *Conversion:* Vaega *Penalty Goals:* Vaega (2)

Test Match 11 November, Lansdowne Road, Dublin
Ireland 35 (3G 3PG 1T)   Samoa 8 (1PG 1T)

Ireland: J W Staunton; G E A Murphy, B G O'Driscoll, K M Maggs, T G Howe; R J R O'Gara, P A Stringer; E Byrne, F J Sheahan, J J Hayes, M J Galwey, G W Longwell, E R P Miller, A G Foley *(captain)*, K Dawson *Substitutions:* S H Easterby & T Brennan for Foley & Miller (40 mins); P M Clohessy, M J Mullins & G Easterby for Hayes, O'Driscoll & Stringer (69 mins)

Scorers *Tries:* Sheahan, Staunton, Murphy, Howe *Conversions:* O'Gara (3) *Penalty Goals:* O'Gara (3)

Samoa: T Vili; L Fa'atau, B Lima, V L Tuigamala, A So'oalo; E Va'a, S So'oialo; T Leupolu, J Meredith, J Tomuli, K Viliamu, O Palepoi, S Vaili, G Stowers, S Sititi *(captain) Substitutions:* F Lalomilo for Vaili (temp 13 to 20 mins) and for Tomuli (temp 65 to 72 mins); S Leaega for Va'a (52 mins); A To'oala for Stowers (69 mins); P Segi for Vaili (76 mins); T Vaega for Tuigamala (78 mins)

Scorers *Try:* A So'oalo *Penalty Goal:* Va'a

Referee D I Ramage (Scotland)

Test Match 24 November, Stadio Communale Tommaso Fattori, L'Aquila
Italy 9 (3PG)   Samoa 17 (4PG 1T)

Italy: L Martin; S Pace, W Pozzebon, C Stoica, D Dallan; D Dominguez, A Troncon; G de Carli, A Moscardi *(captain)*, A Muraro, W Visser, M Bortolami, A Benatti, C Checchinato, M Bergamasco *Substitutions:* C Zanoletti for Dallan (temp 18 to 21 mins) and for Martin (21 mins); A Lo Cicero for Muraro (51 mins); A Persico for Benatti (56 mins)

Scorer *Penalty Goals:* Dominguez (3)

Samoa: S Leaega; L Fa'atau, E Seveali'i, V L Tuigamala, B Lima; T Vili, D Tyrell; T Leupolu, J Meredith, J Tomuli, O Palepoi, K Viliamu, S Vaili, S Sititi *(captain)*, F Lalomilo *Substitutions:* M Schwalger for Tomuli (57 mins); P Segi for Vaili (68 mins)

Scorers *Try:* Fa'atau *Penalty Goals:* Vili (2), Leaega (2)

Referee R Davies (Wales)

Fiji to Europe 2001

Tour party

Full-backs: W Serevi (Mont de Marsan, Fra), J Waqa (Nadroga)

Threequarters: M Vunibaka (Canterbury, NZ), V Delasau (Mont de Marsan, Fra), F Lasagavibau (Northland, NZ), V Satala (Mont de Marsan, Fra), I Derenalagi (Montauban, Fra), M Wainibitu (Naitisiri), N Ligairi (Nadi), E Ruivadra (Tailevu), E Tuisese (Naitasiri), S Rokini

Half-backs: N Little (Dax, Fra), A Naiteqe (Naitasiri), S Rabaka (Nadi)

Forwards: I Rasila (Nadroga), A Nagi (Lautka), H Qiodravu (Canberra Vikings, Aust), V Cavubati (Wellington, NZ), R Nyholt (Queensland University, Aust), P Biu (Suva), I Domolailai (Lautoka), E Katalau (Dunvant, Wal), S Raiwalui (Newport, Wales), S Koyamaibole (Suva), J Tuibake (Suva), M Davu (Nadroga), S Niqara (Suva), A Doviverata (Suva) (*captain*), I Male (Suva)

Manager: M Nailumu **Coach:** I Tawake **Assistant Coach:** C Beg

Tour record P 4 W 2 L 2 For 70 Against 181

7 November Won 33-23 v Italia Emergenti XV (Treviso)

10 November Lost 10-66 v ITALY (Treviso)

18 November Won 17-15 v French Barbarians (Toulon)

24 November Lost 10-77 v FRANCE (St Etienne)

Details

7 November, Stadio Communale di Monigo, Treviso
Italia Emergenti XV 23 (2G 3PG)   Fijian XV 33 (2G 3PG 2T)

Italia Emergenti XV scorers *Tries:* Zaffiri, Virgilio *Conversions:* Pilat (2) *Penalty Goals:* Pilat (2), Preo

Fijian XV scorers *Tries:* Serevi (2), Vunibaka, Lasagavibau *Conversions:* Serevi (2) *Penalty Goals:* Serevi (2), Little

Test Match 10 November, Stadio Communale di Monigo, Treviso
Italy 66 (5G 7PG 2T)   Fiji 10 (1G 1PG)

Italy: P Vaccari; M Perziano, W Pozzebon, C Stoica, D Dallan; D Dominguez, A Troncon; A Lo Cicero, A Moscardi (*captain*), A Muraro, C Checchinato, M Bortolami, A Persico C Caione M Bergamasco *Substitutions:* W Visser for Caione (25 mins); L Martin for Vaccari (26 mins); C Paoletti for Muraro (54 mins); G de Carli for Lo Cicero (68 mins); A Benatti for Checchinato (71 mins); F Mazzariol for Dominguez (75 mins); J-M Queirolo for Troncon (78 mins)

Scorers *Tries:* Vaccari, Dallan, Stoica, Martin, Moscardi, Checchinato, Persico *Conversions:* Dominguez (4), Mazzariol *Penalty Goals:* Dominguez (7)

Fiji: J Waqa; M Vunibaka, V Satala, S Rokini, V Delasau; W Serevi, S Rabaka; A Nagi, I Rasila, V Cavubati, S Raiwalui, E Katalau, J Tuibake, M Davu, A Doviverata (*captain*) *Substitutions:* P Biu for Rasila (6 mins); N Little for Rokini (49 mins); H Qiodravu for Cavubati (57 mins); F Lasagavibau for Waqa (65 mins)

Scorer *Try:* Serevi *Conversion:* Serevi *Penalty Goal:* Serevi

Referee A Turner (South Africa)

18 November, Stade Mayol, Toulon
French Barbarians 15 (1G 1PG 1T)   Fijian XV 17 (2G 1PG)

French Barbarians scorers *Tries:* Milhères, Marconnet *Conversion:* Skrela *Penalty Goal:* Skrela

Fijian XV scorers *Tries:* Serevi, Tuisese *Conversions:* Little (2) *Penalty Goal:* Little

Test Match 24 November, Stade Geoffroy-Guichard, St Etienne
France 77 (7G 1PG 5T)   Fiji 10 (1G 1PG)

France: C Poitrenaud; C Dominici, T Marsh, D Traille, D Bory; G Merceron, F Galthié (*captain*); J-J Crenca, R Ibañez, P de Villiers, D Auradou, T Privat, S Betsen, P Tabacco, O Magne *Substitutions:* L Nallet for Auradou (40 mins); A Rougerie, N Jeanjean, F Michalak, S Chabal, Y Bru & J-B Poux for Bory, Poitrenaud, Galthié, Magne, De Villiers & Ibañez (61 mins)

Scorers *Tries:* Betsen (2), Dominici (2), Rougerie (2), Galthié, Bory, Poitrenaud, Magne, Jeanjean, Poux *Conversions:* Merceron (7) *Penalty Goal:* Merceron

Fiji: W Serevi; M Vunibaka, V Satala, I Derenalagi, V Delasau; N Little, S Rabaka; H Qiodravu, P Biu, V Cavubati, I Domolailai, E Katalau, M Davu, J Tuibake, A Doviverata (*captain*) *Substitutions:* F Lasagavibau for Delasau (31 mins); S Koyamaibole for Davu (57 mins); A Nagi for Qiodravu (66 mins); J Waqa & E Tuisese for Derenalagi & Domolailai (71 mins); R Nyholt for Cavubati (81 mins)

Scorers *Try:* Lasagavibau *Conversion:* Little *Penalty Goal:* Little

Referee M Lawrence (South Africa)

England to Argentina 2002

Tour party

Full-backs: M J Horak (London Irish), T R G Stimpson (Leicester)

Threequarters: T D Beim (Gloucester), M Cueto (Sale), P Christophers (Bristol), D L Rees (Bristol), G Appleford (London Irish), B Johnston (Saracens), K J Sorrell (Saracens), T A May (Newcastle)

Half-backs: C Hodgson (Sale), D J H Walder (Newcastle), A C T Gomarsall (Gloucester), N P J Walshe (Sale)

Forwards: S Thompson (Northampton), M P Regan (Bath), D L Flatman (Saracens), R Morris (Northampton), T J Woodman (Gloucester), P J Vickery (Gloucester) (*captain*), B J Kay (Leicester), A Codling (Harlequins), H D Vyvyan (Newcastle), R J Fidler (Gloucester), A Sanderson (Sale), L W Moody (Leicester), D Danaher (London Irish), P Anglesea (Sale), A L Balding (Leicester), J P R Worsley (Wasps)

Head Coach: C R Woodward **Coach:** R A Robinson

Tour record P 2 W 1 L 1 For 50 Against 47

17 June Lost 24-29 v Argentina A (Buenos Aires)

22 June Won 26-18 v ARGENTINA (Buenos Aires)

Details

17 June, Buenos Aires Cricket and Rugby Club
Argentina A 29 (2G 4PG 1DG) England XV 24 (3G 1PG)

Argentina A scorers: *Tries:* Bouza, Giannantonio *Conversions:* Quesada (2) *Penalty Goals:* Quesada (3), J Fernandez-Miranda *Dropped Goal:* Quesada

England XV scorers: *Tries:* Cueto, Morris, Walder *Conversions:* Walder (3) *Penalty Goal:* Walder

Test Match 22 June, Vélez Sarsfield Stadium, Buenos Aires
Argentina 18 (6PG) England 26 (2G 4PG)

Argentina: I Corleto; G F Camardon, J Orengo, F Contepomi, D L Albanese; G Quesada, A Pichot (*captain*); M Reggiardo, F E Mendez, O J Hasan, C I Fernandez Lobbe, R Alvarez, S Phelan, G Longo, R A Martin *Substitutions:* L Ostiglia for Alvarez (temp 43 to 57 mins) and for Phelan (68 mins); D Giannantonio for Quesada (temp 60 to 67 mins); R D Grau for Reggiardo (66 mins); M E Ledesma for Mendez (72 mins)

Scorer *Penalty Goals:* Quesada (6)

England: M J Horak; T R G Stimpson, G Appleford, B Johnston, P Christophers; C Hodgson, A C T Gomarsall; D L Flatman, S Thompson, P J Vickery (*captain*), A Codling, B J Kay, A Sanderson, J P R Worsley, L W Moody

Scorers *Tries:* Kay, Christophers *Conversions:* Hodgson (2) *Penalty Goals:* Hodgson (3), Stimpson

Referee A C Rolland (Ireland)

France to Argentina and Australia 2002

Tour party

Full-backs: N Brusque (Biarritz), P Elhorga (Agen)

Threequarters: A Rougerie (Montferrand), N Jeanjean (Toulouse), C Heymans (Toulouse)*, T Marsh (Montferrand), D Traille (Pau), Y Jauzion (Colomiers)

Half-backs: G Merceron (Montferrand), F Gelez (Agen), F Michalak (Toulouse), P Mignoni (Béziers)

Forwards: R Ibañez (Castres), O Azam (Gloucester, Eng), J-J Crenca (Agen), J-B Poux (Narbonne), S Marconnet (Stade Francais), A Martinez (Narbonne), F Pelous (Toulouse), O Brouzet (Northampton, Eng), C Porcu (Agen), S Chabal (Bourgoin), O Magne (Montferrand), S Betsen (Biarritz), I Harinordoquy (Pau), C Labit (Toulouse)

Manager: J Maso **Coach:** B Laporte **Assistant Coaches:** B Viviès, J Brunel, D Ellis

* Replacement from A team simultaneously touring Australia

Tour record P 3 L 3 For 69 Against 88

15 June Lost 27-28 v ARGENTINA (Buenos Aires)

22 June Lost 17-29 v AUSTRALIA (Melbourne)

29 June Lost 25-31 v AUSTRALIA (Sydney)

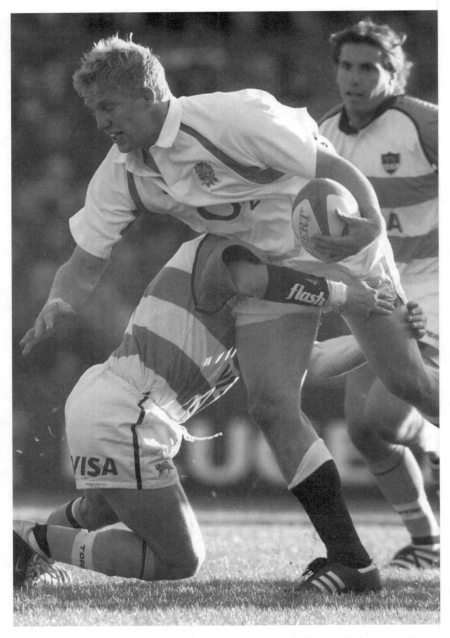

Lewis Moody in action for England against Argentina in the Test at the Velez Sarsfield Stadium in Buenos Aires in June.

Details

Test Match 15 June, Vélez Sarsfield Stadium, Buenos Aires
Argentina 28 (2G 2PG 1DG 1T)   France 27 (3G 2PG)

Argentina: I Corleto; G F Camardon, J Orengo, L Arbizu (*captain*), D L Albanese; F Contepomi, A Pichot; M Reggiardo, F E Mendez, O J Hasan, C I Fernandez Lobbe, R Alvarez, S Phelan, G Longo, R A Martin *Substitutions:* G Quesada for Arbizu (40 mins); R D Grau & M E Ledesma for Reggiardo & Mendez (70 mins); M Durand for Phelan (79 mins)

Scorers *Tries:* Mendez, Albanese, Contepomi *Conversions:* Contepomi (2) *Penalty Goals:* Contepomi (2) *Dropped Goal:* Quesada

France: N Brusque; A Rougerie, T Marsh, D Traille, N Jeanjean; G Merceron, P Mignoni; J-J Crenca, R Ibañez (*captain*), J-B Poux, F Pelous, O Brouzet, S Betsen, C Labit, O Magne *Substitutions:* C Porcu & S Chabal for Brouzet & Labit (66 mins); S Marconnet for Poux (75 mins); O Azam for Chabal (80 mins)

Scorers *Tries:* Brusque, Jeanjean, Marsh *Conversions:* Merceron (3) *Penalty Goals:* Merceron (2)

Referee P R Marshall (Australia)

First Test Match 22 June, Colonial Stadium, Melbourne
Australia 29 (2G 5PG)   France 17 (4PG 1T)

Australia: C E Latham; W J Sailor, M C Burke, D J Herbert, S A Mortlock; S J Larkham, G M Gregan (*captain*); W K Young, J A Paul, E P Noriega, N C Sharpe, J B G Harrison, O D A Finegan, R S T Kefu, G B Smith *Substitutions:* B J Cannon for Paul (33 mins); M J Cockbain for Finegan (60 mins); D J Lyons & R C Moore for Smith & Noriega (64 mins); M S Rogers & E J Flatley for Herbert & Larkham (72 mins)

Scorers *Tries:* Latham, Larkham *Conversions:* Burke (2) *Penalty Goals:* Burke (5)

France: P Elhorga; A Rougerie, T Marsh, D Traille, N Jeanjean; F Gelez, F Michalak; A Martinez, O Azam, S Marconnet, F Pelous (*captain*), C Porcu, S Betsen, I Harinordoquy, O Magne *Substitutions:* Y Jauzion for Jeanjean (51 mins); J-B Poux & O Brouzet for Marconnet & Porcu (58 mins); R Ibañez & C Labit for Martinez & Harinordoquy (75 mins)

Scorers *Try:* Poux *Penalty Goals:* Gelez (3), Traille

Referee C White (England)

Second Test Match 29 June, Stadium Australia, Sydney
Australia 31 (1G 2PG 1DG 3T)   France 25 (2G 2PG 1T)

Australia: C E Latham; W J Sailor, M C Burke, D J Herbert, S A Mortlock; S J Larkham, G M Gregan (*captain*); W K Young, B J Cannon, E P Noriega, N C Sharpe, J B G Harrison, O D A Finegan, D J Lyons, G B Smith *Substitutions:* M S Rogers for Burke (40 mins); S P Hardman for Cannon (43 mins); D J Vickerman for Sharpe (54 mins); M J Cockbain for Smith (63 mins); R C Moore for Noriega (70 mins); E J Flatley for Larkham (72 mins)

Scorers *Tries:* Mortlock (2), Burke, Herbert *Conversion:* Mortlock *Penalty Goals:* Burke, Mortlock *Dropped Goal:* Gregan

France: N Brusque; A Rougerie, T Marsh, D Traille, P Elhorga; G Merceron, F Michalak; J-J Crenca, R Ibañez *(captain)*, S Marconnet, F Pelous, O Brouzet, S Betsen, I Harinordoquy, S Chabal *Substitutions:* C Heymans for Elhorga (12 mins); O Magne for Betsen (39 mins); C Porcu for Pelous (61 mins); J-B Poux for Marconnet (67 mins); Y Jauzion for Traille (68 mins); P Mignoni for Michalak (77 mins)

Scorers *Tries:* Rougerie (2), Marconnet *Conversions:* Merceron (2) *Penalty Goals:* Merceron (2)

Referee P G Honiss (New Zealand)

Scotland to Canada and United States 2002

Tour party

Full-backs: B J Laney (Edinburgh Rugby), G H Metcalfe (Glasgow Rugby)

Threequarters: A Craig (Orrell), M P Di Rollo (Edinburgh Rugby), A R Henderson (Glasgow Rugby), B G Hinshelwood (Worcester), R C Kerr (Glasgow Rugby), M D Leslie (Edinburgh Rugby), C D Paterson (Edinburgh Rugby), T K Philip (Edinburgh Rugby), N Walker (The Borders)

Half-backs: G G Burns (Edinburgh Rugby), M R L Blair (Edinburgh Rugby), D W Hodge (Edinburgh Rugby), G Ross (Edinburgh Rugby)

Forwards: J D Brannigan (Edinburgh Rugby), S J Brotherstone (Newcastle), G C Bulloch (Glasgow Rugby), A K Dall* (Edinburgh Rugby), B A F Douglas (The Borders), S B Grimes (Newcastle), A J A Hall (Glasgow Rugby), N J Hines (Edinburgh Rugby), A Hogg (Edinburgh Rugby), A F Jacobsen (Edinburgh Rugby), D J H Macfadyen (Glasgow Rugby), E W Peters* (unattached), J M Petrie (Glasgow Rugby), N D Ross* (Glasgow Rugby), S J Scott (The Borders), C J Smith (Edinburgh Rugby), M J Stewart (Northampton), S M Taylor (Edinburgh Rugby), J P R White (Glasgow Rugby)

Manager: D W Morgan **Coach:** I R McGeechan **Assistant Coaches:** M Byrne, H Campbell, P Lam, A V Tait

* Replacements during tour

Tour record P 6 W 5 L 1 For 197 Against 82

5 June Won 38-8 v Canada East (Kingston)

8 June Won 33-8 v Rugby Canada (Toronto)

11 June Won 14-9 v Canada West (Victoria)

15 June Lost 23-26 v CANADA (Vancouver)

18 June Won 24-8 v United States A (Portland, Oregon)

22 June Won 65-23 v UNITED STATES (San Francisco)

Details

5 June, Richardson Stadium, Kingston
Canada East 8 (1PG 1T)   Scotland XV 38 (5G 1PG)

Canada East scorers *Try:* Wirachowski *Penalty Goal:* Luke

Scotland XV scorers *Tries:* Di Rollo (2), Hogg, Walker, Burns *Conversions:* G Ross (5) *Penalty Goal:* G Ross

8 June, Fletcher's Field, Markham, Toronto
Rugby Canada 8 (1PG 1T)   Scotland XV 33 (1G 2PG 4T)

Rugby Canada scorers *Try:* Snow *Penalty Goal:* Ross
Scotland XV scorers *Tries:* Kerr (2), Blair, Craig, Hodge *Conversion:* Laney *Penalty Goals:* Laney (2)

11 June, Centennial Stadium, Victoria
Canada West 9 (2PG 1DG)   Scotland XV 14 (3PG 1T)

Canada West scorers *Penalty Goals:* Danskin (2) *Dropped Goal:* Danskin.
Scotland XV scorers *Try:* Jacobsen *Penalty Goals:* G Ross (3)

Test Match 15 June, Thunderbird Stadium, Vancouver
Canada 26 (2G 4PG)   Scotland 23 (1G 2PG 2T)

Canada: W U Stanley; F C Asselin, N Witkowski, J Cannon, S Fauth; J Barker, M Williams; R G A Snow, P Dunkley, J Thiel, A J Charron (*captain*), M B James, R Banks, P Murphy, D Baugh *Substitutions:* C Yukes for Murphy (45 mins); E R P Knaggs for Banks (66 mins); K S Nichols for Asselin (68 mins); K M Wirachowski for Thiel (76 mins)
Scorers *Tries:* Murphy, Thiel *Conversions:* Barker (2) *Penalty Goals:* Barker (4)
Scotland: G H Metcalfe; R C Kerr, A Craig, B J Laney, C D Paterson; D W Hodge, M R L Blair; M J Stewart, G C Bulloch, C J Smith, N J Hines, S B Grimes (*captain*), J P R White, J M Petrie, S M Taylor *Substitutions:* D J H Macfadyen for Petrie (51 mins); A F Jacobsen for Stewart (68 mins); B G Hinshelwood for Metcalfe (76 mins); S J Brotherstone for Bulloch (76 mins)
Scorers *Tries:* Blair, Paterson, Taylor *Conversion:* Laney *Penalty Goals:* Laney (2)
Referee D T M McHugh (Ireland)

18 June, Tualatin Hills Sports Complex, Portland, Oregon
United States A 8 (1PG 1T)   Scotland XV 24 (1G 4PG 1T)

United States A scorers *Try:* Satchwell *Penalty Goal:* Wells
Scotland XV scorers *Tries:* Burns, Hogg *Conversion:* G Ross *Penalty Goals:* G Ross (4)

Test Match 22 June, Balboa Park, San Francisco
United States 23 (2G 3PG)   Scotland 65 (6G 1PG 4T)

United States: J Buchholz; M Timoteo, P Eloff, L Wilfley, J Keyter; M Hercus, K Dalzell; M MacDonald, K Khasigian, D Dorsey, E Reed, L Gross, A Satchwell, D Hodges (*captain*), K Schubert *Substitutions:* C Hodgson for Hodges (temp 29 to 40 mins) and for Satchwell (67 mins); D Anderson for Satchwell (temp 37 to 40 mins); J Naqica for Eloff (41 mins); J Tarpoff for Satchwell (temp 57 to 67 mins) and for Dorsey (67 mins); K Kjar for Dalzell (67 mins); A McGarry for MacDonald (70 mins)
Scorers *Tries:* Keyter, Timoteo *Conversions:* Wilfley (2) *Penalty Goals:* Wilfley (3)
Scotland: G H Metcalfe; R C Kerr, A Craig, B J Laney, C D Paterson; D W Hodge, M R L Blair; A F Jacobsen, G C Bulloch, M J Stewart, N J Hines,

S B Grimes (*captain*), J P R White, S M Taylor, D J H Macfadyen *Substitutions:*
A R Henderson for Metcalfe (30 mins); C J Smith for Jacobsen (39 mins);
A F Jacobsen for Stewart (63 mins); M P Di Rollo for Kerr (68 mins); G G Burns
for Blair (72 mins); S Scott for Bulloch (75 mins); A J A Hall for White (77 mins)

Scorers *Tries:* Hodge (2), Paterson (2), Craig, Kerr, Henderson, Hines, Laney,
White *Conversions:* Laney (6) *Penalty Goal:* Laney

Referee P C Deluca (Argentina)

Wales to South Africa 2002

Tour party

Full-back: K A Morgan (Swansea)

Threequarters: G R Williams (Cardiff), D R James (Bridgend), M Taylor
(Swansea), J Robinson (Cardiff), A W N Marinos (Newport), T Shanklin
(Saracens), C S Morgan (Cardiff)

Half-backs: N R Jenkins (Cardiff), S M Jones (Llanelli), D Peel (Llanelli),
R Powell (Cardiff)

Forwards: R C McBryde (Llanelli), M Davies (Pontypridd), G Jenkins
(Pontypridd), I D Thomas (Llanelli), M Madden (Llanelli), B R Evans (Swansea),
S M Williams (Northampton), R Sidoli (Pontypridd), G O Llewellyn (Neath),
M Owen (Pontypridd), R Parks (Pontypridd), M E Williams (Cardiff), G Thomas
(Bath), C L Charvis (Swansea) (*captain*)

Manager: A J Phillips **Assistant manager:** C Griffiths **Coach:** S Hansen **Assistant
Coach:** S P Johnson

Tour record P 2 L 2 Points for 27 Against 53

8 June Lost 19-34 v SOUTH AFRICA (Bloemfontein)

15 June Lost 8-19 v SOUTH AFRICA (Cape Town)

Details

First Test Match 8 June, Vodacom Free State Stadium, Bloemfontein
South Africa 34 (3G 1PG 2T)   Wales 19 (2PG 1DG 2T)

South Africa: R I P Loubscher; C S Terblanche, M C Joubert, A H Snyman,
B J Paulse; A S Pretorius, J H Conradie; D C F Human, J Dalton, W Meyer,
J J Labuschagne, V Matfield, W K Britz, R B Skinstad (*captain*), A J Venter
Substitutions: B Russell for Loubscher (48 mins); F Rautenbach for Meyer (57
mins); J C van Niekerk for Britz (63 mins); A-H le Roux for Dalton (70 mins);
A A Jacobs for Snyman (73 mins)

Scorers *Tries:* Joubert, Skinstad, Matfield, pen try (Paulse), Rautenbach *Conversions:*
Pretorius (3) *Penalty Goal:* Pretorius

Wales: K A Morgan; G R Williams, M Taylor, A W N Marinos, C S Morgan;
S M Jones, D Peel; I D Thomas, R C McBryde, B R Evans, G O Llewellyn,
S M Williams, M Owen, C L Charvis (*captain*), M E Williams *Substitutions:*
R Parks & R Sidoli for M Williams & Llewellyn (62 mins); T Shanklin for
Marinos (71 mins); N R Jenkins & M Madden for S Jones and Evans (76 mins);
R Powell for Peel (78 mins)

Brent Russell dives over for a try during the Cape Town Test between South Africa and Wales.

Scorers *Tries:* C Morgan, R Williams *Penalty Goals:* S Jones (2) *Dropped Goal:* S Jones

Referee K M Deaker (New Zealand)

Second Test Match 15 June, Newlands, Cape Town
South Africa 19 (3PG 2T)   Wales 8 (1PG 1T)

South Africa: B Russell; C S Terblanche, M C Joubert, D W Barry, B J Paulse; A S Pretorius, J H Conradie; D C F Human, J Dalton, W Meyer, Q Davids, J J Labuschagne, C P J Krige, R B Skinstad (*captain*), A J Venter *Substitutions:* F Rautenbach for Venter (temp 23 to 33 mins) and for Meyer (51 mins); C D Davidson for Conradie (51 mins); A-H le Roux for Human (59 mins); J C van Niekerk & F H Louw for Venter & Davids (63 mins)

Scorers *Tries:* Russell, Davidson *Penalty Goals:* Pretorius (3)

Wales: K A Morgan; G R Williams, M Taylor, A W N Marinos, C S Morgan; S M Jones, D Peel; I D Thomas, R C McBryde, B R Evans, G O Llewellyn, S M Williams, M Owen, C L Charvis (*captain*), M E Williams *Substitutions:* R Powell for Peel (12 mins); T Shanklin & Gavin Thomas for Marinos & M Williams (69 mins); R Sidoli for Llewellyn (71 mins); N R Jenkins and Mefin Davies for C Morgan & McBryde (80 mins)

Scorers *Try:* Charvis *Penalty Goal:* S Jones

Referee A J Spreadbury (England)

Italy to New Zealand 2002

Tour party

Full-back: G Peens (Piacenza)

Threequarters: G-J Canale (Benetton Treviso), N Mazzucato (Benetton Treviso), D Dallan (Benetton Treviso), W Pozzebon (Benetton Treviso), C Zanoletti (Calvisano), M Barbini (Petrarca Padova), G Raineri (Lottomatica Roma)

Half-backs: F Mazzariol (Benetton Treviso), M Mazzantini (Benetton Treviso), A Scanavacca (Rovigo), J-M Queirolo (Dax, Fra)

Forwards: A Matteralia (Petraraca Padova), M-L Castrogiovanni (Calvisano), G Faliva (Benetton Treviso), S Saviozzi (Overmach Parma), R Martinez-Frugoni (Lottomatica Roma), A Moretti (Calvisano), F Ongaro (Benetton Treviso), M Bortolami (Petrarca Padova) (*captain*), E Pavanello (Benetton Treviso), S Dellape (Arix Viadana), M Giacheri (Sale), A Persico (Arix Viadana), A Benatti (Arix Viadana), M Bergamasco (Benetton Treviso), A Mannato (La Guardiense Sannio), S Parisse (Benetton Treviso), A de Rossi (Calvisano), M Phillips (Arix Viadana)

Manager: M Bollesan **Assistant manager:** L Liussi **Coach:** J J Kirwan **Assistant coach:** L M Rutledge

Tour record P 3 W 1 D 1 L 1 For 82 Against 112

29 May Won 37-13 v Manawatu (Palmerston North)

2 June Drew 35-35 v Regional XV (Taupo)

8 June Lost 10-64 v NEW ZEALAND (Hamilton)

Details

29 May, Arena Manawatu, Palmerston North
Manawatu 13 (1G 2PG)   Italian XV 37 (4G 3PG)

Manawatu scorer *Try:* Guise *Conversion:* Guise *Penalty Goals:* Guise (2)

Italian XV scorers *Tries:* Barbini (2), D Dallan, Mazzariol *Conversions:* Peens (4) *Penalty Goals:* Peens (3)

2 June, Owen Delaney Park, Taupo
Divisional XV 35 (2G 2PG 3T)   Italian XV 35 (3G 3PG 1T)

Divisional XV scorers *Tries:* Leawere, Alofa, Fifita, Leung-Wai, Manawatu *Conversions:* Flutey (2) *Penalty Goals:* Flutey (2)

Italian XV scorers *Tries:* Peens, Pozzebon, Mazzariol, Zanoletti *Conversions:* Peens (3) *Penalty Goals:* Peens (3)

Test Match 8 June, Waikato Stadium, Rugby Park, Hamilton
New Zealand 64 (8G 1PG 1T)   Italy 10 (1G 1PG)

New Zealand: C M Cullen; D C Howlett, M P Robinson, D P E Gibson, C S Ralph; A P Mehrtens, B T Kelleher; J M McDonnell, T E Willis, K J Meeuws, T S Maling, N M C Maxwell, R D Thorne (*captain*), T C Randell, M R Holah *Substitutions:* D N Hewett for Meeuws (52 mins); J T Lomu for Howlett (53 mins); M G Hammett for Willis (59 mins); A J D Mauger for Robinson (69 mins)

Scorers *Tries:* Ralph (3), McDonnell, Meeuws, Kelleher, Lomu, Cullen, Hewett *Conversions:* Mehrtens (8) *Penalty Goal:* Mehrtens

Italy: G Peens; N Mazzucato, G Raineri, C Zanoletti, D Dallan; F Mazzariol, M Mazzantini; G Faliva, A Moretti, R Martinez-Frugoni, M Bortolami (*captain*), M Giacheri, A de Rossi, S Parisse, A Persico *Substitutions:* M Bergamasco for De Rossi (temp 20 to 30 mins and 46 mins); M-L Castrogiovanni & J-M Queirolo for Martinez-Frugoni & Mazzantini (52 mins); W Pozzebon for Dallan (55 mins); S Dellape for Giacheri (58 mins); M Barbini & S Saviozzi for Zanoletti & Moretti (74 mins)

Scorers *Try:* Bortolami *Conversion:* Peens *Penalty Goal:* Peens

Referee N Williams (Wales)

Ireland to New Zealand 2002

Tour party

Full-back: G T Dempsey (Terenure College & Leinster)

Threequarters: G E A Murphy (Leicester), J P Bishop (London Irish), B G O'Driscoll (Blackrock College & Leinster), J P Kelly (Cork Constitution & Munster), M Deane (Sale), T G Howe (Dungannon & Ulster), J O'Neill (Munster)

Half-backs: D G Humphreys (Dungannon & Ulster), R J R O'Gara (Cork Constitution) & Munster), G Easterby (Llanelli), P A Stringer (Shannon & Munster)

Forwards: K G M Wood (Harlequins) (*captain*), J S Byrne (Blackrock College & Leinster), R Corrigan (Lansdowne & Leinster), J J Hayes (Shannon & Munster), M J Horan (Shannon & Munster), P S Wallace (Blackrock College & Leinster), M E O'Kelly (St Mary's College & Leinster), G W Longwell (Ballymena & Ulster), P J O'Connell (Young Munster & Munster), L F M Cullen (Leinster), E R P Miller (Terenure College & Munster), A Quinlan (Shannon & Munster), K D Gleeson (St Mary's College & Leinster), A G Foley (Shannon & Munster), S H Easterby (Llanelli)

Manager: B O'Brien **Coach:** E O'Sullivan

Tour record P 3 W 1 L 2 For 70 Against 58

8 June Won 56-3 v NZ Divisional XV (Timaru)

15 June Lost 6-15 v NEW ZEALAND (Dunedin)

22 June Lost 8-40 v NEW ZEALAND (Auckland)

Details

8 June, Alpine Energy Stadium, Timaru
NZ Divisional XV 3 (1PG)   Ireland XV 56 (4G 1PG 5T)

NZ Divisional XV scorer *Penalty Goal:* Flutey

Ireland XV scorers *Tries:* O'Driscoll (3), Humphreys, Bishop, Dempsey, Foley, Deane, Murphy *Conversions:* Humphreys (4) *Penalty Goal:* Humphreys

First Test Match 15 June, Carisbrook, Dunedin
New Zealand 15 (1G 1PG 1T)   Ireland 6 (1PG 1DG)

New Zealand: L R MacDonald; D C Howlett, J F Umaga, A J D Mauger, C S Ralph; A P Mehrtens, J W Marshall; D N Hewett, M G Hammett, G M Somerville, C R Jack, N M C Maxwell, R D Thorne (*captain*), S M Robertson, R H McCaw *Substitutions:* D P E Gibson for Umaga (56 mins); J M McDonnell for Hewett (64 mins); J T Lomu for Howlett (67 mins)

Scorers *Tries:* Howlett, MacDonald *Conversion:* Mehrtens *Penalty Goal:* Mehrtens

Ireland: G T Dempsey; G E A Murphy, B G O'Driscoll, J P Kelly, J P Bishop; R J R O'Gara, P A Stringer; R Corrigan, K G M Wood (*captain*), J J Hayes, G W Longwell, P J O'Connell, S H Easterby, A G Foley, K D Gleeson *Substitutions:* M E O'Kelly for O'Connell (58 mins); D G Humphreys for O'Gara (69 mins)

Scorers *Penalty Goal:* O'Gara *Dropped Goal:* O'Driscoll

Referee J Jutge (France)

Second Test Match 22 June, Eden Park, Auckland
New Zealand 40 (3G 3PG 2T)   Ireland 8 (1DG 1T)

New Zealand: L R MacDonald; J T Lomu, M P Robinson, A J D Mauger, C S Ralph; A P Mehrtens, J W Marshall; D N Hewett, M G Hammett, G M Somerville, C R Jack, N M C Maxwell, R D Thorne (*captain*), S M Robertson, R H McCaw *Substitutions:* B T Kelleher & J M MacDonnell for

Marshall & Hewett (65 mins); D C Howlett for Ralph (67 mins); D P E Gibson & M R Holah for Robinson & McCaw (68 mins); T S Maling for Jack (77 mins)

Scorers *Tries:* MacDonald (2), Ralph, Kelleher, Holah *Conversions:* Mehrtens (3) *Penalty Goals:* Mehrtens (3)

Ireland: G T Dempsey; G E A Murphy, B G O'Driscoll, J P Kelly, J P Bishop; R J R O'Gara, P A Stringer; R Corrigan, K G M Wood (*captain*), J J Hayes, G W Longwell, M E O'Kelly, S H Easterby, A G Foley, K D Gleeson *Substitutions:* D G Humphreys for O'Gara (67 mins); A Quinlan for Gleeson (68 mins); L F M Cullen for O'Kelly (70 mins); P S Wallace for Corrigan (72 mins); J S Byrne for Wood (77 mins)

Scorers *Try:* Longwell *Dropped Goal:* O'Driscoll

Referee W T S Henning (South Africa)

Argentina to South Africa 2002

Tour party

Full-backs: I Corleto (Narbonne, Fra), B Stortoni (CASI)

Threequarters: G F Camardon (Roma, Ita), J Orengo (Perpignan, Fra), F Contepomi (Bristol, Eng), D L Albanese (Leeds, Eng), J N Piossek (Huirapuca), D Giannantonio (La Rochelle, Fra), H Senillosa (Hindu), F Soler (Tala RC)

Half-backs: J de la C Fernandez Miranda (Hindu), N Fernandez Miranda (Hindu), G Quesada (Narbonne, Fra), A Pichot (Bristol, Eng)

Forwards: F Mendez (Mendoza RC), M E Ledesma (Narbonne, Fra), R D Grau (Liceo), M Reggiardo (Castres, Fra), O J Hasan (Agen, Fra), J Garcia (Perpignan, Fra), C I Fernandez Lobbe (Castres, Fra), R Alvarez (Perpignan, Fra), P L Sporleder (Curupayti), M Sambucetti (BACRC), L Ostiglia (Hindu), S Phelan (CASI), R A Martin (SIC), M Durand (Champagnat), G Longo (Narbonne, Fra), P Bouza (Duendes)

Manager: E Perasso **Coach:** M Loffreda **Assistant Coach:** D Baetti

Tour record P 2 L 2 For 65 Against 91

26 June Lost 36-42 v South Africa A (Witbank)

29 June Lost 29-49 v SOUTH AFRICA (Springs)

Details

26 June, Puma Stadium, Witbank
South Africa A 42 (4G 3PG 1T) Argentinian XV 36 (4G 1PG 1T)

South Africa A scorers *Tries:* Hall (2), Coetzee, Scholtz, Sephaka *Conversions:* James (3) Du Toit *Penalty Goals:* James (2), Du Toit

Argentinian XV scorers *Tries:* Durand, Giannantonio, Piossek, Senillosa, Sporleder *Conversions:* Giannantonio (4) *Penalty Goal:* Quesada

Test Match 29 June, P A M Brink Stadium, Springs
South Africa 49 (5G 3PG 1T)   Argentina 29 (2G 5PG)

South Africa: B Russell; C S Terblanche, A A Jacobs, D W Barry, B J Paulse; A S Pretorius, C D Davidson; A-H le Roux, J Dalton, W Meyer, F H Louw, J J Labuschagne, C P J Krige *(captain)*, R B Skinstad, A J Venter *Substitutions:* W W Greeff for Russell (38 mins); D C F Human & F Rautenbach for Dalton & Meyer (55 mins); J C van Niekerk for Venter (62 mins); J H Conradie for Davidson (68 mins); M C Joubert for Barry (73 mins); Q Davids for Labuschagne (77 mins)

Scorers *Tries:* Terblanche (2), Jacobs, Davidson, Pretorius, Conradie *Conversions:* Pretorius (5) *Penalty Goals:* Pretorius (3)

Argentina: I Corleto; G F Camardon, J Orengo, F Contepomi, D L Albanese; G Quesada, A Pichot *(captain)*; R D Grau, F E Mendez, M Reggiardo, C I Fernandez Lobbe, R Alvarez, S Phelan, G Longo, R A Martin *Substitutions:* O J Hasan for Reggiardo (56 mins); M E Ledesma for Mendez (59 mins); L Ostiglia for Phelan (75 mins); M Durand for Martin (79 mins)

Scorers *Tries:* Fernandez Lobbe, pen try (Corleto) *Conversions:* Quesada (2) *Penalty Goals:* Quesada (5)

Referee W J Erickson (Australia)

Fiji to New Zealand 2002

Tour party

Full-backs: A Uluinayau (Suntory, Jap), J Narruhn (Hino, Jap)

Threequarters: N Ligairi (Nawaka, Nadi), V Delasau (Mont de Marsan, Fra), V Satala (Mont de Marsan, Fra), S Rabeni (Otago Univ, NZ), D Baleinadogo (Toyota, Jap)

Half-backs: N Little (Pontypridd, Wal), J Rauluni (Queensland, Aus), S Rabaka (Nadi)

Forwards: G J Smith (Waikato, NZ) *(captain)*, I Rasila (Nadroga), B Gadolo (Suva), P Biu (Nadoga), R Nyholt (Queensland Univ, Aus), V Cavubati (Masterton, NZ), S Raiwalui (Newport, Wal), S Koyamaibole (Toyota, Jap), S Tawake (Brothers, Queensland, Aus), K Sewabu (Gloucester, Eng), A Doviverata (Yamaha, Jap), A Mocelutu (Neath, Wal), H Rawaqa (Lautoka)

Manager: J Browne **Coach:** M McCallion

Tour record P 1 L 1 For 18 Against 68

29 June Lost 18-68 v NEW ZEALAND (Wellington)

Details

Test Match 29 June, WestpacTrust Stadium, Wellington
New Zealand 68 (5G 1PG 6T)   Fiji 18 (1G 2PG 1T)

New Zealand: C M Cullen; D C Howlett, J F Umaga, D P E Gibson, J T Lomu; A J D Mauger, B T Kelleher; J M McDonnell, T E Willis, K J Meeuws, T S Maling, N M C Maxwell, R D Thorne *(captain)*, T C Randell, S Harding

Substitutions: L R MacDonald for Umaga (22 mins); S M Robertson for Randell (51 mins); A P Mehrtens for MacDonald (57 mins); J W Marshall for Mehrtens (63 mins)

Scorers *Tries:* Cullen (3), Meeuws (2), Maxwell (2), MacDonald, Howlett, Mauger, Robertson *Conversions:* Mauger (5) *Penalty Goal:* Mauger

Fiji: A Uluinayau; N Ligairi, V Satala, S Rabeni, V Delasau; N Little, J Rauluni; R Nyholt, G J Smith (*captain*), V Cavubati, S Raiwalui, S Koyamaibole, S Tawake, A Doviverata, K Sewabu *Substitutions:* I Rasila for Smith (40 mins); S Rabaka for Rauluni (52 mins); A Mocelutu for Sewabu (57 mins); P Biu for Tawake (temp 69 to 72 mins) and for Cavubati (72 mins); I Rawaqa for Doviverata (62 mins); J Narruhn for Uluinayau (75 mins)

Scorers *Tries:* Ligairi (2) *Conversion:* Little *Penalty Goals:* Little (2)

Referee S M Young (Australia)

Samoa to South Africa 2002

Tour party

Full-back: S Leaega (Bologna, Ita)

Threequarters: L Fa'atau (Wellington, NZ), B Lima (Swansea, Wal), A So'oalo (Canterbury, NZ), E Seveali'i (Wellington, NZ), C Manu (Gloucester, Eng), D Tausili (Christchurch HSOB, NZ), F Tuilagi (Leicester, Eng), A Tuilagi (Marist St Joseph's)

Half-backs: E Va'a (Southland, NZ), A Toleafoa (Marist St Jospeh's), S So'oialo (Wellington, NZ), D Tyrell (Taranaki, NZ)

Forwards: J Meredith (Auckland, NZ), M Schwalger (Hawkes Bay, NZ), T Leota (Wasps, Eng), K Lealamanua (Marist St Patrick's, NZ), T Leupolu (Auckland), J Tomuli (Colomiers, Fra), O Palepoi (Wellington, NZ), L Leafailai'i (Sanyo, Japan), P Leavasa (Apia), K Viliamu (Waikato, NZ), P Segi (Auckland, NZ), S Sititi (Cardiff, Wal) (*captain*), E Fa'atau (Marist St Patrick's, NZ) , S Vaili (Auckland, NZ), H Tuilagi (Marist St Joseph's), M Fa'asavalu (Northcote, NZ), P Tapelu (Apia), R Fanuafanu (Marist St Joseph's)

Manager L K Tunau **Coach** T J Boe **Assistant coach** M N Jones

Tour record P 3 W 1 L 2 For 75 Against 117

6 July Lost 18-60 v SOUTH AFRICA (Pretoria)

10 July Won 24-17 v Mpumalanga Pumas (Nelspruit)

13 July Lost 33-40 v Free State Cheetahas (Bloemfontein)

Details

6 July, Loftus Versfeld, Pretoria
South Africa 60 (7G 2PG 1T) Samoa 18 (1PG 3T)

South Africa: W W Greeff; C S Terblanche, M C Joubert, D W Barry, D B Hall; A S Pretorius, J H Conradie; L D Sephaka, D Coetzee, S J Rautenbach, F H Louw, V Matfield, C P J Krige (*captain*), R B Skinstad, J C van Niekerk *Substitutions:* B J Paulse for Greef (46 mins); G J D du Preez for Coetzee (64 mins); R S Sowerby & D C F Human for Krige & Sephaka (66 mins); A A Jacobs & Q Davids for Barry & Matfield (71 mins); N A de Kock for Conradie (75 mins)

Scorers *Tries:* Barry (2), Hall (2), Greeff, Matfield, Du Preez, Van Niekerk *Conversions:* Pretorius (7) *Penalty Goals:* Pretorius (2)

Samoa: S Leaega; L Fa'atau, E Seveali'i, F Tuilagi, A Tuilagi; E Va'a, S So'oialo; T Leupolu, T Leota, J Tomuli, O Polepoi, L Lafaiali'i, K Viliamu, S Sititi (*captain*), M Fa'asavalu *Substitutions:* P Leavasa for Lafaiali'i (53 mins); K Lealamanua for Tomuli (57 mins); P Tapelu & D Tyrell for Fa'asavalu & So'oialo (69 mins); J Meredith for Leota (71mins); C Manu & A Toleafoa for Fa'atau & Va'a (72 mins)

Scorers *Tries:* F Tuilagi, Sititi, Viliamu *Penalty Goal:* Va'a

Referee A J Cole (Australia)

10 July, Nelspruit
Mpumalanga Pumas 17 (1G 2T) Samoan XV 24 (3PG 3T)

Mpumalanga Pumas scorers *Tries:* Husselman (2), Ahlers *Conversion:* Van Zyl
Samoan XV scorers *Tries:* Manu (2), Fanuafanu *Penalty Goals:* Tyrell (3)

13 July, Free State Stadium, Bloemfontein
Free State Cheetahs 40 (4G 4PG) Samoan XV 33 (3G 4PG)

Free State Cheetahs scorers *Tries:* Erasmus, Pitout, Du Plooy, Shimange *Conversions:* K Tsimba (3), Barnard *Penalty Goals:* K Tsimba (3), Barnard
Samoan XV scorers *Tries:* A Tuigali (2), Leaega *Conversions:* Va'a (3) *Penalty Goals:* Va'a (4)

THE EUROPEAN NATIONS TOURNAMENT 2001-02

European Nations Cup

Championnat Européen des Nations

Romania's Return to Respectability

Chris Thau

The advance of Eastern Europe in the FIRA-AER Championship, the Continental promotion-relegation competition known as the European Nations Cup, Plate and Bowl, continued unabated, with Romania, Georgia and Russia, in this order, dominating the proceedings of the first division (the Cup), the Czech Republic and to a lesser extent Poland and Ukraine ruling the roost in the second (the Plate). The Romanians won the Cup with the Czechs winning the Plate and the right to play in the elite section next year.

The promotion-relegation process – frozen for a year due to the qualifying rounds for the 2003 Rugby World Cup (RWC) – was duly reinstated at the end of the 2002 season, with the Czechs replacing the bottom-placed Netherlands, who although considerably improved, failed to reach the level of organisation and quality required at this level. The Czech advance brings to four the number of East European teams in the Cup section. With Poland, under new coach Polish legend Gregor Kacala, making considerable strides forward, it may well grow to five in 2004.

Called by the participating unions – perhaps prematurely – the European Championship, the FIRA-AER Tournament, which has provided Continental rugby with a viable playing framework since the late 1960s, took off spectacularly once the IRB stepped in to fund it three years ago. The vision of the IRB to underwrite the continental elite tournament is paying off as the quality of ENC has been rising, with the competition evolving into a second division to the Six Nations.

Romania won the inaugural European Nations Cup (ENC) by beating Georgia in Tbilisi in 2000, and the two nations have been dominating the six-nation elite section ever since. As far as the Home Unions are concerned, the ENC is still one of the best best-kept secrets of European rugby. However, with England having now joined the FIRA-AER (Wales and Ireland have been members for a couple of years) and Scotland about to join – not to mention of course the support of the IRB – the competition is likely to gain in status and significance.

Last season, the ENC had the added incentive of acting as a seeding criterion for the final round of the European qualifying zone for the 2003 RWC, while the European Nations Plate (ENP) matches were suspended to enable the Czech Republic, Poland, Germany, Sweden, Ukraine and Latvia to compete in Round Two of the RWC qualifiers. Eventually Romania and

Georgia, the ENC winners and runners-up respectively, won byes into the fourth round, with Russia, Spain, Portugal and the Netherlands having to battle their way through Round Three alongside the Czech Republic and Poland, who are the two dominant forces of the ENP section.

In the end Russia and Spain, the latter performing a genuine act of escapism against plucky Portugal – arguably one of the success stories of the season – managed to reach the final round of the RWC 2003 European qualifiers involving Ireland, Italy, Romania and Georgia.

Owing to the RWC 2003 qualifying rounds, there was no outright winner of the Cup section in 2001. Instead the ENC was played home and away over two seasons, with Georgia – unexpectedly, but deservedly winning in Bucharest – leading the table at the halfway stage.

The matches of the Cup and Plate are played during Six Nations weekends to enable the continental professional players who ply their trade for clubs in the West to join their national teams without further disruption for their employers. Virtually the entire Georgian squad, about 70% of the Romanians, half-a-dozen Russians and a handful of Czechs, Germans, Poles, Spaniards, Dutch and Portuguese play in France, Italy and in the UK and Ireland.

The Russians, determined to break into the lucrative RWC 2003 elite, abandoned tradition and for the first time ever selected (according to IRB eligibility rules) several foreign nationals for their team. Three experienced South African players, Conrad Breytenbach (Pumas), Tenk Hendriks (Leopards) and Bloues Volschenk (Leopards), made their debuts for Russia in the ENC, and more are expected to follow suit. So far, the majority of the continental nations have used more restrictive eligibility rules, allowing only passport holders to play for their country.

Arguably, the minor miracle of the 2001-02 continental season was Romania's return to respectability after the Twickenham debacle, when the players meekly threw in the towel. The decision of the newly elected FRR President Octavian Morariu to appoint as national coach Bernard Charryere, the FFR's Regional Technical Director for Languedoc Roussillon, paid off.

Charryere's achievement in turning an inept and self-important Romanian team into something akin to a genuine fighting force in less than six months is nothing short of miraculous. Romania, humbled and humiliated at Twickenham last November, managed to find resources of pride and character to turn the tables on Russia and Georgia and finish top of the continental hierarchy.

As a result, Georgia's plans to celebrate the first-ever continental title were thwarted. The first chinks in the Georgian armour had been exposed by brave Portugal, who were unlucky to lose to the visitors from Tbilisi in the dying minutes of a tense and furious game in Lisbon. Russia's search for talent abroad and the decision to import South African players of Russian descent was less productive than coach James Stoffberg would have hoped for, though it definitely added quality to the Russian effort and may in the long term significantly alter the balance of power on the continent.

Russia, though visibly under par against both Spain and Portugal, managed nevertheless to win, but their 12-all draw in Tbilisi, where the Georgians escaped defeat in the dying seconds of a try-less game, gave them high expectations for the crucial clash with Romania in Krasnodar. In the end the Romanian revival upset the plans of both Russia and Georgia.

Perhaps less spectacular, but equally impressive has been Portugal's coming of age. Coached by the capable Tomas Morais, the Portuguese made vast progress and only bad luck and some minor errors prevented them from finishing among the top four. Desperately short of finance, the Portuguese opted against recalling the expensive French-based brigade and relied instead on their home players – a move that might prove to have an impact for the long-term development of Portuguese rugby. Finally, a word for the majestic Rohan Hoffman – probably the most valuable amateur player in Europe. His contribution to Portugal's progress has been described by the pundits as providential.

Results and scorers 2002

3 February in Bucharest

Romania 44 (*Tries:* M Bejan, G Brezoianu, M Dumitru, V Maftei, P Balan, R Gontineac, A Petrache *Conversions:* I Tofan 3 *Penalty Goal:* I Tofan) **Portugal 17** (*Try:* N Garvão *Penalty Goals:* R Hoffman 4)

3 February in Krasnodar

Russia 35 (*Tries:* V Grachov 3, V Simonov 2, S Ilarionov *Conversion:* V Simonov *Penalty Goal:* V Simonov) **Spain 25** (*Try:* F Velazco *Conversion:* A Martinez *Penalty Goals:* A Martinez 4, F Velazco *Dropped Goal:* F Velazco)

3 February in Tbilisi

Georgia 88 (*Tries:* I Zedeguinidze 2, S Modebadze 2, B Kamashuridze 2, L Tsabadze, B Khekhelashvili, M Urjukashvili, A Guiorgadze, G Schvelidze, T Zibzibadze, I Machkhaneli, A.Eloshvili *Conversions:* P Jimsheladze 9) **The Netherlands 0**

17 February in Lisbon

Portugal 23 (*Tries:* G Vareiro, P Goncalves, N Garvão *Conversion:* R Hoffman *Penalty Goals:* R Hoffman 2) **Georgia 27** (*Tries:* A Guiorgadze 2, B Khekhelashvili, M Urjukashvili *Converions:* P Jimsheladze 2 *Penalty Goal:* M Urjukashvili)

17 February in Constanta

Romania 34 (*Tries:* P Balan, R Gontineac, A Petrache, I Tofan, F Corodeanu *Conversions:* I Tofan 3 *Penalty Goal:* I Tofan) **Spain 12** (*Tries:* O Ripol, R Ripol *Conversion:* A Martinez)

17 February in Krasnodar

Russia 73 (*Tries:* V Simonov 2, S Sergeev 2, K Rachkov 2, V Ilarionov, V Grachov V Zykov, A Diatlov *Conversions:* V Simonov 4, I Budnikov 3 *Penalty Goals:* I Budnikov 2, V Simonov) **The Netherlands 10** (*Try:* J Keulemans *Conversion:* G Meek *Penalty Goal:* G Meek)

3 March in Tbilisi

Georgia 12 (*Penalty Goals:* P Jimsheladze 4) **Russia 12** (*Penalty Goals:* V Simonov 3, K Rachkov)

3 March in Caldas da Rainha

Portugal 13 (*Tries:* A Aguilar, M Portela *Penalty Goal:* R Hoffman) **Spain 10** (*Tries:* C Souto, F de la Calle)

3 March in Amsterdam

The Netherlands 3 (*Penalty Goal:* H Kuijer) **Romania 49** (*Tries:* M Tincu 2, A Petrache, M Picoiu, G Chiriac, A Manta, M Dumitru, G Brezoianu, P Toderasc *Conversions:* R Lungu, I Dumitras)

24 March in Madrid

Spain 18 (*Tries:* C Souto 2, I Criado-Garachana *Penalty Goal:* F Diez) **Georgia 34** (*Tries:* B Kamashuridze 2, T Zibzibadze, V Katsadze, G Labadze *Conversions:* P Jimsheladze 3 *Penalty Goal:* P Jimsheladze)

24 March in Krasnodar

Russia 22 (*Tries:* V Simonov, A Kuzin, V Zykov *Conversions:* V Simonov 2 *Penalty Goal:* V Simonov) **Romania 27** (*Tries:* G Brezoianu, I Tofan *Conversion:* I Tofan *Penalty Goals:* I Tofan 5)

24 March in Amsterdam

The Netherlands 11 (*Try:* C Breynburg *Penalty Goals:* H Kuijer 2) **Portugal 27** (*Tries:* R Hoffman 2, A Aguilar, M Portela, P Goncalves *Conversion:* R Hoffman)

6 April in Tbilisi

Georgia 23 (*Tries:* M Urjukashvili, G. Chkhaidze *Conversions:* M Urjukashvili 2 *Penalty Goals:* M Urjukashvili 3) **Romania 31** (*Tries:* M Tincu, G Brezoianu, C Sauan *Conversions:* I Tofan 2 *Penalty Goals:* I Tofan 3 *Dropped Goal:* I Tofan)

7 April in Lousa

Portugal 13 (*Tries:* N Garvão, R Cordeiro *Penalty Goal:* R Hoffman) **Russia 38** (*Tries:* K Rachkov 2, V Fedchenko, T Hendriks, V Simonov *Conversions:* V Simonov 2 *Penalty Goals:* V Simonov 3)

7 April in Madrid

Spain 63 (*Tries:* F Velazco 3, N Macias 2, V Trillo, M Abril, J-I Zapatero, C Souto *Conversions:* A Martinez 4, F Velazco 2 *Penalty Goals:* A Martinez 2) **The Netherlands 3** (*Penalty Goal:* H Kuijer)

Final European Nations Cup Composite Table For 2001 & 2002

	P	W	D	L	For	Against	Pts
Romania	10	9	0	1	373	148	28
Georgia	10	8	1	1	351	152	27
Russia	10	6	1	3	332	230	23
Spain	10	3	0	7	246	247	16
Portugal	10	3	0	7	170	295	16
Netherlands	10	0	0	10	84	484	10

Three points for a win, two for a draw and one for a defeat.

Previous European Nations Cup Winners: 1999-2000 Romania; 2000-01 Georgia (*interim leaders*); 2001-02 Romania

Plate Results 2001-02

The European Round Two Pools A and B and Round Three Pools A and B of the Rugby World Cup section took the place of the Plate competition in 2002-03. The Czech Republic are promoted to the ENC for 2002-03 where they will replace the Dutch. Latvia are relegated to Pool A of the Third Division for 2002-03 and will be replaced in the Plate by Slovenia.

Other European Results 2001-02

Nations eliminated early from the 2003 Rugby World Cup competed in three pools:

Pool A: Austria 16, Slovenia 24; Andorra 56, Austria 3; Moldova 36, Yugoslavia 16; Slovenia 26, Andorra 16; Andorra 5, Yugoslavia 19; Yugoslavia 26, Austria 8; Austria 14, Moldova 27; Yugoslavia 27, Slovenia 21; Slovenia 42, Moldova 0; Andorra were unable to fulfil their fixture with Moldova.

Slovenia promoted to the Plate competition for 2002-03, Austria relegated to Pool B

Pool B: Luxembourg 17, Hungary 19; Hungary 26, Lithuania 16; Bosnia 13, Luxembourg 12; Israel 24, Hungary 39; Luxembourg 31, Israel 13; Luxembourg 7, Lithuania 26; Bosnia 19, Israel 11; Lithuania 33, Israel 24; Lithuania 12, Bosnia 9; Hungary 37, Bosnia 0

Hungary promoted to Pool A for 2002-03, Israel relegated to Pool C

Pool C: Malta 8, Monaco 0; Monaco 60, Norway 3; Bulgaria 14, Malta 27; Monaco 53, Bulgaria 5; Bulgaria 11, Norway 3; Norway 10, Malta 10

Malta promoted to Pool C for 2002-03

Other result: Norway 37, Finland 3

Finland join Pool C for 2002-03

AFRICA TOP SIX 2001

Another South Africa – Morocco Final

Paul Dobson

The Confederation of African Nations competition – now called the Africa Top Six – completed its second year in November 2001. The tournament embraces the South Africa Under 23 side and the leading countries among the rest of the African rugby-playing nations. The young South Africans – previously known as the Gazelles – again won the final, again against Morocco and again in Casablanca.

The six teams that competed were divided into two geographical divisions. In the Northern Division were Côte d'Ivoire, Morocco and Tunisia, with Namibia, South Africa Under 23 and Zimbabwe competing in the Southern Division. The Northerners played first, between March and May 2001. The South Division started in May and the final was played in November.

Morocco did not have it all its own way in winning the Northern Division, played on a home-and-away basis. They won all their matches, but struggled against both opponents, especially away from home. The Ivoreans came second in the division, drawing with Tunisia in Tunis and thrashing them in Abidjan.

The Southern Division was always a matter of who would come second. It was a doddle for South Africa Under 23 who scored a total of 264 points including 42 tries in their four league matches. In the battle for second place, Zimbabwe won at home as did Namibia, though Namibia were fortunate to beat the Sables at Windhoek's Independence Stadium. Each nation ended with five points (to South Africa Under-23's 20) but Namibia had a slightly superior points difference.

The competition was to prove a springboard to senior honours for several of the Gazelles. Backs Marius Joubert, Bolla Conradie and André Pretorius shone in the Divisional matches and came through to cement places in the South African Test side in 2002, while young forwards such as Lawrence Sephaka and Shaun Sowerby, a No 8 in the classic South African mould, showed that they too would soon press for permanent recognition in the Springbok squad.

Africa Top Six Results

Northern Division
17 March Tunisia 14, Morocco 17 (Tunis); **7 April** Côte d'Ivoire 11, Morocco 18 (Abidjan); **21 April** Morocco 20, Côte d'Ivoire 18 (Casablanca); **28 April** Tunisia 11, Côte d'Ivoire 11 (Tunis); **12 May** Côte d'Ivoire 46, Tunisia 0 (Abidjan); **19 May** Morocco 30, Tunisia 3 (Casablanca)

Southern Division

26 May Namibia 15, SA Under-23 60 (Windhoek); **2 June** Zimbabwe 20, SA Under-23 71 (Bulawayo); **16 June** SA Under-23 55, Namibia 13 (Johannesburg); **23 June** SA Under-23 78, Zimbabwe 29 (Durban); **7 July** Zimbabwe 27, Namibia 26 (Bulawayo); **14 July** Namibia 19, Zimbabwe 15 (Windhoek)

Final Standings

Northern Division

	P	W	D	L	For	Against	Bonus	Pts
Morocco	4	4	0	0	85	46	1	17
Côte d'Ivoire	4	1	1	2	86	49	3	9
Tunisia	4	0	1	3	28	104	0	2

Southern Division

	P	W	D	L	For	Against	Bonus	Pts
SA Under-23	4	4	0	0	264	77	4	20
Namibia	4	1	0	3	73	157	1	5
Zimbabwe	4	1	0	3	91	194	1	5

Points: win 4; draw 2; four or more tries, or defeat by seven or fewer points 1

Final

11 November Club Olympique, Casablanca
South Africa Under 23s 36 (4G 1PG 1T)   Morocco 20 (2G 2PG)

The South African Under 23s had beaten Morocco 44-14 in the 2000 final. In 2001, on a cool Casablanca November afternoon in a steady drizzle they won 36-20 after leading 28-3 at half-time.

The South Africans started strongly, running rings around their bigger opponents and proving simply too fast for them whenever the ball went wide. In the first half the South Africans eschewed kicks at goal in pursuit of tries and scored four of them, all converted by Jaco van der Westhuyzen. Hendro Scholtz, the tough Free State flank, led the way crossing twice for the Gazelles while Morocco's only points in the half came from a penalty by Thomas Garcia.

The bigger, older Moroccan pack responded with a physical onslaught that surprised the South African forwards in the second half. Most of the Moroccans play their rugby in the tough French Club Championship and had honed their skills for the final with a fortnight's preparation in France. By contrast, few of the young South Africans had any Currie Cup experience.

The South Africans were happy to kick a penalty at goal in the second half to keep their position secure while big No 8 Mikal Mokhtar and lock

Khalid Benazzi went over for tries for the Moroccans. In the end, however, the fitness and speed of the South Africans overcame their determined opponents.

Mokhtar, measuring 1.92m and scaling 100kg, has played for several French clubs in the First Division, as did Benazzi, the brother of Abdel, before he joined his brother at Saracens in England. The Moroccans took considerable heart from a match that was excellent preparation for their forthcoming World Cup qualifiers.

Morocco: Y Belkhous; Y Derraz, T Garcia, K El Oula, Y Faik; J Semlali, J Eziyar; M Gouasmia, J Narjissi, M Hamdini *(captain)*, J Hilmi, K Benazzi, H Arif, M Mokhtar, F Boukanoucha *Substitutes:* R El Hafid; Y Ouali; N Salmi, M Garcia; M Dermiouni; M Jaadi; H Amiona

Scorers *Tries:* Benazzi, Mokhtar *Conversions:* Garcia (2) *Penalty Goals:* Garcia (2)

South Africa Under 23: F Lombard; W A Human, G Bobo, W Julies, B F Welsh; J N B van der Westhuyzen *(captain)*, J H Conradie; E L Coetzee, H M Shimange, P D Carstens, H Hancke, J P Botha, H Scholtz, R S Sowerby, W van Heerden *Substitutes:* R S Badenhorst; A A A Winter; A J Badenhorst; C A Groenewald; H C Kruger; E Botha; I Job

Scorers *Tries:* Scholtz (2), van Heerden, Welsh, Shimange *Conversions:* Van der Westhuyzen (4) *Penalty Goal:* Kruger

Referee J Hogg (Scotland)

Previous Africa Top Six Championship Finals: 2000 South Africa Under 23s 44, Morocco 14 (Casablanca); 2001 South Africa Under 23s 36, Morocco 20 (Casablanca)

COMMONWEALTH GAMES SEVENS 2002

Gold for Inspired New Zealand

Brendan Gallagher

New Zealand, guided and inspired in equal measure by the ageless Eric Rush, retained their Commonwealth Games title in some style at the City of Manchester Stadium in August with a 33-15 victory over perennial rivals Fiji in a riveting final that was closer than the score might suggest. Rush actually ended up watching the final from the sidelines having damaged a rib in the semi-final, but the former All Black had played superbly prior to that and his calming influence throughout the three-day competition was a key factor for his young squad.

The hard working South Africa squad took the bronze medal, defeating Samoa 19-12 in the play-off in a game that will have left England green with envy after a tournament in which Joe Lydon's men only engaged top gear on the final day. Along with Fiji they were the only team truly capable of challenging the New Zealanders but the intensity of the occasion, in front of a massive home crowd, initially seemed to inhibit them.

Only on the final day with thumping wins over Canada and then Australia, did they show their true form to take the Plate, consolation of sorts for a determined campaign. Henry Paul was the pick of their team with Josh Lewsey and Nick Duncombe not far behind. If only they could replay their 7-5 quarter-final defeat against Fiji. You would settle for only conceding one try to Fiji in any match, but England's potentially high-powered offence failed to create anything except for a Paul Sampson try. Captain Phil Greening's wayward line-out throw virtually gifted Fiji their score but although the Wasps hooker was inconsolable afterwards, one defensive slip was not the sum of the England deficiencies.

The other losing quarter-finalist were Australia who flattered to deceive before losing 12-10 to Samoa, Wales who were outclassed 24-0 by New Zealand and a brave Canadian outfit, who lost 17-12 to South Africa.

Elsewhere Scotland looked an improving outfit and after taking the Bowl, with a 40-26 win over Tonga, might be encouraged to participate in the World Series more often. The Scots have a pool of young players who would clearly benefit from a prolonged Sevens campaign.

Kenya, who defeated Samoa in their opening pool game and performed well against England, were terrific value, and the IRB would be well advised to invest both financially and in manpower in the East African state. Judging by this tournament, Kenya possess some highly talented individuals waiting to be developed.

Though lacking one or two of the epic encounters of Kuala Lumpur four years ago, the Sevens was another stunning success. The organisation was slick, the action unrelenting and over 130,000 spectators attended throughout the three days. All grist to the mill as rugby continues to argue its case for re-admittance to the Olympic movement.

Pool Results (2nd/3rd August 2002)

Pool A: New Zealand 28, Canada 7; Scotland 54, Niue Island 5; New Zealand 66, Niue Island 0; Canada 7, Scotland 0; Canada 31, Niue Island 5; New Zealand 26, Scotland 12

Pool B: South Africa 26, Tonga 12; Wales 55, Sri Lanka 7; South Africa 82, Sri Lanka 0; Wales 31, Tonga 10; Tonga 47, Sri Lanka 12; South Africa 19, Wales 12

Pool C: England 24, Cook Islands 12; Samoa 20, Kenya 28; England 33, Kenya 12; Samoa 43, Cook Islands 5; Cook Islands 14, Kenya 12; England 19, Samoa 7

Pool D: Fiji 73, Malaysia 0; Australia 59, Trinidad & Tobago 0; Fiji 75, Trinidad & Tobago 0; Australia 55, Malaysia 0; Malaysia 45, Trinidad & Tobago 7; Fiji 12, Australia 19

Finals Day (4th August 2002)

Bowl Quarter-Finals: Scotland 57, Sri Lanka 0; Malaysia 52, Cook Islands 0; Trinidad & Tobago 40, Kenya 0; Tonga 59, Niue Island 5 **Semi-Finals** Tonga 41, Kenya 10; Scotland 26, Cook Islands 7 **BOWL FINAL:** Scotland 40, Tonga 26

Plate Semi-Finals: Australia 7, Wales 5; England 29, Canada 0

PLATE FINAL: England 36, Australia 12

Medal Quarter-Finals: New Zealand 24, Wales 0; Samoa 12, Australia 10; Fiji 7, England 5; South Africa 17, Canada 12 **Semi-Finals:** New Zealand 31, Samoa 12; Fiji 17, South Africa 7

Commonwealth Games Gold Medal Final 2002

4 August, City Of Manchester Stadium
New Zealand 33 (4G 1T) **Fiji 15** (1G 1PG 1T)

Reduced to six men after Saiasi Fuli was red-carded for a late challenge with seven minutes of the final to play, Fiji responded positively and even took the lead 15-14 after a crafty penalty from skipper Waisale Serevi, the three points of course coming from a drop-kick.

New Zealand, World Series winners for the last three years, kept cool and replied with a try from acting skipper Craig de Goldi with less than two minutes on the clock. Fiji enjoyed one last throw of the dice when Waisale Serevi, surely making his final appearance on the Sevens arena, wriggled through in characteristic fashion but threw out a poor pass to Bill Satala with the try-line beckoning. Two more late tries to New Zealand – the last after Jope Tuikabe had been sin-binned thus reducing Fiji to five men – bloated the scoreline in what had been a fiercely and closely fought final.

'We're always disappointed to lose a final, but we're proud of our silver medals,' said Serevi afterwards. 'It's always difficult to play with six men. I think we would have won had we had seven men.'

So it was Rush who stepped forward with his team to accept the gold medals and the accolades and, to the surprise of many, did not use the auspicious occasion to announce his retirement. At the venerable age of 37 Rush, who missed the final with a rib injury after starring throughout the pool and knock-out stages, still feels he has a lot to offer.

'It's a lot of travelling on the World Series – I'm away from home for 150 days of the year – but I'll sit and discuss it with my wife and family,' said the New Zealand captain. 'As long as they are OK about it I'm keen to stay on. I'm delighted with our win. The entire squad dedicated the three months leading into the tournament to the Commonwealth Games – preparing and focusing. It was thoroughly deserved. We won it the hard way, playing all the top teams except England. As with Kuala Lumpur it was a very special atmosphere, representing your country and New Zealand rugby at the Commonwealth Games.'

New Zealand: B T Reihana, B R M Fleming; M Muliaina, A Valence; C A Newby, C D de Goldi (*captain*), M C Masoe *Substitutions:* R So'oialo for Masoe (17 mins); R Q Randle for Fleming (17 mins); A S Tuitavake for Reihana (22 mins)

Scorers *Tries:* Muliaina, Newby, De Goldi, Reihana, Randle *Conversions:* Reihana (4)

Fiji: V Delasau, S Fuli; N Ligairi, W Serevi (*captain*); M Saukawa, V Satala, J Tuikabe *Substitution:* J Uluivuda for Saukawa (12 mins)

Scorers *Tries:* Tuikabe, Satala *Conversion:* Serevi *Penalty Goal:* Serevi

Referee S J Dickinson (Australia)

Previous Commonwealth Games Sevens Finals: 1998 New Zealand 21, Fiji 12 (Kuala Lumpur); 2002 New Zealand 33, Fiji 15 (Manchester)

IRB WORLD SEVENS SERIES 2002

New Zealand Complete The Hat Trick

John Griffiths

New Zealand dominated the third IRB World Sevens Series (WSS). They won the opening legs staged in Durban and Santiago, led the tournament points table from start to finish and were outright winners of seven of the eleven events, including the last four. Indeed, the side coached by Gordon Tietjens opened such a commanding lead that the overall title was secured in Kuala Lumpur, at which stage there were still two more legs of the series to be completed. New Zealand have now won all three of the IRB Sevens tournaments since the series was inaugurated in 2000 and their 62-point winning margin in 2002 set a new record that will take some beating.

The continued success of the New Zealanders is the more remarkable for the fact that their management has to select a squad from outside the pools of the Super Twelve franchises. Yet year in, year out Tietjens and his back-up team have brought together a talented team that is a bold mixture of youth and experience.

From Eric Rush, who is arguably the veteran of sevens rugby with more than 50 international tournaments on his cv, to the exciting teenagers Joe Rokocoko and Anthony Tuitavake, New Zealand have players who can and do dominate at sevens. At 37, Rush returned to lead the side with inspiration in 2002, having recovered from the World Cup injury that shortened his sevens activities the previous year. The two 19-year-olds, Rokocoko and Tuitavake, were outstanding in the London event staged at Twickenham in front of nearly 25,000 spectators and on the same weekend as the Heineken Cup and Parker Pen Shield finals. Rokocoko was that tournament's leading try scorer and a week later in Cardiff set the New Zealanders on their way to victory over England in the final final of the series.

It is interesting to see how the challenges to New Zealand's superiority have evolved in the short history of the Sevens Series. Fiji, the former kings of the shortened game, were serious contenders in 2000, coming within six points of toppling the New Zealanders. Then Australia came close to upsetting the apple-cart in 2001.

The surprise packet of 2002, however, was South Africa. In 2001, they had suffered a shock defeat by the Cook Islands at the Wellington stage of the tournament, but a year later, and with former Springbok legend Chester Williams now in charge, a young Springbok squad powered through to beat the New Zealanders 26-10 in the semi-final of the corresponding Wellington leg. One of the stars of South Africa's side was Brent Russell, who was to

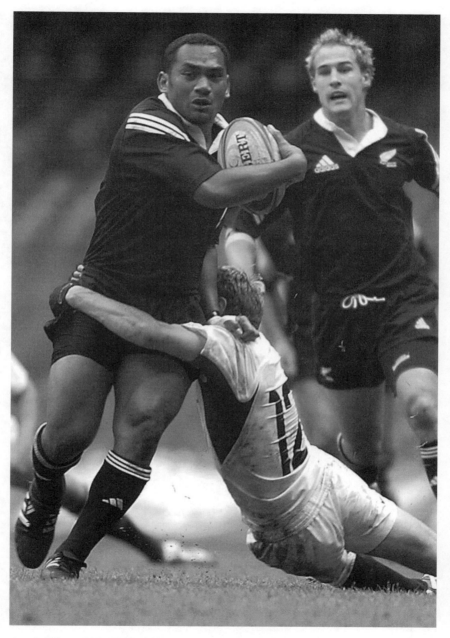

Amasio Valence of New Zealand slips a tackle at Cardiff in the last final of the 2002 IRB World Sevens series.

make a name for himself in the full Springbok Test line-up barely months later. Williams's side went on to beat Samoa in the Wellington final to record its first WSS title and were runners-up in Beijing, Kuala Lumpur and at Twickenham. South Africa thus finished in second place on overall final rankings that were to provide the basis for the Commonwealth Games Sevens seedings in Manchester in August.

England and Wales, too, had reason to celebrate new sevens successes in 2002. Hong Kong remains the premier event on the circuit and it was there that England, coached by Joe Lydon, won their first ever title. They defeated a plucky Welsh side in the semi-finals and overcame Fiji 33-20 in the final when Gloucester's James Simpson-Daniel grabbed a hat-trick of tries. However, it was his club-mate Henry Paul who was the star of the England show. The former League man displayed a dazzling array of skills as England's play-maker in Hong Kong and was again to the fore at the London event. At Twickenham his breaks set up tries for Paul Sampson and Josh Lewsey in a quarter-final win against Australia that accelerated England into third place ahead of Fiji on the IRB sevens table.

IRB World Sevens Series Results from the 2001-02 Tournaments

Team	1	2	3	4	5	6	7	8	9	10	11	Points
New Zealand	20 (W)	20 (W)	12	16 (R)	12	20 (W)	18	20 (W)	20 (W)	20 (W)	20 (W)	198
South Africa	12	12	16 (R)	12	20 (W)	16 (R)	4	4	16 (R)	16 (R)	8	136
England	12	6	6	4	12	8	30 (W)	12	8	12	16 (R)	126
Fiji	6	12	20 (W)	8	4	12	24 (R)	8	12	4	12	122
Australia	8	4	8	20 (W)	4	12	8	12	4	8	12	100
Samoa	16 (R)	8	4	12	16 (R)	6	8	6	12	6	4	98
Argentina	4	16 (R)	12	6	8	4	8	16 (R)	6	4	2	86
Wales	0	4	4	0	6	0	18	2	4	12	0	50
France	4	0	2	0	2	2	2	0	0	2	6	20
Scotland	0	0	0	0	0	0	3	4	2	0	4	13
United States	0	2	0	4	0	4	2	0	0	0	0	12
Canada	0	0	0	0	0	0	8	0	0	0	0	8
Namibia	2	0	0	0	0	0	0	0	0	0	0	2
Cook Islands	0	0	0	2	0	0	0	0	0	0	0	2
Morocco	0	0	0	0	0	0	1	0	0	0	0	1

Key to the tournaments in the table above: 1 Durban; 2 Santiago; 3 Mar del Plata; 4 Brisbane; 5 Wellington; 6 Beijing; 7 Hong Kong; 8 Singapore; 9 Kuala Lumpur; 10 London; 11 Cardiff

(W) winners; (R) runners-up

Previous IRB-World Sevens Series Winners: 1999-2000 New Zealand; 2000-01 New Zealand; 2001-02 New Zealand

Action from the New Zealand-England Sevens final at Cardiff.

IRB/FIRA–AER WORLD JUNIOR CHAMPIONSHIP 2002

Third Title for Talented Junior Blacks

Chris Thau

The annual U19 World Championship has become the cornerstone of the IRB elite development providing the age group programmes in the member unions with a sound base. Unlike the senior Rugby World Cup, which allows the victorious team to bask in the glory of being World Champions for four long years, the time for celebration after an U19 World Championship is uncannily short, while the criteria for success vary considerably among the 32-participating nations. In fact, the work for the next Championship, both in the Host Union and among the participants, would have commenced long before the matches of the current one had come to an end.

The organisers of the 35th IRB/FIRA-AER World U19 Championship have already put in place the infrastructure of the 10-day, 64-match marathon to be held in Ile de France, Paris, during the Easter week. The matches of the U18 zonal qualifying tournaments are already being played in all IRB Regions, while the Unions already qualified have triggered off their own selection programmes to identify the pool of talent available for the 2003 Championship. Underneath that age group the U17s provide the elite developmental pyramid with a wider base. The introduction of the U21 World Championship and the equivalent U20 feeder system has provided the world of rugby with an uninterrupted conveyor belt for talent.

The experiences the players and coaches absorb from such a high-pressure event are going to serve them well in the future, and the lesson of each tournament is that, winning aside, ultimately it is the talent supplied to the U21 set-up that counts.

Some coaches also feel that the developmental value of four matches of such intensity in ten days is questionable, yet the majority of the participants who have accepted the vagaries of the knockout system swear by it. A genuine overall improvement at the tackle area has been observed, with the players showing concern for continuity and the finer aspects of the law.

The IRB has been using the U19 tournament to train and develop a new generation of referees, and equally significant to upgrade refereeing standards in the developing world.

However, there is a virtually unanimous view that success in the U19 World Championship is measured, in the majority of the participating nations, by the number of talented youngsters supplied to the elite U21 programme and not by medals and cups, though winning remains the objective of any participant. An old FIRA hand suggested that a system must be found to reward teams for the number of quality players graduating to U21 age group and then senior ranks, as in many of the IRB member unions the competition has a wider role as a catalyst for the game.

It is perhaps significant that, while in the ten leading rugby-playing nations players can reach the top via different channels and development structures, in the majority of the 90-odd IRB member Unions the age-group development centred round the World U19 Championships is key to the success, and sometimes sheer survival, of their senior rugby. In many of the IRB member Unions the talent identification and selection programmes set in place for the U19 World Championship feed the entire system by increasing both the number and the quality of the players reaching the higher echelons of the game.

However, for a number of reasons the 34th World Junior Championship, held in the Northern Italian region of Treviso near Venice, will be remembered for the remarkable quality displayed by the 32-strong field, with many of the participating nations notably Scotland, England, Russia, Ireland, Georgia, Japan, Italy, Romania, Canada, Spain, newcomers Namibia, the United States, Paraguay, Chile and Uruguay making vast strides forward in terms of talent identification, skill acquisition, team organisation and game comprehension.

In this respect the opinion of the IRB Development manager for Oceania, Lee Smith, is edifying. He observes that the overall quality of the participants has gone up and that quality coaching has now become the norm rather than an exception among the 32 participating Unions.

'Having missed the 2001 U19 World Championship, the immediate impact the tournament has had on me was to note the vast improvement in the standard of play in the lower reaches of Division One and the upper echelons of Division Two. This was enhanced by a great improvement in the fitness of teams, in spite of a very taxing playing schedule over two weeks,' Smith said.

'The level of fitness resulted in greater accuracy in the performance of the skills of the game, in particular passing, tackling and ball retention. The contest for possession, especially at the lineout, was particularly pleasing, and the tackle area was well managed. It takes a lot of work for teams to ensure scrum stability and to develop the skills to compete for the ball in the lineout and not just concede possession and contest territory.'

However, for the 10,000 plus spectators gathered in Treviso's main rugby stadium the lasting memory of the 34th Tournament will be the win over France by arguably the most outrageously talented New Zealand youth team in years. The fact that New Zealand acquired the coveted U19 shield for the third time in four appearances was less of a surprise. After all, the young Blacks were the reigning champions, having won the world title the previous year in Santiago.

What surprised the pundits, was the outstanding ability of the young Blacks to clinically dismantle seemingly locked defences, glide through tackles and defensive platforms with frightening ease and score at will. Coaches Aussie McLean and Leicester Rutledge deserve credit for preparing a New Zealand Youth team that produced a sizzling mix of pace, power, skill and sheer footballing nous that set them apart in Italy. Only in their semi-final against South Africa were the Junior Blacks stretched.

The only time New Zealand looked rattled was when South African captain Luke Watson and his colleagues laboured their way up field with an interminable series of driving mauls and rushes close to the pack. But instead of persevering and battering their way into the New Zealand in-goal, they spun the ball wide in an attempt to play the expansive game to which they were accustomed. Virtually every time the ball left the hands of the South African forwards the ball invariably ended in New Zealand hands and reasonably often behind South Africa's line. This was by and large the story of every single New Zealand match in the tournament.

Smith said: 'The success of the New Zealand team must give confidence to all unions because they proved that skill, fitness and a willingness to support the ball carrier are the ingredients of winning rugby, and that size is not that important. Other unions could also learn that sequencing of play in a deliberate way can be very successful in players of this age group. While the result of the final may lead one to think that the tournament was one-sided, this was an exceptional New Zealand team and they are needed, if only to set the standard to which others can aspire. Mind you, South Africa were pretty good as well. The standard of play of all teams has resulted in a higher level of competition amongst those just below the top three and throughout the remainder of the competition.'

But all this is now history and the whole world of rugby has commenced working for the next tournament scheduled for March 2003. This is perhaps both the magic and the curse of the Junior (U19) World Championship. There is no time to pontificate, savour wins, gold medals and success. The work for the next tournament starts as soon as the medal ceremony of the previous one comes to an end.

Group B Results (20th/29th March 2002)

Round One: Canada 54, Czech Republic 3; Germany 24, Portugal 28; Ukraine 32, Chinese Taipei 27; United States 19, The Netherlands 18; Poland 14, Namibia 21; Lithuania 0, Paraguay 13; Morocco 0, Tunisia 20; Spain 89, Trinidad & Tobago 0

Quarter-finals: Canada 63, Portugal 7; Ukraine 23, United States 27; Namibia 8, Paraguay 8 (Namibia won 5-4 in penalty shoot-out); Spain 21, Tunisia 13

Semi-finals: Canada 44, United States 6; Namibia 13, Spain 6

Final: Canada 38, Namibia 22

Group B Final Rankings: 1st Canada; 2nd Namibia; 3rd Spain; 4th United States; 5th Tunisia; 6th Portugal; 7th Paraguay; 8th Ukraine; 9th Germany; 10th Morocco; 11th Chinese Taipei; 12th Lithuania; 13th The Netherlands; 14th Poland; 15th Czech Republic; 16 Trinidad & Tobago

Group A Results (21st/30th March 2002)

Round One: New Zealand 83, Korea 10; Ireland 24, Italy 27; South Africa 48, Chile 3; England 59, Romania 6; Wales 13, Georgia 3; Argentina 50, Japan 5; Uruguay 13, Scotland 54; France 15, Russia 0

Quarter-finals: New Zealand 80, Italy 8; South Africa 17, England 8; Wales 3, Argentina 3 (Argentina won 3-2 in penalty shoot-out); Scotland 17, France 26

Semi-finals: New Zealand 41, South Africa 9; Argentina 6, France 20

Final 30 March, Stadio di Monigo, Treviso
New Zealand 71 (9G 1PG 1T) **France 18** (1G 2PG 1T)

New Zealand: B Atiga; P Williams, C Aporo, T Ellison, P Te Whare; L McAllister, T Morland; B Nolan, T Paulo (*captain*), J Afoa, G Alaese, J Ryan, J Kaino, T Waldrom, R Tuivaiti *Substitutions:* B Smith for Williams (53 mins); W Crockett for Afoa (53 mins); C Clarke for Alaesi (55 mins); S Cowan for Morland (58 mins); B Stanley for Ellison (59 mins); J Pareanga for Paulo (64 mins); C Moke for Tuivaiti (64 mins)

Scorers *Tries:* Te Whare (2), Aporo (2), Kaino (2), McAllister, Waldrom, Atiga, Smith *Conversions:* McAllister (8), Aporo *Penalty Goal:* McAllister

France: A Floch; J Arias, D Lison, B Baby, J Saubade; N Rondet, A Aguirre; R Vaquin, R Carmignani, Y Nyanga (*captain*), R Millo-Chlusky, A Marchois, G Bergos, D Szarzewski, L Fior *Substitutions:* P-M Garcia for Rondet (43 mins); J Dupuy for Aguirre (43 mins); A Vigouroux for Szarzewski (50 mins); M Gouagout for Fior (58 mins); Y Dessème for Saubade (64 mins); M Dridi for Vaquin (64 mins); Roques for Millo-Chlusky (70 mins)

Scorers *Tries:* Marchois, Saubade *Conversion:* Floch *Penalty Goals:* Floch (2)

Referee D van Blommestein (South Africa)

Group A Final Rankings: 1st New Zealand; 2nd France; 3rd South Africa; 4th Argentina; 5th Scotland; 6th England; 7th Wales; 8th Italy; 9th Ireland; 10th Georgia; 11th Russia; 12th Romania; 13th Japan; 14th Korea; 15th Uruguay; 16 Chile

Previous IRB-FIRA World Junior Championship Winners: 1969 France (Barcelona); 1970 France (Vichy), 1971 France (Casablanca); 1972 Romania

(Rome); 1973 Romania (Bucharest); 1974 France (Heidelberg); 1975 France (Madrid); 1976 France (Albi); 1977 France (Hilversum); 1978 France (Parma); 1979 France (Lisbon); 1980 France (Tunis); 1981 France (Madrid); 1982 France (Geneva); 1983 France (Casablanca); 1984 Italy (Warsaw); 1985 France (Brussels); 1986 France (Bucharest); 1987 Argentina (Berlin); 1988 France (Makarska); 1989 Argentina (Lisbon); 1990 Argentina (Brescia); 1991 France (Toulouse); 1992 France (Madrid); 1993 Argentina (Lille); 1994 South Africa (Lyon); 1995 France (Bucharest); 1996 Argentina (Brescia); 1997 Argentina (Buenos Aires); 1998 Ireland (Toulouse); 1999 New Zealand (Llanelli); 2000 France (Burgundy); 2001 New Zealand (Santiago de Chile); 2002 New Zealand (Treviso)

IRB UNDER 21 WORLD CUP 2002

Resounding Success of Inaugural Event
Michelle Treacy

The resounding success of the inaugural IRB U21 World Cup included a superb semi-final and a final that will long live in the memories of those who saw it. However, it wasn't only the display of the top four teams that stood out in the tournament. Romania gave a gutsy performance in arguably the outstanding match of the third round to defeat Fiji by 28-26, while players from the so-called smaller unions gained invaluable experience competing against their peers in an age group that sits just beneath full Test level.

This competition is a very important and necessary step for world rugby. Since its forerunner, the SANZAR/UAR U21 tournament, began in 1995, more than 150 U21 players (including Christian Cullen, Ben Cohen and Toutai Kefu) have progressed to full international status. Many among this year's crop of talent will no doubt be added to that list. Certainly the energy and zeal of the coming generation of Test players were evident in the exciting talents of Tamaiti Horua (Australia), Mathieu Siro (France), Sam Tuitupou (New Zealand), Ashley Willemse (South Africa), Jim Scaysbrook (England), Roland Barnard (South Africa), Patricio Albacete (Argentina), Martín Castrogiovani (Italy) and Eoghan Hickey (Ireland).

Hosts South Africa opened their World Cup challenge in dramatic fashion with a 135-0 win over Romania at Ellis Park. New Zealand, Australia, Wales and France were also impressive with wins over England, Ireland, Italy and Fiji respectively. Argentina began their campaign in Ellis Park with a 46-24 win over Japan.

Argentina, despite taking an early lead, were then beaten by Wales 45-34 in a physical encounter at the Rand Afrikaans University Stadium on the second day's play, while New Zealand survived an early scare from Japan to record their expected win. South Africa encountered tough opposition from France, but the Junior Boks had sufficient resources to maintain their 100% record with a 28-9 victory. England defeated Italy 41-12, Australia continued their impressive start to the tournament with a win over Romania, and Ireland's fly-half Eoghan Hickey claimed 33 points in his side's 63-10 win over of Fiji.

After the third day's play the seedings were re-set for the final stages. Top seeds New Zealand were matched with South Africa, and Australia were to play Wales in the main tournament semi-finals. There were two more pairs of semi-finals to determine the lower rankings: Argentina v France and England v Ireland for fifth-eighth place, and Italy v Romania and Fiji v Japan for ninth-12th place.

In a pulsating semi-final in front of a huge crowd, Francois Swart kicked an angled penalty to give South Africa a last-minute one-point win against New Zealand. South Africa's full-back, Jorrie Muller, had earlier seen his drop-kick charged down only for New Zealand to break out and score at the other end of the field. The New Zealanders scored two tries, but Swart's steadiness with the boot – he landed five kicks from seven attempts – was the deciding factor that put his side into the final. In the other main semi-final Australia confirmed their potential with a comfortable 43-7 win against Wales.

The final day exceeded all expectations with spectators exposed to an effervescent display of nail-biting rugby. Much to the delight of the crowd South Africa beat Australia 24-21 to become the first IRB U21 World Champions. The wounded New Zealanders rounded off their participation with a solid 59-7 win over Wales to secure third position overall, full-back Ben Atiga scoring a brace in an eight-try performance. Team manager Sean Fitzpatrick said afterwards: 'They played really well. This tournament is about development and this win shows how much they developed in the last five weeks.'

France secured fifth place with a comeback win over Ireland, who changed over with what seemed an unassailable 26-7 lead. France turned the game around in the final 40 minutes, scoring five converted tries to win by 40-29. Irish coach Ciaran Fitzgerald concluded: 'This tournament has been great, and a quality examination for the players. Playing five games in two weeks allowed us to see how they cope with the pressure of high level rugby. On that account, it was a very positive tournament for us.'

England saved their best for last, beating Argentina 74-14 with wings Simon Hunt and John Rudd each scoring try hat-tricks. At Wits University Stadium, Fiji avenged their earlier loss to Romania with a 19-9 win to secure 11th place overall and Italy went down to Japan 41-29.

Captains agreed that the tournament was a huge learning curve, a great challenge and produced memorable, awe-inspiring rugby of the highest standard.

Results (14th/28th June 2002)

First round: France 80, Fiji 10; Argentina 46, Japan 24; Australia 51, Ireland 18; Wales 82, Italy 18; New Zealand 67, England 23; South Africa 135, Romania 0

Second round: Australia 135, Romania 3; Ireland 63, Fiji 10; South Africa 28, France 9; New Zealand 99, Japan 8; Wales 45, Argentina 34; England 41, Italy 12

Third round: England 20, Argentina 17; Romania 28, Fiji 26; New Zealand 73, Wales 19; Japan 34, Italy 13; South Africa 42, Ireland 22; Australia 64, France 15

Fourth round: Italy 23, Romania 22; France 29, Argentina 17; Japan 25, Fiji 21; Ireland 28, England 15; Australia 43, Wales 7; South Africa 19, New Zealand 18

Play-off finals: Fiji 19, Romania 9; Japan 49, Italy 29; England 74, Argentina 14; France 40, Ireland 29; New Zealand 59, Wales 7

Final 28 June, Ellis Park, Johannesburg
South Africa 24 (1G 4PG 1T)   Australia 21 (1G 3PG 1T)

A dozen teams had originally nursed aspirations and dreams of making it all the way to the final. Four rounds, 14 days and 24 matches later South Africa, the most consistent and unyielding team in the tournament, beat Australia 24-21 in front of an ecstatic crowd of 25,000 to become the first IRB U21 World Cup holders.

South Africa's Francois Swart opened the scoring with a seventh-minute penalty goal from the half-way line and added the second of his four penalties seven minutes later. Australia's Brock James narrowed the margin to 6-3 when South Africa conceded a penalty for playing the ball in the ruck, before Swart's third success on 24 minutes restored the South Africans' six-point lead. A minute later, Rathbone broke the first line of defence and passed to Jorrie Muller who sent Ashwin Willemse in for the first try of the final. The conversion and two more penalties from Swart, and another penalty by James for Australia, left South Africa firmly in charge at the break.

The second half opened with a fine try from Rathbone before South Africa's Roland Bernard was sin-binned. Australia now capitalised on having an extra player and launched a series of attacks that culminated in prop Anthony Mathison crossing the line. With ten minutes remaining, Australia were still pounding the South African try-line and deservedly narrowed the margin to 24-21 when wing Peter Hynes ran in for an unconverted try that completed the scoring.

South Africa's Francois Swart, the tournament's leading points scorer, said: 'To describe how I feel I could use all the adjectives – ecstatic, exciting, exhilarating, exhausted you name it. The truth is you have to experience it to understand the feeling.'

Winning Coach Jake White acknowledged the support his team had enjoyed. 'SA Rugby gave us all we needed to have a successful campaign and the crowd support was unbelievable. We came to this tournament seeded seventh and we had to take the long road to win it. Having to beat New Zealand and Australia within four days was a huge task and the players should take all the credit.'

Australian captain Tamaiti Horua said: 'We are disappointed, we set the goal of winning this World Cup and didn't. But we had to be proud of our performance throughout. Had it not been for a few mistakes and the fact that South Africa adapted better to the circumstances we could have won it. We will still celebrate a good tournament.'

South Africa: G P Muller; J de Villiers, C Rathbone (*captain*), D F Swartbooi, A K Willemse; F J Swart, E Januarie; G G Steenkamp, G Botha, P Barnard, S van Rooyen, J Smith, R Bernard, J Cronjé, P J Wannenberg *Substitutions:* P F du Preez for Januarie (59 mins); J P Nel for Rathbone (67 mins); S Burger for Bernard

(67 mins); Q Geldenhuys for Van Rooyen (72 mins); R Gerber for Barnard (75 mins)

Scorers *Tries:* Willemse, Rathbone *Conversion:* Swart *Penalty Goals:* Swart (4)

Australia: M Tabrett; L Sweeney, M Gerrard, M Turinui, P Hynes; B James, M Henjak; N Henderson, J Mann-Rea, A Mathison, D Heenan, M Chisholm, J Tawake, T Horua *(captain)*, M Hodgson *Substitutions:* A Whalley for Tawake (63 mins); M Kefu for Turinui (67 mins); M Giteau for James (75 mins)

Scorers *Tries:* Mathison, Hynes *Conversion:* James *Penalty Goals:* James (3)

Referee S McDowell (Ireland)

Final Rankings: 1st South Africa; 2nd Australia; 3rd New Zealand; 4th Wales; 5th France; 6th Ireland; 7th England; 8th Argentina; 9th Japan; 10th Italy; 11th Fiji; 12th Romania

Previous SANZAR/UAR Under-21 World Cup Winners: 1995 New Zealand (Buenos Aires); 1996 Australia (Takapuna); 1997 Australia (Sydney); 1998 Australia (Cape Town); 1999 South Africa (Buenos Aires); 2000 New Zealand (Auckland); 2001 New Zealand (Sydney)

Previous IRB Under-21 World Cup Finals: 2002 South Africa 24, Australia 21 (Johannesburg)

ENGLAND TEST SEASON REVIEW 2001-02

Grand Slam Woodward's Holy Grail

Mick Cleary

They were an unfamiliar looking lot that trotted down the Vélez Sarsfield tunnel in mid-June to be greeted with typical respect and reverence by the locals. The cacophony of jeers, whistles and firecrackers indicated that the 40,000 packed into the stadium that afternoon didn't care one jot that the men in white were not the household names that had represented the red rose of England throughout the season. This was England and opportunities to claim a famous scalp were to be treasured. This was the real thing. Hence the boos. Hence the respect.

That was pretty much how Clive Woodward saw it too. No matter that only four Six Nations regulars started that Test – tight-head Phil Vickery, hooker Steve Thompson, lock Ben Kay and No 8 Joe Worsley. Leicester flanker Lewis Moody and fly-half Charlie Hodgson, who also tuned into the Buenos Aires reception committee that afternoon, deserve honourable mentions as they too had been key members of the England squad throughout the season with regular game time as substitutes.

But there was a cast of stars that did not make the trip: players such as Martin Johnson, Jonny Wilkinson, Neil Back, Will Greenwood, Dan Luger, Ben Cohen, Jason Robinson, Kyran Bracken, Matt Dawson and Lawrence Dallaglio, all either injured or rested. All told, 23 front-line players were missing. Instead there were five debutants in Buenos Aires: London Irish duo, full-back Michael Horak and centre Geoff Appleford, Bristol wing, Phil Christophers, Saracens centre, Ben Johnston and Harlequins lock, Alex Codling.

Dallaglio had been due to captain the tour party after recovering from the cruciate knee injury that had blighted his Lions tour and sidelined him for nine months. He recovered in time to make a try-scoring cameo appearance in England's last Six Nations game against Italy in Rome but then picked up a hand injury that ruled him out of the tour. Vickery stepped into the fold, the first Gloucester player in 131 years of Test rugby to captain England and their fifth captain within a 12-month period – Bracken, Johnson, Back and Dallaglio being the others.

If such a change of personnel suggests uncertainty and mishap then it is entirely misleading. That was not the story of England's year. Woodward was more than happy to have the chance to shuffle his resources and fully intends to carry on with such a policy right through to the World Cup. The 2001 Lions tour gave him a chance to run the rule over several players jockeying for recognition who had shown what they had to offer on the trip

Clive Woodward celebrates the win against Scotland at Murrayfield.

that summer to North America. The two-match, one-Test trip to Argentina served the same purpose albeit Woodward was disappointed that one newcomer, Gloucester wing James Simpson-Daniel, was forced to pull out of the tour at the last minute. Simpson-Daniel was a star of England's unexpected victory at the Hong Kong Sevens, the 20-year-old wing scoring a hat-trick in the 33-20 victory over Fiji in the final. He then went on to show Jonah Lomu a clean pair of heels in England's 53-29 victory over the Barbarians in May.

Woodward got a good chance to run the rule over many other contenders in the course of a fascinating year which saw his team win eight of their nine matches after the 20-14 defeat against Ireland in October in the held-over 2001 Six Nations match. France won 20-15 in Paris in the game that effectively settled the 2002 championship. England averaged over 40 points, albeit that healthy return was distorted by the 134-0 drubbing handed out to the unfortunate Romanians in November, a record score for England and a sobering day for all concerned as a proud rugby nation was publicly humbled by what was not much more than a mix n'match England side. For the second year in succession England also managed to see off the southern hemisphere challenge, beating Australia, 21-15, as well as South Africa, 29-9.

In the course of the year new names came to the fore: Leicester lock, Ben Kay, now the mainstay of the England second-row; Northampton hooker, Steve Thompson; flanker Lewis Moody, who managed the impressive feat of overshadowing club-mates Neil Back and former All Black open-side Josh Kronfeld during Leicester's gallop to honours; Wasps No 8 Joe Worsley, who finally managed to emerge from the shadows of Dallaglio and play with conviction during his extended run in England colours; Hodgson, too, came through as not just an understudy to the ever-improving Jonny Wilkinson but also as a challenger to his position. Hodgson scored a record 44 points in that rout of Romania.

There were many other heartening signs for Woodward. Jason Robinson was switched to full-back as the troubling decline of Iain Balshaw continued. It was a spectacular success. Among the highlights were four tries against Romania, one a bewitching 75-metre effort, and a brace against Scotland, tries that killed that game stone dead within the opening quarter of an hour. Robinson scared the living daylights out of the opposition, and occasionally his own team as they looked on in bewilderment when he set off from the rear on his unorthodox angles. He not only gave England a dangerous cutting edge, he also made the opposition reconsider their own strategies. A kicking game had to be subtle and accurate. Robinson punished any aberration with the kick or any complacency with the chase.

Will Greenwood re-established himself as a world-class inside-centre, to the eventual detriment of Mike Catt, who was dropped to make way for Greenwood. Ben Cohen, after a disappointing Lions tour, came back strongly, so much so that the Northampton wing was one of the first names on Woodward's team-sheet by the end of the season.

It was not all sunshine and roses. Balshaw, a class act during the previous year's Six Nations, fell off the radar as his confidence plummeted after a dispiriting Lions tour. Rugby league convert Henry Paul struggled to really make a mark, flitting between positions and looking out of his depth when he came on to make his England debut as a substitute against France. He played a prominent role in the Sevens success, but has yet to master the ever-changing landscape of a union field. Still, great faith has been placed in him to perhaps fill the troublesome outside-centre berth, although the rejuvenation of Mike Tindall and the emergence of Simpson-Daniel will enliven that debate.

Woodward, although troubled by the continuing battle to secure greater player release from the clubs during the season, was a contented man as he clocked off for a brief summer respite following the 26-18 victory over a Pumas outfit that had seen off Grand Slam France seven days earlier. There was also an Argentina A victory over their England counterparts to take into account.

Woodward had been criticised for taking such an under-strength side to Argentina. The doubters were proved wrong and he was proved right. His main men were given a chance to recharge and get stuck into some heavy-duty training. Several of them would need every last second of that summer respite if they were to hold off the challenge from some of those who came through on the Argentina trip. Kay matured not just as a second-row but as a future leader, while Hodgson confirmed his obvious talent. Moody put himself in the frame for starting honours on the open-side while Gloucester scrum-half Andy Gomarsall indicated the scrap for the No 9 shirt will not be a straightforward tussle between just Bracken and Dawson. Competition for places is a boon for any coach.

Woodward's whole coaching department enjoyed a good year – all that is bar Brian Ashton, who parted company with the elite squad just before the end of the Six Nations owing to personal problems. Ashton was reassigned to work with the under 21s and under 19s. But for Andy Robinson, Phil Larder and Dave Alred, the front-line coaches, there was real evidence that all the hard labour is paying off. Sure, there were blips, notably against France, but at so many other times there was evidence of genuine class. The opening hour in the February match against Ireland saw some of the finest rugby ever produced at Twickenham. Jonny Wilkinson gave a master-class in fly-half play that day.

And yet still Woodward had to ward off the back-biters. There were some murmurings even during the autumn when England completed a clean sweep. Critics noted that Woodward's England had yet to win anything. True, the sting of the Grand Slam defeat against Ireland was still in the air. But to beat both Australia and South Africa for the second year running is no mean feat. England, even with Robinson at full-back for the first time, did not manage to score a try in their 21-15 win over the world champion Wallabies, but they deserved their victory. Johnson was absent through injury so Back led the side, a role he was to take on at various stages through the year.

Johnson was back in harness for the South Africa match but was forced to step down midway through the Six Nations. The Leicester lock looked set to miss the crucial showdown with France after receiving a three week ban for punching Saracens hooker, Robbie Russell. The incident, spotted at the time but only deemed worthy of a yellow card, became a *cause célèbre*. Johnson was cleared to play in Paris only after lodging an appeal. Back carried the captain's armband for the remaining two games against Wales and then Italy, even though Johnson was available for the final game. He only made it as far as the bench, a calculated bit of selection for Woodward as he reviewed his options. Johnson was none too impressed by the move and was chomping at the bit to get into the action. He eventually got on to the field at the Stadio Flaminio as one of a quartet of England captains coming off the replacements' bench – Dallaglio, Dawson and Jason Leonard being the others.

England won the Triple Crown for the 22nd time when they demolished Wales 50-10 in March. It was little consolation for England, who had set their sights once again on the Grand Slam. For all the good vibrations emanating from England's season there was a hollow feel about the relative successes. Woodward's England made many gains during another demanding campaign. The Grand Slam still eludes them. That failing will keep them honest and hungry through the next 12 months.

England's Test Record in 2001-2002: Played 9, won 8, lost 1.

Opponents	Date	Venue	Result
Argentina	22nd June 2002	A	Won 26-18
Italy	7th April 2002	A	Won 45-9
Wales	23rd March 2002	H	Won 50-10
France	2nd March 2002	A	Lost 15-20
Ireland	16th February 2002	H	Won 45-11
Scotland	2nd February 2002	A	Won 29-3
South Africa	24th November 2001	H	Won 29-9
Romania	17th November 2001	H	Won 134-0
Australia	10th November 2001	H	Won 21-15

ENGLAND INTERNATIONAL STATISTICS

(to 31 August 2002)

Match Records

MOST CONSECUTIVE TEST WINS

11 2000 *SA 2, A, Arg, SA 3*, 2001 *W, It, S, F, C 1,2, US*

10 1882 *W*, 1883 *I, S*, 1884 *W, I, S*, 1885 *W, I*, 1886 *W, I*

10 1994 *R, C*, 1995 *I, F, W, S, Arg, It, WS, A*

MOST CONSECUTIVE TESTS WITHOUT DEFEAT

Matches	Wins	Draws	Period
12	10	2	1882 to 1887
11	10	1	1922 to 1924
11	11	0	2000 to 2001

MOST POINTS IN A MATCH
by the team

Pts	Opponents	Venue	Year
134	Romania	Twickenham	2001
110	Netherlands	Huddersfield	1998
106	United States	Twickenham	1999
101	Tonga	Twickenham	1999
80	Italy	Twickenham	2001
67	Italy	Twickenham	1999
60	Japan	Sydney	1987
60	Canada	Twickenham	1994
60	Wales	Twickenham	1998

by a player

Pts	Player	Opponents	Venue	Year
44	C Hodgson	Romania	Twickenham	2001
36	P J Grayson	Tonga	Twickenham	1999
35	J P Wilkinson	Italy	Twickenham	2001
32	J P Wilkinson	Italy	Twickenham	1999
30	C R Andrew	Canada	Twickenham	1994
30	P J Grayson	Netherlands	Huddersfield	1998
30	J P Wilkinson	Wales	Twickenham	2002
29	D J H Walder	Canada	Burnaby	2001
27	C R Andrew	South Africa	Pretoria	1994
27	J P Wilkinson	South Africa	Bloemfontein	2000
26	J P Wilkinson	United States	Twickenham	1999

MOST TRIES IN A MATCH
by the team

Tries	Opponents	Venue	Year
20	Romania	Twickenham	2001
16	Netherlands	Huddersfield	1998
16	United States	Twickenham	1999
13	Wales	Blackheath	1881
13	Tonga	Twickenham	1999
10	Japan	Sydney	1987
10	Fiji	Twickenham	1989
10	Italy	Twickenham	2001
9	France	Paris	1906
9	France	Richmond	1907
9	France	Paris	1914
9	Romania	Bucharest	1989

by a player

Tries	Player	Opponents	Venue	Year
5	D Lambert	France	Richmond	1907
5	R Underwood	Fiji	Twickenham	1989
4	G W Burton	Wales	Blackheath	1881
4	A Hudson	France	Paris	1906
4	R W Poulton	France	Paris	1914
4	C Oti	Romania	Bucharest	1989
4	J C Guscott	Netherlands	Huddersfield	1998
4	N A Back	Netherlands	Huddersfield	1998
4	J C Guscott	United States	Twickenham	1999
4	J Robinson	Romania	Twickenham	2001

MOST CONVERSIONS IN A MATCH
by the team

Cons	Opponents	Venue	Year
15	Netherlands	Huddersfield	1998
14	Romania	Twickenham	2001
13	United States	Twickenham	1999
12	Tonga	Twickenham	1999
9	Italy	Twickenham	2001
8	Romania	Bucharest	1989
7	Wales	Blackheath	1881
7	Japan	Sydney	1987
7	Argentina	Twickenham	1990
7	Wales	Twickenham	1998

by a player

Cons	Player	Opponents	Venue	Year
15	P J Grayson	Netherlands	Huddersfield	1998
14	C Hodgson	Romania	Twickenham	2001
13	J P Wilkinson	United States	Twickenham	1999
12	P J Grayson	Tonga	Twickenham	1999
9	J P Wilkinson	Italy	Twickenham	2001
8	S D Hodgkinson	Romania	Bucharest	1989
7	J M Webb	Japan	Sydney	1987
7	S D Hodgkinson	Argentina	Twickenham	1990
7	P J Grayson	Wales	Twickenham	1998

MOST PENALTIES IN A MATCH
by the team

Penalties	Opponents	Venue	Year
8	South Africa	Bloemfontein	2000
7	Wales	Cardiff	1991
7	Scotland	Twickenham	1995
7	France	Twickenham	1999
7	Fiji	Twickenham	1999
7	South Africa	Paris	1999
7	South Africa	Twickenham	2001
6	Wales	Twickenham	1986
6	Canada	Twickenham	1994
6	Argentina	Durban	1995
6	Scotland	Murrayfield	1996
6	Ireland	Twickenham	1996
6	South Africa	Twickenham	2000

by a player

Penalties	Player	Opponents	Venue	Year
8	J P Wilkinson	South Africa	Bloemfontein	2000
7	S D Hodgkinson	Wales	Cardiff	1991
7	C R Andrew	Scotland	Twickenham	1995
7	J P Wilkinson	France	Twickenham	1999
7	J P Wilkinson	Fiji	Twickenham	1999
7	J P Wilkinson	South Africa	Twickenham	2001
6	C R Andrew	Wales	Twickenham	1986
6	C R Andrew	Canada	Twickenham	1994
6	C R Andrew	Argentina	Durban	1995
6	P J Grayson	Scotland	Murrayfield	1996
6	P J Grayson	Ireland	Twickenham	1996
6	P J Grayson	South Africa	Paris	1999
6	J P Wilkinson	South Africa	Twickenham	2000

MOST DROPPED GOALS IN A MATCH
by the team

Drops	Opponents	Venue	Year
2	Ireland	Twickenham	1970
2	France	Paris	1978
2	France	Paris	1980
2	Romania	Twickenham	1985
2	Fiji	Suva	1991
2	Argentina	Durban	1995
2	France	Paris	1996
2	Australia	Twickenham	2001

by a player

Drops	Player	Opponents	Venue	Year
2	R Hiller	Ireland	Twickenham	1970
2	A G B Old	France	Paris	1978
2	J P Horton	France	Paris	1980
2	C R Andrew	Romania	Twickenham	1985
2	C R Andrew	Fiji	Suva	1991
2	C R Andrew	Argentina	Durban	1995
2	P J Grayson	France	Paris	1996
2	J P Wilkinson	Australia	Twickenham	2001

Career Records
MOST CAPPED PLAYERS

Caps	Player	Career Span
97	J Leonard	1990 to 2002
85	R Underwood	1984 to 1996
72	W D C Carling	1988 to 1997
71	C R Andrew	1985 to 1997
67	M O Johnson	1993 to 2002
65	J C Guscott	1989 to 1999
64	B C Moore	1987 to 1995
58	P J Winterbottom	1982 to 1993
56	M J Catt	1994 to 2001
55	W A Dooley	1985 to 1993
50	N A Back	1994 to 2002
49	R A Hill	1997 to 2002
48	D Richards	1986 to 1996
48	L B N Dallaglio	1995 to 2002

MOST CONSECUTIVE TESTS

Tests	Player	Span
44	W D C Carling	1989 to 1995
40	J Leonard	1990 to 1995
36	J V Pullin	1968 to 1975
33	W B Beaumont	1975 to 1982
30	R Underwood	1992 to 1996

MOST TESTS AS CAPTAIN

Tests	Captain	Span
59	W D C Carling	1988 to 1996
23	M O Johnson	1998 to 2002
21	W B Beaumont	1978 to 1982
14	L B N Dallaglio	1997 to 1999
13	W W Wakefield	1924 to 1926
13	N M Hall	1949 to 1955

| 13 | R E G Jeeps | 1960 to 1962 |
| 13 | J V Pullin | 1972 to 1975 |

MOST TESTS IN INDIVIDUAL POSITIONS

Position	Player	Tests	Span
Full-back	M B Perry	35	1997 to 2001
Wing	R Underwood	85	1984 to 1996
Centre	W D C Carling	72	1988 to 1997
Fly-half	C R Andrew	70	1985 to 1997
Scrum-half	M J S Dawson	44	1995 to 2002
Prop	J Leonard	97	1990 to 2002
Hooker	B C Moore	63*	1987 to 1995
Lock	M O Johnson	67	1993 to 2002
Flanker	P J Winterbottom	58	1982 to 1993
No 8	D Richards	47*	1986 to 1996

excludes an appearance as a temporary replacement

MOST POINTS IN TESTS

Points	Player	Tests	Career
533	J P Wilkinson	35	1998 to 2002
396	C R Andrew	71	1985 to 1997
310	P J Grayson	23	1995 to 1999
296	J M Webb	33	1987 to 1993
240	W H Hare	25	1974 to 1984
210	R Underwood	85	1984 to 1996

MOST TRIES IN TESTS

Tries	Player	Tests	Career
49	R Underwood	85	1984 to 1996
30	J C Guscott	65	1989 to 1999
19	W J H Greenwood	30	1997 to 2002
19	D D Luger	27	1998 to 2002

18	C N Lowe	25	1913 to 1923
15	B C Cohen	18	2000 to 2002
15	A S Healey	47	1997 to 2002
13	T Underwood	27	1992 to 1998
13	N A Back	50	1994 to 2002
13	M J S Dawson	44	1995 to 2002

MOST CONVERSIONS IN TESTS

Cons	Player	Tests	Career
90	J P Wilkinson	35	1998 to 2002
52	P J Grayson	23	1995 to 1999
41	J M Webb	33	1987 to 1993
35	S D Hodgkinson	14	1989 to 1991
33	C R Andrew	71	1985 to 1997
17	L Stokes	12	1875 to 1881
17	C Hodgson	5	2001 to 2002

MOST PENALTY GOALS IN TESTS

Penalties	Player	Tests	Career
105	J P Wilkinson	35	1998 to 2002
86	C R Andrew	71	1985 to 1997
67	W H Hare	25	1974 to 1984
66	J M Webb	33	1987 to 1993
61	P J Grayson	23	1995 to 1999
43	S D Hodgkinson	14	1989 to 1991

MOST DROPPED GOALS IN TESTS

Drops	Player	Tests	Career
21	C R Andrew	71	1985 to 1997
6	P J Grayson	23	1995 to 1999
6	J P Wilkinson	35	1998 to 2002
4	J P Horton	13	1978 to 1984

International Championship Records

Record	Detail		Set
Most points in season	229	in five matches	2001
Most tries in season	29	in five matches	2001
Highest Score	80	80-23 v Italy	2001
Biggest win	57	80-23 v Italy	2001
Highest score conceded	37	12-37 v France	1972
Biggest defeat	27	6-33 v Scotland	1986
Most appearances	50	R Underwood	1984 – 1996
	50	J Leonard	1991 – 2002
Most points in matches	302	J P Wilkinson	1998-2002
Most points in season	89	J P Wilkinson	2001
Most points in match	35	J P Wilkinson	v Italy, 2001
Most tries in matches	18	C N Lowe	1913 – 1923
	18	R Underwood	1984 – 1996

Most tries in season	8	C N Lowe	1914
Most tries in match	4	R W Poulton	v France, 1914
Most cons in matches	61	J P Wilkinson	1998 – 2002
Most cons in season	24	J P Wilkinson	2001
Most cons in match	9	J P Wilkinson	v Italy, 2001
Most pens in matches	54	J P Wilkinson	1998 – 2002
Most pens in season	18	S D Hodgkinson	1991
	18	J P Wilkinson	2000
Most pens in match	7	S D Hodgkinson	v Wales, 1991
	7	C R Andrew	v Scotland, 1995
	7	J P Wilkinson	v France, 1999
Most drops in matches	9	C R Andrew	1985 – 1997
Most drops in season	3	P J Grayson	1996
Most drops in match	2	R Hiller	v Ireland, 1970
	2	A G B Old	v France, 1978
	2	J P Horton	v France, 1980
	2	P J Grayson	v France, 1996

Miscellaneous Records

Record	Holder	Detail
Longest Test Career	G S Pearce	14 seasons, 1978-79 to 1991-92
Youngest Test Cap	H C C Laird	18 yrs 134 days in 1927
Oldest Test Cap	F Gilbert	38 yrs in 1923

Career Records Of England International Players
(up to 31 August 2002)

PLAYER	Debut	Caps	T	C	P	D	Pts
Backs:							
G Appleford	2002 v Arg	1	0	0	0	0	0
I R Balshaw	2000 v I	14	5	0	0	0	25
O Barkley	2001 v US	1	0	0	0	0	0
T D Beim	1998 v NZ	2	1	0	0	0	5
S Benton	1998 v A	1	0	0	0	0	0
K P P Bracken	1993 v NZ	41	3	0	0	0	15
M J Catt	1994 v W	56	5	14	22	3	128
P Christophers	2002 v Arg	1	1	0	0	0	5
B C Cohen	2000 v I	18	15	0	0	0	75
M J S Dawson	1995 v WS	44	13	4	3	0	82
N Duncombe	2002 v S	2	0	0	0	0	0
W J H Greenwood	1997 v A	30	19	0	0	0	95
A C T Gomarsall	1996 v It	8	4	0	0	0	20
A S Healey	1997 v I	47	15	0	0	0	75
C Hodgson	2001 v R	5	2	17	5	0	59
M J Horak	2002 v Arg	1	0	0	0	0	0
B Johnston	2002 v Arg	1	0	0	0	0	0
A D King	1997 v Arg	4	1	1	0	0	7
O J Lewsey	1998 v NZ	6	4	0	0	0	20
L D Lloyd	2000 v SA	5	2	0	0	0	10
D D Luger	1998 v H	27	19	0	0	0	95
B-J Mather	1999 v W	1	0	0	0	0	0
J Noon	2001 v C	3	1	0	0	0	5
H Paul	2002 v F	1	0	0	0	0	0

M B Perry	1997 v A	36	10	0	0	0	50
D L Rees	1997 v A	11	3	0	0	0	15
J Robinson	2001 v It	11	8	0	0	0	40
P C Sampson	1998 v SA	3	0	0	0	0	0
M Stephenson	2001 v C	3	0	0	0	0	0
T R G Stimpson	1996 v It	18	2	3	5	0	31
M J Tindall	2000 v I	18	4	0	0	0	20
T Voyce	2001 v US	1	0	0	0	0	0
D J H Walder	2001 v C	3	2	10	3	0	39
F H H Waters	2001 v US	1	0	0	0	0	0
J P Wilkinson	1998 v I	35	4	90	105	6	533
M B Wood	2001 v C	2	1	0	0	0	5
Forwards:							
G S Archer	1996 v S	21	0	0	0	0	0
N A Back	1994 v S	50	13	0	0	1	68
S W Borthwick	2001 v F	5	0	0	0	0	0
A Codling	2002 v Arg	1	0	0	0	0	0
M E Corry	1997 v Arg	25	2	0	0	0	10
L B N Dallaglio	1995 v SA	48	11	0	0	0	55
D L Flatman	2000 v SA	8	0	0	0	0	0
D J Garforth	1997 v W	25	0	0	0	0	0
P B T Greening	1996 v It	24	6	0	0	0	30
D J Grewcock	1997 v Arg	33	1	0	0	0	5
R A Hill	1997 v S	49	10	0	0	0	50
M O Johnson	1993 v F	67	2	0	0	0	10
B J Kay	2001 v C	11	2	0	0	0	10
J Leonard	1990 v Arg	97	1	0	0	0	5
L W Moody	2001 v C	10	3	0	0	0	15
T Palmer	2001 v US	1	0	0	0	0	0
M P Regan	1995 v SA	23	2	0	0	0	10
G C Rowntree	1995 v S	38	0	0	0	0	0
A Sanderson	2001 v R	2	1	0	0	0	5
P H Sanderson	1998 v NZ	6	1	0	0	0	5
S D Shaw	1996 v It	19	2	0	0	0	10
S Thompson	2002 v S	6	0	0	0	0	0
P J Vickery	1998 v W	26	0	0	0	0	0
D E West	1998 v F	16	2	0	0	0	10
J M White	2000 v SA	13	0	0	0	0	0
S White-Cooper	2001 v C	2	0	0	0	0	0
T J Woodman	1999 v US	5	0	0	0	0	0
J P R Worsley	1999 v Tg	20	5	0	0	0	25

ENGLISH INTERNATIONAL PLAYERS

(up to 31 August 2002)

Note: Years given for International Championship matches are for second half of season; eg 1972 means season 1971-72. Years for all other matches refer to the actual year of the match. When a series has taken place, figures have been used to denote the particular matches in which players have featured. Thus 1984 *SA* 2 indicates that a player appeared in the second Test of the series.

Aarvold, C D (Cambridge U, W Hartlepool, Headingley, Blackheath) 1928 *A, W, I, F, S,* 1929 *W, I, F,* 1931 *W, S, F,* 1932 *SA, W, I, S,* 1933 *W*
Ackford, P J (Harlequins) 1988 *A,* 1989 *S, I, F, W, R, Fj,* 1990 *I, F, W, S, Arg* 3, 1991 *W, S, I, F, A, [NZ, It, F, S, A]*
Adams, A A (London Hospital) 1910 *F*
Adams, F R (Richmond) 1875 *I, S,* 1876 *S,* 1877 *I,* 1878 *S,* 1879 *S, I*
Adebayo, A A (Bath) 1996, *It,* 1997 *Arg* 1,2, *A* 2, *NZ* 1, 1998 *S*
Adey, G J (Leicester) 1976 *I, F*
Adkins, S J (Coventry) 1950 *I, F, S,* 1953 *W, I, F, S*
Agar, A E (Harlequins) 1952 *SA, W, S, I, F,* 1953 *W, I*
Alcock, A (Guy's Hospital) 1906 *SA*
Alderson, F H R (Hartlepool R) 1891 *W, I, S,* 1892 *W, S,* 1893 *W*
Alexander, H (Richmond) 1900 *I, S,* 1901 *W, I, S,* 1902 *W, I*
Alexander, W (Northern) 1927 *F*
Allison, D F (Coventry) 1956 *W, I, S, F,* 1957 *W,* 1958 *W, S*
Allport, A (Blackheath) 1892 *W,* 1893 *I,* 1894 *W, I, S*
Anderson, S (Rockcliff) 1899 *I*
Anderson, W F (Orrell) 1973 *NZ* 1
Anderton, C (Manchester FW) 1889 *M*
Andrew, C R (Cambridge U, Nottingham, Wasps, Toulouse, Newcastle) 1985 *R, F, S, I, W,* 1986 *W, S, I, F,* 1987 *I, F, W, [J* (R), *US],* 1988 *S, I* 1,2, *A* 1,2, *Fj, A,* 1989 *S, I, F, W, R, Fj,* 1990 *I, F, W, S, Arg* 3, 1991 *W, S, I, F, Fj, A, [NZ, It, US, F, S, A],* 1992 *S, I, F, W, C, SA,* 1993 *F, W, NZ,* 1994 *S, I, F, W, SA* 1,2, *R, C,* 1995 *I, F, W, S, [Arg, It, A, NZ, F],* 1997 *W* (R)
Appleford, G (London Irish) 2002 *Arg*
Archer, G S (Bristol, Army, Newcastle) 1996 *S, I,* 1997 *A* 2, *NZ* 1, *SA, NZ* 2, 1998 *F, W, S, I, A* 1, *NZ* 1, *H, It,* 1999 *Tg, Fj,* 2000 *I, F, W, It, S*
Archer, H (Bridgwater A) 1909 *W, F, I*
Armstrong, R (Northern) 1925 *W*
Arthur, T G (Wasps) 1966 *W, I*
Ashby, R C (Wasps) 1966 *I, F,* 1967 *A*
Ashcroft, A (Waterloo) 1956 *W, I, S, F,* 1957 *W, I, F, S,* 1958 *W, A, I, F, S,* 1959 *I, F, S*
Ashcroft, A H (Birkenhead Park) 1909 *A*
Ashford, W (Richmond) 1897 *W, I,* 1898 *S, W*
Ashworth, A (Oldham) 1892 *I*
Askew, J G (Cambridge U) 1930 *W, I, F*
Aslett, A R (Richmond) 1926 *W, I, F, S,* 1929 *S, F*
Assinder, E W (O Edwardians) 1909 *A, W*
Aston, R L (Blackheath) 1890 *S, I*
Auty, J R (Headingley) 1935 *S*

Back, N A (Leicester) 1994 *S, I,* 1995 *[Arg* (t), *It, WS],* 1997 *NZ* 1(R), *SA, NZ* 2, 1998 *F, W, S, I, H, It, A* 2, *SA* 2, 1999 *S, I, F, W, A, US, C, [It, NZ, Fj, SA],* 2000 *I, F, W, It, S, SA* 1,2, *A, Arg, SA* 3(R), 2001 *W, It, S, F, I, A, R, SA,* 2002 *S, I, F, W, It*
Bailey, M D (Cambridge U, Wasps) 1984 *SA* 1,2, 1987 *[US],* 1989 *Fj,* 1990 *I, F, S* (R)
Bainbridge, S (Gosforth, Fylde) 1982 *F, W,* 1983 *F, W, S, I, NZ,* 1984 *S, I, F, W,* 1985 *NZ* 1,2, 1987 *F, W, S, [J, US]*
Baker, D G S (OMTs) 1955 *W, I, F, S*
Baker, E M (Moseley) 1895 *W, I, S,* 1896 *W, I, S,* 1897 *W*
Baker, H C (Clifton) 1887 *W*
Balshaw, I R (Bath) 2000 *I* (R), *F* (R), *It* (R), *S* (R), *A* (R), *Arg, SA* 3(R), 2001 *W, It, S, F, I,* 2002 *S* (R), *I* (R)
Bance, J F (Bedford) 1954 *S*
Barkley, O (Bath) 2001 *US* (R)
Barley, B (Wakefield) 1984 *I, F, W, A,* 1988 *A* 1,2, *Fj*
Barnes, S (Bristol, Bath) 1984 *A,* 1985 *R* (R), *NZ* 1,2, 1986 *S* (R), *F* (R), 1987 *I* (R), 1988 *Fj,* 1993 *S, I*
Barr, R J (Leicester) 1932 *SA, W, I*
Barrett, E I M (Lennox) 1903 *S*
Barrington, T J M (Bristol) 1931 *W, I*
Barrington-Ward, L E (Edinburgh U) 1910 *W, I, F, S*
Barron, J H (Bingley) 1896 *S,* 1897 *W, I*

Bartlett, J T (Waterloo) 1951 *W*
Bartlett, R M (Harlequins) 1957 *W, I, F, S,* 1958 *I, F, S*
Barton, J (Coventry) 1967 *I, F, W,* 1972 *F*
Batchelor, T B (Oxford U) 1907 *F*
Bates, S M (Wasps) 1989 *R*
Bateson, A H (Otley) 1930 *W, I, F, S*
Bateson, H D (Liverpool) 1879 *I*
Batson, T (Blackheath) 1872 *S,* 1874 *S,* 1875 *I*
Batten, J M (Cambridge U) 1874 *S*
Baume, J L (Northern) 1950 *S*
Baxendell, J J N (Sale) 1998 *NZ* 2, *SA* 1
Baxter, J (Birkenhead Park) 1900 *W, I, S*
Bayfield, M C (Northampton) 1991 *Fj, A,* 1992 *S, I, F, W, C, SA,* 1993 *F, W, S, I,* 1994 *S, I, SA* 1,2, *R, C,* 1995 *I, F, W, S, [Arg, It, A, NZ, F], SA, WS,* 1996 *F, W*
Bazley, R C (Waterloo) 1952 *I, F,* 1953 *W, I, F, S,* 1955 *W, I, F, S*
Beal, N D (Northampton) 1996 *Arg,* 1997 *A* 1, 1998 *NZ* 1,2, *SA* 1, *H* (R), *SA* 2, 1999 *S, F* (R), *A* (t), *C* (R), *[It* (R), *Tg* (R), *Fj, SA]*
Beaumont, W B (Fylde) 1975 *I, A* 1(R),2, 1976 *A, W, S, I, F,* 1977 *S, I, F, W,* 1978 *F, W, S, I, NZ,* 1979 *S, I, F, W, NZ,* 1980 *I, F, W, S,* 1981 *W, S, I, F, Arg* 1,2, 1982 *A, S*
Bedford, H (Morley) 1889 *M,* 1890 *S, I*
Bedford, L L (Headingley) 1931 *W, I*
Beer, I D S (Harlequins) 1955 *F, S*
Beese, M C (Liverpool) 1972 *W, I, F*
Beim, T D (Sale) 1998 *NZ* 1(R),2
Bell, F J (Northern) 1900 *W*
Bell, H (New Brighton) 1884 *I*
Bell, J L (Darlington) 1878 *I*
Bell, P J (Blackheath) 1968 *W, I, F, S*
Bell, R W (Northern) 1900 *W, I, S*
Bendon, G J (Wasps) 1959 *W, I, F, S*
Bennett, N O (St Mary's Hospital, Waterloo) 1947 *W, S, F,* 1948 *A, W, I, S*
Bennett, W N (Bedford, London Welsh) 1975 *S, A*1, 1976 *S* (R), 1979 *S, I, F, W*
Bennetts, B B (Penzance) 1909 *A, W*
Bentley, J (Sale, Newcastle) 1988 *I* 2, *A* 1, 1997 *A* 1, *SA*
Bentley, J E (Gipsies) 1871 *S,* 1872 *S*
Benton, S (Gloucester) 1998 *A* 1
Berridge, M J (Northampton) 1949 *W, I*
Berry, H (Gloucester) 1910 *W, I, F, S*
Berry, J (Tyldesley) 1891 *W, I, S*
Berry, J T W (Leicester) 1939 *W, I, S*
Beswick, E (Swinton) 1882 *I, S*
Biggs, J M (UCH) 1878 *S,* 1879 *I*
Birkett, J G G (Harlequins) 1906 *S, F, SA,* 1907 *F, W, S,* 1908 *F, W I, S,* 1910 *W, I, S,* 1911 *W, F, I, S,* 1912 *W, I, S, F*
Birkett L (Clapham R) 1875 *S,* 1877 *I, S*
Birkett, R H (Clapham R) 1871 *S,* 1875 *S,* 1876 *S,* 1877 *I*
Bishop, C C (Blackheath) 1927 *F*
Black, B H (Blackheath) 1930 *W, I, F, S,* 1931 *W, I, S, F,* 1932 *S,* 1933 *W*
Blacklock, J H (Aspatria) 1898 *I,* 1899 *I*
Blakeway, P J (Gloucester) 1980 *I, F, W, S,* 1981 *W, S, I, F,* 1982 *I, F, W,* 1984 *I, F, W, SA* 1, 1985 *R, F, S, I*
Blakiston, A F (Northampton) 1920 *S,* 1921 *W, I, S, F,* 1922 *W,* 1923 *S, F,* 1924 *W, I, F, S,* 1925 *NZ, W, I, S, F*
Blatherwick, T (Manchester) 1878 *I*
Body, J A (Gipsies) 1872 *S,* 1873 *S*
Bolton, C A (United Services) 1909 *F*
Bolton, R (Harlequins) 1933 *W,* 1936 *S,* 1937 *S,* 1938 *W, I*
Bolton, W N (Blackheath) 1882 *I, S,* 1883 *W, I, S,* 1884 *W, I, S,* 1885 *I,* 1887 *I, S*
Bonaventura, M S (Blackheath) 1931 *W*
Bond, A M (Sale) 1978 *NZ,* 1979 *S, I, NZ,* 1980 *I,* 1982 *I*
Bonham-Carter, E (Oxford U) 1891 *S*
Bonsor, F (Bradford) 1886 *W, I, S,* 1887 *W, S,* 1889 *M*

Coop, T (Leigh) 1892 *S*
Cooper, J G (Moseley) 1909 *A, W*
Cooper, M J (Moseley) 1973 *F, S, NZ* 2(R), 1975 *F, W*, 1976 *A, W*, 1977 *S, I, F, W*
Coopper, S F (Blackheath) 1900 *W*, 1902 *W, I*, 1905 *W, I, S*, 1907 *W*
Corbett, L J (Bristol) 1921 *F*, 1923 *W, I*, 1924 *W, I, F, S*, 1925 *NZ, W, I, S, F*, 1927 *W, I, S, F*
Corless, B J (Coventry, Moseley) 1976 *A, I* (R), 1977 *S, I, F, W*, 1978 *F, W, S, I*
Corry, M E (Bristol, Leicester) 1997 *Arg* 1,2, 1998 *H, It, SA* 2(t), 1999 *F*(R), *A, C* (t), [*It* (R), *NZ* (t+R), *SA* (R)], 2000 *I* (R), *F* (R), *W* (R), *It* (R), *S (R), Arg* (R), *SA* 3(t), 2001 *W* (R), *It* (R), *F* (t), *C* 1, *I*, 2002 *F* (t+R), *W* (t)
Cotton, F E (Loughborough Colls, Coventry, Sale) 1971 *S* (2[1C]), *P*, 1973 *W, I, F, S, NZ* 2, *A*, 1974 *S, I*, 1975 *I, F, W*, 1976 *A, W, S, I, F*, 1977 *S, I, F, W*, 1978 *S, I*, 1979 *NZ*, 1980 *I, F, W, S*, 1981 *W*
Coulman, M J (Moseley) 1967 *A, I, F, S, W*, 1968 *W, I, F, S*
Coulson, T J (Coventry) 1927 *W*, 1928 *A, W*
Court, E D (Blackheath) 1885 *W*
Coverdale, H (Blackheath) 1910 *F*, 1912 *I, F*, 1920 *W*
Cove-Smith, R (OMTs) 1921 *S, F*, 1922 *I, F, S*, 1923 *W, I, S, F*, 1924 *W, I, S, F*, 1925 *NZ, W, I, S, F*, 1927 *W, I, S, F*, 1928 *A, W, I, F, S*, 1929 *W, I*
Cowling, R J (Leicester) 1977 *S, I, F, W*, 1978 *F, NZ*, 1979 *S, I*
Cowman, A R (Loughborough Colls, Coventry) 1971 *S* (2[1C]), *P*, 1973 *W, I*
Cox, N S (Sunderland) 1901 *S*
Cranmer, P (Richmond, Moseley) 1934 *W, I, S*, 1935 *W, I, S*, 1936 *NZ, W, I, S*, 1937 *W, I, S*, 1938 *W, I, S*
Creed, R N (Coventry) 1971 *P*
Cridlan, A G (Blackheath) 1935 *W, I, S*
Crompton, C A (Blackheath) 1871 *S*
Crosse, C W (Oxford U) 1874 *S*, 1875 *I*
Cumberlege, B S (Blackheath) 1920 *W, I, S*, 1921 *W, I, S, F*, 1922 *W*
Cumming, D C (Blackheath) 1925 *S, F*
Cunliffe, F L (RMA) 1874 *S*
Currey, F I (Marlborough N) 1872 *S*
Currie, J D (Oxford U, Harlequins, Bristol) 1956 *W, I, S, F*, 1957 *W, I, F, S*, 1958 *W, A, I, F, S*, 1959 *W, I, F, S*, 1960 *W, I, F, S*, 1961 *SA*, 1962 *W, I, F*
Cusani, D A (Orrell) 1987 *I*
Cusworth, L (Leicester) 1979 *NZ*, 1982 *F, W*, 1983 *F, W, NZ*, 1984 *S, I, F, W*, 1988 *F, W*

D'Aguilar, F B G (Royal Engineers) 1872 *S*
Dallaglio, L B N (Wasps) 1995 *SA* (R), *WS*, 1996 *F, W, S, I, It, Arg*, 1997 *S, I, F*, 1997 *A* 1,2, *NZ* 1, *SA, NZ* 2, 1998 *F, W, S, I, A* 2, *SA* 2, 1999 *S, I, F, W, US, C*, [*It, NZ, Tg, Fj, SA*], 2000 *I, F, W, It, S, SA* 1,2, *A, Arg, SA* 3, 2001 *W, It, S, F*, 2002 *It* (R)
Dalton, T J (Coventry) 1969 *S*(R)
Danby, T (Harlequins) 1949 *W*
Daniell, J (Richmond) 1899 *W*, 1900 *I, S*, 1902 *I, S*, 1904 *I, S*
Darby, A J L (Birkenhead Park) 1899 *I*
Davenport, A (Ravenscourt Park) 1871 *S*
Davey, J (Redruth) 1908 *S*, 1909 *W*
Davey, R F (Teignmouth) 1931 *W*
Davidson, Jas (Aspatria) 1897 *S*, 1898 *S, W*, 1899 *I, S*
Davidson, Jos (Aspatria) 1899 *W, S*
Davies, G H (Cambridge U, Coventry, Wasps) 1981 *S, I, F, Arg* 1,2, 1982 *A, S, I*, 1983 *F, W, S*, 1984 *S, SA* 1,2, 1985 *R* (R), *NZ* 1,2, 1986 *W, S, I, F*
Davies, P H (Sale) 1927 *I*
Davies, V G (Harlequins) 1922 *W*, 1925 *NZ*
Davies, W J A (United Services, RN) 1913 *SA, W, F, I, S*, 1914 *I, S, F*, 1920 *F, I, S*, 1921 *W, I, S, F*, 1922 *I, F, S*, 1923 *W, I, S, F*
Davies, W P C (Harlequins) 1953 *S*, 1954 *NZ, I*, 1955 *W, I, F, S*, 1956 *W*, 1957 *F, S*, 1958 *W*
Davis, A M (Torquay Ath, Harlequins) 1963 *W, I, S, NZ* 1,2, 1964 *NZ, W, I, F, S*, 1966 *W*, 1967 *A*, 1969 *SA*, 1970 *I, W, S*
Dawe, R G R (Bath) 1987 *I, F, W, [US]*, 1995 *[WS]*
Dawson, E F (RIEC) 1878 *I*
Dawson, M J S (Northampton) 1995 *WS*, 1996 *F, W, S, I*, 1997 *A* 1, *SA, NZ* 2(R), 1998 *W* (R), *S, I, NZ* 1,2, *SA* 1, *H, It, A* 2, *SA* 2, 1999 *S, F*(R), *W, A*(R), *US, C*, [*It, NZ, Tg, Fj* (R), *SA*], 2000 *I, F, W, It, S, A* (R), *Arg, SA* 3, 2001 *W, It, S, F, I*, 2002 *W* (R), *It* (R)
Day, H L V (Leicester) 1920 *W*, 1922 *W, F*, 1926 *S*
Dean, G J (Harlequins) 1931 *I*

Dee, J M (Hartlepool R) 1962 *S*, 1963 *NZ* 1
Devitt, Sir T G (Blackheath) 1926 *I, F*, 1928 *A, W*
Dewhurst, J H (Richmond) 1887 *W, I, S*, 1890 *W*
De Glanville, P R (Bath) 1992 *SA* (R), 1993 *W* (R), *NZ*, 1994 *S, I, F, W, SA* 1,2, *C* (R), 1995 [*Arg* (R), *It, WS*], *SA* (R), 1996 *W* (R), *I* (R), *It*, 1997 *S, I, F, W, Arg* 1,2, *A* 1,2, *NZ* 1,2, 1998 *W* (R), *S* (R), *I* (R), *A* 2, *SA* 2, 1999 *A* (R), *US*, [*It, NZ, Fj* (R), *SA*]
De Winton, R F C (Marlborough N) 1893 *W*
Dibble, R (Bridgwater A) 1906 *S, F, SA*, 1908 *F, W, I, S*, 1909 *A, W, F, I, S*, 1910 *S*, 1911 *W, F, S*, 1912 *W, I, S*
Dicks, J (Northampton) 1934 *W, I, S*, 1935 *W, I, S*, 1936 *S*, 1937 *I*
Dillon, E W (Blackheath) 1904 *W, I, S*, 1905 *W*
Dingle, A J (Hartlepool R) 1913 *I*, 1914 *S, F*
Diprose, A J (Saracens) 1997 *Arg* 1,2, *A* 2, *NZ* 1, 1998 *W* (R), *S* (R), *I, A* 1, *NZ* 2, *SA* 1
Dixon, P J (Harlequins, Gosforth) 1971 *P*, 1972 *W, I, F, S*, 1973 *I, F, S*, 1974 *S, I, F, W*, 1975 *I*, 1976 *F*, 1977 *S, I, F, W*, 1978 *F, S, I, NZ*
Dobbs, G E B (Devonport A) 1906 *W, I*
Doble, S A (Moseley) 1972 *SA*, 1973 *NZ* 1, *W*
Dobson, D D (Newton Abbot) 1902 *W, I, S*, 1903 *W, I, S*
Dobson, T H (Bradford) 1895 *S*
Dodge, P W (Leicester) 1978 *W, S, I, NZ*, 1979 *S, I, F, W*, 1980 *W, S*, 1981 *W, S, I, F, Arg* 1,2, 1982 *A, S, F, W*, 1983 *F, W, S, I, NZ*, 1985 *R, F, S, I, W, NZ* 1,2
Donnelly, M P (Oxford U) 1947 *I*
Dooley, W A (Preston Grasshoppers, Fylde) 1985 *R, F, S, I, W, NZ* 2(R), 1986 *W, S, I, F*, 1987 *F, W*, [*A, US, W*], 1988 *F, W, S, I* 1,2, *A* 1,2, *Fj, A*, 1989 *S, I, F, W, R, Fj*, 1990 *I, F, W, S, Arg* 1,2,3, 1991 *W, S, I, F*, [*NZ, US, F, S, A*], 1992 *S, I, F, W, C, SA*, 1993 *W, S, I*
Dovey, B A (Rosslyn Park) 1963 *W, I*
Down, P J (Bristol) 1909 *A*
Dowson, A O (Moseley) 1899 *S*
Drake-Lee, N J (Cambridge U, Leicester) 1963 *W, I, F, S*, 1964 *NZ, W, I*, 1965 *W*
Duckett, H (Bradford) 1893 *I, S*
Duckham, D J (Coventry) 1969 *I, F, S, W, SA*, 1970 *I, W, S, F*, 1971 *W, I, F, S* (2[1C]), *P*, 1972 *W, I, F, S*, 1973 *NZ* 1, *W, I, F, S, NZ* 2, *A*, 1974 *S, I, F, W*, 1975 *I, F, W*, 1976 *A, W, S*
Dudgeon, H W (Richmond) 1897 *S*, 1898 *I, S, W*, 1899 *W, I, S*
Dugdale, J M (Ravenscourt Park) 1871 *S*
Dun, A F (Wasps) 1984 *W*
Duncan, R F H (Guy's Hospital) 1922 *I, F, S*
Duncombe, N (Harlequins) 2002 *S* (R), *I* (R)
Dunkley, P E (Harlequins) 1931 *I, S*, 1936 *NZ, W, I, S*
Duthie, J (W Hartlepool) 1903 *W*
Dyson, J W (Huddersfield) 1890 *S*, 1892 *S*, 1893 *I, S*

Ebdon, P J (Wellington) 1897 *W, I*
Eddison, J H (Headingley) 1912 *W, I, S, F*
Edgar, C S (Birkenhead Park) 1901 *S*
Edwards, R (Newport) 1921 *W, I, S, F*, 1922 *W, F*, 1923 *W*, 1924 *W, F, S*, 1925 *NZ*
Egerton, D W (Bath) 1988 *I* 2, *A* 1, *Fj* (R), *A*, 1989 *Fj*, 1990 *I, Arg* 2(R)
Elliot, C H (Sunderland) 1886 *W*
Elliot, E W (Sunderland) 1901 *W, I, S*, 1904 *W*
Elliot, W (United Services, RN) 1932 *I, S*, 1933 *W, I, S*, 1934 *W, I*
Elliott, A E (St Thomas's Hospital) 1894 *S*
Ellis, J (Wakefield) 1939 *S*
Ellis, S S (Queen's House) 1880 *I*
Emmott, C (Bradford) 1892 *W*
Enthoven, H J (Richmond) 1878 *I*
Estcourt, N S D (Blackheath) 1955 *S*
Evans, B J (Leicester) 1988 *A* 2, *Fj*
Evans, E (Sale) 1948 *A*, 1950 *W*, 1951 *I, F, S*, 1952 *SA, W, S, I, F*, 1953 *I, F, S*, 1954 *W, NZ, I, F*, 1956 *W, I, S, F*, 1957 *W, I, F, S*, 1958 *W, A, I, F, S*
Evans, G W (Coventry) 1972 *S*, 1973 *W (R), F, S, NZ* 2, 1974 *S, I, F, W*
Evans, N L (RNEC) 1932 *W, I, S*, 1933 *W, I*
Evanson, A M (Richmond) 1883 *W, I, S*, 1884 *S*
Evanson, W A D (Richmond) 1875 *S*, 1877 *S*, 1878 *S*, 1879 *S, I*
Evershed, F (Blackheath) 1889 *M*, 1890 *W, S, I*, 1892 *W, I, S*, 1893 *W, I, S*
Eyres, W C T (Richmond) 1927 *I*

163

Fagan, A R St L (Richmond) 1887 *I*
Fairbrother, K E (Coventry) 1969 *I, F, S, W, SA*, 1970 *I, W, S, F*, 1971 *W, I, F*
Faithfull, C K T (Harlequins) 1924 *I*, 1926 *F, S*
Fallas, H (Wakefield T) 1884 *I*
Fegan, J H C (Blackheath) 1895 *W, I, S*
Fernandes, C W L (Leeds) 1881 *I, W, S*
Fidler, J H (Gloucester) 1981 *Arg* 1,2, 1984 *SA* 1,2
Fidler, R J (Gloucester) 1998 *NZ* 2, *SA* 1
Field, E (Middlesex W) 1893 *W, I*
Fielding, K J (Moseley, Loughborough Colls) 1969 *I, F, S, SA*, 1970 *I, W, F*, 1972 *W, I, F, S*
Finch, R T (Cambridge U) 1880 *S*
Finlan, J F (Moseley) 1967 *I, F, S, W, NZ*, 1968 *W, I*, 1969 *I, F, S, W*, 1970 *F*, 1973 *NZ* 1
Finlinson, H W (Blackheath) 1895 *W, I, S*
Finney, S (RIE Coll) 1872 *S*, 1873 *S*
Firth, F (Halifax) 1894 *W, I, S*
Flatman, D L (Saracens) 2000 *SA* 1(t),2(t+R), *A* (t), *Arg* (t+R), 2001 *F* (t), *C* 2(t+R), *US* (t+R), 2002 *Arg*
Fletcher, N C (OMTs) 1901 *W, I, S*, 1903 *S*
Fletcher, T (Seaton) 1897 *W*
Fletcher, W R B (Marlborough N) 1873 *S*, 1875 *S*
Fookes, E F (Sowerby Bridge) 1896 *W, I, S*, 1897 *W, I, S*, 1898 *I, W*, 1899 *I, S*
Ford, P J (Gloucester) 1964 *W, I, F, S*
Forrest, J W (United Services, RN) 1930 *W, I, F, S*, 1931 *W, I, S, F*, 1934 *I, S*
Forrest, R (Wellington) 1899 *W*, 1900 *S*, 1902 *I, S*, 1903 *I, S*
Foulds, R T (Waterloo) 1929 *W, I*
Fowler, F D (Manchester) 1878 *S*, 1879 *S*
Fowler, H (Oxford U) 1878 *S*, 1881 *W, S*
Fowler, R H (Leeds) 1877 *I*
Fox, F H (Wellington) 1890 *W, S*
Francis, T E S (Cambridge U) 1926 *W, I, F, S*
Frankcom, G P (Cambridge U, Bedford) 1965 *W, I, F, S*
Fraser, E C (Blackheath) 1875 *I*
Fraser, G (Richmond) 1902 *W, I, S*, 1903 *W, I*
Freakes, H D (Oxford U) 1938 *W*, 1939 *W, I*
Freeman, H (Marlborough N) 1872 *S*, 1873 *S*, 1874 *S*
French, R J (St Helens) 1961 *W, I, F, S*
Fry, H A (Liverpool) 1934 *W, I, S*
Fry, T W (Queen's House) 1880 *I, S*, 1881 *W*
Fuller, H G (Cambridge U) 1882 *I, S*, 1883 *W, I, S*, 1884 *W*

Gadney, B C (Leicester, Headingley) 1932 *I, S*, 1933 *I, S*, 1934 *W, I, S*, 1935 *S*, 1936 *NZ, W, I, S*, 1937 *S*, 1938 *W*
Gamlin, H T (Blackheath) 1899 *W, S*, 1900 *W, I, S*, 1901 *S*, 1902 *W, I, S*, 1903 *W, I, S*, 1904 *W, I, S*
Gardner, E R (Devonport Services) 1921 *W, I, S*, 1922 *W, I, F*, 1923 *W, I, S, F*
Gardner, H P (Richmond) 1878 *I*
Garforth, D J (Leicester) 1997 *W* (R), *Arg* 1,2, *A* 1, *NZ* 1, *SA, NZ* 2, 1998 *F, W* (R), *S, I, H, It, A* 2, *SA* 2, 1999 *S, I, F, W, A, C* (R), [*It* (R), *NZ* (R), *Fj*], 2000 *It*
Garnett, H W T (Bradford) 1877 *S*
Gavins, M N (Leicester) 1961 *W*
Gay, D J (Bath) 1968 *W, I, F, S*
Gent, D R (Gloucester) 1905 *NZ*, 1906 *W, I*, 1910 *W, I*
Genth, J S M (Manchester) 1874 *S*, 1875 *S*
George, J T (Falmouth) 1947 *S, F*, 1949 *I*
Gerrard, R A (Bath) 1932 *SA, W, I, S*, 1933 *W, I, S*, 1934 *W, I, S*, 1936 *NZ, W, I, S*
Gibbs, G A (Bristol) 1947 *F*, 1948 *I*
Gibbs, J C (Harlequins) 1925 *NZ, W*, 1926 *F*, 1927 *W, I, S, F*
Gibbs, N (Harlequins) 1954 *S, F*
Giblin, L F (Blackheath) 1896 *W, I*, 1897 *S*
Gibson, A S (Manchester) 1871 *S*
Gibson, C O P (Northern) 1901 *W*
Gibson, G R (Northern) 1899 *W*, 1901 *S*
Gibson, T A (Northern) 1905 *W, S*
Gilbert, F G (Devonport Services) 1923 *W, I*
Gilbert, R (Devonport A) 1908 *W, I, S*
Giles, J L (Coventry) 1935 *W, I*, 1937 *W, I*, 1938 *I, S*
Gittings, W J (Coventry) 1967 *NZ*
Glover, P B (Bath) 1967 *A*, 1971 *F, P*
Godfray, R E (Richmond) 1905 *NZ*
Godwin, H O (Coventry) 1959 *F, S*, 1963 *S, NZ* 1,2, *A*, 1964 *NZ, I, F, S*, 1967 *NZ*
Gomarsall, A C T (Wasps, Bedford) 1996 *It, Arg*, 1997 *S, I, F, Arg* 2(R) 2000 *It* (R), 2002 *Arg*
Gordon-Smith, G W (Blackheath) 1900 *W, I, S*
Gotley, A L H (Oxford U) 1910 *F, S*, 1911 *W, F, I, S*

Graham, D (Aspatria) 1901 *W*
Graham, H J (Wimbledon H) 1875 *I, S*, 1876 *I, S*
Graham, J D G (Wimbledon H) 1876 *I*
Gray, A (Otley) 1947 *W, I, S*
Grayson, P J (Northampton) 1995 *WS*, 1996 *F, W, S, I*, 1997 *S, I, F, A* 2(t), *SA* (R), *NZ* 2, 1998 *F, W, S, I, H, It, A* 2, 1999 *I, [NZ* (R), *Tg, Fj* (R), *SA*]
Green, J (Skipton) 1905 *I*, 1906 *S, F, SA*, 1907 *F, W, I, S*
Green, J F (West Kent) 1871 *S*
Green, W R (Wasps) 1997 *A* 2, 1998 *NZ* 1(t+R), 1999 *US* (R)
Greening, P B T (Gloucester, Wasps) 1996 *It* (R), 1997 *W* (R), *Arg* 1 1998 *NZ* 1(R),2(R), 1999 *A* (R), *US, C*, [*It* (R), *NZ* (R), *Tg, Fj, SA*], 2000 *I, F, W, It, S, SA* 1,2, *A, SA* 3, 2001 *F, I*
Greenstock, N J J (Wasps) 1997 *Arg* 1,2, *A* 1, *SA*
Greenwell, J H (Rockcliff) 1893 *W, I*
Greenwood, J E (Cambridge U, Leicester) 1912 *F*, 1913 *SA, W, F, I, S*, 1914 *W, S, F*, 1920 *W, F, I, S*
Greenwood, J R H (Waterloo) 1966 *I, F, S*, 1967 *A*, 1969 *I*
Greenwood, W J H (Leicester, Harlequins) 1997 *A* 2, *NZ* 1, *SA, NZ* 2, 1998 *F, W, S, I, H, It*, 1999 *C*, [*It, Tg, Fj, SA*], 2000 *Arg* (R), *SA* 3, 2001 *W, It, S, F, I, A, R, SA*, 2002 *S, I, F, W, It*
Greg, W (Manchester) 1876 *I, S*
Gregory, G G (Bristol) 1931 *I, S, F*, 1932 *SA, W, I, S*, 1933 *W, I, S*, 1934 *W, I, S*
Gregory, J A (Blackheath) 1949 *W*
Grewcock, D J (Coventry, Saracens, Bath) 1997 *Arg* 2, *SA*, 1998 *W* (R), *S* (R), *I* (R), *A* 1, *NZ* 1, *SA* 2(R), 1999 *S* (R), *A* (R), *US, C*, [*It, NZ, Tg* (R), *SA*], 2000 *SA* 1,2, *A, Arg, SA* 3, 2001 *W, It, S, I, A, R* (R), *SA*, 2002 *S, F* (R), *W, It*
Grylls, W M (Redruth) 1905 *I*
Guest, R H (Waterloo) 1939 *W, I, S*, 1947 *W, I, S, F*, 1948 *A, W, I, S*, 1949 *F, S*
Guillemard, A G (West Kent) 1871 *S*, 1872 *S*
Gummer, C H A (Plymouth A) 1929 *F*
Gunner, C R (Marlborough N) 1876 *I*
Gurdon, C (Richmond) 1880 *I, S*, 1881 *I, W, S*, 1882 *I, S*, 1883 *S*, 1884 *W, S*, 1885 *I*, 1886 *W, I, S*
Gurdon, E T (Richmond) 1878 *S*, 1879 *I*, 1880 *S*, 1881 *I, W, S*, 1882 *S*, 1883 *W, I, S*, 1884 *W, I, S*, 1885 *W, I*, 1886 *S*
Guscott, J C (Bath) 1989 *R, Fj*, 1990 *I, F, S, Arg* 3, 1991 *W, S, I, F, Fj, A*, [*NZ, It, F, S, A*], 1992 *S, I, F, W, C, SA*, 1993 *F, W, S, I*, 1994 *R, C*, 1995 *I, F, W, S*, [*Arg, It, A, NZ, F*], *SA, WS*, 1996 *F, W, S, I, Arg*, 1997 *I* (R), *W* (R), 1998 *F, W, S, I, H, It, A* 2, *SA* 2, 1999 *S, I, F, A, US, C*, [*It* (R), *NZ, Tg*]

Haag, M (Bath) 1997 *Arg* 1,2
Haigh, L (Manchester) 1910 *W, I, S*, 1911 *W, F, I, S*
Hale, P M (Moseley) 1969 *SA*, 1970 *I, W*
Hall, C (Gloucester) 1901 *I, S*
Hall, J (N Durham) 1894 *W, I, S*
Hall, J P (Bath) 1984 *S* (R), *I, F, SA* 1,2, *A*, 1985 *R, F, S, I, W, NZ* 1,2, 1986 *W, S*, 1987 *I, F, W, S*, 1990 *Arg* 3, 1994 *S*
Hall, N M (Richmond) 1947 *W, I, S, F*, 1949 *W, I*, 1952 *SA, W, S, I, F*, 1953 *W, I, F, S*, 1955 *W, I*
Halliday, S J (Bath, Harlequins) 1986 *W, S*, 1987 *S*, 1988 *S, I* 1,2, *A* 1, *A*, 1989 *S, I, F, W, R, Fj* (R), 1990 *W, S*, 1991 [*US, S, A*], 1992 *S, I, F, W*
Hamersley, A St G (Marlborough N) 1871 *S*, 1872 *S*, 1873 *S*, 1874 *S*
Hamilton-Hill, E A (Harlequins) 1936 *NZ, W, I*
Hamilton-Wickes, R H (Cambridge U) 1924 *I*, 1925 *NZ,* *W, I, S, F*, 1926 *W, I, S*, 1927 *W*
Hammett, E D G (Newport) 1920 *W, F, S*, 1921 *W, I, S, F*, 1922 *W*
Hammond, C E L (Harlequins) 1905 *NZ*, 1906 *W, I, S, F*, 1908 *W, I*
Hancock, A W (Northampton) 1965 *F, S*, 1966 *F*
Hancock, G E (Birkenhead Park) 1939 *W, I, S*
Hancock, J H (Newport) 1955 *W, I*
Hancock, P F (Blackheath) 1886 *W, I*, 1890 *W*
Hancock, P S (Richmond) 1904 *W, I, S*
Handford, F G (Manchester) 1909 *W, F, I, S*
Hands, R H M (Blackheath) 1910 *F, S*
Hanley, J (Plymouth A) 1927 *W, S, F*, 1928 *W, I, F, S*
Hanley, S M (Sale) 1999 *W*
Hannaford, R C (Bristol) 1971 *W, I, F*
Hanvey, R J (Aspatria) 1926 *W, I, F, S*
Harding, E H (Devonport Services) 1931 *I*
Harding, R M (Bristol) 1985 *R, F, S*, 1987 *S*, [*A, J, W*], 1988 *I* 1(R),2, *A* 1,2, *Fj*
Harding, V S J (Saracens) 1961 *F, S*, 1962 *W, I, F, S*

Hardwick, P F (Percy Park) 1902 *I, S*, 1903 *W, I, S*, 1904 *W, I, S*
Hardwick, R J K (Coventry) 1996 *It* (R)
Hardy, E M P (Blackheath) 1951 *I, F, S*
Hare, W H (Nottingham, Leicester) 1974 *W*, 1978 *F, NZ*, 1979 *NZ*, 1980 *I, F, W, S*, 1981 *W, S, Arg* 1,2, 1982 *F, W*, 1983 *F, W, S, I, NZ*, 1984 *S, I, F, W, SA* 1,2
Harper, C H (Exeter) 1899 *W*
Harriman, A T (Harlequins) 1988 *A*
Harris, S W (Blackheath) 1920 *I, S*
Harris, T W (Northampton) 1929 *S*, 1932 *I*
Harrison, A C (Hartlepool R) 1931 *I, S*
Harrison, A L (United Services, RN) 1914 *I, F*
Harrison, G (Hull) 1877 *I, S*, 1879 *S, I*, 1880 *S*, 1885 *W, I*
Harrison, H C (United Services, RN) 1909 *S*, 1914 *I, S, F*
Harrison, M E (Wakefield) 1985 *NZ* 1,2, 1986 *S, I, F*, 1987 *I, F, W, S, [A, J, US, W]*, 1988 *F, W*
Hartley, B C (Blackheath) 1901 *S*, 1902 *S*
Haslett, L W (Birkenhead Park) 1926 *I, F*
Hastings, G W D (Gloucester) 1955 *W, I, F, S*, 1957 *W, I, F, S*, 1958 *W, A, I, F, S*
Havelock, H (Hartlepool R) 1908 *F, W, I*
Hawcridge, J J (Bradford) 1885 *W, I*
Hayward, L W (Cheltenham) 1910 *I*
Hazell, D St G (Leicester) 1955 *W, I, F, S*
Healey, A S (Leicester) 1997 *I* (R), *W, A* 1(R),2(R), *NZ* 1(R), *SA* (R), *NZ* 2, 1998 *F, W, S, I, A* 1, *NZ* 1,2, *H, It, A* 2, *SA* 2(R), 1999 *US, C, [It, NZ, Tg, Fj, SA* (R)], 2000 *I, F, W, It, S, SA* 1,2, *A, SA* 3(R), 2001 *W* (R), *It, S, F, I* (R), *A, R, SA*, 2002 *S, I, F, W, It* (R)
Hearn, R D (Bedford) 1966 *F, S*, 1967 *I, F, S, W*
Heath, A H (Oxford U) 1876 *S*
Heaton, J (Waterloo) 1935 *W, I, S*, 1939 *W, I, S*, 1947 *I, S, F*
Henderson, A P (Edinburgh Wands) 1947 *W, I, S, F*, 1948 *I, S, F*, 1949 *W, I*
Henderson, R S F (Blackheath) 1883 *W, S*, 1884 *W, S*, 1885 *W*
Heppell, W G (Devonport A) 1903 *I*
Herbert, A J (Wasps) 1958 *F, S*, 1959 *W, I, F, S*
Hesford, R (Bristol) 1981 *S* (R), 1982 *A, S, F* (R), 1983 *F* (R), 1985 *R, F, S, I, W*
Heslop, N J (Orrell) 1990 *Arg* 1,2,3, 1991 *W, S, I, F, [US, F],* 1992 *W* (R)
Hetherington, J G G (Northampton) 1958 *A, I*, 1959 *W, I, F, S*
Hewitt, E N (Coventry) 1951 *W, I, F*
Hewitt, W W (Queen's House) 1881 *I, W, S*, 1882 *I*
Hickson, J L (Bradford) 1887 *W, I, S*, 1890 *W, S, I*
Higgins, R (Liverpool) 1954 *W, NZ, I, S*, 1955 *W, I, F, S*, 1957 *W, I, F, S*, 1959 *W*
Hignell, A J (Cambridge U, Bristol) 1975 *A* 2, 1976 *A, W, S, I*, 1977 *S, I, F, W*, 1978 *W*, 1979 *S, I, F, W*
Hill, B A (Blackheath) 1903 *I, S*, 1904 *W, I*, 1905 *W, NZ*, 1906 *SA*, 1907 *F, W*
Hill, R A (Saracens) 1997 *S, I, F, W, A* 1,2, *NZ* 1, *SA, NZ* 2, 1998 *F, W, H* (R), *It* (R), *A* 2, *SA* 2, 1999 *S, I, F, W, A, US, C, [It, NZ, Tg, Fj* (R), *SA*], 2000 *I, F, W, It, S, SA* 1,2, *A, Arg, SA* 3, 2001 *W, It, S, F, I, A, SA*, 2002 *S, I, F, W*
Hill, R J (Bath) 1984 *SA* 1,2, 1985 *I* (R), *NZ* 2(R), 1986 *F* (R), 1987 *I, F, W, [US]*, 1989 *Fj*, 1990 *I, F, W, S, Arg* 1,2,3, 1991 *W, S, I, F, Fj, A, [NZ, It, US, F, S, A]*
Hillard, R J (Oxford U) 1925 *NZ*
Hiller, R (Harlequins) 1968 *W, I, F, S*, 1969 *I, F, S, W, SA*, 1970 *I, W, S*, 1971 *I, F, S* (2[1C]), *P*, 1972 *W, I*
Hind, A E (Leicester) 1905 *NZ*, 1906 *W*
Hind, G R (Blackheath) 1910 *S*, 1911 *I*
Hobbs, R F A (Blackheath) 1899 *S*, 1903 *W*
Hobbs, R G S (Richmond) 1932 *SA, W, I, S*
Hodges, H A (Nottingham) 1906 *W, I*
Hodgkinson, S D (Nottingham) 1989 *R, Fj*, 1990 *I, F, W, S, Arg* 1,2,3, 1991 *W, S, I, F, [US]*
Hodgson, C (Sale) 2001 *R*, 2002 *S* (R), *I* (R), *It* (R), *Arg*
Hodgson, J McD (Northern) 1932 *SA, W, I, S*, 1934 *W, I*, 1936 *I*
Hodgson, S A M (Durham City) 1960 *W, I, F, S*, 1961 *SA, W*, 1962 *W, I, F, S*, 1964 *W*
Hofmeyr, M B (Oxford U) 1950 *W, F, S*
Hogarth, T B (Hartlepool R) 1906 *F*
Holford, G (Gloucester) 1920 *W, F*
Holland, D (Devonport A) 1912 *W, I, S*
Holliday, T E (Aspatria) 1923 *S, F*, 1925 *I, S, F*, 1926 *F, S*
Holmes, C B (Manchester) 1947 *S*, 1948 *I, F*
Holmes, E (Manningham) 1890 *S, I*

Holmes, W A (Nuneaton) 1950 *W, I, F, S*, 1951 *W, I, F, S*, 1952 *SA, S, I, F*, 1953 *W, I, F, S*
Holmes, W B (Cambridge U) 1949 *W, I, F, S*
Hook, W G (Gloucester) 1951 *S*, 1952 *SA, W*
Hooper, C A (Middlesex W) 1894 *W, I, S*
Hopley, D P (Wasps) 1995 *[WS* (R)], *SA, WS*
Hopley, F J V (Blackheath) 1907 *F, W*, 1908 *I*
Horak, M J (London Irish) 2002 *Arg*
Hordern, P C (Gloucester) 1931 *I, S, F*, 1934 *W*
Horley, C H (Swinton) 1885 *I*
Hornby, A N (Manchester) 1877 *I, S*, 1878 *S, I*, 1880 *I*, 1881 *I, S*, 1882 *I, S*
Horrocks-Taylor, J P (Cambridge U, Leicester, Middlesbrough) 1958 *W, A*, 1961 *S*, 1962 *S*, 1963 *NZ* 1,2, *A*, 1964 *NZ, W*
Horsfall, E L (Harlequins) 1949 *W*
Horton, A L (Blackheath) 1965 *W, I, F, S*, 1966 *F, S*, 1967 *NZ*
Horton, J P (Bath) 1978 *W, S, I, NZ*, 1980 *I, F, W, S*, 1981 *W*, 1983 *S, I*, 1984 *SA* 1,2
Horton, N E (Moseley, Toulouse) 1969 *I, F, S, W*, 1971 *I, F, S*, 1974 *S*, 1975 *W*, 1977 *S, I, F, W*, 1978 *F, W*, 1979 *S, I, F, W*, 1980 *I*
Hosen, R W (Bristol, Northampton) 1963 *NZ* 1,2, *A*, 1964 *F, S*, 1967 *A, I, F, S, W*
Hosking, G R d'A (Devonport Services) 1949 *W, I, F, S*, 1950 *W*
Houghton, S (Runcorn) 1892 *I*, 1896 *W*
Howard, P D (O Millhillians) 1930 *W, I, F, S*, 1931 *W, I, S, F*
Hubbard, G C (Blackheath) 1892 *W, I*
Hubbard, J C (Harlequins) 1930 *S*
Hudson, A (Gloucester) 1906 *W, I, F*, 1908 *F, W, I, S*, 1910 *F*
Hughes, G E (Barrow) 1896 *S*
Hull, P A (Bristol, RAF) 1994 *SA* 1,2, *R, C*
Hulme, F C (Birkenhead Park) 1903 *W, I*, 1905 *W, I*
Hunt, J T (Manchester) 1882 *I, S*, 1884 *W*
Hunt, R (Manchester) 1880 *I*, 1881 *W, S*, 1882 *I*
Hunt, W H (Manchester) 1876 *S*, 1877 *I, S*, 1878 *I*
Hunter, I (Northampton) 1992 *C*, 1993 *F, W*, 1994 *F, W*, 1995 *[WS, F]*
Huntsman, R P (Headingley) 1985 *NZ* 1,2
Hurst, A C B (Wasps) 1962 *S*
Huskisson, T F (OMTs) 1937 *W, I, S*, 1938 *W, I*, 1939 *W, I, S*
Hutchinson, F (Headingley) 1909 *F, I, S*
Hutchinson, J E (Durham City) 1906 *I*
Hutchinson, W C (RIE Coll) 1876 *S*, 1877 *I*
Hutchinson, W H H (Hull) 1875 *I*, 1876 *I*
Huth, H (Huddersfield) 1879 *S*
Hyde, J P (Northampton) 1950 *F, S*
Hynes, W B (United Services, RN) 1912 *F*

Ibbitson, E D (Headingley) 1909 *W, F, I, S*
Imrie, H M (Durham City) 1906 *NZ*, 1907 *I*
Inglis, R E (Blackheath) 1886 *W, I, S*
Irvin, S H (Devonport A) 1905 *W*
Isherwood, F W (Ravenscourt Park) 1872 *S*

Jackett, E J (Leicester, Falmouth) 1905 *NZ*, 1906 *W, I, S, F, SA*, 1907 *W, I, S*, 1909 *W, F, I, S*
Jackson, A H (Blackheath) 1878 *I*, 1880 *I*
Jackson, B S (Broughton Park) 1970 *S* (R), *F*
Jackson, P B (Coventry) 1956 *W, I, F*, 1957 *W, I, F, S*, 1958 *W, A, F, S*, 1959 *W, I, F, S*, 1961 *S*, 1963 *W, I, F, S*
Jackson, W J (Halifax) 1894 *S*
Jacob, F (Cambridge U) 1897 *W, I, S*, 1898 *I, S, W*, 1899 *W, I*
Jacob, H P (Blackheath) 1924 *W, I, F, S*, 1930 *F*
Jacob, P G (Blackheath) 1898 *I*
Jacobs, C R (Northampton) 1956 *W, I, S, F*, 1957 *W, I, F, S*, 1958 *W, A, I, F, S*, 1960 *W, I, F, S*, 1961 *SA, W, I, F, S*, 1963 *NZ* 1,2, *A*, 1964 *W, I, F, S*
Jago, R A (Devonport A) 1906 *W, I, SA*, 1907 *W, I*
Janion, J P A G (Bedford) 1971 *W, I, F, S* (2[1C]), *P*, 1972 *W, S, SA*, 1973 *A*, 1975 *A* 1,2
Jarman, J W (Bristol) 1900 *W*
Jeavons, N C (Moseley) 1981 *S, I, F, Arg* 1,2, 1982 *A, S, I, F, W*, 1983 *F, W, S, I*
Jeeps, R E G (Northampton) 1956 *W, I, F, S*, 1957 *W, I, F, S*, 1958 *W, A, I, F, S*, 1959 *I, F, S*, 1960 *W, I, F, S*, 1961 *SA, W, I, F, S*, 1962 *W, I, F, S*
Jeffery, G L (Blackheath) 1886 *W, I, S*, 1887 *W, I, S*
Jennins, C R (Waterloo) 1967 *A, I, F*
Jewitt, J (Hartlepool R) 1902 *W*
Johns, W A (Gloucester) 1909 *W, F, I, S*, 1910 *W, I, F*

Johnson, M O (Leicester) 1993 *F, NZ,* 1994 *S, I, F, W, R, C,* 1995 *I, F, W, S,* [*Arg, It, WS, A, NZ, F*], *SA, WS,* 1996 *F, W, S, I, It, Arg,* 1997 *S, I, F, W, A* 2, *NZ* 1,2, 1998 *F, W, S, I, H, It, A* 2, *SA* 2, 1999 *S, I, F, W, A, US, C,* [*It, NZ, Tg, Fj, SA*], 2000 *SA* 1,2, *A, Arg, SA* 3, 2001 *W, It, S, F, SA,* 2002 *S, I, F, It* (t+R)
Johnston, B (Saracens) 2002 *Arg*
Johnston, W R (Bristol) 1910 *W, I, S,* 1912 *W, I, S, F,* 1913 *SA, W, F, I, S,* 1914 *W, I, S, F*
Jones, F P (New Brighton) 1893 *S*
Jones, H A (Barnstaple) 1950 *W, I, F*
Jorden, A M (Cambridge U, Blackheath, Bedford) 1970 *F,* 1973 *I, F, S,* 1974 *F,* 1975 *W, S*
Jowett, D (Heckmondwike) 1889 *M,* 1890 *S, I,* 1891 *W, I, S*
Judd, P E (Coventry) 1962 *W, I, F, S,* 1963 *S, NZ* 1,2, *A,* 1964 *NZ,* 1965 *I, F, S,* 1966 *W, I, F, S,* 1967 *A, I, F, S, W, NZ*

Kay, B J (Leicester) 2001 *C* 1,2, *A, R, SA* (t+R), 2002 *S, I, F, W, It, Arg*
Kayll, H E (Sunderland) 1878 *S*
Keeling, J H (Guy's Hospital) 1948 *A, W*
Keen, B W (Newcastle U) 1968 *W, I, F, S*
Keeton, G H (Leicester) 1904 *W, I, S*
Kelly, G A (Bedford) 1947 *W, I, S,* 1948 *W*
Kelly, T S (London Devonians) 1906 *W, I, S, F, SA,* 1907 *F, W, I, S,* 1908 *F, I, S*
Kemble, A T (Liverpool) 1885 *W, I,* 1887 *I*
Kemp, D T (Blackheath) 1935 *W*
Kemp, T A (Richmond) 1937 *W, I,* 1939 *S,* 1948 *A, W*
Kendall, P D (Birkenhead Park) 1901 *S,* 1902 *W, I,* 1903 *S*
Kendall-Carpenter, J MacG K (Oxford U, Bath) 1949 *I, F, S,* 1950 *W, I, F, S,* 1951 *I, F, S,* 1952 *SA, W, S, I, F,* 1953 *W, I, F, S,* 1954 *W, NZ, I, F*
Kendrew, D A (Leicester) 1930 *W, I,* 1933 *I, S,* 1934 *S,* 1935 *W, I,* 1936 *NZ, W, I*
Kennedy, R D (Camborne S of M) 1949 *I, F, S*
Kent, C P (Rosslyn Park) 1977 *S, I, F, W,* 1978 *F* (R)
Kent, T (Salford) 1891 *W, I, S,* 1892 *W, I, S*
Kershaw, C A (United Services, RN) 1920 *W, F, I, S,* 1921 *W, I, S, F,* 1922 *W, I, F, S,* 1923 *W, I, S, F*
Kewley, E (Liverpool) 1874 *S,* 1875 *S,* 1876 *I, S,* 1877 *I, S,* 1878 *S*
Kewney, A L (Leicester) 1906 *W, I, S, F,* 1909 *A, W, F, I, S,* 1911 *W, F, I, S,* 1912 *I, S,* 1913 *SA*
Key, A (O Cranleighans) 1930 *I,* 1933 *W*
Keyworth, M (Swansea) 1976 *A, W, S, I*
Kilner, B (Wakefield T) 1880 *I*
Kindersley, R S (Exeter) 1883 *W,* 1884 *S,* 1885 *W*
King, A D (Wasps) 1997 *Arg* 2(R), 1998 *SA* 2(R), 2000 *It* (R), 2001 *C* 2(R)
King, I (Harrogate) 1954 *W, NZ, I*
King, J A (Headingley) 1911 *W, F, I, S,* 1912 *W, I, S,* 1913 *SA, W, F, I, S*
King, Q E M A (Army) 1921 *S*
Kingston, P (Gloucester) 1975 *A* 1,2, 1979 *I, F, W*
Kitching, A E (Blackheath) 1913 *I*
Kittermaster, H R J (Harlequins) 1925 *NZ, W, I,* 1926 *W, I, F, S*
Knight, F (Plymouth) 1909 *A*
Knight, P M (Bristol) 1972 *F, S, SA*
Knowles, E (Millom) 1896 *S,* 1897 *S*
Knowles, T C (Birkenhead Park) 1931 *S*
Krige, J A (Guy's Hospital) 1920 *W*

Labuschagne, N A (Harlequins, Guy's Hospital) 1953 *W,* 1955 *W, I, F, S*
Lagden, R O (Richmond) 1911 *S*
Laird, H C C (Harlequins) 1927 *W, I, S,* 1928 *A, W, I, F, S,* 1929 *F, I*
Lambert, D (Harlequins) 1907 *F,* 1908 *F, W, S,* 1911 *W, F, I*
Lampkowski, M S (Headingley) 1976 *A, W, S, I*
Lapage, W N (United Services, RN) 1908 *F, W, I, S*
Larter, P J (Northampton, RAF) 1967 *A, NZ,* 1968 *W, I, F, S,* 1969 *I, F, S, W, SA,* 1970 *I, W, F, S,* 1971 *W, I, F, S* (2[1C]), *P,* 1972 *SA,* 1973 *NZ* 1, *W*
Law, A F (Richmond) 1877 *S*
Law, D E (Birkenhead Park) 1927 *I*
Lawrence, Hon H A (Richmond) 1873 *S,* 1874 *S,* 1875 *I, S*
Lawrie, P W (Leicester) 1910 *S,* 1911 *S*
Lawson, R G (Workington) 1925 *I*
Lawson, T M (Workington) 1928 *A, W*
Leadbetter, M M (Broughton Park) 1970 *F*
Leadbetter, V H (Edinburgh Wands) 1954 *S, F*
Leake, W R M (Harlequins) 1891 *W, I, S*
Leather, G (Liverpool) 1907 *I*

Lee, F H (Marlborough N) 1876 *S,* 1877 *I*
Lee, H (Blackheath) 1907 *F*
Le Fleming, J (Blackheath) 1887 *W*
Leonard, J (Saracens, Harlequins) 1990 *Arg* 1,2,3, 1991 *W, S, I, F, Fj, A,* [*NZ, It, US, F, S, A*], 1992 *S, I, F, W, C, SA,* 1993 *F, W, S, I, NZ,* 1994 *S, I, F, W, SA* 1,2, *R, C,* 1995 *I, F, W, S,* [*Arg, It, A, NZ, F*], *SA, WS,* 1996 *F, W, S, I, It, Arg,* 1997 *S, I, F, W, A* 2, *NZ* 1, *SA, NZ* 2, 1998 *F, W, S, I, H, It, A* 2, *SA* 1,2, *A, Arg, SA* 3, 2001 *W, It, S, F, I, R,* 2002 *S* (R), *I* (R), *F* (R), *It* (R)
Leslie-Jones, F A (Richmond) 1895 *W, I*
Lewis, A O (Bath) 1952 *SA, W, S, I, F,* 1953 *W, I, F, S,* 1954 *F*
Lewsey, O J (Wasps) 1998 *NZ* 1,2, *SA* 1, 2001 *C* 1,2, *US*
Leyland, R (Waterloo) 1935 *W, I, S*
Linnett, M S (Moseley) 1989 *Fj*
Livesay, R O'H (Blackheath) 1898 *W,* 1899 *W*
Lloyd, L D (Leicester) 2000 *SA* 1(R),2(R), 2001 *C* 1,2, *US*
Lloyd, R H (Harlequins) 1967 *NZ,* 1968 *W, I, F, S*
Locke, H M (Birkenhead Park) 1923 *S, F,* 1924 *W, F, S,* 1925 *W, I, S, F,* 1927 *W, I, S*
Lockwood, R E (Heckmondwike) 1887 *W, I, S,* 1889 *M,* 1891 *W, I, S,* 1892 *W, I, S,* 1893 *W, I,* 1894 *W, I*
Login, S H M (RN Coll) 1876 *I*
Lohden, F C (Blackheath) 1893 *W*
Long, A E (Bath) 1997 *A* 2, 2001 *US* (R)
Longland, R J (Northampton) 1932 *S,* 1933 *W, S,* 1934 *W, I, S,* 1935 *W, I, S,* 1936 *NZ, W, I, S,* 1937 *W, I, S,* 1938 *W, I, S*
Lowe, C N (Cambridge U, Blackheath) 1913 *SA, W, F, I, S,* 1914 *W, I, S, F,* 1920 *W, F, I, S,* 1921 *W, I, F, S,* 1922 *W, I, F, S,* 1923 *W, I, S, F*
Lowrie, F (Wakefield T) 1889 *M,* 1890 *W*
Lowry, W M (Birkenhead Park) 1920 *F*
Lozowski, R A P (Wasps) 1984 *A*
Luddington, W G E (Devonport Services) 1923 *W, I, S, F,* 1924 *W, I, F, S,* 1925 *W, I, S, F,* 1926 *W*
Luger, D D (Harlequins, Saracens) 1998 *H, It, SA* 2, 1999 *S, I, F, W, A, US, C,* [*It, NZ, Tg, Fj, SA*], 2000 *SA* 1, *A, Arg, SA* 3, 2001 *W, I, A, R, SA,* 2002 *F* (R), *W, It*
Luscombe, F (Gipsies) 1872 *S,* 1873 *S,* 1875 *I,* 1876 *I, S*
Luscombe, J H (Gipsies) 1871 *S*
Luxmoore, A F C C (Richmond) 1900 *S,* 1901 *W*
Luya, H F (Waterloo, Headingley) 1948 *W, I, S, F,* 1949 *W*
Lyon, A (Liverpool) 1871 *S*
Lyon, G H d'O (United Services, RN) 1908 *S,* 1909 *A*

McCanlis, M A (Gloucester) 1931 *W, I*
McCarthy, N (Gloucester) 1999 *I* (t), *US* (R), 2000 *It* (R)
McFadyean, C W (Moseley) 1966 *I, F, S,* 1967 *A, I, F, S, W, NZ,* 1968 *W, I*
MacIlwaine, A H (United Services, Hull & E Riding) 1912 *W, I, S, F,* 1920 *I*
Mackie, O G (Wakefield T, Cambridge U) 1897 *S,* 1898 *I*
Mackinlay, J E H (St George's Hospital) 1872 *S,* 1873 *S,* 1875 *I*
MacLaren, W (Manchester) 1871 *S*
MacLennan, R R F (OMTs) 1925 *I, S, F*
McLeod, N F (RIE Coll) 1879 *S, I*
Madge, R J P (Exeter) 1948 *A, W, I, S*
Malir, F W S (Otley) 1930 *W, I, S*
Mallett, J A (Bath) 1995 [*WS* (R)]
Mallinder, J (Sale) 1997 *Arg* 1,2
Mangles, R H (Richmond) 1897 *W, I*
Manley, D C (Exeter) 1963 *W, I, F, S*
Mann, W E (United Services, Army) 1911 *W, F, I*
Mantell, N D (Rosslyn Park) 1975 *A* 1
Mapletoft, M S (Gloucester) 1997 *Arg* 2
Markendale, E T (Manchester R) 1880 *I*
Marques, R W D (Cambridge U, Harlequins) 1956 *W, I, S, F,* 1957 *W, I, F, S,* 1958 *W, A, I, F, S,* 1959 *W, I, F, S,* 1960 *W, I, F, S,* 1961 *SA, W*
Marquis, J C (Birkenhead Park) 1900 *I, S*
Marriott, C J B (Blackheath) 1884 *W, I, S,* 1886 *W, I, S,* 1887 *I*
Marriott, E E (Manchester) 1876 *I*
Marriott, V R (Harlequins) 1963 *NZ* 1,2, *A,* 1964 *NZ*
Marsden, G H (Morley) 1900 *W, I, S*
Marsh, H (RIE Coll) 1873 *S*
Marsh, J (Swinton) 1892 *I*
Marshall, H (Blackheath) 1893 *W*
Marshall, M W (Blackheath) 1873 *S,* 1874 *S,* 1875 *I, S,* 1876 *I, S,* 1877 *I, S,* 1878 *S, I*
Marshall, R M (Oxford U) 1938 *I, S,* 1939 *W, I, S*
Martin, C R (Bath) 1985 *F, S, I, W*

Martin, N O (Harlequins) 1972 *F* (R)
Martindale, S A (Kendal) 1929 *F*
Massey, E J (Leicester) 1925 *W, I, S*
Mather, B-J (Sale) 1999 *W*
Mathias, J L (Bristol) 1905 *W, I, S, NZ*
Matters, J C (RNE Coll) 1899 *S*
Matthews, J R C (Harlequins) 1949 *F, S,* 1950 *I, F, S,* 1952 *SA, W, S, I, F*
Maud, P (Blackheath) 1893 *W, I*
Maxwell, A W (New Brighton, Headingley) 1975 *A* 1, 1976 *A, W, S, I, F,* 1978 *F*
Maxwell-Hyslop, J E (Oxford U) 1922 *I, F, S*
Maynard, A F (Cambridge U) 1914 *W, I, S*
Meikle, G W C (Waterloo) 1934 *W, I, S*
Meikle, S S C (Waterloo) 1929 *S*
Mellish, F W (Blackheath) 1920 *W, F, I, S,* 1921 *W, I*
Melville, N D (Wasps) 1984 *A,* 1985 *I, W, NZ* 1,2, 1986 *W, S, I, F,* 1988 *F, W, S, I* 1
Merriam, L P B (Blackheath) 1920 *W, F*
Michell, A T (Oxford U) 1875 *I, S,* 1876 *I*
Middleton, B B (Birkenhead Park) 1882 *I,* 1883 *I*
Middleton, J A (Richmond) 1922 *S*
Miles, J H (Leicester) 1903 *W*
Millett, H (Richmond) 1920 *F*
Mills, F W (Marlborough N) 1872 *S,* 1873 *S*
Mills, S G F (Gloucester) 1981 *Arg* 1,2, 1983 *W,* 1984 *SA* 1, *A*
Mills, W A (Devonport A) 1906 *W, I, S, F, SA,* 1907 *F, W, I, S,* 1908 *F, W*
Milman, D L K (Bedford) 1937 *W,* 1938 *W, I, S*
Milton, C H (Camborne S of M) 1906 *I*
Milton, J G (Camborne S of M) 1904 *W, I, S,* 1905 *S,* 1907 *I*
Milton, W H (Marlborough N) 1874 *S,* 1875 *I*
Mitchell, F (Blackheath) 1895 *W, I, S,* 1896 *W, I, S*
Mitchell, W G (Richmond) 1890 *W, S, I,* 1891 *W, I, S,* 1893 *S*
Mobbs, E R (Northampton) 1909 *A, W, F, I, S,* 1910 *I, F*
Moberley, W O (Ravenscourt Park) 1872 *S*
Moody, L W (Leicester) 2001 *C* 1,2, *US, I* (R), *R, SA* (R), 2002 *I* (R), *W, It, Arg*
Moore, B C (Nottingham, Harlequins) 1987 *S, [A, J, W],* 1988 *F, W, S, I* 1,2, *A* 1, 2, *Fj, A,* 1989 *S, I, F, W, R, Fj,* 1990 *I, F, W, S, Arg* 1,2, 1991 *W, S, I, F, Fj, A, [NZ, It, F, S, A],* 1992 *S, I, F, W, SA,* 1993 *F, W, S, I, NZ,* 1994 *S, I, F, W, SA* 1,2, *R, C,* 1995 *I, F, W, S, [Arg, It, WS* (R), *A, NZ, F]*
Moore, E J (Blackheath) 1883 *I, S*
Moore, N J N H (Bristol) 1904 *W, I, S*
Moore, P B C (Blackheath) 1951 *W*
Moore, W K T (Leicester) 1947 *W, I,* 1949 *F, S,* 1950 *I, F, S*
Mordell, R J (Rosslyn Park) 1978 *W*
Morfitt, S (W Hartlepool) 1894 *W, I, S,* 1896 *W, I, S*
Morgan, J R (Hawick) 1920 *W*
Morgan, W G D (Medicals, Newcastle) 1960 *W, I, F, S,* 1961 *SA, W, I, F, S*
Morley, A J (Bristol) 1972 *SA,* 1973 *NZ* 1, *W, I,* 1975 *S, A* 1,2
Morris, A D W (United Services, RN) 1909 *A, W, F*
Morris, C D (Liverpool St Helens, Orrell) 1988 *A,* 1989 *S, I, F, W,* 1992 *S, I, F, W, C, SA,* 1993 *F, W, S, I,* 1994 *F, W, SA* 1,2, *R,* 1995 *S* (t), *[Arg, WS, A, NZ, F]*
Morrison, P H (Cambridge U) 1890 *W, S, I,* 1891 *I*
Morse, S (Marlborough N) 1873 *S,* 1874 *S,* 1875 *S*
Mortimer, W (Marlborough N) 1899 *W*
Morton, H J S (Blackheath) 1909 *I, S,* 1910 *W, I*
Moss, F (Broughton) 1885 *W, I,* 1886 *W*
Mullins, A R (Harlequins) 1989 *Fj*
Mycock, J (Sale) 1947 *W, I, S, F,* 1948 *A*
Myers, E (Bradford) 1920 *I, S,* 1921 *W, I,* 1922 *W, I, F, S,* 1923 *W, I, S, F,* 1924 *W, I, F, S,* 1925 *S, F*
Myers, H (Keighley) 1898 *I*

Nanson, W M B (Carlisle) 1907 *F, W*
Nash, E H (Richmond) 1875 *I*
Neale, B A (Rosslyn Park) 1951 *I, F, S*
Neale, M E (Blackheath) 1912 *F*
Neame, S (O Cheltonians) 1879 *S, I,* 1880 *I, S*
Neary, A (Broughton Park) 1971 *W, I, F, S* (2[1C]), *P,* 1972 *W, I, F, SA,* 1973 *NZ* 1, *W, I, F, S, NZ* 2, *A,* 1974 *S, I, F, W,* 1975 *I, F, W, S, A* 1, 1976 *A, W, S, I, F,* 1977 *I,* 1978 *F* (R), 1979 *S, I, F, W, NZ,* 1980 *I, F, W, S*
Nelmes, B G (Cardiff) 1975 *A* 1,2, 1978 *W, S, I, NZ*
Newbold, C J (Blackheath) 1904 *W, I, S,* 1905 *W, I, S*
Newman, S C (Oxford U) 1947 *F,* 1948 *A, W*
Newton, A W (Blackheath) 1907 *S*
Newton, P A (Blackheath) 1882 *S*

Newton-Thompson, J O (Oxford U) 1947 *S, F*
Nichol, W (Brighouse R) 1892 *W, S*
Nicholas, P L (Exeter) 1902 *W*
Nicholson, B E (Harlequins) 1938 *W, I*
Nicholson, E S (Leicester) 1935 *W, I, S,* 1936 *NZ, W*
Nicholson, E T (Birkenhead Park) 1900 *W, I*
Nicholson, T (Rockcliff) 1893 *I*
Ninnes, B F (Coventry) 1971 *W*
Noon, J (Newcastle) 2001 *C* 1,2, *US*
Norman, D J (Leicester) 1932 *SA, W*
North, E H G (Blackheath) 1891 *W, I, S*
Northmore, S (Millom) 1897 *I*
Novak, M J (Harlequins) 1970 *W, S, F*
Novis, A L (Blackheath) 1929 *S, F,* 1930 *W, I, F,* 1933 *I, S*

Oakeley, F E (United Services, RN) 1913 *S,* 1914 *I, S, F*
Oakes, R F (Hartlepool R) 1897 *W, I, S,* 1898 *I, S, W,* 1899 *W, S*
Oakley, L F L (Bedford) 1951 *W*
Obolensky, A (Oxford U) 1936 *NZ, W, I, S*
Ojomoh, S O (Bath, Gloucester) 1994 *I, F, SA* 1(R),2, *R,* 1995 *S* (R), *[Arg, WS, A* (t), *F],* 1996 *F,* 1998 *NZ* 1
Old, A G B (Middlesbrough, Leicester, Sheffield) 1972 *W, I, F, S, SA,* 1973 *NZ* 2, *A,* 1974 *S, I, F, W,* 1975 *I, A* 2, 1976 *S, I,* 1978 *F*
Oldham, W L (Coventry) 1908 *S,* 1909 *A*
Olver, C J (Northampton) 1990 *Arg* 3, 1991 *[US],* 1992 *C*
O'Neill, A (Teignmouth, Torquay A) 1901 *W, I, S*
Openshaw, W E (Manchester) 1879 *I*
Orwin, J (Gloucester, RAF, Bedford) 1985 *R, F, S, I, W, NZ* 1,2, 1988 *F, W, S, I* 1,2, *A* 1,2
Osborne, R R (Manchester) 1871 *S*
Osborne, S H (Oxford U) 1905 *S*
Oti, C (Cambridge U, Nottingham, Wasps) 1988 *S, I* 1, 1989 *S, I, F, W, R,* 1990 *Arg* 1,2, 1991 *Fj, A, [NZ, It]*
Oughtred, B (Hartlepool R) 1901 *S,* 1902 *W, I, S,* 1903 *W, I*
Owen, J E (Coventry) 1963 *W, I, F, S, A,* 1964 *NZ,* 1965 *W, I, F, S,* 1966 *I, F, S,* 1967 *NZ*
Owen-Smith, H G O (St Mary's Hospital) 1934 *W, I, S,* 1936 *NZ, W, I, S,* 1937 *W, I, S*

Page, J J (Bedford, Northampton) 1971 *W, I, F, S,* 1975 *S*
Pallant, J N (Notts) 1967 *I, F, S*
Palmer, A C (London Hospital) 1909 *I, S*
Palmer, F H (Richmond) 1905 *W*
Palmer, G V (Richmond) 1928 *I, F, S*
Palmer, J A (Bath) 1984 *SA* 1,2, 1986 *I* (R)
Palmer, T (Leeds) 2001 *US* (R)
Pargetter, T A (Coventry) 1962 *S,* 1963 *F, NZ* 1
Parker, G W (Gloucester) 1938 *I, S*
Parker, Hon S (Liverpool) 1874 *S,* 1875 *S*
Parsons, E I (RAF) 1939 *S*
Parsons, M J (Northampton) 1968 *W, I, F, S*
Patterson, W M (Sale) 1961 *SA, S*
Pattisson, R M (Blackheath) 1883 *I, S*
Paul, H (Gloucester) 2002 *F* (R)
Paul, J E (RIE Coll) 1875 *S*
Payne, A T (Bristol) 1935 *I, S*
Payne, C M (Harlequins) 1964 *I, F, S,* 1965 *I, F, S,* 1966 *W, I, F, S*
Payne, J H (Broughton) 1882 *S,* 1883 *W, I, S,* 1884 *I,* 1885 *W, I*
Pearce, G S (Northampton) 1979 *S, I, F, W,* 1981 *Arg* 1,2, 1982 *A, S,* 1983 *F, W, S, I, NZ,* 1984 *S, A* 1,2, 1985 *R, F, S, I, W, NZ* 1,2, 1986 *W, S, I, F,* 1987 *I, F, W, S, [A, US, W],* 1988 *Fj,* 1991 *[US]*
Pears, D (Harlequins) 1990 *Arg* 1,2, 1992 *F* (R), 1994 *F*
Pearson, A W (Blackheath) 1875 *I, S,* 1876 *I, S,* 1877 *S,* 1878 *S, I*
Peart, T G A H (Hartlepool R) 1964 *F, S*
Pease, F E (Hartlepool R) 1887 *I*
Penny, S H (Leicester) 1909 *A*
Penny, W J (United Hospitals) 1878 *I,* 1879 *S, I*
Percival, L J (Rugby) 1891 *I,* 1892 *I,* 1893 *S*
Periton, H G (Waterloo) 1925 *W,* 1926 *W, I, F, S,* 1927 *W, I, S, F,* 1928 *A, I, F, S,* 1929 *W, I, F, S,* 1930 *W, I, F, S*
Perrott, E S (O Cheltonians) 1875 *I*
Perry, D G (Bedford) 1963 *F, S, NZ* 1,2, *A* 1964 *NZ, W, I,* 1965 *W, I, F, S,* 1966 *W, I, F*
Perry, M B (Bath) 1997 *A* 2, *NZ* 1, *SA, NZ* 2, 1998 *W, S, I, A* 1, *NZ* 1,2, *SA* 1, *H, It, A* 2, 1999 *I, F, W, A US, C, [It, NZ, Tg, Fj, SA],* 2000 *I, F, W, It, S, SA* 1,2, *A, SA* 3, 2001 *W* (R), *F* (R)

Lewis Moody is tackled by Iestyn Harris during England's record 50-10 defeat of Wales at Twickenham.

Perry, S V (Cambridge U, Waterloo) 1947 *W, I*, 1948 *A, W, I, S, F*
Peters, J (Plymouth) 1906 *S, F*, 1907 *I, S*, 1908 *W*
Phillips, C (Birkenhead Park) 1880 *S*, 1881 *I, S*
Phillips, M S (Fylde) 1958 *A, I, F, S*, 1959 *W, I, F, S*, 1960 *W, I, F, S*, 1961 *W*, 1963 *W, I, F, S, NZ* 1,2, *A*, 1964 *NZ, W, I, F, S*
Pickering, A S (Harrogate) 1907 *I*
Pickering, R D A (Bradford) 1967 *I, F, S, W*, 1968 *F, S*
Pickles, R C W (Bristol) 1922 *I, F*
Pierce, R (Liverpool) 1898 *I*, 1903 *S*
Pilkington, W N (Cambridge U) 1898 *S*
Pillman, C H (Blackheath) 1910 *W, I, F, S*, 1911 *W, F, I, S*, 1912 *W, F*, 1913 *SA, W, F, I, S*, 1914 *W, I, S*
Pillman, R L (Blackheath) 1914 *F*
Pinch, J (Lancaster) 1896 *W, I*, 1897 *S*
Pinching, W W (Guy's Hospital) 1872 *S*
Pitman, I J (Oxford U) 1922 *S*
Plummer, K C (Bristol) 1969 *W*, 1976 *S, I, F*
Pool-Jones, R J (Stade Francais) 1998 *A* 1
Poole, F O (Oxford U) 1895 *W, I, S*
Poole, R W (Hartlepool R) 1896 *S*
Pope, E B (Blackheath) 1931 *W, S, F*
Portus, G V (Blackheath) 1908 *F, I*
Potter, S (Leicester) 1998 *A* 1(t)
Poulton, R W (later Poulton Palmer) (Oxford U, Harlequins, Liverpool) 1909 *F, I, S*, 1910 *W*, 1911 *S*, 1912 *W, I, S*, 1913 *SA, W, F, I, S*, 1914 *W, I, S, F*
Powell, D L (Northampton) 1966 *W, I*, 1969 *I, F, S, W*, 1971 *W, I, F, S* (2[1C])
Pratten, W E (Blackheath) 1927 *S, F*
Preece, I (Coventry) 1948 *I, S, F*, 1949 *F, S*, 1950 *W, I, F, S*, 1951 *W, I, F*
Preece, P S (Coventry) 1972 *SA*, 1973 *NZ* 1, *W, I, F, S, NZ* 2, 1975 *I, F, W, A* 2, 1976 *W* (R)
Preedy, M (Gloucester) 1984 *SA* 1
Prentice, F D (Leicester) 1928 *I, F, S*
Prescott, R E (Harlequins) 1937 *W, I*, 1938 *I*, 1939 *W, I, S*
Preston, N J (Richmond) 1979 *NZ*, 1980 *I, F*
Price, H L (Harlequins) 1922 *I, S*, 1923 *W, I*
Price, J (Coventry) 1961 *I*
Price, P L A (RIE Coll) 1877 *I, S*, 1878 *S*
Price, T W (Cheltenham) 1948 *S, F*, 1949 *W, I, F, S*
Probyn, J A (Wasps, Askeans) 1988 *F, W, S, I* 1,2, *A* 1, 2, *A*, 1989 *S, I, R* (R), 1990 *I, F, W, S, Arg* 1,2,3, 1991 *W, S, I, F, Fj, A*, [*NZ, It, F, S, A*], 1992 *S, I, F, W*, 1993 *F, W, S, I*
Prout, D H (Northampton) 1968 *W, I*
Pullin, J V (Bristol) 1966 *W*, 1968 *W, I, F, S*, 1969 *I, F, S, W, SA*, 1970 *I, W, S, F*, 1971 *W, I, F, S* (2[1C]), *P*, 1972 *W, I, F, S, SA*, 1973 *NZ* 1, *W, I, F, S, NZ* 2, *A*, 1974 *S, I, F, W*, 1975 *I, W* (R), *S, A* 1,2, 1976 *F*
Purdy, S J (Rugby) 1962 *S*
Pyke, J (St Helens Recreation) 1892 *W*
Pym, J A (Blackheath) 1912 *W, I, S, F*

Quinn, J P (New Brighton) 1954 *W, NZ, I, S, F*

Rafter, M (Bristol) 1977 *S, F, W*, 1978 *F, W, S, I, NZ*, 1979 *S, I, F, W, NZ*, 1980 *W*(R), 1981 *W, Arg* 1,2
Ralston, C W (Richmond) 1971 *S* (C), *P*, 1972 *W, I, F, S, SA*, 1973 *NZ* 1, *W, I, F, S, NZ* 2, *A*, 1974 *S, I, F, W*, 1975 *I, F, W, S*
Ramsden, H E (Bingley) 1898 *W, S*
Ranson, J M (Rosslyn Park) 1963 *NZ* 1,2, *A*, 1964 *W, I, F, S*
Raphael, J E (OMTs) 1902 *W, I, S*, 1905 *W, S, NZ*, 1906 *W, S, F*
Ravenscroft, J (Birkenhead Park) 1881 *I*
Ravenscroft, S C W (Saracens) 1998 *A* 1, *NZ* 2(R)
Rawlinson, W C W (Blackheath) 1876 *S*
Redfern, S (Leicester) 1984 *I* (R)
Redman, N C (Bath) 1984 *A*, 1986 *S* (R), 1987 *I, S, [A, J, W]*, 1988 *Fj*, 1990 *Arg* 1,2, 1991 *Fj, [It, US]*, 1993 *NZ*, 1994 *F, W, SA* 1,2, 1997 *Arg* 1, *A* 1
Redmond, G F (Cambridge U) 1970 *F*
Redwood, B W (Bristol) 1968 *W, I*
Rees, D L (Sale) 1997 *A* 2, *NZ* 1, *SA, NZ* 2, 1998 *F, W, SA* 2(R), 1999 *S, I, F, A*
Rees, G W (Nottingham) 1984 *SA* 2(R), *A*, 1986 *I, F*, 1987 *F, W, S, [A, J, US, W]*, 1988 *S* (R), *I* 1,2, *A* 1,2, *Fj*, 1989 *W* (R), *R* (R), *Fj* (R), 1990 *Arg* 3(R), 1991 *Fj, [US]*
Reeve, J S R (Harlequins) 1929 *F*, 1930 *W, I, F, S*, 1931 *W, I, S*
Regan, M (Liverpool) 1953 *W, I, F, S*, 1954 *W, NZ, I, S, F*, 1956 *I, S, F*
Regan, M P (Bristol, Bath) 1995 *SA, WS*, 1996 *F, W, S, I, It, Arg*, 1997 *S, I, F, W, A* 1, *NZ* 2(R), 1998 *F*, 2000 *SA* 1(t), *A* (R), *Arg, SA* 3(t), 2001 *It* (R), *S* (R), *C* 2(R), *R*
Rendall, P A G (Wasps, Askeans) 1984 *W, SA* 2, 1986 *W, S*, 1987 *I, F, S, [A, J, W]*, 1988 *F, W, S, I* 1,2, *A* 1,2, 1989 *S, I, F, W, R*, 1990 *I, F, W, S*, 1991 *[It* (R)]
Rew, H (Blackheath) 1929 *S, F*, 1930 *F, S*, 1931 *W, S, F*, 1934 *W, I, S*
Reynolds, F J (O Cranleighans) 1937 *S*, 1938 *I, S*
Reynolds, S (Richmond) 1900 *W, I, S*, 1901 *I*
Rhodes, J (Castleford) 1896 *W, I, S*
Richards, D (Leicester) 1986 *I, F*, 1987 *S, [A, J, US, W]*, 1988 *F, W, S, I* 1, *A* 1,2, *Fj, A*, 1989 *S, I, F, W, R*, 1990 *Arg* 3, 1991 *W, S, I, F, Fj, A, [NZ, It, US]*, 1992 *S* (R), *F, W, C*, 1993 *NZ*, 1994 *W, SA* 1, *C*, 1995 *I, F, W, S, [WS, A, NZ]*, 1996 *F* (t), *S, I*
Richards, E E (Plymouth A) 1929 *S, F*
Richards, J (Bradford) 1891 *W, I, S*
Richards, S B (Richmond) 1965 *W, I, F, S*, 1967 *A, I, F, S, W*
Richardson, J V (Birkenhead Park) 1928 *A, W, I, F, S*
Richardson, W R (Manchester) 1881 *I*
Rickards, C H (Gipsies) 1873 *S*
Rimmer, G (Waterloo) 1949 *W, I*, 1950 *W*, 1951 *W, I, F*, 1952 *SA, W*, 1954 *W, NZ, I, S*
Rimmer, L I (Bath) 1961 *SA, W, I, F, S*
Ripley, A G (Rosslyn Park) 1972 *W, I, F, S, SA*, 1973 *NZ* 1, *W, I, F, S, NZ* 2, *A*, 1974 *S, I, F, W*, 1975 *I, F, S, A* 1,2, 1976 *A, W, S*
Risman, A B W (Loughborough Coll) 1959 *W, I, F, S*, 1961 *SA, W, I, F*
Ritson, J A S (Northern) 1910 *F, S*, 1912 *F*, 1913 *SA, W, F, I, S*
Rittson-Thomas, G C (Oxford U) 1951 *W, I, F*
Robbins, G L (Coventry) 1986 *W, S*
Robbins, P G D (Oxford U, Moseley, Coventry) 1956 *W, I, S, F*, 1957 *W, I, F, S*, 1958 *W, A, I, S*, 1960 *W, I, F, S*, 1961 *SA, W*, 1962 *S*
Roberts, A D (Northern) 1911 *W, F, I, S*, 1912 *I, S, F*, 1914 *I*
Roberts, E W (RNE Coll) 1901 *W, I*, 1905 *NZ*, 1906 *W, I*, 1907 *S*
Roberts, G D (Harlequins) 1907 *S*, 1908 *F, W*
Roberts, J (Sale) 1960 *W, I, F, S*, 1961 *SA, W, I, F, S*, 1962 *W, I, F, S*, 1963 *W, I, F, S*, 1964 *NZ*
Roberts, R S (Coventry) 1932 *I*
Roberts, S (Swinton) 1887 *W, I*
Roberts, V G (Penryn, Harlequins) 1947 *F*, 1949 *W, I, F, S*, 1950 *I, F, S*, 1951 *W, I, F, S*, 1956 *W, I, S, F*
Robertshaw, A R (Bradford) 1886 *W, I, S*, 1887 *W, S*
Robinson, A (Blackheath) 1889 *M*, 1890 *W, S, I*
Robinson, E T (Coventry) 1954 *S*, 1961 *I, F, S*
Robinson, G C (Percy Park) 1897 *I, S*, 1898 *I*, 1899 *W*, 1900 *I, S*, 1901 *I, S*
Robinson, J (Sale) 2001 *It* (R), *S* (R), *F*(R), *I, A, R, SA*, 2002 *S, I, F, It*
Robinson, J J (Headingley) 1893 *S*, 1902 *W, I, S*
Robinson, R A (Bath) 1988 *A* 2, *Fj, A*, 1989 *S, I, F, W*, 1995 *SA*
Robson, A (Northern) 1924 *W, I, F, S*, 1926 *W*
Robson, M (Oxford U) 1930 *W, I, F, S*
Rodber, T A K (Army, Northampton) 1992 *S, I*, 1993 *NZ*, 1994 *I, F, W, SA* 1,2, *R, C*, 1995 *I, F, W, S, [Arg, It, WS* (R), *A, NZ, F]*, *SA, WS*, 1996 *W, S* (R), *I* (t), *It, Arg*, 1997 *S, I, F, W, A* 1, 1998 *H* (R), *It* (R), *A* 2, *SA* 2, 1999 *S, I, F, W, A, US* (R), *[NZ* (R), *Fj* (R)]
Rogers, D P (Bedford) 1961 *I, F, S*, 1962 *W, I, F*, 1963 *W, I, F, S, NZ* 1,2, *A*, 1964 *NZ, W, I, F, S*, 1965 *W, I, F, S*, 1966 *W, I, F, S*, 1967 *A, S, W, NZ*, 1969 *I, F, S, W*
Rogers, J H (Moseley) 1890 *W, S, I*, 1891 *S*
Rogers, W L Y (Blackheath) 1905 *W, I*
Rollitt, D M (Bristol) 1967 *I, F, S, W*, 1969 *I, F, S, W*, 1975 *S, A* 1,2
Roncoroni, A D S (West Herts, Richmond) 1933 *W, I, S*
Rose, W M H (Cambridge U, Coventry, Harlequins) 1981 *I, F*, 1982 *A, S, I*, 1987 *I, F, W, S, [A]*
Rossborough, P A (Coventry) 1971 *W*, 1973 *NZ* 2, *A*, 1974 *S, I*, 1975 *I, F*
Rosser, D W A (Wasps) 1965 *W, I, F, S*, 1966 *W*
Rotherham, Alan (Richmond) 1883 *W, S*, 1884 *W, S*, 1885 *W, I*, 1886 *W, I, S*, 1887 *W, I, S*
Rotherham, Arthur (Richmond) 1898 *S, W*, 1899 *W, I, S*
Roughley, D (Liverpool) 1973 *A*, 1974 *S, I*
Rowell, R E (Leicester) 1964 *W*, 1965 *W*
Rowley, A J (Coventry) 1932 *SA*

Rowley, H C (Manchester) 1879 *S, I,* 1880 *I, S,* 1881 *I, W, S,* 1882 *I, S*
Rowntree, G C (Leicester) 1995 *S* (t), [*It, WS*], *WS,* 1996 *F, W, S, I, It, Arg,* 1997 *S, I, F, W, A* 1, 1998 *A* 1, *NZ* 1, 2, *SA* 1, *H* (R), *It* (R), 1999 *US, C,* [*It* (R), *Tg, Fj* (R)], 2001 *C* 1,2, *US, I* (R), *A, R, SA,* 2002 *S, I, F, W, It*
Royds, P M R (Blackheath) 1898 *S, W,* 1899 *W*
Royle, A V (Broughton R) 1889 *M*
Rudd, E L (Liverpool) 1965 *W, I, S,* 1966 *W, I, S*
Russell, R F (Leicester) 1905 *NZ*
Rutherford, D (Percy Park, Gloucester) 1960 *W, I, F, S,* 1961 *SA,* 1965 *W, I, F, S,* 1966 *W, I, F, S,* 1967 *NZ*
Ryalls, H J (New Brighton) 1885 *W, I*
Ryan, D (Wasps, Newcastle) 1990 *Arg* 1,2, 1992 *C,* 1998 *S*
Ryan, P H (Richmond) 1955 *W, I*

Sadler, E H (Army) 1933 *I, S*
Sagar, J W (Cambridge U) 1901 *W, I*
Salmon, J L B (Harlequins) 1985 *NZ* 1,2, 1986 *W, S,* 1987 *I, F, W, S,* [*A, J, US, W*]
Sample, C H (Cambridge U) 1884 *I,* 1885 *I,* 1886 *S*
Sampson, P C (Wasps) 1998 *SA* 1, 2001 *C* 1,2
Sanders, D L (Harlequins) 1954 *W, NZ, I, S, F,* 1956 *W, I, S, F*
Sanders, F W (Plymouth A) 1923 *I, S, F*
Sanderson, A (Sale) 2001 *R* (R), 2002 *Arg*
Sanderson, P H (Sale, Harlequins) 1998 *NZ* 1,2, *SA* 1, 2001 *C* 1(R),2(R), *US* (t+R)
Sandford, J R P (Marlborough N) 1906 *I*
Sangwin, R D (Hull and E Riding) 1964 *NZ, W*
Sargent, G A F (Gloucester) 1981 *I* (R)
Savage, K F (Northampton) 1966 *W, I, F, S,* 1967 *A, I, F, S, W, NZ,* 1968 *W, F, S*
Sawyer, C M (Broughton) 1880 *S,* 1881 *I*
Saxby, L E (Gloucester) 1932 *SA, W*
Schofield, J W (Manchester) 1880 *I*
Scholfield, J A (Preston Grasshoppers) 1911 *W*
Schwarz, R O (Richmond) 1899 *S,* 1901 *W, I*
Scorfield, E S (Percy Park) 1910 *F*
Scott, C T (Blackheath) 1900 *W, I,* 1901 *W, I*
Scott, E K (St Mary's Hospital, Redruth) 1947 *W,* 1948 *A, W, I, S*
Scott, F S (Bristol) 1907 *W*
Scott, H (Manchester) 1955 *F*
Scott, J P (Rosslyn Park, Cardiff) 1978 *F, W, S, I, NZ,* 1979 *S* (R), *I, F, W, NZ,* 1980 *I, F, W, S,* 1981 *W, S, I, F, Arg* 1,2, 1982 *I, F, W,* 1983 *F, W, S, I, NZ,* 1984 *S, I, F, W, SA* 1,2
Scott, J S M (Oxford U) 1958 *F*
Scott, M T (Cambridge U) 1887 *I,* 1890 *S, I*
Scott, W M (Cambridge U) 1889 *M*
Seddon, R L (Broughton R) 1887 *W, I, S*
Sellar, K A (United Services, RN) 1927 *W, I, S,* 1928 *A, W, I, F*
Sever, H S (Sale) 1936 *NZ, W, I, S,* 1937 *W, I, S,* 1938 *W, I, S*
Shackleton, I R (Cambridge U) 1969 *SA,* 1970 *I, W, S*
Sharp, R A W (Oxford U, Wasps, Redruth) 1960 *W, I, F, S,* 1961 *I, F,* 1962 *W, I, F,* 1963 *W, I, S,* 1967 *A*
Shaw, C H (Moseley) 1906 *S, SA,* 1907 *F, W, I, S*
Shaw, F (Cleckheaton) 1898 *I*
Shaw, J F (RNE Coll) 1898 *S, W*
Shaw, S D (Bristol, Wasps) 1996 *It, Arg,* 1997 *S, I, F, W, A* 1, *SA* (R), 2000 *I, F, W, It, S, SA* 1(R),2(R), 2001 *C* 1(R), 2, *US, I*
Sheasby, C M A (Wasps) 1996 *It, Arg,* 1997 *W* (R), *Arg* 1(R),2(R), *SA* (R), *NZ* 2(t)
Sheppard, A (Bristol) 1981 *W* (R), 1985 *W*
Sherrard, C W (Blackheath) 1871 *S,* 1872 *S*
Sherriff, G A (Saracens) 1966 *S,* 1967 *A, NZ*
Shewring, H E (Bristol) 1905 *I, NZ,* 1906 *W, S, F, SA,* 1907 *F, W, I, S*
Shooter, J H (Morley) 1899 *I, S,* 1900 *I, S*
Shuttleworth, D W (Headingley) 1951 *S,* 1953 *S*
Sibree, H J H (Harlequins) 1908 *F,* 1909 *I, S*
Silk, N (Harlequins) 1965 *W, I, F, S*
Simms, K G (Cambridge U, Liverpool, Wasps) 1985 *R, F, S, I, W,* 1986 *I, F,* 1987 *I, F, W,* [*A, J, W*], 1988 *F, W*
Simpson, C P (Harlequins) 1965 *W*
Simpson, P D (Bath) 1983 *NZ,* 1984 *S,* 1987 *I*
Simpson, T (Rockcliff) 1902 *S,* 1903 *W, I, S,* 1904 *I, S,* 1905 *I, S,* 1906 *S, SA,* 1909 *F*
Sims, D (Gloucester) 1998 *NZ* 1(R),2, *SA* 1
Skinner, M G (Harlequins) 1988 *F, W, S, I* 1,2, 1989 *Fj,* 1990 *I, F, W, S, Arg* 1,2, 1991 *Fj* (R), [*US, F, S, A*], 1992 *S, I, F, W*

Sladen, G M (United Services, RN) 1929 *W, I, S*
Sleightholme, J M (Bath) 1996 *F, W, S, I, It, Arg,* 1997 *S, I, F, W, Arg* 1,2
Slemen, M A C (Liverpool) 1976 *I, F,* 1977 *S, I, F, W,* 1978 *F, W, S, I, NZ,* 1979 *S, I, F, W, NZ,* 1980 *I, F, W, S,* 1981 *W, S, I, F,* 1982 *A, S, I, F, W,* 1983 *NZ,* 1984 *S*
Slocock, L A N (Liverpool) 1907 *F, W, I, S,* 1908 *F, W, I, S*
Slow, C F (Leicester) 1934 *S*
Small, H D (Oxford U) 1950 *W, I, F, S*
Smallwood, A M (Leicester) 1920 *F, I,* 1921 *W, I, S, F,* 1922 *I, S,* 1923 *W, I, S, F,* 1925 *I, S*
Smart, C E (Newport) 1979 *F, W, NZ,* 1981 *S, I, F, Arg* 1,2, 1982 *A, S, I, F, W,* 1983 *F, W, S, I*
Smart, S E J (Gloucester) 1913 *SA, W, F, I, S,* 1914 *W, I, S, F,* 1920 *W, I, S*
Smeddle, R W (Cambridge U) 1929 *W, I, S,* 1931 *F*
Smith, C C (Gloucester) 1901 *W*
Smith, D F (Richmond) 1910 *W, I*
Smith, J V (Cambridge U, Rosslyn Park) 1950 *W, I, F, S*
Smith, K (Roundhay) 1974 *F, W,* 1975 *W, S*
Smith, M J K (Oxford U) 1956 *W*
Smith, S J (Sale) 1973 *I, F, S, A,* 1974 *I, F,* 1975 *W* (R), 1976 *F,* 1977 *F* (R), 1979 *NZ,* 1980 *I, F, W, S,* 1981 *W, S, I, F, Arg* 1,2, 1982 *A, S, I, F, W,* 1983 *F, W, S*
Smith, S R (Richmond) 1959 *W, F, S,* 1964 *F, S*
Smith, S T (Wasps) 1985 *R, F, S, I, W, NZ* 1,2, 1986 *W, S*
Smith, T H (Northampton) 1951 *W*
Soane, F (Bath) 1893 *S,* 1894 *W, I, S*
Sobey, W H (O Millhillians) 1930 *W, F, S,* 1932 *SA, W*
Solomon, B (Redruth) 1910 *W*
Sparks, R H W (Plymouth A) 1928 *I, F, S,* 1929 *W, I, S,* 1931 *I, S, F*
Speed, H (Castleford) 1894 *W, I, S,* 1896 *S*
Spence, F W (Birkenhead Park) 1890 *I*
Spencer, J (Harlequins) 1966 *W*
Spencer, J S (Cambridge U, Headingley) 1969 *I, F, S, W, SA,* 1970 *I, W, S, F,* 1971 *W, I, S* (2[1C]), *P*
Spong, R S (O Millhillians) 1929 *F,* 1930 *W, I, F, S,* 1931 *F,* 1932 *SA, W*
Spooner, R H (Liverpool) 1903 *W*
Springman, H H (Liverpool) 1879 *S,* 1887 *S*
Spurling, A (Blackheath) 1882 *I*
Spurling, N (Blackheath) 1886 *I, S,* 1887 *W*
Squires, P J (Harrogate) 1973 *F, S, NZ* 2, *A,* 1974 *S, I, F, W,* 1975 *I, F, W, S, A* 1,2, 1976 *A, W,* 1977 *S, I, F, W,* 1978 *F, W, S, I, NZ,* 1979 *S, I, F, W*
Stafford, R C (Bedford) 1912 *W, I, S, F*
Stafford, W F H (RE) 1874 *S*
Stanbury, E (Plymouth A) 1926 *W, I, S,* 1927 *W, I, S, F,* 1928 *A, W, I, F, S,* 1929 *W, I, S, F*
Standing, G (Blackheath) 1883 *W, I*
Stanger-Leathes, C F (Northern) 1905 *I*
Stark, K J (O Alleynians) 1927 *W, I, S, F,* 1928 *A, W, I, F, S*
Starks, A (Castleford) 1896 *W, I*
Starmer-Smith, N C (Harlequins) 1969 *SA,* 1970 *I, W, S, F,* 1971 *S* (C), *P*
Start, S P (United Services, RN) 1907 *S*
Steeds, J H (Saracens) 1949 *F, S,* 1950 *I, F, S*
Steele-Bodger, M R (Cambridge U) 1947 *W, I, S, F,* 1948 *A, W, I, S, F*
Steinthal, F E (Ilkley) 1913 *W, F*
Stephenson, M (Newcastle) 2001 *C* 1,2, *US*
Stevens, C B (Penzance-Newlyn, Harlequins) 1969 *SA,* 1970 *I, W, S,* 1971 *P,* 1972 *W, I, F, S, SA,* 1973 *NZ* 1, *W, I, F, S, NZ* 2, *A,* 1974 *S, I, F, W,* 1975 *I, F, W, S*
Still, E R (Oxford U, Ravenscourt P) 1873 *S*
Stimpson, T R G (Newcastle, Leicester) 1996 *It,* 1997 *S, I, F, W, A* 1, *NZ* 2(t+R), 1998 *A* 1, *NZ* 1,2(R), *SA* 1(R), 1999 *US* (R), *C* (R), 2000 *SA* 1, 2001 *C* 1(t),2(R), 2002 *W* (R), *Arg*
Stirling, R V (Leicester, RAF, Wasps) 1951 *W, I, F,* 1952 *SA, W, S, I, F,* 1953 *W, I, F, S,* 1954 *W, NZ, I, S, F*
Stoddart, A E (Blackheath) 1885 *W, I,* 1886 *W, I, S,* 1889 *M,* 1890 *W, I,* 1893 *W, S*
Stoddart, W B (Liverpool) 1897 *W, I, S*
Stokes, F (Blackheath) 1871 *S,* 1872 *S,* 1873 *S*
Stokes, L (Blackheath) 1875 *I,* 1876 *S,* 1877 *I, S,* 1878 *S,* 1879 *S, I,* 1880 *I, S,* 1881 *I, W, S*
Stone, F le S (Blackheath) 1914 *F*
Stoop, A D (Harlequins) 1905 *S,* 1906 *S, F, SA,* 1907 *F, W,* 1910 *W, I, S,* 1911 *W, F, I, S,* 1912 *W, S*
Stoop, F M (Harlequins) 1910 *S,* 1911 *F, I,* 1913 *SA*
Stout, F M (Richmond) 1897 *W, I,* 1898 *I, S, W,* 1899 *I, S,* 1903 *S,* 1904 *W, I, S,* 1905 *W, I, S*

Stout, P W (Richmond) 1898 *S, W*, 1899 *W, I, S*
Stringer, N C (Wasps) 1982 *A* (R), 1983 *NZ* (R), 1984 *SA* 1(R), *A*, 1985 *R*
Strong, E L (Oxford U) 1884 *W, I, S*
Sturnham B (Saracens) 1998 *A* 1, *NZ* 1(t),2(t)
Summerscales, G E (Durham City) 1905 *NZ*
Sutcliffe, J W (Heckmondwike) 1889 *M*
Swarbrick, D W (Oxford U) 1947 *W, I, F*, 1948 *A, W*, 1949 *I*
Swayne, D H (Oxford U) 1931 *W*
Swayne, J W R (Bridgwater) 1929 *W*
Swift, A H (Swansea) 1981 *Arg* 1,2, 1983 *F, W, S*, 1984 *SA* 2
Syddall, J P (Waterloo) 1982 *I*, 1984 *A*
Sykes, A R V (Blackheath) 1914 *F*
Sykes, F D (Northampton) 1955 *F, S*, 1963 *NZ* 2, *A*
Sykes, P W (Wasps) 1948 *F*, 1952 *S, I, F*, 1953 *W, I, F*
Syrett, R E (Wasps) 1958 *W, A, I, F*, 1960 *W, I, F, S*, 1962 *W, I, F*

Tallent, J A (Cambridge U, Blackheath) 1931 *S, F*, 1932 *SA, W*, 1935 *I*
Tanner, C C (Cambridge U, Gloucester) 1930 *S*, 1932 *SA, W, I, S*
Tarr, F N (Leicester) 1909 *A, W, F*, 1913 *S*
Tatham, W M (Oxford U) 1882 *S*, 1883 *W, I, S*, 1884 *W, I, S*
Taylor, A S (Blackheath) 1883 *W, I*, 1886 *W, I*
Taylor, E W (Rockcliff) 1892 *I*, 1893 *I*, 1894 *W, I, S*, 1895 *W, I, S*, 1896 *W, I*, 1897 *W, I, S*, 1899 *I*
Taylor, F (Leicester) 1920 *F, I*
Taylor, F M (Leicester) 1914 *W*
Taylor, H H (Blackheath) 1879 *S*, 1880 *S*, 1881 *I, W*, 1882 *S*, 1902 *W, I, S*, 1903 *W, I*, 1905 *S*
Taylor, J T (W Hartlepool) 1897 *I*, 1899 *I*, 1900 *I*, 1901 *W, I*, 1902 *W, I, S*, 1903 *W, I*, 1905 *S*
Taylor, P J (Northampton) 1955 *W, I*, 1962 *W, I, F, S*
Taylor, R B (Northampton) 1966 *W*, 1967 *I, F, S, W, NZ*, 1969 *F, S, W, SA*, 1970 *I, W, S, F*, 1971 *S* (2[1C])
Taylor, W J (Blackheath) 1928 *A, W, I, F, S*
Teague, M C (Gloucester, Moseley) 1985 *F* (R), *NZ* 1, 2, 1989 *S, I, F, W, R*, 1990 *F, W, S*, 1991 *W, S, I, F, Fj, A*, [*NZ, It, F, S, A*], 1992 *SA*, 1993 *F, W, S, I*
Teden, D E (Richmond) 1939 *W, I, S*
Teggin, A (Broughton R) 1884 *I*, 1885 *W*, 1886 *I, S*, 1887 *I, S*
Tetley, T S (Bradford) 1876 *S*
Thomas, C (Barnstaple) 1895 *W, I, S*, 1899 *I*
Thompson, P H (Headingley, Waterloo) 1956 *W, I, S, F*, 1957 *W, I, F, S*, 1958 *W, A, I, F, S*, 1959 *W, I, F, S*
Thompson, S (Northampton) 2002 *S, I, F, W, It, Arg*
Thomson, G T (Halifax) 1878 *S*, 1882 *I, S*, 1883 *W, I, S*, 1884 *I, S*, 1885 *I*
Thomson, W B (Blackheath) 1892 *W*, 1895 *W, I, S*
Thorne, J D (Bristol) 1963 *W, I, F*
Tindall, M J (Bath) 2000 *I, F, W, It, S, SA* 1,2, *A, Arg, SA* 3, 2001 *W* (R), *SA* (R), 2002 *S, I, F, W, It*
Tindall, V R (Liverpool U) 1951 *W, I, F, S*
Tobin, F (Liverpool) 1871 *S*
Todd, A F (Blackheath) 1900 *I, S*
Todd, R (Manchester) 1877 *S*
Toft, H B (Waterloo) 1936 *S*, 1937 *W, I, S*, 1938 *W, I, S*, 1939 *W, I, S*
Toothill, J T (Bradford) 1890 *S, I*, 1891 *W, I*, 1892 *W, I, S*, 1893 *W, I, S*, 1894 *W, I*
Tosswill, L R (Exeter) 1902 *W, I, S*
Touzel, C J C (Liverpool) 1877 *I, S*
Towell, A C (Bedford) 1948 *F*, 1951 *S*
Travers, B H (Harlequins) 1947 *W, I*, 1948 *A, W*, 1949 *F, S*
Treadwell, W T (Wasps) 1966 *I, F, S*
Trick, D M (Bath) 1983 *I*, 1984 *SA* 1
Tristram, H B (Oxford U) 1883 *S*, 1884 *W, S*, 1885 *W*, 1887 *S*
Troop, C L (Aldershot S) 1933 *I, S*
Tucker, J S (Bristol) 1922 *W*, 1925 *NZ, W, I, S, F*, 1926 *W, I, F, S*, 1927 *W, I, S, F*, 1928 *A, W, I, F, S*, 1929 *W, I, F*, 1930 *W, I, F, S*, 1931 *W*
Tucker, W E (Blackheath) 1894 *W, I*, 1895 *W, I, S*
Tucker, W E (Blackheath) 1926 *I*, 1930 *W, I*
Turner, D P (Richmond) 1871 *S*, 1872 *S*, 1873 *S*, 1874 *S*, 1875 *I, S*
Turner, E B (St George's Hospital) 1876 *I*, 1877 *I*, 1878 *I*
Turner, G R (St George's Hospital) 1876 *S*
Turner, H J C (Manchester) 1871 *S*
Turner, M F (Blackheath) 1948 *S, F*
Turquand-Young, D (Richmond) 1928 *A, W*, 1929 *I, S, F*
Twynam, H T (Richmond) 1879 *I*, 1880 *I*, 1881 *W*, 1882 *I*, 1883 *I*, 1884 *W, I, S*

Ubogu, V E (Bath) 1992 *C, SA*, 1993 *NZ*, 1994 *S, I, F, W, SA* 1,2, *R, C*, 1995 *I, F, W, S*, [*Arg, WS, A, NZ, F*], *SA*, 1999 *F* (R), *W* (R), *A* (R)
Underwood, A M (Exeter) 1962 *W, I, F, S*, 1964 *I*
Underwood, R (Leicester, RAF) 1984 *I, F, W, A*, 1985 *R, F, S, I, W*, 1986 *W, I, F*, 1987 *I, F, W, S*, [*A, J, W*], 1988 *F, W, S, I* 1,2, *A* 1,2, *Fj, A*, 1989 *S, I, F, W, R, Fj*, 1990 *I, F, W, S, Arg* 3, 1991 *W, S, I, F, Fj, A*, [*NZ, It, US, F, S, A*], 1992 *S, I, F, W, SA*, 1993 *F, W, S, I, NZ*, 1994 *S, I, F, W, SA* 1,2, *R, C*, 1995 *I, F, W, S*, [*Arg, It, WS, A, NZ, F*], *SA, WS*, 1996 *F, W, S, I*
Underwood, T (Leicester, Newcastle) 1992 *C, SA*, 1993 *S, I, NZ*, 1994 *S, I, W, SA* 1,2, *R, C*, 1995 *I, F, W, S*, [*Arg, It, A, NZ*], 1996 *Arg*, 1997 *S, I, F, W*, 1998 *A* 2, *SA* 2
Unwin, E J (Rosslyn Park, Army) 1937 *S*, 1938 *W, I, S*
Unwin, G T (Blackheath) 1898 *S*
Uren, R (Waterloo) 1948 *I, S, F*, 1950 *I*
Uttley, R M (Gosforth) 1973 *I, F, S, NZ* 2, *A*, 1974 *I, F, W*, 1975 *F, W, S, A* 1,2, 1977 *S, I, F, W*, 1978 *NZ* 1979 *S*, 1980 *I, F, W, S*

Valentine J (Swinton) 1890 *W*, 1896 *W, I, S*
Vanderspar, C H R (Richmond) 1873 *S*
Van Ryneveld, C B (Oxford U) 1949 *W, I, F, S*
Varley, H (Liversedge) 1892 *S*
Vassall, H (Blackheath) 1881 *W, S*, 1882 *I, S*, 1883 *W*
Vassall, H H (Blackheath) 1908 *I*
Vaughan, D B (Headingley) 1948 *A, W, I, S*, 1949 *I, F, S*, 1950 *W*
Vaughan-Jones, A (Army) 1932 *I, S*, 1933 *W*
Verelst, C L (Liverpool) 1876 I, 1878 *I*
Vernon, G F (Blackheath) 1878 *S, I*, 1880 *I, S*, 1881 *I*
Vickery, G (Aberavon) 1905 *I*
Vickery, P J (Gloucester) 1998 *W, A* 1, *NZ* 1,2, *SA* 1, 1999 *US, C*, [*It, NZ, Tg, SA*], 2000 *I, F, W, S, A, Arg* (R), *SA* 3(R), 2001 *W, It, S, A, SA*, 2002 *I, F, Arg*
Vivyan, E J (Devonport A) 1901 *W*, 1904 *W, I, S*
Voyce, A T (Gloucester) 1920 *I, S*, 1921 *W, I, S, F*, 1922 *W, I, F, S*, 1923 *W, I, S, F*, 1924 *W, I, F, S*, 1925 *NZ, W, I, S, F*, 1926 *W, I, F, S*
Voyce, T (Bath) 2001 *US* (R)

Wackett, J A S (Rosslyn Park) 1959 *W, I*
Wade, C G (Richmond) 1883 *W, I, S*, 1884 *W, S*, 1885 *W*, 1886 *W, I*
Wade, M R (Cambridge U) 1962 *W, I, F*
Wakefield, W W (Harlequins) 1920 *W, F, I, S*, 1921 *W, I, S, F*, 1922 *W, I, F, S*, 1923 *W, I, S, F*, 1924 *W, I, F, S*, 1925 *NZ, W, I, S, F*, 1926 *W, I, F, S*, 1927 *S, F*
Walder, D J H (Newcastle) 2001 *C* 1,2, *US*
Walker, G A (Blackheath) 1939 *W, I*
Walker, H W (Coventry) 1947 *W, I, S, F*, 1948 *A, W, I, S, F*
Walker, R (Manchester) 1874 *S*, 1875 *I*, 1876 *S*, 1879 *S*, 1880 *S*
Wallens, J N S (Waterloo) 1927 *F*
Walton, E J (Castleford) 1901 *W, I*, 1902 *I, S*
Walton, W (Castleford) 1894 *S*
Ward, G (Leicester) 1913 *W, F, S*, 1914 *W, I, S*
Ward, H (Bradford) 1895 *W*
Ward, J I (Richmond) 1881 *I*, 1882 *I*
Ward, J W (Castleford) 1896 *W, I, S*
Wardlow, C S (Northampton) 1969 *SA* (R), 1971 *W, I, F, S* (2[1C])
Warfield, P J (Rosslyn Park, Durham U) 1973 *NZ* 1, *W, I*, 1975 *I, F, S*
Warr, A L (Oxford U) 1934 *W, I*
Waters, F H H (Wasps) 2001 *US*
Watkins, J A (Gloucester) 1972 *SA*, 1973 *NZ* 1, *W, NZ* 2, *A*, 1975 *F, W*
Watkins, J K (United Services, RN) 1939 *W, I, S*
Watson, F B (United Services, RN) 1908 *S*, 1909 *S*
Watson, J H D (Blackheath) 1914 *W, S, F*
Watt, D E J (Bristol) 1967 *I, F, S, W*
Webb, C S H (Devonport Services, RN) 1932 *SA, W, I, S*, 1933 *W, I, S*, 1935 *S*, 1936 *NZ, W, I, S*
Webb, J M (Bristol, Bath) 1987 [*A* (R), *J, US, W*], 1988 *F, W, S, I* 1,2, *A* 2, 1989 *S, I, F, W*, 1991 *Fj, A*, [*NZ, It, F, S, A*], 1992 *S, I, F, W, C, SA*, 1993 *F, W, S, I*
Webb, J W G (Northampton) 1926 *F, S*, 1929 *S*
Webb, R E (Coventry) 1967 *S, W, NZ*, 1968 *I, F, S*, 1969 *I, F, S, W*, 1972 *I, F*
Webb, St L H (Bedford) 1959 *W, I, F, S*
Webster, J G (Moseley) 1972 *W, I, SA*, 1973 *NZ* 1, *W, NZ* 2, 1974 *S, W*, 1975 *I, F, W*

Wedge, T G (St Ives) 1907 *F*, 1909 *W*
Weighill, R H G (RAF, Harlequins) 1947 *S, F*, 1948 *S, F*
Wells, C M (Cambridge U, Harlequins) 1893 *S*, 1894 *W, S*, 1896 *S*, 1897 *W, S*
West, B R (Loughborough Colls, Northampton) 1968 *W, I, F, S*, 1969 *SA*, 1970 *I, W, S*
West, D E (Leicester) 1998 *F* (R), *S* (R), 2000 *Arg* (R), 2001 *W, It, S, F* (t), *C* 1,2, *US, I* (R), *A, SA*, 2002 *F* (R), *W* (R), *It* (R)
West, R (Gloucester) 1995 *[WS]*
Weston, H T F (Northampton) 1901 *S*
Weston, L E (W of Scotland) 1972 *F, S*
Weston, M P (Richmond, Durham City) 1960 *W, I, F, S*, 1961 *SA, W, I, F, S*, 1962 *W, I, F*, 1963 *W, I, F, S, NZ* 1,2, *A*, 1964 *NZ, W, I, F, S*, 1965 *F, S*, 1966 *S*, 1968 *F, S*
Weston, W H (Northampton) 1933 *I, S*, 1934 *I, S*, 1935 *W, I, S*, 1936 *NZ, W, S*, 1937 *W, I, S*, 1938 *W, I, S*
Wheatley, A A (Coventry) 1937 *W, I, S*, 1938 *W, S*
Wheatley, H F (Coventry) 1936 *I*, 1937 *S*, 1938 *W, S*, 1939 *W, I, S*
Wheeler, P J (Leicester) 1975 *F, W*, 1976 *A, W, S, I*, 1977 *S, I, F, W*, 1978 *F, W, S, I, NZ*, 1979 *S, I, F, W, NZ*, 1980 *I, F, W, S*, 1981 *W, S, I, F*, 1982 *A, S, I, F, W*, 1983 *F, S, I, NZ*, 1984 *S, I, F, W*
White, C (Gosforth) 1983 *NZ*, 1984 *S, I, F*
White, D F (Northampton) 1947 *W, I, S*, 1948 *I, F*, 1951 *S*, 1952 *SA, W, S, I, F*, 1953 *W, I, S*
White, J (Saracens, Bristol) 2000 *SA* 1,2, *Arg, SA* 3, 2001 *F, C* 1,2, *US, I, R* (R), 2002 *S, W, It*
White-Cooper, S (Harlequins) 2001 *C* 2, *US*
Whiteley, E C P (O Alleynians) 1931 *S, F*
Whiteley, W (Bramley) 1896 *W*
Whitely, H (Northern) 1929 *W*
Wightman, B J (Moseley, Coventry) 1959 *W*, 1963 *W, I, NZ* 2, *A*
Wigglesworth, H J (Thornes) 1884 *I*
Wilkins, D T (United Services, RN, Roundhay) 1951 *W, I, F, S*, 1952 *SA, W, S, I, F*, 1953 *W, I, F, S*
Wilkinson, E (Bradford) 1886 *W, I, S*, 1887 *W, S*
Wilkinson, H (Halifax) 1929 *W, I, S*, 1930 *F*
Wilkinson, H J (Halifax) 1889 *M*
Wilkinson, J P (Newcastle) 1998 *I* (R), *A* 1, *NZ* 1, 1999 *S, I, F, W, A, US, C, [It, NZ, Fj, SA]* (R)], 2000 *I, F, W, It, S, SA* 2, *A, Arg, SA* 3, 2001 *W, It, S, F, I, A, SA*, 2002 *S, I, F, W, It*
Wilkinson, P (Law Club) 1872 *S*
Wilkinson, R M (Bedford) 1975 *A* 2, 1976 *A, W, S, I, F*
Willcocks, T J (Plymouth) 1902 *W*
Willcox, J G (Oxford U, Harlequins) 1961 *I, F, S*, 1962 *W, I, F, S*, 1963 *W, I, F, S*, 1964 *NZ, W, I, F, S*
William-Powlett, P B R W (United Services, RN) 1922 *S*
Williams, C G (Gloucester, RAF) 1976 *F*
Williams, C S (Manchester) 1910 *F*
Williams, J E (O Millhilians, Sale) 1954 *F*, 1955 *W, I, F, S*, 1956 *I, S, F*, 1965 *W*
Williams, J M (Penzance-Newlyn) 1951 *I, S*
Williams, P N (Orrell) 1987 *S, [A, J, W]*
Williams, S G (Devonport A) 1902 *W, I, S*, 1903 *I, S*, 1907 *I, S*
Williams, S H (Newport) 1911 *W, F, I, S*
Williamson, R H (Oxford U) 1908 *W, I, S*, 1909 *A, F*
Wilson, A J (Camborne S of M) 1909 *I*
Wilson, C E (Blackheath) 1898 *I*
Wilson, C P (Cambridge U, Marlborough N) 1881 *W*
Wilson, D S (Met Police, Harlequins) 1953 *F*, 1954 *W, NZ, I, S, F*, 1955 *F, S*

Wilson, G S (Tyldesley) 1929 *W, I*
Wilson, K J (Gloucester) 1963 *F*
Wilson, R P (Liverpool OB) 1891 *W, I, S*
Wilson, W C (Richmond) 1907 *I, S*
Winn, C E (Rosslyn Park) 1952 *SA, W, S, I, F*, 1954 *W, S, F*
Winterbottom, P J (Headingley, Harlequins) 1982 *A, S, I, F, W*, 1983 *F, W, S, I, NZ*, 1984 *S, F, W, SA* 1,2, 1986 *W, S, I, F*, 1987 *I, F, W, [A, J, US, W]*, 1988 *F, W, S*, 1989 *R, Fj*, 1990 *I, F, W, S, Arg* 1,2,3, 1991 *W, S, I, F, A, [NZ, It, F, S, A]*, 1992 *S, I, F, W, C, SA*, 1993 *F, W, S, I*
Wintle, T C (Northampton) 1966 *S*, 1969 *I, F, S, W*
Wodehouse, N A (United Services, RN) 1910 *F*, 1911 *W, F, I, S*, 1912 *W, I, S, F*, 1913 *SA, W, F, I, S*
Wood, A (Halifax) 1884 *I*
Wood, A E (Gloucester, Cheltenham) 1908 *F, W, I*
Wood, G W (Leicester) 1914 *W*
Wood, M B, (Wasps) 2000 *C* 2(R), *US* (R)
Wood, R (Liversedge) 1894 *I*
Wood, R D (Liverpool OB) 1901 *I*, 1903 *W, I*
Woodgate, E E (Paignton) 1952 *W*
Woodhead, E (Huddersfield) 1880 *I*
Woodman, T J, (Gloucester) 1999 *US* (R), 2000 *I* (R), *It* (R), 2001 *W* (R), *It* (R)
Woodruff, C G (Harlequins) 1951 *W, I, F, S*
Woods, S M J (Cambridge U, Wellington) 1890 *W, S, I*, 1891 *W, I, S*, 1892 *I, S*, 1893 *W, I*, 1895 *W, I, S*
Woods, T (Bridgwater) 1908 *S*
Woods, T (United Services, RN) 1920 *S*, 1921 *W, I, S, F*
Woodward, C R (Leicester) 1980 *I* (R), *F, W, S*, 1981 *W, S, I, F, Arg* 1,2, 1982 *A, S, I, F, W*, 1983 *I, NZ*, 1984 *S, I, F, W*
Woodward, J E (Wasps) 1952 *SA, W, S*, 1953 *W, I, F, S*, 1954 *W, NZ, I, S, F*, 1955 *W, I*, 1956 *S*
Wooldridge, C S (Oxford U, Blackheath) 1883 *W, I, S*, 1884 *W, I, S*, 1885 *I*
Wordsworth, A J (Cambridge U) 1975 *A* 1(R)
Worsley, J P R (Wasps) 1999 *[Tg, Fj]*, 2000 *It* (R), *S* (R), *SA* 1(R),2(R), 2001 *It* (R), *S* (R), *F* (R), *C* 1,2, *US, A, R, SA*, 2002 *S, I, F, W* (t+R), *Arg*
Worton, J R B (Harlequins, Army) 1926 *W*, 1927 *W*
Wrench, D F B (Harlequins) 1964 *F, S*
Wright, C C G (Cambridge U, Blackheath) 1909 *I, S*
Wright, F T (Edinburgh Acady, Manchester) 1881 *S*
Wright, I D (Northampton) 1971 *W, I, F, S* (R)
Wright. J C (Met Police) 1934 *W*
Wright, J F (Bradford) 1890 *W*
Wright, T P (Blackheath) 1960 *W, I, F, S*, 1961 *SA, W, I, F, S*, 1962 *W, I, F*
Wright, W H G (Plymouth) 1920 *W, F*
Wyatt, D M (Bedford) 1976 *S* (R)

Yarranton, P G (RAF, Wasps) 1954 *W, NZ, I*, 1955 *F, S*
Yates, K P (Bath) 1997 *Arg* 1,2
Yiend, W (Hartlepool R, Gloucester) 1889 *M*, 1892 *W, I, S*, 1893 *I, S*
Young, A T (Cambridge U, Blackheath, Army) 1924 *W, I, F, S*, 1925 *NZ, F*, 1926 *I, F, S*, 1927 *I, S, F*, 1928 *A, W, I, F, S*, 1929 *I*
Young, J R C (Oxford U, Harlequins) 1958 *I*, 1960 *W, I, F, S*, 1961 *SA, F*
Young, M (Gosforth) 1977 *S, I, F, W*, 1978 *F, W, S, I, NZ*, 1979 *S*
Young, P D (Dublin Wands) 1954 *W, NZ, I, S, F*, 1955 *W, I, F, S*
Youngs, N G (Leicester) 1983 *I, NZ*, 1984 *S, I, F, W*

SCOTLAND TEST SEASON REVIEW 2001-02

Scotland Fade After Bright Start

Bill McMurtrie

Scotland had roared into September 2001 in flamboyant style. Their 32-10 victory against Ireland at Murrayfield in the hangover match from the 2000-01 season laid down what should have been a clear marker for the new international season. But the signs that it posted were not followed.

True, Scotland won their next international, opening Murrayfield's November series against Tonga. That game, however, was to be Scotland's only home win of the 2001-02 season. They had to look farther afield for their three other successes – in Rome, Cardiff, and San Francisco. The Cardiff result saved face in what would otherwise have been a sorry campaign in the Six Nations Championship, and a 65-23 victory against the United States, closing the season, was in sharp contrast to the dire defeat a week earlier against Canada.

It was as if the September match against Ireland was a bright lighthouse beacon in a troubled sea. Of course, that international had been delayed from the previous April because of the foot-and-mouth disasters on the mainland.

Come September, the agricultural communities had picked themselves up. Scotland's rugby team did likewise. They had gleaned only a draw with Wales and a win against Italy – both at Murrayfield – from their truncated Six Nations Championship programme earlier in the year, whereas Ireland had had away victories against Italy and France. Scotland, however, ignored that the Irish were still in the hunt for the Grand Slam. It was as if the Scots were the championship chasers as they ran in four tries to Ireland's one.

Exhilarating rugby, especially by Glenn Metcalfe, Chris Paterson, and James McLaren, quickly stated the Scottish case, though it was 23 minutes into the game before Budge Pountney crossed for the first of the home tries. Tom Smith added one before half-time, when the Scots led 17-0, and second-half tries followed from John Leslie and his centre replacement, Andy Henderson. The latter was on the field for only a few minutes before he scored his debut try. It was a truly dramatic introduction to the international game for the 21-year-old Glasgow centre only a few weeks into his first season as a full-time professional.

Gordon Ross had an even more startling international debut when Scotland opened their autumn series against Tonga. The 23-year-old Edinburgh stand-off recorded no fewer than 23 points with four conversions and five penalty goals in Scotland's 43-20 win. His tally was a record for a Scotland debutant.

The Scotland team and replacements that faced England at Murrayfield.

Another newcomer, Roland Reid, emulated his Glasgow colleague, Henderson, by scoring a try on his debut. His was with his first touch of the ball as a second-half replacement. Metcalfe and McLaren, who had been among Ireland's tormentors, each had a try. Gordon Simpson had the other.

Scotland were then unbeaten at home in 2001 with a record of three wins and a draw. It seemed that fortress Murrayfield was being rebuilt. But a week later the Pumas broke down the walls in beating Scotland by 25-16. It was the second successive time Argentina had won at Murrayfield – they had done so two years earlier, also by nine points (31-22). It was not enough that Scotland won the try-count, with scores by Gregor Townsend and Derrick Lee, the Edinburgh full back who, replacing the injured Metcalfe, answered a late call to return to the fold after three years' absence from international rugby.

Scotland introduced five newcomers during the autumn series – Henderson, Ross, Reid, Andrew Mower and Brendan Laney. None was more controversial than Laney, the former Otago Highlanders full-back who, seeking new fame in his grandmother's homeland, had joined Edinburgh. He had not long shaken off jet-lag when he made his international debut against none other than the representatives of his native New Zealand.

However, it was to be no dream debut for Laney. The All Blacks won by 37-6, and Laney had to wait until the February visit to Rome before he made his mark for his new country by scoring no fewer than 24 points, a championship record for a Scot.

Before then, the Scots had to take on the Auld Enemy at Murrayfield, opening the 2002 Six Nations Championship. The Calcutta Cup, of course, was at stake, as it has been when those two countries have met in championship matches for more than a century. In recent times that trophy has been almost permanently held in Twickenham, though two years earlier Scotland had broken English domination with an unexpected 19-13 win at Murrayfield. Duncan Hodge scored all of the home points that soaking Sunday, denying England a Grand Slam, and he was again at stand-off for Scotland this year. Scots dreamed of a repetition, but it was not to be: England won 29-3, their widest winning margin at Murrayfield.

A fortnight later the Scots were at Stadio Flaminio, where two years earlier as defending champions they had stumbled to defeat as Italy celebrated their introduction to the Six Nations Championship. This time the Scots came home with a 29-12 victory, Laney contributing a try, two conversions and five penalty goals. Yet it was a nervous performance by the Scots, who led only 15-12 after an hour. However, they were settled by an interception try by Gregor Townsend. Belatedly, Laney made sure with his try.

Then came the re-match with Ireland at Lansdowne Road, and revenge was swift and sweet for the Shamrock against the Thistle. The losing margin (43-22) was only fractionally better for Scotland than it had been two years earlier (44-22), and Laney had a 100% kicking return with five penalty goals and the conversion of Martin Leslie's try. Neither of those points was any solace, and even Scots will remember the match for Brian O'Driscoll's treble. Nor could Scots find straws to clutch in the Friday evening preambles. Ireland won the A international by 60-3 as well as notching victories in the under-21 and students' matches.

France, with a Paris win over England in the bag, came to Murrayfield in March, and they duly claimed the fourth win of what was to be the first Grand Slam of the Six Nations era. Although Laney gave Scotland an early lead with a penalty goal, the French ground out a 22-10 win – two tries to one. France led 22-3 just six minutes into the second half, and Bryan Redpath's try nine minutes later gave the Scots hope, though nothing more.

Scotland had to visit Cardiff needing a result to save their championship season, and they did it by winning 27-22, though they had to recover from a nine-point deficit that Stephen Jones inflicted with three penalty goals in the first quarter. Gordon Bulloch's two close-range tries and Laney's conversion and penalty goal lifted the Scots to a 15-9 lead at half-time. A Rhys Williams try and Jones's conversion edged Wales a point ahead four minutes after the interval, but, like boxers trading punches, Laney and Jones swapped penalty goals in the final 25 minutes. Five times the lead changed hands, the pace of the blows quickening towards the close of the contest – three in all to the Scot, two to the Welshman. Laney was injured after he had lifted Scotland to 24-22 and the *coup de grâce* was delivered by Hodge, who was sent on as replacement to slot another penalty goal. Laney, however, was not to be denied another record. His haul of 60 points was a Scottish record for the championship, beating the 56 by Gavin Hastings in 1995.

Scotland went to North America for a six-match tour in June, but even then, after their Cardiff success, they squandered a rare chance to register two away wins in successive matches. They lost to Canada by 23-26 at the Thunderbird Stadium, Vancouver.

With prominent personalities missing, Scotland fielded no fewer than seven new caps, three as replacements. Yet the Scots ought to have won, not least because they scored three tries to two. An early try by Chris Paterson should have settled them, and, tightly bracketing the interval, further tries by Mike Blair, the newcomer at scrum-half, and Simon Taylor carried the Scots to a 23-13 lead. The tourists, however, could not deny the Canadians' final surge.

A week later the Scots picked themselves up to run in 10 tries in beating the United States by 65-23 in San Francisco. Six of the tries were scored in the second half while the tourists were short-handed after Nathan Hines had become the first Scot to be sent off in a cap international.

Scotland's Test Record in 2001-2002: Played 10, won 4, lost 6.

Opponents	Date	Venue	Result
United States	22nd June 2002	A	Won 65-23
Canada	15th June 2002	A	Lost 23-26
Wales	6th April 2002	A	Won 27-22
France	23rd March 2002	H	Lost 10-22
Ireland	2nd March 2002	A	Lost 22-43
Italy	16th February 2002	A	Won 29-12
England	2nd February 2002	H	Lost 3-29
New Zealand	24th November 2001	H	Lost 6-37
Argentina	18th November 2001	H	Lost 16-25
Tonga	10th November 2001	H	Won 43-20

SCOTLAND INTERNATIONAL STATISTICS

(to 31 August 2002)

Match Records

MOST CONSECUTIVE TEST WINS

6 1925 *F, W, I, E,* 1926 *F, W*
6 1989 *Fj, R,* 1990 *I, F, W, E*

MOST CONSECUTIVE TESTS WITHOUT DEFEAT

Matches	Wins	Draws	Period
9	6*	3	1885 to 1887
6	6	0	1925 to 1926
6	6	0	1989 to 1990
6	4	2	1877 to 1880
6	5	1	1983 to 1984

* includes an abandoned match

MOST POINTS IN A MATCH
by the team

Pts	Opponents	Venue	Year
89	Ivory Coast	Rustenburg	1995
65	United States	San Francisco	2002
60	Zimbabwe	Wellington	1987
60	Romania	Hampden Park	1999
55	Romania	Dunedin	1987
53	United States	Murrayfield	2000
51	Zimbabwe	Murrayfield	1991
49	Argentina	Murrayfield	1990
49	Romania	Murrayfield	1995

by a player

Pts	Player	Opponents	Venue	Year
44	A G Hastings	Ivory Coast	Rustenburg	1995
33	G P J Townsend	United States	Murrayfield	2000
31	A G Hastings	Tonga	Pretoria	1995
27	A G Hastings	Romania	Dunedin	1987
26	K M Logan	Romania	Hampden Park	1999
24	B J Laney	Italy	Rome	2002
23	G Ross	Tonga	Murrayfield	2001
21	A G Hastings	England	Murrayfield	1986
21	A G Hastings	Romania	Bucharest	1986

MOST TRIES IN A MATCH
by the team

Tries	Opponents	Venue	Year
13	Ivory Coast	Rustenburg	1995
12	Wales	Raeburn Place	1887
11	Zimbabwe	Wellington	1987

10	United States	San Francisco	2002
9	Romania	Dunedin	1987
9	Argentina	Murrayfield	1990

by a player

Tries	Player	Opponents	Venue	Year
5	G C Lindsay	Wales	Raeburn Place	1887
4	W A Stewart	Ireland	Inverleith	1913
4	I S Smith	France	Inverleith	1925
4	I S Smith	Wales	Swansea	1925
4	A G Hastings	Ivory Coast	Rustenburg	1995

MOST CONVERSIONS IN A MATCH
by the team

Cons	Opponents	Venue	Year
9	Ivory Coast	Rustenburg	1995
8	Zimbabwe	Wellington	1987
8	Romania	Dunedin	1987

by a player

Cons	Player	Opponents	Venue	Year
9	A G Hastings	Ivory Coast	Rustenburg	1995
8	A G Hastings	Zimbabwe	Wellington	1987
8	A G Hastings	Romania	Dunedin	1987

MOST PENALTIES IN A MATCH
by the team

Penalties	Opponents	Venue	Year
8	Tonga	Pretoria	1995
6	France	Murrayfield	1986

by a player

Penalties	Player	Opponents	Venue	Year
8	A G Hastings	Tonga	Pretoria	1995
6	A G Hastings	France	Murrayfield	1986

MOST DROPPED GOALS IN A MATCH
by the team

Drops	Opponents	Venue	Year
3	Ireland	Murrayfield	1973
2	on several occasions		

by a player

Drops	Player	Opponents	Venue	Year
2	R C MacKenzie	Ireland	Belfast	1877
2	N J Finlay	Ireland	Glasgow	1880
2	B M Simmers	Wales	Murrayfield	1965
2	D W Morgan	Ireland	Murrayfield	1973
2	B M Gossman	France	Parc des Princes	1983
2	J Y Rutherford	New Zealand	Murrayfield	1983
2	J Y Rutherford	Wales	Murrayfield	1985
2	J Y Rutherford	Ireland	Murrayfield	1987
2	C M Chalmers	England	Twickenham	1995

Career Records

MOST CAPPED PLAYERS

Caps	Player	Career Span
66	G P J Townsend	1993 to 2002
65	S Hastings	1986 to 1997
61	A G Hastings	1986 to 1995
61	G W Weir	1990 to 2000
60	C M Chalmers	1989 to 1999
56	K M Logan	1992 to 2002
52	J M Renwick	1972 to 1984
52	C T Deans	1978 to 1987
52	A G Stanger	1989 to 1998
52	A P Burnell	1989 to 1999
51	A R Irvine	1972 to 1982
51	G Armstrong	1988 to 1999
50	A B Carmichael	1967 to 1978
48	A J Tomes	1976 to 1987

MOST CONSECUTIVE TESTS

Tests	Player	Span
49	A B Carmichael	1967 to 1978
40	H F McLeod	1954 to 1962
37	J M Bannerman	1921 to 1929
35	A G Stanger	1989 to 1994

MOST TESTS AS CAPTAIN

Tests	Captain	Span
25	D M B Sole	1989 to 1992
20	A G Hastings	1993 to 1995
19	J McLauchlan	1973 to 1979
16	R I Wainwright	1995 to 1998
15	M C Morrison	1899 to 1904
15	A R Smith	1957 to 1962
15	A R Irvine	1980 to 1982

MOST TESTS IN INDIVIDUAL POSITIONS

Position	Player	Tests	Span
Full-back	A G Hastings	61	1986 to 1995
Wing	K M Logan	54	1992 to 2002
Centre	S Hastings	63	1986 to 1997
Fly-half	C M Chalmers	55	1989 to 1999
Scrum-half	G Armstrong	51	1988 to 1999
Prop	A P Burnell	52	1989 to 1999
Hooker	C T Deans	52	1978 to 1987
Lock	G W Weir	50	1990 to 2000
Flanker	J Jeffrey	40	1984 to 1991
No 8	D B White	29	1982 to 1992
	E W Peters	29	1995 to 1999

MOST POINTS IN TESTS

Points	Player	Tests	Career
667	A G Hastings	61	1986 to 1995
273	A R Irvine	51	1972 to 1982
215	K M Logan	56	1992 to 2002
210	P W Dods	23	1983 to 1991
166	C M Chalmers	60	1989 to 1999
157	G P J Townsend	66	1993 to 2002
123	D W Hodge	26	1997 to 2002
106	A G Stanger	52	1989 to 1998

MOST TRIES IN TESTS

Tries	Player	Tests	Career
24	I S Smith	32	1924 to 1933
24	A G Stanger	52	1989 to 1998
17	A G Hastings	61	1986 to 1995
17	A V Tait	27	1987 to 1999
16	G P J Townsend	66	1993 to 2002
15	I Tukalo	37	1985 to 1992
12	A R Smith	33	1955 to 1962
12	K M Logan	56	1992 to 2002

MOST CONVERSIONS IN TESTS

Cons	Player	Tests	Career
86	A G Hastings	61	1986 to 1995
34	K M Logan	56	1992 to 2002
26	P W Dods	23	1983 to 1991
25	A R Irvine	51	1972 to 1982
19	D Drysdale	26	1923 to 1929
15	D W Hodge	26	1997 to 2002
14	F H Turner	15	1911 to 1914
14	R J S Shepherd	20	1995 to 1998

MOST PENALTY GOALS IN TESTS

Penalties	Player	Tests	Career
140	A G Hastings	61	1986 to 1995
61	A R Irvine	51	1972 to 1982
50	P W Dods	23	1983 to 1991
32	C M Chalmers	60	1989 to 1999
29	K M Logan	56	1992 to 2002
21	M Dods	8	1994 to 1996
21	R J S Shepherd	20	1995 to 1998

MOST DROPPED GOALS IN TESTS

Drops	Player	Tests	Career
12	J Y Rutherford	42	1979 to 1987
9	C M Chalmers	60	1989 to 1999
7	I R McGeechan	32	1972 to 1979
7	G P J Townsend	66	1993 to 2002
6	D W Morgan	21	1973 to 1978
5	H Waddell	15	1924 to 1930

International Championship Records

Record	Detail	Holder	Set
Most points in season	120	in four matches	1999
Most tries in season	17	in four matches	1925
Highest Score	38	38-10 v Ireland	1997
Biggest win	28	31-3 v France	1912
	28	38-10 v Ireland	1997
Highest score conceded	51	16-51 v France	1998
Biggest defeat	40	3-43 v England	2001
Most appearances	42	J M Renwick	1972 – 1983
Most points in matches	288	A G Hastings	1986 – 1995
Most points in season	60	B J Laney	2002
Most points in match	24	B J Laney	v Italy, 2002
Most tries in matches	24	I S Smith	1924 – 1933
Most tries in season	8	I S Smith	1925
Most tries in match	5	G C Lindsay	v Wales, 1887
Most cons in matches	20	A G Hastings	1986 – 1995
Most cons in season	11	K M Logan	1999
Most cons in match	5	F H Turner	v France, 1912
	5	J W Allan	v England, 1931
	5	R J S Shepherd	v Ireland, 1997
Most pens in matches	77	A G Hastings	1986 – 1995
Most pens in season	15	B J Laney	2002
Most pens in match	6	A G Hastings	v France, 1986
Most drops in matches	8	J Y Rutherford	1979 – 1987
	8	C M Chalmers	1989-98
Most drops in season	3	J Y Rutherford	1987
Most drops in match	2	on several	occasions

Miscellaneous Records

Record	Holder	Detail
Longest Test Career	W C W Murdoch	14 seasons, 1934-35 to 1947-48
Youngest Test Cap	N J Finlay	17 yrs 36 days in 1875*
Oldest Test Cap	J McLauchlan	37 yrs 210 days in 1979

* C Reid, also 17 yrs 36 days on debut in 1881, was a day *older* than Finlay, having lived through an extra leap-year day.

Career Records Of Scotland International Players
(up to 31 August 2002)

PLAYER	Debut	Caps	T	C	P	D	Pts
Backs:							
G Beveridge	2000 v NZ	3	0	0	0	0	0
M R L Blair	2002 v C	2	1	0	0	0	5
A J Bulloch	2000 v US	5	1	0	0	0	5
G G Burns	1999 v It	4	0	0	0	0	0
A Craig	2002 v C	2	1	0	0	0	5
J M Craig	1997 v A	4	0	0	0	0	0
M P di Rollo	2002 v US	1	0	0	0	0	0
I T Fairley	1999 v It	3	0	0	0	0	0
A R Henderson	2001 v I	6	2	0	0	0	10
B G Hinshelwood	2002 v C	1	0	0	0	0	0
D W Hodge	1997 v F	26	6	15	20	1	123
R C Kerr	2002 v C	2	1	0	0	0	5
B J Laney	2001 v NZ	8	2	12	18	0	88
D J Lee	1998 v I	9	1	4	7	0	34
J A Leslie	1998 v SA	23	4	0	0	0	20
K M Logan	1992 v A	56	12	34	29	0	215
S L Longstaff	1998 v F	15	2	0	0	0	10
J G McLaren	1999 v Arg	20	4	0	0	0	20
M J M Mayer	1998 v SA	8	0	0	0	0	0
G H Metcalfe	1998 v A	27	4	0	0	0	20
C C Moir	2000 v W	3	0	0	0	0	0
C A Murray	1998 v E	26	7	0	0	0	35
A D Nicol	1992 v E	23	2	0	0	0	9
C D Paterson	1999 v Sp	22	6	3	6	0	54
B W Redpath	1993 v NZ	45	1	0	0	0	5
R E Reid	2001 v Tg	2	1	0	0	0	5
G Ross	2001 v Tg	1	0	4	5	0	23
J F Steel	2000 v US	5	0	0	0	0	0
G P J Townsend	1993 v E	66	16	7	14	7	157
Forwards:							
R S Beattie	2000 v NZ	3	0	0	0	0	0
S J Brotherstone	1999 v I	8	0	0	0	0	0
G C Bulloch	1997 v SA	41	4	0	0	0	20
S J Campbell	1995 v C	17	0	0	0	0	0
I A Fullarton	2000 v NZ	3	0	0	0	0	0
G Graham	1997 v A	25	1	0	0	0	5
S B Grimes	1997 v A	41	2	0	0	0	10
A J A Hall	2002 v US	1	0	0	0	0	0
N J Hines	2000 v NZ	3	1	0	0	0	5
A F Jacobsen	2002 v C	2	0	0	0	0	0
M D Leslie	1998 v SA	26	9	0	0	0	45
D J H Macfadyen	2002 v C	2	0	0	0	0	0
G R McIlwham	1998 v Fj	11	0	0	0	0	0
C G Mather	1999 v R	4	2	0	0	0	10
R Metcalfe	2000 v E	9	1	0	0	0	5
A L Mower	2001 v Tg	3	0	0	0	0	0
S Murray	1997 v A	40	2	0	0	0	10
J M Petrie	2000 v NZ	13	1	0	0	0	5

A C Pountney	1998 v SA	28	3	0	0	0	15
M C Proudfoot	1998 v Fj	3	0	0	0	0	0
A J Roxburgh	1997 v A	8	0	0	0	0	0
R R Russell	1999 v R	9	1	0	0	0	5
S Scott	2000 v NZ	7	0	0	0	0	0
G L Simpson	1998 v A	15	3	0	0	0	15
C J Smith	2002 v C	2	0	0	0	0	0
T J Smith	1997 v E	37	5	0	0	0	25
B D Stewart	1996 v NZ	4	0	0	0	0	0
M J Stewart	1996 v It	33	0	0	0	0	0
S M Taylor	2000 v US	13	1	0	0	0	5
J P R White	2000 v E	18	1	0	0	0	5

SCOTTISH INTERNATIONAL PLAYERS

(up to 31 August 2002)

Note: Years given for International Championship matches are for second half of season; eg 1972 means season 1971-72. Years for all other matches refer to the actual year of the match. When a series has taken place, figures have been used to denote the particular matches in which players have featured. Thus 1981 *NZ* 1,2 indicates that a player appeared in the first and second Tests of the series.

Abercrombie, C H (United Services) 1910 *I, E,* 1911 *F, W,* 1913 *F, W*
Abercrombie, J G (Edinburgh U) 1949 *F, W, I,* 1950 *F, W, I, E*
Agnew, W C C (Stewart's Coll FP) 1930 *W, I*
Ainslie, R (Edinburgh Inst FP) 1879 *I, E,* 1880 *I, E,* 1881 *E,* 1882 *I, E*
Ainslie, T (Edinburgh Inst FP) 1881 *E,* 1882 *I, E,* 1883 *W, I, E,* 1884 *W, I, E,* 1885 *W, I* 1,2
Aitchison, G R (Edinburgh Wands) 1883 *I*
Aitchison, T G (Gala) 1929 *W, I, E*
Aitken, A I (Edinburgh Inst FP) 1889 *I*
Aitken, G G (Oxford U) 1924 *W, I, E,* 1925 *F, W, I, E,* 1929 *F*
Aitken, J (Gala) 1977 *E, I, F,* 1981 *F, W, E, I, NZ* 1,2, *R, A,* 1982 *E, I, F, W,* 1983 *F, W, E, NZ,* 1984 *W, E, I, F, R*
Aitken, R (London Scottish) 1947 *W*
Allan, B (Glasgow Acads) 1881 *I*
Allan, J (Edinburgh Acads) 1990 *NZ* 1, 1991, *W, I, R,* [*J, I, WS, E, NZ*]
Allan, J L (Melrose) 1952 *F, W, I,* 1953 *W*
Allan, J L F (Cambridge U) 1957 *I, E*
Allan, J W (Melrose) 1927 *F,* 1928 *I,* 1929 *F, W, I, E,* 1930 *F, E,* 1931 *F, W, I, E,* 1932 *SA, W, I,* 1934 *I, E*
Allan, R C (Hutchesons' GSFP) 1969 *I*
Allardice, W D (Aberdeen GSFP) 1947 *A,* 1948 *F, W, I,* 1949 *F, W, I, E*
Allen, H W (Glasgow Acads) 1873 *E*
Anderson, A H (Glasgow Acads) 1894 *I*
Anderson, D G (London Scottish) 1889 *I,* 1890 *W, I, E,* 1891 *W, E,* 1892 *W, E*
Anderson, E (Stewart's Coll FP) 1947 *I, E*
Anderson, J W (W of Scotland) 1872 *E*
Anderson, T (Merchiston) 1882 *I*
Angus, A W (Watsonians) 1909 *W,* 1910 *F, W, E,* 1911 *W, I,* 1912 *F, W, I, E, SA,* 1913 *F, W,* 1914 *E,* 1920 *F, W, I, E*
Anton, P A (St Andrew's U) 1873 *E*
Armstrong, G (Jedforest, Newcastle) 1988 *A,* 1989 *W, E, I, F, Fj, R,* 1990 *I, F, W, E, NZ* 1,2, *Arg,* 1991 *F, W, E, I, R,* [*J, I, WS, E, NZ*], 1993 *I, F, W, E,* 1994 *E, I,* 1996 *NZ,* 1,2, *A,* 1997 *W, SA* (R), 1998 *It, I, F, W, E, SA* (R), 1999 *W, E, I, F, Arg, R,* [*SA, U, Sm, NZ*]
Arneil, R J (Edinburgh Acads, Leicester and Northampton) 1968 *I, E, A,* 1969 *F, W, I, E, SA,* 1970 *F, W, I, E, A,* 1971 *F, W, I, E* (2[1C]), 1972 *F, W, E, NZ*
Arthur, A (Glasgow Acads) 1875 *E,* 1876 *E*
Arthur, J W (Glasgow Acads) 1871 *E,* 1872 *E*
Asher, A G G (Oxford U) 1882 *I,* 1884 *W, I, E,* 1885 *W,* 1886 *I, E*
Auld, W (W of Scotland) 1889 *W,* 1890 *W*
Auldjo, L J (Abertay) 1878 *E*

Bain, D McL (Oxford U) 1911 *E,* 1912 *F, W, E, SA,* 1913 *F, W, I, E,* 1914 *W, I*
Baird, G R T (Kelso) 1981 *A,* 1982 *E, I, F, W, A* 1,2, 1983 *I, F, W, E, NZ,* 1984 *W, E, I, F, A,* 1985 *I, W, E,* 1986 *F, W, E, I, R,* 1987 *E,* 1988 *I*
Balfour, A (Watsonians) 1896 *W, I, E,* 1897 *E*
Balfour, L M (Edinburgh Acads) 1872 *E*
Bannerman, E M (Edinburgh Acads) 1872 *E,* 1873 *E*
Bannerman, J M (Glasgow HSFP) 1921 *F, W, I, E,* 1922 *F, W, I, E,* 1923 *F, W, I, E,* 1924 *F, W, I, E,* 1925 *F, W, I, E,* 1926 *F, W, I, E,* 1927 *F, W, I, E,* 1928 *F, W, I, E,* 1929 *F, W, I, E*
Barnes, I A (Hawick) 1972 *W,* 1974 *F* (R), 1975 *E* (R), *NZ,* 1977 *I, F, W*
Barrie, R W (Hawick) 1936 *E*
Bearne, K R F (Cambridge U, London Scottish) 1960 *F, W*
Beattie, J A (Hawick) 1929 *F, W,* 1930 *W,* 1931 *F, W, I, E,* 1932 *SA, W, I,* 1933 *W, E, I,* 1934 *I, E,* 1935 *W, I, E, NZ,* 1936 *W, I, E*

Beattie, J R (Glasgow Acads) 1980 *I, F, W, E,* 1981 *F, W, E, I,* 1983 *F, W, E, NZ,* 1984 *E* (R), *R, A,* 1985 *I,* 1986 *F, W, E, I, R,* 1987 *I, F, W, E*
Beattie, R S (Newcastle) 2000 *NZ* 1,2(R), *Sm* (R)
Bedell-Sivright, D R (Cambridge U, Edinburgh U) 1900 *W,* 1901 *W, I, E,* 1902 *W, I, E,* 1903 *W, I,* 1904 *W, I, E,* 1905 *NZ,* 1906 *W, I, E, SA,* 1907 *W, I, E,* 1908 *W, I*
Bedell-Sivright, J V (Cambridge U) 1902 *W*
Begbie, T A (Edinburgh Wands) 1881 *I, E*
Bell, D L (Watsonians) 1975 *I, F, W, E*
Bell, J A (Clydesdale) 1901 *W, I, E,* 1902 *W, I, E*
Bell, L H I (Edinburgh Acads) 1900 *E,* 1904 *W, I*
Berkeley, W V (Oxford U) 1926 *F,* 1929 *F, W, I*
Berry, C W (Fettesian-Lorettonians) 1884 *I, E,* 1885 *W, I* 1, 1887 *I, W, E,* 1888 *W, I*
Bertram, D M (Watsonians) 1922 *F, W, I, E,* 1923 *F, W, I, E,* 1924 *W, I, E*
Beveridge, G (Glasgow) 2000 *NZ* 2(R), *US* (R), *Sm* (R)
Biggar, A G (London Scottish) 1969 *SA,* 1970 *F, I, E, A,* 1971 *F, W, I, E* (2[1C]), 1972 *F, W*
Biggar, M A (London Scottish) 1975 *I, F, W, E,* 1976 *W, E, I,* 1977 *I, F, W,* 1978 *I, F, W, E, NZ,* 1979 *W, E, I, F, NZ,* 1980 *I, F, W, E*
Birkett, G A (Harlequins, London Scottish) 1975 *NZ*
Bishop, J M (Glasgow Acads) 1893 *I*
Bisset, A A (RIE Coll) 1904 *W*
Black, A W (Edinburgh U) 1947 *F, W,* 1948 *E,* 1950 *W, I, E*
Black, W P (Glasgow HSFP) 1948 *F, W, I, E,* 1951 *E*
Blackadder, W F (W of Scotland) 1938 *E*
Blaikie, C F (Heriot's FP) 1963 *I, E,* 1966 *E,* 1968 *A,* 1969 *F, W, I, E*
Blair, M R L (Edinburgh) 2002 *C, US*
Blair, P C B (Cambridge U) 1912 *SA,* 1913 *F, W, I, E*
Bolton, W H (W of Scotland) 1876 *E*
Borthwick, J B (Stewart's Coll FP) 1938 *W, I*
Bos, F H ten (Oxford U, London Scottish) 1959 *E,* 1960 *F, W, SA,* 1961 *F, SA, W, I, E,* 1962 *F, W, I, E,* 1963 *F, W, I, E*
Boswell, J D (W of Scotland) 1889 *W, I,* 1890 *W, I, E,* 1891 *W, I, E,* 1892 *W, I, E,* 1893 *I, E,* 1894 *I, E*
Bowie, T C (Watsonians) 1913 *I, E,* 1914 *I, E*
Boyd, G M (Glasgow HSFP) 1926 *E*
Boyd, J L (United Services) 1912 *E, SA*
Boyle, A C W (London Scottish) 1963 *F, W, I*
Boyle, A H W (St Thomas's Hospital, London Scottish) 1966 *A,* 1967 *F, NZ,* 1968 *F, W, I*
Brash, J C (Cambridge U) 1961 *E*
Breakey, R W (Gosforth) 1978 *E*
Brewis, N T (Edinburgh Inst FP) 1876 *E,* 1878 *E,* 1879 *I, E,* 1880 *I, E*
Brewster, A K (Stewart's-Melville FP) 1977 *E,* 1980 *I, F,* 1986 *E, I, R*
Brotherstone, S J (Melrose, Brive, Newcastle) 1999 *I* (R), 2000 *F, W, E, US, A, Sm,* 2002 *C* (R)
Brown, A H (Heriot's FP) 1928 *E,* 1929 *F, W*
Brown, A R (Gala) 1971 *E* (2[1C]), 1972 *F, W, E*
Brown, C H C (Dunfermline) 1929 *E*
Brown, D I (Cambridge U) 1933 *W, E, I*
Brown, G L (W of Scotland) 1969 *SA,* 1970 *F, W* (R), *I, E, A,* 1971 *F, W, I, E* (2[1C]), 1972 *F, W, E, NZ,* 1973 *E* (R), *P,* 1974 *W, I, F,* 1975 *I, F, W, E, A,* 1976 *F, W, E, I*
Brown, J A (Glasgow Acads) 1908 *W, I*
Brown, J B (Glasgow Acads) 1879 *I, E,* 1880 *I, E,* 1881 *I, E,* 1882 *I, E,* 1883 *W, I, E,* 1884 *W, I, E,* 1885 *I* 1,2, 1886 *W, I, E*
Brown, P C (W of Scotland, Gala) 1964 *F, NZ, W, I, E,* 1965 *I, E, SA,* 1966 *A,* 1969 *I, E,* 1970 *W, E,* 1971 *F, W, I, E* (2[1C]), 1972 *F, W, E, NZ,* 1973 *F, W, I, E, P*
Brown, T G (Heriot's FP) 1929 *W*
Brown, W D (Glasgow Acads) 1871 *E,* 1872 *E,* 1873 *E,* 1874 *E,* 1875 *E*
Brown, W S (Edinburgh Inst FP) 1880 *I, E,* 1882 *I, E,* 1883 *W, E*

Browning, A (Glasgow HSFP) 1920 *I*, 1922 *F, W, I*, 1923 *W, I, E*

Bruce, C R (Glasgow Acads) 1947 *F, W, I, E*, 1949 *F, W, I, E*

Bruce, N S (Blackheath, Army and London Scottish) 1958 *F, A, I, E*, 1959 *F, W, I, E*, 1960 *F, W, I, E, SA*, 1961 *F, SA, W, I, E*, 1962 *F, W, I, E*, 1963 *F, W, I, E*, 1964 *F, NZ, W, I, E*

Bruce, R M (Gordonians) 1947 *A*, 1948 *F, W, I*

Bruce-Lockhart, J H (London Scottish) 1913 *W*, 1920 *E*

Bruce-Lockhart, L (London Scottish) 1948 *E*, 1950 *F, W*, 1953 *I, E*

Bruce-Lockhart, R B (Cambridge U and London Scottish) 1937 *I*, 1939 *I, E*

Bryce, C C (Glasgow Acads) 1873 *E*, 1874 *E*

Bryce, R D H (W of Scotland) 1973 *I* (R)

Bryce, W E (Selkirk) 1922 *W, I, E*, 1923 *F, W, I, E*, 1924 *F, W, I, E*

Brydon, W R C (Heriot's FP) 1939 *W*

Buchanan, A (Royal HSFP) 1871 *E*

Buchanan, F G (Kelvinside Acads and Oxford U) 1910 *F*, 1911 *F, W*

Buchanan, J C R (Stewart's Coll FP) 1921 *W, I, E*, 1922 *W, I, E*, 1923 *F, W, I, E*, 1924 *F, W, I, E*, 1925 *F, I*

Buchanan-Smith, G A E (London Scottish, Heriot's FP) 1989 *Fj* (R), 1990 *Arg*

Bucher, A M (Edinburgh Acads) 1897 *E*

Budge, G M (Edinburgh Wands) 1950 *F, W, I, E*

Bullmore, H H (Edinburgh U) 1902 *I*

Bulloch, A J (Glasgow) 2000 *US, A, Sm*, 2001 *F* (t+R), *E*

Bulloch, G C (West of Scotland, Glasgow) 1997 *SA*, 1998 *It, I, F, W, E, Fj, A* 1, *SA*, 1999 *W, E, It, I, F, Arg, [SA, U, Sm, NZ]*, 2000 *It, I, W* (R), *NZ* 1,2, *A* (R), *Sm* (R), 2001 *F, W, E, It, I, Tg, Arg, NZ*, 2002 *E, It, I, F, W, C, US*

Burnell, A P (London Scottish, Montferrand) 1989 *E, I, F, Fj, R*, 1990 *I, F, W, E, Arg*, 1991 *F, W, E, I, R, [J, Z, I, WS, E, NZ]*, 1992 *E, I, F, W*, 1993 *I, F, W, E, NZ*, 1994 *W, E, I, F, Arg* 1,2, *SA*, 1995 *[Iv, Tg* (R), *F* (R)]*, WS*, 1998 *E, SA*, 1999 *W, E, It, I, F, Arg, [Sp, Sm* (R), *NZ]*

Burnet, P J (London Scottish and Edinburgh Acads) 1960 *SA*

Burnet, W (Hawick) 1912 *E*

Burnet, W A (W of Scotland) 1934 *W*, 1935 *W, I, E, NZ*, 1936 *W, I, E*

Burnett, J N (Heriot's FP) 1980 *I, F, W, E*

Burns, G G (Watsonians, Edinburgh) 1999 *It* (R), 2001 *Tg* (R), *NZ* (R), 2002 *US* (R)

Burrell, G (Gala) 1950 *F, W, I*, 1951 *SA*

Cairns, A G (Watsonians) 1903 *W, I, E*, 1904 *W, I, E*, 1905 *W, I, E*, 1906 *W, I, E*

Calder, F (Stewart's-Melville FP) 1986 *F, W, E, I, R*, 1987 *I, F, W, E, [F, Z, R, NZ]*, 1988 *I, F, W, E*, 1989 *W, E, I, F, R*, 1990 *I, F, W, E, NZ* 1,2, 1991 *R, [J, I, WS, E, NZ]*

Calder, J H (Stewart's-Melville FP) 1981 *F, W, E, I, NZ* 1,2, *R, A*, 1982 *E, I, F, W, A* 1,2, 1983 *I, F, W, E, NZ*, 1984 *W, E, I, F, A*, 1985 *I, F, W*

Callander, G J (Kelso) 1984 *R*, 1988 *I, F, W, E, A*

Cameron, A (Glasgow HSFP) 1948 *W*, 1950 *I, E*, 1951 *F, W, I, E, SA*, 1953 *I, E*, 1955 *F, W, I, E*, 1956 *F, W, I*

Cameron, A D (Hillhead HSFP) 1951 *F*, 1954 *F, W*

Cameron, A W (Watsonians) 1887 *W*, 1893 *W*, 1894 *I*

Cameron, D (Glasgow HSFP) 1953 *I, E*, 1954 *F, NZ, I, E*

Cameron, N W (Glasgow U) 1952 *E*, 1953 *F, W*

Campbell, A J (Hawick) 1984 *I, F, R*, 1985 *I, F, W, E*, 1986 *F, W, E, I, R*, 1988 *F, W, A*

Campbell, G T (London Scottish) 1892 *W, I, E*, 1893 *I, E*, 1894 *W, I, E*, 1895 *W, I, E*, 1896 *W, I, E*, 1897 *I*, 1899 *I*, 1900 *E*

Campbell, H H (Cambridge U, London Scottish) 1947 *I, E*, 1948 *I, E*

Campbell, J A (W of Scotland) 1878 *E*, 1879 *I, E*, 1881 *I, E*

Campbell, J A (Cambridge U) 1900 *I*

Campbell, N M (London Scottish) 1956 *F, W*

Campbell, S J (Dundee HSFP) 1995 *C, I, F, W, E, R, [Iv, NZ* (R)]*, WS* (t), 1996 *I, F, W, E*, 1997 *A, SA*, 1998 *Fj* (R), *A* 2(R)

Campbell-Lamerton, J R E (London Scottish) 1986 *F*, 1987 *[Z, R(R)]*

Campbell-Lamerton, M J (Halifax, Army, London Scottish) 1961 *F, SA, W, I*, 1962 *F, W, I, E*, 1963 *F, W, I, E*, 1964 *I, E*, 1965 *F, W, I, E, SA*, 1966 *F, W, I, E*

Carmichael, A B (W of Scotland) 1967 *I, NZ*, 1968 *F, W, I, E, A*, 1969 *F, W, I, E, SA*, 1970 *F, W, I, E, A*, 1971 *F, W, I, E*

(2[1C]), 1972 *F, W, E, NZ*, 1973 *F, W, I, E, P*, 1974 *W, E, I, F*, 1975 *I, F, W, E, NZ, A*, 1976 *F, W, E, I*, 1977 *E, I* (R), *F, W*, 1978 *I*

Carmichael, J H (Watsonians) 1921 *F, W, I*

Carrick, J S (Glasgow Acads) 1876 *E*, 1877 *E*

Cassels, D Y (W of Scotland) 1880 *E*, 1881 *I*, 1882 *I, E*, 1883 *W, I, E*

Cathcart, C W (Edinburgh U) 1872 *E*, 1873 *E*, 1876 *E*

Cawkwell, G L (Oxford U) 1947 *F*

Chalmers, C M (Melrose) 1989 *W, E, I, F, Fj*, 1990 *I, F, W, E, NZ* 1,2, *Arg*, 1991 *F, W, E, I, R, [J, Z* (R), *I, WS, E, NZ]*, 1992 *E, I, F, W, A* 1,2, 1993 *I, F, W, E, NZ*, 1994 *W, SA*, 1995 *C, I, F, W, E, R, [Iv, Tg, F, NZ]*, *WS*, 1996 *A, It*, 1997 *W, I, F, A* (R), *SA*, 1998 *It, I, F, W, E*, 1999 *Arg* (R)

Chalmers, T (Glasgow Acads) 1871 *E*, 1872 *E*, 1873 *E*, 1874 *E*, 1875 *E*, 1876 *E*

Chambers, H F T (Edinburgh U) 1888 *W, I*, 1889 *W, I*

Charters, R (Hawick) 1955 *W, I, E*

Chisholm, D H (Melrose) 1964 *I, E*, 1965 *E, SA*, 1966 *F, I, E, A*, 1967 *F, W, NZ*, 1968 *F, W, I*

Chisholm, R W T (Melrose) 1955 *I, E*, 1956 *F, W, I, E*, 1958 *F, W, A, I*, 1960 *SA*

Church, W C (Glasgow Acads) 1906 *W*

Clark, R L (Edinburgh Wands, Royal Navy) 1972 *F, W, E, NZ*, 1973 *F, W, I, E, P*

Clauss, P R A (Oxford U) 1891 *W, I, E*, 1892 *W, E*, 1895 *I*

Clay, A T (Edinburgh Acads) 1886 *W, I, E*, 1887 *I, W, E*, 1888 *W*

Clunies-Ross, A (St Andrew's U) 1871 *E*

Coltman, S (Hawick) 1948 *I*, 1949 *F, W, I, E*

Colville, A G (Merchistonians, Blackheath) 1871 *E*, 1872 *E*

Connell, G C (Trinity Acads and London Scottish) 1968 *E, A*, 1969 *F, E*, 1970 *F*

Cooper, M McG (Oxford U) 1936 *W, I*

Corcoran, I (Gala) 1992 *A* 1(R)

Cordial, I F (Edinburgh Wands) 1952 *F, W, I, E*

Cotter, J L (Hillhead HSFP) 1934 *I, E*

Cottington, G S (Kelso) 1934 *I, E*, 1935 *W, I*, 1936 *E*

Coughtrie, S (Edinburgh Acads) 1959 *F, W, I, E*, 1962 *W, I, E*, 1963 *F, W, I, E*

Couper, J H (W of Scotland) 1896 *W, I*, 1899 *I*

Coutts, F H (Melrose, Army) 1947 *W, I, E*

Coutts, I D F (Old Alleynians) 1951 *F*, 1952 *E*

Cowan, R C (Selkirk) 1961 *F*, 1962 *F, W, I, E*

Cowie, W L K (Edinburgh Wands) 1953 *E*

Cownie, W B (Watsonians) 1893 *W, I, E*, 1894 *W, I, E*, 1895 *W, I, E*

Crabbie, G E (Edinburgh Acads) 1904 *W*

Crabbie, J E (Edinburgh Acads, Oxford U) 1900 *W*, 1902 *I*, 1903 *W, I*, 1904 *E*, 1905 *W*

Craig, A (Orrell) 2002 *C, US*

Craig, J B (Heriot's FP) 1939 *W*

Craig, J M (West of Scotland, Glasgow) 1997 *A*, 2001 *W* (R), *E* (R), *It*

Cramb, R I (Harlequins) 1987 *[R(R)]*, 1988 *I, F, A*

Cranston, A G (Hawick) 1976 *W, E, I*, 1977 *E, W*, 1978 *F* (R), *W, E, NZ*, 1981 *NZ* 1,2

Crawford, J A (Army, London Scottish) 1934 *I*

Crawford, W H (United Services, RN) 1938 *W, I, E*, 1939 *W, E*

Crichton-Miller, D (Gloucester) 1931 *W, I, E*

Crole, G B (Oxford U) 1920 *F, W, I, E*

Cronin, D F (Bath, London Scottish, Bourges, Wasps) 1988 *I, F, W, E, A*, 1989 *W, E, I, F, Fj, R*, 1990 *I, F, W, E, NZ* 1,2, 1991 *F, W, E, I, R, [Z]*, 1992 *A* 2, 1993 *I, F, W, E, NZ*, 1995 *C, I, F, [Tg, F, NZ]*, *WS*, 1996 *NZ* 1,2, *A, It*, 1997 *F* (R), 1998 *I, F, W, E*

Cross, M (Merchistonians) 1875 *E*, 1876 *E*, 1877 *I, E*, 1878 *E*, 1879 *I, E*, 1880 *I, E*

Cross, W (Merchistonians) 1871 *E*, 1872 *E*

Cumming, R S (Aberdeen U) 1921 *F, W*

Cunningham, G (Oxford U) 1908 *W, I*, 1909 *W, E*, 1910 *F, I, E*, 1911 *E*

Cunningham, R F (Gala) 1978 *NZ*, 1979 *W, E*

Currie, L R (Dunfermline) 1947 *A*, 1948 *F, W, I*, 1949 *F, W, I, E*

Cuthbertson, W (Kilmarnock, Harlequins) 1980 *I*, 1981 *W, E, I, NZ* 1,2, *R, A*, 1982 *E, I, F, W, A* 1,2, 1983 *I, F, W, NZ*, 1984 *W, E, A*

Dalgleish, A (Gala) 1890 *W, E*, 1891 *W, I*, 1892 *W*, 1893 *W*, 1894 *W, I*

Dalgleish, K J (Edinburgh Wands, Cambridge U) 1951 *I, E*, 1953 *F, W*

Dallas, J D (Watsonians) 1903 *E*
Davidson, J A (London Scottish, Edinburgh Wands) 1959 *E*, 1960 *I, E*
Davidson, J N G (Edinburgh U) 1952 *F, W, I, E*, 1953 *F, W,* 1954 *F*
Davidson, J P (RIE Coll) 1873 *E*, 1874 *E*
Davidson, R S (Royal HSFP) 1893 *E*
Davies, D S (Hawick) 1922 *E, W, I, E*, 1923 *F, W, I, E*, 1924 *F, E*, 1925 *W, I, E*, 1926 *F, W, I, E*, 1927 *F, W, I*
Dawson, J C (Glasgow Acads) 1947 *A*, 1948 *F, W*, 1949 *F, W, I*, 1950 *F, W, I, E*, 1951 *F, W, I, E, SA*, 1952 *F, W, I, E*, 1953 *E*
Deans, C T (Hawick) 1978 *F, W, E, NZ*, 1979 *W, E, I, F, NZ*, 1980 *I, F*, 1981 *F, W, E, I, NZ* 1,2, *R, A*, 1982 *E, I, F, W, A* 1,2, 1983 *I, F, W, E, NZ*, 1984 *W, E, I, F, A*, 1985 *I, F, W, E*, 1986 *F, W, E, I, R*, 1987 *I, F, W, E*, [*F, Z, R, NZ*]
Deans, D T (Hawick) 1968 *E*
Deas, D W (Heriot's FP) 1947 *F, W*
Dick, L G (Loughborough Colls, Jordanhill, Swansea) 1972 *W* (R), *E*, 1974 *W, E, I, F*, 1975 *I, F, W, E, NZ, A*, 1976 *F*, 1977 *E*
Dick, R C S (Cambridge U, Guy's Hospital) 1934 *W, I, E*, 1935 *W, I, E, NZ*, 1936 *W, I, E*, 1937 *W*, 1938 *W, I, E*
Dickson, G (Gala) 1978 *NZ*, 1979 *W, E, I, F, NZ*, 1980 *W*, 1981 *F*, 1982 *W* (R)
Dickson, M R (Edinburgh U) 1905 *I*
Dickson, W M (Blackheath, Oxford U) 1912 *F, W, E, SA*, 1913 *F, W, I*
Di Rollo, M P (Edinburgh) 2002 *US* (R)
Dobson, J (Glasgow Acads) 1911 *E*, 1912 *F, W, I, E, SA*
Dobson, J D (Glasgow Acads) 1910 *I*
Dobson, W G (Heriot's FP) 1922 *W, I, E*
Docherty, J T (Glasgow HSFP) 1955 *F, W*, 1956 *F*, 1958 *F, W, A, I, E*
Dods, F P (Edinburgh Acads) 1901 *I*
Dods, J H (Edinburgh Acads) 1895 *W, I, E*, 1896 *W, I, E*, 1897 *I, E*
Dods, M (Gala, Northampton) 1994 *I* (t), *Arg* 1,2, 1995 *WS*, 1996 *I, F, W, E*
Dods, P W (Gala) 1983 *I, F, W, E, NZ*, 1984 *W, E, I, F, R, A*, 1985 *I, F, W, E*, 1989 *W, E, I, F*, 1991 *I* (R), *R*, [*Z, NZ* (R)]
Donald, D G (Oxford U) 1914 *W, I*
Donald, R L H (Glasgow HSFP) 1921 *W, I, E*
Donaldson, W P (Oxford U, W of Scotland) 1893 *I*, 1894 *I*, 1895 *E*, 1896 *I, E*, 1899 *I*
Don-Wauchope, A R (Fettesian-Lorettonians) 1881 *E*, 1882 *E*, 1883 *W, I, E*, 1884 *W, I, E*, 1885 *W, I* 1,2, 1886 *W, I, E*, 1888 *I*, 1886 *W*, 1887 *I, W, E*
Don-Wauchope, P H (Fettesian-Lorettonians) 1885 *I* 1,2, 1886 *W*, 1887 *I, W, E*
Dorward, A F (Cambridge U, Gala) 1950 *F*, 1951 *SA*, 1952 *W, I, E*, 1953 *F, W, E*, 1955 *F, W, E*, 1956 *F, E*, 1957 *F, W, I, E*
Dorward, T F (Gala) 1938 *W, I, E*, 1939 *I, E*
Douglas, G (Jedforest) 1921 *W*
Douglas, J (Stewart's Coll FP) 1961 *F, SA, W, I, E*, 1962 *F, W, I, E*, 1963 *F, W, I*
Douty, P S (London Scottish) 1927 *A*, 1928 *F, W*
Drew, D (Glasgow Acads) 1871 *E*, 1876 *E*
Druitt, W A H (London Scottish) 1936 *W, I, E*
Drummond, A H (Kelvinside Acads) 1938 *W, I*
Drummond, C W (Melrose) 1947 *F, W, I, E*, 1948 *F, I, E*, 1950 *F, W, I, E*
Drybrough, A S (Edinburgh Wands, Merchistonians) 1902 *I*, 1903 *I*
Dryden, R H (Watsonians) 1937 *E*
Drysdale, D (Heriot's FP) 1923 *F, W, I, E*, 1924 *F, W, I, E*, 1925 *F, W, I, E*, 1926 *F, W, I, E*, 1927 *F, W, I, E, A*, 1928 *F, W, I, E*, 1929 *F*
Duff, P L (Glasgow Acads) 1936 *W, I*, 1938 *W, I, E*, 1939 *W*
Duffy, H (Jedforest) 1955 *F*
Duke, A (Royal HSFP) 1888 *W, I*, 1889 *W, I*, 1890 *W, I*
Duncan, A W (Edinburgh U) 1901 *W, I, E*, 1902 *W, I, E*
Duncan, D D (Oxford U) 1920 *F, W, I, E*
Duncan, M D F (W of Scotland) 1986 *F, W, E, R*, 1987 *I, F, W, E*, [*F, Z, R, NZ*], 1988 *I, F, W, E, A*, 1989 *W*
Duncan, M M (Fettesian-Lorettonians) 1888 *W*
Dunlop, J W (W of Scotland) 1875 *E*
Dunlop, Q (W of Scotland) 1971 *E* (2[1C])
Dykes, A S (Glasgow Acads) 1932 *E*
Dykes, J C (Glasgow Acads) 1922 *F, E*, 1924 *I*, 1925 *F, W, I*, 1926 *F, W, I, E*, 1927 *F, W, I, E, A*, 1928 *F, I*, 1929 *F, W, I*
Dykes, J M (Clydesdale, Glasgow HSFP) 1898 *I, E*, 1899 *W, E*, 1900 *W, I*, 1901 *W, I, E*, 1902 *E*

Edwards, D B (Heriot's FP) 1960 *I, E, SA*
Edwards, N G B (Harlequins, Northampton) 1992 *E, I, F, W, A* 1, 1994 *W*
Elgie, M K (London Scottish) 1954 *NZ, I, E, W*, 1955 *F, W, I, E*
Elliot, C (Langholm) 1958 *E*, 1959 *F*, 1960 *F*, 1963 *E*, 1964 *F, NZ, W, I, E*, 1965 *F, W, I*
Elliot, M (Hawick) 1895 *W*, 1896 *E*, 1897 *I, E*, 1898 *I, E*
Elliot, T (Gala) 1905 *E*
Elliot, T (Gala) 1955 *W, I, E*, 1956 *F, W, I, E*, 1957 *F, W, I, E*, 1958 *W, A, I*
Elliot, T G (Langholm) 1968 *W, A*, 1969 *F, W*, 1970 *E*
Elliot, W I D (Edinburgh Acads) 1947 *F, W, E, A*, 1948 *F, W, I, E*, 1949 *F, W, I, E*, 1950 *F, W, I, E*, 1951 *F, W, I, E, SA*, 1952 *F, W, I, E*, 1954 *NZ, I, E, W*
Ellis, D G (Currie) 1997 *W, E, I, F*
Emslie, W D (Royal HSFP) 1930 *F*, 1932 *I*
Eriksson, B R S (London Scottish) 1996 *NZ* 1, *A*, 1997 *E*
Evans, H L (Edinburgh U) 1885 *I* 1,2
Ewart, E N (Glasgow Acads) 1879 *E*, 1880 *I, E*

Fahmy, Dr E C (Abertillery) 1920 *F, W, I, E*
Fairley, I T (Kelso, Edinburgh) 1999 *It, I* (R), [*Sp* (R)]
Fasson, F H (London Scottish, Edinburgh Wands) 1900 *W*, 1901 *W, I*, 1902 *W, E*
Fell, A N (Edinburgh U) 1901 *W, I, E*, 1902 *W, E*, 1903 *W, E*
Ferguson, J H (Gala) 1928 *W*
Ferguson, W G (Royal HSFP) 1927 *A*, 1928 *F, W, I, E*
Fergusson, E A J (Oxford U) 1954 *F, NZ, I, E, W*
Finlay, A B (Edinburgh Acads) 1875 *E*
Finlay, J F (Edinburgh Acads) 1871 *E*, 1872 *E*, 1874 *E*, 1875 *E*
Finlay, N J (Edinburgh Acads) 1875 *E*, 1876 *E*, 1878 *E*, 1879 *I, E*, 1880 *I, E*, 1881 *I, E*
Finlay, R (Watsonians) 1948 *E*
Fisher, A T (Waterloo, Watsonians) 1947 *I, E*
Fisher, C D (Waterloo) 1975 *NZ, A*, 1976 *W, E, I*
Fisher, D (W of Scotland) 1893 *I*
Fisher, J P (Royal HSFP, London Scottish) 1963 *E*, 1964 *F, NZ, W, I, E*, 1965 *F, W, I, E, SA*, 1966 *F, W, I, E, A*, 1967 *F, W, I, E, NZ*, 1968 *F, W, I, E*
Fleming, C J N (Edinburgh Wands) 1896 *I, E*, 1897 *I*
Fleming, G R (Glasgow Acads) 1875 *E*, 1876 *E*
Fletcher, H N (Edinburgh U) 1904 *E*, 1905 *W*
Flett, A B (Edinburgh U) 1901 *W, I, E*, 1902 *W, I*
Forbes, J L (Watsonians) 1905 *W*, 1906 *I, E*
Ford, D St C (United Services, RN) 1930 *I, E*, 1931 *E*, 1932 *W, I*
Ford, J R (Gala) 1893 *I*
Forrest, J E (Glasgow Acads) 1932 *SA*, 1935 *E, NZ*
Forrest, J G S (Cambridge U) 1938 *W, I, E*
Forrest, W T (Hawick) 1903 *W, I, E*, 1904 *W, I, E*, 1905 *W, I*
Forsayth, H H (Oxford U) 1921 *F, W, I, E*, 1922 *W, I, E*
Forsyth, I W (Stewart's Coll FP) 1972 *NZ*, 1973 *F, W, I, E, P*
Forsyth, J (Edinburgh U) 1871 *E*
Foster, R A (Hawick) 1930 *W*, 1932 *SA, I, E*
Fox, J (Gala) 1952 *F, W, I, E*
Frame, J N M (Edinburgh U, Gala) 1967 *NZ*, 1968 *F, W, I, E*, 1969 *F, I, E, SA*, 1970 *F, W, I, E, A*, 1971 *F, W, I, E* (2[1C]), 1972 *F, W, E*, 1973 *P* (R)
France, C (Kelvinside Acads) 1903 *I*
Fraser, C F P (Glasgow U) 1888 *W*, 1889 *W*
Fraser, J W (Edinburgh Inst FP) 1881 *E*
Fraser, R (Cambridge U) 1911 *F, W, I, E*
French, J (Glasgow Acads) 1886 *W*, 1887 *I, W, E*
Frew, A (Edinburgh U) 1901 *W, I, E*
Frew, G M (Glasgow HSFP) 1906 *SA*, 1907 *W, I, E*, 1908 *W, I, E*, 1909 *W, I, E*, 1910 *F, W, I*, 1911 *I, E*
Friebe, J P (Glasgow HSFP) 1952 *E*
Fullarton, I A (Edinburgh) 2000 *NZ* 1(R),2, 2001 *NZ* (R)
Fulton, A K (Edinburgh U, Dollar Acads) 1952 *F*, 1954 *F*
Fyfe, K C (Cambridge U, Sale, London Scottish) 1933 *W, E*, 1934 *E*, 1935 *W, I, E, NZ*, 1936 *W, E*, 1939 *I*

Gallie, G H (Edinburgh Acads) 1939 *W*
Gallie, R A (Glasgow Acads) 1920 *F, W, I, E*, 1921 *F, W, I, E*
Gammell, W B B (Edinburgh Wands) 1977 *I, F, W*, 1978 *W, E*
Geddes, I C (London Scottish) 1906 *SA*, 1907 *W, I, E*, 1908 *W, E*
Geddes, K I (London Scottish) 1947 *F, W, I, E*
Gedge, H T S (Oxford U, London Scottish, Edinburgh Wands) 1894 *W, I, E*, 1896 *E*, 1899 *W, E*

Gedge, P M S (Edinburgh Wands) 1933 *I*
Gemmill, R (Glasgow HSFP) 1950 *F, W, I, E,* 1951 *F, W, I*
Gibson, W R (Royal HSFP) 1891 *I, E,* 1892 *W, I, E,* 1893 *W, I, E,* 1894 *W, I, E,* 1895 *W, I, E*
Gilbert-Smith, D S (London Scottish) 1952 *E*
Gilchrist, J (Glasgow Acads) 1925 *F*
Gill, A D (Gala) 1973 *P,* 1974 *W, E, I, F*
Gillespie, J I (Edinburgh Acads) 1899 *E,* 1900 *W, E,* 1901 *W, I, E,* 1902 *W, I,* 1904 *I, E*
Gillies, A C (Watsonians) 1924 *W, I, E,* 1925 *F, W, E,* 1926 *F, W,* 1927 *F, W, I, E*
Gilmour, H R (Heriot's FP) 1998 *Fj*
Gilray, C M (Oxford U, London Scottish) 1908 *E,* 1909 *W, E,* 1912 *I*
Glasgow, I C (Heriot's FP) 1997 *F* (R)
Glasgow, R J C (Dunfermline) 1962 *F, W, I, E,* 1963 *I, E,* 1964 *I, E,* 1965 *W, I*
Glen, W S (Edinburgh Wands) 1955 *W*
Gloag, L G (Cambridge U) 1949 *F, W, I, E*
Goodfellow, J (Langholm) 1928 *W, I, E*
Goodhue, F W J (London Scottish) 1890 *W, I, E,* 1891 *W, I, E,* 1892 *W, I, E*
Gordon, R (Edinburgh Wands) 1951 *W,* 1952 *F, W, I, E,* 1953 *W*
Gordon, R E (Royal Artillery) 1913 *F, W, I*
Gordon, R J (London Scottish) 1982 *A* 1,2
Gore, A C (London Scottish) 1882 *I*
Gossman, B M (W of Scotland) 1980 *W,* 1983 *F, W*
Gossman, J S (W of Scotland) 1980 *E* (R)
Gowans, J J (Cambridge U, London Scottish) 1893 *W,* 1894 *W, E,* 1895 *W, I, E,* 1896 *I, E*
Gowland, G C (London Scottish) 1908 *W,* 1909 *W, E,* 1910 *F, W, I, E*
Gracie, A L (Harlequins) 1921 *F, W, I, E,* 1922 *F, W, I, E,* 1923 *F, W, I, E,* 1924 *F*
Graham, G (Newcastle) 1997 *A* (R), *SA* (R), 1998 *I, F* (R), *W* (R), 1999 *F* (R), *Arg* (R), *R,* [*SA, U, Sm, NZ* (R)], 2000 *I* (R), *US, A, Sm,* 2001 *I* (R), *Tg* (R), *Arg* (R), *NZ* (R), 2002 *E* (R), *It* (R), *I* (R), *F* (R), *W* (R)
Graham, I N (Edinburgh Acads) 1939 *I, E*
Graham, J (Kelso) 1926 *I, E,* 1927 *F, W, I, E, A,* 1928 *F, W, I, E,* 1930 *I, E,* 1932 *SA, W*
Graham, J H S (Edinburgh Acads) 1876 *E,* 1877 *I, E,* 1878 *E,* 1879 *I, E,* 1880 *I, E,* 1881 *I, E*
Grant, D (Hawick) 1965 *F, E, SA,* 1966 *F, W, I, E, A,* 1967 *F, W, I, E, NZ,* 1968 *F*
Grant, D M (East Midlands) 1911 *W, I*
Grant, M L (Harlequins) 1955 *F,* 1956 *F, W,* 1957 *F*
Grant, T O (Hawick) 1960 *I, E, SA,* 1964 *F, NZ, W*
Grant, W St C (Craigmount) 1873 *E,* 1874 *E*
Gray, C A (Nottingham) 1989 *W, E, I, F, Fj, R,* 1990 *I, F, W, E, NZ* 1,2, *Arg,* 1991 *F, W, E, I,* [*J, I, WS, E, NZ*]
Gray, D (W of Scotland) 1978 *E,* 1979 *I, F, NZ,* 1980 *I, F, W, E,* 1981 *F*
Gray, G L (Gala) 1935 *NZ,* 1937 *W, I, E*
Gray, T (Northampton, Heriot's FP) 1950 *E,* 1951 *F, E*
Greenlees, H D (Leicester) 1927 *A,* 1928 *F, W,* 1929 *I, E,* 1930 *E*
Greenlees, J R C (Cambridge U, Kelvinside Acads) 1900 *I,* 1902 *W, I, E*
Greenwood, J T (Dunfermline and Perthshire Acads) 1952 *F,* 1955 *F, W, I, E,* 1956 *F, W, I, E,* 1957 *F, W, E,* 1958 *F, W, A, I, E,* 1959 *F, W, I*
Greig, A (Glasgow HSFP) 1911 *I*
Greig, L L (Glasgow Acads, United Services) 1905 *NZ,* 1906 *SA,* 1907 *W,* 1908 *W, I*
Greig, R C (Glasgow Acads) 1893 *W,* 1897 *I*
Grieve, C F (Oxford U) 1935 *W,* 1936 *E*
Grieve, R M (Kelso) 1935 *W, I, E, NZ,* 1936 *W, I, E*
Grimes, S B (Watsonians, Newcastle) 1997 *A* (t+R), 1998 *I* (R), *F* (R), *W* (R), *E* (R), *Fj, A* 1, 2, 1999 *W* (R), *E, It, I, F, Arg, R,* [*SA, U, Sm* (R), *NZ* (R)], 2000 *It, I, F* (R), *W, US, A, Sm* (R), 2001 *F* (R), *W* (R), *E* (R), *It, I* (R), *Tg, Arg, NZ,* 2002 *E, It, I, F* (R), *W* (R), *C, US*
Gunn, A W (Royal HSFP) 1912 *F, W, I, SA,* 1913 *F*

Hall, A J A (Glasgow) 2002 *US* (R)
Hamilton, A S (Headingley) 1914 *W,* 1920 *F*
Hamilton, H M (W of Scotland) 1874 *E,* 1875 *E*
Hannah, R S M (W of Scotland) 1971 *I*
Harrower, P R (London Scottish) 1885 *W*
Hart, J G M (London Scottish) 1951 *SA*
Hart, T M (Glasgow U) 1930 *W, I*

Hart, W (Melrose) 1960 *SA*
Harvey, L (Greenock Wands) 1899 *I*
Hastie, A J (Melrose) 1961 *W, I, E,* 1964 *I, E,* 1965 *E, SA,* 1966 *F, W, I, E, A,* 1967 *F, W, I, NZ,* 1968 *F, W*
Hastie, I R (Kelso) 1955 *F,* 1958 *F, E,* 1959 *F, W, I*
Hastie, J D H (Melrose) 1938 *W, I, E*
Hastings, A G (Cambridge U, Watsonians, London Scottish) 1986 *F, W, E, I, R,* 1987 *I, F, W,* [*F, Z, R, NZ*], 1988 *I, F, W, E, A,* 1989 *Fj, R,* 1990 *I, F, W, E, NZ* 1,2, *Arg,* 1991 *F, W, E, I,* [*J, I, WS, E, NZ*], 1992 *E, I, F, W, A* 1, 1993 *I, F, W, E, NZ,* 1994 *W, E, I, F, SA,* 1995 *C, I, F, W, E, R,* [*Iv, Tg, F, NZ*]
Hastings, S (Watsonians) 1986 *F, W, E, I, R,* 1987 *I, F, W,* [*R*], 1988 *I, F, W, A,* 1989 *W, E, I, F, Fj, R,* 1990 *I, F, W, E, NZ* 1,2, *Arg,* 1991 *F, W, E, I,* [*J, Z, I, WS, E, NZ*], 1992 *E, I, F, W, A* 1,2, 1993 *I, F, W, E, NZ,* 1994 *E, I, F, SA,* 1995 *W, E, R* (R), [*Tg, F, NZ*], 1996 *I, F, W, E, NZ* 2, *It,* 1997 *W, E* (R)
Hay, B H (Boroughmuir) 1975 *NZ, A,* 1976 *F,* 1978 *I, F, W, E, NZ,* 1979 *W, E, I, F, NZ,* 1980 *I, F, W, E,* 1981 *F, W, E, I, NZ* 1,2
Hay, J A (Hawick) 1995 *WS*
Hay-Gordon, J R (Edinburgh Acads) 1875 *E,* 1877 *I, E*
Hegarty, C B (Hawick) 1978 *I, F, W, E*
Hegarty, J J (Hawick) 1951 *F,* 1953 *F, W, I, E,* 1955 *F*
Henderson, A R (Glasgow) 2001 *I* (R), *Tg* (R), *NZ* (R), 2002 *It, I, US* (R)
Henderson, B C (Edinburgh Wands) 1963 *E,* 1964 *F, I, E,* 1965 *F, W, I, E,* 1966 *F, W, I, E*
Henderson, F W (London Scottish) 1900 *W, I*
Henderson, I C (Edinburgh Acads) 1939 *I, E,* 1947 *F, W, E, A,* 1948 *I, E*
Henderson, J H (Oxford U, Richmond) 1953 *F, W, I, E,* 1954 *F, NZ, I, E, W*
Henderson, J M (Edinburgh Acads) 1933 *W, E, I*
Henderson, J Y M (Watsonians) 1911 *E*
Henderson, M M (Dunfermline) 1937 *W, I, E*
Henderson, N F (London Scottish) 1892 *I*
Henderson, R G (Newcastle Northern) 1924 *I, E*
Hendrie, K G P (Heriot's FP) 1924 *F, W, I*
Hendry, T L (Clydesdale) 1893 *W, I, E,* 1895 *I*
Henriksen, E H (Royal HSFP) 1953 *I*
Hepburn, D P (Woodford) 1947 *A,* 1948 *F, W, I, E,* 1949 *F, W, I, E*
Heron, G (Glasgow Acads) 1874 *E,* 1875 *E*
Hill, C C P (St Andrew's U) 1912 *F, I*
Hilton, D I W (Bath, Glasgow) 1995 *C, I, F, W, E, R,* [*Tg, F, NZ*], *WS,* 1996 *I, F, W, E, NZ* 1,2, *A, It,* 1997 *W, A, SA,* 1998 *It, I* (R), *F, W, E, A* 1,2, *SA* (R), 1999 *W, E* (R), *It* (R), *I* (R), *F, R* (R), [*SA* (R), *U* (R), *Sp*], 2000 *It* (R), *F* (R), *W* (R)
Hines, N J (Edinburgh) 2000 *NZ* 2(R), 2002 *C, US*
Hinshelwood, A J W (London Scottish) 1966 *F, W, I, E, A,* 1967 *F, W, I, E, NZ,* 1968 *F, W, I, E, A,* 1969 *F, W, I, SA,* 1970 *F, W*
Hinshelwood, B G (Worcester) 2002 *C* (R)
Hodge D W (Watsonians, Edinburgh) 1997 *F* (R), *A, SA* (t+R), 1998 *A* 2(R), *SA,* 1999 *W, Arg, R,* [*Sp, Sm* (R)], 2000 *F* (R), *W, E, NZ* 1,2, *US* (R), *Sm* (R), 2001 *F* (R), *W, E, It, I* (R), 2002 *E, W* (R), *C, US*
Hodgson, C G (London Scottish) 1968 *I, E*
Hogg, C D (Melrose) 1992 *A* 1,2, 1993 *NZ* (R), 1994 *Arg* 1,2
Hogg, C G (Boroughmuir) 1978 *F* (R), *W* (R)
Holmes, S D (London Scottish) 1998 *It, I, F*
Holms, W F (RIE Coll) 1886 *W, E,* 1887 *I, E,* 1889 *W, I*
Horsburgh, G B (London Scottish) 1937 *W, I, E,* 1938 *W, I, E,* 1939 *W, I, E*
Howie, D D (Kirkcaldy) 1912 *F, W, I, E, SA,* 1913 *F, W*
Howie, R A (Kirkcaldy) 1924 *F, W, I, E,* 1925 *W, I, E*
Hoyer-Millar, G C (Oxford U) 1953 *I*
Huggan, J L (London Scottish) 1914 *E*
Hume, J (Royal HSFP) 1912 *F,* 1920 *F,* 1921 *F, W, I, E,* 1922 *F*
Hume, J W G (Oxford U, Edinburgh Wands) 1928 *I,* 1930 *F*
Hunter, F (Edinburgh U) 1882 *I*
Hunter, I G (Selkirk) 1984 *I* (R), 1985 *F* (R), *W, E*
Hunter, J M (Cambridge U) 1947 *F*
Hunter, M D (Glasgow High) 1974 *F*
Hunter, W J (Hawick) 1964 *F, NZ, W,* 1967 *F, W, I, E*
Hutchison, W R (Glasgow HSFP) 1911 *E*
Hutton, A H M (Dunfermline) 1932 *I*
Hutton, J E (Harlequins) 1930 *E,* 1931 *F*

Inglis, H M (Edinburgh Acads) 1951 *F, W, I, E, SA,* 1952 *W, I*
Inglis, J M (Selkirk) 1952 *E*

Inglis, W M (Cambridge U, Royal Engineers) 1937 *W, I, E,* 1938 *W, I, E*
Innes, J R S (Aberdeen GSFP) 1939 *W, I, E,* 1947 *A,* 1948 *F, W, I, E*
Ireland, J C H (Glasgow HSFP) 1925 *W, I, E,* 1926 *F, W, I, E,* 1927 *F, W, I, E*
Irvine, A R (Heriot's FP) 1972 *NZ,* 1973 *F, W, I, E, P,* 1974 *W, E, I, F,* 1975 *I, F, W, E, NZ, A,* 1976 *F, W, E, I,* 1977 *E, I, F, W,* 1978 *I, F, E, NZ,* 1979 *W, E, I, F, NZ,* 1980 *I, F, W, E,* 1981 *F, W, E, I, NZ* 1,2, *R, A,* 1982 *E, I, F, W, A* 1,2
Irvine, D R (Edinburgh Acads) 1878 *E,* 1879 *I, E*
Irvine, R W (Edinburgh Acads) 1871 *E,* 1872 *E,* 1873 *E,* 1874 *E,* 1875 *E,* 1876 *E,* 1877 *I, E,* 1878 *E,* 1879 *I, E,* 1880 *I, E*
Irvine T W (Edinburgh Acads) 1885 *I* 1,2, 1886 *W, I, E,* 1887 *I, W, E,* 1888 *W, I,* 1889 *I*

Jackson, K L T (Oxford U) 1933 *W, E, I,* 1934 *W*
Jackson, T G H (Army) 1947 *F, W, E, A,* 1948 *F, W, I, E,* 1949 *F, W, I, E*
Jackson, W D (Hawick) 1964 *I,* 1965 *E, SA,* 1968 *A,* 1969 *F, W, I, E*
Jacobsen, A F (Edinburgh) 2002 *C* (R), *US*
Jamieson, J (W of Scotland) 1883 *W, I, E,* 1884 *W, I, E,* 1885 *W, I* 1,2
Jardine, I C (Stirling County) 1993 *NZ,* 1994 *W, E* (R), *Arg* 1,2, 1995 *C, I, F, [Tg, F* (t & R), *NZ* (R)], 1996 *I, F, W, E, NZ* 1,2, 1998 *Fj*
Jeffrey, J (Kelso) 1984 *A,* 1985 *I, E,* 1986 *F, W, E, I, R,* 1987 *I, F, W, E, [F, Z, R],* 1988 *I, W, A,* 1989 *W, E, I, F, Fj, R,* 1990 *I, F, W, E, NZ* 1,2, *Arg,* 1991 *F, W, E, I, [J, I, WS, E, NZ]*
Johnston, D I (Watsonians) 1979 *NZ,* 1980 *I, F, W, E,* 1981 *R, A,* 1982 *E, I, F, W, A* 1,2, 1983 *I, F, W, NZ,* 1984 *W, E, I, F, R,* 1986 *F, W, E, I, R*
Johnston, H H (Edinburgh Collegian FP) 1877 *I, E*
Johnston, J (Melrose) 1951 *SA,* 1952 *F, W, I, E*
Johnston, W C (Glasgow HSFP) 1922 *F*
Johnston, W G S (Cambridge U) 1935 *W, I,* 1937 *W, I, E*
Joiner, C A (Melrose, Leicester) 1994 *Arg* 1,2, 1995 *C, I, F, W, E, R, [Iv, Tg, F, NZ],* 1996 *I, F, W, E, NZ* 1, 1997 *SA,* 1998 *It, I, A* 2(R), 2000 *NZ* 1(R),2, *US* (R)
Jones, P M (Gloucester) 1992 *W* (R)
Junor, J E (Glasgow Acads) 1876 *E,* 1877 *I, E,* 1878 *E,* 1879 *E,* 1881 *I*

Keddie, R R (Watsonians) 1967 *NZ*
Keith, G J (Wasps) 1968 *F, W*
Keller, D H (London Scottish) 1949 *F, W, I, E,* 1950 *F, W, I*
Kelly, R F (Watsonians) 1927 *A,* 1928 *F, W, E*
Kemp, J W Y (Glasgow HSFP) 1954 *W,* 1955 *F, W, I, E,* 1956 *F, W, I, E,* 1957 *F, W, I, E,* 1958 *F, W, A, I, E,* 1959 *F, W, I, E,* 1960 *F, W, I, E, SA*
Kennedy, A E (Watsonians) 1983 *NZ,* 1984 *W, E, A*
Kennedy, F (Stewart's Coll FP) 1920 *F, W, I, E,* 1921 *E*
Kennedy, N (W of Scotland) 1903 *W, I, E*
Ker, A B M (Kelso) 1988 *W, E*
Ker, H T (Glasgow Acads) 1887 *I, W, E,* 1888 *I,* 1889 *W,* 1890 *I, E*
Kerr, D S (Heriot's FP) 1923 *F, W,* 1924 *F,* 1926 *I, E,* 1927 *W, I, E,* 1928 *I, E*
Kerr, G C (Old Dunelmians, Edinburgh Wands) 1898 *I, E,* 1899 *I, W, E,* 1900 *W, I, E*
Kerr, J M (Heriot's FP) 1935 *NZ,* 1936 *I, E,* 1937 *W, I*
Kerr, R C (Glasgow) 2002 *C, US*
Kerr, W (London Scottish) 1953 *E*
Kidston, D W (Glasgow Acads) 1883 *W, E*
Kidston, W H (W of Scotland) 1874 *E*
Kilgour, I J (RMC Sandhurst) 1921 *F*
King, J H F (Selkirk) 1953 *F, W, E,* 1954 *E*
Kininmonth, P W (Oxford U, Richmond) 1949 *F, W, I, E,* 1950 *F, W, I, E,* 1951 *F, W, I, E, SA,* 1952 *F, W, I,* 1954 *F, NZ, I, E, W*
Kinnear, R M (Heriot's FP) 1926 *F, W, I*
Knox, J (Kelvinside Acads) 1903 *W, I, E*
Kyle, W E (Hawick) 1902 *W, I, E,* 1903 *W, I, E,* 1904 *W, I, E,* 1905 *W, I, E, NZ,* 1906 *W, I, E,* 1908 *E, I,* 1909 *W, I, E,* 1910 *W*

Laidlaw, A S (Hawick) 1897 *I*
Laidlaw, F A L (Melrose) 1965 *F, W, I, E, SA,* 1966 *F, W, I, E, A,* 1967 *F, W, I, E, NZ,* 1968 *F, W, I, A,* 1969 *F, W, I, E, SA,* 1970 *F, W, I, E, A,* 1971 *F, W, I*

Laidlaw, R J (Jedforest) 1980 *I, F, W, E,* 1981 *F, W, E, I, NZ* 1,2, *R, A,* 1982 *E, I, F, W, A* 1,2, 1983 *I, F, W, E, NZ,* 1984 *W, E, I, F, R, A,* 1985 *I, F,* 1986 *F, W, E, I, R,* 1987 *I, F, W, E, [F, R, NZ],* 1988 *I, F, W, E*
Laing, A D (Royal HSFP) 1914 *W, I, E,* 1920 *F, W, I,* 1921 *F*
Lambie, I K (Watsonians) 1978 *NZ* (R), 1979 *W, E, NZ*
Lambie, L B (Glasgow HSFP) 1934 *W, I, E,* 1935 *W, I, E, NZ*
Lamond, G A W (Kelvinside Acads) 1899 *W, E,* 1905 *E*
Laney, B J (Edinburgh) 2001 *NZ,* 2002 *E, It, I, F, W, C, US*
Lang, D (Paisley) 1876 *E,* 1877 *I*
Langrish, R W (London Scottish) 1930 *F,* 1931 *F, W, I*
Lauder, W (Neath) 1969 *I, E, SA,* 1970 *F, W, I, A,* 1973 *F,* 1974 *W, E, I, F,* 1975 *I, F, NZ, A,* 1976 *F,* 1977 *F*
Laughland, I H P (London Scottish) 1959 *F,* 1960 *F, W, I, E,* 1961 *SA, W, I, E,* 1962 *F, W, I, E,* 1963 *F, W, I,* 1964 *F, NZ, W, I, E,* 1965 *F, W, I, E, SA,* 1966 *F, W, I, E,* 1967 *E*
Lawrie, J R (Melrose) 1922 *F, W, I, E,* 1923 *F, W, I, E,* 1924 *W, I, E*
Lawrie, K G (Gala) 1980 *F* (R), *W, E*
Lawson, A J M (Edinburgh Wands, London Scottish) 1972 *F* (R), *E,* 1973 *F,* 1974 *W, E,* 1976 *E, I,* 1977 *E,* 1978 *NZ,* 1979 *W, E, I, F, NZ,* 1980 *W* (R)
Lawther, T H B (Old Millhillians) 1932 *SA, W*
Ledingham, G A (Aberdeen GSFP) 1913 *F*
Lee, D J (London Scottish, Edinburgh) 1998 *I* (R), *F, W, E, Fj, A* 1,2, *SA,* 2001 *Arg*
Lees, J B (Gala) 1947 *I, A,* 1948 *F, W, E*
Leggatt, H T O (Watsonians) 1891 *W, I, E,* 1892 *W, I,* 1893 *W, E,* 1894 *I, E*
Lely, W G (Cambridge U, London Scottish) 1909 *I*
Leslie, D G (Dundee HSFP, W of Scotland, Gala) 1975 *I, F, W, E, NZ, A,* 1976 *F, W, E, I,* 1978 *NZ,* 1980 *E,* 1981 *W, E, I, NZ* 1,2, *R, A,* 1982 *E,* 1983 *I, F, W, E,* 1984 *W, E, I, F, R,* 1985 *F, W, E*
Leslie, J A (Glasgow, Northampton) 1998 *SA,* 1999 *W, E, It, I, F, [SA],* 2000 *It, F, W, US, A, Sm,* 2001 *F, W, E, It, I, Tg, Arg, NZ,* 2002 *F, W*
Leslie, M D (Glasgow, Edinburgh) 1998 *SA* (R), 1999 *W, E, It, I, F, R, [SA, U, Sm, NZ],* 2000 *It, I, F, W, E, NZ* 1,2, 2001 *F, W, E, It,* 2002 *It* (R), *I* (R), *F, W*
Liddell, E H (Edinburgh U) 1922 *F, W, I,* 1923 *F, W, I, E*
Lind, H (Dunfermline) 1928 *I,* 1931 *F, W, I, E,* 1932 *SA, W, E,* 1933 *W, E, I,* 1934 *W, I, E,* 1935 *I,* 1936 *E*
Lindsay, A B (London Hospital) 1910 *I,* 1911 *I*
Lindsay, G C (London Scottish) 1884 *W,* 1885 *I* 1, 1887 *W, E*
Lindsay-Watson, R H (Hawick) 1909 *I*
Lineen, S R P (Boroughmuir) 1989 *W, E, I, F, Fj, R,* 1990 *I, F, W, E, NZ* 1,2, *Arg,* 1991 *F, W, E, I, R, [J, Z, I, E, NZ],* 1992 *E, I, F, W, A* 1,2
Little, A W (Hawick) 1905 *W*
Logan, K M (Stirling County, Wasps) 1992 *A* 2, 1993 *E* (R), *NZ* (t), 1994 *W, E, I, F, Arg* 1,2, *SA,* 1995 *C, I, F, W, E, R, [Iv, Tg, F, NZ], WS,* 1996 *W* (R), *NZ* 1,2, *A, It,* 1997 *W, E, I, F, A,* 1998 *I, F, SA* (R), 1999 *W, E, It, I, F, Arg, R, [SA, U, Sm, NZ],* 2000 *It, I, F, Sm,* 2001 *F, W, E, It,* 2002 *I* (R), *F* (R), *W*
Logan, W R (Edinburgh U, Edinburgh Wands) 1931 *E,* 1932 *SA, W, I,* 1933 *W, E, I,* 1934 *W, I, E,* 1935 *W, I, E, NZ,* 1936 *W, I, E,* 1937 *W, I, E*
Longstaff, S L (Dundee HSFP, Glasgow) 1998 *F* (R), *W, E, Fj, A* 1,2 1999 *It* (R), *I* (R), *Arg* (R), *R, [U* (R), *Sp],* 2000 *It, I, NZ* 1
Lorraine, H D B (Oxford U) 1933 *W, E, I*
Loudoun-Shand, E G (Oxford U) 1913 *E*
Lowe, J D (Heriot's FP) 1934 *W*
Lumsden, I J M (Bath, Watsonians) 1947 *F, W, A,* 1949 *F, W, I, E*
Lyall, G G (Gala) 1947 *A,* 1948 *F, W, I, E*
Lyall, W J C (Edinburgh Acads) 1871 *E*

Mabon, J T (Jedforest) 1898 *I, E,* 1899 *I,* 1900 *I*
Macarthur, J P (Waterloo) 1932 *E*
MacCallum, J C (Watsonians) 1905 *E, NZ,* 1906 *W, I, E, SA,* 1907 *W, I, E,* 1908 *W, I, E,* 1909 *W, I, E,* 1910 *F, W, I, E,* 1911 *F, I, E,* 1912 *F, W, I, E*
McClung, T (Edinburgh Acads) 1956 *I, E,* 1957 *F, I, E,* 1959 *F, W, I,* 1960 *W*
McClure, G B (W of Scotland) 1873 *E*
McClure, J H (W of Scotland) 1872 *E*
McCowan, D (W of Scotland) 1880 *I, E,* 1881 *F, I, E,* 1882 *I, E,* 1883 *I, E,* 1884 *I, E*
McCowat, R H (Glasgow Acads) 1905 *I*

Brendan Laney sets a new Scotland Championship record scoring 24 points in the match against Italy in Rome.

McCrae, I G (Gordonians) 1967 *E*, 1968 *I*, 1969 *F* (R), *W*, 1972 *F, NZ*
McCrow, J W S (Edinburgh Acads) 1921 *I*
Macdonald, A E D (Heriot's FP) 1993 *NZ*
McDonald, C (Jedforest) 1947 *A*
Macdonald, D C (Edinburgh U) 1953 *E, F, W*, 1958 *I, E*
Macdonald, D S M (Oxford U, London Scottish, W of Scotland) 1977 *E, I, F, W*, 1978 *I, W, E*
Macdonald, J D (London Scottish, Army) 1966 *F, W, I, E*, 1967 *F, W, I, E*
Macdonald, J M (Edinburgh Wands) 1911 *W*
Macdonald, J S (Edinburgh U) 1903 *E*, 1904 *W, I, E*, 1905 *W*
Macdonald, K R (Stewart's Coll FP) 1956 *F, W, I*, 1957 *W, I, E*
Macdonald, R (Edinburgh U) 1950 *F, W, I, E*
McDonald, W A (Glasgow U) 1889 *W*, 1892 *I, E*
Macdonald, W G (London Scottish) 1969 *I* (R)
Macdougall, J B (Greenock Wands, Wakefield) 1913 *F*, 1914 *I*, 1921 *F, I, E*
McEwan, M C (Edinburgh Acads) 1886 *E*, 1887 *I, W, E*, 1888 *W, I*, 1889 *W I*, 1890 *W, I, E*, 1891 *W, I, E*, 1892 *E*
MacEwan, N A (Gala, Highland) 1971 *F, W, I, E* (2[1C]), 1972 *F, W, E, NZ*, 1973 *F, W, I, E, P*, 1974 *W, E, I, F*, 1975 *W, E*
McEwan, W M C (Edinburgh Acads) 1894 *W, E*, 1895 *W, E*, 1896 *W, I, E*, 1897 *I, E*, 1898 *I, E*, 1899 *I, W, E*, 1900 *W, E*
MacEwen, R K G (Cambridge U, London Scottish) 1954 *F, NZ, I, W*, 1956 *F, W, I, E*, 1957 *F, W, I, E*, 1958 *W*
Macfadyen, D J H (Glasgow) 2002 *C* (R), *US*
Macfarlan, D J (London Scottish) 1883 *W*, 1884 *W, I, E*, 1886 *W, I*, 1887 *I*, 1888 *I*
McFarlane, J L H (Edinburgh U) 1871 *E*, 1872 *E*, 1873 *E*
McGaughey, S K (Hawick) 1984 *R*
McGeechan, I R (Headingley) 1972 *NZ*, 1973 *F, W, I, E, P*, 1974 *W, E, I, F*, 1975 *I, F, W, E, NZ, A*, 1976 *F, W, E, I*, 1977 *E, I, F, W*, 1978 *I, F, W, NZ*, 1979 *W, E, I, F*
McGlashan, T P L (Royal HSFP) 1947 *F, I, E*, 1954 *F, NZ, I, E, W*
MacGregor, D G (Watsonians, Pontypridd) 1907 *W, I, E*
MacGregor, G (Cambridge U) 1890 *W, I, E*, 1891 *W, I, E*, 1893 *W, I, E*, 1894 *W, I, E*, 1896 *E*
MacGregor, I A A (Hillhead HSFP, Llanelli) 1955 *I, E*, 1956 *F, W, I, E*, 1957 *W, I*
MacGregor, J R (Edinburgh U) 1909 *I*
McGuinness, G M (W of Scotland) 1982 *A* 1,2, 1983 *I*, 1985 *I, F, W, E*
McHarg, A F (W of Scotland, London Scottish) 1968 *I, E, A*, 1969 *F, W, I, E*, 1971 *F, W, I, E* (2[1C]), 1972 *F, E, NZ*, 1973 *F, W, I, E, P*, 1974 *W, E, I, F*, 1975 *I, F, W, E, NZ, A*, 1976 *F, W, E, I*, 1977 *E, I, F, W*, 1978 *F, W, NZ*, 1979 *W, E*
McIlwham, G R (Glasgow Hawks, Glasgow) 1998 *Fj, A* 2(R), 2000 *E* (R), *NZ* 2(R), *US* (R), *A* (R), *Sm* (R), 2001 *F* (R), *W* (R), *E* (R), *It* (R)
McIndoe, F (Glasgow Acads) 1886 *W, I*
MacIntyre, I (Edinburgh Wands) 1890 *W, I, E*, 1891 *W, I, E*
McIvor, D J (Edinburgh Acads) 1992 *E, I, F, W*, 1993 *NZ*, 1994 *SA*
Mackay, E B (Glasgow Acads) 1920 *W*, 1922 *E*
McKeating, E (Heriot's FP) 1957 *F, W*, 1961 *SA, W, I, E*
McKelvey, G (Watsonians) 1997 *A*
McKendrick, J G (W of Scotland) 1889 *I*
Mackenzie, A D G (Selkirk) 1984 *A*
Mackenzie, C J G (United Services) 1921 *E*
Mackenzie, D D (Edinburgh U) 1947 *W, I, E*, 1948 *F, W, I*
Mackenzie, D K A (Edinburgh Wands) 1939 *I, E*
Mackenzie, J M (Edinburgh U) 1905 *NZ*, 1909 *W, I, E*, 1910 *W, I, E*, 1911 *W, I*
McKenzie, K D (Stirling County) 1994 *Arg* 1,2, 1995 *R*, [*Iv*], 1996 *I, F, W, E, NZ* 1,2, *A, It*, 1998 *A* 1(R), 2
Mackenzie, R C (Glasgow Acads) 1877 *I, E*, 1881 *I, E*
Mackie, G Y (Highland) 1975 *A*, 1976 *F, W*, 1978 *F*
MacKinnon, A (London Scottish) 1898 *I, E*, 1899 *I, W, E*, 1900 *E*
Mackintosh, C E W C (London Scottish) 1924 *F*
Mackintosh, H S (Glasgow U, W of Scotland) 1929 *F, W, I, E*, 1930 *F, W, I, E*, 1931 *F, W, I, E*, 1932 *SA, W, I, E*
MacLachlan, L P (Oxford U, London Scottish) 1954 *NZ, I, E, W*
Maclagan, W E (Edinburgh Acads) 1878 *E*, 1879 *I, E*, 1880 *I, E*, 1881 *I, E*, 1882 *I, E*, 1883 *W, I, E*, 1884 *W, I, E*, 1885 *W, I* 1,2, 1887 *I, W, E*, 1888 *W, I*, 1890 *W, I, E*
McLaren, A (Durham County) 1931 *F*

McLaren, E (London Scottish, Royal HSFP) 1923 *F, W, I, E*, 1924 *F*
McLaren, J G (Bourgoin, Glasgow) 1999 *Arg, R*, [*Sp, Sm*], 2000 *It* (R), *F, E, NZ* 1, 2001 *F, W, E* (R), *I, Tg, Arg, NZ*, 2002 *E, It, I, F, W*
McLauchlan, J (Jordanhill) 1969 *E, SA*, 1970 *F, W*, 1971 *F, W, I, E* (2[1C]), 1972 *F, W, E, NZ*, 1973 *F, W, I, E, P*, 1974 *W, E, I, F*, 1975 *I, F, W, E, NZ, A*, 1976 *F, W, E, I*, 1977 *W, 1978 I, F, W, E, NZ*, 1979 *W, E, I, F, NZ*
McLean, D I (Royal HSFP) 1947 *I, E*
Maclennan, W D (Watsonians) 1947 *F, I*
MacLeod, D A (Glasgow U) 1886 *I, E*
MacLeod, G (Edinburgh Acads) 1878 *E*, 1882 *I*
McLeod, H F (Hawick) 1954 *F, NZ, I, E, W*, 1955 *F, W, I, E*, 1956 *F, W, I, E*, 1957 *F, W, I, E*, 1958 *F, W, A, I, E*, 1959 *F, W, I, E*, 1960 *F, W, I, E, SA*, 1961 *F, SA, W, I, E*, 1962 *F, W, I, E*
MacLeod, K G (Cambridge U) 1905 *NZ*, 1906 *W, I, E, SA*,1907 *W, I, E*, 1908 *I, E*
MacLeod, L M (Cambridge U) 1904 *W, I, E*, 1905 *W, I, NZ*
Macleod, W M (Fettesian-Lorettonians, Edinburgh Wands) 1886 *W, I*
McMillan, K H D (Sale) 1953 *F, W, I, E*
MacMillan, R G (London Scottish) 1887 *W, I, E*, 1890 *W, I, E*, 1891 *W, E*, 1892 *W, I, E*, 1893 *W, E*, 1894 *W, I, E*, 1895 *W, I, E*, 1897 *I, E*
MacMyn, D J (Cambridge U, London Scottish) 1925 *F, W, I, E*, 1926 *F, W, I, E*, 1927 *E, A*, 1928 *F*
McNeil, A S B (Watsonians) 1935 *I*
McPartlin, J J (Harlequins, Oxford U) 1960 *F, W*, 1962 *F, W, I, E*
Macphail, J A R (Edinburgh Acads) 1949 *E*, 1951 *SA*
Macpherson, D G (London Hospital) 1910 *I, E*
Macpherson, G P S (Oxford U, Edinburgh Acads) 1922 *F, W, I, E*, 1924 *W, E*, 1925 *F, W, E*, 1927 *F, W, I, E*, 1928 *F, W, E*, 1929 *I, E*, 1930 *F, W, I, E*, 1931 *W, E*, 1932 *SA, E*
Macpherson, N C (Newport) 1920 *W, I, E*, 1921 *F, E*, 1923 *I, E*
McQueen, S B (Waterloo) 1923 *F, W, I, E*
Macrae, D J (St Andrew's U) 1937 *W, I, E*, 1938 *W, I, E*, 1939 *W, I, E*
Madsen, D F (Gosforth) 1974 *W, E, I, F*, 1975 *I, F, W, E*, 1976 *F*, 1977 *E, I, F, W*, 1978 *I*
Mair, N G R (Edinburgh U) 1951 *F, W, I, E*
Maitland, G (Edinburgh Inst FP) 1885 *W, I* 2
Maitland, R (Edinburgh Inst FP) 1881 *E*, 1882 *I, E*, 1884 *W*, 1885 *W*
Maitland, R P (Royal Artillery) 1872 *E*
Malcolm, A G (Glasgow U) 1888 *I*
Manson, J J (Dundee HSFP) 1995 *E* (R)
Marsh, J (Edinburgh Inst FP) 1889 *W, I*
Marshall, A (Edinburgh Acads) 1875 *E*
Marshall, G R (Selkirk) 1988 *A* (R), 1989 *Fj*, 1990 *Arg*, 1991 [*Z*]
Marshall, J C (London Scottish) 1954 *F, NZ, I, E, W*
Marshall, K W (Edinburgh Acads) 1934 *W, I, E*, 1935 *W, I, E*, 1936 *W*, 1937 *E*
Marshall, T R (Edinburgh Acads) 1871 *E*, 1872 *E*, 1873 *E*, 1874 *E*
Marshall, W (Edinburgh Acads) 1872 *E*
Martin, H (Edinburgh Acads, Oxford U) 1908 *W, I, E*, 1909 *W, E*
Masters, W H (Edinburgh Inst FP) 1879 *I*, 1880 *I, E*
Mather, C G (Edinburgh) 1999 *R* (R), [*Sp, Sm* (R)], 2000 *F* (t)
Maxwell, F T (Royal Engineers) 1872 *E*
Maxwell, G H H P (Edinburgh Acads, RAF, London Scottish) 1913 *I, E*, 1914 *W, I, E*, 1920 *W, E*, 1921 *F, W, I, E*, 1922 *F, E*
Maxwell, J M (Langholm) 1957 *I*
Mayer, M J M (Watsonians, Edinburgh) 1998 *SA*, 1999 [*SA* (R), *U, Sp, Sm, NZ*], 2000 *It, I*
Mein, J (Edinburgh Acads) 1871 *E*, 1872 *E*, 1873 *E*, 1874 *E*, 1875 *E*
Melville, C L (Army) 1937 *W, I, E*
Menzies, H F (W of Scotland) 1893 *W, I*, 1894 *W, E*
Metcalfe, G H (Glasgow Hawks, Glasgow) 1998 *A* 1,2, 1999 *W, E, It, I, F, Arg, R*, [*SA, U, Sm, NZ*], 2000 *It, I, F, W, E*, 2001 *I, Tg*, 2002 *E, It, I, F, W* (R), *C, US*
Metcalfe, R (Northampton, Edinburgh) 2000 *E, NZ* 1,2, *US* (R), *A* (R), *Sm*, 2001 *F, W, E*
Methuen, A (London Scottish) 1889 *W, I*
Michie, E J S (Aberdeen U, Aberdeen GSFP) 1954 *F, NZ, I, E*, 1955 *W, I, E*, 1956 *F, W, I, E*, 1957 *F, W, I, E*

Millar, J N (W of Scotland) 1892 *W, I, E*, 1893 *W*, 1895 *I, E*
Millar, R K (London Scottish) 1924 *I*
Millican, J G (Edinburgh U) 1973 *W, I, E*
Milne, C J B (Fettesian-Lorettonians, W of Scotland) 1886 *W, I, E*
Milne, D F (Heriot's FP) 1991 [*J*(R)]
Milne, I G (Heriot's FP, Harlequins) 1979 *I, F, NZ*, 1980 *I, F*, 1981 *NZ* 1,2, *R, A*, 1982 *E, I, F, W, A* 1,2, 1983 *I, F, W, E, NZ*, 1984 *W, E, I, F, W, E*, 1986 *F, W, E, I, F, NZ*, 1987 *I, F, W, E*, [*F, Z, NZ*], 1988 *A*, 1989 *W*, 1990 *NZ* 1,2
Milne, K S (Heriot's FP) 1989 *W, E, I, F, Fj, R*, 1990 *I, F, W, E, NZ* 2, *Arg*, 1991 *F, W* (R), *E*, [*Z*], 1992 *E, I, F, W, A* 1, 1993 *I, F, W, E, NZ*, 1994 *W, E, I, F, SA*, 1995 *C, I, F, W, E*, [*Tg, F, NZ*]
Milne, W M (Glasgow Acads) 1904 *I, E*, 1905 *W, I*
Milroy, E (Watsonians) 1910 *W*, 1911 *E*, 1912 *W, I, E, SA*, 1913 *F, W, I, E*, 1914 *I, E*
Mitchell, G W E (Edinburgh Wands) 1967 *NZ*, 1968 *F, W*
Mitchell, J G (W of Scotland) 1885 *W, I* 1,2
Moir, C C (Northampton) 2000 *W, E, NZ* 1
Moncreiff, F J (Edinburgh Acads) 1871 *E*, 1872 *E*, 1873 *E*
Monteith, H G (Cambridge U, London Scottish) 1905 *E*, 1906 *W, I, E, SA*, 1907 *W, I*, 1908 *E*
Monypenny, D B (London Scottish) 1899 *I, W, E*
Moodie, A R (St Andrew's) 1909 *E*, 1910 *F*, 1911 *F*
Moore, A (Edinburgh Acads) 1990 *NZ* 2, *Arg*, 1991 *F, W, E*
Morgan, D W (Stewart's-Melville FP) 1973 *W, I, E, P*, 1974 *I, F*, 1975 *I, F, W, E, NZ, A*, 1976 *F, W*, 1977 *I, F, W*, 1978 *I, F, W, E*
Morrison, I R (London Scottish) 1993 *I, F, W, E*, 1994 *W, SA*, 1995 *C, I, F, W, E, R*, [*Tg, F, NZ*]
Morrison, M C (Royal HSFP) 1896 *W, I, E*, 1897 *I, E*, 1898 *I, E*, 1899 *I, W, E*, 1900 *W, E*, 1901 *W, I, E*, 1902 *W, I, E*, 1903 *W, I*, 1904 *W, I, E*
Morrison, R H (Edinburgh U) 1886 *W, I, E*
Morrison, W H (Edinburgh Acads) 1900 *W*
Morton, D S (W of Scotland) 1887 *I, W, E*, 1888 *W, I*, 1889 *W, I*, 1890 *I, E*
Mowat, J G (Glasgow Acads) 1883 *W, E*
Mower, A L (Newcastle) 2001 *Tg, Arg, NZ*, 2002 *It*
Muir, D E (Heriot's FP) 1950 *F, W, I, E*, 1952 *W, I, E*
Munnoch, N M (Watsonians) 1952 *F, W, I*
Munro, D S (Glasgow High Kelvinside) 1994 *W, E, I, F, Arg* 1,2, 1997 *W* (R)
Munro, P (Oxford U, London Scottish) 1905 *W, I, E, NZ*, 1906 *W, I, E, SA*, 1907 *I, E*, 1911 *F, W, I*
Munro, R (St Andrew's U) 1871 *E*
Munro, S (Ayr, W of Scotland) 1980 *I, F*, 1981 *F, W, E, I, NZ* 1,2, *R*, 1984 *W*
Munro, W H (Glasgow HSFP) 1947 *I, E*
Murdoch, W C W (Hillhead HSFP) 1935 *E, NZ*, 1936 *W, I*, 1939 *E*, 1948 *F, W, I, E*
Murray, C A (Hawick, Edinburgh) 1998 *E* (R), *Fj, A* 1,2, *SA*, 1999 *W, E, It, I, F, Arg*, [*SA, U, Sp, Sm, NZ*], 2000 *NZ* 2, *US, A, Sm*, 2001 *F, W, E, It* (R), *Tg, Arg*
Murray, G M (Glasgow Acads) 1921 *I*, 1926 *W*
Murray, H M (Glasgow U) 1936 *W, I*
Murray, K T (Hawick) 1985 *I, F, W*
Murray, R O (Cambridge U) 1935 *W, E*
Murray, S (Bedford, Saracens) 1997 *A, SA*, 1998 *It, Fj, A* 1,2, *SA*, 1999 *W, E, It, I, F, Arg, R*, [*SA, U, Sm, NZ*], 2000 *It, I, F, W, E, NZ* 1, *US, A, Sm*, 2001 *F, W, E, It, I, Tg, Arg, NZ*, 2002 *E, It, I, F, W*
Murray, W A K (London Scottish) 1920 *F, I*, 1921 *F*

Napier, H M (W of Scotland) 1877 *I, E*, 1878 *E*, 1879 *I, E*
Neill, J B (Edinburgh Acads) 1963 *E*, 1964 *F, NZ, W, I, E*, 1965 *F*
Neill, R M (Edinburgh Acads) 1901 *E*, 1902 *I*
Neilson, G T (W of Scotland) 1891 *W, I, E*, 1892 *W, E*, 1893 *W*, 1894 *W, I*, 1895 *W, I, E*, 1896 *W, I, E*
Neilson, J A (Glasgow Acads) 1878 *E*, 1879 *E*
Neilson, R T (W of Scotland) 1898 *I, E*, 1899 *I, W*, 1900 *I, E*
Neilson, T (W of Scotland) 1874 *E*
Neilson, W (Merchiston, Cambridge U, London Scottish) 1891 *W, E*, 1892 *W, I, E*, 1893 *I, E*, 1894 *E*, 1895 *W, I, E*, 1896 *I*, 1897 *I, E*
Neilson, W G (Merchistonians) 1894 *E*
Nelson, J B (Glasgow Acads) 1925 *F, W, I, E*, 1926 *F, W, I, E*, 1927 *F, W, I, E*, 1928 *I, E*, 1929 *F, W, I, E*, 1930 *F, W, I, E*, 1931 *F, W, I*
Nelson, T A (Oxford U) 1898 *E*
Nichol, J A (Royal HSFP) 1955 *W, I, E*

Nichol, S A (Selkirk) 1994 *Arg* 2(R)
Nicol, A D (Dundee HSFP, Bath, Glasgow) 1992 *E, I, F, W, A* 1,2, 1993 *NZ*, 1994 *W*, 1997 *A, SA*, 2000 *I* (R), *F, W, E, NZ* 1,2, 2001 *F, W, E, I* (R), *Tg, Arg, NZ*
Nimmo, C S (Watsonians) 1920 *E*

Ogilvy, C (Hawick) 1911 *I, E*, 1912 *I*
Oliver, G H (Hawick) 1987 [*Z*], 1990 *NZ* 2(R), 1991 [*Z*]
Oliver, G K (Gala) 1970 *A*
Orr, C E (W of Scotland) 1887 *I, E, W*, 1888 *W, I*, 1889 *W, I*, 1890 *W, I, E*, 1891 *W, I, E*, 1892 *W, I, E*
Orr, H J (London Scottish) 1903 *W, I, E*, 1904 *W, I*
Orr, J E (W of Scotland) 1889 *I*, 1890 *W, I, E*, 1891 *W, I, E*, 1892 *W, I, E*, 1893 *I, E*
Orr, J H (Edinburgh City Police) 1947 *F, W*
Osler, F L (Edinburgh U) 1911 *F, W*

Park, J (Royal HSFP) 1934 *W*
Paterson, C D (Edinburgh) 1999 [*Sp*], 2000 *F, W, E, NZ* 1,2, *US, A, Sm*, 2001 *F, W, E, It, I, NZ*, 2002 *E, It, I, F, W, C, US*
Paterson, D S (Gala) 1969 *SA*, 1970 *I, E, A*, 1971 *F, W, I, E* (2[1C]), 1972 *W*
Paterson, G Q (Edinburgh Acads) 1876 *E*
Paterson, J R (Birkenhead Park) 1925 *F, W, I, E*, 1926 *F, W, I, E*, 1927 *F, W, I, E, A*, 1928 *F, W, I, E*, 1929 *F, W, I, E*
Patterson, D (Hawick) 1896 *W*
Patterson, D W (West Hartlepool) 1994 *SA*, 1995 [*Tg*]
Pattullo, G L (Panmure) 1920 *F, W, I, E*
Paxton, I A M (Selkirk) 1981 *NZ* 1,2, *R, A*, 1982 *E, I, F, W, A* 1,2, 1983 *I, E, NZ*, 1984 *W, E, I, F*, 1985 *I* (R), *F, W, E*, 1986 *W, E, I, R*, 1987 *I, F, W, E*, [*F, Z, R, NZ*], 1988 *I, F, E, A*
Paxton, R E (Kelso) 1982 *I, A* 2(R)
Pearson, J (Watsonians) 1909 *I, E*, 1910 *F, W, I, E*, 1911 *F*, 1912 *F, W, SA*, 1913 *I, E*
Pender, I M (London Scottish) 1914 *E*
Pender, N E K (Hawick) 1977 *I*, 1978 *F, W, E*
Penman, W M (RAF) 1939 *I*
Peterkin, W A (Edinburgh U) 1881 *E*, 1883 *I*, 1884 *W, I, E*, 1885 *W, I* 1,2
Peters, E W (Bath) 1995 *C, I, F, W, E, R*, [*Tg, F, NZ*], 1996 *I, W, E, NZ* 1,2, *A, It*, 1997 *A, SA*, 1998 *W, E, Fj, A* 1,2, *SA*, 1999 *W, E, It, I*
Petrie, A G (Royal HSFP) 1873 *E*, 1874 *E*, 1875 *E*, 1876 *E*, 1877 *I, E*, 1878 *E*, 1879 *I, E*, 1880 *I, E*
Petrie, J M (Glasgow) 2000 *NZ* 2, *US, A, Sm*, 2001 *F, W, It* (R), *I* (R), *Tg, Arg*, 2002 *F* (t), *W* (R), *C*
Philp, A (Edinburgh Inst FP) 1882 *E*
Pocock, E I (Edinburgh Wands) 1877 *I, E*
Pollock, J A (Gosforth) 1982 *W*, 1983 *E, NZ*, 1984 *E* (R), *I, F, R*, 1985 *F*
Polson, A H (Gala) 1930 *E*
Pountney, A C (Northampton) 1998 *SA*, 1999 *W* (t+R), *E* (R), *It* (t+R), *I* (R), *F, Arg*, [*SA, U, Sm, NZ*], 2000 *It, I, F, W, E, NZ* 1, *US, A, Sm*, 2001 *F, W, E, It, I*, 2002 *E, I, F, W*
Proudfoot, M C (Melrose) 1998 *Fj, A* 1,2
Purdie, W (Jedforest) 1939 *W, I, E*
Purves, A B H L (London Scottish) 1906 *W, I, E, SA*, 1907 *W, I, E*, 1908 *W, I, E*
Purves, W D C L (London Scottish) 1912 *F, W, I, SA*, 1913 *I, E*

Rea, C W W (W of Scotland, Headingley) 1968 *A*, 1969 *F, W, I, SA*, 1970 *F, W, I, A*, 1971 *F, W, E* (2[1C])
Redpath, B W (Melrose, Narbonne, Sale) 1993 *NZ* (t), 1994 *E* (t), *F, Arg* 1,2, 1995 *C, I, F, W, E, R*, [*Iv, F, NZ*], *WS*, 1996 *I, F, W, E, A* (R), *It*, 1997 *I, E, F, Fj, A* 1,2, *SA*, 1999 *R* (R), [*U* (R), *Sp*], 2000 *It, I, US, A, Sm*, 2001 *F* (R), *E* (R), *It, I*, 2002 *E, It, I, F, W*
Reed, A I (Bath, Wasps) 1993 *I, F, W, E*, 1994 *E, I, F, Arg* 1,2, *SA*, 1996 *It*, 1997 *W, E, I, F*, 1999 *It* (R), *F* (R), [*Sp*]
Reid, C (Edinburgh Acads) 1881 *I, E*, 1882 *I, E*, 1883 *W, I, E*, 1884 *W, I, E*, 1885 *W, I* 1,2, 1886 *W, I, E*, 1887 *I, W, E*, 1888 *W, I*
Reid, J (Edinburgh Wands) 1874 *E*, 1875 *E*, 1876 *E*, 1877 *I, E*
Reid, J M (Edinburgh Acads) 1898 *I, E*, 1899 *I*
Reid, M F (Loretto) 1883 *I, E*
Reid, R E (Glasgow) 2001 *Tg* (R), *Arg*
Reid, S J (Boroughmuir, Leeds, Narbonne) 1995 *WS*, 1999 *F, Arg*, [*Sp*], 2000 *It* (t), *F, W, E* (t)
Reid-Kerr, J (Greenock Wand) 1909 *E*
Relph, W K L (Stewart's Coll FP) 1955 *F, W, I, E*
Renny-Tailyour, H W (Royal Engineers) 1872 *E*

Renwick, J M (Hawick) 1972 *F, W, E, NZ*, 1973 *F*, 1974 *W, E, I, F*, 1975 *I, F, W, E, NZ, A*, 1976 *F, W, E* (R), 1977 *I, F, W*, 1978 *I, F, W, E, NZ*, 1979 *W, E, I, F, NZ*, 1980 *I, F, W, E*, 1981 *F, W, E, I, NZ* 1,2, *R, A*, 1982 *E, I, F, W*, 1983 *I, F, W, E*, 1984 *R*
Renwick, W L (London Scottish) 1989 *R*
Renwick, W N (London Scottish, Edinburgh Wands) 1938 *E*, 1939 *W*
Richardson, J F (Edinburgh Acads) 1994 *SA*
Ritchie, G (Merchistonians) 1871 *E*
Ritchie, G F (Dundee HSFP) 1932 *E*
Ritchie, J M (Watsonians) 1933 *W, E, I*, 1934 *W, I, E*
Ritchie, W T (Cambridge U) 1905 *I, E*
Robb, G H (Glasgow U) 1881 *I*, 1885 *W*
Roberts, G (Watsonians) 1938 *W, I, E*, 1939 *W, E*
Robertson, A H (W of Scotland) 1871 *E*
Robertson, A W (Edinburgh Acads) 1897 *E*
Robertson, D (Edinburgh Acads) 1875 *E*
Robertson, D D (Cambridge U) 1893 *W*
Robertson, I (London Scottish, Watsonians) 1968 *E*, 1969 *E, SA*, 1970 *F, W, I, E, A*
Robertson, I P M (Watsonians) 1910 *F*
Robertson, J (Clydesdale) 1908 *E*
Robertson, K W (Melrose) 1978 *NZ*, 1979 *W, E, I, F, NZ*, 1980 *W, E*, 1981 *F, W, E, I, R, A*, 1982 *E, I, F, A* 1,2, 1983 *I, F, W, E*, 1984 *E, I, F, R, A*, 1985 *I, F, W, E*, 1986 *I, F, W, E*, 1987 *F* (R), *W, E, [F, Z, NZ]*, 1988 *E, A*, 1989 *I, F*
Robertson, L (London Scottish United Services) 1908 *E*, 1911 *W*, 1912 *W, I, E, SA*, 1913 *W, I, E*
Robertson, M A (Gala) 1958 *F*
Robertson, R D (London Scottish) 1912 *F*
Robson, A (Hawick) 1954 *F*, 1955 *F, W, I, E*, 1956 *F, W, I, E*, 1957 *F, W, I, E*, 1958 *W, A, I, E*, 1959 *F, W, I, E*, 1960 *F*
Rodd, J A T (United Services, RN, London Scottish) 1958 *F, W, A, I, E*, 1960 *F, W*, 1962 *F*, 1964 *F, NZ, W*, 1965 *F, W, I*
Rogerson, J (Kelvinside Acads) 1894 *W*
Roland, E T (Edinburgh Acads) 1884 *I, E*
Rollo, D M D (Howe of Fife) 1959 *F*, 1960 *F, W, I, E, SA*, 1961 *F, SA, W, I, E*, 1962 *F, W, E*, 1963 *F, W, I, E*, 1964 *F, NZ, W, I, E*, 1965 *F, W, I, E, SA*, 1966 *F, W, I, E, A*, 1967 *F, W, E, NZ*, 1968 *F, W, I*
Rose, D M (Jedforest) 1951 *F, W, I, E, SA*, 1953 *F, W*
Ross, A (Kilmarnock) 1924 *F, W*
Ross, A (Royal HSFP) 1905 *W, I, E*, 1909 *W, I*
Ross, A R (Edinburgh U) 1911 *W*, 1914 *W, I, E*
Ross, E J (London Scottish) 1904 *W*
Ross, G (Edinburgh) 2001 *Tg*
Ross, G T (Watsonians) 1954 *NZ, I, E, W*
Ross, I A (Hillhead HSFP) 1951 *F, W, I, E*
Ross, J (London Scottish) 1901 *W, I, E*, 1902 *W*, 1903 *E*
Ross, K I (Boroughmuir FP) 1961 *SA, W, I, E*, 1962 *F, W, I, E*, 1963 *F, W, E*
Ross, W A (Hillhead HSFP) 1937 *W, E*
Rottenburg, H (Cambridge U, London Scottish) 1899 *W, E*, 1900 *W, I, E*
Roughead, W N (Edinburgh Acads, London Scottish) 1927 *A*, 1928 *F, W, I, E*, 1930 *I, E*, 1931 *F, W, I, E*, 1932 *W*
Rowan, N A (Boroughmuir) 1980 *W, E*, 1981 *F, W, E, I*, 1984 *R*, 1985 *I*, 1987 *[R]*, 1988 *I, F, W, E*
Rowand, R (Glasgow HSFP) 1930 *F, W*, 1932 *E*, 1933 *W, E, I*, 1934 *W*
Roxburgh, A J (Kelso) 1997 *A*, 1998 *It, F* (R), *W, E, Fj, A* 1(R),2(R)
Roy, A (Waterloo) 1938 *W, I, E*, 1939 *W, I, E*
Russell, R R (Saracens) 1999 *R, [U* (R), *Sp, Sm* (R), *NZ* (R)], 2000 *I* (R), 2001 *F* (R), 2002 *F* (R), *W* (R)
Russell, W L (Glasgow Acads) 1905 *NZ*, 1906 *W, I, E*
Rutherford, J Y (Selkirk) 1979 *W, E, I, F, NZ*, 1980 *I, F, E*, 1981 *F, W, E, I, NZ* 1,2, 1982 *E, I, F, W, A* 1,2, 1983 *E, NZ*, 1984 *W, E, I, F, R*, 1985 *I, F, W, E*, 1986 *F, W, E, I, R*, 1987 *F, W, E, [F]*

Sampson, R W F (London Scottish) 1939 *W*, 1947 *W*
Sanderson, G A (Royal HSFP) 1907 *W, I, E*, 1908 *I*
Sanderson, J L P (Edinburgh Acads) 1873 *E*
Schulze, D G (London Scottish) 1905 *E*, 1907 *I, E*, 1908 *W, I, E*, 1909 *W, I, E*, 1910 *W, I, E*, 1911 *W, E*
Scobie, R M (Royal Military Coll) 1914 *W, I, E*
Scotland, K J F (Heriot's FP, Cambridge U, Leicester) 1957 *F, W, I, E*, 1958 *E*, 1959 *F, W, I, E*, 1960 *F, W, I, E*, 1961 *F, SA, W, I, E*, 1962 *F, W, I, E*, 1963 *F, W, I, E*, 1965 *F*
Scott, D M (Langholm, Watsonians) 1950 *I, E*, 1951 *W, I, E*, 1952 *F, W, I*, 1953 *F*

Scott, J M B (Edinburgh Acads) 1907 *E*, 1908 *W, I, E*, 1909 *W, I, E*, 1910 *F, W, I, E*, 1911 *F, W, I*, 1912 *W, I, E, SA*, 1913 *W, I, E*
Scott, J S (St Andrew's U) 1950 *E*
Scott, J W (Stewart's Coll FP) 1925 *F, W, I, E*, 1926 *F, W, I, E*, 1927 *F, W, I, E, A*, 1928 *F, W, E*, 1929 *E*, 1930 *F*
Scott, M (Dunfermline) 1992 *A* 2
Scott, R (Hawick) 1898 *I*, 1900 *I, E*
Scott, S (Edinburgh, Borders) 2000 *NZ* 2 (R), *US* (t+R), 2001 *It* (R), *I* (R), *Tg* (R), *NZ* (R), 2002 *US* (R)
Scott, T (Langholm, Hawick) 1896 *W*, 1897 *I, E*, 1898 *I, E*, 1899 *I, E*, 1900 *W, I, E*
Scott, T M (Hawick) 1893 *E*, 1895 *W, I, E*, 1896 *W, E*, 1897 *I, E*, 1898 *I, E*, 1900 *W, I*
Scott, W P (W of Scotland) 1900 *I, E*, 1902 *I, E*, 1903 *W, I, E*, 1904 *W, I, E*, 1905 *W, I, E, NZ*, 1906 *W, I, E, SA*, 1907 *W, I, E*
Scoular, J G (Cambridge U) 1905 *NZ*, 1906 *W, I, E, SA*
Selby, J A R (Watsonians) 1920 *W, I*
Shackleton, J A P (London Scottish) 1959 *E*, 1963 *F, W*, 1964 *NZ, W*, 1965 *I, SA*
Sharp, A V (Bristol) 1994 *E, I, F, Arg* 1,2 *SA*
Sharp, G (Stewart's FP, Army) 1960 *F*, 1964 *F, NZ, W*
Shaw, G D (Sale) 1935 *NZ*, 1936 *W*, 1937 *W, I, E*, 1939 *I*
Shaw, I (Glasgow HSFP) 1937 *I*
Shaw, J N (Edinburgh Acads) 1921 *W, I*
Shaw, R W (Glasgow HSFP) 1934 *W, I, E*, 1935 *W, I, E, NZ*, 1936 *W, I, E*, 1937 *W, I, E*, 1938 *W, I, E*, 1939 *W, I, E*
Shedden, D (W of Scotland) 1972 *NZ*, 1973 *F, W, I, E, P*, 1976 *W, E, I*, 1977 *I, F, W*, 1978 *I, F, W*
Shepherd, R J S (Melrose) 1995 *WS*, 1996 *I, F, W, E, NZ* 1,2, *A, It*, 1997 *W, E, I, F, SA*, 1998 *It, I, W* (R), *Fj* (t), *A* 1,2
Shiel, A G (Melrose, Edinburgh) 1991 *[I* (R), *WS*], 1993 *I, F, W, E, NZ*, 1994 *Arg* 1,2, *SA*, 1995 *R, [Iv, F, NZ]*, *WS*, 2000 *I, NZ* 1(R),2
Shillinglaw, R B (Gala, Army) 1960 *I, E, SA*, 1961 *F, SA*
Simmers, B M (Glasgow Acads) 1965 *F, W*, 1966 *A*, 1967 *F, W, I*, 1971 *F* (R)
Simmers, W M (Glasgow Acads) 1926 *W, I, E*, 1927 *F, W, I, E, A*, 1928 *F, W, I, E*, 1929 *F, W, I, E*, 1930 *F, W, I, E*, 1931 *F, W, I, E*, 1932 *SA, W, I, E*
Simpson, G L (Kirkcaldy, Glasgow) 1998 *A* 1,2, 1999 *Arg* (R), *R, [SA, U, Sm, NZ]*, 2000 *It, I, NZ* 1(R), 2001 *I, Tg* (R), *Arg* (R), *NZ*
Simpson, J W (Royal HSFP) 1893 *I, E*, 1894 *W, I, E*, 1895 *W, I, E*, 1896 *W, I*, 1897 *E*, 1899 *W, E*
Simpson, R S (Glasgow Acads) 1923 *I*
Simson, E D (Edinburgh U, London Scottish) 1902 *E*, 1903 *W, I, E*, 1904 *W, I, E*, 1905 *W, I, E, NZ*, 1906 *W, I, E*, 1907 *W, I, E*
Simson, J T (Watsonians) 1905 *NZ*, 1909 *W, I*, 1910 *F, W, I*, 1911 *I*
Simson, R F (London Scottish) 1911 *E*
Sloan, A T (Edinburgh Acads) 1914 *W, I*, 1920 *F, W, I, E*, 1921 *F, W, I, E*
Sloan, D A (Edinburgh Acads, London Scottish) 1950 *F, W, E*, 1951 *W, I, E*, 1953 *F*
Sloan, T (Glasgow Acads, Oxford U) 1905 *NZ*, 1906 *W, SA*, 1907 *W, E*, 1908 *W*, 1909 *I*
Smeaton, P W (Edinburgh Acads) 1881 *I*, 1883 *I, E*
Smith, A R (Oxford U) 1895 *W, I, E*, 1896 *W, I*, 1897 *I, E*, 1898 *I, E*, 1900 *I, E*
Smith, A R (Cambridge U, Gosforth, Ebbw Vale, Edinburgh Wands) 1955 *W, I, E*, 1956 *F, W, I, E*, 1957 *F, W, I, E*, 1958 *F, W, A, I*, 1959 *F, W, I, E*, 1960 *F, W, I, E, SA*, 1961 *F, SA, W, I, E*, 1962 *F, W, I, E*
Smith, C J (Edinburgh) 2002 *C, US* (R)
Smith, D W C (London Scottish) 1949 *F, W, I, E*, 1950 *F, W, I*, 1953 *I*
Smith, E R (Edinburgh Acads) 1879 *I*
Smith, G K (Kelso) 1957 *I, E*, 1958 *F, W, A*, 1959 *F, W, I, E*, 1960 *F, W, I, E*, 1961 *F, SA, W, I, E*
Smith, H O (Watsonians) 1895 *W*, 1896 *W, I, E*, 1898 *I, E*, 1899 *W, I, E*, 1900 *E*, 1902 *E*
Smith, I R (Gloucester, Moseley) 1992 *E, I, W, A* 1,2, 1994 *E* (R), *I, F, Arg* 1,2, 1995 *[Iv]*, *WS*, 1996 *I, F, W, E, NZ* 1,2, *A, It*, 1997 *E, I, F, A, SA*
Smith, I S (Oxford U, Edinburgh U) 1924 *W, I, E*, 1925 *F, W, I, E*, 1926 *F, W, I, E*, 1927 *F, I, E*, 1929 *F, W, I, E*, 1930 *F, W, I*, 1931 *F, W, I, E*, 1932 *SA, W, I, E*, 1933 *W, E, I*
Smith I S G (London Scottish) 1969 *SA*, 1970 *F, W, I, E*, 1971 *F, W, E*
Smith, M A (London Scottish) 1970 *W, I, E, A*

Smith, R T (Kelso) 1929 *F, W, I, E*, 1930 *F, W, I*
Smith, S H (Glasgow Acads) 1877 *I*, 1878 *E*
Smith, T J (Gala) 1983 *E, NZ*, 1985 *I, F*
Smith T J (Watsonians, Dundee HSFP, Glasgow, Brive, Northampton) 1997 *E, I, F*, 1998 *SA*, 1999 *W, E, It, I, Arg, R, [SA, U, Sm, NZ]*, 2000 *It, I, F, W, E, NZ* 1,2, *US, A, Sm*, 2001 *F, W, E, It, I, Tg, Arg, NZ*, 2002 *E, It, I, F, W*
Sole, D M B (Bath, Edinburgh Acads) 1986 *F, W*, 1987 *I, F, W, E, [F, Z, R, NZ]*, 1988 *I, F, W, E, A*, 1989 *W, E, I, F, Fj, R*, 1990 *I, F, W, E, NZ* 1,2, *Arg*, 1991 *F, W, E, I, R, [J, I, WS, E, NZ]*, 1992 *E, I, F, W, A* 1,2
Somerville, D (Edinburgh Inst FP) 1879 *I*, 1882 *I*, 1883 *W, I, E*, 1884 *W*
Speirs, L M (Watsonians) 1906 *SA*, 1907 *W, I, E*, 1908 *W, I, E*, 1910 *F, W, E*
Spence, K M (Oxford U) 1953 *I*
Spencer, E (Clydesdale) 1898 *I*
Stagg, P K (Sale) 1965 *F, W, E, SA*, 1966 *F, W, I, E, A*, 1967 *F, W, I, E, NZ*, 1968 *F, W, I, E, A*, 1969 *F, W, I* (R), *SA*, 1970 *F, W, I, E, A*
Stanger, A G (Hawick) 1989 *Fj, R*, 1990 *I, F, W, E, NZ* 1,2, *Arg*, 1991 *F, W, E, I, R, [J, Z, I, WS, E, NZ]*, 1992 *E, I, F, W, A* 1,2, 1993 *I, F, W, E, NZ*, 1994 *W, E, I, F, SA*, 1995 *R, [Iv]*, 1996 *NZ* 2, *A, It*, 1997 *W, E, I, F, A, SA*, 1998 *It, I* (R), *F, W, E*
Stark, D A (Boroughmuir, Melrose, Glasgow Hawks) 1993 *I, F, W, E*, 1996 *NZ* 2(R), *It* (R), 1997 *W* (R), *E, SA*
Steel, J F (Glasgow) 2000 *US, A*, 2001 *I, Tg, NZ*
Steele, W C C (Langholm, Bedford, RAF, London Scottish) 1969 *E*, 1971 *F, W, I, E* (2[1C]), 1972 *F, W, E, NZ*, 1973 *F, W, I, E*, 1975 *I, F, W, E, NZ* (R), 1976 *W, E, I*, 1977 *E*
Stephen, A E (W of Scotland) 1885 *W*, 1886 *I*
Steven, P D (Heriot's FP) 1984 *A*, 1985 *F, W, E*
Steven, R (Edinburgh Wands) 1962 *I*
Stevenson, A K (Glasgow Acads) 1922 *F*, 1923 *F, W, E*
Stevenson, A M (Glasgow U) 1911 *F*
Stevenson, G D (Hawick) 1956 *E*, 1957 *F*, 1958 *F, W, A, I, E*, 1959 *W, I, E*, 1960 *W, I, E, SA*, 1961 *F, SA, W, I, E*, 1963 *F, W, I*, 1964 *E*, 1965 *F*
Stevenson, H J (Edinburgh Acads) 1888 *W, I*, 1889 *W, I*, 1890 *W, I, E*, 1891 *W, I, E*, 1892 *W, I, E*, 1893 *I, E*
Stevenson, L E (Edinburgh U) 1888 *W*
Stevenson, R C (London Scottish) 1897 *I, E*, 1898 *E*, 1899 *I, W, E*
Stevenson, R C (St Andrew's U) 1910 *F, I, E*, 1911 *F, W, I*
Stevenson, W H (Glasgow Acads) 1925 *F*
Stewart, A K (Edinburgh U) 1874 *E*, 1876 *E*
Stewart, A M (Edinburgh Acads) 1914 *W*
Stewart, B D (Edinburgh Acads, Edinburgh) 1996 *NZ* 2, *A*, 2000 *NZ* 1,2
Stewart, C A R (W of Scotland) 1880 *I, E*
Stewart, C E B (Kelso) 1960 *W*, 1961 *F*
Stewart, J (Glasgow HSFP) 1930 *F*
Stewart, J L (Edinburgh Acads) 1921 *I*
Stewart M J (Northampton) 1996 *It*, 1997 *W, E, I, F, A, SA*, 1998 *It, I, F, W, Fj* (R), 2000 *It, I, F, W, E, NZ* 1(R), 2001 *F, W, E, It, I, Tg, Arg, NZ*, 2002 *E, It, I, F, W, C, US*
Stewart, M S (Stewart's Coll FP) 1932 *SA, W, I*, 1933 *W, E, I*, 1934 *W, I, E*
Stewart, W A (London Hospital) 1913 *F, W, I*, 1914 *W*
Steyn, S S L (Oxford U) 1911 *E*, 1912 *I*
Strachan, G M (Jordanhill) 1971 *E* (C) (R), 1973 *W, I, E, P*
Stronach, R S (Glasgow Acads) 1901 *W, E*, 1905 *W, I, E*
Stuart, C D (W of Scotland) 1909 *I*, 1910 *F, W, I, E*, 1911 *I, E*
Stuart, L M (Glasgow HSFP) 1923 *F, W, I, E*, 1924 *F*, 1928 *E*, 1930 *I, E*
Suddon, N (Hawick) 1965 *W, I, E, SA*, 1966 *A*, 1968 *E, A*, 1969 *F, W, I*, 1970 *I, E, A*
Sutherland, W R (Hawick) 1910 *W, E*, 1911 *F, E*, 1912 *F, W, E, SA*, 1913 *F, W, I, E*, 1914 *W*
Swan, J S (Army, London Scottish, Leicester) 1953 *E*, 1954 *F, NZ, I, E, W*, 1955 *F, W, I, E*, 1956 *F, W, I, E*, 1957 *F, W*, 1958 *F*
Swan, M W (Oxford U, London Scottish) 1958 *F, W, A, I, E*, 1959 *F, W, I*
Sweet, J B (Glasgow HSFP) 1913 *E*, 1914 *I*
Symington, A W (Cambridge U) 1914 *W, E*

Tait, A V (Kelso, Newcastle, Edinburgh) 1987 *[F(R), Z, R, NZ]*, 1988 *I, F, W, E*, 1997 *I, F, A*, 1998 *It, I, F, W, E, SA*, 1999 *W* (R), *E, It, I, F, Arg, R, [A, U, NZ]*
Tait, J G (Edinburgh Acads) 1880 *I*, 1885 *I* 2
Tait, P W (Royal HSFP) 1935 *E*

Taylor, E G (Oxford U) 1927 *W, A*
Taylor, R C (Kelvinside-West) 1951 *W, I, E, SA*
Taylor, S M (Edinburgh) 2000 *US, A*, 2001 *E, It, I, NZ* (R), 2002 *E, It, I, F, W, C, US*
Telfer, C M (Hawick) 1968 *A*, 1969 *F, W, I, E*, 1972 *F, W, E*, 1973 *W, I, E, P*, 1974 *W, E, I*, 1975 *A*, 1976 *F*
Telfer, J W (Melrose) 1964 *F, NZ, W, I, E*, 1965 *F, W, I*, 1966 *F, W, I, E*, 1967 *W, I, E*, 1968 *E, A*, 1969 *F, W, I, E, SA*, 1970 *F, W, I*
Tennent, J M (W of Scotland) 1909 *W, I, E*, 1910 *F, W, E*
Thom, D A (London Scottish) 1934 *W*, 1935 *W, I, E, NZ*
Thom, G (Kirkcaldy) 1920 *F, W, I, E*
Thom, J R (Watsonians) 1933 *W, E, I*
Thomson, A E (United Services) 1921 *F, W, E*
Thomson, A M (St Andrew's U) 1949 *I*
Thomson, B E (Oxford U) 1953 *F, W, I*
Thomson, I H M (Heriot's FP, Army) 1951 *W, I*, 1952 *F, W, I*, 1953 *I, E*
Thomson, J S (Glasgow Acads) 1871 *E*
Thomson, R H (London Scottish, PUC) 1960 *I, E, SA*, 1961 *F, SA, W, I, E*, 1963 *F, W, I, E*, 1964 *F, NZ, W*
Thomson, W H (W of Scotland) 1906 *SA*
Thomson, W J (W of Scotland) 1899 *W, E*, 1900 *W*
Timms, A B (Edinburgh U, Edinburgh Wands) 1896 *W*, 1900 *W, I*, 1901 *W, I, E*, 1902 *W, E*, 1903 *W, E*, 1904 *I, E*, 1905 *I, E*
Tod, H B (Gala) 1911 *F*
Tod, J (Watsonians) 1884 *W, I, E*, 1885 *W, I* 1,2, 1886 *W, I, E*
Todd, J K (Glasgow Acads) 1874 *E*, 1875 *E*
Tolmie, J M (Glasgow HSFP) 1922 *E*
Tomes, A J (Hawick) 1976 *E, I*, 1977 *E*, 1978 *I, F, W, E, NZ*, 1979 *W, E, I, F, NZ*, 1980 *F, W, E*, 1981 *F, W, E, I, NZ* 1,2, *R*, 1982 *E, I, F, W, A* 1,2, 1983 *I, F, W*, 1984 *W, E, I, F, R, A*, 1985 *W, E*, 1987 *I, F, E* (R), *[F, Z, R, NZ]*
Torrie, T J (Edinburgh Acads) 1877 *E*
Townsend, G P J (Gala, Northampton, Brive, Castres) 1993 *E* (R), 1994 *W, E, I, F, Arg* 1,2, 1995 *C, I, F, W, E, WS*, 1996 *I, F, W, E, NZ* 1,2, *A, It*, 1997 *W, I, E, A, SA*, 1998 *I, F, W, E, Fj, A* 1,2, *SA* (R), 1999 *W, E, It, I, F, [SA, U, Sp* (R), *Sm, NZ]*, 2000 *It, I, F, W, E, NZ* 1,2, *US, A, Sm*, 2001 *F, It, I, Arg, NZ*, 2002 *E, It, I, F, W*
Tukalo, I (Selkirk) 1985 *I*, 1987 *I, F, W, E, [F, Z, R, NZ]*, 1988 *F, W, E, A*, 1989 *W, E, I, F, Fj*, 1990 *I, F, W, E, NZ* 1, 1991 *I, R, [J, Z, I, WS, E, NZ]*, 1992 *E, I, F, W, A* 1,2
Turk, A S (Langholm) 1971 *E* (R)
Turnbull, D J (Hawick) 1987 *[NZ]*, 1988 *F, E*, 1990 *E* (R), 1991 *F, W, E, I, R, [Z]*, 1993 *I, F, W, E*, 1994 *W*
Turnbull, F O (Kelso) 1951 *F, SA*
Turnbull, G O (W of Scotland) 1896 *I, E*, 1897 *I, E*, 1904 *W*
Turnbull, P (Edinburgh Acads) 1901 *W, I, E*, 1902 *W, I, E*
Turner, F H (Oxford U, Liverpool) 1911 *F, W, I, E*, 1912 *F, W, I, E, SA*, 1913 *F, W, I, E*, 1914 *I, E*
Turner, J W C (Gala) 1966 *W, A*, 1967 *F, W, I, E, NZ*, 1968 *F, W, I, E, A*, 1969 *F, W, I, E* (2[1C])

Usher, C M (United Services, Edinburgh Wands) 1912 *E*, 1913 *F, W, I, E*, 1914 *E*, 1920 *F, W, I, E*, 1921 *W, E*, 1922 *F, W, I, E*

Valentine, A R (RNAS, Anthorn) 1953 *F, W, I*
Valentine, D D (Hawick) 1947 *I, E*
Veitch, J P (Royal HSFP) 1882 *E*, 1883 *I*, 1884 *W, I, E*, 1885 *I* 1,2, 1886 *E*
Villar, C (Edinburgh Wands) 1876 *E*, 1877 *I, E*

Waddell, G H (London Scottish, Cambridge U) 1957 *E*, 1958 *F, W, A, I, E*, 1959 *F, W, I, E*, 1960 *I, E, SA*, 1961 *F*, 1962 *F, W, I, E*
Waddell, H (Glasgow Acads) 1924 *F, W, I, E*, 1925 *I, E*, 1926 *F, W, I, E*, 1927 *F, W, I, E*, 1930 *W*
Wade, A L (London Scottish) 1908 *E*
Wainwright, R I (Edinburgh Acads, West Hartlepool, Watsonians, Army, Dundee HSFP) 1992 *I* (R), *F, A* 1,2, 1993 *NZ*, 1994 *W, E*, 1995 *C, I, F, W, E, R, [Iv, Tg, F, NZ]*, *WS*, 1996 *I, F, W, E, NZ* 1,2, 1997 *W, E, I, F, SA*, 1998 *It, I, F, W, E, Fj, A* 1,2
Walker, A (W of Scotland) 1881 *I*, 1882 *E*, 1883 *W, I, E*
Walker, A W (Cambridge U, Birkenhead Park) 1931 *F, W, I, E*, 1932 *I*
Walker, J G (W of Scotland) 1882 *E*, 1883 *W*
Walker, M (Oxford U) 1952 *F*
Wallace, A C (Oxford U) 1923 *F*, 1924 *F, W, E*, 1925 *F, W, I, E*, 1926 *F*

Wallace, W M (Cambridge U) 1913 *E*, 1914 *W, I, E*
Wallace, M I (Glasgow High Kelvinside) 1996 *A, It*, 1997 *W*
Walls, W A (Glasgow Acads) 1882 *E*, 1883 *W, I, E*, 1884 *W, I, E*, 1886 *W, I, E*
Walter, M W (London Scottish) 1906 *I, E, SA*, 1907 *W, I*, 1908 *W, I*, 1910 *I*
Walton, P (Northampton, Newcastle) 1994 *E, I, F, Arg* 1,2, 1995 *[Iv]*, 1997 *W, E, I, F, SA* (R), 1998 *I, F, SA*, 1999 *W, E, It, I, F* (R), *Arg, R, [SA* (R), *U* (R), *Sp]*
Warren, J R (Glasgow Acads) 1914 *I*
Warren, R C (Glasgow Acads) 1922 *W, I*, 1930 *W, I, E*
Waters, F H (Cambridge U, London Scottish) 1930 *F, W, I, E*, 1932 *SA, W, I*
Waters, J A (Selkirk) 1933 *W, E, I*, 1934 *W, I, E*, 1935 *W, I, E, NZ*, 1936 *W, I, E*, 1937 *W, I, E*
Waters, J B (Cambridge U) 1904 *I, E*
Watherston, J G (Edinburgh Wands) 1934 *I, E*
Watherston, W R A (London Scottish) 1963 *F, W, I*
Watson, D H (Glasgow Acads) 1876 *E*, 1877 *I, E*
Watson, W S (Boroughmuir) 1974 *W, E, I, F*, 1975 *NZ*, 1977 *I, F, W*, 1979 *I, F*
Watt, A G J (Glasgow High Kelvinside) 1991 *[Z]*, 1993 *I, NZ*, 1994 *Arg* 2(t & R)
Watt, A G M (Edinburgh Acads) 1947 *F, W, I, A*, 1948 *F, W*
Weatherstone, T G (Stewart's Coll FP) 1952 *E*, 1953 *I, E*, 1954 *F, NZ, I, E, W*, 1955 *F*, 1958 *W, A, I, E*, 1959 *W, I, E*
Weir, G W (Melrose, Newcastle) 1990 *Arg*, 1991 *R, [J, Z, I, WS, E, NZ]*, 1992 *E, I, F, W, A* 1,2, 1993 *I, F, W, E, NZ*, 1994 *W* (R), *E, I, F, SA*, 1995 *F* (R), *W, E, R, [Iv, Tg, F, NZ]*, *WS*, 1996 *I, F, W, E, NZ* 1,2, *A, It* (R), 1997 *W, E, I, F*, 1998 *It, I, F, W, E, SA*, 1999 *W, Arg* (R), *R* (R), *[SA* (R), *Sp, Sm, NZ]*, 2000 *It* (R), *I* (R), *F*
Welsh, R (Watsonians) 1895 *W, I, E*, 1896 *W*
Welsh, R B (Hawick) 1967 *I, E*
Welsh, W B (Hawick) 1927 *A*, 1928 *F, W, I*, 1929 *I, E*, 1930 *F, W, I, E*, 1931 *F, W, I, E*, 1932 *SA, W, I, E*, 1933 *W, E, I*
Welsh, W H (Edinburgh U) 1900 *I, E*, 1901 *W, I, E*, 1902 *W, I, E*
Wemyss, A (Gala, Edinburgh Wands) 1914 *W, I*, 1920 *F, E*, 1922 *F, W, I*
West, L (Edinburgh U, West Hartlepool) 1903 *W, I, E*, 1905 *I, E, NZ*, 1906 *W, I, E*
Weston, V G (Kelvinside Acads) 1936 *I, E*
White, D B (Gala, London Scottish) 1982 *F, W, A* 1,2, 1987 *W, E, [F, R, NZ]*, 1988 *I, F, W, E, A*, 1989 *W, E, I, F, Fj, R*, 1990 *I, F, W, E, NZ* 1,2, 1991 *F, W, E, I, R, [J, Z, I, WS, E, NZ]*, 1992 *E, I, F, W*

White, D M (Kelvinside Acads) 1963 *F, W, I, E*
White, J P R (Glasgow) 2000 *E, NZ* 1,2, *US* (R), *A* (R), *Sm*, 2001 *F* (R), *I, Tg, Arg, NZ*, 2002 *E, It, I, F, W, C, US*
White, T B (Edinburgh Acads) 1888 *W, I*, 1889 *W*
Whittington, T P (Merchistonians) 1873 *E*
Whitworth, R J E (London Scottish) 1936 *I*
Whyte, D J (Edinburgh Wands) 1965 *W, I, E, SA*, 1966 *F, W, I, E, A*, 1967 *F, W, I, E*
Will, J G (Cambridge U) 1912 *F, W, I, E*, 1914 *W, I, E*
Wilson, A W (Dunfermline) 1931 *F, I, E*
Wilson, G A (Oxford U) 1949 *F, W, E*
Wilson, G R (Royal HSFP) 1886 *E*, 1890 *W, I, E*, 1891 *I*
Wilson, J H (Watsonians) 1953 *I*
Wilson, J S (St Andrew's U) 1931 *F, W, I, E*, 1932 *E*
Wilson, J S (United Services, London Scottish) 1908 *I*, 1909 *W*
Wilson, R (London Scottish) 1976 *E, I*, 1977 *E, I, F*, 1978 *I, F*, 1981 *F*, 1983 *I*
Wilson, R L (Gala) 1951 *F, W, I, E, SA*, 1953 *F, W, E*
Wilson, R W (W of Scotland) 1873 *E*, 1874 *E*
Wilson, S (Oxford U, London Scottish) 1964 *F, NZ, W, I, E*, 1965 *W, I, E, SA*, 1966 *F, W, I, A*, 1967 *F, W, I, E, NZ*, 1968 *F, W, I, E*
Wood, A (Royal HSFP) 1873 *E*, 1874 *E*, 1875 *E*
Wood, G (Gala) 1931 *W, I*, 1932 *W, I, E*
Woodburn, J C (Kelvinside Acads) 1892 *I*
Woodrow, A N (Glasgow Acads) 1887 *I, W, E*
Wotherspoon, W (W of Scotland) 1891 *I*, 1892 *I*, 1893 *W, E*, 1894 *W, I, E*
Wright, F A (Edinburgh Acads) 1932 *E*
Wright, H B (Watsonians) 1894 *W*
Wright, K M (London Scottish) 1929 *F, W, I, E*
Wright, P H (Boroughmuir) 1992 *A* 1,2, 1993 *F, W, E*, 1994 *W*, 1995 *C, I, F, W, E, R, [Iv, Tg, F, NZ]*, 1996 *W, E, NZ* 1
Wright, R W J (Edinburgh Wands) 1973 *F*
Wright, S T H (Stewart's Coll FP) 1949 *E*
Wright, T (Hawick) 1947 *A*
Wyllie, D S (Stewart's-Melville FP) 1984 *A*, 1985 *W* (R), *E*, 1987 *I, F, [F, Z, R, NZ]*, 1989 *R*, 1991 *R, [J* (R), *Z]*, 1993 *NZ* (R), 1994 *W* (R), *E, I, F*

Young, A H (Edinburgh Acads) 1874 *E*
Young, E T (Glasgow Acads) 1914 *E*
Young, R G (Watsonians) 1970 *W*
Young, T E B (Durham) 1911 *F*
Young, W B (Cambridge U, London Scottish) 1937 *W, I, E*, 1938 *W, I, E*, 1939 *W, I, E*, 1948 *E*

IRELAND TEST SEASON REVIEW 2001-02

A Search for Consistency

Peter O'Reilly

With neat symmetry, Ireland's season featured November and June Test matches against New Zealand, thus affording a means of gauging the team's progress over a seven-month period. Our controlled experiment sees a 40-29 defeat at one end of the season, a 40-8 defeat at the other. Conclusion: Ireland have regressed. If only it were all so simple.

This was one of the most turbulent periods in recent Irish rugby history, on and off the field. Consider the events that led to Warren Gatland's dismissal as national coach at the end of November. Following on from the momentous Grand Slam-denying win over England at Lansdowne Road (and a relatively humdrum defeat of Samoa), Gatland's team proceeded to give the All Blacks the hurry-up at the same venue, actually leading 21-7 at the break. Even if the tourists eventually recovered to win, Gatland could enter his contract review meeting with the IRFU in confident mood. Ireland had 10 wins from the previous 16 outings and their best International Championship finish in 16 years. It made for pretty impressive reading.

Not impressive enough, however. To general astonishment (not least Gatland's), the IRFU announced that his assistant Eddie O'Sullivan would be taking over, with Munster's Declan Kidney being installed as O'Sullivan's second in command. A confidentiality clause in Gatland's severance agreement meant that no official explanation was forthcoming. Certain conclusions can be drawn, however, and they serve to put the subsequent performance of the new management team into some sort of context.

Gatland's apologists claimed he had been hounded out by committee-men who merely wanted an Irish-born coach. Yet even they would have to accept the Kiwi's biggest failing – Ireland under Gatland lacked consistency. While there were historic back-to-back wins over France and that unforgettable victory over England, there were also debacles in Lens, Twickenham and more than once at Murrayfield. At times, there were wild fluctuations of form even within a single game, as against New Zealand, when Ireland's defence simply crumbled in the second half.

It hardly came as a surprise when O'Sullivan's first act as new coach was to hire a defence specialist from rugby league, Mike Ford. In fact, he assembled a team of specialists, with Niall O'Donovan (also of Munster) being enlisted for his forwards expertise. Irish training sessions suddenly became far more rigorously organised affairs. Now all the new management needed were some results.

They couldn't have had a better start. Despite disrupted preparations and injuries to Keith Wood, Shane Horgan and Malcolm O'Kelly, Ireland walloped a woeful Welsh side by a record margin – 54-10. There were 24 points for David Humphreys, two tries for Geordan Murphy and one for lock Paul O'Connell, whose international debut ended unfortunately with concussion sustained before the interval. But it was one of very few disappointments on the first championship Sunday at Lansdowne Road.

Wisely, O'Sullivan had avoided setting targets for himself, preferring to talk of consistency of performance – after all, he knew he had to travel to London and Paris. But he cannot have foreseen the utter devastation of Twickenham.

England, sparked by Jonny Wilkinson, were outstandingly good, especially before the break. But Ireland's flaws were equally striking. The line-out was a liability, with England's jumpers mercilessly targeting Frankie Sheahan's throw. Meanwhile the new defensive system simply unravelled under pressure. England scored six tries in all, with just one in response from Ronan O'Gara – and this in a fairly meaningless final quarter.

A fortnight later, Ireland set about restoring some meaning to their season and did so impressively, on the scoreboard at least. A 43-22 home victory over the Scots was seriously flawed – once again, the Irish line-out was shambolic, with the unfortunate Sheahan having to be called ashore after 35 minutes (his replacement, Shane Byrne, also had his problems). Ireland relied heavily on the individual brilliance of Brian O'Driscoll, who recorded his second Six Nations hat-trick. And without wishing to detract from this achievement, it has to be put into the context of Scotland's dreadful midfield defence, which was directly responsible for two of O'Drsicoll's tries.

It had been generally accepted that to win all three home games would constitute a reasonable championship. This was achieved with a 33-17 win over the Italians, which was notable for three things – David Humphreys passed Michael Kiernan's points-scoring record of 308, Munster wing John Kelly celebrated his international debut by scoring a brace of tries and veteran prop Peter Clohessy bade Lansdowne Road an emotional farewell. Yet something was still missing.

Once again, Ireland struggled in the set-pieces – this time, the scrum took a battering from the Italians – while the handling of the backs was substandard. It was not the sort of performance to engender a sense of optimism for the final game in Paris, where France were preparing for their grand slam celebrations. Sure enough, even with the returned Wood, Ireland failed abysmally to spoil the party on this occasion.

The details of the *Tricolores'* 44-5 win are recounted elsewhere in this yearbook so it's enough to say that Ireland had an embarrassing afternoon. For O'Sullivan, there was also the awareness that he had been brought in on the understanding that he could prevent the scale of reversal that occurred at Twickenham and the Stade de France. His response was to plead for patience – this was a new management team finding its feet, and the defensive system in particular would need time.

As punishment, O'Sullivan and Co were sent to New Zealand for a couple of Test matches. At the end of a season already cluttered by the knock-on effects of foot-and-mouth, here was an assignment to the toughest touring environment imaginable – especially for the large Munster contingent, who had just been through the disappointment of another European Cup final defeat. And yet the three weeks in New Zealand (without a clutch of first-choice players) was in some respects the most rewarding phase of the season.

To everyone's surprise, Ireland came within a whisker of breaking their duck against New Zealand. A reconstructed team put in a wonderfully committed and well-organised defensive performance at Carisbrook, where a clearly rattled home team secured a 15-6 victory with a late try by full-back Leon MacDonald. Ireland were left to rue the errant place-kicking of Ronan O'Gara, promoted ahead of Humphreys. The Munster out-half landed just one successful kick from four attempts with the All Blacks' controversial Adidas ball.

And O'Gara was to suffer at Eden Park a week later. Once again, Ireland created all sorts of problems for their hosts before the break and would have been on level terms had O'Gara not missed three shots at goal, two of them straightforward. Fatigue finally caught up with the tourists in the second half, during which New Zealand ran in four tries.

It was an unfortunate note on which to end a decidedly mixed season, yet the management insisted the tour had been beneficial. Apart from having the opportunity to work on set-piece and defence – the team's most obvious problem areas – several players had considerably benefited. After David Wallace's surprise omission from the tour party, Keith Gleeson had shone as an open-side flanker, particularly in the first Test. As a scrummager and general contributor in the loose, Reggie Corrigan had made a plausible case as Clohessy's successor. From Geordan Murphy, there were flashes of his brilliant form for Leicester. All of which was encouraging for O'Sullivan – with another dense 14-Test season ahead, the one thing he needs is some strength in depth. That, and some consistency.

Ireland's Test Record in 2001–2002: Played 9, won 4, lost 5.

Opponents	Date	Venue	Result
New Zealand	22nd June 2002	A	Lost 8-40
New Zealand	15th June 2002	A	Lost 6-15
France	6th April 2002	A	Lost 5-44
Italy	23rd March 2002	H	Won 32-17
Scotland	2nd March 2002	H	Won 43-22
England	16th February 2002	A	Lost 11-45
Wales	3rd February 2002	H	Won 54-10
New Zealand	17th November 2001	H	Lost 29-40
Samoa	11th November 2001	H	Won 35-8

IRELAND INTERNATIONAL STATISTICS

(up to 31 August 2002)

Match Records

MOST CONSECUTIVE TEST WINS

6 1968 *S, W, A*, 1969 *F, E, S*

MOST CONSECUTIVE TESTS WITHOUT DEFEAT

Matches	Wins	Draws	Period
7	6	1	1968 to 1969
5	4	1	1972 to 1973

MOST POINTS IN A MATCH
by the team

Pts	Opponents	Venue	Year
83	United States	Manchester (NH)	2000
78	Japan	Dublin	2000
70	Georgia	Dublin	1998
60	Romania	Dublin	1986
60	Italy	Dublin	2000
55	Zimbabwe	Dublin	1991
54	Wales	Dublin	2002
53	Romania	Dublin	1998
53	United States	Dublin	1999
50	Japan	Bloemfontein	1995

by a player

Pts	Player	Opponents	Venue	Year
30	R J R O'Gara	Italy	Dublin	2000
24	P A Burke	Italy	Dublin	1997
24	D G Humphreys	Argentina	Lens	1999
23	R P Keyes	Zimbabwe	Dublin	1991
23	R J R O'Gara	Japan	Dublin	2000
22	D G Humphreys	Wales	Dublin	2002
21	S O Campbell	Scotland	Dublin	1982
21	S O Campbell	England	Dublin	1983
21	R J R O'Gara	Italy	Rome	2001
20	M J Kiernan	Romania	Dublin	1986
20	E P Elwood	Romania	Dublin	1993
20	S J P Mason	Samoa	Dublin	1996
20	E P Elwood	Georgia	Dublin	1998
20	K G M Wood	United States	Dublin	1999

MOST TRIES IN A MATCH
by the team

Tries	Opponents	Venue	Year
13	United States	Manchester (NH)	2000
11	Japan	Dublin	2000
10	Romania	Dublin	1986
10	Georgia	Dublin	1998
8	Western Samoa	Dublin	1988
8	Zimbabwe	Dublin	1991
7	Japan	Bloemfontein	1995
7	Romania	Dublin	1998
7	United States	Dublin	1999

by a player

Tries	Player	Opponents	Venue	Year
4	B F Robinson	Zimbabwe	Dublin	1991
4	K G M Wood	United States	Dublin	1999
3	R Montgomery	Wales	Birkenhead	1887
3	J P Quinn	France	Cork	1913
3	E O'D Davy	Scotland	Murrayfield	1930
3	S J Byrne	Scotland	Murrayfield	1953
3	K D Crossan	Romania	Dublin	1986
3	B J Mullin	Tonga	Brisbane	1987
3	M R Mostyn	Argentina	Dublin	1999
3	B G O'Driscoll	France	Paris	2000
3	M J Mullins	United States	Manchester (NH)	2000
3	D A Hickie	Japan	Dublin	2000
3	R A J Henderson	Italy	Rome	2001
3	B G O'Driscoll	Scotland	Dublin	2002

MOST CONVERSIONS IN A MATCH
by the team

Cons	Opponents	Venue	Year
10	Georgia	Dublin	1998
10	Japan	Dublin	2000
9	United States	Manchester (NH)	2000
7	Romania	Dublin	1986
6	Japan	Bloemfontein	1995
6	Romania	Dublin	1998
6	United States	Dublin	1999
6	Italy	Dublin	2000

by a player

Cons	Player	Opponents	Venue	Year
10	E P Elwood	Georgia	Dublin	1998
10	R J R O'Gara	Japan	Dublin	2000
8	R J R O'Gara	United States	Manchester (NH)	2000
7	M J Kiernan	Romania	Dublin	1986
6	P A Burke	Japan	Bloemfontein	1995
6	R J R O'Gara	Italy	Dublin	2000
5	M J Kiernan	Canada	Dunedin	1987
5	E P Elwood	Romania	Dublin	1999

MOST PENALTIES IN A MATCH
by the team

Penalties	Opponents	Venue	Year
8	Italy	Dublin	1997
7	Argentina	Lens	1999
6	Scotland	Dublin	1982
6	Romania	Dublin	1993
6	United States	Atlanta	1996
6	Western Samoa	Dublin	1996
6	Italy	Dublin	2000
6	Wales	Dublin	2002

by a player

Penalties	Player	Opponents	Venue	Year
8	P A Burke	Italy	Dublin	1997
7	D G Humphreys	Argentina	Lens	1999
6	S O Campbell	Scotland	Dublin	1982
6	E P Elwood	Romania	Dublin	1993
6	S J P Mason	Western Samoa	Dublin	1996
6	R J R O'Gara	Italy	Dublin	2000
6	D G Humphreys	Wales	Dublin	2002

MOST DROPPED GOALS IN A MATCH
by the team

Drops	Opponents	Venue	Year
2	Australia	Dublin	1967
2	France	Dublin	1975
2	Australia	Sydney	1979
2	England	Dublin	1981
2	Canada	Dunedin	1987
2	England	Dublin	1993
2	Wales	Wembley	1999
2	New Zealand	Dublin	2001

by a player

Drops	Player	Opponents	Venue	Year
2	C M H Gibson	Australia	Dublin	1967
2	W M McCombe	France	Dublin	1975
2	S O Campbell	Australia	Sydney	1979
2	E P Elwood	England	Dublin	1993
2	D G Humphreys	Wales	Wembley	1999
2	D G Humphreys	New Zealand	Dublin	2001

Career Records

MOST CAPPED PLAYERS

Caps	Player	Career Span
69	C M H Gibson	1964 to 1979
63	W J McBride	1962 to 1975
61	J F Slattery	1970 to 1984

59	P S Johns	1990 to 2000
58	P A Orr	1976 to 1987
55	B J Mullin	1984 to 1995
54	T J Kiernan	1960 to 1973
54	P M Clohessy	1993 to 2002
52	D G Lenihan	1981 to 1992
51	M I Keane	1974 to 1984
50	K G M Wood	1994 to 2002
48	N J Popplewell	1989 to 1998

MOST CONSECUTIVE TESTS

Tests	Player	Span
52	W J McBride	1964 to 1975
49	P A Orr	1976 to 1986
43	D G Lenihan	1981 to 1989
39	M I Keane	1974 to 1981
37	G V Stephenson	1920 to 1929

MOST TESTS AS CAPTAIN

Tests	Captain	Span
28	K G M Wood	1996 to 2002
24	T J Kiernan	1963 to 1973
19	C F Fitzgerald	1982 to 1986
17	J F Slattery	1979 to 1981
17	D G Lenihan	1986 to 1990

MOST TESTS IN INDIVIDUAL POSITIONS

Position	Player	Tests	Span
Full-back	T J Kiernan	54	1960 to 1973
Wing	K D Crossan	41	1982 to 1992
Centre	B J Mullin	55	1984 to 1995
Fly-half	J W Kyle	46	1947 to 1958
Scrum-half	M T Bradley	40	1984 to 1995
Prop	P A Orr	58	1976 to 1987
Hooker	K G M Wood	49	1994 to 2002
Lock	W J McBride	63	1962 to 1975
Flanker	J F Slattery	61	1970 to 1984
No 8	W P Duggan	39	1975 to 1984

MOST POINTS IN TESTS

Points	Player	Tests	Career
325	D G Humphreys	43	1996 to 2002
308	M J Kiernan	43	1982 to 1991
296	E P Elwood	35	1993 to 1999
217	S O Campbell	22	1976 to 1984
200	R J R O'Gara	22	2000 to 2002
158	T J Kiernan	54	1960 to 1973
113	A J P Ward	19	1978 to 1987

MOST TRIES IN TESTS

Tries	Player	Tests	Career
17	B J Mullin	55	1984 to 1995
14	G V Stephenson	42	1920 to 1930
13	D A Hickie	29	1997 to 2002
13	B G O'Driscoll	27	1999 to 2002
13	K G M Wood	50	1994 to 2002
12	K D Crossan	41	1982 to 1992
11	A T A Duggan	25	1963 to 1972
11	S P Geoghegan	37	1991 to 1996

MOST PENALTY GOALS IN TESTS

Penalties	Player	Tests	Career
75	D G Humphreys	43	1996 to 2002
68	E P Elwood	35	1993 to 1999
62	M J Kiernan	43	1982 to 1991
54	S O Campbell	22	1976 to 1984
35	R J R O'Gara	22	2000 to 2002
31	T J Kiernan	54	1960 to 1973
29	A J P Ward	19	1978 to 1987

MOST CONVERSIONS IN TESTS

Cons	Player	Tests	Career
43	E P Elwood	35	1993 to 1999
40	M J Kiernan	43	1982 to 1991
40	R J R O'Gara	22	2000 to 2002
32	D G Humphreys	43	1996 to 2002
26	T J Kiernan	54	1960 to 1973
16	R A Lloyd	19	1910 to 1920
15	S O Campbell	22	1976 to 1984

MOST DROPPED GOALS IN TESTS

Drops	Player	Tests	Career
7	R A Lloyd	19	1910 to 1920
7	S O Campbell	22	1976 to 1984
7	D G Humphreys	43	1996 to 2002
6	C M H Gibson	69	1964 to 1979
6	B J McGann	25	1969 to 1976
6	M J Kiernan	43	1982 to 1991

International Championship Records

Record	Detail		Set
Most points in season	168	in five matches	2000
Most tries in season	17	in five matches	2000
Highest Score	60	60-13 v Italy	2000
Biggest win	47	60-13 v Italy	2000
Highest score conceded	50	18-50 v England	2000
Biggest defeat	40	6-46 v England	1997
Most appearances	56	C M H Gibson	1964 – 1979
Most points in matches	207	M J Kiernan	1982 – 1991
Most points in season	58	R J R O'Gara	2000
Most points in match	30	R J R O'Gara	v Italy, 2000
Most tries in matches	14	G V Stephenson	1920 – 1930
Most tries in season	5	J E Arigho	1928
	5	B G O'Driscoll	2000
Most tries in match	3	R Montgomery	v Wales, 1887
	3	J P Quinn	v France, 1913
	3	E O'D Davy	v Scotland, 1930
	3	S J Byrne	v Scotland, 1953
	3	B G O'Driscoll	v France, 2000
	3	R A J Henderson	v Italy, 2001
	3	B G O'Driscoll	v Scotland, 2002
Most cons in matches	21	M J Kiernan	1982 – 1991
Most cons in season	11	R J R O'Gara	2000
Most cons in match	6	R J R O'Gara	v Italy, 2000
Most pens in matches	48	S O Campbell	1980 – 1984
Most pens in season	16	D G Humphreys	2002
Most pens in match	6	S O Campbell	v Scotland, 1982
	6	R J R O'Gara	v Italy, 2000
	6	D G Humphreys	v Wales, 2002
Most drops in matches	7	R A Lloyd	1910 – 1920

Most drops in season	2	on several	occasions
Most drops in match	2	W M McCombe	v France, 1975
	2	E P Elwood	v England, 1993
	2	D G Humphreys	v Wales, 1999

Miscellaneous Records

Record	Holder	Detail
Longest Test Career	A J F O'Reilly	16 seasons, 1954-55 to 1969-70
	C M H Gibson	16 seasons, 1963-64 to 1979
Youngest Test Cap	F S Hewitt	17 yrs 157 days in 1924
Oldest Test Cap	C M H Gibson	36 yrs 195 days in 1979

Career Records of Ireland International Players
(up to 31 August 2002)

PLAYER	Debut	Caps	T	C	P	D	Pts
Backs:							
J C Bell	1994 v A	33	7	0	0	0	35
J P Bishop	1998 v SA	21	7	0	0	0	35
P A Burke	1995 v E	11	0	12	26	1	105
D J Crotty	1996 v A	5	0	0	0	0	0
G M D'Arcy	1999 v R	1	0	0	0	0	0
G T Dempsey	1998 v Gg	26	5	0	0	0	25
G Easterby	2000 v US	8	2	0	0	0	10
R A J Henderson	1996 v WS	24	5	0	0	0	25
D A Hickie	1997 v W	29	13	0	0	0	65
S P Horgan	2000 v S	15	8	0	0	0	40
T G Howe	2000 v US	8	4	0	0	0	20
D G Humphreys	1996 v F	43	3	32	75	7	325
J P Kelly	2002 v It	3	2	0	0	0	10
K M Maggs	1997 v NZ	39	8	0	0	0	40
M J Mullins	1999 v Arg	14	3	0	0	0	15
G E A Murphy	2000 v US	10	6	0	0	0	30
B G O'Driscoll	1999 v A	27	13	0	0	3	74
R J R O'Gara	2000 v S	22	3	40	35	0	200
J W Staunton	2001 v Sm	1	1	0	0	0	5
P A Stringer	2000 v S	23	1	0	0	0	5
Forwards:							
T Brennan	1998 v SA	12	0	0	0	0	0
E Byrne	2001 v It	7	0	0	0	0	0
J S Byrne	2001 v R	6	0	0	0	0	0
R E Casey	1999 v A	5	0	0	0	0	0
P M Clohessy	1993 v F	54	4	0	0	0	20
R Corrigan	1997 v C	12	0	0	0	0	0
V C P Costello	1996 v US	22	3	0	0	0	15
L F M Cullen	2002 v NZ	1	0	0	0	0	0
J W Davidson	1995 v Fj	32	0	0	0	0	0
K Dawson	1997 v NZ	17	1	0	0	0	5
S H Easterby	2000 v S	16	3	0	0	0	15
A G Foley	1995 v E	33	2	0	0	0	10
M J Galwey	1991 v F	41	3	0	0	0	15

K D Gleeson	2002 v W	4	1	0	0	0	5
J J Hayes	2000 v S	23	0	0	0	0	0
M J Horan	2000 v US	1	0	0	0	0	0
P S Johns	1990 v Arg	59	4	0	0	0	20
G W Longwell	2000 v J	14	1	0	0	0	5
E R P Miller	1997 v It	29	2	0	0	0	10
P J O'Connell	2002 v W	4	1	0	0	0	5
M O'Driscoll	2001 v R	1	0	0	0	0	0
M E O'Kelly	1997 v NZ	40	3	0	0	0	15
A Quinlan	1999 v R	4	0	0	0	0	0
F J Sheahan	2000 v US	8	1	0	0	0	5
D P Wallace	2000 v Arg	14	0	0	0	0	0
P S Wallace	1995 v J	43	5	0	0	0	25
A J Ward	1998 v F	28	3	0	0	0	15
K G M Wood	1994 v A	50	13	0	0	0	65

NB Humphreys's figures include a penalty try awarded against Scotland in 1999

IRISH INTERNATIONAL PLAYERS
(up to 31 August 2002)

Note: Years given for International Championship matches are for second half of season; eg 1972 means season 1971-72. Years for all other matches refer to the actual year of the match. When a series has taken place, figures have been used to denote the particular matches in which players have featured. Thus 1981 *SA* 2 indicates that a player appeared in the second Test of the series.

Abraham, M (Bective Rangers) 1912 *E, S, W, SA*, 1914 *W*
Adams, C (Old Wesley), 1908 *E*, 1909 *E, F*, 1910 *F*, 1911 *E, S, W, F*, 1912 *S, W, SA*, 1913 *W, F*, 1914 *F, E, S*
Agar, R D (Malone) 1947 *F, E, S, W*, 1948 *F*, 1949 *S, W*, 1950 *F, E, W*
Agnew, P J (CIYMS) 1974 *F* (R), 1976 *A*
Ahearne, T (Queen's Coll, Cork) 1899 *E*
Aherne, L F P (Dolphin, Lansdowne) 1988 *E* 2, *WS, It*, 1989 *F, W, E, S, NZ*, 1990 *E, S, F, W* (R), 1992 *E, S, F, A*
Alexander, R (NIFC, Police Union) 1936 *E, S, W*, 1937 *E, S, W*, 1938 *E, S*, 1939 *E, S, W*
Allen, C E (Derry, Liverpool) 1900 *E, S, W*, 1901 *E, S, W*, 1903 *S, W*, 1904 *E, S, W*, 1905 *E, S, W, NZ*, 1906 *E, S, W, SA*, 1907 *S, W*
Allen, G G (Derry, Liverpool) 1896 *E, S, W*, 1897 *E, S*, 1898 *E, S*, 1899 *E, W*
Allen, T C (NIFC) 1885 *E, S* 1
Allen, W S (Wanderers) 1875 *E*
Allison, J B (Edinburgh U) 1899 *E, S*, 1900 *E, S, W*, 1901 *E, S, W*, 1902 *E, S, W*, 1903 *S*
Anderson, F E (Queen's U, Belfast, NIFC) 1953 *F, E, S, W*, 1954 *NZ, F, E, S, W*, 1955 *F, E, S, W*
Anderson, H J (Old Wesley) 1903 *E, S*, 1906 *E, S*
Anderson, W A (Dungannon) 1984 *A*, 1985 *S, F, W, E*, 1986 *F, S, R*, 1987 *E, S, F, W*, [*W, C, Tg, A*], 1988 *S, F, W, E* 1,2, 1989 *F, W, E, NZ*, 1990 *E, S*
Andrews, G (NIFC) 1875 *E*, 1876 *E*
Andrews, H W (NIFC) 1888 *M*, 1889 *S, W*
Archer, A M (Dublin U, NIFC) 1879 *S*
Arigho, J E (Lansdowne) 1928 *F, E, W*, 1929 *F, E, S, W*, 1930 *F, E, S, W*, 1931 *F, E, S, W, SA*
Armstrong, W K (NIFC) 1960 *SA*, 1961 *E*
Arnott, D T (Lansdowne) 1876 *E*
Ash, W H (NIFC) 1875 *E*, 1876 *E*, 1877 *S*
Aston, H R (Dublin U) 1908 *E, W*
Atkins, A P (Bective Rangers) 1924 *F*
Atkinson, J M (NIFC) 1927 *F, A*
Atkinson, J R (Dublin U) 1882 *W, S*

Bagot, J C (Dublin U, Lansdowne) 1879 *S, E*, 1880 *E, S*, 1881 *S*
Bailey, A H (UC Dublin, Lansdowne) 1934 *W*, 1935 *E, S, W, NZ*, 1936 *E, S, W*, 1937 *E, S, W*, 1938 *E, S*
Bailey, N (Northampton) 1952 *E*
Bardon, M E (Bohemians) 1934 *E*
Barlow, M (Wanderers) 1875 *E*
Barnes, R J (Dublin U, Armagh) 1933 *W*
Barr, A (Methodist Coll, Belfast) 1898 *W*, 1899 *S*, 1901 *E, S*
Barry, N J (Garryowen) 1991 *Nm* 2(R)
Beamish, C E St J (RAF, Leicester) 1933 *W, S*, 1934 *S, W*, 1935 *E, S, W, NZ*, 1936 *E, S, W*, 1938 *W*
Beamish, G R (RAF, Leicester) 1925 *E, S, W*, 1928 *F, E, S, W*, 1929 *F, E, S, W*, 1930 *F, S, W*, 1931 *F, E, S, W, SA*, 1932 *E, S, W*, 1933 *E, W, S*
Beatty, W J (NIFC, Richmond) 1910 *F*, 1912 *F, W*
Becker, V A (Lansdowne) 1974 *F, W*
Beckett, G G P (Dublin U) 1908 *E, S, W*
Bell, J C (Ballymena, Northampton, Dungannon) 1994 *A* 1,2, *US*, 1995 *S, It*, [*NZ, W, F*], *Fj*, 1996 *US, S, F, W, E, WS, A*, 1997 *It* 1, *F, W, E, S*, 1998 *Gg, R, SA* 3, 1999 *F, W, S It* (R), [*US* (R), *A* 3(R), *R*], 2001 *R* (R)
Bell, R J (NIFC) 1875 *E*, 1876 *E*
Bell, W E (Belfast Collegians) 1953 *F, E, S, W*
Bennett, F (Belfast Collegians) 1913 *S*
Bent, G C (Dublin U) 1882 *W, E*
Berkery, P J (Lansdowne) 1954 *W*, 1955 *W*, 1956 *S, W*, 1957 *F, E, S, W*, 1958 *A, E, S*
Bermingham, J J C (Blackrock Coll) 1921 *E, S, W, F*
Bishop, J P (London Irish) 1998 *SA* 1,2, *Gg, R, SA* 3, 1999 *F, W, E, S, It, A* 1,2, *Arg* 1, [*US, A* 3, *Arg* 2], 2000 *E, Arg, C*, 2002 *NZ* 1,2

Blackham, J C (Queen's Coll, Cork) 1909 *S, W, F*, 1910 *E, S, W*
Blake-Knox, S E F (NIFC) 1976 *E, S*, 1977 *F* (R)
Blayney, J J (Wanderers) 1950 *S*
Bond, A T W (Derry) 1894 *S, W*
Bornemann, W W (Wanderers) 1960 *E, S, W, SA*
Bowen, D St J (Cork Const) 1977 *W, E, S*
Boyd, C A (Dublin U) 1900 *S*, 1901 *S, W*
Boyle, C V (Dublin U) 1935 *NZ*, 1936 *E, S, W*, 1937 *E, S, W*, 1938 *W*, 1939 *W*
Brabazon, H M (Dublin U) 1884 *E*, 1885 *S* 1, 1886 *E*
Bradley, M J (Dolphin) 1920 *W, F*, 1922 *E, S, W, F*, 1923 *E, S, W, F*, 1925 *F, S, W*, 1926 *F, E, S, W*, 1927 *F, W*
Bradley, M T (Cork Constitution) 1984 *A*, 1985 *S, F, W, E*, 1986 *F, W, E, S, R*, 1987 *E, S, F, W*, [*W, C, Tg, A*], 1988 *S, F, W, E* 1, 1990 *W*, 1992 *NZ* 1,2, 1993 *S, F, W, E, R*, 1994 *F, W, E, S, A* 1,2, *US*, 1995 *S, F*, [*NZ*]
Bradshaw, G (Belfast Collegians) 1903 *W*
Bradshaw, R M (Wanderers) 1885 *E, S* 1,2
Brady, A M (UC Dublin, Malone) 1966 *S*, 1968 *E, S, W*
Brady, J A (Wanderers) 1976 *E, S*
Brady, J R (CIYMS) 1951 *S, W*, 1953 *F, E, S, W*, 1954 *W*, 1956 *W*, 1957 *F, E, S, W*
Bramwell, T (NIFC) 1928 *F*
Brand, T N (NIFC) 1924 *NZ*
Brennan, J I (CIYMS) 1957 *S, W*
Brennan, T (St Mary's Coll, Barnhall) 1998 *SA* 1(R),2(R), 1999 *F, S* (R), *It, A* 2, *Arg* 1, [*US, A* 3], 2000 *E* (R), 2001 *W* (R), *E* (R), *Sm* (R)
Bresnihan, F P K (UC Dublin, Lansdowne, London Irish) 1966 *E, W*, 1967 *A* 1, *E, S, W, F*, 1968 *F, E, S, W, A*, 1969 *F, E, S, W*, 1970 *SA, F, E, S, W*, 1971 *F, E, S, W*
Brett, J T (Monkstown) 1914 *W*
Bristow, J R (NIFC) 1879 *E*
Brophy, N H (Blackrock Coll, UC Dublin, London Irish) 1957 *F, E*, 1959 *E, S, W, F*, 1960 *F, SA*, 1961 *S, W*, 1962 *E, S, W*, 1963 *E, W*, 1967 *E, S, W, F, A* 2
Brown, E L (Instonians) 1958 *F*
Brown, G S (Monkstown, United Services) 1912 *S, W, SA*
Brown, H (Windsor) 1877 *E*
Brown, T (Windsor) 1877 *E, S*
Brown, W H (Dublin U) 1899 *E*
Brown, W J (Malone) 1970 *SA, F, S, W*
Brown, W S (Dublin U) 1893 *S, W*, 1894 *E, S, W*
Browne, A W (Dublin U) 1951 *SA*
Browne, D (Blackrock Coll) 1920 *F*
Browne, H C (United Services and RN) 1929 *E, S, W*
Browne, W F (United Services and Army) 1925 *E, S, W*, 1926 *S, W*, 1927 *F, E, S, W, A*, 1928 *E, S*
Browning, D R (Wanderers) 1881 *E, S*
Bruce, S A M (NIFC) 1883 *E, S*, 1884 *E*
Brunker, A A (Lansdowne) 1895 *E, W*
Bryant, C H (Cardiff) 1920 *E, S*
Buchanan, A McM (Dublin U) 1926 *E, S, W*, 1927 *S, W, A*
Buchanan, J W B (Dublin U) 1882 *S*, 1884 *E, S*
Buckley, J H (Sunday's Well) 1973 *E, S*
Bulger, L Q (Lansdowne) 1896 *E, S, W*, 1897 *E, S*, 1898 *E, S, W*
Bulger, M J (Dublin U) 1888 *M*
Burges, J H (Rosslyn Park) 1950 *F, E*
Burgess, R B (Dublin U) 1912 *SA*
Burke, P A (Cork Constitution, Bristol, Harlequins) 1995 *E, S, W* (R), *It*, [*J*], *Fj*, 1996 *US* (R), *A*, 1997 *It* 1, *S* (R), 2001 *R* (R)
Burkitt, J C S (Queen's Coll, Cork) 1881 *E*
Burns, I J (Wanderers) 1980 *E* (R)
Butler, L G (Blackrock Coll) 1960 *W*
Butler, N (Bective Rangers) 1920 *E*
Byers, R M (NIFC) 1928 *S, W*, 1929 *E, S, W*
Byrne, E (St Mary's Coll) 2001 *It* (R), *F* (R), *S* (R), *W* (R), *E* (R), *Sm, NZ* (R)

Byrne, E M J (Blackrock Coll) 1977 *S, F*, 1978 *F, W, E, NZ*
Byrne, N F (UC Dublin) 1962 *F*
Byrne, S J (UC Dublin, Lansdowne) 1953 *S, W*, 1955 *F*
Byrne, S J (Blackrock Coll) 2001 *R* (R), 2002 *W* (R), *E* (R), *S* (R), *It, NZ* 2(R)
Byron, W G (NIFC) 1896 *E, S, W*, 1897 *E, S*, 1898 *E, S, W*, 1899 *E, S, W*

Caddell, E D (Dublin U, Wanderers) 1904 *S*, 1905 *E, S, W, NZ*, 1906 *E, S, W, SA*, 1907 *E, S*, 1908 *S, W*
Cagney, S J (London Irish) 1925 *W*, 1926 *F, E, S, W*, 1927 *F*, 1928 *E, S, W*, 1929 *F, E, S, W*
Callan, C P (Lansdowne) 1947 *F, E, S, W*, 1948 *F, E, S, W*, 1949 *F, E*
Cameron, E D (Bective Rangers) 1891 *S, W*
Campbell, C E (Old Wesley) 1970 *SA*
Campbell, E F (Monkstown) 1899 *S, W*, 1900 *E, W*
Campbell, S B B (Derry) 1911 *E, S, W, F*, 1912 *F, E, S, W, SA*, 1913 *E, S, F*
Campbell, S O (Old Belvedere) 1976 *A*, 1979 *A* 1,2, 1980 *E, S, F, W*, 1981 *F, W, E, S*, *SA* 1, 1982 *W, E, S, F*, 1983 *S, F, W, E*, 1984 *F, W*
Canniffe, D M (Lansdowne) 1976 *W, E*
Cantrell, J L (UC Dublin, Blackrock Coll) 1976 *A, F, W, E, S*, 1981 *SA* 1,2, *A*
Carey, R W (Dungannon) 1992 *NZ* 1,2
Carpendale, M J (Monkstown) 1886 *S*, 1887 *W*, 1888 *W, S*
Carr, N J (Ards) 1985 *S, F, W, E*, 1986 *W, E, S, R*, 1987 *E, S, W*
Carroll, C (Bective Rangers) 1930 *F*
Carroll, R (Lansdowne) 1947 *F*, 1950 *S, W*
Casement, B N (Dublin U) 1875 *E*, 1876 *E*, 1879 *E*
Casement, F (Dublin U) 1906 *E, S, W*
Casey, J C (Young Munster) 1930 *S*, 1932 *E*
Casey, P J (UC Dublin, Lansdowne) 1963 *F, E, S, W, NZ*, 1964 *E, S, W, F*, 1965 *F, E, S*
Casey, R E (Blackrock Coll) 1999 [*A* 3(t), *Arg* 2(R)], 2000 *E, US* (R), *C* (R)
Chambers, J (Dublin U) 1886 *E, S*, 1887 *E, S, W*
Chambers, R R (Instonians) 1951 *F, E, S, W*, 1952 *F, W*
Clancy, T P J (Lansdowne) 1988 *W, E* 1,2, *WS, It*, 1989 *F, W, E, S*
Clarke, A T H (Northampton, Dungannon) 1995 *Fj* (R), 1996 *W, E, WS*, 1997 *F* (R), *It* 2(R), 1998 *Gg* (R), *R*
Clarke, C P (Terenure Coll) 1993 *F, W, E*, 1998 *W, E*
Clarke, D J (Dolphin) 1991 *W, Nm* 1,2, [*J, A*], 1992 *NZ* 2(R)
Clarke, J A B (Bective Rangers) 1922 *S, W, F*, 1923 *F*, 1924 *E, S, W*
Clegg, R J (Bangor) 1973 *F*, 1975 *E, S, F, W*
Clifford, J T (Young Munster) 1949 *F, E, S, W*, 1950 *F, E, S, W*, 1951 *F, E, SA*, 1952 *F, S, W*
Clinch, A D (Dublin U, Wanderers) 1892 *S*, 1893 *W*, 1895 *E, S, W*, 1896 *E, S, W*, 1897 *E, S*
Clinch, J D (Wanderers, Dublin U) 1923 *W*, 1924 *F, E, S, W, NZ*, 1925 *F, E, S*, 1926 *E, S, W*, 1927 *F*, 1928 *F, E, S, W*, 1929 *F, E, S, W*, 1930 *F, E, S, W*, 1931 *F, E, S, W, SA*
Clohessy, P M (Young Munster) 1993 *F, W, E*, 1994 *F, W, E, S, A* 1,2, *US*, 1995 *E, S, F, W*, 1996 *S, F*, 1997 *It* 2, 1998 *F* (R), *W* (R), *SA* 2(R), *Gg, R, SA* 3, 1999 *F, W, E, S, It, A* 1,2 *Arg* 1, [*US, A* 3(R)], 2000 *E, S, It, F, W, Arg, J, SA*, 2001 *It, F, R, S, W, E, Sm* (R), *NZ*, 2002 *W, E, S, It, F*
Clune, J J (Blackrock Coll) 1912 *SA*, 1913 *W, F*, 1914 *F, E, W*
Coffey, J J (Lansdowne) 1900 *E*, 1901 *W*, 1902 *E, S, W*, 1903 *E, S, W*, 1905 *E, S, W, NZ*, 1906 *E, S, W, SA*, 1907 *E*, 1908 *W*, 1910 *F*
Cogan, W St J (Queen's Coll, Cork) 1907 *E, S*
Collier, S R (Queen's Coll, Belfast) 1883 *S*
Collins, P C (Lansdowne, London Irish) 1987 [*C*], 1990 *S* (R)
Collis, W R F (KCH, Harlequins) 1924 *F, W, NZ*, 1925 *F, E, S*, 1926 *F*
Collis, W S (Wanderers) 1884 *W*
Collopy, G (Bective Rangers) 1891 *S*, 1892 *S*
Collopy, R (Bective Rangers) 1923 *E, S, W, F*, 1924 *F, E, S, W, NZ*, 1925 *F, E, S, W*
Collopy, W P (Bective Rangers) 1914 *F, E, S, W*, 1921 *E, S, W, F*, 1922 *E, S, W, F*, 1923 *S, W, F*, 1924 *F, E, S, W*
Combe, A (NIFC) 1875 *E*
Condon, H C (London Irish) 1984 *S* (R)
Cook, H G (Lansdowne) 1884 *W*
Coote, P B (RAF, Leicester) 1933 *S*
Corcoran, J C (London Irish) 1947 *A*, 1948 *F*

Corken, T S (Belfast Collegians) 1937 *E, S, W*
Corkery, D S (Cork Constitution, Bristol) 1994 *A* 1,2, *US*, 1995 *E*, [*NZ, J, W, F*], *Fj*, 1996 *US, S, F, W, E, WS, A*, 1997 *It* 1, *F, W, E, S*, 1998 *S, F, W, E*, 1999 *A* 1(R),2(R)
Corley, H H (Dublin U, Wanderers) 1902 *E, S, W*, 1903 *E, S, W*, 1904 *E, S*
Cormac, H S T (Clontarf) 1921 *E, S, W*
Corrigan, R (Greystones, Lansdowne) 1997 *C* (R), *It* 2, 1998 *S, F, W, E, SA* 3(R), 1999 *A* 1(R),2(R), [*Arg* 2], 2002 *NZ* 1,2
Costello, P (Bective Rangers) 1960 *F*
Costello, R A (Garryowen) 1993 *S*
Costello, V C P (St Mary's Coll, London Irish) 1996 *US, F, W, E, WS* (R), 1997 *C, It* 2(R), 1998 *S* (R), *F, W, E, SA* 1,2, *Gg, R, SA* 3, 1999 *F, W* (R), *E, S* (R), *It, A* 1
Cotton, J (Wanderers) 1889 *W*
Coulter, H H (Queen's U, Belfast) 1920 *E, S, W*
Courtney, A W (UC Dublin) 1920 *S, W, F*, 1921 *E, S, W, F*
Cox, H L (Dublin U) 1875 *E*, 1876 *E*, 1877 *E, S*
Craig, R G (Queen's U, Belfast) 1938 *S, W*
Crawford, E C (Dublin U) 1885 *E, S* 1
Crawford, W E (Lansdowne) 1920 *E, S, W, F*, 1921 *E, S, W, F*, 1922 *E, S*, 1923 *E, S, W, F*, 1924 *F, E, W, NZ*, 1925 *F, E, S, W*, 1926 *F, E, S, W*, 1927 *F, E, S, W*
Crean, T J (Wanderers) 1894 *E, S, W*, 1895 *E, S, W*, 1896 *E, S, W*
Crichton, R Y (Dublin U) 1920 *E, S, W, F*, 1921 *F*, 1922 *E*, 1923 *W, F*, 1924 *F, E, S, W, NZ*, 1925 *E, S*
Croker, E W D (Limerick) 1878 *E*
Cromey, C F (Queen's U, Belfast) 1937 *E, S, W*, 1938 *E, S, W*, 1939 *E, S, W*
Cronin, B M (Garryowen) 1995 *S*, 1997 *S*
Cronyn, A P (Dublin U, Lansdowne) 1875 *E*, 1876 *E*, 1880 *S*
Crossan, K D (Instonians) 1982 *S*, 1984 *F, W, E, S*, 1985 *S, F, W, E*, 1986 *E, S, R*, 1987 *E, S, F, W*, [*W, C, Tg, A*], 1988 *S, F, W, E* 1, *WS, It*, 1989 *W, S, NZ*, 1990 *E, S, F, W, Arg*, 1991 *E, S, Nm* 2 [*Z, J, S*], 1992 *W*
Crotty, D J (Garryowen) 1996 *A*, 1997 *It* 1, *F, W*, 2000 *C*
Crowe, J F (UC Dublin) 1974 *NZ*
Crowe, L (Old Belvedere) 1950 *E, S, W*
Crowe, M P (Lansdowne) 1929 *W*, 1930 *E, S, W*, 1931 *F, S, W, SA*, 1932 *S, W*, 1933 *W, S*, 1934 *E*
Crowe, P M (Blackrock Coll) 1935 *E*, 1938 *E*
Cullen, L F M (Blackrock Coll) 2002 *NZ* 2(R)
Cullen, T J (UC Dublin) 1949 *F*
Cullen, W J (Monkstown and Manchester) 1920 *E*
Culliton, M G (Wanderers) 1959 *E, S, W, F*, 1960 *E, S, W, F, SA*, 1961 *E, S, W, F*, 1962 *S, F*, 1964 *E, S, W, F*
Cummins, W E A (Queen's Coll, Cork) 1879 *S*, 1881 *E*, 1882 *E*
Cunningham, D McC (NIFC) 1923 *E, S, W*, 1925 *F, E, W*
Cunningham, M J (UC Cork) 1955 *F, E, S, W*, 1956 *F, S, W*
Cunningham, V J G (St Mary's Coll) 1988 *E* 2, *It*, 1990 *Arg* (R), 1991 *Nm* 1,2, [*Z, J*(R)], 1992 *NZ* 1,2, *A*, 1993 *S, F, W, E, R*, 1994 *F*
Cunningham, W A (Lansdowne) 1920 *W*, 1921 *E, S, W, F*, 1922 *E*, 1923 *S, W*
Cuppaidge, J L (Dublin U) 1879 *E*, 1880 *E, S*
Currell, J (NIFC) 1877 *S*
Curtis, A B (Oxford U) 1950 *F, E, S*
Curtis, D M (London Irish) 1991 *W, E, S, Nm* 1,2, [*Z, J, S, A*], 1992 *W, E, S* (R), *F*
Cuscaden, W A (Dublin U, Bray) 1876 *E*
Cussen, D J (Dublin U) 1921 *E, S, W, F*, 1922 *E*, 1923 *E, S, W, F*, 1926 *F, E, S, W*, 1927 *F, E*

Daly, J C (London Irish) 1947 *F, E, S, W*, 1948 *E, S, W*
Daly, M J (Harlequins) 1938 *E*
Danaher, P P A (Lansdowne, Garryowen) 1988 *S, F, W, WS, It*, 1989 *F, NZ* (R), 1990 *F*, 1992 *S, F, NZ* 1, *A*, 1993 *S, F, W, E, R*, 1994 *F, W, E, S, A* 1,2, *US*, 1995 *E, S, F, W*
D'Arcy, G M (Lansdowne) 1999 [*R* (R)]
Dargan, M J (Old Belvedere) 1952 *S, W*
Davidson, C T (NIFC) 1921 *F*
Davidson, I G (NIFC) 1899 *E*, 1900 *S, W*, 1901 *E, S, W*, 1902 *E, S, W*
Davidson, J C (Dungannon) 1969 *F, E, S, W*, 1973 *NZ*, 1976 *NZ*
Davidson, J W (Dungannon, London Irish, Castres) 1995 *Fj*, 1996 *S, F, W, E, WS, A*, 1997 *F, E, S, W*, 1998 *Gg* (R), *R* (R), *SA* 3(R), 1999 *F, W, E, S, It, A* 1,2(R), *Arg* 1, [*US,R* (R), *Arg* 2], 2000 *S* (R), *W* (R), *US, C*, 2001 *It* (R), *S*
Davies, F E (Lansdowne) 1892 *S, W*, 1893 *E, S, W*
Davis, J L (Monkstown) 1898 *E, S*

Davis, W J N (Edinburgh U, Bessbrook) 1890 *S, W, E*, 1891 *E, S, W*, 1892 *E, S*, 1895 *S*
Davison, W (Belfast Academy) 1887 *W*
Davy, E O'D (UC Dublin, Lansdowne) 1925 *W*, 1926 *F, E, S, W*, 1927 *F, E, S, W, A*, 1928 *F, E, S, W*, 1929 *F, E, S, W*, 1930 *F, E, S, W*, 1931 *F, E, S, W, SA*, 1932 *E, S, W*, 1933 *E, W, S*, 1934 *E*
Dawson, A R (Wanderers) 1958 *A, E, S, W, F*, 1959 *E, S, W, F*, 1960 *F, SA*, 1961 *E, S, W, F, SA*, 1962 *S, F, W*, 1963 *F, E, S, W, NZ*, 1964 *E, S, F*
Dawson, K (London Irish) 1997 *NZ, C*, 1998 *S*, 1999 [*R, Arg* 2], 2000 *E, S, It, F, W, J, SA*, 2001 *R, S, W* (R), *E* (R), *Sm*
Dean, P M (St Mary's Coll) 1981 *SA* 1,2, *A*, 1982 *W, E, S, F*, 1984 *A*, 1985 *S, F, W, E*, 1986 *F, W, R*, 1987 *E, S, F, W, [W, A]*, 1988 *S, F, W, E* 1,2, *WS, It*, 1989 *F, W, E, S*
Deane, E C (Monkstown) 1909 *E*
Deering, M J (Bective Rangers) 1929 *W*
Deering, S J (Bective Rangers) 1935 *E, S, W, NZ*, 1936 *E, S, W*, 1937 *E, S*
Deering, S M (Garryowen, St Mary's Coll) 1974 *W*, 1976 *F, W, E, S*, 1977 *W, E*, 1978 *NZ*
de Lacy, H (Harlequins) 1948 *E, S*
Delany, M G (Bective Rangers) 1895 *W*
Dempsey, G T (Terenure Coll) 1998 *Gg* (R). *SA* 3, 1999 *F, E, S, It, A* 2, 2000 *E* (R), *S, It, F, W, SA*, 2001 *It, F, S, W, E, NZ*, 2002 *W, E, S, It, F, NZ* 1,2
Dennison, S P (Garryowen) 1973 *F*, 1975 *E, S*
Dick, C J (Ballymena) 1961 *W, F, SA*, 1962 *W*, 1963 *F, E, S, W*
Dick, J S (Queen's U, Belfast) 1962 *E*
Dick, J S (Queen's U, Cork) 1887 *E, S, W*
Dickson, J A N (Dublin U) 1920 *E, W, F*
Doherty, A E (Old Wesley) 1974 *P* (R)
Doherty, W D (Guy's Hospital) 1920 *E, S, W*, 1921 *E, S, W, F*
Donaldson, J A (Belfast Collegians) 1958 *A, E, S, W*
Donovan, T M (Queen's Coll, Cork) 1889 *S*
Dooley, J F (Galwegians) 1959 *E, S, W*
Doran, B R W (Lansdowne) 1900 *S, W*, 1901 *E, S, W*, 1902 *E, S, W*
Doran, E F (Lansdowne) 1890 *S, W*
Doran, G P (Lansdowne) 1899 *S, W*, 1900 *E, S*, 1902 *S, W*, 1903 *W*, 1904 *E*
Douglas, A C (Instonians) 1923 *F*, 1924 *E, S*, 1927 *A*, 1928 *S*
Downing, A J (Dublin U) 1882 *W*
Dowse, J C A (Monkstown) 1914 *F, S, W*
Doyle, J A P (Greystones) 1984 *E, S*
Doyle, J T (Bective Rangers) 1935 *W*
Doyle, M G (Blackrock Coll, UC Dublin, Cambridge U, Edinburgh Wands) 1965 *F, E, S, W, SA*, 1966 *F, E, S, W*, 1967 *A* 1, *E, S, W, F, A* 2, 1968 *F, E, S, W, A*
Doyle, T J (Wanderers) 1968 *E, S, W*
Duggan, A T A (Lansdowne) 1963 *NZ*, 1964 *F*, 1966 *W*, 1967 *A* 1, *S, W, A* 2, 1968 *F, E, S, W*, 1969 *F, E, S, W*, 1970 *SA, F, E, S, W*, 1971 *F, E, S, W*, 1972 *F* 2
Duggan, W (UC Cork) 1920 *S, W*
Duggan, W P (Blackrock Coll) 1975 *E, S, F, W*, 1976 *A, F, W, S, NZ*, 1977 *W, E, S, F*, 1978 *F, W, E, NZ*, 1979 *E, S, A* 1,2, 1980 *E*, 1981 *F, W, E, S, SA* 1,2, *A*, 1982 *W, E, S*, 1983 *S, F, W, E*, 1984 *F, W, E, S*
Duignan, P (Galwegians) 1998 *Gg, R*
Duncan, W R (Malone) 1984 *W, E*
Dunlea, F J (Lansdowne) 1989 *W, E, S*
Dunlop, R (Dublin U) 1889 *W*, 1890 *S, W, E*, 1891 *E, S, W*, 1892 *E, S*, 1893 *W*, 1894 *W*
Dunn, P E F (Bective Rangers) 1923 *S*
Dunn, T B (NIFC) 1935 *NZ*
Dunne, M J (Lansdowne) 1929 *F, E, S*, 1930 *F, E, S, W*, 1932 *E, S, W*, 1933 *E, W, S*, 1934 *E, S, W*
Dwyer, P J (UC Dublin) 1962 *W*, 1963 *F, NZ*, 1964 *S, W*

Easterby, G (Ebbw Vale, Ballynahinch, Llanelli) 2000 *US, C* (R), 2001 *R* (R), *S, W* (R), *Sm* (R), 2002 *W* (R), *S* (R)
Easterby, S H (Llanelli) 2000 *S, It, F, W, Arg, US, C*, 2001 *S, Sm* (R), 2002 *W, E* (R), *S* (R), *It, F, NZ* 1,2
Edwards, H G (Dublin U) 1877 *E*, 1878 *E*
Edwards, R W (Malone) 1904 *W*
Edwards, T (Lansdowne) 1888 *M*, 1890 *S, W, E*, 1892 *W*, 1893 *E*
Edwards, W V (Malone) 1912 *F, E*
Egan, J D (Bective Rangers) 1922 *S*
Egan, J T (Cork Constitution) 1931 *F, E, SA*
Egan, M S (Garryowen) 1893 *E*, 1895 *S*

Ekin, W (Queen's Coll, Belfast) 1888 *W, S*
Elliott, W R J (Bangor) 1979 *S*
Elwood, E P (Lansdowne, Galwegians) 1993 *W, E, R*, 1994 *F, W, E, S, A* 1,2, 1995 *F, W, [NZ, W, F]*, 1996 *US, S*, 1997 *F, W, E, NZ, C, It* 2(R), 1998 *F, W, E, SA* 1,2, *Gg, R, SA* 3, 1999 *It, Arg* 1(R), [*US* (R), *A* 3(R), *R*]
English, M A F (Lansdowne, Limerick Bohemians) 1958 *W, F*, 1959 *E, S, F*, 1960 *E, S*, 1961 *S, W, F*, 1962 *F, W*, 1963 *E, S, W, NZ*
Ennis, F N G (Wanderers) 1979 *A* 1(R)
Ensor, A H (Wanderers) 1973 *W, F*, 1974 *F, W, E, S, P, NZ*, 1975 *E, S, F, W*, 1976 *A, F, W, E, NZ*, 1977 *E*, 1978 *S, F, W, E*
Entrican, J C (Queen's U, Belfast) 1931 *S*
Erskine, D J (Sale) 1997 *NZ* (R), *C, It* 2

Fagan, G L (Kingstown School) 1878 *E*
Fagan, W B C (Wanderers) 1956 *F, E, S*
Farrell, J L (Bective Rangers) 1926 *F, E, S, W*, 1927 *F, E, S, W, A*, 1928 *F, E, S, W*, 1929 *F, E, S, W*, 1930 *F, E, S, W*, 1931 *F, E, S, W, SA*, 1932 *E, S, W*
Feddis, N (Lansdowne) 1956 *E*
Feighery, C F P (Lansdowne) 1972 *F* 1, *E, F* 2
Feighery, T A O (St Mary's Coll) 1977 *W, E*
Ferris, H H (Queen's Coll, Belfast) 1901 *W*
Ferris, J H (Queen's Coll, Belfast) 1900 *E, S, W*
Field, M J (Malone) 1994 *E, S, A* 1(R), 1995 *F* (R), *W* (t), *It* (R), *[NZ(t + R), J]*, *Fj*, 1996 *F* (R), *W, E, A* (R), 1997 *F, W, E, S*
Finlay, J E (Queen's Coll, Belfast) 1913 *E, S, W*, 1920 *E, S, W*
Finlay, W (NIFC) 1876 *E*, 1877 *E, S*, 1878 *E*, 1879 *S, E*, 1880 *S*, 1882 *S*
Finn, M C (UC Cork, Cork Constitution) 1979 *E*, 1982 *W, E, S, F*, 1983 *S, F, W, E*, 1984 *E, S, A*, 1986 *F, W*
Finn, R G A (UC Dublin) 1977 *F*
Fitzgerald, C C (Glasgow U, Dungannon) 1902 *E*, 1903 *E, S*
Fitzgerald, C F (St Mary's Coll) 1979 *A* 1,2, 1980 *E, S, F, W*, 1982 *W, E, S, F*, 1983 *S, F, W, E*, 1984 *F, W, A*, 1985 *S, F, W, E*, 1986 *F, W, E, S*
Fitzgerald, D C (Lansdowne, De La Salle Palmerston) 1984 *E, S*, 1986 *W, E, S*, 1987 *E, S, F, W, [W, C, A]*, 1988 *S, F, W, E* 1, 1989 *NZ* (R), 1990 *E, S, F, W, Arg*, 1991 *F, W, E, S, Nm* 1,2, *[Z, S, A]*, 1992 *W, J, S* (R)
Fitzgerald, J (Wanderers) 1884 *W*
Fitzgerald, J J (Young Munster) 1988 *S, F*, 1990 *S, F, W*, 1991 *F, W, E, S, [J]*, 1994 *A* 1,2
Fitzgibbon, M J J (Shannon) 1992 *W, E, S, F, NZ* 1,2
Fitzpatrick, J M (Dungannon) 1998 *SA* 1,2 *Gg* (R), *R* (R), *SA* 3, 1999 *F* (R), *W* (R), *E* (R), *It, Arg* 1(R), *[US* (R), *A* 3, *R, Arg* 2(t&R)], 2000 *S* (R), *It* (R), *Arg* (R), *US, C, SA* (t&R), 2001 *R* (R)
Fitzpatrick, M P (Wanderers) 1978 *S*, 1980 *S, F, W*, 1981 *F, W, E, S, A*, 1985 *F* (R)
Flavin, P (Blackrock Coll) 1997 *F* (R), *S*
Fletcher, W W (Kingstown) 1882 *W, S*, 1883 *E*
Flood, R S (Dublin U) 1925 *W*
Flynn, M K (Wanderers) 1959 *F*, 1960 *F*, 1962 *E, S, F, W*, 1964 *E, S, W, F*, 1965 *F, E, S, W, SA*, 1966 *F, E, S*, 1972 *F* 1, *E, F* 2, 1973 *NZ*
Fogarty, T (Garryowen) 1891 *W*
Foley, A G (Shannon) 1995 *E, S, F, W, It, [J(t + R)]*, 1996 *A*, 1997 *It* 1, *E* (R), 2000 *E, S, It, F, W, Arg, C, J, SA*, 2001 *It, F, R, S, W, E, Sm, NZ*, 2002 *W, E, S, It, F, NZ* 1,2
Foley, B O (Shannon) 1976 *F, E*, 1977 *W* (R), 1980 *F, W*, 1981 *F, E, S, SA* 1,2, *A*
Forbes, R E (Malone) 1907 *E*
Forrest, A J (Wanderers) 1880 *E, S*, 1881 *E, S*, 1882 *W, E*, 1883 *E*, 1885 *S* 2
Forrest, E G (Wanderers) 1888 *M*, 1889 *S, W*, 1890 *S, E*, 1891 *E*, 1893 *S*, 1894 *E, S, W*, 1895 *W*, 1897 *E, S*
Forrest, H (Wanderers) 1893 *S, W*
Fortune, J J (Clontarf) 1963 *NZ*, 1964 *E*
Foster, A R (Derry) 1910 *E, S, F*, 1911 *E, S, W, F*, 1912 *F, E, S, W*, 1914 *E, S, W*, 1921 *E, S, W*
Francis, N P J (Blackrock Coll, London Irish, Old Belvedere) 1987 *[Tg, A]*, 1988 *WS, It*, 1989 *S*, 1990 *E, F, W*, 1991 *E, S, Nm* 1,2, *[Z, J, S, A]*, 1992 *W, E, S*, 1993 *F, W*, 1994 *F, W, E, S, A* 1,2, *US*, 1995 *E, [NZ, J, W, F]*, *Fj*, 1996 *US, S*
Franks, J G (Dublin U) 1898 *E, S, W*
Frazer, E F (Bective Rangers) 1891 *S*, 1892 *S*
Freer, A E (Lansdowne) 1901 *E, S, W*

Fulcher, G M (Cork Constitution, London Irish) 1994 *A* 2, *US*, 1995 *E* (R), *S, F, W, It*, [*NZ, W, F*], 1996 *US, S, F, W, E, A*, 1997 *It* 1, *W* (R), 1998 *SA* 1(R)
Fulton, J (NIFC) 1895 *S, W*, 1896 *E*, 1897 *E*, 1898 *W*, 1899 *E*, 1900 *W*, 1901 *E*, 1902 *E, S, W*, 1903 *E, S, W*, 1904 *E, S*
Furlong, J N (UC Galway) 1992 *NZ* 1,2

Gaffikin, W (Windsor) 1875 *E*
Gage, J H (Queen's U, Belfast) 1926 *S, W*, 1927 *S, W*
Galbraith, E (Dublin U) 1875 *E*
Galbraith, H T (Belfast Acad) 1890 *W*
Galbraith, R (Dublin U) 1875 *E*, 1876 *E*, 1877 *E*
Galwey, M J (Shannon) 1991 *F, W, Nm* 2(R), [*J*], 1992 *E, S, F, NZ* 1,2, *A*, 1993 *F, W, E, R*, 1994 *F, W, E, S, A* 1, *US* (R), 1995 *E*, 1996 *WS*, 1998 *F* (R), 1999 *W* (R), 2000 *E* (R), *S, It, F, W, Arg, C*, 2001 *It, F, R, W, E, Sm, NZ*, 2002 *W, E, S*
Ganly, J B (Monkstown) 1927 *F, E, S, W, A*, 1928 *F, E, S, W*, 1929 *F, S*, 1930 *F*
Gardiner, F (NIFC) 1900 *E, S*, 1901 *E, W*, 1902 *E, S, W*, 1903 *E, W*, 1904 *E, S, W*, 1906 *E, S, W*, 1907 *S, W*, 1908 *S, W*, 1909 *S, F*
Gardiner, J B (NIFC) 1923 *E, S, W, F*, 1924 *F, E, S, W, NZ*, 1925 *F, E, S, W*
Gardiner, S (Belfast Albion) 1893 *E, S*
Gardiner, W (NIFC) 1892 *E, S*, 1893 *E, S, W*, 1894 *E, S, W*, 1895 *E, S, W*, 1896 *E, S, W*, 1897 *E, S*, 1898 *W*
Garry, M G (Bective Rangers) 1909 *E, S, W, F*, 1911 *E, S, W*
Gaston, J T (Dublin U) 1954 *NZ, F, E, S, W*, 1955 *W* 1956 *F, E*
Gavin, T J (Moseley, London Irish) 1949 *F, E*
Geoghegan, S P (London Irish, Bath) 1991 *F, W, E, S, Nm* 1, [*Z, S, A*], 1992 *E, S, F, A*, 1993 *S, F, W, E, R*, 1994 *F, W, E, S, A* 1,2, *US*, 1995 *E, S, F, W*, [*NZ, J, W, F*], *Fj*, 1996 *US, S, W, E*
Gibson, C M H (Cambridge U, NIFC) 1964 *E, S, W, F*, 1965 *F, E, S, W, SA*, 1966 *F, E, S, W*, 1967 *A* 1, *E, S, W, F, A* 2, 1968 *E, S, W, A*, 1969 *E, S, W*, 1970 *SA, F, E, S, W*, 1971 *F, E, S, W*, 1972 *F* 1, *E, F* 2, 1973 *NZ, E, S, W, F*, 1974 *F, W, E, S, P*, 1975 *E, S, F, W*, 1976 *A, F, W, E, S, NZ*, 1977 *W, E, S, F*, 1978 *F, W, E, NZ*, 1979 *S, A* 1,2
Gibson, M E (Lansdowne, London Irish) 1979 *F, W, E, S*, 1981 *W* (R), 1986 *R*, 1988 *S, F, W, E* 2
Gifford, H P (Wanderers) 1890 *S*
Gillespie, J C (Dublin U) 1922 *W, F*
Gilpin, F G (Queen's U, Belfast) 1962 *E, S, F*
Glass, D C (Belfast Collegians) 1958 *F*, 1960 *W*, 1961 *W, SA*
Gleeson, K D (St Mary's Coll) 2002 *W* (R), *F* (R), *NZ* 1,2
Glennon, B T (Lansdowne) 1993 *F* (R)
Glennon, J J (Skerries) 1980 *E, S*, 1987 *E, S, F*, [*W* (R)]
Godfrey, R P (UC Dublin) 1954 *S, W*
Goodall, K G (City of Derry, Newcastle U) 1967 *A* 1, *E, S, W, F, A* 2, 1968 *F, E, S, W, A*, 1969 *F, E, S*, 1970 *SA, F, E, S, W*
Gordon, A (Dublin U) 1884 *S*
Gordon, T G (NIFC) 1877 *E, S*, 1878 *E*
Gotto, R P C (NIFC) 1906 *SA*
Goulding, W J (Cork) 1879 *S*
Grace, T O (UC Dublin, St Mary's Coll) 1972 *F* 1, *E*, 1973 *NZ, E, S, W*, 1974 *E, S, P, NZ*, 1975 *E, S, F, W*, 1976 *A, F, W, E, S, NZ*, 1977 *W, E, S, F*, 1978 *S*
Graham, R I (Dublin U) 1911 *F*
Grant, E L (CIYMS) 1971 *F, E, S, W*
Grant, P J (Bective Rangers) 1894 *S, W*
Graves, C R A (Wanderers) 1934 *E, S, W*, 1935 *E, S, W, NZ*, 1936 *E, S, W*, 1937 *E, S*, 1938 *E, S, W*
Gray, R D (Old Wesley) 1923 *E, S*, 1925 *F*, 1926 *F*
Greene, E H (Dublin U, Kingstown) 1882 *W*, 1884 *W*, 1885 *E, S* 2, 1886 *E*
Greer, R (Kingstown) 1876 *E*
Greeves, T J (NIFC) 1907 *E, S, W*, 1909 *W, F*
Gregg, R J (Queen's U, Belfast) 1953 *F, E, S, W*, 1954 *F, E, S*
Griffin, C S (London Irish) 1951 *F, E*
Griffin, J L (Wanderers) 1949 *S, W*
Griffiths, W (Limerick) 1878 *E*
Grimshaw, C (Queen's U, Belfast) 1969 *E* (R)
Guerin, B N (Galwegians) 1956 *S*
Gwynn, A P (Dublin U) 1895 *W*
Gwynn, L H (Dublin U) 1893 *S*, 1894 *E, S, W*, 1897 *S*, 1898 *E, S*

Hakin, R F (CIYMS) 1976 *W, S, NZ*, 1977 *W, E, F*
Hall, R O N (Dublin U) 1884 *W*
Hall, W H (Instonians) 1923 *E, S, W, F*, 1924 *F, S*
Hallaran, C F G T (Royal Navy) 1921 *E, S, W*, 1922 *E, S, W*, 1923 *E, F*, 1924 *F, E, S, W*, 1925 *F*, 1926 *F, E*

Halpin, G F (Wanderers, London Irish) 1990 *E*, 1991 [*J*], 1992 *E, S, F*, 1993 *R*, 1994 *F* (R), 1995 *It*, [*NZ, W, F*]
Halpin, T (Garryowen) 1909 *S, W, F*, 1910 *E, S, W*, 1911 *E, S, W, F*, 1912 *F, E, S*
Halvey, E O (Shannon) 1995 *F, W, It*, [*J, W* (t), *F* (R)], 1997 *NZ, C* (R)
Hamilton, A J (Lansdowne) 1884 *W*
Hamilton, G F (NIFC) 1991 *F, W, E, S, Nm* 2, [*Z, J, S, A*], 1992 *A*
Hamilton, R L (NIFC) 1926 *F*
Hamilton, R W (Wanderers) 1893 *W*
Hamilton, W J (Dublin U) 1877 *E*
Hamlet, G T (Old Wesley) 1902 *E, S, W*, 1903 *E, S, W*, 1904 *S, W*, 1905 *E, S, W, NZ*, 1906 *SA*, 1907 *E, S, W*, 1908 *E, S, W*, 1909 *E, S, W, F*, 1910 *E, S, F*, 1911 *E, S, W, F*
Hanrahan, C J (Dolphin) 1926 *S, W*, 1927 *E, S, W, A*, 1928 *F, E, S*, 1929 *F, E, S, W*, 1930 *F, E, S, W*, 1931 *F*, 1932 *S, W*
Harbison, H T (Bective Rangers) 1984 *W* (R), *E, S*, 1986 *R*, 1987 *E, S, F, W*
Hardy, G G (Bective Rangers) 1962 *S*
Harman, G R A (Dublin U) 1899 *E, W*
Harper, J (Instonians) 1947 *F, E, S*
Harpur, T G (Dublin U) 1908 *E, S, W*
Harrison, T (Cork) 1879 *S*, 1880 *S*, 1881 *E*
Harvey, F M W (Wanderers) 1907 *W*, 1911 *F*
Harvey, G A D (Wanderers) 1903 *E, S*, 1904 *W*, 1905 *E, S*
Harvey, T A (Dublin U) 1900 *W*, 1901 *S, W*, 1902 *E, S, W*, 1903 *E, W*
Haycock, P P (Terenure Coll) 1989 *E*
Hayes, J J (Shannon) 2000 *S, It, F, W, Arg, C, J, SA*, 2001 *It, F, R, S, W, E, Sm, NZ*, 2002 *W, E, S, It, F, NZ* 1,2
Headon, T A (UC Dublin) 1939 *S, W*
Healey, P (Limerick) 1901 *E, S, W*, 1902 *E, S, W*, 1903 *E, S, W*, 1904 *S*
Heffernan, M R (Cork Constitution) 1911 *E, S, W, F*
Hemphill, R (Dublin U) 1912 *F, E, S, W*
Henderson, N J (Queen's U, Belfast, NIFC) 1949 *S, W*, 1950 *F*, 1951 *F, E, S, W, SA*, 1952 *F, S, W, E*, 1953 *F, E, S, W*, 1954 *NZ, F, E, S, W*, 1955 *F, E, S, W*, 1956 *S, W*, 1957 *F, E, S, W*, 1958 *A, E, S, W, F*, 1959 *E, S, W, F*
Henderson R A J (London Irish, Wasps, Young Munster) 1996 *WS*, 1997 *NZ, C*, 1998 *F, W, SA* 1(R),2(R), 1999 *F* (R), *E, S* (R), *It*, 2000 *S* (R), *It* (R), *F, W, Arg, US, J* (R), *SA*, 2001 *It, F*, 2002 *W* (R), *E* (R), *F*
Henebrey, G J (Garryowen) 1906 *E, S, W, SA*, 1909 *W, F*
Heron, A G (Queen's Coll, Belfast) 1901 *E*
Heron, J (NIFC) 1877 *S*, 1879 *E*
Heron, W T (NIFC) 1880 *E, S*
Herrick, R W (Dublin U) 1886 *S*
Heuston, F S (Kingstown) 1882 *W*, 1883 *E, S*
Hewitt, D (Queen's U, Belfast, Instonians) 1958 *A, E, S, F*, 1959 *S, W, F*, 1960 *E, S, W, F*, 1961 *E, S, W, F*, 1962 *S, F*, 1965 *W*
Hewitt, F S (Instonians) 1924 *W, NZ*, 1925 *F, E, S*, 1926 *E*, 1927 *E, S, W*
Hewitt, J A (NIFC) 1981 *SA* 1(R),2(R)
Hewitt, T R (Queen's U, Belfast) 1924 *W, NZ*, 1925 *F, E, S*, 1926 *F, E, S, W*
Hewitt, V A (Instonians) 1935 *S, W, NZ*, 1936 *E, S, W*
Hewitt, W J (Instonians) 1954 *E*, 1956 *S*, 1959 *W*, 1961 *SA*
Hewson, F T (Wanderers) 1875 *E*
Hickie, D A (St Mary's Coll) 1997 *W, E, S, NZ, C, It* 2, 1998 *S, F, W, E, SA* 1,2, 2000 *S, It, F, W, J, SA*, 2001 *F, R, S, W, E, NZ*, 2002 *W, E, S, It, F*
Hickie, D J (St Mary's Coll) 1971 *F, E, S, W*, 1972 *F* 1, *E*
Higgins, J A D (Civil Service) 1947 *S, W, A*, 1948 *F, S, W*
Higgins, W W (NIFC) 1884 *E, S*
Hillary, M F (UC Dublin) 1952 *E*
Hingerty, D J (UC Dublin) 1947 *F, E, S, W*
Hinton, W P (Old Wesley) 1907 *W*, 1908 *E, S, W*, 1909 *E, S*, 1910 *E, S, W, F*, 1911 *E, S, W*, 1912 *F, E, W*
Hipwell, M L (Terenure Coll) 1962 *E, S*, 1968 *F, A*, 1969 *F* (R), *S* (R), *W*, 1971 *F, E, S, W*, 1972 *F* 2
Hobbs, T H M (Dublin U) 1884 *S*, 1885 *E*
Hobson, E W (Dublin U) 1876 *E*
Hogan, N A (Terenure Coll, London Irish) 1995 *E, W*, [*J, W, F*], 1996 *F, W, E, WS*, 1997 *F, W, E, It* 2
Hogan, P (Garryowen) 1992 *F*
Hogg, W (Dublin U) 1885 *S* 2
Holland, J J (Wanderers) 1981 *SA* 1,2, 1986 *W*
Holmes, G W (Dublin U) 1912 *SA*, 1913 *E, S*
Holmes, L J (Lisburn) 1889 *S, W*

Lytle, J N (NIFC) 1888 *M*, 1889 *W*, 1890 *E*, 1891 *E, S*, 1894 *E, S, W*
Lyttle, V J (Collegians, Bedford) 1938 *E*, 1939 *E, S*

McAleese, D R (Ballymena) 1992 *F*
McAllan, G H (Dungannon) 1896 *S, W*
Macauley, J (Limerick) 1887 *E, S*
McBride, W D (Malone) 1988 *W, E* 1, *WS, It*, 1989 *S*, 1990 *F, W, Arg*, 1993 *S, F, W, E, R*, 1994 *W, E, S, A* 1(R), 1995 *S, F, [NZ, W, F], Fj* (R), 1996 *W, E, WS, A*, 1997 *It* 1(R), *F, W, E, S*
McBride, W J (Ballymena) 1962 *E, S, F, W*, 1963 *F, E, S, W, NZ*, 1964 *E, S, F*, 1965 *F, E, S, W, SA*, 1966 *F, E, S, W*, 1967 *A* 1, *E, S, W, F, A* 2, 1968 *F, E, S, W, A*, 1969 *F, E, S, W*, 1970 *SA, F, E, S, W*, 1971 *F, E, S, W*, 1972 *F* 1, *E, F* 2, 1973 *NZ, E, S, W, F*, 1974 *F, W, E, S, P, NZ*, 1975 *E, S, F, W*
McCahill, S A (Sunday's Well) 1995 *Fj* (t)
McCall, B W (London Irish) 1985 *F* (R), 1986 *E, S*
McCall, M C (Bangor, Dungannon, London Irish) 1992 *NZ* 1(R),2, 1994 *W*, 1996 *E* (R), *A*, 1997 *It* 1, *NZ, C, It* 2, 1998 *S, E, SA* 1,2
McCallan, B (Ballymena) 1960 *E, S*
McCarten, R J (London Irish) 1961 *E, W, F*
McCarthy, E A (Kingstown) 1882 *W*
McCarthy, J S (Dolphin) 1948 *F, E, S, W*, 1949 *F, E, S, W*, 1950 *W*, 1951 *F, E, S, W, SA*, 1952 *F, S, W, E*, 1953 *F, E, S*, 1954 *NZ, F, E, S, W*, 1955 *F, E*
McCarthy, P D (Cork Const) 1992 *NZ* 1,2, *A*, 1993 *S, R* (R)
MacCarthy, St G (Dublin U) 1882 *W*
McCarthy, T (Cork) 1898 *W*
McClelland, T A (Queen's U, Belfast) 1921 *E, S, W, F*, 1922 *E, W, F*, 1923 *E, S, W, F*, 1924 *F, E, S, W, NZ*
McClenahan, R O (Instonians) 1923 *E, S, W*
McClinton, A N (NIFC) 1910 *W, F*
McCombe, W McM (Dublin U, Bangor) 1968 *F*, 1975 *E, S, F, W*
McConnell, A A (Collegians) 1947 *A*, 1948 *F, E, S, W*, 1949 *F, E*
McConnell, G (Derry, Edinburgh U) 1912 *F, E*, 1913 *W, F*
McConnell, J W (Lansdowne) 1913 *S*
McCormac, F M (Wanderers) 1909 *W*, 1910 *W, F*
McCormick, W J (Wanderers) 1930 *E*
McCoull, H C (Belfast Albion) 1895 *E, S, W*, 1899 *E*
McCourt, D (Queen's U, Belfast) 1947 *A*
McCoy, J J (Dungannon, Bangor, Ballymena) 1984 *W, A*, 1985 *S, F, W, E*, 1986 *F*, 1987 *[Tg]*, 1988 *E* 2, *WS, It*, 1989 *F, W, E, S, NZ*
McCracken, H (NIFC) 1954 *W*
McDermott, S J (London Irish) 1955 *S, W*
Macdonald, J A (Methodist Coll, Belfast) 1875 *E*, 1876 *E*, 1877 *S*, 1878 *E*, 1879 *S*, 1880 *E*, 1881 *S*, 1882 *E, S*, 1883 *E, S*, 1884 *E, S*
McDonald, J P (Malone) 1987 *[C]*, 1990 *E* (R), *S, Arg*
McDonnell, A C (Dublin U) 1889 *W*, 1890 *S, W*, 1891 *E*
McDowell, J C (Instonians) 1924 *F, NZ*
McFarland, B A T (Derry) 1920 *S, W, F*, 1922 *W*
McGann, B J (Lansdowne) 1969 *F, E, S, W*, 1970 *SA, F, E, S, W*, 1971 *F, E, S, W*, 1972 *F* 1, *E, F* 2, 1973 *NZ, E, S, W*, 1976 *F, W, E, S, NZ*
McGowan, A N (Blackrock Coll) 1994 *US*
McGown, T M W (NIFC) 1899 *E, S*, 1901 *S*
McGrath, D G (UC Dublin, Cork Const) 1984 *S*, 1987 *[W, C, Tg, A]*
McGrath, N F (Oxford U, London Irish) 1934 *W*
McGrath, P J (UC Cork) 1965 *E, S, W, SA*, 1966 *F, E, S, W*, 1967 *A* 1, *A* 2
McGrath, R J M (Wanderers) 1977 *W, E, F* (R), 1981 *SA* 1,2, *A*, 1982 *W, E, S, F*, 1983 *S, F, W, E*, 1984 *F, W*
McGrath, T (Garryowen) 1956 *W*, 1958 *F, E*, 1960 *E, S, W, F*, 1961 *SA*
McGuinness, C D (St Mary's Coll) 1997 *NZ, C*, 1998 *F, W, E, SA* 1,2, *Gg, R* (R), *SA* 3, 1999 *F, W, E, S*
McGuire, E P (UC Galway) 1963 *E, S, W, NZ*, 1964 *E, S, W, F*
MacHale, S (Lansdowne) 1965 *F, E, S, W, SA*, 1966 *F, E, S, W*, 1967 *S, W, F*
McIldowie, G (Malone) 1906 *SA*, 1910 *E, S, W*
McIlrath, J A (Ballymena) 1976 *A, F, NZ*, 1977 *W, E*
McIlwaine, E H (NIFC) 1895 *S, W*
McIlwaine, E N (NIFC) 1875 *E*, 1876 *E*
McIlwaine, J E (NIFC) 1897 *E, S*, 1898 *E, S, W*, 1899 *E, W*
McIntosh, L M (Dublin U) 1884 *S*
MacIvor, C V (Dublin U) 1912 *F, E, S, W*, 1913 *E, S, F*
McIvor, S C (Garryowen) 1996 *A*, 1997 *It* 1, *S* (R)

McKay, J W (Queen's U, Belfast) 1947 *F, E, S, W, A*, 1948 *F, E, S, W*, 1949 *F, E, S, W*, 1950 *F, E, S, W*, 1951 *F, E, S, W, SA*, 1952 *F*
McKee, W D (NIFC) 1947 *A*, 1948 *F, E, S, W*, 1949 *F, E, S, W*, 1950 *F, E*, 1951 *SA*
McKeen, A J W (Lansdowne) 1999 *[R* (R)]
McKelvey, J M (Queen's U, Belfast) 1956 *F, E*
McKenna, P (St Mary's Coll) 2000 *Arg*
McKibbin, A R (Instonians, London Irish) 1977 *W, E, S*, 1978 *S, F, W, E, NZ*, 1979 *F, W, E, S*, 1980 *E, S*
McKibbin, C H (Instonians) 1976 *S* (R)
McKibbin, D (Instonians) 1950 *F, E, S, W*, 1951 *F, E, S, W*
McKibbin, H R (Queen's U, Belfast) 1938 *W*, 1939 *E, S, W*
McKinney, S A (Dungannon) 1972 *F* 1, *E, F* 2, 1973 *W, F*, 1974 *F, E, S, P, NZ*, 1975 *E, S*, 1976 *A, F, W, E, S, NZ*, 1977 *W, E, S*, 1978 *S* (R), *F, W, E*
McLaughlin, J H (Derry) 1887 *E, S*, 1888 *W, S*
McLean, R E (Dublin U) 1881 *S*, 1882 *W, E, S*, 1883 *E, S*, 1884 *E, S*, 1885 *E, S* 1
Maclear, B (Cork County, Monkstown) 1905 *E, S, W, NZ*, 1906 *E, S, W, SA*, 1907 *E, S, W*
McLennan, A C (Wanderers) 1977 *F*, 1978 *S, F, W, E, NZ*, 1979 *F, W, E, S*, 1980 *E, F*, 1981 *F, W, E, S, SA* 1,2
McLoughlin, F M (Northern) 1976 *A*
McLoughlin, G A J (Shannon) 1979 *F, W, E, S, A* 1,2, 1980 *E*, 1981 *SA* 1,2, 1982 *W, E, S, F*, 1983 *S, F, W, E*, 1984 *F*
McLoughlin, R J (UC Dublin, Blackrock Coll, Gosforth) 1962 *E, S, F*, 1963 *E, S, W, NZ*, 1964 *E, S*, 1965 *F, E, S, W, SA*, 1966 *F, E, S, W*, 1971 *F, E, S, W*, 1972 *F* 1, *E, F* 2, 1973 *NZ, E, S, W, F*, 1974 *F, W, E, S, P, NZ*, 1975 *E, S, F, W*
McMahon, L B (Blackrock Coll, UC Dublin) 1931 *E, SA*, 1933 *E*, 1934 *E*, 1936 *E, S, W*, 1937 *E, S, W*, 1938 *E, S*
McMaster, A W (Ballymena) 1972 *F* 1, *E, F* 2, 1973 *NZ, E, S, W, F*, 1974 *F, E, S, P*, 1975 *F, W*, 1976 *A, F, W, NZ*
McMordie, J (Queen's Coll, Belfast) 1886 *S*
McMorrow, A (Garryowen) 1951 *W*
McMullen, A R (Cork) 1881 *E, S*
McNamara, V (UC Cork) 1914 *E, S, W*
McNaughton, P P (Greystones) 1978 *S, F, W, E*, 1979 *F, W, E, S, A* 1,2, 1980 *E, S, F, W*, 1981 *F*
MacNeill, H P (Dublin U, Oxford U, Blackrock Coll, London Irish) 1981 *F, W, E, S, A*, 1982 *W, E, S, F*, 1983 *S, F, W, E*, 1984 *F, W, E, A*, 1985 *S, F, W, E*, 1986 *F, W, E, S, R*, 1987 *E, S, F, W, [W, C, Tg, A]*, 1988 *S* (R), *E* 1,2
McQuilkin, K P (Bective Rangers, Lansdowne) 1996 *US, S, F*, 1997 *F* (t & R), *S*
MacSweeney, D A (Blackrock Coll) 1955 *S*
McVicker, H (Army, Richmond) 1927 *E, S, W, A*, 1928 *F*
McVicker, J (Collegians) 1924 *F, E, S, W, NZ*, 1925 *F, E, S, W*, 1926 *F, E, S, W*, 1927 *F, E, S, W, A*, 1928 *W*, 1930 *F*
McVicker, S (Queen's U, Belfast) 1922 *E, S, W, F*
McWeeney, J P J (St Mary's Coll) 1997 *NZ*
Madden, M N (Sunday's Well) 1955 *E, S, W*
Magee, J T (Bective Rangers) 1895 *E, S*
Magee, A M (Louis) (Bective Rangers, London Irish) 1895 *E, S, W*, 1896 *E, S, W*, 1897 *E, S*, 1898 *E, S, W*, 1899 *E, S, W*, 1900 *E, S, W*, 1901 *E, S, W*, 1902 *E, S, W*, 1903 *E, S, W*, 1904 *W*
Maggs, K M (Bristol, Bath) 1997 *NZ* (R), *C, It* 2, 1998 *S, F, W, E, SA* 1,2, *Gg, R* (R), *SA* 3, 1999 *F, W, E, S, It, A* 1, *Arg* 1, *[US, A* 3, *Arg* 2], 2000 *E, F, Arg, US* (R), *C*, 2001 *It* (R), *F* (R), *R, S* (R), *W, E, Sm, NZ*, 2002 *W, E, S*
Maginiss, R M (Dublin U) 1875 *E*, 1876 *E*
Magrath, R M (Cork Constitution) 1909 *S*
Maguire, J F (Cork) 1884 *S*
Mahoney, J (Dolphin) 1923 *E*
Malcolmson, G L (RAF, NIFC) 1935 *NZ*, 1936 *E, S, W*, 1937 *E, S, W*
Malone, N G (Oxford U, Leicester) 1993 *S, F*, 1994 *US* (R)
Mannion, N P (Corinthians, Lansdowne, Wanderers) 1988 *WS, It*, 1989 *F, W, E, S, NZ*, 1990 *E, S, F, W, Arg*, 1991 *Nm* 1(R),2, *[J]*, 1993 *S*
Marshall, B D E (Queen's U, Belfast) 1963 *E*
Mason, S J P (Orrell, Richmond) 1996 *W, E, WS*
Massey-Westropp, R H (Limerick, Monkstown) 1886 *E*
Matier, R N (NIFC) 1878 *E*, 1879 *S*
Matthews, P M (Ards, Wanderers) 1984 *A*, 1985 *S, F, W, E*, 1986 *R*, 1987 *E, S, F, W, [W, Tg, A]*, 1988 *S, F, W, E* 1,2, *WS, It*, 1989 *F, W, E, S, NZ*, 1990 *E, S*, 1991 *F, W, E, S, Nm* 1 *[Z, S, A]*, 1992 *W, E, S*
Mattsson, J (Wanderers) 1948 *E*
Mayne, R B (Queen's U, Belfast) 1937 *W*, 1938 *E, W*, 1939 *E, S, W*

Mayne, R H (Belfast Academy) 1888 *W, S*
Mayne, T (NIFC) 1921 *E, S, F*
Mays, K M A (UC Dublin) 1973 *NZ, E, S, W*
Meares, A W D (Dublin U) 1899 *S, W,* 1900 *E, W*
Megaw, J (Richmond, Instonians) 1934 *W,* 1938 *E*
Millar, A (Kingstown) 1880 *E, S,* 1883 *E*
Millar, H J (Monkstown) 1904 *W,* 1905 *E, S, W*
Millar, S (Ballymena) 1958 *F,* 1959 *E, S, W, F,* 1960 *E, S, W, F, SA,* 1961 *E, S, W, F, SA,* 1962 *E, S, F,* 1963 *F, E, S, W,* 1964 *F,* 1968 *F, E, S, W, A,* 1969 *F, E, S, W,* 1970 *SA, F, E, S, W*
Millar, W H J (Queen's U, Belfast) 1951 *E, S, W,* 1952 *S, W*
Miller, E R P (Leicester, Tererure Coll) 1997 *It* 1, *F, W, E, NZ, It* 2, 1998 *S, W* (R), *Gg, R,* 1999 *F, W, E* (R), *S, Arg* 1(R), [*US* (R), *A* 3(t&R), *Arg* 2(R)], 2000 *US, C* (R), *SA,* 2001 *R, W, E, Sm, NZ,* 2002 *E, S, It* (R)
Miller, F H (Wanderers) 1886 *S*
Milliken, R A (Bangor) 1973 *E, S, W, F,* 1974 *F, W, E, S, P, NZ,* 1975 *E, S, F, W*
Millin, T J (Dublin U) 1925 *W*
Minch, J B (Bective Rangers) 1912 *SA,* 1913 *E, S,* 1914 *E, S*
Moffat, J (Belfast Academy) 1888 *W, S, M,* 1889 *S,* 1890 *S, W,* 1891 *S*
Moffatt, J E (Old Wesley) 1904 *S,* 1905 *E, S, W*
Moffett, J W (Ballymena) 1961 *E, S*
Molloy, M G (UC Galway, London Irish) 1966 *F, E,* 1967 *A* 1, *E, S, W, F, A* 2, 1968 *F, E, S, W, A,* 1969 *F, E, S, W,* 1970 *F, E, S, W,* 1971 *F, E, S, W,* 1973 *F,* 1976 *A*
Moloney, J J (St Mary's Coll) 1972 *F* 1, *E, F* 2, 1973 *NZ, E, S, W, F,* 1974 *F, W, E, S, P, NZ,* 1975 *E, S, F, W,* 1976 *S,* 1978 *S, F, W, E,* 1979 *A* 1,2, 1980 *S, W*
Moloney, L A (Garryowen) 1976 *W* (R), *S,* 1978 *S* (R), *NZ*
Molony, J U (UC Dublin) 1950 *S*
Monteith, J D E (Queen's U, Belfast) 1947 *E, S, W*
Montgomery, A (NIFC) 1895 *S*
Montgomery, F P (Queen's U, Belfast) 1914 *E, S, W*
Montgomery, R (Cambridge U) 1887 *E, S, W,* 1891 *E,* 1892 *W*
Moore, C M (Dublin U) 1887 *S,* 1888 *W, S*
Moore, D F (Wanderers) 1883 *E, S,* 1884 *E, W*
Moore, F W (Wanderers) 1884 *W,* 1885 *E, S* 2, 1886 *S*
Moore, H (Windsor) 1876 *S,* 1877 *S*
Moore, H (Queen's U, Belfast) 1910 *S, W,* 1911 *W, F,* 1912 *F, E, S, W, SA*
Moore, T A P (Highfield) 1967 *A* 2, 1973 *NZ, E, S, W, F,* 1974 *F, W, E, S, P, NZ*
Moore, W D (Queen's Coll, Belfast) 1878 *E*
Moran, F G (Clontarf) 1936 *E,* 1937 *E, S, W,* 1938 *S, W,* 1939 *E, S, W*
Morell, H B (Dublin U) 1881 *E, S,* 1882 *W, E*
Morgan, G J (Clontarf) 1934 *E, S, W,* 1935 *E, S, W, NZ,* 1936 *E, S, W,* 1937 *E, S, W,* 1938 *E, S, W,* 1939 *E, S, W*
Moriarty, C C H (Monkstown) 1899 *W*
Moroney, J C M (Garryowen) 1968 *W, A,* 1969 *F, E, S, W*
Moroney, R J M (Lansdowne) 1984 *F, W,* 1985 *F*
Moroney, T A (UC Dublin) 1964 *W,* 1967 *A* 1, *E*
Morphy, E McG (Dublin U) 1908 *E*
Morris, D P (Bective Rangers) 1931 *W,* 1932 *E,* 1935 *E, S, W, NZ*
Morrow, J W R (Queen's Coll, Belfast) 1882 *S,* 1883 *E, S,* 1884 *E, W,* 1885 *S* 1,2, 1886 *E, S,* 1888 *S*
Morrow, R D (Bangor) 1986 *F, E, S*
Mortell, M (Bective Rangers, Dolphin) 1953 *F, E, S, W,* 1954 *NZ, F, E, S, W*
Morton, W A (Dublin U) 1888 *S*
Mostyn, M R (Galwegians) 1999 *A* 1, *Arg* 1, [*US, A* 3, *R, Arg* 2]
Moyers, L W (Dublin U) 1884 *W*
Moylett, M M F (Shannon) 1988 *E* 1
Mulcahy, W A (UC Dublin, Bective Rangers, Bohemians) 1958 *A, E, S, W, F,* 1959 *E, S, W, F,* 1960 *E, S, W, SA,* 1961 *E, S, W, SA,* 1962 *E, S, F, W,* 1963 *F, E, S, W, NZ,* 1964 *E, S, W, F,* 1965 *F, E, S, W, SA*
Mullan, B (Clontarf) 1947 *F, E, S, W,* 1948 *F, E, S, W*
Mullane, J P (Limerick Bohemians) 1928 *W,* 1929 *F*
Mullen, K D (Old Belvedere) 1947 *F, E, S, W, A,* 1948 *F, E, S, W,* 1949 *F, E, S, W,* 1950 *F, E, S, W,* 1951 *F, E, S, W, SA,* 1952 *F, S, W*
Mulligan, A A (Wanderers) 1956 *F, E,* 1957 *F, E, S, W,* 1958 *A, E, S, F,* 1959 *E, S, W, F,* 1960 *E, S, W, F, SA,* 1961 *W, F, SA*
Mullin, B J (Dublin U, Oxford U, Blackrock Coll, London Irish) 1984 *A,* 1985 *S, W, E,* 1986 *F, W, E, S,* 1987 *E, S, F, W,* [*W, C, Tg, A*], 1988 *S, F, W, E* 1,2, *WS, It,* 1989 *F, W, E, S,*

NZ, 1990 *E, S, W, Arg,* 1991 *F, W, E, S, Nm* 1,2, [*J, S, A*], 1992 *W, E, S,* 1994 *US,* 1995 *E, S, F, W, It,* [*NZ, J, W, F*]
Mullins, M J (Young Munster) 1999 *Arg* 1(R), [*R*], 2000 *E, S, It, Arg* (t&R), *US, C,* 2001 *It, R, W* (R), *E* (R), *Sm* (R), *NZ* (R)
Murphy, C J (Lansdowne) 1939 *E, S, W,* 1947 *F, E*
Murphy, G E A (Leicester) 2000 *US, C* (R), *J,* 2001 *R, S, Sm,* 2002 *W, E, NZ* 1,2
Murphy, J G M W (London Irish) 1951 *SA,* 1952 *S, W, E,* 1954 *NZ,* 1958 *W*
Murphy, J J (Greystones) 1981 *SA* 1, 1982 *W* (R), 1984 *S*
Murphy, J N (Greystones) 1992 *A*
Murphy, K J (Cork Constitution) 1990 *E, S, F, W, Arg,* 1991 *F, W* (R), *S* (R), 1992 *S, F, NZ* 2(R)
Murphy, N A A (Cork Constitution) 1958 *A, E, S, W, F,* 1959 *E, S, W, F,* 1960 *E, S, W, F, SA,* 1961 *E, S, W,* 1962 *E,* 1963 *NZ,* 1964 *E, S, W, F,* 1965 *F, E, S, W, SA,* 1966 *F, E, S, W,* 1967 *A* 1, *E, S, W, F,* 1969 *F, E, S, W*
Murphy, N F (Cork Constitution) 1930 *E, W,* 1931 *F, E, S, W, SA,* 1932 *E, S, W,* 1933 *E*
Murphy-O'Connor, J (Bective Rangers) 1954 *E*
Murray, H W (Dublin U) 1877 *S,* 1878 *E,* 1879 *E*
Murray, J B (UC Dublin) 1963 *F*
Murray, P F (Wanderers) 1927 *F,* 1929 *F, E, S,* 1930 *F, E, S, W,* 1931 *F, E, S, W, SA,* 1932 *E, S, W,* 1933 *E, W, S*
Murtagh, C W (Portadown) 1977 *S*
Myles, J (Dublin U) 1875 *E*

Nash, L C (Queen's Coll, Cork) 1889 *S,* 1890 *W, E,* 1891 *E, S, W*
Neely, M R (Collegians) 1947 *F, E, S, W*
Neill, H J (NIFC) 1885 *E, S* 1,2, 1886 *S,* 1887 *E, S, W,* 1888 *W, S*
Neill, J McF (Instonians) 1926 *F*
Nelson, J E (Malone) 1947 *A,* 1948 *E, S, W,* 1949 *F, E, S, W,* 1950 *F, E, S, W,* 1951 *F, E, W,* 1954 *F*
Nelson, R (Queen's Coll, Belfast) 1882 *E, S,* 1883 *S,* 1886 *S*
Nesdale, R P (Newcastle) 1997 *W, E, S, NZ* (R), *C,* 1998 *F* (R), *W* (R), *Gg, SA* 3(R), 1999 *It, A* 2(R), [*US* (R), *R*]
Nesdale, T J (Garryowen) 1961 *F*
Neville, W C (Dublin U) 1879 *S, E*
Nicholson, P C (Dublin U) 1900 *E, S, W*
Norton, G W (Bective Rangers) 1949 *F, E, S, W,* 1950 *F, E, S, W,* 1951 *F, E, S*
Notley, J R (Wanderers) 1952 *F, S*
Nowlan, K W (St Mary's Coll) 1997 *NZ, C, It* 2

O'Brien, B (Derry) 1893 *S, W*
O'Brien, B A P (Shannon) 1968 *F, E, S*
O'Brien, D J (London Irish, Cardiff, Old Belvedere) 1948 *E, S, W,* 1949 *F, E, S, W,* 1950 *F, E, S, W, SA,* 1951 *F, E, S, W, SA,* 1952 *F, S, W, E*
O'Brien, K A (Broughton Park) 1980 *E,* 1981 *SA* 1(R),2
O'Brien-Butler, P E (Monkstown) 1897 *S,* 1898 *E, S,* 1899 *S, W,* 1900 *E*
O'Callaghan, C T (Carlow) 1910 *W, F,* 1911 *E, S, W, F,* 1912 *F*
O'Callaghan, M P (Sunday's Well) 1962 *W,* 1964 *E, F*
O'Callaghan, P (Dolphin) 1967 *A* 1, *E, A* 2, 1968 *F, E, S, W,* 1969 *F, E, S, W,* 1970 *SA, F, E, S, W,* 1976 *F, W, E, S, NZ*
O'Connell, K D (Sunday's Well) 1994 *F, E* (t)
O'Connell, P (Bective Rangers) 1913 *W, F,* 1914 *F, E, S, W*
O'Connell, P J (Young Munster) 2002 *W, It* (R), *F* (R), *NZ* 1
O'Connell, W J (Lansdowne) 1955 *F*
O'Connor, H S (Dublin U) 1957 *F, E, S, W*
O'Connor, J (Garryowen) 1895 *S*
O'Connor, J H (Bective Rangers) 1888 *M,* 1890 *S, W, E,* 1891 *E, S,* 1892 *E, W,* 1893 *E, S,* 1894 *E, S, W,* 1895 *E, S, W,* 1896 *E, S, W*
O'Connor, J J (Garryowen) 1909 *F*
O'Connor, J J (UC Cork) 1933 *S,* 1934 *E, S, W,* 1935 *E, S, W, NZ,* 1936 *S, W,* 1938 *S*
O'Connor, P J (Lansdowne) 1887 *W*
O'Cuinneagain, D (Sale, Ballymena) 1998 *SA* 1,2, *Gg* (R), *R* (R), *SA* 3, 1999 *F, W, E, S, It, A* 1,2, *Arg* 1, [*US, A* 3, *R, Arg* 2], 2000 *E, It* (R)
Odbert, R V M (RAF) 1928 *F*
O'Donnell, R C (St Mary's Coll) 1979 *A* 1,2, 1980 *S, F, W*
O'Donoghue, P J (Bective Rangers) 1955 *F, E, S, W,* 1956 *W,* 1957 *F, E,* 1958 *A, E, S, W*
O'Driscoll, B G (Blackrock Coll) 1999 *A* 1,2, *Arg* 1, [*US, A* 3, *R* (R), *Arg* 2], 2000 *E, S, It, F, W, J, SA,* 2001 *F, S, W, E, Sm, NZ,* 2002 *W, E, It, F, NZ* 1,2
O'Driscoll, B J (Manchester) 1971 *F* (R), *E, S, W*

O'Driscoll, J B (London Irish, Manchester) 1978 *S*, 1979 *A* 1,2, 1980 *E, S, F, W*, 1981 *F, W, E, S, SA* 1,2, *A*, 1982 *W, E, S, F*, 1983 *S, F, W, E*, 1984 *F, W, E, S*
O'Driscoll, M (Cork Const) 2001 *R* (R)
O'Flanagan, K P (London Irish) 1947 *A*
O'Flanagan, M (Lansdowne) 1948 *S*
O'Gara, R J R (Cork Const) 2000 *S, It, F, W, Arg* (R), *US, C* (R), *J, SA*, 2001 *It, F, S, W* (R), *E* (R), *Sm*, 2002 *W* (R), *E* (R), *S* (R), *It* (t), *F* (R), *NZ* 1,2
O'Grady, D (Sale) 1997 *It* 2
O'Hanlon, B (Dolphin) 1947 *E, S, W*, 1948 *F, E, S, W*, 1949 *F, E, S, W*, 1950 *F*
O'Hara, P T J (Sunday's Well, Cork Const) 1988 *WS* (R), 1989 *F, W, E, NZ*, 1990 *E, S, F, W*, 1991 *Nm* 1, [*J*], 1993 *F, W, E*, 1994 *US*
O'Kelly, M E (London Irish, St Mary's Coll) 1997 *NZ, C, It* 2, 1998 *S, F, W, E, SA* 1,2, *Gg, R, SA* 3, 1999 *A* 1(R),2, *Arg* 1(R), [*US* (R), *A* 3, *R, Arg* 2], 2000 *E, S, It, F, W, Arg, US, J, SA*, 2001 *It, F, S, W, E, NZ*, 2002 *E, S, It, F, NZ* 1(R),2
O'Leary, A (Cork Constitution) 1952 *S, W, E*
O'Loughlin, D B (UC Cork) 1938 *E, S, W*, 1939 *E, S, W*
O'Mahony, D W (UC Dublin, Moseley, Bedford) 1995 *It*, [*F*], 1997 *It* 2, 1998 *R*
O'Mahony, David (Cork Constitution) 1995 *It*
O'Meara, B T (Cork Constitution) 1997 *E* (R), *S, NZ* (R), 1998 *S*, 1999 [*US* (R), *R* (R)], 2001 *R* (R)
O'Meara, J A (UC Cork, Dolphin) 1951 *F, E, S, W, SA*, 1952 *F, S, W, E*, 1953 *F, E, S, W*, 1954 *NZ, F, E, S*, 1955 *F, E*, 1956 *S, W*, 1958 *W*
O'Neill, H O'H (Queen's U, Belfast, UC Cork) 1930 *E, S, W*, 1933 *E, S, W*
O'Neill, J B (Queen's U, Belfast) 1920 *S*
O'Neill, W A (UC Dublin, Wanderers) 1952 *E*, 1953 *F, E, S, W*, 1954 *NZ*
O'Reilly, A J F (Old Belvedere, Leicester) 1955 *F, E, S, W*, 1956 *F, E, S, W*, 1957 *F, E, S, W*, 1958 *A, E, S, W, F*, 1959 *E, S, W, F*, 1960 *E*, 1961 *E, F, SA*, 1963 *F, S, W*, 1970 *E*
Orr, P A (Old Wesley) 1976 *F, W, E, S, NZ*, 1977 *W, E, S, F*, 1978 *S, F, W, E, NZ*, 1979 *F, W, E, S, A* 1,2, 1980 *E, S, F, W*, 1981 *F, W, E, S, SA* 1,2, *A*, 1982 *W, E, S*, 1983 *S, F, W, E*, 1984 *F, W, E, S, A*, 1985 *S, F, W, E*, 1986 *F, S, R*, 1987 *E, S, F, W*, [*W, C, A*]
O'Shea, C M P (Lansdowne, London Irish) 1993 *R*, 1994 *F, W, E, S, A* 1,2, *US*, 1995 *E, S*, [*J, W, F*], 1997 *It* 1, *F, S* (R), 1998 *F, SA* 1,2, *Gg, R, SA* 3, 1999 *F, W, E, S, It, A* 1, *Arg* 1, [*US, A* 3, *R, Arg* 2], 2000 *E*
O'Sullivan, A C (Dublin U) 1882 *S*
O'Sullivan, J M (Limerick) 1884 *S*, 1887 *S*
O'Sullivan, P J A (Galwegians) 1957 *F, E, S, W*, 1959 *E, S, W, F*, 1960 *SA*, 1961 *E, S*, 1962 *F, W*, 1963 *F, NZ*
O'Sullivan, W (Queen's Coll, Cork) 1895 *S*
Owens, R H (Dublin U) 1922 *E, S*

Parfrey, P (UC Cork) 1974 *NZ*
Parke, J C (Monkstown) 1903 *W*, 1904 *E, S, W*, 1905 *W, NZ*, 1906 *E, S, W, SA*, 1907 *E, S, W*, 1908 *E, S, W*, 1909 *E, S, W, F*
Parr, J S (Wanderers) 1914 *F, E, S, W*
Patterson, C S (Instonians) 1978 *NZ*, 1979 *F, W, E, S, A* 1,2, 1980 *E, S, F, W*
Patterson, R d'A (Wanderers) 1912 *F, S, W, SA*, 1913 *E, S, W, F*
Payne, C T (NIFC) 1926 *E*, 1927 *F, E, S, A*, 1928 *F, E, S, W*, 1929 *F, E, W*, 1930 *F, E, S, W*
Pedlow, A C (CIYMS) 1953 *W*, 1954 *NZ, F, E*, 1955 *F, E, S, W*, 1956 *F, E, S, W*, 1957 *F, E, S, W*, 1958 *A, E, S, W, F*, 1959 *E*, 1960 *E, S, W, F, SA*, 1961 *S*, 1962 *W*, 1963 *F*
Pedlow, J (Bessbrook) 1882 *S*, 1884 *W*
Pedlow, R (Bessbrook) 1891 *W*
Pedlow, T B (Queen's Coll, Belfast) 1889 *S, W*
Peel, T (Limerick) 1892 *E, S, W*
Peirce, W (Cork) 1881 *E*
Phipps, G C (Army) 1950 *E, W*, 1952 *F, W, E*
Pike, T O (Lansdowne) 1927 *E, S, W, A*, 1928 *F, E, S, W*
Pike, V J (Lansdowne) 1931 *E, S, W, SA*, 1932 *E, S, W*, 1933 *E, W, S*, 1934 *E, S, W*
Pike, W W (Kingstown) 1879 *E*, 1881 *E, S*, 1882 *E*, 1883 *S*
Pinion, G (Belfast Collegians) 1909 *E, S, W, F*
Piper, O J S (Cork Constitution) 1909 *E, S, W, F*, 1910 *E, S, W, F*
Polden, S E (Clontarf) 1913 *W, F*, 1914 *F*, 1920 *F*
Popham, I (Cork Constitution) 1922 *W, F*, 1923 *F*
Popplewell, N J (Greystones, Wasps, Newcastle) 1989 *NZ*, 1990 *Arg*, 1991 *Nm* 1,2, [*Z, S, A*], 1992 *W, E, S, F, NZ* 1,2, *A*,

1993 *S, F, W, E, R*, 1994 *F, W, E, S, US*, 1995 *E, S, F, W, It*, [*NZ, J, W, F*], *Fj*, 1996 *US, S, F, W, E, A*, 1997 *It* 1, *F, W, E, NZ, C*, 1998 *S* (t), *F* (R)
Potterton, H N (Wanderers) 1920 *W*
Pratt, R H (Dublin U) 1933 *E, W, S*, 1934 *E, S*
Price, A H (Dublin U) 1920 *S, F*
Pringle, J C (NIFC) 1902 *S, W*
Purcell, N M (Lansdowne) 1921 *E, S, W, F*
Purdon, H (NIFC) 1879 *S, E*, 1880 *E*, 1881 *E, S*
Purdon, W B (Queen's Coll, Belfast) 1906 *E, S, W*
Purser, F C (Dublin U) 1898 *E, S, W*

Quinlan, A (Shannon) 1999 [*R* (R)], 2001 *It, F*, 2002 *NZ* 2(R)
Quinlan, S V J (Blackrock Coll) 1956 *F, E, W*, 1958 *W*
Quinn, B T (Old Belvedere) 1947 *F*
Quinn, F P (Old Belvedere) 1981 *F, W, E*
Quinn, J P (Dublin U) 1910 *E, S*, 1911 *E, S, W, F*, 1912 *E, S, W*, 1913 *E, W, F*, 1914 *F, E, S*
Quinn, K (Old Belvedere) 1947 *F, A*, 1953 *F, E, S*
Quinn, M A M (Lansdowne) 1973 *F*, 1974 *F, W, E, S, P, NZ*, 1977 *S, F*, 1981 *SA* 2
Quirke, J M T (Blackrock Coll) 1962 *E, S*, 1968 *S*

Rainey, P I (Ballymena) 1989 *NZ*
Rambaut, D F (Dublin U) 1887 *E, S, W*, 1888 *W*
Rea, H H (Edinburgh U) 1967 *A* 1, 1969 *F*
Read, H M (Dublin U) 1910 *E, S*, 1911 *E, S, W, F*, 1912 *F, E, S, W, SA*, 1913 *E, S*
Reardon, J V (Cork Constitution) 1934 *E, S*
Reid, C (NIFC) 1899 *S, W*, 1900 *E*, 1903 *W*
Reid, J L (Richmond) 1934 *S, W*
Reid, P J (Garryowen) 1947 *A*, 1948 *F, E, W*
Reid, T E (Garryowen) 1953 *E, S, W*, 1954 *NZ, F*, 1955 *E, S*, 1956 *F, E*, 1957 *F, E, S, W*
Reidy, C J (London Irish) 1937 *W*
Reidy, G F (Dolphin, Lansdowne) 1953 *W*, 1954 *F, E, S, W*
Richey, H A (Dublin U) 1889 *W*, 1890 *S*
Ridgeway, E C (Wanderers) 1932 *S, W*, 1935 *E, S, W*
Rigney, B J (Greystones) 1991 *F, W, E, S, Nm* 1, 1992 *F, NZ* 1(R),2
Ringland, T M (Queen's U, Belfast, Ballymena) 1981 *A*, 1982 *W, E, F*, 1983 *S, F, W, E*, 1984 *F, W, E, S, A*, 1985 *S, F, W, E*, 1986 *F, W, E, S, R*, 1987 *E, S, F, W*, [*W, C, Tg, A*], 1988 *S, F, W, E* 1
Riordan, W F (Cork Constitution) 1910 *E*
Ritchie, J S (London Irish) 1956 *F, E*
Robb, C G (Queen's Coll, Belfast) 1904 *E, S, W*, 1905 *NZ*, 1906 *S*
Robbie, J C (Dublin U, Greystones) 1976 *A, F, NZ*, 1977 *S, F*, 1981 *F, W, E, S*
Robinson, B F (Ballymena, London Irish) 1991 *F, W, E, S, Nm* 1,2, [*Z, S, A*], 1992 *W, E, S, F, NZ* 1,2, *A*, 1993 *W, E, R*, 1994 *F, W, E, S, A* 1,2
Robinson, T T H (Wanderers) 1904 *E, S*, 1905 *E, S, W, NZ*, 1906 *SA*, 1907 *E, S, W*
Roche, J (Wanderers) 1890 *S, W, E*, 1891 *E, S, W*, 1892 *W*
Roche, R E (UC Galway) 1955 *E, S*, 1957 *S, W*
Roche, W J (UC Cork) 1920 *E, S, F*
Roddy, P J (Bective Rangers) 1920 *S, F*
Roe, R (Lansdowne) 1952 *E*, 1953 *F, E, S, W*, 1954 *F, E, S, W*, 1955 *F, E, S, W*, 1956 *F, E, S, W*, 1957 *F, E, S, W*
Rolland, A C (Blackrock Coll) 1990 *Arg*, 1994 *US* (R), 1995 *It* (R)
Rooke, C V (Dublin U) 1891 *E, W*, 1892 *E, S, W*, 1893 *E, S, W*, 1894 *E, S, W*, 1895 *E, S, W*, 1896 *E, S, W*, 1897 *E, S*
Ross, D J (Belfast Academy) 1884 *E*, 1885 *S* 1,2, 1886 *E, S*
Ross, G R P (CIYMS) 1955 *W*
Ross, J F (NIFC) 1886 *S*
Ross, J P (Lansdowne) 1885 *E, S* 1,2, 1886 *E, S*
Ross, N G (Malone) 1927 *F, E*
Ross, W McC (Queen's U, Belfast) 1932 *E, S, W*, 1933 *E, W, S*, 1934 *E, S*, 1935 *NZ*
Russell, J (UC Cork) 1931 *F, E, S, W, SA*, 1933 *E, W, S*, 1934 *E, S, W*, 1935 *E, S, W*, 1936 *E, S, W*, 1937 *E, S*
Russell, P (Instonians) 1990 *E*, 1992 *NZ* 1,2, *A*
Rutherford, W G (Tipperary) 1884 *E, S*, 1885 *E, S* 1, 1886 *E, S*, 1888 *W*
Ryan, E (Dolphin) 1937 *W*, 1938 *E, S*
Ryan, J (Rockwell Coll) 1897 *E*, 1898 *E, S, W*, 1899 *E, S, W*, 1900 *S, W*, 1901 *E, S, W*, 1902 *E*, 1904 *E*
Ryan, J G (UC Dublin) 1939 *E, S, W*

Ryan, M (Rockwell Coll) 1897 *E, S*, 1898 *E, S, W*, 1899 *E, S, W*, 1900 *E, S, W*, 1901 *E, S, W*, 1903 *E*, 1904 *E, S*

Saunders, R (London Irish) 1991 *F, W, E, S, Nm* 1,2, [*Z, J, S, A*], 1992 *W*, 1994 *F* (t)
Saverimutto, C (Sale) 1995 *Fj*, 1996 *US, S*
Sayers, H J M (Lansdowne) 1935 *E, S, W*, 1936 *E, S, W*, 1938 *W*, 1939 *E, S, W*
Scally, C J (U C Dublin) 1998 *Gg* (R), *R*, 1999 *S* (R), *It*
Schute, F (Wanderers) 1878 *E*, 1879 *E*
Schute, F G (Dublin U) 1912 *SA*, 1913 *E, S*
Scott, D (Malone) 1961 *F, SA*, 1962 *S*
Scott, R D (Queen's U, Belfast) 1967 *E, F*, 1968 *F, E, S*
Scovell, R H (Kingstown) 1883 *E*, 1884 *E*
Scriven, G (Dublin U) 1879 *S, E*, 1880 *E, S*, 1881 *E*, 1882 *S*, 1883 *E, S*
Sealy, J (Dublin U) 1896 *E, S, W*, 1897 *S*, 1899 *E, S, W*, 1900 *E, S*
Sexton, J F (Dublin U, Lansdowne) 1988 *E* 2, *WS, It*, 1989 *F*
Sexton, W J (Garryowen) 1984 *A*, 1988 *S, E* 2
Shanahan, T (Lansdowne) 1885 *E, S* 1,2, 1886 *E*, 1888 *S, W*
Shaw, G M (Windsor) 1877 *S*
Sheahan, F J (Cork Const) 2000 *US* (R), 2001 *It* (R), *R, W* (R), *Sm*, 2002 *W, E, S*
Sheehan, M D (London Irish) 1932 *E*
Sherry, B F (Terenure Coll) 1967 *A* 1, *E, S, A* 2, 1968 *F, E*
Sherry, M J A (Lansdowne) 1975 *F, W*
Siggins, J A E (Belfast Collegians) 1931 *F, E, S, W, SA*, 1932 *E, S, W*, 1933 *E, S, W*, 1934 *E, S, W*, 1935 *E, S, W, NZ*, 1936 *E, S, W*, 1937 *E, S, W*
Slattery, J F (UC Dublin, Blackrock Coll) 1970 *SA, F, E, S, W*, 1971 *F, E, S, W*, 1972 *F* 1, *E, F* 2, 1973 *NZ, E, S, W, F*, 1974 *F, W, E, S, P, NZ*, 1975 *E, S, F, W*, 1976 *A*, 1977 *S, F*, 1978 *S, F, W, E, NZ*, 1979 *F, W, E, S, A* 1,2, 1980 *E, S, F, W*, 1981 *F, W, E, S, SA* 1,2, *A*, 1982 *W, E, S, F*, 1983 *S, F, W, E*, 1984 *F*
Smartt, F N B (Dublin U) 1908 *E, S*, 1909 *E*
Smith, B A (Oxford U, Leicester) 1989 *NZ*, 1990 *S, F, W, Arg*, 1991 *F, W, E, S*
Smith, J H (London Irish) 1951 *F, E, S, W, SA*, 1952 *F, S, W, E*, 1954 *NZ, W, F*
Smith, R E (Lansdowne) 1892 *E*
Smith, S J (Ballymena) 1988 *E* 2, *WS, It*, 1989 *F, W, E, S, NZ*, 1990 *E*, 1991 *F, W, E, S, Nm* 1,2, [*Z, S, A*], 1992 *W, E, S, F, NZ* 1,2, 1993 *S*
Smithwick, F F S (Monkstown) 1898 *S, W*
Smyth, J T (Queen's U, Belfast) 1920 *F*
Smyth, P J (Belfast Collegians) 1911 *E, S, F*
Smyth, R S (Dublin U) 1903 *E, S*, 1904 *E*
Smyth, T (Malone, Newport) 1908 *E, S, W*, 1909 *E, S, W*, 1910 *E, S, W, F*, 1911 *E, S, W*, 1912 *E*
Smyth, W S (Belfast Collegians) 1910 *W, F*, 1920 *E*
Solomons, B A H (Dublin U) 1908 *E, S, W*, 1909 *E, S, W, F*, 1910 *E, S, W*
Spain, A W (UC Dublin) 1924 *NZ*
Sparrow, W (Dublin U) 1893 *W*, 1894 *E*
Spillane, B J (Bohemians) 1985 *S, F, W, E*, 1986 *F, W, E*, 1987 *F, W*, [*W, C, A* (R)], 1989 *E* (R)
Spring, D E (Dublin U) 1978 *S, NZ*, 1979 *S*, 1980 *S, F, W*, 1981 *W*
Spring, R M (Lansdowne) 1979 *F, W, E*
Spunner, H F (Wanderers) 1881 *E, S*, 1884 *W*
Stack, C R R (Dublin U) 1889 *S*
Stack, G H (Dublin U) 1875 *E*
Staples, J E (London Irish, Harlequins) 1991 *W, E, S, Nm* 1,2, [*Z, J, S, A*], 1992 *W, E, NZ* 1,2, *A*, 1995 *F, W, It*, [*NZ*], *Fj*, 1996 *US, S, F, A*, 1997 *W, E, S*
Staunton, J W (Garryowen) 2001 *Sm*
Steele, H W (Ballymena) 1976 *E*, 1977 *F*, 1978 *F, W, E*, 1979 *F, W, E, A* 1,2
Stephenson, G V (Queen's U, Belfast, London Hosp) 1920 *F*, 1921 *E, S, W, F*, 1922 *E, S, W, F*, 1923 *E, S, W, F*, 1924 *F, E, S, W*, *NZ*, 1925 *F, E, S, W*, 1926 *F, E, S, W*, 1927 *F, E, S, W, A*, 1928 *F, E, S, W*, 1929 *F, E, W*, 1930 *F, E, S, W*
Stephenson, H W V (United Services) 1922 *S, W, F*, 1924 *F, E, S, W, NZ*, 1925 *F, E, S, W*, 1927 *A*, 1928 *E*
Stevenson, J (Dungannon) 1888 *M*, 1889 *S*
Stevenson, J B (Instonians) 1958 *A, E, S, W, F*
Stevenson, R (Dungannon) 1887 *E, S, W*, 1888 *M*, 1889 *S, W*, 1890 *S, W, E*, 1891 *W*, 1892 *W*, 1893 *E, S, W*
Stevenson, T H (Belfast Acad) 1895 *E, W*, 1896 *E, S, W*, 1897 *E, S*
Stewart, A L (NIFC) 1913 *W, F*, 1914 *F*

Stewart, W J (Queen's U, Belfast, NIFC) 1922 *F*, 1924 *S*, 1928 *F, E, S, W*, 1929 *F, E, S, W*
Stoker, E W (Wanderers) 1888 *W, S*
Stoker, F O (Wanderers) 1886 *S*, 1888 *W, M*, 1889 *S*, 1891 *W*
Stokes, O S (Cork Bankers) 1882 *E*, 1884 *E*
Stokes, P (Garryowen) 1913 *E, S*, 1914 *F*, 1920 *E, S, W, F*, 1921 *E, S, F*, 1922 *W, F*
Stokes, R D (Queen's Coll, Cork) 1891 *S, W*
Strathdee, E (Queen's U, Belfast) 1947 *E, S, W, A*, 1948 *W, F*, 1949 *E, S, W*
Stringer, P A (Shannon) 2000 *S, It, F, W, Arg, C, J, SA*, 2001 *It, F, R, S* (R), *W, E, Sm, NZ*, 2002 *W, E, S, It, F, NZ* 1,2
Stuart, C P (Clontarf) 1912 *SA*
Stuart, I M B (Dublin U) 1924 *E, S*
Sugars, H S (Dublin U) 1905 *NZ*, 1906 *SA*, 1907 *S*
Sugden, M (Wanderers) 1925 *F, E, S, W*, 1926 *F, E, S, W*, 1927 *E, S, W, A*, 1928 *F, E, S, W*, 1929 *F, E, S, W*, 1930 *F, E, S, W*, 1931 *F, E, S, W*
Sullivan, D B (UC Dublin) 1922 *E, S, W, F*
Sweeney, J A (Blackrock Coll) 1907 *E, S, W*
Symes, G R (Monkstown) 1895 *E*
Synge, J S (Lansdowne) 1929 *S*

Taggart, T (Dublin U) 1887 *W*
Taylor, A S (Queen's Coll, Belfast) 1910 *E, S, W*, 1912 *F*
Taylor, D R (Queen's Coll, Belfast) 1903 *E*
Taylor, J (Belfast Collegians) 1914 *E, S, W*
Taylor, J W (NIFC) 1879 *S*, 1880 *E, S*, 1881 *S*, 1882 *E, S*, 1883 *E, S*
Tector, W R (Wanderers) 1955 *F, E, S*
Tedford, A (Malone) 1902 *E, S, W*, 1903 *E, S, W*, 1904 *E, S, W*, 1905 *E, S, W, NZ*, 1906 *E, S, W, SA*, 1907 *E, S, W*, 1908 *E, S, W*
Teehan, C (UC Cork) 1939 *E, S, W*
Thompson, C (Belfast Collegians) 1907 *E, S*, 1908 *E, S, W*, 1909 *E, S, W, F*, 1910 *E, S, W, F*
Thompson, J A (Queen's Coll, Belfast) 1885 *S* 1,2
Thompson, J K S (Dublin U) 1921 *W*, 1922 *E, S, F*, 1923 *E, S, W, F*
Thompson, R G (Lansdowne) 1882 *W*
Thompson, R H (Instonians) 1951 *SA*, 1952 *F*, 1954 *NZ, F, E, S, W*, 1955 *F, S, W*, 1956 *W*
Thornhill, T (Wanderers) 1892 *E, S, W*, 1893 *E*
Thrift, H (Dublin U) 1904 *W*, 1905 *E, S, W, NZ*, 1906 *E, W, SA*, 1907 *E, S, W*, 1908 *E, S, W*, 1909 *E, S, W, F*
Tierney, D (UC Cork) 1938 *S, W*, 1939 *E*
Tierney, T A (Garryowen) 1999 *A* 1,2, *Arg* 1, [*US, A* 3, *R, Arg* 2], 2000 *E*
Tillie, C R (Dublin U) 1887 *E, S*, 1888 *W, S*
Todd, A W P (Dublin U) 1913 *W, F*, 1914 *F*
Topping, J A (Ballymena) 1996 *WS, A*, 1997 *It* 1, *F, E*, 1999 [*R*], 2000 *US*
Torrens, J D (Bohemians) 1938 *W*, 1939 *E, S, W*
Tucker, C C (Shannon) 1979 *F, W*, 1980 *F* (R)
Tuke, B B (Bective Rangers) 1890 *E*, 1891 *E, S*, 1892 *E*, 1894 *E, S, W*, 1895 *E, S*
Turley, N (Blackrock Coll) 1962 *E*
Tweed, D A (Ballymena) 1995 *F, W, It*, [*J*]
Tydings, J J (Young Munster) 1968 *A*
Tyrrell, W (Queen's U, Belfast) 1910 *F*, 1913 *E, S, W, F*, 1914 *F, E, S, W*

Uprichard, R J H (Harlequins, RAF) 1950 *S, W*

Waide, S L (Oxford U, NIFC) 1932 *E, S, W*, 1933 *E, W*
Waites, J (Bective Rangers) 1886 *S*, 1888 *M*, 1889 *W*, 1890 *S, W, E*, 1891 *E*
Waldron, O C (Oxford U, London Irish) 1966 *S, W*, 1968 *A*
Walker, S (Instonians) 1934 *E, S*, 1935 *E, S, W, NZ*, 1936 *E, S, W*, 1937 *E, S, W*, 1938 *E, S, W*
Walkington, D B (NIFC) 1887 *E, W*, 1888 *W*, 1890 *W, E*, 1891 *E, S, W*
Walkington, R B (NIFC) 1875 *E*, 1876 *E*, 1877 *E, S*, 1878 *E*, 1879 *S*, 1880 *E, S*, 1882 *E, S*
Wall, H (Dolphin) 1965 *S, W*
Wallace, D P (Garryowen) 2000 *Arg, US*, 2001 *It, F, R* (R), *S* (R), *W, E, NZ*, 2002 *W, E, S, It, F*
Wallace, Jas (Wanderers) 1904 *E, S*
Wallace, Jos (Wanderers) 1903 *S, W*, 1904 *E, S, W*, 1905 *E, S, W, NZ*, 1906 *W*
Wallace, P S (Blackrock Coll, Saracens) 1995 [*J*], *Fj*, 1996 *US, W, E, WS, A*, 1997 *It* 1, *F, W, E, S, NZ, C*, 1998 *S, F, W, E,*

SA 1,2, *Gg, R*, 1999 *F, W, E, S, It* (R), 1999 *A* 1,2, *Arg* 1, [*US, A* 3, *R, Arg* 2], 2000 *E, US, C* (R), 2002 *W* (R), *E* (R), *S* (R), *It* (R), *F* (R), *NZ* 2(R)

Wallace, R M (Garryowen, Saracens) 1991 *Nm* 1(R), 1992 *W, E, S, F, A*, 1993 *S, F, W, E, R*, 1994 *F, W, E, S*, 1995 *W, It*, [*NZ, J, W*], *Fj*, 1996 *US, S, F, WS*, 1998 *S, F, W, E*

Wallace, T H (Cardiff) 1920 *E, S, W*

Wallis, A K (Wanderers) 1892 *E, S, W*, 1893 *E, W*

Wallis, C O'N (Old Cranleighans, Wanderers) 1935 *NZ*

Wallis, T G (Wanderers) 1921 *F*, 1922 *E, S, W, F*

Wallis, W A (Wanderers) 1880 *S*, 1881 *E, S*, 1882 *W*, 1883 *S*

Walmsley, G (Bective Rangers) 1894 *E*

Walpole, A (Dublin U) 1888 *S, M*

Walsh, E J (Lansdowne) 1887 *E, S, W*, 1892 *E, S, W*, 1893 *E*

Walsh, H D (Dublin U) 1875 *E*, 1876 *E*

Walsh, J C (UC Cork, Sunday's Well) 1960 *S, SA*, 1961 *E, S, F, SA*, 1963 *E, S, W, NZ*, 1964 *E, S, W, F*, 1965 *F, S, W, SA*, 1966 *F, S, W*, 1967 *E, S, W, F, A* 2

Ward, A J (Ballynahinch) 1998 *F, W, E, SA* 1,2, *Gg, R, SA* 3, 1999 *W, E, S, It* (R), *A* 1,2, *Arg* 1, [*US, A* 3, *R, Arg* 2], 2000 *F* (R), *W* (t&R), *Arg* (R), *US* (R), *C, J, SA* (R), 2001 *It* (R), *F* (R)

Ward, A J P (Garryowen, St Mary's Coll, Greystones) 1978 *S, F, W, E, NZ*, 1979 *F, W, E, S*, 1981 *W, E, S, A*, 1983 *E* (R), 1984 *E, S*, 1986 *S*, 1987 [*C, Tg*]

Warren, J P (Kingstown) 1883 *E*

Warren, R G (Lansdowne) 1884 *W*, 1885 *E, S* 1,2, 1886 *E*, 1887 *E, S, W*, 1888 *W, S, M*, 1889 *S, W*, 1890 *S, W, E*

Watson, R (Wanderers) 1912 *SA*

Wells, H G (Bective Rangers) 1891 *S, W*, 1894 *E, S*

Westby, A J (Dublin U) 1876 *E*

Wheeler, G H (Queen's Coll, Belfast) 1884 *S*, 1885 *E*

Wheeler, J R (Queen's U, Belfast) 1922 *E, S, W, F*, 1924 *E*

Whelan, P C (Garryowen) 1975 *E, S*, 1976 *NZ*, 1977 *W, E, S, F*, 1978 *S, F, W, E, NZ*, 1979 *F, W, E, S*, 1981 *F, W, E*

White, M (Queen's Coll, Cork) 1906 *E, S, W, SA*, 1907 *E, W*

Whitestone, A M (Dublin U) 1877 *E*, 1879 *S, E*, 1880 *E*, 1883 *S*

Whittle, D (Bangor) 1988 *F*

Wilkinson, C R (Malone) 1993 *S*

Wilkinson, R W (Wanderers) 1947 *A*

Williamson, F W (Dolphin) 1930 *E, S, W*

Willis, W J (Lansdowne) 1879 *E*

Wilson, F (CIYMS) 1977 *W, E, S*

Wilson, H G (Glasgow U, Malone) 1905 *E, S, W, NZ*, 1906 *E, S, W, SA*, 1907 *E, S, W*, 1908 *E, S, W*, 1909 *E, S, W*, 1910 *W*

Wilson, W H (Bray) 1877 *E, S*

Withers, H H C (Army, Blackheath) 1931 *F, E, S, W, SA*

Wolfe, E J (Armagh) 1882 *E*

Wood, G H (Dublin U) 1913 *W*, 1914 *F*

Wood, B G M (Garryowen) 1954 *E, S*, 1956 *F, E, S, W*, 1957 *F, E, S, W*, 1958 *A, E, S, W, F*, 1959 *E, S, W, F*, 1960 *E, S, W, F, SA*, 1961 *E, S, W, F, SA*

Wood, K G M (Garryowen, Harlequins) 1994 *A* 1,2, *US*, 1995 *E, S,* [*J*], 1996 *A*, 1997 *It* 1, *F*, 1997 *NZ, It* 2, 1998 *S, F, W, E, SA* 1,2, *R* (R), *SA* 3, 1999 *F, W, E, S, It* (R), *A* 1,2, *Arg* 1, [*US, A* 3, *R* (R), *Arg* 2], 2000 *E, S, It, F, W, Arg, US, C, J, SA*, 2001 *It, F, S, W, E, NZ*, 2002 *F, NZ* 1,2

Woods, D C (Bessbrook) 1888 *M*, 1889 *S*

Woods, N K P J (Blackrock Coll, London Irish) 1994 *A* 1,2, 1995 *E, F*, 1996 *F, W, E*, 1999 *W*

Wright, R A (Monkstown) 1912 *S*

Yeates, R A (Dublin U) 1889 *S, W*

Young, G (UC Cork) 1913 *E*

Young, R M (Collegians) 1965 *F, E, S, W, SA*, 1966 *F, E, S, W*, 1967 *W, F*, 1968 *W, A*, 1969 *F, E, S, W*, 1970 *SA, F, E, S, W*, 1971 *F, E, S, W*

WALES TEST SEASON REVIEW 2001-02

Desperate days on and off the Field

John Billot

'The Gatling's jammed and the Colonel dead.' Sir Henry Newbolt's dramatic words from his heroic poem faithfully illustrate the situation that afflicted Wales on and off the field during a desperate season. Only once before had Wales lost two International Championship matches by 50 points or more. Never had national squad players threatened to strike unless the WRU supported the six major clubs for whom they played and who demanded substantially increased funding and a reduction in the top division from nine to six teams. Never had the WRU been compelled to call two extraordinary general meetings in the space of seven weeks. Some alleged that never had so little emerged from both. It appeared that Wales had become a Never, Never Land!

Graham Henry, the national coach who had been hailed as The Great Redeemer when Wales won 10 matches in succession, including a first ever victory over South Africa, left 'by mutual consent' after Ireland had made it a day of doom in Dublin by a humiliating 54-10 margin. Henry indicated he was suffering from 'burn-out' after the disappointment of the Lions' defeats in Australia. Later, Nick Bishop, who co-authored Graham Henry's book on events Down Under, explained that Henry, 'Did not want to be associated with the incestuous, mediocre rugby culture fostered by the WRU any longer.'

Another New Zealander with an impressive pedigree, Steve Hansen, succeeded to the role of Wales supremo, though the poisoned chalice was sweetened somewhat with an increase of salary by £50,000. Considering the WRU were strapped for cash, with debts of around £70m on the Millennium Stadium, this was indeed a generous gesture, giving Hansen annual payment of some £200,000 virtually before he had dipped his toe into the whirlpool of Welsh rugby and all that goes with it.

He was tasked with the job of freeing players from the restrictive painting-by-numbers, pod system of Graham Henry, and reintroducing freedom of expression, which is the key to Welsh flair. There can be no doubt that Graham Henry was handicapped by the paucity of talent and experience available and, as well as fragile tackling, there was obvious lack of fitness. Too often the team flagged in the second half. Leighton Samuel, the owner of Bridgend RFC, bluntly blamed it on the 'beer culture.' All these criticisms and observations had valid foundations. Someone has to repair that jammed Gatling gun!

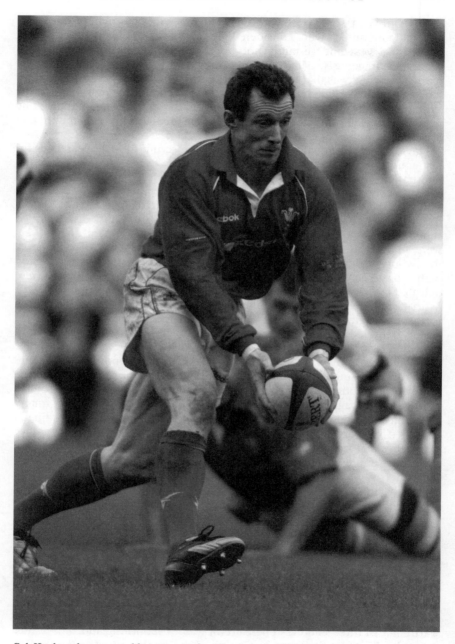

Rob Howley, who announced his retirement from Test rugby in 2002, makes a break against England at Twickenham.

Graham Henry cut no ice with Les Williams, vice-chairman of the WRU general committee, who considered no coach in the world was worth £250,000 a year and certainly not when his team were losing by record scores. Courageously, Mr Williams outlined feelings that were shared by many. The view was that the coach had lost the plot and should go. He did, four days after the Dublin disaster. The general committee reprimanded Mr Williams for speaking out and, with deteriorating health, he announced he would retire. He should have been commended for his perception and honesty.

David Young, renowned cornerstone of the scrum in 51 appearances for his country (and veteran of the three Lions tours), retired from the international scene after Argentina defeated Wales by 30-16 in Cardiff. Welsh players had been booed from the field after the game and missiles hurled at the team bus as they left the stadium. He felt the fallout was too hurtful for him and his family. The scorn of so many disenchanted supporters was difficult to endure. Then, when management and players were an hour late for a team release announcement before the Tonga game, the fed-up media responded to the customary question-and-answer session with stony silence. Matters were going from bad to worse. Tonga were defeated by 51-7, which was as expected.

Scott Quinnell was accorded the captaincy and proceeded to do his best to inspire, mainly through his trademark charge down the middle. Neil Jenkins required further surgery on a knee and missed 10 Wales games until returning against South Africa in the summer of 2002. In his absence, Stephen Jones proved a notable kicker of goals and for position, but there was no real cutting edge behind the scrum. Mark Taylor, strong man in the middle, was another who missed most of the Six Nations with knee trouble.

It was jeers again for the team after losing by 21-13 to what many considered a grimly poor Wallaby side, who failed to cross the Wales line in Cardiff. To Dublin to launch the Six Nations was a seriously scary experience and Ireland made it a record success by 54-10. Next, Wales gave their most impressive performance in losing by 37-33 to France in Cardiff. Surrender was not on the agenda that time and victory followed by 44-20 over Italy, although too many substitutes disrupted fluency.

After the Italian fixture, six major clubs – Bridgend, Cardiff, Swansea, Llanelli, Pontypridd and Newport – submitted their demand for more funding and fewer teams in the top division. They warned they would not release their players for the visit to Twickenham unless their claims were addressed. One club official sombrely stated, 'The professional game in Wales is in a mess. The game is bust. We are pointing the gun and starting to pull the trigger.'

England's record margin of success against Wales by 50-10 came as little surprise. Wales made an explosive start and dominated for the heart-warming first three minutes! Thereafter it was all about England. Then, after defeat by 27-22 to Scotland in Cardiff, Rob Howley received a standing ovation as he left the field to play international rugby no more. The Human

Eel will be remembered for many outrageous tries for club and country as Wales's most-capped scrum-half with 59 appearances.

Wales splashed out to buy in rugby league big name Iestyn Harris at a cost of around £1.5m, shared between the WRU and Cardiff, though it proved ambitious to expect him to embrace the union code after only a few club games. He withdrew from the Wales squad to visit South Africa in June 2002 because of injury, and a number of other leading players were absent for a variety of reasons. There were no great expectations of what might be achieved and memories of the horrendous defeat by 96-13 in Pretoria in 1998 were still all too fresh. Yet Wales surprised everyone, and certainly the Springboks, before losing the first Test by 34-19 in Bloemfontein, where Pontypridd flanker Michael Owen became the 1,000th Welsh international player to win his spurs since 1881. Wales dominated the first 35 minutes to lead 11-3. A week later, in heavy rain in Cape Town, Wales lasted the pace better and defeat by 19-8 was no disgrace. Perhaps happier days are ahead.

What happened at those two EGMs called by the WRU? The clubs voted by 207 to 204 to accept the main proposal by the Sir Tasker Watkins working party, but it failed to obtain the 75 per cent majority required by the constitution. The general committee were renamed the board of directors and slimmed down by 11 members to 18. In addition, a six-man executive was to be set up, headed by a professional chief executive, to conduct the day-to-day running of affairs. Perhaps the 'Colonel' was only wounded after all!

Glanmor Griffiths, WRU chairman and treasurer, stressed at the July 2002 AGM, 'If we all tighten our belts and become more financially astute, we will emerge from these hard times in better shape. We must find ways of increasing income and cutting costs.' He also warned that the country's international playing results must improve if Wales are to be taken seriously on the world stage. Sir Tasker Watkins, the Union's president, emphasised his concern at the threat of burn-out if leading players are burdened with too many games.

Wales's Test Record in 2001-2002:
Played 10, won 2, lost 8.

Opponents	Date	Venue	Result
South Africa	15th June 2002	A	Lost 8-19
South Africa	8th June 2002	A	Lost 19-34
Scotland	6th April 2002	H	Lost 22-27
England	23rd March 2002	A	Lost 10-50
Italy	2nd March 2002	H	Won 44-20
France	16th February 2002	H	Lost 33-37
Ireland	3rd February 2002	A	Lost 10-54
Australia	25th November 2001	H	Lost 13-21
Tonga	17th November 2001	H	Won 51-7
Argentina	10th November 2001	H	Lost 16-30

WALES INTERNATIONAL STATISTICS

(up to 31 August 2002)

Match Records

MOST CONSECUTIVE TEST WINS

11 1907 *I*, 1908 *E, S, F, I, A*, 1909 *E, S, F, I*, 1910 *F*
10 1999 *F1, It, E, Arg 1,2, SA, C, F2, Arg 3, J*
8 1970 *F*, 1971 *E, S, I, F*, 1972 *E, S, F*

MOST CONSECUTIVE TESTS WITHOUT DEFEAT

Matches	Wins	Draws	Period
11	11	0	1907 to 1910
10	10	0	1999 to 1999
8	8	0	1970 to 1972

MOST POINTS IN A MATCH
by the team

Pts	Opponents	Venue	Year
102	Portugal	Lisbon	1994
81	Romania	Cardiff	2001
70	Romania	Wrexham	1997
64	Japan	Cardiff	1999
64	Japan	Osaka	2001
60	Italy	Treviso	1999
57	Japan	Bloemfontein	1995
55	Japan	Cardiff	1993

by a player

Pts	Player	Opponents	Venue	Year
30	N R Jenkins	Italy	Treviso	1999
29	N R Jenkins	France	Cardiff	1999
28	N R Jenkins	Canada	Cardiff	1999
28	N R Jenkins	France	Paris	2001
27	N R Jenkins	Italy	Cardiff	2000
26	S M Jones	Romania	Cardiff	2001
24	N R Jenkins	Canada	Cardiff	1993
24	N R Jenkins	Italy	Cardiff	1994
23	A C Thomas	Romania	Wrexham	1997
23	N R Jenkins	Argentina	Llanelli	1998
23	N R Jenkins	Scotland	Murrayfield	2001
22	N R Jenkins	Portugal	Lisbon	1994
22	N R Jenkins	Japan	Bloemfontein	1995
22	N R Jenkins	England	Wembley	1999

MOST TRIES IN A MATCH
by the team

Tries	Opponents	Venue	Year
16	Portugal	Lisbon	1994
11	France	Paris	1909
11	Romania	Wrexham	1997
11	Romania	Cardiff	2001
10	France	Swansea	1910
10	Japan	Osaka	2001
9	France	Cardiff	1908
9	Japan	Cardiff	1993
9	Japan	Cardiff	1999
9	Japan	Tokyo	2001

by a player

Tries	Player	Opponents	Venue	Year
4	W Llewellyn	England	Swansea	1899
4	R A Gibbs	France	Cardiff	1908
4	M C R Richards	England	Cardiff	1969
4	I C Evans	Canada	Invercargill	1987
4	N Walker	Portugal	Lisbon	1994
4	G Thomas	Italy	Treviso	1999
4	S M Williams	Japan	Osaka	2001

MOST CONVERSIONS IN A MATCH
by the team

Cons	Opponents	Venue	Year
11	Portugal	Lisbon	1994
10	Romania	Cardiff	2001
8	France	Swansea	1910
8	Japan	Cardiff	1999
7	France	Paris	1909
7	Japan	Osaka	2001

by a player

Cons	Player	Opponents	Venue	Year
11	N R Jenkins	Portugal	Lisbon	1994
10	S M Jones	Romania	Cardiff	2001
8	J Bancroft	France	Swansea	1910
8	N R Jenkins	Japan	Cardiff	1999
7	S M Jones	Japan	Osaka	2001
6	J Bancroft	France	Paris	1909

MOST PENALTIES IN A MATCH
by the team

Penalties	Opponents	Venue	Year
9	France	Cardiff	1999
8	Canada	Cardiff	1993
7	Italy	Cardiff	1994
7	Canada	Cardiff	1999
7	Italy	Cardiff	2000
6	France	Cardiff	1982
6	Tonga	Nuku'alofa	1994
6	England	Wembley	1999

by a player

Penalties	Player	Opponents	Venue	Year
9	N R Jenkins	France	Cardiff	1999
8	N R Jenkins	Canada	Cardiff	1993
7	N R Jenkins	Italy	Cardiff	1994
7	N R Jenkins	Canada	Cardiff	1999
7	N R Jenkins	Italy	Cardiff	2000
6	G Evans	France	Cardiff	1982
6	N R Jenkins	Tonga	Nuku'alofa	1994
6	N R Jenkins	England	Wembley	1999

MOST DROPPED GOALS IN A MATCH
by the team

Drops	Opponents	Venue	Year
3	Scotland	Murrayfield	2001
2	Scotland	Swansea	1912
2	Scotland	Cardiff	1914
2	England	Swansea	1920
2	Scotland	Swansea	1921
2	France	Paris	1930
2	England	Cardiff	1971
2	France	Cardiff	1978
2	England	Twickenham	1984
2	Ireland	Wellington	1987
2	Scotland	Cardiff	1988
2	France	Paris	2001

by a player

Drops	Player	Opponents	Venue	Year
3	N R Jenkins	Scotland	Murrayfield	2001
2	J Shea	England	Swansea	1920
2	A Jenkins	Scotland	Swansea	1921
2	B John	England	Cardiff	1971
2	M Dacey	England	Twickenham	1984
2	J Davies	Ireland	Wellington	1987
2	J Davies	Scotland	Cardiff	1988
2	N R Jenkins	France	Paris	2001

Career Records
MOST CAPPED PLAYERS

Caps	Player	Career Span
86	N R Jenkins	1991 to 2002
72	I C Evans	1987 to 1998
67	G O Llewellyn	1989 to 2002
59	R Howley	1996 to 2002
58	G R Jenkins	1991 to 2000
57	G Thomas	1995 to 2002
55	J P R Williams	1969 to 1981
54	R N Jones	1986 to 1995
53	G O Edwards	1967 to 1978
53	I S Gibbs	1991 to 2001
51	D Young	1987 to 2001
50	L S Quinnell	1993 to 2002
46	T G R Davies	1966 to 1978
46	P T Davies	1985 to 1995
46	C L Charvis	1996 to 2002
44	K J Jones	1947 to 1957
42	M R Hall	1988 to 1995

MOST CONSECUTIVE TESTS

Tests	Player	Span
53	G O Edwards	1967 to 1978
43	K J Jones	1947 to 1956
39	G Price	1975 to 1983
38	T M Davies	1969 to 1976
33	W J Bancroft	1890 to 1901

MOST TESTS AS CAPTAIN

Tests	Captain	Span
28	I C Evans	1991 to 1995
22	R Howley	1998 to 1999
18	A J Gould	1889 to 1897
17	J M Humphreys	1995 to 1997
14	D C T Rowlands	1963 to 1965
14	W J Trew	1907 to 1913

MOST TESTS IN INDIVIDUAL POSITIONS

Position	Player	Tests	Span
Full-back	J P R Williams	54	1969 to 1981
Wing	I C Evans	72	1987 to 1998
Centre	I S Gibbs	53	1991 to 2001
Fly-half	N R Jenkins	69	1991 to 2002
Scrum-half	R Howley	59	1996 to 2002
Prop	D Young	51	1987 to 2002
Hooker	G R Jenkins	57	1991 to 2000
Lock	G O Llewellyn	66	1989 to 2002
Flanker	C L Charvis	40	1996 to 2002
No 8	L S Quinnell	49	1993 to 2002

MOST POINTS IN TESTS

Points	Player	Tests	Career
1029	N R Jenkins	86	1991 to 2002
304	P H Thorburn	37	1985 to 1991
211	A C Thomas	23	1996 to 2000
166	P Bennett	29	1969 to 1978
158	S M Jones	21	1998 to 2002
157	I C Evans	72	1987 to 1998

MOST TRIES IN TESTS

Tries	Player	Tests	Career
33	I C Evans	72	1987 to 1998
26	G Thomas	57	1995 to 2002
20	G O Edwards	53	1967 to 1978
20	T G R Davies	46	1966 to 1978
17	R A Gibbs	16	1906 to 1911
17	J L Williams	17	1906 to 1911
17	K J Jones	44	1947 to 1957

MOST CONVERSIONS IN TESTS

Cons	Player	Tests	Career
126	N R Jenkins	86	1991 to 2002
43	P H Thorburn	37	1985 to 1991

38	J Bancroft	18	1909 to 1914
35	S M Jones	21	1998 to 2002
30	A C Thomas	23	1996 to 2000
20	W J Bancroft	33	1890 to 1901

MOST PENALTY GOALS IN TESTS

Penalties	Player	Tests	Career
231	N R Jenkins	86	1991 to 2002
70	P H Thorburn	37	1985 to 1991
36	P Bennett	29	1969 to 1978
35	S P Fenwick	30	1975 to 1981
32	A C Thomas	23	1996 to 2000
25	S M Jones	21	1998 to 2002
22	G Evans	10	1981 to 1983

MOST DROPPED GOALS IN TESTS

Drops	Player	Tests	Career
13	J Davies	32	1985 to 1997
10	N R Jenkins	86	1991 to 2002
8	B John	25	1966 to 1972
7	W G Davies	21	1978 to 1985

International Championship Records

Record	Detail		Set
Most points in season	125	in five matches	2001
Most tries in season	21	in four matches	1910
Highest Score	49	49-14 v France	1910
Biggest win	35	49-14 v France	1910
Highest score conceded	60	26-60 v England	1998
Biggest defeat	51	0-51 v France	1998
Most appearances	45	G O Edwards	1967 – 1978
Most points in matches	406	N R Jenkins	1991 – 2001
Most points in season	74	N R Jenkins	2001
Most points in match	28	N R Jenkins	v France, 2001
Most tries in matches	18	G O Edwards	1967 – 1978
Most tries in season	6	M C R Richards	1969
Most tries in match	4	W Llewellyn	v England, 1899
	4	M C R Richards	v England, 1969
Most cons in matches	41	N R Jenkins	1991 – 2001
Most cons in season	10	S M Jones	2002
Most cons in match	8	J Bancroft	v France, 1910
Most pens in matches	93	N R Jenkins	1991 – 2001
Most pens in season	16	P H Thorburn	1986
	16	N R Jenkins	1999
Most pens in match	7	N R Jenkins	v Italy, 2000
Most drops in matches	8	J Davies	1985 – 1997
Most drops in season	5	N R Jenkins	2001
Most drops in match	3	N R Jenkins	v Scotland, 2001

Miscellaneous Records

Record	Holder	Detail
Longest Test Career	D Young	15 seasons, 1987 to 2001
Youngest Test Cap	N Biggs	18 yrs 49 days in 1888
Oldest Test Cap	T H Vile	38 yrs 152 days in 1921

Career Records of Wales International Players
(up to 31 August 2002)

PLAYER	Debut	Caps	T	C	P	D	Pts
Backs:							
A G Bateman	1990 v S	35	10	0	0	0	50
M.D.Cardey	2000 v S	1	0	0	0	0	0
G J Cooper	2001 v F	3	1	0	0	0	5
I R Harris	2001 v Arg	7	1	6	11	0	50
R Howley	1996 v E	59	10	0	0	0	50
D R James	1996 v A	40	13	0	0	0	65
N R Jenkins	1991 v E	86	11	126	231	10	1029
M A Jones	2001 v E	3	1	0	0	0	5
S M Jones	1998 v SA	21	2	35	25	1	158
A W N Marinos	2002 v I	7	1	0	0	0	5
C S Morgan	2002 v I	7	2	0	0	0	10
K A Morgan	1997 v US	22	5	0	0	0	25
D Peel	2001 v J	9	0	0	0	0	0
R D Powell	2002 v SA	2	0	0	0	0	0
J P Robinson	2001 v J	6	2	0	0	0	10
T Shanklin	2001 v J	5	2	0	0	0	10
A C Sullivan	2001 v Arg	2	0	0	0	0	0
M Taylor	1994 v SA	33	8	0	0	0	40
Gareth Thomas	1995 v J	57	26	0	0	0	130
G R Williams	2000 v I	18	5	0	0	0	25
S M Williams	2000 v F	10	10	0	0	0	50
Forwards:							
C T Anthony	1997 v US	16	1	0	0	0	5
N J Budgett	2000 v S	12	2	0	0	0	10
C L Charvis	1996 v A	46	8	0	0	0	40
Mefin Davies	2002 v SA	1	0	0	0	0	0
B R Evans	1998 v SA	15	0	0	0	0	0
I M Gough	1998 v SA	20	1	0	0	0	5
S C John	1995 v S	18	0	0	0	0	0
Duncan Jones	2001 v A	3	0	0	0	0	0
Steve Jones	2001 v J	1	0	0	0	0	0
A L P Lewis	1996 v It	27	0	0	0	0	0
G Lewis	1998 v SA	16	0	0	0	0	0
G O Llewellyn	1989 v NZ	67	5	0	0	0	24
R C McBryde	1994 v Fj	20	0	0	0	0	0
M Madden	2002 v SA	1	0	0	0	0	0
A P Moore	1995 v SA	26	0	0	0	0	0
D R Morris	1998 v Z	15	1	0	0	0	5
M Owen	2002 v SA	2	0	0	0	0	0
R Parks	2002 v SA	1	0	0	0	0	0
J C Quinnell	1995 v Fj	32	5	0	0	0	25

L S Quinnell	1993 v C	50	10	0	0	0	50
P J D Rogers	1999 v F	18	0	0	0	0	0
R Sidoli	2002 v SA	2	0	0	0	0	0
B D Sinkinson	1999 v F	20	1	0	0	0	5
Gavin Thomas	2001 v J	9	3	0	0	0	15
I D Thomas	2000 v Sm	14	0	0	0	0	0
Barry Williams	1996 v F	24	5	0	0	0	25
M E Williams	1996 v Bb	25	0	0	0	0	0
S M Williams	1994 v Tg	22	1	0	0	0	5
C P Wyatt	1998 v Z	33	2	0	0	0	10
D Young	1987 v E	51	1	0	0	0	4

WELSH INTERNATIONAL PLAYERS
(up to 31 August 2002)

Note: Years given for International Championship matches are for second half of season; eg 1972 means season 1971-72. Years for all other matches refer to the actual year of the match. When a series has taken place, figures have been used to denote the particular matches in which players have featured. Thus 1969 *NZ* 2 indicates that a player appeared in the second Test of the series.

Ackerman, R A (Newport, London Welsh) 1980 *NZ*, 1981 *E, S, A*, 1982 *I, F, E, S*, 1983 *S, I, F, R*, 1984 *S, I, F, E, A*, 1985 *S, I, F, E, Fj*
Alexander, E P (Llandovery Coll, Cambridge U) 1885 *S*, 1886 *E, S*, 1887 *E, I*
Alexander, W H (Llwynypia) 1898 *I, E*, 1899 *E, S, I*, 1901 *S, I*
Allen, A G (Newbridge) 1990 *F, E, I*
Allen, C P (Oxford U, Beaumaris) 1884 *E, S*
Andrews, F (Pontypool) 1912 *SA*, 1913 *E, S, I*
Andrews, F G (Swansea) 1884 *E, S*
Andrews, G E (Newport) 1926 *E, S*, 1927 *E, F, I*
Anthony, C T (Swansea, Newport) 1997 *US* 1(R),2(R), C (R), *Tg* (R), 1998 *SA* 2, *Arg*, 1999 *S, I* (R), 2001 *J* 1,2, *I* (R), 2002 *I, F, It, E, S*
Anthony, L (Neath) 1948 *E, S, F*
Appleyard, R C (Swansea) 1997 *C, R, Tg, NZ*, 1998 *It, E* (R), *S, I, F*
Arnold, P (Swansea) 1990 *Nm* 1, 2, *Bb*, 1991 *E, S, I, F* 1, *A*, [*Arg, A*], 1993 *F* (R), *Z* 2, 1994 *Sp, Fj*, 1995 *SA*, 1996 *Bb* (R)
Arnold, W R (Swansea) 1903 *S*
Arthur, C S (Cardiff) 1888 *I, M*, 1891 *E*
Arthur, T (Neath) 1927 *S, F, I*, 1929 *E, S, F, I*, 1930 *E, S, I, F*, 1931 *E, S, F, I, SA*, 1933 *E, S*
Ashton, C (Aberavon) 1959 *E, S, I*, 1960 *E, S, I*, 1962 *I*
Attewell, S L (Newport) 1921 *E, S, F*

Back, M J (Bridgend) 1995 *F* (R), *E* (R), *S, I*
Badger, O (Llanelli) 1895 *E, S, I*, 1896 *E*
Baker, A (Neath) 1921 *I*, 1923 *E, S, F, I*
Baker, A M (Newport) 1909 *S, F*, 1910 *S*
Bancroft, J (Swansea) 1909 *E, S, F, I*, 1910 *F, E, S, I*, 1911 *E, F, I*, 1912 *E, S, I*, 1913 *I*, 1914 *E, S, F*
Bancroft, W J (Swansea) 1890 *S, E, I*, 1891 *E, S, I*, 1892 *E, S, I*, 1893 *E, S, I*, 1894 *E, S, I*, 1895 *E, S, I*, 1896 *E, S, I*, 1897 *E*, 1898 *I, E*, 1899 *E, S, I*, 1900 *E, S, I*, 1901 *E, S, I*
Barlow, T M (Cardiff) 1884 *I*
Barrell, R J (Cardiff) 1929 *S, F, I*, 1933 *I*
Bartlett, J D (Llanelli) 1927 *S*, 1928 *E, S*
Bassett, A (Cardiff) 1934 *I*, 1935 *E, S, I*, 1938 *E, S*
Bassett, J A (Penarth) 1929 *E, S, F, I*, 1930 *E, S, I*, 1931 *E, S, F, I, SA*, 1932 *E, S, I*
Bateman, A G (Neath, Richmond, Northampton) 1990 *S, I, Nm* 1,2, 1996 *SA*, 1997 *US, S, F, E, R, NZ*, 1998 *It, E, S, I*, 1999 *S, Arg* 1,2, *SA, C,* [*J, A* (R)], 2000 *It, E, S, I, Sm, US, SA*, 2001 *E* (R), *It* (t), *R, I, Art* (R), *Tg*
Bayliss, G (Pontypool) 1933 *S*
Bebb, D I E (Carmarthen TC, Swansea) 1959 *E, S, I, F*, 1960 *E, S, I, F, SA*, 1961 *E, S, I, F*, 1962 *E, S, F, I*, 1963 *E, F, NZ*, 1964 *E, S, F, SA*, 1965 *E, S, I, F*, 1966 *F, A*, 1967 *S, I, F, E*
Beckingham, G (Cardiff) 1953 *E, S*, 1958 *F*
Bennett, A M (Cardiff) 1995 [*NZ*] *SA, Fj*
Bennett, I (Aberavon) 1937 *I*
Bennett, P (Cardiff Harlequins) 1891 *E, S*, 1892 *S, I*
Bennett, P (Llanelli) 1969 *F* (R), 1970 *SA, S, F*, 1972 *S* (R), *NZ*, 1973 *E, S, I, F, A*, 1974 *S, I, F, E*, 1975 *S* (R), *I*, 1976 *E, S, I, F*, 1977 *I, F, E, S*, 1978 *E, S, I, F*
Bergiers, R T E (Cardiff Coll of Ed, Llanelli) 1972 *E, S, F, NZ*, 1973 *E, S, I, F, A*, 1974 *E*, 1975 *I*
Bevan, G W (Llanelli) 1947 *E*
Bevan, J A (Cambridge U) 1881 *E*
Bevan, J C (Cardiff, Cardiff Coll of Ed) 1971 *E, S, I, F*, 1972 *E, S, F, NZ*, 1973 *E, S*
Bevan, J D (Aberavon) 1975 *F, E, S, A*
Bevan, S (Swansea) 1904 *I*
Beynon, B (Swansea) 1920 *E, S*
Beynon, G E (Swansea) 1925 *F, I*
Bidgood, R A (Newport) 1992 *S*, 1993 *Z* 1,2, *Nm, J* (R)
Biggs, N W (Cardiff) 1888 *M*, 1889 *I*, 1892 *I*, 1893 *E, S, I*, 1894 *E, I*

Biggs, S H (Cardiff) 1895 *E, S*, 1896 *S*, 1897 *E*, 1898 *I, E*, 1899 *S, I*, 1900 *I*
Birch, J (Neath) 1911 *S, F*
Birt, F W (Newport) 1911 *E, S*, 1912 *E, S, I, SA*, 1913 *E*
Bishop, D J (Pontypool) 1984 *A*
Bishop, E H (Swansea) 1889 *S*
Blackmore, J H (Abertillery) 1909 *E*
Blackmore, S W (Cardiff) 1987 *I*, [*Tg* (R), *C, A*]
Blake, J (Cardiff) 1899 *E, S, I*, 1900 *E, S, I*, 1901 *E, S, I*
Blakemore, R E (Newport) 1947 *E*
Bland, A F (Cardiff) 1887 *E, S, I*, 1888 *S, I, M*, 1890 *S, E, I*
Blyth, L (Swansea) 1951 *SA*, 1952 *E, S*
Blyth, W R (Swansea) 1974 *E*, 1975 *S* (R), 1980 *F, E, S, I*
Boobyer, N (Llanelli) 1993 *Z* 1(R),2, *Nm*, 1994 *Fj, Tg*, 1998 *F*, 1999 *It* (R)
Boon, R W (Cardiff) 1930 *S, F*, 1931 *E, S, F, I, SA*, 1932 *E, S, I*, 1933 *E, I*
Booth, J (Pontymister) 1898 *I*
Boots, J G (Newport) 1898 *I, E*, 1899 *I*, 1900 *E, S, I*, 1901 *E, S, I*, 1902 *E, S, I*, 1903 *E, S, I*, 1904 *E*
Boucher, A W (Newport) 1892 *E, S, I*, 1893 *E, S, I*, 1894 *E, S, I*, 1895 *E, S, I*, 1896 *E, I*, 1897 *E*
Bowcott, H M (Cardiff, Cambridge U) 1929 *S, F, I*, 1930 *E, I*, 1931 *E, S*, 1933 *E, I*
Bowdler, F A (Cross Keys) 1927 *A*, 1928 *E, S, I, F*, 1929 *E, S, F, I*, 1930 *I, SA*, 1932 *E, S, I*, 1933 *I*
Bowen, B (S Wales Police, Swansea) 1983 *R*, 1984 *S, I, F, E*, 1985 *Fj*, 1986 *E, S, I, F, Fj, Tg, WS*, 1987 [*C, E, NZ*], *US*, 1988 *E, S, I, F, WS*, 1989 *S, I*
Bowen, C A (Llanelli) 1896 *E, S, I*, 1897 *E*
Bowen, D H (Llanelli) 1883 *E*, 1886 *E, S*, 1887 *E*
Bowen, G E (Swansea) 1887 *S, I*, 1888 *S, I*
Bowen, W (Swansea) 1921 *S, F*, 1922 *E, S, I, F*
Bowen, Wm A (Swansea) 1886 *E, S*, 1887 *E, S, I*, 1888 *M*, 1889 *S, I*, 1890 *S, E, I*, 1891 *E, S*
Brace, D O (Llanelli, Oxford U) 1956 *E, S, I, F*, 1957 *E*, 1960 *S, I, F*, 1961 *I*
Braddock, K J (Newbridge) 1966 *A*, 1967 *S, I*
Bradshaw, K (Bridgend) 1964 *E, S, I, F, SA*, 1966 *E, S, I, F*
Brewer, T J (Newport) 1950 *E*, 1955 *E, S*
Brice, A B (Aberavon) 1899 *E, S, I*, 1900 *E, S, I*, 1901 *E, S, I*, 1902 *E, S, I*, 1903 *E, S, I*, 1904 *E, S, I*
Bridges, C J (Neath) 1990 *Nm* 1,2, *Bb*, 1991 *E* (R), *I, F* 1, *A*
Bridie, R H (Newport) 1882 *I*
Britton, G R (Newport) 1961 *S*
Broughton, A S (Treorchy) 1927 *A*, 1929 *S*
Brown, A (Newport) 1921 *I*
Brown, J (Cardiff) 1925 *I*
Brown, J A (Cardiff) 1907 *E, S, I*, 1908 *E, S, F*, 1909 *E*
Brown, M (Pontypool) 1983 *R*, 1986 *E, S, Fj* (R), *Tg, WS*
Bryant, D J (Bridgend) 1988 *NZ* 1,2, *WS, R*, 1989 *S, I, F, E*
Buchanan, A (Llanelli) 1987 [*Tg, E, NZ, A*], 1988 *I*
Buckett, I M (Swansea) 1994 *Tg*, 1997 *US* 2, *C*
Budgett, N J (Ebbw Vale, Bridgend) 2000 *S, I, Sm* (R), *US, SA*, 2001 *J* 1(R),2, 2002 *I, F, It, E, S*
Burcher, D H (Newport) 1977 *I, F, E, S*
Burgess, R C (Ebbw Vale) 1977 *I, F, E, S*, 1981 *I, F*, 1982 *F, E, S*
Burnett, R (Newport) 1953 *E*
Burns, J (Cardiff) 1927 *F, I*
Bush, P F (Cardiff) 1905 *NZ*, 1906 *E, SA*, 1907 *I*, 1908 *E, S*, 1910 *S, I*
Butler, E T (Pontypool) 1980 *F, E, S, I, NZ* (R), 1982 *S*, 1983 *E, S, I, F, R*, 1984 *S, I, F, E, A*

Cale, W R (Newbridge, Pontypool) 1949 *E, S, I, F*, 1950 *E, S, I, F*

Cardey, M D (Llanelli) 2000 *S*
Carter, A J (Newport) 1991 *E, S*
Cattell, A (Llanelli) 1883 *E, S*
Challinor, C (Neath) 1939 *E*

Charvis, C L (Swansea) 1996 *A* 3(R), *SA*, 1997 *US*, *S*, *I*, *F*, 1998 *It* (R), *E*, *S*, *I*, *F*, *Z* (R), *SA* 1,2, *Arg*, 1999 *S*, *I*, *F* 1, *It*, *E*, *Arg* 1, *SA*, *F* 2, [*Arg* 3, *A*], 2000 *F*, *It* (R), *E*, *S*, *I*, *Sm*, *US*, *SA*, 2001 *E*, *S*, *F*, *It*, *R*, *I*, *Arg*, *Tg*, *A*, 2002 *E* (R), *S*, *SA* 1,2
Clapp, T J S (Newport) 1882 *I*, 1883 *E*, *S*, 1884 *E*, *S*, *I*, 1885 *E*, *S*, 1886 *S*, 1887 *E*, *S*, *I*, 1888 *S*, *I*
Clare, J (Cardiff) 1883 *E*
Clark, S S (Neath) 1882 *I*, 1887 *I*
Cleaver, W B (Cardiff) 1947 *E*, *S*, *F*, *I*, *A*, 1948 *E*, *S*, *F*, *I*, 1949 *I*, 1950 *E*, *S*, *I*, *F*
Clegg, B G (Swansea) 1979 *F*
Clement, A (Swansea) 1987 *US* (R), 1988 *E*, *NZ* 1, *WS* (R), *R*, 1989 *NZ*, 1990 *S* (R), *I* (R), *Nm* 1,2, 1991 *S* (R), *A* (R), *F* 2, [*WS*, *A*], 1992 *I*, *F*, *E*, *S*, 1993 *I* (R), *F*, *J*, *C*, 1994 *S*, *I*, *F*, *Sp*, *C* (R), *Tg*, *WS*, *It*, *SA*, 1995 *F*, *E*, [*J*, *NZ*, *F*]
Clement, W H (Llanelli) 1937 *E*, *S*, *I*, 1938 *E*, *S*, *I*
Cobner, T J (Pontypool) 1974 *S*, *I*, *F*, *E*, 1975 *F*, *E*, *S*, *I*, *A*, 1976 *E*, *S*, 1977 *F*, *E*, *S*, 1978 *E*, *S*, *I*, *F*, *A* 1
Coldrick, A P (Newport) 1911 *E*, *S*, *I*, 1912 *E*, *S*, *F*
Coleman, E (Newport) 1949 *E*, *S*
Coles, F C (Pontypool) 1960 *S*, *I*, *F*
Collins, J (Aberavon) 1958 *A*, *E*, *S*, *F*, 1959 *E*, *S*, *I*, *F*, 1960 *E*, 1961 *F*
Collins, R G (S Wales Police, Cardiff, Pontypridd) 1987 *E* (R), *I*, [*I*, *E*, *NZ*], *US*, 1988 *E*, *S*, *I*, *F*, *R*, 1990 *E*, *S*, *I*, 1991 *A*, *F* 2, [*WS*], 1994 *C*, *Fj*, *Tg*, *WS*, *R*, *It*, *SA*, 1995 *F*, *E*, *S*, *I*
Collins, T (Mountain Ash) 1923 *I*
Conway-Rees, J (Llanelli) 1892 *S*, 1893 *E*, 1894 *E*
Cook, T (Cardiff) 1949 *S*, *I*
Cooper, G J (Bath) 2001 *F*, *J* 1,2
Cope, W (Cardiff, Blackheath) 1896 *S*
Copsey, A H (Llanelli) 1992 *I*, *F*, *E*, *S*, *A*, 1993 *E*, *S*, *I*, *J*, *C*, 1994 *E* (R), *Pt*, *Sp* (R), *Fj*, *Tg*, *WS* (R)
Cornish, F H (Cardiff) 1897 *E*, 1898 *I*, *E*, 1899 *I*
Cornish, R A (Cardiff) 1923 *E*, *S*, 1924 *E*, 1925 *E*, *S*, *F*, 1926 *E*, *S*, *I*, *F*
Coslett, K (Aberavon) 1962 *E*, *S*, *F*
Cowey, B T V (Welch Regt, Newport) 1934 *E*, *S*, *I*, 1935 *E*
Cresswell, B (Newport) 1960 *E*, *S*, *I*, *F*
Cummins, W (Treorchy) 1922 *E*, *S*, *I*, *F*
Cunningham, L J (Aberavon) 1960 *E*, *S*, *I*, *F*, 1962 *E*, *S*, *F*, *I*, 1963 *NZ*, 1964 *E*, *S*, *I*, *F*, *SA*

Dacey, M (Swansea) 1983 *E*, *S*, *I*, *F*, *R*, 1984 *S*, *I*, *F*, *E*, *A*, 1986 *Fj*, *Tg*, *WS*, 1987 *F* (R), [*Tg*]
Daniel, D J (Llanelli) 1891 *S*, 1894 *E*, *S*, *I*, 1898 *I*, *E*, 1899 *E*, *I*
Daniel, L T D (Newport) 1970 *S*
Daniels, P C T (Cardiff) 1981 *A*, 1982 *I*
Darbishire, G (Bangor) 1881 *E*
Dauncey, F H (Newport) 1896 *E*, *S*, *I*
Davey, C (Swansea) 1930 *F*, 1931 *E*, *S*, *F*, *I*, *SA*, 1932 *E*, *S*, *I*, 1933 *E*, *S*, 1934 *E*, *S*, *I*, 1935 *E*, *S*, *I*, *NZ*, 1936 *S*, 1937 *E*, *I*, 1938 *E*, *I*
David, R J (Cardiff) 1907 *I*
David, T P (Llanelli, Pontypridd) 1973 *F*, *A*, 1976 *I*, *F*
Davidge, G D (Newport) 1959 *F*, 1960 *S*, *I*, *F*, *SA*, 1961 *E*, *S*, *I*, 1962 *F*
Davies, A (Cambridge U, Neath, Cardiff) 1990 *Bb* (R), 1991 *A*, 1993 *Z* 1,2, *J*, *C*, 1994 *Fj*, 1995 [*J*, *I*]
Davies, A C (London Welsh) 1889 *I*
Davies, A E (Llanelli) 1984 *A*
Davies, B (Llanelli) 1895 *E*, 1896 *E*
Davies, C (Cardiff) 1947 *S*, *F*, *I*, *A*, 1948 *E*, *S*, *F*, *I*, 1949 *F*, 1950 *E*, *S*, *I*, *F*, 1951 *E*, *S*, *I*
Davies, C (Llanelli) 1988 *WS*, 1989 *S*, *I* (R), *F*
Davies, C H A (Llanelli, Cardiff) 1957 *I*, 1958 *A*, *E*, *S*, *I*, 1960 *SA*, 1961 *E*
Davies, C L (Cardiff) 1956 *E*, *S*, *I*
Davies, C R (Bedford, RAF) 1934 *E*
Davies, D (Bridgend) 1921 *I*, 1925 *I*
Davies, D B (Llanelli) 1907 *E*
Davies, D B (Llanelli) 1962 *I*, 1963 *E*, *S*
Davies, D G (Cardiff) 1923 *E*, *S*
Davies, D H (Neath) 1904 *S*
Davies, D H (Aberavon) 1924 *E*
Davies, D I (Swansea) 1939 *E*
Davies, D J (Neath) 1962 *I*
Davies, D M (Somerset Police) 1950 *E*, *S*, *I*, *F*, 1951 *E*, *S*, *I*, *F*, *SA*, 1952 *E*, *S*, *I*, *F*, 1953 *I*, *F*, *NZ*, 1954 *E*
Davies, E (Aberavon) 1947 *A*, 1948 *I*
Davies, E (Maesteg) 1919 *NZA*
Davies, E G (Cardiff) 1912 *E*, *F*

Davies, E G (Cardiff) 1928 *F*, 1929 *E*, 1930 *S*
Davies, G (Swansea) 1900 *E*, *S*, *I*, 1901 *E*, *S*, *I*, 1905 *E*, *S*, *I*
Davies, G (Cambridge U, Pontypridd) 1947 *S*, *A*, 1948 *E*, *S*, *F*, *I*, 1949 *E*, *S*, *F*, 1951 *E*, *S*
Davies, G (Llanelli) 1921 *F*, *I*, 1925 *F*
Davies, H (Swansea) 1898 *I*, *E*, 1901 *S*, *I*
Davies, H (Swansea, Llanelli) 1939 *S*, *I*, 1947 *E*, *S*, *F*, *I*
Davies, H (Neath) 1912 *E*, *S*
Davies, H (Bridgend) 1984 *S*, *I*, *F*, *E*
Davies, H J (Cambridge U, Aberavon) 1959 *E*, *S*
Davies, H J (Newport) 1924 *S*
Davies, I T (Llanelli) 1914 *S*, *F*, *I*
Davies, J (Neath, Llanelli, Cardiff) 1985 *E*, *Fj*, 1986 *E*, *S*, *I*, *F*, *Fj*, *Tg*, *WS*, 1987 *F*, *E*, *S*, *I*, [*I*, *Tg* (R), *C*, *E*, *NZ*, *A*], 1988 *E*, *S*, *I*, *F*, *NZ* 1,2, *WS*, *R*, 1996 *A* 3, 1997 *US* (t), *S* (R), *F* (R), *E*
Davies, Rev J A (Swansea) 1913 *S*, *F*, *I*, 1914 *E*, *S*, *F*, *I*
Davies, J D (Neath, Richmond) 1991 *I*, *F* 1, 1993 *F* (R), *Z* 2, *J*, *C*, 1994 *S*, *I*, *F*, *E*, *Pt*, *Sp*, *C*, *WS*, *R*, *It*, *SA*, 1995 *F*, *E*, [*J*, *NZ*, *I*] *SA*, 1996 *It*, *E*, *S*, *I*, *F* 1, *A* 1, *Bb*, *F* 2, *It*, 1998 *Z*, *SA* 1
Davies, J H (Aberavon) 1923 *I*
Davies, L (Swansea) 1939 *S*, *I*
Davies, L (Bridgend) 1966 *E*, *S*, *I*
Davies, L B (Neath, Cardiff, Llanelli) 1996 *It*, *E*, *S*, *I*, *F* 1, *A* 1, *Bb*, *F* 2, *It* (R), 1997 *US* 1,2, *C*, *R*, *Tg*, *NZ* (R), 1998 *E* (R), *I*, *F*, 1999 *C*, 2001 *I*
Davies, L M (Llanelli) 1954 *F*, *S*, 1955 *I*
Davies, M (Swansea) 1981 *A*, 1982 *I*, 1985 *Fj*
Davies, Mefin (Pontypridd) 2002 *SA* 2(R)
Davies, M J (Blackheath) 1939 *S*, *I*
Davies, N G (London Welsh) 1955 *E*
Davies, N G (Llanelli) 1988 *NZ* 2, *WS*, 1989 *S*, *I*, 1993 *F*, 1994 *S*, *I*, *E*, *Pt*, *Sp*, *C*, *Fj*, *Tg* (R), *WS*, *R*, *It*, 1995 *E*, *S*, *I*, *Fj*, 1996 *E*, *S*, *I*, *F* 1, *A* 1,2, *Bb*, *F* 2, 1997 *E*
Davies, P T (Llanelli) 1985 *E*, *Fj*, 1986 *E*, *S*, *I*, *F*, *Fj*, *Tg*, *WS*, 1987 *F*, *E*, *I*, [*Tg*, *C*, *NZ*], 1988 *WS*, *R*, 1989 *S*, *I*, *F*, *E*, *NZ*, 1990 *F*, *E*, *S*, 1991 *I*, *F* 1, *A*, *F* 2, [*WS*, *Arg*, *A*], 1993 *F*, *Z* 1, *Nm*, 1994 *S*, *I*, *F*, *E*, *C*, *Fj* (R), *WS*, *R*, *It*, 1995 *F*, *I*
Davies, R H (Oxford U, London Welsh) 1957 *S*, *I*, *F*, 1958 *A*, 1962 *E*, *S*
Davies, S (Treherbert) 1923 *I*
Davies, S (Swansea) 1992 *I*, *F*, *E*, *S*, *A*, 1993 *E*, *S*, *I*, *Z* 1(R),2, *Nm*, *J*, 1995 *F*, [*J*, *I*], 1998 *I* (R), *F*
Davies, T G R (Cardiff, London Welsh) 1966 *A*, 1967 *S*, *I*, *F*, *E*, 1968 *E*, *S*, 1969 *S*, *I*, *F*, *NZ* 1,2, *A*, 1971 *E*, *S*, *I*, *F*, 1972 *E*, *S*, *F*, *NZ*, 1973 *E*, *S*, *I*, *F*, *A*, 1974 *S*, *F*, *E*, 1975 *F*, *E*, *S*, *I*, 1976 *E*, *S*, *I*, *F*, 1977 *I*, *F*, *E*, *S*, 1978 *E*, *S*, *I*, *A* 1,2
Davies, T J (Devonport Services, Swansea, Llanelli) 1953 *E*, *S*, *I*, *F*, 1957 *E*, *S*, *I*, *F*, 1958 *A*, *E*, *S*, *F*, 1959 *E*, *S*, *I*, *F*, 1960 *E*, *SA*, 1961 *E*, *S*, *F*
Davies, T M (London Welsh, Swansea) 1969 *S*, *I*, *F*, *E*, *NZ* 1,2, *A*, 1970 *SA*, *S*, *E*, *I*, *F*, 1971 *E*, *S*, *I*, *F*, 1972 *E*, *S*, *F*, *NZ*, 1973 *E*, *S*, *I*, *F*, *A*, 1974 *S*, *I*, *F*, *E*, 1975 *F*, *E*, *S*, *I*, *A*, 1976 *E*, *S*, *I*, *F*
Davies, W (Cardiff) 1896 *S*
Davies, W (Swansea) 1931 *SA*, 1932 *E*, *S*, *I*
Davies, W A (Aberavon) 1912 *S*, *I*
Davies, W G (Cardiff) 1978 *A* 1,2, *NZ*, 1979 *S*, *I*, *F*, *E*, 1980 *F*, *E*, *S*, *NZ*, 1981 *E*, *S*, *A*, 1982 *I*, *F*, *E*, *S*, 1985 *S*, *I*, *F*
Davies, W T H (Swansea) 1936 *I*, 1937 *E*, *I*, 1939 *E*, *S*, *I*
Davis, C E (Newbridge) 1978 *A* 2, 1981 *E*, *S*
Davis, M (Newport) 1991 *A*
Davis, W E N (Cardiff) 1939 *E*, *S*, *I*
Dawes, S J (London Welsh) 1964 *I*, *F*, *SA*, 1965 *E*, *S*, *I*, *F*, 1966 *A*, 1968 *I*, *F*, 1969 *E*, *NZ* 2, *A*, 1970 *SA*, *S*, *E*, *I*, *F*, 1971 *E*, *S*, *I*, *F*
Day, H C (Newport) 1930 *S*, *I*, *F*, 1931 *E*, *S*
Day, H T (Newport) 1892 *I*, 1893 *E*, *S*, 1894 *S*, *I*
Day, T B (Swansea) 1931 *E*, *S*, *F*, *I*, *SA*, 1932 *E*, *S*, *I*, 1934 *S*, *I*, 1935 *E*, *S*, *I*
Deacon, J T (Swansea) 1891 *I*, 1892 *E*, *S*, *I*
Delahay, W J (Bridgend) 1922 *E*, *S*, *I*, *F*, 1923 *E*, *S*, *F*, *I*, 1924 *NZ*, 1925 *E*, *S*, *F*, *I*, 1926 *E*, *S*, *I*, *F*, 1927 *S*
Delaney, L (Llanelli) 1989 *I*, *F*, *E*, 1990 *E*, 1991 *F* 2, [*WS*, *Arg*, *A*], 1992 *I*, *F*, *E*
Devereux, D (Neath) 1958 *A*, *E*, *S*
Devereux, J A (S Glamorgan Inst, Bridgend) 1986 *E*, *S*, *I*, *F*, *Fj*, *Tg*, *WS*, 1987 *F*, *E*, *S*, *I*, [*I*, *C*, *E*, *NZ*, *A*], 1988 *NZ* 1,2, *R*, 1989 *S*, *I*
Diplock, R (Bridgend) 1988 *R*
Dobson, G (Cardiff) 1900 *S*
Dobson, T (Cardiff) 1898 *I*, *E*, 1899 *E*, *S*
Donovan, A J (Swansea) 1978 *A* 2, 1981 *I* (R), *A*, 1982 *E*, *S*
Donovan, R (S Wales Police) 1983 *F* (R)

Douglas, M H J (Llanelli) 1984 *S, I, F*
Douglas, W M (Cardiff) 1886 *E, S*, 1887 *E, S*
Dowell, W H (Newport) 1907 *E, S, I*, 1908 *E, S, F, I*
Durston, A (Bridgend) 2001 *J* 1,2
Dyke, J C M (Penarth) 1906 *SA*
Dyke, L M (Penarth, Cardiff) 1910 *I*, 1911 *S, F, I*

Edmunds, D A (Neath) 1990 *I* (R), *Bb*
Edwards, A B (London Welsh, Army) 1955 *E, S*
Edwards, B O (Newport) 1951 *I*
Edwards, D (Glynneath) 1921 *E*
Edwards, G O (Cardiff, Cardiff Coll of Ed) 1967 *F, E, NZ,* 1968 *E, S, I, F,* 1969 *S, I, F, E, NZ* 1,2, *A,* 1970 *SA, S, E, I, F,* 1971 *E, S, I, F,* 1972 *E, S, F, NZ,* 1973 *E, S, I, F, A,* 1974 *S, I, F, E,* 1975 *F, E, S, I, A,* 1976 *E, S, I, F,* 1977 *I, F, E, S,* 1978 *E, S, I, F*
Eidman, I H (Cardiff) 1983 *S, R,* 1984 *I, F, E, A,* 1985 *S, I, Fj,* 1986 *E, S, I, F*
Elliott, J E (Cardiff) 1894 *I,* 1898 *I, E*
Elsey, W J (Cardiff) 1895 *E*
Emyr, Arthur (Swansea) 1989 *E, NZ,* 1990 *F, E, S, I, Nm* 1,2, 1991 *F* 1,2, *[WS, Arg, A]*
Evans, A (Pontypool) 1924 *E, I, F*
Evans, B (Swansea) 1933 *S*
Evans, B (Llanelli) 1933 *E, S,* 1936 *E, S, I,* 1937 *E*
Evans, B R (Swansea) 1998 *SA* 2(R), 1999 *F* 1, *It, E, Arg* 1,2, *C, [J* (R), *Sm* (R), *A* (R)], 2000 *Sm, US,* 2001 *J* 1(R), 2002 *SA* 1,2
Evans, B S (Llanelli) 1920 *E,* 1922 *E, S, I, F*
Evans, C (Pontypool) 1960 *E*
Evans, D (Penygraig) 1896 *S, I,* 1897 *E,* 1898 *E*
Evans, D B (Swansea) 1926 *E*
Evans, D D (Cheshire, Cardiff U) 1934 *E*
Evans, D P (Llanelli) 1960 *SA*
Evans, D W (Cardiff) 1889 *S, I,* 1890 *E, I,* 1891 *E*
Evans, D W (Oxford U, Cardiff, Treorchy) 1989 *F, E, NZ,* 1990 *F, E, S, I, Bb,* 1991 *A* (R), *F* 2(R), *[A* (R)], 1995 *[J* (R)]
Evans, E (Llanelli) 1937 *E,* 1939 *S, I*
Evans, F (Llanelli) 1921 *S*
Evans, G (Cardiff) 1947 *E, S, F, I, A,* 1948 *E, S, F, I,* 1949 *E, S, I*
Evans, G (Maesteg) 1981 *S* (R), *I, F, A,* 1982 *I, F, E, S,* 1983 *F, R*
Evans, G L (Newport) 1977 *F* (R), 1978 *F, A* 2(R)
Evans, G R (Llanelli) 1998 *SA* 1
Evans, I (London Welsh) 1934 *S, I*
Evans, I (Swansea) 1922 *E, S, I, F*
Evans, I C (Llanelli, Bath) 1987 *F, E, S, I, [I, C, E, NZ, A],* 1988 *E, S, I, F, NZ* 1,2, 1989 *I, F, E,* 1991 *E, S, I, F* 1, *A, F* 2, *[WS, Arg, A],* 1992 *I, F, E, S, A,* 1993 *E, S, I, F, J, C,* 1994 *S, I, E, Pt, Sp, C, Fj, Tg, WS, R,* 1995 *S, I, [J, NZ, I], SA, Fj,* 1996 *It, E, S, I, F* 1, *A* 1,2, *Bb, F* 2, *A* 3, *SA,* 1997 *US, S, I, F,* 1998 *It*
Evans, I L (Newport) 1991 *F* 2(R)
Evans, J (Llanelli) 1896 *S, I,* 1897 *E*
Evans, J (Blaina) 1904 *E*
Evans, J (Pontypool) 1907 *E, S, I*
Evans, J D (Cardiff) 1958 *I, F*
Evans, J E (Llanelli) 1924 *S*
Evans, J R (Newport) 1934 *E*
Evans, O J (Cardiff) 1887 *E, S,* 1888 *S, I*
Evans, P D (Llanelli) 1951 *E, F*
Evans, R (Cardiff) 1889 *S*
Evans, R (Bridgend) 1963 *S, I, F*
Evans, R L (Llanelli) 1993 *E, S, I, F,* 1994 *S, I, F, E, Pt, Sp, C, Fj, WS, R, It, SA,* 1995 *F, [NZ, I* (R)]
Evans, R T (Newport) 1947 *F, I,* 1950 *E, S, I, F,* 1951 *E, S, I, F*
Evans, S (Swansea, Neath) 1985 *F, E,* 1986 *Fj, Tg, WS,* 1987 *F, E, [I, Tg]*
Evans, T (Swansea) 1924 *I*
Evans, T G (London Welsh) 1970 *SA, S, E, I,* 1972 *E, S, F*
Evans, T H (Llanelli) 1906 *I,* 1907 *E, S, I,* 1908 *I, A,* 1909 *E, S, F, I,* 1910 *F, E, S, I,* 1911 *E, S, F, I*
Evans, T P (Swansea) 1975 *F, E, S, I, A,* 1976 *E, S, I, F,* 1977 *I*
Evans, V (Neath) 1954 *I, F, S*
Evans, W (Llanelli) 1958 *A*
Evans, W F (Rhymney) 1882 *I,* 1883 *S*
Evans, W G (Brynmawr) 1911 *I*
Evans, W H (Llwynypia) 1914 *E, S, F, I*
Evans, W J (Pontypool) 1947 *S*

Evans, W R (Bridgend) 1958 *A, E, S, I, F,* 1960 *SA,* 1961 *E, S, I, F,* 1962 *E, S, I*
Everson, W A (Newport) 1926 *S*

Faulkner, A G (Pontypool) 1975 *F, E, S, I, A,* 1976 *E, S, I, F,* 1978 *E, S, I, F, A* 1,2, *NZ,* 1979 *S, I, F*
Faull, J (Swansea) 1957 *I, F,* 1958 *A, E, S, I, F,* 1959 *E, S, I,* 1960 *E, F*
Fauvel, T J (Aberavon) 1988 *NZ* 1(R)
Fear, A G (Newport) 1934 *S, I,* 1935 *S, I*
Fender, N H (Cardiff) 1930 *I, F,* 1931 *E, S, F, I*
Fenwick, S P (Bridgend) 1975 *F, E, S, A,* 1976 *E, S, I, F,* 1977 *I, F, E, S,* 1978 *E, S, I, F, A* 1,2, *NZ,* 1979 *S, I, F, E,* 1980 *F, E, S, I, NZ,* 1981 *E, S*
Finch, E (Llanelli) 1924 *F, NZ,* 1925 *F, I,* 1926 *F,* 1927 *A,* 1928 *I*
Finlayson, A A J (Cardiff) 1974 *I, F, E*
Fitzgerald, D (Cardiff) 1894 *S, I*
Ford, F J V (Welch Regt, Newport) 1939 *E*
Ford, I (Newport) 1959 *E, S*
Ford, S P (Cardiff) 1990 *I, Nm* 1,2, *Bb,* 1991 *E, S, I, A*
Forward, A (Pontypool, Mon Police) 1951 *S, SA,* 1952 *E, S, I, F*
Fowler, I J (Llanelli) 1919 *NZA*
Francis, D G (Llanelli) 1919 *NZA,* 1924 *S*
Francis, P (Maesteg) 1987 *S*
Funnell, J S (Ebbw Vale) 1998 *Z* (R), *SA* 1

Gabe, R T (Cardiff, Llanelli) 1901 *I,* 1902 *E, S, I,* 1903 *E, S, I,* 1904 *E, S, I,* 1905 *E, S, I, NZ,* 1906 *E, I, SA,* 1907 *E, S, I,* 1908 *E, S, F, I*
Gale, N R (Swansea, Llanelli) 1960 *I,* 1963 *E, S, I, NZ,* 1964 *E, S, I, F, SA,* 1965 *E, S, I, F,* 1966 *E, S, I, F, A,* 1967 *E, NZ,* 1968 *E,* 1969 *NZ* 1(R),2, *A*
Gallacher, I S (Llanelli) 1970 *F*
Garrett, R M (Penarth) 1888 *M,* 1889 *S,* 1890 *S, E, I,* 1891 *S, I,* 1892 *E*
Geen, W P (Oxford U, Newport) 1912 *SA,* 1913 *E, I*
George, E E (Pontypridd, Cardiff) 1895 *S, I,* 1896 *E*
George, G M (Newport) 1991 *E, S*
Gething, G I (Neath) 1913 *F*
Gibbs, A (Newbridge) 1995 *I, SA,* 1996 *A* 2, 1997 *US* 1,2, *C*
Gibbs, I S (Neath, Swansea) 1991 *E, S, I, F* 1, *A, F* 2, *[WS, Arg, A],* 1992 *I, F, E, S, A,* 1993 *E, S, I, C,* 1996 *It, A* 3, *SA,* 1997 *US, S, I, F, Tg, NZ,* 1998 *It, E, S, SA* 2, *Arg,* 1999 *S, I, F* 1, *It, E, C, F* 2, *[Arg* 3, *J, Sm, A],* 2000 *I, Sm, US, SA,* 2001 *E, S, F, It*
Gibbs, R A (Cardiff) 1906 *S, I,* 1907 *E, S,* 1908 *E, S, F, I,* 1910 *F, E, S, I,* 1911 *E, S, F, I*
Giles, R (Aberavon) 1983 *R,* 1985 *Fj* (R), 1987 *[C]*
Girling, B E (Cardiff) 1881 *E*
Goldsworthy, S J (Swansea) 1884 *I,* 1885 *E, S*
Gore, J H (Blaina) 1924 *I, F, NZ,* 1925 *E*
Gore, W (Newbridge) 1947 *S, F, I*
Gough, I M (Newport, Pontypridd) 1998 *SA* 1, 1999 *S,* 2000 *F, It* (R), *E* (R), *S, I, Sm, US, SA,* 2001 *E, S, F, It, Tg, A,* 2002 *I* (R), *F* (R), *It, S*
Gould, A J (Newport) 1885 *E, S,* 1886 *E, S,* 1887 *E, S, I,* 1888 *S,* 1889 *I,* 1890 *S, E, I,* 1892 *E, S, I,* 1893 *E, S, I,* 1894 *E, S,* 1895 *E, S, I,* 1896 *E, S, I,* 1897 *E*
Gould, G H (Newport) 1892 *I,* 1893 *S, I*
Gould, R (Newport) 1882 *I,* 1883 *E, S,* 1884 *E, S, I,* 1885 *E, S,* 1886 *E,* 1887 *E, S*
Graham, T C (Newport) 1890 *I,* 1891 *S, I,* 1892 *E, S,* 1893 *E, S, I,* 1894 *E, S,* 1895 *E, S*
Gravell, R W R (Llanelli) 1975 *F, E, S, I, A,* 1976 *E, S, I, F,* 1978 *E, S, I, F, A* 1,2, *NZ,* 1979 *S, I,* 1981 *I, F,* 1982 *F, E, S*
Gray, A J (London Welsh) 1968 *E, S*
Greenslade, D (Newport) 1962 *S*
Greville, H G (Llanelli) 1947 *A*
Griffin, Dr J (Edinburgh U) 1883 *S*
Griffiths, C (Llanelli) 1979 *E* (R)
Griffiths, D (Llanelli) 1888 *M,* 1889 *I*
Griffiths, G (Llanelli) 1889 *I*
Griffiths, G M (Cardiff) 1953 *E, S, I, F, NZ,* 1954 *I, F, S,* 1955 *I, F,* 1957 *E, S*
Griffiths, J (Swansea) 2000 *Sm* (R)
Griffiths, J L (Llanelli) 1988 *NZ* 2, 1989 *S*
Griffiths, M (Bridgend, Cardiff, Pontypridd) 1988 *WS, R,* 1989 *S, I, F, E, NZ,* 1990 *F, E, Nm* 1,2, *Bb,* 1991 *I, F* 1,2, *[WS, Arg, A],* 1992 *I, F, E, S, A,* 1993 *Z* 1,2, *Nm, J, C,* 1995 *F* (R), *E, S, I, [J, I],* 1998 *SA* 1
Griffiths, V M (Newport) 1924 *S, I, F*

Gronow, B (Bridgend) 1910 *F, E, S, I*
Gwilliam, J A (Cambridge U, Newport) 1947 *A*, 1948 *I*, 1949 *E, S, I, F*, 1950 *E, S, I, F*, 1951 *E, S, I, SA*, 1952 *E, S, I, F*, 1953 *E, I, F, NZ*, 1954 *E*
Gwynn, D (Swansea) 1883 *E*, 1887 *S*, 1890 *E, I*, 1891 *E, S*
Gwynn, W H (Swansea) 1884 *E, S, I*, 1885 *E, S*

Hadley, A M (Cardiff) 1983 *R*, 1984 *S, I, F, E*, 1985 *F, E, Fj*, 1986 *E, S, I, F, Fj, Tg*, 1987 *S* (R), *I, [I, Tg, C, E, NZ, A]*, *US*, 1988 *E, S, I, F*
Hall, I (Aberavon) 1967 *NZ*, 1970 *SA, S, E*, 1971 *S*, 1974 *S, I, F*
Hall, M R (Cambridge U, Bridgend, Cardiff) 1988 *NZ* 1(R),2, *WS, R*, 1989 *S, I, F, E, NZ*, 1990 *F, E, S*, 1991 *A, F* 2, [*WS, Arg, A*], 1992 *I, F, E, S, A*, 1993 *E, S, I*, 1994 *S, I, F, E, Pt, Sp, C, Tg, R, It, SA*, 1995 *F, S, I*, [*J, NZ, I*]
Hall, W H (Bridgend) 1988 *WS*
Hancock, F E (Cardiff) 1884 *I*, 1885 *E, S*, 1886 *S*
Hannan, J (Newport) 1888 *M*, 1889 *S, I*, 1890 *S, E, I*, 1891 *E*, 1892 *E, S, I*, 1893 *E, S, I*, 1894 *E, S, I*, 1895 *E, S, I*
Harding, A F (London Welsh) 1902 *E, S, I*, 1903 *E, S, I*, 1904 *E, S, I*, 1905 *E, S, I, NZ*, 1906 *E, S, I, SA*, 1907 *I*, 1908 *E, S*
Harding, G F (Newport) 1881 *E*, 1882 *I*, 1883 *E, S*
Harding, R (Swansea, Cambridge U) 1923 *E, S, F, I*, 1924 *I, F, NZ*, 1925 *F, I*, 1926 *E, I, F*, 1927 *E, S, F, I*, 1928 *E*
Harding, T (Newport) 1888 *M*, 1889 *S, I*
Harris, D J E (Pontypridd, Cardiff) 1959 *I, F*, 1960 *S, I, F, SA*, 1961 *E, S*
Harris, I R (Cardiff) 2001 *Arg, Tg, A*, 2002 *I, It* (R), *E, S* (R)
Harris, T (Aberavon) 1927 *A*
Hathway, G F (Newport) 1924 *I, F*
Havard, Rev W T (Llanelli) 1919 *NZA*
Hawkins, F (Pontypridd) 1912 *I, F*
Hayward, B I (Ebbw Vale) 1998 *Z* (R), *SA* 1
Hayward, D (Newbridge) 1949 *E, F*, 1950 *E, S, I, F*, 1951 *E, S, I, F, SA*, 1952 *E, S, I, F*
Hayward, D J (Cardiff) 1963 *E, NZ*, 1964 *S, I, F, SA*
Hayward, G (Swansea) 1908 *S, F, I, A*, 1909 *E*
Hellings, R (Llwynypia) 1897 *E*, 1898 *I, E*, 1899 *S, I*, 1900 *E, I*, 1901 *E, S*
Henson, G L (Swansea) 2001 *J* 1(R), *R*
Herrerá, R C (Cross Keys) 1925 *S, F, I*, 1926 *E, S, I, F*, 1927 *E*
Hiams, H (Swansea) 1912 *I, F*
Hickman, A (Neath) 1930 *E*, 1933 *S*
Hiddlestone, D D (Neath) 1922 *E, S, I, F*, 1924 *NZ*
Hill, A F (Cardiff) 1885 *S*, 1886 *E, S*, 1888 *S, I, M*, 1889 *S*, 1890 *S, I*, 1893 *E, S, I*, 1894 *E, S, I*
Hill, S D (Cardiff) 1993 *Z* 1,2, *Nm*, 1994 *I* (R), *F, SA*, 1995 *F, SA*, 1996 *A* 2, *F* 2(R), *It*, 1997 *E*
Hinam, S (Cardiff) 1925 *I*, 1926 *E, S, I, F*
Hinton, J T (Cardiff) 1884 *I*
Hirst, G L (Newport) 1912 *S*, 1913 *S*, 1914 *E, S, F, I*
Hodder, W (Pontypool) 1921 *E, S, F*
Hodges, J J (Newport) 1899 *E, S, I*, 1900 *E, S, I*, 1901 *E, S*, 1902 *E, S, I*, 1903 *E, S, I*, 1904 *E, S*, 1905 *E, S, I, NZ*, 1906 *E, S, I*
Hodgson, G T R (Neath) 1962 *I*, 1963 *E, S, I, F, NZ*, 1964 *E, S, I, F, SA*, 1966 *S, I, F*, 1967 *I*
Hollingdale, H (Swansea) 1912 *SA*, 1913 *E*
Hollingdale, T H (Neath) 1927 *A*, 1928 *E, S, I, F*, 1930 *E*
Holmes, T D (Cardiff) 1978 *A* 2, *NZ*, 1979 *S, I, F, E*, 1980 *F, E, S, I, NZ*, 1981 *A*, 1982 *I, F, E*, 1983 *E, S, I, F*, 1984 *E*, 1985 *S, I, F, E, Fj*
Hopkin, W H (Newport) 1937 *S*
Hopkins, K (Cardiff, Swansea) 1985 *E*, 1987 *F, E, S*, [*Tg, C* (R)], *US*
Hopkins, P L (Swansea) 1908 *A*, 1909 *E, I*, 1910 *E*
Hopkins, R (Maesteg) 1970 *E* (R)
Hopkins, T (Swansea) 1926 *E, S, I, F*
Hopkins, W J (Aberavon) 1925 *E, S*
Howarth, S P (Sale, Newport) 1998 *SA* 2, *Arg*, 1999 *S, I, F* 1, *It, E, Arg* 1,2, *SA, C, F* 2, [*Arg* 3, *J, Sm, A*], 2000 *F, It, E*
Howells, B (Llanelli) 1934 *E*
Howells, W G (Llanelli) 1957 *E, S, I, F*
Howells, W H (Swansea) 1888 *S, I*
Howley, R (Bridgend, Cardiff) 1996 *E, S, I, F* 1, *A* 1,2, *Bb, F* 2, *It, A* 3, *SA*, 1997 *US, S, I, F, E, Tg* (R), *NZ*, 1998 *It, E, S, I, F, Z, SA* 2, *Arg*, 1999 *S, I, F* 1, *It, E, Arg* 1,2, *SA, C, F* 2, [*Arg* 3, *J, Sm, A*], 2000 *F, It, E, Sm, US, SA*, 2001 *E, S, F, R, I, Arg, Tg, A*, 2002 *I, F, It, E, S*
Hughes, D (Newbridge) 1967 *NZ*, 1969 *NZ* 2, 1970 *SA, S, E, I*

Hughes, G (Penarth) 1934 *E, S, I*
Hughes, H (Cardiff) 1887 *S*, 1889 *S*
Hughes, K (Cambridge U, London Welsh) 1970 *I*, 1973 *A*, 1974 *S*
Hullin, W (Cardiff) 1967 *S*
Humphreys, J M (Cardiff) 1995 [*NZ, I*], *SA, Fj*, 1996 *It, E, S, I, F* 1, *A* 1,2, *Bb, It, A* 3, *SA*, 1997 *S, I, F, E, Tg* (R), *NZ* (R), 1998 *It* (R), *E* (R), *S* (R), *I* (R), *F* (R), *SA* 2, *Arg*, 1999 *S, Arg* 2(R), *SA* (R), *C*, [*J* (R)]
Hurrell, J (Newport) 1959 *F*
Hutchinson, F (Neath) 1894 *I*, 1896 *S, I*
Huxtable, R (Swansea) 1920 *F, I*
Huzzey, H V P (Cardiff) 1898 *I, E*, 1899 *E, S, I*
Hybart, A J (Cardiff) 1887 *E*

Ingledew, H M (Cardiff) 1890 *I*, 1891 *E, S*
Isaacs, I (Cardiff) 1933 *E, S*

Jackson, T H (Swansea) 1895 *E*
James, B (Bridgend) 1968 *E*
James, C R (Llanelli) 1958 *A, F*
James, D (Swansea) 1891 *I*, 1892 *S, I*, 1899 *E*
James, D R (Treorchy) 1931 *F, I*
James, D R (Bridgend, Pontypridd, Llanelli) 1996 *A* 2(R), *It, A* 3, *SA*, 1997 *I, Tg* (R), 1998 *F* (R), *Z, SA* 1,2, *Arg*, 1999 *S, I, F* 1, *It, E, Arg* 1,2, *SA, F* 2, [*Arg* 3, *Sm, A*], 2000 *F, It* (R), *I* (R), *Sm* (R), *US, SA*, 2001 *E, S, F, It, R, I*, 2002 *I, F, It, E, S* (R)
James, E (Swansea) 1890 *S*, 1891 *I*, 1892 *S, I*, 1899 *E*
James, M (Cardiff) 1947 *A*, 1948 *E, S, F, I*
James, T O (Aberavon) 1935 *I*, 1937 *S*
James, W J (Aberavon) 1983 *E, S, I, F, R*, 1984 *S*, 1985 *S, I, F, E, Fj*, 1986 *E, S, I, F, Fj, Tg, WS*, 1987 *E, S, I*
James, W P (Aberavon) 1925 *E, S*
Jarman, H (Newport) 1910 *E, S, I*, 1911 *E*
Jarrett, K S (Newport) 1967 *E*, 1968 *E, S*, 1969 *S, I, F, E, NZ* 1,2, *A*
Jarvis, L (Cardiff) 1997 *R* (R)
Jeffery, J J (Cardiff Coll of Ed, Newport) 1967 *NZ*
Jenkin, A M (Swansea) 1895 *I*, 1896 *E*
Jenkins, A (Llanelli) 1920 *E, S, F, I*, 1921 *S, F*, 1922 *F*, 1923 *E, S, F, I*, 1924 *S, I*, 1928 *S, I*
Jenkins, D M (Treorchy) 1926 *E, S, I, F*
Jenkins, D R (Swansea) 1927 *A*, 1929 *E*
Jenkins, E (Newport) 1910 *S, I*
Jenkins, E M (Aberavon) 1927 *S, F, I, A*, 1928 *E, S, I, F*, 1929 *F*, 1930 *E, S, I, F*, 1931 *E, S, F, I, SA*, 1932 *E, S, I*
Jenkins, G R (Pontypool, Swansea) 1991 *F* 2, [*WS* (R), *Arg, A*], 1992 *I, F, E, S, A*, 1993 *C*, 1994 *S, I, F, E, Pt, Sp, C, Tg, WS, R, It, SA*, 1995 *F, E, S, I*, [*J*], *SA* (R), *Fj* (t), 1996 *E* (R), 1997 *US, US* 1, *C*, 1998 *S, I, F, Z, SA* 1(R), 1999 *I* (R), *F* 1, *It, E, Arg* 1,2, *SA, F* 2, [*Arg* 3, *J, Sm, A*], 2000 *F, It, E, S, I, Sm, US, SA*
Jenkins, J C (London Welsh) 1906 *SA*
Jenkins, J L (Aberavon) 1923 *S, F*
Jenkins, L H (Mon TC, Newport) 1954 *I*, 1956 *E, S, I, F*
Jenkins, N R (Pontypridd, Cardiff) 1991 *E, S, I, F* 1, 1992 *I, F, E, S*, 1993 *E, S, F, Z* 1,2, *Nm, J, C*, 1994 *S, I, F, E, Pt, Sp, C, Tg, WS, R, It, SA*, 1995 *F, E, S, I*, [*J, NZ, I*], *SA, Fj*, 1996 *F* 1, *A* 1,2, *Bb, F* 2, *It, A* 3(R), *SA*, 1997 *S, I, F, E, Tg, NZ*, 1998 *It, E, S, I, F, SA* 2, *Arg*, 1999 *S, I, F* 1, *It, E, Arg* 1,2, *SA, C, F* 2, [*Arg* 3, *J, Sm, A*], 2000 *F, It, E, I* (R), *Sm* (R), *US* (R), *SA*, 2001 *E, S, F, It*, 2002 *SA* 1(R),2(R)
Jenkins, V G J (Oxford U, Bridgend, London Welsh) 1933 *E, I*, 1934 *S, I*, 1935 *E, S, NZ*, 1936 *E, S, I*, 1937 *E*, 1938 *E, S*, 1939 *E*
Jenkins, W (Cardiff) 1912 *I, F*, 1913 *S, I*
John, B (Llanelli, Cardiff) 1966 *A*, 1967 *S, NZ*, 1968 *E, S, I, F*, 1969 *E, I, E, NZ* 1,2, *A*, 1970 *SA, S, E, I*, 1971 *E, S, I, F*, 1972 *E, S, F*
John, D A (Llanelli) 1925 *I*, 1928 *E, S, I*
John, D E (Llanelli) 1923 *F, I*, 1928 *E, S, I*
John, E R (Neath) 1950 *E, S, I, F*, 1951 *E, S, I, F, SA*, 1952 *E, S, I, F*, 1953 *E, S, I, F, NZ*, 1954 *E*
John G (St Luke's Coll, Exeter) 1954 *E, F*
John, J H (Swansea) 1926 *E, S, I, F*, 1927 *E, S, F, I*
John, P (Pontypridd) 1994 *Tg*, 1996 *Bb* (t), 1997 *US* (R), *US* 1,2, *C, R, Tg*, 1998 *Z* (R), *SA* 1
John, S C (Llanelli, Cardiff) 1995 *S, I*, 1997 *E* (R), *Tg, NZ* (R), 2000 *F* (R), *It* (R), *E* (R), *Sm* (R), *SA* (R), 2001 *E* (R), *S* (R), *Tg* (R), *A*, 2002 *I, F, It* (R), *S* (R)
Johnson, A (Cardiff) 1921 *E, F, I*, 1923 *E, S, F*, 1924 *E, S, NZ*, 1925 *E, S, F*
Johnson, W D (Swansea) 1953 *E*
Jones, A H (Cardiff) 1933 *E, S*

Jones, B (Abertillery) 1914 *E, S, F, I*
Jones, Bert (Llanelli) 1934 *S, I*
Jones, Bob (Llwynypia) 1901 *I*
Jones, B J (Newport) 1960 *I, F*
Jones, B Lewis (Devonport Services, Llanelli) 1950 *E, S, I, F,*
1951 *E, S, SA,* 1952 *E, I, F*
Jones, C W (Cambridge U, Cardiff) 1934 *E, S, I,* 1935 *E, S, I,*
NZ, 1936 *E, S, I,* 1938 *E, S, I*
Jones, C W (Bridgend) 1920 *E, S, F*
Jones, D (Neath) 1927 *A*
Jones, D (Aberavon) 1897 *E*
Jones, D (Swansea) 1947 *E, F, I,* 1949 *E, S, I, F*
Jones, D (Treherbert) 1902 *E, S, I,* 1903 *E, S, I,* 1905 *E, S, I,*
NZ, 1906 *E, S, SA*
Jones, D (Newport) 1926 *E, S, I, F,* 1927 *E*
Jones, D (Llanelli) 1948 *E*
Jones, D (Cardiff) 1994 *SA,* 1995 *F, E, S, [J, NZ, I], SA, Fj,*
1996 *It, E, S, I, F* 1, *A* 1,2, *Bb, It, A* 3
Jones, Duncan (Neath) 2001 *A* (R), 2002 *I* (R), *F* (R)
Jones, D K (Llanelli, Cardiff) 1962 *E, S, F, I,* 1963 *E, F, NZ,*
1964 *E, S, SA,* 1966 *E, S, I, F*
Jones, D L (Ebbw Vale) 2000 *Sm*
Jones, D P (Pontypool) 1907 *I*
Jones, E H (Neath) 1929 *E, S*
Jones, E L (Llanelli) 1930 *F,* 1933 *E, S, I,* 1935 *E*
Jones, Elvet L (Llanelli) 1939 *S*
Jones, G (Ebbw Vale) 1963 *S, I, F*
Jones, G (Llanelli) 1988 *NZ* 2, 1989 *F, E, NZ,* 1990 *F*
Jones, G G (Cardiff) 1930 *S,* 1933 *I*
Jones, G H (Bridgend) 1995 *SA*
Jones, H (Penygraig) 1902 *S, I*
Jones, H (Neath) 1904 *I*
Jones, H (Swansea) 1930 *I, F*
Jones, Iorwerth (Llanelli) 1927 *A,* 1928 *E, S, I, F*
Jones, I C (London Welsh) 1968 *I*
Jones, Ivor E (Llanelli) 1924 *E, S,* 1927 *S, F, I, A,* 1928 *E, S,*
I, F, 1929 *E, S, F, I,* 1930 *E, S*
Jones, J (Aberavon) 1901 *E*
Jones, J (Swansea) 1924 *F*
Jones, Jim (Aberavon) 1919 *NZA,* 1920 *E, S,* 1921 *S, F, I*
Jones, J A (Cardiff) 1883 *S*
Jones, J P (Tuan) (Pontypool) 1913 *S*
Jones, J P (Pontypool) 1908 *A,* 1909 *E, S, F, I,* 1910 *F, E,*
1912 *E, F,* 1913 *F, I,* 1920 *F, I,* 1921 *E*
Jones, K D (Cardiff) 1960 *SA,* 1961 *E, S, I,* 1962 *E, F,* 1963
E, S, I, NZ
Jones, K J (Newport) 1947 *E, S, F, I, A,* 1948 *E, S, F, I,* 1949
E, S, I, F, 1950 *E, S, I, F,* 1951 *E, S, I, F, SA,* 1952 *E, S, I, F,*
1953 *E, S, I, F, NZ,* 1954 *E, I, F, S,* 1955 *E, S, I, F,* 1956 *E, S,*
I, F, 1957 *S*
Jones, K P (Ebbw Vale) 1996 *Bb, F* 2, *It, A* 3, 1997 *I* (R), *E,*
1998 *S, I, F*(R), *SA* 1
Jones, K W J (Oxford U, London Welsh) 1934 *E*
Jones, M A (Neath, Ebbw Vale) 1987 *S,* 1988 *NZ* 2(R), 1989
S, I, F, E, NZ, 1990 *F, E, S, I, Nm* 1,2, *Bb,* 1998 *Z*
Jones, M A (Llanelli) 2001 *E* (R), *S, J* 1
Jones, P (Newport) 1912 *SA,* 1913 *E, S, F,* 1914 *E, S, F, I*
Jones, P B (Newport) 1921 *S*
Jones, R (Swansea) 1901 *I,* 1902 *E,* 1904 *E, S, I,* 1905 *E,*
1908 *F, I, A,* 1909 *E, S, F, I,* 1910 *F, E*
Jones, R (London Welsh) 1929 *E*
Jones, R (Northampton) 1926 *E, S, F*
Jones, R (Swansea) 1927 *A,* 1928 *F*
Jones, R B (Cambridge U) 1933 *E, S*
Jones, R E (Coventry) 1967 *F, E,* 1968 *S, I, F*
Jones, R G (Llanelli, Cardiff) 1996 *It, E, S, I, F* 1, *A* 1, 1997
US (R), *S* (R), *US* 1,2, *R, Tg, NZ*
Jones, R L (Llanelli) 1993 *Z* 1,2, *Nm, J, C*
Jones, R N (Swansea) 1986 *E, S, I, F, Fj, Tg, WS,* 1987 *F, E, S,*
I, [I, Tg, E, NZ, A], US, 1988 *S, I, F, NZ* 1, *WS, R,* 1989 *I, F,*
E, NZ, 1990 *F, E, S, I,* 1991 *E, S, F, [WS, Arg, A],* 1992 *I, F,*
E, S, A, 1993 *E, S, I,* 1994 *I* (R), *Pt,* 1995 *F, E, S, I, [NZ, I]*
Jones, S (Neath) 2001 *J* 1(R)
Jones, S M (Llanelli) 1998 *SA* 1(R), 1999 *C* (R), *[J* (R)], 2000
It (R), *S, I,* 2001 *E, F*(R), *J* 1,2, *R, I, Arg, Tg, A,* 2002 *I, F, It,*
S, SA 1,2
Jones, S T (Pontypool) 1983 *S, I, F, R,* 1984 *S,* 1988 *E, S, F,*
NZ 1,2
Jones, Tom (Newport) 1922 *E, S, I, F,* 1924 *E, S*
Jones, T B (Newport) 1882 *I,* 1883 *E, S,* 1884 *S,* 1885 *E, S*
Jones, W (Cardiff) 1898 *I, E*
Jones, W (Mountain Ash) 1905 *I*
Jones, W I (Llanelli, Cambridge U) 1925 *E, S, F, I*

Jones, W J (Llanelli) 1924 *I*
Jones, W K (Cardiff) 1967 *NZ,* 1968 *E, S, I, F*
Jones-Davies, T E (London Welsh) 1930 *E, I,* 1931 *E, S*
Jones-Hughes, J (Newport) 1999 *[Arg* 3(R), *J],* 2000 *F*
Jordan, H M (Newport) 1885 *E, S,* 1889 *S*
Joseph, W (Swansea) 1902 *E, S, I,* 1903 *E, S, I,* 1904 *E, S,*
1905 *E, S, I, NZ,* 1906 *E, S, I, SA*
Jowett, W F (Swansea) 1903 *E*
Judd, S (Cardiff) 1953 *E, S, I, F, NZ,* 1954 *E, F, S,* 1955 *E, S*
Judson, J H (Llanelli) 1883 *E, S*

Kedzlie, Q D (Cardiff) 1888 *S, I*
Keen, L (Aberavon) 1980 *F, E, S, I*
Knight, P (Pontypridd) 1990 *Nm* 1,2, *Bb* (R), 1991 *E, S*
Knill, F M D (Cardiff) 1976 *F* (R)

Lamerton, A E H (Llanelli) 1993 *F, Z* 1,2, *Nm, J*
Lane, S M (Cardiff) 1978 *A* 1(R),2, 1979 *I* (R), 1980 *S, I*
Lang, J (Llanelli) 1931 *F, I,* 1934 *S, I,* 1935 *E, S, I, NZ,* 1936
E, S, I, 1937 *E*
Lawrence, S (Bridgend) 1925 *S, I,* 1926 *S, I, F,* 1927 *E*
Law, V J (Newport) 1939 *I*
Legge, W S G (Newport) 1937 *I,* 1938 *I*
Leleu, J (London Welsh, Swansea) 1959 *E, S,* 1960 *F, SA*
Lemon, A (Neath) 1929 *I,* 1930 *S, I, F,* 1931 *E, S, F, I, SA,*
1932 *E, S, I,* 1933 *I*
Lewis, A J L (Ebbw Vale) 1970 *F,* 1971 *E, I, F,* 1972 *E, S, F,*
1973 *E, S, I, F*
Lewis, A L P (Cardiff) 1996 *It, E, S, I, A* 2(t), 1998 *It, E, S, I,*
F, SA 2, *Arg,* 1999 *F* 1(R), *E* (R), *Arg* 1(R),2(R), *SA* (R), *C* (R),
[J (R), *Sm* (R), *A* (R)], 2000 *Sm* (R), *US* (R), *SA* (R), 2001 *F*
(R), *J* 1,2
Lewis, A R (Abertillery) 1966 *E, S, I, F, A,* 1967 *I*
Lewis, B R (Swansea, Cambridge U) 1912 *I,* 1913 *I*
Lewis, C P (Llandovery Coll) 1882 *I,* 1883 *E, S,* 1884 *E, S*
Lewis, D H (Cardiff) 1886 *E, S*
Lewis, E J (Llandovery) 1881 *E*
Lewis, E W (Llanelli, Cardiff) 1991 *I, F* 1, *A, F* 2, *[WS, Arg,*
A], 1992 *I, F, S, A,* 1993 *E, S, I, F, Z* 1,2, *Nm, J, C,* 1994 *S, I, F,*
E, Pt, Sp, Fj, WS, R, It, SA, 1995 *E, S, I, [J, I],* 1996 *It, E, S, I,*
F 1
Lewis, G (Pontypridd, Swansea) 1998 *SA* 1(R), 1999 *It* (R),
Arg 2, *C, [J],* 2000 *F* (R), *It, S, I, Sm, US* (t+R), 2001 *F* (R), *J*
1,2, *R, I*
Lewis, G W (Richmond) 1960 *E, S*
Lewis, H (Swansea) 1913 *S, F, I,* 1914 *E*
Lewis, J G (Llanelli) 1887 *I*
Lewis, J M C (Cardiff, Cambridge U) 1912 *E,* 1913 *S, F, I,*
1914 *E, S, F, I,* 1921 *I,* 1923 *E, S*
Lewis, J R (S Glam Inst, Cardiff) 1981 *E, S, I, F,* 1982 *F, E, S*
Lewis, M (Treorchy) 1913 *F*
Lewis, P I (Llanelli) 1984 *A,* 1985 *S, I, F, E,* 1986 *E, S, I*
Lewis, T W (Cardiff) 1926 *E,* 1927 *E, S*
Lewis, W (Llanelli) 1925 *F*
Lewis, W H (London Welsh, Cambridge U) 1926 *I,* 1927 *E,*
F, I, A, 1928 *F*
Llewelyn, D B (Newport, Llanelli) 1970 *SA, S, E, I, F,* 1971
E, S, I, F, 1972 *E, S, F, NZ*
Llewellyn, D S (Ebbw Vale, Newport) 1998 *SA* 1(R), 1999 *F*
1(R), *It* (R), *[J* (R)]
Llewellyn, G D (Neath) 1990 *Nm* 1,2, *Bb,* 1991 *E, S, I, F* 1,
A, F 2
Llewellyn, G O (Neath, Harlequins) 1989 *NZ,* 1990 *E, S, I,*
1991 *E, S, A* (R), 1992 *I, F, E, S, A,* 1993 *E, S, I, F, Z* 1,2, *Nm,*
J, C, 1994 *S, I, F, E, Pt, Sp, C, Tg, WS, R, It, SA,* 1995 *F, E, S, I,*
[J, NZ, I], 1996 *It, E, S, I, F* 1, *A* 1,2, *Bb, F* 2, *It, A* 3, *SA,* 1997
US, S, I, F, E, US 1,2, *NZ,* 1998 *It, E,* 1999 *C* (R), *[Sm],* 2002
E (R), *SA* 1,2
Llewellyn, P D (Swansea) 1973 *I, F, A,* 1974 *S, E*
Llewellyn, W (Llwynypia) 1899 *E, S, I,* 1900 *E, S, I,* 1901 *E,*
S, I, 1902 *E, S, I,* 1903 *I,* 1904 *E, S, I,* 1905 *E, S, I, NZ*
Lloyd, A (Bath) 2001 *J* 1
Lloyd, D J (Bridgend) 1966 *E, S, I, F, A,* 1967 *S, I, F, E,* 1968
S, I, F, 1969 *S, I, F, E, NZ* 1, *A,* 1970 *F, I,* 1972 *E, S, F,* 1973 *E,*
S
Lloyd, E (Llanelli) 1895 *S*
Lloyd, G L (Newport) 1896 *I,* 1899 *S, I,* 1900 *E, S,* 1901 *E, S,*
1902 *S, I,* 1903 *E, S, I*
Lloyd, P (Llanelli) 1890 *S, E,* 1891 *E, I*
Lloyd, R A (Pontypool) 1913 *S, F, I,* 1914 *E, S, F, I*
Lloyd, T (Maesteg) 1953 *I, F*
Lloyd, T C (Neath) 1909 *F,* 1913 *F, I,* 1914 *E, S, F, I*

Loader, C D (Swansea) 1995 *SA, Fj,* 1996 *F* 1, *A* 1,2, *Bb, F* 2, *It, A, 3, SA,* 1997 *US, S, I, F, E, US* 1, *R, Tg, NZ*
Lockwood, T W (Newport) 1887 *E, S, I*
Long, E C (Swansea) 1936 *E, S, I,* 1937 *E, S,* 1939 *S, I*
Lyne, H S (Newport) 1883 *S,* 1884 *E, S, I,* 1885 *E*

McBryde, R C (Swansea, Llanelli) 1994 *Fj, SA* (t), 1997 *US* 2, 2000 *I* (R), 2001 *E, S, F, It, R, I, Arg, Tg, A,* 2002 *I, F, It, E, S* (R), *SA* 1,2
McCall, B E W (Welch Regt, Newport) 1936 *E, S, I*
McCarley, A (Neath) 1938 *E, S, I*
McCutcheon, W M (Swansea) 1891 *S,* 1892 *E, S,* 1893 *E, S, I,* 1894 *E*
McIntosh, D L M (Pontypridd) 1996 *SA,* 1997 *E* (R)
Madden, M (Llanelli) 2002 *SA* 1(R)
Maddock, H T (London Welsh) 1906 *E, S, I,* 1907 *E, S,* 1910 *F*
Maddocks, K (Neath) 1957 *E*
Main, D R (London Welsh) 1959 *E, S, I, F*
Mainwaring, H J (Swansea) 1961 *F*
Mainwaring, W T (Aberavon) 1967 *S, I, F, E, NZ,* 1968 *E*
Major, W C (Maesteg) 1949 *F,* 1950 *S*
Male, B O (Cardiff) 1921 *F,* 1923 *S,* 1924 *S, I,* 1927 *E, S, F, I,* 1928 *S, I, F*
Manfield, L (Mountain Ash, Cardiff) 1939 *S, I,* 1947 *A,* 1948 *E, S, F, I*
Mann, B B (Cardiff) 1881 *E*
Mantle, J T (Loughborough Colls, Newport) 1964 *E, SA*
Margrave, F L (Llanelli) 1884 *E, S*
Marinos, A W N (Newport) 2002 *I* (R), *F, It, E, S, SA* 1,2
Marsden-Jones, D (Cardiff) 1921 *E,* 1924 *NZ*
Martin, A J (Aberavon) 1973 *A,* 1974 *S, I,* 1975 *F, E, S, I, A,* 1976 *E, S, I, F,* 1977 *I, F, E, S,* 1978 *E, S, I, F, A* 1,2, *NZ,* 1979 *S, I, F, E,* 1980 *F, E, S, I, NZ,* 1981 *I, F*
Martin, W J (Newport) 1912 *I, F,* 1919 *NZA*
Mason, J (Pontypridd) 1988 *NZ* 2(R)
Mathews, Rev A A (Lampeter) 1886 *S*
Mathias, R (Llanelli) 1970 *F*
Matthews, C (Bridgend) 1939 *I*
Matthews, J (Cardiff), 1947 *E, A,* 1948 *E, S, F,* 1949 *E, S, I, F,* 1950 *E, S, I, F,* 1951 *E, S, I, F*
May, P S (Llanelli) 1988 *E, S, I, F, NZ* 1,2, 1991 [*WS*]
Meek, N N (Pontypool) 1993 *E, S, I*
Meredith, A (Devonport Services) 1949 *E, S, I*
Meredith, B V (St Luke's Coll, London Welsh, Newport) 1954 *I, F, S,* 1955 *E, S, I, F,* 1956 *E, S, I, F,* 1957 *E, S, I, F,* 1958 *A, E, S, I,* 1959 *E, S, I, F,* 1960 *E, S, F, SA,* 1961 *E, S, I,* 1962 *E, S, F, I*
Meredith, C C (Neath) 1953 *S, NZ,* 1954 *E, I, F, S,* 1955 *E, S, I, F,* 1956 *E, I,* 1957 *E, S*
Meredith, J (Swansea) 1888 *S, I,* 1890 *S, E*
Merry, A E (Pill Harriers) 1912 *I, F*
Michael, G (Swansea) 1923 *E, S, F*
Michaelson, R C B (Aberavon, Cambridge U) 1963 *E*
Miller, F (Mountain Ash) 1896 *I,* 1900 *E, S, I,* 1901 *E, S, I*
Mills, F M (Swansea, Cardiff) 1892 *E, S, I,* 1893 *E, S, I,* 1894 *E, S, I,* 1895 *E, S, I,* 1896 *E*
Moon, R H StJ B (Llanelli) 1993 *F, Z* 1,2, *Nm, J, C,* 1994 *S, I, F, E, Sp, C, Fj, WS, R, It, SA,* 1995 *E, SA, Sm* (R), *US* (R), 2001 *E* (R), *S* (R)
Moore, A P (Cardiff) 1995 [*J*], *SA, Fj,* 1996 *It*
Moore, A P (Swansea) 1995 *SA* (R), *Fj,* 1998 *S, I, F, Z, SA* 1, 1999 *C,* 2000 *S, I, US* (R), 2001 *E* (R), *S, F, It, J* 1,2, *R, I, Arg, Tg, A,* 2002 *F, It, E, S*
Moore, S J (Swansea, Moseley) 1997 *C, R, Tg*
Moore, W J (Bridgend) 1933 *I*
Morgan, C H (Llanelli) 1957 *I, F*
Morgan, C I (Cardiff) 1951 *I, F, SA,* 1952 *E, S, I,* 1953 *S, I, F, NZ,* 1954 *E, I, S,* 1955 *E, S, I, F,* 1956 *E, S, I, F,* 1957 *E, S, I, F,* 1958 *E, S, I, F*
Morgan, C S (Cardiff) 2002 *I, F, It, E, S, SA* 1,2
Morgan, D (Swansea) 1885 *S,* 1886 *E, S,* 1887 *E, S, I,* 1889 *I*
Morgan, D (Llanelli) 1895 *I,* 1896 *E*
Morgan, D R R (Llanelli) 1962 *E, S, F, I,* 1963 *E, S, I, F, NZ*
Morgan, E (Llanelli) 1920 *I,* 1921 *E, S, F*
Morgan, Edgar (Swansea) 1914 *E, S, F, I*
Morgan, E T (London Welsh) 1902 *E, S, I,* 1903 *I,* 1904 *E, S, I,* 1905 *E, S, I, NZ,* 1906 *E, S, I, SA,* 1908 *F*
Morgan, F L (Llanelli) 1938 *E, S, I,* 1939 *E*
Morgan, H J (Abertillery) 1958 *E, S, I, F,* 1959 *I, F,* 1960 *E, 1961 *E, S, I, F,* 1962 *E, S, F, I,* 1963 *S, I, F,* 1965 *E, S, I, F,* 1966 *E, S, I, F, A*
Morgan, H P (Newport) 1956 *E, S, I, F*

Morgan, I (Swansea) 1908 *A,* 1909 *E, S, F, I,* 1910 *F, E, S, I,* 1911 *E, F, I,* 1912 *S*
Morgan, J L (Llanelli) 1912 *SA,* 1913 *E*
Morgan, K A (Pontypridd, Swansea) 1997 *US* 1,2, *C, R, NZ,* 1998 *S, I, F,* 2001 *J* 1,2, *R, I, Arg, Tg, A,* 2002 *I, F, It, E, S, SA* 1,2
Morgan, M E (Swansea) 1938 *E, S, I,* 1939 *E*
Morgan, N (Newport) 1960 *S, I, F*
Morgan, P E J (Aberavon) 1961 *E, S, F*
Morgan, P J (Llanelli) 1980 *S* (R), *I, NZ* (R), 1981 *I*
Morgan, R (Newport) 1984 *S*
Morgan, T (Llanelli) 1889 *I*
Morgan, W G (Cambridge U) 1927 *F, I,* 1929 *E, S, F, I,* 1930 *I, F*
Morgan, W L (Cardiff) 1910 *S*
Moriarty, R D (Swansea) 1981 *A,* 1982 *I, F, E, S,* 1983 *E,* 1984 *S, I, F, E,* 1985 *S, I, F,* 1986 *Fj, Tg, WS,* 1987 [*I, Tg, C* (R), *E, NZ, A*]
Moriarty, W P (Swansea) 1986 *I, F, Fj, Tg, WS,* 1987 *F, E, S, I,* [*I, Tg, C, E, NZ, A*], *US,* 1988 *E, S, I, F, NZ* 1
Morley, J C (Newport) 1929 *E, S, F, I,* 1930 *E, I,* 1931 *E, S, F, I, SA,* 1932 *E, S, I*
Morris, D R (Neath, Swansea) 1998 *Z, SA* 1(R),2(R), 1999 *S, I, It* (R), 2000 *US, SA,* 2001 *E, S, F, It, Arg, Tg, A*
Morris, G L (Swansea) 1882 *I,* 1883 *E, S,* 1884 *E, S*
Morris, H T (Cardiff) 1951 *F,* 1955 *I, F*
Morris, J I T (Swansea) 1924 *E, S*
Morris, M S (S Wales Police, Neath) 1985 *S, I, F,* 1990 *I, Nm* 1,2, *Bb,* 1991 *I, F* 1, [*WS* (R)], 1992 *E*
Morris, R R (Swansea, Bristol) 1933 *S,* 1937 *S*
Morris, S (Cross Keys) 1920 *E, S, F, I,* 1922 *E, S, I, F,* 1923 *E, S, F, I,* 1924 *E, S, F, NZ,* 1925 *E, S, F*
Morris, W (Abertillery) 1919 *NZA,* 1920 *F,* 1921 *I*
Morris, W (Llanelli) 1896 *S, I,* 1897 *E*
Morris, W D (Neath) 1967 *F, E,* 1968 *E, S, I, F,* 1969 *S, I, F, E, NZ* 1,2, *A,* 1970 *SA, S, E, I, F,* 1971 *E, S, I, F,* 1972 *E, S, F, NZ,* 1973 *E, S, I, A,* 1974 *S, I, F, E*
Morris, W J (Newport) 1965 *S,* 1966 *F*
Morris, W J (Pontypool) 1963 *S, I*
Moseley, K (Pontypool, Newport) 1988 *NZ* 2, *R,* 1989 *S, I,* 1990 *F,* 1991 *F* 2, [*WS, Arg, A*]
Murphy, C D (Cross Keys) 1935 *E, S, I*
Mustoe, L (Cardiff) 1995 *Fj,* 1996 *A* 1(R),2, 1997 *US* 1,2, *C, R* (R), 1998 *E* (R), *I* (R), *F* (R)

Nash, D (Ebbw Vale) 1960 *SA,* 1961 *E, S, I, F,* 1962 *F*
Newman, C H (Newport) 1881 *E,* 1882 *I,* 1883 *E, S,* 1884 *E, S,* 1885 *E, S,* 1886 *E,* 1887 *E*
Nicholas, D L (Llanelli) 1981 *E, S, I, F*
Nicholas, T J (Cardiff) 1919 *NZA*
Nicholl, C B (Cambridge U, Llanelli) 1891 *I,* 1892 *E, S, I,* 1893 *E, S, I,* 1894 *E, S,* 1895 *E, S, I,* 1896 *E, S, I*
Nicholl, D W (Llanelli) 1894 *I*
Nicholls, E G (Cardiff) 1896 *S, I,* 1897 *E,* 1898 *I, E,* 1899 *E, S, I,* 1900 *S, I,* 1901 *E, S, I,* 1902 *E, S, I,* 1903 *I,* 1904 *E,* 1905 *I, NZ,* 1906 *E, S, I, SA*
Nicholls, F E (Cardiff Harlequins) 1892 *I*
Nicholls, H (Cardiff) 1958 *I*
Nicholls, S H (Cardiff) 1888 *M,* 1889 *S, I,* 1891 *S*
Norris, C H (Cardiff) 1963 *F,* 1966 *F*
Norster, R L (Cardiff) 1982 *S,* 1983 *E, S, I, F,* 1984 *S, I, F, E, A,* 1985 *S, I, F, E, Fj,* 1986 *Fj, Tg, WS,* 1987 *F, E, S, I,* [*I, C, E*], *US,* 1988 *E, S, I, F, NZ* 1, *WS,* 1989 *F, E*
Norton, W B (Cardiff) 1882 *I,* 1883 *E, S,* 1884 *E, S, I*

O'Connor, A (Aberavon) 1960 *SA,* 1961 *E, S,* 1962 *F, I*
O'Connor, R (Aberavon) 1957 *E*
O'Neill, W (Cardiff) 1904 *S, I,* 1905 *E, S, I,* 1907 *E, I,* 1908 *E, S, F, I*
O'Shea, J P (Cardiff) 1967 *S, I,* 1968 *S, I, F*
Oliver, G (Pontypool) 1920 *E, S, F, I*
Osborne, W T (Mountain Ash) 1902 *E, S, I,* 1903 *E, S, I*
Ould, W J (Cardiff) 1924 *E, S*
Owen, A (Swansea) 1924 *E*
Owen, G D (Newport) 1955 *I, F,* 1956 *E, S, I, F*
Owen, M (Pontypridd) 2002 *SA* 1,2
Owen, R M (Swansea) 1901 *I,* 1902 *E, S, I,* 1903 *E, S, I,* 1904 *E, S, I,* 1905 *E, S, I, NZ,* 1906 *E, S, I, SA,* 1907 *E, S,* 1908 *F, I, A,* 1909 *E, S, F, I,* 1910 *F, E,* 1911 *E, S, F, I,* 1912 *E, S*

Packer, H (Newport) 1891 *E,* 1895 *S, I,* 1896 *E, S, I,* 1897 *E*
Palmer, F (Swansea) 1922 *E, S, I*

Parfitt, F C (Newport) 1893 *E, S, I*, 1894 *E, S, I*, 1895 *S*, 1896 *S, I*
Parfitt, S A (Swansea) 1990 *Nm* 1(R), *Bb*
Parker, D S (Swansea) 1924 *I, F, NZ*, 1925 *E, S, F, I*, 1929 *F, I*, 1930 *E*
Parker, T (Swansea) 1919 *NZA*, 1920 *E, S, I*, 1921 *E, S, F, I*, 1922 *E, S, I, F*, 1923 *E, S, F*
Parker, W (Swansea) 1899 *E, S*
Parks, R (Pontypridd) 2002 *SA* 1(R)
Parsons, G W (Newport) 1947 *E*
Pascoe, D (Bridgend) 1923 *F, I*
Pask, A E I (Abertillery) 1961 *F*, 1962 *E, S, F, I*, 1963 *E, S, I, F, NZ*, 1964 *E, S, I, F, SA*, 1965 *E, S, I, F*, 1966 *E, S, I, F, A*, 1967 *S, I*
Payne, G W (Army, Pontypridd) 1960 *E, S, I*
Payne, H (Swansea) 1935 *NZ*
Peacock, H (Newport) 1929 *S, F, I*, 1930 *S, I, F*
Peake, E (Chepstow) 1881 *E*
Pearce, G P (Bridgend) 1981 *I, F*, 1982 *I* (R)
Pearson, T W (Cardiff, Newport) 1891 *E, I*, 1892 *E, S*, 1894 *S, I*, 1895 *E, S, I*, 1897 *E*, 1898 *I, E*, 1903 *E*
Peel, D (Llanelli) 2001 *J* 2(R), *R* (R), *Tg* (R), 2002 *I* (R), *It* (R), *E* (R), *S* (R), *SA* 1,2
Pegge, E V (Neath) 1891 *E*
Perego, M A (Llanelli) 1990 *S*, 1993 *F, Z* 1, *Nm* (R), 1994 *S, I, F, E, Sp*
Perkins, S J (Pontypool) 1983 *S, I, F, R*, 1984 *S, I, F, E, A*, 1985 *S, I, F, E, Fj*, 1986 *E, S, I, F*
Perrett, F L (Neath) 1912 *SA*, 1913 *E, S, F, I*
Perrins, V C (Newport) 1970 *SA, S*
Perry, W (Neath) 1911 *E*
Phillips, A J (Cardiff) 1979 *E*, 1980 *F, E, S, I, NZ*, 1981 *E, S, I, F, A*, 1982 *I, F, E, S*, 1987 *[C, E, A]*
Phillips, B (Aberavon) 1925 *E, S, F, I*, 1926 *E*
Phillips, D H (Swansea) 1952 *F*
Phillips, H P (Newport) 1892 *E*, 1893 *E, S, I*, 1894 *E, S*
Phillips, H T (Newport) 1927 *E, S, F, I, A*, 1928 *E, S, I, F*
Phillips, K H (Neath) 1987 *F, [I, Tg, NZ]*, *US*, 1988 *E, NZ* 1, 1989 *NZ*, 1990 *F, E, S, I, Nm* 1,2, *Bb*, 1991 *E, S, I, F* 1, *A*
Phillips, L A (Newport) 1900 *E, S, I*, 1901 *S*
Phillips, R (Neath) 1987 *US*, 1988 *E, S, I, F, NZ* 1,2, *WS*, 1989 *S, I*
Phillips, W D (Cardiff) 1881 *E*, 1882 *I*, 1884 *E, S, I*
Pickering, D F (Llanelli) 1983 *E, S, I, F, R*, 1984 *S, I, F, E, A*, 1985 *S, I, F, E, Fj*, 1986 *E, S, I, F, Fj*, 1987 *F, E, S*
Plummer, R C S (Newport) 1912 *S, I, F, SA*, 1913 *E*
Pook, T (Newport) 1895 *S*
Powell, G (Ebbw Vale) 1957 *I, F*
Powell, J (Cardiff) 1906 *I*
Powell, J (Cardiff) 1923 *I*
Powell, R D (Cardiff) 2002 *SA* 1(R),2(R)
Powell, R W (Newport) 1888 *S, I*
Powell, W C (London Welsh) 1926 *S, I, F*, 1927 *E, F, I*, 1928 *S, I, F*, 1929 *E, S, F, I*, 1930 *S, I, F*, 1931 *E, S, F, I, SA*, 1932 *E, S, I*, 1935 *E, S, I*
Powell, W J (Cardiff) 1920 *E, S, F, I*
Price, B (Newport) 1961 *I, F*, 1962 *E, S*, 1963 *E, S, F, NZ*, 1964 *E, S, I, F, SA*, 1965 *E, S, I, F*, 1966 *E, S, I, F, A*, 1967 *S, I, F, E*, 1969 *S, I, F, NZ* 1,2, *A*
Price, G (Pontypool) 1975 *F, E, S, I, A*, 1976 *E, S, I, F*, 1977 *I, F, E, S*, 1978 *E, S, I, F, A* 1,2, *NZ*, 1979 *S, I, F, E*, 1980 *F, E, S, I, NZ*, 1981 *E, S, I, F, A*, 1982 *I, F, E, S*, 1983 *E, I, F*
Price, M J (Pontypool, RAF) 1959 *E, S, I, F*, 1960 *E, S, I, F*, 1962 *E*
Price, R E (Weston-s-Mare) 1939 *S, I*
Price, T G (Llanelli) 1965 *E, S, I, F*, 1966 *E, A*, 1967 *S, F*
Priday, A J (Cardiff) 1958 *I*, 1961 *I*
Pritchard, C (Pontypool) 1928 *E, S, I, F*, 1929 *E, S, F, I*
Pritchard, C C (Newport, Pontypool) 1904 *S, I*, 1905 *NZ*, 1906 *E, S*
Pritchard, C M (Newport) 1904 *I*, 1905 *E, S, NZ*, 1906 *E, S, I, SA*, 1907 *E, S, I*, 1908 *E, I*, 1910 *F, E, A* 1,2, *Bb, F* 2, *It, A* 3, 1997 *E* (R)
Proctor, W T (Llanelli) 1992 *A*, 1993 *E, S, Z* 1,2, *Nm, C*, 1994 *I, C, Fj, WS, R, It, SA*, 1995 *S, I, [NZ], Fj*, 1996 *It, E, S, I, A* 1,2, *Bb, F* 2, *It, A* 3, 1997 *E*(R), *US* 1,2, *C, R*, 1998 *E* (R), *S, I, F, Z*, 2001 *A*
Prosser, D R (Neath) 1934 *S, I*
Prosser, G (Neath) 1934 *E, S, I*, 1935 *NZ*
Prosser, G (Pontypridd) 1995 *[NZ]*
Prosser, J (Cardiff) 1921 *I*
Prosser, T R (Pontypool) 1956 *S, F*, 1957 *E, S, I, F*, 1958 *A, E, S, I, F*, 1959 *E, S, I, F*, 1960 *E, S, I, F, SA*, 1961 *I, F*

Prothero, G J (Bridgend) 1964 *S, I, F*, 1965 *E, S, I, F*, 1966 *E, S, I, F*
Pryce-Jenkins, T J (London Welsh) 1888 *S, I*
Pugh, C (Maesteg) 1924 *E, S, I, F, NZ*, 1925 *E, S*
Pugh, J D (Neath) 1987 *US*, 1988 *S* (R), 1990 *S*
Pugh, P (Neath) 1989 *NZ*
Pugsley, J (Cardiff) 1910 *E, S, I*, 1911 *E, S, F, I*
Pullman, J J (Neath) 1910 *F*
Purdon, F T (Newport) 1881 *E*, 1882 *I*, 1883 *E, S*

Quinnell, D L (Llanelli) 1972 *F* (R), *NZ*, 1973 *E, S, A*, 1974 *S, F*, 1975 *E* (R), 1977 *I* (R), *F, E, S*, 1978 *E, S, I, F, A* 1, *NZ*, 1979 *S, I, F, E*, 1980 *NZ*
Quinnell, J C (Llanelli, Richmond, Cardiff) 1995 *Fj*, 1996 *A* 3(R), 1997 *US* (R), *S* (R), *I* (R), *E* (R), 1998 *SA* 2, *Arg*, 1999 *I, F* 1, *It, E, Arg* 1,2, *SA, C, F* 2, *[Arg 3, J, A]*, 2000 *It, E*, 2001 *S* (R), *F* (R), *It* (R), *J* 1,2, *R* (R), *I* (R), *Arg*, 2002 *I, F*
Quinnell, L S (Llanelli, Richmond) 1993 *C*, 1994 *S, I, F, E, Pt, Sp, C, WS*, 1997 *US, S, I, F, E*, 1998 *It, E, S* (R), *Z, SA* 2, *Arg*, 1999 *S, I, F* 1, *It, E, Arg* 1,2, *SA, C, F* 2, *[Arg 3, Sm, A]*, 2000 *F, It, E, Sm, US, SA*, 2001 *E, S, F, It, Arg, Tg, A*, 2002 *I, F, It, E*

Radford, W J (Newport) 1923 *I*
Ralph, A R (Newport) 1931 *F, I, SA*, 1932 *E, S, I*
Ramsey, S H (Treorchy) 1896 *E*, 1904 *E*
Randell, R (Aberavon) 1924 *I, F*
Raybould, W H (London Welsh, Cambridge U, Newport) 1967 *S, I, F, E, NZ*, 1968 *I, F*, 1970 *SA, E, I, F* (R)
Rayer, M A (Cardiff) 1991 *[WS* (R), *Arg, A* (R)], 1992 *E* (R), *A*, 1993 *E, S, I, Z* 1, *Nm, J* (R), 1994 *S* (R), *I* (R), *F, E, Pt, C, Fj, WS, R, It*
Rees, Aaron (Maesteg) 1919 *NZA*
Rees, Alan (Maesteg) 1962 *E, S, F*
Rees, A M (London Welsh) 1934 *E*, 1935 *E, S, I, NZ*, 1936 *E, S, I*, 1937 *E, S, I*, 1938 *E, S*
Rees, B I (London Welsh) 1967 *S, I, F*
Rees, C F W (London Welsh) 1974 *I*, 1975 *A*, 1978 *NZ*, 1981 *F, A*, 1982 *I, F, E, S*, 1983 *E, S, I, F*
Rees, D (Swansea) 1968 *S, I, F*
Rees, Dan (Swansea) 1900 *E*, 1903 *E, S*, 1905 *E, S*
Rees, E B (Swansea) 1919 *NZA*
Rees, H (Cardiff) 1937 *S, I*, 1938 *E, S, I*
Rees, H E (Neath) 1979 *S, I, F, E*, 1980 *F, E, S, I, NZ*, 1983 *E, S, I, F*
Rees, J (Swansea) 1920 *E, S, F, I*, 1921 *E, S, I*, 1922 *E*, 1923 *E, F, I*, 1924 *E*
Rees, J I (Swansea) 1934 *E, S, I*, 1935 *S, NZ*, 1936 *E, S, I*, 1937 *E, S, I*, 1938 *E, S, I*
Rees, L M (Cardiff) 1933 *I*
Rees, P (Llanelli) 1947 *F, I*
Rees, P M (Newport) 1961 *E, S, I*, 1964 *I*
Rees, R (Swansea) 1998 *Z*
Rees, T (Newport) 1935 *S, I, NZ*, 1936 *E, S, I*, 1937 *E, S*
Rees, T A (Llandovery) 1881 *E*
Rees, T E (London Welsh) 1926 *I, F*, 1927 *A*, 1928 *E*
Rees-Jones, G R (Oxford U, London Welsh) 1934 *E, S*, 1935 *I, NZ*, 1936 *E*
Reeves, F (Cross Keys) 1920 *F, I*, 1921 *E*
Reynolds, A (Swansea) 1990 *Nm* 1,2(R), 1992 *A* (R)
Rhapps, J (Penygraig) 1897 *E*
Rice-Evans, W (Swansea) 1890 *S*, 1891 *E, S*
Richards, B (Swansea)1960 *F*
Richards, C (Pontypool) 1922 *E, S, I, F*, 1924 *I*
Richards, D S (Swansea) 1979 *F, E*, 1980 *F, E, S, I, NZ*, 1981 *E, S, I, F*, 1982 *I, F*, 1983 *I, R* (R)
Richards, E G (Cardiff) 1927 *S*
Richards, E S (Swansea) 1885 *E*, 1887 *S*
Richards, H D (Neath) 1986 *Tg* (R), 1987 *[Tg, E* (R), *NZ]*
Richards, I (Cardiff) 1925 *E, S, F*
Richards, K H L (Bridgend) 1960 *SA*, 1961 *E, S, I, F*
Richards, M C R (Cardiff) 1968 *I, F*, 1969 *S, I, F, E, NZ* 1,2, *A*
Richards, R (Aberavon) 1913 *S, F, I*
Richards, R (Cross Keys) 1956 *F*
Richards, T L (Maesteg) 1923 *I*
Richardson, S J (Aberavon) 1978 *A* 2(R), 1979 *E*
Rickards, A F (Cardiff) 1924 *F*
Ring, J (Aberavon) 1921 *E*
Ring, M G (Cardiff, Pontypool) 1983 *E*, 1984 *A*, 1985 *S, I, F*, 1987 *I, [I, Tg, A]*, *US*, 1988 *E, S, I, F, NZ* 1,2, 1989 *NZ*, 1990 *F, E, S, I, Nm* 1,2, *Bb*, 1991 *E, S, I, F* 1,2, *[WS, Arg, A]*
Ringer, J (Bridgend) 2001 *J* 1(R),2(R)

Ringer, P (Ebbw Vale, Llanelli) 1978 *NZ*, 1979 *S, I, F, E,*
1980 *F, E, NZ*
Roberts, C (Neath) 1958 *I, F*
Roberts, D E A (London Welsh) 1930 *E*
Roberts, E (Llanelli) 1886 *E*, 1887 *I*
Roberts, E J (Llanelli) 1888 *S, I*, 1889 *I*
Roberts, G J (Cardiff) 1985 *F* (R), *E*, 1987 [*I, Tg, C, E, A*]
Roberts, H M (Cardiff) 1960 *SA*, 1961 *E, S, I, F*, 1962 *S, F,*
1963 *I*
Roberts, J (Cardiff) 1927 *E, S, F, I, A*, 1928 *E, S, I, F*, 1929 *E,*
S, F, I
Roberts, M G (London Welsh) 1971 *E, S, I, F*, 1973 *I, F,*
1975 *S*, 1979 *E*
Roberts, T (Newport, Risca) 1921 *S, F, I*, 1922 *E, S, I, F,*
1923 *E, S*
Roberts, W (Cardiff) 1929 *E*
Robins, J D (Birkenhead Park) 1950 *E, S, I, F*, 1951 *E, S, I, F,*
1953 *E, I, F*
Robins, R J (Pontypridd) 1953 *S*, 1954 *F, S*, 1955 *E, S, I, F,*
1956 *E, F*, 1957 *E, S, I, F*
Robinson, I R (Cardiff) 1974 *F, E*
Robinson, J P (Cardiff) 2001 *J* 1(R),2(R), *Arg* (R), *Tg* (R), *A,*
2002 *I*
Robinson, M F D (Swansea) 1999 *S, I, F* 1, *Arg* 1
Rocyn-Jones, D N (Cambridge U) 1925 *I*
Roderick, W B (Llanelli) 1884 *I*
Rogers, P J D (London Irish, Newport, Cardiff) 1999 *F* 1, *It,*
E, Arg 1,2, *SA, C, F* 2, [*Arg* 3, *J, Sm, A*], 2000 *F, It, E, S, I, SA*
Rosser, M A (Penarth) 1924 *S, F*
Rowland, E M (Lampeter) 1885 *E*
Rowlands, C F (Aberavon) 1926 *I*
Rowlands, D C T (Pontypool) 1963 *E, S, I, F, NZ*, 1964 *E, S,*
I, F, SA, 1965 *E, S, I, F*
Rowlands, G (RAF, Cardiff) 1953 *NZ*, 1954 *E, F*, 1956 *F*
Rowlands, K A (Cardiff) 1962 *F, I*, 1963 *I*, 1965 *I, F*
Rowles, G R (Penarth) 1892 *E*
Rowley, M (Pontypridd) 1996 *SA*, 1997 *US, S, I, F, R*
Roy, W S (Cardiff) 1995 [*J* (R)]
Russell, S (London Welsh) 1987 *US*

Samuel, D (Swansea) 1891 *I*, 1893 *I*
Samuel, F (Mountain Ash) 1922 *S, I, F*
Samuel, J (Swansea) 1891 *I*
Scourfield, T (Torquay) 1930 *F*
Scrine, G F (Swansea) 1899 *E, S*, 1901 *I*
Shanklin, J L (London Welsh) 1970 *F*, 1972 *NZ*, 1973 *I, F*
Shanklin, T (Saracens) 2001 *J* 2, 2002 *F, It, SA* 1(R),2(R)
Shaw, G (Neath) 1972 *NZ*, 1973 *E, S, I, F, A*, 1974 *S, I, F, E,*
1977 *I, F*
Shaw, T W (Newbridge) 1983 *R*
Shea, J (Newport) 1919 *NZA*, 1920 *E, S*, 1921 *E*
Shell, R C (Aberavon) 1973 *A* (R)
Sidoli, R (Pontypridd) 2002 *SA* 1(R),2(R)
Simpson, H J (Cardiff) 1884 *E, S, I*
Sinkinson, B D (Neath) 1999 *F* 1, *It, E, Arg* 1,2, *SA, F* 2, [*Arg*
3, *J, Sm, A*], 2000 *F, It, E*, 2001 *R* (R), *I, Arg* (R), *Tg, A*, 2002
It (R)
Skirmshire, R T (Newport) 1899 *E, S, I*
Skym, A (Llanelli) 1928 *E, S, I, F*, 1930 *E, S, I, F*, 1931 *E, S,*
F, I, SA, 1932 *E, S, I*, 1933 *E, S, I*, 1935 *F*
Smith, J S (Cardiff) 1884 *E, I*, 1885 *E*
Smith, R (Ebbw Vale) 2000 *F* (R)
Sparks, B (Neath) 1954 *I*, 1955 *E, F*, 1956 *E, S, I*, 1957 *S*
Spiller, W J (Cardiff) 1910 *S, I*, 1911 *E, S, F, I*, 1912 *E, F, SA,*
1913 *E*
Squire, J (Newport, Pontypool) 1977 *I, F*, 1978 *E, S, I, F, A*,
NZ, 1979 *I, F*, 1980 *F, E, S, I, NZ*, 1981 *E, S, I, F, A*, 1982
I, F, E, 1983 *E, S, I, F*
Stadden, W J W (Cardiff) 1884 *I*, 1886 *E, S*, 1887 *I*, 1888 *S,*
M, 1890 *S, E*
Stephens, C (Bridgend) 1998 *E* (R), 2001 *J* 2(R)
Stephens, C J (Llanelli) 1992 *I, F, E, A*
Stephens, G (Neath) 1912 *E, S, I, F, SA*, 1913 *E, S, F, I*, 1919
NZA
Stephens, I (Bridgend) 1981 *E, S, I, F, A*, 1982 *I, F, E, S*, 1984
I, F, E, A
Stephens, Rev J G (Llanelli) 1922 *E, S, I, F*
Stephens, J R G (Neath) 1947 *E, S, F, I*, 1948 *I*, 1949 *S, I, F,*
1951 *F, SA*, 1952 *E, S, I, F*, 1953 *E, S, I, F, NZ*, 1954 *E, I*, 1955
E, S, I, F, 1956 *S, I, F*, 1957 *E, S, I, F*
Stock, A (Newport) 1924 *F, NZ*, 1926 *E, S*
Stone, P (Llanelli) 1949 *F*
Strand-Jones, J (Llanelli) 1902 *E, S, I*, 1903 *E, S*

Sullivan, A C (Cardiff) 2001 *Arg, Tg*
Summers, R H B (Haverfordwest) 1881 *E*
Sutton, S (Pontypool, S Wales Police) 1982 *F, E*, 1987 *F, E,*
S, I, [*C, NZ* (R), *A*]
Sweet-Escott, R B (Cardiff) 1891 *S*, 1894 *I*, 1895 *I*

Tamplin, W E (Cardiff) 1947 *S, F, I, A*, 1948 *E, S, F*
Tanner, H (Swansea, Cardiff) 1935 *NZ*, 1936 *E, S, I*, 1937 *E,*
S, I, 1938 *E, S, I*, 1939 *E, S, I*, 1947 *E, S, F, I*, 1948 *E, S, F, I,*
1949 *E, S, I, F*
Tarr, D J (Swansea, Royal Navy) 1935 *NZ*
Taylor, A R (Cross Keys) 1937 *I*, 1938 *I*, 1939 *E*
Taylor, C G (Ruabon) 1884 *E, S, I*, 1885 *E, S*, 1886 *E, S,*
1887 *E, I*
Taylor, H T (Cardiff) 1994 *Pt, C, Fj, Tg, WS* (R), *R, It, SA,*
1995 *E, S*, [*J, NZ, I*], *SA, Fj*, 1996 *It, E, S, I, F* 1, *A* 1,2, *It, A* 3
Taylor, J (London Welsh) 1967 *S, I, F, E, NZ*, 1968 *I, F*, 1969
S, I, F, E, NZ 1, *A*, 1970 *F*, 1971 *E, S, I, F*, 1972 *E, S, F, NZ,*
1973 *E, S, I, F*
Taylor, M (Pontypool, Swansea) 1994 *SA*, 1995 *F, E, SA* (R),
1998 *Z, SA* 1,2, *Arg*, 1999 *I, F* 1, *It, E, Arg* 1,2, *SA, F* 2, [*Arg* 3,
J, Sm, A], 2000 *F, It, E, S, Sm, US*, 2001 *E, S, F, It*, 2002 *S, SA*
1,2
Thomas, A (Newport) 1963 *NZ*, 1964 *E*
Thomas, A C (Bristol, Swansea) 1996 *It, E, S, I, F* 2(R), *SA,*
1997 *US, S, I, F, US* 1,2, *C, R, NZ* (t), 1998 *It, E, S* (R), *Z, SA*
1, 2000 *Sm, US, SA* (R)
Thomas, A G (Swansea, Cardiff) 1952 *E, S, I, F*, 1953 *S, I, F,*
1954 *E, I, F*, 1955 *S, I, F*
Thomas, Bob (Swansea) 1900 *E, S, I*, 1901 *E*
Thomas, Brian (Neath, Cambridge U) 1963 *E, S, I, F, NZ,*
1964 *E, S, I, F, SA*, 1965 *E, S, I*, 1966 *E, S, I*, 1967 *NZ*, 1969 *S, I, F,*
E, NZ 1,2
Thomas, C (Bridgend) 1925 *E, S*
Thomas, C J (Newport) 1888 *I, M*, 1889 *S, I*, 1890 *S, E, I,*
1891 *E, I*
Thomas, D (Aberavon) 1961 *I*
Thomas, D (Llanelli) 1954 *I*
Thomas, Dick (Mountain Ash) 1906 *SA*, 1908 *F, I*, 1909 *S*
Thomas, D J (Swansea) 1904 *E*, 1908 *A*, 1910 *E, S, I*, 1911 *E,*
S, F, I, 1912 *E*
Thomas, D J (Swansea) 1930 *S, I*, 1932 *E, S, I*, 1933 *E, S,*
1934 *E*, 1935 *E, S, I*
Thomas, D L (Neath) 1937 *E*
Thomas, E (Newport) 1904 *S, I*, 1909 *S, F, I*, 1910 *F*
Thomas, G (Llanelli) 1923 *E, S, F, I*
Thomas, G (Newport) 1888 *M*, 1890 *I*, 1891 *S*
Thomas, G (Bridgend, Cardiff) 1995 [*J, NZ, I*], *SA, Fj*, 1996 *F*
1, *A* 1,2, *Bb, F* 2, *It, A* 3, 1997 *US, S, I, F, E, US* 1,2, *C, R, Tg,*
NZ, 1998 *It, E, S, I, F, SA* 2, *Arg*, 1999 *F* 1(R), *It, E, Arg* 2, *SA,*
F 2, [*Arg* 3, *J* (R), *Sm, A*], 2000 *F, It, E, S, I, US* (R), *SA*, 2001
E, F, It, J 1,2, *R, Arg, Tg, A*, 2002 *E*
Thomas, G (Bath) 2001 *J* 1,2, *R, I* (R), *Arg, Tg* (R), *A* (R),
2002 *S* (R), *SA* 2(R)
Thomas, H (Llanelli) 1912 *F*
Thomas, H (Neath) 1936 *E, S, I*, 1937 *E, S, I*
Thomas, H W (Swansea) 1912 *SA*, 1913 *E*
Thomas, I (Bryncethin) 1924 *E*
Thomas, I D (Ebbw Vale, Llanelli) 2000 *Sm, US* (R), *SA* (R),
2001 *J* 1,2, *R, I, Arg* (R), *Tg*, 2002 *It, E, S, SA* 1,2
Thomas, L C (Cardiff) 1885 *E, S*
Thomas, M C (Newport, Devonport Services) 1949 *F*, 1950
E, S, I, F, 1951 *E, S, I, F, SA*, 1952 *E, S, I, F*, 1953 *E*, 1956 *E,*
S, I, F, 1957 *E, S*, 1958 *E, S, I, F*, 1959 *I, F*
Thomas, M G (St Bart's Hospital) 1919 *NZA*, 1921 *S, F, I,*
1923 *F*, 1924 *E*
Thomas, N (Bath) 1996 *SA* (R), 1997 *US* 1(R),2, *C* (R), *R, Tg,*
NZ, 1998 *Z, SA* 1
Thomas, R (Pontypool) 1909 *F, I*, 1911 *S, F*, 1912 *E, S, SA,*
1913 *E*
Thomas, R C C (Swansea) 1949 *F*, 1952 *I, F*, 1953 *S, I, F,*
NZ, 1954 *E, I, F, S*, 1955 *S, I*, 1956 *E, S, I*, 1957 *E*, 1958 *A, E,*
S, I, F, 1959 *E, S, I, F*
Thomas, R L (London Welsh) 1889 *S, I*, 1890 *I*, 1891 *E, S, I,*
1892 *E*
Thomas, S (Llanelli) 1890 *S, E*, 1891 *I*
Thomas, W D (Llanelli) 1966 *A*, 1968 *S, I, F*, 1969 *E, NZ* 2,
A, 1970 *SA, S, E, I, F*, 1971 *E, S, I, F*, 1972 *E, S, F, NZ*, 1973
E, S, I, F, 1974 *E*
Thomas, W G (Llanelli, Waterloo, Swansea) 1927 *E, S, F, I,*
1929 *E*, 1931 *E, S, SA*, 1932 *E, S, I*, 1933 *E, S, I*
Thomas, W H (Llandovery Coll, Cambridge U) 1885 *S,*
1886 *E, S*, 1887 *E, S*, 1888 *S, I*, 1890 *E, I*, 1891 *S, I*

Thomas, W J (Cardiff) 1961 *F*, 1963 *F*
Thomas, W J L (Llanelli, Cardiff) 1995 *SA, Fj*, 1996 *It, E, S, I, F* 1, 1996 *Bb* (R), 1997 *US*
Thomas, W L (Newport) 1894 *S*, 1895 *E, I*
Thomas, W T (Abertillery) 1930 *E*
Thompson, J F (Cross Keys) 1923 *E*
Thorburn, P H (Neath) 1985 *F, E, Fj*, 1986 *E, S, I, F*, 1987 *F, [I, Tg, C, E, NZ, A], US*, 1988 *S, I, F, WS, R* (R), 1989 *S, I, F, E, NZ*, 1990 *F, E, S, I, Nm* 1,2, *Bb*, 1991 *E, S, I, F* 1, *A*
Titley, M H (Bridgend, Swansea) 1983 *R*, 1984 *S, I, F, E, A*, 1985 *S, I, Fj*, 1986 *F, Fj, Tg, WS*, 1990 *F, E*
Towers, W H (Swansea) 1887 *I*, 1888 *M*
Travers, G (Pill Harriers) 1903 *E, S, I*, 1905 *E, S, I, NZ*, 1906 *E, S, I, SA*, 1907 *E, S, I*, 1908 *E, S, F, I, A*, 1909 *E, S, I*, 1911 *S, F, I*
Travers, W H (Newport) 1937 *S, I*, 1938 *E, S, I*, 1939 *E, S, I*, 1949 *E, S, I, F*
Treharne, E (Pontypridd) 1881 *E*, 1883 *E*
Trew, W J (Swansea) 1900 *E, S, I*, 1901 *E, S*, 1903 *S*, 1905 *S*, 1906 *S*, 1907 *E, S*, 1908 *E, S, F, I, A*, 1909 *E, S, F, I*, 1910 *F, E, S*, 1911 *E, S, F, I*, 1912 *S*, 1913 *S, F*
Trott, R F (Cardiff) 1948 *E, S, F, I*, 1949 *E, S, I, F*
Truman, W H (Llanelli) 1934 *E*, 1935 *E*
Trump, L C (Newport) 1912 *E, S, I*
Turnbull, B R (Cardiff) 1925 *I*, 1927 *E, S*, 1928 *E, F*, 1930 *S*
Turnbull, M J L (Cardiff) 1933 *E, I*
Turner, P (Newbridge) 1989 *I* (R), *F, E*

Uzzell, H (Newport) 1912 *E, S, I, F*, 1913 *S, F, I*, 1914 *E, S, F, I*, 1920 *E, S, F, I*
Uzzell, J R (Newport) 1963 *NZ*, 1965 *E, S, I, F*

Vickery, W E (Aberavon) 1938 *E, S, I*, 1939 *E*
Vile, T H (Newport) 1908 *E, S*, 1910 *I*, 1912 *I, F, SA*, 1913 *E*, 1921 *S*
Vincent, H C (Bangor) 1882 *I*
Voyle, M J (Newport, Llanelli, Cardiff) 1996 *A* 1(t), *F* 2, 1997 *E, US* 1,2, *C, Tg, NZ*, 1998 *It, E, S, I, F, Arg* (R), 1999 *S* (R), *I* (t), *It* (R), *SA* (R), *F* 2(R), *[J, A* (R)], 2000 *F* (R)

Wakeford, J D M (S Wales Police) 1988 *WS, R*
Waldron, R (Neath) 1965 *E, S, I, F*
Walker, N (Cardiff) 1993 *I, F, J*, 1994 *S, F, E, Sp, Pt, Sp*, 1995 *F, E*, 1997 *US* 1,2, *C, R* (R), *Tg, NZ*, 1998 *E*
Waller, P D (Newport) 1908 *A*, 1909 *E, S, F, I*, 1910 *F, E*
Walne, N J (Richmond, Cardiff) 1999 *It* (R), *E* (R), *C*
Walters, N (Llanelli) 1902 *E*
Wanbon, R (Aberavon) 1968 *E*
Ward, W S (Cross Keys) 1934 *S, I*
Warlow, J (Llanelli) 1962 *I*
Waters, D R (Newport) 1986 *E, S, I, F*
Waters, K (Newbridge) 1991 *[WS]*
Watkins, D (Newport) 1963 *E, S, I, F, NZ*, 1964 *E, S, I, F, SA*, 1965 *E, S, I, F*, 1966 *E, S, I, F*, 1967 *I, F, E*
Watkins, E (Neath) 1924 *E, S, I, F*
Watkins, E (Blaina) 1926 *S, I, F*
Watkins, E (Cardiff) 1935 *NZ*, 1937 *S, I*, 1938 *E, S, I*, 1939 *E, S*
Watkins, H (Llanelli) 1904 *S, I*, 1905 *E, S, I*, 1906 *E*
Watkins, I J (Ebbw Vale) 1988 *E* (R), *S, I, F, NZ* 2, *R*, 1989 *S, I, F, E*
Watkins, L (Oxford U, Llandaff) 1881 *E*
Watkins, M J (Newport) 1984 *I, F, E, A*
Watkins, S J (Newport, Cardiff) 1964 *S, I, F*, 1965 *E, S, I, F*, 1966 *E, S, I, F, A*, 1967 *S, I, F, E, NZ*, 1968 *E, S*, 1969 *S, I, F, E, NZ* 1, 1970 *E, I*
Watkins, W R (Newport) 1959 *F*
Watts, D (Maesteg) 1914 *E, S, F, I*
Watts, J (Llanelli) 1907 *E, S, I*, 1908 *E, S, F, I, A*, 1909 *S, F, I*
Watts, W (Llanelli) 1914 *E*
Watts, W H (Newport) 1892 *E, S, I*, 1893 *E, S, I*, 1894 *E, S, I*, 1895 *E, I*, 1896 *E*
Weatherley, D J (Swansea) 1998 *Z*
Weaver, D (Swansea) 1964 *E*
Webb, J (Abertillery) 1907 *S*, 1908 *E, S, F, I, A*, 1909 *E, S, F, I*, 1910 *F, E, S, I*, 1911 *E, S, F, I*, 1912 *E, S*
Webb, J E (Newport) 1888 *M*, 1889 *S*
Webbe, G M C (Bridgend) 1986 *Tg* (R), *WS*, 1987 *F, E, S, [Tg]*, *US*, 1988 *F* (R), *NZ* 1, *R*
Webster, R E (Swansea) 1987 *[A]*, 1990 *Bb*, 1991 *[Arg, A]*, 1992 *I, F, E, S, A*, 1993 *E, S, I, F*
Wells, G T (Cardiff) 1955 *E, S*, 1957 *I, F*, 1958 *A, E, S*
Westacott, D (Cardiff) 1906 *I*

Wetter, H (Newport) 1912 *SA*, 1913 *E*
Wetter, J J (Newport) 1914 *S, F, I*, 1920 *E, S, F, I*, 1921 *E*, 1924 *I, NZ*
Wheel, G A D (Swansea) 1974 *I, E* (R), 1975 *F, E, I, A*, 1976 *E, S, I, F*, 1977 *I, E, S*, 1978 *E, S, I, F, A* 1,2, *NZ*, 1979 *S, I*, 1980 *F, E, S, I*, 1981 *E, S, I, F, A*, 1982 *I*
Wheeler, P J (Aberavon) 1967 *NZ*, 1968 *E*
Whitefoot, J (Cardiff) 1984 *A* (R), 1985 *S, I, F, E, Fj*, 1986 *E, S, I, F, Fj, Tg, WS*, 1987 *F, E, S, I, [I, C]*
Whitfield, J (Newport) 1919 *NZA*, 1920 *E, S, F, I*, 1921 *E*, 1922 *E, S, I, F*, 1924 *S, I*
Whitson, G K (Newport) 1956 *F*, 1960 *S, I*
Wilkins, G (Bridgend) 1994 *Tg*
Williams, A (Bridgend, Swansea) 1990 *Nm* 2(R), 1995 *Fj* (R)
Williams, B (Llanelli) 1920 *S, F, I*
Williams, B H (Neath, Richmond, Bristol) 1996 *F* 2, 1997 *R, Tg, NZ*, 1998 *It, E, Z* (R), *SA* 1, *Arg* (R), 1999 *S* (R), *I, It* (R), 2000 *F* (R), *It* (R), *E* (t+R), 2001 *R* (R), *I* (R), *Tg* (R), *A* (R), 2002 *I* (R), *F* (R), *It* (R), *E* (R), *S*
Williams, B L (Cardiff) 1947 *E, S, F, I, A*, 1948 *E, S, F, I*, 1949 *E, S, I*, 1951 *I, SA*, 1952 *S*, 1953 *E, S, I, F, NZ*, 1954 *S*, 1955 *E*
Williams, B R (Neath) 1990 *S, I, Bb*, 1991 *E, S*
Williams, C (Llanelli) 1924 *NZ*, 1925 *E*
Williams, C (Aberavon, Swansea) 1977 *E, S*, 1980 *F, E, S, I, NZ*, 1983 *E*
Williams, C D (Cardiff, Neath) 1955 *F*, 1956 *F*
Williams, D (Llanelli) 1998 *SA* 1(R)
Williams, D (Ebbw Vale) 1963 *E, S, I, F*, 1964 *E, S, I, F, SA*, 1965 *E, S, I, F*, 1966 *E, S, I, A*, 1967 *F, E, NZ*, 1968 *E*, 1969 *S, I, F, E, NZ* 1,2, *A*, 1970 *SA, S, E, I*, 1971 *E, S, I, F*
Williams, D B (Newport, Swansea) 1978 *A* 1, 1981 *E, S*
Williams, E (Neath) 1924 *NZ*, 1925 *F*
Williams, E (Aberavon) 1925 *E, S*
Williams, F L (Cardiff) 1929 *S, F, I*, 1930 *E, S, I, F*, 1931 *F, I, SA*, 1932 *E, S, I*, 1933 *I*
Williams, G (Aberavon) 1936 *E, S, I*
Williams, G (London Welsh) 1950 *I, F*, 1951 *E, S, I, F, SA*, 1952 *E, S, I, F*, 1953 *NZ*, 1954 *E*
Williams, G (Bridgend) 1981 *I, F*, 1982 *E* (R), *S*
Williams, G P (Bridgend) 1980 *NZ*, 1981 *E, S, A*, 1982 *I*
Williams, R (Cardiff) 2000 *I, Sm, US, SA*, 2001 *S, F, It, R* (R), *I* (R), *Arg, Tg* (R), *A* (R), 2002 *F* (R), *It* (R), *E* (R), *S, SA* 1,2
Williams, J (Blaina) 1920 *E, S, F, I*, 1921 *S, F, I*
Williams, J F (London Welsh) 1905 *I, NZ*, 1906 *S, SA*
Williams, J J (Llanelli) 1973 *F* (R), *A*, 1974 *S, I, F, E*, 1975 *F, E, S, I, A*, 1976 *E, S, I, F*, 1977 *I, F, E, S*, 1978 *E, S, I, F, A* 1,2, *NZ*, 1979 *S, I, F, E*
Williams, J L (Cardiff) 1906 *SA*, 1907 *E, S, I*, 1908 *E, S, I, A*, 1909 *E, S, F, I*, 1910 *I*, 1911 *E, S, F, I*
Williams, J P R (London Welsh, Bridgend) 1969 *S, I, F, E, NZ* 1,2, *A*, 1970 *SA, S, E, I, F*, 1971 *E, S, I, F*, 1972 *E, S, F, NZ*, 1973 *E, S, I, F, A*, 1974 *S, I, F*, 1975 *F, E, S, I, A*, 1976 *E, S, I, F*, 1977 *I, F, E, S*, 1978 *E, S, I, F, A* 1,2, *NZ*, 1979 *S, I, F, E*, 1980 *NZ*, 1981 *E, S*
Williams, L (Llanelli, Cardiff) 1947 *E, S, F, I, A*, 1948 *I*, 1949 *E*
Williams, L H (Cardiff) 1957 *S, I, F*, 1958 *E, S, I, F*, 1959 *E, S, I*, 1961 *F*, 1962 *E, S*
Williams, M (Newport) 1923 *F*
Williams, M E (Pontypridd, Cardiff) 1996 *Bb, F* 2, *It* (t), 1998 *It, E, Z, SA* 2, *Arg*, 1999 *S, I, C, J, [Sm]*, 2000 *E* (R), 2001 *E, S, F, It*, 2002 *I, F, It, E, S, SA* 1,2
Williams, O (Bridgend) 1990 *Nm* 2
Williams, O (Llanelli) 1947 *E, S, A*, 1948 *E, S, F, I*
Williams, R (Llanelli) 1954 *S*, 1957 *F*, 1958 *A*
Williams, R D G (Newport) 1881 *E*
Williams, R F (Cardiff) 1912 *SA*, 1913 *E, S*, 1914 *I*
Williams, R H (Llanelli) 1954 *I, F, S*, 1955 *S, I, F*, 1956 *E, S, I*, 1957 *E, S, I, F*, 1958 *A, E, S, I, F*, 1959 *E, S, I, F*, 1960 *E*
Williams, S (Llanelli) 1947 *E, S, F, I*, 1948 *S, F*
Williams, S A (Aberavon) 1939 *E, S, I*
Williams, S M (Neath, Cardiff, Northampton) 1994 *Tg*, 1996 *E* (t), *A* 1,2, *Bb, F* 2, *It, A* 3, *SA*, 1997 *US, S, I, F, E, US* 1,2(R), *C, R* (R), *Tg* (R), *NZ* (t+R), 2002 *SA* 1,2
Williams, S M (Neath) 2000 *F* (R), *It, E, S, I, Sm, SA* (R), 2001 *J* 1,2, *I*
Williams, T (Pontypridd) 1882 *I*
Williams, T (Swansea) 1888 *S, I*
Williams, T (Swansea) 1912 *I*, 1913 *F*, 1914 *E, S, F, I*
Williams, Tudor (Swansea) 1921 *F*

Williams, T G (Cross Keys) 1935 *S, I, NZ*, 1936 *E, S, I*, 1937 *S, I*

Williams, W A (Crumlin) 1927 *E, S, F, I*

Williams, W A (Newport) 1952 *I, F*, 1953 *E*

Williams, W E O (Cardiff) 1887 *S, I*, 1889 *S*, 1890 *S, E*

Williams, W H (Pontymister) 1900 *E, S, I*, 1901 *E*

Williams, W O G (Swansea, Devonport Services) 1951 *F, SA*, 1952 *E, S, I, F*, 1953 *E, S, I, F, NZ*, 1954 *E, I, F, S*, 1955 *E, S, I, F*, 1956 *E, S, I*

Williams, W P J (Neath) 1974 *I, F*

Williams-Jones, H (S Wales Police, Llanelli) 1989 *S* (R), 1990 *F* (R), *I*, 1991 *A*, 1992 *S, A*, 1993 *E, S, I, F, Z* 1, *Nm*, 1994 *Fj, Tg, WS* (R), *It* (t), 1995 *E* (R)

Willis, W R (Cardiff) 1950 *E, S, I, F*, 1951 *E, S, I, F, SA*, 1952 *E, S*, 1953 *S, NZ*, 1954 *E, I, F, S*, 1955 *E, S, I, F*

Wiltshire, M L (Aberavon) 1967 *NZ*, 1968 *E, S, F*

Windsor, R W (Pontypool) 1973 *A*, 1974 *S, I, F, E*, 1975 *F, E, S, I, A*, 1976 *E, S, I, F*, 1977 *I, F, E, S*, 1978 *E, S, I, F, A* 1,2, *NZ*, 1979 *S, I, F*

Winfield, H B (Cardiff) 1903 *I*, 1904 *E, S, I*, 1905 *NZ*, 1906 *E, S, I*, 1907 *S, I*, 1908 *E, S, F, I, A*

Winmill, S (Cross Keys) 1921 *E, S, F, I*

Wintle, M E (Llanelli) 1996 *It*

Wintle, R V (London Welsh) 1988 *WS* (R)

Wooller, W (Sale, Cambridge U, Cardiff) 1933 *E, S, I*, 1935 *E, S, I, NZ*, 1936 *E, S, I*, 1937 *E, S, I*, 1938 *S, I*, 1939 *E, S, I*

Wyatt, C P (Llanelli) 1998 *Z* (R), *SA* 1(R),2, *Arg*, 1999 *S, I, F* 1, *It, E, Arg* 1,2, *SA, C* (R), *F* 2, [*Arg* 3, *J* (R), *Sm, A*], 2000 *F, It, E, US, SA*, 2001 *E, R, I, Arg* (R), *Tg* (R), *A* (R), 2002 *I, It* (R), *E, S* (R)

Wyatt, G (Pontypridd) 1997 *Tg*

Wyatt, M A (Swansea) 1983 *E, S, I, F*, 1984 *A*, 1985 *S, I*, 1987 *E, S, I*

Young, D (Swansea, Cardiff) 1987 [*E, NZ*], *US*, 1988 *E, S, I, F, NZ* 1,2, *WS, R*, 1989 *S, NZ*, 1990 *F*, 1996 *A* 3, *SA*, 1997 *US, S, I, F, E, R, NZ*, 1998 *It, E, S, I, F*, 1999 *I, E* (R), *Arg* 1(R),2(R), *SA, C* (R), *F* 2, [*Arg* 3, *J, Sm, A*], 2000 *F, It, E, S, I*, 2001 *E, S, F, It, R, I, Arg*

Young, G A (Cardiff) 1886 *E, S*

Young, J (Harrogate, RAF, London Welsh) 1968 *S, I, F*, 1969 *S, I, F, E, NZ* 1, 1970 *E, I, F*, 1971 *E, S, I, F*, 1972 *E, S, F, NZ*, 1973 *E, S, I, F*

FRANCE TEST SEASON REVIEW 2001-2002

Few Blues for Les Bleus

Ian Borthwick

This was another eventful year for France in the international arena, and although it ended on a negative note with three losses from three Tests on their end of season tour, it was undoubtedly a year of progress for the *Tricolores*.

They not only triumphed in Europe, winning the first ever Grand Slam of the Six Nations Championship, and the seventh Grand Slam of their history, but under the guiding hand of coach Bernard Laporte they also took aspects of their game to new levels, stringing together eight wins in a row and a series of performances which, a year out from the 2003 World Cup, undoubtedly place them amongst the favourites.

Admittedly, there was still a degree of inconsistency throughout the season and *Les Bleus* only really hit full form when they picked themselves up for the big games, notably the win (20-15) over England, remarkable after the previous year's 48-19 thrashing at Twickenham, and the rollicking 44-5 demolition of Ireland at the Stade de France. Against Italy, for instance, in the first game of the Six Nations Championship, the French lacked direction and conviction and, despite the final score-line of 33-12, were largely unconvincing; against Wales, they were lucky to escape with a four-point winning margin, and the game in Cardiff could easily have tipped in favour of the Welsh. But above all, the 2002 French side showed that when they really tried, their discipline, their commitment, their defensive alignment and their *sang-froid* could be as good, if not better than their Anglo-Saxon rivals. In some games, they gave away as few as eight penalties, and the fact that England's kicker, Jonny Wilkinson, was restricted to only one shot at goal was a major factor in the historic French win in Paris.

With the team spirit still on a high after the impressive 32-23 victory against the Springboks in Johannesburg in June 2001, the season started very much where the previous one had left off, with two wins against Southern Hemisphere opponents in France. First France beat South Africa 20-10 in Paris, then a week later in Marseilles they added a precious Wallaby scalp to their belt, with an emphatic, if close, win (14-13). In both cases, especially against Australia, the final score-lines flattered the opponents, but what was most remarkable was that Laporte had once again successfully taken a punt on introducing new players into the team.

Against South Africa on November 10th, the French side featured eight new players (second row Thibault Privat, No 8 Francis Ntamack, fly-half François Gelez, the centres Damien Traille and Tony Marsh, winger

The French Grand Slam side that beat Ireland in Paris in April.

Aurélien Rougerie, full-back Clément Poitrenaud and replacement scrum-half, the 19-year-old Frédéric Michalak) winning their first caps for their country. Of these, Gelez, Rougerie, Poitrenaud and Michalak are certain to figure strongly in France's World Cup campaign, while Traille and the New Zealand-born Marsh quickly established themselves as the unshakeable pair in France's mid-field, winning their first eight Tests in a row before losing the next three on the summer tour.

After confidently beating the Springboks, the *Tricolores* added to the mystique of the Stade Vélodrome in Marseilles, following up their surprise win there over the All Blacks in 2000 with an equally surprising win over the world-champion Australians. The Wallabies were no doubt suffering from end-of-season fatigue, but the intensity and control of France's overall performance enabled the team to gain in confidence and the Marseilles result became the spring-board for what was to follow in the Six Nations. The game against Fiji, played in freezing conditions in Saint-Etienne, was a mere formality, remarkable only for the fact that 1999 World Cup hero Christophe Dominici made a fleeting return to the side.

In the New Year, Laporte made no secret that his priority in 2002 was to win the Six Nations. 'Two years ago we said our ambition was to be able to compete with Southern Hemisphere teams on their own terms. With wins over New Zealand, Australia and South Africa in the past twelve months, we have now crossed that hurdle,' he said in early January. 'Our main aim is now to compete with our Northern Hemisphere neighbours.' With captain Fabien Galthié out with a knee injury, the French struggled against Italy and Wales, but for the match against England, the return of France's influential scrum-half finally nudged France into top gear. Unofficially billed as the Six Nations final, this was no doubt the turning point of the season for France. Their discipline was remarkable, their defence equally so, and thanks notably to an outstanding performance from Biarritz flanker Serge Betsen, who hounded Jonny Wilkinson out of the game, they successfully closed the English down.

One of the revelations of the season, Betsen was once again proof of the depth of talent available in France, as was another back-rower, Imanol Harinordoquy. Plucked seemingly out of nowhere after injury sidelined the find of the 2001 season Patrick Tabacco, the brilliant Basque No 8 had a superb international debut, while Nicolas Brusque, the elegant full-back from Biarritz, cemented his place in the team after starting the season as France's third-choice full-back.

After starting as one of French rugby's most successful seasons ever, the international year ended on a less enthusiastic note with three losses in Buenos Aires, Melbourne and Sydney. This tour, along with its suicidal travel itinerary – there was a Test against the Pumas only a week after the French club final – once again highlighted the problem of player burn-out, questioning the relevance of these end of season trips.

Despite the losses, however, French optimism remained high as, despite their physical lassitude, in all three games Laporte's men showed considerable mental strength and determination. Trailing 28-13 against the Pumas, they clawed their way back to 28-27 with two tries in the last five minutes and could easily have won if Gérald Merceron's last-minute penalty had gone over. Then, despite being well-beaten in the jet-lagged Melbourne Test, in the final game of the season in Sydney they pushed the Wallabies every step of the way, twice overcoming a 13-point deficit and coming desperately close to scoring a sensational match-winning try in the dying seconds.

'Two years ago, teams like Australia would have scored 50 points against us,' noted Bernard Laporte. 'But we have shown that our game plan works and that we can compete with the world champions on their own grounds.' An encouraging end to a satisfying season.

France's Test Record in 2001-2002: Played 11, won 8, lost 3.

Opponents	Date	Venue	Result
Australia	29th June 2002	A	Lost 25-31
Australia	22nd June 2002	A	Lost 17-29
Argentina	15th June 2002	A	Lost 27-28
Ireland	6th April 2002	H	Won 44-5
Scotland	23rd March 2002	A	Won 22-10
England	2nd March 2002	H	Won 20-15
Wales	16th February 2002	A	Won 37-33
Italy	2nd February 2002	H	Won 33-12
Fiji	24th November 2001	H	Won 77-10
Australia	17th November 2001	H	Won 14-13
South Africa	10th November 2001	H	Won 20-10

FRANCE INTERNATIONAL STATISTICS

(to 31 August 2002)

Match Records

MOST CONSECUTIVE TEST WINS

10 1931 *E, G,* 1932 *G,* 1933 *G,* 1934 *G,* 1935
G, 1936 *G 1,2,* 1937 *G, It*
8 1998 *E, S, I, W, Arg 1,2, Fj, Arg 3*
8 2001 *SA 3 A, Fj* 2002 *It, W, E, S, I*

MOST CONSECUTIVE TESTS WITHOUT DEFEAT

Matches	Wins	Draws	Period
10	10	0	1931 to 1938
10	8	2	1958 to 1959
10	9	1	1986 to 1987

MOST POINTS IN A MATCH
by the team

Pts	Opponents	Venue	Year
77	Fiji	Saint Etienne	2001
70	Zimbabwe	Auckland	1987
67	Romania	Bucharest	2000
64	Romania	Aurillac	1996
62	Romania	Castres	1999
60	Italy	Toulon	1967
59	Romania	Paris	1924
55	Romania	Wellington	1987

by a player

Pts	Player	Opponents	Venue	Year
30	D Camberabero	Zimbabwe	Auckland	1987
28	C Lamaison	New Zealand	Twickenham	1999
27	G Camberabero	Italy	Toulon	1967
27	C Lamaison	New Zealand	Marseilles	2000
27	G Merceron	South Africa	Johannesburg	2001
26	T Lacroix	Ireland	Durban	1995
25	J-P Romeu	United States	Chicago	1976
25	P Berot	Romania	Agen	1987
25	T Lacroix	Tonga	Pretoria	1995

MOST TRIES IN A MATCH
by the team

Tries	Opponents	Venue	Year
13	Romania	Paris	1924
13	Zimbabwe	Auckland	1987
12	Fiji	Saint Etienne	2001
11	Italy	Toulon	1967
10	Romania	Aurillac	1996
10	Romania	Bucharest	2000

by a player

Tries	Player	Opponents	Venue	Year
4	A Jauréguy	Romania	Paris	1924
4	M Celhay	Italy	Paris	1937

MOST CONVERSIONS IN A MATCH
by the team

Cons	Opponents	Venue	Year
9	Italy	Toulon	1967
9	Zimbabwe	Auckland	1987
8	Romania	Wellington	1987

by a player

Cons	Player	Opponents	Venue	Year
9	G Camberabero	Italy	Toulon	1967
9	D Camberabero	Zimbabwe	Auckland	1987
8	G Laporte	Romania	Wellington	1987

MOST PENALTIES IN A MATCH
by the team

Penalties	Opponents	Venue	Year
8	Ireland	Durban	1995
7	Wales	Paris	2001
7	Italy	Paris	2002
6	Argentina	Buenos Aires	1977
6	Scotland	Paris	1997
6	Italy	Auch	1997
6	Ireland	Paris	2000
6	South Africa	Johannesburg	2001

by a player

Penalties	Player	Opponents	Venue	Year
8	T Lacroix	Ireland	Durban	1995
7	G Merceron	Italy	Paris	2002
6	J-M Aguirre	Argentina	Buenos Aires	1977
6	C Lamaison	Scotland	Paris	1997
6	C Lamaison	Italy	Auch	1997
6	G Merceron	Ireland	Paris	2000
6	G Merceron	South Africa	Johannesburg	2001

MOST DROPPED GOALS IN A MATCH

by the team

Drops	Opponents	Venue	Year
3	Ireland	Paris	1960
3	England	Twickenham	1985
3	New Zealand	Christchurch	1986
3	Australia	Sydney	1990
3	Scotland	Paris	1991
3	New Zealand	Christchurch	1994

by a player

Drops	Player	Opponents	Venue	Year
3	P Albaladejo	Ireland	Paris	1960
3	J-P Lescarboura	England	Twickenham	1985
3	J-P Lescarboura	New Zealand	Christchurch	1986
3	D Camberabero	Australia	Sydney	1990

Career Records

MOST CAPPED PLAYERS

Caps	Player	Career Span
111	P Sella	1982 to 1995
93	S Blanco	1980 to 1991
78	A Benazzi	1990 to 2001
71	J-L Sadourny	1991 to 2001
69	R Bertranne	1971 to 1981
69	P Saint-André	1990 to 1997
69	F Pelous	1995 to 2002
66	C Califano	1994 to 2001
63	M Crauste	1957 to 1966
63	B Dauga	1964 to 1972
61	J Condom	1982 to 1990
61	O Roumat	1989 to 1996

MOST CONSECUTIVE TESTS

Tests	Player	Span
46	R Bertranne	1973 to 1979
45	P Sella	1982 to 1987
44	M Crauste	1960 to 1966
35	B Dauga	1964 to 1968

MOST TESTS AS CAPTAIN

Tests	Captain	Span
34	J-P Rives	1978 to 1984
34	P Saint-André	1994 to 1997
26	R Ibanez	1998 to 2002
25	D Dubroca	1986 to 1988
24	G Basquet	1948 to 1952
22	M Crauste	1961 to 1966

MOST TESTS IN INDIVIDUAL POSITIONS

Position	Player	Tests	Span
Full-back	S Blanco	81	1980 to 1991
Wing	P Saint-André	67	1990 to 1997
Centre	P Sella	104	1982 to 1995
Fly-half	J-P Romeu	33	1972 to 1977
Scrum-half	P Berbizier	56	1981 to 1991
Prop	C Califano	66	1994 to 2001
Hooker	R Ibañez	53	1997 to 2002
Lock	J Condom	61	1982 to 1990
Flanker	J-P Rives	59	1975 to 1984
No 8	G Basquet	33	1945 to 1952

MOST POINTS IN TESTS

Points	Player	Tests	Career
380	C Lamaison	37	1996 to 2001
367	T Lacroix	43	1989 to 1997
354	D Camberabero	36	1982 to 1993
265	J-P Romeu	34	1972 to 1977
233	S Blanco	93	1980 to 1991
227	G Merceron	19	1999 to 2002
222	T Castaignède	35	1995 to 2000
200	J-P Lescarboura	28	1982 to 1990

MOST TRIES IN TESTS

Tries	Player	Tests	Career
38	S Blanco	93	1980 to 1991
33	P Saint-André	69	1990 to 1997
30	P Sella	111	1982 to 1995
26	E Ntamack	46	1994 to 2000
26	P Bernat Salles	41	1992 to 2001
23	C Darrouy	40	1957 to 1967

MOST CONVERSIONS IN TESTS

Cons	Player	Tests	Career
59	C Lamaison	37	1996 to 2001
48	D Camberabero	36	1982 to 1993
45	M Vannier	43	1953 to 1961
41	T Castaignède	35	1995 to 2000
36	R Dourthe	31	1995 to 2001
32	T Lacroix	43	1989 to 1997
29	P Villepreux	34	1967 to 1972

MOST PENALTY GOALS IN TESTS

Penalties	Player	Tests	Career
89	T Lacroix	43	1989 to 1997
78	C Lamaison	37	1996 to 2001
59	D Camberabero	36	1982 to 1993
56	J-P Romeu	34	1972 to 1977
49	G Merceron	19	1999 to 2002
33	P Villepreux	34	1967 to 1972
33	P Bérot	19	1986 to 1989

MOST DROPPED GOALS IN TESTS

Drops	Player	Tests	Career
15	J-P Lescarboura	28	1982 to 1990
12	P Albaladejo	30	1954 to 1964
11	G Camberabero	14	1961 to 1968
11	D Camberabero	36	1982 to 1993
9	J-P Romeu	34	1972 to 1977

International Championship Records

Record	Detail		Set
Most points in season	156	in five matches	2002
Most tries in season	18	in four matches	1998
Highest Score	51	51-16 v Scotland	1998
	51	51 – 0 v Wales	1998
Biggest win	51	51 – 0 v Wales	1998
Highest score conceded	49	14-49 v Wales	1910
Biggest defeat	37	0-37 v England	1911
Most appearances	50	P Sella	1983 – 1995
Most points in matches	144	C Lamaison	1997 – 2001
Most points in season	80	G Merceron	2002
Most points in match	24	S Viars	v Ireland, 1992
	24	C Lamaison	v Scotland, 1997
Most tries in matches	14	S Blanco	1981 – 1991
	14	P Sella	1983 – 1995
Most tries in season	5	P Estève	1983
	5	E Bonneval	1987
	5	E Ntamack	1999
	5	P Bernat Salles	2001
Most tries in match	3	M Crauste	v England, 1962
	3	C Darrouy	v Ireland, 1963
	3	E Bonneval	v Scotland, 1987
	3	D Venditti	v Ireland, 1997
	3	E Ntamack	v Wales, 1999
Most cons in matches	23	C Lamaison	1997 – 2001
Most cons in season	9	C Lamaison	1998
	9	G Merceron	2002
Most cons in match	5	P Villepreux	v England, 1972
	5	S Viars	v Ireland, 1992
	5	T Castaignède	v Ireland, 1996
	5	C Lamaison	v Wales, 1998
Most pens in matches	34	G Merceron	2000 – 2002
Most pens in season	18	G Merceron	2002
Most pens in match	7	G Merceron	v Italy, 2002
Most drops in matches	9	J-P Lescarboura	1982 – 1988
Most drops in season	5	G Camberabero	1967
Most drops in match	3	P Albaladejo	v Ireland, 1960
	3	J-P Lescarboura	v England, 1985

Miscellaneous Records

Record	Holder	Detail
Longest Test Career	F Haget	14 seasons, 1974 to 1987
Youngest Test Cap	C Dourthe	18 yrs 7 days in 1966
Oldest Test Cap	A Roques	37 yrs 329 days in 1963

Career Records of France International Players
(up to 31 August 2002)

PLAYER	Debut	Caps	T	C	P	D	Pts
Backs:							
A Albouy	2002 v It	1	0	0	0	0	0
D Bory	2000 v I	15	1	0	0	0	5
N Brusque	1997 v R	7	3	0	0	0	15
T Castaignède	1995 v R	35	13	41	21	4	222
C Dominici	1998 v E	26	12	0	0	0	60
P Elhorga	2001 v NZ	3	0	0	0	0	0
F Galthié	1991 v R	49	9	0	0	0	44
X Garbajosa	1998 v I	24	7	0	0	0	35
F Gelez	2001 v SA	3	0	0	8	0	24
C Heymans	2000 v It	3	0	0	0	0	0
Y Jauzion	2001 v SA	5	0	0	0	0	0
N Jeanjean	2001 v SA	9	2	0	0	0	10
C Lamaison	1996 v SA	37	2	59	78	6	380
J Marlu	1998 v Fj	3	0	0	0	0	0
T Marsh	2001 v SA	11	6	0	0	0	30
G Merceron	1999 v R	19	3	28	49	3	227
F Michalak	2001 v SA	6	0	0	1	0	3
P Mignoni	1997 v R	13	3	0	0	0	15
C Poitrenaud	2001 v SA	3	1	0	0	0	5
A Rougerie	2001 v SA	11	6	0	0	0	30
D Skrela	2001 v NZ	1	0	0	4	0	12
J-M Souverbie	2000 v R	1	1	0	0	0	5
D Traille	2001 v SA	11	1	0	5	0	20
Forwards:							
A Audebert	2000 v R	2	0	0	0	0	0
D Auradou	1999 v E	24	0	0	0	0	0
O Azam	1995 v R	10	0	0	0	0	0
S Betsen	1997 v It	21	5	0	0	0	25
O Brouzet	1994 v S	57	2	0	0	0	10
Y Bru	2001 v A	3	0	0	0	0	0
S Chabal	2000 v S	7	0	0	0	0	0
A Costes	1994 v C	14	1	0	0	0	5
J-J Crenca	1996 v SA	18	1	0	0	0	5
P de Villiers	1999 v W	26	0	0	0	0	0
S Hall	2002 v It	2	0	0	0	0	0
I Harinordoquy	2002 v W	6	1	0	0	0	5
R Ibañez	1996 v W	55	5	0	0	0	25
C Labit	1999 v S	7	0	0	0	0	0
T Lièvremont	1996 v W	21	2	0	0	0	10
O Magne	1997 v W	55	8	0	0	0	40
S Marconnet	1998 v Arg	20	1	0	0	0	5

R Martin	2002 v E	3	0	0	0	0	0
A Martinez	2002 v A	1	0	0	0	0	0
F Ntamack	2001 v SA	1	0	0	0	0	0
F Pelous	1995 v R	69	5	0	0	0	25
C Porcu	2002 v Arg	3	0	0	0	0	0
J-B Poux	2001 v Fj	6	2	0	0	0	10
T Privat	2001 v SA	6	0	0	0	0	0
P Tabacco	2001 v SA	6	0	0	0	0	0
E Vermeulen	2001 v SA	2	0	0	0	0	0

FRENCH INTERNATIONAL PLAYERS

(up to 31 August 2002)

Note: Years given for International Championship matches are for second half of season, eg 1972 refers to season 1971-72. Years for all other matches refer to the actual year of the match. When a series has taken place, or more than one match has been played against a country in the same year, figures have been used to denote the particular matches in which players have featured. Thus 1967 *SA* 2,4 indicates that a player appeared in the second and fourth Tests of the 1967 series against South Africa. This list includes only those players who have appeared in FFR International Matches '*donnant droit au titre d'international*'.

Abadie, A (Pau) 1964 *I*

Abadie, A (Graulhet) 1965 *R*, 1967 *SA* 1,3,4, *NZ*, 1968 *S, I*

Abadie, L (Tarbes) 1963 *R*

Accoceberry, G (Bègles) 1994 *NZ* 1,2, *C* 2, 1995 *W, E, S, I, R* 1, [*Iv, S*], *It*, 1996 *I, W* 1, *R, Arg* 1, *W* 2(R), *SA* 2, 1997 *S, It* 1

Aguerre, R (Biarritz O) 1979 *S*

Aguilar, D (Pau) 1937 *G*

Aguirre, J-M (Bagnères) 1971 *A* 2, 1972 *S*, 1973 *W, I, J, R*, 1974 *I, W, Arg* 2, *R, SA* 1, 1976 *W* (R), *E, US, A* 2, *R*, 1977 *W, E, S, I, Arg* 1,2, *NZ* 1,2, *R*, 1978 *E, S, I, W, R*, 1979 *I, W, E, S, NZ* 1,2, *R*, 1980 *W, I*

Ainciart, E (Bayonne) 1933 *G*, 1934 *G*, 1935 *G*, 1937 *G, It*, 1938 *G* 1

Albaladejo, P (Dax) 1954 *E, It*, 1960 *W, I, It, R*, 1961 *S, SA, E, W, I, NZ* 1,2, *A*, 1962 *S, E, W, I*, 1963 *S, I, E, W, It*, 1964 *S, NZ, W, It, I, SA, Fj*

Albouy, A (Castres) 2002 *It* (R)

Alvarez, A-J (Tyrosse) 1945 *B*2, 1946 *B, I, K, W*, 1947 *S, I, W, E*, 1948 *I, A, S, W, E*, 1949 *I, E, W*, 1951 *S, E, W*

Amand, H (SF) 1906 *NZ*

Ambert, A (Toulouse) 1930 *S, I, E, G, W*

Amestoy, J-B (Mont-de-Marsan) 1964 *NZ, E*

André, G (RCF) 1913 *SA, E, W, I*, 1914 *I, W, E*

Andrieu, M (Nîmes) 1986 *Arg* 2, *NZ* 1, *R* 2, *NZ* 2, 1987 [*R, Z*], *R*, 1988 *E, S, I, W, Arg* 1,2,3,4, *R*, 1989 *I, W, E, S, NZ* 2, *B, A* 2, 1990 *W, E, I* (R)

Anduran, J (SCUF) 1910 *W*

Aqua, J-L (Toulon) 1999 *R, Tg, NZ* 1(R)

Araou, R (Narbonne) 1924 *R*

Arcalis, R (Brive) 1950 *S, I*, 1951 *I, E, W*

Arino, M (Agen) 1962 *R*

Aristouy, P (Pau) 1948 *S*, 1949 *Arg* 2, 1950 *S, I, E, W*

Arlettaz, P (Perpignan) 1995 *R* 2

Armary, L (Lourdes) 1987 [*R*], *R*, 1988 *S, I, W, Arg* 3,4, *R*, 1989 *W, S, A* 1,2, 1990 *W, E, S, I, A* 1,2,3, *NZ* 1, 1991 *W* 2, 1992 *S, I, R, Arg* 1,2, *SA* 1,2, *Arg*, 1993 *E, S, I, W, SA* 1,2, *R* 2, *A* 1,2, 1994 *I, W, NZ* 1(t),2(t), 1995 *I, R* 1 [*Tg, I, SA*]

Arnal, J-M (RCF) 1914 *I, W*

Arnaudet, M (Lourdes) 1964 *I*, 1967 *It, W*

Arotca, R (Bayonne) 1938 *R*

Arrieta, J (SF) 1953 *E, W*

Arthapignet, P (see Harislur-Arthapignet)

Artiguste, E (Castres) 1999 *WS*

Astre, R (Béziers) 1971 *R*, 1972 *I* 1, 1973 *E* (R), 1975 *E, S, I, SA* 1,2, *Arg* 2, 1976 *A* 2, *R*

Aucagne, D (Pau) 1997 *W* (R), *S, It* 1, *R* 1(R), *A* 1, *R* 2(R), *SA* 2(R), 1998 *S* (R), *W* (R), *Arg* 2(R), *Fj* (R), *Arg* 3, *A*, 1999 *W* 1(R), *S* (R)

Audebert, A (Montferrand) 2000 *R*, 2002 *W* (R)

Aué, J-M (Castres) 1998 *W* (R)

Augé, J (Dax) 1929 *S, W*

Augras-Fabre, L (Agen) 1931 *I, S, W*

Auradou, D (SF) 1999 *E* (R), *S* (R), *WS* (R), *Tg, NZ* 1, *W* 2(R), [*Arg* (R)], 2000 *A* (R), *NZ* 1,2, 2001 *S, I, It, W, E* (R), *SA* 1,2, *NZ* (R), *SA* 3, *A, Fj*, 2002 *It, E, I* (R)

Averous, J-L (La Voulte) 1975 *S, I, SA* 1,2, 1976 *I, W, E, US, A* 1,2, *R*, 1977 *W, E, S, I, Arg* 1, *R*, 1978 *E, S, I*, 1979 *NZ* 1,2, 1980 *E, S*, 1981 *A* 2

Azam, O (Montferrand, Gloucester) 1995 *R* 2, *Arg* (R), 2000 *A* (R), *NZ* 2(R), 2001 *SA* 2(R), *NZ*, 2002 *E* (R), *I* (R), *Arg* (R), *A* 1

Azarete, J-L (Dax, St Jean-de-Luz) 1969 *W, R*, 1970 *S, I, W, R*, 1971 *S, I, E, SA* 1,2, *A* 1, 1972 *E, W, I* 2, *A* 1, *R*, 1973 *NZ, W, I, R*, 1974 *I, R, SA* 1,2, 1975 *W*

Bacqué, N (Pau) 1997 *R* 2

Bader, E (Primevères) 1926 *M*, 1927 *I, S*

Badin, C (Chalon) 1973 *W, I*, 1975 *Arg* 1

Baillette, M (Perpignan) 1925 *I, NZ, S*, 1926 *W, M*, 1927 *I, W, G* 2, 1929 *G*, 1930 *S, I, E, G*, 1931 *I, S, E*, 1932 *G*

Baladie, G (Agen) 1945 *B* 1,2, *W*, 1946 *B, I, K*

Ballarin, J (Tarbes) 1924 *E*, 1925 *NZ, S*

Baquey, J (Toulouse) 1921 *I*

Barbazanges, A (Roanne) 1932 *G*, 1933 *G*

Barrau, M (Beaumont, Toulouse) 1971 *S, E, W*, 1972 *E, W, A* 1,2, 1973 *S, NZ, E, I, J, R*, 1974 *I, S*

Barrère, P (Toulon) 1929 *G*, 1931 *W*

Barrière, R (Béziers) 1960 *R*

Barthe, E (SBUC) 1925 *W, E*

Barthe, J (Lourdes) 1954 *Arg* 1,2, 1955 *S*, 1956 *I, W, It, E, Cz*, 1957 *S, I, E, W, R* 1,2, 1958 *S, E, A, W, It, I, SA* 1,2, 1959 *S, E, It, W*

Basauri, R (Albi) 1954 *Arg* 1

Bascou, P (Bayonne) 1914 *E*

Basquet, G (Agen) 1945 *W*, 1946 *B, I, K, W*, 1947 *S, I, W, E*, 1948 *I, A, S, W, E*, 1949 *I, E, W, Arg* 1, 1950 *S, I, E, W*, 1951 *S, I, E, W*, 1952 *S, I, SA, W, E, It*

Bastiat, J-P (Dax) 1969 *R*, 1970 *S, I, W*, 1971 *S, I, SA* 2, 1972 *A* 1, 1973 *E*, 1974 *Arg* 1,2, *SA* 2, 1975 *W, Arg* 1,2, *R*, 1976 *S, I, W, E, A* 1,2, *R*, 1977 *W, E, S, I*, 1978 *E, S, I, W*

Baudry, N (Montferrand) 1949 *S, I, W, Arg* 1,2

Baulon, R (Vienne, Bayonne) 1954 *S, NZ, W, E, It*, 1955 *I, E, W, It*, 1956 *I, W, It, E, Cz*, 1957 *S, I, It*

Baux, J-P (Lannemezan) 1968 *NZ* 1,2, *SA* 1,2

Bavozet, J (Lyon) 1911 *S, E, W*

Bayard, J (Toulouse) 1923 *S, W, E*, 1924 *W, R, US*

Bayardon, J (Chalon) 1964 *S, NZ, E*

Beaurin-Gressier, C (SF) 1907 *E*, 1908 *E*

Bégu, J (Dax) 1982 *Arg* 2(R), 1984 *E, S*

Béguerie, C (Agen) 1979 *NZ* 1

Beguet, L (RCF) 1922 *I*, 1923 *S, W, E, I*, 1924 *S, I, E, R, US*

Behoteguy, A (Bayonne, Cognac) 1923 *E*, 1924 *S, I, E, W, R, US*, 1926 *E*, 1927 *E, G* 1,2, 1928 *A, I, E, G, W*, 1929 *S, W, E*

Behoteguy, H (RCF, Cognac) 1923 *W*, 1928 *A, I, E, G, W*

Belascain, C (Bayonne) 1977 *R*, 1978 *E, S, I, W, R*, 1979 *I, W, E, S*, 1982 *W, E, S, I*, 1983 *E, S, I, W*

Belletante, G (Nantes) 1951 *I, E, W*

Belot, F (Toulouse) 2000 *I* (R)

Benazzi, A (Agen) 1990 *A* 1,2,3, *NZ* 1,2, 1991 *E, US* 1(R),2, [*R, Fj, C*], 1992 *SA* 1(R),2, *Arg*, 1993 *E, S, I, W, A* 1,2, 1994 *I, W, E, S, C* 1, *NZ* 1,2, *C* 2, 1995 *W, E, S, I*, [*Tg, Iv, S, I, SA, E*], *NZ* 1,2, 1996 *E, S, I, W* 1, *Arg* 1,2, *W* 2, *SA* 1,2, 1997 *I, W, E, S, R* 1, *A* 1,2, *NZ* 2(R), *Arg, SA* 1,2, 1999 *R, WS, W* 2, [*C, Nm* (R), *Fj, Arg, NZ* 2, *A*], 2000 *W, E, I, It* (R), *R*, 2001 *S* (R), *I* (t&R), *E*

Bénésis, R (Narbonne) 1969 *W, R*, 1970 *S, I, W, E, R*, 1971 *S, I, E, W, A* 2, *R*, 1972 *S, I* 1, *E, W, I* 2, *A* 1, *R*, 1973 *NZ, E, W, I, J, R*, 1974 *I, W, E, S*

Benetière, J (Roanne) 1954 *It, Arg* 1

Benetton, P (Agen) 1989 *B*, 1990 *NZ* 2, 1991 *US* 2, 1992 *Arg* 1,2(R), *SA* 1(R),2, *Arg*, 1993 *E, S, I, W, SA* 1,2, *R* 2, *A* 1,2, 1994 *I, W, E, S, C* 1, *NZ* 1,2, *C* 2, 1995 *W, E, S, I*, [*Tg, Iv* (R), *S*], *It, R* 2(R), *Arg, NZ* 1,2, 1996 *Arg* 1,2, *W* 2, *SA* 1,2, 1997 *I, It* 1,2(R), *R* 2, *Arg, SA* 1,2, 1998 *E, S* (R), *I* (R), *W* (R), *Arg* 1(R),2(R), *Fj* (R), 1999 *I, W* 1, *S* (R)

Benezech, L (RCF) 1994 *E, S, C* 1, *NZ* 1,2, *C* 2, 1995 *W, E*, [*Iv, S, E*], *R* 2, *Arg, NZ* 1,2

Berbizier, P (Lourdes, Agen) 1981 *S, I, W, E, NZ* 1,2, 1982 *I, R*, 1983 *S, I*, 1984 *S* (R), *NZ* 1,2, 1985 *Arg* 1,2, 1986 *S, I, W, E, R* 1, *Arg* 1, *A, NZ* 1, *R* 2, *NZ* 2,3, 1987 *W, E, S, I*, [*S, R, Fj, A, NZ*], *R*, 1988 *E, S, I, W, Arg* 1,2, 1989 *I, W, E, S, NZ* 1,2, *B, A* 1, 1990 *W, E*, 1991 *S, I, W* 1, *E*

Berejnoi, J-C (Tulle) 1963 *R*, 1964 *S, W, It, I, SA, Fj, R*, 1965 *S, I, E, W, It, R*, 1966 *S, I, E, W, It, R*, 1967 *S, A, E, It, W, I, R*

Berges, B (Toulouse) 1926 *I*

Berges-Cau, R (Lourdes) 1976 *E* (R)

Bergese, F (Bayonne) 1936 *G* 2, 1937 *G, It*, 1938 *G* 1, *R, G* 2

Bergougnan, Y (Toulouse) 1945 *B* 1, *W*, 1946 *B, I, K, W*, 1947 *S, I, W, E*, 1948 *S, W, E*, 1949 *S, E, Arg* 1,2
Bernard, R (Bergerac) 1951 *S, I, E, W*
Bernat-Salles, P (Pau, Bègles-Bordeaux, Biarritz) 1992 *Arg*, 1993 *R* 1, *SA* 1,2, *R* 2, *A* 1,2, 1994 *I*, 1995 *E, S*, 1996 *E* (R), 1997 *R* 1, *A* 1,2, 1998 *E, S, I, W, Arg* 1,2, *Fj, Arg* 3(R), *A* 1999 *I, W* 1, *R, Tg*, [*Nm, Fj, Arg, NZ* 2, *A*], 2000 *I, It, NZ* 1(R),2, 2001 *S, I, It, W, E*
Bernon, J (Lourdes) 1922 *I*, 1923 *S*
Bérot, J-L (Toulouse) 1968 *NZ* 3, *A*, 1969 *S, I*, 1970 *E, R*, 1971 *S, I, E, W, SA* 1,2, *A* 1,2, *R*, 1972 *S, I* 1, *E, W, A* 1, 1974 *I*
Bérot, P (Agen) 1986 *R* 2, *NZ* 2,3, 1987 *W, E, S, I, R*, 1988 *E, S, I, Arg* 1,2,3,4, *R*, 1989 *S, NZ* 1,2
Bertrand, P (Bourg) 1951 *I, E, W*, 1953 *S, I, E, W, It*
Bertranne, R (Bagnères) 1971 *E, W, SA* 2, *A* 1,2, 1972 *S, I* 1, 1973 *NZ, E, J, R*, 1974 *I, W, E, S, Arg* 1,2, *R, SA* 1,2, 1975 *W, E, S, I, SA* 1,2, *Arg* 1,2, *R*, 1976 *S, I, W, E, US, A* 1,2, *R*, 1977 *W, E, S, I, Arg* 1,2, *NZ* 1,2, *R*, 1978 *E, S, I, W, R*, 1979 *I, W, E, S, R*, 1980 *W, E, S, I, SA, R*, 1981 *S, I, W, E, R, NZ* 1,2
Berty, D (Toulouse) 1990 *NZ* 2, 1992 *R* (R), 1993 *R* 2, 1995 *NZ* 1(R), 1996 *W* 2(R), *SA* 1
Besset, E (Grenoble) 1924 *S*
Besset, L (SCUF) 1914 *W, E*
Besson, M (CASG) 1924 *I*, 1925 *I, E*, 1926 *S, W*, 1927 *I*
Besson, P (Brive) 1963 *S, I, E*, 1965 *R*, 1968 *SA* 1
Betsen, S (Biarritz) 1997 *It* 1(R), 2000 *W* (R), *E* (R), *A* (R), *NZ* 1(R),2(R), 2001 *S* (R), *I* (R), *It* (R), *W* (R), *SA* 3(R), *A, Fj*, 2002 *It, W, E, S, I, Arg, A* 1,2
Bianchi, J (Toulon) 1986 *Arg* 1
Bichindaritz, J (Biarritz O) 1954 *It, Arg* 1,2
Bidart, L (La Rochelle) 1953 *W*
Biemouret, P (Agen) 1969 *E, W*, 1970 *I, W, E*, 1971 *W, SA* 1,2, *A* 1, 1972 *E, W, I* 2, *A* 2, *R*, 1973 *S, NZ, E, W, I*
Biénès, R (Cognac) 1950 *S, I, E, W*, 1951 *S, I, E, W*, 1952 *S, I, SA, W, E, It*, 1953 *S, I, E*, 1954 *S, I, NZ, W, E, Arg* 1,2, 1956 *S, I, W, It, E*
Bigot, C (Quillan) 1930 *S, E*, 1931 *I, S*
Bilbao, L (St Jean-de-Luz) 1978 *I*, 1979 *I*
Billac, E (Bayonne) 1920 *S, E, W, I, US*, 1921 *S, W*, 1922 *W*, 1923 *E*
Billière, M (Toulouse) 1968 *NZ* 3
Bioussa, A (Toulouse) 1924 *W, US*, 1925 *I, NZ, S, E*, 1926 *S, I, E*, 1928 *E, G, W*, 1929 *I, S, W, E*, 1930 *S, I, E, G, W*
Bioussa, C (Toulouse) 1913 *W, I*, 1914 *I*
Biraben, M (Dax) 1920 *W, I, US*, 1921 *S, W, E, I*, 1922 *S, E, I*
Blain, A (Carcassonne) 1934 *G*
Blanco, S (Biarritz O) 1980 *SA, R*, 1981 *S, W, E, A* 1,2, *R, NZ* 1,2, 1982 *W, E, S, I, R, Arg* 1,2, 1983 *E, S, I, W*, 1984 *I, W, E, S, NZ* 1,2, *R*, 1985 *E, S, I, W, Arg* 1,2, 1986 *S, I, W, E, R* 1, *Arg* 2, *A, NZ* 1, *R* 2, *NZ* 2,3, 1987 *W, E, S, R, Fj, A, NZ*, *R*, 1988 *E, S, I, W, Arg* 1,2,3,4, *R*, 1989 *I, W, E, S, NZ* 1,2, *B, A* 1, 1990 *E, S, I, R, A* 1,2,3, *NZ* 1,2, 1991 *S, I, W* 1, *E, R, US* 1,2, *W* 2, [*R, Fj, C, E*]
Blond, J (SF) 1935 *G*, 1936 *G* 2, 1937 *G*, 1938 *G* 1, *R, G* 2
Blond, X (RCF) 1990 *A* 3, 1991 *S, I, W* 1, *E*, 1994 *NZ* 2(R)
Boffelli, V (Aurillac) 1971 *A* 2, *R*, 1972 *S, I* 1, 1973 *J, R*, 1974 *I, W, E, S, Arg* 1,2, *R, SA* 1,2, 1975 *W, S, I*
Bonal, J-M (Toulouse) 1968 *E, W, Cz, NZ* 2,3, *SA* 1,2, *R*, 1969 *S, I, E*, 1970 *W, E*
Bonamy, R (SB) 1928 *A, I*
Bondouy, P (Narbonne, Toulouse) 1997 *S* (R), *It* 1, *A* 2(R), *R* 2, 2000 *R* (R)
Bonetti, S (Biarritz) 2001 *It, W, NZ* (R)
Boniface, A (Mont-de-Marsan) 1954 *I, NZ, W, E, It, Arg* 1,2, 1955 *S, I*, 1956 *S, I, W, E, Cz*, 1957 *S, I, W, R* 2, 1958 *S, E*, 1959 *E*, 1961 *NZ* 1,3, *A, R*, 1962 *E, W, I, It, R*, 1963 *S, I, E, W, It, R*, 1964 *S, NZ, E, W, It*, 1965 *W, It, R*, 1966 *S, I, E, W*
Boniface, G (Mont-de-Marsan) 1960 *W, I, It, R, Arg* 1,2,3, 1961 *S, SA, E, W, It, I, NZ* 1,2,3, *R*, 1962 *R*, 1963 *S, I, E, W, It, R*, 1964 *S, NZ* 1,5, *W, It, R*, 1966 *S, I, E, W*
Bonnes, E (Narbonne) 1924 *W, R, US*
Bonneval, E (Toulouse) 1984 *NZ* 2(R), 1985 *W, Arg* 1, 1986 *W, E, R* 1, *Arg* 1,2, *A, R* 2, *NZ* 2,3, 1987 *W, E, S, I*, [*Z*], 1988 *E*
Bonnus, F (Toulon) 1950 *S, I, E, W*
Bonnus, M (Toulon) 1937 *It*, 1938 *G* 1, *R, G* 2, 1940 *B*
Bontemps, D (La Rochelle) 1968 *SA* 2
Borchard, P (RCF) 1908 *E*, 1909 *E, W, I*, 1911 *I*
Borde, F (RCF) 1920 *I, US*, 1921 *S, W, E*, 1922 *S, W*, 1923 *S, I*, 1924 *I*, 1925 *I*, 1926 *E*
Bordenave, L (Toulon) 1948 *A, S, W, E*, 1949 *S*
Bory, D (Montferrand) 2000 *I, It, A, NZ* 1, 2001 *S, I, SA* 1,2,3, *A, Fj*, 2002 *It, E, S, I*

Boubée, J (Tarbes) 1921 *S, E, I*, 1922 *E, W*, 1923 *E, I*, 1925 *NZ, S*
Boudreaux, R (SCUF) 1910 *W, S*
Bouet, D (Dax) 1989 *NZ* 1,2, *B, A* 2, 1990 *A* 3
Bouguyon, G (Grenoble) 1961 *SA, E, W, It, I, NZ* 1,2,3, *A*
Bouic, G (Agen) 1996 *SA* 1
Bouilhou, J (Toulouse) 2001 *NZ*
Boujet, C (Grenoble) 1968 *NZ* 2, *A* (R), *SA* 1
Bouquet, J (Bourgoin, Vienne) 1954 *S*, 1955 *E*, 1956 *S, I, W, It, E, Cz*, 1957 *S, E, W, R* 2, 1958 *S, E*, 1959 *S, It, W, I*, 1960 *S, E, W, I, R*, 1961 *SA, E, W, It, I, R*, 1962 *S, E, W, I*
Bourdeu, J R (Lourdes) 1952 *S, I, SA, W, E, It*, 1953 *S, I, E*
Bourgarel, R (Toulouse) 1969 *R*, 1970 *S, I, E, R*, 1971 *W, SA* 1,2, 1973 *E*
Bourguignon, G (Narbonne) 1988 *Arg* 3, 1989 *I, E, B, A* 1, 1990 *R*
Bousquet, A (Béziers) 1921 *E, I*, 1924 *R*
Bousquet, R (Albi) 1926 *M*, 1927 *I, S, W, E, G* 1, 1929 *W, E*, 1930 *W*
Boyau, M (SBUC) 1912 *I, S, W, E*, 1913 *W, I*
Boyer, P (Toulon) 1935 *G*
Branca, G (SF) 1928 *S*, 1929 *I, S*
Branlat, A (RCF) 1906 *NZ, E*, 1908 *W*
Brejassou, R (Tarbes) 1952 *S, I, SA, W, E*, 1953 *W, E*, 1954 *S, I, NZ*, 1955 *S, I, E, W, It*
Brethes, R (St Sever) 1960 *Arg* 2
Bringeon, A (Biarritz O) 1925 *W*
Brouzet, O (Grenoble, Bègles, Northampton) 1994 *S, NZ* 2(R), 1995 *E, S, I, R* 1, [*Tg, Iv, E* (t)], *It, Arg* (R), 1996 *W* 1(R), 1997 *R* 1, *A* 1,2, *It* 2, *Arg, SA* 1,2, 1998 *E, S, I, W, Arg* 1,2, *Fj, Arg* 3, *A*, 1999 *I, W* 1, *E, S, R*, [*C* (R), *Nm, Fj* (R), *Arg, NZ* 2(R), *A* (R)], 2000 *W, E, S, I, It, A, NZ* 1(R),2(R), 2001 *SA* 1,2, *NZ*, 2002 *W, E, S, I, Arg, A* 1(R),2
Bru, Y (Toulouse) 2001 *A* (R), *Fj* (R), 2002 *It*
Brun, G (Vienne) 1950 *E, W*, 1951 *S, E, W*, 1952 *S, I, SA, W, E, It*, 1953 *E, W, It*
Bruneau, M (SBUC) 1910 *W, E*, 1913 *SA, E*
Brunet, Y (Perpignan) 1975 *SA* 1, 1977 *Arg* 1
Bruno, S (Béziers) 2002 *W* (R)
Brusque, N (Pau, Biarritz) 1997 *R* 2(R), 2002 *W, E, S, I, Arg, A* 2
Buchet, E (Nice) 1980 *R*, 1982 *E, R* (R), *Arg* 1,2
Buisson, H (see Empereur-Buisson)
Buonomo, Y (Béziers) 1971 *A* 2, *R*, 1972 *I* 1
Burgun, M (RCF) 1909 *I*, 1910 *W, S, I*, 1911 *S, E*, 1912 *I, S*, 1913 *S, E*, 1914 *E*
Bustaffa, D (Carcassonne) 1977 *Arg* 1,2, *NZ* 1,2, 1978 *W, R*, 1980 *W, E, S, SA, R*
Buzy, C-E (Lourdes) 1946 *K, W*, 1947 *S, I, W, E*, 1948 *I, A, S, W, E*, 1949 *S, I, E, W, Arg* 1,2

Cabanier, J-M (Montauban) 1963 *R*, 1964 *S, Fj*, 1965 *S, I, W, It, R*, 1966 *S, I, E, W, It, R*, 1967 *S, A, E, It, W, I, SA* 1,3, *NZ, R*, 1968 *S, I*
Cabannes, L (RCF, Harlequins) 1990 *NZ* 2(R), 1991 *S, I, W* 1, *E, US* 2, *W* 2, [*R, Fj, C, E*], 1992 *W, E, S, I, R, Arg* 2, *SA* 1,2, 1993 *E, S, I, W, R* 1, *SA* 1,2, 1994 *E, S, C* 1, *NZ* 1,2, 1995 *W, E, S, R* 1, [*Tg* (R), *Iv, S, I, SA, E*], 1996 *E, S, I, W* 1, 1997 *It* 2, *Arg, SA* 1,2
Cabrol, H (Béziers) 1972 *A* 1(R),2, 1973 *J*, 1974 *SA* 2
Cadenat, J (SCUF) 1910 *S, E*, 1911 *W, I*, 1912 *W, E*, 1913 *I*
Cadieu, J-M (Toulouse) 1991 *R, US* 1, [*R, Fj, C, E*], 1992 *W, I, R, Arg* 1,2, *SA* 1
Cahuc, F (St Girons) 1922 *S*
Califano, C (Toulouse) 1994 *NZ* 1,2, *C* 2, 1995 *W, E, S, I*, [*Iv, S, I, SA, E*], *It, Arg, NZ* 1,2, 1996 *E, S, I, W* 1, *R, Arg* 1,2, *SA* 1,2, 1997 *I, W, E, A* 1,2, *It* 2, *R* 2(R), *Arg, SA* 1,2, 1998 *E, S, I, W*, 1999 *I, W* 1, *E* (R), *S, WS, Tg* (R), *NZ* 1, *W* 2, [*C, Nm, Fj*], 2000 *W, E, S, I, It, R, A, NZ* 1,2(R), 2001 *S* (R), *I* (R), *It, W, SA* 1(R),2(R), *NZ*
Cals, R (RCF) 1938 *G* 1
Calvo, G (Lourdes) 1961 *NZ* 1,3
Camberabero, D (La Voulte, Béziers) 1982 *R, Arg* 1,2, 1983 *E, W*, 1987 [*R* (R), *Z, Fj* (R), *A, NZ*], 1988 *I*, 1989 *B, A* 1, 1990 *W, S, I, R, A* 1,2,3, *NZ* 1,2, 1991 *S, I, W* 1, *E, R, US* 1,2, *W* 2, [*R, Fj, C*], 1993 *E, S, I*
Camberabero, G (La Voulte) 1961 *NZ* 3, 1962 *R*, 1964 *R*, 1967 *A, E, It, W, I, SA* 1,3,4, 1968 *S, E, W*
Camberabero, L (La Voulte) 1964 *R*, 1965 *S, I*, 1966 *E, W*, 1967 *A, E, It, W, I*, 1968 *S, E, W*
Cambré, T (Oloron) 1920 *E, W, I, US*
Camel, A (Toulouse) 1928 *S, A, I, E, G, W*, 1929 *W, E, G*, 1930 *S, I, E, G, W*, 1935 *G*

Camel, M (Toulouse) 1929 *S, W, E*
Camicas, F (Tarbes) 1927 *G* 2, 1928 *S, I, E, G, W*, 1929 *I, S, W, E*
Camo, E (Villeneuve) 1931 *I, S, W, E, G*, 1932 *G*
Campaes, A (Lourdes) 1965 *W*, 1967 *NZ*, 1968 *S, I, E, W, Cz, NZ* 1,2, *A*, 1969 *S, W*, 1972 *R*, 1973 *NZ*
Campan, O (Agen) 1993 *SA* 1(R),2(R), *R* 2(R), 1996 *I, W* 1, *R*
Cantoni, J (Béziers) 1970 *W, R*, 1971 *S, I, E, W, SA* 1,2, *R*, 1972 *S, I* 1, 1973 *S, NZ, W, I*, 1975 *W* (R)
Capdouze, J (Pau) 1964 *SA, Fj, R*, 1965 *S, I, E*
Capendeguy, J-M (Bègles) 1967 *NZ, R*
Capitani, P (Toulon) 1954 *Arg* 1,2
Capmau, J-L (Toulouse) 1914 *E*
Carabignac, G (Agen) 1951 *S, I*, 1952 *SA, W, E*, 1953 *S, I*
Carbonne, J (Perpignan) 1927 *W*
Carbonneau, P (Toulouse, Brive, Pau) 1995 *R* 2, *Arg, NZ* 1,2, 1996 *E, S, R* (R), *Arg* 2, *W* 2, *SA* 1, 1997 *I* (R), *W, E, S* (R), *R* 1(R), *A* 1,2, 1998 *E, S, I, W, Arg* 1,2, *Fj, Arg* 3, *A*, 1999 *I, W* 1, *E, S*, 2000 *NZ* 2(R), 2001 *I*
Carminati, A (Béziers, Brive) 1986 *R* 2, *NZ* 2, 1987 [*R, Z*], 1988 *I, W, Arg* 1,2, 1989 *I, W, S, NZ* 1(R),2, *A* 2, 1990 *S*, 1995 *It, R* 2, *Arg, NZ* 1,2
Caron, L (Lyon O, Castres) 1947 *E*, 1948 *I, A, W, E*, 1949 *S, I, E, W, Arg* 1
Carpentier, M (Lourdes) 1980 *E, SA, R*, 1981 *S, I, A* 1, 1982 *E, S*
Carrère, C (Toulon) 1966 *R*, 1967 *S, A, E, W, I, SA* 1,3,4, *NZ, R*, 1968 *S, I, E, W, Cz, NZ* 3, *A, R*, 1969 *S, I*, 1970 *S, I, W, E*, 1971 *E, W*
Carrère, J (Vichy, Toulon) 1956 *S*, 1957 *E, W, R* 2, 1958 *S, SA* 1,2, 1959 *I*
Carrère, R (Mont-de-Marsan) 1953 *E, It*
Casadei, D (Brive) 1997 *S, R* 1, *SA* 2(R)
Casaux, L (Tarbes) 1959 *I, It*, 1962 *S*
Cassagne, P (Pau) 1957 *It*
Cassayet-Armagnac, A (Tarbes, Narbonne) 1920 *S, E, W, US*, 1921 *W, E, I*, 1922 *S, E, W*, 1923 *S, W, E, I*, 1924 *S, E, W, R, US*, 1925 *I, NZ, S, W*, 1926 *S, I, E, W, M*, 1927 *I, S, W*
Cassiède, M (Dax) 1961 *NZ* 3, *A, R*
Castaignède, S (Mont-de-Marsan) 1999 *W* 2, [*C* (R), *Nm* (R), *Fj, Arg NZ* 2(R), *A* (R)]
Castaignède, T (Toulouse, Castres) 1995 *R* 2, *Arg, NZ* 1,2, 1996 *E, S, I, W* 1, *Arg* 1,2, 1997 *I, A* 1,2, *It* 2, 1998 *E, S, I, W, Arg* 1,2, *Fj*, 1999 *I, W* 1, *E, S, R, WS, Tg* (R), *NZ* 1, *W* 2, [*C*], 2000 *W, E, S, It*
Castel, R (Toulouse, Béziers) 1996 *I, W* 1, *W* 2, *SA* 1(R),2, 1997 *I* (R), *W, E* (R), *SA* (R), *A* 1(R), 1998 *Arg* 3(R), *A* (R), 1999 *W* 1(R), *E, S*
Castets, J (Toulon) 1923 *W, E, I*
Caujolle, J (Tarbes) 1909 *E*, 1913 *SA, E*, 1914 *W, E*
Caunègre, R (SB) 1938 *R, G* 2
Caussade, A (Lourdes) 1978 *R*, 1979 *I, W, E, NZ* 1,2, *R*, 1980 *W, E, S*, 1981 *S* (R), *I*
Caussarieu, G (Pau) 1929 *I*
Cayrefourcq, E (Tarbes) 1921 *E*
Cazalbou, J (Toulouse) 1997 *It* 2(R), *R* 2, *Arg, SA* 2(R)
Cazals, P (Mont-de-Marsan) 1961 *NZ* 1, *A, R*
Cazenave, A (Pau) 1927 *E, G* 1, 1928 *S, A, G*
Cazenave, F (RCF) 1950 *E, NZ* 2, 1952 *S*, 1954 *I, NZ, W, E*
Cecillon, M (Bourgoin) 1988 *I, W, Arg* 2,3,4, *R*, 1989 *I, E, NZ* 1,2, *A* 1, 1991 *S, I, E* (R), *R, US* 1, *W* 2, [*E*], 1992 *W, E, S, I, R, Arg* 1,2, *SA* 1,2, 1993 *E, S, I, W, R* 1, *SA* 1,2, *R* 2, *A* 1,2, 1994 *I, W, NZ* 1(R), 1995 *I, R* 1, [*Tg, S* (R), *I, SA*]
Celaya, M (Biarritz O, SBUC) 1953 *E, W, It*, 1954 *I, E, It, Arg* 1,2, 1955 *S, I, E, W, It*, 1956 *S, I, W, It, E, Cz* 1957 *S, I, E, W, R* 2, 1958 *S, E, A, W, It, R*, 1959 *S, E*, 1960 *S, E, W, I, R, Arg* 1,2,3, 1961 *S, SA, E, W, It, I, NZ* 1,2,3, *A, R*
Celhay, M (Bayonne) 1935 *G*, 1936 *G* 1, 1937 *G, It*, 1938 *G* 1, 1940 *B*
Cermeno, F (Perpignan) 2000 *R*
Cessieux, R (Lyon) 1906 *NZ*
Cester, E (TOEC, Valence) 1966 *S, I, E*, 1967 *W*, 1968 *S, I, E, W, Cz, NZ* 1,3, *A, SA* 1,2, *R*, 1969 *S, I, E, W, I, R*, 1971 *A* 1, 1972 *R*, 1973 *S, NZ, W, I, J, R*, 1974 *I, W, E, S*
Chabal, S (Bourgoin) 2000 *S*, 2001 *SA* 1,2, *NZ* (R), *Fj* (R), 2002 *Arg* (R), *A* 2
Chaban-Delmas, J (CASG) 1945 *B* 2
Chabowski, H (Nice, Bourgoin) 1985 *Arg* 2, 1986 *R* 2, *NZ* 2, 1989 *B* (R)
Chadebech, P (Brive) 1982 *R, Arg* 1,2, 1986 *S, I*

Champ, E (Toulon) 1985 *Arg* 1,2, 1986 *I, W, E, R* 1, *Arg* 1,2, *A, NZ* 1, *R* 2, *NZ* 2,3, 1987 *W, E, S, I*, [*S, R, Fj, A, NZ*], *R*, 1988 *E, S, Arg* 1,3,4, *R*, 1989 *W, S, A* 1,2, 1990 *W, E, NZ* 1, 1991 *R, US* 1, [*R, Fj, C, E*]
Chapuy, L (SF) 1926 *S*
Charpentier, G (SF) 1911 *E*, 1912 *W, E*
Charton, P (Montferrand) 1940 *B*
Charvet, D (Toulouse) 1986 *W, E, R* 1, *Arg* 1, *A, NZ* 1,3, 1987 *W, E, S, I*, [*S, R, Z, Fj, A, NZ*], *R*, 1989 *E* (R), 1990 *W, E*, 1991 *S, I*
Chassagne, J (Montferrand) 1938 *G* 1
Chatau, A (Bayonne) 1913 *SA*
Chaud, E (Toulon) 1932 *G*, 1934 *G*, 1935 *G*
Chazalet, A (Bourgoin) 1999 *Tg*
Chenevay, C (Grenoble) 1968 *SA* 1
Chevallier, B (Montferrand) 1952 *S, I, SA, W, E, It*, 1953 *E, W, It*, 1954 *S, I, NZ, W, Arg* 1, 1955 *S, I, E, W, It*, 1956 *S, I, W, It, E, Cz*, 1957 *S*
Chiberry, J (Chambéry) 1955 *It*
Chilo, A (RCF) 1920 *S, W*, 1925 *I, NZ*
Cholley, G (Castres) 1975 *E, S, I, SA* 1,2, *Arg* 1,2, *R*, 1976 *S, I, W, E, A* 1,2, *R*, 1977 *W, E, S, I, Arg* 1,2, *NZ* 1,2, *R*, 1978 *E, S, I, W, R*, 1979 *I, S*
Choy J (Narbonne) 1930 *S, I, E, G, W*, 1931 *I*, 1933 *G*, 1934 *G*, 1935 *G*, 1936 *G* 2
Cigagna, A (Toulouse) 1995 [*E*]
Cimarosti, J (Castres) 1976 *US* (R)
Cistacq, J-C (Agen) 2000 *R* (R)
Clady, A (Lezignan) 1929 *G*, 1931 *I, S, E, G*
Clarac, H (St Girons) 1938 *G* 1
Claudel, R (Lyon) 1932 *G*, 1934 *G*
Clauzel, F (Béziers) 1924 *E, W*, 1925 *W*
Clavé, J (Agen) 1936 *G* 2, 1938 *R, G* 2
Claverie, H (Lourdes) 1954 *NZ, W*
Cléda, T (Pau) 1998 *E* (R), *S* (R), *I* (R), *W* (R), *Arg* 1(R), *Fj* (R), *Arg* 3(R), 1999 *I* (R), *S*
Clément, G (RCF) 1931 *W*
Clément, J (RCF) 1921 *S, W, E*, 1922 *S, E, W, I*, 1923 *S, W, I*
Clemente, M (Oloron) 1978 *R*, 1980 *S, I*
Cluchague, L (Biarritz O) 1924 *S*, 1925 *E*
Coderc, J (Chalon) 1932 *G*, 1933 *G*, 1934 *G*, 1935 *G*, 1936 *G* 1
Codorniou, D (Narbonne) 1979 *NZ* 1,2, *R*, 1980 *W, E, S, I*, 1981 *S, W, E, A* 2, 1983 *E, S, I, W, A* 1,2, 1984 *I, W, E, S, NZ* 1,2, *R*, 1985 *E, S, I, W, Arg* 1,2
Coeurveille, C (Agen) 1992 *Arg* 1(R),2
Cognet, L (Montferrand) 1932 *G*, 1936 *W* 1,2, 1937 *G, It*
Collazo, P (Bègles) 2000 *R*
Colombier, J (St Junien) 1952 *SA, W, E*
Colomine, G (Narbonne) 1979 *NZ* 1
Comba, F (SF) 1998 *Arg* 1,2, *Fj, Arg* 3, 1999 *I, W* 1, *E, S*, 2000 *A, NZ* 1,2, 2001 *S, I*
Combe, J (SF) 1910 *S, E, I*, 1911 *S*
Combes, G (Fumel) 1945 *B* 2
Communeau, M (SF) 1906 *NZ, E*, 1907 *E*, 1908 *E, W*, 1909 *E, W, I*, 1910 *S, E, I*, 1911 *S, E, I*, 1912 *I, S, W, E*, 1913 *SA, E, W*
Condom, J (Boucau, Biarritz O) 1982 *R*, 1983 *E, S, I, W, A* 1,2, *R*, 1984 *I, W, E, S, NZ* 1,2, *R*, 1985 *E, S, I, W, Arg* 1,2, 1986 *S, I, W, E, R* 1, *Arg* 1,2, *NZ* 1, *R* 2, *NZ* 2,3, 1987 *W, E, S, I*, [*S, R, Z, A, NZ*], *R*, 1988 *E, S, W, Arg* 1,2,3,4, 1989 *I, W, E, S, NZ* 1,2, *A* 1, 1990 *I, R, A* 2,3(R)
Conilh de Beyssac, J-J (SBUC) 1912 *I, S*, 1914 *I, W, E*
Constant, G (Perpignan) 1920 *W*
Coscolla, G (Béziers) 1921 *S, W*
Costantino, J (Montferrand) 1973 *R*
Costes, A (Montferrand) 1994 *C* 2, 1995 *R* 1, [*Iv*], 1997 *It* 1, 1999 *WS, Tg* (R), *NZ* 1, [*Nm* (R), *Fj* (R), *Arg* (R), *NZ* 2(R), *A* (t&R)], 2000 *S* (R), *I*
Costes, F (Montferrand) 1979 *E, S, NZ* 1,2, *R*, 1980 *W, I*
Couffignal, H (Colomiers) 1993 *R* 1
Coulon, E (Grenoble) 1928 *S*
Courtiols, M (Bègles) 1991 *R, US* 1, *W* 2
Crabos, R (RCF) 1920 *S, E, W, I, US*, 1921 *S, W, E, I*, 1922 *S, E, W, I*, 1923 *S, I*, 1924 *S, I*
Crampagne, J (Bègles) 1967 *SA* 4
Crancee, R (Lourdes) 1960 *Arg* 3, 1961 *S*
Crauste, M (RCF, Lourdes) 1957 *R* 1,2, 1958 *S, E, A, W, It, I*, 1959 *E, It, W, I*, 1960 *S, E, W, I, It, R, Arg* 1,3, 1961 *S, SA, E, W, It, I, NZ* 1,2,3, *A, R*, 1962 *S, E, W, I, It, R*, 1963 *S, I, E, W, It, R*, 1964 *S, NZ, E, W, It, I, SA, Fj, R*, 1965 *S, I, E, W, It, R*, 1966 *S, I, E, W, It*

Cremaschi, M (Lourdes) 1980 *R*, 1981 *R, NZ* 1,2, 1982 *W, S*, 1983 *A* 1,2, *R*, 1984 *I, W*
Crenca, J-J (Agen) 1996 *SA* 2(R), 1999 *R, Tg, WS* (R), *NZ* 1(R), 2001 *SA* 1,2, *NZ* (R), *SA* 3, *A, Fj*, 2002 *It, W, E, S, I, Arg, A* 2
Crichton, W H (Le Havre) 1906 *NZ, E*
Cristina, J (Montferrand) 1979 *R*
Cussac, P (Biarritz O) 1934 *G*
Cutzach, A (Quillan) 1929 *G*

Daguerre, F (Biarritz O) 1936 *G* 1
Daguerre, J (CASG) 1933 *G*
Dal Maso, M (Mont-de-Marsan, Agen, Colomiers) 1988 *R* (R), 1990 *NZ* 2, 1996 *SA* 1(R),2, 1997 *I, W, E, S, It* 1, *R* 1(R), *A* 1,2, *It* 2, *Arg, SA* 1,2, 1998 *W* (R), *Arg* 1(t), *Fj* (R), 1999 *R* (R), *WS* (R), *Tg, NZ* 1(R), *W* 2(R), [*Nm* (R), *Fj* (R), *Arg* (R), *A* (R)], 2000 *W, E, S, I, It*
Danion, J (Toulon) 1924 *I*
Danos, P (Toulon, Béziers) 1954 *Arg* 1,2, 1957 *R* 2, 1958 *S, E, W, It, I, SA* 1,2, 1959 *S, E, It, W, I*, 1960 *S, E*
Dantiacq, D (Pau) 1997 *R* 1
Darbos, P (Dax) 1969 *R*
Darracq, R (Dax) 1957 *It*
Darrieussecq, A (Biarritz O) 1973 *E*
Darrieussecq, J (Mont-de-Marsan) 1953 *It*
Darrouy, C (Mont-de-Marsan) 1957 *I, E, W, It, R* 1, 1959 *E*, 1961 *R*, 1963 *S, I, E, W, It*, 1964 *NZ, E, W, It, I, SA, Fj, R*, 1965 *S, I, E, It, R*, 1966 *S, I, E, W, It, R*, 1967 *S, A, E, It, W, I, SA* 1,2,4
Daudé, J (Bourgoin) 2000 *S*
Daudignon, G (SF) 1928 *S*
Dauga, B (Mont-de-Marsan) 1964 *S, NZ, E, W, It, I, SA, Fj, R*, 1965 *S, I, E, W, It, R*, 1966 *S, I, E, W, It, R*, 1967 *S, A, E, It, W, I, SA* 1,2,3,4, *NZ, R*, 1968 *S, I, NZ* 1,2,3, *A, SA* 1,2, *R*, 1969 *S, I, E, R*, 1970 *S, I, W, E, R*, 1971 *S, I, E, W, SA* 1,2, *A* 1,2, *R*, 1972 *S, I* 1, *W*
Dauger, J (Bayonne) 1945 *B* 1,2, 1953 *S*
Daulouede, P (Tyrosse) 1937 *G, It*, 1938 *G* 1, 1940 *B*
De Besombes, S (Perpignan) 1998 *Arg* 1(R), *Fj* (R)
Decamps, P (RCF) 1911 *S*
Dedet, J (SF) 1910 *S, E, I*, 1911 *W, I*, 1912 *S*, 1913 *E, I*
Dedeyn, P (RCF) 1906 *NZ*
Dedieu, P (Béziers) 1963 *E, It*, 1964 *W, It, I, SA, Fj, R*, 1965 *S, I, E, W*
De Gregorio, J (Grenoble) 1960 *S, E, W, I, It, R, Arg* 1,2, 1961 *S, SA, E, W, I, It*, 1962 *S, E, W*, 1963 *S, W, It*, 1964 *NZ, E*
Dehez, J-L (Agen) 1967 *SA* 2, 1969 *R*
De Jouvencel, E (SF) 1909 *W, I*
De Laborderie, M (RCF) 1921 *I*, 1922 *I*, 1925 *W, E*
Delage, C (Agen) 1983 *S, I*
De Malherbe, H (CASG) 1932 *G*, 1933 *G*
De Malmann, R (RCF) 1908 *E, W*, 1909 *E, W, I*, 1910 *E, I*
De Muizon, J J (SF) 1910 *I*
Delaigue, G (Toulon) 1973 *J, R*
Delaigue, Y (Toulon) 1994 *S, NZ* 2(R), *C* 2, 1995 *I, R* 1, [*Tg, Iv*], *It, R* 2(R), 1997 *It* 1
Delmotte, G (Toulon) 1999 *R, Tg*
Delque, A (Toulouse) 1937 *It*, 1938 *G* 1, *R, G* 2
De Rougemont, M (Toulon) 1995 *E* (t), *R* 1(t), [*Iv*], *NZ* 1,2, 1996 *I* (R), *Arg* 1,2, *W* 2, *SA* 1, 1997 *E* (R), *S* (R), *It* 1
Desbrosse, C (Toulouse) 1999 [*Nm* (R)], 2000 *I*
Descamps, P (SB) 1927 *G* 2
Desclaux, F (RCF) 1949 *Arg* 1,2, 1953 *It*
Desclaux, J (Perpignan) 1934 *G*, 1935 *G*, 1936 *G* 1,2, 1937 *G, It*, 1938 *G* 1, *R, G* 2, 1945 *B* 1
Deslandes, C (RCF) 1990 *A* 1, *NZ* 2, 1991 *W* 1, 1992 *R, Arg* 1,2
Desnoyer, L (Brive) 1974 *R*
Destarac, L (Tarbes) 1926 *S, I, E, W, M*, 1927 *W, E, G* 1,2
Desvouges, R (SF) 1914 *W*
Detrez, P-E (Nîmes) 1983 *A* 2(R), 1986 *Arg* 1(R),2, *A* (R), *NZ* 1
Devergie, T (Nîmes) 1988 *R*, 1989 *NZ* 1,2, *B, A* 2, 1990 *W, E, S, I, R, A* 1,2,3, 1991 *US* 2, *W* 2, 1992 *R, A, Arg* 2(R)
De Villiers, P (SF) 1999 *W* 2, [*Arg* (R), *NZ* 2(R), *A* (R)], 2000 *W* (R), *E* (R), *S* (R), *I* (R), *It, NZ* 1,2, 2001 *S, I, It, W, E, SA* 1,2, *NZ* (R), *SA* 3, *A, Fj*, 2002 *It, W, E, I*
Deygas, M (Vienne) 1937 *It*
Deylaud, C (Toulouse) 1992 *R, Arg* 1,2, *SA* 1, 1994 *C* 1, *NZ* 1,2, 1995 *W, E, S*, [*Iv* (R), *S, I, SA*], *It, Arg*
Dintrans, P (Tarbes) 1979 *NZ* 1,2, *R*, 1980 *E, S, I, SA, R*, 1981 *S, I, W, E, A* 1,2, *R, NZ* 1,2, 1982 *W, E, S, I, R, Arg* 1,2,

1983 *E, W, A* 1,2, *R*, 1984 *I, W, E, S, NZ* 1,2, *R*, 1985 *E, S, I, W, Arg* 1,2, 1987 [*R*], 1988 *Arg* 1,2,3, 1989 *W, E, S*, 1990 *R*
Dispagne, S (Toulouse) 1996 *I* (R), *W* 1
Dizabo, P (Tyrosse) 1948 *A, S, E*, 1949 *S, I, E, W, Arg* 2, 1950 *S, I*, 1960 *Arg* 1,2,3
Domec, A (Carcassonne) 1929 *W*
Domec, H (Lourdes) 1953 *W, It*, 1954 *S, I, NZ, W, E, It*, 1955 *S, I, E, W*, 1956 *I, W, It*, 1958 *E, A, W, It, I*
Domenech, A (Vichy, Brive) 1954 *W, E, It*, 1955 *S, I, E, W*, 1956 *S, I, W, It, E, Cz*, 1957 *S, I, E, W, It, R* 1,2, 1958 *S, E, It*, 1959 *It*, 1960 *S, E, W, I, It, R, Arg* 1,2,3, 1961 *S, SA, E, W, It, I, NZ* 1,2,3, *A, R*, 1962 *S, E, W, I, It, R*, 1963 *W, It*
Domercq, J (Bayonne) 1912 *I, S*
Dominici, C (SF) 1998 *E, S, Arg* 1,2, 1999 *E, S, WS, NZ* 1, *W* 2, [*C, Fj, Arg, NZ* 2, *A*], 2000 *W, E, S, R*, 2001 *I* (R), *It, W, E, SA* 1,2, *NZ, Fj*
Dorot, J (RCF) 1935 *G*
Dospital, P (Bayonne) 1977 *R*, 1980 *I*, 1981 *S, I, W, E*, 1982 *I, R, Arg* 1,2, 1983 *E, S, I, W*, 1984 *E, S, NZ* 1,2, *R*, 1985 *E, S, I, W, Arg* 1
Dourthe, C (Dax) 1966 *R*, 1967 *S, A, E, W, I, SA* 1,2,3, *NZ*, 1968 *W, NZ* 3, *SA* 1,2, 1969 *W*, 1971 *SA* 2(R), *R*, 1972 *I* 1,2, *A* 1,2, *R*, 1973 *S, NZ, E*, 1974 *I, Arg* 1,2, *SA* 1,2, 1975 *W, E, S*
Dourthe, M (Dax) 2000 *NZ* 2(t)
Dourthe, R (Dax, SF, Béziers) 1995 *R* 2, *Arg, NZ* 1,2, 1996 *E, R*, 1996 *Arg* 1,2, *W* 2, *SA* 1,2, 1997 *W, A* 1, 1999 *I, W* 1,2, [*C, Nm, Fj, Arg, NZ* 2, *A*], 2000 *W, E, It, R, A, NZ* 1,2, 2001 *S, I*
Doussau, E (Angoulême) 1938 *R*
Droitecourt, M (Montferrand) 1972 *R*, 1973 *NZ* (R), *E*, 1974 *E, S, Arg* 1, *SA* 2, 1975 *SA* 1,2, *Arg* 1,2, *R*, 1976 *S, I, W, A* 1, 1977 *Arg* 2
Dubertrand, A (Montferrand) 1971 *A* 1,2, *R*, 1972 *I* 2, 1974 *I, W, E, SA* 2, 1975 *Arg* 1,2, *R*, 1976 *S, US*
Dubois, D (Bègles) 1971 *S*
Dubroca, D (Agen) 1979 *NZ* 2, 1981 *NZ* 2(R), 1982 *E, S*, 1984 *W, E*, 1985 *Arg* 2, 1986 *S, I, W, E, I, Arg* 2, *A, NZ* 1, *R* 2, *NZ* 2,3, 1987 *W, E, S, I*, [*S, Z, Fj, A, NZ*], *R*, 1988 *E, S, I, W*
Duché, A (Limoges) 1929 *G*
Duclos, A (Lourdes) 1931 *S*
Ducousso, J (Tarbes) 1925 *S, W, E*
Dufau, G (RCF) 1948 *I, A*, 1949 *I, W*, 1950 *S, E, W*, 1951 *S, I, E, W*, 1952 *SA, W*, 1953 *S, I, E, W*, 1954 *S, I, NZ, W, E, It*, 1955 *S, I, E, W, It*, 1956 *S, I, W, It*, 1957 *S, I, E, W, It, R* 1
Dufau, J (Biarritz) 1912 *I, S, W, E*
Duffaut, Y (Agen) 1954 *Arg* 1,2
Duffour, R (Tarbes) 1911 *W*
Dufourcq, J (SBUC) 1906 *NZ, E*, 1907 *E*, 1908 *W*
Duhard, Y (Bagnères) 1980 *E*
Duhau, J (SF) 1928 *I*,1930 *I, G*, 1931 *I, S, W*, 1933 *G*
Dulaurens, C (Toulouse) 1926 *I*, 1928 *S*, 1929 *W*
Duluc, A (Béziers) 1934 *E*
Du Manoir, Y le P (RCF) 1925 *I, NZ, S, W, E*, 1926 *S*, 1927 *I, S*
Dupont, C (Lourdes) 1923 *S, W, I*, 1924 *S, I, W, R, US*, 1925 *S*, 1927 *E, G* 1,2, 1928 *A, G, W*, 1929 *I*
Dupont, J-L (Agen) 1983 *E*
Dupont, L (RCF) 1934 *G*, 1935 *G*, 1936 *G* 1,2, 1938 *R, G* 2
Dupouy, A (SB) 1924 *W, R*
Duprat, B (Bayonne) 1966 *E, W, It, R*, 1967 *S, A, E, SA* 2,3, 1968 *S, I*, 1972 *E, W, I* 2, *A* 1
Dupré, P (RCF) 1909 *W*
Dupuy, J (Tarbes) 1956 *S, I, W, It, E, Cz*, 1957 *S, I, E, W, It, R* 2, 1958 *S, E, SA* 1,2, 1959 *S, E, It, W, I*, 1960 *W, I, It, Arg* 1,3, 1961 *S, SA, E, NZ* 2, *R*, 1962 *S, E, W, I, It*, 1963 *W, It, R*, 1964 *S*
Du Souich, C J (see Judas du Souich)
Dutin, B (Mont-de-Marsan) 1968 *NZ* 2, *A, SA* 2, *R*
Dutour, F X (Toulouse) 1911 *E, I*, 1912 *S, W, E*, 1913 *S*
Dutrain, H (Toulouse) 1945 *W*, 1946 *B, I*, 1947 *E*, 1949 *I, E, W, Arg* 1
Dutrey, J (Lourdes) 1940 *B*
Duval, R (SF) 1908 *E, W*, 1909 *E*, 1911 *E, W, I*

Echavé, L (Agen) 1961 *S*
Elhorga, P (Agen) 2001 *NZ*, 2002 *A* 1,2
Elissalde, E (Bayonne) 1936 *G* 2, 1940 *B*
Elissalde, J-B (La Rochelle) 2000 *S* (R), *R* (R)
Elissalde, J-P (La Rochelle) 1980 *SA, W*, 1981 *A* 1,2, *R*
Empereur-Buisson, H (Béziers) 1931 *E, G*
Erbani, D (Agen) 1981 *A* 1,2, *NZ* 1,2, 1982 *Arg* 1,2, 1983 *S* (R), *I, W, A* 1,2, *R*, 1984 *W, E, R*, 1985 *E, W* (R), *Arg* 2, 1986

S, I, W, E, R 1, *Arg* 2, *NZ* 1,2(R),3, 1987 W, E, S, I, [S, R, Fj, A, NZ], 1988 E, S, 1989 I (R), W, E, S, NZ 1, A 2, 1990 W, E
Escaffre, P (Narbonne) 1933 G, 1934 G
Escommier, M (Montelimar) 1955 *It*
Esponda, J-M (RCF) 1967 *SA* 1,2, R, 1968 *NZ* 1,2, *SA* 2, R, 1969 S, I (R), E
Estève, A (Béziers) 1971 *SA* 1, 1972 I 1, E, W, I 2, A 2, R, 1973 S, NZ, E, I, 1974 I, W, E, S, R, SA 1,2, 1975 W, E
Estève, P (Narbonne, Lavelanet) 1982 R, *Arg* 1,2, 1983 E, S, I, W, A 1,2, R, 1984 I, W, E, S, NZ 1,2, R, 1985 E, S, I, W, 1986 S, I 1987 [S, Z]
Etcheberry, J (Rochefort, Cognac) 1923 W, I, 1924 S, I, E, W, R, US, 1926 S, I, E, M, 1927 I, S, W, G 2
Etchenique, J-M (Biarritz O) 1974 R, SA 1, 1975 E, *Arg* 2
Etchepare, A (Bayonne) 1922 I
Etcheverry, M (Pau) 1971 S, I
Eutrope, A (SCUF) 1913 I

Fabre, E (Toulouse) 1937 *It*, 1938 G 1,2
Fabre, J (Toulouse) 1963 S, I, E, W, *It*, 1964 S, NZ, E
Fabre, L (Lezignan) 1930 G
Fabre, M (Béziers) 1981 A 1, R, NZ 1,2, 1982 I, R
Failliot, P (RCF) 1911 S, W, I, 1912 I, S, E, 1913 E, W
Fargues, G (Dax) 1923 I
Fauré, F (Tarbes) 1914 I, W, E
Fauvel, J-P (Tulle) 1980 R
Favre, M (Lyon) 1913 E, W
Ferrand, L (Chalon) 1940 B
Ferrien, R (Tarbes) 1950 S, I, E, W
Finat, R (CASG) 1932 G, 1933 G
Fite, R (Brive) 1963 W, *It*
Forestier, J (SCUF) 1912 W
Forgues, F (Bayonne) 1911 S, E, W, 1912 I, W, E, 1913 S, SA, W, 1914 I, E
Fort, J (Agen) 1967 *It*, W, I, SA 1,2,3,4
Fourcade, G (BEC) 1909 E, W
Foures, H (Toulouse) 1951 S, I, E, W
Fournet, F (Montferrand) 1950 W
Fouroux, J (La Voulte) 1972 I 2, R, 1974 W, E, *Arg* 1,2, R, SA 1,2, 1975 W, *Arg* 1, R, 1976 S, I, W, E, US, A 1, 1977 W, E, S, I, *Arg* 1,2, NZ 1,2, R
Francquenelle, A (Vaugirard) 1911 S, 1913 W, I
Furcade, R (Perpignan) 1952 S

Gabernet, S (Toulouse) 1980 E, S, 1981 S, I, W, E, A 1,2, R, NZ 1,2, 1982 I, 1983 A 2, R
Gachassin, J (Lourdes) 1961 S, I, 1963 R, 1964 S, NZ, E, W, *It*, I, SA, Fj, R, 1965 S, I, E, W, *It*, R, 1966 S, I, E, W, 1967 S, A, I, W, I, 1968 I, E, 1969 S, I
Galasso, A (Toulon, Montferrand) 2000 R (R), 2001 E (R)
Galau, H (Toulouse) 1924 S, I, E, W, US
Galia, J (Quillan) 1927 E, G 1,2, 1928 S, A, I, E, W, 1929 I, E, G, 1930 S, I, E, G, W, 1931 S, W, E, G
Gallart, P (Béziers) 1990 R, A 1,2(R),3, 1992 S, I, R, *Arg* 1,2, SA 1,2, 1994 I, W, E, 1995 I (t), R 1, [Tg]
Gallion, J (Toulon) 1978 E, S, I, W, 1979 I, W, E, S, NZ 2, R, 1980 W, E, S, I, 1983 A 1,2, R, 1984 I, W, E, S, R, 1985 E, S, I, W, 1986 *Arg* 2
Galthié, F (Colomiers, SF) 1991 R, US 1, [R, Fj, C, E], 1992 W, E, S, R, *Arg*, 1994 I, W, E, 1995 [SA, E], 1996 W 1(R), 1997 I, *It* 2, SA 1,2, 1998 W (R), Fj (R), 1999 R, WS (R), Tg, NZ 1(R), [Fj (R), *Arg*, NZ 2, A], 2000 W, E, A, NZ 1,2, 2001 S, *It*, W, E, SA 1,2, NZ, SA 3, A, Fj, 2002 E, S, I
Galy, J (Perpignan) 1953 W
Garbajosa, X (Toulouse) 1998 I, W, *Arg* 2(R), Fj, 1999 W 1(R), E, S, WS, NZ 1, W 2, [C, Nm (R), Fj (R), *Arg*, NZ 2, A], 2000 A, NZ 1,2, 2001 S, I, E, 2002 *It* (R), W
Garuet-Lempirou, J-P (Lourdes) 1983 A 1,2, R, 1984 I, NZ 1,2, R, 1985 E, S, I, W, *Arg* 1, 1986 S, I, W, E, R 1, *Arg* 1, NZ 1, R 2, NZ 2,3, 1987 W, E, S, I, [S, R, Fj, A, NZ], 1988 E, S, *Arg* 1, R, 1989 E (R), S, NZ 1,2, 1990 W, E
Gasc, J (Graulhet) 1977 NZ 2
Gasparotto, G (Montferrand) 1976 A 2, R
Gauby, G (Perpignan) 1956 Cz
Gaudermen, P (RCF) 1906 E
Gayraud, W (Toulouse) 1920 I
Gelez, F (Agen) 2001 SA 3, 2002 I (R), A 1
Geneste, R (BEC) 1945 B 1, 1949 *Arg* 2
Genet, J-P (RCF) 1992 S, I, R
Gensane, R (Béziers) 1962 S, E, W, I, *It*, R, 1963 S
Gerald, G (RCF) 1927 E, G 2, 1928 S, 1929 I, S, W, E, G, 1930 S, I, E, G, W, 1931 I, S, E, G
Gérard, D (Bègles) 1999 Tg

Gerintes, G (CASG) 1924 R, 1925 I, 1926 W
Geschwind, P (RCF) 1936 G 1,2
Giacardy, M (SBUC) 1907 E
Gimbert, P (Bègles) 1991 R, US 1, 1992 W, E
Giordani, P (Dax) 1999 E, S
Glas, S (Bourgoin) 1996 S (t), I (R), W 1, R, *Arg* 2(R), W 2, SA 1,2, 1997 I, W, E, S, *It* 2(R), R 2, *Arg*, SA 1,2, 1998 E, S, I, W, *Arg* 1,2, Fj, *Arg* 3, A, 1999 W 2, [C,Nm, *Arg* (R), NZ 2(R), A (t&R)], 2000 I, 2001 E, SA 1,2, NZ
Gomès, A (SF) 1998 *Arg* 1,2, Fj, *Arg* 3, A, 1999 I (R)
Gommes, J (RCF) 1910 I
Gonnet, C-A (Albi) 1921 E, I, 1922 E, W, 1924 S, E, 1926 S, I, E, W, M, 1927 I, S, W, G 1
Gonzalez, J-M (Bayonne) 1992 *Arg* 1,2, SA 1,2, *Arg*, 1993 R 1, SA 1,2, R 2, A 1,2, 1994 I, W, E, S, C 1, NZ 1,2, C 2, 1995 W, E, S, I, R 1, [Tg, S, I, SA, E], *It*, *Arg*, 1996 E, S, I, W 1
Got, R (Perpignan) 1920 I, US, 1921 S, W, 1922 S, E, W, I, 1924 I, E, W, R, US
Gourdon, J-F (RCF, Bagnères) 1974 S, *Arg* 1,2, R, SA 1,2, 1975 W, E, S, I, R, 1976 S, I, W, E, 1978 E, S, 1979 W, E, S, R, 1980 I
Gourragne, J-F (Béziers) 1990 NZ 2, 1991 W 1
Goyard, A (Lyon U) 1936 G 1,2, 1937 G, *It*, 1938 G 1, R, G 2
Graciet, R (SBUC) 1926 I, W, 1927 S, G 1, 1929 E, 1930 W
Graou, S (Auch, Colomiers) 1992 *Arg* (R), 1993 SA 1,2, R 2, A 2(R), 1995 R 2, *Arg* (t), NZ 2(R)
Gratton, J (Agen) 1984 NZ 2, R, 1985 E, S, I, W, *Arg* 1,2, 1986 S, NZ 1
Graule, V (Arl Perpignan) 1926 I, E, W, 1927 S, W, 1931 G
Greffe, M (Grenoble) 1968 W, Cz, NZ 1,2, SA 1
Griffard, J (Lyon U) 1932 G, 1933 G, 1934 G
Gruarin, A (Toulon) 1964 W, *It*, I, SA, Fj, R, 1965 S, I, E, W, *It*, 1966 S, I, W, *It*, R, 1967 S, A, E, *It*, W, I, NZ, 1968 S, I
Guelorget, P (RCF) 1931 E, G
Guichemerre, A (Dax) 1920 E, 1921 E, I, 1923 S
Guilbert, A (Toulon) 1975 E, S, I, SA 1,2, 1976 A 1, 1977 *Arg* 1,2, NZ 1,2, R, 1979 I, W, E
Guillemin, P (RCF) 1908 E, W, 1909 E, I, 1910 W, S, E, I, 1911 S, E, W
Guilleux, P (Agen) 1952 SA, *It*
Guiral, M (Agen) 1931 G, 1932 G, 1933 G
Guiraud, H (Nîmes) 1996 R

Haget, A (PUC) 1953 E, 1954 I, NZ, E, *Arg* 2, 1955 E, W, *It*, 1957 I, E, *It*, R 1, 1958 *It*, SA 2
Haget, F (Agen, Biarritz O) 1974 *Arg* 1,2, 1975 SA 2, *Arg* 1,2, R, 1976 S, 1978 S, I, W, 1979 I, W, E, S, NZ 1,2, R, 1980 W, S, I, 1984 S, NZ 1,2, R, 1985 E, S, I, 1986 S, I, W, E, R 1, *Arg* 1, A, NZ 1, 1987 S, I, [R, Fj]
Haget, H (CASG) 1928 S, 1930 G
Halet, R (Strasbourg) 1925 NZ, S, W
Hall, S (Béziers) 2002 *It*, W
Harinordoquy, I (Pau) 2002 W, E, S, I, A 1,2
Harislur-Arthapignet, P (Tarbes) 1988 *Arg* 4(R)
Harize, D (Cahors, Toulouse) 1975 SA 1,2, 1976 A 1,2, R, 1977 W, E, S, I
Hauc, J (Toulon) 1928 E, G, 1929 I, S, G
Hauser, M (Lourdes) 1969 E
Hedembaigt, M (Bayonne) 1913 S, SA, 1914 W
Hericé, D (Bègles) 1950 I
Herrero, A (Toulon) 1963 R, 1964 NZ, E, W, *It*, I, SA, Fj, R, 1965 S, I, E, W, 1966 W, *It*, R, 1967 S, A, E, *It*, I, R
Herrero, B (Nice) 1983 I, 1986 *Arg* 1
Heyer, F (Montferrand) 1990 A 2
Heymans, C (Agen) 2000 *It* (R) R, 2002 A 2(R)
Hiquet, J-C (Agen) 1964 E
Hoche, M (PUC) 1957 I, E, W, *It*, R 1
Hondagné-Monge, M (Tarbes) 1988 *Arg* 2(R)
Hontas, P (Biarritz) 1990 S, I, R, 1991 R, 1992 *Arg*, 1993 E, S, I, W
Hortoland, J-P (Béziers) 1971 A 2
Houblain, H (SCUF) 1909 E, 1910 W
Houdet, R (SF) 1927 S, W, G 1, 1928 G, W, 1929 I, S, E, 1930 S, E
Hourdebaigt, A (SBUC) 1909 I, 1910 W, S, E, I
Hubert, A (ASF) 1906 E, 1907 E, 1908 E, W, 1909 E, W, I
Hueber, A (Lourdes, Toulon) 1990 A 3, NZ 1, 1991 US 2, 1992 I, *Arg* 1,2, SA 1,2, 1993 E, S, I, W, SA 1,2, R 2, A 1,2, 1995 [Tg, S (R), J], 2000 *It*, W
Hutin, R (CASG) 1927 I, S, W
Hyardet, A (Castres) 1995 *It*, *Arg* (R)

Ibanez, R (Dax, Perpignan, Castres) 1996 *W* 1(R), 1997 *It* 1(R), *R* 1, *It* 2(R), *R* 2, *SA* 2(R), 1998 *E, S, I, W, Arg* 1,2, *Fj, Arg* 3, *A*, 1999 *I, W* 1, *E, S, R, WS, Tg* (R), *NZ* 1, *W* 2, [*C, Nm, Fj, Arg, NZ* 2, *A*], 2000 *W* (R), *E* (R), *S* (R), *I* (R), *It* (R), *R*, 2001 *S, I, It, W, E, SA* 1,2, *NZ* (R), *SA* 3, *A, Fj*, 2002 *It* (R), *W, E, S, I, Arg, A* 1(R),2
Icard, J (SF) 1909 *E, W*
Iguiniz, E (Bayonne) 1914 *E*
Ihingoué, D (BEC) 1912 *I, S*
Imbernon, J-F (Perpignan) 1976 *I, W, E, US, A* 1, 1977 *W, E, S, I, Arg* 1,2, *NZ* 1,2, 1978 *E, R*, 1979 *I*, 1981 *S, I, W, E*, 1982 *I*, 1983 *I, W*
Iraçabal, J (Bayonne) 1968 *NZ* 1,2, *SA* 1, 1969 *S, I, W, R*, 1970 *S, I, W, E, R*, 1971 *W, SA* 1,2, *A* 1, 1972 *E, W, I* 2, *A* 2, *R*, 1973 *S, NZ, E, W, I, J*, 1974 *I, W, E, S, Arg* 1,2, *SA* 2(R)
Isaac, H (RCF) 1907 *E*, 1908 *E*
Ithurra, E (Biarritz O) 1936 *G* 1,2, 1937 *G*

Janeczek, T (Tarbes) 1982 *Arg* 1,2, 1990 *R*
Janik, K (Toulouse) 1987 *R*
Jarasse, A (Brive) 1945 *B* 1
Jardel, J (SB) 1928 *I, E*
Jaureguy, A (RCF, Toulouse, SF) 1920 *S, E, W, I, US*, 1922 *S, W*, 1923 *W, E, I*, 1924 *S, W, R, US*, 1925 *I, NZ*, 1926 *S, E, W, M*, 1927 *I, E*, 1928 *S, A, E, G, W*, 1929 *I, S, E*
Jaureguy, P (Toulouse) 1913 *S, SA, W, I*
Jauzion, Y (Colomiers) 2001 *SA* 1,2, *NZ*, 2002 *A* 1(R),2(R)
Jeangrand, M-H (Tarbes) 1921 *I*
Jeanjean, N (Toulouse) 2001 *SA* 1,2, *NZ, SA* 3(R), *A* (R), *Fj* (R), 2002 *It, Arg, A* 1
Jeanjean, P (Toulon) 1948 *I*
Jérôme, J (SF) 1906 *NZ, E*
Joinel, J-L (Brive) 1977 *NZ* 1, 1978 *R*, 1979 *I, W, E, S, NZ* 1,2, *R*, 1980 *W, E, S, I, SA*, 1981 *S, I, W, E, R, NZ* 1,2, 1982 *E, S, I, R*, 1983 *E, S, I, W, A* 1,2, *R*, 1984 *I, W, E, S, NZ* 1,2, 1985 *S, I, W, Arg* 1, 1986 *S, I, W, E, R* 1, *Arg* 1,2, *A*, 1987 [*Z*]
Jol, M (Biarritz O) 1947 *S, I, W, E*, 1949 *S, I, E, W, Arg* 1,2
Jordana, J-L (Pau, Toulouse) 1996 *R* (R), *Arg* 1(t),2, *W* 2, 1997 *I* (t), *W, S* (R)
Judas du Souich, C (SCUF) 1911 *W, I*
Juillet, C (Montferrand, SF) 1995 *R* 2, *Arg*, 1999 *E, S, WS, NZ* 1, [*C, Fj, Arg, NZ* 2, *A*], 2000 *A, NZ* 1,2, 2001 *S, I, It, W, E, SA* 1,2
Junquas, L (Tyrosse) 1945 *B* 1,2, *W*, 1946 *B, I, K, W*, 1947 *S, I, W, E*, 1948 *S, W*

Kaczorowski, D (Le Creusot) 1974 *I* (R)
Kaempf, A (St Jean-de-Luz) 1946 *B*

Labadie, P (Bayonne) 1952 *S, I, SA, W, E, It*, 1953 *S, I, It*, 1954 *S, I, NZ, W, E, Arg* 2, 1955 *S, I, E, W*, 1956 *I*, 1957 *I*
Labarthete, R (Pau) 1952 *S*
Labazuy, A (Lourdes) 1952 *I*, 1954 *S, W*, 1956 *E*, 1958 *A, W, I*, 1959 *S, E, It, W*
Labit, C (Toulouse) 1999 *S, R* (R), *WS* (R), *Tg*, 2000 *R* (R), 2002 *Arg, A* 1(R)
Laborde, C (RCF) 1962 *It, R*, 1963 *R*, 1964 *SA*, 1965 *E*
Labrousse, T (Brive) 1996 *R, SA* 1
Lacans, P (Béziers) 1980 *SA*, 1981 *W, E, A* 2, *R*, 1982 *W*
Lacassagne, H (SBUC) 1906 *NZ*, 1907 *E*
Lacaussade, R (Bègles) 1948 *A, S*
Lacaze, C (Lourdes, Angoulême) 1961 *NZ* 2,3, *A, R*, 1962 *E, W, I, It*, 1963 *W, R*, 1964 *S, NZ, E*, 1965 *It, R*, 1966 *S, I, E, W, It, R*, 1967 *S, E, SA* 1,3,4, *R*, 1968 *S, E, W, Cz, NZ* 1, 1969 *E*
Lacaze, H (Périgueux) 1928 *I, G, W*, 1929 *I, W*
Lacaze, P (Lourdes) 1958 *SA* 1,2, 1959 *S, E, It, W, I*
Lacazedieu, C (Dax) 1923 *W, I*, 1928 *A, I*, 1929 *S*
Lacombe, B (Agen) 1989 *B*, 1990 *A* 2
Lacome, M (Pau) 1960 *Arg* 2
Lacoste, R (Tarbes) 1914 *I, W, E*
Lacrampe, F (Béziers) 1949 *Arg* 2
Lacroix, P (Mont-de-Marsan, Agen) 1958 *A*, 1960 *W, I, It, R, Arg* 1,2,3, 1961 *S, SA, E, W, I, NZ* 1,2,3, *A, R*, 1962 *S, E, W, I, R*, 1963 *I, E, W*
Lacroix, T (Dax, Harlequins) 1989 *A* 1(R),2, 1991 *W* 1(R),2(R), [*R, C* (R), *E*], 1992 *SA* 2, 1993 *E, S, I, W, SA* 1,2, *R* 2, *A* 1,2, 1994 *I, W, E, S, C* 1, *NZ* 1,2, *C* 2, 1995 *W, E, S, R* 1, [*Tg, Iv, S, I, SA, E*], 1996 *E, S, I*, 1997 *It* 2, *R* 2, *Arg, SA* 1,2
Lafarge, Y (Montferrand) 1978 *R*, 1979 *NZ* 1, 1981 *I* (R)
Laffitte, R (SCUF) 1910 *W, S*
Laffont, H (Narbonne) 1926 *W*
Lafond, A (Bayonne) 1922 *E*

Lafond, J-B (RCF) 1983 *A* 1, 1985 *Arg* 1,2 1986 *S, I, W, E, R* 1, 1987 *I* (R), 1988 *W*, 1989 *I, W, E*, 1990 *W, A* 3(R), *NZ* 2, 1991 *S, I, W* 1, *E, R, US* 1, *W* 2, [*R* (R), *Fj, C, E*], 1992 *W, E, S, I* (R), *SA* 2, 1993 *E, S, I, W*
Lagisquet, P (Bayonne) 1983 *A* 1,2, *R*, 1984 *I, W, NZ* 1,2, 1986 *R* 1(R), *Arg* 1,2, *A, NZ* 1, 1987 [*S, R, Fj, A, NZ*], 1988 *S, I, W, Arg* 1,2,3,4, *R*, 1989 *I, W, E, S, NZ* 1,2, *B, A* 1,2, 1990 *W, E, S, I, A* 1,2,3, 1991 *S, I, US* 2, [*R*]
Lagrange, J-C (RCF) 1966 *It*
Lalande, M (RCF) 1923 *S, W, I*
Lalanne, F (Mont-de-Marsan) 2000 *R*
Lamaison, C (Brive, Agen) 1996 *SA* 1(R),2, 1997 *W, E, S, R* 1, *A* 2, *It* 2, *R* 2, *Arg, SA* 1,2, 1998 *E, S, I, W, Arg* 3(R), *A*, 1999 *R, WS* (R), *Tg, NZ* 1(R), *W* 2(R), [*C* (R), *Nm, Fj, Arg, NZ* 2, *A*], 2000 *W, A, NZ* 1,2, 2001 *S, I, It, W* (R)
Landreau, F (SF) 2000 *A, NZ* 1,2, 2001 *E* (R)
Lane, G (RCF) 1906 *NZ, E*, 1907 *E*, 1908 *E, W*, 1909 *E, W, I*, 1910 *W, E*, 1911 *S, W*, 1912 *I, W, E*, 1913 *S*
Langlade, J-C (Hyères) 1990 *R, A* 1, *NZ* 1
Laperne, D (Dax) 1997 *R* 1(R)
Laporte, G (Graulhet) 1981 *I, W, E, R, NZ* 1,2, 1986 *S, I, W, E, R* 1, *Arg* 1, *A* (R), 1987 [*R, Z* (R), *Fj*]
Larreguy, P (Bayonne) 1954 *It*
Larribau, J (Périgueux) 1912 *I, S, W, E*, 1913 *S*, 1914 *I, E*
Larrieu, J (Tarbes) 1920 *I, US*, 1921 *W*, 1923 *S, W, E, I*
Larrieux, M (SBUC) 1927 *G* 2
Larrue, H (Carmaux) 1960 *W, I, It, R, Arg* 1,2,3
Lasaosa, P (Dax) 1950 *I*, 1952 *S, I, E, It*, 1955 *It*
Lascubé, G (Agen) 1991 *S, I, W* 1, *E, US* 2, *W* 2, [*R, Fj, C, E*], 1992 *W, E*
Lassegue, J-B (Toulouse) 1946 *W*, 1947 *S, I, W*, 1948 *W*, 1949 *I, E, W, Arg* 1
Lasserre, F (René) (Bayonne, Cognac, Grenoble) 1914 *I*, 1920 *S*, 1921 *S, W, I*, 1922 *S, E, W, I*, 1923 *W, E, I*, 1924 *S, I, R, US*
Lasserre, J-C (Dax) 1963 *It*, 1964 *S, NZ, E, W, It, I, Fj*, 1965 *W, It, R*, 1966 *R*, 1967 *S*
Lasserre, M (Agen) 1967 *SA* 2,3, 1968 *E, W, Cz, NZ* 3, *A, SA* 1,2, 1969 *S, I, E*, 1970 *E*, 1971 *E, W*
Laterrade, G (Tarbes) 1910 *E, I*, 1911 *S, E, I*
Laudouar, J (Soustons, SBUC) 1961 *NZ* 1,2, *R*, 1962 *I, R*
Lauga, P (Vichy) 1950 *S, I, E, W*
Laurent, A (Biarritz O) 1925 *NZ, S, W, E*, 1926 *W*
Laurent, J (Bayonne) 1920 *S, E, W*
Laurent, M (Auch) 1932 *G*, 1933 *G*, 1934 *G*, 1935 *G*, 1936 *G* 1
Lassucq, C (SF) 1999 *S* (R), 2000 *W* (R), *S, I*
Lavail, G (Perpignan) 1937 *G*, 1940 *B*
Lavaud, R (Carcassonne) 1914 *I, W*
Lavergne, P (Limoges) 1950 *S*
Lavigne, B (Agen) 1984 *R*, 1985 *E*
Lavigne, J (Dax) 1920 *E, W*
Lazies, H (Auch) 1954 *Arg* 2, 1955 *It*, 1956 *E*, 1957 *S*
Le Bourhis, R (La Rochelle) 1961 *R*
Lecointre, M (Nantes) 1952 *It*
Le Droff, J (Auch) 1963 *It*, 1964 *S, NZ, E*, 1970 *E, R*, 1971 *S, I*
Lefevre, R (Brive) 1961 *NZ* 2
Leflamand, L (Bourgoin) 1996 *SA* 2, 1997 *W, E, S, It* 2, *Arg, SA* 1,2(R)
Lefort, J-B (Biarritz O) 1938 *G* 1
Le Goff, R (Métro) 1938 *R, G* 2
Legrain, M (SF) 1909 *I*, 1910 *I*, 1911 *S, E, W, I*, 1913 *S, SA, E, I*, 1914 *I, W*
Lemeur, Y (RCF) 1993 *R* 1
Lenient, J-J (Vichy) 1967 *R*
Lepatey, J (Mazamet) 1954 *It*, 1955 *S, I, E, W*
Lepatey, L (Mazamet) 1924 *S, I, E*
Lescarboura, J-P (Dax) 1982 *W, E, S, I*, 1983 *A* 1,2, *R*, 1984 *I, W, E, S, NZ* 1,2, *R*, 1985 *E, S, I, W, Arg* 1,2, 1986 *Arg* 2, *A, NZ* 1, *R* 2, 1988 *S, W*, 1990 *R*
Lesieur, E (SF) 1906 *E*, 1908 *E, W*, 1909 *E, W, I*, 1910 *S, E, I*, 1911 *E, I*, 1912 *W*
Leuvielle, M (SBUC) 1908 *W*, 1913 *S, SA, E, W*, 1914 *W, E*
Levasseur, R (SF) 1925 *W, E*
Levée, H (RCF) 1906 *NZ*
Lewis, E W (Le Havre) 1906 *E*
Lhermet, J-M (Montferrand) 1990 *S, I*, 1993 *R* 1
Libaros, G (Tarbes) 1936 *G* 1, 1940 *B*
Lievremont, M (Perpignan, SF) 1995 *It, R* 2, *Arg* (R), *NZ* 2(R), 1996 *R, Arg* 1(R), *SA* 2(R), 1997 *R* 1, *A* 2(R), 1998 *E* (R), *S, I, W, Arg* 1,2, *Fj, Arg* 3, *A*, 1999 *W* 2, [*C, Nm, Fj, Arg, NZ* 2, *A*]

Lievremont, T (Perpignan, SF, Biarritz) 1996 *W* 2(R), 1998 *E, S, I, W, Arg* 1,2, *Fj, Arg* 3, *A*, 1999 *I, W* 1, *E, W* 2, [*Nm*], 2000 *W* (R), *E* (R), *S* (R), *I, It,* 2001 *E* (R)
Lira, M (La Voulte) 1962 *R*, 1963 *I, E, W, It, R*, 1964 *W, It, I, SA*, 1965 *S, I, R*
Llari, R (Carcassonne) 1926 *S*
Lobies, J (RCF) 1921 *S, W, E*
Lombard, F (Narbonne) 1934 *G*, 1937 *It*
Lombard, T (SF) 1998 *Arg* 3, *A*, 1999 *I, W* 1, *S* (R), 2000 *W, E, S, A, NZ* 1, 2001 *It, W*
Lombarteix, R (Montferrand) 1938 *R, G* 2
Londios, J (Montauban) 1967 *SA* 3
Loppy, L (Toulon) 1993 *R* 2
Lorieux, A (Grenoble, Aix) 1981 *A* 1, *R, NZ* 1,2, 1982 *W*, 1983 *A* 2, *R*, 1984 *I, W, E*, 1985 *Arg* 1,2(R), 1986 *R* 2, *NZ* 2,3, 1987 *W, E,* [*S, Z, Fj, A, NZ*], 1988 *S, I, W, Arg* 1,2,4, 1989 *W, A* 2
Loury, A (RCF) 1927 *E, G* 1,2, 1928 *S, A, I*
Loustau, M (Dax) 1923 *E*
Lubin-Lebrère, M-F (Toulouse) 1914 *I, W, E*, 1920 *S, E, W, I, US*, 1921 *S*, 1922 *S, E, W*, 1924 *W, US*, 1925 *I*
Lubrano, A (Béziers) 1972 *A* 2, 1973 *S*
Lux, J-P (Tyrosse, Dax) 1967 *E, It, W, I, SA* 1,2,4, *R*, 1968 *I, E, Cz, NZ* 3, *A, SA* 1,2, 1969 *S, I, E*, 1970 *S, I, W, E, R*, 1971 *S, I, E, W, A* 1,2, 1972 *S I* 1, *E, W I* 2, *A* 1,2, *R*, 1973 *S, NZ, E*, 1974 *I, W, E, S, Arg* 1,2, 1975 *W*

Macabiau, A (Perpignan) 1994 *S, C* 1
Maclos, P (SF) 1906 *E*, 1907 *E*
Magne, O (Dax, Brive, Montferrand) 1997 *W* (R), *E, S, R* 1(R), *A* 1,2, *It* 2(R), *R* 2, *Arg* (R), 1998 *E, S, I, W, Arg* 1,2, *Fj, Arg* 3, *A*, 1999 *I, R, WS, NZ* 1, *W* 2, [*C, Nm, Fj, Arg, NZ* 2, *A*], 2000 *W, E, S, It, R, A, NZ* 1,2, 2001 *S, I, It, W, E, SA* 1,2, *NZ, SA* 3, *A, Fj*, 2002 *It, E, S, I, Arg, A* 1,2(R)
Magnanou, C (RCF) 1923 *E*, 1925 *W, E*, 1926 *S*, 1929 *S, W*, 1930 *S, I, E, W*
Magnol, L (Toulouse) 1928 *S*, 1929 *S, W, E*
Magois, H (La Rochelle) 1968 *SA* 1,2, *R*
Majerus, R (SF) 1928 *W*, 1929 *I, S*, 1930 *S, I, E, G, W*
Malbet, J-C (Agen) 1967 *SA* 2,4
Maleig, A (Oloron) 1979 *W, E, NZ* 2, 1980 *W, E, SA, R*
Mallier, L (Brive) 1999 *R, W* 2(R), [*C R*)], 2000 *I* (R), *It*
Malquier, Y (Narbonne) 1979 *S*
Manterola, T (Lourdes) 1955 *It*, 1957 *R* 1
Mantoulan, C (Pau) 1959 *I*
Marcet, J (Albi) 1925 *I, NZ, S, W, E*, 1926 *I, E*
Marchal, J-F (Lourdes) 1979 *S, R*, 1980 *W, S, I*
Marconnet, S (SF) 1998 *Arg* 3, *A*, 1999 *I* (R), *W* 1(R), *E, S* (R), *R, Tg*, 2000 *A, NZ* 1,2, 2001 *S, I, It* (R), *W* (R), *E*, 2002 *S* (R), *Arg* (R), *A* 1,2
Marchand, R (Poitiers) 1920 *S, W*
Marfaing, M (Toulouse) 1992 *R, Arg* 1
Marlu, J (Montferrand) 1998 *Fj* (R), 2002 *S* (R), *I* (R)
Marocco, P (Montferrand) 1968 *S, I, W, E, R* 1, *Arg* 1,2, *A*, 1988 *Arg* 4, 1989 *I*, 1990 *E* (R), *NZ* 1(R), 1991 *S, I, W* 1, *E, US* 2, [*R, Fj, C, E*]
Marot, A (Brive) 1969 *R*, 1970 *S, I, W*, 1971 *SA* 1, 1972 *I* 2, 1976 *A* 1
Marquesuzaa, A (RCF) 1958 *It, SA* 1,2, 1959 *E, It, W*, 1960 *S, E, Arg* 1
Marracq, H (Pau) 1961 *R*
Marsh, T (Montferrand) 2001 *SA* 3, *A, Fj*, 2002 *It, W, E, S, I, Arg, A* 1,2
Martin, C (Lyon) 1909 *I*, 1910 *W, S*
Martin, H (SBUC) 1907 *E*, 1908 *W*
Martin, J-L (Béziers) 1971 *A* 2, *R*, 1972 *S, I* 1
Martin, L (Pau) 1948 *I, A, S, W, E*, 1950 *S*
Martin, R (SF) 2002 *E* (t+R), *S* (R), *I* (R)
Martine, R (Lourdes) 1952 *S, I, It*, 1953 *It*, 1954 *S, I, NZ, W, E, It, Arg* 2, 1955 *S, I, W*, 1958 *A, W, It, I, SA* 1,2, 1960 *S, E, Arg* 3, 1961 *S, It*
Martinez, A (Narbonne) 2002 *A* 1
Martinez, G (Toulouse) 1982 *W, E, S, Arg* 1,2, 1983 *E, W*
Mas, F (Béziers) 1962 *R*, 1963 *S, I, E, W*
Maso, J (Perpignan, Narbonne) 1966 *It, R*, 1967 *S, R*, 1968 *S, W, Cz, NZ* 1,2,3, *A, R*, 1969 *S, I, W*, 1971 *SA* 1,2, *R*, 1972 *E, W, A* 2, 1973 *W, I, J, R*
Massare, J (PUC) 1945 *B* 1,2, *W*, 1946 *B, I, W*
Massé, A (SBUC) 1908 *W*, 1909 *E, W*, 1910 *W, S, E, I*
Masse, H (Grenoble) 1937 *G*
Matheu-Cambas, J (Agen) 1945 *W*, 1946 *B, I, K, W*, 1947 *S, I, W, E*, 1948 *I, A, S, W, E*, 1949 *S, I, E, W, Arg* 1,2, 1950 *E, W*, 1951 *S, I*

Matiu, L (Biarritz) 2000 *W, E*
Mauduy, G (Périgueux) 1957 *It, R* 1,2, 1958 *S, E*, 1961 *W, It*
Mauran, J (Castres) 1952 *SA, W, E, It*, 1953 *I, E*
Mauriat, P (Lyon) 1907 *E*, 1908 *E, W*, 1909 *W, I*, 1910 *W, S, E, I*, 1911 *S, E, W, I*, 1912 *I, S*, 1913 *S, SA, W, I*
Maurin, G (ASF) 1906 *E*
Maury, A (Toulouse) 1925 *I, NZ, S, W, E*, 1926 *S, I, E*
Mayssonnié, A (Toulouse) 1908 *E, W*, 1910 *W*
Mazas, L (Colomiers, Biarritz) 1992 *Arg*, 1996 *SA* 1
Melville, E (Toulon) 1990 *I* (R), *A* 1,2,3, *NZ* 1, 1991 *US* 2
Menrath, R (SCUF) 1910 *W*
Menthiller, Y (Romans) 1964 *W, It, SA, R*, 1965 *E*
Merceron, G (Montferrand) 1999 *R* (R), *Tg*, 2000 *S, I, R*, 2001 *S* (R), *W, E, SA* 1,2, *NZ* (R), *Fj*, 2002 *It, W, E, S, I, Arg, A* 2
Meret, F (Tarbes) 1940 *B*
Mericq, S (Agen) 1959 *I*, 1960 *S, E, W*, 1961 *I*
Merle, O (Grenoble, Montferrand) 1993 *SA* 1,2, *R* 2, *A* 1,2, 1994 *I, W, E, S, C* 1, *NZ* 1,2, *C* 2, 1995 *W, I, R* 1, [*Tg, S, I, SA, E*], *It, R* 2, *Arg, NZ* 1,2, 1996 *E, S, R, Arg* 1, *NZ* 2, *SA* 2, 1997 *I, W, E, S, It* 1, *R* 1, *A* 1,2, *It* 2, *R* 2, *SA* 1(R),2
Merquey, J (Toulouse)1950 *S, I, E, W*
Mesnel, F (RCF) 1986 *NZ* 2(R),3, 1987 *W, E, S, I*, [*S, Z, Fj, A, NZ*], *R*, 1988 *E, Arg* 1,2,3,4, *R*, 1989 *I, W, E, S, NZ* 1, *A* 1,2, 1990 *E, S, I, A* 2,3, *NZ* 1,2, 1991 *S, I, W* 1, *E, R, US* 1,2, *W* 2, [*R, Fj, C, E*], 1992 *W, E, S, I, SA* 1,2, 1993 *E* (R), *W*, 1995 *I, R* 1, [*Iv, E*]
Mesny, P (RCF, Grenoble) 1979 *NZ* 1,2, 1980 *SA, R*, 1981 *I, W* (R), *A* 1,2, *R, NZ* 1,2, 1982 *I, Arg* 1,2
Meyer, G-S (Périgueux) 1960 *S, E, It, R, Arg* 2
Meynard, J (Cognac) 1954 *Arg* 1, 1956 *Cz*
Mias, L (Mazamet) 1951 *S, I, E, W*, 1952 *I, SA, W, E, It*, 1953 *S, I, W, It*, 1954 *S, I, NZ, W*, 1957 *R* 2, 1958 *S, E, A, W, I, SA* 1,2, 1959 *S, It, W, I*
Michalak, F (Toulouse) 2001 *SA* 3(R), *A, Fj* (R), 2002 *It, A* 1,2
Mignoni, P (Béziers) 1997 *R* 2(R), *Arg* (t), 1999 *R* (R), *WS, NZ* 1, *W* 2(R), [*C, Nm*], 2002 *W, E* (R), *I* (R), *Arg, A* 2(R)
Milhères, C (Biarritz) 2001 *E*
Milliand, P (Grenoble) 1936 *G* 2, 1937 *G, It*
Milloud, O (Bourgoin) 2000 *R* (R), 2001 *NZ*, 2002 *W* (R), *E* (R)
Minjat, R (Lyon) 1945 *B* 1
Miorin, H (Toulouse) 1996 *R, SA* 1, 1997 *I, W, E, S, It* 1, 2000 *It* (R), *W* (R)
Mir, J-H (Lourdes) 1967 *R*, 1968 *I*
Mir, J-P (Lourdes) 1967 *A*
Modin, R (Brive) 1987 [*Z*]
Moga, A-M-A (Bègles) 1945 *B* 1,2, *W*, 1946 *B, I, K, W*, 1947 *S, I, W, E*, 1948 *I, A, S, W, E*, 1949 *S, I, E, W, Arg* 1,2
Mola, U (Dax, Castres) 1997 *S* (R), 1999 *R* (R), *WS, Tg* (R), *NZ* 1, *W* 2, [*C, Nm, Fj, Arg* (R), *NZ* 2(R), *A* (R)]
Mommejat, B (Cahors, Albi) 1958 *It, I, SA* 1,2, 1959 *S, E, It, W, I*, 1960 *S, E, I, R*, 1963 *S, I, W*, 1963 *S, I, W*
Moncla, F (RCF, Pau) 1956 *Cz*, 1957 *I, E, W, It, R* 1, 1958 *SA* 1,2, 1959 *S, E, It, W, I*, 1960 *S, E, W, I, It, R, Arg* 1,2,3, 1961 *S, SA, E, W, It, I, NZ* 1,2,3
Moni, C (Nice, SF) 1996 *R*, 2000 *A, NZ* 1,2, 2001 *S, I, It, W*
Monié, R (Perpignan) 1956 *Cz*, 1957 *E*
Monier, R (SBUC) 1911 *I*, 1912 *S*
Monniot, M (RCF) 1912 *W, E*
Montade, A (Perpignan) 1925 *I, NZ, S, W*, 1926 *W*
Montlaur, P (Agen) 1992 *E* (R), 1994 *S* (R)
Moraitis, B (Toulon) 1969 *E, W*
Morel, A (Grenoble) 1954 *Arg* 2
Morere, J (Toulouse) 1927 *E, G* 1, 1928 *S, A*
Moscato, V (Bègles) 1991 *R, US* 1, 1992 *W, E*
Mougeot, C (Bègles) 1992 *W, E, Arg*
Mouniq, P (Toulouse) 1911 *S, E, W, I,*1912 *I, E*, 1913 *S, SA, E*
Moure, H (SCUF) 1908 *E*
Moureu, P (Béziers) 1920 *I, US*, 1921 *W, E, I*, 1922 *S, W, I*, 1923 *S, W, E, I*, 1924 *S, I, E, W*, 1925 *E*
Mournet, A (Bagnères) 1981 *A* 1(R)
Mouronval, F (SF) 1909 *I*
Muhr, A H (RCF) 1906 *NZ, E*, 1907 *E*
Murillo, G (Dijon) 1954 *It, Arg* 1

Nallet, L (Bourgoin) 2000 *R*, 2001 *E, SA* 1(R),2(R), *NZ, SA* 3(R), *A* (R), *Fj* (R)
Namur, R (Toulon) 1931 *E, G*
Noble, J-C (La Voulte) 1968 *E, W, Cz, NZ* 3, *A, R*
Normand, A (Toulouse) 1957 *R* 1
Novès, G (Toulouse) 1977 *NZ* 1,2, *R*, 1978 *W, R*, 1979 *I, W*

Olivier Magne, the outstanding French flanker, sets up another phase in an attack against Italy in the opening match of last season's Six Nations Championship.

Ntamack, E (Toulouse) 1994 *W, C* 1, *NZ* 1,2, *C* 2, 1995 *W, I, R* 1, [*Tg, S, I, SA, E*], *It, R* 2, *Arg, NZ* 1,2, 1996 *E, S, I, W* 1, *R* (R), *Arg* 1,2, *W* 2, 1997 *I*, 1998 *Arg* 3, 1999 *I, W* 1, *E, WS, NZ* 1, *W* 2(R), [*C* (R), *Nm, Fj, Arg, NZ* 2, *A*], 2000 *W, E, S, I, It*
Ntamack F (Colomiers) 2001 *SA* 3

Olive, D (Montferrand) 1951 *I*, 1952 *I*
Ondarts, P (Biarritz O) 1986 *NZ* 3, 1987 *W, E, S, I,* [*S, Z, Fj, A, NZ*], *R*, 1988 *E, I, W, Arg* 1,2,3,4, *R*, 1989 *I, W, E, NZ* 1,2, *A* 2, 1990 *W, E, S, I, R* (R), *NZ* 1,2, 1991 *S, I, W* 1, *E, US* 2, *W* 2, [*R, Fj, C, E*]
Orso, J-C (Nice, Toulon) 1982 *Arg* 1,2, 1983 *E, S, A* 1, 1984 *E* (R), *S, NZ* 1, 1985 *I* (R), *W*, 1988 *I*
Othats, J (Dax) 1960 *Arg* 2,3
Ougier, S (Toulouse) 1992 *R, Arg* 1, 1993 *E* (R), 1997 *It* 1

Paco, A (Béziers) 1974 *Arg* 1,2, *R, SA* 1,2, 1975 *W, E, Arg* 1,2, *R*, 1976 *S, I, W, E, US, A* 1,2, *R*, 1977 *W, E, S, I, NZ* 1,2, *R*, 1978 *S, I, W, R*, 1979 *I, W, E, S*, 1980 *W*
Palat, J (Perpignan) 1938 *G* 2
Palmié, M (Béziers) 1975 *SA* 1,2, *Arg* 1,2, *R*, 1976 *S, I, W, E, US*, 1977 *W, E, S, I, Arg* 1,2, *NZ* 1,2, *R*, 1978 *E, S, I, W*
Paoli, R (see Simonpaoli)
Paparemborde, R (Pau) 1975 *SA* 1,2, *Arg* 1,2, *R*, 1976 *S, I, W, E, US, A* 1,2, *R*, 1977 *W, E, S, I, Arg* 1, *NZ* 1,2, 1978 *E, S, I, W, R*, 1979 *I, W, E, S, NZ* 1,2, *R*, 1980 *W, E, S, SA, R*, 1981 *S, I, W, E, A* 1,2, *R, NZ* 1,2, 1982 *W, I, R, Arg* 1,2 1983 *E, S, I, W*
Pardo, L (Hendaye) 1924 *I, E*
Pardo, L (Bayonne) 1980 *SA, R*, 1981 *S, I, W, E, A* 1, 1982 *W, E, S*, 1983 *A* 1(R), 1985 *S, I, Arg* 2
Pargade, J-H (Lyon U) 1953 *It*
Paries, L (Biarritz O) 1968 *SA* 2, *R*, 1970 *S, I, W*, 1975 *E, S, I*
Pascalin, P (Mont-de-Marsan) 1950 *I, E, W*, 1951 *S, I, E, W*
Pascarel, J-R (TOEC) 1912 *W, E*, 1913 *S, SA, E, I*
Pascot, J (Perpignan) 1922 *S, E, I*, 1923 *S*, 1926 *I*, 1927 *G* 2
Paul, R (Montferrand) 1940 *B*
Pauthe, G (Graulhet) 1956 *E*
Pebeyre, E-J (Fumel, Brive) 1945 *W*, 1946 *I, K, W*, 1947 *S, I, W, E*
Pebeyre, M (Vichy, Montferrand) 1970 *E, R*, 1971 *I, SA* 1,2, *A* 1, 1973 *W*
Pecune, J (Tarbes) 1974 *W, E, S*, 1975 *Arg* 1,2, *R*, 1976 *I, W, E, US*
Pedeutour, P (Begles) 1980 *I*
Pellissier, L (RCF) 1928 *A, I, E, G, W*
Pelous, F (Dax, Toulouse) 1995 *R* 2, *Arg, NZ* 1,2, 1996 *E, S, I, R* (R), *Arg* 1,2, *W* 2, *SA* 1,2, 1997 *I, W, E, S, It* 1, *R* 1, *A* 1,2, *It* 2, *R* 2, *Arg, SA* 1,2(R), 1998 *E, S, I, W, Arg* 1,2, *Fj, Arg* 3, *A*, 1999 *I, W* 1, *E, R* (R), *WS, Tg* (R), *NZ* 1, *W* 2, [*C, Nm, Fj, NZ* 2, *A*], 2000 *W, E, S, I, It, A, NZ* 1,2, 2001 *S, I, It, W, E*, 2002 *It* (R), *W* (R), *E* (R), *S, I, Arg, A* 1,2
Penaud, A (Brive, Toulouse) 1992 *W, E, S, I, R, Arg* 1,2, *SA* 1,2, *Arg*, 1993 *R* 1, *SA* 1,2, *R* 2, *A* 1,2, 1994 *I, W, E*, 1995 *NZ* 1,2, 1996 *S, R, Arg* 1,2, *W* 2, 1997 *I, E, R* 1, *A* 2, 2000 *W* (R), *It*
Périé, M (Toulon) 1996 *E, S, I* (R)
Peron, P (RCF) 1975 *SA* 1,2
Perrier, P (Bayonne) 1982 *W, E, S, I* (R)
Pesteil, J-P (Béziers) 1975 *SA* 1, 1976 *A* 2, *R*
Petit, C (Lorrain) 1931 *W*
Peyrelade, H (Tarbes) 1940 *B*
Peyroutou, G (Périgueux) 1911 *S, E*
Phliponeau, J-F (Montferrand) 1973 *W, I*
Piazza, A (Montauban) 1968 *NZ* 1, *A*
Picard, T (Montferrand) 1985 *Arg* 2, 1986 *R* 1(R), *Arg* 2
Pierrot, G (Pau) 1914 *I, W, E*
Pilon, J (Périgueux) 1949 *E*, 1950 *E*
Piqué, J (Pau) 1961 *NZ* 2,3, *A*, 1962 *S, It*, 1964 *NZ, E, W, It, I, SA, Fj, R*, 1965 *S, I, E, W, It*
Piquemal, M (Tarbes) 1927 *I, S*, 1929 *I, G*, 1930 *S, I, E, G, W*
Piquiral, E (RCF) 1924 *S, I, E, W, R, US*, 1925 *E*, 1926 *S, I, E, W, M*, 1927 *I, S, W, E, G* 1,2, 1928 *E*
Piteu, R (Pau) 1921 *S, W, E, I*, 1922 *S, E, W, I*, 1923 *E*, 1924 *I, E, S, W*, 1925 *I, NZ, W, E*, 1926 *E*
Plantefol, A (RCF) 1967 *SA* 2,3,4, *NZ, R*, 1968 *E, W, Cz, NZ* 2, 1969 *E, W*
Plantey, S (RCF) 1961 *A*, 1962 *It*
Podevin, G (SF) 1913 *W, I*
Poeydebasque, F (Bayonne) 1914 *I, W*
Poirier, A (SCUF) 1907 *E*

Poitrenaud, C (Toulouse) 2001 *SA* 3, *A, Fj*
Pomathios, M (Agen, Lyon U, Bourg) 1948 *I, A, S, W, E*, 1949 *S, I, E, W, Arg* 1,2, 1950 *S, I, W*, 1951 *S, I, E, W*, 1952 *W, E*, 1953 *S, I, W*, 1954 *S*
Pons, P (Toulouse) 1920 *S, E, W*, 1921 *S, W*, 1922 *S*
Porcu, C (Agen) 2002 *Arg* (R), *A* 1,2(R)
Porra, M (Lyon) 1931 *I*
Porthault, A (RCF) 1951 *S, E, W*, 1952 *I*, 1953 *S, I, It*
Portolan, C (Toulouse) 1986 *A*, 1989 *I, E*
Potel, A (Begles) 1932 *G*
Poux, J-B (Narbonne) 2001 *Fj* (R), 2002 *S, I* (R), *Arg, A* 1(R),2(R)
Prat, J (Lourdes) 1945 *B* 1,2, *W*, 1946 *B, I, K, W*, 1947 *S, I, W, E*, 1948 *I, A, S, W, E*, 1949 *S, I, E, W, Arg* 1,2, 1950 *S, I, E, W*, 1951 *S, E, W*, 1952 *S, I, SA, W, E, It*, 1953 *S, I, E, W, It*, 1954 *S, I, NZ, W, E, It*, 1955 *S, I, E, W, It*
Prat, M (Lourdes) 1951 *I*, 1952 *S, I, SA, W, E*, 1953 *S, I, E*, 1954 *I, NZ, W, E, It*, 1955 *S, I, E, W, It*, 1956 *I, W, It, Cz*, 1957 *S, I, W, It, R* 1, 1958 *A, W, I*
Prevost, A (Albi) 1926 *M*, 1927 *I, S, W*
Prin-Clary, J (Cavaillon, Brive) 1945 *B* 1,2, *W*, 1946 *B, I, K, W*, 1947 *S, I, W*
Privat, T (Béziers) 2001 *SA* 3, *A, Fj*, 2002 *It, W, S* (R)
Puech, L (Toulouse) 1920 *S, E, I*, 1921 *E, I*
Puget, M (Toulouse) 1961 *It*, 1966 *S, I, It*, 1967 *SA* 1,3,4, *NZ*, 1968 *Cz, NZ* 1,2, *SA* 1,2, *R*, 1969 *E, R*, 1970 *W*
Puig, A (Perpignan) 1926 *S, E*
Pujol, A (SOE Toulouse) 1906 *NZ*
Pujolle, M (Nice) 1989 *B, A* 1, 1990 *S, I, R, A* 1,2, *NZ* 2

Quaglio, A (Mazamet) 1957 *R* 2, 1958 *S, E, A, W, I, SA* 1,2, 1959 *S, E, It, W, I*
Quilis, A (Narbonne) 1967 *SA* 1,4, *NZ*, 1970 *R*, 1971 *I*

Ramis, R (Perpignan) 1922 *E, I*, 1923 *W*
Rancoule, H (Lourdes, Toulon, Tarbes) 1955 *E, W, It*, 1958 *A, W, It, I, SA* 1, 1959 *S, It, W*, 1960 *I, It, R, Arg* 1,2, 1961 *SA, E, W, It, NZ* 1,2, 1962 *S, E, W, I, It*
Rapin, A (SBUC) 1938 *R*
Raymond, F (Toulouse) 1925 *S*, 1927 *W*, 1928 *I*
Raynal, F (Perpignan) 1935 *G*, 1936 *G* 1,2, 1937 *G, It*
Raynaud, F (Carcassonne) 1933 *G*
Raynaud, M (Narbonne) 1999 *W* 1, *E* (R)
Razat, J-P (Agen) 1962 *R*, 1963 *S, I, R*
Rebujent, R (RCF) 1963 *E*
Revailler, D (Graulhet) 1981 *S, I, W, E, A* 1,2, *R, NZ* 1,2, 1982 *W, S, I, R, Arg* 1
Revillon, J (RCF) 1926 *I, E*, 1927 *S*
Ribère, E (Perpignan, Quillan) 1924 *I*, 1925, *I, NZ, S*, 1926 *S, I, W, M*, 1927 *I, S, W, E, G* 1,2, 1928 *S, A, I, E, G, W*, 1929 *I, E, G*, 1930 *S, I, E, W*, 1931 *I, S, W, E, G*, 1932 *G*, 1933 *G*
Rives, J-P (Toulouse, RCF) 1975 *E, S, I, Arg* 1,2, *R*, 1976 *S, I, W, E, US, A* 1,2, *R*, 1977 *W, E, S, I, Arg* 1,2, *R*, 1978 *E, S, I, W, R*, 1979 *I, W, E, S, NZ* 1,2, *R*, 1980 *W, E, S, I, SA*, 1981 *S, I, W, E, A* 2, 1982 *W, E, S, I, R*, 1983 *E, S, I, W, A* 1,2, *R*, 1984 *I, W, E, S*
Rochon, A (Montferrand) 1936 *G* 1
Rodrigo, M (Mauléon) 1931 *I, W*
Rodriguez, L (Mont-de-Marsan, Montferrand, Dax) 1981 *A* 1,2, *R, NZ* 1,2, 1982 *W, E, S, I, R*, 1983 *E, S*, 1984 *I, NZ* 1,2, *R*, 1985 *E, S, I, W*, 1986 *Arg* 1, *A, R* 2, *NZ* 2,3, 1987 *W, E, S, I*, [*S, Z, Fj, A, NZ*], *R*, 1988 *E, S, I, W, Arg* 1,2,3,4, *R*, 1989 *I, E, S, NZ* 1,2, *B, A* 1, 1990 *W, E, S, I, NZ* 1
Rogé, L (Béziers) 1952 *It*, 1953 *E, W, It*, 1954 *S, Arg* 1,2, 1955 *S, I*, 1956 *W, It, E*, 1957 *S*, 1960 *S, E*
Rollet, J (Bayonne) 1960 *Arg* 3, 1961 *NZ* 3, *A*, 1962 *It*, 1963 *I*
Romero, H (Montauban) 1962 *S, E, W, I, It, R*, 1963 *E*
Romeu, J-P (Montferrand) 1972 *R*, 1973 *S, NZ, E, W, I, R*, 1974 *W, E, S, Arg* 1,2, *R, SA* 1,2(R), 1975 *W, Arg* 1,2, *R*, 1976 *S, I, W, E, US*, 1977 *W, E, S, I, Arg* 1,2, *NZ* 1,2, *R*
Roques, A (Cahors) 1958 *A, W, It, I, SA* 1,2, 1959 *S, E, W, I*, 1960 *S, E, W, I, It, Arg* 1,2,3, 1961 *S, SA, E, W, I, It*, 1962 *S, E, W, I, It*, 1963 *S*
Roques, J-C (Brive) 1966 *S, I, It, R*
Rossignol, J-C (Brive) 1972 *A* 2
Rouan, J (Narbonne) 1953 *S, I*
Roucaries, G (Perpignan) 1956 *S*
Rouffia, L (Narbonne) 1945 *B* 2, *W*, 1946 *W*, 1948 *I*
Rougerie, A (Montferrand) 2001 *SA* 3, *A, Fj* (R), 2002 *It, W, E, S, I, Arg, A* 1,2
Rougerie, J (Montferrand) 1973 *J*
Rougé-Thomas, P (Toulouse) 1989 *NZ* 1,2

Roujas, F (Tarbes) 1910 *I*
Roumat, O (Dax) 1989 *NZ* 2(R), *B*, 1990 *W, E, S, I, R, A* 1,2,3, *NZ* 1,2, 1991 *S, I, W* 1, *E, R, US* 1, *W* 2, [*R, Fj, C, E*], 1992 *W* (R), *E* (R), *S, I, SA* 1,2, *Arg*, 1993 *E, S, I, W, R* 1, *SA* 1,2, *R* 2, *A* 1,2, 1994 *I, W, E, C* 1, *NZ* 1,2, *C* 2, 1995 *W, E, S,* [*Iv, S, I, SA, E*], 1996 *E, S, I, W* 1, *Arg* 1,2
Rousie, M (Villeneuve) 1931 *S, G*, 1932 *G*, 1933 *G*
Rousset, G (Béziers) 1975 *SA* 1, 1976 *US*
Ruiz, A (Tarbes) 1968 *SA* 2, *R*
Rupert, J-J (Tyrosse) 1963 *R*, 1964 *S, Fj*, 1965 *E, W, It*, 1966 *S, I, E, W, It*, 1967 *It, R*, 1968 *S*

Sadourny, J-L (Colomiers) 1991 *W* 2(R), [*C* (R)], 1992 *E* (R), *S, I, Arg* 1(R),2, *SA* 1,2, 1993 *R* 1, *SA* 1,2, *R* 2, *A* 1,2, 1994 *I, W, E, S, C* 1, *NZ* 1,2, *C* 2, 1995 *W, E, S, I, R* 1, [*Tg, S, I, SA, E*], *It, R* 2, *Arg, NZ* 1,2, 1996 *E, S, I, W* 1, *Arg* 1,2, *W* 2, *SA* 1,2, 1997 *I, W, E, S, It* 1, *R* 1, *A* 1,2, *It* 2, *R* 2, *Arg, SA* 1,2, 1998 *E, S, I, W*, 1999 *R, Tg, NZ* 1(R), 2000 *NZ* 2, 2001 *It, W, E*
Sagot, P (SF) 1906 *NZ*, 1908 *E*, 1909 *W*
Sahuc, A (Métro) 1945 *B* 1,2
Sahuc, F (Toulouse) 1936 *G* 2
Saint-André, P (Montferrand, Gloucester) 1990 *R, A* 3, *NZ* 1,2, 1991 *I* (R), *W* 1, *E, US* 1,2, *W* 2, [*R, Fj, C, E*], 1992 *W, E, S, I, R, Arg* 1,2, *SA* 1,2, 1993 *E, S, I, W, SA* 1,2, *A* 1,2, 1994 *I, W, E, S, C* 1, *NZ* 1,2, *C* 2, 1995 *W, E, S, I, R* 1, [*Tg, Iv, S, I, SA, E*], *It, R* 2, *Arg, NZ* 1,2, 1996 *E, S, I, W* 1, *R, Arg* 1,2, *W* 2, 1997 *It* 1,2, *R* 2, *Arg, SA* 1,2
Saisset, O (Béziers) 1971 *R*, 1972 *S, I* 1, *A* 1,2, 1973 *S, NZ, E, W, I, R*, 1974 *I, Arg* 2, *SA* 1,2, 1975 *W*
Salas, P (Narbonne) 1979 *NZ* 1,2, *R*, 1980 *W, E*, 1981 *A* 1, 1982 *Arg* 2
Salinié, R (Perpignan) 1923 *E*
Sallefranque, M (Dax) 1981 *A* 2, 1982 *W, E, S*
Salut, J (TOEC) 1966 *R*, 1967 *S*, 1968 *I, E, Cz, NZ* 1, 1969 *I*
Samatan, R (Agen) 1930 *S, I, E, G, W*, 1931 *I, S, W, E, G*
Sanac, A (Perpignan) 1952 *It*, 1953 *I, S*, 1954 *E*, 1956 *Cz*, 1957 *S, I, E, W, It*
Sangalli, F (Narbonne) 1975 *I, SA* 1,2, 1976 *S, A* 1,2, *R*, 1977 *W, E, S, I, Arg* 1,2, *NZ* 1,2
Sanz, H (Narbonne) 1988 *Arg* 3,4, *R*, 1989 *A* 2, 1990 *S, I, R, A* 1,2, *NZ* 2, 1991 *W* 2
Sappa, M (Nice) 1973 *J, R*, 1977 *R*
Sarrade, R (Pau) 1929 *I*
Sarraméa, O (Castres) 1999 *R, WS* (R), *Tg, NZ* 1
Saux, J-P (Pau) 1960 *W, It, Arg* 1,2, 1961 *SA, E, W, It, I, NZ* 1,2,3, *A*, 1962 *S, E, W, I, It*, 1963 *S, I, E, It*
Savitsky, M (La Voulte) 1969 *R*
Savy, M (Montferrand) 1931 *I, S, W, E*, 1936 *G* 1
Sayrou, J (Perpignan) 1926 *W, M*, 1928 *E, G, W*, 1929 *S, W, E, G*
Scohy, R (BEC) 1931 *S, W, E, G*
Sébedio, J (Tarbes) 1913 *S, E*, 1914 *I*, 1920 *S, I, US*, 1922 *S, E*, 1923 *S*
Seguier, N (Béziers) 1973 *J, R*
Seigne, L (Agen, Merignac) 1989 *B, A* 1, 1990 *NZ* 1, 1993 *E, S, I, W, R* 1, *A* 1,2, 1994 *S, C* 1, 1995 *E* (R), *S*
Sella, P (Agen) 1982 *R, Arg* 1,2, 1983 *E, S, I, W, A* 1,2, *R*, 1984 *I, W, E, S, NZ* 1,2, *R*, 1985 *E, S, I, W, Arg* 1,2, 1986 *S, I, W, E, R, I, Arg* 1,2, *A, NZ* 1, *R* 2, *NZ* 2,3, 1987 *W, E, S, I,* [*S, R, Z* (R), *Fj, A, NZ*], 1988 *E, S, I, W, Arg* 1,2,3,4, *R*, 1989 *I, W, E, S, NZ* 1,2, *B, A* 1,2, 1990 *W, E, S, I, A* 1,2,3, 1991 *W* 1, *E, R, US* 1,2, *W* 2, [*Fj, C, E*], 1992 *W, E, S, I, Arg*, 1993 *E, S, I, W, R* 1, *SA* 1,2, *R* 2, *A* 1,2, 1994 *I, W, E, S, C* 1, *NZ* 1,2, *C* 2, 1995 *W, E, S, I,* [*Tg, S, I, SA, E*]
Semmartin, J (SCUF) 1913 *W, I*
Senal, G (Béziers) 1974 *Arg* 1,2, *R, SA* 1,2, 1975 *W*
Sentilles, J (Tarbes) 1912 *W, E*, 1913 *S, SA*
Serin, L (Béziers) 1928 *E*, 1929 *W, E, G*, 1930 *S, I, E, G, W*, 1931 *I, W, E*
Serre, P (Perpignan) 1920 *S, E*
Serrière, P (RCF) 1986 *A*, 1987 *R*, 1988 *E*
Servole, L (Toulon) 1931 *I, S, W, E, G*, 1934 *G*, 1935 *G*
Sicart, N (Perpignan) 1922 *I*
Sillières, J (Tarbes) 1968 *R*, 1970 *S, I*, 1971 *S, I, E*, 1972 *E, W*
Siman, M (Montferrand) 1948 *E*, 1949 *S*, 1950 *S, I, E, W*
Simon, S (Bègles) 1991 *R, US* 1
Simonpaoli, R (SF) 1911 *I*, 1912 *I, S*
Sitjar, M (Agen) 1964 *W, It, I, R*, 1965 *It, R*, 1967 *A, E, It, W, I, SA* 1,2
Skrela, D (Colomiers) 2001 *NZ*
Skrela, J-C (Toulouse) 1971 *SA* 2, *A* 1,2, 1972 *I* 1(R), *E, W, I* 2, *A* 1, 1973 *W, J, R*, 1974 *W, E, S, Arg* 1, *R*, 1975 *W* (R), *E, S,*

I, SA 1,2, *Arg* 1,2, *R*, 1976 *S, I, W, E, US, A* 1,2, *R*, 1977 *W, E, S, I, Arg* 1,2, *NZ* 1,2, *R*, 1978 *E, S, I, W*
Soler, M (Quillan) 1929 *G*
Soro, R (Lourdes, Romans) 1945 *B* 1,2, *W*, 1946 *B, I, K*, 1947 *S, I, W, E*, 1948 *I, A, S, W, E*, 1949 *S, I, E, W, Arg* 1,2
Sorondo, L-M (Montauban) 1946 *K*, 1947 *S, I, W, E*, 1948 *I*
Soulette, C (Béziers, Toulouse) 1997 *R* 2, 1998 *S* (R), *I* (R), *W* (R), *Arg* 1,2, *Fj*, 1999 *W* 2(R), [*C* (R), *Nm* (R), *Arg, NZ* 2, *A*]
Soulié, E (CASG) 1920 *E, I, US*, 1921 *S, E, I*, 1922 *E, W, I*
Sourgens, J (Bègles) 1926 *M*
Souverbie, J-M (Bègles) 2000 *R*
Spanghero, C (Narbonne) 1971 *E, W, SA* 1,2, *A* 1,2, 1972 *S, E, W, I* 2, *A* 1,2, 1974 *I, W, E, S, R, SA* 1, 1975 *E, S, I*
Spanghero, W (Narbonne) 1964 *SA, Fj, R*, 1965 *S, I, E, W, It, R*, 1966 *S, I, E, W, It, R*, 1967 *S, A, E, SA* 1,2,3,4, *NZ*, 1968 *S, I, E, W, NZ* 1,2,3, *A, SA* 1,2, 1969 *S, I, W*, 1970 *R*, 1971 *E, W, SA* 1, 1972 *E, I* 2, *A* 1,2, 1973 *S, NZ, E, W, I*
Stener, G (PUC) 1956 *S, I, E*, 1958 *SA* 1,2
Struxiano, P (Toulouse) 1913 *W, I*, 1920 *S, E, W, I, US*
Sutra, G (Narbonne) 1967 *SA* 2, 1969 *W*, 1970 *S, I*
Swierczinski, C (Bègles) 1969 *E*, 1977 *Arg* 2

Tabacco, P (SF) 2001 *SA* 1,2, *NZ, SA* 3, *A, Fj*
Tachdjian, M (RCF) 1991 *S, I, E*
Taffary, M (RCF) 1975 *W, E, S, I*
Taillantou, J (Pau) 1930 *I, G, W*
Tarricq, P (Lourdes) 1958 *A, W, It, I*
Tavernier, H (Toulouse) 1913 *I*
Techoueyres, W (SBUC) 1994 *E, S*, 1995 [*Iv*]
Terreau, M-M (Bourg) 1945 *W*, 1946 *B, I, K, W*, 1947 *S, I, W, E*, 1948 *I, A, W, E*, 1949 *S, Arg* 1,2, 1951 *S*
Theuriet, A (SCUF) 1909 *E, W*, 1910 *S, I*, 1911 *W*, 1913 *E*
Thevenot, M (SCUF) 1910 *W, E, I*
Thierry, R (RCF) 1920 *S, E, W, US*
Thiers, P (Montferrand) 1936 *G* 1,2, 1937 *G, It*, 1938 *G* 1,2, 1940 *B*, 1945 *B,* 1,2
Tignol, P (Toulouse) 1953 *S, I*
Tilh, H (Nantes) 1912 *W, E*, 1913 *S, SA, E, W*
Tolot, J-L (Agen) 1987 [*Z*]
Tordo, J-F (Nice) 1991 *US* 1(R), 1992 *W, E, S, I, R, Arg* 1,2, *SA* 1, *Arg*, 1993 *E, S, I, W, R* 1
Torossian, F (Pau) 1997 *R* 1
Torreilles, S (Perpignan) 1956 *S*
Tournaire, F (Narbonne, Toulouse) 1995 *It*, 1996 *I, W* 1, *R, Arg* 1,2(R), *W* 2, *SA* 1,2, 1997 *I, E, S, It* 1, *R* 1, *A* 1,2, *It* 2, *R* 2, *Arg, SA* 1,2, 1998 *S, I, W, Arg* 1,2, *Fj, Arg* 3, *A*, 1999 *I, W* 1, *E, S, R* (R), *WS, NZ* 1, [*C, Nm, Fj, Arg, NZ* 2, *A*], 2000 *W, E, S, I, It, A* (R)
Tourte, R (St Girons) 1940 *B*
Traille, D (Pau) 2001 *SA* 3, *A, Fj*, 2002 *It, W, E, S, I, Arg, A* 1,2
Trillo, J (Bègles) 1967 *SA* 3,4, *NZ, R*, 1968 *S, I, NZ* 1,2,3, *A*, 1969 *I, E, W, R*, 1970 *E, R*, 1971 *S, I, SA* 1,2, *A* 1,2, 1972 *S, A* 1,2, *R*, 1973 *S, E*
Triviaux, R (Cognac) 1931 *E, G*
Tucco-Chala, M (PUC) 1940 *B*

Ugartemendia, J-L (St Jean-de-Luz) 1975 *S, I*

Vaills, G (Perpignan) 1928 *A*, 1929 *G*
Vallot, C (SCUF) 1912 *S*
Van Heerden, A (Tarbes) 1992 *E, S*
Vannier, M (RCF, Chalon) 1953 *W*, 1954 *S, I, Arg* 1,2, 1955 *S, I, E, W, It*, 1956 *S, I, W, It, E*, 1957 *S, I, E, W, It, R* 1,2, 1958 *S, E, A, W, It, I*, 1960 *S, E, W, I, It, R, Arg* 1,3, 1961 *SA, E, W, It, I, NZ* 1, *A*
Vaquer, F (Perpignan) 1921 *S, W*, 1922 *W*
Vaquerin, A (Béziers) 1971 *R*, 1972 *S, I* 1, *A* 1, 1973 *S*, 1974 *W, E, S, Arg* 1,2, *R, SA* 1,2, 1975 *W, E, S, I*, 1976 *US, A* 1(R),2, *R*, 1977 *Arg* 2, 1979 *W, E*, 1980 *S, I*
Vareilles, C (SF) 1907 *E*, 1908 *E, W*, 1910 *S, E*
Varenne, F (RCF) 1952 *S*
Varvier, T (RCF) 1906 *E*, 1909 *E, W*, 1911 *E, W*, 1912 *I*
Vassal, G (Carcassonne) 1938 *R, G* 2
Vaysse, J (Albi) 1924 *US*, 1926 *M*
Vellat, E (Grenoble) 1927 *I, E, G* 1,2, 1928 *A*
Venditti, D (Bourgoin, Brive) 1996 *R, SA* 1(R),2, 1997 *I, W, E, S, R* 1, *A* 1, *SA* 2, 2000 *W* (R), *E, S, It* (R)
Vergé, L (Bègles) 1993 *R* 1(R)
Verger, A (SF) 1927 *W, E, G* 1, 1928 *I, E, G, W*
Verges, S-A (SF) 1906 *NZ, E*, 1907 *E*
Vermeulen, E (Brive) 2001 *SA* 1(R),2(R)

Viard, G (Narbonne) 1969 *W*, 1970 *S, R*, 1971 *S, I*
Viars, S (Brive) 1992 *W, E, I, R, Arg* 1,2, *SA* 1,2(R), *Arg*, 1993 *R* 1, 1994 *C* 1(R), *NZ* 1(t), 1995 *E* (R), [*Iv*], 1997 *R* 1(R), *A* 1(R),2
Vigerie, M (Agen) 1931 *W*
Vigier, R (Montferrand) 1956 *S, W, It, E, Cz*, 1957 *S, E, W, It, R* 1,2, 1958 *S, E, A, W, It, I, SA* 1,2, 1959 *S, E, It, W, I*
Vigneau, A (Bayonne) 1935 *G*
Vignes, C (RCF) 1957 *R* 1,2, 1958 *S, E*
Vila, E (Tarbes) 1926 *M*
Vilagra, J (Vienne) 1945 *B* 2

Villepreux, P (Toulouse) 1967 *It, I, SA* 2, *NZ*, 1968 *I, Cz, NZ* 1,2,3, *A*, 1969 *S, I, E, W, R*, 1970 *S, I, W, E, R*, 1971 *S, I, E, W, A* 1,2, *R*, 1972 *S, I* 1, *E, W, I* 2, *A* 1,2
Viviès, B (Agen) 1978 *E, S, I, W*, 1980 *SA, R*, 1981 *S, A* 1, 1983 *A* 1(R)
Volot, M (SF) 1945 *W*, 1946 *B, I, K, W*

Weller, S (Grenoble) 1989 *A* 1,2, 1990 *A* 1, *NZ* 1
Wolf, J-P (Béziers) 1980 *SA, R*, 1981 *A* 2, 1982 *E*

Yachvili, M (Tulle, Brive) 1968 *E, W, Cz, NZ* 3, *A, R*, 1969 *S, I, R*, 1971 *E, SA* 1,2 *A* 1, 1972 *R*, 1975 *SA* 2

Zago, F (Montauban) 1963 *I, E*

ITALY TEST SEASON REVIEW 2001-02

Italy's Annus Horribilis

Paolo Pacitti

Less than 18 months before the 2003 Rugby World Cup kicks off, Italy went through an internal revolution. Despite last November's first win against Fiji in Treviso, the "annus horribilis" of Italian rugby reached its nadir when Brad Johnstone was forced to resign from his coaching position three weeks after the final Championship game of the season against England at the Flaminio Stadium in Rome.

The story had begun when the former All Black John Kirwan was appointed as Johnstone's assistant. The expectation was that his knowledge of Italian rugby would help Johnstone to improve on the previous season's performance. Unfortunately, the appointing committee didn't take into account the two Kiwis' differing rugby philosophies.

On the one hand, Johnstone stood by his ideas that rugby should be built essentially on set pieces, driving the ball forward with rucks and mauls an essential part of the game. On the other hand, Kirwan, strongly influenced by the defensive philosophy Wayne Smith used during his All Black days, wanted to introduce new patterns reminiscent of the defensive lines Georges Coste had employed during the glory days of the *azzurri* between 1993 and 1999.

Initially, the change in coaching staff seemed to be successful. Italy shocked Fiji, beating them 66-10 in their Test meeting in Treviso. Physically it was a very demanding game for the Italians as the Fijians approached the game in a robust manner that resulted in one red card (for skipper Alivereti Doviverata) and three sin-binned players (Waisale Serevi, Vili Satala and Setoki Niqara). Undoubtedly this helped Italy to win a match that provided a springboard to preparations for the game against South Africa in Genoa.

The Italians went into the Test brimful of confidence, particularly after the disaster the Springboks had suffered in losing against the French. At the Luigi Ferraris Stadium the early stages of the first half confirmed the Italian expectations, but then careless mistakes gave South Africa possession and Braam van Straaten converted penalties into points. In the second half, Italy showed that they were not yet ready to beat a relaxed South African side that made international rugby look so easy. They moved the ball wide at great speed to stretch the Italian defence and eventually won by 54-26, turning Italian hopes to despair.

The last Test of the autumn was on a cold evening in L'Aquila, against John Boe's Samoans. Boe had been considered by Italy before preferring Johnstone as their coach and it was felt that both sides had a point to prove.

The Italian players, however, were in no mood for a rugby match. They had spent the entire week before the Samoan match discussing their playing contracts without a final decision being reached. When they arrived for the match, their minds were far away from the game and Samoa punished them with a splendid display of aggressive defence, hard but fair tackling and controlled rugby in midfield. They scored a try that reflected their clear superiority, while Italy could only manage three penalties from the boot of Diego Dominguez.

Rumours abounded about Johnstone's faults but these were buried under the excitement of the club season, although it was clear to all that the 2002 Six Nations would be a story of the Italians involved in a desperate battle to avoid the wooden spoon.

The adventure started in Arezzo with a warm-up match against an Italian League XV. Italy beat an all-stars selection and Johnstone had the opportunity to blood a new No 8, the New Zealand-born Matthew Phillips. Under the Tuscany clouds the Viadana captain did not impress, but the Italian coaching staff were still confident about his potential.

The Championship opened in Paris where for the entire match the Italian play was littered with mistakes. They yielded too many penalties which the French fly-half, Gérald Merceron, was grateful to convert into points. The Italians also exhibited attacking weaknesses through faulty alignment. Diego Dominguez in particular was unable to get his threequarter line moving and the French defence had an easy afternoon. The result – France 33, Italy 12 – hardly punished the Italian team as much as it might have done, and there were still hopes that against Scotland the music would be different.

The Scots came for their Roman weekend with the intention of taking revenge for the defeat they suffered two years earlier in the inaugural Six Nations Championship match. This time they played a perfect game. Gregor Townsend showed Dominguez how to play modern rugby, taking the pressure off his outsides before spreading the ball wide. For Italy, there were yellow cards, more mistakes and a defence which ran out of steam by the interval.

It was this 29-12 defeat that precipitated a players' showdown with Johnstone. Several announced that they would not play if Johnstone remained in charge of the coaching staff. John Kirwan did not take a stand, but it was clear that the majority of the players were with the former Auckland wing. The executive board then confirmed Johnstone as the head coach, but only until the end of the championship. It was clear that the coach was on the verge of being sacked : no longer a question of if, more a question of when.

Now came Johnstone's revenge. Alessandro Troncon was relegated to the A side, a scandal that forced the FIR president, Giancarlo Dondi, to travel from Parma to the training camp to talk with Johnstone and persuade him to change his mind. It was under this cloud that Italy faced Wales in the next match. The electric atmosphere of the Millennium Stadium helped

Italy to play with more pride, but it was not enough for the critics to change their views. The result was another defeat (20-44), though Italy did score their first tries of the tournament.

Ireland were next. At Lansdowne Road, Dominguez was near to his best but Ireland were so consistent throughout the game that Italy couldn't sustain their tempo. The referee sin-binned Salvatore Perugini (which meant a suspension for him in the next game) after he had stamped on Peter Stringer. Johnstone punished him further by not allowing him back in the game after ten minutes. The final score (17-32) did not give a fair reflection of the game. Ireland should have scored more points but for once the wall in the midfield was not easy for Brian O'Driscoll and Shane Horgan to penetrate.

The final game against England was one-way traffic. Clive Woodward's team arrived at the Flaminio knowing that France had won the Championship. It was the perfect chance for England to blood new players – at least in the first half. It was very strange to see the former captains Lawrence Dallaglio, Matthew Dawson and Martin Johnston on the bench. However, once they came onto the field in the second half the story was over. England completely dominated the game, from the set pieces to the rucks and mauls, and it was very easy for Jason Robinson to turn the defence around.

The England game proved to be Brad Johnstone's last as coach. His record was five matches won and 22 lost before a new era began under John Kirwan, whose target is to win the Six Nations within five years. That's a tall order – even for the most optimistic Italian rugby fan. To help him reach that target he has called upon another Kiwi, Leicester Rutledge.

Their first game in charge together was on the tour to New Zealand in June. They had a very young and inexperienced team for such a difficult visit. Italy won 37-13 in a game against Manawatu before drawing 35-35 with a Divisional XV. But in the Test against John Mitchell's All Blacks, Italy were well beaten by 64-10. Even so, it provided very good experience for Italian rugby as it prepares for the 2003 Rugby World Cup. New players like No 8 Sergio Parisse, Argentine-born prop Ramiro Martinez-Frugoni and centre Matteo Barbini joined the team together with Mirco Bergamasco, (Mauro's younger brother) and Gert Peens, a South African by birth who has lived in Italy for more than five years.

Peens and Martinez-Frugoni may well be the last eligible foreign players to appear for Italy as the FIR has changed policy and will no longer look overseas for its players. This may prove to be a good move for a team that now has a future. In September, the RWC qualifying matches take place against Romania and Spain, and these will be followed by autumn Tests against Australia in Genoa and Argentina in Rome. All will be approached with a new coach and new hopes.

Italy's Test Record in 2001-2002:
Played 9, won 1, lost 8.

Opponents	Date	Venue	Result
New Zealand	8th June 2002	A	Lost 10-64
England	7th April 2002	H	Lost 9-45
Ireland	23rd March 2002	A	Lost 17-32
Wales	2nd March 2002	A	Lost 20-44
Scotland	16th February 2002	H	Lost 12-29
France	2nd February 2002	A	Lost 12-33
Samoa	24th November 2001	H	Lost 9-17
South Africa	17th November 2001	H	Lost 26-54
Fiji	10th November 2001	H	Won 66-10

ITALY INTERNATIONAL STATISTICS

(to 31 August 2002)

Match Records

MOST CONSECUTIVE TEST WINS

6 1968 *Pt, G,Y,* 1969 *Bu, Sp, Be*

MOST CONSECUTIVE TESTS WITHOUT DEFEAT

Matches	Wins	Draws	Period
6	6	0	1968-69
5	4	1	1982-83

MOST POINTS IN A MATCH
by the team

Pts	Opponents	Venue	Year
104	Czech Republic	Viadana	1994
78	Croatia	Perpignan	1993
70	Morocco	Carcassonne	1993
67	Netherlands	Huddersfield	1998
66	Fiji	Treviso	2001
64	Portugal	Lisbon	1996

by a player

Pts	Player	Opponents	Venue	Year
29	S Bettarello	Canada	Toronto	1983
29	D Dominguez	Scotland	Rome	2000
29	D Dominguez	Fiji	Treviso	2001
28	D Dominguez	Netherlands	Calvisano	1994
27	D Dominguez	Ireland	Bologna	1997
25	D Dominguez	Romania	Tarbes	1997
24	L Troiani	Spain	Parma	1994

MOST TRIES IN A MATCH
by the team

Tries	Opponents	Venue	Year
16	Czech Republic	Viadana	1994
11	Croatia	Perpignan	1993
11	Netherlands	Huddersfield	1998
10	Belgium	Paris	1937
10	Morocco	Carcassonne	1993
10	Portugal	Lisbon	1996

by a player

Tries	Player	Opponents	Venue	Year
4	R Cova	Belgium	Paris	1937
4	I Francescato	Morocco	Carcassonne	1993

MOST CONVERSIONS IN A MATCH
by the team

Cons	Opponents	Venue	Year
12	Czech Republic	Viadana	1994
10	Croatia	Perpignan	1993
10	Morocco	Carcassonne	1993
8	Spain	Parma	1994

by a player

Cons	Player	Opponents	Venue	Year
12	L Troiani	Czech Reuplic	Viadana	1994
10	L Troiani	Croazia	Perpignan	1993
10	G Filizzola	Morocco	Carcassonne	1993
8	L Troiani	Spain	Parma	1994

MOST PENALTIES IN A MATCH
by the team

Penalties	Opponents	Venue	Year
8	Romania	Catania	1994
7	Fiji	Treviso	2001
6	Scotland	Rovigo	1993
6	Argentina	Lourdes	1997
6	Ireland	Bologna	1997
6	Scotland	Treviso	1998
6	Tonga	Leicester	1999
6	Scotland	Rome	2000

by a player

Penalties	Player	Opponents	Venue	Year
8	D Dominguez	Romania	Catania	1994
7	D Dominguez	Fiji	Treviso	2001
6	D Dominguez	Scotland	Rovigo	1993
6	D Dominguez	Argentina	Lourdes	1997
6	D Dominguez	Ireland	Bologna	1997
6	D Dominguez	Scotland	Treviso	1998
6	D Dominguez	Tonga	Leicester	1999
6	D Dominguez	Scotland	Rome	2000

MOST DROPPED GOALS IN A MATCH
by the team

Drops	Opponents	Venue	Year
3	Transvaal	Johannesburg	1973
3	Scotland	Rome	2000

by a player

Drops	Player	Opponents	Venue	Year
3	R Caligiuri	Tranvaal	Johannesburg	1973
3	D Dominguez	Scotland	Rome	2000

Career Records

MOST CAPPED PLAYERS

Caps	Player	Career Span
73	C Checchinato	1990-2002
71	D Dominguez	1991-2002
69	Massimo Cuttitta	1990-2000
67	A Troncon	1994-2002
60	S Ghizzoni	1977-87
60	M Giovanelli	1989-2000
57	P Vaccari	1991-2002
55	S Bettarello	1979-88
54	M Mascioletti	1977-90
54	Marcello Cuttitta	1987-99
54	F Properzi-Curti	1990-2001
53	G Pivetta	1979-93

MOST CONSECUTIVE TESTS

Tests	Player	Span
31	A Moscardi	1999-2002
29	M Bollesan	1968-72
27	Massimo Cuttitta	1991-94
25	C Orlandi	1995-98
24	D Dominguez	1995-99
23	A Sgorlon	1995-98
23	C Stoica	1999-2001

MOST TESTS AS CAPTAIN

Tests	Captain	Span
37	M Giovanelli	1992-99
34	M Bollesan	1969-75
22	Massimo Cuttitta	1993-99
20	M Innocenti	1985-88

MOST TESTS IN INDIVIDUAL POSITIONS

Position	Player	Tests	Span
Full-back	L Troiani	41	1985-95
Wing	Marcello Cuttitta	54	1987-99
Centre	N Francescato	39	1972-82
Fly-half	D Dominguez	65	1991-2002
Scrum-half	A Troncon	67	1994-2002
Prop	M Cuttitta	69	1990-2000
Hooker	A Moscardi	44	1993-2002
Lock	R Favaro	42	1988-96

Flanker	M Giovanelli	60	1989-2000
No 8	C Checchinato	42	1991-2002

MOST POINTS IN TESTS

Points	Player	Tests	Career
959	D Dominguez	71	1991-2002
483	S Bettarello	55	1979-88
296	L Troiani	47	1985-95
133	E Ponzi	20	1973-77
110	Marc Cuttitta	54	1987-99

MOST TRIES IN TESTS

Tries	Player	Tests	Career
25	Marc Cuttitta	54	1987-99
22	P Vaccari	57	1991-2002
21	M Marchetto	43	1972-81
20	C Checchinato	73	1990-2002
17	S Ghizzoni	60	1977-87
17	M Mascioletti	54	1977-90

MOST CONVERSIONS IN TESTS

Cons	Player	Tests	Career
124	D Dominguez	71	1991-2002
58	L Troiani	47	1985-95
46	S Bettarello	55	1979-88
17	E Ponzi	20	1973-77
16	G Filizzola	12	1993-95

MOST PENALTY GOALS IN TESTS

Penalties	Player	Tests	Career
205	D Dominguez	71	1991-2002
104	S Bettarello	55	1979-88
57	L Troiani	47	1985-95
31	E Ponzi	20	1973-77

MOST DROPPED GOALS IN TESTS

Drops	Player	Tests	Career
17	S Bettarello	55	1979-88
17	D Dominguez	71	1991-2002
5	M Bonomi	34	1988-96
5	O Collodo	15	1977-87

International Championship Records

Record	Detail		Set
Most points in season	106	in five matches	2000
	106	in five matches	2001
Most tries in season	9	in five matches	2000
Highest Score	34	34-20 v Scotland	2000
Biggest win	14	34-20 v Scotland	2000
Highest score conceded	80	23-80 v England	2001
Biggest defeat	57	23-80 v England	2001
Most appearances	15	C Stoica	2000 – 2002
	15	A Moscardi	2000 – 2002
	15	M Bergamasco	2000 – 2002
Most points in matches	144	D Dominguez	2000 – 2002
Most points in season	61	D Dominguez	2000
Most points in match	29	D Dominguez	v Scotland, 2000
Most tries in matches	4	C Checchinato	2000 – 2002
Most tries in season	3	C Checchinato	2001
Most tries in match	2	A Troncon	v France, 2000
Most cons in matches	12	D Dominguez	2000 – 2002
Most cons in season	8	D Dominguez	2000
Most cons in match	4	D Dominguez	v France, 2000
Most pens in matches	34	D Dominguez	2000 – 2002
Most pens in season	13	D Dominguez	2001
Most pens in match	6	D Dominguez	v Scotland, 2000
Most drops in matches	6	D Dominguez	2000 – 2002
Most drops in season	5	D Dominguez	2000
Most drops in match	3	D Dominguez	v Scotland, 2000

Miscellaneous Records

Record	Holder	Detail
Longest Test Career	S Lanfranchi	16 seasons, 1949 to 1964

Career Records Of Italy International Players
(up to 31 August 2002)

PLAYER	Debut	Caps	T	C	P	D	Pts
Backs:							
J A Antoni	2001 v Nm	2	0	0	0	0	0
M Barbini	2002 v NZ	1	0	0	0	0	0
M Baroni	1999 v F	6	1	0	0	0	5
Mirco Bergamasco	2002 v F	3	0	0	0	0	0
A Ceppolino	1999 v U	5	1	0	0	0	5
D Dallan	1999 v F	23	2	0	0	0	10
M Dallan	1997 v Arg	13	3	0	0	0	15
D Dominguez	1991 v F	71	9	124	205	17	959
J S Francesio	2000 v W	4	0	0	0	0	0
F Frati	2000 v C	4	0	0	0	0	0
E Galon	2001 v I	1	0	0	0	0	0
L Martin	1997 v F	38	9	0	0	0	45
A Masi	1999 v Sp	1	1	0	0	0	5
M Mazzantini	2000 v S	5	0	0	0	0	0
F Mazzariol	1995 v F	26	2	12	14	0	76

G Mazzi	1998 v H	5	1	0	0	0	5
N Mazzucato	1995 v SA	20	3	0	0	0	15
S Pace	2001 v SA	2	0	0	0	0	0
R Pedrazzi	2001 v Nm	5	0	0	0	0	0
G Peens	2002 v W	4	0	2	2	1	13
M Perziano	2000 v NZ	10	3	0	0	0	15
R Pez	2000 v Sm	9	1	6	7	1	41
C Pilat	1997 v I	7	2	0	1	0	13
W Pozzebon	2001 v I	13	2	0	0	0	10
G Preo	1999 v I	7	0	1	0	0	2
J-M Queirolo	2000 v Sm	6	0	0	0	0	0
G Raineri	1998 v H	16	2	0	1	0	13
M Rivaro	2000 v S	4	0	0	0	0	0
F Roselli	1995 v F	16	5	0	0	0	25
A Scanavacca	1999 v U	2	0	2	3	0	13
C Stoica	1997 v I	43	9	0	0	0	45
A Troncon	1994 v Sp	67	13	0	0	0	65
P Vaccari	1991 v Nm	57	22	0	0	0	107
L Villagra	2000 v Sm	2	0	0	0	0	0
C Zanoletti	2001 v Sm	3	0	0	0	0	0
N Zisti	1999 v E	4	0	0	0	0	0
Forwards:							
A Benatti	2001 v Fj	4	1	0	0	0	5
Mauro Bergamasco	1998 v H	24	5	0	0	0	25
M Birtig	1998 v H	2	0	0	0	0	0
M Bortolami	2001 v Nm	11	1	0	0	0	5
C Caione	1995 v R	25	3	0	0	0	15
A Castellani	1994 v Cz	20	1	0	0	0	5
M-L Castrogiovanni	2002 v NZ	1	0	0	0	0	0
C Checchinato	1990 v Sp	73	20	0	0	0	100
L Cornella	1999 v Sp	1	0	0	0	0	0
D Dal Maso	2000 v Sm	4	0	0	0	0	0
G P de Carli	1996 v W	29	4	0	0	0	20
A de Rossi	1999 v U	16	1	0	0	0	5
S Dellape	2002 v F	5	0	0	0	0	0
G Faliva	1999 v SA	2	0	0	0	0	0
S Garozzo	2001 v U	2	0	0	0	0	0
M Giacheri	1992 v R	43	0	0	0	0	0
A Gritti	1996 v Pt	15	0	0	0	0	0
G Lanzi	1998 v Arg	8	0	0	0	0	0
A Lo Cicero	2000 v E	18	2	0	0	0	10
R Martinez-Frugoni	2002 v NZ	1	0	0	0	0	0
L Mastrodomenico	2000 v Sm	5	0	0	0	0	0
A Moreno	1999 v Tg	4	0	0	0	0	0
A Moretti	1997 v R	8	0	0	0	0	0
A Moscardi	1993 v Pt	44	6	0	0	0	30
A Muraro	2000 v C	13	0	0	0	0	0
C Nieto	2002 v E	1	0	0	0	0	0
F Ongaro	2000 v C	5	0	0	0	0	0
C Paoletti	2000 v S	15	0	0	0	0	0
S Parisse	2002 v NZ	1	0	0	0	0	0
A Persico	2000 v S	22	1	0	0	0	5
S Perugini	2000 v I	12	0	0	0	0	0

M Phillips	2002 v F	5	0	0	0	0	0
R Piovan	1996 v Pt	4	0	0	0	0	0
F Pucciariello	1999 v Sp	7	1	0	0	0	5
R Rampazzo	1996 v W	2	0	0	0	0	0
S Saviozzi	1998 v Ru	13	2	0	0	0	10
S Stocco	1998 v H	4	1	0	0	0	5
L Travini	1999 v SA	5	0	0	0	0	0
W Visser	1999 v I	22	1	0	0	0	5
M Zaffiri	2000 v Fj	4	0	0	0	0	0

SOUTH AFRICA TEST SEASON REVIEW 2001-02

A hint of brighter things to come

Dan Retief

For South African rugby a period that marked the 10th year since the end of isolation contained enough incident to have filled an entire decade. For a start, the Springbok team ended up with yet another new coach – the ninth since re-admission in 1992 – while a significant re-structuring of the way in which the game is run in the Republic took place. Along the way there were also some significant victories, some heart-wrenching losses, some disciplinary issues, a spate of injuries to big-name players, victory in the IRB Under 21 World Cup and the departure to foreign fields of more major players taking advantage of the parlous state of the South African Rand.

While steps were being taken at administrative level to split the running of the game into 'amateur' and 'professional' arms with the creation of a new commercial entity to be known as SA Rugby (Pty) Ltd, the Springboks were in the throes of preparing for their by-now obligatory tour to the northern hemisphere taking in internationals against France, Italy, England and the United States. Rian Oberholzer, the former chief executive of the SA Rugby Football Union, became managing director of SA Rugby (Pty) Ltd charged with the running of the financial aspects of rugby – including the Springbok team – and answering to a board that for the first time would include directors drawn from the wider business community.

In a significant move Songezo Nayo was appointed as deputy MD of SA Rugby as part of a concerted effort to transform South African rugby and make it more representative of the national demographics; a process carefully monitored by the ministry of sport. The SA Rugby Football Union remained in place to control all the administrative aspects of the game and Mveleli Ncula, an official from Eastern Province, became its first black chief executive. Silas Nkanunu became chairman of both bodies.

Far-reaching as these decisions were, they went almost unnoticed against the intense interest that surrounded the doings of the Springbok team. For coach Harry Viljoen, after a promising Tri Nations in 2001 when the Springboks had beaten and drawn (away) with the Wallabies while running the All Blacks close, the end-of-year overseas tour represented a watershed. Doubts had begun to arise about the 'process' he claimed would take South Africa to success in the World Cup in 2003 and the public were looking for signs that all was well with their beloved Springbok team. That, in South Africa, meant only one thing; the team had to start winning. But they didn't. Up against what appeared to be a callow French team full of untried players the Boks lost 10-20 in Paris, looked unconvincing in subduing Italy 54-26 in Genoa and were comprehensively out-thought, out-played and out-muscled 29-9 by England at Twickenham.

Dissatisfaction with Viljoen was starting to bubble over at home and the young coach was clearly facing a crisis when his team, making their first visit to America since playing a Test on a polo field in upstate New York during the 1981 'demo' tour, made heavy weather of beating the United States 43-20 in Houston in December. The summer holidays and strong messages of support from SA Rugby brought some respite for Viljoen and his position seemed entrenched when he played a key role in the naming of the country's four regional squads to take part in the Super Twelve competition.

These squads, sending a signal that the national coach would have a strong hand in the Super Twelve, were announced on January 14 and there was no inkling of the bombshell that would burst just four days later. Viljoen, citing off-field media pressures as his reason, took even his closest confidants by surprise when he resigned on January 18, saying: 'The media are unrelenting in South Africa. Frankly, I could not deal with the constant negatives.'

Under pressure to rectify what had become an embarrassing sequence of hiring and firing, SA Rugby decided to call for applications – only South Africans eligible – for the position and eventually settled on a short-list of four, Rudolf Straeuli, Rudi Joubert, Allister Coetzee and Jake White. The foursome were called to interviews, during which input was enlisted from former Springbok captain Morné du Plessis and former coach André Markgraaff, and on March 1, at the height of the Super Twelve season, former Test No 8 and the current Sharks coach, Rudolf Straeuli, was named to succeed Viljoen.

Straeuli had been a member of the side that won the Rugby World Cup in 1995 and had had a spell in England before returning to South Africa to take up a position with Border before, soon afterwards, moving to the Natal Sharks. He immediately set about putting in place his 'back to the basics' programme aimed at restoring discipline among the players, regaining the trust of the public and rekindling pride in the traditions of Springbok rugby.

Straeuli's methods immediately found favour among rugby supporters; more so because just days before he took over the reins former Springbok captain André Vos, South Africa's Player of the Year for 2001, had caused even more reverberations by announcing that he was leaving South Africa to join Harlequins. Others, such as Pieter Rossouw, Robbie Kempson and Percy Montgomery, would soon follow. The new coach came in hard. He re-instituted national trials and also scrapped plans for the annual Springbok training camp at a luxury hotel in Plettenberg Bay, an east coast holiday resort, instead announcing his squad would gather in the Spartan surroundings of the SA Police Training College in Pretoria.

In the event the trial game, held at Loftus Versfeld, turned out to be a masterstroke for it brought to the fore in Jannes Labuschagne the hard-working lock that Straeuli had been looking for, while also providing the stage for the exceptional skills of Sevens star Brent Russell. When it came to naming his first team, Straeuli overturned notions of his being conservative by including Russell as well as exciting youngsters such as flanker Joe van Niekerk and half-backs André Pretorius and Johannes 'Bolla' Conradie. Straeuli, unlike some of his predecessors, was more inclusive of the national selectors Francois Davids and Wynand Claassen and willing to consult with the like of national Sevens coach Chester Williams while involving Naas Botha to smarten up the team's kicking skills.

His tenure started successfully enough with a series victory over Wales, seeing off Argentina and routing Samoa, but everyone knew the acid test would be the Tri Nations. The Springboks showed glimpses of an exciting new attacking style which led to spectacular tries. But still they lost.

Then came the series deciding match against Australia at Ellis Park, almost 10 years to the day since the Springboks were welcomed back into the fold by playing the All Blacks at the same venue in 1992. With the final hooter already having sounded, full-back Werner Greeff cut in on the angle to score the try and conversion that gave the Springboks a 33-31 victory and, most South Africans believe, cast the die for a bright new passage in Springbok history.

South Africa's Test Record in 2001-2002: Played 12, won 7, lost 5

Opponents	Date	Venue	Result
Australia	17th August 2002	H	Won 33-31
New Zealand	10th August 2002	H	Lost 23-30
Australia	27th July 2002	A	Lost 27-38
New Zealand	20th July 2002	A	Lost 20-41
Samoa	29th June 2002	H	Won 60-18
Argentina	22nd June 2002	H	Won 49-29
Wales	15th June 2002	H	Won 19-8
Wales	8th June 2002	H	Won 34-19
United States	1st December 2001	A	Won 43-20
England	24th November 2001	A	Lost 9-29
Italy	17th November 2001	A	Won 54-26
France	10th November 2001	A	Lost 10-20

SOUTH AFRICA INTERNATIONAL STATISTICS
(up to 31 August 2002)

Match Records

MOST CONSECUTIVE TEST WINS

17 1997 *A*2, *It*, *F* 1,2, *E*, *S*, 1998 *I* 1,2, *W* 1, *E* 1, *A* 1, *NZ* 1, 2, *A* 2, *W* 2, *S*, *I* 3
15 1994 *Arg* 1,2, *S*, *W* 1995 *WS*, *A*, *R*, *C*, *WS*, *F*, *NZ*, *W*, *It*, *E*, 1996 *Fj*

MOST CONSECUTIVE TESTS WITHOUT DEFEAT

Matches	Wins	Draws	Period
17	17	0	1997 to 1998
16	15	1	1994 to 1996
15	12	3	1960 to 1963

MOST POINTS IN A MATCH
by the team

Pts	Opponents	Venue	Year
101	Italy	Durban	1999
96	Wales	Pretoria	1998
74	Tonga	Cape Town	1997
74	Italy	Port Elizabeth	1999
68	Scotland	Murrayfield	1997
62	Italy	Bologna	1997
61	Australia	Pretoria	1997

by a player

Pts	Player	Opponents	Venue	Year
34	J H de Beer	England	Paris	1999
31	P C Montgomery	Wales	Pretoria	1998
29	G S du Toit	Italy	Port Elizabeth	1999
28	G K Johnson	W Samoa	Johannesburg	1995
26	J H de Beer	Australia	Pretoria	1997
26	P C Montgomery	Scotland	Murrayfield	1997
25	J T Stransky	Australia	Bloemfontein	1996
25	C S Terblanche	Italy	Durban	1999

MOST TRIES IN A MATCH
by the team

Tries	Opponents	Venue	Year
15	Wales	Pretoria	1998
15	Italy	Durban	1999
12	Tonga	Cape Town	1997
11	Italy	Port Elizabeth	1999
10	Ireland	Dublin	1912
10	Scotland	Murrayfield	1997

by a player

Tries	Player	Opponents	Venue	Year
5	C S Terblanche	Italy	Durban	1999
4	C M Williams	W Samoa	Johannesburg	1995
4	P W G Rossouw	France	Parc des Princes	1997
4	C S Terblanche	Ireland	Bloemfontein	1998

MOST CONVERSIONS IN A MATCH
by the team

Cons	Opponents	Venue	Year
13	Italy	Durban	1999
9	Scotland	Murrayfield	1997
9	Wales	Pretoria	1998
8	Italy	Port Elizabeth	1999
7	Scotland	Murrayfield	1951
7	Tonga	Cape Town	1997
7	Italy	Bologna	1997
7	France	Parc des Princes	1997
7	Italy	Genoa	2001
7	Samoa	Pretoria	2002

by a player

Cons	Player	Opponents	Venue	Year
9	P C Montgomery	Wales	Pretoria	1998
8	P C Montgomery	Scotland	Murrayfield	1997
8	G S du Toit	Italy	Port Elizabeth	1999
8	G S du Toit	Italy	Durban	1999
7	A Geffin	Scotland	Murrayfield	1951
7	E Lubbe	Tonga	Cape Town	1997
7	H W Honiball	Italy	Bologna	1997
7	H W Honiball	France	Parc des Princes	1997
7	A S Pretorius	Samoa	Pretoria	2002

MOST PENALTIES IN A MATCH
by the team

Penalties	Opponents	Venue	Year
7	France	Pretoria	1975
6	Australia	Bloemfontein	1996
6	Australia	Twickenham	1999
6	England	Pretoria	2000
6	Australia	Durban	2000
6	France	Johannesburg	2001

by a player

Penalties	Player	Opponents	Venue	Year
6	G R Bosch	France	Pretoria	1975
6	J T Stransky	Australia	Bloemfontein	1996
6	J H de Beer	Australia	Twickenham	1999
6	A J J van Straaten	England	Pretoria	2000
6	A J J van Straaten	Australia	Durban	2000
6	P C Montgomery	France	Johannesburg	2001
5	A Geffin	N Zealand	Cape Town	1949
5	R Blair	World XV	Pretoria	1977
5	H E Botha	N Zealand	Wellington	1981
5	J W Heunis	England	Port Elizabeth	1984
5	H E Botha	NZ Cavaliers	Johannesburg	1986
5	J T J van Rensburg	France	Durban	1993
5	A J Joubert	England	Pretoria	1994
5	P C Montgomery	Australia	Johannesburg	1998
5	J H de Beer	England	Paris	1999
5	A D James	France	Durban	2001
5	A J J van Straaten	Australia	Pretoria	2001
5	A J J van Straaten	New Zealand	Auckland	2001

MOST DROPPED GOALS IN A MATCH
by the team

Drops	Opponents	Venue	Year
5	England	Paris	1999
3	S America	Durban	1980
3	Ireland	Durban	1981

by a player

Drops	Player	Opponents	Venue	Year
5	J H de Beer	England	Paris	1999
3	H E Botha	S America	Durban	1980
3	H E Botha	Ireland	Durban	1981
2	B L Osler	N Zealand	Durban	1928
2	H E Botha	NZ Cavaliers	Cape Town	1986
2	J T Stransky	N Zealand	Johannesburg	1995

Career Records
MOST CAPPED PLAYERS

Caps	Player	Career Span
79	J H van der Westhuizen	1993 to 2001
77	M G Andrews	1994 to 2001
66	A G Venter	1996 to 2001
54	A-H le Roux	1994 to 2002
50	P C Montgomery	1997 to 2001
47	J T Small	1992 to 1997
42	G H Teichmann	1995 to 1999
42	P W G Rossouw	1997 to 2001
41	J Dalton	1994 to 2002
39	J P du Randt	1994 to 1999

38	F C H du Preez	1961 to 1971
38	J H Ellis	1965 to 1976
38	K Otto	1995 to 2000

MOST CONSECUTIVE TESTS

Tests	Player	Span
39	G H Teichmann	1996 to 1999
26	A N Vos	1999 to 2001
25	S H Nomis	1967 to 1972
25	A G Venter	1997 to 1999
24	P C Montgomery	1997 to 1999
24	P W G Rossouw	1997 to 1999

MOST TESTS AS CAPTAIN

Tests	Captain	Span
36	G H Teichmann	1996 to 1999
29	J F Pienaar	1993 to 1996
22	D J de Villiers	1965 to 1970
16	A N Vos	1999 to 2001
15	M du Plessis	1975 to 1980
11	J F K Marais	1971 to 1974

MOST TESTS IN INDIVIDUAL POSITIONS

Position	Player	Tests	Span
Full-back	P C Montgomery	36	1997 to 2001
Wing	J T Small	43*	1992 to 1997
Centre	J C Mulder	34	1994 to 2001
Fly-half	H E Botha	28	1980 to 1992
Scrum-half	J H van der Westhuizen	77	1993 to 2001
Prop	A-H Le Roux	52	1994 to 2002
Hooker	J Dalton	41	1994 to 2002
Lock	M G Andrews	75	1994 to 2001
Flanker	A G Venter	56	1996 to 2001
No 8	G H Teichmann	42	1995 to 1999

* excludes an appearance as a temporary replacement

MOST POINTS IN TESTS

Points	Player	Tests	Career
312	H E Botha	28	1980 to 1992
261	P C Montgomery	50	1997 to 2001
240	J T Stransky	22	1993 to 1996
221	A J J van Straaten	21	1999 to 2001
181	J H de Beer	13	1997 to 1999
175	J H van der Westhuizen	79	1993 to 2001
156	H W Honiball	35	1993 to 1999
130	P J Visagie	25	1967 to 1971

MOST TRIES IN TESTS

Tries	Player	Tests	Career
35	J H van der Westhuizen	79	1993 to 2001
21	P W G Rossouw	42	1997 to 2001
20	J T Small	47	1992 to 1997
19	D M Gerber	24	1980 to 1992
17	C S Terblanche	29	1998 to 2002
17	B J Paulse	36	1999 to 2002
15	P C Montgomery	50	1997 to 2001
14	C M Williams	27	1993 to 2000

MOST CONVERSIONS IN TESTS

Cons	Player	Tests	Career
50	H E Botha	28	1980 to 1992
42	P C Montgomery	50	1997 to 2001
38	H W Honiball	35	1993 to 1999
33	J H de Beer	13	1997 to 1999
30	J T Stransky	22	1993 to 1996
23	A J J van Straaten	21	1999 to 2001
21	A S Pretorius	7	2002
20	P J Visagie	25	1967 to 1971
20	G S du Toit	6	1998 to 1999

MOST PENALTY GOALS IN TESTS

Penalties	Player	Tests	Career
55	A J J van Straaten	21	1999 to 2001
50	H E Botha	28	1980 to 1992
47	J T Stransky	22	1993 to 1996
31	P C Montgomery	50	1997 to 2001
27	J H de Beer	13	1997 to 1999
25	H W Honiball	35	1993 to 1999
23	G R Bosch	9	1974 to 1976
19	P J Visagie	25	1967 to 1971

MOST DROPPED GOALS IN TESTS

Drops	Player	Tests	Career
18	H E Botha	28	1980 to 1992
8	J H de Beer	13	1997 to 1999
5	J D Brewis	10	1949 to 1953
5	P J Visagie	25	1967 to 1971
4	B L Osler	17	1924 to 1933

Tri Nations Records

Record	Detail		Set
Most points in season	148	in four matches	1997
Most tries in season	18	in four matches	1997
Highest Score	61	61-22 v Australia (h)	1997
Biggest win	39	61-22 v Australia (h)	1997
Highest score conceded	55	35-55 v N Zealand (a)	1997
Biggest defeat	28	0-28 v N Zealand (a)	1999
Most points in matches	94	A J J van Straaten	1999 to 2001
Most points in season	64	J H de Beer	1997
Most points in match	26	J H de Beer	v Australia (h),1997
Most tries in matches	4	J H vd Westhuizen	1996 to 2001
	4	R B Skinstad	1998 to 2002
Most tries in season	3	P C Montgomery	1997
	3	M C Joubert	2002
Most tries in match	2	P C Montgomery	v Australia (h),1997
	2	R F Fleck	v New Zealand (h) 2000
	2	W Swanepoel	v New Zealand (h) 2000
	2	M C Joubert	v Australia (a) 2002
	2	B J Paulse	v Australia (h) 2002
Most cons in matches	13	J H de Beer	1997 to 1999
Most cons in season	12	J H de Beer	1997
Most cons in match	6	J H de Beer	v Australia (h),1997
Most pens in matches	28	A J J van Straaten	1999 to 2001
Most pens in season	13	A J J van Straaten	2000
	13	A J J van Straaten	2001
Most pens in match	6	J T Stransky	v Australia (h),1996
	6	A J J van Straaten	v Australia (h),2000

Series Records

Record	Holder	Detail
Most tries	P W G Rossouw	8 in Europe, 1997
Most points	H E Botha	69 v NZ Cavaliers, 1986

Miscellaneous Records

Record	Holder	Detail
Longest Test Career	J M Powell/B H Heatlie/	13 seasons, 1891-1903/1891-1903/
	D M Gerber/H E Botha	1980-1992/1980-1992
Youngest Test Cap	A J Hartley	17 yrs 18 days in 1891
Oldest Test Cap	W H Morkel	36 yrs 258 days in 1921

Career Records Of South Africa International Players
(up to 31 August 2002)

PLAYER	Debut	Caps	T	C	P	D	Pts
Backs:							
D W Barry	2000 v C	16	3	0	0	0	15
J H Conradie	2002 v W	8	1	0	0	0	5
C D Davidson	2002 v W	2	2	0	0	0	10
D de Kock	2001 v It	2	0	0	0	0	0
N A de Kock	2001 v It	5	1	0	0	0	5
W W Greeff	2002 v Arg	6	3	4	0	1	26
D B Hall	2001 v F	13	4	0	0	0	20
T M Halstead	2001 v F	4	2	0	0	0	10
A A Jacobs	2001 v It	7	1	0	0	0	5
C A Jantjes	2001 v It	8	2	1	0	0	12
M C Joubert	2001 v NZ	9	4	0	0	0	20
L J Koen	2000 v A	4	0	8	3	0	25
R I P Loubscher	2002 v W	1	0	0	0	0	0
P C Montgomery	1997 v BI	50	15	42	31	3	261
B J Paulse	1999 v It	36	17	0	0	0	85
A S Pretorius	2002 v W	7	2	21	13	1	94
P W G Rossouw	1997 v BI	42	21	0	0	0	105
R B Russell	2002 v W	6	3	0	0	0	15
A H Snyman	1996 v NZ	34	9	0	0	0	45
C S Terblanche	1998 v I	29	17	0	0	0	85
J H van der Westhuizen	1993 v Arg	79	35	0	0	0	175
J N B van der Westhuyzen	2000 v NZ	2	0	0	0	0	0
A J J van Straaten	1999 v It	21	2	23	55	0	221
Forwards:							
M G Andrews	1994 v E	77	12	0	0	0	60
W K Britz	2002 v W	1	0	0	0	0	0
D Coetzee	2002 v Sm	1	0	0	0	0	0
J Dalton	1994 v Arg	41	5	0	0	0	25
Q Davids	2002 v W	3	0	0	0	0	0
G J D du Preez	2002 v Sm	2	1	0	0	0	5
D C F Human	2002 v W	4	0	0	0	0	0
C P J Krige	1999 v It	28	2	0	0	0	10
J J Labuschagne	2000 v NZ	8	0	0	0	0	0
A-H le Roux	1994 v E	54	1	0	0	0	5

F H Louw	2002 v W	3	0	0	0	0	0
V Matfield	2001 v It	13	3	0	0	0	15
W Meyer	1997 v S	25	1	0	0	0	5
S J Rautenbach	2002 v W	8	1	0	0	0	5
L D Sephaka	2001 v US	6	0	0	0	0	0
H Scholtz	2002 v A	3	0	0	0	0	0
R B Skinstad	1997 v E	33	10	0	0	0	50
W J Smit	2000 v C	21	1	0	0	0	5
R S Sowerby	2002 v Sm	1	0	0	0	0	0
L van Biljon	2001 v It	9	1	0	0	0	5
P A van den Berg	1999 v It	24	2	0	0	0	10
A van der Linde	1995 v It	7	0	0	0	0	0
J C van Niekerk	2001 v NZ	14	2	0	0	0	10
A G Venter	1996 v NZ	66	9	0	0	0	45
A J Venter	2000 v W	12	0	0	0	0	0
I J Visagie	1999 v It	26	0	0	0	0	0
A N Vos	1999 v It	33	5	0	0	0	25

NB Paulse's figures include a penalty try awarded against Wales in 2002

SOUTH AFRICAN INTERNATIONAL PLAYERS

(up to 31 August 2002)

Ackermann, D S P (WP) 1955 *BI* 2,3,4, 1956 *A* 1,2, *NZ* 1,3, 1958 *F* 2
Ackermann, J N (NT, BB) 1996 *Fj, A* 1, *NZ* 1, *A* 2, 2001 *F* 2(R), *It* 1, *NZ* 1(R), *A* 1
Aitken, A D (WP) 1997 *F* 2(R), *E*, 1998 *I* 2(R), *W* 1(R), *NZ* 1,2(R), *A* 2(R)
Albertyn, P K (SWD) 1924 *BI* 1,2,3,4
Alexander, F A (GW) 1891 *BI* 1,2
Allan, J (N) 1993 *A* 1(R), *Arg* 1,2(R), 1994 *E* 1,2, *NZ* 1,2,3, 1996 *Fj, A* 1, *NZ* 1, *A* 2, *NZ* 2
Allen, P B (EP) 1960 *S*
Allport, P H (WP) 1910 *BI* 2,3
Anderson, J W (WP) 1903 *BI* 3
Anderson, J H (WP) 1896 *BI* 1,3,4
Andrew, J B (Tvl) 1896 *BI* 2
Andrews, K S (WP) 1992 *E*, 1993 *F* 1,2, *A* 1(R), 2,3, *Arg* 1(R), 2, 1994 *NZ* 3
Andrews, M G (N) 1994 *E* 2, *NZ* 1,2,3, *Arg* 1,2, *S*, *W*, 1995 *WS*, [*A*, *WS*, *F*, *NZ*], *W*, *It*, *E*, 1996 *Fj, A* 1, *NZ* 1, *A* 2, *NZ* 2,3,4,5, *Arg* 1,2, *F* 1,2, *W*, 1997 *Tg* (R), *BI* 1,2, *NZ* 1, *A* 1, *NZ* 2, *A* 2, *It*, *F* 1,2, *E*, *S*, 1998 *I* 1,2, *W* 1, *E* 1, *A* 1, *NZ* 1,2, *A* 2, *W* 2, *S*, *I* 3, *E* 2, 1999 *NZ* 1,2(R), *A* 2(R), [*S*, *U*, *E*, *A* 3, *NZ* 3], 2000 *A* 2, *NZ* 2, *A* 3, *Arg*, *I*, *W*, 2001 *F* 1,2, *It* 1, *NZ* 1, *A* 1,2, *NZ* 2, *F* 3, *E*
Antelme, M J G (Tvl) 1960 *NZ* 1,2,3,4, 1961 *F*
Apsey, J T (WP) 1933 *A* 4,5, 1938 *BI* 2
Ashley, S (WP) 1903 *BI* 2
Aston, F T D (Tvl) 1896 *BI* 1,2,3,4
Atherton, S (N) 1993 *Arg* 1,2, 1994 *E* 1,2, *NZ* 1,2,3, 1996 *NZ* 2
Aucamp, J (WT) 1924 *BI* 1,2

Baard, A P (WP) 1960 *I*
Babrow, L (WP) 1937 *A* 1,2, *NZ* 1,2,3
Badenhorst, C (OFS) 1994 *Arg* 2, 1995 *WS* (R)
Barnard, A S (EP) 1984 *S Am* 1,2, 1986 *Cv* 1,2
Barnard, J H (Tvl) 1965 *S*, *A* 1,2, *NZ* 3,4
Barnard, R W (Tvl) 1970 *NZ* 2(R)
Barnard, W H M (NT) 1949 *NZ* 4, 1951 *W*
Barry, D W (WP) 2000 *C*, *E* 1,2, *A* 1(R), *NZ* 1, *A* 2, 2001 *F* 1,2, *US* (R), 2002 *W* 2, *Arg*, *Sm*, *NZ* 1, *A* 1, *NZ* 2, *A* 2
Barry, J (WP) 1903 *BI* 1,2,3
Bartmann, W J (Tvl, N) 1986 *Cv* 1,2,3,4, 1992 *NZ*, *A*, *F*, 1,2
Bastard, W E (N) 1937 *A* 1, *NZ* 1,2,3, 1938 *BI* 1,3
Bates, A J (WT) 1969 *E*, 1970 *NZ* 1,2, 1972 *E*
Bayvel, P C R (Tvl) 1974 *BI* 2,4, *F* 1,2, 1975 *F* 1,2, 1976 *NZ* 1,2,3,4
Beck, J J (WP) 1981 *NZ* 2(R), 3(R), *US*
Bedford, T P (N) 1963 *A* 1,2,3,4, 1964 *W*, *F*, 1965 *I*, *A* 1,2, 1968 *BI* 1,2,3,4, *F* 1,2, 1969 *A* 1,2,3,4, *S*, *E*, 1970 *I*, *W*, 1971 *F* 1,2
Bekker, H J (WP) 1981 *NZ* 1,3
Bekker, H P J (NT) 1952 *E*, *F*, 1953 *A* 1,2,3,4, 1955 *BI* 2,3,4, 1956 *A* 1,2, *NZ* 1,2,3,4
Bekker, M J (NT) 1960 *S*
Bekker, R P (NT) 1953 *A* 3,4
Bekker, S (NT) 1997 *A* 2(t)
Bennett, R G (Border) 1997 *Tg* (R), *BI* 1(R), 3, *NZ* 1, *A* 1, *NZ* 2
Bergh, W F (SWD) 1931 *W*, *I*, 1932 *E*, *S*, 1933 *A* 1,2,3,4,5, 1937 *A* 1,2, *NZ* 1,2,3, 1938 *BI* 1,2,3
Bestbier, A (OFS) 1974 *F* 2(R)
Bester, J J N (WP) 1924 *BI* 2,4
Bester, J L A (WP) 1938 *BI* 2,3
Beswick, A M (Bor) 1896 *BI* 2,3,4
Bezuidenhoudt, C E (NT) 1962 *BI* 2,3,4
Bezuidenhoudt, N S E (NT) 1972 *E*, 1974 *BI* 2,3,4, *F* 1,2, 1975 *F* 1,2, 1977 *Wld*
Bierman, J N (Tvl) 1931 *I*
Bisset, W M (WP) 1891 *BI* 1,3
Blair, R (WP) 1977 *Wld*
Boome, C S (WP) 1999 *It* 1,2, *W*, *NZ* 1(R), *A* 1, *NZ* 2, *A* 2, 2000 *C*, *E* 1,2
Bosch, G R (Tvl) 1974 *BI* 2, *F* 1,2, 1975 *F* 1,2, 1976 *NZ* 1,2,3,4
Bosman, N J S (Tvl) 1924 *BI* 2,3,4
Botha, D S (NT) 1981 *NZ* 1

Botha, H E (NT) 1980 *S Am* 1,2, *BI* 1,2,3,4, *S Am* 3,4, *F*, 1981 *I* 1,2, *NZ* 1,2,3, *US*, 1982 *S Am* 1,2, 1986 *Cv* 1,2,3,4, 1989 *Wld* 1,2, 1992 *NZ*, *A*, *F* 1,2, *E*
Botha, J A (Tvl) 1903 *BI* 3
Botha, J P F (NT) 1962 *BI* 2,3,4
Botha, P H (Tvl) 1965 *A* 1,2
Boyes, H C (GW) 1891 *BI* 1,2
Brand, G H (WP) 1928 *NZ* 2,3, 1931 *W*, *I*, 1932 *E*, *S*, 1933 *A* 1,2,3,4,5, 1937 *A* 1,2, *NZ* 2,3, 1938 *BI* 1
Bredenkamp, M J (GW) 1896 *BI* 1,3
Breedt, J C (Tvl) 1986 *Cv* 1,2,3,4, 1989 *Wld* 1,2, 1992 *NZ*, *A*
Brewis, J D (NT) 1949 *NZ* 1,2,3,4, 1951 *S*, *I*, *W*, 1952 *E*, *F*, 1953 *A* 1
Briers, T P D (WP) 1955 *BI* 1,2,3,4, 1956 *NZ* 2,3,4
Brink, D J (WP) 1906 *S*, *W*, *E*
Brink, R (WP) 1995 [*R*, *C*]
Britz, W K (N) 2002 *W* 1
Brooks, D (Bor) 1906 *S*
Brosnihan, W (GL, N) 1997 *A* 2, 2000 *NZ* 1(t+R), *A* 2(t+R), *NZ* 2(R), *A* 3(R), *E* 3(R)
Brown, C B (WP) 1903 *BI* 1,2,3
Brynard, G S (WP) 1965 *A* 1, *NZ* 1,2,3,4, 1968 *BI* 3,4
Buchler, J U (Tvl) 1951 *S*, *I*, *W*, 1952 *E*, *F*, 1953 *A* 1,2,3,4, 1956 *A* 2
Burdett, A F (WP) 1906 *S*, *I*
Burger, J M (WP) 1989 *Wld* 1,2
Burger, M B (NT) 1980 *BI* 2(R), *S Am* 3, 1981 *US* (R)
Burger, S W P (WP) 1984 *E* 1,2, 1986 *Cv* 1,2,3,4
Burger, W A G (Bor) 1906 *S*, *I*, *W*, 1910 *BI* 2

Carelse, G (EP) 1964 *W*, *F*, 1965 *I*, *S*, 1967 *F* 1,2,3, 1968 *F* 1,2, 1969 *A* 1,2,3,4, *S*
Carlson, R A (WP) 1972 *E*
Carolin, H W (WP) 1903 *BI* 3, 1906 *S*, *I*
Castens, H H (WP) 1891 *BI* 1
Chignell, T W (WP) 1891 *BI* 3
Cilliers, G D (OFS) 1963 *A* 1,3,4
Cilliers, N V (WP) 1996 *NZ* 3(t)
Claassen, J T (WT) 1955 *BI* 1,2,3,4, 1956 *A* 1,2, *NZ* 1,2,3,4, 1958 *F* 1,2, 1960 *S*, *NZ* 1,2,3, *W*, *I*, 1961 *E*, *S*, *F*, *I*, *A* 1,2, 1962 *BI* 1,2,3,4
Claassen, W (N) 1981 *I* 1,2, *NZ* 2,3, *US*, 1982 *S Am* 1,2
Clark, W H G (Tvl) 1933 *A* 3
Clarkson, W A (N) 1921 *NZ* 1,2, 1924 *BI* 1
Cloete, H A (WP) 1896 *BI* 4
Cockrell, C H (WP) 1969 *S*, 1970 *I*, *W*
Cockrell, R J (WP) 1974 *F* 1,2, 1975 *F* 1,2, 1976 *NZ* 1,2, 1977 *Wld*, 1981 *NZ* 1,2(R), 3, *US*
Coetzee, D (BB) 2002 *Sm*
Coetzee, J H H (WP) 1974 *BI* 1, 1975 *F* 2(R), 1976 *NZ* 1,2,3,4
Conradie, J H (WP) 2002 *W* 1,2, *Arg* (R), *Sm*, *NZ* 1, *A* 1, *NZ* 2(R), *A* 2(R)
Cope, D K (Tvl) 1896 *BI* 2
Cotty, W (GW) 1896 *BI* 3
Crampton, G (GW) 1903 *BI* 2
Craven, D H (WP) 1931 *W*, *I*, 1932 *S*, 1933 *A* 1,2,3,4,5, 1937 *A* 1,2, *NZ* 1,2,3, 1938 *BI* 1,2,3,
Cronje, P A (Tvl) 1971 *F* 1,2, *A* 1,2,3, 1974 *BI* 3,4
Crosby, J H (Tvl) 1896 *BI* 2
Crosby, N J (Tvl) 1910 *BI* 1,3
Currie, C (GW) 1903 *BI* 2

D'Alton, G (WP) 1933 *A* 1
Dalton, J (Tvl, GL, Falcons) 1994 *Arg* 1(R), 1995 [*A*, *C*], *W*, *It*, *E*, 1996 *NZ* 4(R),5, *Arg* 1,2, *F* 1,2, *W*, 1997 *Tg* (R), *BI* 3, *NZ* 2, *A* 2, *It*, *F* 1,2, *E*, *S*, 1998 *I* 1,2, *W* 1, *E* 1, *A* 1, *NZ* 1,2, *A* 2, *W* 2, *S*, *I* 3, *E* 2, 2002 *W* 1,2, *Arg*, *NZ* 1, *A* 1, *NZ* 2, *A* 2
Daneel, G M (WP) 1928 *NZ* 1,2,3,4, 1931 *W*, *I*, 1932 *E*, *S*
Daneel, H J (WP) 1906 *S*, *I*, *W*, *E*
Davidson, C D (N) 2002 *W* 2(R), *Arg*
Davids, Q (WP) 2002 *W* 2, *Arg* (R), *Sm* (R)
Davison, P M (EP) 1910 *BI* 1
De Beer, J H (OFS) 1997 *BI* 3, *NZ* 1, *A* 1, *NZ* 2, *A* 2, *F* 2(R), *S*, 1999 *A* 2, [*S*, *Sp*, *U*, *E*, *A* 3]
De Bruyn, J (OFS) 1974 *BI* 3
De Jongh, H P K (WP) 1928 *NZ* 3

De Klerk, I J (Tvl) 1969 *E*, 1970 *I, W*
De Klerk, K B H (Tvl) 1974 *BI* 1,2,3(R), 1975 *F* 1,2, 1976 *NZ* 2(R), 3,4, 1980 *S Am* 1,2, *BI* 2, 1981 *I* 1,2
De Kock, A N (GW) 1891 *BI* 2
De Kock, D (Falcons) 2001 *It* 2(R), *US*
De Kock, J S (WP) 1921 *NZ* 3, 1924 *BI* 3
De Kock, N A (WP) 2001 *It* 1, 2002 *Sm* (R), *NZ* 1(R),2, *A* 2
Delport, G M (GL) 2000 *C* (R), *E* 1(t+R), *A* 1, *NZ* 1, *A* 2, *NZ* 2, *A* 3, *Arg, I, W*, 2001 *F* 2, *It* 1
Delport, W H (EP) 1951 *S, I, W*, 1952 *E, F*, 1953 *A* 1,2,3,4
De Melker, S C (GW) 1903 *BI* 2, 1906 *E*
Devenish, C E (GW) 1896 *BI* 2
Devenish, G St L (Tvl) 1896 *BI* 2
Devenish, G E (Tvl) 1891 *BI* 1
De Villiers, D I (Tvl) 1910 *BI* 1,2,3
De Villiers, D J (WP, Bol) 1962 *BI* 2,3, 1965 *I, NZ* 1,3,4, 1967 *F* 1,2,3,4, 1968 *BI* 1,2,3,4, *F* 1,2, 1969 *A* 1,4, *E*, 1970 *I, W, NZ* 1,2,3,4
De Villiers, H A (WP) 1906 *S, W, E*
De Villiers, H O (WP) 1967 *F* 1,2,3,4, 1968 *F* 1,2, 1969 *A* 1,2,3,4, *S, E*, 1970 *I, W*
De Villiers, P du P (WP) 1928 *NZ* 1,3,4, 1932 *E*, 1933 *A* 4, 1937 *A* 1,2, *NZ* 1
Devine, D (Tvl) 1924 *BI* 3, 1928 *NZ* 2
De Vos, D J J (WP) 1965 *S*, 1969 *A* 3, *S*
De Waal, A N (WP) 1967 *F* 1,2,3,4
De Waal, P J (WP) 1896 *BI* 4
De Wet, A E (WP) 1969 *A* 3,4, *E*
De Wet, P J (WP) 1938 *BI* 1,2,3
Dinkelmann, E E (NT) 1951 *S, I*, 1952 *E, F*, 1953 *A* 1,2
Dirksen, C W (NT) 1963 *A* 4, 1964 *W*, 1965 *I, S*, 1967 *F* 1,2,3,4, 1968 *BI* 1,2
Dobbin, F J (GW) 1903 *BI* 1,2, 1906 *S, W, E*, 1910 *BI* 1, 1912 *S, I, W*
Dobie, J A R (Tvl) 1928 *NZ* 2
Dormehl, P J (WP) 1896 *BI* 3,4
Douglass, F W (EP) 1896 *BI* 1
Drotské, A E (OFS) 1993 *Arg* 2, 1995 [*WS* (R)], 1996 *A* 1(R), 1997 *Tg, BI* 1,2,3(R), *NZ* 1, *A* 1, *NZ* 2(R), 1998 *I* 2(R), *W* 1(R), *I* 3(R), 1999 *It* 1,2, *W, NZ* 1, *A* 1, *NZ* 2, *A* 2, [*S, Sp* (R), *U, E, A* 3, *NZ* 3]
Dryburgh, R G (WP) 1955 *BI* 2,3,4, 1956 *A* 2, *NZ* 1,4, 1960 *NZ* 1,2
Duff, B R (WP) 1891 *BI* 1,2,3
Duffy, B A (Bor) 1928 *NZ* 1
Du Plessis, C J (WP) 1982 *S Am* 1,2, 1984 *E* 1,2, *S Am* 1,2, 1986 *Cv* 1,2,3,4, 1989 *Wld* 1,2
Du Plessis, D C (NT) 1977 *Wld*, 1980 *S Am* 2
Du Plessis, F (Tvl) 1949 *NZ* 1,2,3
Du Plessis, M (WP) 1971 *A* 1,2,3, 1974 *BI* 1,2, *F* 1,2, 1975 *F* 1,2, 1976 *NZ* 1,2,3,4, 1977 *Wld*, 1980 *S Am* 1,2, *BI* 1,2,3,4, *S Am* 4, *F*
Du Plessis, M J (WP) 1984 *S Am* 1,2, 1986 *Cv* 1,2,3,4, 1989 *Wld* 1,2
Du Plessis, N J (WT) 1921 *NZ* 2,3, 1924 *BI* 1,2,3
Du Plessis, P G (NT) 1972 *E*
Du Plessis, T D (NT) 1980 *S Am* 1,2
Du Plessis, W (WP) 1980 *S Am* 1,2, *BI* 1,2,3,4, *S Am* 3,4, *F*, 1981 *NZ* 1,2,3, 1982 *S Am* 1,2
Du Plooy, A J J (EP) 1955 *BI* 1
Du Preez, F C H (NT) 1961 *E, S, A* 1,2, 1962 *BI* 1,2,3,4, 1963 *A* 1, 1964 *W, F*, 1965 *A* 1,2, *NZ* 1,2,3,4, 1967 *F* 4, 1968 *BI* 1,2,3,4, *F* 1,2, 1969 *A* 1,2, *S*, 1970 *I, W, NZ* 1,2,3,4, 1971 *F* 1,2, *A* 1,2,3
Du Preez, G J D (GL) 2002 *Sm* (R), *A* 1(R)
Du Preez, J G H (WP) 1956 *NZ* 1
Du Preez, R J (N) 1992 *NZ, A*, 1993 *F* 1,2, *A* 1,2,3
Du Rand, J A (R, NT) 1949 *NZ* 2,3, 1951 *S, I, W*, 1952 *E, F*, 1953 *A* 1,2,3,4, 1955 *BI* 1,2,3,4, 1956 *A* 1,2, *NZ* 1,2,3,4
Du Randt, J P (OFS) 1994 *Arg* 1,2, *S, W*, 1995 *WS*, [*A, WS, F, NZ*], 1996 *Fj, A* 1, *NZ* 1, *A* 2, *NZ* 2,3,4, 1997 *Tg, BI* 1,2,3, *NZ* 1, *A* 1, *NZ* 2, *A* 2, *It, F* 1,2, *E, S*, 1999 *NZ* 1, *A* 1, *NZ* 2, *A* 2, [*S, Sp* (R), *U, E, A* 3, *NZ* 3]
Du Toit, A F (WP) 1928 *NZ* 3,4
Du Toit, B A (Tvl) 1938 *BI* 1,2,3
Du Toit, G S (GW) 1998 *I* 1, 1999 *It* 1,2, *W* (R), *NZ* 1,2
Du Toit, P A (NT) 1949 *NZ* 2,3,4, 1951 *S, I, W*, 1952 *E, F*
Du Toit, P G (WP) 1981 *NZ* 1, 1982 *S Am* 1,2, 1984 *E* 1,2
Du Toit, P S (WP) 1958 *F* 1,2, 1960 *NZ* 1,2,3,4, *W, I*, 1961 *E, S, F, I, A* 1,2
Duvenhage, F P (GW) 1949 *NZ* 1,3

Edwards, P (NT) 1980 *S Am* 1,2
Ellis, J H (SWA) 1965 *NZ* 1,2,3,4, 1967 *F* 1,2,3,4, 1968 *BI* 1,2,3,4, *F* 1,2, 1969 *A* 1,2,3,4, *S*, 1970 *I, W, NZ* 1,2,3,4, 1971 *F* 1,2, *A* 1,2,3, 1972 *E*, 1974 *BI* 1,2,3,4, *F* 1,2, 1976 *NZ* 1
Ellis, M C (Tvl) 1921 *NZ* 2,3, 1924 *BI* 1,2,3,4
Els, W W (OFS) 1997 *A* 2(R)
Engelbrecht, J P (WP) 1960 *S, W, I*, 1961 *E, S, F, A* 1,2, 1962 *BI* 2,3,4, 1963 *A* 2,3,4, 1964 *W, F*, 1965 *I, S, A* 1,2, *NZ* 1,2,3,4, 1967 *F* 1,2,3,4, 1968 *BI* 1,2, *F* 1,2, 1969 *A* 1,2
Erasmus, F H (EP) 1986 *Cv* 3,4, 1989 *Wld* 2
Erasmus, J C (OFS, GL) 1997 *BI* 3, *A* 2, *It, F* 1,2, *S*, 1998 *I* 1,2, *W* 1, *E* 1, *A* 1, *NZ* 2, *A* 2, *S, W* 2, *I* 3, *E* 2, 1999 *It* 1,2, *W, A* 1, *NZ* 2, *A* 2, [*S, U, E, A* 3, *NZ* 3], 2000 *C, E* 1, *A* 1, *NZ* 1,2, *A* 3, 2001 *F* 1,2
Esterhuizen, G (GL) 2000 *NZ* 1(R),2, *A* 3, *Arg, I, W* (R), *E* 3(t)
Etlinger, T E (WP) 1896 *BI* 4

Ferreira, C (OFS) 1986 *Cv* 1,2
Ferreira, P S (WP) 1984 *S Am* 1,2
Ferris, H H (Tvl) 1903 *BI* 3
Fleck R F (WP) 1999 *It* 1,2, *NZ* 1(R), *A* 1, *NZ* 2(R), *A* 2, [*S, U, E, A* 3, *NZ* 3], 2000 *C, E* 1,2, *A* 1, *NZ* 1, *A* 2, *NZ* 2, *A* 3, *Arg, I, W, E* 3, 2001 *F* 1(R),2, *It* 1, *NZ* 1, *A* 1,2
Forbes, H H (Tvl) 1896 *BI* 2
Fourie, C (EP) 1974 *F* 1,2, 1975 *F* 1,2
Fourie, T T (SET) 1974 *BI* 3
Fourie, W L (SWA) 1958 *F* 1,2
Francis, J A J (Tvl) 1912 *S, I, W*, 1913 *E, F*
Frederickson, C A (Tvl) 1974 *BI* 2, 1980 *S Am* 1,2
Frew, A (Tvl) 1903 *BI* 1
Froneman, D C (OFS) 1977 *Wld*
Froneman, I L (Bor) 1933 *A* 1
Fuls, H T (Tvl, EP) 1992 *NZ* (R), 1993 *F* 1,2, *A* 1,2,3, *Arg* 1,2
Fry, S P (WP) 1951 *S, I, W*, 1952 *E, F*, 1953 *A* 1,2,3,4, 1955 *BI* 1,2,3,4
Fynn, E E (N) 2001 *F* 1, *It* 1(R)
Fyvie, W (N) 1996 *NZ* 4(t & R), 5(R), *Arg* 2(R)

Gage, J H (OFS) 1933 *A* 1
Gainsford, J L (WP) 1960 *S, NZ* 1,2,3,4, *W, I*, 1961 *E, S, F, A* 1,2, 1962 *BI* 1,2,3,4, 1963 *A* 1,2,3,4, 1964 *W, F*, 1965 *I, S, A* 1,2, *NZ* 1,2,3,4, 1967 *F* 1,2,3
Garvey, A C (N) 1996 *Arg* 1,2, *F* 1,2, *W*, 1997 *Tg, BI* 1,2,3(R), *A* 1(t), *It, F* 1,2, *E, S*, 1998 *I* 1,2, *W* 1, *E*1, *A* 1, *NZ* 1, *A* 2, *W* 2, *S, I* 3, *E* 2, 1999 [*Sp*]
Geel, P J (OFS) 1949 *NZ* 3
Geere, V (Tvl) 1933 *A* 1,2,3,4,5
Geffin, A O (Tvl) 1949 *NZ* 1,2,3,4, 1951 *S, I, W*
Geldenhuys, A (EP) 1992 *NZ, A, F* 1,2
Geldenhuys, S B (NT) 1981 *NZ* 2,3, *US*, 1982 *S Am* 1,2, 1989 *Wld* 1,2
Gentles, T A (WP) 1955 *BI* 1,2,4, 1956 *NZ* 2,3, 1958 *F* 2
Geraghty, E M (Bor) 1949 *NZ* 4
Gerber, D M (EP, WP) 1980 *S Am* 3,4, *F*, 1981 *I* 1,2, *NZ* 1,2,3, *US*, 1982 *S Am* 1,2, 1984 *E* 1,2, *S Am* 1,2, 1986 *Cv* 1,2,3,4, 1992 *NZ, A, F* 1,2, *E*
Gerber, M C (EP) 1958 *F* 1,2, 1960 *S*
Gericke, F W (Tvl) 1960 *S*
Germishuys, J S (OFS, Tvl) 1974 *BI* 2, 1976 *NZ* 1,2,3,4, 1977 *Wld*, 1980 *S Am* 1,2, *BI* 1,2,3,4, *S Am* 3,4, *F*, 1981 *I* 1,2, *NZ* 2,3, *US*
Gibbs, B (GW) 1903 *BI* 2
Goosen, C P (OFS) 1965 *NZ* 2
Gorton, H C (Tvl) 1896 *BI* 1
Gould, R L (N) 1968 *BI* 1,2,3,4
Gray, B G (WP) 1931 *W*, 1932 *E, S*, 1933 *A* 5
Greeff, W W (WP) 2002 *Arg* (R), *Sm, NZ* 1, *A* 1, *NZ* 2, *A* 2
Greenwood, C M (WP) 1961 *I*
Greyling, P J F (OFS) 1967 *F* 1,2,3,4, 1968 *BI* 1, *F* 1,2, 1969 *A* 1,2,3,4, *S, E*, 1970 *I, W, NZ* 1,2,3,4, 1971 *F* 1,2, *A* 1,2,3, 1972 *E*
Grobler, C J (OFS) 1974 *BI* 4, 1975 *F* 1,2
Guthrie, F H (WP) 1891 *BI* 1,3, 1896 *BI* 1

Hahn, C H L (Tvl) 1910 *BI* 1,2,3
Hall, D B (GL) 2001 *F* 1,2, *NZ* 1, *A* 1,2, *NZ* 2, *It* 2, *E, US*, 2002 *Sm, NZ* 1,2, *A* 2
Halstead, T M (N) 2001 *F* 3, *It* 2, *E, US* (R)
Hamilton, F (EP) 1891 *BI* 1
Harris, T A (Tvl) 1937 *NZ* 2,3, 1938 *BI* 1,2,3
Hartley, A J (WP) 1891 *BI* 3
Hattingh, H (NT) 1992 *A* (R), *F* 2(R), *E*, 1994 *Arg* 1,2

269

Hattingh, L B (OFS) 1933 *A* 2
Heatlie, B H (WP) 1891 *BI* 2,3, 1896 *BI* 1,4, 1903 *BI* 1,3
Hendricks, M (Bol) 1998 *I* 2(R), *W* 1(R)
Hendriks, P (Tvl) 1992 *NZ, A*, 1994 *S, W*, 1995 [*A, R, C*], 1996 *A* 1, *NZ* 1, *A* 2, *NZ* 2,3,4,5
Hepburn, T B (WP) 1896 *BI* 4
Heunis, J W (NT) 1981 *NZ* 3(R), *US*, 1982 *S Am* 1,2, 1984 *E* 1,2, *S Am* 1,2, 1986 *Cv* 1,2,3,4, 1989 *Wld* 1,2
Hill, R A (R) 1960 *W, I*, 1961 *I, A* 1,2, 1962 *BI* 4, 1963 *A* 3
Hills, W G (NT) 1992 *F* 1,2, *E*, 1993 *F* 1,2, *A* 1
Hirsch, J G (EP) 1906 *I*, 1910 *BI* 1
Hobson, T E C (WP) 1903 *BI* 3
Hoffman, R S (Bol) 1953 *A* 3
Holton, D N (EP) 1960 *S*
Honiball, H W (N) 1993 *A* 3(R), *Arg* 2, 1995 *WS* (R), 1996 *Fj, A* 1, *NZ* 5, *Arg* 1,2, *F* 1,2, *W*, 1997 *Tg, BI* 1,2,3(R), *NZ* 1(R), *A* 1(R), *NZ* 2, *A* 2, *It, F* 1,2, *E*, 1998 *W* 1(R), *E* 1, *A* 1, *NZ* 1,2, *A* 2, *W* 2, *S, I* 3, *E* 2, 1999 [*A* 3(R), *NZ* 3]
Hopwood, D J (WP) 1960 *S, NZ* 3,4, *W*, 1961 *E, S, F, I, A* 1,2, 1962 *BI* 1,2,3,4, 1963 *A* 1,2,4, 1964 *W, F*, 1965 *S, NZ* 3,4
Howe, B F (Bor) 1956 *NZ* 1,4
Howe-Browne, N R F G (WP) 1910 *BI* 1,2,3
Hugo, D P (WP) 1989 *Wld* 1,2
Human, D C F (WP) 2002 *W* 1,2, *Arg* (R), *Sm* (R)
Hurter, M H (NT) 1995 [*R, C*], *W*, 1996 *Fj, A* 1, *NZ* 1,2,3,4,5, 1997 *NZ* 1,2, *A* 2

Immelman, J H (WP) 1913 *F*

Jackson, D C (WP) 1906 *I, W, E*
Jackson, J S (WP) 1903 *BI* 2
Jacobs, A A (Falcons) 2001 *It* 2(R), *US*, 2002 *W* 1(R), *Arg, Sm* (R), *NZ* 1(t+R), *A* 1(R)
James, A D (N) 2001 *F* 1,2, *NZ* 1, *A* 1,2, *NZ* 2
Jansen, E (OFS) 1981 *NZ* 1
Jansen, J S (OFS) 1970 *NZ* 1,2,3,4, 1971 *F* 1,2, *A* 1,2,3, 1972 *E*
Jantjes, C A (GL) 2001 *It* 1, *A* 1,2, *NZ* 2, *F* 3, *It* 2, *E, US*
Jennings, C B (Bor) 1937 *NZ* 1
Johnson, G K (Tvl) 1993 *Arg* 2, 1994 *NZ* 3, *Arg* 1, 1995 *WS*, [*R, C, WS*]
Johnstone, P G A (WP) 1951 *S, I, W*, 1952 *E, F*, 1956 *A* 1, *NZ* 1,2,4
Jones, C H (Tvl) 1903 *BI* 1,2
Jones, P S T (WP) 1896 *BI* 1,3,4
Jordaan, R P (NT) 1949 *NZ* 1,2,3,4
Joubert, A J (OFS, N) 1989 *Wld* 1(R), 1993 *A* 3, *Arg* 1, 1994 *E* 1,2, *NZ* 1,2(R), 3, *Arg* 2, *S, W*, 1995 [*A, C, WS, F, NZ*], *W, It, E*, 1996 *Fj, A* 1, *NZ* 1,3,4,5, *Arg* 1,2, *F* 1,2, *W*, 1997 *Tg, BI* 1,2, *A* 2
Joubert, M C (Bol, WP) 2001 *NZ* 1, 2002 *W* 1,2, *Arg* (R), *Sm, NZ* 1, *A*1, *NZ* 2, *A* 2
Joubert, S J (WP) 1906 *I, W, E*
Julies, W (Bol) 1999 [*Sp*]

Kahts, W J H (NT) 1980 *BI* 1,2,3, 1981 *I* 1,2, *NZ* 2, 1982 *S Am* 1,2
Kaminer, J (Tvl) 1958 *F* 2
Kayser, D J (EP, N) 1999 *It* 2(R), *A* 1(R), *NZ* 2, *A* 2, [*S, Sp* (R), *U, E, A* 3], 2001 *It* 1(R), *NZ* 1(R), *A* 2(R), *NZ* 2(R)
Kebble, G R (N) 1993 *Arg* 1,2, 1994 *NZ* 1(R), 2
Kelly, E W (GW) 1896 *BI* 3
Kempson, R (N, WP) 1998 *I* 2(R), *W* 1, *E* 1, *A* 1, *NZ* 1,2 *A* 2, *W* 2, *S, I* 3, *E* 2, 1999 *It* 1,2, *W*, 2000 *C, E* 1,2, *A* 1, *NZ* 1, *A* 2,3, *Arg, I, W, E* 3, 2001 *F* 1,2(R), *NZ* 1, *A* 1,2, *NZ* 2
Kenyon, B J (Bor) 1949 *NZ* 4
Kipling, H G (GW) 1931 *W, I*, 1932 *E, S*, 1933 *A* 1,2,3,4,5
Kirkpatrick, A I (GW) 1953 *A* 2, 1956 *NZ* 2, 1958 *F* 1, 1960 *S, NZ* 1,2,3,4, *W, I*, 1961 *E, S, F*
Knight, A S (Tvl) 1912 *S, I, W*, 1913 *E, F*
Knoetze, F (WP) 1989 *Wld* 1,2
Koch, A C (Bol) 1949 *NZ* 2,3,4, 1951 *S, I, W*, 1952 *E, F*, 1953 *I* 1,2,4,5, 1955 *BI* 1,2,3,4, 1956 *A* 1, *NZ* 2,3, 1958 *F* 1,2, 1960 *NZ* 1,2
Koch, H V (WP) 1949 *NZ* 1,2,3,4
Koen, L J (GL) 2000 *A* 1, 2001 *It* 2, *E, US*
Kotze, G J M (WP) 1967 *F* 1,2,3,4
Krantz, E F W (OFS) 1976 *NZ* 1, 1981 *I* 1,
Krige, C P J (WP) 1999 *It* 2, *NZ* 1, 2000 *C* (R), *E* 1(R),2, *A* 1(R), *NZ* 1, *A* 2, *NZ* 2, *A* 3, *Arg, I, W, E* 3, 2001 *F* 1,2, *It* 1(R), *A* 1(t+R), *It* 2(R), *E* (R), 2002 *W* 2, *Arg, Sm, NZ* 1, *A* 1, *NZ* 2, *A* 2
Krige, J D (WP) 1903 *BI* 1,3, 1906 *S, I, W*

Kritzinger, J L (Tvl) 1974 *BI* 3,4, *F* 1,2, 1975 *F* 1,2, 1976 *NZ* 4
Kroon, C M (EP) 1955 *BI* 1
Kruger, P E (Tvl) 1986 *Cv* 3,4
Kruger, R J (NT, BB) 1993 *Arg* 1,2, 1994 *S, W*, 1995 *WS*, [*A, R, WS, F, NZ*], *W, It, E*, 1996 *Fj, A* 1, *NZ* 1, *A* 2, *NZ* 2,3,4,5, *Arg* 1,2, *F* 1,2, *W*, 1997 *Tg, BI* 1,2, *NZ* 1, *A* 1, *NZ* 2, 1999 *NZ* 2, *A* 2(R), [*Sp, NZ* 3(R)]
Kruger, T L (Tvl) 1921 *NZ* 1,2, 1924 *BI* 1,2,3,4, 1928 *NZ* 1,2
Kuhn, S P (Tvl) 1960 *NZ* 3,4, *W, I*, 1961 *E, S, F, I, A* 1,2, 1962 *BI* 2,3,4, 1963 *A* 1,2,3, 1965 *I, S*

Labuschagne, J J (GL) 2000 *NZ* 1(R), 2002 *W* 1,2, *Arg, NZ* 1, *A* 1, *NZ* 2, *A*2
La Grange, J B (WP) 1924 *BI* 3,4
Larard, A (Tvl) 1896 *BI* 2,4
Lategan, M T (WP) 1949 *NZ* 1,2,3,4, 1951 *S, I, W*, 1952 *E, F*, 1953 *A* 1,2
Laubscher, T G (WP) 1994 *Arg* 1,2, *S, W*, 1995 *It, E*
Lawless, M J (WP) 1964 *F*, 1969 *E* (R), 1970 *I, W*
Ledger, S H (GW) 1912 *S, I*, 1913 *E, F*
Leonard, A (WP, SWD) 1999 *A* 1, [*Sp*]
Le Roux, A H (OFS, N) 1994 *E* 1, 1998 *I* 1,2, *W* 1(R), *E* 1(R), *A* 1(R), *NZ* 1,2(R), *A* 2(R), *W* 2(R), *S* (R), *I* 3(R), *E* 2(t+R), 1999 *It* 1(R),2(R), *W* (R), *NZ* 1(R), *A* 1(R), *NZ* 2(R), *A* 2(R), [*S*(R), *Sp, U* (R), *E* (R), *A* 3(R), *NZ* 3(R)], 2000 *E* 1(t+R),2(R), *A* 1(R),2(R), *NZ* 2, *A* 3(R), *Arg* (R), *I* (t), *W* (R), *E* 3(R), 2001 *F* 1(R),2, *It* 1, *NZ* 1(R), *A* 1(R),2(R), *NZ* 2(R), *F* 3, *It* 2, *E, US* (R), 2002 *W* 1(R),2(R), *Arg, NZ* 1(R), *A* 1(R), *NZ* 2(R), *A* 2(R)
Le Roux, H P (Tvl) 1993 *F* 1,2, 1994 *E* 1,2, *NZ* 1,2,3, *Arg* 2, *S, W*, 1995 *WS* [*A, R, C* (R), *WS, F, NZ*], *W, It, E*, 1996 *Fj, NZ* 2, *Arg* 1,2, *F* 1,2, *W*
Le Roux, J H S (Tvl) 1994 *E* 2, *NZ* 1,2
Le Roux, M (OFS) 1980 *BI* 1,2,3,4, *S Am* 3,4, *F*, 1981 *I* 1
Le Roux, P A (WP) 1906 *I, W, E*
Little, E M (GW) 1891 *BI* 1,3
Lochner, G P (WP) 1955 *BI* 3, 1956 *A* 1,2, *NZ* 1,2,3,4, 1958 *F* 1,2
Lochner, G P (EP) 1937 *NZ* 3, 1938 *BI* 1,2
Lockyear, R J (GW) 1960 *NZ* 1,2,3,4, 1960 *I*, 1961 *F*
Lombard, A C (EP) 1910 *BI* 2
Lötter, D (Tvl) 1993 *F* 2, *A* 1,2
Lotz, J W (Tvl) 1937 *A* 1,2, *NZ* 1,2,3, 1938 *BI* 1,2,3
Loubscher, R I P (Elephants) 2002 *W* 1
Loubser, J A (WP) 1903 *BI* 3, 1906 *S, I, W, E*, 1910 *BI* 1,3
Lourens, M J (NT) 1968 *BI* 2,3,4
Louw, F H (WP) 2002 *W* 2(R), *Arg, Sm*
Louw, J S (Tvl) 1891 *BI* 1,2,3
Louw, M J (Tvl) 1971 *A* 2,3
Louw, M M (WP) 1928 *NZ* 3,4, 1931 *W, I*, 1932 *E, S*, 1933 *A* 1,2,3,4,5, 1937 *A* 1,2, *NZ* 2,3, 1938 *BI* 1,2,3
Louw, R J (WP) 1980 *S Am* 1,2, *BI* 1,2,3,4 *S Am* 3,4, *F*, 1981 *I* 1,2, *NZ* 1,3, 1982 *S Am* 1,2, 1984 *E* 1,2, *S Am* 1,2
Louw, S C (WP) 1933 *A* 1,2,3,4,5, 1937 *A* 1, *NZ* 1,2,3, 1938 *BI* 1,2,3
Lubbe, E (GW) 1997 *Tg, BI* 1
Luyt, F P (WP) 1910 *BI* 1,2,3, 1912 *S, I, W*, 1913 *E*
Luyt, J D (EP) 1912 *S, W*, 1913 *E, F*
Luyt, R R (W P) 1910 *BI* 2,3, 1912 *S, I, W*, 1913 *E, F*
Lyons, D J (EP) 1896 *BI* 1
Lyster, P J (N) 1933 *A* 2,5, 1937 *NZ* 1

McCallum, I D (WP) 1970 *NZ* 1,2,3,4, 1971 *F* 1,2, *A* 1,2,3, 1974 *BI* 1,2
McCallum, R J (WP) 1974 *BI* 1
McCulloch, J D (GW) 1913 *E, F*
MacDonald, A W (R) 1965 *A* 1, *NZ* 1,2,3,4
Macdonald, D A (WP) 1974 *BI* 2
Macdonald, I (Tvl) 1992 *NZ, A*, 1993 *F* 1, *A* 3, 1994 *E* 2, 1995 *WS* (R)
McDonald, J A J (WP) 1931 *W, I*, 1932 *E, S*
McEwan, W M C (Tvl) 1903 *BI* 1,3
McHardy, E E (OFS) 1912 *S, I, W*, 1913 *E, F*
McKendrick, J A (WP) 1891 *BI* 3
Malan, A S (Tvl) 1960 *NZ* 1,2,3,4, *W, I*, 1961 *E, S, F*, 1962 *BI* 1, 1963 *A* 1,2,3, 1964 *W*, 1965 *I, S*
Malan, A W (NT) 1989 *Wld* 1,2, 1992 *NZ, A, F* 1,2, *E*
Malan, E (NT) 1980 *BI* 3(R)
Malan, G F (WP) 1958 *F* 2, 1960 *NZ* 1,3,4, 1961 *E, S, F*, 1962 *BI* 1,2,3, 1963 *A* 1,2,4, 1964 *W*, 1965 *A* 1,2, *NZ* 1,2
Malan, P (Tvl) 1949 *NZ* 4
Mallett, N V H (WP) 1984 *S Am* 1,2

Malotana K (Bor) 1999 [*Sp*]
Mans, W J (WP) 1965 *I, S*
Marais, C F (WP) 1999 *It* 1(R),2(R), 2000 *C, E* 1,2, *A* 1, *NZ* 1, *A* 2, *NZ* 2, *A* 3, *Arg* (R), *W* (R)
Marais, F P (Bol) 1949 *NZ* 1,2, 1951 *S*, 1953 *A* 1,2
Marais, J F K (WP) 1963 *A* 3, 1964 *W, F*, 1965 *I, S, A* 2, 1968 *BI*, 1,2,3,4, *F* 1,2, 1969 *A* 1,2,3,4, *S, E*, 1970 *I, W, NZ* 1,2,3,4, 1971 *F* 1,2, *A* 1,2,3, 1974 *BI* 1,2,3,4, *F* 1,2
Maré, D S (Tvl) 1906 *S*
Marsberg, A F W (GW) 1906 *S, W, E*
Marsberg, P A (GW) 1910 *BI* 1
Martheze, W C (GW) 1903 *BI* 2, 1906 *I, W*
Martin, H J (Tvl) 1937 *A* 2
Matfield, V (BB) 2001 *It* 1(R), *NZ* 1, *A* 2, *NZ* 2, *F* 3, *It* 2, *E, US*, 2002 *W* 1, *Sm, NZ* 1, *A* 1, *NZ* 2(R)
Mellet, T B (GW) 1896 *BI* 2
Mellish, F W (WP) 1921 *NZ* 1,3, 1924 *BI* 1,2,3,4
Merry, J (EP) 1891 *BI* 1
Metcalf, H D (Bor) 1903 *BI* 2
Meyer, C du P (WP) 1921 *NZ* 1,2,3
Meyer, P J (GW) 1896 *BI* 1
Meyer, W (OFS, GL) 1997 *S* (R), 1999 *It* 2, *NZ* 1(R), *A* 1(R), 2000 *C* (R), *E* 1, *NZ* 1(R),2(R), *Arg, I, W, E* 3, 2001 *F* 1(R),2, *It* 1, *F* 3(R), *It* 2, *E, US* (t+R), 2002 *W* 1,2, *Arg, NZ* 1,2, *A* 2
Michau, J M (Tvl) 1921 *NZ* 1
Michau, J P (WP) 1921 *NZ* 1,2,3
Millar, W A (WP) 1906 *E*, 1910 *BI* 2,3, 1912 *I, W*, 1913 *F*
Mills, W J (WP) 1910 *BI* 2
Moll, T (Tvl) 1910 *BI* 2
Montini, P E (WP) 1956 *A* 1,2
Montgomery, P C (WP) 1997 *BI* 2,3, *NZ* 1, *A* 1, *NZ* 2, *A* 2, *F* 1,2, *E, S*, 1998 *I* 1,2, *W* 1, *E* 1, *A* 1, *NZ* 1,2, *A* 2, *W* 2, *S, I* 3, *E* 2, 1999 *It* 1,2, *W, NZ* 1, *A* 1, *NZ* 2, *A* 2, [*S, U, E, A* 3, *NZ* 3], 2000 *C, E* 1,2, *A* 1, *NZ* 1, *A* 2(R), *Arg, I, W, E* 3, 2001 *F* 1, 2(t), *It* 1, *NZ* 1, *F* 3(R), *It* 2(R)
Moolman, L C (NT) 1977 *Wld*, 1980 *S Am* 1,2, *BI* 1,2,3,4, *S Am* 3,4, *F*, 1981 *I* 1,2, *NZ* 1,2,3, *US*, 1982 *S Am* 1,2, 1984 *S Am* 1,2, 1986 *Cv* 1,2,3,4
Mordt, R H (Z-R, NT) 1980 *S Am* 1,2, *BI* 1,2,3,4, *S Am* 3,4, *F*, 1981 *I* 2, *NZ* 1,2,3, *US*, 1982 *S Am* 1,2, 1984 *S Am* 1,2
Morkel, D A (Tvl) 1903 *BI* 1
Morkel, D F T (Tvl) 1906 *I, E*, 1910 *BI* 1,3, 1912 *S, I, W*, 1913 *E, F*
Morkel, H J (WP) 1921 *NZ* 1
Morkel, H W (WP) 1921 *NZ* 1,2
Morkel, J A (WP) 1921 *NZ* 2,3
Morkel, J W H (WP) 1912 *S, I, W*, 1913 *E, F*
Morkel, P G (WP) 1912 *S, I, W*, 1913 *E, F*, 1921 *NZ* 1,2,3
Morkel, P K (WP) 1928 *NZ* 4
Morkel, W H (WP) 1910 *BI* 3, 1912 *S, I, W*, 1913 *E, F*, 1921 *NZ* 1,2,3
Morkel, W S (Tvl) 1906 *S, I, W, E*
Moss, C (N) 1949 *NZ* 1,2,3,4
Mostert, P J (WP) 1921 *NZ* 1,2,3, 1924 *BI* 1,2,4, 1928 *NZ* 1,2,3,4, 1931 *W, I*, 1932 *E, S*
Mulder, J C (Tvl, GL) 1994 *NZ* 2,3, *S, W*, 1995 *WS*, [*A, WS, F, NZ*], *W, It, E*, 1996 *Fj, A* 1, *NZ* 1, *A* 2, *NZ* 2,5, *Arg* 1,2, *F* 1,2, *W*, 1997 *Tg, BI* 1, 1999 *It* 1(R),2, *W, NZ* 1, 2000 *C*(R), *A* 1, *E* 3, 2001 *F* 1, *It* 1
Muller, G H (WP) 1969 *A* 3,4, *S*, 1970 *W, NZ* 1,2,3,4, 1971 *F* 1,2, 1972 *E*, 1974 *BI* 1,3,4
Muller, H L (OFS) 1986 *Cv* 4(R), 1989 *Wld* 1(R)
Muller, H S V (Tvl) 1949 *NZ* 1,2,3,4, 1951 *S, I, W*, 1952 *E, F*, 1953 *A* 1,2,3,4
Muller, L J J (N) 1992 *NZ, A*
Muller, P G (N) 1992 *NZ, A, F* 1,2, *E*, 1993 *F* 1,2, *A* 1,2,3, *Arg* 1,2, 1994 *E* 1,2, *NZ* 1, *S, W*, 1998 *I* 1,2, *W* 1, *E* 1, *A* 1, *NZ* 1,2, *A* 2, 1999 *It* 1, *W, NZ* 1, *A* 1, [*Sp, A* 3, *NZ* 3]
Muir, D J (WP) 1997 *It, F* 1,2, *E, S*
Myburgh, F R (EP) 1896 *BI* 1
Myburgh, J L (NT) 1962 *BI* 1, 1963 *A* 4, 1964 *W, F*, 1968 *BI* 1,2,3, *F* 1,2, 1969 *A* 1,2,3,4, *E*, 1970 *I, W, NZ* 3,4
Myburgh, W H (WT) 1924 *BI* 1

Naude, J P (WP) 1963 *A* 4, 1965 *A* 1,2, *NZ* 1,3,4, 1967 *F* 1,2,3,4, 1968 *BI* 1,2,3,4
Neethling, J B (WP) 1967 *F* 1,2,3,4, 1968 *BI* 4, 1969 *S*, 1970 *NZ* 1,2
Nel, J A (Tvl) 1960 *NZ* 1,2, 1963 *A* 1,2, 1965 *A* 2, *NZ* 1,2,3,4, 1970 *NZ* 3,4
Nel, J J (WP) 1956 *A* 1,2, *NZ* 1,2,3,4, 1958 *F* 1,2
Nel, P A R O (Tvl) 1903 *BI* 1,2,3

Nel, P J (N) 1928 *NZ* 1,2,3,4, 1931 *W, I*, 1932 *E, S*, 1933 *A* 1,3,4,5, 1937 *A* 1,2, *NZ* 2,3
Nimb, C F (WP) 1961 *I*
Nomis, S H (Tvl) 1967 *F* 4, 1968 *BI* 1,2,3,4, *F* 1,2, 1969 *A* 1,2,3,4, *S, E*, 1970 *I, W, NZ* 1,2,3,4, 1971 *F* 1,2, *A* 1,2,3, 1972 *E*
Nykamp, J L (Tvl) 1933 *A* 2

Ochse, J K (WP) 1951 *I, W*, 1952 *E, F*, 1953 *A* 1,2,4
Oelofse, J S A (Tvl) 1953 *A* 1,2,3,4
Oliver, J F (Tvl) 1928 *NZ* 3,4
Olivier, E (WP) 1967 *F* 1,2,3,4, 1968 *BI* 1,2,3,4, *F* 1,2, 1969 *A* 1,2,3,4, *S, E*
Olivier, E (NT) 1992 *F* 1,2, *E*, 1993 *F* 1,2 *A* 1,2,3, *Arg* 1, 1995 *W, It* (R), *E*, 1996 *Arg* 1,2, *F* 1,2, *W*
Olver, E (EP) 1896 *BI* 1
Oosthuizen, J J (WP) 1974 *BI* 1, *F* 1,2, 1975 *F* 1,2, 1976 *NZ* 1,2,3,4
Oosthuizen, O W (NT, Tvl) 1981 *I* 1(R), 2, *NZ* 2,3, *US*, 1982 *S Am* 1,2, 1984 *E* 1,2
Osler, B L (WP) 1924 *BI* 1,2,3,4, 1928 *NZ* 1,2,3,4, 1931 *W, I*, 1932 *E, S*, 1933 *A* 1,2,3,4,5
Osler, S G (WP) 1928 *NZ* 1
Otto, K (NT, BB) 1995 [*R, C* (R), *WS* (R)], 1997 *BI* 3, *A* 1, *NZ* 2, *A* 2, *It, F* 1,2, *E, S*, 1998 *I* 1,2, *W* 1, *E* 1, *A* 1, *NZ* 1,2, *A* 2, *W* 2, *S, I* 3, *E* 2, 1999 *It* 1, *W, NZ* 1, *A* 1, [*S* (R), *Sp, U, E, A* 3, *NZ* 3], 2000 *C, E* 1,2, *A* 1
Oxlee, K (N) 1960 *NZ* 1,2,3,4, *W, I*, 1961 *S, A* 1,2, 1962 *BI* 1,2,3,4, 1963 *A* 1,2,4, 1964 *W*, 1965 *NZ* 1,2

Pagel, G L (WP) 1995 [*A* (R), *R, C, NZ* (R)], 1996 *NZ* 5(R)
Parker, W H (EP) 1965 *A* 1,2
Partridge, J E C (Tvl) 1903 *BI* 1
Paulse, B J (WP) 1999 *It* 1,2, *NZ* 1, *A* 1,2(R), [*S* (R), *Sp, NZ* 3], 2000 *C, E* 1,2, *A* 1, *NZ* 1, *A* 2, *NZ* 2, *A* 3, *Arg, W, E* 3, 2001 *F* 1,2, *It* 1, *NZ* 1, *A* 1,2, *NZ* 2, *F* 3, *It* 2, *E*, 2002 *W* 1,2, *Arg, Sm* (R), *A* 1, *NZ* 2, *A* 2
Payn, C (N) 1924 *BI* 1,2
Pelser, H J M (Tvl) 1958 *F* 1, 1960 *NZ* 1,2,3,4, *W, I*, 1961 *F, I, A* 1,2
Pfaff, B D (WP) 1956 *A* 1
Pickard, J A J (WP) 1953 *A* 3,4, 1956 *NZ* 2, 1958 *F* 2
Pienaar, J F (Tvl) 1993 *F* 1,2, *A* 1,2,3, *Arg* 1,2, 1994 *E* 1,2, *NZ* 2,3, *Arg* 1,2, *S, W*, 1995 *WS*, [*A, C, WS, F, NZ*], *W, It, E*, 1996 *Fj* 1,2, *A* 1, *NZ* 2, *A* 2
Pienaar, Z M J (OFS) 1980 *S Am* 2(R), *BI* 1,2,3,4, *S Am* 3,4, *F*, 1981 *I* 1,2, *NZ* 1,2,3
Pitzer, G (NT) 1967 *F* 1,2,3,4, 1968 *BI* 1,2,3,4, *F* 1,2, 1969 *A* 3,4
Pope, C F (WP) 1974 *BI* 1,2,3,4, 1975 *F* 1,2, 1976 *NZ* 2,3,4
Potgieter, H J (OFS) 1928 *NZ* 1,2
Potgieter, H L (OFS) 1977 *Wld*
Powell, A W (GW) 1896 *BI* 3
Powell, J M (GW) 1891 *BI* 2, 1896 *BI* 3, 1903 *BI* 1,2
Prentis, R B (Tvl) 1980 *S Am* 1,2, *BI* 1,2,3,4, *S Am* 3,4, *F*, 1981 *I* 1,2
Pretorius, A S (GL) 2002 *W* 1,2, *Arg, Sm, NZ* 1, *A* 1, *NZ* 2
Pretorius, N F (Tvl) 1928 *NZ* 1,2,3,4
Prinsloo, J (Tvl) 1958 *F* 1,2
Prinsloo, J (NT) 1963 *A* 3
Prinsloo, J P (Tvl) 1928 *NZ* 1
Putter, D J (WT) 1963 *A* 1,2,4

Raaff, J W E (GW) 1903 *BI* 1,2, 1906 *S, W, E*, 1910 *BI* 1
Ras, W J de Wet (OFS) 1976 *NZ* 1(R), 1980 *S Am* 2(R)
Rautenbach, S J (WP) 2002 *W* 1(R),2(t+R), *Arg* (R), *Sm, NZ* 1(R), *A* 1, *NZ* 2(R), *A* 2(R)
Reece-Edwards, H (N) 1992 *F* 1,2, 1993 *A* 2
Reid, A (WP) 1903 *BI* 3
Reid, B C (Bor) 1933 *A* 4
Reinach, J (OFS) 1986 *Cv* 1,2,3,4
Rens, I J (Tvl) 1953 *A* 3,4
Retief, D F (NT) 1955 *BI* 1,2,4, 1956 *A* 1,2, *NZ* 1,2,3,4
Reyneke, H J (WP) 1910 *BI* 3
Richards, A R (WP) 1891 *BI* 1,2,3
Richter, A (NT) 1992 *F* 1,2, *E*, 1994 *E* 2, *NZ* 1,2,3, 1995 [*R, C, WS* (R)]
Riley, N M (ET) 1963 *A* 3
Riordan, C A (Tvl) 1910 *BI* 1,2
Robertson, I W (R) 1974 *F* 1,2, 1976 *NZ* 1,2,4
Rodgers, P H (NT, Tvl) 1989 *Wld* 1,2, 1992 *NZ, F* 1,2
Rogers, C D (Tvl) 1984 *E* 1,2, *S Am* 1,2
Roos, G D (WP) 1910 *BI* 2,3

Roos, P J (WP) 1903 *BI* 3, 1906 *I, W, E*
Rosenberg, W (Tvl) 1955 *BI* 2,3,4, 1956 *NZ* 3, 1958 *F* 1
Rossouw, C L C (Tvl, N) 1995 *WS*, [*R, WS, F, NZ*], 1999 *NZ* 2(R), *A* 2(t), [*Sp, NZ* 3(R)]
Rossouw, D H (WP) 1953 *A* 3, 4
Rossouw, P W G (WP) 1997 *BI* 2,3, *NZ* 1, *A* 1, *NZ* 2(R), *A* 2(R), *It, F* 1,2, *E, S*, 1998 *I* 1,2, *W* 1, *E* 1, *A* 1, *NZ* 1,2, *A* 2, *W* 2, *S, I* 3, *E* 2, 1999 *It* 1, *W, NZ* 1, *A* 1(R), *NZ* 2, *A* 2, [*S, U, E, A* 3], 2000 *C, E* 1,2, *A* 2, *Arg* (R), *I, W*, 2001 *F* 3, *US*
Rousseau, W P (WP) 1928 *NZ* 3,4
Roux, F du T (WP) 1960 *W*, 1961 *A* 1,2, 1962 *BI* 1,2,3,4, 1963 *A* 2, 1965 *A* 1,2, *NZ* 1,2,3,4, 1968 *BI* 3,4, *F* 1,2 1969 *A* 1,2,3,4, 1970 *I, NZ* 1,2,3,4
Roux, J P (Tvl) 1994 *E* 2, *NZ* 1,2,3, *Arg* 1, 1995 [*R, C, F*(R)], 1996 *A* 1(R), *NZ* 1, *A* 2, *NZ* 3
Roux, O A (NT) 1969 *S, E*, 1970 *I, W*, 1972 *E*, 1974 *BI* 3,4
Russell, R B (Pumas) 2002 *W* 1(R),2, *Arg, A* 1(R), *NZ* 2(R), *A* 2

Samuels, T A (GW) 1896 *BI* 2,3,4
Sauermann, J T (Tvl) 1971 *F* 1,2, *A* 1, 1972 *E*, 1974 *BI* 1
Schlebusch, J J J (OFS) 1974 *BI* 3,4, 1975 *F* 2
Schmidt, L U (NT) 1958 *F* 2, 1962 *BI* 2
Schmidt, U L (NT, Tvl) 1986 *Cv* 1,2,3,4, 1989 *Wld* 1,2, 1992 *NZ, A*, 1993 *F* 1,2, *A* 1,2,3, 1994 *Arg* 1,2, *S, W*
Schoeman, J (WP) 1963 *A* 3,4, 1965 *I, S, A* 1, *NZ* 1,2
Scholtz, C P (WP, Tvl) 1994 *Arg* 1, 1995 [*R, C, WS*]
Scholtz, H (FSC) 2002 *A* 1(R), *NZ* 2(R), *A* 2(R)
Scholtz, H H (WP) 1921 *NZ* 1,2
Schutte, P J W (Tvl) 1994 *S, W*
Scott, P A (Tvl) 1896 *BI* 1,2,3,4
Sendin, W D (GW) 1921 *NZ* 2
Sephaka, L D (GL) 2001 *US*, 2002 *Sm, NZ* 1, *A* 1, *NZ* 2, *A* 2
Serfontein, D J (WP) 1980 *BI* 1,2,3,4, *S Am* 3,4, *F*, 1981 *I* 1,2, *NZ* 1,2,3, *US*, 1982 *S Am* 1,2, 1984 *E* 1,2
Shand, R (GW) 1891 *BI* 2,3
Sheriff, A R (Tvl) 1938 *BI* 1,2,3
Shum, E H (Tvl) 1913 *E*
Sinclair, D J (Tvl) 1955 *BI* 1,2,3,4
Sinclair, J H (Tvl) 1903 *BI* 1
Skene, A L (WP) 1958 *F* 2
Skinstad, R B (WP) 1997 *E* (t), 1998 *W* 1(R), *E* 1(t), *NZ* 1(R),2(R), *A* 2(R), *W* 2(R), *S, I* 3, *E* 2, 1999 [*S, Sp* (R), *U, E, A* 3], 2001 *F* 1(R),2(R), *It* 1, *NZ* 1, *A* 1,2, *NZ* 2, *F* 3, *It* 2, *E*, 2002 *W* 1,2, *Arg, Sm, NZ* 1, *A* 1, *NZ* 2, *A* 2
Slater, J T (EP) 1924 *BI* 3,4, 1928 *NZ* 1
Smal, G P (WP) 1986 *Cv* 1,2,3,4, 1989 *Wld* 1,2
Small, J T (Tvl, N, WP) 1992 *NZ, A, F* 1,2, *E*, 1993 *F* 1,2, *A* 1,2,3, *Arg* 1,2, 1994 *E* 1,2, *NZ* 1,2,3(t), *Arg* 1, 1995 *WS*, [*A, R, F, NZ*], *W, It, E* (R), 1996 *Fj, A* 1, *NZ* 1, *A* 2, *NZ* 2, *Arg* 1,2, *F* 1,2, *W*, 1997 *Tg, BI* 1, *NZ* 1(R), *A* 1(R), *NZ* 2, *A* 2, *It, F* 1,2, *E, S*
Smit, F C (WP) 1992 *E*
Smit, W J (N) 2000 *C* (t), *A* 1(R), *NZ* 1(t+R), *A* 2(R), *NZ* 2(R), *A* 3(R), *Arg, I, W, E* 3, 2001 *F* 1,2, *It* 1, *NZ* 1(R), *A* 1(R),2(R), *NZ* 2(R), *F* 3(R), *It* 2, *E, US* (R)
Smith, C M (OFS) 1963 *A* 3,4, 1964 *W, F*, 1965 *A* 1,2, *NZ* 2
Smith, C W (GW) 1891 *BI* 2, 1896 *BI* 2,3
Smith, D (GW) 1891 *BI* 2
Smith D J (Z-R) 1980 *BI* 1,2,3,4
Smith, G A C (EP) 1938 *BI* 3
Smith, P F (GW) 1997 *S* (R), 1998 *I* 1(t),2, *W* 1, *NZ* 1(R),2(R), *A* 2(R), *W* 2, 1999 *NZ* 2
Smollan, F C (Tvl) 1933 *A* 3,4,5
Snedden, R C D (GW) 1891 *BI* 2
Snyman, A H (NT, BB) 1996 *NZ* 3,4, *Arg* 2(R), *W* (R), 1997 *Tg, BI* 1,2,3, *NZ* 1, *A* 1, *NZ* 2, *A* 2, *It, F* 1,2, *E, S*, 1998 *I* 1,2, *W* 1, *E* 1, *A* 1, *NZ* 1,2, *A* 2, *W* 2, *S, I* 3, *E* 2, 1999 *NZ* 2, 2001 *NZ* 2, *F* 3, *US*, 2002 *W* 1
Snyman, D S L (WP) 1972 *E*, 1974 *BI* 1,2(R), *F* 1,2, 1975 *F* 1,2, 1976 *NZ* 2,3, 1977 *Wld*
Snyman, J C P (OFS) 1974 *BI* 2,3,4
Sonnekus, G H H (OFS) 1974 *BI* 3, 1984 *E* 1,2
Sowerby, R S (N) 2002 *Sm* (R)
Spies, J J (NT) 1970 *NZ* 1,2,3,4
Stander, J C J (OFS) 1974 *BI* 4(R), 1976 *NZ* 1,2,3,4
Stapelberg, W P (NT) 1974 *F* 1,2
Starke, J J (WP) 1956 *NZ* 4
Starke, K T (WP) 1924 *BI* 1,2,3,4
Steenekamp, J G A (Tvl) 1958 *F* 1
Stegmann, A C (WP) 1906 *S, I*
Stegmann, J A (Tvl) 1912 *S, I, W*, 1913 *E, F*
Stewart, C (WP) 1998 *S, I* 3, *E* 2

Stewart, D A (WP) 1960 *S*, 1961 *E, S, F, I*, 1963 *A* 1,3,4, 1964 *W, F*, 1965 *I*
Stofberg, M T S (OFS, NT, WP) 1976 *NZ* 2,3, 1977 *Wld*, 1980 *S Am* 1,2, *BI* 1,2,3,4, *S Am* 3,4, *F*, 1981 *I* 1,2, *NZ* 1,2, *US*, 1982 *S Am* 1,2, 1984 *E* 1,2
Strachan, L C (Tvl) 1932 *E, S*, 1937 *A* 1,2, *NZ* 1,2,3, 1938 *BI* 1,2,3
Stransky, J (N, WP) 1993 *A* 1,2,3, *Arg* 1, 1994 *Arg* 1,2, 1995 *WS*, [*A, R* (t), *C, F, NZ*], *W, It, E*, 1996 *Fj* (R), *NZ* 1, *A* 2, *NZ* 2,3,4,5(R)
Straeuli, R A W (Tvl) 1994 *NZ* 1, *Arg* 1,2, *S, W*, 1995 *WS*, [*A, WS, NZ* (R)], *E* (R)
Strauss, C P (WP) 1992 *F* 1,2, *E*, 1993 *F* 1,2, *A* 1,2,3, *Arg* 1,2, 1994 *E* 1, *NZ* 1,2, *Arg* 1,2
Strauss, J A (WP) 1984 *S Am* 1,2
Strauss, J H P (Tvl) 1976 *NZ* 3,4, 1980 *S Am* 1
Strauss, S S F (GW) 1921 *NZ* 3
Strydom, C F (OFS) 1955 *BI* 3, 1956 *A* 1,2, *NZ* 1,4, 1958 *F* 1,
Strydom, J J (Tvl, GL) 1993 *F* 2, *A* 1,2,3, *Arg* 1,2, 1994 *E* 1, 1995 [*A, C, F, NZ*], 1996 *A* 2(R), *NZ* 2(R), 3,4, *W* (R), 1997 *Tg, BI* 1,2,3, *A* 2
Strydom, L J (NT) 1949 *NZ* 1,2
Styger, J J (OFS) 1992 *NZ* (R), *A, F* 1,2, *E*, 1993 *F* 2(R), *A* 3(R)
Suter, M R (N) 1965 *I, S*
Swanepoel, W (OFS, GL) 1997 *BI* 3(R), *A* 2(R), *F* 1(R), 2, *E, S*, 1998 *I* 2(R), *W* 1(R), *E* 2(R), 1999 *It* 1,2(R), *W, A* 1, [*Sp, NZ* 3(t)], 2000 *A* 1, *NZ* 1, *A* 2, *NZ* 2, *A* 3
Swart, J (WP) 1996 *Fj, NZ* 1(R), *A* 2, *NZ* 2,3,4,5, 1997 *BI* 3(R), *It, S* (R)
Swart, J J N (SWA) 1955 *BI* 1
Swart, I S (Tvl) 1993 *A* 1,2,3, *Arg* 1, 1994 *E* 1,2, *NZ* 1,3, *Arg* 2(R), 1995 *WS*, [*A, WS, F, NZ*], *W*, 1996 *A* 2

Taberer, W S (GW) 1896 *BI* 2
Taylor, O B (N) 1962 *BI* 1
Terblanche, C S (Bol, N) 1998 *I* 1,2, *W* 1, *E* 1, *A* 1, *NZ* 1,2, *A* 2, *W* 2, *S, I* 3, *E* 2, 1999 *It* 1(R),2, *W, A* 1, *NZ* 2(R), [*Sp, E* (R), *A* 3(R), *NZ* 3], 2000 *E* 3, 2002 *W* 1,2, *Arg, Sm, NZ* 1, *A* 1,2(R)
Teichmann, G H (N) 1995 *W*, 1996 *Fj, A* 1, *NZ* 1, *A* 2, *NZ* 2,3,4,5, *Arg* 1,2, *F* 1,2, *W*, 1997 *Tg, BI* 1,2,3, *NZ* 1, *A* 1, *NZ* 2, *A* 2, *It, F* 1,2, *E, S*, 1998 *I* 1,2, *W* 1, *E* 1, *A* 1, *NZ* 1,2, *A* 2, *W* 2, *S, I* 3, *E* 2, 1999 *It* 1, *W, NZ* 1
Theron, D F (GW) 1996 *A* 2(R), *NZ* 2(R), 5, *Arg* 1,2, *F* 1,2, *W*, 1997 *BI* 2(R), 3, *NZ* 1(R), *A* 1, *NZ* 2(R)
Theunissen, D J (GW) 1896 *BI* 3
Thompson, G (WP) 1912 *S, I, W*
Tindall, J C (WP) 1924 *BI* 1, 1928 *NZ* 1,2,3,4
Tobias, E G (SARF, Bol) 1981 *I* 1,2, 1984 *E* 1,2, *S Am* 1,2
Tod, N S (N) 1928 *NZ* 2
Townsend, W H (N) 1921 *NZ* 1
Trenery, W E (GW) 1891 *BI* 2
Tromp, H (NT) 1996 *NZ* 3,4, *Arg* 2(R), *F* 1(R)
Truter, D R (WP) 1924 *BI* 2,4
Truter, J T (N) 1963 *A* 1, 1964 *F*, 1965 *A* 2
Turner, F G (EP) 1933 *A* 1,2,3, 1937 *A* 1,2, *NZ* 1,2,3, 1938 *BI* 1,2,3
Twigge, R J (NT) 1960 *S*

Ulyate, C A (Tvl) 1955 *BI* 1,2,3,4, 1956 *NZ* 1,2,3
Uys, P de W (NT) 1960 *W*, 1961 *E, S, I, A* 1,2, 1962 *BI* 1,4, 1963 *A* 1,2, 1969 *A* 1(R), 2

Van Aswegen, H J (WP) 1981 *NZ* 1, 1982 *S Am* 2(R)
Van Biljon, L (N) 2001 *It* 1(R), *NZ* 1, *A* 1,2, *NZ* 2, *F* 3, *It* 2(R), *E* (R), *US*
Van Broekhuizen, H D (WP) 1896 *BI* 4
Van Buuren, M C (Tvl) 1891 *BI* 1
Van de Vyver, D F (WP) 1937 *A* 2
Van den Berg, D S (N) 1975 *F* 1,2, 1976 *NZ* 1,2
Van den Berg, M A (WP) 1937 *A* 1, *NZ* 1,2,3
Van den Berg, P A (WP, GW, N) 1999 *It* 1(R),2, *NZ* 2, *A* 2, [*S, U* (t+R), *E* (R), *A* 3(R), *NZ* 3(R)], 2000 *E* 1(R), *A* 1, *NZ* 1, *A* 2, *NZ* 2(R), *A* 3(t+R), *Arg, I, W, E* 3, 2001 *F* 1(R),2, *A* 2(R), *NZ* 2(R), *US*
Van den Bergh, E (EP) 1994 *Arg* 2(t & R)
Van der Linde, A (WP) 1995 *It, E*, 1996 *Arg* 1(R), 2(R), *F* 1(R), *W* (R), 2001 *F* 3(R)
Van der Merwe, A J (Bol) 1955 *BI* 2,3,4, 1956 *A* 1,2, *NZ* 1,2,3,4, 1958 *F* 1, 1960 *S, NZ* 2
Van der Merwe, A V (WP) 1931 *W*

Van der Merwe, B S (NT) 1949 *NZ* 1
Van der Merwe, H S (NT) 1960 *NZ* 4, 1963 *A* 2,3,4, 1964 *F*
Van der Merwe, J P (WP) 1970 *W*
Van der Merwe, P R (SWD, WT, GW) 1981 *NZ* 2,3, *US*, 1986 *Cv* 1,2, 1989 *Wld* 1
Vanderplank, B E (N) 1924 *BI* 3,4
Van der Schyff, J H (GW) 1949 *NZ* 1,2,3,4, 1955 *BI* 1
Van der Watt, A E (WP) 1969 *S* (R), *E*, 1970 *I*
Van der Westhuizen, J C (WP) 1928 *NZ* 2,3,4, 1931 *I*
Van der Westhuizen, J H (WP) 1931 *I*, 1932 *E, S*
Van der Westhuizen, J H (NT, BB) 1993 *Arg* 1,2, 1994 *E* 1,2(R), *Arg* 2, *S, W*, 1995 *WS*, [*A, C* (R), *WS, F, NZ*], *W, It, E*, 1996 *Fj, A* 1,2(R), *NZ* 2,3(R), 4,5, *Arg* 1,2, *F* 1,2, *W*, 1997 *Tg, BI* 1,2,3, *NZ* 1, *A* 1, *NZ* 2, *A* 2, *It, F* 1, 1998 *I* 1,2, *W* 1, *E* 1, *A* 1, *NZ* 1,2, *A* 2, *W* 2, *S, I* 3, *E* 2, 1999 *NZ* 2, *A* 2, [*S, Sp* (R), *U, E, A* 3, *NZ* 3], 2000 *C, E* 1,2, *A* 1(R); *NZ* 1(R), *A* 2(R), *Arg, I, W, E* 3, 2001 *F* 1,2, *It* 1(R); *NZ* 1, *A* 1,2, *NZ* 2, *F* 3, *It* 2, *E, US* (R)
Van der Westhuyzen, J N B (Mp) 2000 *NZ* 2(R), 2001 *It* 1(R)
Van Druten, N J V (Tvl) 1924 *BI* 1,2,3,4, 1928 *NZ* 1,2,3,4
Van Heerden, A J (Tvl) 1921 *NZ* 1,3
Van Heerden, F J (WP) 1994 *E* 1,2(R), *NZ* 3, 1995 *It, E*, 1996 *NZ* 5(R), *Arg* 1(R),2(R), 1997 *Tg, NZ* 2(t+R),3(R), *NZ* 1(R),2(R), 1999 [*Sp*]
Van Heerden, J L (NT, Tvl) 1974 *BI* 3,4, *F* 1,2, 1975 *F* 1,2, 1976 *NZ* 1,2,3,4, 1977 *Wld*, 1980 *BI* 1,3,4, *S Am* 3,4, *F*
Van Jaarsveld, C J (Tvl) 1949 *NZ* 1
Van Jaarsveldt, D C (R) 1960 *S*
Van Niekerk, J A (WP) 1928 *NZ* 4
Van Niekerk, J C (GL) 2001 *NZ* 1(R), *A* 1(R), *NZ* 2(t+R), *F* 3(R), *It*2, *US*, 2002 *W* 1(R),2(R), *Arg* (R), *Sm, NZ* 1, *A* 1, *NZ* 2, *A* 2
Van Reenen, G L (WP) 1937 *A* 2, *NZ* 1
Van Renen, C G (WP) 1891 *BI* 3, 1896 *BI* 1,4
Van Renen, W (WP) 1903 *BI* 1,3
Van Rensburg, J T J (Tvl) 1992 *NZ, A, E*, 1993 *F* 1,2, *A* 1, 1994 *NZ* 2
Van Rooyen, G W (Tvl) 1921 *NZ* 2,3
Van Ryneveld, R C B (WP) 1910 *BI* 2,3
Van Schalkwyk, D (NT) 1996 *Fj* (R), *NZ* 3,4,5, 1997 *BI* 2,3, *NZ* 1, *A* 1
Van Schoor, R A M (R) 1949 *NZ* 2,3,4, 1951 *S, I, W*, 1952 *E, F*, 1953 *A* 1,2,3,4
Van Straaten, A J J (WP) 1999 *It* 2(R), *W, NZ* 1(R), *A* 1, 2000 *C, E* 1,2, *NZ* 1, *A* 2, *A* 3, *Arg* (R), *I* (R), *W, E* 3, 2001 *A* 1,2, *NZ* 2, *F* 3, *It* 2, *E*
Van Vollenhoven, K T (NT) 1955 *BI* 1,2,3,4, 1956 *A* 1,2, *NZ* 3
Van Vuuren, T F (EP) 1912 *S, I, W*, 1913 *E, F*
Van Wyk, C J (Tvl) 1951 *S, I, W*, 1952 *E, F*, 1953 *A* 1,2,3,4, 1955 *BI* 1
Van Wyk, J F B (NT) 1970 *NZ* 1,2,3,4, 1971 *F* 1,2, *A* 1,2,3, 1972 *E*, 1974 *BI* 1,3,4, 1976 *NZ* 3,4
Van Wyk, S P (WP) 1928 *NZ* 1,2
Van Zyl, B P (WP) 1961 *I*
Van Zyl, C G P (OFS) 1965 *NZ* 1,2,3,4
Van Zyl, D J (WP) 2000 *E* 3(R)
Van Zyl, G H (WP) 1958 *F* 1, 1960 *S, NZ* 1,2,3,4, *W, I*, 1961 *E, S, F, I, A* 1,2, 1962 *BI* 1,3,4
Van Zyl, H J (Tvl) 1960 *NZ* 1,2,3,4, *I*, 1961 *E, S, I, A* 1,2
Van Zyl, P J (Bol) 1961 *I*
Veldsman, P E (WP) 1977 *Wld*
Venter, A G (OFS) 1996 *NZ* 3,4,5, *Arg* 1,2, *F* 1,2, *W*, 1997 *Tg, BI* 1,2,3, *NZ* 1, *A* 1, *NZ* 2, *It, F* 1,2, *E, S*, 1998 *I* 1,2, *W* 1,

E 1, *A* 1, *NZ* 1,2, *A* 2, *W* 2, *S* (R), *I* 3(R), *E* 2(R), 1999 *It* 1,2(R), *W* (R), *NZ* 1, *A* 1, *NZ* 2, *A* 2, [*S, U, E, A* 3, *NZ* 3], 2000 *C, E* 1,2, *A* 1, *NZ* 1, *A* 2, *NZ* 2, *A* 3, *Arg, I, W, E* 3, 2001 *F* 1, *It* 1, *NZ* 1, *A* 1,2, *NZ* 2, *F* 3(R), *It* 2(R), *E* (t+R), *US* (R)
Venter, A J (N) 2000 *W* (R), *E* 3(R), 2001 *F* 3, *It* 2, *E, US*, 2002 *W* 1,2, *Arg, NZ* 1(R),2, *A* 2
Venter, B (OFS) 1994 *E* 1,2, *NZ* 1,2,3, *Arg* 1,2, 1995 [*R, C, WS* (R), *NZ* (R)], 1996 *A* 1, *NZ* 1, *A* 2, 1999 *A* 2, [*S, U*]
Venter, F D (Tvl) 1931 *W*, 1932 *S*, 1933 *A* 3
Versfeld, C (WP) 1891 *BI* 3
Versfeld, M (WP) 1891 *BI* 1,2,3
Vigne, J T (Tvl) 1891 *BI* 1,2,3
Viljoen, J F (WP) 1971 *F* 1,2, *A* 1,2,3, 1972 *E*
Viljoen, J T (N) 1971 *A* 1,2,3
Villet, J (WP) 1984 *E* 1,2
Visagie, I J (WP) 1999 *It* 1, *W, NZ* 1, *A* 1, *NZ* 2, *A* 2, [*S, U, E, A* 3, *NZ* 3], 2000 *C, E* 2, *A* 1, *NZ* 1, *A* 2, *NZ* 2, *A* 3, 2001 *NZ* 1, *A* 1,2, *NZ* 2, *F* 3, *It* 2(R), *E* (t+R), *US*
Visagie, P J (GW) 1967 *F* 1,2,3,4, 1968 *BI* 1,2,3,4, *F* 1,2, 1969 *A* 1,2,3,4, *S, E*, 1970 *NZ* 1,2,3,4, 1971 *F* 1,2, *A* 1,2,3
Visagie, R G (OFS, N) 1984 *E* 1,2, *S Am* 1,2, 1993 *F* 1
Visser, J de V (WP) 1981 *NZ* 2, *US*
Visser, M (WP) 1995 *WS* (R)
Visser, P J (Tvl) 1933 *A* 2
Viviers, S S (OFS) 1956 *A* 1,2, *NZ* 2,3,4
Vogel, M L (OFS) 1974 *BI* 2(R)
Von Hoesslin, D J B (GW) 1999 *It* 1(R),2, *W* (R), *NZ* 1, *A* 1(R)
Vos, A N (GL) 1999 *It* 1(t+R),2, *NZ* 1(R),2(R), *A* 2, [*S* (R), *Sp, E* (R), *A* 3(R), *NZ* 3], 2000 *C, E* 1,2, *A* 1, *NZ* 1, *A* 2, *NZ* 2, *A* 3, *Arg, I, W, E* 3, 2001 *F* 1,2, *It* 1, *NZ* 1, *A* 1,2, *NZ* 2, *F* 3, *It* 2, *E, US*

Wagenaar, C (NT) 1977 *Wld*
Wahl, J J (WP) 1949 *NZ* 1
Walker, A P (N) 1921 *NZ* 1,3, 1924 *BI* 1,2,3,4
Walker, H N (OFS) 1953 *A* 3, 1956 *A* 2, *NZ* 1,4
Walker, H W (Tvl) 1910 *BI* 1,2,3
Walton, D C (N) 1964 *F*, 1965 *I, S, NZ* 3,4, 1969 *A* 1,2, *E*
Waring, F W (WP) 1931 *I*, 1932 *E*, 1933 *A* 1,2,3,4,5
Wegner, N (WP) 1993 *F* 2, *A* 1,2,3
Wessels, J J (WP) 1896 *BI* 1,2,3
Whipp, P J M (WP) 1974 *BI* 1,2, 1975 *F* 1, 1976 *NZ* 1,3,4, 1980 *S Am* 1,2
White, J (Bor) 1931 *W*, 1933 *A* 1,2,3,4,5, 1937 *A* 1,2, *NZ* 1,2
Wiese, J J (Tvl) 1993 *F* 1, 1995 *WS*, [*R, C, WS, F, NZ*], *W, It, E*, 1996 *NZ* 3(R), 4(R), 5, *Arg* 1,2, *F* 1,2, *W*
Williams, A E (GW) 1910 *BI* 1
Williams, A P (WP) 1984 *E* 1,2
Williams, C M (WP, GL) 1993 *Arg* 2, 1994 *E* 1,2, *NZ* 1,2,3, *Arg* 1,2, *S, W*, 1995 *WS*, [*WS, F, NZ*], *It, E*, 1998 *A* 1(t), *NZ* 1(t), 2000 *C* (R), *E* 1(t),2(R), *A* 1(R), *NZ* 2, *A* 3, *Arg, I, W* (R)
Williams, D O (WP) 1937 *A* 1,2, *NZ* 1,2,3, 1938 *BI* 1,2,3
Williams, J G (NT) 1971 *F* 1,2, *A* 1,2,3, 1972 *E*, 1974 *BI* 1,2,4, *F* 1,2, 1976 *NZ* 1,2
Wilson, L G (WP) 1960 *NZ* 3,4, *W, I*, 1961 *E, F, I, A* 1,2, 1962 *BI* 1,2,3,4, 1963 *A* 1,2,3,4, 1964 *W, F*, 1965 *I, S, A* 1,2, *NZ* 1,2,3,4
Wolmarans, B J (OFS) 1977 *Wld*
Wright, G D (EP, Tvl) 1986 *Cv* 3,4, 1989 *Wld* 1,2, 1992 *F* 1,2, *E*
Wyness, M R K (WP) 1962 *BI* 1,2,3,4, 1963 *A* 2

Zeller, W C (N) 1921 *NZ* 2,3
Zimerman, M (WP) 1931 *W, I*, 1932 *E, S*

NEW ZEALAND TEST SEASON REVIEW 2001-02

Closer to the Front of the Queue

Don Cameron

Viewed in comfortable isolation – ignoring that there was more distracting rugby news made off the New Zealand playing fields than on them – John Mitchell would have earned at least a B+ rating for his All Blacks over the last 11 internationals stretching back to November 2001.The report card might also have carried a note at the bottom saying there was room, and a distinct possibility, for improvement in the future.

No-one was quite sure about Mitchell when he took the All Blacks on their Ireland-Scotland-Argentina tour late in 2001, only a matter of weeks after Wayne Smith had stepped away from the job and Mitchell was suddenly promoted on the basis of his solid playing record, and his coaching times in England and more recently with Waikato. Mitchell gave the impression of having a hard-nosed attitude to rugby and its coaching, that he had his own opinions about players and tactics, and was not likely to be diverted from these.

His early away steps were uncertain – a win over Ireland, a spotty defeat of Scotland, a last-minute escape from defeat by Argentina – but New Zealanders were prepared to give Mitchell a fresh start in 2002. Four months later the unforgiving New Zealand critics were prepared to give Mitchell, and themselves, a pat on the back. His 11 matches since the start in 2001 had brought ten victories (which resulted in New Zealand regaining the Tri Nations Trophy) and one loss, a last-minute 14-16 loss to Australia which denied New Zealand the reward of the Bledisloe Cup, Ireland had been defeated thrice, with varying degrees of comfort. Italy and Fiji had been cannon-fodder, as usual, Scotland and Argentina defeated with less confidence. After these aperitifs, the All Blacks had a double helping of success against South Africa (41-20 and 30-23), the agonising loss (14-16) to Australia at Sydney balancing the out-playing of the Wallabies (12-6) under Antarctic conditions at Christchurch.

Even with their limited backline attack, the All Blacks averaged just under five tries and 35 points a match. The defensive figures were even more impressive, and represented the solid foundation that Mitchell and his men have slowly been building. In their 11 matches the All Blacks conceded 15 tries. They let in three in the first match against Ireland, otherwise no team scored more than two in a match. Three sides – Scotland, Ireland and Australia – went try-less in matches against New Zealand. It said much for the All Blacks' ability to play in their opponents' half – another Mitchell mantra – that, in these days of fickle referees and expert goal-kickers, the All Blacks offered up only 19 penalty goals, and never more than two a match.

Going into a three-match European expedition at the end of 2002 Mitchell was planning to rest some of his leading players. This was a matter of caution laced with confidence. During the 11 matches Mitchell used 34 players in internationals. Of these, Doug Howlett and Andrew Mehrtens appeared in all 11, Aaron Mauger, Scott Robertson and Reuben Thorne in 10, Richard McCaw (grown so quickly to loose-forward stardom), Chris Jack, Dave Hewett, Greg Somerville in nine, Jonah Lomu in eight, Leon MacDonald, Tana Umaga, Norm Maxwell, Byron Kelleher, Caleb Ralph, Justin Marshall and Simon Maling in seven. Mitchell might regard those 17 as already invested in the 2003 World Cup bank account. Immediately after the Tri Nations win Mitchell made the traditional comment that other World Cup candidates might appear during the home domestic championship in late 2002 and the early international engagements in 2003.

The big question is whether Lomu will remain among the front-line All Black candidates. Lomu made only one Tri Nations appearance, from the reserves' bench. Mitchell and his main assistant Robbie Deans denied that Lomu was unfit or unwanted. The flow of waffling rugby-speak was extraordinary: 'Jonah is training very well; we have plans for Jonah; Jonah did not quite fit into our plans for this match or that.' And so on. Yet the plain fact was that Lomu is still regarded as a defensive risk, and that a journeyman wing, Ralph, was a better Test-match fit because he was an expert cover-defender and quick-witted opportunist. Ralph is not especially fast nor determined heading for the corner, but Mitchell worked out, quite accurately, that Ralph's basic values far exceeded Lomu's reputation.

New Zealanders were horrified that Lomu should be used as an advertisement for the Commonwealth Games at Manchester, when there was never a prospect that the giant would be in the New Zealand gold-medal sevens team. There are even whispers that Lomu remains a member of Mitchell's enlarged squad, and sometimes sits on the reserves' bench to keep *Adidas*, major separate sponsors of the All Blacks and Lomu, content. The continuing confusion about Lomu's playing future – he was a reserve for Wellington in the first match of the National Provincial Championship in mid-August – was so often a talking-point as the All Blacks built up their strengths during the home season.

Then, approaching the height that was the Tri Nations and New Zealand's urgent quest to regain the Bledisloe Cup from Australia, the All Blacks were swept off the sports and front pages of the newspapers by the unholy row that erupted over New Zealand's clumsy handling of its proposed sub-host role in the 2003 Rugby World Cup where Australia would be the major organiser. The All Blacks were forgotten as the bitter trans-Tasman battle raged. They remained in the background as the New Zealand Rugby Football Union (NZRFU) board, after making what looked like token damage-control by removing its chief executive and chairman, suddenly found the rest of the country setting off on a march to the Bastille of rugby control in Wellington. A special meeting of the NZRFU resulted in the removal of all nine board members.

So, almost unnoticed, the All Blacks moved into their best form of Mitchell's reign so far. New Zealand were lucky to have the rain and chilling wind at Jade Stadium in Christchurch stifling the skill and confidence of the Wallabies. The All Black forwards, not unused to wet and windy rugby, played magnificently and there was no complaint from either side at the result, or the complete absence of tries. A week later the All Blacks, completely unaffected by their crumbling administration, reached close to their best form with a 41-20 win over the Springboks at Wellington. The Boks struck quickly and hard, but Mitchell's men showed a new composure which slowly gave their pack some advantage over a bruising Springbok pack. Best of all, the spritely play of Marshall at half-back, Mehrtens at five-eighths and Howlett on the wing lifted the quality of the All Black attacking play to new heights. There were five tries for the All Blacks on that splendid night, and with four points from the Australian slip-and-slither and five from the Springboks, the All Blacks took a dominant position in the Tri Nations race.

There was a stumble, another of those heart-breaking losses to Australia, when at Sydney Matt Burke nudged over a second penalty to give Australia a 16-14 verdict when the All Blacks had a not undeserved victory in sight. But it was the final measure of the stability and confidence that Mitchell had been establishing that the All Blacks climbed straight onto a plane from Sydney to Durban, and a week later outplayed a lively South African side by four tries to two.

This was the final flourish that Mitchell had hoped for. He is not the most outgoing of coaches, and tends to fall back on rather worn clichés. But the more confident walk of the man, the sharper smile in his eye, suggested that he was climbing steadily up the mountain he started to scale 12 months before, and could see a winning path ahead of him.

However, there were public image glitches in the All Black attitudes which still annoyed the home folk. Mitchell might have been permitted his growing unwillingness to be quoted at length, if at all, but he was part of a foolish affair when he and the rest of the All Blacks marched through the Sydney airport terminal with every lip buttoned-shut. The All Black manager, Andrew Martin, added to his rather quaint habits by busily searching among the undergrowth surrounding the field on which the All Blacks were having a "secret" training run. When the All Blacks hid in Hamner, an up-country Canterbury hamlet, the All Black minders tried to prevent a photographer moving into the town. The town fathers of Palmerston North questioned the money they had put into the well-appointed rugby academy in their town when the All Blacks instead took their off-duty breaks at Whangamata (an old Mitchell stamping ground), Hamner and Nelson. But New Zealanders are learning to live with these public relations wrecks and mono-syllabic statements when they realise that, on the basis of one win over Australia and two from two against South Africa, New Zealand rugby is steadily climbing up through the strange climate of professionalism.

New Zealand may not be leading the way in rugby trends and tactics as they were accustomed to do in the old amateur days, but Mitchell has taken them much closer to the front of the queue after his first year in command.

New Zealand's Test Record in 2001–2002: Played 11, won 10, lost 1

Opponents	Date	Venue	Result
South Africa	10th August 2002	A	Won 30-23
Australia	3rd August 2002	A	Lost 14-16
South Africa	20th July 2002	H	Won 41-20
Australia	13th July 2002	H	Won 12-6
Fiji	29th June 2002	H	Won 68-18
Ireland	22nd June 2002	H	Won 40-8
Ireland	15th June 2002	H	Won 15-6
Italy	8th June 2002	H	Won 64-10
Argentina	1st December 2001	A	Won 24-20
Scotland	24th November 2001	A	Won 37-6
Ireland	17th November 2001	A	Won 40-29

NEW ZEALAND INTERNATIONAL STATISTICS

(up to 31 August 2002)

Match Records

MOST CONSECUTIVE TEST WINS

17 1965 *SA* 4, 1966 *BI* 1,2,3,4, 1967 *A, E, W, F, S,* 1968 *A* 1,2, *F* 1,2,3, 1969 *W* 1,2
12 1988 *A* 3, 1989 *F* 1,2, *Arg* 1,2, *A, W, I,* 1990 *S* 1,2, *A* 1,2

MOST CONSECUTIVE TESTS WITHOUT DEFEAT

Matches	Wins	Draws	Period
23	22	1	1987 to 1990
17	15	2	1961 to 1964
17	17	0	1965 to 1969

MOST POINTS IN A MATCH
by the team

Pts	Opponents	Venue	Year
145	Japan	Bloemfontein	1995
102	Tonga	Albany	2000
101	Italy	Huddersfield	1999
93	Argentina	Wellington	1997
74	Fiji	Christchurch	1987
73	Canada	Auckland	1995
71	Fiji	Albany	1997
71	Samoa	Albany	1999

by a player

Pts	Player	Opponents	Venue	Year
45	S D Culhane	Japan	Bloemfontein	1995
36	T E Brown	Italy	Huddersfield	1999
33	C J Spencer	Argentina	Wellington	1997
33	A P Mehrtens	Ireland	Dublin	1997
32	T E Brown	Tonga	Albany	2000
30	M C G Ellis	Japan	Bloemfontein	1995
30	T E Brown	Samoa	Albany	2001
29	A P Mehrtens	Australia	Auckland	1999
29	A P Mehrtens	France	Paris	2000
28	A P Mehrtens	Canada	Auckland	1995

MOST TRIES IN A MATCH
by the team

Tries	Opponents	Venue	Year
21	Japan	Bloemfontein	1995
15	Tonga	Albany	2000
14	Argentina	Wellington	1997
14	Italy	Huddersfield	1999
13	U S A	Berkeley	1913
12	Italy	Auckland	1987
12	Fiji	Christchurch	1987

by a player

Tries	Player	Opponents	Venue	Year
6	M C G Ellis	Japan	Bloemfontein	1995
5	J W Wilson	Fiji	Albany	1997
4	D McGregor	England	Crystal Palace	1905
4	C I Green	Fiji	Christchurch	1987
4	J A Gallagher	Fiji	Christchurch	1987
4	J J Kirwan	Wales	Christchurch	1988
4	J T Lomu	England	Cape Town	1995
4	C M Cullen	Scotland	Dunedin	1996
4	J W Wilson	Samoa	Albany	1999

MOST CONVERSIONS IN A MATCH
by the team

Cons	Opponents	Venue	Year
20	Japan	Bloemfontein	1995
12	Tonga	Albany	2000
11	Italy	Huddersfield	1999
10	Fiji	Christchurch	1987
10	Argentina	Wellington	1997
8	Italy	Auckland	1987
8	Wales	Auckland	1988
8	Fiji	Albany	1997
8	Italy	Hamilton	2002

by a player

Cons	Player	Opponents	Venue	Year
20	S D Culhane	Japan	Bloemfontein	1995
12	T E Brown	Tonga	Albany	2000
11	T E Brown	Italy	Huddersfield	1999
10	G J Fox	Fiji	Christchurch	1987
10	C J Spencer	Argentina	Wellington	1997
8	G J Fox	Italy	Auckland	1987
8	G J Fox	Wales	Auckland	1988
8	A P Mehrtens	Italy	Hamilton	2002

MOST PENALTIES IN A MATCH
by the team

Penalties	Opponents	Venue	Year
9	Australia	Auckland	1999
9	France	Paris	2000
7	Western Samoa	Auckland	1993
7	South Africa	Pretoria	1999
6	British/Irish Lions	Dunedin	1959
6	England	Christchurch	1985
6	Argentina	Wellington	1987
6	Scotland	Christchurch	1987
6	France	Paris	1990
6	South Africa	Auckland	1994
6	Australia	Brisbane	1996
6	Ireland	Dublin	1997
6	South Africa	Cardiff	1999
6	Scotland	Murrayfield	2001

by a player

Penalties	Player	Opponents	Venue	Year
9	A P Mehrtens	Australia	Auckland	1999
9	A P Mehrtens	France	Paris	2000
7	G J Fox	Western Samoa	Auckland	1993
7	A P Mehrtens	South Africa	Pretoria	1999
6	D B Clarke	British/Irish Lions	Dunedin	1959
6	K J Crowley	England	Christchurch	1985
6	G J Fox	Argentina	Wellington	1987
6	G J Fox	Scotland	Christchurch	1987
6	G J Fox	France	Paris	1990
6	S P Howarth	South Africa	Auckland	1994
6	A P Mehrtens	Australia	Brisbane	1996
6	A P Mehrtens	Ireland	Dublin	1997
6	A P Mehrtens	South Africa	Cardiff	1999
6	A P Mehrtens	Scotland	Murrayfield	2001

MOST DROPPED GOALS IN A MATCH
by the team

Drops	Opponents	Venue	Year
3	France	Christchurch	1986

by a player

Drops	Player	Opponents	Venue	Year
2	O D Bruce	Ireland	Dublin	1978
2	F M Botica	France	Christchurch	1986
2	A P Mehrtens	Australia	Auckland	1995

Career Records
MOST CAPPED PLAYERS

Caps	Player	Career Span
92	S B T Fitzpatrick	1986 to 1997
79	I D Jones	1990 to 1999
63	J J Kirwan	1984 to 1994
63	A P Mehrtens	1995 to 2002
62	R M Brooke	1992 to 1999
60	C W Dowd	1993 to 2001
60	J W Wilson	1993 to 2001
60	J T Lomu	1994 to 2002
60	J W Marshall	1995 to 2002
58	G W Whetton	1981 to 1991
58	Z V Brooke	1987 to 1997
57	C M Cullen	1996 to 2002
56	O M Brown	1992 to 1998
55	C E Meads	1957 to 1971
55	F E Bunce	1992 to 1997
55	M N Jones	1987 to 1998
54	J A Kronfeld	1995 to 2000

MOST CONSECUTIVE TESTS

Tests	Player	Span
63	S B T Fitzpatrick	1986 to 1995
51	C M Cullen	1996 to 2000
49	R M Brooke	1995 to 1999
41	J W Wilson	1996 to 1999
40	G W Whetton	1986 to 1991

MOST TESTS AS CAPTAIN

Tests	Captain	Span
51	S B T Fitzpatrick	1992 to 1997
30	W J Whineray	1958 to 1965
19	G N K Mourie	1977 to 1982
19	T C Randell	1998 to 1999
18	B J Lochore	1966 to 1970
17	A G Dalton	1981 to 1985

MOST TESTS IN INDIVIDUAL POSITIONS

Position	Player	Tests	Span
Full-back	C M Cullen	44	1996 to 2002
Wing	J J Kirwan	63	1984 to 1994
Centre	F E Bunce	55	1992 to 1997
Fly-half	A P Mehrtens	63	1995 to 2002
Scrum-half	J W Marshall	59	1995 to 2002
Prop	C W Dowd	58	1993 to 2000
Hooker	S B T Fitzpatrick	92	1986 to 1997
Lock	I D Jones	79	1990 to 1999
Flanker	J A Kronfeld	54	1995 to 2000
No 8	Z V Brooke	52	1990 to 1997

MOST POINTS IN TESTS

Points	Player	Tests	Career
895	A P Mehrtens	63	1995 to 2002
645	G J Fox	46	1985 to 1993
236	C M Cullen	57	1996 to 2002
234	J W Wilson	60	1993 to 2001
207	D B Clarke	31	1956 to 1964
201	A R Hewson	19	1981 to 1984
177	C J Spencer	14	1997 to 2000

MOST TRIES IN TESTS

Tries	Player	Tests	Career
46	C M Cullen	57	1996 to 2002
44	J W Wilson	60	1993 to 2001
35	J J Kirwan	63	1984 to 1994
35	J T Lomu	60	1994 to 2002
24	J F Umaga	42	1999 to 2002
22	J W Marshall	60	1995 to 2002
20	F E Bunce	55	1992 to 1997
19	S S Wilson	34	1977 to 1983
19	T J Wright	30	1986 to 1991

MOST CONVERSIONS IN TESTS

Cons	Player	Tests	Career
154	A P Mehrtens	63	1995 to 2002
118	G J Fox	46	1985 to 1993

43	T E Brown	18	1999 to 2001
39	C J Spencer	14	1997 to 2000
33	D B Clarke	31	1956 to 1964
32	S D Culhane	6	1995 to 1996

MOST PENALTY GOALS IN TESTS

Penalties	Player	Tests	Career
174	A P Mehrtens	63	1995 to 2002
128	G J Fox	46	1985 to 1993
43	A R Hewson	19	1981 to 1984
38	D B Clarke	31	1956 to 1964
24	W F McCormick	16	1965 to 1971

MOST DROPPED GOALS IN TESTS

Drops	Player	Tests	Career
10	A P Mehrtens	63	1995 to 2002
7	G J Fox	46	1985 to 1993
5	D B Clarke	31	1956 to 1964
5	M A Herewini	10	1962 to 1967
5	O D Bruce	14	1976 to 1978

Tri Nations Records

Record	Detail	Holder	Set
Most points in season	159	in four matches	1997
Most tries in season	17	in four matches	1997
Highest Score	55	55-35 v S Africa (h)	1997
Biggest win	37	43-6 v Australia (h)	1996
Highest score conceded	46	40-46 v S Africa (a)	2000
Biggest defeat	21	7-28 v Australia (a)	1999
Most points in matches	309	A P Mehrtens	1996 to 2002
Most points in season	84	C J Spencer	1997
Most points in match	29	A P Mehrtens	v Australia (h) 1999
Most tries in matches	16	C M Cullen	1996 to 2002
Most tries in season	7	C M Cullen	2000
Most tries in match	2	F E Bunce	v S Africa (a) 1997
	2	C M Cullen	v S Africa (h) 1997
	2	C M Cullen	v S Africa (a) 1999
	2	C M Cullen	v S Africa (h) 2000
	2	C M Cullen	v Australia (h) 2000
	2	C M Cullen	v S Africa (a) 2000
	2	J F Umaga	v S Africa (a) 2000
Most cons in matches	32	A P Mehrtens	1996 to 2002
Most cons in season	13	C J Spencer	1997
Most cons in match	4	C J Spencer	v S Africa (h) 1997
	4	A P Mehrtens	v Australia (a) 2000

	4	A P Mehrtens	v S Africa (a) 2000
Most pens in matches	77	A P Mehrtens	1996 to 2002
Most pens in season	19	A P Mehrtens	1996
	19	A P Mehrtens	1999
Most pens in match	9	A P Mehrtens	v Australia (h) 1999

Series Records

Record	Holder	Detail
Most tries	C M Cullen	7 v Tri Nations 2000
Most points	C J Spencer	84 v Tri Nations 1997

Miscellaneous Records

Record	Holder	Detail
Longest Test Career	E Hughes/C E Meads	15 seasons, 1907-21/1957-71
Youngest Test Cap	J T Lomu	19 yrs 45 days in 1994
Oldest Test Cap	E Hughes	40 yrs 123 days in 1921

Career Records Of New Zealand International Players
(up to 31 August 2002)

	Debut	Caps	T	C	PG	DG	Pts
Backs:							
B A Blair	2001 v S	2	0	0	0	0	0
C M Cullen	1996 v WS	57	46	3	0	0	236
D P E Gibson	1999 v WS	19	1	0	0	0	5
D C Howlett	2000 v Tg	21	14	0	0	0	70
B T Kelleher	1999 v WS	23	4	0	0	0	20
J T Lomu	1994 v F	60	35	0	0	0	175
L R MacDonald	2000 v S	18	7	0	0	0	35
J W Marshall	1995 v F	60	22	0	0	0	110
A J D Mauger	2001 v I	11	3	5	1	0	28
A P Mehrtens	1995 v C	63	7	154	174	10	895
C S Ralph	1998 v E	8	4	0	0	0	20
M D Robinson	1998 v E	3	1	0	0	0	5
M P Robinson	2000 v S	6	1	0	0	0	5
J F Umaga	1997 v Fj	42	24	0	0	0	120
J W Wilson	1993 v S	60	44	1	3	1	234
Forwards:							
S R Broomhall	2002 v SA	2	0	0	0	0	0
G E Feek	1999 v WS	10	0	0	0	0	0
M G Hammett	1999 v F	21	3	0	0	0	15
S Harding	2002 v Fj	1	0	0	0	0	0
C J Hayman	2001 v Sm	6	0	0	0	0	0
D N Hewett	2001 v I	10	2	0	0	0	10
M R Holah	2001 v Sm	10	2	0	0	0	10
C R Jack	2001 v Arg	13	2	0	0	0	10
R H McCaw	2001 v I	9	1	0	0	0	5
J M McDonnell	2002 v It	6	1	0	0	0	5
T S Maling	2002 v It	7	0	0	0	0	0
N M C Maxwell	1999 v WS	34	5	0	0	0	25

K J Meeuws	1998 v A	21	3	0	0	0	15
A D Oliver	1997 v Fj	39	2	0	0	0	10
T C Randell	1997 v Fj	48	12	0	0	0	60
S M Robertson	1998 v A	23	4	0	0	0	20
G M Somerville	2000 v Tg	22	0	0	0	0	0
R D Thorne	1999 v SA	27	3	0	0	0	15
D A G Waller	2001 v Arg	1	0	0	0	0	0
R K Willis	1998 v SA	12	0	0	0	0	0
T E Willis	2002 v It	5	0	0	0	0	0

NB MacDonald's figures include a penalty try awarded against South Africa in 2001 and Umaga's a penalty try awarded against South Africa in 2002

NEW ZEALAND INTERNATIONAL PLAYERS
(up to 31 August 2002)

Abbott, H L (Taranaki) 1906 *F*
Aitken, G G (Wellington) 1921 *SA* 1,2
Aitken, G G (Wellington) 1921 *SA* 1,2
Alatini, P F (Otago) 1999 *F* 1(R), [*It, SA* 3(R)], 2000 *Tg, S* 1, *A* 1, *SA* 1, *A* 2, *SA* 2, *It*, 2001 *Sm, Arg* 1, *F, SA* 1, *A* 1, *SA* 2, *A* 2
Allen, M R (Taranaki, Manawatu) 1993 *WS* (t), 1996 *S* 2 (t), 1997 *Arg* 1(R),2(R), *SA* 2(R), *A* 3(R), *E* 2, *W* (R)
Allen, N H (Counties) 1980 *A* 3, *W*
Alley, G T (Canterbury) 1928 *SA* 1,2,3
Anderson, A (Canterbury) 1983 *S, E*, 1984 *A* 1,2,3, 1987 [*Fj*]
Anderson, B L (Wairarapa-Bush) 1986 *A* 1
Archer, W R (Otago, Southland) 1955 *A* 1,2, 1956 *SA* 1,3
Argus, W G (Canterbury) 1946 *A* 1,2, 1947 *A* 1,2
Arnold, D A (Canterbury) 1963 *I, W*, 1964 *E, F*
Arnold, K D (Waikato) 1947 *A* 1,2
Ashby, D L (Southland) 1958 *A* 2
Asher, A A (Auckland) 1903 *A*
Ashworth, B G (Auckland) 1978 *A* 1,2
Ashworth, J C (Canterbury, Hawke's Bay) 1978 *A* 1,2,3, 1980 *A* 1,2,3, 1981 *SA* 1,2,3, 1982 *A* 1,2, 1983 *BI* 1,2,3,4, *A*, 1984 *F* 1,2, *A* 1,2,3, 1985 *E* 1,2, *A*
Atkinson, H (West Coast) 1913 *A* 1
Avery, H E (Wellington) 1910 *A* 1,2,3

Bachop, G T M (Canterbury) 1989 *W, I*, 1990 *S* 1,2, *A* 1,2,3, *F* 1,2, 1991 *Arg* 1,2, *A* 1,2, [*E, US, C, A, S*], 1992 *Wld* 1, 1994 *SA* 1,2,3, *A*, 1995 *C*, [*I, W, S, E, SA*], *A* 1,2
Bachop, S J (Otago) 1994 *F* 2, *SA* 1,2,3, *A*
Badeley, C E O (Auckland) 1921 *SA* 1,2
Baird, J A S (Otago) 1913 *A* 2
Ball, N (Wellington) 1931 *A*, 1932 *A* 2,3, 1935 *W*, 1936 *E*
Barrett, J (Auckland) 1913 *A* 2,3
Barry, E F (Wellington) 1934 *A* 2
Barry, L J (North Harbour) 1995 *F* 2
Batty, G B (Wellington, Bay of Plenty) 1972 *W, S*, 1973 *E* 1, *I, F, E* 2, 1974 *A* 1,3, *I*, 1975 *S*, 1976 *SA* 1,2,3,4, 1977 *BI* 1
Batty, W (Auckland) 1930 *BI* 1,3,4, 1931 *A*
Beatty, G E (Taranaki) 1950 *BI* 1
Bell, R H (Otago) 1951 *A* 3, 1952 *A* 1,2
Bellis, E A (Wanganui) 1921 *SA* 1,2,3
Bennet, R (Otago) 1905 *A*
Berghan, T (Otago) 1938 *A* 1,2,3
Berry, M J (Wairarapa-Bush) 1986 *A* 3(R)
Berryman, N R (Northland) 1998 *SA* 2(R)
Bevan, V D (Wellington) 1949 *A* 1,2, 1950 *BI* 1,2,3,4
Birtwistle, W M (Canterbury) 1965 *SA* 1,2,3,4, 1967 *E, W, S*
Black, J E (Canterbury) 1977 *F* 1, 1979 *A*, 1980 *A* 3
Black, N W (Auckland) 1949 *SA* 3
Black, R S (Otago) 1914 *A* 1
Blackadder, T J (Canterbury) 1998 *E* 1(R),2, 2000 *Tg, S* 1,2, *A* 1, *SA* 1, *A* 2, *SA* 2, *F* 1,2, *It*
Blair, B A (Canterbury) 2001 *S* (R), *Arg* 2
Blake, A W (Wairarapa) 1949 *A* 1
Blowers, A F (Auckland) 1996 *SA* 2(R),4(R), 1997 *I, E* 1(R), *W* (R), 1999 *F* 1(R), *SA* 1, *A* 1(R), *SA* 2, *A* 2(R), [*It*]
Boggs, E G (Auckland) 1946 *A* 2, 1949 *SA* 1
Bond, J G (Canterbury) 1949 *A* 2
Booth, E E (Otago) 1906 *F*, 1907 *A* 1,3
Boroevich, K G (Wellington) 1986 *F* 1, *A* 1, *F* 3(R)
Botica, F M (North Harbour) 1986 *F* 1, *A* 1,2,3, *F* 2,3, 1989 *Arg* 1(R)
Bowden, N J G (Taranaki) 1952 *A* 2
Bowers, R G (Wellington) 1954 *I, F*
Bowman, A W (Hawke's Bay) 1938 *A* 1,2,3
Braid, G J (Bay of Plenty) 1983 *S, E*
Bremner, S G (Auckland, Canterbury) 1952 *A* 2, 1956 *SA* 2
Brewer, M R (Otago, Canterbury) 1986 *F* 1, *A* 1,2,3, *F* 2,3, 1988 *A* 1, 1989 *A, W, I*, 1990 *S* 1,2, *A* 1,2,3, *F* 1,2, 1992 *I* 2, *A* 1, 1994 *F* 1,2, *SA* 1,2,3, *A*, 1995 *C*, [*I, W, E, SA*], *A* 1,2
Briscoe, K C (Taranaki) 1959 *BI* 2, 1960 *SA* 1,2,3,4, 1963 *I, W*, 1964 *E, S*
Brooke, R M (Auckland) 1992 *I* 2, *A* 1,2,3, *SA*, 1993 *BI* 1,2,3, *A, WS*, 1994 *SA* 2,3, 1995 *C*, [*J, S, E, SA*], *A* 1,2, *It, F* 1,2, 1996 *WS, S* 1,2, *A* 1, *SA* 1, *A* 2, *SA* 2,3,4,5, 1997 *Fj, Arg*

1,2, *A* 1, *SA* 1, *A* 2, *SA* 2, *A* 3, *I, E* 1, *W, E* 2, 1998 *E* 1,2, *A* 1, *SA* 1, *A* 2, *SA* 2, *A* 3, 1999 *WS, F* 1, *SA* 1, *A* 1, *SA* 2, *A* 2, [*Tg, E, It* (R), *S, F* 2]
Brooke, Z V (Auckland) 1987 [*Arg*], 1989 *Arg* 2(R), 1990 *A* 1,2,3, *F* 1(R), 1991 *Arg* 2, *A* 1,2, [*E, It, C, A, S*], 1992 *A* 2,3, *SA*, 1993 *BI* 1,2,3(R), *WS* (R), *S, E*, 1994 *F* 2, *SA* 1,2,3, *A*, 1995 [*J, S, E, SA*], *A* 1,2, *It, F* 1,2, 1996 *WS, S* 1,2, *A* 1, *SA* 1, *A* 2, *SA* 2,3,4,5, 1997 *Arg* 1,2, *A* 1, *SA* 1, *A* 2, *SA* 2, *A* 3, *I, E* 1, *W, E* 2
Brooke-Cowden, M (Auckland) 1986 *F* 1, *A* 1, 1987 [*W*]
Broomhall, S R (Canterbury) 2002 *SA* 1(R),2(R)
Brown, C (Taranaki) 1913 *A* 2,3
Brown, O M (Auckland) 1992 *I* 2, *A* 1,2,3, *SA*, 1993 *BI* 1,2,3, *A, S, E*, 1994 *F* 1,2, *SA* 1,2,3, *A*, 1995 *C*, [*I, W, S, E, SA*], *A* 1,2, *It, F* 1,2, 1996 *WS, S* 1,2, *A* 1, *SA* 1, *A* 2, *SA* 2,3,4,5, 1997 *Fj, Arg* 1,2, *A* 1, *SA* 1, *A* 2, *SA* 2, *A* 3, *I, E* 1, *W, E* 2, 1998 *E* 1,2, *A* 1, *SA* 1, *A* 2, *SA* 2
Brown, R H (Taranaki) 1955 *A* 3, 1956 *SA* 1,2,3,4, 1957 *A* 1,2, 1958 *A* 1,2,3, 1959 *BI* 1,3, 1961 *F* 1,2,3, 1962 *A* 1
Brown, T E (Otago) 1999 *WS, F* 1(R), *SA* 1(R), *A* 1(R),2(R), [*E* (R), *It, S* (R)], 2000 *Tg, S* 2(R), *A* 1(R), *SA* 1(R), *A* 2(R), 2001 *Sm, Arg* 1(R), *F, SA* 1, *A* 1
Brownlie, C J (Hawke's Bay) 1924 *W*, 1925 *E, F*
Brownlie, M J (Hawke's Bay) 1924 *I, W*, 1925 *E, F*, 1928 *SA* 1,2,3,4
Bruce, J A (Auckland) 1914 *A* 1,2
Bruce, O D (Canterbury) 1976 *SA* 1,2,4, 1977 *BI* 2,3,4, *F* 1,2, 1978 *A* 1,2, *I, W, E, S*
Bryers, R F (King Country) 1949 *A* 1
Budd, T A (Southland) 1946 *A* 2, 1949 *A* 2
Bullock-Douglas, G A H (Wanganui) 1932 *A* 1,2,3, 1934 *A* 1,2
Bunce, F E (North Harbour) 1992 *Wld* 1,2,3, *I* 1,2, *A* 1,2,3, *SA*, 1993 *BI* 1,2,3, *A, WS, S, E*, 1994 *F* 1,2, *SA* 1,2,3, *A*, 1995 *C*, [*I, W, S, E, SA*], *A* 1,2, *It, F* 1,2, 1996 *WS, S* 1,2, *A*1, *SA* 1, *A* 2, *SA* 2,3,4,5, 1997 *Fj, Arg* 1,2, *A* 1, *SA* 1, *A* 2, *SA* 2, *A* 3, *I, E* 1, *W, E* 2
Burgess, G A J (Auckland) 1981 *SA* 2
Burgess, G F (Southland) 1905 *A*
Burgess, R E (Manawatu) 1971 *BI* 1,2,3, 1972 *A* 3, *W*, 1973 *I, F*
Burke, P S (Taranaki) 1955 *A* 1, 1957 *A* 1,2
Burns, P J (Canterbury) 1908 *AW* 2, 1910 *A* 1,2,3, 1913 *A* 3
Bush, R G (Otago) 1931 *A*
Bush, W K (Canterbury) 1974 *A* 1,2, 1975 *S*, 1976 *I, SA*, 2,4, 1977 *BI* 2,3,4(R), 1978 *I, W*, 1979 *A*
Buxton, J B (Canterbury) 1955 *A* 3, 1956 *SA* 1

Cain, M J (Taranaki) 1913 *US*, 1914 *A* 1,2,3
Callesen, J A (Manawatu) 1974 *A* 1,2,3, 1975 *S*
Cameron, D (Taranaki) 1908 *AW* 1,2,3
Cameron, L M (Manawatu) 1980 *A* 3, 1981 *SA* 1(R),2,3, *R*
Carleton, S R (Canterbury) 1928 *SA* 1,2,3, 1929 *A* 1,2,3
Carrington, K R (Auckland) 1971 *BI* 1,3,4
Carter, M P (Auckland) 1991 *A* 2, [*It, A*], 1997 *Fj* (R), *A* 1(R), 1998 *E* 2(R), *A* 2
Casey, S T (Otago) 1905 *S, I, E, W*, 1907 *A* 1,2,3, 1908 *AW* 1
Cashmore, A R (Auckland) 1996 *S* 2(R), 1997 *A* 2(R)
Catley, E H (Waikato) 1946 *A* 1, 1947 *A* 1,2, 1949 *SA* 1,2,3,4
Caughey, T H C (Auckland) 1932 *A* 1,3, 1934 *A* 1,2, 1935 *S, I*, 1936 *E, A* 1, 1937 *SA* 3
Caulton, R W (Wellington) 1959 *BI* 2,3,4, 1960 *SA* 1,4, 1961 *F* 2, 1963 *E* 1,2, *I, W*, 1964 *E, S, F, A* 1,2,3
Cherrington, N P (North Auckland) 1950 *BI* 1
Christian, D L (Auckland) 1949 *SA* 4
Clamp, M (Wellington) 1984 *A* 2,3
Clark, D W (Otago) 1964 *A* 1,2
Clark, W H (Wellington) 1953 *W*, 1954 *I, E, S*, 1955 *A* 1,2, 1956 *SA* 2,3,4
Clarke, A H (Auckland) 1958 *A* 3, 1959 *BI* 4, 1960 *SA* 1
Clarke, D B (Waikato) 1956 *SA* 3,4, 1957 *A* 1,2, 1958 *A* 1,3, 1959 *BI* 1,2,3,4, 1960 *SA* 1,2,3,4, 1961 *F* 1,2,3, 1962 *A* 1,2,3,4,5, 1963 *E* 1,2, *I, W*, 1964 *E, S, F, A* 2,3
Clarke, E (Auckland) 1992 *Wld* 2,3, *I* 1,2, 1993 *BI* 1,2, *S* (R), *E*, 1998 *SA* 2, *A* 3

Clarke, I J (Waikato) 1953 *W*, 1955 *A* 1,2,3, 1956 *SA* 1,2,3,4, 1957 *A* 1,2, 1958 *A* 1,3, 1959 *BI* 1,2, 1960 *SA* 2,4, 1961 *F* 1,2,3, 1962 *A* 1,2,3, 1963 *E* 1,2
Clarke, R L (Taranaki) 1932 *A* 2,3
Cobden, D G (Canterbury) 1937 *SA* 1
Cockerill, M S (Taranaki) 1951 *A* 1,2,3
Cockroft, E A P (South Canterbury) 1913 *A* 3, 1914 *A* 2,3
Codlin, B W (Counties) 1980 *A* 1,2,3
Collins, A H (Taranaki) 1932 *A* 2,3, 1934 *A* 1
Collins, J (Wellington) 2001 *Arg* 1
Collins, J L (Poverty Bay) 1964 *A* 1, 1965 *SA* 1,4
Colman, J T H (Taranaki) 1907 *A* 1,2, 1908 *AW* 1,3
Connor, D M (Auckland) 1961 *F* 1,2,3, 1962 *A* 1,2,3,4,5, 1963 *E* 1,2, 1964 *A* 2,3
Conway, R J (Otago, Bay of Plenty) 1959 *BI* 2,3,4, 1960 *SA* 1,3,4, 1965 *SA* 1,2,3,4
Cooke, A E (Auckland, Wellington) 1924 *I*, *W*, 1925 *E*, *F*, 1930 *BI* 1,2,3,4
Cooke, R J (Canterbury) 1903 *A*
Cooksley, M S B (Counties, Waikato) 1992 *Wld* 1, 1993 *BI* 2,3(R), *A*, 1994 *F* 1,2, *SA* 1,2, *A*, 2001 *A* 1(R), *SA* 2(t&R)
Cooper, G J L (Auckland, Otago) 1986 *F* 1, *A* 1,2, 1992 *Wld* 1,2,3, *I* 1
Cooper, M J A (Waikato) 1992 *I* 2, *SA* (R), 1993 *BI* 1(R),3(t), *WS* (t), *S*, 1994 *F* 1,2
Corner, M M N (Auckland) 1930 *BI* 2,3,4, 1931 *A*, 1934 *A* 1, 1936 *E*
Cossey, R R (Counties) 1958 *A* 1
Cottrell, A I (Canterbury) 1929 *A* 1,2,3, 1930 *BI* 1,2,3,4, 1931 *A*, 1932 *A* 1,2,3
Cottrell, W D (Canterbury) 1968 *A* 1,2, *F* 2,3, 1970 *SA* 1, 1971 *BI* 1,2,3,4
Couch, M B R (Wairarapa) 1947 *A* 1, 1949 *A* 1,2
Coughlan, T D (South Canterbury) 1958 *A* 1
Creighton, J N (Canterbury) 1962 *A* 4
Cribb, R T (North Harbour) 2000 *S* 1,2, *A* 1, *SA* 1, *A* 2, *SA* 2, *F* 1,2, *It*, 2001 *Sm*, *F*, *SA* 1, *A* 1, *SA* 2, *A* 2
Crichton, S (Wellington) 1983 *S*, *E*
Cross, T (Canterbury) 1904 *BI*, 1905 *A*
Crowley, K J (Taranaki) 1985 *E* 1,2, *A*, *Arg* 1,2, 1986 *A* 3, *F* 2,3, 1987 [*Arg*], 1990 *S* 1,2, *A* 1,2,3, *F* 1,2, 1991 *Arg* 1,2, [*A*]
Crowley, P J B (Auckland) 1949 *SA* 3,4, 1950 *BI* 1,2,3,4
Culhane, S D (Southland) 1995 [*J*], *It*, *F* 1,2, 1996 *SA* 3,4
Cullen C M (Manawatu, Central Vikings, Wellington) 1996 *WS*, *S* 1,2, *A* 1, *SA* 1, *A* 2, *SA* 2,3,4,5, 1997 *Fj*, *Arg* 1,2, *A* 1, *SA* 1, *A* 2, *SA* 2, *A* 3, *I*, *E* 1, *W*, *E* 2, 1998 *E* 1,2, *A* 1, *SA* 1, *A* 2, *SA* 2, *A* 3, 1999 *WS*, *F* 1, *SA* 1, *A* 1, *SA* 2, *A* 2, [*Tg*, *E*, *It* (R), *S*, *F* 2, *SA* 3], 2000 *Tg*, *S* 1,2, *A* 1, *SA* 1, *A* 2, *SA* 2, *F* 1,2, *It*, 2001 *A* 2(R), 2002 *It*, *Fj*, *A* 1, *SA* 1, *A2*
Cummings, W (Canterbury) 1913 *A* 2,3
Cundy, R T (Wairarapa) 1929 *A* 2(R)
Cunningham, G R (Auckland) 1979 *A*, *S*, *E*, 1980 *A* 1,2
Cunningham, W (Auckland) 1905 *S*, *I*, 1906 *F*, 1907 *A* 1,2,3, 1908 *AW* 1,2,3
Cupples, L F (Bay of Plenty) 1924 *I*, *W*
Currie, C J (Canterbury) 1978 *I*, *W*
Cuthill, J E (Otago) 1913 *A* 1, *US*

Dalley, W C (Canterbury) 1924 *I*, 1928 *SA* 1,2,3,4
Dalton, A G (Counties) 1977 *F* 2, 1978 *A* 1,2,3, *I*, *W*, *E*, *S*, 1979 *F* 1,2, *S*, 1981 *S* 1,2, *SA* 1,2,3, *R*, *F* 1,2, 1982 *A* 1,2,3, 1983 *BI* 1,2,3,4, *A*, 1984 *F* 1,2, *A* 1,2,3, 1985 *E* 1,2, *A*
Dalton, D (Hawke's Bay) 1935 *I*, *W*, 1936 *A* 1,2, 1937 *SA* 1,2,3, 1938 *A* 1,2
Dalton, R A (Wellington) 1947 *A* 1,2
Dalzell, G N (Canterbury) 1953 *W*, 1954 *I*, *E*, *S*, *F*
Davie, M G (Canterbury) 1983 *E* (R)
Davies, W A (Auckland, Otago) 1960 *SA* 4, 1962 *A* 4,5
Davis, K (Auckland) 1952 *A* 2, 1953 *W*, 1954 *I*, *E*, *S*, *F*, 1955 *A* 2, 1958 *A* 1,2,3
Davis, L J (Canterbury) 1976 *I*, 1977 *BI* 3,4
Davis, W L (Hawke's Bay) 1967 *A*, *E*, *W*, *F*, *S*, 1968 *A* 1,2, *F* 1, 1969 *W* 1,2, 1970 *SA* 2
Deans, I B (Canterbury) 1988 *A* 1,2, *A* 1,2,3, 1989 *F* 1,2, *Arg* 1,2, *A*
Deans, R G (Canterbury) 1905 *S*, *I*, *E*, *W*, 1908 *AW* 3
Deans, R M (Canterbury) 1983 *S*, *E*, 1984 *A* 1(R),2,3
Delamore, G W (Wellington) 1949 *SA* 4
Dewar, H (Taranaki) 1913 *A* 1, *US*
Diack, E S (Otago) 1959 *BI* 2
Dick, J (Auckland) 1937 *SA* 1,2, 1938 *A* 3
Dick, M J (Auckland) 1963 *I*, *W*, 1964 *E*, *S*, *F*, 1965 *SA* 3, 1966 *BI* 4, 1967 *A*, *E*, *W*, *F*, 1969 *W* 1,2, 1970 *SA* 1,4

Dixon, M J (Canterbury) 1954 *I*, *E*, *S*, *F*, 1956 *SA* 1,2,3,4, 1957 *A* 1,2
Dobson, R L (Auckland) 1949 *A* 1
Dodd, E H (Wellington) 1905 *A*
Donald, A J (Wanganui) 1983 *S*, *E*, 1984 *F* 1,2, *A* 1,2,3
Donald, J G (Wairarapa) 1921 *SA* 1,2
Donald, Q (Wairarapa) 1924 *I*, *W*, 1925 *E*, *F*
Donaldson, M W (Manawatu) 1977 *F* 1,2, 1978 *A* 1,2,3, *I*, *E*, *S*, 1979 *F* 1,2, *A*, *S* (R), 1981 *SA* 3(R)
Dougan, J P (Wellington) 1972 *A* 1, 1973 *E* 2
Dowd, C W (Auckland) 1993 *BI* 1,2,3, *A*, *WS*, *S*, *E*, 1994 *SA* 1(R), 1995 *C*, [*I*, *W*, *J*, *E*, *SA*], *A* 1,2, *It*, *F* 1,2, 1996 *WS*, *S* 1,2, *A* 1, *SA* 1, *A* 2, *SA* 2,3,4,5, 1997 *Fj*, *Arg* 1,2, *A* 1, *SA* 1, *A* 2, *SA* 2, *A* 3, *I*, *E* 1, *W*, 1998 *E* 1,2, *A* 1, *SA* 1, *A* 2,3(R), 1999 *SA* 2(R), *A* 2(R), [*Tg* (R), *E*, *It*, *S*, *F* 2, *SA* 3], 2000 *Tg*, *S* 1(R),2(R), *A* 1(R), *SA* 1(R), *A* 2(R)
Dowd, G W (North Harbour) 1992 *I* 1(R)
Downing, A J (Auckland) 1913 *A* 1, *US*, 1914 *A* 1,2,3
Drake, J A (Auckland) 1986 *F* 2,3, 1987 [*Fj*, *Arg*, *S*, *W*, *F*], *A* 2,3, 1956 *SA* 1,2,3,4
Duff, R H (Canterbury) 1951 *A* 1,2,3, 1952 *A* 1,2, 1955 *A* 2,3, 1956 *SA* 1,2,3,4
Duggan, R J L (Waikato) 1999 [*It* (R)]
Duncan, J (Otago) 1903 *A*
Duncan, M G (Hawke's Bay) 1971 *BI* 3(R),4
Duncan, W D (Otago) 1921 *SA* 1,2,3
Dunn, E J (North Auckland) 1979 *S*, 1981 *S* 1
Dunn, I T W (North Auckland) 1983 *BI* 1,4, *A*
Dunn, J M (Auckland) 1946 *A* 1

Earl, A T (Canterbury) 1986 *F* 1, *A* 1, *F* 3(R), 1987 [*Arg*], 1989 *W*, *I*, 1991 *Arg* 1(R),2, *A* 1, [*E* (R), *US*, *S*], 1992 *A* 2,3(R)
Eastgate, B P (Canterbury) 1952 *A* 1,2, 1954 *S*
Elliott, K G (Wellington) 1946 *A* 1,2
Ellis, M C G (Otago) 1993 *S*, *E*, 1995 *C*, [*I* (R), *W*, *J*, *S*, *SA* (R)]
Elsom, A E G (Canterbury) 1952 *A* 1,2, 1953 *W*, 1955 *A* 1,2,3
Elvidge, R R (Otago) 1946 *A* 1,2, 1949 *SA* 1,2,3,4, 1950 *BI* 1,2,3
Erceg, C P (Auckland) 1951 *A* 1,2,3, 1952 *A* 1
Evans, D A (Hawke's Bay) 1910 *A* 2
Eveleigh, K A (Manawatu) 1976 *SA* 2,4, 1977 *BI* 1,2

Fanning, A H N (Canterbury) 1913 *A* 3
Fanning, B J (Canterbury) 1903 *A*, 1904 *BI*
Farrell, C P (Auckland) 1977 *BI* 1,2
Fawcett, C L (Auckland) 1976 *SA* 2,3
Fea, W R (Otago) 1921 *SA* 3
Feek, G E (Canterbury) 1999 *WS* (R), *A* 1(R), *SA* 2, [*E* (t), *It*], 2000 *F* 1,2, *It*, 2001 *I*, *S*
Finlay, B E L (Manawatu) 1959 *BI* 1
Finlay, J (Manawatu) 1946 *A* 1
Finlayson, I (North Auckland) 1928 *SA* 1,2,3,4, 1930 *BI* 1,2
Fitzgerald, J T (Wellington) 1952 *A* 1
Fitzpatrick, B B J (Wellington) 1953 *W*, 1954 *I*, *F*
Fitzpatrick, S B T (Auckland) 1986 *F* 1, *A* 1, *F* 2,3, 1987 [*It*, *Fj*, *Arg*, *S*, *W*, *F*], *A*, 1988 *W* 1,2, *A* 1,2,3, 1989 *F* 1,2, *Arg* 1,2, *A*, *W*, *I*, 1990 *S* 1,2, *A* 1,2,3, *F* 1,2, 1991 *Arg* 1,2, *A* 1,2, [*E*, *US*, *It*, *C*, *A*, *S*], 1992 *Wld* 1,2,3, *I* 1,2, *A* 1,2,3, *SA*, 1993 *BI* 1,2,3, *A*, *WS*, *S*, *E*, 1994 *F* 1,2, *SA* 1,2,3, *A*, 1995 *C*, [*I*, *W*, *S*, *E*, *SA*], *A* 1,2, *It*, *F* 1,2, 1996 *WS*, *S* 1,2, *A* 1, *SA* 1, *A* 2, *SA* 2,3,4,5, 1997 *Fj*, *Arg* 1,2, *A* 1, *SA* 1, *A* 2, *SA* 2, *A* 3, *W* (R)
Flavell, T V (North Harbour) 2000 *Tg*, *S* 1(R), *A* 1(R), *SA* 1,2(t), *F* 1(R),2(R), *It*, 2001 *Sm*, *Arg* 1, *F*, *SA* 1, *A* 1, *SA* 2, *A* 2
Fleming, J K (Wellington) 1979 *S*, *E*, 1980 *A* 1,2,3
Fletcher, C J C (North Auckland) 1921 *SA* 3
Fogarty, R (Taranaki) 1921 *SA* 1,3
Ford, B R (Marlborough) 1977 *BI* 3,4, 1978 *I*, 1979 *E*
Forster, S T (Otago) 1993 *S*, *E*, 1994 *F* 1,2, 1995 *It*, *F* 1
Fox, G J (Auckland) 1985 *Arg* 1, 1987 [*It*, *Fj*, *Arg*, *S*, *W*, *F*], *A*, 1988 *W* 1,2, *A* 1,2,3, 1989 *F* 1,2, *Arg* 1,2, *A*, *W*, *I*, 1990 *S* 1,2, *A* 1,2,3, *F* 1,2, 1991 *Arg* 1,2, *A* 1,2, [*E*, *It*, *C*, *A*], 1992 *Wld* 1,2(R), *A* 1,2,3, *SA*, 1993 *BI* 1,2,3, *A*, *WS*
Francis, A R H (Auckland) 1905 *A*, 1907 *A* 1,2,3, 1908 *AW* 1,2,3, 1910 *A* 1,2,3
Francis, W C (Wellington) 1913 *A* 2,3, 1914 *A* 1,2,3
Fraser, B G (Wellington) 1979 *S*, *E*, 1980 *A* 3, *W*, 1981 *S* 1,2, *SA* 1,2,3, *R*, *F* 1,2, 1982 *A* 1,2,3, 1983 *BI* 1,2,3,4, *A*, *S*, *E*, 1984 *A* 1
Frazer, H F (Hawke's Bay) 1946 *A* 1,2, 1947 *A* 1,2, 1949 *SA* 2
Fryer, F C (Canterbury) 1907 *A* 1,2,3, 1908 *AW* 2
Fuller, W B (Canterbury) 1910 *A* 1,2

Furlong, B D M (Hawke's Bay) 1970 *SA* 4

Gallagher, J A (Wellington) 1987 [*It, Fj, S, W, F*], *A*, 1988 *W* 1,2, *A* 1,2,3, 1989 *F* 1,2, *Arg* 1,2, *A, W, I*
Gallaher, D (Auckland) 1903 *A*, 1904 *BI*, 1905 *S, E, W*, 1906 *F*
Gard, P C (North Otago) 1971 *BI* 4
Gardiner, A J (Taranaki) 1974 *A* 3
Geddes, J H (Southland) 1929 *A* 1
Geddes, W McK (Auckland) 1913 *A* 2
Gemmell, B McL (Auckland) 1974 *A* 1,2
George, V L (Southland) 1938 *A* 1,2,3
Gibson, D P E (Canterbury) 1999 *WS, F* 1, *SA* 1, *A* 1, *SA* 2, *A* 2, [*Tg* (R), *E* (R), *It, S* (R), *F* 2(R)], 2000 *F* 1,2, 2002 *It, I* 1(R),2(R), *Fj, A* 2(R), *SA* 2(R)
Gilbert, G D M (West Coast) 1935 *S, I, W*, 1936 *E*
Gillespie, C T (Wellington) 1913 *A* 2
Gillespie, W D (Otago) 1958 *A* 3
Gillett, G A (Canterbury, Auckland) 1905 *S, I, E, W*, 1907 *A* 2,3, 1908 *AW* 1,3
Gillies, C C (Otago) 1936 *A* 2
Gilray, C M (Otago) 1905 *A*
Glasgow, F T (Taranaki, Southland) 1905 *S, I, E, W*, 1906 *F*, 1908 *AW* 3
Glenn, W S (Taranaki) 1904 *BI*, 1906 *F*
Goddard, M P (South Canterbury) 1946 *A* 2, 1947 *A* 1,2, 1949 *SA* 3,4
Going, S M (North Auckland) 1967 *A, F*, 1968 *F* 3, 1969 *W* 1,2, 1970 *SA* 1(R),4, 1971 *BI* 1,2,3,4, 1972 *A* 1,2,3, *W, S*, 1973 *E* 1, *I, F, E* 2, 1974 *I*, 1975 *S*, 1976 *I* (R), *SA* 1,2,3,4, 1977 *BI* 1,2
Gordon, S B (Waikato) 1993 *S, E*
Graham, D J (Canterbury) 1958 *A* 1,2, 1960 *SA* 2,3, 1961 *F* 1,2,3, 1962 *A* 1,2,3,4,5, 1963 *E* 1,2, *I, W*, 1964 *E, S, F, A* 1,2,3
Graham, J B (Otago) 1913 *US*, 1914 *A* 1,3
Graham, W G (Otago) 1979 *F* 1(R)
Grant, L A (South Canterbury) 1947 *A* 1,2, 1949 *SA* 1,2
Gray, G D (Canterbury) 1908 *AW* 2, 1913 *A* 1, *US*
Gray, K F (Wellington) 1963 *I, W*, 1964 *E, S, F, A* 1,2,3, 1965 *SA* 1,2,3,4, 1966 *BI* 1,2,3,4, 1967 *W, F, S*, 1968 *A* 1, *F* 2,3, 1969 *W* 1,2
Gray, W N (Bay of Plenty) 1955 *A* 2,3, 1956 *SA* 1,2,3,4
Green, C I (Canterbury) 1983 *S* (R), *E*, 1984 *A* 1,2,3, 1985 *E* 1,2, *A, Arg* 1,2, 1986 *A* 2,3, *F* 2,3, 1987 [*It, Fj, S, W, F*], *A*
Grenside, B A (Hawke's Bay) 1928 *SA* 1,2,3,4, 1929 *A* 2,3
Griffiths, J L (Wellington) 1934 *A* 2, 1935 *S, I, W*, 1936 *A* 1,2, 1938 *A* 3
Guy, R A (North Auckland) 1971 *BI* 1,2,3,4

Haden, A M (Auckland) 1977 *BI* 1,2,3,4, *F* 1,2, 1978 *A* 1,2,3, *I, W, E, S*, 1979 *F* 1,2, *A, S, E*, 1980 *A* 1,2,3, *W*, 1981 *S* 2, *SA* 1,2,3, *R, F* 1,2, 1982 *A* 1,2,3, *W*, 1983 *BI* 1,2,3,4, *A*, 1984 *F* 1,2, 1985 *Arg* 1,2
Hadley, S (Auckland) 1928 *SA* 1,2,3,4
Hadley, W E (Auckland) 1934 *A* 1,2, 1935 *S, I, W*, 1936 *E, A* 1,2
Haig, J S (Otago) 1946 *A* 1,2
Haig, L S (Otago) 1950 *BI* 2,3,4, 1951 *A* 1,2,3, 1953 *W*, 1954 *E, S*
Hales, D A (Canterbury) 1972 *A* 1,2,3, *W*
Hamilton, D C (Southland) 1908 *AW* 2
Hammett, MG (Canterbury) 1999 *F* 1(R), *SA* 2(R), [*It, S* (R), *SA* 3], 2000 *Tg, S* 1(R),2(t&R), *A* 1(R), *SA* (R), *A* 2(R), *SA* 2(R), *F* 2(R), *It* (R), 2001 *Arg* 1(t), 2002 *It* (R), *I* 1,2, *A* 1, *SA* 1,2(R)
Hammond, I A (Marlborough) 1952 *A* 2
Harper, E T (Canterbury) 1904 *BI*, 1906 *F*
Harding, S (Otago) 2002 *Fj*
Harris, P C (Manawatu) 1976 *SA* 3
Hart, A H (Taranaki) 1924 *I*
Hart, G F (Canterbury) 1930 *BI* 1,2,3,4, 1931 *A*, 1934 *A* 1, 1935 *S, I, W*, 1936 *A* 1,2
Harvey, B A (Wairarapa-Bush) 1986 *F* 1
Harvey, I H (Wairarapa) 1928 *SA* 4
Harvey, L R (Otago) 1949 *SA* 1,2,3,4, 1950 *BI* 1,2,3,4
Harvey, P (Canterbury) 1904 *BI*
Hasell, E W (Canterbury) 1913 *A* 2,3
Hayman, C J (Otago) 2001 *Sm* (R), *Arg* 1, *F* (R), *A* 1(R), *SA* 2(R), *A* 2(R)
Hayward, H O (Auckland) 1908 *AW* 3
Hazlett, E J (Southland) 1966 *BI* 1,2,3,4, 1967 *A, E*
Hazlett, W E (Southland) 1928 *SA* 1,2,3,4, 1930 *BI* 1,2,3,4
Heeps, T R (Wellington) 1962 *A* 1,2,3,4,5

Heke, W R (North Auckland) 1929 *A* 1,2,3
Hemi, R C (Waikato) 1953 *W*, 1954 *I, E, S, F*, 1955 *A* 1,2,3, 1956 *SA* 1,3,4, 1957 *A* 1,2, 1959 *BI* 1,3,4
Henderson, P (Wanganui) 1949 *SA* 1,2,3,4, 1950 *BI* 2,3,4
Henderson, P W (Otago) 1991 *Arg* 1, [*C*], 1992 *Wld* 1,2,3, *I* 1, 1995 [*J*]
Herewini, M A (Auckland) 1962 *A* 5, 1963 *I*, 1964 *S, F*, 1965 *SA* 4, 1966 *BI* 1,2,3,4, 1967 *A*
Hewett, D N (Canterbury) 2001 *I* (R), *S* (R), *Arg* 2, 2002 *It* (R), *I* 1,2, *A* 1, *SA* 1, *A* 2, *SA* 2
Hewett, J A (Auckland) 1991 [*It*]
Hewitt, N J (Southland) 1995 [*I* (t), *J*], 1996 *A* 1(R), 1997 *SA* 1(R), *I, E* 1, *W, E* 2, 1998 *E* 2(t + R)
Hewson, A R (Wellington) 1981 *S* 1,2, *SA* 1,2,3, *R, F* 1,2, 1982 *A* 1,2,3, 1983 *BI* 1,2,3,4, *A*, 1984 *F* 1,2, *A* 1
Higginson, G (Canterbury, Hawke's Bay) 1980 *W*, 1981 *S* 1, *SA* 1, 1982 *A* 1,2, 1983 *A*
Hill, S F (Canterbury) 1955 *A* 3, 1956 *SA* 1,3,4, 1957 *A* 1,2, 1958 *A* 3, 1959 *BI* 1,2,3,4
Hines, G R (Waikato) 1980 *A* 3
Hobbs, M J B (Canterbury) 1983 *BI* 1,2,3,4, *A, S, E*, 1984 *F* 1,2, *A* 1,2,3, 1985 *E* 1,2, *A, Arg* 1,2, 1986 *A* 2,3, *F* 2,3
Hoeft, C H (Otago) 1998 *E* 2(t + R), *A* 2(R), *SA* 2, *A* 3, 1999 *WS, F* 1, *SA* 1, *A* 1,2, [*Tg,E, S, F* 2, *SA* 3(R)], 2000 *S* 1,2, *A* 1, *SA* 1, *A* 2, *SA* 2, 2001 *Sm, Arg* 1, *F, SA* 1, *A* 1, *SA* 2, *A* 2
Holah, M R (Waikato) 2001 *Sm, Arg* 1(t&R), *F* (R), *SA* 1(R), *A* 1(R), *SA* 2(R), *A* 2(R), 2002 *It, I* 2(R), *A* 2(t)
Holder, E C (Buller) 1934 *A* 2
Hook, L S (Auckland) 1929 *A* 1,2,3
Hooper, J A (Canterbury) 1937 *SA* 1,2,3
Hopkinson, A E (Canterbury) 1967 *S*, 1968 *A* 2, *F* 1,2,3, 1969 *W* 2, 1970 *SA* 1,2,3
Hore, J (Otago) 1930 *BI* 2,3,4, 1932 *A* 1,2, 1934 *A* 1,2, 1935 *S*, 1936 *E*
Horsley, R H (Wellington) 1960 *SA* 2,3,4
Hotop, J (Canterbury) 1952 *A* 1,2, 1955 *A* 3
Howarth, S P (Auckland) 1994 *SA* 1,2,3, *A*
Howlett, D C (Auckland) 2000 *Tg* (R), *F* 1,2, *It*, 2001 *Sm, Arg* 1(R), *F* (R), *SA* 1, *A* 1,2, *I, S, Arg* 2, 2002 *It, I* 1,2(R), *Fj, A* 1, *SA* 1, *A* 2, *SA* 2
Hughes, A M (Auckland) 1949 *A* 1,2, 1950 *BI* 1,2,3,4
Hughes, E (Southland, Wellington) 1907 *A* 1,2,3, 1908 *AW* 1, 1921 *SA* 1,2
Hunter, B A (Otago) 1971 *BI* 1,2,3
Hunter, J (Taranaki) 1905 *S, I, E, W*, 1906 *F*, 1907 *A* 1,2,3, 1908 *AW* 1,2,3
Hurst, I A (Canterbury) 1973 *I, F, E* 2, 1974 *A* 1,2

Ieremia, A (Wellington) 1994 *SA* 1,2,3, 1995 [*J*], 1996 *SA* 2(R),5(R), 1997 *A* 1(R), *SA* 1(R), *A* 2, *SA* 2, *A* 3, *I, E* 1, 1999 *WS, F* 1, *SA* 1, *A* 1, *SA* 2, *A* 2, [*Tg, E, S, F* 2, *SA* 3], 2000 *Tg, S* 1,2, *A* 1,2, *SA* 2
Ifwersen, K D (Auckland) 1921 *SA* 3
Innes, C R (Auckland) 1989 *W, I*, 1990 *A* 1,2,3, *F* 1,2, 1991 *Arg* 1,2, *A* 1,2, [*E, US, It, C, A, S*]
Innes, G D (Canterbury) 1932 *A* 2
Irvine, I B (North Auckland) 1952 *A* 1
Irvine, J G (Otago) 1914 *A* 1,2,3
Irvine, W R (Hawke's Bay, Wairarapa) 1924 *I, W*, 1925 *E, F*, 1930 *BI* 1
Irwin, M W (Otago) 1955 *A* 1,2, 1956 *SA* 1, 1958 *A* 2, 1959 *BI* 3,4, 1960 *SA* 1

Jack, C R (Canterbury) 2001 *Arg* 1(R), *SA* 1(R),2, *A* 2, *I, S, Arg* 2, 2002 *I* 1,2, *A* 1, *SA* 1, *A* 2, *SA* 2
Jackson, E S (Hawke's Bay) 1936 *A* 1,2, 1937 *SA* 1,2,3, 1938 *A* 3
Jaffray, J L (Otago, South Canterbury) 1972 *A* 2, 1975 *S*, 1976 *I, SA* 1, 1977 *BI* 2, 1979 *F* 1,2
Jarden, R A (Wellington) 1951 *A* 1,2, 1952 *A* 1,2, 1953 *W*, 1954 *I, E, S, F*, 1955 *A* 1,2,3, 1956 *SA* 1,2,3,4
Jefferd, A C R (East Coast) 1981 *S* 1,2, *SA* 1
Jessep, E M (Wellington) 1931 *A*, 1932 *A* 1
Johnson, L M (Wellington) 1928 *SA* 1,2,3,4
Johnston, W (Otago) 1907 *A* 1,2,3
Johnstone, B R (Auckland) 1976 *SA* 2, 1977 *BI* 1,2, *F* 1,2, 1978 *I, W, E, S*, 1979 *F* 1,2, *S, E*
Johnstone, P (Otago) 1949 *SA* 2,4, 1950 *BI* 1,2,3,4, 1951 *A* 1,2,3
Jones, I D (North Auckland, North Harbour) 1990 *S* 1,2, *A* 1,2,3, *F* 1,2, 1991 *Arg* 1,2, *A* 1,2, [*E, US, It, C, A, S*], 1992 *Wld* 1,2,3, *I* 1,2, *A* 1,2,3, *SA*, 1993 *BI* 1,2(R),3, *WS, S, E*, 1994 *F* 1,2, *SA* 1,3, *A*, 1995 *C*, [*I, W, S, E, SA*], *A* 1,2, *It, F* 1,2, 1996

WS, S 1,2, *A* 1, *SA* 1, *A* 2, *SA* 2,3,4,5, 1997 *Fj, Arg* 1,2, *A* 1, *SA* 1, *A* 2, *SA* 2, *A* 3, *I, E* 1, *W, E* 2, 1998 *E* 1,2, *A* 1, *SA* 1, *A* 2,3,(R), 1999 *F* 1(R), [*It, S* (R)]
Jones, M G (North Auckland) 1973 *E* 2
Jones, M N (Auckland) 1987 [*It, Fj, S, F*], *A,* 1988 *W* 1,2, *A* 2,3, 1989 *F* 1,2, *Arg* 1,2, 1990 *F* 1,2, 1991 *A* 1,2, [*E, US, S*], 1992 *Wld* 1,3, *I* 2, *A* 1,3, *SA,* 1993 *BI* 1,2,3, *A, WS,* 1994 *SA* 3(R), *A,* 1995 *A* 1(R),2, *I, F* 1,2, 1996 *WS, S* 1,2, *A* 1, *SA* 1, *A* 2, *SA* 2,3,4,5, 1997 *Fj,* 1998 *E* 1, *A* 1, *SA* 1, *A* 2
Jones, P F H (North Auckland) 1954 *E, S,* 1955 *A* 1,2, 1956 *SA* 3,4, 1958 *A* 1,2,3, 1959 *BI* 1, 1960 *SA* 1
Joseph, H T (Canterbury) 1971 *BI* 2,3
Joseph, J W (Otago) 1992 *Wld* 2,3(R), *I* 1, *A* 1(R),3, *SA,* 1993 *BI* 1,2,3, *A, WS, S, E,* 1994 *SA* 2(t), 1995 *C,* [*I, W, J* (R), *S, SA* (R)]

Karam, J F (Wellington, Horowhenua) 1972 *W, S,* 1973 *E* 1, *I, F,* 1974 *A* 1,2,3, *I,* 1975 *S*
Katene, T (Wellington) 1955 *A* 2
Kearney, J C (Otago) 1947 *A* 2, 1949 *SA* 1,2,3
Kelleher, B T (Otago) 1999 *WS* (R), *SA* 1(R), *A* 2(R), [*Tg* (R), *E* (R), *It, F* 2], 2000 *S* 1, *A* 1(R),2(R), *It* (R), 2001 *Sm, F* (R), *A* 1(R), *SA* 2, *A* 2, *I, S,* 2002 *It, I* 2(R), *Fj, SA* 1(R),2(R)
Kelly, J W (Auckland) 1949 *A* 1,2
Kember, G F (Wellington) 1970 *SA* 4
Ketels, R C (Counties) 1980 *W,* 1981 *S* 1,2, *R, F* 1
Kiernan, H A D (Auckland) 1903 *A*
Kilby, F D (Wellington) 1932 *A* 1,2,3, 1934 *A* 2
Killeen, B A (Auckland) 1936 *A* 1
King, R R (West Coast) 1934 *A* 2, 1935 *S, I, W,* 1936 *E, A* 1,2, 1937 *SA* 1,2,3, 1938 *A* 1,2,3
Kingstone, C N (Taranaki) 1921 *SA* 1,2,3
Kirk, D E (Auckland) 1985 *E* 1,2, *A, Arg* 1, 1986 *F* 1, *A* 1,2,3, *F* 2,3, 1987 [*It, Fj, Arg, S, W, F*], *A*
Kirkpatrick, I A (Canterbury, Poverty Bay) 1967 *F,* 1968 *A* 1(R),2, *F* 1,2,3, 1969 *W* 1,2, 1970 *SA* 1,2,3,4, 1971 *BI* 1,2,3,4, 1972 *A* 1,2,3, *W, S,* 1973 *E* 1, *I, F, E* 2, 1974 *A* 1,2,3, *I* 1975 *S,* 1976 *I, SA* 1,2,3,4, 1977 *BI* 1,3,4
Kirton, E W (Otago) 1967 *E, W, F, S,* 1968 *A* 1,2, *F* 1,2,3, 1969 *W* 1,2, 1970 *SA* 2,3
Kirwan, J J (Auckland) 1984 *F* 1,2, 1985 *E* 1,2, *A, Arg* 1,2, 1986 *F* 1, *A* 1,2,3, *F* 2,3, 1987 [*It, Fj, Arg, S, W, F*], *A,* 1988 *W* 1,2, *A* 1,2,3, 1989 *F* 1,2, *Arg* 1,2, *A,* 1990 *S* 1,2, *A* 1,2,3, *F* 1,2, 1991 *Arg* 2, *A* 1,2, [*E, It, C, A, S*], 1992 *Wld* 1,2(R),3, *I* 1,2, *A* 1,2,3, *SA,* 1993 *BI* 2,3, *A, WS,* 1994 *F* 1,2, *SA* 1,2,3
Kivell, A L (Taranaki) 1929 *A* 2,3
Knight, A (Auckland) 1934 *A* 1
Knight, G A (Manawatu) 1977 *F* 1,2, 1978 *A* 1,2,3, *E, S,* 1979 *F* 1,2, *A,* 1980 *A* 1,2,3, *W,* 1981 *S* 1,2, *SA* 1,3, 1982 *A* 1,2,3, 1983 *BI* 1,2,3,4, *A,* 1984 *F* 1,2, *A* 1,2,3, 1985 *E* 1,2, *A,* 1986 *A* 2,3
Knight, L G (Poverty Bay) 1977 *BI* 1,2,3,4, *F* 1,2
Koteka, T T (Waikato) 1981 *F* 2, 1982 *A* 3
Kreft, A J (Otago) 1968 *A* 2
Kronfeld, J A (Otago) 1995 *C,* [*I, W, S, E, SA*], *A* 1,2(R) 1996 *WS, S* 1,2, *A* 1, *SA* 1, *A* 2, *SA* 2,3,4,5, 1997 *Fj, Arg* 1,2, *A* 1, *SA* 1, *A* 2, *SA* 2, *A* 3, *I* (R), *E* 1, *W, E* 2, 1998 *E* 1,2, *A* 1, *SA* 1,2, *A* 3, 1999 *WS, F* 1, *SA* 1, *A* 1,2, [*Tg, E, S, F* 2, *SA* 3], 2000 *Tg, S* 1(R),2, *A* 1(R), *SA* 1, *A* 2, *SA* 2, *A* 4(R)
Le Lievre, J M (Canterbury) 1962 *A* 4
Lendrum, R N (Counties) 1973 *E* 2
Leslie, A R (Wellington) 1974 *A* 1,2,3, *I,* 1975 *S,* 1976 *I, SA* 1,2,3,4
Leys, E T (Wellington) 1929 *A* 3
Lilburne, H T (Canterbury, Wellington) 1928 *SA* 3,4, 1929 *A* 1,2,3, 1930 *BI* 1,4, 1931 *A,* 1932 *A* 1, 1934 *A* 2
Lindsay, D F (Otago) 1928 *SA* 1,2,3
Lineen, T R (Auckland) 1957 *A* 1,2, 1958 *A* 1,2,3, 1959 *BI* 1,2,3,4, 1960 *SA* 1,2,3
Lister, T N (South Canterbury) 1968 *A* 1,2, *F* 1, 1969 *W* 1,2, 1970 *SA* 1,4, 1971 *BI* 4

Little, P F (Auckland) 1961 *F* 2,3, 1962 *A* 2,3,5, 1963 *I, W,* 1964 *E, S, F*
Little, W K (North Harbour) 1990 *S* 1,2, *A* 1,2,3, *F* 1,2, 1991 *Arg* 1,2, *A* 1, [*It, S*], 1992 *Wld* 1,2,3, *I* 1,2, *A* 1,2,3, *SA,* 1993 *BI* 1, *WS* (R), 1994 *SA* 2(R), *A,* 1995 *C,* [*I, W, S, E, SA*], *A* 1,2, *It, F* 1,2, 1996 *S* 2, *A* 1, *SA* 1, *A* 2, *SA* 2,3,4,5, 1997 *W, E* 2, 1998 *E* 1, *A* 1, *SA* 1, *A* 2
Loader, C J (Wellington) 1954 *I, E, S, F*
Lochore, B J (Wairarapa) 1964 *E, S,* 1965 *SA* 1,2,3,4, 1966 *BI* 1,2,3,4, 1967 *A, E, W, F, S,* 1968 *A* 1, *F* 2,3, 1969 *W* 1,2, 1970 *SA* 1,2,3,4, 1971 *BI* 3
Loe, R W (Waikato, Canterbury) 1987 [*It, Arg*], 1988 *W* 1,2, *A* 1,2,3, 1989 *F* 1,2, *Arg* 1,2, *A, W, I,* 1990 *S* 1,2, *A* 1,2,3, *F* 1,2, 1991 *Arg* 1,2, *A* 1,2, [*E, It, C, A, S*], 1992 *Wld* 1,2,3, *I* 1, *A* 1,2,3, *SA,* 1994 *SA* 1,2,3, *A,* 1995 [*J, S, SA* (R)], *A* 1,2(t), *F* 2(R)
Lomu, J T (Counties Manukau, Wellington) 1994 *F* 1,2, 1995 [*I, W, S, E, SA*], *A* 1,2, *It, F* 1,2, 1996 *WS, S* 1, *A* 1, *SA* 1, *A* 2, 1997 *E* 1, *W, E* 2, 1998 *E* 1,2, *A* 1(R), *SA* 1, *A* 2, *SA* 2, *A* 3, 1999 *WS* (R), *SA* 1(R), *A* 1(R), *SA* 2(R), *A* 2(R), [*Tg, E, It, S, F* 2, *SA* 3], 2000 *Tg, S* 1,2, *A* 1, *SA* 1, *A* 2, *SA* 2, *F* 1, 2001 *Arg* 1, *F, SA* 1, *A* 1, *SA* 2, *A* 2, *I, S, Arg* 2, 2002 *It* (R), *I* 1(R),2, *Fj, SA* 1(R)
Long, A J (Auckland) 1903 *A*
Loveridge, D S (Taranaki) 1978 *W,* 1979 *S, E,* 1980 *A* 1,2,3, *W,* 1981 *S* 1,2,3, *R, F* 1,2, 1982 *A* 1,2,3, 1983 *BI* 1,2,3,4, *A,* 1985 *Arg* 2
Lucas, F W (Auckland) 1924 *I,* 1925 *F,* 1928 *SA* 4, 1930 *BI* 1,2,3,4
Lunn, W A (Otago) 1949 *A* 1,2
Lynch, T W (South Canterbury) 1913 *A* 1, 1914 *A* 1,2,3
Lynch, T W (Canterbury) 1951 *A* 1,2,3

McAtamney, F S (Otago) 1956 *SA* 2
McCahill, B J (Auckland) 1987 [*Arg, S* (R), *W* (R)], 1989 *Arg* 1(R),2(R), 1991 *A* 2, [*E, US, C, A*]
McCaw, R H (Canterbury) 2001 *I, S, Arg* 2, 2002 *I* 1,2, *A* 1, *SA* 1, *A* 2, *SA* 2
McCaw, W A (Southland) 1951 *A* 1,2,3, 1953 *W,* 1954 *F*
McCool, M J (Wairarapa-Bush) 1979 *A*
McCormick, W F (Canterbury) 1965 *SA* 4, 1967 *E, W, F, S,* 1968 *A* 1,2, *F* 1,2,3, 1969 *W* 1,2, 1970 *SA* 1,2,3, 1971 *BI* 1
McCullough, J F (Taranaki) 1959 *BI* 2,3,4
McDonald, A (Otago) 1905 *S, I, E, W,* 1907 *A* 1, 1908 *AW* 1, 1913 *A* 1, *US*
Macdonald, H H (Canterbury, North Auckland) 1972 *W, S,* 1973 *E* 1, *I, F, E* 2, 1974 *I,* 1975 *S,* 1976 *I, SA* 1,2,3
MacDonald, L R (Canterbury) 2000 *S* 1(R),2(R), *SA* 1(t),2(R), 2001 *Sm, Arg* 1, *F, SA* 1(R), *A* 1(R), *SA* 2, *A* 2, *I, S,* 2002 *I* 1,2, *Fj* (R), *A* 2(R), *SA* 2
McDonnell, J M (Otago) 2002 *It, I* 1(R),2(R), *Fj, SA* 1(R), *A* 2(R)
McDowell, S C (Auckland, Bay of Plenty) 1985 *Arg* 1,2, 1986 *A* 2,3, *F* 2,3, 1987 [*It, Fj, S, W, F*], *A,* 1988 *W* 1,2, *A* 1,2,3, 1989 *F* 1,2, *Arg* 1,2, *A, W, I,* 1990 *S* 1,2, *A* 1,2,3, *F* 1,2, 1991 *Arg* 1,2, [*E, US, It, C, A, S*], 1992 *Wld* 1,2,3, *I* 1,2
McEldowney, J T (Taranaki) 1977 *BI* 3,4
MacEwan, I N (Wellington) 1956 *SA* 2, 1957 *A* 1,2, 1958 *A* 1,2,3, 1959 *BI* 2,3, 1960 *SA* 1,2,3,4, 1961 *F* 1,2,3, 1962 *A* 1,2,3,4
McGrattan, B (Wellington) 1983 *S, E,* 1985 *Arg* 1,2, 1986 *F* 1, *A* 1
McGregor, A J (Auckland) 1913 *A* 1, *US*
McGregor, D (Canterbury, Southland) 1903 *A,* 1904 *BI,* 1905 *E, W*
McGregor, N P (Canterbury) 1924 *W,* 1925 *E*
McGregor, R W (Auckland) 1903 *A,* 1904 *BI*
McHugh, M J (Auckland) 1946 *A* 1,2, 1949 *SA* 3
McIntosh, D N (Wellington) 1956 *SA* 1,2, 1957 *A* 1,2
McKay, D W (Auckland) 1961 *F* 1,2,3, 1963 *E* 1,2
McKechnie, B J (Southland) 1977 *F* 1,2, 1978 *A* 2(R),3, *W* (R), *E, S,* 1979 *A,* 1981 *SA* 1(R), *F* 1
McKellar, G F (Wellington) 1910 *A* 1,2,3
McKenzie, R J (Wellington) 1913 *A* 1, *US,* 1914 *A* 2,3
McKenzie, R McC (Manawatu) 1934 *A* 1, 1935 *S,* 1936 *A* 1, 1937 *SA* 1,2,3, 1938 *A* 1,2,3
McLachlan, J S (Auckland) 1974 *A* 2
McLaren, H C (Waikato) 1952 *A* 1
McLean, A L (Bay of Plenty) 1921 *SA* 2,3
McLean, H F (Wellington, Auckland) 1930 *BI* 3,4, 1932 *A* 1,2,3, 1934 *A* 1, 1935 *I, W,* 1936 *E*
McLean, J K (King Country, Auckland) 1947 *A* 1, 1949 *A* 2

McLeod, B E (Counties) 1964 *A* 1,2,3, 1965 *SA* 1,2,3,4, 1966 *BI* 1,2,3,4, 1967 *E, W, F, S,* 1968 *A* 1,2, *F* 1,2,3, 1969 *W* 1,2, 1970 *SA* 1,2
McLeod, S J (Waikato) 1996 *WS, S* 1, 1997 *Fj* (R), *Arg* 2(t + R), *I* (R), *E* 1(R), *W* (t), *E* 2(R), 1998 *A* 1, *SA* 1(R)
McMinn, A F (Wairarapa, Manawatu) 1903 *A*, 1905 *A*
McMinn, F A (Manawatu) 1904 *BI*
McMullen, R F (Auckland) 1957 *A* 1,2, 1958 *A* 1,2,3, 1959 *BI* 1,2,3, 1960 *SA* 2,3,4
McNab, J R (Otago) 1949 *SA* 1,2,3, 1950 *BI* 1,2,3
McNaughton, A M (Bay of Plenty) 1971 *BI* 1,2,3
McNeece, J (Southland) 1913 *A* 2,3, 1914 *A* 1,2,3
McPhail, B E (Canterbury) 1959 *BI* 1,4
Macpherson, D G (Otago) 1905 *A*
MacPherson, G L (Otago) 1986 *F* 1
MacRae, I R (Hawke's Bay) 1966 *BI* 1,2,3,4, 1967 *A, E, W, F, S,* 1968 *F* 1,2, 1969 *W* 1,2, 1970 *SA* 1,2,3,4
McRae, J A (Southland) 1946 *A* 1(R),2
McWilliams, R G (Auckland) 1928 *SA* 2,3,4, 1929 *A* 1,2,3, 1930 *BI* 1,2,3,4
Mackrell, W H C (Auckland) 1906 *F*
Macky, J V (Auckland) 1913 *A* 2
Maguire, J R (Auckland) 1910 *A* 1,2,3
Mahoney, A (Bush) 1935 *S, I, W,* 1936 *E*
Mains, L W (Otago) 1971 *BI* 2,3,4, 1976 *I*
Major, J (Taranaki) 1967 *A*
Maka, I (Otago) 1998 *E* 2(R), *A* 1(R), *SA* 1(R),2
Maling, T S (Otago) 2002 *It, I* 2(R), *Fj, A* 1, *SA* 1, *A* 2, *SA* 2
Manchester, J E (Canterbury) 1932 *A* 1,2,3, 1934 *A* 1,2, 1935 *S, I, W,* 1936 *E*
Mannix, S J (Wellington) 1994 *F* 1
Marshall, J W (Southland, Canterbury) 1995 *F* 2, 1996 *WS, S* 1,2, *A* 1, *SA* 1, *A* 2, *SA* 2,3,4,5, 1997 *Fj, Arg* 1,2, *A* 1, *SA* 1, *A* 2, *SA* 2, *A* 3, *I, E* 1, *W, E* 2, 1998 *A* 1, *SA* 1, *A* 2, *SA* 2, *A* 3, 1999 *WS, F* 1, *SA* 1, *A* 1, *SA* 2, *A* 2, [*Tg, E, S, F* 2(R), *SA* 3], 2000 *Tg, S* 2, *A* 1, *SA* 1, *A* 2, *SA* 2, *F* 1,2, *It,* 2001 *Arg* 1, *F, SA* 1, *A* 1,2(R), 2002 *I* 1,2, *Fj* (R), *A* 1, *SA* 1, *A* 2, *SA* 2
Mason, D F (Wellington) 1947 *A* 2(R)
Masters, R R (Canterbury) 1924 *I, W,* 1925 *E, F*
Mataira, H K (Hawke's Bay) 1934 *A* 2
Matheson, J D (Otago) 1972 *A* 1,2,3, *W, S*
Mauger, A J D (Canterbury) 2001 *I, S, Arg* 2, 2002 *It* (R), *I* 1,2, *Fj, A* 1, *SA* 1, *A* 2, *SA* 2
Max, D S (Nelson) 1931 *A*, 1934 *A* 1,2
Maxwell, N M C (Canterbury) 1999 *WS, F* 1, *SA* 1, *A* 1, *SA* 2, *A* 2, [*Tg, E, S, F* 2, *SA* 3], 2000 *S* 1,2, *A* 1, *SA* 1(R), *A* 2, *SA* 2, *F* 1,2, *It* (R), 2001 *Sm, Arg* 1, *SA* 1, *A* 1, *SA* 2, *A* 2, *A* 2, *I, S, Arg* 2, 2002 *It, I* 1,2, *Fj*
Mayerhofler, M A (Canterbury) 1998 *E* 1,2, *SA* 1, *A* 2, *SA* 2, *A* 3
Meads, C E (King Country) 1957 *A* 1,2, 1958 *A* 1,2,3, 1959 *BI* 2,3,4, 1960 *SA* 1,2,3,4, 1961 *F* 1,2,3, 1962 *A* 1,2,3,5, 1963 *E* 1,2, *I, W,* 1964 *E, S, F, A* 1,2,3, 1965 *SA* 1,2,3,4, 1966 *BI* 1,2,3,4, 1967 *A, E, W, F, S,* 1968 *A* 1,2, *F* 1,2,3, 1969 *W* 1,2, 1970 *SA* 3,4, 1971 *BI* 1,2,3,4
Meads, S T (King Country) 1961 *F* 1, 1962 *A* 4,5, 1963 *I,* 1964 *A* 1,2,3, 1965 *SA* 1,2,3,4, 1966 *BI* 1,2,3,4
Meates, K F (Canterbury) 1952 *A* 1,2
Meates, W A (Otago) 1949 *SA* 2,3,4, 1950 *BI* 1,2,3,4
Meeuws, K J (Otago) 1998 *A* 3, 1999 *WS, F* 1, *SA* 1, *A* 1, *SA* 2, *A* 2, [*Tg, It* (R), *S* (R), *F* 2(R), *SA* 3], 2000 *Tg* (R), *S* 2, *A* 1, *SA* 1, *A* 2, 2001 *Arg* 2, 2002 *It, Fj*
Mehrtens, A P (Canterbury) 1995 *C,* [*I, W, S, E, SA*], *A* 1,2, 1996 *WS, S* 1,2, *A* 1, *SA* 1, *A* 2, *SA* 2,5, 1997 *Fj, SA* 2(R), *I, E* 1, *W, E* 2, 1998 *E* 1,2, *A* 1, *SA* 1(R), *A* 2, *SA* 2, *A* 3, 1999 *F* 1, *SA* 1, *A* 1, *SA* 2, *A* 2, [*Tg, E, S, F* 2, *SA* 3], 2000 *S* 1,2, *A* 1, *SA* 1, *A* 2, *SA* 2, *F* 1,2, *It* (R), 2001 *Arg* 1, *A* 1(R), 2002 *I* 1,2, *Fj* (R), *A* 1, *SA* 1, *A* 2, *SA* 2
Metcalfe, T C (Southland) 1931 *A*, 1932 *A* 1
Mexted, G G (Wellington) 1950 *BI* 4
Mexted, M G (Wellington) 1979 *S, E,* 1980 *A* 1,2,3, *W,* 1981 *S* 1,2, *SA* 1,2,3, *R, F* 1,2, 1982 *A* 1,2,3, 1983 *BI* 1,2,3,4, *A, S, E,* 1984 *F* 1, *A* 1,2,3, 1985 *E* 1,2, *A, Arg* 1,2
Mika, D G (Auckland) 1999 *WS, F* 1, *SA* 1(R), *A* 1,2, [*It, SA* 3(R)]
Mill, J J (Hawke's Bay, Wairarapa) 1924 *W,* 1925 *E, F,* 1930 *BI* 1
Milliken, H M (Canterbury) 1938 *A* 1,2,3
Milner, H P (Wanganui) 1970 *SA* 3
Mitchell, N A (Southland, Otago) 1935 *S, I, W,* 1936 *E, A* 2, 1937 *SA* 3, 1938 *A* 1,2
Mitchell, T W (Canterbury) 1976 *SA* 4(R)
Mitchell, W J (Canterbury) 1910 *A* 2,3

Mitchinson, F E (Wellington) 1907 *A* 1,2,3, 1908 *AW* 1,2,3, 1910 *A* 1,2,3, 1913 *A* 1(R), *US*
Moffitt, J E (Wellington) 1921 *SA* 1,2,3
Moore, G J T (Otago) 1949 *A* 1
Moreton, R C (Canterbury) 1962 *A* 3,4, 1964 *A* 1,2,3, 1965 *SA* 2,3
Morgan, J E (North Auckland) 1974 *A* 3, *I,* 1976 *SA* 2,3,4
Morris, T J (Nelson Bays) 1972 *A* 1,2,3
Morrison, T C (South Canterbury) 1938 *A* 1,2,3
Morrison, T G (Otago) 1973 *E* 2(R)
Morrissey, P J (Canterbury) 1962 *A* 3,4,5
Mourie, G N K (Taranaki) 1977 *BI* 3,4, *F* 1,2, 1978 *I, W, E, S,* 1979 *F* 1,2, *A, S, E,* 1980 *W,* 1981 *S* 1,2, *F* 1,2, 1982 *A* 1,2,3
Muller, B L (Taranaki) 1967 *A, E, W, F,* 1968 *A* 1, *F* 1, 1969 *W* 1, 1970 *SA* 1,2,4, 1971 *BI* 1,2,3,4
Mumm, W J (Buller) 1949 *A* 1
Murdoch, K (Otago) 1970 *SA* 4, 1972 *A* 3, *W*
Murdoch, P H (Auckland) 1964 *A* 2,3, 1965 *SA* 1,2,3
Murray, H V (Canterbury) 1913 *A* 1, *US,* 1914 *A* 2,3
Murray, P C (Wanganui) 1908 *AW* 2
Myers, R G (Waikato) 1978 *A* 3
Mynott, H J (Taranaki) 1905 *I, W,* 1906 *F,* 1907 *A* 1,2,3, 1910 *A* 1,3

Nathan, W J (Auckland) 1962 *A* 1,2,3,4,5, 1963 *E* 1,2, *W,* 1964 *F,* 1966 *BI* 1,2,3,4, 1967 *A*
Nelson, K A (Otago) 1962 *A* 4,5
Nepia, G (Hawke's Bay, East Coast) 1924 *I, W,* 1925 *E, F,* 1929 *A* 1, 1930 *BI* 1,2,3,4
Nesbit, S R (Auckland) 1960 *SA* 2,3
Newton, F (Canterbury) 1905 *E, W,* 1906 *F*
Nicholls, H E (Wellington) 1921 *SA* 1
Nicholls, M F (Wellington) 1921 *SA* 1,2,3, 1924 *I, W,* 1925 *E, F,* 1928 *SA* 4, 1930 *BI* 2,3
Nicholson, G W (Auckland) 1903 *A,* 1904 *BI,* 1907 *A* 2,3
Norton, R W (Canterbury) 1971 *BI* 1,2,3,4, 1972 *A* 1,2,3, *W, S,* 1973 *E* 1, *I, F, E* 2, 1974 *A* 1,2,3, *I,* 1975 *S,* 1976 *I, SA* 1,2,3,4, 1977 *BI* 1,2,3,4

O'Brien, J G (Auckland) 1914 *A* 1
O'Callaghan, M W (Manawatu) 1968 *F* 1,2,3
O'Callaghan, T R (Wellington) 1949 *A* 2
O'Donnell, D H (Wellington) 1949 *A* 2
O'Halloran, J D (Wellington) 2000 *It* (R)
Old, G H (Manawatu) 1981 *SA* 3, *R* (R), 1982 *A* 1(R)
O'Leary, M J (Auckland) 1910 *A* 1,3, 1913 *A* 2,3
Oliver, A D (Otago) 1997 *Fj* (t), 1998 *E* 1,2, *A* 1, *SA* 1, *A* 2, *SA* 2, *A* 3, 1999 *WS, F* 1, *SA* 1, *A* 1, *SA* 2, *A* 2, [*Tg, E, S, F* 2, *SA* 3(R)], 2000 *Tg* (R), *S* 1,2, *A* 1, *SA* 1, *A* 2, *SA* 2, *F* 1,2, *It,* 2001 *Sm, Arg* 1, *F, SA* 1, *A* 1, *SA* 2, *A* 2, *I, S, Arg* 2
Oliver, C J (Canterbury) 1929 *A* 1,2, 1934 *A* 1, 1935 *S, I, W,* 1936 *E*
Oliver, D J (Wellington) 1930 *BI* 1,2
Oliver, D O (Otago) 1954 *I, F*
Oliver, F J (Southland, Otago, Manawatu) 1976 *SA* 4, 1977 *BI* 1,2,3,4, *F* 1,2, 1978 *A* 1,2,3, *I, W, E, S,* 1979 *F* 1,2, 1981 *SA* 2
Orr, R W (Otago) 1949 *A* 1
Osborne, G M (North Harbour) 1995 *C,* [*I, W, J, E, SA*], *A* 1,2, *F* 1(R),2, 1996 *SA* 2,3,4,5, 1997 *Arg* 1(R), *A* 2,3, *I,* 1999 [*It*]
Osborne, W M (Wanganui) 1975 *S,* 1976 *SA* 2(R),4(R), 1977 *BI* 1,2,3,4, *F* 1(R),2, 1978 *I, W, E, S,* 1980 *W,* 1982 *A* 1,3
O'Sullivan, J M (Taranaki) 1905 *S, I, E, W,* 1907 *A* 3
O'Sullivan, T P A (Taranaki) 1960 *SA* 1, 1961 *F* 1, 1962 *A* 1,2

Page, J R (Wellington) 1931 *A,* 1932 *A* 1,2,3, 1934 *A* 1,2
Palmer, B P (Auckland) 1929 *A* 2, 1932 *A* 2,3
Parker, J H (Canterbury) 1924 *I, W,* 1925 *E*
Parkhill, A A (Otago) 1937 *SA* 1,2,3, 1938 *A* 1,2,3
Parkinson, R M (Poverty Bay) 1972 *A* 1,2,3, *W, S,* 1973 *E* 1,2
Paterson, A M (Otago) 1908 *AW* 2,3, 1910 *A* 1,2,3
Paton, H (Otago) 1910 *A* 1,3
Pene, A R B (Otago) 1992 *Wld* 1(R),2,3, *I* 1,2, *A* 1,2(R), 1993 *BI* 3, *A, WS, S, E,* 1994 *F* 1,2(R), *SA* 1(R)
Phillips, W J (King Country) 1937 *SA* 2, 1938 *A* 1,2
Philpott, S (Canterbury) 1991 [*It* (R), *S* (R)]
Pickering, E A R (Waikato) 1958 *A* 2, 1959 *BI* 1,4

Pierce, M J (Wellington) 1985 *E* 1,2, *A, Arg* 1, 1986 *A* 2,3, *F* 2,3, 1987 [*It, Arg, S, W, F*], *A*, 1988 *W* 1,2, *A*, 1,2,3, 1989 *F* 1,2, *Arg* 1,2, *A, W, I*
Pokere, S T (Southland, Auckland) 1981 *SA* 3, 1982 *A* 1,2,3, 1983 *BI* 1,2,3,4, *A, S, E*, 1984 *F* 1,2, *A* 2,3, 1985 *E* 1,2, *A*
Pollock, H R (Wellington) 1932 *A* 1,2,3, 1936 *A* 1,2
Porter, C G (Wellington) 1925 *F*, 1929 *A* 2,3, 1930 *BI* 1,2,3,4
Preston, J P (Canterbury, Wellington) 1991 [*US, S*], 1992 *SA* (R), 1993 *BI* 2,3, *A, WS*, 1996 *SA* 4(R), 1997 *I* (R), *E* 1(R)
Procter, A C (Otago) 1932 *A* 1
Purdue, C A (Southland) 1905 *A*
Purdue, E (Southland) 1905 *A*
Purdue, G B (Southland) 1931 *A*, 1932 *A* 1,2,3
Purvis, G H (Waikato) 1991 [*US*], 1993 *WS*
Purvis, N A (Otago) 1976 *I*

Quaid, C E (Otago) 1938 *A* 1,2

Ralph, C S (Auckland, Canterbury) 1998 *E* 2, 2002 *It, I* 1,2, *A* 1, *SA* 1, *A* 2, *SA* 2
Ranby, R M (Waikato) 2001 *Sm* (R)
Randell, T C (Otago) 1997 *Fj, Arg* 1,2, *A* 1, *SA* 1, *A* 2, *SA* 2, *A* 3, *I, E* 1, *W, E* 2, 1998 *E* 1,2, *A* 1, *SA* 1, *A* 2, *SA* 2, *A* 3, 1999 *WS, F* 1, *SA* 1, *A* 1, *SA* 2, *A* 2, [*Tg, E, It, S, F, SA* 3], 2000 *Tg, S* 1,2(R), *A* 1, *SA* 1, *A* 2, *SA* 2, *F* 2(R), *It* (R), 2001 *Arg* 1, *F, SA* 1, *A* 1, *SA* 2, *A* 2, 2002 *It, Fj*
Rangi, R E (Auckland) 1964 *A* 2,3, 1965 *SA* 1,2,3,4, 1966 *BI* 1,2,3,4
Rankin, J G (Canterbury) 1936 *A* 1,2, 1937 *SA* 2
Reedy, W J (Wellington) 1908 *AW* 2,3
Reid, A R (Waikato) 1952 *A* 1, 1956 *SA* 3,4, 1957 *A* 1,2
Reid, H R (Bay of Plenty) 1980 *A* 1,2, *W*, 1983 *S, E*, 1985 *Arg* 1,2, 1986 *A* 2,3
Reid, K H (Wairarapa) 1929 *A* 1,2
Reid, S T (Hawke's Bay) 1935 *S, I, W*, 1936 *E, A* 1,2, 1937 *SA* 1,2,3
Reihana, B T (Waikato) 2000 *F* 2, *It*
Reside, W B (Wairarapa) 1929 *A* 1
Rhind, P K (Canterbury) 1946 *A* 1,2
Richardson, J (Otago, Southland) 1921 *SA* 1,2,3, 1924 *I, W*, 1925 *E, F*
Rickit, H (Waikato) 1981 *S* 1,2
Riechelmann, C C (Auckland) 1997 *Fj* (R), *Arg* 1(R), *A* 1(R), *SA* 2(t), *I* (R), *E* 2(t)
Ridland, A J (Southland) 1910 *A* 1,2,3
Roberts, E J (Wellington) 1914 *A* 1,2,3, 1921 *SA* 2,3
Roberts, F (Wellington) 1905 *S, I, E, W*, 1907 *A* 1,2,3, 1908 *AW* 1,3, 1910 *A* 1,2,3
Roberts, R W (Taranaki) 1913 *A* 1, *US*, 1914 *A* 1,2,3
Robertson, B J (Counties) 1972 *A* 1,3, *S*, 1973 *E* 1, *I, F*, 1974 *A* 1,2,3, *I*, 1976 *I*, 1,2,3,4, 1977 *BI* 1,3,4, *F* 1,2, 1978 *A* 1,2,3, *W, E, S*, 1979 *F* 1,2, *A*, 1980 *A* 2,3, *W*, 1981 *S* 1,2
Robertson, D J (Otago) 1974 *A* 1,2,3, *I*, 1975 *S*, 1976 *I, SA* 1,3,4, 1977 *BI* 1
Robertson, S M (Canterbury) 1998 *A* 2(R), *SA* 2(R), *A* 3(R), 1999 [*It* (R)], 2000 *Tg* (R), *S* 1,2(R), *A* 1, *SA* 1(R),2(R), *F* 1,2, *It*, 2001 *S, Arg* 2, 2002 *I* 1,2, *Fj* (R), *A* 1, *SA* 1, *A* 2, *SA* 2
Robilliard, A C C (Canterbury) 1928 *A* 1,2,3,4
Robinson, C E (Southland) 1951 *A* 1,2,3, 1952 *A* 1,2
Robinson, M D (North Harbour) 1998 *E* 1(R), 2001 *S* (R), *Arg* 2
Robinson, M P (Canterbury) 2000 *S* 2, *SA* 1, 2002 *It, I* 2, *A* 1, *SA* 1
Rollerson, D L (Manawatu) 1980 *W*, 1981 *S* 2, *SA* 1,2,3, *R*, *F* 1(R),2
Roper, R A (Taranaki) 1949 *A* 2, 1950 *BI* 1,2,3,4
Rowley, H C B (Wanganui) 1949 *A* 2
Rush, E J (North Harbour) 1995 [*W* (R), *J*], *It, F* 1,2, 1996 *S* 1(R),2, *A* 1(t), *SA* 1(R)
Rush, X J (Auckland) 1998 *A* 3
Rutledge, L M (Southland) 1978 *A* 1,2,3, *I, W, E, S*, 1979 *F* 1,2, *A*, 1980 *A* 1,2,3
Ryan, J (Wellington) 1910 *A* 2, 1914 *A* 1,2,3

Sadler, B S (Wellington) 1935 *S, I, W*, 1936 *A* 1,2
Salmon, J L B (Wellington) 1981 *R, F* 1,2(R)
Savage, L T (Canterbury) 1949 *SA* 1,2,4
Saxton, C K (South Canterbury) 1938 *A* 1,2,3
Schuler, K J (Manawatu, North Harbour) 1990 *A* 2(R), 1992 *A* 2, 1995 [*I* (R), *J*]
Schuster, N J (Wellington) 1988 *F* 1,2, 1989 *F* 1,2, *Arg* 1,2, *A, W, I*

Scott, R W H (Auckland) 1946 *A* 1,2, 1947 *A* 1,2, 1949 *SA* 1,2,3,4, 1950 *BI* 1,2,3,4, 1953 *W*, 1954 *I, E, S, F*
Scown, A I (Taranaki) 1972 *A* 1,2,3, *W* (R), *S*
Scrimshaw, G (Canterbury) 1928 *SA* 1
Seear, G A (Otago) 1977 *F* 1,2, 1978 *A* 1,2,3, *I, W, E, S*, 1979 *F* 1,2, *A*
Seeling, C E (Auckland) 1904 *BI*, 1905 *S, I, E, W*, 1906 *F*, 1907 *A* 1,2, 1908 *AW* 1,2,3
Sellars, G M V (Auckland) 1913 *A* 1, *US*
Shaw, M W (Manawatu, Hawke's Bay) 1980 *A* 1,2,3(R), *W*, 1981 *S* 1,2, *A* 1, *R, F* 1,2, 1982 *A* 1,2,3, 1983 *BI* 1,2,3,4, *A, S, E*, 1984 *F* 1,2, *A* 1, 1985 *E* 1,2, *A*, *Arg* 1,2, 1986 *A* 3
Shelford, F N K (Bay of Plenty) 1981 *SA* 3, *R*, 1984 *A* 2,3
Shelford, W T (North Harbour) 1986 *F* 2,3, 1987 [*It, Fj, S, W, F*], *A*, 1988 *W* 1,2, *A* 1,2,3, 1989 *F* 1,2, *Arg* 1,2, *A, W, I*, 1990 *S* 1,2
Siddells, S K (Wellington) 1921 *SA* 3
Simon, H J (Otago) 1937 *SA* 1,2,3
Simpson, J G (Auckland) 1947 *A* 1,2, 1949 *SA* 1,2,3,4, 1950 *BI* 1,2,3
Simpson, V L J (Canterbury) 1985 *Arg* 1,2
Sims, G S (Otago) 1972 *A* 2
Skeen, J R (Auckland) 1952 *A* 2
Skinner, K L (Otago, Counties) 1949 *SA* 1,2,3,4, 1950 *BI* 1,2,3,4, 1951 *A* 1,2,3, 1952 *A* 1,2, 1953 *W*, 1954 *I, E, S, F*, 1956 *SA* 3,4
Skudder, G R (Waikato) 1969 *W* 2
Slater, G L (Taranaki) 2000 *F* 1(R),2(R), *It* (R)
Sloane, P H (North Auckland) 1979 *E*
Smith, A E (Taranaki) 1969 *W* 1,2, 1970 *SA* 1
Smith, B W (Waikato) 1984 *F* 1,2, *A* 1
Smith, G W (Auckland) 1905 *S, I*
Smith, I S T (Otago, North Otago) 1964 *A* 1,2,3, 1965 *SA* 1,2,4, 1966 *BI* 1,2,3
Smith, J B (North Auckland) 1946 *A* 1, 1947 *A* 2, 1949 *A* 1,2
Smith, R M (Canterbury) 1955 *A* 1
Smith, W E (Nelson) 1905 *A*
Smith, W R (Canterbury) 1980 *A* 1, 1982 *A* 1,2,3, 1983 *BI* 2,3, *S, E*, 1984 *F* 1,2, *A* 1,2,3, 1985 *E* 1,2, *A, Arg* 2
Snow, E M (Nelson) 1929 *A* 1,2,3
Solomon, F (Auckland) 1931 *A*, 1932 *A* 2,3
Somerville, G M (Canterbury) 2000 *Tg, S* 1, *SA* 2(R), *F* 1,2, *It*, 2001 *Sm, Arg* 1(R), *F, SA* 1, *A* 1, *SA* 2, *A* 2, *I, S, Arg* 2(t+R), 2002 *I* 1,2, *A* 1, *SA* 1, *A* 2, *SA* 2
Sonntag, W T C (Otago) 1929 *A* 1,2,3
Speight, M W (Waikato) 1986 *A* 1
Spencer, C J (Auckland) 1997 *Arg* 1,2, *A* 1, *SA* 1, *A* 2, *SA* 2, *A* 3, *E* 2(R), 1998 *E* 2(R), *A* 1(R), *SA* 1, *A* 3(R), 2000 *F* 1(t&R), *It*
Spencer, J C (Wellington) 1905 *A*, 1907 *A* 1(R)
Spiers, J E (Counties) 1979 *S, E*, 1981 *R, F* 1,2
Spillane, A P (South Canterbury) 1913 *A* 2,3
Stanley, J T (Auckland) 1986 *F* 1, *A* 1,2,3, *F* 2,3, 1987 [*It, Fj, Arg, S, W, F*], *A*, 1988 *W* 1,2, *A* 1,2,3, 1989 *F* 1,2, *Arg* 1,2, *A, W, I*, 1990 *S* 1,2
Stead, J W (Southland) 1904 *BI*, 1905 *S, I, E*, 1906 *F*, 1908 *AW* 1,3
Steel, A G (Canterbury) 1966 *BI* 1,2,3,4, 1967 *A, F, S*, 1968 *A* 1,2
Steel, J (West Coast) 1921 *SA* 1,2,3, 1924 *W*, 1925 *E, F*
Steele, L B (Wellington) 1951 *A* 1,2,3
Steere, E R G (Hawke's Bay) 1930 *BI* 1,2,3,4, 1931 *A*, 1932 *A* 1
Stensness, L (Auckland) 1993 *BI* 3, *A, WS*, 1997 *Fj, Arg* 1,2, *A* 1, *SA* 1
Stephens, O G (Wellington) 1968 *F* 3
Stevens, I N (Wellington) 1972 *S*, 1973 *E* 1, 1974 *A* 3
Stewart, A J (Canterbury, South Canterbury) 1963 *E* 1,2, *I, W*, 1964 *E, S, F, A* 3
Stewart, J D (Auckland) 1913 *A*
Stewart, K W (Southland) 1973 *E* 2, 1974 *A* 1,2,3, *I*, 1975 *S*, 1976 *I, SA* 1,3, 1979 *S, E*, 1981 *SA* 1,2
Stewart, R T (South Canterbury, Canterbury) 1928 *SA* 1,2,3,4, 1930 *BI* 2
Stohr, L B (Taranaki) 1910 *A* 1,2,3
Stone, A M (Waikato, Bay of Plenty) 1981 *F* 1,2, 1983 *BI* 3(R), 1984 *A* 3, 1986 *F* 1, *A* 1,3, *F* 2,3
Storey, P W (South Canterbury) 1921 *SA* 1,2
Strachan, A D (Auckland, North Harbour) 1992 *Wld* 2,3, *I* 1,2, *A* 1,2,3, 1995 [*J, SA* (t)]
Strahan, S C (Manawatu) 1967 *A, E, W, F, S*, 1968 *A* 1,2, *F* 1,2,3, 1970 *SA* 1,2,3, 1972 *A* 1,2,3, 1973 *E* 2

Strang, W A (South Canterbury) 1928 *SA* 1,2, 1930 *BI* 3,4, 1931 *A*
Stringfellow, J C (Wairarapa) 1929 *A* 1(R),3
Stuart, K C (Canterbury) 1955 *A* 1
Stuart, R C (Canterbury) 1949 *A* 1,2, 1953 *W*, 1954 *I, E, S, F*
Stuart, R L (Hawke's Bay) 1977 *F* 1(R)
Sullivan, J L (Taranaki) 1937 *SA* 1,2,3, 1938 *A* 1,2,3
Sutherland, A R (Marlborough) 1970 *SA* 2,4, 1971 *BI* 1, 1972 *A* 1,2,3, *W*, 1973 *E* 1, *I, F*
Svenson, K S (Wellington) 1924 *I, W*, 1925 *E, F*
Swain, J P (Hawke's Bay) 1928 *SA* 1,2,3,4

Tanner, J M (Auckland) 1950 *BI* 4, 1951 *A* 1,2,3, 1953 *W*
Tanner, K J (Canterbury) 1974 *A* 1,2,3, *I*, 1975 *S*, 1976 *I, SA* 1
Taylor, G L (Northland) 1996 *SA* 5(R)
Taylor, H M (Canterbury) 1913 *A* 1, *US*, 1914 *A* 1,2,3
Taylor, J M (Otago) 1937 *SA* 1,2,3, 1938 *A* 1,2,3
Taylor, M B (Waikato) 1979 *F* 1,2, *A, S, E*, 1980 *A* 1,2
Taylor, N M (Bay of Plenty, Hawke's Bay) 1977 *BI* 2,4(R), *F* 1,2, 1978 *A* 1,2,3, *I*, 1982 *A* 2
Taylor, R (Taranaki) 1913 *A* 2,3
Taylor, W T (Canterbury) 1983 *BI* 1,2,3,4, *A, S*, 1984 *F* 1,2, *A* 1,2, 1985 *E* 1,2, *A, Arg* 1,2, 1986 *A* 2, 1987 *[It, Fj, S, W, F]*, *A*, 1988 *W* 1,2
Tetzlaff, P L (Auckland) 1947 *A* 1,2
Thimbleby, N W (Hawke's Bay) 1970 *SA* 3
Thomas, B T (Auckland, Wellington) 1962 *A* 5, 1964 *A* 1,2,3
Thomson, H D (Wellington) 1908 *AW* 1
Thorne, G S (Auckland) 1968 *A* 1,2, *F* 1,2,3, 1969 *W* 1, 1970 *SA* 1,2,3,4
Thorne, R D (Canterbury) 1999 *SA* 2(R), *[Tg, E, S, F* 2, *SA* 3], 2000 *Tg, S* 2, *A* 2(R), *F* 1,2, 2001 *Sm, Arg* 1, *F, SA* 1, *A* 1, *I, S, Arg* 2, 2002 *It, I* 1,2, *Fj, A* 1, SA 1, *A* 2, *SA* 2
Thornton, N H (Auckland) 1947 *A* 1,2, 1949 *SA* 1
Tiatia, F I (Wellington) 2000 *Tg* (R), *It*
Tilyard, J T (Wellington) 1913 *A* 3
Timu, J K R (Otago) 1991 *Arg* 1, *A* 1,2, *[E, US, C, A]*, 1992 *Wld* 2, *I* 2, *A* 1,2,3, *SA*, 1993 *BI* 1,2,3, *A, WS, S, E*, 1994 *F* 1,2, *SA* 1,2,3, *A*
Tindill, E W T (Wellington) 1936 *E*
Tonu'u, O F J (Auckland) 1997 *Fj* (R), *A* 3(R), 1998 *E* 1,2, *SA* 1(R)
Townsend, L J (Otago) 1955 *A* 1,3
Tremain, K R (Canterbury, Hawke's Bay) 1959 *BI* 2,3,4, 1960 *SA* 1,2,3,4, 1961 *F* 2,3 1962 *A* 1,2,3, 1963 *E* 1,2, *I, W*, 1964 *E, S, F, A* 1,2,3, 1965 *SA* 1,2,3,4, 1966 *BI* 1,2,3,4, 1967 *A, E, W, S*, 1968 *A* 1, *F* 1,2,3
Trevathan, D (Otago) 1937 *SA* 1,2,3
Tuck, J M (Waikato) 1929 *A* 1,2,3
Tuigamala, V L (Auckland) 1991 *[US, It, C, S]*, 1992 *Wld* 1,2,3, *I* 1, *A* 1,2,3, *SA*, 1993 *BI* 1,2,3, *A, WS, S, E*
Turner, R S (North Harbour) 1992 *Wld* 1,2(R)
Turtill, H S (Canterbury) 1905 *A*
Twigden, T M (Auckland) 1980 *A* 2,3
Tyler, G A (Auckland) 1903 *A*, 1904 *BI*, 1905 *S, I, E, W*, 1906 *F*

Udy, D K (Wairarapa) 1903 *A*
Umaga, J F (Wellington) 1997 *Fj, Arg* 1,2, *A* 1, *SA* 1,2, 1999 *WS, F* 1, *SA* 1, *A* 1, *SA* 2, *A* 2, *[Tg, E, S, F* 2, *SA* 3], 2000 *Tg, S* 1,2, *A* 1, SA 1, *A* 2, *SA* 2, *F* 1,2, *It*, 2001 *Sm, Arg* 1, *F, SA* 1, *A* 1, *SA* 2, *A* 2, *I, S, Arg* 2, 2002 *I* 1, *Fj, SA* 1(R), *A* 2, *SA* 2
Urbahn, R J (Taranaki) 1959 *BI* 1,3,4
Urlich, R A (Auckland) 1970 *SA* 3,4
Uttley, I N (Wellington) 1963 *E* 1,2

Vidiri, J (Counties Manukau) 1998 *E* 2(R), *A* 1
Vincent, P B (Canterbury) 1956 *SA* 1,2
Vodanovich, I M H (Wellington) 1955 *A* 1,2,3

Wallace, W J (Wellington) 1903 *A*, 1904 *BI*, 1905 *S, I, E, W*, 1906 *F*, 1907 *A* 1,2,3, 1908 *AW* 2
Waller, D A G (Wellington) 2001 *Arg* 2(t)
Walsh, P T (Counties) 1955 *A* 1,2,3, 1956 *SA* 1,2,4, 1957 *A* 1,2, 1958 *A* 1,2,3, 1959 *BI* 1, 1963 *E* 2
Ward, R H (Southland) 1936 *A* 2, 1937 *SA* 1,3
Waterman, A C (North Auckland) 1929 *A* 1,2

Watkins, E L (Wellington) 1905 *A*
Watt, B A (Canterbury) 1962 *A* 1,4, 1963 *E* 1,2, *W*, 1964 *E, S, A* 1
Watt, J M (Otago) 1936 *A* 1,2
Watt, J R (Wellington) 1958 *A* 2, 1960 *SA* 1,2,3,4, 1961 *F* 1,3, 1962 *A* 1,2
Watts, M G (Taranaki) 1979 *F* 1,2, 1980 *A* 1,2,3(R)
Webb, D S (North Auckland) 1959 *BI* 2
Wells, J (Wellington) 1936 *A* 1,2
West, A H (Taranaki) 1921 *SA* 2,3
Whetton, A J (Auckland) 1984 *A* 1(R),3(R), 1985 *A* (R), *Arg* 1(R), 1986 *A* 2, 1987 *[It, Fj, Arg, S, W, F]*, *A*, 1988 *W* 1,2, *A* 1,2,3, 1989 *F* 1,2, *Arg* 1,2, *A*, 1990 *S* 1,2, *A* 1,2,3, *F* 1,2, 1991 *Arg* 1, *[E, US, It, C, A]*
Whetton, G W (Auckland) 1981 *SA* 3, *R, F* 1,2, 1982 *A* 3, 1983 *BI* 1,2,3,4, 1984 *F* 1,2, *A* 1,2,3, 1985 *E* 1,2, *A, Arg* 2, 1986 *A* 2,3, *F* 2,3, 1987 *[It, Fj, Arg, S, W, F]*, *A*, 1988 *W* 1,2, *A* 1,2,3, 1989 *F* 1,2, *Arg* 1,2, *A, W, I*, 1990 *S* 1,2, *A* 1,2,3, *F* 1,2, 1991 *Arg* 1,2, *A* 1,2, *[E, US, It, C, A, S]*
Whineray, W J (Canterbury, Waikato, Auckland) 1957 *A* 1,2, 1958 *A* 1,2,3, 1959 *BI* 1,2,3,4, 1960 *SA* 1,2,3,4, 1961 *F* 1,2,3, 1962 *A* 1,2,3,4,5, 1963 *E* 1,2, *I, W*, 1964 *E, S, F*, 1965 *SA* 1,2,3,4
White, A (Southland) 1921 *SA* 1, 1924 *I*, 1925 *E, F*
White, H L (Auckland) 1954 *I, E, F*, 1955 *A* 3
White, R A (Poverty Bay) 1949 *A* 1,2, 1950 *BI* 1,2,3,4, 1951 *A* 1,2,3, 1952 *A* 1,2, 1953 *W*, 1954 *I, E, S, F*, 1955 *A* 1,2,3, 1956 *SA* 1,2,3,4
White, R M (Wellington) 1946 *A* 1,2, 1947 *A* 1,2
Whiting, G J (King Country) 1972 *A* 1,2, *S*, 1973 *E* 1, *I, F*
Whiting, P J (Auckland) 1971 *BI* 1,2,4, 1972 *A* 1,2,3, *W, S*, 1973 *E* 1, *I, F*, 1974 *A* 1,2,3, *I*, 1976 *I, SA* 1,2,3,4
Williams, B G (Auckland) 1970 *SA* 1,2,3,4, 1971 *BI* 1,2,4, 1972 *A* 1,2,3, *W, S*, 1973 *E* 1, *I, F, E* 2, 1974 *A* 1,2,3, *I*, 1975 *S*, 1976 *I, SA* 1,2,3,4, 1977 *BI* 1,2,3,4, *F* 1, 1978 *A* 1,2,3, *I* (R), *W, E, S*
Williams, G C (Wellington) 1967 *E, W, F, S*, 1968 *A* 2
Williams, P (Otago) 1913 *A* 1
Williment, M (Wellington) 1964 *A* 1, 1965 *SA* 1,2,3, 1966 *BI* 1,2,3,4, 1967 *A*
Willis, R K (Waikato) 1998 *SA* 2, *A* 3, 1999 *SA* 1(R), *A* 1(R), *SA* 2(R), *A* 2(R), *[Tg* (R), *E* (R), *It, F* 2(R), *SA* 3], 2002 *SA* 1(R)
Willis, T E (Otago) 2002 *It, Fj, SA* 2(R), *A* 2, *SA* 2
Willocks, C (Otago) 1946 *A* 1,2, 1949 *SA* 1,3,4
Wilson, B W (Otago) 1977 *BI* 3,4, 1978 *A* 1,2,3, 1979 *F* 1,2, *A*
Wilson, D D (Canterbury) 1954 *E, S*
Wilson, H W (Otago) 1949 *A* 1, 1950 *BI* 4, 1951 *A* 1,2,3
Wilson, J W (Otago) 1993 *S, E*, 1994 *A*, 1995 *C, [I, J, S, E, SA]*, *A* 1,2, *It, F* 1, 1996 *WS, S* 1,2, *A* 1, *SA* 1, *A* 2, *SA* 2,3,4,5, 1997 *Fj, Arg* 1,2, *A* 1, *SA* 1, *A* 2, *SA* 2, *A* 3, *I, E* 1, *W, E* 2, 1998 *E* 1,2, *A* 1, *SA* 1, *A* 2, *SA* 2, *A* 3, 1999 *WS, F* 1, *SA* 1, *A* 1, *SA* 2, *A* 2, *[Tg, E, It, S, F* 2, *SA* 3], 2001 *Sm, Arg* 1, *F, SA* 1, *A* 1, *SA* 2
Wilson, N A (Wellington) 1908 *AW* 1,2, 1910 *A* 1,2,3, 1913 *A* 2,3, 1914 *A* 1,2,3
Wilson, N L (Otago) 1951 *A* 1,2,3
Wilson, R G (Canterbury) 1979 *S, E*
Wilson, S S (Wellington) 1977 *F* 1,2, 1978 *A* 1,2,3, *I, W, E, S*, 1979 *F* 1,2, *A, S, E*, 1980 *A* 1, *W*, 1981 *S* 1,2, *SA* 1,2,3, *R, F* 1,2, 1982 *A* 1,2,3, 1983 *BI* 1,2,3,4, *A, S, E*
Wolfe, T N (Wellington, Taranaki) 1961 *F* 1,2,3, 1962 *A* 2,3, 1963 *E* 1
Wood, M E (Canterbury, Auckland) 1903 *A*, 1904 *BI*
Woodman, F A (North Auckland) 1981 *SA* 1,2, *F* 2
Wrigley, E (Wairarapa) 1905 *A*
Wright, T J (Auckland) 1986 *F* 1, *A* 1, 1987 *[Arg]*, 1988 *W* 1,2, *A* 1,2,3, 1989 *F* 1,2, *Arg* 1,2, *A, W, I*, 1990 *S* 1,2, *A* 1,2,3, *F* 1,2, 1991 *Arg* 1,2, *A* 1,2, *[E, US, It, S]*
Wylie, J T (Auckland) 1913 *A* 1, *US*
Wyllie, A J (Canterbury) 1970 *SA* 2,3, 1971 *BI* 2,3,4, 1972 *W, S*, 1973 *E* 1, *I, F, E* 2

Yates, V M (North Auckland) 1961 *F* 1,2,3
Young, D (Canterbury) 1956 *SA* 2, 1958 *A* 1,2,3, 1960 *SA* 1,2,3,4, 1961 *F* 1,2,3, 1962 *A* 1,2,3,5, 1963 *E* 1,2, *I, W*, 1964 *E, S, F*

AUSTRALIA TEST SEASON REVIEW 2001-02

Houdini Act Keeps Bledisloe Cup in its Place

Peter Jenkins

Houdini had nothing on these Wallaby escape freaks. Before Matthew Burke landed a heart-stopping penalty after the siren at the Olympic Stadium on August 3rd to ensure the Bledisloe Cup made its home in Australia for a record fifth season, the Wallabies were on the bottom of the harbour in a chest covered by chains.

Burke had already wasted a chance to pick the locks. Super-sub Mat Rogers, a prized recruit from rugby league, scored a solo try in the 73rd minute to seal what was surely another last-gasp victory. Australia trailed just 14-13. But Burke missed the conversion from close range. His attempt, against all expectation, struck the left upright – thudding into the pole with all the force of imaginary stakes piercing Australian hearts in the crowd of 80,000. Finally, surely, the Australians had emptied their bag of tricks.

Then the All Blacks, clock ticking down, were penalised on their quarter. Fourteen metres from the left touchline, Burke banged over the match-winner. Another great escape. Just like the year before when Toutai Kefu stuck out a paw to deny the All Blacks with an injury time try. Just like the year 2000, when John Eales kicked the penalty goal to decide another titanic Bledisloe Cup game and, a couple of weeks later, Stirling Mortlock repeated the Eales feat and won Australia the Tri Nations trophy.

If the mark of a great side is the making of their own luck, then the Australian side, circa 2000-2002, is one of the greatest the country has produced. Eventually, however, the gods have to smile elsewhere. And so they did a fortnight after the Sydney thriller when the Wallabies went to Johannesburg needing to win by 26 points to retain the Tri Nations silverware. That was never going to happen, but the Wallabies were determined simply to win at Ellis Park. They had only done so once in history, with an against-the-odds victory in 1963, winning 11-9.

With just 12 minutes to play in the Tri Nations decider, the Australians were struggling to avoid embarrassment. They trailed 26-9 before launching the comeback that could have topped their 'best of' album. Rogers shimmied his way through for a try, powerhouse No 8 Toutai Kefu strolled across and when flanker George Smith grabbed a wayward Springbok line-out throw and raced 60 metres before providing the last pass for replacement hooker Brendan Cannon, the impossible was unfolding. Australia led 31-26.

Into the final minute now and the South Africans are on the attack. Full-back Werner Greeff works back on the angle, takes a pass as first receiver at full tilt, breaks through two Australian forwards and scores. Then kicks the conversion. Houdini has finally swapped sides. The Springboks win 33-31.

The earlier matches in the Tri Nations had also been memorable, but for far less exhilarating reasons. The Wallabies kicked off their defence against the All Blacks in Christchurch, at night, in rain and sleet, in what would be labelled the Ice-Box Test. No tries were scored and very little rugby was played, but with plenty of teeth chattering the All Blacks emerged with a 12-6 victory courtesy of fly-half Andrew Mehrtens's right boot.

On then to balmy Brisbane for the Wallabies where the Ben Tune drugs scandal broke. It was revealed that the Australian Rugby Union (ARU) and the Queensland Rugby Union (QRU) covered up a doctor's bungle from the previous year when Tune was treated for an infected knee with a banned drug, probenecid, which can be used as a masking agent for steroids. The blunder was spotted because the doctors involved presumed the drug could be prescribed provided drug authorities are notified in case it turns up on a test.

The Australian Sports Drug Agency, having received the paperwork detailing Tune's treatment, immediately informed the QRU and ARU that the Test speedster had been treated with a prohibited drug. Tune was stood down until clean and the story went to sleep for more than a year. The Springboks, understandably, were concerned about Tune playing. He offered to take a test on the eve of the game to prove he is not a drugs user, and eventually scored the first try of the game.

Then, at the 32-minute mark of the first half, with Australia three tries to the good and cruising, an all-in brawl broke out. Players were sin binned, others would be cited later and the entire episode was a shameful exhibition of foul play from both sides. But not a single player was punished by suspension. Work that one out. The Wallabies won the Test 38-27. But the same Boks side would deny the Australians the Tri Nations trophy, which headed to New Zealand.

For Wallaby coach Eddie Jones, it was the hand-over of another trophy from a once-bulging cabinet. Jones took over from Rod Macqueen after the Lions series the previous year and brought home the bacon in his first Tri Nations championship. But then came the 2001 end-of-season tour to Europe, and a reality check for the Australians.

They breezed past Spain 92-10 in Madrid, scoring a record number of points, with Chris Latham picking up three tries and Joe Roff two. Hardly the testing pre-cursor, however, to a Twickenham clash with England. Clive Woodward's side had won the Cook Cup the previous year on the back of a dubious Dan Luger try. No controversies this time though, with England winning 21-15, despite Australia scoring two tries to nil. Daniel Herbert broke a thumb in the defeat, ending his tour.

A week later Graeme Bond was called up for the showdown in Marseilles with France. In effect, this was a watershed match for the Wallabies under Jones. They were outpaced, out-muscled and outplayed in the forwards, with the athleticism of the French back-row ramming home the need for future surgery to the Australian side. France won 14-13, both sides scoring a try apiece. But privately Jones was conceding the Macqueen team that had been so successful was in need of an overhaul when 2002 came around.

And so it would happen, even if injury (Nathan Grey, Phil Waugh, David Giffin), retirement (Michael Foley) and a European sojourn (Joe Roff) would combine to rip a third of the team that lost to France from Test contention in the season just passed. Bond and Stiles also departed, their omissions the result of the selectors' falling axe. Before the Wallabies left Europe, they beat Wales 21-13 but were unable to score a try. The only five pointer went to the home side. Jones was not amused.

Australia opened the 2002 international season with a non-cap match against New Zealand Maori. The match ushered two former league internationals, wing Wendell Sailor and utility back Rogers, on to the international stage. The Wallabies survived a late three-try blitz from the Maori to win 27-23.

Two Tests against France followed, with Sailor holding his spot and Rogers being used off the bench. As the French experimented, Jones took a steady approach to selection leading into the Tri Nations. Australia won the first Test 29-17 in Melbourne with Kefu breaking a bone in his hand. He missed the second Test, played to 64,000 at the Olympic Stadium in Sydney, as Australia won a pulse-racing encounter 31-25. From there the Wallabies prepared to defend their Tri Nations title. But as the Houdini protégés learned in the tournament finale, Johannesburg is not the place to try for miracles.

Australia's Test Record in 2001–2002:
Played 10, won 6, lost 4

Opponents	Date	Venue	Result
South Africa	17th August 2002	A	Lost 31-33
New Zealand	3rd August 2002	H	Won 16-14
South Africa	27th July 2002	H	Won 38-27
New Zealand	13th July 2002	A	Lost 6-12
France	29th June 2002	H	Won 31-25
France	22nd June 2002	H	Won 29-17
Wales	25th November 2001	A	Won 21-13
France	17th November 2001	A	Lost 13-14
England	10th November 2001	A	Lost 15-21
Spain	1st November 2001	A	Won 92-10

AUSTRALIA INTERNATIONAL STATISTICS

(up to 31 August 2002)

Match Records

MOST CONSECUTIVE TEST WINS

10 1991 *Arg, WS, W, I, NZ, E,* 1992 *S* 1,2, *NZ* 1,2

10 1998 *NZ 3, Fj, Tg, Sm, F, E 2,* 1999 *I* 1,2, *E, SA 1*

10 1999 *NZ 2, R, I 3, US, W, SA 3, F,* 2000 *Arg 1,2, SA 1*

MOST CONSECUTIVE TESTS WITHOUT DEFEAT

Matches	Wins	Draws	Period
10	10	0	1991 to 1992
10	10	0	1998 to 1999
10	10	0	1999 to 2000

MOST POINTS IN A MATCH
by the team

Pts	Opponents	Venue	Year
92	Spain	Madrid	2001
76	England	Brisbane	1998
74	Canada	Brisbane	1996
74	Tonga	Canberra	1998
73	Western Samoa	Sydney	1994
67	United States	Brisbane	1990

by a player

Pts	Player	Opponents	Venue	Year
39	M C Burke	Canada	Brisbane	1996
29	S A Mortlock	South Africa	Melbourne	2000
28	M P Lynagh	Argentina	Brisbane	1995
25	M C Burke	Scotland	Sydney	1998
25	M C Burke	France	Cardiff	1999
25	M C Burke	British/Irish Lions	Melbourne	2001
24	M P Lynagh	United States	Brisbane	1990
24	M P Lynagh	France	Brisbane	1990
24	M C Burke	New Zealand	Melbourne	1998
24	M C Burke	South Africa	Twickenham	1999

MOST TRIES IN A MATCH
by the team

Tries	Opponents	Venue	Year
13	South Korea	Brisbane	1987
13	Spain	Madrid	2001
12	United States	Brisbane	1990
12	Wales	Brisbane	1991
12	Tonga	Canberra	1998
11	Western Samoa	Sydney	1994
11	England	Brisbane	1998

by a player

Tries	Player	Opponents	Venue	Year
4	G Cornelsen	New Zealand	Auckland	1978
4	D I Campese	United States	Sydney	1983
4	J S Little	Tonga	Canberra	1998
4	C E Latham	Argentina	Brisbane	2000
3	A D McLean	NZ Maori	Palmerston N	1936
3	J R Ryan	Japan	Brisbane	1975
3	M P Burke	Canada	Brisbane	1985
3	M P Burke	South Korea	Brisbane	1987
3	D I Campese	Italy	Rome	1988
3	A S Nuiqila	Italy	Rome	1988
3	D I Campese	Canada	Calgary	1993
3	M Burke	Canada	Brisbane	1996
3	S J Larkham	England	Brisbane	1998
3	B N Tune	England	Brisbane	1998
3	C P Strauss	Ireland	Brisbane	1999
3	R S T Kefu	Romania	Belfast	1999
3	C E Latham	Spain	Madrid	2001

MOST CONVERSIONS IN A MATCH
by the team

Cons	Opponents	Venue	Year
12	Spain	Madrid	2001
9	Canada	Brisbane	1996
9	Fiji	Parramatta	1998
8	Italy	Rome	1988
8	United States	Brisbane	1990
7	Canada	Sydney	1985
7	Tonga	Canberra	1998

by a player

Cons	Player	Opponents	Venue	Year
10	M C Burke	Spain	Madrid	2001
9	M C Burke	Canada	Brisbane	1996
9	J A Eales	Fiji	Parramatta	1998
8	M P Lynagh	Italy	Rome	1988
8	M P Lynagh	United States	Brisbane	1990
7	M P Lynagh	Canada	Sydney	1985

MOST PENALTIES IN A MATCH
by the team

Penalties	Opponents	Venue	Year
8	South Africa	Twickenham	1999
7	New Zealand	Sydney	1999
7	France	Cardiff	1999
7	Wales	Cardiff	2001
6	New Zealand	Sydney	1984
6	France	Sydney	1986
6	England	Brisbane	1988
6	Argentina	Buenos Aires	1997
6	Ireland	Perth	1999
6	France	Paris	2000
6	British/Irish Lions	Melbourne	2001

by a player

Penalties	Player	Opponents	Venue	Year
8	M C Burke	South Africa	Twickenham	1999
7	M C Burke	New Zealand	Sydney	1999
7	M C Burke	France	Cardiff	1999
7	M C Burke	Wales	Cardiff	2001
6	M P Lynagh	France	Sydney	1986
6	M P Lynagh	England	Brisbane	1988
6	D J Knox	Argentina	Buenos Aires	1997
6	M C Burke	France	Paris	2000
6	M C Burke	British/Irish Lions	Melbourne	2001

MOST DROPPED GOALS IN A MATCH
by the team

Drops	Opponents	Venue	Year
3	England	Twickenham	1967
3	Ireland	Dublin	1984
3	Fiji	Brisbane	1985

by a player

Drops	Player	Opponents	Venue	Year
3	P F Hawthorne	England	Twickenham	1967
2	M G Ella	Ireland	Dublin	1984
2	D J Knox	Fiji	Brisbane	1985

CAREER RECORDS
MOST CAPPED PLAYERS

Caps	Player	Career Span
101	D I Campese	1982 to 1996
86	J A Eales	1991 to 2001
80	T J Horan	1989 to 2000
79	D J Wilson	1992 to 2000
78	G M Gregan	1994 to 2002
75	J S Little	1989 to 2000
72	M P Lynagh	1984 to 1995
72	J W C Roff	1995 to 2001
67	P N Kearns	1989 to 1999
64	M C Burke	1993 to 2002
63	N C Farr Jones	1984 to 1993
63	D J Herbert	1994 to 2002
59	S P Poidevin	1980 to 1991

MOST CONSECUTIVE TESTS

Tests	Player	Span
62	J W C Roff	1996 to 2001
46	P N Kearns	1989 to 1995
42	D I Campese	1990 to 1995
37	P G Johnson	1959 to 1968

MOST TESTS AS CAPTAIN

Tests	Captain	Span
55	J A Eales	1996 to 2001
36	N C Farr Jones	1988 to 1992
19	A G Slack	1984 to 1987
16	J E Thornett	1962 to 1967
16	G V Davis	1969 to 1972

MOST TESTS IN INDIVIDUAL POSITIONS

Position	Player	Tests	Span
Full-back	M C Burke	50	1993 to 2002
Wing	D I Campese	85	1982 to 1996
Centre	T J Horan	69	1989 to 2000
Fly-half	M P Lynagh	64	1984 to 1995
Scrum-half	G M Gregan	77*	1994 to 2002
Prop	E J A McKenzie	51	1990 to 1997
Hooker	P N Kearns	66	1989 to 1999
Lock	J A Eales	84	1991 to 2001
Flanker	D J Wilson	79	1992 to 2000
No 8	R S T Kefu	47	1998 to 2002

* excludes an additional appearance as a temporary replacement

MOST POINTS IN TESTS

Points	Player	Tests	Career
911	M P Lynagh	72	1984 to 1995
790	M C Burke	64	1993 to 2002
315	D I Campese	101	1982 to 1996
260	P E McLean	30	1974 to 1982
173	J A Eales	86	1991 to 2001
173	J W C Roff	72	1995 to 2001

MOST TRIES IN TESTS

Tries	Player	Tests	Career
64	D I Campese	101	1982 to 1996
30	T J Horan	80	1989 to 2000
27	J W C Roff	72	1995 to 2001
25	M C Burke	64	1993 to 2002
24	B N Tune	45	1996 to 2002
21	J S Little	75	1989 to 2000

MOST CONVERSIONS IN TESTS

Cons	Player	Tests	Career
140	M P Lynagh	72	1984 to 1995

94	M C Burke	64	1993 to 2002
31	J A Eales	86	1991 to 2001
27	P E McLean	30	1974 to 1982
19	D J Knox	13	1985 to 1997

MOST PENALTY GOALS IN TESTS

Penalties	Player	Tests	Career
177	M P Lynagh	72	1984 to 1995
159	M C Burke	64	1993 to 2002
62	P E McLean	30	1974 to 1982
34	J A Eales	86	1991 to 2001
25	S A Mortlock	16	2000 to 2002
23	M C Roebuck	23	1991 to 1993

MOST DROPPED GOALS IN TESTS

Drops	Player	Tests	Career
9	P F Hawthorne	21	1962 to 1967
9	M P Lynagh	72	1984 to 1995
8	M G Ella	25	1980 to 1984
4	P E McLean	30	1974 to 1982

TRI NATIONS RECORDS

Record	Detail	Holder	Set
Most points in season	104	in four matches	2000
Most tries in season	13	in four matches	1997
Highest Score	38	38-27 v S Africa (h)	2002
Biggest win	26	32-6 v S Africa (h)	1999
Highest score conceded	61	22-61 v S Africa (a)	1997
Biggest defeat	39	22-61 v S Africa (a)	1997
Most points in matches	245	M C Burke	1996 to 2002
Most points in season	71	S A Mortlock	2000
Most points in match	24	M C Burke	v N Zealand (h) 1998
Most tries in matches	8	J W C Roff	1996 to 2001
Most tries in season	4	S A Mortlock	2000
Most tries in match	2	B N Tune	v S Africa (h) 1997
	2	M C Burke	v N Zealand (h) 1998
	2	J W C Roff	v S Africa (h) 1999
	2	S A Mortlock	v N Zealand (h) 2000
	2	C E Latham	v S Africa (h) 2002
Most cons in matches	16	M C Burke	1996 to 2002
Most cons in season	7	D J Knox	1997
Most cons in match	3	D J Knox	v S Africa (h) 1997
	3	M C Burke	v S Africa (h) 1999
	3	M C Burke	v S Africa (h) 2002
Most pens in matches	61	M C Burke	1996 to 2002
Most pens in season	14	M C Burke	2001
Most pens in match	7	M C Burke	v N Zealand (h) 1999

SERIES RECORDS

Record	Holder	Detail
Most tries	D I Campese	6 in Europe 1988
Most points	M C Burke	74 in Europe 1996

MISCELLANEOUS RECORDS

Record	Holder	Detail
Longest Test Career	G M Cooke/A R Miller	16 seasons, 1932-1947-48/1952-67
Youngest Test Cap	B W Ford	18 yrs 90 days in 1957
Oldest Test Cap	A R Miller	38 yrs 113 days in 1967

Career Records of Australian International Players
(up to 31 August 2002)

PLAYER	Debut	Caps	T	C	P	D	Pts
Backs:							
G S G Bond	2001 v SA	5	1	0	0	0	5
M C Burke	1993 v SA	64	25	94	159	0	790
E J Flatley	1997 v E	17	0	4	0	0	8
G M Gregan	1994 v It	78	11	0	0	2	61
N P Grey	1998 v S	30	5	0	0	0	25
D J Herbert	1994 v I	63	11	0	0	0	55
S Kefu	2001 v W	1	0	0	0	0	0
S J Larkham	1996 v W	52	15	2	0	1	82
C E Latham	1998 v F	32	17	0	0	0	85
S A Mortlock	2000 v Arg	16	10	10	25	0	145
J W C Roff	1995 v C	72	27	10	6	0	173
M S Rogers	2002 v F	6	2	0	0	0	10
W J Sailor	2002 v F	2	0	0	0	0	0
B N Tune	1996 v W	45	24	0	0	0	120
C J Whitaker	1998 v SA	10	2	0	0	0	10
Forwards:							
T M Bowman	1998 v E	16	2	0	0	0	10
B J Cannon	2001 v BI	9	1	0	0	0	5
M J Cockbain	1997 v F	52	1	0	0	0	5
B J Darwin	2001 v BI	13	0	0	0	0	0
O D A Finegan	1996 v W	50	6	0	0	0	30
M A Foley	1995 v C	50	4	0	0	0	20
D T Giffin	1996 v W	34	0	0	0	0	0
S P Hardman	2002 v F	1	0	0	0	0	0
J B G Harrison	2001 v BI	13	0	0	0	0	0
R S T Kefu	1997 v SA	49	9	0	0	0	45
D J Lyons	2000 v Arg	10	0	0	0	0	0
R C Moore	1999 v US	14	0	0	0	0	0
E P Noriega	1998 v F	14	0	0	0	0	0
J A Paul	1998 v S	30	5	0	0	0	25
N C Sharpe	2002 v F	6	1	0	0	0	5
G B Smith	2000 v F	20	1	0	0	0	5
N B Stiles	2001 v BI	11	1	0	0	0	5
D J Vickerman	2002 v F	1	0	0	0	0	0
P R Waugh	2000 v E	8	1	0	0	0	5
W K Young	2000 v F	9	0	0	0	0	0

NB Roff's figures include a penalty try awarded against New Zealand in 2001

AUSTRALIAN INTERNATIONAL PLAYERS

(up to 31 August 2002)

Abrahams, A M F (NSW) 1967 *NZ*, 1968 *NZ* 1, 1969 *W*
Adams, N J (NSW) 1955 *NZ* 1
Adamson, R W (NSW) 1912 *US*
Allan, T (NSW) 1946 *NZ* 1, *M*, *NZ* 2, 1947 *NZ* 2, *S, I, W,* 1948 *E, F,* 1949 *M* 1,2,3, *NZ* 1,2
Anderson, R P (NSW) 1925 *NZ* 1
Anlezark, E A (NSW) 1905 *NZ*
Armstrong, A R (NSW) 1923 *NZ* 1,2
Austin, L R (NSW) 1963 *E*

Baker, R L (NSW) 1904 *BI* 1,2
Baker, W H (NSW) 1914 *NZ* 1,2,3
Ballesty, J P (NSW) 1968 *NZ* 1,2, *F, I, S,* 1969 *W, SA* 2,3,4,
Bannon, D P (NSW) 1946 *M*
Bardsley, E J (NSW) 1928 *NZ* 1,3, *M* (R)
Barker, H S (NSW) 1952 *Fj* 1,2, *NZ* 1,2, 1953 *SA* 4, 1954 *Fj* 1,2
Barnett, J T (NSW) 1907 *NZ* 1,2,3, 1908 *W,* 1909 *E*
Barry, M J (Q) 1971 *SA* 3
Barton, R F D (NSW) 1899 *BI* 3
Batch, P G (Q) 1975 *S, W,* 1976 *E, Fj* 1,2,3, *F* 1,2, 1978 *W* 1,2, *NZ* 1,2,3, 1979 *Arg* 2
Batterham, R P (NSW) 1967 *NZ,* 1970 *S*
Battishall, B R (NSW) 1973 *E*
Baxter, A J (NSW) 1949 *M* 1,2,3, *NZ* 1,2, 1951 *NZ* 1,2, 1952 *NZ* 1,2
Baxter, T J (Q) 1958 *NZ* 3
Beith, B McN (NSW) 1914 *NZ* 3, 1920 *NZ* 1,2,3
Bell, K R (Q) 1968 *S*
Bell, M D (NSW) 1996 *C*
Bennett, W G (Q) 1931 *M,* 1933 *SA* 1,2,3,
Bermingham, J V (Q) 1934 *NZ* 1,2, 1937 *SA* 1
Berne, J E (NSW) 1975 *S*
Besomo, K S (NSW) 1979 *I* 2
Betts, T N (Q) 1951 *NZ* 2,3, 1954 *Fj* 2
Biilmann, R R (NSW) 1933 *SA* 1,2,3,4
Birt, R (Q) 1914 *NZ* 2
Black, J W (NSW) 1985 *C* 1,2, *NZ, Fj* 1
Blackwood, J G (NSW) 1922 *M* 1, *NZ* 1,2,3, 1923 *M* 1, *NZ* 1,2,3, 1924 *NZ* 1,2,3, 1925 *NZ* 1,4, 1926 *NZ* 1,2,3, 1927 *I, W, S,* 1928 *E, F*
Blades, A T (NSW) 1996 *S, I, W* 3, 1997 *NZ* 1(R), *E* 1(R), *NZ* 1(R), *NZ* 3, *SA* 2, *Arg* 1,2, *E* 2, *S,* 1998 *E* 1, *S* 1,2, *NZ* 1, *SA* 1, *NZ* 2, *SA* 2, *NZ* 3, *Fj, WS, F, E* 2, 1999 *I* 1(R), *SA* 2, *NZ* 2, [*R, I* 3, *W, SA* 3, *F*]
Blades, C D (NSW) 1997 *E* 1
Blair, M R (NSW) 1928 *F,* 1931 *M, NZ*
Bland, G V (NSW) 1928 *NZ* 3, *M,* 1932 *NZ* 1,2, 1933 *SA* 1,2,4,5
Blomley, J (NSW) 1949 *M* 1,2,3, *NZ* 1,2, 1950 *BI* 1,2
Boland, S B (Q) 1899 *BI* 3,4, 1903 *NZ*
Bond, G S G (ACT) 2001 *SA* 2(R), *Sp* (R), *E* (R), *F, W*
Bond, J H (NSW) 1920 *NZ* 1,2,3, 1921 *NZ*
Bondfield, C (NSW) 1925 *NZ* 2
Bonis, E T (Q) 1929 *NZ* 1,2,3, 1930 *BI,* 1931 *M, NZ,* 1932 *NZ* 1,2,3, 1933 *SA* 1,2,3,4,5, 1934 *NZ* 1,2, 1936 *NZ* 1,2, *M,* 1937 *SA* 1, 1938 *NZ* 1
Bonner, J E (NSW) 1922 *NZ* 1,2,3, 1923 *M* 1,2,3, 1924 *NZ* 1,2
Bosler, J M (NSW) 1953 *SA* 1
Bouffler, R G (NSW) 1899 *BI* 3
Bourke, T K (Q) 1947 *NZ* 2
Bowden, R (NSW) 1926 *NZ* 4
Bowen, S (NSW) 1993 *SA* 1,2,3, 1995 [*R*], *NZ* 1,2, 1996 *C, NZ* 1, *SA* 2
Bowers, A J A (NSW) 1923 *M* 2(R),3, *NZ,* 3, 1925 *NZ* 1,4, 1926 *NZ* 1, 1927 *I*
Bowman, T M (NSW) 1998 *E* 1, *S* 1,2, *NZ* 1, *SA* 1, *NZ* 2, *SA* 2, *NZ* 3, *Fj, WS, F, E* 2, 1999 *I* 1,2, *SA* 2, [*US*]
Boyce, E S (NSW) 1962 *NZ* 1,2, 1964 *NZ* 1,2,3, 1965 *SA* 1,2, 1966 *W, S,* 1967 *E, I* 1, *F, I* 2
Boyce, J S (NSW) 1962 *NZ* 3,4,5, 1963 *E, SA* 1,2,3,4, 1964 *NZ* 1,3, 1965 *SA* 1,2
Boyd, A (NSW) 1899 *BI* 3
Boyd, A F McC (Q) 1958 *M* 1
Brass, J E (NSW) 1966 *BI* 2, *W, S,* 1967 *E, I* 1, *F, I* 2, *NZ,* 1968 *NZ* 1, *F, I, S*

Breckenridge, J W (NSW) 1925 *NZ* 2(R),3, 1927 *I, W, S,* 1928 *E, F,* 1929 *NZ* 1,2,3, 1930 *BI*
Brial, M C (NSW) 1993 *F* 1(R), 2, 1996 *W* 1(R), 2, *C, NZ* 1, *SA* 1, *NZ* 2, *SA* 2, *It, I, W* 3, 1997 *NZ* 2
Bridle, O L (V) 1931 *M,* 1932 *NZ* 1,2,3, 1933 *SA* 3,4,5, 1934 *NZ* 1,2, 1936 *NZ* 1,2, *M*
Broad, E G (Q) 1949 *M* 1
Brockhoff, J D (NSW) 1949 *M* 2,3, *NZ* 1,2, 1950 *BI* 1,2, 1951 *NZ* 2,3
Brown, B R (Q) 1972 *NZ* 1,3
Brown, J V (NSW) 1956 *SA* 1,2, 1957 *NZ* 1,2, 1958 *W, I, E, S, F*
Brown, R C (NSW) 1975 *E* 1,2
Brown, S W (NSW) 1953 *SA* 2,3,4
Bryant, H (NSW) 1925 *NZ* 1,3,4
Buchan, A J (NSW) 1946 *NZ* 1,2, 1947 *NZ* 1,2, *S, I, W,* 1948 *E, F,* 1949 *M* 3
Buchanan, P N (NSW) 1923 *M* 2(R),3
Bull, D (NSW) 1928 *M*
Buntine, H (NSW) 1923 *NZ* 1(R), 1924 *NZ* 2
Burdon, A (NSW) 1903 *NZ,* 1904 *BI* 1,2, 1905 *NZ*
Burge, A B (NSW) 1907 *NZ* 3, 1908 *W*
Burge, P H (NSW) 1907 *NZ* 1,2,3
Burge, R (NSW) 1928 *NZ* 1,2,3(R), *M* (R)
Burke, B T (NSW) 1988 *S* (R)
Burke, C T (NSW) 1946 *NZ* 2, 1947 *NZ* 1,2, *S, I, W,* 1948 *E, F,* 1949 *M* 2,3, *NZ* 1,2, 1950 *BI* 1,2, 1951 *NZ* 1,2,3, 1953 *SA* 2,3,4, 1954 *Fj* 1, 1955 *NZ* 1,2,3, 1956 *SA* 1,2,
Burke, M C (NSW) 1993 *SA* 3(R), *F* 1, 1994 *I* 1,2, *It* 1,2, 1995 [*C, R, E*], *NZ* 1,2, 1996 *W* 1,2, *C, NZ* 1, *SA* 1, *NZ* 2, *SA* 2, *It, S, I, W* 3, 1997 *E* 1, *NZ* 2, 1998 *E* 1, *S* 1,2, *NZ* 1, *SA* 1, *NZ* 2, *SA* 2, *NZ* 3, 1999 *I* 2(R), *E* (R), *SA* 1, *NZ* 1, *SA* 2, *NZ* 2, [*R, I* 3, *US, W, SA* 3, *F*], 2000 *F, S, E,* 2001 *BI* 1(R),2,3, *SA* 1, *NZ* 1, *SA* 2, *NZ* 2, *Sp, E, F, W,* 2002 *F* 1,2, *NZ* 1, *SA* 1, *NZ* 2, *SA* 2
Burke, M P (NSW) 1984 *E* (R), *I,* 1985 *C* 1,2, *NZ, Fj* 1,2, 1986 *It* (R), *F, Arg* 1,2, *NZ* 1,2,3, 1987 *SK,* [*US, J, I, F, W*], *NZ, Arg* 1,2
Burnet, D R (NSW) 1972 *F* 1,2, *NZ* 1,2,3, *Fj*
Butler, O F (NSW) 1969 *SA* 1,2, 1970 *S,* 1971 *SA* 2,3, *F* 1,2

Calcraft, W J (NSW) 1985 *C* 1, 1986 *It, Arg* 2
Caldwell, B C (NSW) 1928 *NZ* 3
Cameron, A S (NSW) 1951 *NZ* 1,2,3, 1952 *Fj* 1,2, *NZ* 1,2, 1953 *SA* 1,2,3,4, 1954 *Fj* 1,2, 1955 *NZ* 1,2,3, 1956 *SA* 1,2, 1957 *NZ* 1, 1958 *I*
Campbell, J D (NSW) 1910 *NZ* 1,2,3
Campbell, W A (Q) 1984 *Fj,* 1986 *It, F, Arg* 1,2, *NZ* 1,2,3, 1987 *SK,* [*E, US, J* (R), *I, F*], *NZ,* 1988 *E,* 1989 *BI* 1,2,3, *NZ,* 1990 *NZ* 2,3
Campese, D I (ACT, NSW) 1982 *NZ* 1,2,3, 1983 *US, Arg* 1,2, *NZ, It, F* 1,2, 1984 *Fj, NZ* 1,2,3, *E, I, W, S,* 1985 *Fj* 1,2, 1986 *It, F, Arg* 1,2, *NZ* 1,2,3, 1987 [*E, US, J, I, F, W*], *NZ,* 1988 *E* 1,2, *NZ* 1,2,3, *E, S, It,* 1989 *BI* 1,2,3, *NZ, F* 1,2, 1990 *F* 2,3, *US, NZ* 1,2,3, 1991 *W, E, NZ* 1,2, [*Arg, WS, W, I, NZ, E*], 1992 *S* 1,2, *NZ* 1,2,3, *SA, I, W,* 1993 *Tg, NZ, SA* 1,2,3, *C, F* 1,2, 1994 *I* 1,2, *It* 1,2, *WS, NZ,* 1995 *Arg* 1,2, [*SA, C, E*], *NZ* 2(R), 1996 *W* 1,2, *C, NZ* 1, *SA* 1, *NZ* 2, *SA* 2, *It, W* 3
Canniffe, W D (Q) 1907 *NZ* 2
Cannon, B J (NSW) 2001 *BI* 2(R), *NZ* 1(R), *Sp* (R), *F* (R), *W* (R), 2002 *F* 1(R),2, *SA* 1(t),2(R)
Caputo, M E (ACT) 1996 *W* 1,2, 1997 *F* 1,2, *NZ* 1
Carberry, C M (NSW, Q) 1973 *Tg* 2, *E,* 1976 *I, US, Fj* 1,2,3, 1981 *F* 1,2, *I, W, S,* 1982 *E*
Cardy, A M (NSW) 1966 *BI* 1,2, *W, S,* 1967 *E, I* 1, *F,* 1968 *NZ* 1,2
Carew, P J (Q) 1899 *BI* 1,2,3,4
Carmichael, P (Q) 1904 *BI* 2, 1907 *NZ* 1, 1908 *W,* 1909 *E*
Carozza, P V (Q) 1990 *F* 1,2,3, *NZ* 2,3, 1992 *S* 1,2, *NZ* 1,2,3, *SA, I, W,* 1993 *Tg, NZ*
Carpenter, M G (V) 1938 *NZ* 1,2,
Carr, E T A (NSW) 1913 *NZ* 1,2,3, 1914 *NZ* 1,2,3
Carr, E W (NSW) 1921 *SA* 1,2,3, *NZ* (R)
Carroll, D B (NSW) 1908 *W,* 1912 *US*
Carroll, J C (NSW) 1953 *SA* 1
Carroll, J H (NSW) 1958 *M* 2,3, *NZ* 1,2,3, 1959 *BI* 1,2
Carson, J (NSW) 1899 *BI* 1

297

Carson, P J (NSW) 1979 *NZ*, 1980 *NZ* 3
Carter, D G (NSW) 1988 *E* 1,2, *NZ* 1, 1989 *F* 1,2
Casey, T V (NSW) 1963 *SA* 2,3,4, 1964 *NZ* 1,2,3
Catchpole, K W (NSW) 1961 *Fj* 1,2,3, *SA* 1,2, *F*, 1962 *NZ* 1,2,4, 1963 *SA* 2,3,4, 1964 *NZ* 1,2,3, 1965 *SA* 1,2, 1966 *BI* 1,2, *W*, *S*, 1967 *E*, *I* 1, *F*, *I* 2, *NZ*, 1968 *NZ* 1
Cawsey, R M (NSW) 1949 *M* 1, *NZ* 1,2
Cerutti, W H (NSW) 1928 *NZ* 1,2,3, *M*, 1929 *NZ* 1,2,3, 1930 *BI*, 1931 *M*, *NZ*, 1932 *NZ* 1,2,3, 1933 *SA* 1,2,3,4,5, 1936 *M*, 1937 *SA* 1,2
Challoner, R L (NSW) 1899 *BI* 2
Chambers, R (NSW) 1920 *NZ* 1,3
Chapman, G A (NSW) 1962 *NZ* 3,4,5
Clark, J G (Q) 1931 *M*, *NZ*, 1932 *NZ* 1,2, 1933 *SA* 1
Clarken, J C (NSW) 1905 *NZ*, 1910 *NZ* 1,2,3
Cleary, M A (NSW) 1961 *Fj* 1,2,3, *SA* 1,2, *F*
Clements, P (NSW) 1982 *NZ* 3
Clifford, M (NSW) 1938 *NZ* 3
Cobb, W G (NSW) 1899 *BI* 3,4
Cockbain, M J (Q) 1997 *F* 2(R), *NZ* 1, *SA* 1,2, 1998 *E* 1, *S* 1,2, *NZ* 1, *SA* 1, *NZ* 2, *SA* 2, *NZ* 3, *Fj*, *Tg* (R), *WS*, *F*, *E* 2, 1999 *I* 1,2, *E*, *SA* 1, *NZ* 1, *SA* 2, *NZ* 2, [*US* (t&R), *W*, *SA* 3, *F*], 2000 *Arg* 1,2, *SA* 2(t&R),3(t&R), *F*, *S*, *E* (R), 2001 *BI* 1(R),2(R),3(R), *SA* 1(R), *NZ* 1(R), *SA* 2(R), *NZ* 2(R), *Sp* (R), *E* (R), *F* (t+R), *W*, 2002 *F* 1(R),2(R), *NZ* 1(R), *SA* 1(R), *NZ* 2(R), *SA* 2(R)
Cocks, M R (NSW, Q) 1972 *F* 1,2, *NZ* 2,3, *Fj*, 1973 *Tg* 1,2, *W*, *E*, 1975 *J* 1
Codey, D (NSW Country, Q) 1983 *Arg* 1, 1984 *E*, *W*, *S*, 1985 *C* 2, *NZ*, 1986 *F*, *Arg* 1, 1987 [*US*, *J*, *F* (R), *W*], *NZ*
Cody, E W (NSW) 1913 *NZ* 1,2,3
Coker, T (Q, ACT) 1987 [*E*, *US*, *F*, *W*], 1991 *NZ* 2, [*Arg*, *WS*, *NZ*, *E*], 1992 *NZ* 1,2,3, *W* (R), 1993 *Tg*, *NZ*, 1995 *Arg* 2, *NZ* 1(R), 1997 *F* 1(R), 2, *NZ* 1, *E* 1, *NZ* 2(R), *SA* 1(R), *NZ* 3, *SA* 2, *Arg* 1,2
Colbert, R (NSW) 1952 *Fj* 2, *NZ* 1,2, 1953 *SA* 2,3,4
Cole, J W (NSW) 1968 *NZ* 1,2, *F*, *I*, *S*, 1969 *W*, *SA* 1,2,3,4, 1970 *S*, 1971 *SA* 1,2,3, *F* 1,2, 1972 *NZ* 1,2,3, 1973 *Tg* 1,2, 1974 *NZ* 1,2,3
Collins, P K (NSW) 1937 *SA* 2, 1938 *NZ* 2,3
Colton, A J (Q) 1899 *BI* 1,3
Colton, T (Q) 1904 *BI* 1,2
Comrie-Thomson, I R (NSW) 1926 *NZ* 4, 1928 *NZ* 1,2,3 *M*
Connor, D M (Q) 1958 *W*, *I*, *E*, *S*, *F*, *M* 2,3, *NZ* 1,2,3, 1959 *BI* 1,2
Connors, M R (Q) 1999 *SA* 1(R), *NZ* 1(R), *SA* 2(R), *NZ* 2, [*R* (R), *I* 3, *US*, *W* (R), *SA* 3(R), *F*(R)], 2000 *Arg* 1(R),2(R), *SA* 1, *NZ* 1, *SA* 2, *NZ* 2(t&R), *SA* 3, *F* (R), *S* (R), *E* (R)
Constable, R (Q) 1994 *I* 2(t & R)
Cook, M T (Q) 1986 *F*, 1987 *SK*, [*J*], 1988 *E* 1,2, *NZ* 1,2,3, *E*, *S*, *It*
Cooke, B P (Q) 1979 *I* 1
Cooke, G M (Q) 1932 *NZ* 1,2,3, 1933 *SA* 1,2,3, 1946 *NZ* 2, 1947 *NZ* 2, *S*, *I*, *W*, 1948 *E*, *F*
Coolican, J E (NSW) 1982 *NZ* 1, 1983 *It*, *F* 1,2
Cooney, R C (NSW) 1922 *M* 2
Cordingley, S J (Q) 2000 *Arg* 1(R), *SA* 1(R), *F*, *S*, *E*
Corfe, A C (Q) 1899 *BI* 2
Cornelsen, G (NSW) 1974 *NZ* 2,3, 1975 *J* 2, *S*, *W*, 1976 *E*, *F* 1,2, 1978 *W* 1,2, *NZ* 1,2,3, 1979 *I* 1,2, *NZ*, *Arg* 1,2, 1980 *NZ* 1,2,3, 1981 *I*, *W*, *S*, 1982 *E*
Cornes, J R (Q) 1972 *Fj*
Cornforth, R G W (NSW) 1947 *NZ* 1, 1950 *BI* 2
Cornish, P (ACT) 1990 *F* 2,3, *NZ* 1
Costello, P P S (Q) 1950 *BI* 2
Cottrell, N V (Q) 1949 *M* 1,2,3, *NZ* 1, 1950 *BI* 1,2, 1951 *NZ* 1,2,3, 1952 *Fj* 1,2, *NZ* 1,2
Cowper, D L (V) 1931 *NZ*, 1932 *NZ* 1,2,3, 1933 *SA* 1,2,3,4,5
Cox, B P (NSW) 1952 *Fj* 1,2, *NZ* 1,2, 1954 *Fj* 2, 1955 *NZ* 1, 1956 *SA* 2, 1957 *NZ* 1,2
Cox, M H (NSW) 1981 *W*, *S*
Cox, P A (NSW) 1979 *Arg* 1,2, 1980 *Fj*, *NZ* 1,2, 1981 *W* (R), *S*, 1982 *S* 1,2, *NZ* 1,2,3, 1984 *Fj*, *NZ* 1,2,3
Craig, R R (NSW) 1908 *W*
Crakanthorp, J S (NSW) 1923 *NZ* 3
Cremin, J F (NSW) 1946 *NZ* 1,2, 1947 *NZ* 1
Crittle, C P (NSW) 1962 *NZ* 4,5, 1963 *NZ* 2,3,4, 1964 *NZ* 1,2,3, 1965 *SA* 1,2, 1966 *BI* 1,2, *S*, 1967 *E*, *I*
Croft, B H D (NSW) 1928 *M*
Cross, J R (NSW) 1955 *NZ* 1,2,3
Cross, K A (NSW) 1949 *M* 1, *NZ* 1,2, 1950 *BI* 1,2, 1951 *NZ* 2,3, 1952 *NZ* 1, 1953 *NZ* 1,2,3,4, 1954 *Fj* 1,2, 1955 *NZ* 3, 1956 *NZ* 1,2, 1957 *NZ* 1,2

Crossman, O C (NSW) 1923 *M* 1(R),2,3, 1924, *NZ* 1,2,3, 1925 *NZ* 1,3,4, 1926 *NZ* 1,2,3,4, 1929 *NZ* 2, 1930 *BI*
Crowe, P J (NSW) 1976 *F* 2, 1978 *W* 1,2, 1979 *I* 2, *NZ*, *Arg* 1
Crowley, D J (Q) 1989 *BI* 1,2,3, 1991 [*WS*], 1992 *I*, *W*, 1993 *C* (R), 1995 *Arg* 1,2, [*SA*, *E*], *NZ* 1, 1996 *W* 2(R), *C*, *NZ* 1, *SA* 1,2, *I*, *W* 3, 1998 *E* 1(R), *S* 1(R),2(R), *NZ* 1(R), *SA* 1, *NZ* 2, *SA* 2, *NZ* 3, *Tg*, *WS*, 1999 *I* 1,2(R), *E* (R), *SA* 1, *NZ* 1(R), [*R* (R), *I* 3(t&R), *US*, *F*(R)]
Curley, T G P (NSW) 1957 *NZ* 1,2, 1958 *W*, *I*, *E*, *S*, *F*, *M* 1, *NZ* 1,2,3
Curran, D J (NSW) 1980 *NZ* 3, 1981 *F* 1,2, *W*, 1983 *Arg* 1
Currie, E W (Q) 1899 *BI* 2
Cutler, S A G (NSW) 1982 *NZ* 2(R), 1984 *NZ* 1,2,3, *E*, *I*, *W*, *S*, 1985 *C* 1,2, *NZ*, *Fj* 1,2, 1986 *It*, *F*, *NZ* 1,2,3, 1987 *SK*, [*E*, *J*, *I*, *F*, *W*], *NZ*, *Arg* 1,2, 1988 *E* 1,2, *NZ* 1,2,3, *E*, *S*, *It*, 1989 *BI* 1,2,3, *NZ*, 1991 [*WS*]

Daly, A J (NSW) 1989 *NZ*, *F* 1,2, 1990 *F* 1,2,3, *US*, *NZ* 1,2,3, 1991 *W*, *E*, *NZ* 1,2, [*Arg*, *W*, *I*, *NZ*, *E*], 1992 *S* 1,2, *NZ* 1,2,3, *SA*, 1993 *Tg*, *NZ*, *SA* 1,2,3, *C*, *F* 1,2, 1994 *I* 1,2, *It* 1,2, *WS*, *NZ*, 1995 [*C*, *R*]
D'Arcy, A M (Q) 1980 *Fj*, *NZ* 3, 1981 *F* 1,2, *I*, *W*, *S*, 1982 *E*, *S* 1,2
Darveniza, P (NSW) 1969 *W*, *SA* 2,3,4
Darwin, B J (ACT) 2001 *BI* 1(R), *SA* 1(R), *NZ* 1(R), *SA* 2(R), *NZ* 2(t&R), *Sp*, *E*, *F*, *W*, 2002 *NZ* 1(R), *SA* 1(R), *NZ* 2(R), *SA* 2
Davidson, R A L (NSW) 1952 *Fj* 1,2, *NZ* 1,2, 1953 *SA* 1, 1957 *NZ* 1,2, 1958 *W*, *I*, *E*, *S*, *F*, *M* 1
Davis, C C (NSW) 1949 *NZ* 1, 1951 *NZ* 1,2,3
Davis, E H (V) 1947 *S*, *W*, 1949 *M* 1,2
Davis, G V (NSW) 1963 *E*, *SA* 1,2,3,4, 1964 *NZ* 1,2,3, 1965 *SA* 1, 1966 *BI* 1,2, *W*, *S*, 1967 *E*, *I* 1, *F*, *I* 2, *NZ*, 1968 *NZ* 1,2, *F*, *I*, *S*, 1969 *W*, *SA* 1,2,3,4, 1970 *S*, 1971 *SA* 1,2,3, *F* 1,2, 1972 *F* 1,2, *NZ* 1,2,3
Davis, G W G (NSW) 1955 *NZ* 2,3
Davis, R A (NSW) 1974 *NZ* 1,2,3
Davis, T S R (NSW) 1920 *NZ* 1,2,3, 1921 *SA* 1,2,3, *NZ*, 1922 *M* 1,2,3, *NZ* 1,2,3, 1923 *M* 3, *NZ* 1,2,3, 1924 *NZ* 1,2, 1925 *NZ* 1
Davis, W (NSW) 1899 *BI* 1,3,4
Dawson, W L (NSW) 1946 *NZ* 1,2
Diett, L J (NSW) 1959 *BI* 1,2
Dix, W (NSW) 1907 *NZ* 1,2,3, 1909 *E*
Dixon, E J (Q) 1904 *BI* 3
Donald, K J (Q) 1957 *NZ* 1, 1958 *W*, *I*, *E*, *S*, *M* 2,3, 1959 *BI* 1,2
Dore, E (Q) 1904 *BI* 1
Dore, M J (Q) 1905 *NZ*
Dorr, R W (V) 1936 *M*, 1937 *SA* 1
Douglas, J A (V) 1962 *NZ* 3,4,5
Douglas, W A (NSW) 1922 *NZ* 3(R)
Dowse, J H (NSW) 1961 *Fj* 1,2, *SA* 1,2
Dunbar, A R (NSW) 1910 *NZ* 1,2,3, 1912 *US*
Duncan, J L (NSW) 1926 *NZ* 4
Dunlop, E E (V) 1932 *NZ* 3, 1934 *NZ* 1
Dunn, P K (NSW) 1958 *NZ* 1,2,3, 1959 *BI* 1,2
Dunn, V A (NSW) 1920 *NZ* 1,2,3, 1921 *SA* 1,2,3, *NZ*
Dunworth, D A (Q) 1971 *F* 1,2, 1972 *F* 1,2, 1976 *Fj* 2
Dwyer, L J (NSW) 1910 *NZ* 1,2,3, 1912 *US*, 1913 *NZ* 3, 1914 *NZ* 1,2,3
Dyson, F J (Q) 2000 *Arg* 1,2, *SA* 1, *NZ* 1, *SA* 2, *NZ* 2, *SA* 3, *F*, *S*, *E*

Eales, J A (Q) 1991 *W*, *E*, *NZ* 1,2, [*Arg*, *WS*, *W*, *I*, *NZ*, *E*], 1992 *S* 1,2, *NZ* 1,2,3, *SA*, 1994 *I* 1,2, *It* 1,2, *WS*, *NZ*, 1995 *Arg* 1,2, [*SA*, *C*, *R*, *E*], *NZ* 1,2, 1996 *W* 1,2, *C*, *NZ* 1, *SA* 1, *NZ* 2, *SA* 2, *It*, *S*, *I*, 1997 *F* 1,2, *NZ* 1, *E* 1, *NZ* 2, *SA* 1, *Arg* 1,2, *E* 2, *S*, 1998 *E* 1, *S* 1,2, *NZ* 1, *SA* 2, *NZ* 3, *Fj*, *Tg*, *WS*, *F*, *E* 2, 1999 [*R*, *I* 3, *W*, *SA* 3, *F*], 2000 *Arg* 1,2, *SA* 1, *NZ* 1, *SA* 2, *NZ* 2, *SA* 3, *F*, *S*, *E*, 2001 *BI* 1,2,3, *SA* 1, *NZ* 1, *SA* 2, *NZ* 2
Eastes, C C (NSW) 1946 *NZ* 1,2, 1947 *NZ* 1,2, 1949 *M* 1,2
Edmonds, M H M (NSW) 1998 *Tg*, 2001 *SA* 1(R)
Egerton, R H (NSW) 1991 *W*, *E*, *NZ* 1,2, [*Arg*, *W*, *I*, *NZ*, *E*]
Ella, G A (NSW) 1982 *NZ* 1,2, 1983 *F* 1,2, 1988 *E* 2, *NZ* 1
Ella, G J (NSW) 1982 *S* 1, 1983 *It*, 1985 *C* 2(R), *Fj* 2
Ella, M G (NSW) 1980 *NZ* 1,2,3, 1981 *F* 2, *S*, 1982 *E*, *S* 1, *NZ* 1,2,3, 1983 *US*, *Arg* 1,2, *NZ*, *It*, *F* 1,2, 1984 *NZ* 1,2,3, *E*, *I*, *W*, *S*
Ellem, M A (NSW) 1976 *Fj* 3(R)
Elliott, F M (NSW) 1957 *NZ* 1

Elliott, R E (NSW) 1920 *NZ* 1, 1921 *NZ*, 1922 *M* 1,2, *NZ* 1(R),2,3, 1923 *M* 1,2,3, *NZ* 1,2,3
Ellis, C S (NSW) 1899 *BI* 1,2,3,4
Ellis, K J (NSW) 1958 *NZ* 1,2,3, 1959 *BI* 1,2
Ellwood, B J (NSW) 1958 *NZ* 1,2,3, 1961 *Fj* 2,3, *SA* 1, *F*, 1962 *NZ* 1,2,3,4,5, 1963 *SA* 1,2,3,4, 1964 *NZ* 3, 1965 *SA* 1,2, 1966 *BI* 1
Emanuel, D M (NSW) 1957 *NZ* 2, 1958 *W, I, E, S, F, M* 1,2,3
Emery, N A (NSW) 1947 *NZ* 2, *S, I, W*, 1948 *E, F*, 1949 *M* 2,3, *NZ* 1,2
Erasmus, D J (NSW) 1923 *NZ* 1,2
Erby, A B (NSW) 1923 *M* 1,2, *NZ* 2,3, 1925 *NZ* 2
Evans, L J (Q) 1903 *NZ*, 1904 *BI* 1,3
Evans, W T (Q) 1899 *BI* 1,2

Fahey, E J (NSW) 1912 *US*, 1913 *NZ* 1,2, 1914 *NZ* 3
Fairfax, R L (NSW) 1971 *F* 1,2, 1972 *F* 1,2, *NZ* 1, *Fj*, 1973 *W, E*
Farmer, E H (Q) 1910 *NZ* 1
Farquhar, C R (NSW) 1920 *NZ* 2
Farr-Jones, N C (NSW) 1984 *E, I, W, S*, 1985 *C* 1,2, *NZ, Fj* 1,2, 1986 *It, F, Arg* 1,2, *NZ* 1,2,3, 1987 *SK*, [*E, I, F, W* (R)], *NZ, Arg* 2, 1988 *E* 1,2, *NZ* 1,2,3, *E, S, It*, 1989 *BI* 1,2,3, *NZ, F* 1,2, 1990 *F* 1,2,3, *US, NZ* 1,2,3, 1991 *W, E, NZ* 1,2, [*Arg, WS, I, NZ, E*], 1992 *S* 1,2, *NZ* 1,2,3, *SA*, 1993 *NZ, SA* 1,2,3
Fay, G (NSW) 1971 *SA* 2, 1972 *NZ* 1,2,3, 1973 *Tg* 1,2, *W, E*, 1974 *NZ* 1,2,3, 1975 *E* 1,2, *J* 1, *S, W*, 1976 *I, US*, 1978 *W* 1,2, *NZ* 1,2,3, 1979 *I* 1
Fenwicke, P T (NSW) 1957 *NZ* 1, 1958 *W, I, E*, 1959 *BI* 1,2
Ferguson, R T (NSW) 1922 *M* 3, *NZ* 1, 1923 *M* 3, *NZ* 3
Fihelly, J A (Q) 1907 *NZ* 2
Finau, S P (NSW) 1997 *NZ* 3
Finegan, O D A (ACT) 1996 *W* 1,2, *C, NZ* 1, *SA* 1(t), *S, W* 3, 1997 *SA* 1, *NZ* 3, *SA* 2, *Arg* 1,2, *E* 2, *S*, 1998 *E* 1(R), *S* 1(t + R),2(t + R), *NZ* 1(R), *SA* 1(t),2(R), *NZ* 3(R), *Fj* (R), *Tg, WS* (t + R), *F* (R), *E* 2(R), 1999 *NZ* 2(R), [*R, I* 3(R)], *US, W* (R), *SA* 3(R), *F* (R)], 2001 *BI* 1,2,3, *SA* 1, *NZ* 1, *SA* 2, *NZ* 2, *Sp, E, F, W*, 2002 *F* 1,2, *NZ* 1, *SA* 1, *NZ* 2, *SA* 2
Finlay, A N (NSW) 1926 *NZ* 1,2,3, 1927 *I, W, S*, 1928 *E, F*, 1929 *NZ* 1,2,3, 1930 *BI*
Finley, F G (NSW) 1904 *BI* 3
Finnane, S C (NSW) 1975 *E* 1, *J* 1,2, 1976 *E*, 1978 *W* 1,2
FitzSimons, P (NSW) 1989 *F* 1,2, 1990 *F* 1,2,3, *US, NZ* 1
Flanagan, P (Q) 1907 *NZ* 1,2
Flatley, E J (Q) 1997 *E* 2, *S*, 2000 *S* 2(R), 2001 *BI* 1(R),2(R),3, *SA* 1, *NZ* 1(R),2(R), *Sp* (R), *F* (R), *W*, 2002 *F* 1(R),2(R), *NZ* 1(t+R), *SA* 1(R), *NZ* 2(t)
Flett, J A (NSW) 1990 *US, NZ* 2,3, 1991 [*WS*]
Flynn, J P (Q) 1914 *NZ* 1,2
Fogarty, J R (Q) 1949 *M* 2,3
Foley, M A (Q) 1995 [*C* (R), *R*], 1996 *W* 2(R), *NZ* 1, *SA* 1, *NZ* 2, *SA* 2, *It, S, I, W* 3, 1997 *NZ* 1(R), *E* 1, *NZ* 2, *SA* 1, *NZ* 3, *SA* 2, *Arg* 1,2, *E* 2, *S*, 1998 *Tg* (R), *F* (R), *E* 2(R), 1999 *NZ* 2(R), [*US, W, SA* 3, *F*], 2000 *Arg* 1,2, *SA* 1, *NZ* 1, *SA* 2, *NZ* 2, *SA* 3, *F, S, E*, 2001 *BI* 1(R),2,3, *SA* 1, *NZ* 1, *SA* 2, *NZ* 2, *Sp, E, F, W*
Foote, R H (NSW) 1924 *NZ* 2,3, 1926 *NZ* 2
Forbes, C F (Q) 1953 *SA* 2,3,4, 1954 *Fj* 1, 1956 *SA* 1,2
Ford, B (Q) 1957 *NZ* 2
Ford, E E (NSW) 1927 *I, W, S*, 1928 *E, F*, 1929 *NZ* 1,3
Ford, J A (NSW) 1925 *NZ* 4, 1926 *NZ* 1,2, 1927 *I, W, S*, 1928 *E*, 1929 *NZ* 1,2,3, 1930 *BI*
Forman, T R (NSW) 1968 *I, S*, 1969 *W, SA* 1,2,3,4
Fowles, D G (NSW) 1921 *SA* 1,2,3, 1922 *M* 2,3, 1923 *M* 2,3
Fox, C L (NSW) 1920 *NZ* 1,2,3, 1921 *SA* 1, *NZ*, 1922 *M* 1,2, *NZ* 1, 1924 *NZ* 1,2,3, 1925 *NZ* 1,2,3, 1926 *NZ* 1,3, 1928 *F*
Fox, O G (NSW) 1958 *F*
Francis, E (Q) 1914 *NZ* 1,2
Frawley, D (Q, NSW) 1986 *Arg* 2(R), 1987 *Arg* 1,2, 1988 *E* 1,2, *NZ* 1,2,3, *S, It*
Freedman, J E (NSW) 1962 *NZ* 3,4,5, 1963 *SA* 1
Freeman, E (NSW) 1946 *NZ* 1(R), *M*
Freney, M E (Q) 1972 *NZ* 1,2,3, 1973 *Tg* 1, *W, E* (R)
Friend, W S (NSW) 1920 *NZ* 3, 1921 *SA* 1,2,3, 1922 *NZ* 1,2,3, 1923 *M* 1,2,3
Furness, D C (NSW) 1946 *M*
Futter, F C (NSW) 1904 *BI* 3

Gardner, J M (Q) 1987 *Arg* 2, 1988 *E* 1, *NZ* 1, *E*
Gardner, W C (NSW) 1950 *BI* 1
Garner, R L (NSW) 1949 *NZ* 1,2
Gavin, K A (NSW) 1909 *E*

Gavin, T B (NSW) 1988 *NZ* 2,3, *S, It* (R), 1989 *NZ* (R), *F* 1,2, 1990 *F* 1,2,3, *US, NZ* 1,2,3, 1991 *W, E, NZ* 1, 1992 *S* 1,2, *SA, I, W*, 1993 *Tg, NZ, SA* 1,2,3, *C, F* 1,2, 1994 *I* 1,2, *It* 1,2, *WS, NZ*, 1995 *Arg* 1,2, [*SA, C, R, E*], *NZ* 1,2, 1996 *NZ* 2(R), *SA* 2, *W* 3
Gelling, A M (NSW) 1972 *NZ* 1, *Fj*
George, H W (NSW) 1910 *NZ* 1,2,3, 1912 *US*, 1913 *NZ* 1,3, 1914 *NZ* 1,3
George, W G (NSW) 1923 *M* 1,3, *NZ* 1,2, 1924 *NZ* 3, 1925 *NZ* 2,3, 1926 *NZ* 4, 1928 *NZ* 1,2,3, *M*
Gibbons, E de C (NSW) 1936 *NZ* 1,2, *M*
Gibbs, P R (V) 1966 *S*
Giffin, D T (ACT) 1996 *W* 3, 1997 *F* 1,2, 1999 *I* 1,2, *E, SA* 1, *NZ* 1, *SA* 2, *NZ* 2, [*R, I* 3, *US* (R), *W, SA* 3, *F*], 2000 *Arg* 1,2, *SA* 1, *NZ* 1, *SA* 2, *NZ* 2, *SA* 3, *F, S, E*, 2001 *BI* 1,2, *SA* 1, *NZ* 2, *Sp, E, F, W*
Gilbert, H (NSW) 1910 *NZ* 1,2,3
Girvan, B (ACT) 1988 *E*
Gordon, G C (NSW) 1929 *NZ* 1
Gordon, K M (NSW) 1950 *BI* 1,2
Gould, R G (Q) 1980 *NZ* 1,2,3, 1981 *I, W, S*, 1982 *S* 2, *NZ* 1,2,3, 1983 *US, Arg* 1, *F* 1,2, 1984 *NZ* 1,2,3, *E, I, W, S*, 1985 *NZ*, 1986 *It*, 1987 *SK*, [*E*]
Gourley, S R (NSW) 1988 *S, It*, 1989 *BI* 1,2,3
Graham, C S (Q) 1899 *BI* 2
Graham, R (NSW) 1973 *Tg* 1,2, *W, E*, 1974 *NZ* 2,3, 1975 *E* 2, *J* 1,2, *S, W*, 1976 *I, US, Fj* 1,2,3, *F* 1,2
Gralton, A S I (Q) 1899 *BI* 1,4, 1903 *NZ*
Grant, J C (NSW) 1988 *E* 1, *NZ* 2,3, *E*
Graves, R H (NSW) 1907 *NZ* 1(R)
Greatorex, E N (NSW) 1923 *M* 3, *NZ* 1,2,3, 1925 *NZ* 1, 1928 *E, F*
Gregan, G M (ACT) 1994 *It* 1,2, *WS, NZ*, 1995 *Arg* 1,2, [*SA, C* (R), *R, E*], 1996 *W* 1, *C* (t), *SA* 1, *NZ* 2, *SA* 2, *It, I, W* 3, 1997 *F* 1,2, *NZ* 1, *E* 1, *NZ* 2, *SA* 1, *NZ* 3, *SA* 2, *Arg* 1,2, *E* 2, *S*, 1998 *E* 1, *S* 1,2, *NZ* 1, *SA* 1, *NZ* 2, *SA* 2, *NZ* 3, *Fj, WS, F, E* 2, 1999 *I* 1,2, *E, SA* 1, *NZ* 1, *SA* 2, *NZ* 2, [*R, I* 3, *W, SA* 3, *F*], 2000 *Arg* 1,2, *SA* 1, *NZ* 1, *SA* 2, *NZ* 2, *SA* 3, 2001 *BI* 1,2,3, *SA* 1, *NZ* 1, *SA* 2, *NZ* 2, *Sp, E, F, W*, 2002 *F* 1,2, *NZ* 1, *SA* 1, *NZ* 2, *SA* 2
Gregory, S C (Q) 1968 *NZ* 3, *F, I, S*, 1969 *SA* 1,3, 1971 *SA* 1,3, *F* 1,2, 1972 *F* 1,2, 1973 *Tg* 1,2, *W, E*
Grey, G O (NSW) 1972 *F* 2(R), *NZ* 1,2,3, *Fj* (R)
Grey, N P (NSW) 1998 *S* 2(R), *SA* 2(R), *Fj* (R), *Tg* (R), *F, E* 2, 1999 *I* 1(R),2(R), *E, SA* 1, *NZ* 1, *SA* 2, *NZ* 2(t&R), [*R* (R), *I* 3(R), *US, SA* 3(R), *F* (R)], 2000 *S* (R), *E* (R), 2001 *BI* 1,2,3, *SA* 1, *NZ* 1, *SA* 2, *NZ* 2, *Sp, E, F*
Griffin, T S (NSW) 1907 *NZ* 1,3, 1908 *W*, 1910 *NZ* 1,2, 1912 *US*
Grigg, P C (Q) 1980 *NZ* 3, 1982 *S* 2, *NZ* 1,2,3, 1983 *Arg* 2, *NZ*, 1984 *Fj, W, S*, 1985 *C* 1,2, *NZ, Fj* 1,2, 1986 *Arg* 1,2, *NZ* 1,2, 1987 *SK*, [*E, J, I, F, W*]
Grimmond, D N (NSW) 1964 *NZ* 2
Gudsell, K E (NSW) 1951 *NZ* 1,2,3
Guerassimoff, J (Q) 1963 *SA* 2,3,4, 1964 *NZ* 1,2,3, 1965 *SA* 2, 1966 *BI* 1,2, 1967 *E, I, F*
Gunther, W J (NSW) 1957 *NZ* 2

Hall, D (Q) 1980 *Fj, NZ* 1,2,3, 1981 *F* 1,2, 1982 *S* 1,2, *NZ* 1,2, 1983 *US, Arg* 1,2, *NZ, It*
Hamalainen, H A (Q) 1929 *NZ* 1,2,3
Hamilton, B G (NSW) 1946 *M*
Hammand, C A (NSW) 1908 *W*, 1909 *E*
Hammon, J D C (V) 1937 *SA* 2
Handy, C B (Q) 1978 *NZ* 3, 1979 *NZ, Arg* 1,2, 1980 *NZ* 1,2
Hanley, R G (Q) 1983 *US* (R), *It* (R), 1985 *Fj* 2(R)
Hardcastle, P A (NSW) 1946 *NZ* 1, *M, NZ* 2, 1947 *NZ* 1, 1949 *M* 3
Hardcastle, W R (NSW) 1899 *BI* 4, 1903 *NZ*
Harding, M A (NSW) 1983 *It*
Hardman, S P (Q) 2002 *F* 2(R)
Hardy, M D (ACT) 1997 *F* 1(t), 2(R), *NZ* 1(R), 3(R), *Arg* 1(R), 2(R), 1998 *Tg, WS*
Harrison, J B (ACT) 2001 *BI* 3, *NZ* 1, *SA* 2, *Sp, E, F, W* (R), 2002 *F* 1,2, *NZ* 1, *SA* 1, *NZ* 2, *SA* 2
Harry, R L L (NSW) 1996 *W* 1,2, *NZ* 1, *SA* 1(t), *NZ* 2, *It, S*, 1997 *F* 1,2, *NZ* 1,2, *SA* 1, *NZ* 3, *SA* 2, *Arg* 1,2, *E* 2, *S*, 1998 *E* 1, *S* 1,2, *NZ* 1, *SA* 1, *Fj*, 1999 *SA* 2, *NZ* 2, [*R, I* 3, *W, SA* 3, *F*], 2000 *Arg* 1,2, *SA* 1, *NZ* 1, *SA* 2, *NZ* 2, *SA* 3
Hartill, M N (NSW) 1986 *NZ* 1,2,3, 1987 *SK*, [*J*], *Arg* 1, 1988 *NZ* 1,2, *E, It*, 1989 *BI* 1(R), 2,3, *F* 1,2, 1995 *Arg* 1(R), 2(R), [*C*], *NZ* 1,2
Harvey, P B (Q) 1949 *M* 1,2

Harvey, R M (NSW) 1958 *F, M* 3
Hatherell, W I (Q) 1952 *Fj* 1,2
Hauser, R G (Q) 1975 *J* 1(R), 2, *W* (R), 1976 *E, I, US, Fj* 1,2,3, *F* 1,2, 1978 *W* 1,2, 1979 *I* 1,2
Hawker, M J (NSW) 1980 *Fj, NZ* 1,2,3, 1981 *F* 1,2, *I, W,* 1982 *E, S* 1,2, *NZ* 1,2,3, 1983 *US, Arg* 1,2, *NZ, It, F* 1,2, 1984 *NZ* 1,2,3, 1987 *NZ*
Hawthorne, P F (NSW) 1962 *NZ* 3,4,5, 1963 *E, SA* 1,2,3,4, 1964 *NZ* 1,2,3, 1965 *SA* 1,2, 1966 *BI* 1,2, *W,* 1967 *E, I* 1, *F, I* 2, *NZ*
Hayes, E S (Q) 1934 *NZ* 1,2, 1938 *NZ* 1,2,3
Heath, A (NSW) 1996 *C, SA* 1, *NZ* 2, *SA* 2, *It,* 1997 *NZ* 2, *SA* 1, *E* 2(R)
Heinrich, E L (NSW) 1961 *Fj* 1,2,3, *SA* 2, *F,* 1962 *NZ* 1,2,3, 1963 *E, SA* 1
Heinrich, V W (NSW) 1954 *Fj* 1,2
Heming, R J (NSW) 1961 *Fj* 2,3, *SA* 1,2, *F,* 1962 *NZ* 2,3,4,5, 1963 *SA* 2,3,4, 1964 *NZ* 1,2,3, 1965 *SA* 1,2, 1966 *BI* 1,2, *W,* 1967 *F*
Hemingway, W H (NSW) 1928 *NZ* 2,3, 1931 *M, NZ,* 1932 *NZ* 3
Henry, A R (Q) 1899 *BI* 2
Herbert, A G (Q) 1987 *SK* (R), [*F* (R)], 1990 *F* 1(R), *US, NZ* 2,3, 1991 [*WS*], 1992 *NZ* 3(R), 1993 *NZ* (R), *SA* 2(R)
Herbert, D J (Q) 1994 *I* 2, *It* 1,2, *WS* (R), 1995 *Arg* 1,2, [*SA, R*], 1996 *C, SA* 2, *It, S, I,* 1997 *NZ* 1, 1998 *E* 1, *S* 1,2, *NZ* 1, *SA* 1, *NZ* 2, *SA* 2, *Fj, Tg, WS, F, E* 2, 1999 *I* 1,2, *E, SA* 1, *NZ* 1, *SA* 2, *NZ* 2, [*R, I* 3, *W, SA* 3, *F*], 2000 *Arg* 1,2, *SA* 1, *NZ* 1, *SA* 2, *NZ* 2, *SA* 3, *F, S, E,* 2001 *BI* 1,2,3, *SA* 1, *NZ* 1, *SA* 2, *NZ* 2, *Sp, E,* 2002 *F* 1, *NZ* 1, *SA* 1, *NZ* 2, *SA* 2
Herd, H V (NSW) 1931 *M*
Hickey, J (NSW) 1908 *W,* 1909 *E*
Hill, J (NSW) 1925 *NZ* 1
Hillhouse, D W (Q) 1975 *S,* 1976 *E, Fj* 1,2,3, *F* 1,2, 1978 *W* 1,2, 1983 *US, Arg* 1,2, *NZ, It, F* 1,2
Hills, E F (V) 1950 *BI* 1,2
Hindmarsh, J A (Q) 1904 *BI* 1
Hindmarsh, J C (NSW) 1975 *J* 2, *S, W,* 1976 *US, Fj* 1,2,3, *F* 1,2
Hipwell, J N B (NSW) 1968 *NZ* 1(R), 2, *F, I, S,* 1969 *W, SA* 1,2,3,4, 1970 *S,* 1971 *SA* 1,2, *F* 1,2, 1972 *F* 1,2, 1973 *Tg* 1, *W, E,* 1974 *NZ* 1,2,3, 1975 *E* 1,2, *J* 1, *S, W,* 1978 *NZ* 1,2,3, 1981 *F* 1,2, *I, W,* 1982 *E*
Hirschberg, W A (NSW) 1905 *NZ*
Hodgins, C H (NSW) 1910 *NZ* 1,2,3
Hodgson, A J (NSW) 1933 *SA* 2,3,4, 1934 *NZ* 1, 1936 *NZ* 1,2, *M,* 1937 *SA* 2, 1938 *NZ* 1,2,3
Holbeck, J C (ACT) 1997 *NZ* 1(R), *E* 1, *NZ* 2, *SA* 1, *NZ* 3, *SA* 2, 2001 *BI* 3(R)
Holdsworth, J W (NSW) 1921 *SA* 1,2,3, 1922 *M* 2,3, *NZ* 1(R)
Holt, N C (Q) 1984 *Fj*
Honan, B D (Q) 1968 *NZ* 1(R), 2, *F, I, S,* 1969 *SA* 1,2,3,4
Honan, R E (Q) 1964 *NZ* 1
Horan, T J (Q) 1989 *NZ, F* 1,2, 1990 *F* 1, *NZ* 1,2,3, 1991 *W, E, NZ* 1,2, [*Arg, WS, W, I, NZ, E*], 1992 *S* 1,2, *NZ* 1,2,3, *SA,* 1993 *Tg, NZ, SA* 1,2,3, *C, F* 1,2, 1995 [*C, R, E*], *NZ* 1,2, 1996 *W* 1,2, *C, NZ* 1, *SA* 1, *It, S, I, W* 3, 1997 *F* 1,2, *NZ* 1, *Arg* 1,2, *E* 2, *S,* 1998 *E* 1, *S* 1,2, *NZ* 1, *SA* 1, *NZ* 2, *SA* 2, *NZ* 3, *Fj, Tg, WS,* 1999 *I* 1,2, *E, SA* 1, *NZ* 1, *SA* 2, *NZ* 2, [*R, I* 3, *W, SA* 3, *F*], 2000 *Arg* 1
Horodam, D J (Q) 1913 *NZ* 2
Horsley, G R (Q) 1954 *Fj* 2
Horton, P A (NSW) 1974 *NZ* 1,2,3, 1975 *E* 1,2, *J* 1,2, *S, W,* 1976 *E, F* 1,2, 1978 *W* 1,2, *NZ* 1,2,3, 1979 *NZ, Arg* 1
Hoskins, J E (NSW) 1924 *NZ* 1,2,3
How, R A (NSW) 1967 *I* 2
Howard, J (Q) 1938 *NZ* 1,2
Howard, J L (NSW) 1970 *S,* 1971 *SA* 1, 1972 *F* 1(R), *NZ* 2, 1973 *Tg* 1,2, *W*
Howard, P W (Q, ACT) 1993 *NZ,* 1994 *WS, NZ,* 1995 *NZ* 1(R), 2(t), 1996 *W* 1,2, *SA* 1, *NZ* 2, *SA* 2, *It, S, W* 3, 1997 *F* 1,2, *NZ* 1, *Arg* 1,2, *E* 2, *S*
Howell, M L (NSW) 1946 *NZ* 1(R), 1947 *NZ* 1, *S, I, W*
Hughes, B D (NSW) 1913 *NZ* 2
Hughes, J C (NSW) 1907 *NZ* 1,3
Hughes, N McL (NSW) 1953 *SA* 1,2,3,4, 1955 *NZ* 1,2,3, 1956 *SA* 1,2, 1958 *W, I, E, S, F*
Humphreys, O W (NSW) 1920 *NZ* 3, 1921 *NZ,* 1922 *M* 1,2,3, 1925 *NZ* 1
Hutchinson, E E (NSW) 1937 *SA* 1,2
Hutchinson, F E (NSW) 1936 *NZ* 1,2, 1938 *NZ* 1,3

Ide, W P J (Q) 1938 *NZ* 2,3
Ives, W N (NSW) 1926 *NZ* 1,2,3,4, 1929 *NZ* 3

James, P M (Q) 1958 *M* 2,3
James, S L (NSW) 1987 *SK* (R), [*E* (R)], *NZ, Arg* 1,2, 1988 *NZ* 2(R)
Jamieson, A E (NSW) 1925 *NZ* 3(R)
Jaques, T (ACT) 2000 *SA* 1(R), *NZ* 1(R)
Jessep, E M (V) 1934 *NZ* 1,2
Johnson, A P (NSW) 1946 *NZ* 1, *M*
Johnson, B B (NSW) 1952 *Fj* 1,2, *NZ* 1,2, 1953 *SA* 2,3,4, 1955 *NZ* 1,2
Johnson, P G (NSW) 1959 *BI* 1,2, 1961 *Fj* 1,2,3, *SA* 1,2, *F,* 1962 *NZ* 1,2,3,4,5, 1963 *E, SA* 1,2,3,4, 1964 *NZ* 1,2,3, 1965 *SA* 1,2, 1966 *BI* 1,2, *W, S,* 1967 *E, I* 1, *F, I* 2, *NZ,* 1968 *NZ* 1,2, *F, I, S,* 1970 *S,* 1971 *SA* 1,2, *F* 1,2
Johnstone, B (Q) 1993 *Tg* (R)
Jones, G G (Q) 1952 *Fj* 1,2, 1953 *SA* 1,2,3,4, 1954 *Fj* 1,2, 1955 *NZ* 1,2,3, 1956 *SA* 1
Jones, H (NSW) 1913 *NZ* 1,2,3
Jones, P A (NSW) 1963 *E, SA* 1
Jorgensen, P (NSW) 1992 *S* 1(R), 2(R)
Joyce, J E (NSW) 1903 *NZ*
Judd, H A (NSW) 1903 *NZ,* 1904 *BI* 1,2,3, 1905 *NZ*
Judd, P B (NSW) 1925 *NZ* 4, 1926 *NZ* 1,2,3,4, 1927 *I, W, S,* 1928 *E,* 1931 *M, NZ*
Junee, D K (NSW) 1989 *F* 1(R), 2(R), 1994 *WS* (R), *NZ* (R)

Kafer, R B (ACT) 1999 *NZ* 2, [*R, US* (R)], 2000 *Arg* 1(R),2, *SA* 1, *NZ* 1(t&R), *SA* 2(R),3(R), *F, S, E*
Kahl, P R (Q) 1992 *W*
Kassulke, N (Q) 1985 *C* 1,2
Kay, A R (V) 1958 *NZ* 2, 1959 *BI* 2
Kay, P (NSW) 1988 *E* 2
Kearney, K H (NSW) 1947 *NZ* 1,2, *S, I, W,* 1948 *E, F*
Kearns, P N (NSW) 1989 *NZ, F* 1,2, 1990 *F* 1,2,3, *US, NZ* 1,2,3, 1991 *W, E, NZ* 1,2, [*Arg, WS, W, I, NZ, E*], 1992 *S* 1,2, *NZ* 1,2,3, *SA, I, W,* 1993 *Tg, NZ, SA* 1,2,3, *C, F* 1,2, 1994 *I* 1,2, *It* 1,2, *WS, NZ,* 1995 *Arg* 1,2, [*SA, C, E*], *NZ* 1,2, 1998 *E* 1, *S* 1,2, *NZ* 1, *SA* 1, *NZ* 2, *SA* 2, *NZ* 3, *Fj, WS, F, E* 2, 1999 *I* 2(R), *SA* 1(R),2, *NZ* 2, [*R, I* 3]
Kefu, R S T (Q) 1997 *SA* 2(R), 1998 *E* 1, *S* 1,2, *NZ* 1, *SA* 1, *NZ* 2, *SA* 2, *NZ* 3, *Fj* (R), *Tg, WS* (R), *F, E* 2, 1999 *I* 1,2, *E, SA* 1, *NZ* 1(R), *SA* 2, *NZ* 2, [*R, I* 3, *SA* 3, *F*], 2000 *SA* 1(t&R), *NZ* 1(R), *SA* 2(R), *NZ* 2, *SA* 3(R), *F, S, E,* 2001 *BI* 1,2,3, *SA* 1, *NZ* 1, *SA* 2, *NZ* 2, *Sp, E, F, W,* 2002 *F* 1, *NZ* 1, *SA* 1, *NZ* 2, *SA* 2
Kefu, S (Q) 2001 *W* (R)
Kelaher, J D (NSW) 1933 *SA* 1,2,3,4,5, 1934 *NZ* 1,2, 1936 *NZ* 1,2, *M,* 1937 *SA* 1,2, 1938 *NZ* 3
Kelaher, T P (NSW) 1992 *NZ* 1, *I* (R), 1993 *NZ*
Kelleher, R J (Q) 1969 *SA* 2,3
Keller, D H (NSW) 1947 *NZ* 1, *S, I, W,* 1948 *E, F*
Kelly, A J (NSW) 1899 *BI* 1
Kelly, R L F (NSW) 1936 *NZ* 1,2, *M,* 1937 *SA* 1,2, 1938 *NZ* 1,2
Kent, A (Q) 1912 *US*
Kerr, F R (V) 1938 *NZ* 1
King, S C (NSW) 1926 *NZ* 1,2,3,4(R), 1927 *W, S,* 1928 *E, F,* 1929 *NZ* 1,2,3, 1930 *BI,* 1932 *NZ* 1,2
Knight, M (NSW) 1978 *W* 1,2, *NZ* 1
Knight, S O (NSW) 1969 *SA* 2,4, 1970 *S,* 1971 *SA* 1,2,3
Knox, D J (NSW, ACT) 1985 *Fj* 1,2, 1990 *US* (R), 1994 *WS, NZ,* 1996 *It, S, I,* 1997 *SA* 1, *NZ* 3, *SA* 2, *Arg* 1,2
Kraefft, D F (NSW) 1947 *NZ* 2, *S, I, W,* 1948 *E, F*
Kreutzer, S D (Q) 1914 *NZ* 2

Lamb, J S (NSW) 1928 *NZ* 1,2, *M*
Lambie, J K (NSW) 1974 *NZ* 1,2,3, 1975 *W*
Lane, R E (NSW) 1921 *SA* 1
Lane, T A (Q) 1985 *C* 1,2, *NZ*
Lang, C W P (V) 1938 *NZ* 2,3
Langford, J F (ACT) 1997 *NZ* 3, *SA* 2, *E* 2, *S*
Larkham, S J (ACT) 1996 *W* 2(R), 1997 *F* 1,2, *NZ* 1,2(R), *SA* 1, *NZ* 3, *SA* 2, *Arg* 1,2, *E* 2, *S,* 1998 *E* 1, *S* 1,2, *NZ* 1, *SA* 1, *NZ* 2, *SA* 2, *NZ* 3, *Fj, Tg* (t), *WS, F, E* 2, 1999 [*I* 3, *US, W, SA* 3, *F*], 2000 *Arg* 1,2, *SA* 1, *NZ* 1, *SA* 2, *NZ* 2, *SA* 3, *F,* 2001 *BI* 1,2, *NZ* 1, *SA* 2, *NZ* 2, *Sp, E, F, W,* 2002 *F* 1,2, *NZ* 1, *SA* 1, *NZ* 2, *SA* 2
Larkin, E R (NSW) 1903 *NZ*
Larkin, K K (Q) 1958 *M* 2,3

Latham, C E (Q) 1998 *F, E* 2, 1999 *I* 1,2, *E*, [*US*], 2000 *Arg* 1,2, *SA* 1, *NZ* 1, *SA* 2, *NZ* 2, *SA* 3, *F, S, E*, 2001 *BI* 1,2(R), *SA* 1(R), *NZ* 1(R), *SA* 2, *NZ* 2, *Sp, E, F, W* (R), 2002 *F* 1,2, *NZ* 1, *SA* 1, *NZ* 2, *SA* 2
Latimer, N B (NSW) 1957 *NZ* 2
Lawton, R (Q) 1988 *E* 1, *NZ* 2(R), 3, *S*
Lawton, T (NSW, Q) 1920 *NZ* 1,2, 1925 *NZ* 4, 1927 *I, W, S*, 1928 *E, F*, 1929 *NZ* 1,2,3, 1930 *BI*, 1932 *NZ* 1,2
Lawton, T A (Q) 1983 *F* 1(R), 2, 1984 *Fj, NZ* 1,2,3, *E, I, W, S*, 1985 *C* 1,2, *NZ, Fj* 1, 1986 *It, F, Arg* 1,2, *NZ* 1,2,3, 1987 *SK*, [*E, US, I, F, W*], *NZ, Arg* 1,2, 1988 *E* 1,2, *NZ* 1,2,3, *E, S, It*, 1989 *BI* 1,2,3
Laycock, W M B (NSW) 1925 *NZ* 2,3,4, 1926 *NZ* 2
Leeds, A J (NSW) 1986 *NZ* 3, 1987 [*US, W*], *NZ, Arg* 1,2, 1988 *E* 1,2, *NZ* 1,2,3, *E, S, It*
Lenehan, J K (NSW) 1958 *W, E, S, F, M* 1,2,3, 1959 *BI* 1,2, 1961 *SA* 1,2, *F*, 1962 *NZ* 2,3,4,5, 1965 *SA* 1,2, 1966 *W, S*, 1967 *E, I* 1, *F I* 2
L'Estrange, R D (Q) 1971 *F* 1,2, 1972 *NZ* 1,2,3, 1973 *Tg* 1,2, *W, E*, 1974 *NZ* 1,2,3, 1975 *S, W*, 1976 *I, US*
Lewis, L S (Q) 1934 *NZ* 1,2, 1936 *NZ* 2, 1938 *NZ* 1
Lidbury, S (NSW) 1987 *Arg* 1, 1988 *E* 2
Lillicrap, C P (Q) 1985 *Fj* 2, 1987 [*US, I, F, W*], 1989 *BI* 1, 1991 [*WS*]
Lindsay, R T G (Q) 1932 *NZ* 3
Lisle, R J (NSW) 1961 *Fj* 1,2,3, *SA* 1
Little, J S (Q, NSW) 1989 *F* 1,2, 1990 *F* 1,2,3, *US*, 1991 *W, E, NZ* 1,2, [*Arg, W, I, NZ, E*], 1992 *NZ* 1,2,3, *SA, I, W*, 1993 *Tg, NZ, SA* 1,2,3, *C, F* 1,2, 1994 *WS, NZ*, 1995 *Arg* 1,2, [*SA, C, E*], *NZ* 1,2, 1996 *It* (R), *I, W, S*, 1997 *F* 1,2, *E* 1, *NZ* 2, *SA* 1, *NZ* 2, *SA* 2(R), *NZ* 3, *Fj, Tg, WS, F, E* 2, 1999 *I* 1(R),2, *SA* 2(R), *NZ* 2, [*R, I* 3(t&R), *US, W* (R), *SA* 3(t&R), *F* (R)], 2000 *Arg* 1(R),2(R), *SA* 1(R), *NZ* 1, *SA* 2, *NZ* 2, *SA* 3
Livermore, A E (Q) 1946 *NZ* 1, *M*
Loane, M E (Q) 1973 *Tg* 1,2, 1974 *NZ* 1, 1975 *E* 1,2, *J* 1, 1976 *E, I, Fj* 1,2,3, *F* 1,2, 1978 *W, I*, 1979 *I* 1,2, *NZ, Arg* 1,2, 1981 *F* 1,2, *I, W, S*, 1982 *E, S* 1,2
Logan, D L (NSW) 1958 *M* 1
Loudon, D B (NSW) 1921 *NZ*, 1922 *M* 1,2,3
Loudon, R B (NSW) 1923 *NZ* 1(R), 2,3, 1928 *NZ* 1,2,3, *M*, 1929 *NZ* 2, 1933 *SA* 2,3,4,5, 1934 *NZ* 2
Love, E W (NSW) 1932 *NZ* 1,2,3
Lowth, D R (NSW) 1958 *NZ* 1
Lucas, B C (Q) 1905 *NZ*
Lucas, P W (NSW) 1982 *NZ* 1,2,3
Lutge, D (NSW) 1903 *NZ*, 1904 *BI* 1,2,3
Lynagh, M P (Q) 1984 *Fj, E, I, W, S*, 1985 *C* 1,2, *NZ*, 1986 *It, F, Arg* 1,2, *NZ* 1,2,3, 1987 [*E, US, J, I, F, W*], *Arg* 1,2, 1988 *E* 1,2, *NZ* 1,3(R), *E, S, It*, 1989 *BI* 1,2,3, *NZ, F* 1,2, 1990 *F* 1,2,3, *US, NZ* 1,2,3, 1991 *W, E, NZ* 1,2, [*Arg, WS, W, I, NZ, E*], 1992 *S* 1,2, *NZ* 1,2,3, *SA, I*, 1993 *Tg, C, F* 1,2, 1994 *I* 1,2, *It* 1, 1995 *Arg* 1,2, [*SA, C, E*]
Lyons, D J (NSW) 2000 *Arg* 1(t&R),2(R), 2001 *BI* 1(R), *SA* 1(R), 2002 *F* 1(R),2, *NZ* 1(R), *SA* 1(R), *NZ* 2(R), *SA* 2(t+R)

McArthur, M (NSW) 1909 *E*
McBain, M I (Q) 1983 *It, F* 1, 1985 *Fj* 2, 1986 *It* (R), 1987 [*J*], 1988 *E* 2(R), 1989 *BI* 1(R)
MacBride, J W T (NSW) 1946 *NZ* 1, *M, NZ* 2, 1947 *NZ* 1,2, *S, I, W*, 1948 *E, F*
McCabe, A J M (NSW) 1909 *E*
McCall, R J (Q) 1989 *F* 1,2, 1990 *F* 1,2,3, *US, NZ* 1,2,3, 1991 *W, E, NZ* 1,2, [*Arg, W, I, NZ, E*], 1992 *S* 1,2, *NZ* 1,2,3, *SA, I, W*, 1993 *Tg, NZ, SA* 1,2,3, *C, F* 1,2, 1994 *It* 2, 1995 *Arg* 1,2, [*SA, R, E*]
McCarthy, F J C (Q) 1950 *BI* 1
McCowan, R H (Q) 1899 *BI* 1,2,4
McCue, P A (NSW) 1907 *NZ* 1,3, 1908 *W*, 1909 *E*
McDermott, L C (Q) 1962 *NZ* 1,2
McDonald, B S (NSW) 1969 *SA* 4, 1970 *S*
McDonald, J C (Q) 1938 *NZ* 2,3
Macdougall, D G (NSW) 1961 *Fj* 1, *SA* 1
Macdougall, S G (NSW, ACT) 1971 *SA* 3, 1973 *E*, 1974 *NZ* 1,2,3, 1975 *E* 1,2, 1976 *E*
McGhie, G H (Q) 1929 *NZ* 2,3, 1930 *BI*
McGill, A N (NSW) 1968 *NZ* 1,2, *F*, 1969 *W, SA* 1,2,3,4, 1970 *S*, 1971 *SA* 1,2,3, *F* 1,2, 1972 *F* 1,2, *NZ* 1,2,3, 1973 *Tg* 1,2
McIntyre, A J (Q) 1982 *NZ* 1,2,3, 1983 *F* 1,2, 1984 *Fj, NZ* 1,2,3, *E, I, W, S*, 1985 *C* 1,2, *NZ, Fj* 1,2, 1986 *It, F, Arg* 1,2, 1987 [*E, US, I, F, W*], *NZ, Arg* 2, 1988 *E* 1,2, *NZ* 1,2,3, *E, S, It*, 1989 *NZ*

McKay, G R (NSW) 1920 *NZ* 2, 1921 *SA* 2,3, 1922 *M* 1,2,3
McKenzie, E J A (NSW, ACT) 1990 *F* 1,2,3, *US, NZ* 1,2,3, 1991 *W, E, NZ* 1,2, [*Arg, W, I, NZ, E*], 1992 *S* 1,2, *NZ* 1,2,3, *SA, I, W*, 1993 *Tg, NZ, SA* 1,2,3, *C, F* 1,2, 1994 *I* 1,2, *It* 1,2, *WS, NZ*, 1995 *Arg* 1,2, [*SA, C* (R), *R, E*], *NZ* 2, 1996 *W* 1,2, 1997 *F* 1,2, *NZ* 1, *E* 1
McKid, W A (NSW) 1976 *E, Fj* 1, 1978 *NZ* 2,3, 1979 *I* 1,2
McKinnon, A (Q) 1904 *BI* 2
McKivat, C H (NSW) 1907 *NZ* 1,3, 1908 *W*, 1909 *E*
McLaren, S D (NSW) 1926 *NZ* 4
McLaughlin, R E M (NSW) 1936 *NZ* 1,2
McLean, A D (Q) 1933 *SA* 1,2,3,4,5, 1934 *NZ* 1,2, 1936 *NZ* 1,2, *M*
McLean, J D (Q) 1904 *BI* 2,3, 1905 *NZ*
McLean, J J (Q) 1971 *SA* 2,3, *F* 1,2, 1972 *F* 1,2, *NZ* 1,2,3, *Fj*, 1973 *W, E*, 1974 *NZ* 1
McLean, P E (Q) 1974 *NZ* 1,2,3, 1975 *J* 1,2, *S, W*, 1976 *E, I, Fj* 1,2,3, *F* 1,2, 1978 *W* 1,2, *NZ* 2, 1979 *I* 1,2, *NZ, Arg* 1,2, 1980 *Fj*, 1981 *F* 1,2, *I, W, S*, 1982 *E, S* 2
McLean, P W (Q) 1978 *NZ* 1,2,3, 1979 *I* 1,2, *NZ, Arg* 1,2, 1980 *Fj* (R), *NZ* 3, 1981 *I, W, S*, 1982 *E, S* 1,2
McLean, R A (NSW) 1971 *SA* 1,2,3, *F* 1,2
McLean, W M (Q) 1946 *NZ* 1, *M, NZ* 2, 1947 *NZ* 1,2
McMahon, M (Q) 1913 *NZ* 1
McMaster, R E (Q) 1946 *NZ* 1, *M, NZ* 2, 1947 *NZ* 1,2, *I, W*
MacMillan, D I (Q) 1950 *BI* 1,2
McMullen, K V (NSW) 1962 *NZ* 3,5, 1963 *E, SA* 1
McShane, J M S (NSW) 1937 *SA* 1,2
Mackay, G (NSW) 1926 *NZ* 4
Mackney, W A R (NSW) 1933 *SA* 1,5, 1934 *NZ* 1,2
Magrath, E (NSW) 1961 *Fj* 1, *SA* 2, *F*
Maguire, D J (Q) 1989 *BI* 1,2,3
Malcolm, S J (NSW) 1927 *S*, 1928 *E, F, NZ* 1,2, *M*, 1929 *NZ* 1,2,3, 1930 *BI*, 1931 *NZ*, 1932 *NZ* 1,2,3, 1933 *SA* 4,5, 1934 *NZ* 1,2
Malone, J H (NSW) 1936 *NZ* 1,2, *M*, 1937 *SA* 2
Malouf, B P (NSW) 1982 *NZ* 1
Mandible, E F (NSW) 1907 *NZ* 2,3, 1908 *W*
Manning, J (NSW) 1904 *BI* 2
Manning, R C S (Q) 1967 *NZ*
Mansfield, B W (NSW) 1975 *J* 2
Manu, D T (NSW) 1995 [*R* (t)], *NZ* 1,2, 1996 *W* 1,2(R), *SA* 1, *NZ* 2, *It, S, I*, 1997 *F* 1, *NZ* 1(t), *E* 1, *NZ* 2, *SA* 1
Marks, H (NSW) 1899 *BI* 1,2
Marks, R J P (Q) 1962 *NZ* 4,5, 1963 *E, SA* 2,3,4, 1964 *NZ* 1,2,3, 1965 *SA* 1,2, 1966 *W, S*, 1967 *E, I* 1, *F, I* 2
Marrott, R (NSW) 1920 *NZ* 1,3
Marrott, W J (NSW) 1922 *NZ* 2,3, 1923 *M* 1,2,3, *NZ* 1,2
Marshall, J S (NSW) 1949 *M* 1
Martin, G J (Q) 1989 *BI* 1,2,3, *NZ, F* 1,2, 1990 *F* 1,3(R), *NZ* 1
Martin, M C (NSW) 1980 *Fj, NZ* 1,2, 1981 *F* 1,2, *W* (R)
Massey-Westropp, M (NSW) 1914 *NZ* 3
Mathers, M J (NSW) 1980 *Fj, NZ* 2(R)
Maund, J W (NSW) 1903 *NZ*
Mayne, A V (NSW) 1920 *NZ* 1,2,3, 1922 *M* 1
Meadows, J E C (V, Q) 1974 *NZ* 1, 1975 *S, W*, 1976 *I, US, Fj* 1,3, *F* 1,2, 1978 *NZ* 1,2,3, 1979 *I* 1,2, 1981 *I, S*, 1982 *E, NZ* 2,3, 1983 *US, Arg* 2, *NZ*
Meadows, R W (NSW) 1958 *M* 1,2,3, *NZ* 1,2,3
Meagher, F W (NSW) 1923 *NZ* 3, 1924 *NZ* 3, 1925 *NZ* 4, 1926 *NZ* 1,2,3, 1927 *I, W*
Meibusch, J H (Q) 1904 *BI* 3
Meibusch, L S (Q) 1912 *US*
Melrose, T C (NSW) 1978 *NZ* 3, 1979 *I* 1,2, *NZ, Arg* 1,2
Merrick, S (NSW) 1995 *NZ* 1,2
Messenger, H H (NSW) 1907 *NZ* 2,3
Middleton, S A (NSW) 1909 *E*, 1910 *NZ* 1,2,3
Miller, A R (NSW) 1952 *Fj* 1,2, *NZ* 1,2, 1953 *SA* 1,2,3,4, 1954 *Fj* 1,2, 1955 *NZ* 1,2,3, 1956 *SA* 1,2, 1957 *NZ* 1,2, 1958 *W, E, S, F, M* 1,2,3, 1959 *BI* 1,2, 1961 *Fj* 1,2,3, *SA* 2, *F*, 1962 *NZ* 1,2, 1966 *W, S*, 1967 *I* 1, *F, I* 2, *NZ*
Miller, J M (NSW) 1962 *NZ* 1, 1963 *E, SA* 1, 1966 *W, S*, 1967 *E*
Miller, J S (Q) 1986 *NZ* 2,3, 1987 *SK*, [*US, I, F*], *NZ, Arg* 1,2, 1988 *E* 1,2, *NZ* 2,3, *E, S, It*, 1989 *BI* 1,2,3, *NZ*, 1990 *F* 1,3, 1991 *W*, [*WS, W, I*]
Miller, S W J (NSW) 1899 *BI* 3
Mingey, N (NSW) 1920 *NZ* 3, 1921 *SA* 1,2,3, 1923 *M* 1, *NZ* 1,2
Monaghan, L E (NSW) 1973 *E*, 1974 *NZ* 1,2,3, 1975 *E* 1,2, *S, W*, 1976 *E, I, US, F* 1, 1978 *W* 1,2, *NZ* 1, 1979 *I* 1,2
Monti, C I A (Q) 1938 *NZ* 2

Moon, B J (Q) 1978 *NZ* 2,3, 1979 *I* 1,2, *NZ*, *Arg* 1,2, 1980 *Fj*, *NZ* 1,2,3, 1981 *F* 1,2, *I*, *W*, *S*, 1982 *E*, *S* 1,2, 1983 *US*, *Arg* 1,2, *NZ*, *It*, *F* 1,2, 1984 *Fj*, *NZ* 1,2,3, *E*, 1986 *It*, *F*, *Arg* 1,2
Mooney, T P (Q) 1954 *Fj* 1,2
Moore, R C (ACT, NSW) 1999 [*US*], 2001 *BI* 2,3, *SA* 1, *NZ* 1, *SA* 2, *NZ* 2, *Sp* (R), *E* (R), *F* (R), *W* (R), 2002 *F* 1(R),2(R), *SA* 2(R)
Moran, H M (NSW) 1908 *W*
Morgan, G (Q) 1992 *NZ* 1(R), 3(R), *W*, 1993 *Tg*, *NZ*, *SA* 1,2,3, *C*, *F* 1,2, 1994 *I* 1,2, *It* 1, *WS*, *NZ*, 1996 *W* 1,2, *C*, *NZ* 1, *SA* 1, *NZ* 2, 1997 *E* 1, *NZ* 2
Morrissey, C V (NSW) 1925 *NZ* 2,3,4, 1926 *NZ* 2,3
Morrissey, W (Q) 1914 *NZ* 2
Mortlock, S A (ACT) 2000 *Arg* 1,2, *SA* 1, *NZ* 1, *SA* 2, *NZ* 2, *SA* 3, *F*, *S*, *E*, 2002 *F* 1,2, *NZ* 1, *SA* 1, *NZ* 2, *SA* 2
Morton, A R (NSW) 1957 *NZ* 1,2, 1958 *F*, *M* 1,2,3, *NZ* 1,2,3, 1959 *BI* 1,2
Mossop, R P (NSW) 1949 *NZ* 1,2, 1950 *BI* 1,2, 1951 *NZ* 1
Moutray, I E (NSW) 1963 *SA* 2
Mulligan, P J (NSW) 1925 *NZ* 1(R)
Munsie, A (NSW) 1928 *NZ* 2
Murdoch, A R (NSW) 1993 *F* 1, 1996 *W* 1
Murphy, P J (Q) 1910 *NZ* 1,2,3, 1913 *NZ* 1,2,3, 1914 *NZ* 1,2,3
Murphy, W (Q) 1912 *US*

Nasser, B P (Q) 1989 *F* 1,2, 1990 *F* 1,2,3, *US*, *NZ* 2, 1991 [*WS*]
Newman, E W (NSW) 1922 *NZ* 1
Nicholson, F C (Q) 1904 *BI* 3
Nicholson, F V (Q) 1903 *NZ*, 1904 *BI* 1
Niuqila, A S (NSW) 1988 *S*, *It*, 1989 *BI* 1
Noriega, E P (ACT) 1998 *F*, *E* 2, 1999 *I* 1,2, *E*, *SA* 1, *NZ* 1, *SA* 2(R), *NZ* 2(R), 2002 *F* 1,2, *NZ* 1, *SA* 1, *NZ* 2
Nothling, O E (NSW) 1921 *SA* 1,2,3, *NZ*, 1922 *M* 1,2,3, *NZ* 1,2,3, 1923 *M* 1,2,3, *NZ* 1,2,3, 1924 *NZ* 1,2,3
Nucifora, D V (Q) 1991 [*Arg* (R)], 1993 *C* (R)

O'Brien, F W H (NSW) 1937 *SA* 2, 1938 *NZ* 3
O'Connor, J A (NSW) 1928 *NZ* 1,2,3, *M*
O'Connor, M (ACT) 1994 *I* 1
O'Connor, M D (ACT, Q) 1979 *Arg* 1,2, 1980 *Fj*, *NZ* 1,2,3, 1981 *F* 1,2, *I*, 1982 *E*, *S* 1,2
O'Donnell, C (NSW) 1913 *NZ* 1,2
O'Donnell, I C (NSW) 1899 *BI* 3,4
O'Donnell, J B (NSW) 1928 *NZ* 1,3, *M*
O'Donnell, J M (NSW) 1899 *BI* 4
O'Gorman, J F (NSW) 1961 *Fj* 1, *SA* 1,2, *F*, 1962 *NZ* 2, 1963 *E*, *SA* 1,2,3,4, 1965 *SA* 1,2, 1966 *W*, *S*, 1967 *E*, *I* 1, *F*, *I* 2
O'Neill, D J (Q) 1964 *NZ* 1,2
O'Neill, J M (Q) 1952 *NZ* 1,2, 1956 *SA* 1,2
Ofahengaue, V (NSW) 1990 *NZ* 1,2,3, 1991 *W*, *E*, *NZ* 1,2, [*Arg*, *W*, *I*, *NZ*, *E*], 1992 *S* 1,2, *SA*, *I*, *W*, 1994 *WS*, *NZ*, 1995 *Arg* 1,2(R), [*SA*, *C*, *E*], *NZ* 1,2, 1997 *Arg* 1(t + R), 2(R), *E* 2, *S*, 1998 *E* 1(R), *S* 1(R),2(R), *NZ* 1(R), *SA* 1(R), *NZ* 2(R), *SA* 2(R), *NZ* 3(R), *Fj*, *WS*, *F* (R)
Ormiston, I W L (NSW) 1920 *NZ* 1,2,3
Osborne, D H (V) 1975 *E* 1,2, *J* 1
Outterside, R (NSW) 1959 *BI* 1,2
Oxenham, A McE (Q) 1904 *BI* 2, 1907 *NZ* 2
Oxlade, A M (Q) 1904 *BI* 2,3, 1905 *NZ*, 1907 *NZ* 2
Oxlade, B D (Q) 1938 *NZ* 1,2,3

Palfreyman, J R L (NSW) 1929 *NZ* 1, 1930 *BI*, 1931 *NZ*, 1932 *NZ* 3
Panoho, G M (Q) 1998 *SA* 2(R), *NZ* 3(R), *Fj* (R), *Tg*, *WS* (R), 1999 *I* 2, *E*, *SA* 1(R), *NZ* 1, 2000 *Arg* 1(R),2(R), *SA* 1(R), *NZ* 1(R), *SA* 2(R),3(R), *F* (R), *S* (R), *E* (R), 2001 *BI* 1
Papworth, B (NSW) 1985 *Fj* 1,2, 1986 *It*, *Arg* 1,2, *NZ* 1,2,3, 1987 [*E*, *US*, *J* (R), *I*, *F*], *NZ*, *Arg* 1,2
Parker, A J (Q) 1983 *Arg* 1(R), 2, *NZ*
Parkinson, C E (Q) 1907 *NZ* 2
Paul, J A (ACT) 1998 *S* 1(R), *NZ* 1(R), *SA* 1(t), *Fj* (R), *Tg*, 1999 *I* 1,2, *E*, *SA* 1, *NZ* 1, [*R* (R), *I* 3(R), *W* (t), *F* (R)], 2000 *Arg* 1(R),2(R), *SA* 1(R), *NZ* 1(R), *SA* 2(R), *NZ* 2(R), *SA* 3(R), *F* (R), *S* (R), *E* (R), 2001 *BI* 1, 2002 *F* 1, *NZ* 1, *SA* 1, *NZ* 2, *SA* 2
Pashley, J J (NSW) 1954 *Fj* 1,2, 1958 *M* 1,2,3
Pauling, T P (NSW) 1936 *NZ* 1, 1937 *SA* 1
Payne, S J (NSW) 1996 *W* 2, *C*, *NZ* 1, *S*, 1997 *F* 1(t), *NZ* 2(R), *Arg* 2(t)
Pearse, G K (NSW) 1975 *W* (R), 1976 *I*, *US*, *Fj* 1,2,3, 1978 *NZ* 1,2,3

Penman, A P (NSW) 1905 *NZ*
Perrin, P D (Q) 1962 *NZ* 1
Perrin, T D (NSW) 1931 *M*, *NZ*
Phelps, R (NSW) 1955 *NZ* 2,3, 1956 *SA* 1,2, 1957 *NZ* 1,2, 1958 *W*, *I*, *E*, *S*, *F*, *M* 1, *NZ* 1,2,3, 1961 *Fj* 1,2,3, *SA* 1,2, *F*, 1962 *NZ* 1,2
Phipps, J A (NSW) 1953 *SA* 1,2,3,4, 1954 *Fj* 1,2, 1955 *NZ* 1,2,3, 1956 *SA* 1,2
Phipps, W J (NSW) 1928 *NZ* 2
Piggott, H R (NSW) 1922 *M* 3(R)
Pilecki, S J (Q) 1978 *W* 1,2, *NZ* 1,2, 1979 *I* 1,2, *NZ*, *Arg* 1,2, 1980 *Fj*, *NZ* 1,2, 1982 *S* 1,2, 1983 *US*, *Arg* 1,2, *NZ*
Pini, M (Q) 1994 *I* 1, *It* 2, *WS*, *NZ*, 1995 *Arg* 1,2, [*SA*, *R* (t)]
Piper, B J C (NSW) 1946 *NZ* 1, *M*, *NZ* 2, 1947 *NZ* 1, *S*, *I*, *W*, 1948 *E*, *F*, 1949 *M*, 1,2,3
Poidevin, S P (NSW) 1980 *Fj*, *NZ* 1,2,3, 1981 *F* 1,2, *I*, *W*, *S*, 1982 *E*, 1983 *US*, *Arg* 1,2, *NZ*, *It*, *F* 1,2, 1984 *Fj*, *NZ* 1,2,3, *E*, *I*, *W*, *S*, 1985 *C* 1,2, *NZ*, *Fj* 1,2, 1986 *It*, *F*, *Arg* 1,2, *NZ* 1,2,3, 1987 *SK*, [*E*, *J*, *I*, *F*, *W*], *Arg* 1, 1988 *NZ* 1,2,3, 1989 *NZ*, 1991 *E*, *NZ* 1,2, [*Arg*, *W*, *I*, *NZ*, *E*]
Pope, A M (Q) 1968 *NZ* 2(R)
Potter, R T (Q) 1961 *Fj* 2
Potts, J M (NSW) 1957 *NZ* 1,2, 1958 *W*, *I*, 1959 *BI* 1
Prentice, C W (NSW) 1914 *NZ* 3
Prentice, W S (NSW) 1908 *W*, 1909 *E*, 1910 *NZ* 1,2,3, 1912 *US*
Price, R A (NSW) 1974 *NZ* 1,2,3, 1975 *E* 1,2, *J* 1,2, 1976 *US*
Primmer, C J (Q) 1951 *NZ* 1,3
Proctor, I J (NSW) 1967 *NZ*
Prosser, R B (NSW) 1967 *E*, *I* 1,2, *NZ*, 1968 *NZ* 1,2, *F*, *I*, *S*, 1969 *W*, *SA* 1,2,3,4, 1971 *SA* 1,2,3, *F* 1,2, 1972 *F* 1,2, *NZ* 1,2,3, *Fj*
Pugh, G H (NSW) 1912 *US*
Purcell, M P (Q) 1966 *W*, *S*, 1967 *I* 2
Purkis, E M (NSW) 1958 *S*, *M* 1
Pym, J E (NSW) 1923 *M* 1

Rainbow, A E (NSW) 1925 *NZ* 1
Ramalli, C (NSW) 1938 *NZ* 2,3
Ramsay, K M (NSW) 1936 *M*, 1937 *SA* 1, 1938 *NZ* 1,3
Rankin, R (NSW) 1936 *NZ* 1,2, *M*, 1937 *SA* 1,2, 1938 *NZ* 1,2
Rathie, D S (Q) 1972 *F* 1,2
Raymond, R L (NSW) 1920 *NZ* 1,2, 1921 *SA* 2,3, *NZ*, 1922 *M* 1,2,3, *NZ* 1,2,3, 1923 *M* 1,2
Redwood, C (Q) 1903 *NZ*, 1904 *BI* 1,2,3
Reid, E J (NSW) 1925 *NZ* 2,3,4
Reid, T W (NSW) 1961 *Fj* 1,2,3, *SA* 1, 1962 *NZ* 1
Reilly, N P (Q) 1968 *NZ* 1,2, *F*, *I*, *S*, 1969 *W*, *SA* 1,2,3,4
Reynolds, L J (NSW) 1910 *NZ* 2(R), 3
Reynolds, R J (NSW) 1984 *Fj*, *NZ* 1,2,3, 1985 *Fj* 1,2, 1986 *Arg* 1,2, *NZ* 1, 1987 [*J*]
Richards, E W (Q) 1904 *BI* 1,3, 1905 *NZ*, 1907 *NZ* 1(R), 2
Richards, G (NSW) 1978 *NZ* 2(R), 3, 1981 *F* 1
Richards, T J (Q) 1908 *W*, 1909 *E*, 1912 *US*
Richards, V S (NSW) 1936 *NZ* 1,2(R), *M*, 1937 *SA* 1, 1938 *NZ* 1
Richardson, G C (Q) 1971 *SA* 1,2,3, 1972 *NZ* 2,3, *Fj*, 1973 *Tg* 1,2, *W*
Rigney, W A (NSW) 1925 *NZ* 2,4, 1926 *NZ* 4
Riley, S A (NSW) 1903 *NZ*
Ritchie, E V (NSW) 1924 *NZ* 1,3, 1925 *NZ* 2,3
Roberts, B T (NSW) 1956 *SA* 2
Roberts, H F (Q) 1961 *Fj* 1,3, *SA* 2, *F*
Robertson, I J (NSW) 1975 *J* 1,2
Robinson, B J (ACT) 1996 *It* (R), *S* (R), *I* (R), 1997 *F* 1,2, *NZ* 1, *E* 1, *NZ* 2, *SA* 1(R), *NZ* 3(R), *SA* 2(R), *Arg* 1,2, *E* 2, *S*, 1998 *Tg*
Roche, C (Q) 1982 *S* 1,2, *NZ* 1,2,3, 1983 *US*, *Arg* 1,2, *NZ*, *It*, *F* 1,2, 1984 *Fj*, *NZ* 1,2,3, *I*
Rodriguez, E E (NSW) 1984 *Fj*, *NZ* 1,2,3, *E*, *I*, *W*, *S*, 1985 *C* 1,2, *NZ*, *Fj* 1,2, 1986 *It*, *F*, *Arg* 1,2, *NZ* 1,2,3, 1987 *SK*, [*E*, *J*, *W* (R)], *NZ*, *Arg* 1,2
Roebuck, M C (NSW) 1991 *W*, *E*, *NZ* 1,2, [*Arg*, *WS*, *W*, *I*, *NZ*, *E*], 1992 *S* 1,2, *NZ* 2,3, *SA*, *I*, *W*, 1993 *Tg*, *SA* 1,2,3, *C*, *F* 2
Roff, J W C (ACT) 1995 [*C*, *R*], *NZ* 1,2, 1996 *W* 1,2, *NZ* 1, *SA* 1, *NZ* 2, *SA* 2(R), *S*, *I*, *W* 3, 1997 *F* 1,2, *NZ* 1, *E* 1, *NZ* 2, *SA* 1, *NZ* 3, *SA* 2, *Arg* 2, *E* 2, *S*, 1998 *E* 1, *S* 1,2, *NZ* 1, *SA* 1, *NZ* 2, *SA* 2, *NZ* 3, *Fj*, *Tg*, *WS*, *F*, *E* 2, 1999 *I* 1,2, *E*, *SA* 1, *NZ* 1, *SA* 2, *NZ* 2(R), [*R* (R), *I* 3, *US* (R), *W*, *SA* 3, *F*], 2000 *Arg* 1,2, *SA* 1, *NZ* 1, *SA* 2, *NZ* 2, *SA* 3, *F*, *S*, *E*, 2001 *BI* 1,2,3, *SA* 1, *NZ* 1, *SA* 2, *NZ* 2, *Sp*, *E*, *F*, *W*

Rogers, M S (NSW) 2002 *F* 1(R),2(R), *NZ* 1(R), *SA* 1(R), *NZ* 2(R), *SA* 2(t+R)
Rose, H A (NSW), 1967 *I* 2, *NZ*, 1968 *NZ* 1,2, *F, I, S*, 1969 *W, SA* 1,2,3,4, 1970 *S*
Rosenblum, M E (NSW) 1928 *NZ* 1,2,3, *M*
Rosenblum, R G (NSW) 1969 *SA* 1,3, 1970 *S*
Rosewell, J S H (NSW) 1907 *NZ* 1,3
Ross, A W (NSW) 1925 *NZ* 1,2,3, 1926 *NZ* 1,2,3, 1927 *I, W, S*, 1928 *E, F*, 1929 *NZ* 1, 1930 *BI*, 1931 *M, NZ*, 1932 *NZ* 2,3, 1933 *SA* 5, 1934 *NZ* 1,2
Ross, W S (Q) 1979 *I* 1,2, *Arg* 2, 1980 *Fj*, *NZ* 1,2,3, 1982 *S* 1,2, 1983 *US, Arg* 1,2, *NZ*
Rothwell, P R (NSW) 1951 *NZ* 1,2,3, 1952 *Fj* 1
Row, F L (NSW) 1899 *BI* 1,3,4
Row, N E (NSW) 1907 *NZ* 1,3, 1909 *E*, 1910 *NZ* 1,2,3
Rowles, P G (NSW) 1972 *Fj*, 1973 *E*
Roxburgh, J R (NSW) 1968 *NZ* 1,2, *F*, 1969 *W, SA* 1,2,3,4, 1970 *S*
Ruebner, G (NSW) 1966 *BI* 1,2
Russell, C J (NSW) 1907 *NZ* 1,2,3, 1908 *W*, 1909 *E*
Ryan, J R (NSW) 1975 *J* 2, 1976 *I, US, Fj* 1,2,3
Ryan, K J (Q) 1958 *E, M* 1, *NZ* 1,2,3
Ryan, P F (NSW) 1963 *E, SA* 1, 1966 *BI* 1,2
Rylance, M H (NSW) 1926 *NZ* 4(R)

Sailor, W J (Q) 2002 *F* 1,2
Sampson, J H (NSW) 1899 *BI* 4
Sayle, J L (NSW) 1967 *NZ*
Schulte, B G (Q) 1946 *NZ* 1, *M*
Scott, P R I (NSW) 1962 *NZ* 1,2
Scott-Young, S J (Q) 1990 *F* 2,3(R), *US, NZ* 3, 1992 *NZ* 1,2,3
Shambrook, G G (Q) 1976 *Fj* 2,3
Sharpe, N C (Q) 2002 *F* 1,2, *NZ* 1, *SA* 1, *NZ* 2, *SA* 2
Shaw, A A (Q) 1973 *W, E*, 1975 *E* 1,2, *J* 2, *S, W*, 1976 *E, I, US, Fj* 1,2,3, *F* 1,2, 1978 *W* 1,2, *NZ* 1,2,3, 1979 *I* 1,2, *NZ, Arg* 1,2, 1980 *Fj, NZ* 1,2,3, 1981 *F* 1,2, *I, W, S*, 1982 *S* 1,2
Shaw, C (NSW) 1925 *NZ* 2,3,4(R)
Shaw, G A (NSW) 1969 *W, SA* 1(R), 1970 *S*, 1971 *SA* 1,2,3, *F* 1,2, 1973 *W, E*, 1974 *NZ* 1,2,3, 1975 *E* 1,2, *J* 1,2, *W*, 1976 *E, I, US, Fj* 1,2,3, *F* 1,2, 1979 *NZ*
Sheehan, W B J (NSW) 1921 *SA* 1,2,3, 1922 *NZ* 1,2,3, 1923 *M* 1,2, *NZ* 1,2,3, 1924 *NZ* 1,2, 1926 *NZ* 1,2,3, 1927 *W, S*
Shehadie, N M (NSW) 1947 *NZ* 2, 1948 *E, F*, 1949 *M* 1,2,3, *NZ* 1,2, 1950 *BI* 1,2, 1951 *NZ* 1,2,3, 1952 *Fj* 1,2, *NZ* 2, 1953 *SA* 1,2,3,4, 1954 *Fj* 1,2, 1955 *NZ* 1,2,3, 1956 *SA* 1,2, 1957 *NZ* 2, 1958 *W, I*
Sheil, A G R (Q) 1956 *SA* 1
Shepherd, D J (V) 1964 *NZ* 3, 1965 *SA* 1,2, 1966 *BI* 1,2
Shute, J L (NSW) 1920 *NZ* 3, 1922 *M* 2,3
Simpson, R J (NSW) 1913 *NZ* 2
Skinner, A J (NSW) 1969 *W, SA* 4, 1970 *S*
Slack, A G (Q) 1978 *W* 1,2, *NZ* 1,2, 1979 *NZ, Arg* 1,2, 1980 *Fj*, 1981 *I, W, S*, 1982 *E, S* 1, *NZ* 3, 1983 *US, Arg* 1,2 *NZ, It*, 1984 *Fj, NZ* 1,2,3, *E, I, W, S*, 1986 *It, F, NZ* 1,2,3, 1987 *SK, [E, US, J, I, F, W]*
Slater, S H (NSW) 1910 *NZ* 3
Slattery, P J (Q) 1990 *US* (R), 1991 *W* (R), *E* (R), [*WS* (R), *W, I* (R)], 1992 *I, W*, 1993 *Tg, C, F* 1,2, 1994 *I* 1,2, *It* 1(R), 1995 [*C, R* (R)]
Smairl, A M (NSW) 1928 *NZ* 1,2,3
Smith, B A (Q) 1987 *SK*, [*US, J, I* (R), *W*], *Arg* 1
Smith, D P (Q) 1993 *SA* 1,2,3, *C, F* 2, 1994 *I* 1,2, *It* 1,2, *WS, NZ*, 1995 *Arg* 1,2, [*SA, R, E*], *NZ* 1,2, 1998 *SA* 1(R), *NZ* 3(R), *Fj*
Smith, F B (NSW) 1905 *NZ*, 1907 *NZ* 1,2,3
Smith, G B (ACT) 2000 *F, S, E*, 2001 *BI* 1,2,3, *SA* 1, *NZ* 1, *SA* 2, *NZ* 2, *Sp, E, F* (R), *W* (R), 2002 *F* 1,2, *NZ* 1, *SA* 1, *NZ* 2, *SA* 2
Smith, L M (NSW) 1905 *NZ*
Smith, N C (NSW) 1922 *NZ* 2,3, 1923 *NZ* 1, 1924 *NZ* 1,3(R), 1925 *NZ* 2,3
Smith, P V (NSW) 1967 *NZ*, 1968 *NZ* 1,2, *F, I, S*, 1969 *W, SA* 1
Smith, R A (NSW) 1971 *SA* 1,2, 1972 *F* 1,2, *NZ* 1,2(R), 3, *Fj*, 1975 *E* 1,2, *J* 1,2, *S, W*, 1976 *E, I, US, Fj* 1,2,3, *F* 1,2
Smith, T S (NSW) 1921 *SA* 1,2,3, *NZ*, 1922 *M* 2,3, *NZ* 1,2,3, 1925 *NZ* 1,3,4
Snell, H W (NSW) 1925 *NZ* 2,3, 1928 *NZ* 3
Solomon, H J (NSW) 1949 *M* 3, *NZ* 2, 1950 *BI* 1,2, 1951 *NZ* 1,2, 1952 *Fj* 1,2, *NZ* 1,2, 1953 *SA* 1,2,3, 1955 *NZ* 1
Spooner, N R (Q) 1999 *I* 1,2
Spragg, S A (NSW) 1899 *BI* 1,2,3,4
Staniforth, S N G (NSW) 1999 [*US*]

Stanley, R G (NSW) 1921 *NZ*, 1922 *M* 1,2,3, *NZ* 1,2,3, 1923 *M* 2,3, *NZ* 1,2,3, 1924 *NZ* 1,3
Stapleton, E T (NSW) 1951 *NZ* 1,2,3, 1952 *Fj* 1,2, *NZ* 1,2, 1953 *SA* 1,2,3,4, 1954 *Fj* 1, 1955 *NZ* 1,2,3, 1958 *NZ* 1
Steggall, J C (Q) 1931 *M, NZ*, 1932 *NZ* 1,2,3, 1933 *SA* 1,2,3,4,5
Stegman, T R (NSW) 1973 *Tg* 1,2
Stephens, O G (NSW) 1973 *Tg* 1,2, *W*, 1974 *NZ* 2,3
Stewart, A A (NSW) 1979 *NZ, Arg* 1,2
Stiles, N B (Q) 2001 *BI* 1,2,3, *SA* 1, *NZ* 1, *SA* 2, *NZ* 2, *Sp, E, F, W*
Stone, A H (NSW) 1937 *SA* 2, 1938 *NZ* 2,3
Stone, C G (NSW) 1938 *NZ* 1
Stone, J M (NSW) 1946 *M, NZ* 2
Storey, G P (NSW) 1926 *NZ* 4, 1927 *I, W, S*, 1928 *E, F*, 1929 *NZ* 3(R), 1930 *BI*
Storey, K P (NSW) 1936 *NZ* 2
Storey, N J D (NSW) 1962 *NZ* 1
Strachan, D J (NSW) 1955 *NZ* 2,3
Strauss, C P (NSW) 1999 *I* 1(R),2(R), *E* (R), *SA* 1(R), *NZ* 1, *SA* 2(R), *NZ* 2(R), [*R* (R), *I* 3(R), *US, W*]
Street, N O (NSW) 1899 *BI* 2
Streeter, S F (NSW) 1978 *NZ* 1
Stuart, R (NSW) 1910 *NZ* 2,3
Stumbles, B D (NSW) 1972 *NZ* 1(R), 2,3, *Fj*
Sturtridge, G S (V) 1929 *NZ* 2, 1932 *NZ* 1,2,3, 1933 *SA* 1,2,3,4,5
Sullivan, P D (NSW) 1971 *SA* 1,2,3, *F* 1,2, 1972 *F* 1,2, *NZ* 1,2, *Fj*, 1973 *Tg* 1,2, *W*
Summons, A J (NSW) 1958 *W, I, E, S, M* 2, *NZ* 1,2,3, 1959 *BI* 1,2
Suttor, D C (NSW) 1913 *NZ* 1,2,3
Swannell, B I (NSW) 1905 *NZ*
Sweeney, T L (Q) 1953 *SA* 1

Taafe, B S (NSW) 1969 *SA* 1, 1972 *F* 1,2
Tabua, I (Q) 1993 *SA* 2,3, *C, F* 1, 1994 *I* 1,2, *It* 1,2, 1995 [*C, R*]
Tancred, A J (NSW) 1927 *I, W, S*
Tancred, H E (NSW) 1923 *M* 1,2
Tancred, J L (NSW) 1926 *NZ* 3,4, 1928 *F*
Tanner, W H (Q) 1899 *BI* 1,2
Tarleton, K (NSW) 1925 *NZ* 2,3
Tasker, W G (NSW) 1913 *NZ* 1,2,3, 1914 *NZ* 1,2,3
Tate, M J (NSW) 1951 *NZ* 3, 1952 *Fj* 1,2, *NZ* 1,2, 1953 *SA* 1, 1954 *Fj* 1,2
Taylor, D A (Q) 1968 *NZ* 1,2, *F, I, S*
Taylor, H C (NSW) 1923 *NZ* 1,2,3, 1924 *NZ* 4
Taylor, J I (NSW) 1971 *SA* 1, 1972 *F* 1,2, *Fj*
Taylor, J M (NSW) 1922 *M* 1,2
Teitzel, R G (Q) 1966 *W, S*, 1967 *E, I* 1, *F, I* 2, *NZ*
Telford, D G (NSW) 1926 *NZ* 3(R)
Thompson, C E (NSW) 1922 *M* 1, 1923 *M* 1,2, *NZ* 1, 1924 *NZ* 2,3
Thompson, E G (Q) 1929 *NZ* 1,2,3, 1930 *BI*
Thompson, F (NSW) 1913 *NZ* 1,2,3, 1914 *NZ* 1,2,3
Thompson, J (Q) 1914 *NZ* 1
Thompson, P D (Q) 1950 *BI* 1
Thompson, R J (WA) 1971 *SA* 3, *F* 2(R), 1972 *Fj*
Thorn, A M (NSW) 1921 *SA* 1,2,3, *NZ*, 1922 *M* 1,3
Thorn, E J (NSW) 1922 *NZ* 1,2,3, 1923 *NZ* 1,2,3, 1924 *NZ* 1,2,3, 1925 *NZ* 1,2, 1926 *NZ* 1,2,3,4
Thornett, J E (NSW) 1955 *NZ* 1,2,3, 1956 *SA* 1,2, 1958 *W, I, S, F, M* 2,3, *NZ* 2,3, 1959 *BI* 1,2, 1961 *Fj* 2,3, *SA* 1,2, *F*, 1962 *NZ* 2,3,4,5, 1963 *E, SA* 1,2,3,4, 1964 *NZ* 1,2,3, 1965 *SA* 1,2, 1966 *BI* 1,2, 1967 *F*
Thornett, R N (NSW) 1961 *Fj* 1,2,3, *SA* 1,2, *F*, 1962 *NZ* 1,2,3,4,5
Thorpe, A C (NSW) 1929 *NZ* 1(R)
Timbury, F R V (Q) 1910 *NZ* 1,2,
Tindall, E N (NSW) 1973 *Tg* 2
Toby, A E (NSW) 1925 *NZ* 1,4
Tolhurst, H A (NSW) 1931 *M, NZ*
Tombs, R C (NSW) 1992 *S* 1,2, 1994 *I* 2, *It* 1, 1996 *NZ* 2
Tonkin, A E J (NSW) 1947 *S, I, W*, 1948 *E, F*, 1950 *BI* 2
Tooth, R M (NSW) 1951 *NZ* 1,2,3, 1954 *Fj* 1,2, 1955 *NZ* 1,2,3, 1957 *NZ* 1,2
Towers, C H T (NSW) 1926 *NZ* 1,3(R),4, 1927 *I*, 1928 *E, F, NZ* 1,2,3, *M*, 1929 *NZ* 1,3, 1930 *BI*, 1931 *M, NZ*, 1934 *NZ* 1,2, 1937 *SA* 1,2
Trivett, R K (Q) 1966 *BI* 1,2
Tune, B N (Q) 1996 *W* 2, *C, NZ* 1, *SA* 1, *NZ* 2, *SA* 2, 1997 *F* 1,2, *NZ* 1, *E* 1, *NZ* 2, *SA* 1, *NZ* 3, *SA* 2, *Arg*, 1,2, *E* 2, *S*, 1998

E 1, *S* 1,2, *NZ* 1, *SA* 1,2, *NZ* 3, 1999 *I* 1, *E*, *SA* 1, *NZ* 1, *SA* 2, *NZ* 2, [*R*, *I* 3, *W*, *SA* 3, *F*], 2000 *SA* 2(R), *NZ* 2(t&R), *SA* 3(R), 2001 *F* (R), *W*, 2002 *NZ* 1, *SA* 1, *NZ* 2, *SA* 2

Turnbull, A (V) 1961 *Fj* 3

Turnbull, R V (NSW) 1968 *I*

Tuynman, S N (NSW) 1983 *F* 1,2, 1984 *E*, *I*, *W*, *S*, 1985 *C* 1,2, *NZ*, *Fj* 1,2, 1986 *It*, *F*, *Arg* 1,2, *NZ* 1,2,3, 1987 *SK*, [*E*, *US*, *J*, *I*, *W*], *NZ*, *Arg* 1(R), 2, 1988 *E*, *It*, 1989 *BI* 1,2,3, *NZ*, 1990 *NZ* 1

Tweedale, E (NSW) 1946 *NZ* 1,2, 1947 *NZ* 2, *S*, *I*, 1948 *E*, *F*, 1949 *M* 1,2,3

Vaughan, D (NSW) 1983 *US*, *Arg* 1, *It*, *F* 1,2

Vaughan, G N (V) 1958 *E*, *S*, *F*, *M* 1,2,3

Verge, A (NSW) 1904 *BI* 1,2

Vickerman, D J (ACT) 2002 *F* 2(R)

Walden, R J (NSW) 1934 *NZ* 2, 1936 *NZ* 1,2, *M*

Walker, A K (NSW) 1947 *NZ* 1, 1948 *E*, *F*, 1950 *BI* 1,2

Walker, A M (ACT) 2000 *NZ* 1(R), 2001 *BI* 1,2,3, *SA* 1, *NZ* 1,2(R)

Walker, A S B (NSW) 1912 *US*, 1920 *NZ* 1,2, 1921 *SA* 1,2,3, *NZ*, 1922 *M* 1,3, *NZ* 1,2,3, 1923 *M* 2,3, 1924 *NZ* 1,2

Walker, L F (NSW) 1988 *NZ* 2,3, *S*, *It*, 1989 *BI* 1,2,3, *NZ*

Walker, L R (NSW) 1982 *NZ* 2,3

Wallace, A C (NSW) 1921 *NZ*, 1926 *NZ* 3,4, 1927 *I*, *W*, *S*, 1928 *E*, *F*

Wallace, T M (NSW) 1994 *It* 1(R), 2

Wallach, C (NSW) 1913 *NZ* 1,3, 1914 *NZ* 1,2,3

Walsh, J J (NSW) 1953 *SA* 1,2,3,4

Walsh, P B (NSW) 1904 *BI* 1,2,3

Walsham, K P (NSW) 1962 *NZ* 3, 1963 *E*

Ward, P G (NSW) 1899 *BI* 1,2,3,4

Ward, T (Q) 1899 *BI* 2

Watson, G W (Q) 1907 *NZ* 1

Watson, W T (NSW) 1912 *US*, 1913 *NZ* 1,2,3, 1914 *NZ* 1, 1920 *NZ* 1,2,3

Waugh, P R (NSW) 2000 *E* (R), 2001 *NZ* 1(R), *SA* 2(R), *NZ* 2(R), *Sp* (R), *E* (R), *F*, *W*

Waugh, W W (NSW, ACT) 1993 *SA* 1, 1995 [*C*], *NZ* 1,2, 1996 *S*, *I*, 1997 *Arg* 1,2

Weatherstone, L J (ACT) 1975 *E* 1,2, *J* 1,2, *S* (R), 1976 *E*, *I*

Webb, W (NSW) 1899 *BI* 3,4

Welborn J P (NSW) 1996 *SA* 2, *It*, 1998 *Tg*, 1999 *E*, *SA* 1, *NZ* 1

Wells, B G (NSW) 1958 *M* 1

Westfield, R E (NSW) 1928 *NZ* 1,2,3, *M*, 1929 *NZ* 2,3

Whitaker, C J (NSW) 1998 *SA* 2(R), *Fj* (R), *Tg*, 1999 *NZ* 2(R), [*R* (R), *US*, *F* (R)], 2000 *S* (R), 2001 *Sp* (R), *W* (R)

White, C J B (NSW) 1899 *BI* 1, 1903 *NZ*, 1904 *BI* 1

White, J M (NSW) 1904 *BI* 3

White, J P L (NSW) 1958 *NZ* 1,2,3, 1961 *Fj* 1,2,3, *SA* 1,2, *F*, 1962 *NZ* 1,2,3,4,5, 1963 *E*, *SA* 1,2,3,4, 1964 *NZ* 1,2,3, 1965 *SA* 1,2

White, M C (Q) 1931 *M*, *NZ* 1932 *NZ* 1,2, 1933 *SA* 1,2,3,4,5

White, S W (NSW) 1956 *SA* 1,2, 1958 *I*, *E*, *S*, *M* 2,3

White, W G S (Q) 1933 *SA* 1,2,3,4,5, 1934 *NZ* 1,2, 1936 *NZ* 1,2, *M*

White, W J (NSW) 1928 *NZ* 1, *M*, 1932 *NZ* 1

Wickham, S M (NSW) 1903 *NZ*, 1904 *BI* 1,2,3, 1905 *NZ*

Williams, D (Q) 1913 *NZ* 3, 1914 *NZ* 1,2,3

Williams, I M (NSW) 1987 *Arg* 1,2, 1988 *E* 1,2, *NZ* 1,2,3, 1989 *BI* 2,3, *NZ*, *F* 1,2, 1990 *F* 1,2,3, *US*, *NZ* 1

Williams, J L (NSW) 1963 *SA* 1,3,4

Williams, R W (ACT) 1999 *I* 1(t&R),2(t&R), *E* (R), [*US*], 2000 *Arg* 1,2, *SA* 1, *NZ* 1, *SA* 2, *NZ* 2, *SA* 3, *F* (R), *S* (R), *E*

Williams, S A (NSW) 1980 *Fj*, *NZ* 1,2, 1981 *F* 1,2, 1982 *E*, *NZ* 1,2,3, 1983 *US*, *Arg* 1(R), 2, *NZ*, *It*, *F* 1,2, 1984 *NZ* 1,2,3, *E*, *I*, *W*, *S*, 1985 *C* 1,2, *NZ*, *Fj* 1,2

Wilson, B J (NSW) 1949 *NZ* 1,2

Wilson, C R (Q) 1957 *NZ* 1, 1958 *NZ* 1,2,3

Wilson, D J (Q) 1992 *S* 1,2, *NZ* 1,2,3, *SA*, *I*, *W*, 1993 *Tg*, *NZ*, *SA* 1,2,3, *C*, *F* 1,2, 1994 *I* 1,2, *It* 1,2, *WS*, *NZ*, 1995 *Arg* 1,2, [*SA*, *R*, *E*], 1996 *W* 1,2, *C*, *NZ* 1, *SA* 1, *NZ* 2, *SA* 2, *It*, *S*, *I*, *W* 3, 1997 *F* 1,2, *NZ* 1, *E* 1(t + R), *NZ* 2(R), *SA* 1, *NZ* 3, *SA* 2, *E* 2(R), *S* (R), 1998 *E* 1, *S* 1,2, *NZ* 1, *SA* 1, *NZ* 2, *SA* 2, *NZ* 3, *Fj*, *WS*, *F*, *E* 2, 1999 *I* 1,2, *E*, *SA* 1, *NZ* 1, *SA* 2, *NZ* 2, [*R*, *I* 3, *W*, *SA* 3, *F*], 2000 *Arg* 1,2, *SA* 1, *NZ* 1, *SA* 2, *NZ* 2, *SA* 3

Wilson, V W (Q) 1937 *SA* 1,2, 1938 *NZ* 1,2,3

Windon, C J (NSW) 1946 *NZ* 1,2, 1947 *NZ* 1, *S*, *I*, *W*, 1948 *E*, *F*, 1949 *M* 1,2,3, *NZ* 1,2, 1951 *NZ* 1,2,3, 1952 *Fj* 1,2, *NZ* 1,2

Windon, K S (NSW) 1937 *SA* 1,2, 1946 *M*

Windsor, J C (Q) 1947 *NZ* 2

Winning, K C (Q) 1951 *NZ* 1

Wogan, L W (NSW) 1913 *NZ* 1,2,3, 1914 *NZ* 1,2,3, 1920 *NZ* 1,2,3, 1921 *SA* 1,2,3, *NZ*, 1922 *M* 3, *NZ* 1,2,3, 1923 *M* 1,2, 1924 *NZ* 1,2,3

Wood, F (NSW) 1907 *NZ* 1,2,3, 1910 *NZ* 1,2,3, 1913 *NZ* 1,2,3, 1914 *NZ* 1,2,3

Wood, R N (Q) 1972 *Fj*

Woods, H F (NSW) 1925 *NZ* 4, 1926 *NZ* 1,2,3, 1927 *I*, *W*, *S*, 1928 *E*

Wright, K J (NSW) 1975 *E* 1,2, *J* 1, 1976 *US*, *F* 1,2, 1978 *NZ* 1,2,3

Wyld, G (NSW) 1920 *NZ* 2

Yanz, K (NSW) 1958 *F*

Young, W K (ACT) 2000 *F*, *S*, *E*, 2002 *F* 1,2, *NZ* 1, *SA* 1, *NZ* 2, *SA* 2

CANADA TEST SEASON REVIEW 2001-02

A Step in the Right Direction

Peter McMullan

Just as one swallow does not make a summer so Canada's welcome return to winning ways has to be viewed in the context of the opposition. Victory over Scotland, touring below full strength, set the pace for successive wins, over the United States, home and away, and visiting Uruguay and Chile.

With a number of leading performers absent earning a living in the UK and France, Canada stumbled in Montevideo, losing 25-23 to Uruguay, before Chile were overcome 29-11, in Santiago, ensuring first place in the Americas qualifying series for Rugby World Cup 2003.

Canada has come a long way since the upheavals of 2001 brought the dismissal, and subsequent reinstatement, of coach David Clark, a full-blown and unprecedented players' strike on his behalf and cancellation of a Vancouver Test with Australia as well as the November games in Scotland and Ireland. Numerous changes followed in boardroom and administration.

The six wins have given Canadian rugby the morale boost it so badly needed and confirmation of primacy in the Americas. That places Canada in RWC Pool D beside New Zealand and Wales, the second qualifier from Europe and the second repechage entry, from Asia or Oceania.

What a contrast to the chaos of 2001 when two victories were followed by five straight losses. Now with a settled and maturing squad, with Al Charron an inspirational leader whose caps total has reached a record 72 since 1990, and with stability in the back rooms, bleak fears have given way to guarded optimism.

How will Canada fare in Melbourne, Canberra and Wollongong in October of next year? The question will only be answered on the day but there will be a lot more to be learned from the November 16th and 23rd Tests in Wales, first up 2003 RWC opponents in Melbourne, and France.

Strong efforts on foreign soil – and Canada have beaten both Six Nations sides in the past decade – would be the perfect launching pad for what lies ahead. That said, near perfection in selection and overall execution will be needed for a serious challenge in November and to progress in RWC 2003.

Much, of course, will depend on the depth and character of the playing resources available on the day. Canada came to the first five of the seven summer Tests with the majority of its overseas professionals and minimal adjustments to make on account of injuries.

Significant too was the reappearance of outside-half Jared Barker. Missing last year following major knee surgery, Barker returned to kick like the proverbial dream. Just as previous captain Gareth Rees, named as Canada's new Chief Executive Officer in May, had done in another era, so Barker found his target time after time in a remarkable run of 33 successive and successful shots at goals in six Tests. He finished with a final tally of 103 points from 27 penalties and 11 conversions.

Earlier, Canada's 2002 campaign got off to a dreadful start. A three-game trip to Australia lacked the essential quality and experience of scrum-half Morgan Williams and forwards Rod Snow, Al Charron, Mike James, John Tait and Phil Murphy, all seasoned overseas professionals. Australia A ran in 16 tries on the way to Canada's heaviest-ever defeat, 102-8 on June 1st, in Sydney, while earlier games against New South West Country and Sydney ended in 24-6 and 47-24 losses. A 26-6 overall try count told its own story.

Almost immediately Scotland launched their North American tour in Markham with a 33-8 victory over Rugby Canada, a Test XV in all but name, and continued the build-up to the international with wins over Canada East (38-8) and Canada West (14-9), in Kingston and Victoria. It was a very different story in Vancouver, on June 15th. Canada allowed two tries on either side of the interval, when Charron was off for a yellow card offence, but rallied magnificently on his return to win 26-23, two tries, four penalties and two conversions to three tries, a conversion and two penalties.

Scotland, who started with four new caps, came badly unstuck under sustained pressure in the second half, were outplayed forward, missed easy penalties and generally lost focus squandering a 23-13 lead as they gave up 13 points in the final 25 minutes.

Canada's try scorers were forwards James, back from France after a two-year absence, and John Thiel with Barker, who was not selected against Australia A or for Rugby Canada against Scotland, kicking both conversions and four penalties including the winning goal with minutes to play. It was the result Canada needed so badly and it set the agenda for the Rugby World Cup qualifiers.

The United States came first, home and away in Markham and Chicago on June 29th and July 13th. The first game provided a somewhat untidy 26-9 Canadian victory, two converted tries and four penalties to three penalties. Lock James and flanker Dan Baugh took the tries while Barker enjoyed another 16-point afternoon kicking both conversions and the penalties. In Chicago, with centre John Cannon injured and Baugh and John Tait missing for the latter's wedding, the Canadian backs made their mark in a 36-13 victory.

Marco Di Girolamo, a late choice for Cannon, helped himself to two tries and a third went to wing Fred Asselin. Canada were 23-0 ahead at half-time and finished with three tries, three conversions and five penalties with Barker kicking 16 points for the third time. Bob Ross, his replacement and predecessor, had the other points with a conversion and a penalty.

Barker, with 19 points from five penalties and two conversions, was again in flawless kicking form against Uruguay, in Edmonton on August 10th, when Don Whidden was honoured by Rugby Canada on his 50th appointment as team manager.

Canada won this one 51-16, after leading 19-3 at half-time, the backs claiming three of the five tries through full-back Winston Stanley, scrum-half Williams and replacement wing Di Girolamo. Prop Thiel and hooker Pat Dunkley accounted for the other two. Ross added a penalty and two conversions. Uruguay had a converted try, two penalties and a drop goal.

The Chileans proved tougher opposition than anticipated, in Calgary on August 17th, with Canada finally winning 27-6, five Barker penalties and two second half tries by centre Nick Witkowski, one converted by Ross, to a penalty and a drop goal. While a far from dominant display this result assured the winners of a top two finish in the RWC qualifiers.

That left Uruguay and Chile to be faced again on August 24th and 31st, in Montevideo and Santiago. Hooker Pat Dunkley was ruled out by injury and five professionals had returned to their overseas clubs, scrum-half Williams and forwards Baugh, James, Tait and Murphy.

Uruguay, scoring two tries and five penalties, denied Canada 25-23 in Montevideo with Barker responsible for 13 points from three penalties and conversions to tries by Asselin and Ed Fairhurst, who had come in for Williams. Four penalties missed and two tries allowed with the Canadians short-handed made all the difference. That left everything to win or lose in Santiago. It was 8-5 to Canada at the interval before a strong finish brought victory by three tries, a conversion and four penalties (29 points) to a try and two penalties (11 points).

This time, in one of four changes, the more experienced Bob Ross started ahead of Barker, earning his 49th cap since 1989 and kicking the opening penalty before a try by No 8 Ryan Banks. Ross kicked another penalty early in the second half before Barker came on with 27 minutes remaining to finish the job with two more penalties and the conversion to the second of two tries by wings Sean Fauth and Fred Asselin.

One final statistic: in 2002 Canada scored 19 tries against eight in winning six of seven games. In 2000-01 they were outscored 27-8, against Japan (L), Fiji (L), England (L), England (L), Argentina (L), Uruguay (W), United States (W) and Italy (W). Most definitely a step in the right direction but final judgement on 2002 must wait until after Cardiff and Paris.

Canada's Test Record in 2001-2002:
Played 7, won 6, lost 1

Opponents	Date	Venue	Result
Chile	31st August 2002	A	Won 29-11
Uruguay	24th August 2002	A	Lost 23-25
Chile	17th August 2002	H	Won 27-6
Uruguay	10th August 2002	H	Won 51-16
United States	13th July 2002	A	Won 36-13
United States	29th June 2002	H	Won 26-9
Scotland	15th June 2002	H	Won 26-23

CANADA INTERNATIONAL STATISTICS

(up to 31 August 2002)

Match Records

MOST CONSECUTIVE TEST WINS

6 1990 *Arg 2*, 1991 *J, S, US, F, R*
6 1998 *US 1, 2, HK, J, U, US 3*

MOST CONSECUTIVE TESTS WITHOUT DEFEAT

Matches	Wins	Draws	Period
6	6	0	1990 to 1991
6	6	0	1998 to 1998

MOST POINTS IN A MATCH
by the team

Pts	Opponents	Venue	Year
72	Namibia	Toulouse	1999
62	Japan	Markham	2000
57	Hong Kong	Vancouver	1996
53	United States	Vancouver	1997
51	Japan	Vancouver	1996
51	Uruguay	Edmonton	2002

by a player

Pts	Player	Opponents	Venue	Year
27	G L Rees	Namibia	Toulouse	1999
26	R P Ross	Japan	Vancouver	1996
24	M A Wyatt	Scotland	Saint John	1991
23	G L Rees	Argentina	Buenos Aires	1998
22	R P Ross	Hong Kong	Vancouver	1996
22	G L Rees	Japan	Vancouver	1997
22	G L Rees	United States	Burlington	1998
22	J Barker	Japan	Markham	2000

MOST TRIES IN A MATCH
by the team

Tries	Opponents	Venue	Year
9	Namibia	Toulouse	1999
8	Tonga	Napier	1987
8	Japan	Vancouver	1991
8	Japan	Markham	2000
7	Hong Kong	Vancouver	1996
7	United States	Vancouver	1997

by a player

Tries	Player	Opponents	Venue	Year
4	K S Nichols	Japan	Markham	2000
3	S D Gray	United States	Vancouver	1987

MOST CONVERSIONS IN A MATCH
by the team

Cons	Opponents	Venue	Year
9	Namibia	Toulouse	1999
8	Japan	Markham	2000
7	Japan	Vancouver	1991
6	United States	Vancouver	1997
5	Hong Kong	Vancouver	1996

by a player

Cons	Player	Opponents	Venue	Year
9	G L Rees	Namibia	Toulouse	1999
8	J Barker	Japan	Markham	2000
7	M A Wyatt	Japan	Vancouver	1991
6	G L Rees	United States	Vancouver	1997
5	R P Ross	Hong Kong	Vancouver	1996

MOST PENALTIES IN A MATCH
by the team

Penalties	Opponents	Venue	Year
8	Scotland	Saint John	1991
7	Argentina	Buenos Aires	1998
6	United States	Vancouver	1985
6	Ireland	Victoria	1989
6	France	Nepean	1994
6	United States	Burlington	1998

by a player

Penalties	Player	Opponents	Venue	Year
8	M A Wyatt	Scotland	Saint John	1991
7	G L Rees	Argentina	Buenos Aires	1998
6	M A Wyatt	United States	Vancouver	1985
6	M A Wyatt	Ireland	Victoria	1989
6	G L Rees	France	Nepean	1994
6	G L Rees	United States	Burlington	1998

MOST DROPPED GOALS IN A MATCH

by the team

Drops	Opponents	Venue	Year
2	United States	Saranac Lake (NY)	1980
2	United States	Tucson	1986
2	Hong Kong	Hong Kong	1997
2	Fiji	Tokyo	2001

by a player

Drops	Player	Opponents	Venue	Year
2	R P Ross	Hong Kong	Hong Kong	1997
2	R P Ross	Fiji	Tokyo	2001

Career Records

MOST CAPPED PLAYERS

Caps	Player	Career Span
72	A J Charron	1990 to 2002
64	D S Stewart	1989 to 2001
55	G L Rees	1986 to 1999
54	J D Graf	1989 to 1999
54	W U Stanley	1994 to 2002
50	J Hutchinson	1993 to 2000
49	E A Evans	1986 to 1998
49	R P Ross	1989 to 2002
47	S D Gray	1984 to 1997
45	R G A Snow	1995 to 2002

MOST CONSECUTIVE TESTS

Tests	Player	Span
40	J Hutchinson	1995 to 1999
25	J N Tait	1998 to 2001
21	W U Stanley	1998 to 2000
17	R P Ross	1996 to 1997
15	S D Gray	1991 to 1994

MOST TESTS AS CAPTAIN

Tests	Captain	Span
25	G L Rees	1994 to 1999
21	A J Charron	1996 to 2002
16	J D Graf	1995 to 1999
9	M A Wyatt	1990 to 1991
8	M Luke	1974 to 1981
8	H de Goede	1984 to 1987

MOST TESTS IN INDIVIDUAL POSITIONS

Position	Player	Tests	Span
Full-back	D S Stewart	46	1989 to 2001
Wing	W U Stanley	35	1994 to 2002
Centre	S D Gray	31	1984 to 1997
Fly-half	G L Rees	49	1986 to 1999
Scrum-half	J D Graf	39	1989 to 1999
Prop	E A Evans	49	1986 to 1998
Hooker	M E Cardinal	34	1986 to 1998
Lock	M B James	41	1994 to 2002
Flanker	J Hutchinson	46	1995 to 1999
No 8	C McKenzie	25	1992 to 1997

MOST POINTS IN TESTS

Points	Player	Tests	Career
492	G L Rees	55	1986 to 1999
367	R P Ross	49	1989 to 2002
263	M A Wyatt	29	1982 to 1991
145	J Barker	10	2000 to 2002
108	W U Stanley	54	1994 to 2002
90	J D Graf	54	1989 to 1999

MOST TRIES IN TESTS

Tries	Player	Tests	Career
21	W U Stanley	54	1994 to 2002
10	K S Nichols	26	1996 to 2002
9	P Palmer	17	1983 to 1992
9	J D Graf	54	1989 to 1999
9	G L Rees	55	1986 to 1999
9	A J Charron	72	1990 to 2002

MOST CONVERSIONS IN TESTS

Cons	Player	Tests	Career
51	G L Rees	55	1986 to 1999
47	R P Ross	49	1989 to 2002
24	M A Wyatt	29	1982 to 1991
20	J Barker	10	2000 to 2002

MOST PENALTY GOALS IN TESTS

Penalties	Player	Tests	Career
110	G L Rees	55	1986 to 1999
72	R P Ross	49	1989 to 2002
64	M A Wyatt	29	1982 to 1991
34	J Barker	10	2000 to 2002
14	D S Stewart	64	1989 to 2001

MOST DROPPED GOALS IN TESTS

Drops	Player	Tests	Career
9	G L Rees	55	1986 to 1999
9	R P Ross	49	1989 to 2002
5	M A Wyatt	29	1982 to 1991

Career Records Of Canada International Players
(up to 31 August 2002)

PLAYER	Debut	Caps	T	C	P	D	Pts
Backs:							
F C Asselin	1999 v Fj	13	3	0	0	0	15
J Barker	2000 v Tg	10	0	20	34	1	145
J Cannon	2001 v US	12	0	0	0	0	0
J A Cordle	1998 v HK	6	1	0	0	0	5
M Danskin	2001 v J	1	0	0	0	0	0
M di Girolamo	2001 v U	6	3	0	0	0	15
E Fairhurst	2001 v Arg	6	1	0	0	0	5
S Fauth	2000 v Tg	20	5	0	0	0	25
M Irvine	2000 v Tg	8	0	0	0	0	0
M King	2002 v US	1	0	0	0	0	0
K S Nichols	1996 v U	26	9	1	3	0	56
C B Robertson	1997 v HK	7	3	0	0	0	15
R P Ross	1989 v I	49	6	47	72	9	367
W U Stanley	1994 v US	54	21	0	0	1	108
S Thompson	2001 v Fj	2	0	0	0	0	0
J Williams	2001 v US	5	0	0	0	0	0
M Williams	1999 v Tg	22	5	0	0	0	25
N Witkowski	1998 v US	20	4	0	0	0	20
Forwards:							
R Banks	1999 v J	27	3	0	0	0	15
D R Baugh	1998 v J	27	5	0	0	0	25
D Burleigh	2001 v U	4	0	0	0	0	0
L Carlson	2002 v U	1	0	0	0	0	0
A J Charron	1990 v Arg	72	9	0	0	0	44
J Cudmore	2002 v US	2	0	0	0	0	0
G G Cooke	2000 v Tg	4	0	0	0	0	0
G A Dixon	2000 v US	11	0	0	0	0	0
P Dunkley	1998 v J	31	3	0	0	0	15
M B James	1994 v US	41	2	0	0	0	10
R Johnstone	2001 v U	6	0	0	0	0	0
E R P Knaggs	2000 v Tg	14	0	0	0	0	0
M Lawson	2002 v US	5	0	0	0	0	0
B Major	2001 v Fj	2	0	0	0	0	0
D Major	1999 v E	10	0	0	0	0	0
P Murphy	2000 v Tg	14	5	0	0	0	25
M R Schmid	1996 v U	24	2	0	0	0	10
R G A Snow	1995 v Arg	45	7	0	0	0	35
B Stoikos	2001 v U	1	0	0	0	0	0
J N Tait	1997 v US	32	1	0	0	0	5

J Thiel	1998 v HK	27	3	0	0	0	15
K Tkachuk	2000 v Tg	11	0	0	0	0	0
H Toews	1998 v J	11	1	0	0	0	5
J B Tomlinson	1996 v A	2	0	0	0	0	0
A van Staveren	2000 v Tg	9	0	0	0	0	0
K M Wirachowski	1992 v E	16	3	0	0	0	15
C Yukes	2001 v U	7	0	0	0	0	0

ARGENTINA TEST SEASON REVIEW 2001-02

Pumas Show their Claws

Frankie Deges

The past year for Argentine rugby can be divided into two similar periods – the autumn European season and the spring season. Both brought wins to Los Pumas, both also saw them lose. But overall, there was enough to sustain the growth of the international game in Argentina.

Argentina continue to face the same problems as last year – lack of participation in a regular tournament or competition and no professional set-up. With the best players now overseas, domestic competitions desperately miss the stars and so income to the game is mostly dependant on incoming tours. The country, moreover, is in a decline which has left it in its worst ever financial, social and economical situation. Even the optimists have given up on their hopes for the future.

But for all that, rugby has brought many smiles to the worried faces of the *argentinos*. Soccer, the number one sport in the country, crashed out of a World Cup they were supposed to win, leaving rugby to pick up some of the crumbs.

In the autumn, Argentina travelled to Wales and Scotland anxious to prove a point. Last year's headline in this Yearbook was 'Pumas among the best of the rest.' This tour was the right time to prove these words.

With a full squad and the inestimable assistance of former England fly-half and assistant coach Les Cusworth, Argentina trotted on to the Millennium Stadium confident of securing their first win against Wales in Cardiff, four days after a 30-14 win against Wales A. Wales were unveiling their newest recruit, former League star Iestyn Harris, but he was not able to control a rampant Puma side that took the game to them from the first minute and dominated almost throughout the match to win comfortably by 30-16. Incidentally, opposing fly-half Felipe Contepomi scored 25 points (one try, one goal, one drop and five penalties giving him a full-house of scoring actions) and Gonzalo Camardón touched down for the other try.

The squad travelled north to Scotland where they dropped the game against the A side by 35-40, before defeating Scotland at Murrayfield as they had in 1999. Again, Los Pumas' forwards dominated. Contepomi took 20 points and full-back Ignacio Corleto scored the Puma try. History was made and the team's confidence was buoyed by the knowledge that both victories had been by clear margins. Then, to round off a wonderful week Argentina's Development Manager, Jorge Braceras, was rewarded for his work with the presentation of the IRB's first ever Development Award.

Next came New Zealand at a full house at the River Plate Stadium. Never before had Argentina beaten the Men in Black and an expectant crowd of 56,000 spectators turned up to see a fascinating Test unfold. Strangely, Argentina were hot favourites and confidently played that part. New Zealand showed some lapses of concentration, from which Argentina scored its two tries by captain Lisandro Arbizu. The first came when a chip ahead was not cleared, the second when New Zealand made a big blunder behind their try-line. Such was the intensity and the solid defensive pattern of the Pumas that the All Blacks at times looked pedestrian.

With seconds to go and Argentina on track for their most famous ever win, Contepomi, a hero throughout all three of the autumn Tests, missed touch and a quick counter-attack put Scott Robertson in at the corner. A slender two-point lead thus turned into a four-point loss: 20-24. All Black captain Anton Oliver couldn't have described it better when he said after the game: 'They let us out of jail.'

The Argentine Development XV mopped up the prizes at the 22nd South American Championship to bring down the curtain on the autumn international season with wins against Paraguay 69-15, Chile 42-23 and Uruguay 63-7.

Mar del Plata again successfully hosted a round of the IRB World Sevens Series with Los Pumas (who would eventually finish seventh overall) reaching the semi-final in front of their own supporters. A week earlier, at the Santiago Sevens, they had reached their first final in three seasons of the IRB World Sevens Series. Theirs was a good season under coach Hernán Rouco Oliva and for a second year Los Pumas achieved points in every round of the tournament. Since 1981, 178 players have represented Argentina at sevens, 103 also played for Los Pumas while 57 of them represented their country at sevens before winning full honours. These numbers reflect the importance that is placed on the development of players through exposure to the game's shortened version.

Even so, when Marcelo Loffreda reconvened his squad for a three-Test spree in June, he turned to the usual suspects. His starting line-up against France on June 15 was identical to the unchanged fifteens that had featured in the three November Tests. 'It is always very hard for us as coaches and selectors as the players are overseas and we have no real chance of seeing them week-in week-out,' explained Loffreda. 'For the June series we only got together four days before the first Test, and in such a short period we can only do so much.'

As in the previous season, Loffreda and his assistant coach Daniel Baetti travelled to France for a get-together with the European-based Pumas. That was followed by a national team, with the best players rested, taking home the 23rd South American Championship in April. They beat Uruguay 35-21 and Chile 57-13. In between, they humiliated Paraguay 152-0, scoring 24 tries and 16 goals to establish a new world record for a winning margin in a cap match.

France were the first opponents in June and in one of Argentina's best performances of the season, Los Pumas beat the recent Grand Slam champions by 28-27. A flurry of three tries (Contepomi, Federico Méndez and Diego Albanese) in ten minutes during the second half showed how well Argentina can play the game. They did lose concentration to allow France back into the match, before Gérald Merceron fluffed a late penalty that would have given France an undeserved win.

With Clive Woodward's England in Buenos Aires minus most of the usual starting fifteen, Los Pumas had a dip in concentration having led 12-3 at the end of the first half. They lost the plot to allow England to come back at them with far more hunger. England turned the game around and secured a much celebrated 26-18 win. Argentina seemed at times rudderless without captain Lisandro Arbizu, who had been injured the previous weekend.

'We lost because we made too many mistakes,' said makeshift captain Agustín Pichot just 26 hours before leading the team overseas for a two-match tour of South Africa. 'It will be very demanding for us, a small nation, to come to South Africa and be expected to perform at altitude,' said Puma coach Loffreda on arrival.

But after only two days of acclimatising, Argentina were very unlucky to lose to South Africa A by 42-36, conceding the last score after the hooter for full time had blown. Still, it was the full international at the unlikely venue of Springs – an hour's drive from Johannesburg – where the stiffest examination came. Even in losing 29-49, the Pumas showed that they could be a far stronger force if a few things fell into place. 'It is not that we play a one-dimensional game. The amount of time I have to work with the players is very limited,' said coach Loffreda.

The bylaws that regulate the game in Argentina have been altered to permit professionalism, but the sad state of the country means that, for most, earning a decent living from the game in Argentina remains a pipedream. With Rugby World Cup 2003 fast approaching, the players know they must redouble their efforts to match the achievement of 1999 when Argentina reached the quarter-finals. They do know, though, that the non-financial rewards will make the effort worthwhile. So, expect the Pumas to be hungry in 2002-2003.

Argentina's Test Record in 2001–2002: Played 9, won 6, lost 3.

Opponents	Date	Venue	Result
South Africa	29th June 2002	A	Lost 29-49
England	22nd June 2002	H	Lost 18-26
France	15th June 2002	H	Won 28-27
Chile	4th May 2002	H	Won 57-13
Paraguay	1st May 2002	H	Won 152-0
Uruguay	28th April 2002	H	Won 35-21
New Zealand	1st December 2001	H	Lost 20-24
Scotland	18th November 2001	A	Won 25-16
Wales	10th November 2001	A	Won 30-16

ARGENTINA INTERNATIONAL STATISTICS

(up to 31 August 2002)

Match Records

MOST CONSECUTIVE TEST WINS

10 1992 *Sp 1,2, R, F,* 1993 *J 1,2, Br, Ch, P, U*
7 1972 *Gz 2,* 1973 *P, U, Br, Ch, R 1,2*

MOST CONSECUTIVE TESTS WITHOUT DEFEAT

Matches	Wins	Draws	Period
10	10	0	1992 to 1993
7	7	0	1972 to 1973

MOST POINTS IN A MATCH
by the team

Pts	Opponents	Venue	Year
152	Paraguay	Mendoza	2002
114	Brazil	Sao Paulo	1993
109	Brazil	Santiago	1979
103	Paraguay	Asuncion	1995
103	Brazil	Montevideo	1989
102	Paraguay	Asuncion	1985
98	Paraguay	San Pablo	1973
96	Brazil	San Pablo	1973

by a player

Pts	Player	Opponents	Venue	Year
50	E Morgan	Paraguay	San Pablo	1973
40	G M Jorge	Brazil	Sao Paulo	1993
32	M Sansot	Brazil	Tucuman	1977
32	J-L Cilley	Paraguay	Mendoza	2002
31	E Morgan	Uruguay	San Pablo	1973
31	E De Forteza	Paraguay	Asuncion	1975
31	J Luna	Romania	Buenos Aires	1995
30	J Capalbo	Uruguay	Tucuman	1977
29	P Guarrochena	Paraguay	Tucuman	1977
29	S E Meson	Canada	Buenos Aires	1995
29	G Quesada	Canada	Buenos Aires	1998
28	E Morgan	Chile	San Pablo	1973
27	G Quesada	Samoa	Llanelli	1999

MOST TRIES IN A MATCH
by the team

Tries	Opponents	Venue	Year
24	Paraguay	Mendoza	2002
19	Brazil	Santiago	1979
19	Paraguay	Asuncion	1985
18	Paraguay	San Pablo	1973
18	Brazil	San Pablo	1973
18	Brazil	Sao Paulo	1993
17	Brazil	Buenos Aires	1991
16	Paraguay	Asuncion	1995
15	Paraguay	Asuncion	1975
14	Paraguay	Montevideo	1989
14	Brazil	Montevideo	1961

by a player

Tries	Player	Opponents	Venue	Year
8	G M Jorge	Brazil	Sao Paulo	1993
6	E Morgan	Paraguay	San Pablo	1973
6	G M Jorge	Brazil	Montevideo	1989
5	H Goti	Brazil	Montevideo	1961
5	M Rodriguez Jurado	Brazil	Montevideo	1971
5	P Grande	Paraguay	Asuncion	1998

MOST CONVERSIONS IN A MATCH
by the team

Cons	Opponents	Venue	Year
16	Paraguay	Mendoza	2002
15	Brazil	Santiago	1979
13	Paraguay	San Pablo	1973
13	Paraguay	Asuncion	1985
12	Paraguay	Asuncion	1975
12	Brazil	Buenos Aires	1993
10	Paraguay	Tucuman	1977
10	Brazil	Montevideo	1989

by a player

Cons	Player	Opponents	Venue	Year
16	J-L Cilley	Paraguay	Mendoza	2002
13	E Morgan	Paraguay	San Pablo	1973
13	H Porta	Paraguay	Asuncion	1985
11	E De Forteza	Paraguay	Asuncion	1975
10	P Guarrochena	Paraguay	Tucuman	1977
10	S E Meson	Brazil	Montevideo	1989
10	S E Meson	Brazil	Sao Paulo	1993

MOST PENALTIES IN A MATCH
by the team

Penalties	Opponents	Venue	Year
8	Canada	Buenos Aires	1995
8	Samoa	Llanelli	1999
7	France	Buenos Aires	1974
7	France	Nantes	1992
7	Canada	Buenos Aires	1998
7	Japan	Cardiff	1999
7	Ireland	Lens	1999

by a player

Penalties	Player	Opponents	Venue	Year
8	S E Meson	Canada	Buenos Aires	1995
8	G Quesada	Samoa	Llanelli	1999
7	H Porta	France	Buenos Aires	1974
7	S E Meson	France	Nantes	1992
7	G Quesada	Canada	Buenos Aires	1998
7	G Quesada	Japan	Cardiff	1999
7	G Quesada	Ireland	Lens	1999

MOST DROPPED GOALS IN A MATCH
by the team

Drops	Opponents	Venue	Year
3	SA Gazelles	Pretoria	1971
3	Uruguay	Asuncion	1975
3	Australia	Buenos Aires	1979
3	New Zealand	Buenos Aires	1985
3	Canada	Markham	2001
2	SA Gazelles	Buenos Aires	1966
2	Scotland	Buenos Aires	1969
2	Uruguay	Montevideo	1971
2	Chile	Asuncion	1975
2	New Zealand	Dunedin	1979
2	Australia	Buenos Aires	1987
2	Chile	Santiago	1991
2	Australia	Llanelli	1991

by a player

Drops	Player	Opponents	Venue	Year
3	T Harris Smith	SA Gazelles	Pretoria	1971
3	H Porta	Australia	Buenos Aires	1979
3	H Porta	New Zealand	Buenos Aires	1985
3	J D Fernandez Miranda	Canada	Markham	2001
2	E Poggi	SA Gazelles	Buenos Aires	1966
2	T Harris Smith	Scotland	Buenos Aires	1969
2	H Porta	Uruguay	Montevideo	1971
2	E De Forteza	Chile	Asuncion	1975
2	H Porta	New Zealand	Dunedin	1979
2	H Porta	Australia	Buenos Aires	1987
2	L Arbizu	Chile	Santiago	1991
2	L Arbizu	Australia	Llanelli	1991

Career Records

MOST CAPPED PLAYERS

Caps	Player	Career Span
78	L Arbizu	1990 to 2002
73	R Martin	1994 to 2002
68	P L Sporleder	1990 to 2002
63	D Cuesta Silva	1983 to 1995
59	F E Mendez	1990 to 2002
58	H Porta	1971 to 1990
46	M Loffreda	1978 to 1994
44	D Albanese	1995 to 2002
43	G A Llanes	1990 to 2000
42	A Pichot	1995 to 2002
40	E Branca	1976 to 1990
39	R Madero	1978 to 1990
39	D M Cash	1985 to 1992
39	G F Camardon	1990 to 2002
39	M Reggiardo	1996 to 2002
38	R D Grau	1993 to 2002
37	S Salvat	1987 to 1995
37	O J Hasan	1995 to 2002

MOST POINTS IN TESTS

Points	Player	Tests	Career
590	H Porta	58	1971 to 1990
411	G Quesada	30	1996 to 2002
364	S E Meson	34	1987 to 1997
181	F Contepomi	26	1998 to 2002
175	L Arbizu	78	1990 to 2002
138	J-L Cilley	13	1994 to 2002
129	J Luna	8	1995 to 1997
127	E Morgan	12	1972 to 1975
125	D Cuesta Silva	63	1983 to 1995

MOST TRIES IN TESTS

Tries	Player	Tests	Career
28	D Cuesta Silva	63	1983 to 1995
23	G M Jorge	22	1989 to 1994
18	F Soler	26	1996 to 2002
15	R Martin	73	1994 to 2002
15	L Arbizu	78	1990 to 2002
13	G Morgan	7	1977 to 1979
13	G Alvarez	9	1975 to 1977

MOST CONVERSIONS IN TESTS

Cons	Player	Tests	Career
84	H Porta	58	1971 to 1990
68	S E Meson	34	1987 to 1997
50	G Quesada	30	1996 to 2002
31	J-L Cilley	13	1994 to 2002
26	E Morgan	12	1972 to 1975
26	J Luna	8	1995 to 1997

MOST PENALTY GOALS IN TESTS

Penalties	Player	Tests	Career
101	H Porta	58	1971 to 1990
92	G Quesada	30	1996 to 2002
63	S E Meson	34	1987 to 1997
39	F Contepomi	26	1998 to 2002
22	J L Cilley	13	1994 to 2002
19	J Luna	8	1995 to 1997

MOST DROPPED GOALS IN TESTS

Drops	Player	Tests	Career
26	H Porta	58	1971 to 1990
10	L Arbizu	78	1990 to 2002
5	J D Fernandez Miranda	12	1997 to 2001
5	T Harris Smith	5	1969 to 1972
5	G Quesada	30	1996 to 2002

Career Records Of Argentina International Players
(up to 31 August 2002)

PLAYER	Debut	Caps	T	C	P	D	Pts
Backs:							
D Albanese	1995 v U	44	9	0	0	0	45
M Albina	2001 v US	1	0	0	0	0	0
L Arbizu	1990 v I	78	15	14	14	10	175
O Bartolucci	1996 v US	17	8	0	0	0	40
G Camardon	1990 v E	39	9	0	0	0	45
J-L Cilley	1994 v SA	13	2	31	22	0	138
F Contepomi	1998 v Ch	26	5	18	39	1	181
I Corleto	1998 v J	12	5	0	0	0	25
J D Fernandez Miranda	1997 v U	12	2	21	8	5	91
N Fernandez Miranda	1994 v US	23	4	0	0	0	20
M Gaitan	2002 v Pg	2	2	0	0	0	10
D Giannantonio	1996 v U	7	2	1	7	0	33
J C Legora	2002 v Pg	2	1	0	0	0	5
M Nannini	2002 v U	3	2	0	0	0	10
J M Nunez Piossek	2001 v U	6	8	0	0	0	40
J Orengo	1996 v U	25	6	0	0	0	30
A Pichot	1995 v A	42	10	0	0	0	50
G Quesada	1996 v US	30	4	50	92	5	411
H Senillosa	2002 v U	3	7	0	0	0	35
E Simone	1996 v US	36	8	0	0	0	40
F Soler	1996 v U	26	18	0	0	0	90
B Stortoni	1998 v J	11	6	1	0	0	32
Forwards:							
R Alvarez	1998 v Pg	11	0	0	0	0	0
A Amuchastegui	2002 v U	3	0	0	0	0	0
E Bergamaschi	2001 v US	1	0	0	0	0	0
S Bonorino	2001 v U	5	0	0	0	0	0
P Bouza	1996 v F	13	2	0	0	0	10
A Canalda	1999 v S	4	0	0	0	0	0
P Cardinali	2002 v U	2	0	0	0	0	0
H Dande	2001 v U	2	1	0	0	0	5
L de Chazal	2001 v U	2	0	0	0	0	0
M Durand	1998 v Ch	16	2	0	0	0	10
R D Grau	1993 v J	38	2	0	0	0	10
O Hasan	1995 v U	37	1	0	0	0	5
M Ledesma	1996 v U	32	0	0	0	0	0

C I Fernandez Lobbe	1996 v US	34	3	0	0	0	15
G Longo	1999 v W	22	1	0	0	0	5
R Martin	1994 v US	73	15	0	0	0	75
F E Mendez	1990 v I	59	11	0	0	0	55
G Morales Olivier	2001 v U	3	0	0	0	0	0
L Ostiglia	1999 v W	13	0	0	0	0	0
S Phelan	1997 v U	31	1	0	0	0	5
M Reggiardo	1996 v U	39	1	0	0	0	5
D Rodriguez	2002 v U	3	0	0	0	0	0
L Roldan	2001 v U	2	1	0	0	0	5
R Roncero	2002 v U	3	1	0	0	0	5
M Ruiz	1997 v NZ	23	0	0	0	0	0
M Sambucetti	2001 v U	4	0	0	0	0	0
P L Sporleder	1990 v I	68	10	0	0	0	50
G Ugartemendia	1991 v U	13	1	0	0	0	5
J J Villar	2001 v U	5	0	0	0	0	0

PACIFIC TEST SEASON REVIEW 2001-02

Japan Full of Eastern Promise; South Sea Islanders on the March

Jeremy Duxbury

Japan underlined once more their status as the kings of Asian rugby after huge wins over South Korea and Chinese Taipei in the final round of the World Cup qualifiers to earn themselves a place in Pool B next year.

Coach Shogo Mukai's team began with a 90-24 romp over the Koreans in Tokyo despite trailing 24-17 after half-an-hour. The rampant Japanese back division ran in 12 of the 13 tries as right-wing Daisuke Ohata grabbed four and left-wing Toru Kurihara collected 35 points. Three weeks later on the same ground, Mugai's men put Chinese Taipei to the sword in a 23-try, 155-3 annihilation, equalling the world record margin for a Test (set by Argentina in their 152-0 mauling of Paraguay earlier in the year). Ohata excelled himself once again, the Sydney-based speedster touching down eight times. For Mugai, it helped somewhat to put to rest the ghosts of 1995 – he was Japan's coach when they lost 145-17 to New Zealand at the World Cup in South Africa, a result that very nearly put Japanese rugby into isolation.

Japan then travelled to Seoul, where they downed the Koreans 55-17, and flew south to Taiwan for another victory over the Taiwanese – 120-3. But while these massive scores might indicate a great advance in Japanese rugby, one needs also to look at the result of May's home friendly against Tonga to get a true picture. Tonga, who finished winless at the bottom of the Oceania qualifiers, defeated Japan 41-29 in Kumagaya, just north of Tokyo. That match came one week after Japan's easy win in their historic first ever Test against Russia.

Japan's Test Record in 2001-2002: Played 6, won 5, lost 1.

Opponents	Date	Venue	Result
Chinese Taipei	21st July 2002	A	Won 120-3
South Korea	14th July 2002	A	Won 55-17
Chinese Taipei	6th July 2002	H	Won 155-3
South Korea	15th June 2002	H	Won 90-24
Tonga	26th May 2002	H	Lost 29-41
Russia	19th May 2002	H	Won 59-19

The major news for the three South Pacific Island powers was the announcement by IRB chairman Vernon Pugh QC that rugby's world governing body fully supported the idea of Fiji, Samoa and Tonga fielding a combined team to make tours along the lines of the British/Irish Lions.

Speaking in Nadi on Fiji's west coast after completing several rounds of talks with members of the Pacific Islanders Rugby Alliance (PIRA), Pugh said: 'It is a great concept that has considerable potential value if managed, promoted and sold properly. It must be very special, akin to the British Lions, and not a team that plays on an *ad hoc* basis.' He indicated that the first tour could take place in 2004 to Europe and/or the SANZAR nations and visits would recur every three or four years.

PIRA's chief executive, Charlie Charters, expressed delight with the progress, after the IRB had earlier intervened to postpone the Islanders' plans to field combined sides in Tests against both New Zealand and South Africa. 'I think the IRB had very legitimate concerns about the whole nature of the endeavour and whether we were sacrificing our individual identities for some sort of combined structure. I hope we've been able to put those concerns to rest. I think the IRB have marked our card and the concept has now come through with their endorsement,' he added.

More encouragement for the Islanders came with the announcement in May that the IRB would provide Fiji, Samoa and Tonga with a development trust fund worth not less than £2 million to help the three rugby nations rise up the ranks. The funds will come from the proceeds of the biennial North versus South match. The IRB intends to lift what they call the "second tier" unions to make them more competitive with the major nations.

'We've got over the best, or the worst, of professionalism with the major nations. That seems reasonably settled now and it's long overdue to see what can be done for Fiji, Tonga and Samoa,' Vernon Pugh said after heading a high level delegation on a three-day visit to Fiji, where they met with rugby officials from all three island nations. 'We've put up a lot of investment here to try and stabilise things and build a five- or six-year plan to ensure they have their best players available so they can be truly competitive again against almost anybody.' Pugh noted that some problems are very common to all three: 'Lack of finance, non-availability of their best players, dreadful poaching of the raw talent: all that has got to change,' he said.

Pugh added that the IRB was 'very impressed' with the new structure of the Fiji Rugby Union (FRU) that came about from Bill Wallace's report of April 2001. The new structure has seen a revised Constitution to meet the requirements of the professional era, the installing of a Board of Directors and the hiring of the FRU's first professional CEO, Pio Bosco Tikoisuva, who skippered Fiji when they beat the British/Irish Lions in 1977. During the week's meetings, Tikoisuva made a presentation outlining the FRU's immediate needs with much emphasis on development at the grassroots level – primary schools, secondary schools, under 19s, under 21s and women's rugby.

On the playing front, Fiji's topsy-turvy year finished on a high in July 2002 with a 47-20 victory over neighbours Tonga in Nadi to finish atop the

Oceania World Cup qualifying group and thus secure a far more favourable pool for Australia 2003. The seven-try-to-two triumph at Prince Charles Park was just enough for Fiji to overcome Samoa on points difference after a fiercely-contested double round-robin pool.

For the Fijians, it completed a remarkable turnaround from the depths of the disastrous tour to Europe of November 2001. They will now play France and Scotland in RWC Pool B, while Samoa go up against South Africa and England in Pool C. Should Tonga progress through the repechage, which also involves Papua New Guinea, the Cook Islands and South Korea, they would enter Pool D with New Zealand and Wales.

Tongan coach Jim Love confessed his admiration for the quick success enjoyed by his Fiji counterpart Mac McCallion, installed just weeks before the qualifiers began. 'I take my hat off to Mac for the work he has done with Fiji in a very short time,' Love said of his former New Zealand Maori team-mate.

Ex-Wallabies coach Greg Smith had put together a Fiji unit that became Pacific Rim champions in 2001, but he departed after falling out with the old management at the Union. The FRU subsequently underwent major restructuring in an effort to move into the professional era. In the interim, former national captain Ifereimi Tawake was unfortunate enough to coach the side to two abominable defeats in France and Italy.

Against Italy, a team that Fiji had thrashed 43-9 one season earlier, Fiji simply disintegrated and lost 66-10 – their worst-ever loss to a European side. A week later in St Etienne, a rampant France blitzed through a quite hapless Fijian defence, running in 12 tries in a 77-10 walloping. As if to rub salt into the wounds, old foes Samoa then visited Italy and won 17-9, despite playing the whole of the second half with 14 men after centre Fara'aoni Lalomilo was red-carded. The margin of victory for Samoa at the Fattori Stadium in Alghero could have been even wider had they not missed nine out of 13 kicks at goal. Two weeks earlier, John Boe's Samoans were forced to field an under-strength team against Ireland at Lansdowne Road and went down 35-8.

Whereas it would seem unthinkable for an All Black, Wallaby or England player to miss a Test match because of club commitments, it remains a sad reality that Pacific Island teams like Samoa still have to defer to the wishes of professional clubs. Despite IRB regulations that require clubs to release players for international duties or have the players "stood down", it is abundantly clear that no-one has been taking much notice.

Tonga, meanwhile, did not disgrace themselves in their tour of Scotland and Wales in November 2001, despite losing all four games. Though almost the entire Scottish media had written off the opening Test as a walkover, Tonga put up a very creditable performance to make Scotland work hard for their 43-20 win at Murrayfield. Ian McGeechan's men ran in three late tries for a somewhat flattering margin, the Tongans having threatened a bit of an upset when trailing by just five points with only 25 minutes to go. The Scotland coach later called their opponents 'the best group of players Tonga have ever put together world-wide. They made us work very hard to keep ball because they were attacking the ball-carrier all the time.'

Tonga's tour ended in disappointment when they conceded a string of late tries (while reduced to 14 men) in a 51-7 defeat against a mediocre Wales team at the Millennium Stadium. An interesting first half saw the Welsh on the back foot as the battle-hardened Tongans pounded them with heavy tackle after heavy tackle. Gareth Thomas scored the opening try but a powerful surge by Inoke Afeaki, who crashed through several Welshmen to reach the line, brought Tonga back into the game. With Wales leading 19-7 at half-time, Tonga still looked capable of scaring their hosts.

But Scottish referee Rob Dickson then had to wave his cards about – he reached for his yellow card twice within four minutes early into the second spell, leaving Tonga to defend their line with 13 men. Notably, the offences by Pierre Hola then Afeaki were not for high nor dangerous tackles but infringements at the breakdown. As Tonga hung on in the hope of some revival, their new cap in the centre, Gus Leger, was red-carded for trying to stamp on Ian Gough's head, and Wales ran in three of their six tries in the final 10 minutes. So, of the three Pacific Island nations on tour, only Samoa managed a Test victory.

Six months later, with World Cup spots on the line, the teams went head-to-head on a home-and-away basis for the first time. Fiji opened with a surprise 17-16 win at Apia Park in Samoa with 22-year-old wing Tevita Latianara scoring the decisive try on his debut. Five days later, Fiji put on another awesome display to defeat hosts Tonga 47-22 at Teufaiva Stadium. Vili Satala, back after missing the win in Samoa, set up Epeli Ruivadra on the wing for the opening try in the fourth minute, then scored a brace of tries himself to give Fiji a 27-0 lead in the opening half-hour.

Tonga had warmed up with a mini-tour to Tokyo where they looked in good shape and downed Japan 41-29. But Fiji's record points scorer Nicky Little had an outstanding day with the boot in Nuku'alofa, converting all five of Fiji's tries and adding four penalty goals. Tonga came back to score two tries just before the break from overlaps when gaps appeared in the Fiji defence. Ma'afu Pale, who came in as a replacement at left-wing, scored the first and right-wing Fepikou Tatafu added the second. On the hour, Isaac Mow made an important interception and raced away to score under the posts to give Fiji a comfortable cushion.

Samoa emulated Fiji's away form by defeating Tonga 25-16 before travelling to Nadi in western Fiji to upset their hosts 22-12 and blow the qualifying group open. Two tries by wing Lome Fa'atau and one by prop Tamato Leupolu in a 25-minute second-half spell overturned the narrow half-time deficit, while Joseph Narruhn's injury-time try was too little to be of help to Fiji. McCallion, disappointed with the way his team failed to gel, said Fiji lost it in all departments. 'We didn't play at all, we struggled at line-outs, scrum time and there was no forward ball for the backs,' he said, adding that Samoa's tight five out-muscled the Fiji pack.

With Samoa then handing Tonga their third consecutive defeat, the qualifying order came down to whether or not Fiji could outscore Tonga by more than 21 points in the final match. Fiji kept the Tongans try-less in the first half with good defence work and support play, and reached the break with a handy 23-6 advantage. Seru Rabeni, playing brilliantly at inside-centre, set up five of Fiji's seven tries, three via crafty chip-kicks over the Tonga line. He also interacted well with centre Vili Satala and full-back Norman Ligairi, who grabbed two glorious tries to add to the brace he scored against the All Blacks the previous weekend. Simon Raiwalui and half-back Jacob Rauluni played well under pressure, showing their experience when needed, while Satala rounded off a superb day for Fiji with his 15th try in his 25th Test after the required winning margin was secured.

'Fiji just had too much pace and experience for us,' Love exclaimed. 'Their backs tore us to pieces while we played like the third-place getters that we were. We fielded too many young boys who haven't played at this level.'

McCallion, who assisted Graham Henry when Auckland won the first two Super 12 competitions, was justifiably relieved: 'I feel very proud to be associated with this team,' he said. 'They made me proud today and they made the whole country proud.'

Either side of the Fiji-Tonga match, the Fijians played a one-off Test against New Zealand (falling 68-18 in Wellington) and the Samoans went down 60-18 to South Africa in Pretoria. Overall, the year underlined the necessity for these second-tier nations to be able to field their strongest sides for Test matches.

A year of optimism for the Pacific/South Seas region was tinged by sadness, however, with the news of the untimely death in September 2002 of former dual international Pat Tuidraki. A utility back, he had developed his rugby skills at St Paul's College in Auckland before representing Otago as a wing in 1990. He toured New Zealand with the 1994 Fijian side soon after he had emigrated to Japan, where he played for the Toyota club. After living for three years overseas and becoming fluent in the language of his adopted land, he made his Japan Test debut against Hong Kong in the 1997 Pacific Rim tournament and was a regular member of the Japanese Test squad up to last year. In 1999, he played for Japan against his native Fiji in Lautoka and scored a try for Japan against Wales in the 1999 Rugby World Cup tie at the Millennium Stadium. He had recently been diagnosed as suffering from a kidney ailment and collapsed and died suddenly in Nadi.

Fiji's Test Record in 2001-2002:
Played 7, won 3, lost 4.

Opponents	Date	Venue	Result
Tonga	6th July 2002	H	Won 47-20
New Zealand	29th June 2002	A	Lost 18-68
Samoa	22nd June 2002	H	Lost 12-22
Tonga	7th June 2002	A	Won 47-22
Samoa	1st June 2002	A	Won 17-16
France	24th November 2001	A	Lost 10-77
Italy	10th November 2001	A	Lost 10-66

Samoa's Test Record in 2001-2002:
Played 7, won 4, lost 3.

Opponents	Date	Venue	Result
South Africa	6th July 2002	A	Lost 18-60
Tonga	28th June 2002	H	Won 31-13
Fiji	22nd June 2002	A	Won 22-12
Tonga	15th June 2002	A	Won 25-16
Fiji	1st June 2002	H	Lost 16-17
Italy	24th November 2001	A	Won 17-9
Ireland	11th November 2001	A	Lost 8-35

Tonga's Test Record in 2001-2002:
Played 7, won 1, lost 6.

Opponents	Date	Venue	Result
Fiji	6th July 2002	A	Lost 20-47
Samoa	28th June 2002	A	Lost 13-31
Samoa	15th June 2002	H	Lost 16-25
Fiji	7th June 2002	H	Lost 22-47
Japan	26th May 2002	A	Won 41-29
Wales	17th November 2001	A	Lost 7-51
Scotland	10th November 2001	A	Lost 20-43

JAPAN INTERNATIONAL STATISTICS

(to 31 August 2002)

Match Records

MOST CONSECUTIVE TEST WINS
5 1980 *SK* 1981 *AU* 1982 *HK, C* 1,2

MOST CONSECUTIVE TESTS WITHOUT DEFEAT

Matches	Wins	Draws	Period
5	5	0	1980 to 1982

POINTS IN A MATCH
by the team

Pts	Opponents	Venue	Year
155	Chinese Taipei	Tokyo	2002
134	Chinese Taipei	Singapore	1998
120	Chinese Taipei	Tainan	2002
90	South Korea	Tokyo	2002
65	Chinese Taipei	Taiwan	2001

by a player

Pts	Player	Opponents	Venue	Year
60	T Kurihara	Chinese Taipei	Tainan	2002
40	D Ohata	Chinese Taipei	Tokyo	2002
35	T Kurihara	South Korea	Tokyo	2002
34	K Hirose	Tonga	Tokyo	1999
29	T Kurihara	Russia	Tokyo	2002

TRIES IN A MATCH
by the team

Tries	Opponents	Venue	Year
23	Chinese Taipei	Tokyo	2002
20	Chinese Taipei	Singapore	1998
18	Chinese Taipei	Tainan	2002
13	South Korea	Tokyo	2002
11	Chinese Taipei	Taiwan	2001

by a player

Tries	Player	Opponents	Venue	Year
8	D Ohata	Chinese Taipei	Tokyo	2002
6	T Kurihara	Chinese Taipei	Tokyo	2002
5	T Masuho	Chinese Taipei	Singapore	1998
4	Y Sakata	NZ Juniors	Wellington	1968
4	T Hirao	Chinese Taipei	Taiwan	2001
4	D Ohata	South Korea	Tokyo	2002

CONVERSIONS IN A MATCH
by the team

Cons	Opponents	Venue	Year
20	Chinese Taipei	Tokyo	2002
17	Chinese Taipei	Singapore	1998
15	Chinese Taipei	Tainan	2002
12	Zimbabwe	Belfast	1991
11	South Korea	Tokyo	2002

by a player

Cons	Player	Opponents	Venue	Year
15	T Kurihara	Chinese Taipei	Tainan	2002
12	A Miller	Chinese Taipei	Tokyo	2002
11	T Kurihara	South Korea	Tokyo	2002
10	K Hirose	Chinese Taipei	Singapore	1998
8	T Kurihara	Chinese Taipei	Tokyo	2002

PENALTIES IN A MATCH
by the team

Penalties	Opponents	Venue	Year
9	Tonga	Tokyo ·	1999
6	Tonga	Tokyo	1990
5	Argentina (1st Test)	Buenos Aires	1993
5	Argentina (2nd Test)	Buenos Aires	1993
5	South Korea	Tokyo	2001

by a player

Penalties	Player	Opponents	Venue	Year
9	K Hirose	Tonga	Tokyo	1999
6	T Hosokawa	Tonga	Tokyo	1990
5	T Hosokawa	Argentina (1st Test)	Buenos Aires	1993
5	T Hosokawa	Argentina (2nd Test)	Buenos Aires	1993
5	T Kurihara	South Korea	Tokyo	2001

DROPPED GOALS IN A MATCH
by the team

Drops	Opponents	Venue	Year
2	Argentina	Tokyo	1998

by a player

Drops	Player	Opponents	Venue	Year
2	K Iwabuchi	Argentina	Tokyo	1998

Career Records

CAPPED PLAYERS

Caps	Player	Career Span
57	Y Motoki	1991 to 2002
47	T Masuho	1991 to 2001
44	Y Sakuraba	1986 to 1999
43	M Kunda	1991 to 1999
42	T Ito	1996 to 2002
38	T Hayashi	1980 to 1992
37	H Tanuma	1996 to 2001
37	T Matsuda	1992 to 2001
36	S Hirao	1983 to 1995
33	W Murata	1991 to 2002
33	S Hasagawa	1997 to 2002

CONSECUTIVE TESTS

Tests	Player	Span
28	Y Motoki	1994 to 1998
26	Y Yoshida	1988 to 1995
18	S Mori	1974 to 1978
18	T Ishizuka	1978 to 1982
17	Y Konishi	1982 to 1986
17	B Ferguson	1993 to 1996

TESTS AS CAPTAIN

Tests	Captain	Span
16	M Kunda	1993 to 1998
16	A McCormick	1998 to 1999
13	T Hayashi	1984 to 1987
13	S Hirao	1989 to 1991
13	Y Motoki	1996 to 1997
10	T Takada	1976 to 1978

TESTS IN INDIVIDUAL POSITIONS

Position	Player	Tests	Span
Full-back	T Matsuda	33	1992 to 2001
Wing	T Masuho	47	1991 to 2001
Centre	Y Motoki	56	1991 to 2002
Fly-half	K Hirose	31	1994 to 2000
Scrum-half	W Murata	33	1991 to 2002
Prop	S Hasagawa	30	1997 to 2002
Hooker	M Kunda	43	1991 to 1999
Lock	Y Sakuraba	44	1986 to 1999
Flanker	H Kajihara	31	1989 to 1997
No 8	Sinali Latu	23	1987 to 1995

POINTS IN TESTS

Points	Player	Tests	Career
313	K Hirose	31	1994 to 2000
273	T Kurihara	17	2000 to 2002
155	D Ohata	28	1996 to 2002
152	T Masuho	47	1991 to 2001
115	T Hosokawa	11	1990 to 1993

TRIES IN TESTS

Tries	Player	Tests	Career
31	D Ohata	28	1996 to 2002
28	T Masuho	47	1991 to 2001
19	T Itoh	19	1963 to 1974
18	Y Yoshida	26	1988 to 1995
16	T Kurihara	17	2000 to 2002

CONVERSIONS IN TESTS

Cons	Player	Tests	Career
62	T Kurihara	17	2000 to 2002
50	K Hirose	31	1994 to 2000
17	Y Yamaguchi	13	1967 to 1973
14	N Ueyama	21	1973 to 1980
14	T Hosokawa	11	1990 to 1993

PENALTY GOALS IN TESTS

Penalties	Player	Tests	Career
65	K Hirose	31	1994 to 2000
24	T Hosokawa	11	1990 to 1993
23	T Kurihara	17	2000 to 2002
18	Y Yamaguchi	13	1967 to 1973
16	N Ueyama	21	1973 to 1980

DROPPED GOALS IN TESTS

Drops	Player	Tests	Career
3	Y Matsuo	24	1974 to 1984
2	K Matsuo	24	1986 to 1995
2	K Iwabuchi	19	1997 to 2002

Career Records Of Japan International Players
(up to 31 August 2002)

PLAYER	Debut	Caps	T	C	P	D	Pts
Backs:							
S Fuchigama	2000 v I	3	1	0	0	0	5
K Iwabuchi	1997 v HK	19	5	3	1	2	40
T Kurihara	2000 v Fj	17	16	62	23	0	273
A Miller	2002 v Ru	5	5	13	0	0	51
R Miki	1999 v Sp	5	7	0	0	0	35
Y Motoki	1991 v US	57	7	0	0	0	35
W Murata	1991 v US	33	5	13	11	0	84
H Nanba	2000 v Fj	16	5	0	0	0	25
D Ohata	1996 v SK	28	31	0	0	0	155
H Onozawa	2001 v W	7	8	0	0	0	40
Y Sonoda	2000 v Fj	8	1	0	0	0	5
S Tsukida	2001 v SK	6	0	0	0	0	0
H Yoshida	2001 v Sm	4	0	0	0	0	0
T Yoshida	2002 v Tg	2	1	0	0	0	5
Forwards:							
D Anglesey	2002 v Tg	3	2	0	0	0	10
S Hasagawa	1997 v HK	33	1	1	1	0	10
Y Hisadomi	2002 v Ru	1	0	0	0	0	0
T Ito	1996 v HK	42	5	0	0	0	25
T Kinoshita	2002 v Tg	1	0	0	0	0	0
K Koizumi	1997 v US	13	0	0	0	0	0
K Kubo	2000 v I	10	3	0	0	0	15
T Miuchi	2002 v Ru	4	1	0	0	0	5
N T Okubo	1999 v Tg	14	0	0	0	0	0
A Parker	2002 v Ru	6	2	0	0	0	10
Y Saito	2001 v CT	9	3	0	0	0	15
M Sakata	1996 v C	27	4	0	0	0	20
M Shichinohe	2002 v CT	1	0	0	0	0	0
M Toyoyama	2000 v Fj	15	2	0	0	0	10
L Vatuvai	2001 v SK	11	7	0	0	0	35
E Yamamoto	2001 v SK	3	0	0	0	0	0
M Yamamoto	2002 v Ru	3	0	0	0	0	0
R Yamamura	2001 v W	4	1	0	0	0	5

SAMOA INTERNATIONAL STATISTICS

(to 31 August 2002)

Match Records

MOST CONSECUTIVE TEST WINS

8 1990 *SK, Tg* 1, *J, Tg* 2, *Fj* 1991 *Tg, Fj, W*

MOST CONSECUTIVE TESTS WITHOUT DEFEAT

Matches	Wins	Draws	Period
8	8	0	1990 to 1991

MOST POINTS IN A MATCH
by the team

Pts	Opponents	Venue	Year
74	South Korea	Tokyo	1990
68	Japan	Apia	2000
62	Tonga	Apia	1997
55	West Germany	Bonn	1989
47	Japan	Tokyo	2001
43	Japan	Apia	1999
43	Italy	Apia	2000

by a player

Pts	Player	Opponents	Venue	Year
23	A Aiolupo	South Korea	Tokyo	1990
23	S Leaega	Japan	Apia	1999
23	T Samania	Italy	Apia	2000
22	D J Kellett	Tonga	Moamoa	1994
21	M Vaea	Fiji	Apia	1991
20	E Seveali'i	Japan	Apia	2000

MOST TRIES IN A MATCH
by the team

Tries	Opponents	Venue	Year
13	South Korea	Tokyo	1990
10	West Germany	Bonn	1989
10	Tonga	Apia	1997
10	Japan	Apia	2000
8	Tonga	Apia	1991
7	Japan	Tokyo	2001
7	Canada	Apia	2000

by a player

Tries	Player	Opponents	Venue	Year
4	T Fa'amasino	Tonga	Apia	1991
4	E Seveali'i	Japan	Apia	2000
3	T Fa'amasino	South Korea	Tokyo	1990
3	B P Lima	Fiji	Apia	1991
3	A So'oalo	Tonga	Apia	1997

MOST CONVERSIONS IN A MATCH
by the team

Cons	Opponents	Venue	Year
8	South Korea	Tokyo	1990
6	West Germany	Bonn	1989
6	Tonga	Apia	1997
6	Japan	Apia	2000
6	Japan	Tokyo	2001
5	Belgium	Brussels	1989
5	Japan	Apia	1990
5	Wales	Cardiff	1999

by a player

Cons	Player	Opponents	Venue	Year
8	A Aiolupo	South Korea	Tokyo	1990
6	T Vili	Japan	Apia	2000
6	E Va'a	Japan	Tokyo	2001
5	A Aiolupo	Belgium	Brussels	1989
5	A Aiolupo	Japan	Apia	1990
5	S Leaega	Tonga	Apia	1997
5	S Leaega	Wales	Cardiff	1999

MOST PENALTIES IN A MATCH
by the team

Penalties	Opponents	Venue	Year
5	Tonga	Moamoa	1994
5	Wales	Moamoa	1994
5	Argentina	East London	1995
5	Japan	Osaka	1999
4	Tonga	Suva	1988
4	Fiji	Apia	1997
4	Japan	Apia	1999
4	Italy	Apia	2000
4	Tonga	Nuku'alofa	2002

by a player

Penalties	Player	Opponents	Venue	Year
5	D J Kellett	Tonga	Moamoa	1994
5	D J Kellett	Wales	Moamoa	1994
5	D J Kellett	Argentina	East London	1995
5	S Leaega	Japan	Osaka	1999
4	A Aiolupo	Tonga	Suva	1988
4	E Va'a	Fiji	Apia	1997
4	S Leaega	Japan	Apia	1999
4	S Leaega	Italy	Apia	2000
4	E Va'a	Tonga	Nuku'alofa	2002

MOST DROPPED GOALS IN A MATCH
by the team

Drops	Opponents	Venue	Year
1	Fiji	Nadi	1981
1	South Korea	Tokyo	1990
1	Fiji	Apia	1991
1	Scotland	Murrayfield	1991
1	Tonga	Moamoa	1994

by a player

Drops	Player	Opponents	Venue	Year
1	A Palamo	Fiji	Nadi	1981
1	J Ah Kuoi	South Korea	Tokyo	1990
1	S J Bachop	Fiji	Apia	1991
1	S J Bachop	Scotland	Murrayfield	1991
1	D J Kellett	Tonga	Moamoa	1994

Career Records
MOST CAPPED PLAYERS

Caps	Player	Career Span
60	T Vaega	1986 to 2001
48	B P Lima	1991 to 2002
37	A Aiolupo	1983 to 1994
35	P R Lam	1991 to 1999
34	P P Fatialofa	1988 to 1996
29	S To'omalatai	1985 to 1995
29	O Palepoi	1998 to 2002
28	S Vaifale	1989 to 1997
28	T Leota	1997 to 2001
27	T Salesa	1979 to 1989
26	P J Paramore	1991 to 2001

MOST POINTS IN TESTS

Points	Player	Tests	Career
180	A Aiolupo	37	1983 to 1994
160	S Leaega	17	1997 to 2002
157	D J Kellett	13	1993 to 1995
124	B P Lima	48	1991 to 2002
114	T Salesa	27	1979 to 1989
111	E Va'a	22	1996 to 2002
75	A So'oalo	19	1996 to 2001
73	T Vili	16	1999 to 2001
66	T Vaega	60	1986 to 2001
64	S J Bachop	18	1991 to 1999

MOST TRIES IN TESTS

Tries	Player	Tests	Career
26	B P Lima	48	1991 to 2002
15	T Vaega	60	1986 to 2001
15	A So'oalo	19	1996 to 2001
13	R Koko	22	1983 to 1994
11	T Fa'amasino	20	1988 to 1996
10	G E Leaupepe	25	1995 to 1999

MOST CONVERSIONS IN TESTS

Cons	Player	Tests	Career
35	A Aiolupo	37	1983 to 1994
26	S Leaega	17	1997 to 2002
18	D J Kellett	13	1993 to 1995
18	E Va'a	22	1996 to 2002
14	T Salesa	27	1979 to 1989
14	T Vili	16	1999 to 2001

MOST PENALTY GOALS IN TESTS

Penalties	Player	Tests	Career
35	D J Kellett	13	1993 to 1995
31	S Leaega	17	1997 to 2002
27	A Aiolupo	37	1983 to 1994
22	T Salesa	27	1979 to 1989
20	E Va'a	22	1996 to 2002

MOST DROPPED GOALS IN TESTS

Drops	Player	Tests	Career
2	S J Bachop	18	1991 to 1999
1	A Palamo	9	1979 to 1982
1	J Ah Kuoi	5	1987 to 1990
1	D J Kellett	13	1993 to 1995

329

Career Records Of Samoa International Players
(up to 31st August 2002)

PLAYER	Debut	Caps	T	C	P	D	Pts
Backs:							
L Fa'atau	2000 v Fj	9	3	0	0	0	15
T Fanolua	1996 v NZ	20	6	0	0	0	30
S Leaega	1997 v Tg	17	3	26	31	0	160
B P Lima	1991 v Tg	48	26	0	0	0	124
C Manu	2002 v Fj	4	0	0	0	0	0
E Seveali'i	2000 v Fj	14	9	0	0	0	45
A So'oalo	1996 v I	19	15	0	0	0	75
S So'oialo	1998 v Tg	22	4	0	0	0	20
A Toleafoa	2000 v W	3	0	0	0	0	0
V Tuigamala	1996 v I	22	3	1	0	0	17
A Tuilagi	2002 v Fj	3	0	0	0	0	0
F Tuilagi	1992 v Tg	16	2	0	0	0	10
D Tyrell	2000 v Fj	7	1	0	0	0	5
E Va'a	1996 v I	22	3	18	20	0	111
T Vili	1999 v C	16	3	14	10	0	73
Forwards:							
M Fa'asavalu	2002 v SA	1	0	0	0	0	0
L Lafaiali'i	2001 v Tg	9	0	0	0	0	0
F Lalomilo	2001 v I	2	0	0	0	0	0
K Lealamanua	2000 v Fj	14	1	0	0	0	5
P Leavasa	1993 v Tg	17	0	0	0	0	0
T Leota	1997 v Tg	28	1	0	0	0	5
T Leupola	2001 v I	7	0	0	0	0	0
J Meredith	2001 v I	7	0	0	0	0	0
O Palepoi	1998 v Tg	29	1	0	0	0	5
P Segi	2001 v Fj	9	1	0	0	0	5
S Sititi	1999 v J	24	6	0	0	0	30
G Stowers	2001 v I	1	0	0	0	0	0
P Tapelu	2002 v SA	1	0	0	0	0	0
J Tomuli	2001 v I	7	0	0	0	0	0
H Tuilagi	2002 v Fj	4	0	0	0	0	0
S Vaili	2002 v Fj	4	0	0	0	0	0
K Viliamu	2001 v I	4	1	0	0	0	5

WOMEN'S TEST SEASON REVIEW 2001-02

World Cup Focuses the Mind

Nicola Goodwin

For Women's rugby players across the world one thing dominated the 2001-2002 season – Barcelona. The fourth Women's World Cup would be staged in Spain and promised to be the biggest, most widely publicised and most well supported tournament the game had ever seen. For many countries, preparation for the event had begun at the previous World Cup in Holland in 1998, where plans were laid down and the wheels of change were set in motion. For many other nations, however, it was a struggle to even make the tournament, so perhaps the 2001-2002 season should be best remembered as a year of dramatic changes and the tale of the haves versus the have-nots.

The 2000-2001 season had ended with the 1998 world champions, New Zealand, being beaten for the first time in ten years as England overcame them 22-17 in the second of two Tests on All Black soil. New Zealand captain Farah Palmer stated in her post-match speech that defeat would have come at some point and they were glad it was then and not at the World Cup. Her words were prophetic. New Zealand subsequently spent the next eleven months making sure they were stronger, fitter and faster than ever before. That defeat in North Harbour in June 2001 was to be their last international before Barcelona and, although their refusal to play Test matches was not well received by neighbours Australia, the ever-improving NPC domestic games in New Zealand were to provide all the preparation that the Black Ferns needed.

Elsewhere across the globe, many countries were given additional funding by their governing bodies as they focused on the World Cup. France appointed their first professional performance director, Richard Gradel, America brought in a new coaching team and drastically re-vamped their squad, while Scotland's years of virtual poverty were improved by increased funding from the SRU and the promise of lottery assistance in the future.

The England squad were arguably the best supported team of 2001-2002 though, increased funding from the National Lottery and Sport England allowing many players to concentrate solely on rugby. The squad enjoyed first class fitness assistance and expertise in the area of performance analysis.

The vast gulf in financial support for the game, however, was evident throughout the season. Ireland struggled in their second season back in international rugby and their barriers were highlighted by the fact that their entire budget for the season was less than France enjoyed for just one fixture.

The international season began early as tours were undertaken to gain much-needed match preparation. Canada and the United States arrived in Britain and, although England could not fit fixtures into their swamped schedule, Wales and Scotland made the most of the visits. Wales notched up positive and encouraging results with a 13-13 draw against Canada and a narrow 17-20 defeat against the United States, while Scotland consolidated on their 2001 European Championships victory with a 13-3 victory over Sweden and a 22-3 win against the United States. Ireland also notched up wins against Holland (13-0) and the British Police (29-0), while Germany and Holland made the most of their close ties.

Four Canadians, Dawn Keim, Christie Thompson, Raquel Eldridge and Lesley Cripps, stayed in England after their winter tour to play a better standard of rugby; an example of how seriously the World Cup was taken by players across the globe.

Although internationals weren't being regularly played in the Southern Hemisphere, teams were certainly not resting on their laurels. Australia gained enormous support from the ARU and were treated on an equal footing to their male equivalents at the national high-performance unit, where they enjoyed the help of Eddie Jones, Glen Ella and national defence coach John Muggleton.

New Zealand coach Darryl Suasua gave his team extra motivation by announcing his six-year stint would end at the World Cup, and emerging nations Samoa and Tonga coaxed players to return from neighbouring Australia and New Zealand. The Samoans made their Test bow with a home match at Apia Park against Japan. The speed and sleight of hand of the lighter Japanese side were a challenge for the Manusiana and an absorbing match ended in a narrow 12-10 triumph for the visitors.

In the absence of a Canada Cup or European Championship, the annual Six Nations was the only major international tournament prior to the World Cup. England and France were the favourites prior to the tournament and, indeed, it proved to be a two-horse race. France's defeat of England signalled that Geoff Richards's side weren't invincible, even though they recovered well to beat Spain convincingly.

Ireland struggled once again, failing to gain a victory in the tournament, but they won themselves much admiration for their gutsy, brave perform-ances. Spain again proved that they are capable of great things while their third-place finish gave notice that they were more than worthy of admission to the tournament and would make a very able host nation for the World Cup.

Wales struggled with injury, losing both captain Rhian Williams and hooker Jamie Kift amongst others for most of the tournament. Their decision not to include full-back Non Evans in the squad owing to her heavy Commonwealth Games commitments also left them without an experi-enced play-maker.

On the domestic scene, England and New Zealand once again demon-strated they had the best competitions in the world, with players from across the globe travelling to play in the RFUW Premiership and

NPC Championship respectively. Clifton became the *Rugby World* Cup winners and Saracens lifted the RFUW Premiership. Wales indicated their strength in depth when UWIC beat Loughborough in the BUSA final at Twickenham.

The 2001-2002 season took the game to new heights and showed that women's rugby had enormous potential, both as a participation sport and as a spectator sport worldwide. The IRB are to be congratulated for the management and organisation of the World Cup which lived up to expectations and, as promised, once more took the game on a stage further.

The final whistle at the Olympic Stadium in Barcelona brought with it many goodbyes to some great names from the world of women's rugby. New Zealand coach Darryl Suasua left his side on top of the world and England's Gill Burns retired after four World Cups. Two Welsh stalwarts, Pip Minto and Liza Burgess, their most-capped player, also hung up their international boots.

As doors close for some, however, they open for others and news of new nations emerging in women's rugby is highly promising. Great strides are being taken in South Africa as the game there gains more support from the traditionally male-dominated clubs and unions. Trinidad, too, are working hard at launching themselves on to the international scene, while another country to watch is Sweden. Despite being able to train on grass for limited months in the year, they have secured a place in the main 2003 European Competition, thanks to victories over Belgium, Holland and Luxembourg. Perhaps unsurprisingly, though, they are coached by a New Zealander – proof that the 2002 World Champions' dominance of women's rugby stretched far beyond their native islands.

Six Nations Results 2002

2 February: Ireland 9, Wales 13; France 24, Spain 0; 3 February: Scotland 8, England 35; 15 February: Wales 0, France 20; 17 February: England 79, Ireland 0; Spain 15, Scotland 17; 1 March: France 22, England 17; 3 March: Ireland 0, Scotland 13; Spain 20, Wales 0; 23 March: Ireland 6, Spain 8; 24 March: Scotland 12, France 22; England 40, Wales 0; 5 April: France 46, Ireland 0 ; 7 April: Wales 31, Scotland 3; Spain 14, England 53

Six Nations 2002: Final Table

	P	W	D	L	F	A	Pts
France	5	5	0	0	134	29	10
England	5	4	0	1	224	44	8
Spain	5	2	0	3	57	100	4
Wales	5	2	0	3	44	92	4
Scotland	5	2	0	3	53	103	4
Ireland	5	0	0	5	15	159	0

INTERNATIONAL RECORDS

Results of International Matches
(up to 31 August 2002)

Cap matches involving senior executive council member unions only.
Years for International Championship matches are for the second half of the season: eg 1972 means season 1971-72. Years for matches against touring teams from the Southern Hemisphere refer to the actual year of the match.

Points-scoring was first introduced in 1886, when an International Board was formed by Scotland, Ireland and Wales. Points values varied between countries until 1890, when England agreed to join the Board, and uniform values were adopted.

Northern Hemisphere seasons	Try	Conversion	Penalty goal	Dropped goal	Goal from mark
1890-91	1	2	2	3	3
1891-92 to 1892-93	2	3	3	4	4
1893-94 to 1904-05	3	2	3	4	4
1905-06 to 1947-48	3	2	3	4	3
1948-49 to 1970-71	3	2	3	3	3
1971-72 to 1991-92	4	2	3	3	3*
1992-93 onwards	5	2	3	3	–

*The goal from mark ceased to exist when the free-kick clause was introduced, 1977-78.
WC indicates a fixture played during the Rugby World Cup finals. LC indicates a fixture played in the Latin Cup. TN indicates a fixture played in the Tri Nations.

ENGLAND v SCOTLAND
Played 119   England won 62, Scotland won 40, Drawn 17
Highest scores England 43-3 in 2001, Scotland 33-6 in 1986
Biggest wins England 43-3 in 2001, Scotland 33-6 in 1986

1871 Raeburn Place (Edinburgh) **Scotland** 1G 1T to 1T	1889 No Match
1872 The Oval (London) **England** 1G 1DG 2T to 1DG	1890 Raeburn Place **England** 1G 1T to 0
1873 Glasgow **Drawn** no score	1891 Richmond (London) **Scotland** 9-3
1874 The Oval **England** 1DG to 1T	1892 Raeburn Place **England** 5-0
1875 Raeburn Place **Drawn** no score	1893 Leeds **Scotland** 8-0
1876 The Oval **England** 1G 1T to 0	1894 Raeburn Place **Scotland** 6-0
1877 Raeburn Place **Scotland** 1 DG to 0	1895 Richmond **Scotland** 6-3
1878 The Oval **Drawn** no score	1896 Glasgow **Scotland** 11-0
1879 Raeburn Place **Drawn** Scotland 1DG England 1G	1897 Manchester **England** 12-3
1880 Manchester **England** 2G 3T to 1G	1898 Powderhall (Edinburgh) **Drawn** 3-3
1881 Raeburn Place **Drawn** Scotland 1G 1T England 1DG 1T	1899 Blackheath **Scotland** 5-0
1882 Manchester **Scotland** 2T to 0	1900 Inverleith (Edinburgh) **Drawn** 0-0
1883 Raeburn Place **England** 2T to 1T	1901 Blackheath **Scotland** 18-3
1884 Blackheath (London) **England** 1G to 1T	1902 Inverleith **England** 6-3
1885 No Match	1903 Richmond **Scotland** 10-6
1886 Raeburn Place **Drawn** no score	1904 Inverleith **Scotland** 6-3
1887 Manchester **Drawn** 1T each	1905 Richmond **Scotland** 8-0
1888 No Match	1906 Inverleith **England** 9-3
	1907 Blackheath **Scotland** 8-3
	1908 Inverleith **Scotland** 16-10
	1909 Richmond **Scotland** 18-8
	1910 Inverleith **England** 14-5

1911	Twickenham **England** 13-8		1965	Twickenham **Drawn** 3-3
1912	Inverleith **Scotland** 8-3		1966	Murrayfield **Scotland** 6-3
1913	Twickenham **England** 3-0		1967	Twickenham **England** 27-14
1914	Inverleith **England** 16-15		1968	Murrayfield **England** 8-6
1920	Twickenham **England** 13-4		1969	Twickenham **England** 8-3
1921	Inverleith **England** 18-0		1970	Murrayfield **Scotland** 14-5
1922	Twickenham **England** 11-5		1971	Twickenham **Scotland** 16-15
1923	Inverleith **England** 8-6		1971	Murrayfield **Scotland** 26-6
1924	Twickenham **England** 19-0			*Special centenary match – non-championship*
1925	Murrayfield **Scotland** 14-11		1972	Murrayfield **Scotland** 23-9
1926	Twickenham **Scotland** 17-9		1973	Twickenham **England** 20-13
1927	Murrayfield **Scotland** 21-13		1974	Murrayfield **Scotland** 16-14
1928	Twickenham **England** 6-0		1975	Twickenham **England** 7-6
1929	Murrayfield **Scotland** 12-6		1976	Murrayfield **Scotland** 22-12
1930	Twickenham **Drawn** 0-0		1977	Twickenham **England** 26-6
1931	Murrayfield **Scotland** 28-19		1978	Murrayfield **England** 15-0
1932	Twickenham **England** 16-3		1979	Twickenham **Drawn** 7-7
1933	Murrayfield **Scotland** 3-0		1980	Murrayfield **England** 30-18
1934	Twickenham **England** 6-3		1981	Twickenham **England** 23-17
1935	Murrayfield **Scotland** 10-7		1982	Murrayfield **Drawn** 9-9
1936	Twickenham **England** 9-8		1983	Twickenham **Scotland** 22-12
1937	Murrayfield **England** 6-3		1984	Murrayfield **Scotland** 18-6
1938	Twickenham **Scotland** 21-16		1985	Twickenham **England** 10-7
1939	Murrayfield **England** 9-6		1986	Murrayfield **Scotland** 33-6
1947	Twickenham **England** 24-5		1987	Twickenham **England** 21-12
1948	Murrayfield **Scotland** 6-3		1988	Murrayfield **England** 9-6
1949	Twickenham **England** 19-3		1989	Twickenham **Drawn** 12-12
1950	Murrayfield **Scotland** 13-11		1990	Murrayfield **Scotland** 13-7
1951	Twickenham **England** 5-3		1991	Twickenham **England** 21-12
1952	Murrayfield **England** 19-3		1991	Murrayfield *WC* **England** 9-6
1953	Twickenham **England** 26-8		1992	Murrayfield **England** 25-7
1954	Murrayfield **England** 13-3		1993	Twickenham **England** 26-12
1955	Twickenham **England** 9-6		1994	Murrayfield **England** 15-14
1956	Murrayfield **England** 11-6		1995	Twickenham **England** 24-12
1957	Twickenham **England** 16-3		1996	Murrayfield **England** 18-9
1958	Murrayfield **Drawn** 3-3		1997	Twickenham **England** 41-13
1959	Twickenham **Drawn** 3-3		1998	Murrayfield **England** 34-20
1960	Murrayfield **England** 21-12		1999	Twickenham **England** 24-21
1961	Twickenham **England** 6-0		2000	Murrayfield **Scotland** 19-13
1962	Murrayfield **Drawn** 3-3		2001	Twickenham **England** 43-3
1963	Twickenham **England** 10-8		2002	Murrayfield **England** 29-3
1964	Murrayfield **Scotland** 15-6			

ENGLAND v IRELAND
Played 115   England won 68, Ireland won 39, Drawn 8
Highest scores England 50-18 in 2000, Ireland 26-21 in 1974
Biggest wins England 46-6 in 1997, Ireland 22-0 in 1947

1875	The Oval (London) **England** 1G 1DG 1T to 0		1887	Dublin **Ireland** 2G to 0
1876	Dublin **England** 1G 1T to 0		1888	No Match
1877	The Oval **England** 2G 2T to 0		1889	No Match
1878	Dublin **England** 2G 1T to 0		1890	Blackheath (London) **England** 3T to 0
1879	The Oval **England** 2G 1DG 2T to 0		1891	Dublin **England** 9-0
1880	Dublin **England** 1G 1T to 1T		1892	Manchester **England** 7-0
1881	Manchester **England** 2G 2T to 0		1893	Dublin **England** 4-0
1882	Dublin **Drawn** 2T each		1894	Blackheath **Ireland** 7-5
1883	Manchester **England** 1G 3T to 1T		1895	Dublin **England** 6-3
1884	Dublin **England** 1G to 0		1896	Leeds **Ireland** 10-4
1885	Manchester **England** 2T to 1T		1897	Dublin **Ireland** 13-9
1886	Dublin **England** 1T to 0		1898	Richmond (London) **Ireland** 9-6
			1899	Dublin **Ireland** 6-0

1900	Richmond **England** 15-4		1959	Dublin **England** 3-0
1901	Dublin **Ireland** 10-6		1960	Twickenham **England** 8-5
1902	Leicester **England** 6-3		1961	Dublin **Ireland** 11-8
1903	Dublin **Ireland** 6-0		1962	Twickenham **England** 16-0
1904	Blackheath **England** 19-0		1963	Dublin **Drawn** 0-0
1905	Cork **Ireland** 17-3		1964	Twickenham **Ireland** 18-5
1906	Leicester **Ireland** 16-6		1965	Dublin **Ireland** 5-0
1907	Dublin **Ireland** 17-9		1966	Twickenham **Drawn** 6-6
1908	Richmond **England** 13-3		1967	Dublin **England** 8-3
1909	Dublin **England** 11-5		1968	Twickenham **Drawn** 9-9
1910	Twickenham **Drawn** 0-0		1969	Dublin **Ireland** 17-15
1911	Dublin **Ireland** 3-0		1970	Twickenham **England** 9-3
1912	Twickenham **England** 15-0		1971	Dublin **England** 9-6
1913	Dublin **England** 15-4		1972	Twickenham **Ireland** 16-12
1914	Twickenham **England** 17-12		1973	Dublin **Ireland** 18-9
1920	Dublin **England** 14-11		1974	Twickenham **Ireland** 26-21
1921	Twickenham **England** 15-0		1975	Dublin **Ireland** 12-9
1922	Dublin **England** 12-3		1976	Twickenham **Ireland** 13-12
1923	Leicester **England** 23-5		1977	Dublin **England** 4-0
1924	Belfast **England** 14-3		1978	Twickenham **England** 15-9
1925	Twickenham **Drawn** 6-6		1979	Dublin **Ireland** 12-7
1926	Dublin **Ireland** 19-15		1980	Twickenham **England** 24-9
1927	Twickenham **England** 8-6		1981	Dublin **England** 10-6
1928	Dublin **England** 7-6		1982	Twickenham **Ireland** 16-15
1929	Twickenham **Ireland** 6-5		1983	Dublin **Ireland** 25-15
1930	Dublin **Ireland** 4-3		1984	Twickenham **England** 12-9
1931	Twickenham **Ireland** 6-5		1985	Dublin **Ireland** 13-10
1932	Dublin **England** 11-8		1986	Twickenham **England** 25-20
1933	Twickenham **England** 17-6		1987	Dublin **Ireland** 17-0
1934	Dublin **England** 13-3		1988	Twickenham **England** 35-3
1935	Twickenham **England** 14-3		1988	Dublin **England** 21-10
1936	Dublin **Ireland** 6-3			*Non-championship match*
1937	Twickenham **England** 9-8		1989	Dublin **England** 16-3
1938	Dublin **England** 36-14		1990	Twickenham **England** 23-0
1939	Twickenham **Ireland** 5-0		1991	Dublin **England** 16-7
1947	Dublin **Ireland** 22-0		1992	Twickenham **England** 38-9
1948	Twickenham **Ireland** 11-10		1993	Dublin **Ireland** 17-3
1949	Dublin **Ireland** 14-5		1994	Twickenham **Ireland** 13-12
1950	Twickenham **England** 3-0		1995	Dublin **England** 20-8
1951	Dublin **Ireland** 3-0		1996	Twickenham **England** 28-15
1952	Twickenham **England** 3-0		1997	Dublin **England** 46-6
1953	Dublin **Drawn** 9-9		1998	Twickenham **England** 35-17
1954	Twickenham **England** 14-3		1999	Dublin **England** 27-15
1955	Dublin **Drawn** 6-6		2000	Twickenham **England** 50-18
1956	Twickenham **England** 20-0		2001	Dublin **Ireland** 20-14
1957	Dublin **England** 6-0		2002	Twickenham **England** 45-11
1958	Twickenham **England** 6-0			

ENGLAND v WALES

Played 108   England won 47, Wales won 49, Drawn 12
Highest scores England 50-10 in 2002, Wales 34-21 in 1967
Biggest wins England 50-10 in 2002, 46-12 in 2000, Wales 25-0 in 1905

1881	Blackheath (London) **England** 7G 1DG 6T to 0		1888	No Match
1882	No Match		1889	No Match
1883	Swansea **England** 2G 4T to 0		1890	Dewsbury **Wales** 1T to 0
1884	Leeds **England** 1G 2T to 1G		1891	Newport **England** 7-3
1885	Swansea **England** 1G 4T to 1G 1T		1892	Blackheath **England** 17-0
1886	Blackheath **England** 1GM 2T to 1G		1893	Cardiff **Wales** 12-11
1887	Llanelli **Drawn** no score		1894	Birkenhead **England** 24-3
			1895	Swansea **England** 14-6

1896	Blackheath **England** 25-0		1957	Cardiff **England** 3-0
1897	Newport **Wales** 11-0		1958	Twickenham **Drawn** 3-3
1898	Blackheath **England** 14-7		1959	Cardiff **Wales** 5-0
1899	Swansea **Wales** 26-3		1960	Twickenham **England** 14-6
1900	Gloucester **Wales** 13-3		1961	Cardiff **Wales** 6-3
1901	Cardiff **Wales** 13-0		1962	Twickenham **Drawn** 0-0
1902	Blackheath **Wales** 9-8		1963	Cardiff **England** 13-6
1903	Swansea **Wales** 21-5		1964	Twickenham **Drawn** 6-6
1904	Leicester **Drawn** 14-14		1965	Cardiff **Wales** 14-3
1905	Cardiff **Wales** 25-0		1966	Twickenham **Wales** 11-6
1906	Richmond (London) **Wales** 16-3		1967	Cardiff **Wales** 34-21
1907	Swansea **Wales** 22-0		1968	Twickenham **Drawn** 11-11
1908	Bristol **Wales** 28-18		1969	Cardiff **Wales** 30-9
1909	Cardiff **Wales** 8-0		1970	Twickenham **Wales** 17-13
1910	Twickenham **England** 11-6		1971	Cardiff **Wales** 22-6
1911	Swansea **Wales** 15-11		1972	Twickenham **Wales** 12-3
1912	Twickenham **England** 8-0		1973	Cardiff **Wales** 25-9
1913	Cardiff **England** 12-0		1974	Twickenham **England** 16-12
1914	Twickenham **England** 10-9		1975	Cardiff **Wales** 20-4
1920	Swansea **Wales** 19-5		1976	Twickenham **Wales** 21-9
1921	Twickenham **England** 18-3		1977	Cardiff **Wales** 14-9
1922	Cardiff **Wales** 28-6		1978	Twickenham **Wales** 9-6
1923	Twickenham **England** 7-3		1979	Cardiff **Wales** 27-3
1924	Swansea **England** 17-9		1980	Twickenham **England** 9-8
1925	Twickenham **England** 12-6		1981	Cardiff **Wales** 21-19
1926	Cardiff **Drawn** 3-3		1982	Twickenham **England** 17-7
1927	Twickenham **England** 11-9		1983	Cardiff **Drawn** 13-13
1928	Swansea **England** 10-8		1984	Twickenham **Wales** 24-15
1929	Twickenham **England** 8-3		1985	Cardiff **Wales** 24-15
1930	Cardiff **England** 11-3		1986	Twickenham **England** 21-18
1931	Twickenham **Drawn** 11-11		1987	Cardiff **Wales** 19-12
1932	Swansea **Wales** 12-5		1987	Brisbane *WC* **Wales** 16-3
1933	Twickenham **Wales** 7-3		1988	Twickenham **Wales** 11-3
1934	Cardiff **England** 9-0		1989	Cardiff **Wales** 12-9
1935	Twickenham **Drawn** 3-3		1990	Twickenham **England** 34-6
1936	Swansea **Drawn** 0-0		1991	Cardiff **England** 25-6
1937	Twickenham **England** 4-3		1992	Twickenham **England** 24-0
1938	Cardiff **Wales** 14-8		1993	Cardiff **Wales** 10-9
1939	Twickenham **England** 3-0		1994	Twickenham **England** 15-8
1947	Cardiff **England** 9-6		1995	Cardiff **England** 23-9
1948	Twickenham **Drawn** 3-3		1996	Twickenham **England** 21-15
1949	Cardiff **Wales** 9-3		1997	Cardiff **England** 34-13
1950	Twickenham **Wales** 11-5		1998	Twickenham **England** 60-26
1951	Swansea **Wales** 23-5		1999	Wembley **Wales** 32-31
1952	Twickenham **Wales** 8-6		2000	Twickenham **England** 46-12
1953	Cardiff **England** 8-3		2001	Cardiff **England** 44-15
1954	Twickenham **England** 9-6		2002	Twickenham **England** 50-10
1955	Cardiff **Wales** 3-0			
1956	Twickenham **Wales** 8-3			

ENGLAND v FRANCE

Played 79   England won 43, France won 29, Drawn 7
Highest scores England 48-19 in 2001, France 37-12 in 1972
Biggest wins England 37-0 in 1911, France 37-12 in 1972

1906	Paris **England** 35-8		1910	Paris **England** 11-3
1907	Richmond (London) **England** 41-13		1911	Twickenham **England** 37-0
1908	Paris **England** 19-0		1912	Paris **England** 18-8
1909	Leicester **England** 22-0		1913	Twickenham **England** 20-0

1914	Paris **England** 39-13	
1920	Twickenham **England** 8-3	
1921	Paris **England** 10-6	
1922	Twickenham **Drawn** 11-11	
1923	Paris **England** 12-3	
1924	Twickenham **England** 19-7	
1925	Paris **England** 13-11	
1926	Twickenham **England** 11-0	
1927	Paris **France** 3-0	
1928	Twickenham **England** 18-8	
1929	Paris **England** 16-6	
1930	Twickenham **England** 11-5	
1931	Paris **France** 14-13	
1947	Twickenham **England** 6-3	
1948	Paris **France** 15-0	
1949	Twickenham **England** 8-3	
1950	Paris **France** 6-3	
1951	Twickenham **France** 11-3	
1952	Paris **England** 6-3	
1953	Twickenham **England** 11-0	
1954	Paris **France** 11-3	
1955	Twickenham **France** 16-9	
1956	Paris **France** 14-9	
1957	Twickenham **England** 9-5	
1958	Paris **England** 14-0	
1959	Twickenham **Drawn** 3-3	
1960	Paris **Drawn** 3-3	
1961	Twickenham **Drawn** 5-5	
1962	Paris **France** 13-0	
1963	Twickenham **England** 6-5	
1964	Paris **England** 6-3	
1965	Twickenham **England** 9-6	
1966	Paris **France** 13-0	
1967	Twickenham **France** 16-12	
1968	Paris **France** 14-9	
1969	Twickenham **England** 22-8	

1970	Paris **France** 35-13
1971	Twickenham **Drawn** 14-14
1972	Paris **France** 37-12
1973	Twickenham **England** 14-6
1974	Paris **Drawn** 12-12
1975	Twickenham **France** 27-20
1976	Paris **France** 30-9
1977	Twickenham **France** 4-3
1978	Paris **France** 15-6
1979	Twickenham **England** 7-6
1980	Paris **England** 17-13
1981	Twickenham **France** 16-12
1982	Paris **England** 27-15
1983	Twickenham **France** 19-15
1984	Paris **France** 32-18
1985	Twickenham **Drawn** 9-9
1986	Paris **France** 29-10
1987	Twickenham **France** 19-15
1988	Paris **France** 10-9
1989	Twickenham **England** 11-0
1990	Paris **England** 26-7
1991	Twickenham **England** 21-19
1991	Paris *WC* **England** 19-10
1992	Paris **England** 31-13
1993	Twickenham **England** 16-15
1994	Paris **England** 18-14
1995	Twickenham **England** 31-10
1995	Pretoria *WC* **France** 19-9
1996	Paris **France** 15-12
1997	Twickenham **France** 23-20
1998	Paris **France** 24-17
1999	Twickenham **England** 21-10
2000	Paris **England** 15-9
2001	Twickenham **England** 48-19
2002	Paris **France** 20-15

ENGLAND v NEW ZEALAND

Played 23   England won 4, New Zealand won 18, Drawn 1
Highest scores England 29-45 in 1995, New Zealand 64-22 in 1998
Biggest wins England 13-0 in 1936, New Zealand 64-22 in 1998

1905	Crystal Palace (London) **New Zealand** 15-0
1925	Twickenham **New Zealand** 17-11
1936	Twickenham **England** 13-0
1954	Twickenham **New Zealand** 5-0
1963	*1* Auckland **New Zealand** 21-11
	2 Christchurch **New Zealand** 9-6
	New Zealand won series 2-0
1964	Twickenham **New Zealand** 14-0
1967	Twickenham **New Zealand** 23-11
1973	Twickenham **New Zealand** 9-0
1973	Auckland **England** 16-10
1978	Twickenham **New Zealand** 16-6
1979	Twickenham **New Zealand** 10-9
1983	Twickenham **England** 15-9

1985	*1* Christchurch **New Zealand** 18-13
	2 Wellington **New Zealand** 42-15
	New Zealand won series 2-0
1991	Twickenham *WC* **New Zealand** 18-12
1993	Twickenham **England** 15-9
1995	Cape Town *WC* **New Zealand** 45-29
1997	*1* Manchester **New Zealand** 25-8
	2 Twickenham **Drawn** 26-26
	New Zealand won series 1-0, with 1 draw
1998	*1* Dunedin **New Zealand** 64-22
	2 Auckland **New Zealand** 40-10
	New Zealand won series 2-0
1999	Twickenham *WC* **New Zealand** 30-16

ENGLAND v SOUTH AFRICA
Played 21   England won 8, South Africa won 12, Drawn 1
Highest scores England 33-16 in 1992, South Africa 44-21 in 1999
Biggest wins England 29-9 in 2001, South Africa 35-9 in 1984

1906 Crystal Palace (London) **Drawn** 3-3	*2* Cape Town **South Africa** 27-9
1913 Twickenham **South Africa** 9-3	*Series drawn 1-1*
1932 Twickenham **South Africa** 7-0	1995 Twickenham **South Africa** 24-14
1952 Twickenham **South Africa** 8-3	1997 Twickenham **South Africa** 29-11
1961 Twickenham **South Africa** 5-0	1998 Cape Town **South Africa** 18-0
1969 Twickenham **England** 11-8	1998 Twickenham **England** 13-7
1972 Johannesburg **England** 18-9	1999 Paris *WC* **South Africa** 44-21
1984 *1* Port Elizabeth **South Africa** 33-15	2000 *1* Pretoria **South Africa** 18-13
2 Johannesburg **South Africa** 35-9	*2* Bloemfontein **England** 27-22
South Africa won series 2-0	*Series drawn 1-1*
1992 Twickenham **England** 33-16	2000 Twickenham **England** 25-17
1994 *1* Pretoria **England** 32-15	2001 Twickenham **England** 29-9

ENGLAND v AUSTRALIA
Played 26   England won 9, Australia won 16, Drawn 1
Highest scores England 28-19 in 1988, Australia 76-0 in 1998
Biggest wins England 20-3 in 1973 & 23-6 in 1976, Australia 76-0 in 1998

1909 Blackheath (London) **Australia** 9-3	*2* Sydney **Australia** 28-8
1928 Twickenham **England** 18-11	*Australia won series 2-0*
1948 Twickenham **Australia** 11-0	1988 Twickenham **England** 28-19
1958 Twickenham **England** 9-6	1991 Sydney **Australia** 40-15
1963 Sydney **Australia** 18-9	1991 Twickenham *WC* **Australia** 12-6
1967 Twickenham **Australia** 23-11	1995 Cape Town *WC* **England** 25-22
1973 Twickenham **England** 20-3	1997 *1* Sydney **Australia** 25-6
1975 *1* Sydney **Australia** 16-9	*2* Twickenham **Drawn** 15-15
2 Brisbane **Australia** 30-21	*Australia won series 1-0, with 1 draw*
Australia won series 2-0	1998 *1* Brisbane **Australia** 76-0
1976 Twickenham **England** 23-6	*2* Twickenham **Australia** 12-11
1982 Twickenham **England** 15-11	*Australia won series 2-0*
1984 Twickenham **Australia** 19-3	1999 Sydney **Australia** 22-15
1987 Sydney *WC* **Australia** 19-6	2000 Twickenham **England** 22-19
1988 *1* Brisbane **Australia** 22-16	2001 Twickenham **England** 21-15

ENGLAND v NEW ZEALAND NATIVES
Played 1   England won 1
Highest score England 7-0 in 1889, NZ Natives 0-7 in 1889
Biggest win England 7-0 in 1889, NZ Natives no win

1889   Blackheath **England** 1G 4T to 0

ENGLAND v RFU PRESIDENT'S XV
Played 1   President's XV won 1
Highest score England 11-28 in 1971, RFU President's XV 28-11 in 1971
Biggest win RFU President's XV 28-11 in 1971

1971   Twickenham **President's XV** 28-11

ENGLAND v ARGENTINA

Played 11   England won 8, Argentina won 2, Drawn 1
Highest scores England 51-0 in 1990, Argentina 33-13 in 1997
Biggest wins England 51-0 in 1990, Argentina 33-13 in 1997

1981 *1* Buenos Aires **Drawn** 19-19
    2 Buenos Aires **England** 12-6
    England won series 1-0 with 1 draw
1990 *1* Buenos Aires **England** 25-12
    2 Buenos Aires **Argentina** 15-13
    Series drawn 1-1
1990 Twickenham **England** 51-0

1995 Durban *WC* **England** 24-18
1996 Twickenham **England** 20-18
1997 *1* Buenos Aires **England** 46-20
    2 Buenos Aires **Argentina** 33-13
    Series drawn 1-1
2000 Twickenham **England** 19-0
2002 Buenos Aires **England** 26-18

ENGLAND v ROMANIA

Played 4   England won 4
Highest scores England 134-0 in 2001, Romania 15-22 in 1985
Biggest win England 134-0 in 2001, Romania no win

1985 Twickenham **England** 22-15
1989 Bucharest **England** 58-3

1994 Twickenham **England** 54-3
2001 Twickenham **England** 134-0

ENGLAND v JAPAN

Played 1   England won 1
Highest score England 60-7 in 1987, Japan 7-60 in 1987
Biggest win England 60-7 in 1987, Japan no win

1987 Sydney *WC* **England** 60-7

ENGLAND v UNITED STATES

Played 4   England won 4
Highest scores England 106-8 in 1999, United States 19-48 in 2001
Biggest win England 106-8 in 1999, United States no win

1987 Sydney *WC* **England** 34-6
1991 Twickenham *WC* **England** 37-9

1999 Twickenham **England** 106-8
2001 San Francisco **England** 48-19

ENGLAND v FIJI

Played 4   England won 4
Highest scores England 58-23 in 1989, Fiji 24-45 in 1999
Biggest win England 58-23 in 1989, Fiji no win

1988 Suva **England** 25-12
1989 Twickenham **England** 58-23

1991 Suva **England** 28-12
1999 Twickenham *WC* **England** 45-24

ENGLAND v ITALY

Played 8   England won 8
Highest scores England 80-23 in 2001, Italy 23-80 in 2001
Biggest win England 67-7 in 1999, Italy no win

1991 Twickenham *WC* **England** 36-6
1995 Durban *WC* **England** 27-20
1996 Twickenham **England** 54-21
1998 Huddersfield **England** 23-15

1999 Twickenham *WC* **England** 67-7
2000 Rome **England** 59-12
2001 Twickenham **England** 80-23
2002 Rome **England** 45-9

Dan Luger scored three tries in England's record 134-0 victory against Romania last November.

ENGLAND v CANADA

Played 5   England won 5
Highest scores England 60-19 in 1994, Canada 20-59 in 2001
Biggest win England 60-19 in 1994, Canada no win

1992	Wembley **England** 26-13		2001	*1* Markham **England** 22-10
1994	Twickenham **England** 60-19			*2* Burnaby **England** 59-20
1999	Twickenham **England** 36-11			*England won series 2-0*

ENGLAND v SAMOA

Played 2   England won 2
Highest scores England 44-22 in 1995, Samoa 22-44 in 1995
Biggest win England 44-22 in 1995, Samoa no win

1995	Durban *WC* **England** 44-22	1995	Twickenham **England** 27-9

ENGLAND v THE NETHERLANDS

Played 1   England won 1
Highest scores England 110-0 in 1998, The Netherlands 0-110 in 1998
Biggest win England 110-0 in 1998, The Netherlands no win

1998   Huddersfield **England** 110-0

ENGLAND v TONGA

Played 1   England won 1
Highest scores England 101-10 in 1999, Tonga 10-101 in 1999
Biggest win England 101-10 in 1999, Tonga no win

1999   Twickenham *WC* **England** 101-10

SCOTLAND v IRELAND

Played 114   Scotland won 61, Ireland won 47, Drawn 5, Abandoned 1
Highest scores Scotland 38-10 in 1997, Ireland 43-22 in 2002
Biggest wins Scotland 38-10 in 1997, Ireland 43-22 in 2002

1877	Belfast **Scotland** 4G 2DG 2T to 0		1895	Raeburn Place **Scotland** 6-0
1878	No Match		1896	Dublin **Drawn** 0-0
1879	Belfast **Scotland** 1G 1DG 1T to 0		1897	Powderhall (Edinburgh) **Scotland** 8-3
1880	Glasgow **Scotland** 1G 2DG 2T to 0		1898	Belfast **Scotland** 8-0
1881	Belfast **Ireland** 1DG to 1T		1899	Inverleith (Edinburgh) **Ireland** 9-3
1882	Glasgow **Scotland** 2T to 0		1900	Dublin **Drawn** 0-0
1883	Belfast **Scotland** 1G 1T to 0		1901	Inverleith **Scotland** 9-5
1884	Raeburn Place (Edinburgh) **Scotland** 2G 2T to 1T		1902	Belfast **Ireland** 5-0
			1903	Inverleith **Scotland** 3-0
1885	Belfast **Abandoned** Ireland 0 Scotland 1T		1904	Dublin **Scotland** 19-3
1885	Raeburn Place **Scotland** 1G 2T to 0		1905	Inverleith **Ireland** 11-5
1886	Raeburn Place **Scotland** 3G 1DG 2T to 0		1906	Dublin **Scotland** 13-6
			1907	Inverleith **Scotland** 15-3
1887	Belfast **Scotland** 1G 1GM 2T to 0		1908	Dublin **Ireland** 16-11
1888	Raeburn Place **Scotland** 1G to 0		1909	Inverleith **Scotland** 9-3
1889	Belfast **Scotland** 1DG to 0		1910	Belfast **Scotland** 14-0
1890	Raeburn Place **Scotland** 1DG 1T to 0		1911	Inverleith **Ireland** 16-10
1891	Belfast **Scotland** 14-0		1912	Dublin **Ireland** 10-8
1892	Raeburn Place **Scotland** 2-0		1913	Inverleith **Scotland** 29-14
1893	Belfast **Drawn** 0-0		1914	Dublin **Ireland** 6-0
1894	Dublin **Ireland** 5-0		1920	Inverleith **Scotland** 19-0

1921	Dublin **Ireland** 9-8	1966	Dublin **Scotland** 11-3
1922	Inverleith **Scotland** 6-3	1967	Murrayfield **Ireland** 5-3
1923	Dublin **Scotland** 13-3	1968	Dublin **Ireland** 14-6
1924	Inverleith **Scotland** 13-8	1969	Murrayfield **Ireland** 16-0
1925	Dublin **Scotland** 14-8	1970	Dublin **Ireland** 16-11
1926	Murrayfield **Ireland** 3-0	1971	Murrayfield **Ireland** 17-5
1927	Dublin **Ireland** 6-0	1972	No Match
1928	Murrayfield **Ireland** 13-5	1973	Murrayfield **Scotland** 19-14
1929	Dublin **Scotland** 16-7	1974	Dublin **Ireland** 9-6
1930	Murrayfield **Ireland** 14-11	1975	Murrayfield **Scotland** 20-13
1931	Dublin **Ireland** 8-5	1976	Dublin **Scotland** 15-6
1932	Murrayfield **Ireland** 20-8	1977	Murrayfield **Scotland** 21-18
1933	Dublin **Scotland** 8-6	1978	Dublin **Ireland** 12-9
1934	Murrayfield **Scotland** 16-9	1979	Murrayfield **Drawn** 11-11
1935	Dublin **Ireland** 12-5	1980	Dublin **Ireland** 22-15
1936	Murrayfield **Ireland** 10-4	1981	Murrayfield **Scotland** 10-9
1937	Dublin **Ireland** 11-4	1982	Dublin **Ireland** 21-12
1938	Murrayfield **Scotland** 23-14	1983	Murrayfield **Ireland** 15-13
1939	Dublin **Ireland** 12-3	1984	Dublin **Scotland** 32-9
1947	Murrayfield **Ireland** 3-0	1985	Murrayfield **Ireland** 18-15
1948	Dublin **Ireland** 6-0	1986	Dublin **Scotland** 10-9
1949	Murrayfield **Ireland** 13-3	1987	Murrayfield **Scotland** 16-12
1950	Dublin **Ireland** 21-0	1988	Dublin **Ireland** 22-18
1951	Murrayfield **Ireland** 6-5	1989	Murrayfield **Scotland** 37-21
1952	Dublin **Ireland** 12-8	1990	Dublin **Scotland** 13-10
1953	Murrayfield **Ireland** 26-8	1991	Murrayfield **Scotland** 28-25
1954	Belfast **Ireland** 6-0	1991	Murrayfield *WC* **Scotland** 24-15
1955	Murrayfield **Scotland** 12-3	1992	Dublin **Scotland** 18-10
1956	Dublin **Ireland** 14-10	1993	Murrayfield **Scotland** 15-3
1957	Murrayfield **Ireland** 5-3	1994	Dublin **Drawn** 6-6
1958	Dublin **Ireland** 12-6	1995	Murrayfield **Scotland** 26-13
1959	Murrayfield **Ireland** 8-3	1996	Dublin **Scotland** 16-10
1960	Dublin **Scotland** 6-5	1997	Murrayfield **Scotland** 38-10
1961	Murrayfield **Scotland** 16-8	1998	Dublin **Scotland** 17-16
1962	Dublin **Scotland** 20-6	1999	Murrayfield **Scotland** 30-13
1963	Murrayfield **Scotland** 3-0	2000	Dublin **Ireland** 44-22
1964	Dublin **Scotland** 6-3	2001	Murrayfield **Scotland** 32-10
1965	Murrayfield **Ireland** 16-6	2002	Dublin **Ireland** 43-22

SCOTLAND v WALES

Played 106   Scotland won 46, Wales won 57, Drawn 3
Highest scores Scotland 35-10 in 1924, Wales 35-12 in 1972
Biggest wins Scotland 35-10 in 1924, Wales 35-12 in 1972 & 29-6 in 1994

1883	Raeburn Place (Edinburgh) **Scotland** 3G to 1G	1899	Inverleith (Edinburgh) **Scotland** 21-10
1884	Newport **Scotland** 1DG 1T to 0	1900	Swansea **Wales** 12-3
1885	Glasgow **Drawn** no score	1901	Inverleith **Scotland** 18-8
1886	Cardiff **Scotland** 2G 1T to 0	1902	Cardiff **Wales** 14-5
1887	Raeburn Place **Scotland** 4G 8T to 0	1903	Inverleith **Scotland** 6-0
1888	Newport **Wales** 1T to 0	1904	Swansea **Wales** 21-3
1889	Raeburn Place **Scotland** 2T to 0	1905	Inverleith **Wales** 6-3
1890	Cardiff **Scotland** 1G 2T to 1T	1906	Cardiff **Wales** 9-3
1891	Raeburn Place **Scotland** 15-0	1907	Inverleith **Scotland** 6-3
1892	Swansea **Scotland** 7-2	1908	Swansea **Wales** 6-5
1893	Raeburn Place **Wales** 9-0	1909	Inverleith **Wales** 5-3
1894	Newport **Wales** 7-0	1910	Cardiff **Wales** 14-0
1895	Raeburn Place **Scotland** 5-4	1911	Inverleith **Wales** 32-10
1896	Cardiff **Wales** 6-0	1912	Swansea **Wales** 21-6
1897	No Match	1913	Inverleith **Wales** 8-0
1898	No Match	1914	Cardiff **Wales** 24-5
		1920	Inverleith **Scotland** 9-5

1921	Swansea **Scotland** 14-8		1966	Cardiff **Wales** 8-3
1922	Inverleith **Drawn** 9-9		1967	Murrayfield **Scotland** 11-5
1923	Cardiff **Scotland** 11-8		1968	Cardiff **Wales** 5-0
1924	Inverleith **Scotland** 35-10		1969	Murrayfield **Wales** 17-3
1925	Swansea **Scotland** 24-14		1970	Cardiff **Wales** 18-9
1926	Murrayfield **Scotland** 8-5		1971	Murrayfield **Wales** 19-18
1927	Cardiff **Scotland** 5-0		1972	Cardiff **Wales** 35-12
1928	Murrayfield **Wales** 13-0		1973	Murrayfield **Scotland** 10-9
1929	Swansea **Wales** 14-7		1974	Cardiff **Wales** 6-0
1930	Murrayfield **Scotland** 12-9		1975	Murrayfield **Scotland** 12-10
1931	Cardiff **Wales** 13-8		1976	Cardiff **Wales** 28-6
1932	Murrayfield **Wales** 6-0		1977	Murrayfield **Wales** 18-9
1933	Swansea **Scotland** 11-3		1978	Cardiff **Wales** 22-14
1934	Murrayfield **Wales** 13-6		1979	Murrayfield **Wales** 19-13
1935	Cardiff **Wales** 10-6		1980	Cardiff **Wales** 17-6
1936	Murrayfield **Wales** 13-3		1981	Murrayfield **Scotland** 15-6
1937	Swansea **Scotland** 13-6		1982	Cardiff **Scotland** 34-18
1938	Murrayfield **Scotland** 8-6		1983	Murrayfield **Wales** 19-15
1939	Cardiff **Wales** 11-3		1984	Cardiff **Scotland** 15-9
1947	Murrayfield **Wales** 22-8		1985	Murrayfield **Wales** 25-21
1948	Cardiff **Wales** 14-0		1986	Cardiff **Wales** 22-15
1949	Murrayfield **Scotland** 6-5		1987	Murrayfield **Scotland** 21-15
1950	Swansea **Wales** 12-0		1988	Cardiff **Wales** 25-20
1951	Murrayfield **Scotland** 19-0		1989	Murrayfield **Scotland** 23-7
1952	Cardiff **Wales** 11-0		1990	Cardiff **Scotland** 13-9
1953	Murrayfield **Wales** 12-0		1991	Murrayfield **Scotland** 32-12
1954	Swansea **Wales** 15-3		1992	Cardiff **Wales** 15-12
1955	Murrayfield **Scotland** 14-8		1993	Murrayfield **Scotland** 20-0
1956	Cardiff **Wales** 9-3		1994	Cardiff **Wales** 29-6
1957	Murrayfield **Scotland** 9-6		1995	Murrayfield **Scotland** 26-13
1958	Cardiff **Wales** 8-3		1996	Cardiff **Scotland** 16-14
1959	Murrayfield **Scotland** 6-5		1997	Murrayfield **Wales** 34-19
1960	Cardiff **Wales** 8-0		1998	Wembley **Wales** 19-13
1961	Murrayfield **Scotland** 3-0		1999	Murrayfield **Scotland** 33-20
1962	Cardiff **Scotland** 8-3		2000	Cardiff **Wales** 26-18
1963	Murrayfield **Wales** 6-0		2001	Murrayfield **Drawn** 28-28
1964	Cardiff **Wales** 11-3		2002	Cardiff **Scotland** 27-22
1965	Murrayfield **Wales** 14-12			

SCOTLAND v FRANCE

Played 74   Scotland won 33, France won 38, Drawn 3
Highest scores Scotland 36-22 in 1999, France 51-16 in 1998
Biggest wins Scotland 31-3 in 1912, France 51-16 in 1998

1910	Inverleith (Edinburgh) **Scotland** 27-0		1947	Paris **France** 8-3
1911	Paris **France** 16-15		1948	Murrayfield **Scotland** 9-8
1912	Inverleith **Scotland** 31-3		1949	Paris **Scotland** 8-0
1913	Paris **Scotland** 21-3		1950	Murrayfield **Scotland** 8-5
1914	No Match		1951	Paris **France** 14-12
1920	Paris **Scotland** 5-0		1952	Murrayfield **France** 13-11
1921	Inverleith **France** 3-0		1953	Paris **France** 11-5
1922	Paris **Drawn** 3-3		1954	Murrayfield **France** 3-0
1923	Inverleith **Scotland** 16-3		1955	Paris **France** 15-0
1924	Paris **France** 12-10		1956	Murrayfield **Scotland** 12-0
1925	Inverleith **Scotland** 25-4		1957	Paris **Scotland** 6-0
1926	Paris **Scotland** 20-6		1958	Murrayfield **Scotland** 11-9
1927	Murrayfield **Scotland** 23-6		1959	Paris **France** 9-0
1928	Paris **Scotland** 15-6		1960	Murrayfield **France** 13-11
1929	Murrayfield **Scotland** 6-3		1961	Paris **France** 11-0
1930	Paris **France** 7-3		1962	Murrayfield **France** 11-3
1931	Murrayfield **Scotland** 6-4		1963	Paris **Scotland** 11-6

1964	Murrayfield **Scotland** 10-0		1985	Paris **France** 11-3
1965	Paris **France** 16-8		1986	Murrayfield **Scotland** 18-17
1966	Murrayfield **Drawn** 3-3		1987	Paris **France** 28-22
1967	Paris **Scotland** 9-8		1987	Christchurch *WC* **Drawn** 20-20
1968	Murrayfield **France** 8-6		1988	Murrayfield **Scotland** 23-12
1969	Paris **Scotland** 6-3		1989	Paris **France** 19-3
1970	Murrayfield **France** 11-9		1990	Murrayfield **Scotland** 21-0
1971	Paris **France** 13-8		1991	Paris **France** 15-9
1972	Murrayfield **Scotland** 20-9		1992	Murrayfield **Scotland** 10-6
1973	Paris **France** 16-13		1993	Paris **France** 11-3
1974	Murrayfield **Scotland** 19-6		1994	Murrayfield **France** 20-12
1975	Paris **France** 10-9		1995	Paris **Scotland** 23-21
1976	Murrayfield **France** 13-6		1995	Pretoria *WC* **France** 22-19
1977	Paris **France** 23-3		1996	Murrayfield **Scotland** 19-14
1978	Murrayfield **France** 19-16		1997	Paris **France** 47-20
1979	Paris **France** 21-17		1998	Murrayfield **France** 51-16
1980	Murrayfield **Scotland** 22-14		1999	Paris **Scotland** 36-22
1981	Paris **France** 16-9		2000	Murrayfield **France** 28-16
1982	Murrayfield **Scotland** 16-7		2001	Paris **France** 16-6
1983	Paris **France** 19-15		2002	Murrayfield **France** 22-10
1984	Murrayfield **Scotland** 21-12			

SCOTLAND v NEW ZEALAND

Played 24   Scotland won 0, New Zealand won 22, Drawn 2
Highest scores Scotland 31-62 in 1996, New Zealand 69-20 in 2000
Biggest wins Scotland no win, New Zealand 69-20 in 2000

1905	Inverleith (Edinburgh) **New Zealand** 12-7		1990	*1* Dunedin **New Zealand** 31-16
1935	Murrayfield **New Zealand** 18-8			*2* Auckland **New Zealand** 21-18
1954	Murrayfield **New Zealand** 3-0			*New Zealand won series 2-0*
1964	Murrayfield **Drawn** 0-0		1991	Cardiff *WC* **New Zealand** 13-6
1967	Murrayfield **New Zealand** 14-3		1993	Murrayfield **New Zealand** 51-15
1972	Murrayfield **New Zealand** 14-9		1995	Pretoria *WC* **New Zealand** 48-30
1975	Auckland **New Zealand** 24-0		1996	*1* Dunedin **New Zealand** 62-31
1978	Murrayfield **New Zealand** 18-9			*2* Auckland **New Zealand** 36-12
1979	Murrayfield **New Zealand** 20-6			*New Zealand won series 2-0*
1981	*1* Dunedin **New Zealand** 11-4		1999	Murrayfield *WC* **New Zealand** 30-18
	2 Auckland **New Zealand** 40-15		2000	*1* Dunedin **New Zealand** 69-20
	New Zealand won series 2-0			*2* Auckland **New Zealand** 48-14
1983	Murrayfield **Drawn** 25-25			*New Zealand won series 2-0*
1987	Christchurch *WC* **New Zealand** 30-3		2001	Murrayfield **New Zealand** 37-6

SCOTLAND v SOUTH AFRICA

Played 12   Scotland won 3, South Africa won 9, Drawn 0
Highest scores Scotland 29-46 in 1999, South Africa 68-10 in 1997
Biggest wins Scotland 6-0 in 1906, South Africa 68-10 in 1997

1906	Glasgow **Scotland** 6-0		1965	Murrayfield **Scotland** 8-5
1912	Inverleith **South Africa** 16-0		1969	Murrayfield **Scotland** 6-3
1932	Murrayfield **South Africa** 6-3		1994	Murrayfield **South Africa** 34-10
1951	Murrayfield **South Africa** 44-0		1997	Murrayfield **South Africa** 68-10
1960	Port Elizabeth **South Africa** 18-10		1998	Murrayfield **South Africa** 35-10
1961	Murrayfield **South Africa** 12-5		1999	Murrayfield *WC* **South Africa** 46-29

SCOTLAND v AUSTRALIA

Played 19   Scotland won 7, Australia won 12, Drawn 0
Highest scores Scotland 24-15 in 1981, Australia 45-3 in 1998
Biggest wins Scotland 24-15 in 1981, Australia 45-3 in 1998

1927	Murrayfield **Scotland** 10-8	1984	Murrayfield **Australia** 37-12
1947	Murrayfield **Australia** 16-7	1988	Murrayfield **Australia** 32-13
1958	Murrayfield **Scotland** 12-8	1992	*1* Sydney **Australia** 27-12
1966	Murrayfield **Scotland** 11-5		*2* Brisbane **Australia** 37-13
1968	Murrayfield **Scotland** 9-3		*Australia won series 2-0*
1970	Sydney **Australia** 23-3	1996	Murrayfield **Australia** 29-19
1975	Murrayfield **Scotland** 10-3	1997	Murrayfield **Australia** 37-8
1981	Murrayfield **Scotland** 24-15	1998	*1* Sydney **Australia** 45-3
1982	*1* Brisbane **Scotland** 12-7		*2* Brisbane **Australia** 33-11
	2 Sydney **Australia** 33-9		*Australia won series 2-0*
	Series drawn 1-1	2000	Murrayfield **Australia** 30-9

SCOTLAND v SRU PRESIDENT'S XV

Played 1   Scotland won 1
Highest scores Scotland 27-16 in 1972, SRU President's XV 16-27 in 1973
Biggest win Scotland 27-16 in 1973, SRU President's XV no win

1973   Murrayfield **Scotland** 27-16

SCOTLAND v ROMANIA

Played 8   Scotland won 6, Romania won 2, Drawn 0
Highest scores Scotland 60-19 in 1999, Romania 28-55 in 1987 & 28-22 in 1984
Biggest wins Scotland 60-19 in 1999, Romania 28-22 in 1984 & 18-12 in 1991

1981	Murrayfield **Scotland** 12-6	1989	Murrayfield **Scotland** 32-0
1984	Bucharest **Romania** 28-22	1991	Bucharest **Romania** 18-12
1986	Bucharest **Scotland** 33-18	1995	Murrayfield **Scotland** 49-16
1987	Dunedin *WC* **Scotland** 55-28	1999	Glasgow **Scotland** 60-19

SCOTLAND v ZIMBABWE

Played 2   Scotland won 2
Highest scores Scotland 60-21 in 1987, Zimbabwe 21-60 in 1987
Biggest win Scotland 60-21 in 1987 & 51-12 in 1991, Zimbabwe no win

1987	Wellington *WC* **Scotland** 60-21	1991	Murrayfield *WC* **Scotland** 51-12

SCOTLAND v FIJI

Played 2   Scotland won 1, Fiji won 1
Highest scores Scotland 38-17 in 1989, Fiji 51-26 in 1998
Biggest win Scotland 38-17 in 1989, Fiji 51-26 in 1998

1989	Murrayfield **Scotland** 38-17	1998	Suva **Fiji** 51-26

SCOTLAND v ARGENTINA

Played 5   Scotland won 1, Argentina won 4, Drawn 0
Highest scores Scotland 49-3 in 1990, Argentina 31-22 in 1999
Biggest wins Scotland 49-3 in 1990, Argentina 31-22 in 1999 and 25-16 in 2001

1990	Murrayfield **Scotland** 49-3	1994	*1* Buenos Aires **Argentina** 16-15

2 Buenos Aires **Argentina** 19-17
Argentina won series 2-0

1999   Murrayfield **Argentina** 31-22
2001   Murrayfield **Argentina** 25-16

SCOTLAND v JAPAN
Played 1   Scotland won 1
Highest scores Scotland 47-9 in 1991, Japan 9-47 in 1991
Biggest win Scotland 47-9 in 1991, Japan no win

1991   Murrayfield *WC* **Scotland** 47-9

SCOTLAND v SAMOA
Played 4   Scotland won 3, Drawn 1
Highest scores Scotland 35-20 in 1999, Samoa 20-35 in 1999
Biggest win Scotland 31-8 in 2000, Samoa no win

1991   Murrayfield *WC* **Scotland** 28-6
1995   Murrayfield **Drawn** 15-15

1999   Murrayfield *WC* **Scotland** 35-20
2000   Murrayfield **Scotland** 31-8

SCOTLAND v CANADA
Played 2   Scotland won 1, Canada won 1
Highest scores Scotland 23-26 in 2002, Canada 26-23 in 2002
Biggest win Scotland 22-6 in 1995, Canada 26-23 in 2002

1995   Murrayfield **Scotland** 22-6

2002   Vancouver **Canada** 26-23

SCOTLAND v IVORY COAST
Played 1   Scotland won 1
Highest scores Scotland 89-0 in 1995, Ivory Coast 0-89 in 1995
Biggest win Scotland 89-0 in 1995, Ivory Coast no win

1995   Rustenburg *WC* **Scotland** 89-0

SCOTLAND v TONGA
Played 2   Scotland won 2
Highest scores Scotland 43-20 in 2001, Tonga 20-43 in 2001
Biggest win Scotland 41-5 in 1995, Tonga no win

1995   Pretoria *WC* **Scotland** 41-5

2001   Murrayfield **Scotland** 43-20

SCOTLAND v ITALY
Played 6   Scotland won 4, Italy won 2
Highest scores Scotland 30-12 in 1999, Italy 34-20 in 2000
Biggest wins Scotland 30-12 in 1999, Italy 34-20 in 2000

1996   Murrayfield **Scotland** 29-22
1998   Treviso **Italy** 25-21
1999   Murrayfield **Scotland** 30-12

2000   Rome **Italy** 34-20
2001   Murrayfield **Scotland** 23-19
2002   Rome **Scotland** 29-12

SCOTLAND v URUGUAY

Played 1   Scotland won 1
Highest scores Scotland 43-12 in 1999, Uruguay 12-43 in 1999
Biggest win Scotland 43-12 in 1999, Uruguay no win

1999   Murrayfield *WC* **Scotland** 43-12

SCOTLAND v SPAIN

Played 1   Scotland won 1
Highest scores Scotland 48-0 in 1999, Spain 0-48 in 1999
Biggest win Scotland 48-0 in 1999, Spain no win

1999   Murrayfield *WC* **Scotland** 48-0

SCOTLAND v UNITED STATES

Played 2   Scotland won 2
Highest scores Scotland 65-23 in 2002, United States 23-65 in 2002
Biggest win Scotland 53-6 in 2000, United States no win

2000   Murrayfield **Scotland** 53-6   2002   San Francisco **Scotland** 65-23

IRELAND v WALES

Played 106   Ireland won 40, Wales won 60, Drawn 6
Highest scores Ireland 54-10 in 2002, Wales 34-9 in 1976
Biggest wins Ireland 54-10 in 2002, Wales 29-0 in 1907

1882	Dublin **Wales** 2G 2T to 0	1913	Swansea **Wales** 16-13
1883	No Match	1914	Belfast **Wales** 11-3
1884	Cardiff **Wales** 1DG 2T to 0	1920	Cardiff **Wales** 28-4
1885	No Match	1921	Belfast **Wales** 6-0
1886	No Match	1922	Swansea **Wales** 11-5
1887	Birkenhead **Wales** 1DG 1T to 3T	1923	Dublin **Ireland** 5-4
1888	Dublin **Ireland** 1G 1DG 1T to 0	1924	Cardiff **Ireland** 13-10
1889	Swansea **Ireland** 2T to 0	1925	Belfast **Ireland** 19-3
1890	Dublin **Drawn** 1G each	1926	Swansea **Wales** 11-8
1891	Llanelli **Wales** 6-4	1927	Dublin **Ireland** 19-9
1892	Dublin **Ireland** 9-0	1928	Cardiff **Ireland** 13-10
1893	Llanelli **Wales** 2-0	1929	Belfast **Drawn** 5-5
1894	Belfast **Ireland** 3-0	1930	Swansea **Wales** 12-7
1895	Cardiff **Wales** 5-3	1931	Belfast **Wales** 15-3
1896	Dublin **Ireland** 8-4	1932	Cardiff **Ireland** 12-10
1897	No Match	1933	Belfast **Ireland** 10-5
1898	Limerick **Wales** 11-3	1934	Swansea **Wales** 13-0
1899	Cardiff **Ireland** 3-0	1935	Belfast **Ireland** 9-3
1900	Belfast **Wales** 3-0	1936	Cardiff **Wales** 3-0
1901	Swansea **Wales** 10-9	1937	Belfast **Ireland** 5-3
1902	Dublin **Wales** 15-0	1938	Swansea **Wales** 11-5
1903	Cardiff **Wales** 18-0	1939	Belfast **Wales** 7-0
1904	Belfast **Ireland** 14-12	1947	Swansea **Wales** 6-0
1905	Swansea **Wales** 10-3	1948	Belfast **Ireland** 6-3
1906	Belfast **Ireland** 11-6	1949	Swansea **Ireland** 5-0
1907	Cardiff **Wales** 29-0	1950	Belfast **Wales** 6-3
1908	Belfast **Wales** 11-5	1951	Cardiff **Drawn** 3-3
1909	Swansea **Wales** 18-5	1952	Dublin **Wales** 14-3
1910	Dublin **Wales** 19-3	1953	Swansea **Wales** 5-3
1911	Cardiff **Wales** 16-0	1954	Dublin **Wales** 12-9
1912	Belfast **Ireland** 12-5	1955	Cardiff **Wales** 21-3

1956	Dublin **Ireland** 11-3	1981	Cardiff **Wales** 9-8
1957	Cardiff **Wales** 6-5	1982	Dublin **Ireland** 20-12
1958	Dublin **Wales** 9-6	1983	Cardiff **Wales** 23-9
1959	Cardiff **Wales** 8-6	1984	Dublin **Wales** 18-9
1960	Dublin **Wales** 10-9	1985	Cardiff **Ireland** 21-9
1961	Cardiff **Wales** 9-0	1986	Dublin **Wales** 19-12
1962	Dublin **Drawn** 3-3	1987	Cardiff **Ireland** 15-11
1963	Cardiff **Ireland** 14-6	1987	Wellington *WC* **Wales** 13-6
1964	Dublin **Wales** 15-6	1988	Dublin **Wales** 12-9
1965	Cardiff **Wales** 14-8	1989	Cardiff **Ireland** 19-13
1966	Dublin **Ireland** 9-6	1990	Dublin **Ireland** 14-8
1967	Cardiff **Ireland** 3-0	1991	Cardiff **Drawn** 21-21
1968	Dublin **Ireland** 9-6	1992	Dublin **Wales** 16-15
1969	Cardiff **Wales** 24-11	1993	Cardiff **Ireland** 19-14
1970	Dublin **Ireland** 14-0	1994	Dublin **Wales** 17-15
1971	Cardiff **Wales** 23-9	1995	Cardiff **Ireland** 16-12
1972	No Match	1995	Johannesburg *WC* **Ireland** 24-23
1973	Cardiff **Wales** 16-12	1996	Dublin **Ireland** 30-17
1974	Dublin **Drawn** 9-9	1997	Cardiff **Ireland** 26-25
1975	Cardiff **Wales** 32-4	1998	Dublin **Wales** 30-21
1976	Dublin **Wales** 34-9	1999	Wembley **Ireland** 29-23
1977	Cardiff **Wales** 25-9	2000	Dublin **Wales** 23-19
1978	Dublin **Wales** 20-16	2001	Cardiff **Ireland** 36-6
1979	Cardiff **Wales** 24-21	2002	Dublin **Ireland** 54-10
1980	Dublin **Ireland** 21-7		

IRELAND v FRANCE

Played 76   Ireland won 27, France won 44, Drawn 5
Highest scores Ireland 27-25 in 2000, France 45-10 in 1996
Biggest wins Ireland 24-0 in 1913, France 44-5 in 2002

1909	Dublin **Ireland** 19-8	1959	Dublin **Ireland** 9-5
1910	Paris **Ireland** 8-3	1960	Paris **France** 23-6
1911	Cork **Ireland** 25-5	1961	Dublin **France** 15-3
1912	Paris **Ireland** 11-6	1962	Paris **France** 11-0
1913	Cork **Ireland** 24-0	1963	Dublin **France** 24-5
1914	Paris **Ireland** 8-6	1964	Paris **France** 27-6
1920	Dublin **France** 15-7	1965	Dublin **Drawn** 3-3
1921	Paris **France** 20-10	1966	Paris **France** 11-6
1922	Dublin **Ireland** 8-3	1967	Dublin **France** 11-6
1923	Paris **France** 14-8	1968	Paris **France** 16-6
1924	Dublin **Ireland** 6-0	1969	Dublin **Ireland** 17-9
1925	Paris **Ireland** 9-3	1970	Paris **France** 8-0
1926	Belfast **Ireland** 11-0	1971	Dublin **Drawn** 9-9
1927	Paris **Ireland** 8-3	1972	Paris **Ireland** 14-9
1928	Belfast **Ireland** 12-8	1972	Dublin **Ireland** 24-14
1929	Paris **Ireland** 6-0		*Non-championship match*
1930	Belfast **France** 5-0	1973	Dublin **Ireland** 6-4
1931	Paris **France** 3-0	1974	Paris **France** 9-6
1947	Dublin **France** 12-8	1975	Dublin **Ireland** 25-6
1948	Paris **Ireland** 13-6	1976	Paris **France** 26-3
1949	Dublin **France** 16-9	1977	Dublin **France** 15-6
1950	Paris **Drawn** 3-3	1978	Paris **France** 10-9
1951	Dublin **Ireland** 9-8	1979	Dublin **Drawn** 9-9
1952	Paris **Ireland** 11-8	1980	Paris **France** 19-18
1953	Belfast **Ireland** 16-3	1981	Dublin **France** 19-13
1954	Paris **France** 8-0	1982	Paris **France** 22-9
1955	Dublin **France** 5-3	1983	Dublin **Ireland** 22-16
1956	Paris **France** 14-8	1984	Paris **France** 25-12
1957	Dublin **Ireland** 11-6	1985	Dublin **Drawn** 15-15
1958	Paris **France** 11-6	1986	Paris **France** 29-9

1987 Dublin **France** 19-13	1995 Durban *WC* **France** 36-12
1988 Paris **France** 25-6	1996 Paris **France** 45-10
1989 Dublin **France** 26-21	1997 Dublin **France** 32-15
1990 Paris **France** 31-12	1998 Paris **France** 18-16
1991 Dublin **France** 21-13	1999 Dublin **France** 10-9
1992 Paris **France** 44-12	2000 Paris **Ireland** 27-25
1993 Dublin **France** 21-6	2001 Dublin **Ireland** 22-15
1994 Paris **France** 35-15	2002 Paris **France** 44-5
1995 Dublin **France** 25-7	

IRELAND v NEW ZEALAND

Played 17   Ireland won 0, New Zealand won 16, Drawn 1
Highest scores Ireland 29-40 in 2001, New Zealand 63-15 in 1997
Biggest win Ireland no win, New Zealand 59-6 in 1992

1905 Dublin **New Zealand** 15-0	1992 *1* Dunedin **New Zealand** 24-21
1924 Dublin **New Zealand** 6-0	*2* Wellington **New Zealand** 59-6
1935 Dublin **New Zealand** 17-9	*New Zealand won series 2-0*
1954 Dublin **New Zealand** 14-3	1995 Johannesburg *WC* **New Zealand** 43-19
1963 Dublin **New Zealand** 6-5	1997 Dublin **New Zealand** 63-15
1973 Dublin **Drawn** 10-10	2001 Dublin **New Zealand** 40-29
1974 Dublin **New Zealand** 15-6	2002 *1* Dunedin **New Zealand** 15-6
1976 Wellington **New Zealand** 11-3	*2* Auckland **New Zealand** 40-8
1978 Dublin **New Zealand** 10-6	*New Zealand won series 2-0*
1989 Dublin **New Zealand** 23-6	

IRELAND v SOUTH AFRICA

Played 14   Ireland won 1, South Africa won 12, Drawn 1
Highest scores Ireland 18-28 in 2000, South Africa 38-0 in 1912
Biggest wins Ireland 9-6 in 1965, South Africa 38-0 in 1912

1906 Belfast **South Africa** 15-12	1981 *1* Cape Town **South Africa** 23-15
1912 Dublin **South Africa** 38-0	*2* Durban **South Africa** 12-10
1931 Dublin **South Africa** 8-3	*South Africa won series 2-0*
1951 Dublin **South Africa** 17-5	1998 *1* Bloemfontein **South Africa** 37-13
1960 Dublin **South Africa** 8-3	*2* Pretoria **South Africa** 33-0
1961 Cape Town **South Africa** 24-8	*South Africa won series 2-0*
1965 Dublin **Ireland** 9-6	1998 Dublin **South Africa** 27-13
1970 Dublin **Drawn** 8-8	2000 Dublin **South Africa** 28-18

IRELAND v AUSTRALIA

Played 20   Ireland won 6, Australia won 14, Drawn 0
Highest scores Ireland 27-12 in 1979, Australia 46-10 in 1999
Biggest wins Ireland 27-12 in 1979, Australia 46-10 in 1999

1927 Dublin **Australia** 5-3	1987 Sydney *WC* **Australia** 33-15
1947 Dublin **Australia** 16-3	1991 Dublin *WC* **Australia** 19-18
1958 Dublin **Ireland** 9-6	1992 Dublin **Australia** 42-17
1967 Dublin **Ireland** 15-8	1994 *1* Brisbane **Australia** 33-13
1967 Sydney **Ireland** 11-5	*2* Sydney **Australia** 32-18
1968 Dublin **Ireland** 10-3	*Australia won series 2-0*
1976 Dublin **Australia** 20-10	1996 Dublin **Australia** 22-12
1979 *1* Brisbane **Ireland** 27-12	1999 *1* Brisbane **Australia** 46-10
2 Sydney **Ireland** 9-3	*2* Perth **Australia** 32-26
Ireland won series 2-0	*Australia won series 2-0*
1981 Dublin **Australia** 16-12	1999 Dublin *WC* **Australia** 23-3
1984 Dublin **Australia** 16-9	

IRELAND v NEW ZEALAND NATIVES
Played 1   New Zealand Natives won 1
Highest scores Ireland 4-13 in 1888, Zew Zealand Natives 13-4 in 1888
Biggest win Ireland no win, New Zealand Natives 13-4 in 1888

1888 Dublin **New Zealand Natives**
    4G 1T to 1G 1T

IRELAND v IRU PRESIDENT'S XV
Played 1   Drawn 1
Highest scores Ireland 18-18 in 1974, IRFU President's XV 18-18 in 1974

1974   Dublin **Drawn** 18-18

IRELAND v ROMANIA
Played 5   Ireland won 5
Highest scores Ireland 60-0 in 1986, Romania 35-53 in 1998
Biggest win Ireland 60-0 in 1986, Romania no win

1986 Dublin **Ireland** 60-0	1999 Dublin *WC* **Ireland** 44-14
1993 Dublin **Ireland** 25-3	2001 Bucharest **Ireland** 37-3
1998 Dublin **Ireland** 53-35	

IRELAND v CANADA
Played 3   Ireland won 2   Drawn 1
Highest scores Ireland 46-19 in 1987, Canada 27-27 in 2000
Biggest win Ireland 46-19 in 1987, Canada no win

1987 Dunedin *WC* **Ireland** 46-19	2000 Markham **Drawn** 27-27
1997 Dublin **Ireland** 33-11	

IRELAND v TONGA
Played 1   Ireland won 1
Highest scores Ireland 32-9 in 1987, Tonga 9-32 in 1987
Biggest win Ireland 32-9 in 1987, Tonga no win

1987   Brisbane *WC* **Ireland** 32-9

IRELAND v SAMOA
Played 3   Ireland won 2, Samoa won 1, Drawn 0
Highest scores Ireland 49-22 in 1988, Samoa 40-25 in 1996
Biggest wins Ireland 49-22 in 1988 and 35-8 in 2001, Samoa 40-25 in 1996

1988 Dublin **Ireland** 49-22	2001 Dublin **Ireland** 35-8
1996 Dublin **Samoa** 40-25	

IRELAND v ITALY
Played 8   Ireland won 5, Italy won 3, Drawn 0
Highest scores Ireland 60-13 in 2000, Italy 37-29 in 1997 & 37-22 in 1997
Biggest wins Ireland 60-13 in 2000, Italy 37-22 in 1997

1988 Dublin **Ireland** 31-15	1997 Dublin **Italy** 37-29
1995 Treviso **Italy** 22-12	1997 Bologna **Italy** 37-22

1999 Dublin **Ireland** 39-30

2000 Dublin **Ireland** 60-13

2001 Rome **Ireland** 41-22

2002 Dublin **Ireland** 32-17

IRELAND v ARGENTINA

Played 4   Ireland won 2   Argentina won 2

Highest scores Ireland 32-24 in 1999, Argentina 34-23 in 2000

Biggest win Ireland 32-24 in 1999, Argentina 34-23 in 2000

1990 Dublin **Ireland** 20-18

1999 Dublin **Ireland** 32-24

1999 Lens *WC* **Argentina** 28-24

2000 Buenos Aires **Argentina** 34-23

IRELAND v NAMIBIA

Played 2   Namibia won 2

Highest scores Ireland 15-26 in 1991, Namibia 26-15 in 1991

Biggest win Ireland no win, Namibia 26-15 in 1991

1991 *1* Windhoek **Namibia** 15-6

     2 Windhoek **Namibia** 26-15

     Namibia won series 2-0

IRELAND v ZIMBABWE

Played 1   Ireland won 1

Highest scores Ireland 55-11 in 1991, Zimbabwe 11-55 in 1991

Biggest win Ireland 55-11 in 1991, Zimbabwe no win

1991 Dublin *WC* **Ireland** 55-11

IRELAND v JAPAN

Played 3   Ireland won 3

Highest scores Ireland 78-9 in 2000, Japan 28-50 in 1995

Biggest win Ireland 78-9 in 2000, Japan no win

1991 Dublin *WC* **Ireland** 32-16

1995 Bloemfontein *WC* **Ireland** 50-28

2000 Dublin **Ireland** 78-9

IRELAND v UNITED STATES

Played 4   Ireland won 4

Highest scores Ireland 83-3 in 2000, United States 18-25 in 1996

Biggest win Ireland 83-3 in 2000, United States no win

1994 Dublin **Ireland** 26-15

1996 Atlanta **Ireland** 25-18

1999 Dublin *WC* **Ireland** 53-8

2000 Manchester (NH) **Ireland** 83-3

IRELAND v FIJI

Played 1   Ireland won 1

Highest scores Ireland 44-8 in 1995, Fiji 8-44 in 1995

Biggest win Ireland 44-8 in 1995, Fiji no win

1995 Dublin **Ireland** 44-8

IRELAND v GEORGIA

Played 1   Ireland won 1
Highest scores Ireland 70-0 in 1998, Georgia 0-70 in 1998
Biggest win Ireland 70-0 in 1998, Georgia no win

1998   Dublin **Ireland** 70-0

WALES v FRANCE

Played 78   Wales won 41, France won 34, Drawn 3
Highest scores Wales 49-14 in 1910, France 51-0 in 1998
Biggest wins Wales 47-5 in 1909, France 51-0 in 1998

1908	Cardiff	**Wales** 36-4
1909	Paris	**Wales** 47-5
1910	Swansea	**Wales** 49-14
1911	Paris	**Wales** 15-0
1912	Newport	**Wales** 14-8
1913	Paris	**Wales** 11-8
1914	Swansea	**Wales** 31-0
1920	Paris	**Wales** 6-5
1921	Cardiff	**Wales** 12-4
1922	Paris	**Wales** 11-3
1923	Swansea	**Wales** 16-8
1924	Paris	**Wales** 10-6
1925	Cardiff	**Wales** 11-5
1926	Paris	**Wales** 7-5
1927	Swansea	**Wales** 25-7
1928	Paris	**France** 8-3
1929	Cardiff	**Wales** 8-3
1930	Paris	**Wales** 11-0
1931	Swansea	**Wales** 35-3
1947	Paris	**Wales** 3-0
1948	Swansea	**France** 11-3
1949	Paris	**France** 5-3
1950	Cardiff	**Wales** 21-0
1951	Paris	**France** 8-3
1952	Swansea	**Wales** 9-5
1953	Paris	**Wales** 6-3
1954	Cardiff	**Wales** 19-13
1955	Paris	**Wales** 16-11
1956	Cardiff	**Wales** 5-3
1957	Paris	**Wales** 19-13
1958	Cardiff	**France** 16-6
1959	Paris	**France** 11-3
1960	Cardiff	**France** 16-8
1961	Paris	**France** 8-6
1962	Cardiff	**Wales** 3-0
1963	Paris	**France** 5-3
1964	Cardiff	**Drawn** 11-11
1965	Paris	**France** 22-13
1966	Cardiff	**Wales** 9-8
1967	Paris	**France** 20-14
1968	Cardiff	**France** 14-9
1969	Paris	**Drawn** 8-8
1970	Cardiff	**Wales** 11-6
1971	Paris	**Wales** 9-5
1972	Cardiff	**Wales** 20-6
1973	Paris	**France** 12-3
1974	Cardiff	**Drawn** 16-16
1975	Paris	**Wales** 25-10
1976	Cardiff	**Wales** 19-13
1977	Paris	**France** 16-9
1978	Cardiff	**Wales** 16-7
1979	Paris	**France** 14-13
1980	Cardiff	**Wales** 18-9
1981	Paris	**France** 19-15
1982	Cardiff	**Wales** 22-12
1983	Paris	**France** 16-9
1984	Cardiff	**France** 21-16
1985	Paris	**France** 14-3
1986	Cardiff	**France** 23-15
1987	Paris	**France** 16-9
1988	Cardiff	**France** 10-9
1989	Paris	**France** 31-12
1990	Cardiff	**France** 29-19
1991	Paris	**France** 36-3
1991	Cardiff	**France** 22-9
	Non-championship match	
1992	Cardiff	**France** 12-9
1993	Paris	**France** 26-10
1994	Cardiff	**Wales** 24-15
1995	Paris	**France** 21-9
1996	Cardiff	**Wales** 16-15
1996	Cardiff	**France** 40-33
	Non-championship match	
1997	Paris	**France** 27-22
1998	Wembley	**France** 51-0
1999	Paris	**Wales** 34-33
1999	Cardiff	**Wales** 34-23
	Non-championship match	
2000	Cardiff	**France** 36-3
2001	Paris	**Wales** 43-35
2002	Cardiff	**France** 37-33

WALES v NEW ZEALAND

Played 17   Wales won 3, New Zealand won 14, Drawn 0
Highest scores Wales 16-19 in 1972, New Zealand 54-9 in 1988
Biggest wins Wales 13-8 in 1953, New Zealand 52-3 in 1988

1905	Cardiff **Wales** 3-0		1978	Cardiff **New Zealand** 13-12
1924	Swansea **New Zealand** 19-0		1980	Cardiff **New Zealand** 23-3
1935	Cardiff **Wales** 13-12		1987	Brisbane *WC* **New Zealand** 49-6
1953	Cardiff **Wales** 13-8		1988	*1* Christchurch **New Zealand** 52-3
1963	Cardiff **New Zealand** 6-0			*2* Auckland **New Zealand** 54-9
1967	Cardiff **New Zealand** 13-6			*New Zealand won series 2-0*
1969	*1* Christchurch **New Zealand** 19-0		1989	Cardiff **New Zealand** 34-9
	2 Auckland **New Zealand** 33-12		1995	Johannesburg *WC* **New Zealand** 34-9
	New Zealand won series 2-0		1997	Wembley **New Zealand** 42-7
1972	Cardiff **New Zealand** 19-16			

WALES v SOUTH AFRICA

Played 16   Wales won 1, South Africa won 14, Drawn 1
Highest scores Wales 29-19 in 1999, South Africa 96-13 in 1998
Biggest win Wales 29-19 in 1999, South Africa 96-13 in 1998

1906	Swansea **South Africa** 11-0		1996	Cardiff **South Africa** 37-20
1912	Cardiff **South Africa** 3-0		1998	Pretoria **South Africa** 96-13
1931	Swansea **South Africa** 8-3		1998	Wembley **South Africa** 28-20
1951	Cardiff **South Africa** 6-3		1999	Cardiff **Wales** 29-19
1960	Cardiff **South Africa** 3-0		2000	Cardiff **South Africa** 23-13
1964	Durban **South Africa** 24-3		2002	*1* Bloemfontein **South Africa** 34-19
1970	Cardiff **Drawn** 6-6			*2* Cape Town **South Africa** 19-8
1994	Cardiff **South Africa** 20-12			*SA won series 2-0*
1995	Johannesburg **South Africa** 40-11			

WALES v AUSTRALIA

Played 21   Wales won 8, Australia won 13, Drawn 0
Highest scores Wales 28-3 in 1975, Australia 63-6 in 1991
Biggest wins Wales 28-3 in 1975, Australia 63-6 in 1991

1908	Cardiff **Wales** 9-6		1984	Cardiff **Australia** 28-9
1927	Cardiff **Australia** 18-8		1987	Rotorua *WC* **Wales** 22-21
1947	Cardiff **Wales** 6-0		1991	Brisbane **Australia** 63-6
1958	Cardiff **Wales** 9-3		1991	Cardiff *WC* **Australia** 38-3
1966	Cardiff **Australia** 14-11		1992	Cardiff **Australia** 23-6
1969	Sydney **Wales** 19-16		1996	*1* Brisbane **Australia** 56-25
1973	Cardiff **Wales** 24-0			*2* Sydney **Australia** 42-3
1975	Cardiff **Wales** 28-3			*Australia won series 2-0*
1978	*1* Brisbane **Australia** 18-8		1996	Cardiff **Australia** 28-19
	2 Sydney **Australia** 19-17		1999	Cardiff *WC* **Australia** 24-9
	Australia won series 2-0		2001	Cardiff **Australia** 21-13
1981	Cardiff **Wales** 18-13			

WALES v NEW ZEALAND NATIVES

Played 1   Wales won 1
Highest scores Wales 5-0 in 1888, New Zealand Natives 0-5 in 1888
Biggest win Wales 5-0 in 1888, New Zealand Natives no win

1888   Swansea **Wales** 1G 2T to 0

WALES v NEW ZEALAND ARMY

Played 1   New Zealand Army won 1
Highest scores Wales 3-6 in 1919, New Zealand Army 6-3 in 1919
Biggest win Wales no win, New Zealand Army 6-3 in 1919

1919 Swansea **New Zealand Army** 6-3

WALES v ROMANIA
Played 5   Wales won 3, Romania won 2
Highest scores Wales 81-9 in 2001, Romania 24-6 in 1983
Biggest wins Wales 81-9 in 2001, Romania 24-6 in 1983

1983 Bucharest **Romania** 24-6	1997 Wrexham **Wales** 70-21
1988 Cardiff **Romania** 15-9	2001 Cardiff **Wales** 81-9
1994 Bucharest **Wales** 16-9	

WALES v FIJI
Played 4   Wales won 4
Highest scores Wales 40-3 in 1985, Fiji 15-22 in 1986 & 15-19 in 1995
Biggest win Wales 40-3 in 1985, Fiji no win

1985 Cardiff **Wales** 40-3	1994 Suva **Wales** 23-8
1986 Suva **Wales** 22-15	1995 Cardiff **Wales** 19-15

WALES v TONGA
Played 5   Wales won 5
Highest scores Wales 51-7 in 2001, Tonga 16-29 in 1987
Biggest win Wales 51-7 in 2001, Tonga no win

1986 Nuku'Alofa **Wales** 15-7	1997 Swansea **Wales** 46-12
1987 Palmerston North *WC* **Wales** 29-16	2001 Cardiff **Wales 51-7**
1994 Nuku'Alofa **Wales** 18-9	

WALES v SAMOA
Played 6   Wales won 3, Samoa won 3, Drawn 0
Highest scores Wales 50-6 in 2000, Samoa 38-31 in 1999
Biggest wins Wales 50-6 in 2000, Samoa 34-9 in 1994

1986 Apia **Wales** 32-14	1994 Moamoa **Samoa** 34-9
1988 Cardiff **Wales** 28-6	1999 Cardiff *WC* **Samoa** 38-31
1991 Cardiff *WC* **Samoa** 16-13	2000 Cardiff **Wales** 50-6

WALES v CANADA
Played 5   Wales won 4, Canada won 1, Drawn 0
Highest scores Wales 40-9 in 1987, Canada 26-24 in 1993
Biggest wins Wales 40-9 in 1987, Canada 26-24 in 1993

1987 Invercargill *WC* **Wales** 40-9	1997 Toronto **Wales** 28-25
1993 Cardiff **Canada** 26-24	1999 Cardiff **Wales** 33-19
1994 Toronto **Wales** 33-15	

WALES v UNITED STATES
Played 5   Wales won 5
Highest scores Wales 46-0 in 1987, United States 23-28 in 1997
Biggest win Wales 46-0 in 1987, United States no win

1987 Cardiff **Wales** 46-0	*2* San Francisco **Wales** 28-23
1997 Cardiff **Wales** 34-14	*Wales won series 2-0*
1997 *1* Wilmington **Wales** 30-20	2000 Cardiff **Wales** 42-11

WALES v NAMIBIA
Played 3 Wales won 3
Highest scores Wales 38-23 in 1993, Namibia 30-34 in 1990
Biggest win Wales 38-23 in 1993, Namibia no win

1990	*1* Windhoek **Wales** 18-9		1993	Windhoek **Wales** 38-23
	2 Windhoek **Wales** 34-30			
	Wales won series 2-0			

WALES v BARBARIANS
Played 2 Wales won 1, Barbarians won 1
Highest scores Wales 31-10 in 1996, Barbarians 31-24 in 1990
Biggest wins Wales 31-10 in 1996, Barbarians 31-24 in 1990

1990 Cardiff **Barbarians** 31-24		1996 Cardiff **Wales** 31-10

WALES v ARGENTINA
Played 6 Wales won 5, Argentina won 1
Highest scores Wales 43-30 in 1998, Argentina 30-43 in 1998 and 30-16 in 2001
Biggest win Wales 43-30 in 1998, Argentina 30-16 in 2001

1991 Cardiff *WC* **Wales** 16-7		1999 Cardiff *WC* **Wales** 23-18
1998 Llanelli **Wales** 43-30		2001 Cardiff **Argentina** 30-16
1999 *1* Buenos Aires **Wales** 36-26		
2 Buenos Aires **Wales** 23-16		
Wales won series 2-0		

WALES v ZIMBABWE
Played 3 Wales won 3
Highest scores Wales 49-11 in 1998, Zimbabwe 14-35 in 1993
Biggest win Wales 49-11 in 1998, Zimbabwe no win

1993 *1* Bulawayo **Wales** 35-14		1998 Harare **Wales** 49-11
2 Harare **Wales** 42-13		
Wales won series 2-0		

WALES v JAPAN
Played 5 Wales won 5
Highest scores Wales 64-15 in 1999 & 64-10 in 2001, Japan 30-53 in 2001
Biggest win Wales 64-10 in 2001, Japan no win

1993 Cardiff **Wales** 55-5		2001 *1* Osaka **Wales** 64-10
1995 Bloemfontein *WC* **Wales** 57-10		*2* Tokyo **Wales** 53-30
1999 Cardiff *WC* **Wales** 64-15		*Wales won series 2-0*

WALES v PORTUGAL
Played 1 Wales won 1
Highest scores Wales 102-11 in 1994, Portugal 11-102 in 1994
Biggest win Wales 102-11 in 1994, Portugal no win

1994 Lisbon **Wales** 102-11

WALES v SPAIN
Played 1   Wales won 1
Highest scores Wales 54-0 in 1994, Spain 0-54 in 1994
Bigegst win Wales 54-0 in 1994, Spain no win

1994   Madrid **Wales** 54-0

WALES v ITALY
Played 8   Wales won 8
Highest scores Wales 60-21 in 1999, Italy 26-31 in 1996
Biggest win Wales 60-21 in 1999, Italy no win

1994	Cardiff **Wales** 29-19	1999	Treviso **Wales** 60-21
1996	Cardiff **Wales** 31-26	2000	Cardiff **Wales** 47-16
1996	Rome **Wales** 31-22	2001	Rome **Wales** 33-23
1998	Llanelli **Wales** 23-20	2002	Cardiff **Wales** 44-20

BRITISH/IRISH ISLES v SOUTH AFRICA
Played 43   British/Irish won 16, South Africa won 21, Drawn 6
Highest scores: British/Irish 28–9 in 1974, South Africa 35–16 in 1997
Biggest wins: British/Irish 28–9 in 1974, South Africa 34–14 in 1962

1891   *1* Port Elizabeth **British/Irish** 4-0
     2 Kimberley **British/Irish** 3-0
     3 Cape Town **British/Irish** 4-0
     British/Irish won series 3-0
1896   *1* Port Elizabeth **British/Irish** 8-0
     2 Johannesburg **British/Irish** 17-8
     3 Kimberley **British/Irish** 9-3
     4 Cape Town **South Africa** 5-0
     British/Irish won series 3-1
1903   *1* Johannesburg **Drawn** 10-10
     2 Kimberley **Drawn** 0-0
     3 Cape Town **South Africa** 8-0
     South Africa won series 1-0 with two drawn
1910   *1* Johannesburg **South Africa** 14–10
     2 Port Elizabeth **British/Irish** 8–3
     3 Cape Town **South Africa** 21–5
     South Africa won series 2-1
1924   *1* Durban **South Africa** 7–3
     2 Johannesburg **South Africa** 17–0
     3 Port Elizabeth **Drawn** 3–3
     4 Cape Town **South Africa** 16–9
     South Africa won series 3-0, with 1 draw
1938   *1* Johannesburg **South Africa** 26–12
     2 Port Elizabeth **South Africa** 19–3
     3 Cape Town **British/Irish** 21–16
     South Africa won series 2-1
1955   *1* Johannesburg **British/Irish** 23–22
     2 Cape Town **South Africa** 25–9

     3 Pretoria **British/Irish** 9–6
     4 Port Elizabeth **South Africa** 22–8
     Series drawn 2-2
1962   *1* Johannesburg **Drawn** 3–3
     2 Durban **South Africa** 3–0
     3 Cape Town **South Africa** 8–3
     4 Bloemfontein **South Africa** 34–14
     South Africa won series 3-0, with 1 draw
1968   *1* Pretoria **South Africa** 25–20
     2 Port Elizabeth **Drawn** 6–6
     3 Cape Town **South Africa** 11–6
     4 Johannesburg **South Africa** 19–6
     South Africa won series 3-0, with 1 draw
1974   *1* Cape Town **British/Irish** 12–3
     2 Pretoria **British/Irish** 28–9
     3 Port Elizabeth **British/Irish** 26–9
     4 Johannesburg **Drawn** 13–13
     British/Irish won series 3-0, with 1 draw
1980   *1* Cape Town **South Africa** 26–22
     2 Bloemfontein **South Africa** 26–19
     3 Port Elizabeth **South Africa** 12–10
     4 Pretoria **British/Irish** 17–13
     South Africa won series 3-1
1997   *1* Cape Town **British/Irish** 25-16
     2 Durban **British/Irish** 18-15
     3 Johannesburg **South Africa** 35-16
     British/Irish won series 2-1

BRITISH/IRISH ISLES v NEW ZEALAND
Played 32   British/Irish won 6, New Zealand won 24, Drawn 2
Highest scores: British/Irish 20–7 in 1993, New Zealand 38–6 in 1983
Biggest wins: British/Irish 20–7 in 1993, New Zealand 38–6 in 1983

1904   Wellington **New Zealand** 9-3   1930   *1* Dunedin **British/Irish** 6–3

2 Christchurch **New Zealand** 13–10
3 Auckland **New Zealand** 15–10
4 Wellington **New Zealand** 22–8
New Zealand won series 3-1

1950 *1* Dunedin **Drawn** 9–9
2 Christchurch **New Zealand** 8–0
3 Wellington **New Zealand** 6–3
4 Auckland **New Zealand** 11–8
New Zealand won series 3-0, with 1 draw

1959 *1* Dunedin **New Zealand** 18–17
2 Wellington **New Zealand** 11–8
3 Christchurch **New Zealand** 22–8
4 Auckland **British/Irish** 9–6
New Zealand won series 3-1

1966 *1* Dunedin **New Zealand** 20–3
2 Wellington **New Zealand** 16–12
3 Christchurch **New Zealand** 19–6
4 Auckland **New Zealand** 24–11
New Zealand won series 4-0

1971 *1* Dunedin **British/Irish** 9–3
2 Christchurch **New Zealand** 22–12
3 Wellington **British/Irish** 13–3
4 Auckland **Drawn** 14–14
British/Irish won series 2-1, with 1 draw

1977 *1* Wellington **New Zealand** 16–12
2 Christchurch **British/Irish** 13–9
3 Dunedin **New Zealand** 19–7
4 Auckland **New Zealand** 10–9
New Zealand won series 3-1

1983 *1* Christchurch **New Zealand** 16–12
2 Wellington **New Zealand** 9–0
3 Dunedin **New Zealand** 15–8
4 Auckland **New Zealand** 38–6
New Zealand won series 4-0

1993 *1* Christchurch **New Zealand** 20–18
2 Wellington **British/Irish** 20–7
3 Auckland **New Zealand** 30–13
New Zealand won series 2-1

ANGLO-WELSH v NEW ZEALAND

Played 3   New Zealand won 2, Drawn 1
Highest scores Anglo Welsh 5-32 in 1908, New Zealand 32-5 in 1908
Biggest win Anglo Welsh no win, New Zealand 29-0 in 1908

1908 *1* Dunedin **New Zealand** 32-5
2 Wellington **Drawn** 3-3

3 Auckland **New Zealand** 29-0
New Zealand won series 2-0 with one drawn

BRITISH/IRISH ISLES v AUSTRALIA

Played 20   British/Irish won 15, Australia won 5, Drawn 0
Highest scores: British/Irish 31–0 in 1966, Australia 35–14 in 2001
Biggest wins: British/Irish 31–0 in 1966, Australia 35–14 in 2001

1899 *1* Sydney **Australia** 13-3
2 Brisbane **British/Irish** 11-0
3 Sydney **British/Irish** 11-10
4 Sydney **British/Irish** 13-0
British/Irish won series 3-1

1904 *1* Sydney **British/Irish** 17-0
2 Brisbane **British/Irish** 17-3
3 Sydney **British/Irish** 16-0
British/Irish won series 3-0

1930 Sydney **Australia** 6–5
1950 *1* Brisbane **British/Irish** 19–6
2 Sydney **British/Irish** 24–3
British/Irish won series 2-0

1959 *1* Brisbane **British/Irish** 17–6

2 Sydney **British/Irish** 24–3
British/Irish won series 2-0

1966 *1* Sydney **British/Irish** 11–8
2 Brisbane **British/Irish** 31–0
British/Irish won series 2-0

1989 *1* Sydney **Australia** 30–12
2 Brisbane **British/Irish** 19–12
3 Sydney **British/Irish** 19–18
British/Irish won series 2-1

2001 *1* Brisbane **British/Irish** 29-13
2 Melbourne **Australia** 35-14
3 Sydney **Australia** 29-23
Australia won series 2-1

FRANCE v NEW ZEALAND

Played 37   France won 10, New Zealand won 27, Drawn 0
Highest scores France 43-31 in 1999, New Zealand 54-7 in 1999
Biggest wins France 22-8 in 1994, New Zealand 54-7 in 1999

1906 Paris **New Zealand** 38-8
1925 Toulouse **New Zealand** 30-6
1954 Paris **France** 3-0
1961 *1* Auckland **New Zealand** 13-6
2 Wellington **New Zealand** 5-3

3 Christchurch **New Zealand** 32-3
New Zealand won series 3-0

1964 Paris **New Zealand** 12-3
1967 Paris **New Zealand** 21-15
1968 *1* Christchurch **New Zealand** 12-9

George Gregan, current Australian captain, spins out a pass during the series against the Lions in 2001.

	2	Wellington **New Zealand** 9-3
	3	Auckland **New Zealand** 19-12
		New Zealand won series 3-0
1973		Paris **France** 13-6
1977	1	Toulouse **France** 18-13
	2	Paris **New Zealand** 15-3
		Series drawn 1-1
1979	1	Christchurch **New Zealand** 23-9
	2	Auckland **France** 24-19
		Series drawn 1-1
1981	1	Toulouse **New Zealand** 13-9
	2	Paris **New Zealand** 18-6
		New Zealand won series 2-0
1984	1	Christchurch **New Zealand** 10-9
	2	Auckland **New Zealand** 31-18
		New Zealand won series 2-0

1986		Christchurch **New Zealand** 18-9
1986	1	Toulouse **New Zealand** 19-7
	2	Nantes **France** 16-3
		Series drawn 1-1
1987		Auckland *WC* **New Zealand** 29-9
1989	1	Christchurch **New Zealand** 25-17
	2	Auckland **New Zealand** 34-20
		New Zealand won series 2-0
1990	1	Nantes **New Zealand** 24-3
	2	Paris **New Zealand** 30-12
		New Zealand won series 2-0
1994	1	Christchurch **France** 22-8
	2	Auckland **France** 23-20
		France won series 2-0
1995	1	Toulouse **France** 22-15

2 Paris **New Zealand** 37-12
Series drawn 1-1
1999 Wellington **New Zealand** 54-7
1999 Twickenham *WC* **France** 43-31

2000 *1* Paris **New Zealand** 39-26
　　 2 Marseilles **France** 42-33
　　 Series drawn 1-1
2001 Wellington **New Zealand** 37-12

FRANCE v SOUTH AFRICA

Played 31　France won 7, South Africa won 19, Drawn 5
Highest scores France 32-36 in 1997 & 32-23 in 2001, South Africa 52-10 in 1997
Biggest wins France 29-16 in 1992, South Africa 52-10 in 1997

1913 Bordeaux **South Africa** 38-5
1952 Paris **South Africa** 25-3
1958 *1* Cape Town **Drawn** 3-3
　　 2 Johannesburg **France** 9-5
　　 France won series 1-0, with 1 draw
1961 Paris **Drawn** 0-0
1964 Springs (SA) **France** 8-6
1967 *1* Durban **South Africa** 26-3
　　 2 Bloemfontein **South Africa** 16-3
　　 3 Johannesburg **France** 19-14
　　 4 Cape Town **Drawn** 6-6
　　 South Africa won series 2-1, with 1 draw
1968 *1* Bordeaux **South Africa** 12-9
　　 2 Paris **South Africa** 16-11
　　 South Africa won series 2-0
1971 *1* Bloemfontein **South Africa** 22-9
　　 2 Durban **Drawn** 8-8
　　 South Africa won series 1-0, with 1 draw
1974 *1* Toulouse **South Africa** 13-4
　　 2 Paris **South Africa** 10-8
　　 South Africa won series 2-0

1975 *1* Bloemfontein **South Africa** 38-25
　　 2 Pretoria **South Africa** 33-18
　　 South Africa won series 2-0
1980 Pretoria **South Africa** 37-15
1992 *1* Lyons **South Africa** 20-15
　　 2 Paris **France** 29-16
　　 Series drawn 1-1
1993 *1* Durban **Drawn** 20-20
　　 2 Johannesburg **France** 18-17
　　 France won series 1-0, with 1 draw
1995 Durban *WC* **South Africa** 19-15
1996 *1* Bordeaux **South Africa** 22-12
　　 2 Paris **South Africa** 13-12
　　 South Africa won series 2-0
1997 *1* Lyons **South Africa** 36-32
　　 2 Paris **South Africa** 52-10
　　 South Africa won series 2-0
2001 *1* Johannesburg **France** 32-23
　　 2 Durban **South Africa** 20-15
　　 Series drawn 1-1
2001 Paris **France** 20-10

FRANCE v AUSTRALIA

Played 33　France won 14, Australia won 17, Drawn 2
Highest scores France 34-6 in 1976, Australia 48-31 in 1990
Biggest wins France 34-6 in 1976, Australia 35-12 in 1999

1928 Paris **Australia** 11-8
1948 Paris **France** 13-6
1958 Paris **France** 19-0
1961 Sydney **France** 15-8
1967 Paris **France** 20-14
1968 Sydney **Australia** 11-10
1971 *1* Toulouse **Australia** 13-11
　　 2 Paris **France** 18-9
　　 Series drawn 1-1
1972 *1* Sydney **Drawn** 14-14
　　 2 Brisbane **France** 16-15
　　 France won series 1-0, with 1 draw
1976 *1* Bordeaux **France** 18-15
　　 2 Paris **France** 34-6
　　 France won series 2-0
1981 *1* Brisbane **Australia** 17-15
　　 2 Sydney **Australia** 24-14
　　 Australia won series 2-0
1983 *1* Clermont-Ferrand **Drawn** 15-15
　　 2 Paris **France** 15-6
　　 France won series 1-0, with 1 draw
1986 Sydney **Australia** 27-14

1987 Sydney *WC* **France** 30-24
1989 *1* Strasbourg **Australia** 32-15
　　 2 Lille **France** 25-19
　　 Series drawn 1-1
1990 *1* Sydney **Australia** 21-9
　　 2 Brisbane **Australia** 48-31
　　 3 Sydney **France** 28-19
　　 Australia won series 2-1
1993 *1* Bordeaux **France** 16-13
　　 2 Paris **Australia** 24-3
　　 Series drawn 1-1
1997 *1* Sydney **Australia** 29-15
　　 2 Brisbane **Australia** 26-19
　　 Australia won series 2-0
1998 Paris **Australia** 32-21
1999 Cardiff *WC* **Australia** 35-12
2000 Paris **Australia** 18-13
2001 Marseilles **France** 14-13
2002 *1* Melbourne **Australia** 29-17
　　 2 Sydney **Australia** 31-25
　　 Australia won series 2-0

FRANCE v UNITED STATES
Played 5   France won 4, United States won 1, Drawn 0
Highest scores France 41-9 in 1991, United States 17-3 in 1924
Biggest wins France 41-9 in 1991, United States 17-3 in 1924

1920	Paris **France** 14-5	
1924	Paris **United States** 17-3	
1976	Chicago **France** 33-14	
1991	*1* Denver **France** 41-9	

2 Colorado Springs **France** 10-3*
*Abandoned after 43 mins
France won series 2-0

FRANCE v ROMANIA
Played 47   France won 37, Romania won 8, Drawn 2
Highest scores France 67-20 in 2000, Romania 21-33 in 1991
Biggest wins France 59-3 in 1924, Romania 15-0 in 1980

1924	Paris **France** 59-3		1980	Bucharest **Romania** 15-0
1938	Bucharest **France** 11-8		1981	Narbonne **France** 17-9
1957	Bucharest **France** 18-15		1982	Bucharest **Romania** 13-9
1957	Bordeaux **France** 39-0		1983	Toulouse **France** 26-15
1960	Bucharest **Romania** 11-5		1984	Bucharest **France** 18-3
1961	Bayonne **Drawn** 5-5		1986	Lille **France** 25-13
1962	Bucharest **Romania** 3-0		1986	Bucharest **France** 20-3
1963	Toulouse **Drawn** 6-6		1987	Wellington *WC* **France** 55-12
1964	Bucharest **France** 9-6		1987	Agen **France** 49-3
1965	Lyons **France** 8-3		1988	Bucharest **France** 16-12
1966	Bucharest **France** 9-3		1990	Auch **Romania** 12-6
1967	Nantes **France** 11-3		1991	Bucharest **France** 33-21
1968	Bucharest **Romania** 15-14		1991	Béziers *WC* **France** 30-3
1969	Tarbes **France** 14-9		1992	Le Havre **France** 25-6
1970	Bucharest **France** 14-3		1993	Bucharest **France** 37-20
1971	Béziers **France** 31-12		1993	Brive **France** 51-0
1972	Constanza **France** 15-6		1995	Bucharest **France** 24-15
1973	Valence **France** 7-6		1995	Tucumán *LC* **France** 52-8
1974	Bucharest **Romania** 15-10		1996	Aurillac **France** 64-12
1975	Bordeaux **France** 36-12		1997	Bucharest **France** 51-20
1976	Bucharest **Romania** 15-12		1997	Lourdes *LC* **France** 39-3
1977	Clermont-Ferrand **France** 9-6		1999	Castres **France** 62-8
1978	Bucharest **France** 9-6		2000	Bucharest **France** 67-20
1979	Montauban **France** 30-12			

FRANCE v NEW ZEALAND MAORIS
Played 1   New Zealand Maoris won 1
Highest scores France 3-12 in 1926, New Zealand Maoris 12-3 in 1926
Biggest win France no win, New Zealand Maoris 12-3 in 1926

1926   Paris **New Zealand Maoris** 12-3

FRANCE v GERMANY
Played 15   France won 13, Germany won 2, Drawn 0
Highest scores France 38-17 in 1933, Germany 17-16 in 1927 & 17-38 in 1933
Biggest wins France 34-0 in 1931, Germany 3-0 in 1938

1927	Paris **France** 30-5		1931	Paris **France** 34-0
1927	Frankfurt **Germany** 17-16		1932	Frankfurt **France** 20-4
1928	Hanover **France** 14-3		1933	Paris **France** 38-17
1929	Paris **France** 24-0		1934	Hanover **France** 13-9
1930	Berlin **France** 31-0		1935	Paris **France** 18-3

1936 *1* Berlin **France** 19-14	1937 Paris **France** 27-6
2 Hanover **France** 6-3	1938 Frankfurt **Germany** 3-0
France won series 2-0	1938 Bucharest **France** 8-5

FRANCE v ITALY

Played 23   France won 22, Italy won 1, Drawn 0
Highest scores France 60-13 in 1967, Italy 40-32 in 1997
Biggest wins France 60-13 in 1967, Italy 40-32 in 1997

1937	Paris **France** 43-5	1963	Grenoble **France** 14-12
1952	Milan **France** 17-8	1964	Parma **France** 12-3
1953	Lyons **France** 22-8	1965	Pau **France** 21-0
1954	Rome **France** 39-12	1966	Naples **France** 21-0
1955	Grenoble **France** 24-0	1967	Toulon **France** 60-13
1956	Padua **France** 16-3	1995	Buenos Aires *LC* **France** 34-22
1957	Agen **France** 38-6	1997	Grenoble **Italy** 40-32
1958	Naples **France** 11-3	1997	Auch *LC* **France** 30-19
1959	Nantes **France** 22-0	2000	Paris **France** 42-31
1960	Treviso **France** 26-0	2001	Rome **France** 30-19
1961	Chambéry **France** 17-0	2002	Paris **France** 33-12
1962	Brescia **France** 6-3		

FRANCE v BRITISH XVs

Played 5   France won 2, British XVs won 3, Drawn 0
Highest scores France 27-29 in 1989, British XV 36-3 in 1940
Biggest wins France 21-9 in 1945, British XV 36-3 in 1940

1940	Paris **British XV** 36-3	1946	Paris **France** 10-0
1945	Paris **France** 21-9	1989	Paris **British XV** 29-27
1945	Richmond **British XV** 27-6		

FRANCE v WALES XVs

Played 2   France won 1, Wales XV won 1
Highest scores France 12-0 in 1946, Wales XV 8-0 in 1945
Biggest win France 12-0 in 1946, Wales XV 8-0 in 1945

1945	Swansea **Wales XV** 8-0	1946	Paris **France** 12-0

FRANCE v IRELAND XVs

Played 1   France won 1
Highest scores France 4-3 in 1946, Ireland XV 3-4 in 1946
Biggest win France 4-3 in 1946, Ireland XV no win

1946	Dublin **France** 4-3

FRANCE v NEW ZEALAND ARMY

Played 1   New Zealand Army won 1
Highest scores France 9-14 in 1946, New Zealand Army 14-9 in 1946
Biggest win France no win, New Zealand Army 14-9 in 1946

1946	Paris **New Zealand Army** 14-9

FRANCE v ARGENTINA

Played 35   France won 29, Argentina won 5, Drawn 1
Highest scores France 47-12 in 1995 & 47-26 in 1999, Argentina 28-27 in 2002
Biggest wins France 47-12 in 1995, Argentina 18-6 in 1988

1949	*1* Buenos Aires **France** 5-0		1986	*1* Buenos Aires **Argentina** 15-13
	2 Buenos Aires **France** 12-3			*2* Buenos Aires **France** 22-9
	France won series 2-0			*Series drawn 1-1*
1954	*1* Buenos Aires **France** 22-8		1988	*1* Buenos Aires **France** 18-15
	2 Buenos Aires **France** 30-3			*2* Buenos Aires **Argentina** 18-6
	France won series 2-0			*Series drawn 1-1*
1960	*1* Buenos Aires **France** 37-3		1988	*1* Nantes **France** 29-9
	2 Buenos Aires **France** 12-3			*2* Lille **France** 28-18
	3 Buenos Aires **France** 29-6			*France won series 2-0*
	France won series 3-0		1992	*1* Buenos Aires **France** 27-12
1974	*1* Buenos Aires **France** 20-15			*2* Buenos Aires **France** 33-9
	2 Buenos Aires **France** 31-27			*France won series 2-0*
	France won series 2-0		1992	Nantes **Argentina** 24-20
1975	*1* Lyons **France** 29-6		1995	Buenos Aires *LC* **France** 47-12
	2 Paris **France** 36-21		1996	*1* Buenos Aires **France** 34-27
	France won series 2-0			*2* Buenos Aires **France** 34-15
1977	*1* Buenos Aires **France** 26-3			*France won series 2-0*
	2 Buenos Aires **Drawn** 18-18		1997	Tarbes *LC* **France** 32-27
	France won series 1-0, with 1 draw		1998	*1* Buenos Aires **France** 35-18
1982	*1* Toulouse **France** 25-12			*2* Buenos Aires **France** 37-12
	2 Paris **France** 13-6			*France won series 2-0*
	France won series 2-0		1998	Nantes **France** 34-14
1985	*1* Buenos Aires **Argentina** 24-16		1999	Dublin *WC* **France** 47-26
	2 Buenos Aires **France** 23-15		2002	Buenos Aires **Argentina** 28-27
	Series drawn 1-1			

FRANCE v CZECHOSLOVAKIA

Played 2   France won 2
Highest scores France 28-3 in 1956, Czechoslovakia 6-19 in 1968
Biggest win France 28-3 in 1956, Czechoslovakia no win

1956 Toulouse **France** 28-3	1968 Prague **France** 19-6

FRANCE v FIJI

Played 6   France won 6
Highest scores France 77-10 in 2001, Fiji 19-28 in 1999
Biggest win France 77-10 in 2001, Fiji no win

1964 Paris **France** 21-3	1998 Suva **France** 34-9
1987 Auckland *WC* **France** 31-16	1999 Toulouse *WC* **France** 28-19
1991 Grenoble *WC* **France** 33-9	2001 Saint Etienne **France** 77-10

FRANCE v JAPAN

Played 1   France won 1
Highest scores France 30-18 in 1973, Japan 18-30 in 1973
Biggest win France 30-18 in 1973, Japan no win

1973 Bordeaux **France** 30-18

FRANCE v ZIMBABWE
Played 1   France won 1
Highest scores France 70-12 in 1987, Zimbabwe 12-70 in 1987
Biggest win France 70-12 in 1987, Zimbabwe no win

1987   Auckland *WC* **France** 70-12

FRANCE v CANADA
Played 4   France won 3, Canada won 1, Drawn 0
Highest scores France 33-20 in 1999, Canada 20-33 in 1999
Biggest wins France 28-9 in 1994, Canada 18-16 in 1994

1991 Agen *WC* **France** 19-13	1994 Besançon **France** 28-9
1994 Nepean **Canada** 18-16	1999 Béziers *WC* **France** 33-20

FRANCE v TONGA
Played 2   France won 1, Tonga won 1
Highest scores France 38-10 in 1995, Tonga 20-16 in 1999
Biggest win France 38-10 in 1995, Tonga 20-16 in 1999

1995 Pretoria *WC* **France** 38-10	1999 Nuku'alofa **Tonga** 20-16

FRANCE v IVORY COAST
Played 1   France won 1
Highest scores France 54-18 in 1995, Ivory Coast 18-54 in 1995
Biggest win France 54-18 in 1995, Ivory Coast no win

1995   Rustenburg *WC* **France** 54-18

FRANCE v SAMOA
Played 1   France won 1
Highest scores France 39-22 in 1999, Samoa 22-39 in 1999
Biggest win France 39-22 in 1999, Samoa no win

1999   Apia **France** 39-22

FRANCE v NAMIBIA
Played 1   France won 1
Highest scores France 47-13 in 1999, Namibia 13-47 in 1999
Biggest win France 47-13 in 1999, Namibia no win

1999   Bordeaux *WC* **France** 47-13

SOUTH AFRICA v NEW ZEALAND
Played 60   New Zealand won 31, South Africa won 26, Drawn 3
Highest scores New Zealand 55-35 in 1997, South Africa 46-40 in 2000
Biggest wins New Zealand 28-0 in 1999, South Africa 17-0 in 1928

1921 *1* Dunedin **New Zealand** 13-5	1928 *1* Durban **South Africa** 17-0
2 Auckland **South Africa** 9-5	*2* Johannesburg **New Zealand** 7-6
3 Wellington **Drawn** 0-0	*3* Port Elizabeth **South Africa** 11-6
Series drawn 1-1, with 1 draw	*4* Cape Town **New Zealand** 13-5
	Series drawn 2-2

1937 *1* Wellington **New Zealand** 13-7
    2 Christchurch **South Africa** 13-6
    3 Auckland **South Africa** 17-6
    South Africa won series 2-1

1949 *1* Cape Town **South Africa** 15-11
    2 Johannesburg **South Africa** 12-6
    3 Durban **South Africa** 9-3
    4 Port Elizabeth **South Africa** 11-8
    South Africa won series 4-0

1956 *1* Dunedin **New Zealand** 10-6
    2 Wellington **South Africa** 8-3
    3 Christchurch **New Zealand** 17-10
    4 Auckland **New Zealand** 11-5
    New Zealand won series 3-1

1960 *1* Johannesburg **South Africa** 13-0
    2 Cape Town **New Zealand** 11-3
    3 Bloemfontein **Drawn** 11-11
    4 Port Elizabeth **South Africa** 8-3
    South Africa won series 2-1, with 1 draw

1965 *1* Wellington **New Zealand** 6-3
    2 Dunedin **New Zealand** 13-0
    3 Christchurch **South Africa** 19-16
    4 Auckland **New Zealand** 20-3
    New Zealand won series 3-1

1970 *1* Pretoria **South Africa** 17-6
    2 Cape Town **New Zealand** 9-8
    3 Port Elizabeth **South Africa** 14-3
    4 Johannesburg **South Africa** 20-17
    South Africa won series 3-1

1976 *1* Durban **South Africa** 16-7
    2 Bloemfontein **New Zealand** 15-9
    3 Cape Town **South Africa** 15-10

    4 Johannesburg **South Africa** 15-14
    South Africa won series 3-1

1981 *1* Christchurch **New Zealand** 14-9
    2 Wellington **South Africa** 24-12
    3 Auckland **New Zealand** 25-22
    New Zealand won series 2-1

1992 Johannesburg **New Zealand** 27-24

1994 *1* Dunedin **New Zealand** 22-14
    2 Wellington **New Zealand** 13-9
    3 Auckland **Drawn** 18-18
    New Zealand won series 2-0, with 1 draw

1995 Johannesburg *WC* **South Africa** 15-12 *(aet)*

1996 Christchurch *TN* **New Zealand** 15-11

1996 Cape Town *TN* **New Zealand** 29-18

1996 *1* Durban **New Zealand** 23-19
    2 Pretoria **New Zealand** 33-26
    3 Johannesburg **South Africa** 32-22
    New Zealand won series 2-1

1997 Johannesbury *TN* **New Zealand** 35-32

1997 Auckland *TN* **New Zealand** 55-35

1998 Wellington *TN* **South Africa** 13-3

1998 Durban *TN* **South Africa** 24-23

1999 Dunedin *TN* **New Zealand** 28-0

1999 Pretoria *TN* **New Zealand** 34-18

1999 Cardiff *WC* **South Africa** 22-18

2000 Christchurch *TN* **New Zealand** 25-12

2000 Johannesburg *TN* **South Africa** 46-40

2001 Cape Town *TN* **New Zealand** 12-3

2001 Auckland *TN* **New Zealand** 26-15

2002 Wellington *TN* **New Zealand** 41-20

2002 Durban *TN* **New Zealand** 30-23

SOUTH AFRICA v AUSTRALIA

Played 49   South Africa won 30, Australia won 18, Drawn 1
Highest scores South Africa 61-22 in 1997, Australia 44-23 in 2000
Biggest wins South Africa 61-22 in 1997, Australia 32-6 in 1999

1933 *1* Cape Town **South Africa** 17-3
    2 Durban **Australia** 21-6
    3 Johannesburg **South Africa** 12-3
    4 Port Elizabeth **South Africa** 11-0
    5 Bloemfontein **Australia** 15-4
    South Africa won series 3-2

1937 *1* Sydney **South Africa** 9-5
    2 Sydney **South Africa** 26-17
    South Africa won series 2-0

1953 *1* Johannesburg **South Africa** 25-3
    2 Cape Town **Australia** 18-14
    3 Durban **South Africa** 18-8
    4 Port Elizabeth **South Africa** 22-9
    South Africa won series 3-1

1956 *1* Sydney **South Africa** 9-0
    2 Brisbane **South Africa** 9-0
    South Africa won series 2-0

1961 *1* Johannesburg **South Africa** 28-3
    2 Port Elizabeth **South Africa** 23-11
    South Africa won series 2-0

1963 *1* Pretoria **South Africa** 14-3
    2 Cape Town **Australia** 9-5
    3 Johannesburg **Australia** 11-9

    4 Port Elizabeth **South Africa** 22-6
    Series drawn 2-2

1965 *1* Sydney **Australia** 18-11
    2 Brisbane **Australia** 12-8
    Australia won series 2-0

1969 *1* Johannesburg **South Africa** 30-11
    2 Durban **South Africa** 16-9
    3 Cape Town **South Africa** 11-3
    4 Bloemfontein **South Africa** 19-8
    South Africa won series 4-0

1971 *1* Sydney **South Africa** 19-11
    2 Brisbane **South Africa** 14-6
    3 Sydney **South Africa** 18-6
    South Africa won series 3-0

1992 Cape Town **Australia** 26-3

1993 *1* Sydney **South Africa** 19-12
    2 Brisbane **Australia** 28-20
    3 Sydney **Australia** 19-12
    Australia won series 2-1

1995 Cape Town *WC* **South Africa** 27-18

1996 Sydney *TN* **Australia** 21-16

1996 Bloemfontein *TN* **South Africa** 25-19

1997 Brisbane *TN* **Australia** 32-20

1997   Pretoria *TN* **South Africa** 61-22
1998   Perth *TN* **South Africa** 14-13
1998   Johannesburg *TN* **South Africa** 29-15
1999   Brisbane *TN* **Australia** 32-6
1999   Cape Town *TN* **South Africa** 10-9
1999   Twickenham *WC* **Australia** 27-21
2000   Melbourne **Australia** 44-23

2000   Sydney *TN* **Australia** 26-6
2000   Durban *TN* **Australia** 19-18
2001   Pretoria *TN* **South Africa** 20-15
2001   Perth *TN* **Drawn** 14-14
2002   Brisbane *TN* **Australia** 38-27
2002   Johannesburg *TN* **South Africa** 33-31

SOUTH AFRICA v WORLD XVs
Played 3   South Africa won 3
Highest scores South Africa 45-24 in 1977, World XV 24-45 in 1977
Biggest win South Africa 45-24 in 1977, World XV no win

1977   Pretoria **South Africa** 45-24
1989   *1* Cape Town **South Africa** 20-19

2 Johannesburg **South Africa** 22-16
South Africa won series 2-0

SOUTH AFRICA v SOUTH AMERICA
Played 8   South Africa won 7, South America won 1, Drawn 0
Highest scores South Africa 50-18 in 1982, South America 21-12 in 1982
Biggest wins South Africa 50-18 in 1982, South America 21-12 in 1982

1980   *1* Johannesburg **South Africa** 24-9
         2 Durban **South Africa** 18-9
         South Africa won series 2-0
1980   *1* Montevideo **South Africa** 22-13
         2 Santiago **South Africa** 30-16
         South Africa won series 2-0

1982   *1* Pretoria **South Africa** 50-18
         2 Bloemfontein **South America** 21-12
         Series drawn 1-1
1984   *1* Pretoria **South Africa** 32-15
         2 Cape Town **South Africa** 22-13
         South Africa won series 2-0

SOUTH AFRICA v UNITED STATES
Played 2   South Africa won 2
Highest scores South Africa 43-20 in 2001, United States 20-43 in 2001
Biggest win South Africa 38-7 in 1981, United States no win

1981   Glenville **South Africa** 38-7

2001   Houston **South Africa** 43-20

SOUTH AFRICA v NEW ZEALAND CAVALIERS
Played 4   South Africa won 3, New Zealand Cavaliers won 1, Drawn 0
Highest scores South Africa 33-18 in 1986, New Zealand Cavaliers 19-18 in 1986
Biggest wins South Africa 33-18 in 1986, New Zealand Cavaliers 19-18 in 1986

1986   *1* Cape Town **South Africa** 21-15
         2 Durban **New Zealand Cavaliers** 19-18
         3 Pretoria **South Africa** 33-18

4 Johannesburg **South Africa** 24-10
South Africa won series 3-1

SOUTH AFRICA v ARGENTINA
Played 8   South Africa won 8
Highest scores South Africa 52-23 in 1993, Argentina 33-37 in 2000
Biggest wins South Africa 46-15 in 1996, Argentina no win

1993   *1* Buenos Aires **South Africa** 29-26
         2 Buenos Aires **South Africa** 52-23
         South Africa won series 2-0
1994   *1* Port Elizabeth **South Africa** 42-22
         2 Johannesburg **South Africa** 46-26
         South Africa won series 2-0

1996   *1* Buenos Aires **South Africa** 46-15
         2 Buenos Aires **South Africa** 44-21
         South Africa win series 2-0
2000   Buenos Aires **South Africa** 37-33
2002   Springs **South Africa** 49-29

SOUTH AFRICA v SAMOA

Played 3   South Africa won 3
Highest scores South Africa 60-8 in 1995 and 60-18 in 2002, Samoa 18-60 in 2002
Biggest win South Africa 60-8 in 1995, Samoa no win

1995	Johannesburg **South Africa** 60-8	2002 Pretoria **South Africa** 60-18
1995	Johannesburg *WC* **South Africa** 42-14	

SOUTH AFRICA v ROMANIA

Played 1   South Africa won 1
Highest score South Africa 21-8 in 1995, Romania 8-21 in 1995
Biggest win South Africa 21-8 in 1995, Romania no win

1995   Cape Town *WC* **South Africa** 21-8

SOUTH AFRICA v CANADA

Played 2   South Africa won 2
Highest scores South Africa 51-18 in 2000, Canada 18-51 in 2000
Biggest win South Africa 51-18 in 2000, Canada no win

1995 Port Elizabeth *WC* **South Africa** 20-0	2000 East London **South Africa** 51-18

SOUTH AFRICA v ITALY

Played 6   South Africa won 6
Highest scores South Africa 101-0 in 1999, Italy 31-62 in 1997
Biggest win South Africa 101-0 in 1999, Italy no win

1995	Rome **South Africa** 40-21	2001 Port Elizabeth **South Africa** 60-14
1997	Bologna **South Africa** 62-31	2001 Genoa **South Africa** 54-26
1999	*1* Port Elizabeth **South Africa** 74-3	
	2 Durban **South Africa** 101-0	
	South Africa won series 2-0	

SOUTH AFRICA v FIJI

Played 1   South Africa won 1
Highest scores South Africa 43-18 in 1996, Fiji 18-43 in 1996
Biggest win South Africa 43-18 in 1996, Fiji no win

1996   Pretoria **South Africa** 43-18

SOUTH AFRICA v TONGA

Played 1   South Africa won 1
Higest scores South Africa 74-10 in 1997, Tonga 10-74 in 1997
Biggest win South Africa 74-10 in 1997, Tonga no win

1997   Cape Town **South Africa** 74-10

SOUTH AFRICA v SPAIN

Played 1   South Africa won 1
Highest scores South Africa 47-3, Spain 3-47 in 1999
Biggest win South Africa 47-3 in 1999, Spain no win

1999   Murrayfield *WC* **South Africa** 47-3

SOUTH AFRICA v URUGUAY
Played 1   South Africa won 1
Highest scores South Africa 39-3 in 1999, Uruguay 3-39 in 1999
Biggest win South Africa 39-3 in 1999, Uruguay no win

1999   Glasgow *WC* **South Africa** 39-3

NEW ZEALAND v AUSTRALIA
Played 116   New Zealand won 76, Australia won 35, Drawn 5
Highest scores New Zealand 43-6 in 1996, Australia 35-39 in 2000
Biggest wins New Zealand 43-6 in 1996, Australia 28-7 in 1999

1903   Sydney **New Zealand** 22-3
1905   Dunedin **New Zealand** 14-3
1907   *1* Sydney **New Zealand** 26-6
      2 Brisbane **New Zealand** 14-5
      3 Sydney **Drawn** 5-5
      New Zealand won series 2-0, with 1 draw
1910   *1* Sydney **New Zealand** 6-0
      2 Sydney **Australia** 11-0
      3 Sydney **New Zealand** 28-13
      New Zealand won series 2-1
1913   *1* Wellington **New Zealand** 30-5
      2 Dunedin **New Zealand** 25-13
      3 Christchurch **Australia** 16-5
      New Zealand won series 2-1
1914   *1* Sydney **New Zealand** 5-0
      2 Brisbane **New Zealand** 17-0
      3 Sydney **New Zealand** 22-7
      New Zealand won series 3-0
1929   *1* Sydney **Australia** 9-8
      2 Brisbane **Australia** 17-9
      3 Sydney **Australia** 15-13
      Australia won series 3-0
1931   Auckland **New Zealand** 20-13
1932   *1* Sydney **Australia** 22-17
      2 Brisbane **New Zealand** 21-3
      3 Sydney **New Zealand** 21-13
      New Zealand won series 2-1
1934   *1* Sydney **Australia** 25-11
      2 Sydney **Drawn** 3-3
      Australia won series 1-0, with 1 draw
1936   *1* Wellington **New Zealand** 11-6
      2 Dunedin **New Zealand** 38-13
      New Zealand won series 2-0
1938   *1* Sydney **New Zealand** 24-9
      2 Brisbane **New Zealand** 20-14
      3 Sydney **New Zealand** 14-6
      New Zealand won series 3-0
1946   *1* Dunedin **New Zealand** 31-8
      2 Auckland **New Zealand** 14-10
      New Zealand won series 2-0
1947   *1* Brisbane **New Zealand** 13-5
      2 Sydney **New Zealand** 27-14
      New Zealand won series 2-0
1949   *1* Wellington **Australia** 11-6
      2 Auckland **Australia** 16-9
      Australia won series 2-0

1951   *1* Sydney **New Zealand** 8-0
      2 Sydney **New Zealand** 17-11
      3 Brisbane **New Zealand** 16-6
      New Zealand won series 3-0
1952   *1* Christchurch **Australia** 14-9
      2 Wellington **New Zealand** 15-8
      Series drawn 1-1
1955   *1* Wellington **New Zealand** 16-8
      2 Dunedin **New Zealand** 8-0
      3 Auckland **Australia** 8-3
      New Zealand won series 2-1
1957   *1* Sydney **New Zealand** 25-11
      2 Brisbane **New Zealand** 22-9
      New Zealand won series 2-0
1958   *1* Wellington **New Zealand** 25-3
      2 Christchurch **Australia** 6-3
      3 Auckland **New Zealand** 17-8
      New Zealand won series 2-1
1962   *1* Brisbane **New Zealand** 20-6
      2 Sydney **New Zealand** 14-5
      New Zealand won series 2-0
1962   *1* Wellington **Drawn** 9-9
      2 Dunedin **New Zealand** 3-0
      3 Auckland **New Zealand** 16-8
      New Zealand won series 2-0, with1 draw
1964   *1* Dunedin **New Zealand** 14-9
      2 Christchurch **New Zealand** 18-3
      3 Wellington **Australia** 20-5
      New Zealand won series 2-1
1967   Wellington **New Zealand** 29-9
1968   *1* Sydney **New Zealand** 27-11
      2 Brisbane **New Zealand** 19-18
      New Zealand won series 2-0
1972   *1* Wellington **New Zealand** 29-6
      2 Christchurch **New Zealand** 30-17
      3 Auckland **New Zealand** 38-3
      New Zealand won series 3-0
1974   *1* Sydney **New Zealand** 11-6
      2 Brisbane **Drawn** 16-16
      3 Sydney **New Zealand** 16-6
      New Zealand won series 2-0, with 1 draw
1978   *1* Wellington **New Zealand** 13-12
      2 Christchurch **New Zealand** 22-6
      3 Auckland **Australia** 30-16
      New Zealand won series 2-1
1979   Sydney **Australia** 12-6

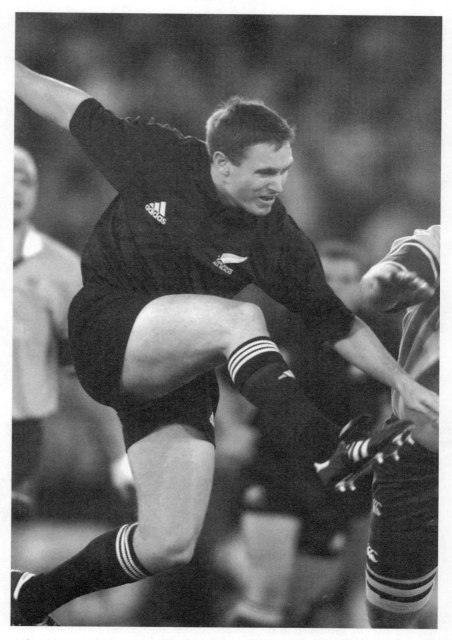

Andrew Mehrtens in action against Australia in Sydney. The New Zealander holds the world record for most conversions in Test matches.

1980	*1* Sydney **Australia** 13-9
	2 Brisbane **New Zealand** 12-9
	3 Sydney **Australia** 26-10
	Australia won series 2-1
1982	*1* Christchurch **New Zealand** 23-16
	2 Wellington **Australia** 19-16
	3 Auckland **New Zealand** 33-18
	New Zealand won series 2-1
1983	Sydney **New Zealand** 18-8
1984	*1* Sydney **Australia** 16-9
	2 Brisbane **New Zealand** 19-15
	3 Sydney **New Zealand** 25-24
	New Zealand won series 2-1
1985	Auckland **New Zealand** 10-9
1986	*1* Wellington **Australia** 13-12
	2 Dunedin **New Zealand** 13-12
	3 Auckland **Australia** 22-9
	Australia won series 2-1
1987	Sydney **New Zealand** 30-16
1988	*1* Sydney **New Zealand** 32-7
	2 Brisbane **Drawn** 19-19
	3 Sydney **New Zealand** 30-9
	New Zealand won series 2-0, with 1 draw
1989	Auckland **New Zealand** 24-12
1990	*1* Christchurch **New Zealand** 21-6
	2 Auckland **New Zealand** 27-17
	3 Wellington **Australia** 21-9
	New Zealand won series 2-1
1991	*1* Sydney **Australia** 21-12
	2 Auckland **New Zealand** 6-3
1991	Dublin *WC* **Australia** 16-6

1992	*1* Sydney **Australia** 16-15
	2 Brisbane **Australia** 19-17
	3 Sydney **New Zealand** 26-23
	Australia won series 2-1
1993	Dunedin **New Zealand** 25-10
1994	Sydney **Australia** 20-16
1995	Auckland **New Zealand** 28-16
1995	Sydney **New Zealand** 34-23
1996	Wellington *TN* **New Zealand** 43-6
1996	Brisbane *TN* **New Zealand** 32-25
	New Zealand won series 2-0
1997	Christchurch **New Zealand** 30-13
1997	Melbourne *TN* **New Zealand** 33-18
1997	Dunedin *TN* **New Zealand** 36-24
	New Zealand won series 3-0
1998	Melbourne *TN* **Australia** 24-16
1998	Christchurch *TN* **Australia** 27-23
1998	Sydney **Australia** 19-14
	Australia won series 3-0
1999	Auckland *TN* **New Zealand** 34-15
1999	Sydney *TN* **Australia** 28-7
	Series drawn 1-1
2000	Sydney *TN* **New Zealand** 39-35
2000	Wellington *TN* **Australia** 24-23
	Series drawn 1-1
2001	Dunedin *TN* **Australia** 23-15
2001	Sydney *TN* **Australia** 29-26
	Australia won series 2-0
2002	Christchurch *TN* **New Zealand** 12-6
2002	Sydney *TN* **Australia** 16-14

NEW ZEALAND v UNITED STATES

Played 2   New Zealand won 2
Highest scores New Zealand 51-3 in 1913, United States 6-46 in 1991
Biggest win New Zealand 51-3 in 1913, United States no win

| 1913 | Berkeley **New Zealand** 51-3 | 1991 | Gloucester *WC* **New Zealand** 46-6 |

NEW ZEALAND v ROMANIA

Played 1   New Zealand won 1
Highest score New Zealand 14-6 in 1981, Romania 6-14 in 1981
Biggest win New Zealand 14-6 in 1981, Romania no win

| 1981 | Bucharest **New Zealand** 14-6 |

NEW ZEALAND v ARGENTINA

Played 11   New Zealand won 10, Drawn 1
Highest scores New Zealand 93-8 in 1997, Argentina 21-21 in 1985
Biggest win New Zealand 93-8 in 1997, Argentina no win

1985	*1* Buenos Aires **New Zealand** 33-20		*2* Wellington **New Zealand** 49-12
	2 Buenos Aires **Drawn** 21-21		*New Zealand won series 2-0*
	New Zealand won series 1-0, with 1 draw	1991	*1* Buenos Aires **New Zealand** 28-14
1987	Wellington *WC* **New Zealand** 46-15		*2* Buenos Aires **New Zealand** 36-6
1989	*1* Dunedin **New Zealand** 60-9		*New Zealand won series 2-0*
		1997	*1* Wellington **New Zealand** 93-8

2 Hamilton **New Zealand** 62-10
New Zealand won series 2-0

2001   Christchurch **New Zealand** 67-19
2001   Buenos Aires **New Zealand** 24-20

NEW ZEALAND v ITALY
Played 6   New Zealand won 6
Highest scores New Zealand 101-3 in 1999, Italy 21-31 in 1991
Biggest win New Zealand 101-3 in 1999, Italy no win

1987   Auckland *WC* **New Zealand** 70-6
1991   Leicester *WC* **New Zealand** 31-21
1995   Bologna **New Zealand** 70-6

1999   Huddersfield *WC* **New Zealand** 101-3
2000   Genoa **New Zealand** 56-19
2002   Hamilton **New Zealand** 64-10

NEW ZEALAND v FIJI
Played 3   New Zealand won 3
Highest scores New Zealand 74-13 in 1987, Fiji 18-68 in 2002
Biggest win New Zealand 71-5 in 1997, Fiji no win

1987   Christchurch *WC* **New Zealand** 74-13
1997   Albany **New Zealand** 71-5

2002   Wellington **New Zealand** 68-18

NEW ZEALAND v CANADA
Played 2   New Zealand won 2
Highest scores New Zealand 73-7 in 1995, Canada 13-29 in 1991
Biggest win New Zealand 73-7 in 1995, Canada no win

1991   Lille *WC* **New Zealand** 29-13

1995   Auckland **New Zealand** 73-7

NEW ZEALAND v WORLD XVs
Played 3   New Zealand won 2, World XV won 1, Drawn 0
Highest scores New Zealand 54-26 in 1992, World XV 28-14 in 1992
Biggest wins New Zealand 54-26 in 1992, World XV 28-14 in 1992

1992   *1* Christchurch **World XV** 28-14
        2 Wellington **New Zealand** 54-26

3 Auckland **New Zealand** 26-15
New Zealand won series 2-1

NEW ZEALAND v SAMOA
Played 4   New Zealand won 4
Highest scores New Zealand 71-13 in 1999, Samoa 13-35 in 1993 & 13-71 in 1999
Biggest win New Zealand 71-13 in 1999, Samoa no win

1993   Auckland **New Zealand** 35-13
1996   Napier **New Zealand** 51-10

1999   Albany **New Zealand** 71-13
2001   Albany **New Zealand** 50-6

NEW ZEALAND v JAPAN
Played 1   New Zealand won 1
Highest scores New Zealand 145-17 in 1995, Japan 17-145 in 1995
Biggest win New Zealand 145-17 in 1995, Japan no win

1995   Bloemfontein *WC* **New Zealand** 145-17

NEW ZEALAND v TONGA

Played 2   New Zealand won 2
Highest scores New Zealand 102-0 in 2000, Tonga 9-45 in 1999
Biggest win New Zealand 102-0 in 2000, Tonga no win

1999 Bristol *WC* **New Zealand** 45-9	2000 Albany **New Zealand** 102-0

AUSTRALIA v UNITED STATES

Played 6   Australia won 6
Highest scores Australia 67-9 in 1990, United States 19-55 in 1999
Biggest win Australia 67-9 in 1990, United States no win

1912 Berkeley **Australia** 12-8	1987 Brisbane *WC* **Australia** 47-12
1976 Los Angeles **Australia** 24-12	1990 Brisbane **Australia** 67-9
1983 Sydney **Australia** 49-3	1999 Limerick *WC* **Australia** 55-19

AUSTRALIA v NEW ZEALAND XVs

Played 24   Australia won 6, New Zealand XVs won 18, Drawn 0
Highest scores Australia 26-20 in 1926, New Zealand XV 38-11 in 1923 and 38-8 in 1924
Biggest win Australia 17-0 in 1921, New Zealand XV 38-8 in 1924

1920 *1* Sydney **New Zealand XV** 26-15	1925 *1* Sydney **New Zealand XV** 26-3
2 Sydney **New Zealand XV** 14-6	*2* Sydney **New Zealand XV** 4-0
3 Sydney **New Zealand XV** 24-13	*3* Sydney **New Zealand XV** 11-3
New Zealand XV won series 3-0	*New Zealand XV won series 3-0*
1921 Christchurch **Australia** 17-0	1925 Auckland **New Zealand XV** 36-10
1922 *1* Sydney **New Zealand XV** 26-19	1926 *1* Sydney **Australia** 26-20
2 Sydney **Australia** 14-8	*2* Sydney **New Zealand XV** 11-6
3 Sydney **Australia** 8-6	*3* Sydney **New Zealand XV** 14-0
Australia won series 2-1	*4* Sydney **New Zealand XV** 28-21
1923 *1* Dunedin **New Zealand XV** 19-9	*New Zealand XV won series 3-1*
2 Christchurch **New Zealand XV** 34-6	1928 *1* Wellington **New Zealand XV** 15-12
3 Wellington **New Zealand XV** 38-11	*2* Dunedin **New Zealand XV** 16-14
New Zealand XV won series 3-0	*3* Christchurch **Australia** 11-8
1924 *1* Sydney **Australia** 20-16	*New Zealand XV won series 2-1*
2 Sydney **New Zealand XV** 21-5	
3 Sydney **New Zealand XV** 38-8	
New Zealand XV won series 2-1	

AUSTRALIA v SOUTH AFRICA XVs

Played 3   South Africa XVs won 3
Highest scores Australia 11-16 in 1921, South Africa XV 28-9 in 1921
Biggest win Australia no win, South Africa XV 28-9 in 1921

1921 *1* Sydney **South Africa XV** 25-10	*3* Sydney **South Africa XV** 28-9
2 Sydney **South Africa XV** 16-11	*South Africa XV won series 3-0*

AUSTRALIA v NEW ZEALAND MAORIS

Played 16   Australia won 8, New Zealand Maoris won 6, Drawn 2
Highest scores Australia 31-6 in 1936, New Zealand Maoris 25-22 in 1922
Biggest wins Australia 31-6 in 1936, New Zealand Maoris 20-0 in 1946

1922 *1* Sydney **New Zealand Maoris** 25-22	1923 *1* Sydney **Australia** 27-23
2 Sydney **Australia** 28-13	*2* Sydney **Australia** 21-16
3 Sydney **New Zealand Maoris** 23-22	*3* Sydney **Australia** 14-12
New Zealand Maoris won series 2-1	*Australia won series 3-0*

1928	Wellington **New Zealand Maoris** 9-8
1931	Palmerston North **Australia** 14-3
1936	Palmerston North **Australia** 31-6
1946	Hamilton **New Zealand Maoris** 20-0
1949	*1* Sydney **New Zealand Maoris** 12-3
	2 Brisbane **Drawn** 8-8

	3 Sydney **Australia** 18-3
	Series drawn 1-1, with 1 draw
1958	*1* Brisbane **Australia** 15-14
	2 Sydney **Drawn** 3-3
	3 Melbourne **New Zealand Maoris** 13-6
	Series drawn 1-1, with 1 draw

AUSTRALIA v FIJI
Played 16   Australia won 13, Fiji won 2, Drawn 1
Highest scores Australia 66-20 in 1998, Fiji 28-52 in 1985
Biggest wins Australia 66-20 in 1998, Fiji 17-15 in 1952 & 18-16 in 1954

1952	*1* Sydney **Australia** 15-9
	2 Sydney **Fiji** 17-15
	Series drawn 1-1
1954	*1* Brisbane **Australia** 22-19
	2 Sydney **Fiji** 18-16
	Series drawn 1-1
1961	*1* Brisbane **Australia** 24-6
	2 Sydney **Australia** 20-14
	3 Melbourne **Drawn** 3-3
	Australia won series 2-0, with 1 draw
1972	Suva **Australia** 21-19

1976	*1* Sydney **Australia** 22-6
	2 Brisbane **Australia** 21-9
	3 Sydney **Australia** 27-17
	Australia won series 3-0
1980	Suva **Australia** 22-9
1984	Suva **Australia** 16-3
1985	*1* Brisbane **Australia** 52-28
	2 Sydney **Australia** 31-9
	Australia won series 2-0
1998	Sydney **Australia** 66-20

AUSTRALIA v TONGA
Played 4   Australia won 3, Tonga won 1, Drawn 0
Highest scores Australia 74-0 in 1998, Tonga 16-11 in 1973
Biggest wins Australia 74-0 in 1998, Tonga 16-11 in 1973

1973	*1* Sydney **Australia** 30-12
	2 Brisbane **Tonga** 16-11
	Series drawn 1-1

1993	Brisbane **Australia** 52-14
1998	Canberra **Australia** 74-0

AUSTRALIA v JAPAN
Played 3   Australia won 3
Highest scores Australia 50-25 in 1975, Japan 25-50 in 1973
Biggest win Australia 50-25 in 1975, Japan no win

1975	*1* Sydney **Australia** 37-7
	2 Brisbane **Australia** 50-25
	Australia won series 2-0

1987	Sydney *WC* **Australia** 42-23

AUSTRALIA v ARGENTINA
Played 15   Australia won 10, Argentina won 4, Drawn 1
Highest scores Australia 53-7 in 1995 & 53-6 in 2000, Argentina 27-19 in 1987
Biggest wins Australia 53-6 in 2000, Argentina 18-3 in 1983

1979	*1* Buenos Aires **Argentina** 24-13
	2 Buenos Aires **Australia** 17-12
	Series drawn 1-1
1983	*1* Brisbane **Argentina** 18-3
	2 Sydney **Australia** 29-13
	Series drawn 1-1
1986	*1* Brisbane **Australia** 39-19
	2 Sydney **Australia** 26-0
	Australia won series 2-0

1987	*1* Buenos Aires **Drawn** 19-19
	2 Buenos Aires **Argentina** 27-19
	Argentina won series 1-0, with 1 draw
1991	Llanelli *WC* **Australia** 32-19
1995	*1* Brisbane **Australia** 53-7
	2 Sydney **Australia** 30-13
	Australia won series 2-0
1997	*1* Buenos Aires **Australia** 23-15

2 Buenos Aires **Argentina** 18-16
Series drawn 1-1
2000 *1* Brisbane **Australia** 53-6

2 Canberra **Australia** 32-25
Australia won series 2-0

AUSTRALIA v SAMOA
Played 3   Australia won 3
Highest scores Australia 73-3 in 1994, Samoa 13-25 in 1998
Biggest win Australia 73-3 in 1994, Samoa no win

1991 Pontypool *WC* **Australia** 9-3
1994 Sydney **Australia** 73-3

1998 Brisbane **Australia** 25-13

AUSTRALIA v ITALY
Played 6   Australia won 6
Highest scores Australia 55-6 in 1988, Italy 20-23 in 1994
Biggest win Australia 55-6 in 1988, Italy no win

1983 Rovigo **Australia** 29-7
1986 Brisbane **Australia** 39-18
1988 Rome **Australia** 55-6
1994 *1* Brisbane **Australia** 23-20

2 Melbourne **Australia** 20-7
Australia won series 2-0
1996 Padua **Australia** 40-18

AUSTRALIA v CANADA
Played 5   Australia won 5
Highest scores Australia 74-9 in 1996, Canada 16-43 in 1993
Biggest win Australia 74-9 in 1996, Canada no win

1985 *1* Sydney **Australia** 59-3
      2 Brisbane **Australia** 43-15
      Australia won series 2-0

1993 Calgary **Australia** 43-16
1995 Port Elizabeth *WC* **Australia** 27-11
1996 Brisbane **Australia** 74-9

AUSTRALIA v KOREA
Played 1   Australia won 1
Highest scores Australia 65-18 in 1987, Korea 18-65 in 1987
Biggest win Australia 65-18 in 1987, Korea no win

1987 Brisbane **Australia** 65-18

AUSTRALIA v ROMANIA
Played 2   Australia won 2
Highest scores Australia 57-9 in 1999, Romania 9-57 in 1999
Biggest win Australia 57-9 in 1999, Romania no win

1995 Stellenbosch *WC* **Australia** 42-3

1999 Belfast *WC* **Australia** 57-9

AUSTRALIA v SPAIN
Played 1   Australia won 1
Highest scores Australia 92-10 in 2001, Spain 10-92 in 2001
Biggest win Australia 92-10 in 2001, Spain no win

2001 Madrid **Australia** 92-10

WORLD INTERNATIONAL RECORDS

*The match and career records cover **official cap matches** played by the dozen Executive Council Member Unions of the International Board (England, Scotland, Ireland, Wales, France, Italy, South Africa, New Zealand, Australia, Argentina, Canada and Japan) from 1871 up to 31 August 2002. Figures include Test performances for the (British/Irish Isles) Lions and (South American) Jaguars (shown in brackets). Where a world record has been set in a cap match played by another nation in membership of the IRB, this is shown as a footnote to the relevant table.*

MATCH RECORDS

MOST CONSECUTIVE TEST WINS

17 by N Zealand 1965 *SA* 4, 1966 *BI* 1,2,3,4, 1967 *A, E, W, F, S,* 1968 *A* 1,2, *F* 1,2,3, 1969 *W* 1,2

17 by S Africa 1997 *A* 2, *It, F* 1,2, *E* , *S,* 1998 *I* 1,2, *W* 1, *E* 1, *A* 1, *NZ* 1,2, *A* 2, *W* 2, *S, I* 3

MOST CONSECUTIVE TESTS WITHOUT DEFEAT

Matches	Wins	Draws	Period
23 by N Zealand	22	1	1987 to 1990
17 by N Zealand	15	2	1961 to 1964
17 by N Zealand	17	0	1965 to 1969
17 by S Africa	17	0	1997 to 1998

MOST POINTS IN A MATCH
by a team

Pts	Opponents	Venue	Year
155 by Japan	Ch Taipei	Tokyo	2002
152 by Argentina	Paraguay	Mendoza	2002
145 by N Zealand	Japan	Bloemfontein	1995
134 by Japan	Ch Taipei	Singapore	1998
134 by England	Romania	Twickenham	2001
120 by Japan	Ch Taipei	Tainan	2002

Hong Kong scored 164 points against Singapore at Kuala Lumpur in 1994

by a player

Pts	Player	Opponents	Venue	Year
60 for Japan	T Kurihara	Ch Taipei	Tainan	2002
50 for Argentina	E Morgan	Paraguay	San Pablo	1973
45 for N Zealand	S D Culhane	Japan	Bloemfontein	1995
44 for England	C Hodgson	Romania	Twickenham	2001
44 for Scotland	A G Hastings	Ivory Coast	Rustenburg	1995

40 for Argentina	G M Jorge	Brazil	Sao Paulo	1993
40 for Japan	D Ohata	Ch Taipei	Tokyo	2002
39 for Australia	M C Burke	Canada	Brisbane	1996

MOST TRIES IN A MATCH
by the team

Tries	Opponents	Venue	Year
24 by Argentina	Paraguay	Mendoza	2002
23 by Japan	Ch Taipei	Tokyo	2002
21 by N Zealand	Japan	Bloemfontein	1995
20 by Japan	Ch Taipei	Singapore	1998
20 by England	Romania	Twickenham	2001
19 by Argentina	Brazil	Santiago	1979
19 by Argentina	Paraguay	Asuncion	1985

Hong Kong scored 26 tries against Singapore at Kuala Lumpur in 1994

by a player

Tries	Player	Opponents	Venue	Year
8 for Argentina	G M Jorge	Brazil	Sao Paulo	1993
8 for Japan	D Ohata	Ch Taipei	Tokyo	2002
6 for Argentina	E Morgan	Paraguay	San Pablo	1973
6 for Argentina	G M Jorge	Brazil	Montevideo	1989
6 for N Zealand	M C G Ellis	Japan	Bloemfontein	1995
6 for Japan	T Kurihara	Ch Taipei	Tainan	2002
5 for Scotland	G C Lindsay	Wales	Raeburn Place	1887
5 for England	D Lambert	France	Richmond	1907
5 for Argentina	H Goti	Brazil	Montevideo	1961
5 for Argentina	M R Jurado	Brazil	Montevideo	1971
5 for England	R Underwood	Fiji	Twickenham	1989
5 for N Zealand	J W Wilson	Fiji	Albany	1997
5 for Japan	T Masuho	Ch Taipei	Singapore	1998
5 for Argentina	P Grande	Paraguay	Asuncion	1998
5 for S Africa	C S Terblanche	Italy	Durban	1999

10 tries were scored for Hong Kong by A Billington against Singapore at Kuala Lumpur in 1994

MOST CONVERSIONS IN A MATCH
by the team

Cons	Opponents	Venue	Year
20 by N Zealand	Japan	Bloemfontein	1995
20 by Japan	Ch Taipei	Tokyo	2002
17 by Japan	Ch Taipei	Singapore	1998
16 by Argentina	Paraguay	Mendoza	2002
15 by Argentina	Brazil	Santiago	1979
15 by England	Holland	Huddersfield	1998
15 by Japan	Ch Taipei	Tainan	2002

by a player

Cons	Player	Opponents	Venue	Year
20 for N Zealand	S D Culhane	Japan	Bloemfontein	1995
16 for Argentina	J-L Cilley	Paraguay	Mendoza	2002
15 for England	P J Grayson	Holland	Huddersfield	1998
15 for Japan	T Kurihara	Ch Taipei	Tainan	2002

MOST PENALTIES IN A MATCH
by the team

Penalties	Opponents	Venue	Year
9 by Japan	Tonga	Tokyo	1999
9 by N Zealand	Australia	Auckland	1999
9 by Wales	France	Cardiff	1999
9 by N Zealand	France	Paris	2000

Portugal scored nine penalties against Georgia at Lisbon in 2000

by a player

Penalties	Player	Opponents	Venue	Year
9 for Japan	K Hirose	Tonga	Tokyo	1999
9 for N Zealand	A P Mehrtens	Australia	Auckland	1999
9 for Wales	N R Jenkins	France	Cardiff	1999
9 for N Zealand	A P Mehrtens	France	Paris	2000

Nine penalties were scored for Portugal by T Teixeira against Georgia at Lisbon in 2000

MOST DROPPED GOALS IN A MATCH
by the team

Drops	Opponents	Venue	Year
5 by South Africa	England	Paris	1999
3 by several nations			

by a player

Drops		Player	Opponents	Venue	Year
5 for S Africa		J H de Beer	England	Paris	1999
3 for several nations					

CAREER RECORDS
MOST CAPPED PLAYERS

Caps	Player	Career Span
111	P Sella (France)	1982 to 1995
102(5)	J Leonard (England/Lions)	1990 to 2002
101	D I Campese (Australia)	1982 to 1996
93	S Blanco (France)	1980 to 1991
92	S B T Fitzpatrick (N Zealand)	1986 to 1997
91(6)	R Underwood (England/Lions)	1984 to 1996

MOST CONSECUTIVE TESTS

Tests	Player	Span
63	S B T Fitzpatrick (N Zealand)	1986 to 1995
62	J W C Roff (Australia)	1996 to 2001
53	G O Edwards (Wales)	1967 to 1978
52	W J McBride (Ireland)	1964 to 1975
51	C M Cullen (N Zealand)	1996 to 2000

MOST TESTS AS CAPTAIN

Tests	Captain	Span
59	W D C Carling (England)	1988 to 1996
55	J A Eales (Australia)	1996 to 2001
51	S B T Fitzpatrick (N Zealand)	1992 to 1997
46 (8)	H Porta (Argentina/Jaguars)	1971 to 1990
41	L Arbizu (Argentina)	1992 to 2002
37	M Giovanelli (Italy)	1992 to 1999
36	N C Farr-Jones (Australia)	1988 to 1992
36	G H Teichmann (S Africa)	1996 to 1999

MOST TESTS IN INDIVIDUAL POSITIONS

Position	Player	Tests	Span
Full-back	S Blanco (France)	81	1980 to 1991
Wing	R Underwood (England/Lions)	91 (6)	1984 to 1996
Centre	P Sella (France)	104	1982 to 1995
Fly-half	C R Andrew (England/Lions)	75 (5)	1985 to 1997
Scrum-half	J H van der Westhuizen (S Africa)	77	1993 to 2001
	G M Gregan (Australia)	77*	1994 to 2002
Prop	J Leonard (England/Lions)	102 (5)	1990 to 2002
Hooker	S B T Fitzpatrick (N Zealand)	92	1986 to 1997
Lock	J A Eales (Australia)	84	1991 to 2001
Flanker	D J Wilson (Australia)	79	1992 to 2000
No 8	D Richards (England/Lions)	53* (6)	1986 to 1996

* excludes an appearance as a temporary replacement

Diego Dominguez, who lies in second place behind Neil Jenkins of Wales on the list of leading points scorers in Test rugby.

MOST POINTS IN TESTS

Points	Player	Tests	Career
1070 (41)	N R Jenkins (Wales/Lions)	90 (4)	1991 to 2002
986 (27)	D Dominguez (Italy/Argentina)	73 (2)	1989 to 2002
911	M P Lynagh (Australia)	72	1984 to 1995
895	A P Mehrtens (N Zealand)	63	1995 to 2002
790	M C Burke (Australia)	64	1993 to 2002
733 (66)	A G Hastings (Scotland/Lions)	67 (6)	1986 to 1995

MOST TRIES IN TESTS

Tries	Player	Tests	Career
64	D I Campese (Australia)	101	1982 to 1996
50 (1)	R Underwood (England/Lions)	91 (6)	1984 to 1996
46	C M Cullen (N Zealand)	57	1996 to 2002
44	J W Wilson (N Zealand)	60	1993 to 2001
38	S Blanco (France)	93	1980 to 1991
35	J J Kirwan (N Zealand)	63	1984 to 1994
35	J H van der Westhuizen (S Africa)	79	1993 to 2001
35	J T Lomu (N Zealand)	60	1994 to 2002
34 (1)	I C Evans (Wales/Lions)	79 (7)	1987 to 1998

MOST CONVERSIONS IN TESTS

Cons	Player	Tests	Career
154	A P Mehrtens (N Zealand)	63	1995 to 2002

140	M P Lynagh (Australia)	72	1984 to 1995
130 (6)	D Dominguez (Italy/Argentina)	73 (2)	1989 to 2002
127 (1)	N R Jenkins (Wales/Lions)	90 (4)	1991 to 2002
118	G J Fox (N Zealand)	46	1985 to 1993

MOST PENALTY GOALS IN TESTS

Penalties	Player	Tests	Career
244 (13)	N R Jenkins (Wales/Lions)	90 (4)	1991 to 2002
210 (5)	D Dominguez (Italy/Argentina)	73 (2)	1989 to 2002
177	M P Lynagh (Australia)	72	1984 to 1995
174	A P Mehrtens (N Zealand)	63	1995 to 2002
160 (20)	A G Hastings (Scotland/Lions)	67 (6)	1986 to 1995
159	M C Burke (Australia)	64	1993 to 2002

MOST DROPPED GOALS IN TESTS

Drops	Player	Tests	Career
28 (2)	H Porta (Argentina/Jaguars)	66 (8)	1971 to 1990
23 (2)	C R Andrew (England/Lions)	76 (5)	1985 to 1997
18	H E Botha (S Africa)	28	1980 to 1992
17	S Bettarello (Italy)	55	1979 to 1988
17 (0)	D Dominguez (Italy/Argentina)	73 (2)	1989 to 2002
15	J-P Lescarboura (France)	28	1982 to 1990

PARTNERSHIP RECORDS

Position	Holders	Detail	Span
Centre threequarters	W D C Carling & J C Guscott	45 (1) for England/Lions	1989 to 1996
Half backs	M P Lynagh & N C Farr-Jones	47 for Australia	1985 to 1992
Front row	A J Daly, P N Kearns & E J A McKenzie	37 for Australia	1990 to 1995
Second row	I D Jones & R M Brooke	49 for N Zealand	1992 to 1999
Back row	R A Hill, L B N Dallaglio & N A Back	31 for England	1997 to 2001

INTERNATIONAL REFEREES

Leading Referees

Up to 31 August 2002 in major international matches. These include all matches for which the eight senior members of the International Board have awarded caps, and also all matches played in the World Cup final stages.

W D Bevan	Wales	43	F A Howard	England	20
J M Fleming	Scotland	39	W J Erickson	Australia	20
E F Morrison	England	30	A J Watson	South Africa	20
C Norling	Wales	25	A M Hosie	Scotland	19
D J Bishop	New Zealand	24	Capt M J Dowling	Ireland	18
K D Kelleher	Ireland	23	A E Freethy	Wales	18
D G Walters	Wales	23	R C Quittenton	England	18
D T M McHugh	Ireland	23	J R West	Ireland	18
M Joseph	Wales	22	J B Anderson	Scotland	18
C J Hawke	New Zealand	22	R Hourquet	France	18
R C Williams	Ireland	21	P D O'Brien	New Zealand	18
K V J Fitzgerald	Australia	21	C Thomas	Wales	18
J Dumé	France	21			

Major international match appearances 2001–02

Matches controlled up to 31 August 2002

2001

Sp v A	J Jutge (France)
W v Arg	J Dumé (France)
E v A	P D O'Brien (New Zealand)
S v Tg	N Whitehouse (Wales)
F v SA	A Lewis (Ireland)
I v Sm	D I Ramage (Scotland)
I v NZ	A J Watson (South Africa)
E v R	P C Deluca (Argentina)
It v SA	W J Erickson (Australia)
W v Tg	R Dickson (Scotland)
F v A	C J Hawke (New Zealand)
S v Arg	J Jutge (France)
E v SA	S J Dickinson (Australia) rep by D T M McHugh (Ireland)
F v Fj	S M Lawrence (South Africa)
S v NZ	P C Deluca (Argentina)
W v A	S J Lander (England)
US v SA	D Mené (France)
Arg v NZ	S Young (Australia)

2002

F v It	A Lewis (Ireland)
S v E	S R Walsh (New Zealand)
I v W	P C Deluca (Argentina)
W v F	D T M McHugh (Ireland)
E v I	P Marshall (Australia)

It v S	K M Deaker (New Zealand)
F v E	A J Watson (South Africa)
W v It	C White (England)
I v S	N Whitehouse (Wales)
I v It	R Dickson (Scotland)
E v W	A Cole (Australia)
S v F	A C Rolland (Ireland)
F v I	P D O'Brien (New Zealand)
W v S	J Jutge (France)
It v E	S M Lawrence (South Africa)
NZ v It	N Williams (Wales)
SA v W	K M Deaker (New Zealand)
NZ v I	J Jutge (France)
SA v W	A J Spreadbury (England)
Arg v F	P Marshall (Australia)
C v S	D T M McHugh (Ireland)
NZ v I	W T S Henning (South Africa)
A v F	C White (England)
Arg v E	A C Rolland (Ireland)
US v S	P C Deluca (Argentina)
NZ v Fj	S Young (Australia)
A v F	P G Honiss (New Zealand)
SA v Arg	W J Erickson (Australia)
SA v Sm	A Cole (Australia)
NZ v A	J I Kaplan (South Africa)
NZ v SA	S J Dickinson (Australia)
A v SA	S J Lander (England)

A v NZ	**A J Watson** (South Africa)	SA v A	**P D O'Brien** (New Zealand)
SA v NZ	**D T M McHugh** (Ireland) rep		
	by **C White** (England)		

Replacement referees in major internationals

F Gardiner (Ireland)	replaced	**J Tulloch** (Scotland)	**I v SA 1912**
B Marie (France)	replaced	**R W Gilliland** (Ireland)	**F v W 1965**
A R Taylor (N Zealand)	replaced	**J P Murphy** (N Zealand)	**NZ v SA 1965**
R F Johnson (England)	replaced	**R Calmet** (France)	**E v W 1970**
F Palmade (France)	replaced	**K A Pattinson** (England)	**F v S 1973**
J M Fleming (Scotland)	replaced	**J B Anderson** (Scotland)	**Arg v WS *1991**
J M Fleming (Scotland)	replaced	**C J Hawke** (N Zealand)	**E v F 1999**
D T M McHugh (Ireland)	replaced	**W T S Henning** (S Africa)	**E v F 2001**
D T M McHugh (Ireland)	replaced	**S J Dickinson** (Australia)	**E v SA 2001**
C White (England)	replaced	**D T M McHugh** (Ireland)	**SA v NZ 2002**

Dismissals in major international matches

A E Freethy	sent off	C J Brownlie (NZ)	E v NZ	1925
K D Kelleher	sent off	C E Meads (NZ)	S v NZ	1967
R T Burnett	sent off	M A Burton (E)	A v E	1975
W M Cooney	sent off	J Sovau (Fj)	A v Fj	1976
N R Sanson	sent off	G A D Wheel (W)	W v I	1977
N R Sanson	sent off	W P Duggan (I)	W v I	1977
D I H Burnett	sent off	P Ringer (W)	E v W	1980
C Norling	sent off	J-P Garuet (F)	F v I	1984
K V J Fitzgerald	sent off	H D Richards (W)	NZ v W	*1987
F A Howard	sent off	D Codey (A)	A v W	*1987
K V J Fitzgerald	sent off	M Taga (Fj)	Fj v E	1988
O E Doyle	sent off	A Lorieux (F)	Arg v F	1988
B W Stirling	sent off	T Vonolagi (Fj)	E v Fj	1989
B W Stirling	sent off	N Nadruku (Fj)	E v Fj	1989
F A Howard	sent off	K Moseley (W)	W v F	1990
F A Howard	sent off	A Carminati (F)	S v F	1990
F A Howard	sent off	A Stoop (Nm)	Nm v W	1990
A J Spreadbury	sent off	A Benazzi (F)	A v F	1990
C Norling	sent off	P Gallart (F)	A v F	1990
C J Hawke	sent off	F E Mendez (Arg)	E v Arg	1990
E F Morrison	sent off	C Cojocariu (R)	R v F	1991
J M Fleming	sent off	P L Sporleder (Arg)	WS v Arg	*1991
J M Fleming	sent off	M G Keenan (WS)	WS v Arg	*1991
S R Hilditch	sent off	G Lascubé (F)	F v E	1992
S R Hilditch	sent off	V Moscato (F)	F v E	1992
D J Bishop	sent off	O Roumat (Wld)	NZ v Wld	1992
E F Morrison	sent off	J T Small (SA)	A v SA	1993
I Rogers	sent off	M E Cardinal (C)	C v F	1994
I Rogers	sent off	P Sella (F)	C v F	1994
D Mené	sent off	J D Davies (W)	W v E	1995
S Lander	sent off	F Mahoni (Tg)	F v Tg	*1995
D T M McHugh	sent off	J Dalton (SA)	SA v C	*1995
D T M McHugh	sent off	R G A Snow (C)	SA v C	*1995
D T M McHugh	sent off	G L Rees (C)	SA v C	*1995
J Dumé	sent off	G R Jenkins (W)	SA v W	1995

W J Erickson	sent off	V B Cavubati (Fj)	NZ v Fj	1997
W D Bevan	sent off	A G Venter (SA)	NZ v SA	1997
C Giacomel	sent off	R Travaglini (Arg)	F v Arg	1997
W J Erickson	sent off	D J Grewcock (E)	NZ v E	1998
S R Walsh	sent off	J Sitoa (Tg)	A v Tg	1998
R G Davies	sent off	M Giovanelli (It)	S v It	1999
C Thomas	sent off	T Leota (Sm)	Sm v F	1999
C Thomas	sent off	G Leaupepe (Sm)	Sm v F	1999
S Dickinson	sent off	J-J Crenca (F)	NZ v F	1999
E F Morrison	sent off	M Vunibaka (Fj)	Fj v C	*1999
A Cole	sent off	D R Baugh (C)	C v Nm	*1999
W J Erickson	sent off	N Ta'ufo'ou (Tg)	E v Tg	*1999
P Marshall	sent off	B D Venter (SA)	SA v U	*1999
P C Deluca	sent off	W Cristofoletto (It)	F v It	2000
J I Kaplan	sent off	A Troncon (It)	It v I	2001
R Dickson	sent off	G Leger (Tg)	W v Tg	2001
P C Deluca	sent off	N J Hines (S)	US v S	2002
P D O'Brien	sent off	M C Joubert (SA)	SA v A	2002

Matches in World Cup final stages

Major international match appointments November/December 2002

Arg v A	**K M Deaker** (New Zealand)	E v A	**P G Honiss** (New Zealand)
W v R	**J Jutge** (France)	F v NZ	**S Young** (Australia)
I v A	**S R Walsh** (New Zealand)	I v Fj	**C White** (England)
F v SA	**A C Rolland** (Ireland)	F v C	**D T M McHugh** (Ireland)
S v R	**A D Turner** (South Africa)	E v SA	**P D O'Brien** (New Zealand)
E v NZ	**J I Kaplan** (South Africa)	It v A	**P C Deluca** (Argentina)
W v Fj	**S Dickinson** (Australia)	I v Arg	**S J Lander** (England)
S v SA	**N Williams** (Wales)	W v NZ	**W T S Henning** (South Africa)
W v C	**G de Santis** (Italy)	S v Fj	**S M Lawrence** (South Africa)

HEINEKEN CUP 2001-02

Champions Again – only Leicester can do this
Mick Cleary

They had pledged themselves to doing it and when Leicester's finest make a pledge it takes a brave man to stop them. Many tried throughout the long, arduous Heineken Cup campaign but the only blemish on Leicester's record was a 24-12 defeat at Stradey Park in the final pool match. And so Leicester became the first side to ever win the Heineken Cup twice, let alone in successive years. One measure of their achievement is to consider how other past champions are now faring. Brive, who shredded Leicester when winning the title in Cardiff in 1997, are in the French second division, a shadow of that imperious outfit of five years ago. Bath, champions in 1998 when they edged out Brive, came close to suffering the same fate as their opponents that day, the west-country side finishing down among the dead men in the Premiership.

But Leicester have withstood all challenges. Once again they proved themselves a cussed, determined lot. They have grown stronger while others have withered; adapted and amended while others have stood still. The one thing that has kept them ahead of the pack is their refusal to stand on their laurels. Complacency may come knocking at Welford Road, but it is turned away in no uncertain fashion. Leicester take nothing for granted, which is just as well as so many teams are looking to knock them off their Heineken pedestal.

My, how those teams tried. Leicester, despite being top seeds, had a tough old group to negotiate. Perpignan were the form side in France in the first half of the season and gave Leicester a rare old roasting at a packed Stade Aimé-Giral. Perpignan had so much to offer yet came up short in one vital ingredient – self-belief. If only they had truly believed that they could have toppled the reigning Heineken champions, then they surely would have done. But they didn't and they couldn't, Tim Stimpson getting his side out of real bother with a late penalty goal to see Leicester to a 31-30 victory.

It was a familiar theme of Leicester's season, their tendency to pull something out of the bag when it really mattered. They did it against Perpignan and again even more dramatically against Llanelli in the semi-final, Stimpson's late, late, long, long winner only going over via crossbar and upright. But good teams make their own luck. These things even out

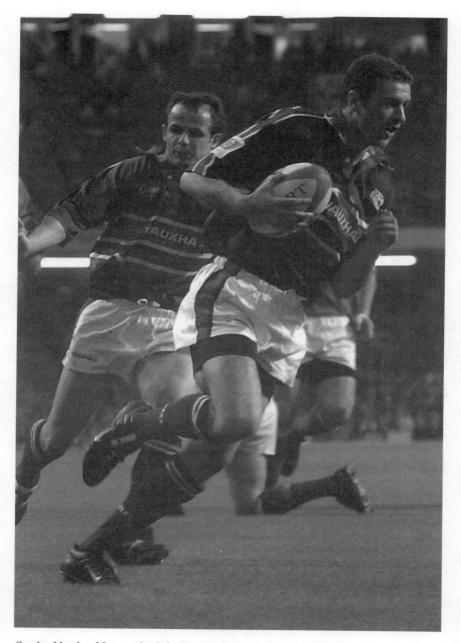

Geordan Murphy of Leicester heads for the line and the opening try of the Heineken Cup Final between Leicester and Munster at Cardiff in May.

across a season. Given that the competition lasted eight months, it's a safe bet that as much will have gone against Leicester as it went for them.

The tournament yet again set new standards. We may not have had as many dazzling matches as in recent years, nor as tense and tight a battle to qualify from the group stages. However, there was no doubting the intense nature of all games, very much the ideal preparation for the Test arena.

Spectators obviously thought so too. The knock-out stages attracted several sell-out crowds and the final itself set a new record for the tournament, 74,000 packing into the Millennium Stadium, a bigger turn-out than for the FA Cup a few weeks earlier. At least the footballers were able to play under natural skies. The roof was closed for the Heineken final. Cardiff had been hit by storms and high winds in the build-up to the game, but quite why the roof can't be opened just for the game itself is a source of real irritation for many. The mechanism takes only 20 minutes to operate. Rugby is a winter sport and adapting to the elements is all part of the challenge.

The scrap for honours was fairly evenly spread among the competing countries. The make-up for the quarter-finals saw three teams from France, two apiece from England and Ireland and one from Wales. Once again neither of the Scottish district sides made the cut, a disturbing trend and one that has to be put to rights. Scottish rugby will never prosper until it has a strong provincial set-up. The rise in Irish rugby is proof of that.

There was a curious backdrop, however, to the quarter-finalists. Bath led the way for England, winning all six games in Pool Three, despite the fact that they were having a desperate time of it in the Premiership. They kicked off well by beating Biarritz 14-6 away from home and never looked back as they did the double over the fancied French side as well as beating disappointing Swansea and Edinburgh outfits. Bath's emphatic defeat by Llanelli in the quarter-final showed that their success had been built on flimsy foundations.

Pool Six threw up some conflicting results and patterns. Toulouse, perennial contenders for honours, were rocked by the devastating bomb blast at a chemical factory that not only damaged their Municipal Stadium but also shattered morale. Toulouse had to do a late switch and play their opening game in Dublin against Leinster. They slumped to a 40-10 defeat and never recovered. Newport staged some memorable games but once more failed to maximise their opportunities. Somehow they contrived to throw away their evident superiority to Leinster at Rodney Parade to lose 26-21.

Stade Français looked comfortable in topping Pool Two, their only hiccup coming at Ravenhill where they lost 19-16 to Ulster. The French side, though, had internal tensions that were only revealed later when Australian coach John Connolly was moved aside for Nick Mallett. The big-spending Parisian club, beaten finalists the year before, crave Heineken success. Wasps, without the injured Lawrence Dallaglio, struggled, losing to Treviso 32-17 which was a real fillip for Italian rugby.

Montferrand were too strong for the most part in Pool Five. They were beaten by Cardiff, 26-20, but once again the Welsh side could not put together a consistent Heineken Cup campaign.

Castres and Munster went at it hammer and tongs in Pool Four, with the match in France particularly explosive. Munster prop Peter Clohessy claimed that he had been bitten on the arm. Castres No 8 Ismaella Lassissi was initially banned for 12 months by ERC, a punishment that was overturned on appeal.

There were few controversies to put the dampener on yet another successful Heineken Cup.

Pool Results

Pool One

Leicester 12 Llanelli 9; Perpignan 56 Calvisano 3; Llanelli 20 Perpignan 6; Calvisano 3 Leicester 37; Calvisano 13 Llanelli 31; Perpignan 30 Leicester 31; Llanelli 93 Calvisano 14; Leicester 54 Perpignan 15; Leicester 29 Calvisano 7; Perpignan 42 Llanelli 10; Calvisano 18 Perpignan 33; Llanelli 24 Leicester 12

Pool One Final Table

	P	W	D	L	For	Against	Pts
Leicester	6	5	0	1	175	88	10
Llanelli	6	4	0	2	187	99	8
Perpignan	6	3	0	3	182	136	6
Amatori & Calvisano	6	0	0	6	58	279	0

Pool Two

Treviso 28 Ulster 33; Wasps 19 Stade Français 25; Ulster 42 Wasps 19; Stade Français 42 Treviso 9; Wasps 29 Treviso 24; Stade Français 40 Ulster 11; Treviso 32 Wasps 17; Ulster 19 Stade Français 16; Treviso 6 Stade Français 59; Wasps 36 Ulster 32; Stade Français 31 Wasps 0; Ulster 59 Treviso 3

Pool Two Final Table

	P	W	D	L	For	Against	Pts
Stade Français	6	5	0	1	213	64	10
Ulster	6	4	0	2	196	142	8
Wasps	6	2	0	4	120	186	4
Benetton Treviso	6	1	0	5	102	239	2

Pool Three

Biarritz 6 Bath 14; Swansea 21 Edinburgh 16; Edinburgh 6 Biarritz 6; Bath 38 Swansea 9; Edinburgh 6 Bath 37; Swansea 15 Biarritz 10; Bath 17 Edinburgh 10; Biarritz 24 Swansea 15; Biarritz 45 Edinburgh 14; Swansea 12 Bath 24; Bath 31 Biarritz 13; Edinburgh 30 Swansea 20

Pool Three Final Table

	P	W	D	L	For	Against	Pts
Bath	6	6	0	0	161	56	12
Biarritz Olympique	6	2	1	3	104	95	5
Swansea	6	2	0	4	92	142	4
Edinburgh Rugby	6	1	1	4	82	146	3

Pool Four

Munster 28 Castres 23; Bridgend 24 Harlequins 30; Harlequins 8 Munster 24;
Castres 35 Bridgend 23; Bridgend 12 Munster 16; Harlequins 17 Castres 39;
Castres 24 Harlequins 18; Munster 40 Bridgend 6; Munster 51 Harlequins 17;
Bridgend 26 Castres 37; Harlequins 29 Bridgend 25; Castres 21 Munster 13

Pool Four Final Table

	P	W	D	L	For	Against	Pts
Castres	6	5	0	1	179	125	10
Munster	6	5	0	1	172	87	10
Harlequins	6	2	0	4	119	187	4
Bridgend	6	0	0	6	116	187	0

Pool Five

Cardiff 25 Northampton 17; Glasgow 19 Montferrand 19; Northampton 30
Glasgow 9; Montferrand 37 Cardiff 10; Cardiff 46 Glasgow 7; Northampton 15
Montferrand 21; Glasgow 47 Cardiff 32; Montferrand 50 Northampton 17; Cardiff
26 Montferrand 20; Glasgow 31 Northampton 27; Montferrand 44 Glasgow 13;
Northampton 26 Cardiff 15

Pool Five Final Table

	P	W	D	L	For	Against	Pts
Montferrand	6	4	1	1	191	100	9
Cardiff	6	3	0	3	154	154	6
Glasgow Rugby	6	2	1	3	126	198	5
Northampton	6	2	0	4	132	151	4

Pool Six

Leinster 40 Toulouse 10; Newcastle 21 Newport 34; Leinster 28 Newcastle 9;
Newport 21 Toulouse 20; Leinster 21 Newport 6; Toulouse 33 Newcastle 13;
Newcastle 42 Toulouse 9; Newport 21 Leinster 26; Toulouse 36 Newport 23;
Newcastle 15 Leinster 17; Newport 53 Newcastle 17; Toulouse 43 Leinster 7

Pool Six Final Table

	P	W	D	L	For	Against	Pts
Leinster	6	5	0	1	139	104	10
Toulouse	6	3	0	3	151	146	6
Newport	6	3	0	3	158	141	6
Newcastle Falcons	6	1	0	5	117	174	2

The Quarter-Finals

26 January, Stade Jean Bouin, Paris
Stade Français 14 (3PG 1T)   Munster 16 (1G 2PG 1DG)

Experience was Munster's greatest ally in this splendid victory, the knowledge born of previous tough European campaigns that the side that pulls together in adversity will come through. And so it proved as Munster withstood a fierce second-half battering to hang on to their half-time advantage and progress to the semi-finals for the third year in succession.

Munster led 16-3 at the interval, a lead built on the elements at their back, a solid performance from their pack and shrewd marshalling of resources from half-backs, Peter Stringer and Ronan O'Gara. O'Gara kicked his goals and Anthony Horgan nipped in for a smart try to send Munster into the half-time break in good heart.

They knew that, in front of 12,000 screaming Parisians, they would have to be disciplined and resilient to survive the second-half. And they were. They barely gave Diego Dominguez a sighting of the posts. Horgan almost scored a second try, just failing to hang on to a pass from Stringer. The Munster scrum-half played a huge part, keeping his pack on the move and also scything down Stade Français centre Franck Comba to save a try. Stade Français gave it everything but it was not enough.

Stade Français: S Jonnet; N Williams, F Comba, N Raffault, R Poulain; D Dominguez, F Galthié (*captain*); S Marconnet, M Blin, P de Villiers, D Auradou, M James, P Rabadan, C Juillet, R Martin *Substitutions:* P Lemoine for Marconnet (66 mins); C Moni for Juillet (78 mins)

Scorers *Try:* Juillet *Penalty Goals:* Dominguez 3

Munster: D Crotty; J Kelly, R Henderson, J Holland, A Horgan; R O'Gara, P Stringer; P Clohessy, F Sheahan, J Hayes, M Galwey (*captain*), P O'Connell, R Williams, A Foley, D Wallace *Substitution:* M Horan for Clohessy (79 mins)

Scorers *Try:* Horgan *Conversion:* O'Gara *Penalty Goals:* O'Gara (2) *Dropped Goal:* O'Gara

Referee N Whitehouse (Wales)

26 January, Stade Pierre-Antoine, Castres
Castres 22 (1G 4PG 1DG)   Montferrand 21 (7PG)

Castres had shown their strong sense of collective purpose when mounting a passionate defence of Ismaella Lassissi, their Ivory Coast No 8 whose 12-month ban for allegedly biting Munster's Peter Clohessy was overturned just two days before this game. That team spirit shone through in this deserved victory in front of 9,500 spectators. Castres were almost hauled back by Montferrand fly-half Gérald Merceron who not only scored all his side's points with seven penalties but launched a last-minute break-out that was only thwarted when Aurélien Rougerie knocked on in the Castres 22.

Castres fluffed two good try-scoring chances. New Zealander Norm Berryman had the ball knocked from his grasp over the line and then a break

Munster's Anthony Horgan takes on Sylvain Jonnet & Franck Comba of Stade Francais during the Heineken Cup quarter-final in Paris. Munster won 16 – 14 and went on to reach the final.

from full-back Romain Teulet was spoiled by a forward pass to centre Eric Artiguste. Teulet did score four penalties and also converted the only try of the game from flanker Romain Froment midway through the second-half. Gregor Townsend also dropped a goal for Castres.

Castres: R Teulet; S Longstaff, N Berryman, E Artiguste, F Plisson; G Townsend (*captain*), A Albouy; M Reggiardo, R Vigneaux, B Moyle, N Spanghero, T Bourdet, R Froment, I Fernandez Lobbe, J Diaz *Substitutions:* I Lassissi for Froment (43 mins); S Chinarro for Bourdet (67 mins); O Sarramea for Teulet (80 mins)

Scorers *Try:* Froment *Conversion:* Teulet *Penalty Goals:* Teulet (4) *Dropped Goal:* Townsend

Montferrand: J Marlu; A Rougerie, J Ngauamo, T Marsh, D Bory; G Merceron, A Troncon; B Reidy, M Caputo, A Galasso, D Barrier (*captain*), S Boome, A Audebert, E Vermeulen, O Magne *Substitutions:* A Tolofua for Reidy (14 mins); L Gomez for Galasso (61 mins); C Dongieu for Audebert (75 mins)

Scorer *Penalty Goals:* Merceron (7)

Referee C White (England)

27 January, Recreation Ground, Bath
Bath 10 (1G 1PG)   Llanelli 27 (8PG 1DG)

Home conditions, despite the support of an 8,200 crowd, did not suit Bath for this traditional Anglo-Welsh clash. A 24-hour postponement for a saturated pitch gave the home side no advantage. They may have scored the only try of the match in the second-half through flanker Gavin Thomas, but they were beaten in almost every phase of play. Certainly Llanelli had by far the better kicking game, fly-half Stephen Jones shrewdly mixing his options. Bath, by contrast, simply hoisted high, hopeful balls downfield. Mike Catt had his poorest game in a long time in a Bath shirt. Jones was also in prime goal-kicking form, landing eight penalties and a drop goal at the death.

Bath could not get any sort of foothold. Their pack was underpowered and their lineout badly malfunctioned. There were far too many unforced errors by Bath who constantly turned over possession. Llanelli made no such mistakes.

Bath: M Perry; I Balshaw, O Barkley, M Tindall, K Maggs; M Catt (*captain*), A Williams; D Barnes, A Long, S Emms, S Borthwick, D Grewcock, G Thomas, N Thomas, M Gabey *Substitutions:* D Lyle for Gabey (41 mins); M Regan for Long (41 mins); G Cooper for Williams (53 mins); R Thirlby for Tindall (53 mins); D Dorsey for Emms (74 mins)

Scorers *Try:* G Thomas *Conversion:* Barkley *Penalty Goal:* Barkley

Llanelli: G Evans; W Proctor, N Boobyer, L Davies, S Finau; S Jones, G Easterby; M Madden, R McBryde, J Davies, V Cooper, C Wyatt, D Hodges, S Quinnell (*captain*), S Easterby *Substitutions:* B Davies for Evans (42 mins); P Booth for Madden (77 mins); D Jones for Hodges (77 mins)

Scorer *Penalty Goals:* Jones (8) *Dropped Goal:* Jones

Referee A Lewis (Ireland)

27 January, Welford Road, Leicester
Leicester 29 (2G 3T) **Leinster 18** (1G 2PG 1T)

A few murmurs of apprehension ran through the capacity crowd of 16,249 when their team went 10-0 down after a quarter-of-an-hour. The Tigers had just been beaten twice in succession and for a few minutes the unthinkable began to take shape. The spectre was smashed apart by a four-try Leicester blitz in the space of 15 minutes just before the interval. Normal service well and truly resumed.

Leicester's fifth try was scored just ten minutes after the restart and the game was as good as over. Four of the five tries came from a variety of driving line-out mauls. Leicester had sensed the Irish side's weak spot and fully exploited it. Lock Malcolm O'Kelly was absent and Leinster were vulnerable. First Neil Back touched down then Leon Lloyd. Austin Healey followed suit in the 33rd minute after the maul had initially skewed right only to be rescued by Martin Corry and Graham Rowntree. Back and Freddie Tuilagi combined well for Geordan Murphy's try. Back got his second just after half-time.

There was a touch of good fortune about both Leinster's tries. Healey looked to have got a hand on the ball when Denis Hickie was awarded a try in the 14th minute and then Ben Willis appeared to have a foot in touch when he scooted down the blindside to score midway through the second-half.

Leicester: G Murphy; F Tuilagi, L Lloyd, R Kafer, O Smith; A Healey, J Hamilton; G Rowntree, R Cockerill, D Garforth, M Johnson (*captain*), B Kay, L Moody, M Corry, N Back *Substitutions:* H Ellis for Hamilton (59 mins); J Kronfeld for Back (68 mins); A Balding for Corry (70 mins)

Scorers *Tries:* Back (2), Lloyd, Healey, Murphy *Conversions:* Murphy (2)

Leinster: G Dempsey; D Hickie, B O'Driscoll, S Horgan, G D'Arcy; N Spooner, B Willis; R Corrigan (*captain*), S Byrne, P Wallace, L Cullen, R Casey, E Miller, V Costello, K Gleeson *Substitutions:* A Magro for Horgan (49 mins); S Keogh for D'Arcy (69 mins); A McCullen for Casey (51 mins); P Coyle for Wallace (70 mins); G Hickie for Byrne (79 mins); T Brennan for Miller (80 mins)

Scorers *Tries:* Hickie, Willis *Conversion:* Spooner *Penalty Goals:* Spooner (2)

Referee J Jutge (France)

The Semi-Finals

27 April, Stade de la Méditerranée, Béziers
Castres 17 (4PG 1T) **Munster 25** (1G 6PG)

On a sun-baked afternoon Munster discovered some new heroes. Old warriors such as Mick Galwey and Peter Clohessy were, for once, upstaged by the likes of young locks Donncha O'Callaghan and Paul O'Connell who sent the opposition on to the back foot from where they rarely managed to regroup. O'Callaghan only came into the action when No 8 Tony Foley was forced off after just 16 minutes with a shoulder injury. Munster were struggling at that point and went 9-0 down shortly afterwards as Romain Teulet landed his third penalty.

Ronan O'Gara pulled his side back into contention with two penalties before half-time. After the break Munster took control, O'Gara knocking over four more goals before John Kelly effectively sealed victory with a try.

Clohessy earned his rapturous acclaim from the sizeable Munster contingent, the Munster prop giving his all despite being badly burned in a domestic accident only three weeks earlier. Attendance: 20,400

Castres: R Teulet; U Mola, E Artiguste, N Berryman, S Longstaff; G Townsend (*captain*), A Albouy; M Reggiardo, R Ibañez, B Moyle, I. Fernandez Lobbe, N Spanghero, R Froment, A Costes, I Lassissi *Substitutions:* R Vignaux for Ibañez (40 mins); G Delmotte for Artiguste (51 mins); D Dima for Froment (temp 22 to 30 mins) and for Reggiardo (69 mins); S Chinarro for Costes (temp 65 to 67 mins) and for Spanghero (69 mins); O Sarramea for Teulet (76 mins); F Plisson for Mola (79 mins);

Scorers *Try:* Longstaff *Penalty Goals:* Teulet (4)

Munster: D Crotty; J Kelly, R Henderson, J Holland, A Horgan; R O'Gara, P Stringer; P Clohessy, F Sheahan, J Hayes, M Galwey (*captain*), P O'Connell, A Quinlan, A Foley, D Wallace *Substitutions:* D O'Callaghan for Foley (15 mins); M Mullins for O'Gara (temp 45 to 51 mins) and for Henderson (78 mins); M Horan for O'Callaghan (temp 22 to 30 mins) and for Clohessy (69 mins)

Scorers *Try:* Kelly *Conversion:* O'Gara *Penalty Goals:* O'Gara (6)

Referee C White (England)

28 April, City Ground, Nottingham
Leicester 13 (1G 2PG)   Llanelli 12 (4PG)

Two licks of paint were all that stood between Llanelli and a famous victory: one on the crossbar and one on the left upright. Tim Stimpson's 60-metre injury-time penalty kick bounced up, then across and finally over. The Leicester fans in the capacity 29,849 were delirious, the Llanelli fans distraught. The infringement had seemed innocuous if not debatable, referee David McHugh adjudging Martyn Madden to have dropped the scrum. Leicester had the rub of the green.

'There was an element of luck about it,' admitted Leicester manager Dean Richards. 'But we work hard for our luck.' They do that. Leicester stuck to their task, confident that a break would come. Llanelli, however, lacked the self-belief and positive attitude to make it happen. They sat on their lead instead of trying to make certain of victory.

Llanelli played a game of damage limitation. They led 9-3 at the break only to be pegged back by a darting try from 19-year-old Leicester scrum-half Harry Ellis four minutes after the restart. Stimpson converted that try to add to his seventh-minute penalty. He had a solid game and held his nerve right to the final whistle.

Leicester: T Stimpson; G Murphy, O Smith, R Kafer, F Tuilagi; A Healey, H Ellis; G Rowntree, D West, D Garforth, M. Johnson (*captain*), B Kay, L Moody, M Corry, N Back *Substitutions:* A Balding for Corry (temp 24 to 30 mins); J Hamilton for Ellis (64 mins); L Lloyd for Tuilagi (71 mins)

Scorers *Try:* H Ellis *Conversion:* Stimpson *Penalty Goals:* Stimpson (2)

Llanelli: G Evans; M. Jones, N. Boobyer, L. Davies, S Finau, S. Jones, G. Easterby, M Madden, R McBryde, J. Davies, V Cooper, C Wyatt, D Hodges, S Quinnell (*captain*), S Easterby *Substitutions:* W Proctor for Evans (71 mins); L Gross for Wyatt (72 mins); I Boobyer for S Easterby (72 mins)

Scorer *Penalty Goals:* S Jones 4

Referee D McHugh (Ireland)

Heineken Cup Final

25 May, Millennium Stadium, Cardiff
Leicester 15 (1G 1PG 1T)   Munster 9 (3PG)

There was much talk in the aftermath of this intense and engaging seventh Heineken Cup final of Neil Back's 'handball.' In the last minute of the game, with Leicester defending their line against a furious late Munster assault, the England flanker flicked the ball out of Peter Stringer's hand at a scrum five metres out from the Tigers' goal-line. The referee was unsighted on the other side of the scrum, the touch-judge failed to spot the incident and for all Stringer's protestations Leicester were able to clear their lines and relieve the pressure.

Back took exception to the word 'cheat' in the post-match interviews. He had no right to. It was a blatant act of interference, a calculated act of defiance against the laws of the game. Teams infringe and foul all the time. However, it was the flagrancy of Back's action that demeaned both him and his side. It's questionable as to whether he even needed to do it, for Leicester had managed to defend their line all afternoon. Even so, the deed was done and Leicester should take the consequences.

It was a pity, for they thoroughly deserved their victory. Munster did as Munster do – they were tight-knit, well-organised and gave body and soul to the cause. However, for all the graft there was not enough craft. There was also a lamentable absence of a line-out. Munster lost eight line-outs according to the official stats of the game. In reality, they barely won a worthwhile ball from the line-out all afternoon. Ben Kay, Martin Corry and Martin Johnson did their damnedest to make life difficult for their opponents and the Irishmen did the rest for them with poor throwing and co-ordination.

Munster did give it a lash in those nail-biting closing stages. Wing John O'Neill was denied by the video referee, Austin Healey's flying tackle deemed to have nudged the Munster wing into touch. Several replays later there was still doubt as to whether the officials had got that one right. In fact there was doubt over many of their decisions. Frenchman Joel Jutge had a poor game.

The same could not be said of the Leicester team. They were inspired by a typically virtuoso performance from Austin Healey. He expressed relief afterwards that he had been chosen at all, so poor had his form been. He repaid the coaches' confidence in him by running the show. He mixed his game intelligently and foxed his opposite number, Ronan O'Gara, when blasting through him for a decisive score in the 59th minute. O'Gara struggled to regain any composure after that.

If that was an individual flourish, then Leicester's opening try in the 26th minute owed much to slick teamwork. Johnson snaffled a Munster throw and Leicester took full advantage. Rod Kafer sent Freddie Tuilagi through the middle, the burly wing finding Tim Stimpson outside him. The full-back sold a dummy before drawing the last two defenders to put Geordan Murphy over the line.

Munster led 6-5 at half-time. O'Gara extended the lead six minutes after the break with his third penalty. The scales were righted with Healey's try and Stimpson's subsequent penalty, even if Back's antics were to scramble the moral radar.

Leicester: T Stimpson; G Murphy, O Smith, R Kafer, F Tuilagi; A Healey, J Hamilton; G Rowntree, D West, D Garforth, M Johnson (*captain*), B Kay, L Moody, M Corry, N Back *Substitutions:* H Ellis for Hamilton (52 mins); P Freshwater for Rowntree (74 mins); G Gelderbloom for Smith (76 mins)

Scorers *Tries:* Murphy, Healey *Conversion:* Stimpson *Penalty Goal:* Stimpson

Munster: D Crotty; J O'Neill, R Henderson, J Holland, J Kelly; R O'Gara, P Stringer; P Clohessy, F Sheahan, J Hayes, M Galwey (*captain*), P O'Connell, A Quinlan, A Foley, D Wallace *Substitutions:* J Blaney for Sheahan (temp 17 to 28 mins); R Williams for Foley (53 mins); M Horan for Clohessy (61 mins); M O'Driscoll for O'Connell (61mins); J Staunton for Crotty (65 mins); M Mullins for Henderson (67 mins)

Scorer *Penalty Goals:* O'Gara (3)

Referee J Jutge (France)

Previous Heineken Cup Finals: 1996 Toulouse 21, Cardiff 18 (Cardiff); 1997 Brive 28, Leicester 9 (Cardiff); 1998 Bath 19, Brive 18 (Bordeaux); 1999 Ulster 21, Colomiers 6 (Dublin); 2000 Northampton 9, Munster 8 (Twickenham); 2001 Leicester 34, Stade Francais 30 (Paris); 2002 Leicester 15, Munster 9 (Cardiff)

HEINEKEN CUP RECORDS 1995-2002

Record	Detail		Set
Most team points in season	379 by Stade Français	in 9 matches	2000-2001
Highest team score	108 by Toulouse	108-16 v Ebbw Vale	1998-1999
Biggest team win	92 by Toulouse	108-16 v Ebbw Vale	1998-1999
Most team tries in match	16 by Toulouse	v Ebbw Vale	1998-1999
Most appearances	45 for Munster	M J Galwey	1995-2002
Most points in matches	552 for Milan/SF	D Dominguez	1995-2002
Most points in season	188 for Stade Français	D Dominguez	2000-2001
Most points in match	37 for Ulster	D G Humphreys v Wasps	2001-2002
Most tries in matches	24 for Toulouse	M Marfaing	1996-2002
Most tries in season	9 for Swansea	M F D Robinson	2000-2001
Most tries in match	5 for Gloucester	T D Beim v Roma	2000-2001
	5 for Llanelli	M D Cardey v Amatori & Calvisano	2001-2002
Most cons in match	12 for Stade Français	D Dominguez v L'Aquila	2000-2001
Most pens in match	9 for Stade Français	D Dominguez v Leicester	2000-2001
Most drops in match	4 for Ulster	D G Humphreys v Wasps	2001-2002

PARKER PEN SHIELD 2001-2002

Sale head the English Charge to Honours

David Llewellyn

It started well, finally gaining a sponsor and consequently a huge chunk of credibility, and it finished proudly in front of 12,000 fans in Oxford's Kassam Stadium. But amid some high quality rugby it also had more than its fair share of controversy. The coup in persuading Parker Pen to come on board for the next two years, albeit at the last minute – the ink was still drying on the contract when the first round of matches got under way – was something else though.

The injection of £3 million suddenly made it worthwhile for clubs to participate, especially since the winners also picked up an automatic qualification for the Heineken European Cup – the Parker Pen Shield's big brother. But Agen had other ideas. They decided they had to drop out of the Parker Pen Shield. They worked out that Ebbw Vale, their Pool One rivals, needed to stick eight more tries on the Frenchmen when the two teams met in the last round-robin match. So Agen contrived, or more correctly, connived, to create the eighth wonder of the world, a victory by the requisite number of tries for Vale.

So the Welsh club ended up with the quarter-final slot and Agen, who had felt that there was too much fixture congestion awaiting them on the European and domestic fronts, seemed happy. But suspicions were aroused. European Rugby Cup's board met and found Agen guilty of 'contriving to achieve a particular result' and initially banned the club from all European competition for two years as well as fining them the best part of £14,000. This penalty was commuted on appeal to a one year ban, but there was a further imposition of a 12-month ban, suspended for three years together with a £60,000 fine, also put in abeyance for three years.

Sale and Overmach Parma also fell foul of the authorities when winter bit briefly into the rugby season. Sale were fined £8,000 for 'failing to protect the pitch' which caused the postponement of their Pool Four tie versus Narbonne, while Parma found themselves banned from European rugby for two years (commuted on appeal to a suspended penalty) after refusing to travel to Gloucester's Kingsholm for a 'home' game against Welsh club Pontypridd after their own Stadio Del Rugby pitch was deemed too hard to play on following freezing temperatures. The Italians argued that they could not finance a trip of 900 miles at such short notice. There was anger too that Kingsholm was almost a home tie for Pontypridd. But it did not prevent ERC from meting out punishment to the Italians, nor from awarding two points to Pontypridd, a gesture which initially had Leeds fulminating.

Pete Anglesea of Sale gets past Richard Parks of Pontypridd during the Parker Pen Shield Final at Oxford's Kassam Stadium.

On the field the competition was dominated throughout by English clubs with five of the six reaching the quarter-finals – the sixth club, Leeds, having lost out when Ponty were awarded those two points for the tie that was never played against Parma. Remarkably there was only one all-English tie and Sale prevailed over Bristol. London Irish powered past Pau, France's sole representatives in a competition that had been dominated by Gallic sides pretty much since its inception – 11 of the first 12 semi-finalists were French and four successive finals were contested by their own clubs. The quarters produced just one shock, Pontypridd's defeat of Saracens at Vicarage Road, and the Welsh club then went on to stun a confident London Irish in the semi-finals in an epic match. Sale then pipped Gloucester by a point to set up an Anglo-Welsh final.

Tables

Pool One Final Table

	P	W	D	L	For	Against	Pts
Ebbw Vale	6	4	0	2	153	90	8
Agen	6	4	0	2	199	119	8
Montauban	6	4	0	2	146	123	8
Rovigo	6	0	0	6	78	244	0

Pool Two Final Table

	P	W	D	L	For	Against	Pts
Pau	6	6	0	0	217	63	12
Colomiers	6	4	0	2	259	105	8
Petrarca Rugby	6	2	0	4	114	223	4
Madrid 2012	6	0	0	6	90	289	0

Pool Three Final Table

	P	W	D	L	For	Against	Pts
Pontypridd	6	4	0	2	139	87	8
Leeds	6	4	0	2	188	154	8
Béziers	6	2	0	4	136	187	4
Overmach Parma	6	2	0	4	127	162	4

Pool Four Final Table

	P	W	D	L	For	Against	Pts
Sale	6	6	0	0	286	79	12
Narbonne	6	3	0	3	128	111	6
Connacht	6	3	0	3	157	140	6
Roma Olimpic	6	0	0	6	57	298	0

Pool Five Final Table

	P	W	D	L	For	Against	Pts
Bristol	6	5	0	1	189	115	10
Neath	6	4	0	2	160	131	8
Viadana	6	2	0	4	120	210	4
Bourgoin	6	1	0	5	160	173	2

Pool Six Final Table

	P	W	D	L	For	Against	Pts
London Irish	6	5	1	0	284	85	11
Dax	6	4	1	1	306	119	9
L'Aquila	6	2	0	4	107	239	4
Valladolid RAC	6	0	0	6	53	307	0

Pool Seven Final Table

	P	W	D	L	For	Against	Pts
Gloucester	6	6	0	0	362	62	12
La Rochelle	6	4	0	2	161	177	8
Caerphilly	6	2	0	4	170	281	4
GR.A.N.Parma	6	0	0	6	104	277	0

Pool Eight Final Table

	P	W	D	L	For	Against	Pts
Saracens	6	6	0	0	435	66	12
Bègles-Bordeaux	6	4	0	2	354	117	8
Dinamo Bucuresti	6	1	0	5	102	403	2
Bologna	6	1	0	5	93	398	2

Quarter-Finals:

25 January, Kingsholm, Gloucester
Gloucester 46 (*T:* O'Leary, Simpson-Daniel, Boer, Forrester *C:* Mercier 4 *PG:* Mercier 6) **Ebbw Vale 11** (*T:* Wagstaff *PG:* Cull 2)

25 January, Heywood Road, Brooklands, Sale
Sale 25 (*T:* Going, Hanley, Redpath *C:* Hodgson 2 *PG:* Hodgson 2) **Bristol 20** (*T:* Christophers, Contepomi *C:* Contepomi 2 *PG:* Contepomi 2)

26 January, Stade Municipal du Hameau, Pau
Pau 9 (*PG:* Traille 2, Pearson) **London Irish 38** (*T:* Sackey, Danaher *C:* Brown 2 *PG:* Everitt 3, Brown 3 *DG:* Everitt, Venter)

27 January, Vicarage Road, Watford
Saracens 15 (*PG:* De Beer 5) **Pontypridd 17** (*T:* Owen, Wyatt *C:* Davey 2 *PG:* Davey)

Semi-Finals:

27 April, The Kassam Stadium, Oxford

London Irish 27 (*T:* Halvey, Kirke, Horak *C:* Everitt 3 *PG:* Everitt 2) **Pontypridd 33** (*T:* Wyatt, Jenkins, M Davies *C:* Davey 3 *PG:* Davey 4)

28 April, Franklin's Gardens, Northampton

Gloucester 27 (*T:* Fanolua 2, Forrester *C:* Mercier 3 *PG:* Mercier *DG:* Mercier) **Sale 28** (*T:* Cueto, Hanley, Marais, Harris *C:* Hodgson *PG:* Hodgson 2)

Parker Pen Shield Final

26 May, 2002, Kassam Stadium, Oxford

Sale 25 (2G 2PG 1T) **Pontypridd 22** (1G 4PG 1DG)

No one who witnessed this fiercely fought final would have imagined that Sale had already qualified for the Heineken Cup. The English club wanted victory just as intensely as did their Welsh opponents. Pontypridd ran themselves to a standstill in an effort to clinch the qualifying place, and had their full-back, Brett Davey, who eight days earlier had secured the Principality Cup for them against Llanelli, been given a shot at goal in the dying minutes the final might have gone into extra time – just as it did the year before when Harlequins emerged as the winners.

As it was, the Pontypridd captain Paul John opted for the kick to touch and a close-range line-out in the hope that they could engineer a try from the resultant driving maul. John later claimed that he was not sure of the extra time ruling – the scores would have been tied at 25-all and the 'tries-scored' ruling only kicked-in after extra time. John added that he was not certain that the kick was in Davey's range anyway. The upshot was that Sale comfortably saw off the line-out threat, and the rest, as they say, is now Shield history.

The English club had been given a psychological boost in the build-up to the final when their England fly-half Charlie Hodgson signed a new four-year contract and the news that their captain Bryan Redpath, the Scotland international scrum-half, had resisted tempting overtures from Leicester.

Early in the match, Sale found themselves knocked repeatedly onto the back foot, as Ponty hit the rucks hard and frequently drove on through. The English side also struggled at the set piece and around the fringes, where the loose forwards Richard Parks and Michael Owen put in a lot of work and came close to forcing the result Pontypridd wanted. Indeed, it needed some sterling defence from Sale to keep the Welshmen at bay. They even managed to keep out the marauding Welshmen when their prop Kevin Yates was sin-binned for up-ending Brent Cockbain at a line-out late in the first half.

Out wide it was a different story. Sale's half-backs Redpath and Hodgson were far more quick-witted, while the midfield and backs packed too much pace, punch and power. Contrary to all expectations Sale's electrifying England full-back-cum-wing Jason Robinson had a quiet day, but he is not the only threat in that team. When Pontypridd lost control of a maul on the halfway line Steve Hanley thundered down the left-hand touchline, where he was badly missed by Gareth Wyatt and Davey, to snaffle the second try, while the first and third tries came from set pieces. Sale's talented lock Chris Jones won clean line-out ball and centre Martin Shaw had a straightforward finish. Then a shuffle and a dummy by Hodgson at a scrum saw Dan Harris, the replacement centre, scuttle through under the posts.

Sale: J Robinson; M Cueto, M Shaw, M Deane, S Hanley; C Hodgson, B Redpath (*captain*); K Yates, C Marais, S Turner, S Lines, C Jones, A Sanderson, P Anglesea, S Pinkerton *Substitutions:* J Baxendell for Hanley (temp 11 to 20 mins); A Black for Sanderson (temp 30 to 39 mins); A Titterell for Marais (66 mins); D Harris for Deane (67 mins)

Scorers *Tries:* Shaw, Hanley, Harris *Conversions:* Hodgson (2) *Penalty Goals:* Hodgson (2)

Pontypridd: B Davey; G Wyatt, S Parker, J Bryant, R Johnston; C Sweeney, P John; G Jenkins, M Davies, D Bell, B Cockbain, R Sidoli, N Kelly, M Owen, R Parks *Substitutions:* G Remnant for Kelly (75 mins); M Rees for Davies (79 mins)

Scorers *Try:* Davies *Conversion:* Davey *Penalty Goals:* Davey (4) *Dropped Goal:* Sweeney

Referee A Lewis (Ireland)

Previous European Shield Finals: 1997 Bourgoin 18, Castres 9 (Béziers); 1998 Colomiers 43, Agen 5 (Toulouse); 1999 Montferrand 35, Bourgoin 16 (Lyons); 2000 Pau 34, Castres 21 (Toulouse); 2001 Harlequins 42, Narbonne 33 (Reading); 2002 Sale 25, Pontypridd 22 (Oxford)

PARKER PEN SHIELD RECORDS 1996-2002

Record	Detail		Set
Most team points in season	450 by Saracens	in seven matches	2001-02
Highest team score	113 by Saracens	113-3 v Bologna	2001-02
	113 by Saracens	113-3 v Dinamo Bucuresti	2001-02
Biggest team win	110 by Saracens	113-3 v Bologna	2001-02
	110 by Saracens	113-3 v Dinamo Bucuresti	2001-02
Most team tries in match	17 by Saracens	113-3 v Bologna	2001-02
	17 by Saracens	113-3 v Dinamo Bucuresti	2001-02
Most points in matches	321 for Connacht	E P Elwood	1996-2002
Most points in match	35 for Colomiers	D Skrela v Petraraca	2001-02
Most tries in matches	16 for Bègles-Bordeaux	A Bouyssie	1996-2002
Most tries in match	6 for Bègles-Bordeaux	A Bouyssie v Bologna	2001-02
Most cons in match	13 for Saracens	J H de Beer v Bologna	2001-02
Most pens in match	9 for Ebbw Vale	J Strange v Toulon	1999-2000
	9 for Bristol	S Vile v Mont-de-Marsan	2000-01
	9 for Narbonne	C Rosalen v Perpignan	2000-01
Most drops in a match	4 for Dax	S Fauque v London Irish	2001-02

THE CELTIC LEAGUE 2001

Irish Provinces Steal the Glory
John Billot & John Griffiths

It was ironic that Wales, who embraced the concept of the Celtic League with such enthusiasm, failed in this inaugural tournament. The four Irish provinces dominated so comprehensively that Welsh clubs managed a meagre two victories in more than 20 engagements with them. The best the Welsh could manage was three teams into the quarter-finals and that was the end of them. Their only successes against the Irish were by Neath (30-22) over Munster at the Gnoll and Llanelli (27-26) over Ulster in Belfast. Inevitably it resulted in an all-Irish final with Leinster defeating Munster by 24-20 at Lansdowne Road.

Ronan O'Gara's 15 points saw Munster account for Ulster by 15-9 in a semi-final that produced no tries. David Humphreys hit over three penalty shots for the losers. But there were tries in the other semi-final which brought Leinster victory by 35-13 to eliminate Glasgow. Girvan Dempsey, Brian O'Driscoll, Shane Horgan and Denis Hickie crossed and Nathan Spooner converted three tries and found the target with three penalty goals. For Glasgow, Tommy Hayes converted Mike Bartlett's try and fired in two penalty goals.

Swansea and Cardiff, the two top teams in the Welsh/Scottish League the previous season, failed to register a win between them against the provinces and Cardiff's rout at Thomond Park by 51-10 was their worst performance of the season. There were eight Munster tries to one and criticism of the Arms Park team's lack of skills and commitment was long and caustic. Connacht had opened the new programme in mid-August with an astonishing success by 6-3 in Cardiff as Eric Elwood found the posts with two penalty kicks to one by Nicky Robinson.

All the provincial teams were expertly drilled defensively and displayed flair that thoroughly rattled the Welsh. Often the Welsh were slipshod in the basics and the Irish, fast, fit and furious, extracted a heavy toll. Swansea went the same way as Cardiff while Newport also fell victims in their two clashes with Irish opponents. Nevertheless, they made it to the quarter-finals only to see Nathan Spooner kick 14 points against them at Donnybrook where Leinster were winners by 34-22.

Llanelli failed to cross the Munster line in a Limerick quarter-final where Stephen Jones's two penalty goals could not save them from defeat by 13-6 as O'Gara converted Mike Prendergast's try and added two penalty goals. Neath certainly fought the good fight in their quarter at Ravenhill before

Ulster took the decision by 38-29. Hayes converted his decisive solo try for Glasgow to go to the semi-finals by 34-29 against Connacht.

The tournament had its knockers. The pool stages were completed by such an early stage of the season (before end-September) that if you blinked you missed them. The competition, moreover, failed to attract a sponsor. Yet the head of steam built up by the successful Irish provinces generated immense interest among Irish fans. The final at Lansdowne Road persuaded nearly 30,000 to put off the Christmas shopping for another week and cheer on their sides in a true rugby occasion. The attendance, as one Irish scribe noted, exceeded the first European Cup Final staged in Cardiff in 1996. Big oaks from small acorns grow.

Pool Results

Pool A

Bridgend 19, Pontypridd 27; Ulster 30, Swansea 13; Leinster 39, Glasgow 11; Llanelli 46, Ebbw Vale 16; Ebbw Vale 18, Pontypridd 13; Llanelli 17, Leinster 19; Glasgow 25, Ulster 25; Swansea 16, Bridgend 25; Leinster 55, Ebbw Vale 13; Pontypridd 6, Swansea 11; Bridgend 50, Glasgow 15; Ulster 26, Llanelli 27; Glasgow 59, Pontypridd 14; Llanelli 36, Bridgend 3; Ebbw Vale 21, Swansea 26; Leinster 31, Ulster 9; Ebbw Vale 27, Ulster 29; Swansea 13, Glasgow 21; Pontypridd 17, Llanelli 19; Bridgend 32, Leinster 51; Leinster 52, Pontypridd 14; Llanelli 21, Swansea 27; Glasgow 58, Ebbw Vale 22; Ulster 46, Bridgend 14; Glasgow 15, Llanelli 9; Ebbw Vale 17, Bridgend 18; Swansea 18, Leinster 34; Pontypridd 20, Ulster 29.

Pool A Final Table

	P	W	D	L	For	Against	Pts
Leinster	7	7	0	0	281	114	21
Ulster	7	4	1	2	194	157	13
Glasgow	7	4	1	2	204	172	13
Llanelli	7	4	0	3	175	123	12
Swansea	7	3	0	4	124	158	9
Bridgend	7	3	0	4	161	208	9
Pontypridd	7	1	0	6	111	207	3
Ebbw Vale	7	1	0	6	134	245	3

Pool B

Edinburgh 22, Munster 25; Cardiff 3, Connacht 6; Caerphilly 13, Neath 43; Neath 25, Cardiff 14; Connacht 21, Edinburgh 30; Newport 50, Caerphilly 22; Edinburgh 20, Neath 32; Munster 40, Connacht 19; Cardiff 20, Newport 14; Neath 30, Munster 22; Caerphilly 15, Cardiff 49; Newport 29, Edinburgh 11; Munster 29, Newport 21; Edinburgh 27, Caerphilly 20; Connacht 28, Neath 10; Cardiff 32, Edinburgh 24; Caerphilly 18, Munster 61; Newport 14, Connacht 16; Munster 51, Cardiff 10; Neath 11, Newport 19; Connacht 62, Caerphilly 0.

Pool B Final Table

	P	W	D	L	For	Against	Pts
Munster	6	5	0	1	228	120	15
Connacht	6	4	0	2	152	97	12
Neath	6	4	0	2	151	116	12
Newport	6	3	0	3	147	109	9
Cardiff	6	3	0	3	128	135	9
Edinburgh	6	2	0	4	134	159	6
Caerphilly	6	0	0	6	88	292	0

Points: win 3; draw 1; defeat nil.

Quarter-Finals:

Munster 13 (*T:* Prendergast *C:* O'Gara *PG:* O'Gara 2) **Llanelli 6** (*PG:* S Jones 2)

Ulster 38 (*T:* Blair, Ward *C:* Humphreys 2 *PG:* Humphreys 8) **Neath 29** (*T:* Moore, Tiueti *C:* Jarvis 2 *PG:* Jarvis 4 *DG:* Jarvis)

Leinster 34 (*T:* Horgan, Dempsey, Hickie, O'Driscoll *C:* Spooner 4 *PG:* Spooner 2) **Newport 22** (*T:* Mostyn, Marinos, Watkins *C:* Howarth 2 *PG:* Howarth)

Connacht 29 (*T:* Robinson, Munn *C:* Elwood 2 *PG:* Elwood 4 *DG:* Elwood) **Glasgow 34** (*T:* McLaren, Hayes, White, Flockhart *C:* Hayes 4 *PG:* Hayes 2)

Semi-Finals:

Munster 15 (*PG:* O'Gara 5) **Ulster 9** (*PG:* Humphreys 3)

Leinster 35 (*T:* Hickie, Horgan, O'Driscoll, Dempsey *C:* Spooner 3 *PG:* Spooner 3) **Glasgow 13** (*T:* Bartlett *C:* Hayes *PG:* Hayes 2)

Celtic League Final

15 December, Lansdowne Road, Dublin
Leinster 24 (1G 4PG 1T) Munster 20 (1G 1PG 2T)

This was a full-blooded contest between two sides determined to stamp their authority on a match that, at times, threatened to boil over into a free for all among the forwards. Welsh referee Nigel Whitehouse had to take a firm hand early on, sending Munster's reserve scrum-half Mike Prendergast to the sin-bin for a professional foul after Shane Horgan had exposed the Munster defence. And with only 25 minutes on the clock, Mr Whitehouse was playing cards again when Leinster's Eric Miller was dismissed for kicking Anthony Foley.

That Leinster, who trailed 15-6 soon after the interval, came back to win with 14 men was a tribute to the industry and skill of their seven remaining forwards. They held up their opponents' much-vaunted pack in the tight and exerted such pressure on them behind the scrum that Munster possession was often turned over. The seven forwards showed magnificent courage and generated such tremendous spirit that Munster were outdone in a depart-ment of the game where they traditionally hold the monopoly.

The turning point of the match came midway through the second half when Munster lost Rob Henderson through a groin strain. The centre had acted as the catalyst for the two first-half tries scored by Anthony Foley and John O'Neill from quickly-taken tapped-penalties. When he departed, Munster were nursing a six-point lead. In the final quarter, however, they leaked 15 points. Nathan Spooner added his fourth penalty for Leinster before Shane Horgan and Brian O'Driscoll took advantage of Henderson's absence to rip through the midfield and set up tries for Gordon D'Arcy and Horgan respectively. Anthony Horgan crossed for a consolation try for Munster in stoppage time, a score that proved too little too late for the men in red.

Leinster: G T Dempsey; D A Hickie, B G O'Driscoll, S P Horgan, G M D'Arcy; N R Spooner, B T O'Meara; R Corrigan (*captain*), J S Byrne, P S Wallace, L F M Cullen, M E O'Kelly, E R P Miller, V C P Costello, K D Gleeson *Substitution:* R E Casey for Cullen (59 mins)
Scorers *Tries:* D'Arcy, S Horgan *Conversion:* Spooner *Penalty Goals:* Spooner (4)

Munster: D J Crotty; J O'Neill, J P Kelly, R A J Henderson, A Horgan; R J R O'Gara, M Prendergast; M Horan, F J Sheahan, P M Clohessy, M J Galwey (*captain*), P J O'Connell, A Quinlan, A G Foley, R W Williams *Substitutions:* M J Mullins for Crotty (temp 3-10 mins and 64 mins); D Hegarty for Kelly (temp 26-33 mins); J Holland for Henderson (58 mins); M Cahill for Clohessy (61 mins); M R O'Driscoll for O'Connell (74 mins); C McMahon for Galwey (74 mins)
Scorers *Tries:* O'Neill, Foley, A Horgan *Conversion:* O'Gara *Penalty Goal:* O'Gara
Referee N Whitehouse (Wales)

SUPER TWELVE SERIES 2002

Crusaders Pick Up Where They Left Off

Paul Dobson

The Crusaders took virtual ownership of the Super Twelves in 2002. They collected their fourth title in five years, and for the seventh time in the eight-season history of the tournament the prize in the southern hemisphere's major sub-international competition went to New Zealand. Normal service as far as New Zealand was concerned was thus resumed after Australia's Brumbies had had the temerity to wrest the title from their hold in 2001.

Super Twelve 2002 started off, as it always has done, with great expectations among teams and supporters. Hope springs everywhere. But pretty soon many of those hopes are dashed. Losing, especially at home, knocks the stuffing out of good sides.

In 2001, the Crusaders were one of those sides. They got off to a bad start and then went from bad to worse. This year they wobbled a bit and were "lucky" against the Chiefs, the Highlanders, the Cats and the Sharks. That's a lot of luck – the sort that really good sides make for themselves. The Crusaders, powered by a great pack and marshalled by Andrew Mehrtens, were a good side, breaking countless records and improving steadily until they reached a crescendo in beating the second-placed team, the Waratahs, by 96-19 – the biggest hiding any team has ever suffered in Super Twelves. Frankly, the Waratahs were fortunate it was not a hundred or more. The Crusaders then went on to win the final against the Brumbies by substantially more than the 31-13 score line suggested.

They were a splendid cohesive side and were rewarded when 15 of the side, including the captain, were selected for the first All Black squad of 2002. 'How do you like the new Crusaders' strip,' they said, 'black with a silver fern?' The Crusaders also became the first team in Super Twelve history to win all 13 of its matches.

The Waratahs, so humiliated at Jade Stadium in Christchurch, had been smoothly successful until then, reaching a semi-final for the first time, and a home one at that as they ended second on the round-robin table. But the Christchurch demolition was too much. The Brumbies, for many of whom Sydney is home, duly shattered the young Waratahs' dream of a final. Earlier in the league phase of the competition the Waratahs had beaten the Brumbies, but in the semi-final the men from ACT thrashed their demoralised hosts 51-10.

The Highlanders, under Laurie Mains, had a good year, reaching the semi-finals after they had bundled out the pedestrian but effective Reds at

Carisbrook's forbidding fortress. They struggled owing to the absence through injury of their play-maker Tony Brown in the semi-final against the Crusaders, which was virtually a final trial for the New Zealand selectors. Jeff Wilson announced his retirement from first-class rugby to concentrate on resurrecting his international cricket career after the defeat. He marked his final match with a try from nothing that closed the Crusaders' lead to five points in the second-half.

The Reds relied almost entirely on Chris Latham's brilliance for sparkle. The Brumbies had been the pre-season favourites but a last-minute drop by Aaron Mauger brought them narrow defeat in Christchurch, which was not good, but then there was that horrible sequence of three round-robin defeats in a row before, classy players that they are, they roared back to reach the final where they fell to a solid defeat. The Stormers could have progressed but, unlike the Crusaders, they narrowly lost where they should have won. They were the best of the South African teams, none of whom reached the semi-finals, a unique occurrence for them.

The Blues started in sparkling fashion but their diamonds gradually turned to gravel. The Hurricanes, despite humiliation by 60-7 by the Blues, sparkled into resolute and unusually disciplined glory in Canberra but then fizzled out. The Chiefs and Sharks had their moments, but the young Cats seemed incapable of winning even when victory looked all theirs. The Bulls, a young side with promise, attacking potential but no defence, outdid themselves in consistency, becoming the first side to lose every match. Still, they did manage what no other side had done for four years – score six tries against the Brumbies.

2002 Round Robin Results

22 Feb: Hurricanes 7, Blues 60 (Wellington); Sharks 18, Stormers 25 (Durban)

23 Feb: Chiefs 25, Waratahs 42 (Rotorua); Crusaders 30, Highlanders 28 (Christchurch); Brumbies 29, Reds 19 (Canberra); Bulls 31, Cats 44 (Pretoria)

1 Mar: Chiefs 27, Crusaders 34 (Hamilton)

2 Mar: Highlanders 45, Sharks 5 (Dunedin); Reds 34, Blues 23 (Brisbane); Bulls 18, Hurricanes 37 (Pretoria); Brumbies 64, Cats 16 (Canberra); Stormers 25, Waratahs 26 (Cape Town)

8 Mar: Highlanders 40, Cats 8 (Dunedin); Stormers 40, Hurricanes 13 (Pretoria); Brumbies 38, Sharks 8 (Canberra)

9 Mar: Crusaders 30, Blues 11 (Christchurch); Reds 27, Chiefs 13 (Brisbane); Bulls 19, Waratahs 51 (Pretoria)

15 Mar: Hurricanes 40, Sharks 17 (Wellington)

16 Mar: Waratahs 44, Cats 21 (Sydney); Bulls 35, Brumbies 45 (Pretoria); Stormers 20, Highlanders 21 (Cape Town)

17 Mar: Reds 27, Crusaders 34 (Brisbane)

22 Mar: Hurricanes 30, Cats 21 (Wellington); Bulls 17, Highlanders 54 (Pretoria)

23 Mar: Blues 37, Chiefs 30 (Auckland); Waratahs 42, Sharks 8 (Sydney); Stormers 15, Brumbies 36 (Cape Town)

29 Mar: Blues 22, Waratahs 20 (Albany)

30 Mar: Hurricanes 22, Reds 18 (Palmerston North); Highlanders 24, Chiefs 29 (Invercargill)

31 Mar: Crusaders 33, Brumbies 32 (Christchurch)

5 Apr: Highlanders 19, Hurricanes 10 (Dunedin)

6 Apr: Crusaders 49, Bulls 15 (Christchurch); Sharks 20, Blues 13 (Durban); Reds 49, Stormers 46 (Brisbane); Cats 25, Chiefs 36 (Bloemfontein)

12 Apr: Crusaders 41, Stormers 21 (Christchuch)

13 Apr: Cats 12, Blues 24 (Bloemfontein); Waratahs 31, Highlanders 13 (Sydney); Sharks 21, Chiefs 18 (Durban); Reds 48, Bulls 12 (Brisbane)

14 Apr: Brumbies 13, Hurricanes 20 (Canberra)

19 Apr: Blues 65, Bulls 24 (Auckland)

20 Apr: Chiefs 33, Stormers 45 (Hamilton); Sharks 34, Crusaders 37 (Durban); Waratahs 19, Brumbies 11 (Sydney); Cats 15, Reds 27 (Johannesburg)

26 Apr: Blues 25, Stormers 6 (Auckland); Brumbies 18, Highlanders 25 (Canberra); Cats 30, Crusaders 37 (Johannesburg)

27 Apr: Waratahs 19, Hurricanes 13 (Sydney); Chiefs 53, Bulls 24 (Hamilton); Sharks 29, Reds 30 (Durban)

3 May: Blues 13, Highlanders 20 (Auckland)

4 May: Hurricanes 20, Crusaders 48 (Wellington); Chiefs 15, Brumbies 42 (Rotorua); Cats 25, Stormers 36 (Johannesburg); Bulls 10, Sharks 23 (Pretoria)

5 May: Reds 31, Waratahs 24 (Brisbane)

10 May: Chiefs 44, Hurricanes 20 (Hamilton); Brumbies 46, Blues 25 (Canberra)

11 May: Highlanders 40, Reds 26 (Dunedin); Crusaders 96, Waratahs 19 (Christchurch); Stormers 31, Bulls 27 (Cape Town); Sharks 38, Cats 11 (Durban)

Super Twelve 2002: Round Robin Table

	P	W	L	Bonus Points	Pts
Crusaders	11	11	0	7	51
Waratahs	11	8	3	7	39
Brumbies	11	7	4	10	38
Highlanders	11	8	3	6	38
Reds	11	7	4	6	34
Blues	11	6	5	5	29
Stormers	11	5	6	7	27
Chiefs	11	4	7	8	24
Hurricanes	11	5	6	3	23
Sharks	11	4	7	4	20
Cats	11	1	10	2	6
Bulls	11	0	11	4	4

Points: win 4; draw 2; four or more tries, or defeat by seven or fewer points 1

First semi-final 18 May Jade Stadium, Lancaster Park, Christchurch
Crusaders 34 (2G 3PG 2DG 1T)   Highlanders 23 (2G 3PG)

Crusaders: L R MacDonald; M Vunibaka, M P Robinson, A J D Mauger,
C S Ralph; A P Mehrtens, J W Marshall; G E Feek, M G Hammett,
G M Somerville, C R Jack, N M C Maxwell, R D Thorne (*captain*),
S M Robertson, R H McCaw *Substitutions:* D N Hewett for Feek (62 mins);
S R Broomhall for Maxwell (71 mins); D P E Gibson for Robinson (75 mins);
C Flynn for Hammett (75 mins); B C Hurst for Marshall (76 mins); J J W Leo'o
for McCaw (76 mins); B A Blair for Vunibaka (78 mins)

Scorers *Tries:* Robinson (2), McCaw *Conversions:* Mehrtens (2) *Penalty Goals:*
Mehrtens (3) *Dropped Goals:* Mehrtens, Mauger

Highlanders: J W Wilson; I Tanivula, T R Nicholas, P Steinmetz, R L L Ropati;
W Walker, B T Kelleher; C H Hoeft, T E Willis, C J Hayman, F Levi,
T S Maling, T C Randell (*captain*), K J Middleton, C Newby *Substitutions:*
S Harding for Newby (6 mins); J M McDonnell for Hoeft (62 mins); P Bowden for
Levi (70 mins); D B Gibson for Kelleher (70 mins)

Scorers *Tries:* Wilson, Walker *Conversions:* Walker (2) *Penalty Goals:* Walker (3)

Referee S J Dickinson (Australia)

Second semi-final 18 May Aussie Stadium, Sydney
Waratahs 10 (1G 1PG)   Brumbies 51 (6G 3PG)

Waratahs: M S Rogers; S N G Staniforth, M C Burke (*captain*), S R Harris,
M Stcherbina; D McRae, C J Whitaker; E P Noriega, B J Cannon, R C Moore,
T M Bowman, V Humphries, D Tuiavi'i, D J Lyons, P R Waugh *Substitutions:*
J Tawake for Tuiavi'i (61 mins); M H M Edmonds for Harris (66 mins); S Talbot
for Bowman (71 mins); T Clark for Whitaker (74 mins); F Cullimore for
Stcherbina (74 mins); H Edmonds for Waugh (74 mins); M Dunning for Noriega
(temp 55 mins to 68 mins)

Scorers *Try:* Staniforth *Conversion:* Burke *Penalty Goal:* Burke

Brumbies: M Bartholomeusz; G S G Bond, S A Mortlock, P W Howard,
A M Walker; S J Larkham, G M Gregan (*captain*); W K Young, J A Paul,
B J Darwin, J B G Harrison, D J Vickerman, O D A Finegan, S Fava, G B Smith
Substitutions: J Huxley for Bartholomeusz (40 mins); D Pusey for Harrison (66
mins); A R Scott for Darwin (69 mins); J Wilson for Mortlock (70 mins); D Flynn
for Paul (71 mins); T S Hall for Gregan (73 mins); T Hora for Vickerman (73
mins)

Scorers *Tries:* Bond (2), Paul, Finegan, Harrison, Howard *Conversions:* Huxley (5),
Walker *Penalty Goals:* Huxley (2), Walker

Referee P D O'Brien (New Zealand)

Final

25 May Jade Stadium, Lancaster Park, Christchurch
Crusaders 31 (2G 3PG 1DG 1T) Brumbies 13 (1G 2PG)

At one stage, ten minutes from time in this liveliest of Super Twelve Finals, only one point separated the sides, but in truth that was the only place where the match was close. In reality the Crusaders raced home, brandishing their skills on a cold, windy night after heavy rain.

The climate was not conducive to good rugby, it would have seemed, but the Crusaders made a mockery of it with a splendid display of running, 15-man rugby. But then they had made a mockery of all other pretenders to the title, including, on this occasion, the noble Brumbies, the 2001 champions, the only non-New Zealand winners of the Super Twelves. Arguably the most telling statistic of the day was that in 80 minutes of playing time the Crusaders missed only two tackles, one a prop's attempt to stop a centre in full stride.

The great Crusader pack may have been short of a really fast loose forward, but they possessed an eight that was full of virtue, especially at lock. Behind them Andrew Mehrtens was able to rule the game from fly-half – a more physical Mehrtens than usual. Out wide they had speed and skill, and a spark of adventure was regularly ignited by Leon MacDonald at full-back.

Playing into the wind in the first half, the Crusaders dominated possession and the whole running of the game, nullifying the Brumbies' phase-control and the strike power of their backs. Stirling Mortlock, so often so incisive in this year's Super Twelve, barely touched the ball in the half.

The Crusaders played the game at speed and with ruthless confidence, unflustered when the Brumbies scored first with a penalty. Mehrtens levelled things in like manner, but by then the Crusaders were already putting the Brumbies to the sword. A sustained attack put Marika Vunibaka over for their first try, which Mehrtens failed to convert – an unusual event worth recording.

Just before half-time Mehrtens kicked a penalty goal and astonishingly hope flickered in the Brumbies' breasts as, into the wind, they played better and began getting their phases going. Andrew Walker kicked a penalty and then, thrillingly, he intercepted a pass from Justin Marshall just inside the Crusaders' half and went galloping off for a try at the posts. Incredibly the Brumbies were only a point behind at 14-13 with only ten minutes to play. That they were that close was more a tribute to their resilience and determination than to a likely outcome to the match.

The Brumbies' challenge ended when Mehrtens dropped a goal and then Aaron Mauger threw a superb pass to send Caleb Ralph over for a try from a line-out. Then, cruelly, just as the Brumbies looked to attack, Ralph intercepted a long pass by Julian Huxley (a first-half replacement when Stephen Larkham suffered an elbow injury) and went skating off for his second try to confirm the Crusaders as champions of Super Twelve.

There was great joy in Jade Stadium as Reuben Thorne hoisted the cup for all to share in the victory. It was the first time in their four triumphs that

Andrew Mehrtens, who spearheaded the Crusaders in their invincible Super Twelve campaign in 2002, is about to engage his threequarter line during the final against the Brumbies at the Jade Stadium, Christchurch, in May.

the Crusaders had won on home turf, before their own fans. It had been a hard final played in an excellent spirit and brilliantly managed by André Watson, who made it a match of few stoppages. In the second half, for example, there were only eleven line-outs, nine scrums and eleven penalties. Praise richly deserved was lavished on the winners and the heroic losers. Both teams would, on their own, have been capable of beating many top international sides.

Crusaders: L R MacDonald; M Vunibaka, M P Robinson, A J D Mauger, C S Ralph; A P Mehrtens, J W Marshall; G E Feek, M G Hammett, G M Somerville, C R Jack, N M C Maxwell, R D Thorne (*captain*), S M Robertson, R H McCaw *Substitutions:* D N Hewett for Feek (50 mins); S R Broomhall for Robertson (74 mins); D P E Gibson for Robinson (74 mins)

Scorers *Tries:* Ralph (2), Vunibaka *Conversions:* Mehrtens (2) *Penalty Goals:* Mehrtens (3) *Dropped Goals:* Mehrtens

Brumbies: M Bartholomeusz; G S G Bond, S A Mortlock, P W Howard, A M Walker; S J Larkham, G M Gregan (*captain*); W K Young, J A Paul, B J Darwin, J B G Harrison, D J Vickerman, O D A Finegan, S Fava, G B Smith *Substitutions:* J Huxley for Larkham (30 mins); P Ryan for Fava (50 mins); D Pusey for Ryan (67 mins)

Scorer *Try:* Walker *Conversion:* Walker *Penalty Goal:* Walker (2)

Referee A Watson (South Africa)

Previous Super Twelve Finals: 1996 Blues 45, Sharks 21 (Auckland); 1997 Blues 23, Brumbies 7 (Auckland); 1998 Crusaders 20, Blues 13 (Auckland); 1999 Crusaders 24, Highlanders 19 (Dunedin); 2000 Crusaders 20, Brumbies 19 (Canberra); 2001 Brumbies 36, Sharks 6 (Canberra); 2002 Crusaders 31, Brumbies 13 (Christchurch)

Super Twelve Draw 2003

21 Feb: Chiefs v Highlanders (Hamilton); Waratahs v Blues Sydney); Cats v Bulls (Bloemfontein); Stormers v Sharks (Cape Town)
22 Feb: Crusaders v Hurricanes (Christchurch); Reds v Brumbies (Brisbane)
28 Feb: Chiefs v Blues (Hamilton)
1 Mar: Highlanders v Stormers (Dunedin); Hurricanes v Bulls (Napier); Crusaders v Reds (Christchurch); Sharks v Brumbies (Durban); Cats v Waratahs (Bloemfontein)
7 Mar: Highlanders v Bulls (Invercargill); Hurricanes v Stormers (Wellington); Cats v Brumbies (Johannesburg)
8 Mar: Chiefs v Reds (Hamilton); Blues v Crusaders (Albany); Sharks v Waratahs (Durban)
14 Mar: Crusaders v Chiefs (Christchurch); Brumbies v Stormers (Canberra); Sharks v Hurricanes (Durban)
15 Mar: Waratahs v Bulls (Sydney); Cats v Highlanders (Johannesburg)
21 Mar: Blues v Reds (Auckland); Waratahs v Stormers (Sydney); Sharks v Highlanders (Durban)
22 Mar: Brumbies v Bulls (Canberra); Cats v Hurricanes (Bloemfontein)
28 Mar: Blues v Brumbies (Auckland)
29 Mar: Highlanders v Crusaders (Dunedin); Hurricanes v Chiefs (Wellington); Waratahs v Reds (Sydney); Cats v Sharks (Johannesburg)
4 Apr: Highlanders v Blues (Dunedin); Reds v Hurricanes (Brisbane)
5 Apr: Waratahs v Crusaders (Sydney); Bulls v Stormers (Pretoria);
6 Apr: Brumbies v Chiefs (Canberra)
11 Apr: Hurricanes v Waratahs (Wellington)

2 Apr: Chiefs v Sharks (Hamilton); Crusaders v Cats (Christchurch); Bulls v Blues (Pretoria); Stormers v Reds (Cape Town)
18 Apr: Crusaders v Sharks (Christchurch); Brumbies v Waratahs (Canberra)
19 Apr: Chiefs v Cats (Rotorua); Hurricanes v Highlanders (New Plymouth); Stormers v Blues (Cape Town); Bulls v Reds (Pretoria)
25 Apr: Highlanders v Brumbies (Dunedin)
26 Apr: Blues v Sharks (Auckland); Reds v Cats (Brisbane); Bulls v Crusaders (Pretoria); Stormers v Chiefs (Cape Town)
2 May: Stormers v Crusaders (Cape Town); Blues v Cats (Auckland)
3 May: Highlanders v Waratahs (Dunedin); Hurricanes v Brumbies (Wellington); Reds v Sharks (Brisbane); Bulls v Chiefs (Pretoria)
9 May: Blues v Hurricanes (Auckland); Brumbies v Crusaders (Canberra)
10 May: Reds v Highlanders (Brisbane); Waratahs v Chiefs (Sydney); Sharks v Bulls (Durban); Stormers v Cats (Cape Town)
17 May: Semi Finals
24 May: FINAL

SUPER TWELVE RECORDS 1996-2002

Record	Detail		Set
Most team points in season	534 by Crusaders	in 13 matches	2002
Most team tries in season	70 by Blues	in 13 matches	1996
Highest team score	96 by Crusaders	96-19 v Waratahs	2002
Biggest team win	77 by Crusaders	96-19 v Waratahs	2002
Most team tries in match	14 by Crusaders	v Waratahs	2002
Most appearances	79 for Sharks	A-H le Roux	1996-2002
	79 for Brumbies	G M Gregan	1996-2002
Most points in matches	883 for Crusaders	A P Mehrtens	1997-2002
Most points in season	206 for Crusaders	A P Mehrtens	1998
Most points in match	50 for Sharks	G Lawless v Highlanders	1997
Most tries in matches	48 for Hurricanes	C M Cullen	1996-2002
Most tries in season	15 for Brumbies	J W C Roff	1997
Most tries in match	4 for Brumbies	J W C Roff v Sharks	1997
	4 for Sharks	G Lawless v Highlanders	1997
	4 for Sharks	C S Terblanche v Chiefs	1998
	4 for Blues	J Vidiri v Bulls	2000
	4 for Blues	D C Howlett v Hurricanes	2002
	4 for Blues	M Muliaina v Bulls	2002
	4 for Crusaders	C S Ralph v Waratahs	2002
Most cons in matches	128 for Waratahs	M C Burke	1996-2002
Most cons in season	39 for Brumbies	S A Mortlock	2000
Most cons in match	13 for Crusaders	A P Mehrtens v Waratahs	2002
Most pens in matches	188 for Crusaders	A P Mehrtens	1997-2002
Most pens in season	43 for Crusaders	A P Mehrtens	1999
Most pens in match	8 for Bulls	J Kruger v Highlanders	1997
Most drops in matches	16 for Crusaders	A P Mehrtens	1997-2002
Most drops in season	4 for Crusaders	A P Mehrtens	1998
	4 for Bulls	J H de Beer	2000
	4 for Crusaders	A P Mehrtens	2002
Most drops in match	3 for Crusaders	A P Mehrtens v Highlanders	1998

THE ORANGE CUP 2002

Battle of Champions goes England's Way

John Griffiths

23 August 2002, Stade Jean Dauger, Bayonne
Biarritz 13 (1G 2PG)   **Leicester 14** (2G)

Leicester began the 2002-03 season where they had left off the previous June: lifting trophies. The Orange Cup, the prize awarded to the winners of the challenge match between the reigning French and English champions, went to the Tigers after an indifferent match that was more pre-season friendly than cut-and-thrust final.

Each side was forced through injuries to field a young and inexperienced back division. Leicester, who were without their first-choice centres, could take heart from the creative play of two of their stand-ins, teenager Danny Hipkiss and Sam Vesty. Hipkiss in particular impressed, playing with the confidence and skill of a seasoned campaigner.

He also inspired Leicester with a try three minutes before the end of a rather insipid first half. Philippe Bernat-Salles, who throughout the match was a danger to the Englishmen, showed in the 33rd minute that he is still among the best finishers in Europe when he opened the scoring from a Biarritz counter-attack after a tapped penalty. Hipkiss then made a classic break for the converted try that levelled the scores, though a Julien Peyrelongue penalty in injury time put Biarritz 10-7 ahead at the break.

Vesty was given his opportunity when Austin Healey was substituted on the hour. Peyrelongue nosed Biarritz six points ahead with a penalty after 65 minutes, but five minutes from time, after a flurry of substitutions, Leicester's never-say-die attitude surfaced among its youngsters. Vesty was first prominent in the 60-metre surge that culminated in a try by Steve Booth near the posts. Then he calmly converted Leicester into their winning one-point lead.

Biarritz might have won the match with the final kick after Freddie Tuilagi was penalised. Stuart Legg, however, missed with the attempt from the touchline to give Leicester their first pre-season victory for three years.

Organisers are hoping that this fixture will become a regular event marking the start of the domestic season in Europe. 'It's a good idea, but like all things you have to find a date that's suitable for everyone. We haven't said yes and we haven't said no either,' commented Howard Thomas, the acting chief executive of England's Premier Rugby, on the eve of the game. Leicester had originally been due to meet Toulouse in a pre-season friendly, but the 2002 clash of the champions was hastily arranged by France's Ligue Nationale de Rugby and sponsored to the tune of £18,000 courtesy of the Orange Group. The fixture attracted more than 5,000 spectators to Bayonne.

Biarritz's home ground, the Stade Municipal d'Aguiléra, was undergoing refurbishment, but both sides were happy to decamp four miles down the road for a match that was broadcast live on satellite television in Britain and France.

Biarritz: M Etcheverria; P Bernat-Salles, G Bousses, J-E Cassin, P Bidabe; J Peyrelongue, D Yachvili; E Menieu, J-M Gonzalez (*captain*), D Avril, J-P Versailles, D Couzinet, S Betsen, D Chouchan, C Milhères *Substitutions:* S Legg for Bidabe (temp 14 to 17 mins and 25 mins); M Fitzgerald for Avril (42 mins); O Roumat for Versailles (51 mins); J Dupuy for Yachvili (63 mins); M Diebolt for Betsen (65 mins); J Campo for Gonzalez (temp 7 to 11 mins and 68 mins); L Mazas for Etcheverria (74 mins)

Scorers *Try:* Bernat-Salles *Conversion:* Peyrelongue *Penalty Goals:* Peyrelongue (2)

Leicester: T Stimpson; J Holtby, F Tuilagi, D Hipkiss, H Ellis; A Healey, J Hamilton; P Freshwater, D West, R Nebbett, M Johnson (*captain*), B Kay, J Kronfeld, M Corry, N Back *Substitutions:* F Tournaire for Nebbett (23 mins); T Tierney for Hamilton (41 mins); G Chuter for West (41 mins); W Johnson for Kay (temp 53 to 68 mins) and for Kronfled (74 mins); S Vesty for Healey (61 mins); S Booth for Stimpson (65 mins); P Short for Corry (74 mins)

Scorers *Tries:* Hipkiss, Booth *Conversions:* Healey, Vesty

Referee J Dumé (France)

Previous Orange Cup Winners: 2001 Toulouse; 2002 Leicester

DOMESTIC RUGBY IN ENGLAND 2001-02

Honours for Leicester and Gloucester: The Zurich Premiership & Championship

Mick Cleary

If it was climax and a sense of drama you wanted then there was little point following Leicester through the Zurich Premiership. They had their fourth successive title all but wrapped up by early New Year. No wobbles, no slumps and no surprises. On the other hand, if quality, class and substance were your fancy, then Leicester gave you plenty to cheer about.

The Tigers' achievement was a landmark one. Below them the Premiership had never been more competitive. All the pre-season forecasts were turned on their head as the likes of Bath, Saracens and, for a time, Wasps struggled. Wasps hauled themselves clear of all the relegation kerfuffle long before the board of England Rugby Ltd took all the sting out of that intriguing contest by declaring that Rotherham were not fit to lace the boots of the Premiership elite, rejecting their bid for promotion on the grounds that they had failed the entry criteria. Sighs of relief all round at Leeds and Bath. Harlequins were in charge of their own breathing by dint of just doing enough to pull clear of the bottom two clubs during that final, frantic week of competition. It was compelling stuff.

Standards had levelled out, or perhaps 'up' would be a more apt preposition, for the likes of Sale, Gloucester and London Irish fully deserved their places in the top four. They may have been distant finishers behind Leicester, with Sale 14 points behind in second place and Gloucester a point behind that, but there was no doubting their right to be there. All three teams, all unheralded to a greater or lesser extent at the beginning of the season, played with brash purpose right through the Premiership campaign. And yet none of them could do enough on a sustained basis to deny Leicester.

It says so much for Leicester that where others have tailed off they have grown stronger. Complacency is simply not in their vocabulary. They have never taken anything for granted and will already be at an advanced stage of planning for the inevitable retirements in the next few years of Martin Johnson, Neil Back, Graham Rowntree and Darren Garforth. Success is not a God-given right and Leicester have made a virtue of that thinking on and off the field. That sense of fighting for every last inch of turf on the pitch, every last detail in coaching and selection, every last spectator through the turnstiles, imbues everything that they do.

An example. Former All Black flanker Josh Kronfeld, one of the great figures of the international game over the last decade, arrived at Welford

2002 was the Year of the Tiger in England. Austin Healey heads for the try line despite the tackle of Ludovic Mercier in the Tigers' 27-10 Zurich Premiership win against Gloucester.

Road in the summer of 2001. The Tigers already had Back and the promising Lewis Moody on their books. Moody thought about a move. Harlequins were interested. But Moody was persuaded to stay by manager Dean Richards on the grounds that he would learn far more in the season from training alongside these guys than playing against them twice a year in someone else's colours. It was an effective sales pitch. Moody not only stayed, he thrived. He was one of the star turns of Leicester's entire season. Kronfeld, plagued by injury, stayed in the background. His presence was nonetheless an important factor.

So too the consistent form of full-back Tim Stimpson, a rock of reliability with the boot as well as threatening when moving forward. Centre Rod Kafer, the replacement for fellow Australian Pat Howard, was not as conspicuous as Howard had been, but his steadying hand was significant.

Leicester did have their occasional alarming moments. They began the defence of their Premiership title with a 19-16 defeat at Newcastle. If they needed any consolation they could have found it on their journey home by calling in at Headingley where newly-promoted Leeds had beaten Bath, 10-6. The season didn't get any better for Bath. For Leicester, it was a different story even though they, too, tasted defeat against Leeds. Deprived of their substantial international contingent, Leicester lost 37-16 there in mid-November.

There were to be only two more setbacks, Leicester going down 36-24 at Wasps and 38-21 at Bristol in early May. By then, though, the Premiership die was well and truly cast.

The rise to prominence of both Sale and London Irish was especially heartening. Given that Sale had not finished above 10th in their three previous Premiership campaigns, there was little reason to suppose that they would improve much on that standing. Their own ambitions were circumspect.

'Our target was to finish around seventh,' said director of rugby, Jim Mallinder. A fount of common sense, Mallinder was one of the season's most impressive figures. Along with coach and former Sale hooker, Steve Diamond, he brought a sense of stability and direction back to Sale. They traded wisely and unobtrusively in the transfer market, bolstering the pack through the signings of Scotland lock Iain Fullarton, prop Kevin Yates and back-row forward Stu Pinkerton from Australia. Sale provided two of the top five try-scorers in the league. Wing Mark Cueto out-scored everyone with 13 tries while wing-cum-full-back Jason Robinson tied alongside Bristol's Felipe Contepomi and Geordan Murphy of Leicester on nine tries.

Sale delivered all-round excellence, spurred by the shrewd promptings of half-backs Bryan Redpath and Charlie Hodgson. Hodgson was the third highest scorer in the Premiership with 273 points, trailing Gloucester's Ludovic Mercier on 334 points with London Irish fly-half Barry Everitt in top slot on 343 points.

Everitt was a vital cog in London Irish's drive to the top. They fell away somewhat after their stunning triumph over Northampton in the Powergen

Cup final. They lost their last four league games, eventually finishing only one point clear of the chasing duo of Northampton and Newcastle in fifth and sixth place. London Irish prided themselves on their close-knit togetherness and relentless work ethic, epitomised by player-coach and former Springbok centre, Brendan Venter. Their pack grafted hard with captain and second-row Ryan Strudwick leading the way. Veteran No 8 Chris Sheasby defied the years while alongside young flanker Declan Danaher announced himself to a wider public.

Northampton's season turned around with the arrival of former All Black coach, Wayne Smith, at Christmas. Up to that point they had won only four games. Their second-half charge saw them take the final Premiership Heineken Cup spot. Newcastle, who finished level with the Saints on 56 points, were to just miss out as Bristol, eighth in the Premiership, qualified by dint of winning through to the final of the Zurich Championship.

That tournament is struggling to find a proper identity. London Irish fielded a weakened team in their first round game against Northampton, much to the disgust of visiting coach, Wayne Smith. Leicester also lost on that opening weekend, Bristol turning them over for the second time in a few weeks. The sponsors' blushes were partially saved when Gloucester avenged their Parker Pen Shield defeat by winning at Sale. With Bristol overcoming Northampton, the west-country match-up ensured a decent crowd of 28,500 for the final.

Final Zurich Premiership Table 2001-02

	P	W	D	L	For	Against	Bonus	Pts
Leicester	22	18	0	4	658	349	11	83
Sale	22	14	1	7	589	517	11	69
Gloucester	22	14	0	8	692	485	12	68
London Irish	22	11	3	8	574	465	7	57
Northampton	22	12	1	9	506	426	6	56
Newcastle	22	12	1	9	490	458	6	56
Wasps	22	12	0	10	519	507	6	54
Bristol	22	9	1	12	591	632	12	50
Harlequins	22	5	3	14	434	507	9	35
Saracens	22	7	0	15	425	671	6	34
Bath	22	7	0	15	311	524	5	33
Leeds	22	6	0	16	406	654	4	28

Four points awarded for a win; two for a draw and none for a defeat.

Previous English Club League Winners: 1987-88 Leicester; 1988-89 Bath; 1989-90 Wasps; 1990-91 Bath; 1991-92 Bath; 1992-93 Bath; 1993-94 Bath; 1994-95 Leicester; 1995-96 Bath; 1996-97 Wasps; 1997-98 Newcastle; 1998-99 Leicester; 1999-2000 Leicester; 2000-01 Leicester; 2001-02 Leicester

Zurich Championship Final

8 June, 2002, Twickenham
Gloucester 28 (1G 7PG)   **Bristol 23** (2G 3PG)

Both teams flopped across the finishing line, strong of heart but jaded in body after the longest of all domestic seasons. Bristol had begun their pre-season training some 13 months earlier. It was no surprise that the two sides were running on empty.

Gloucester came through to win in the closing stages of this Championship Final for the very reason that they had prevailed during the Premiership. There was more composure and patience in their game, fewer tendencies to give away silly penalties. Bristol had clawed themselves right back into contention in the 73rd minute when substitute prop, Paul Johnstone, blazed a 30-metre trail of glory to the try-line. Felipe Contepomi's conversion brought Bristol to within two points at 22-20. But then their Achilles heel showed as they allowed Ludovic Mercier two further shots at goal, both of which he took. The Gloucester fly-half finished with 23 points from seven penalty goals and the conversion of Jake Boer's try just before half-time.

Pumas scrum-half, Agustin Pichot, tried all he knew to get his side moving forward. His smart-thinking brought its own reward three minutes into the second-half when he raced upfield to take a quick tap penalty and bolt past a dozy Gloucester defence.

The Championship play-offs had been much-derided. That view cut little ice with Gloucester skipper, Phil Vickery. 'This will be our trophy in our cabinet in our clubhouse,' said Vickery, proud that the Cherry-and-Whites had something tangible to show for all their fine efforts.

Gloucester: H Paul; D O'Leary, T L Fanolua, R Todd, T D Beim; L Mercier, A C T Gomarsall; P Collazo, O Azam, P J Vickery (*captain*), R J Fidler, E Pearce, J Forrester, P J Paramore, J Boer *Substitutions:* T J Woodman for Forrester (temp 26 mins to 32 mins) and for Collazo (61 mins); C Gillies for Pearce (64 mins); C P Fortey for Azam (75 mins); K Sewabu for Forrester (75 mins); C E Catling for Fanolua (79 mins)

Scorers *Try:* Boer *Conversion:* Mercier *Penalty Goals:* Mercier (7)

Bristol: L Best; J Williams, D L Rees, J S Little (*captain*), P Christophers; F Contepomi, A Pichot; D E Crompton, N McCarthy, J White, G S Archer, A Brown, C L Short, B Sturnham, M Lipman *Substitutions:* R Beattie for Short (41 mins); A Sheridan for Sturnham (50 mins); P D Johnstone for Crompton (64 mins); S Drahm for Williams (71 mins)

Scorers *Tries:* Pichot, Johnstone *Conversions:* Contepomi (2) *Penalty Goals:* Contepomi (3)

Referee R Maybank (RFU)

Previous English Championship Finals: 2001 Leicester 22, Bath 10 (Twickenham); 2002 Gloucester 28, Bristol 23 (Twickenham)

ZURICH PREMIERSHIP CLUB DIRECTORY

Bath

Year of formation 1865
Ground Recreation Ground, London Road, Bath BA2 4BQ
Contacts Web: www.bathrugby.com Tel: Bath (01225) 325200
Colours Blue, white and black shirts; royal blue shorts
Captain 2001-02 Dan Lyle
Zurich Premiership League 2001-02 11th
Zurich Championship Record 2001-02 Did not qualify
Powergen Cup 2001-02 Lost 12-20 to London Irish (6th round)

Zurich League Record 2001-02

Date	Venue	Opponents	Result	Scorers
2 Sep	A	Leeds	6-10	*PG:* Thirlby 2
8 Sep	A	Northampton	7-26	*T:* Cooper *C:* Barkley
15 Sep	H	Saracens	20-27	*T:* Danielli *PG:* Barkley 5
22 Sep	A	Leicester	9-48	*PG:* Barkley 3
13 Oct	H	Sale	20-17	*T:* Perry *PG:* Perry 4 *DG:* Perry
20 Oct	A	Harlequins	8-15	*T:* Williams *PG:* Barkley
11 Nov	H	London Irish	19-11	*T:* Tindall *C:* Perry *PG:* Perry 4
18 Nov	A	Bristol	17-31	*T:* Cooper, Barkley *C:* Perry 2 *PG:* Perry
25 Nov	H	Newcastle	24-9	*T:* Perry, Maggs *C:* Perry *PG:* Perry 4
2 Dec	A	Wasps	10-23	*T:* Thomas *C:* Perry *PG:* Perry
8 Dec	H	Gloucester	12-9	*PG:* Perry 3 *DG:* Balshaw
29 Dec	H	Bristol	15-9	*PG:* Barkley 5
9 Feb	H	Harlequins	18-9	*T:* Catt, Lyle *C:* Barkley *PG:* Barkley *DG:* Perry
23 Feb	A	Sale	14-20	*T:* Dalzell *PG:* Barkley 3
9 Mar	H	Leicester	9-27	*PG:* Barkley 3
17 Mar	A	Saracens	11-33	*T:* Tindall *PG:* Barkley 2
30 Mar	H	Northampton	11-29	*T:* Voyce *PG:* Barkley, Tindall
10 Apr	A	London Irish	15-31	*PG:* Barkley 3 *DG:* Balshaw 2
13 Apr	H	Leeds	23-12	*T:* Danielli, Barkley *C:* Barkley 2 *PG:* Barkley 3
28 Apr	A	Newcastle	9-36	*PG:* Barkley 3
4 May	A	Gloucester	12-68	*T:* Cox, Delve *C:* Barkley
12 May	H	Wasps	22-24	*T:* G Thomas, Long *PG:* Barkley 2, Thirlby 2

Bristol

Year of formation 1888
Ground Memorial Stadium, Filton Avenue, Horfield, Bristol, BS7 0AQ
Contacts Web: www.bristolshoguns.co.uk Tel: Bristol (0117) 3111461
Colours Navy blue and white
Captain 2001-02 Jason Little
Zurich Premiership League 2001-02 8th
Zurich Championship Record 2001-02 Lost 23-28 to Gloucester in final
Powergen Cup 2001-02 Lost 23-37 to Gloucester (6th round)

Zurich League Record 2001-02

Date	Venue	Opponents	Result	Scorers
2 Sep	H	Sale	25-35	*T:* Little *C:* Drahm *PG:* Drahm 6
8 Sep	A	Harlequins	38-32	*T:* Little 2, Salter, Sturnham *C:* Drahm 3 *PG:* Drahm 4
16 Sep	H	London Irish	19-19	*T:* Rees, S Brown *PG:* Drahm 2, Contepomi

23 Sep	H	Leeds	34-29	*T:* Contepomi 2, Christophers *C:* Contepomi 2 *PG:* Contepomi 5
14 Oct	A	Newcastle	20-37	*T:* Little, Carrington *C:* Drahm 2 *PG:* Drahm 2
21 Oct	H	Wasps	43-22	*T:* Contepomi 2, pen try, Nabarro *C:* Contepomi 3, Drahm *PG:* Drahm 3, Contepomi *DG:* Drahm
10 Nov	A	Gloucester	17-51	*T:* Rees, Sheridan *C:* Drahm 2 *PG:* Drahm
18 Nov	H	Bath	31-17	*T:* Archer, McCarthy, S Brown *C:* Drahm 2 *PG:* Drahm 4
25 Nov	A	Northampton	23-20	*T:* Contepomi, Best *C:* Contepomi 2 *PG:* Contepomi 3
2 Dec	H	Saracens	22-25	*T:* Vander *C:* Drahm *PG:* Drahm 5
8 Dec	A	Leicester	19-26	*T:* Contepomi *C:* Best *PG:* Contepomi 3 *DG:* Contepomi
29 Dec	A	Bath	9-15	*PG:* Contepomi 3
10 Feb	A	Wasps	16-34	*T:* Christophers *C:* Contepomi *PG:* Contepomi 3
24 Feb	H	Newcastle	33-17	*T:* Vander, White, Christophers, Williams *C:* Drahm 2 *PG:* Drahm 3
10 Mar	A	Leeds	6-24	*PG:* Contepomi *DG:* Contepomi
16 Mar	A	London Irish	13-24	*T:* Rees *C:* Contepomi *PG:* Contepomi 2
31 Mar	H	Harlequins	43-27	*T:* Christophers 2, Contepomi, Best, Sheridan, Higgins *C:* Contepomi 5 *PG:* Contepomi
13 Apl	A	Sale	47-53	*T:* Best, Rees, Little, Lipman, Drahm *C:* Contepomi 3, Drahm 2 *PG:* Contepomi 4
21 Apl	H	Gloucester	40-41	*T:* Christophers, Contepomi, Best, Williams *C:* Contepomi 4 *PG:* Contepomi 4
5 May	H	Leicester	38-21	*T:* Christophers, Contepomi, Little, Higgins *C:* Contepomi 3 *PG:* Contepomi 4
8 May	H	Northampton	27-37	*T:* Rees, Pichot *C:* Contepomi *PG:* Contepomi 4 *DG:* Pichot
12 May	A	Saracens	28-26	*T:* Cadwallader, Daniel, Best *C:* Carrington 2 *PG:* Carrington 2, Contepomi

Zurich Championship Record 2001-02

Date	Venue	Opponents	Result	Scorers
18 May	A	Leicester (¼-finals)	27-13	*T:* Rees, Williams, Lipman *C:* Contepomi 3 *PG:* Contepomi 2
1 Jun	H	Northampton (½-final	32-24	*T:* Contepomi 2 *C:* Contepomi 2 *PG:* Contepomi 6
8 Jun	-	Gloucester (FINAL)	23-28	*T:* Johnstone, Pichot *C:* Contepomi 2 *PG:* Contepomi 3

Gloucester

Year of formation 1873
Ground Kingsholm, Kingsholm Road, Gloucester, GL1 3AX
Contacts Web: www.gloucesterrugbyclub.com Tel: Gloucester (01452) 422422
Colours Cherry and white
Captain 2001-02 Phil Vickery
Zurich Premiership League 2001-02 3rd
Zurich Championship Record 2001-02 Winners – Won 28-23 against Bristol (FINAL)
Powergen Cup 2001-02 Lost 10-25 to London Irish (quarter-final)

Zurich League Record 2001-02

Date	Venue	Opponents	Result	Scorers
1 Sep	H	Northampton	22-9	*T:* Paramore *C:* Mercier *PG:* Mercier 5
8 Sep	A	Saracens	30-34	*T:* Azam, O'Leary *C:* Mercier *PG:* Mercier 6
15 Sep	H	Leicester	18-40	*PG:* Mercier 6
22 Sep	A	Sale	44-21	*T:* Yachvili, Woodman, Pucciariello, Fanolua *C:* Mercier 3 *PG:* Mercier 3 *DG:* Mercier 3

13 Oct	H	Harlequins	33-7	T: Albanese, pen try, Paramore C: Mercier 3 PG: Mercier 3 DG: Mercier
21 Oct	A	London Irish	15-19	PG: Mercier 5
10 Nov	H	Bristol	51-17	T: Catling, Hazell, Paramore, Fortey, Gomarsall, Simpson-Daniel C: Mercier 5, Paul PG: Mercier 3
18 Nov	A	Newcastle	16-18	T: Gomarsall C: Mercier PG: Mercier 3
23 Nov	H	Wasps	43-13	T: Azam 2, pen try, Boer C: Mercier 3, Paul PG: Paul 2, Mercier DG: Mercier 2
1 Dec	H	Leeds	58-17	T: Simpson-Daniel 2, Mercier, Todd, Eustace, Garvey, O'Leary, Paul C: Mercier 5, Paul PG: Mercier 2
8 Dec	A	Bath	9-12	PG: Mercier DG: Mercier 2
29 Dec	H	Newcastle	29-25	T: Eustace, O'Leary, Fanolua C: Paul PG: Paul 4
9 Feb	H	London Irish	29-22	T: Azam, Fanolua C: Mercier 2 PG: Mercier 5
23 Feb	A	Harlequins	18-6	T: Azam, Albanese C: Mercier PG: Mercier 2
9 Mar	H	Sale	42-14	T: Paramore, Pucciariello, Gomarsall, Simpson-Daniel, Forrester C: Mercier 4 PG: Mercier 3
16 Mar	A	Leicester	10-27	T: Mercier C: Mercier PG: Mercier
30 Mar	H	Saracens	36-13	T: Todd, Fanolua, Gomarsall C: Mercier 2, Paul PG: Mercier 5
10 Apr	A	Wasps	9-44	PG: Mercier 3
13 Apr	A	Northampton	21-58	T: Paramore, Sewabu C: Mercier PG: Mercier 2 DG: Mercier
21 Apr	A	Bristol	41-40	T: Paramore 2, Sewabu, Gomarsall, Vickery C: Mercier 2 PG: Mercier 2 DG: Mercier 2
4 May	H	Bath	68-12	T: Simpson-Daniel 3, Fanolua 2, Paramore, Todd, Collard, Paul C: Mercier 7 PG: Mercier 2 DG: Mercier
12 May	A	Leeds	50-17	T: Simpson-Daniel 2, Forrester, Paramore, Woodman, O'Leary, Sewabu C: Mercier 6 PG: Mercier

Zurich Championship Record 2001-02

Date	Venue	Opponents	Result	Scorers
18 May	H	Newcastle (¼-finals)	60-9	T: Todd, Forrester, Beim, Paramore, Vickery, O'Leary, Fanolua, Mercier, Paul C: Mercier 4, Paul 2 PG: Mercier
2 Jun	A	Sale (½-finals)	33-11	T: Sewabu, Gomarsall, Beim C: Mercier 3 PG: Mercier 3 DG: Mercier
8 Jun	-	Bristol (FINAL)	28-23	T: Boer C: Mercier PG: Mercier 7

Harlequins

Year of formation 1866
Ground Stoop Memorial Ground, Langhorn Drive, Twickenham, Middlesex, TW2 7SX
Contacts Web: www.quins.co.uk Tel: 0208 410 6000
Colours Light blue, magenta, chocolate, French grey, black and light green; white shorts
Captain 2001-02 David Wilson/Garrick Morgan
Zurich Premiership League 2001-02 9th
Zurich Championship Record 2001-02 Did not qualify
Powergen Cup 2001-02 Lost 27-32 to London Irish (semi-final)

Zurich League Record 2001-02

Date	Venue	Opponents	Result	Scorers
1 Sep	H	London Irish	21-32	PG: Burke 7
8 Sep	H	Bristol	32-38	T: Burke, Luger, Greenstock, Bemand C: Burke 3 PG: Burke 2
16 Sep	A	Newcastle	6-6	PG: Burke DG: Burke
22 Sep	H	Wasps	33-13	T: Moore, Mapletoft C: Burke PG: Burke 7
13 Oct	A	Gloucester	7-33	T: Greenwood C: Mapletoft
20 Oct	H	Bath	15-8	PG: Burke 4, Mapletoft

9 Nov	A	Northampton	13-13	*T:* Gollings *C:* Burke *PG:* Burke 2
16 Nov	H	Saracens	43-6	*T:* Burke, Gollings, Olver, Tamarua *C:* Burke 4 *PG:* Burke 5
23 Nov	A	Leicester	18-23	*PG:* Burke 5 *DG:* Burke
1 Dec	H	Sale	16-23	*T:* Leonard *C:* Burke *PG:* Burke 3
9 Dec	A	Leeds	18-23	*T:* Luger 2 *C:* Burke *PG:* Burke 2
22 Dec	H	Leicester	21-38	*T:* Burke, Bemand *C:* Burke *PG:* Burke 3
30 Dec	A	Saracens	25-39	*T:* Greenwood *C:* Burke *PG:* Burke 5 *DG:* Burke
26 Jan	H	Northampton	16-24	*T:* Bell *C:* Burke *PG:* Burke 3
9 Feb	A	Bath	9-18	*PG:* Burke 2 *DG:* Burke
23 Feb	H	Gloucester	6-18	*PG:* Burke 2
16 Mar	H	Newcastle	33-19	*T:* Olver, White-Cooper, Bell, Sherriff *C:* Burke 2 *PG:* Burke 3
31 Mar	A	Bristol	27-43	*T:* Greenstock 2, pen try, Wood *C:* Burke 2 *PG:* Burke
14 Apr	A	London Irish	18-18	*PG:* Burke 2, Slemen *DG:* Slemen 2, Gollings
26 Apr	A	Wasps	6-16	*PG:* Slemen 2
3 May	H	Leeds	40-16	*T:* Wood 2, Greenstock, Greenwood, Moore *C:* Burke 3 *PG:* Burke 2 *DG:* Burke
12 May	A	Sale	11-40	*T:* Moore *PG:* Burke, Mapletoft

Leeds

Year of formation 1991
Ground Headingley Stadium, St Michael's Lane, Headingley, Leeds, LS6 3BR
Contacts Web: www.leedsrugby.com Tel: 01132 786181
Colours White and blue
Captain 2001-02 Carl Hogg
Zurich Premiership League 2001-02 12th
Zurich Championship Record 2001-02 Did not qualify
Powergen Cup 2001-02 Lost 24-41 to Newcastle (quarter-final)

Zurich League Record 2001-02

Date	*Venue*	*Opponents*	*Result*	*Scorers*
2 Sep	H	Bath	10-6	*T:* Mather *C:* Benson *PG:* Benson
9 Sep	A	London Irish	14-42	*T:* Mather, Woof *C:* Benson 2
16 Sep	H	Northampton	6-26	*PG:* Benson 2
22 Sep	A	Bristol	29-34	*T:* Mather, C Murphy, Benson, Scarbrough *C:* Parks 3 *PG:* Parks
14 Oct	H	Saracens	27-14	*T:* Hogg, Scarbrough *C:* Parks *PG:* Parks 3 *DG:* Parks, Clarke
21 Oct	A	Newcastle	8-19	*T:* Jones *PG:* Parks
11 Nov	H	Leicester	37-16	*T:* Emmerson, Kerr, Scarbrough, Palmer *C:* Benson 4 *PG:* Benson 2 *DG:* Parks
18 Nov	A	Wasps	14-64	*T:* Parks, Jones *C:* Parks 2
25 Nov	H	Sale	20-47	*T:* Mackay, Woof *C:* Parks 2 *PG:* Parks 2
1 Dec	A	Gloucester	17-58	*T:* Emmerson, Bachop *C:* Benson 2 *PG:* Benson
9 Dec	H	Harlequins	23-18	*T:* Scarbrough 2 *C:* Van Straaten 2 *PG:* Van Straaten 3
30 Dec	H	Wasps	18-28	*PG:* Van Straaten 6
10 Feb	H	Newcastle	9-19	*PG:* Van Straaten 3
24 Feb	A	Saracens	37-15	*T:* Mulder, Hyde, Hall *C:* Van Straaten 2 *PG:* Van Straaten 6
10 Mar	H	Bristol	24-6	*T:* Emmerson, Scarbrough *C:* Van Straaten *PG:* Van Straaten 4
16 Mar	A	Northampton	14-34	*T:* Scarbrough 2 *C:* Van Straaten 2
31 Mar	A	London Irish	24-29	*T:* Scarbrough 2, Benton *C:* Van Straaten 3 *PG:* Van Straaten
13 Apr	A	Bath	12-23	*PG:* Van Straaten 4

19 Apr	A	Leicester	10-31	*T:* Scarbrough *C:* Van Straaten *PG:* Van Straaten
3 May	A	Harlequins	16-40	*T:* Benton *C:* Van Straaten *PG:* Van Straaten 2 *DG:* Van Straaten
8 May	A	Sale	20-35	*T:* Mulder, Hall *C:* Van Straaten 2 *PG:* Van Straaten
12 May	H	Gloucester	17-50	*T:* Scarbrough, Hall *C:* Van Straaten, Benson *PG:* Van Straaten

Leicester

Year of formation 1880
Ground Welford Stadium, Aylestone Road, Leicester, LE2 7TR
Contacts Web: www.tigers.co.uk Tel: Leicester (0116) 254 1607
Colours Scarlet, green and white shirts; white shorts
Captain 2001-02 Martin Johnson
Zurich Premiership League 2001-02 Winners
Zurich Championship Record 2001-02 Lost 13-27 to Bristol (quarter-final)
Powergen Cup 2001-02 Lost 20-22 to Harlequins (quarter-final)

Zurich League Record 2001-02

Date	Venue	Opponents	Result	Scorers
2 Sep	A	Newcastle	16-19	*T:* Goode, Tuilagi *PG:* Goode 2
8 Sep	H	Wasps	45-15	*T:* Stimpson 2, Murphy 2, Kay, Gelderbloom *C:* Goode 3 *PG:* Stimpson 2 *DG:* Goode
15 Sep	A	Gloucester	40-18	*T:* Moody 2, Booth, Murphy *C:* Stimpson 4 *PG:* Stimpson 2 *DG:* Goode 2
22 Sep	H	Bath	48-9	*T:* Moody, Healey, Goode, Booth, Stimpson *C:* Stimpson 4 *PG:* Stimpson 5
13 Oct	A	Northampton	21-11	*T:* Kafer, Healey *C:* Stimpson *PG:* Stimpson *DG:* Goode, Booth
20 Oct	H	Saracens	36-10	*T:* Booth 2, Kafer, Jelley *C:* Stimpson 2 *PG:* Stimpson 3 *DG:* Goode
11 Nov	A	Leeds	16-37	*T:* Kronfeld *C:* Stimpson *PG:* Stimpson 3
17 Nov	A	Sale	37-3	*T:* Murphy 2, Goode, Booth *C:* Goode 4 *PG:* Goode 3
23 Nov	H	Harlequins	23-18	*T:* Stimpson 2 *C:* Stimpson 2 *PG:* Stimpson 3
2 Dec	A	London Irish	30-15	*T:* Moody, Hamilton, Lloyd *C:* Stimpson 3 *PG:* Stimpson 3
8 Dec	H	Bristol	26-19	*T:* Moody, Booth *C:* Goode, Stimpson *PG:* Stimpson 3, Goode
22 Dec	A	Harlequins	38-21	*T:* Healey 2, M Johnson 2, Murphy *C:* Murphy 4, Stimpson *PG:* Murphy
27 Dec	H	Sale	33-10	*T:* Lloyd, Garforth, Murphy, Booth *C:* Goode, Murphy *PG:* Goode 2 *DG:* Booth
9 Feb	A	Saracens	48-7	*T:* Back, Goode, Kafer, Smith, Booth, Murphy, Tuilagi *C:* Goode 5 *PG:* Goode
23 Feb	H	Northampton	17-6	*T:* Freshwater *PG:* Goode 4
9 Mar	A	Bath	27-9	*T:* Deacon, Smith *C:* Stimpson *PG:* Stimpson 5
16 Mar	H	Gloucester	27-10	*T:* Back, Healey, West *C:* Stimpson 3 *PG:* Stimpson 2
31 Mar	A	Wasps	24-36	*T:* Booth, Tuilagi *C:* Stimpson *PG:* Stimpson 4
13 Apr	H	Newcastle	20-12	*T:* Tuilagi *PG:* Stimpson 5
19 Apr	H	Leeds	31-10	*T:* Back 3, Smith *C:* Stimpson 4 *PG:* Stimpson
5 May	A	Bristol	21-38	*T:* Murphy, Kronfeld, Gelderbloom *PG:* Goode 2
12 May	H	London Irish	34-16	*T:* Lloyd 2, Back, pen try, Corry *C:* Goode 2, Stimpson *PG:* Stimpson

Zurich Championship Record 2001-02

Date	Venue	Opponents	Result	Scorers
18 May	H	Bristol (¼-finals)	13-27	T: Goode C: Goode PG: Goode 2

London Irish

Year of formation 1898
Ground Madejski Stadium, Reading, RG2 0FL
Contacts Web: www.london-irish.com Tel: Reading (0118) 968 1000
Colours Green and black
Captain 2001-02 Ryan Strudwick
Zurich Premiership League 2001-02 4th
Zurich Championship Record 2001-02 Lost 14-38 to Northampton (quarter-final)
Powergen Cup 2001-02 Winners Won 38-7 against Northampton (FINAL)

Zurich League Record 2001-02

Date	Venue	Opponents	Result	Scorers
1 Sep	A	Harlequins	32-21	T: Dawson, Cunningham C: Everitt 2 PG: Everitt 5 DG: Everitt
9 Sep	H	Leeds	42-14	T: Sheasby, Venter, Bates C: Everitt 3 PG: Everitt 7
16 Sep	A	Bristol	19-19	T: Bishop C: Everitt PG: Everitt 4
23 Sep	H	Newcastle	18-22	PG: Everitt 5 DG: Everitt
14 Oct	A	Wasps	20-15	T: Sackey PG: Everitt 4 DG: Everitt
21 Oct	H	Gloucester	19-15	T: Cockle C: Everitt PG: Everitt 4
11 Nov	A	Bath	11-19	T: Sackey PG: Cunningham 2
18 Nov	H	Northampton	48-12	T: Hatley, Edwards, Horak, Danaher, Strudwick, Dawson, Bishop C: Everitt 5 PG: Everitt
22 Nov	A	Saracens	55-13	T: Sackey, Drotské, Thrower, Wright, Sheasby, Bishop, Everitt C: Everitt 4 PG: Everitt 4
2 Dec	H	Leicester	15-30	PG: Everitt 5
8 Dec	A	Sale	19-19	T: Strudwick C: Everitt PG: Everitt 4
23 Dec	H	Saracens	30-23	T: Fahrenson, pen try, Sackey C: Everitt 3 PG: Everitt 3
29 Dec	A	Northampton	15-24	PG: Everitt 4 DG: Everitt
9 Feb	A	Gloucester	22-29	T: Worsley, Sheasby PG: Everitt 2 DG: Everitt 2
24 Feb	H	Wasps	31-17	T: Worsley, Martens, Bishop C: Everitt 2 PG: Everitt 3 DG: Everitt
16 Mar	H	Bristol	24-13	T: Gustard 2 C: Everitt PG: Everitt 4
31 Mar	A	Leeds	29-24	T: Sackey, Everitt, Worsley C: Everitt PG: Everitt 3 DG: Everitt
10 Apr	H	Bath	31-15	T: Horak C: Everitt PG: Everitt 8
14 Apr	H	Harlequins	18-18	T: Horak, Ezulike C: Brown PG: Everitt, Brown
5 May	H	Sale	32-36	T: Horak, Bishop, Delaney, Halvey C: Everitt 3 PG: Everitt 2
8 May	A	Newcastle	28-33	T: Sheasby C: Everitt PG: Everitt 7
12 May	A	Leicester	16-34	T: pen try C: Everitt PG: Everitt 3

Zurich Championship Record 2001-02

Date	Venue	Opponents	Result	Scorers
19 May	H	Northampton (¼-finals)	14-38	T: Pfister, Barrett C: Brown 2

Newcastle

Year of formation 1877, reformed in 1995
Ground Kingston Park, Brunton Road, Kenton Bank Foot, Newcastle upon Tyne NE13 8AF
Contacts Web: www.newcastle-falcons.co.uk Tel: Newcastle (0191) 214 5588
Colours Black
Captain 2001-02 Pat Lam

Zurich Premiership League 2001-02 6th
Zurich Championship Record 2001-02 Lost 9-60 to Gloucester (quarter-final)
Powergen Cup 2001-02 Lost 7-38 to Northampton (semi-final)

Zurich League Record 2001-02

Date	Venue	Opponents	Result	Scorers
2 Sep	H	Leicester	19-16	*T:* Walder *C:* Wilkinson *PG:* Wilkinson 4
8 Sep	A	Sale	11-37	*T:* Vyvyan *PG:* Wilkinson, Walder
16 Sep	H	Harlequins	6-6	*PG:* Wilkinson 2
23 Sep	A	London Irish	22-18	*T:* May *C:* Wilkinson *PG:* Wilkinson 5
14 Oct	H	Bristol	37-20	*T:* Grimes 2, May, Noon *C:* Wilkinson 4 *PG:* Wilkinson 3
21 Oct	H	Leeds	19-8	*T:* Grimes, Stephenson *PG:* Walder 2 *DG:* Walder
11 Nov	A	Wasps	33-30	*T:* Weir, Walder, Noon *C:* Walder 3 *PG:* Walder 4
18 Nov	H	Gloucester	18-16	*PG:* Walder 6
25 Nov	A	Bath	9-24	*PG:* Walder, Richardson *DG:* Walder
2 Dec	H	Northampton	13-28	*T:* May *C:* Walder *PG:* Walder 2
9 Dec	A	Saracens	24-19	*T:* May, Stephenson, Graham *C:* Wilkinson 3 *DG:* Walder
29 Dec	A	Gloucester	25-29	*T:* Wilkinson, pen try, Noon *C:* Wilkinson 2 *PG:* Wilkinson 2
27 Jan	H	Wasps	22-23	*T:* Armstrong *C:* Wilkinson *PG:* Wilkinson 5
10 Feb	A	Leeds	19-9	*T:* Grimes *C:* Wilkinson *PG:* Wilkinson 4
24 Feb	A	Bristol	17-33	*T:* Tuigamala, Stephenson *C:* Wilkinson 2 *DG:* Wilkinson
16 Mar	A	Harlequins	19-33	*T:* Stephenson *C:* Wilkinson *PG:* Wilkinson 2 *DG:* Wilkinson 2
31 Mar	H	Sale	30-10	*T:* Wilkinson, Grimes, May *C:* Wilkinson 3 *PG:* Wilkinson 3
13 Apr	A	Leicester	12-20	*PG:* Wilkinson 4
28 Apr	H	Bath	36-9	*T:* May, Stephenson, Noon, Taione, Tuigamala *C:* Wilkinson 4 *PG:* Wilkinson
5 May	H	Saracens	47-18	*T:* Charlton 2, Stephenson 2, Dunbar, Hurter, Vyvyan *C:* Wilkinson 5, Botham
8 May	H	London Irish	33-28	*T:* Noon 2, Stephenson *C:* Wilkinson 3 *PG:* Wilkinson 4
12 May	A	Northampton	19-24	*T:* Vyvyan *C:* Wilkinson *PG:* Wilkinson 4

Zurich Championship Record 2001-02

Date	Venue	Opponents	Result	Scorers
18 May	A	Gloucester(¼-finals)	9-60	*PG:* Walder 3

Northampton

Year of formation 1880
Ground Franklins Gardens, Weedon Road, St James, Northampton, NN5 5BG
Contacts Web: www.northamptonsaints.co.uk Tel: Northampton (01604) 751543
Colours Black, green and gold
Captain 2001-02 Budge Pountney
Zurich Premiership League 2001-02 5th
Zurich Championship Record 2001-02 Lost 24-32 to Bristol (semi-final)
Powergen Cup 2001-02 Lost 7-38 to London Irish (FINAL)

Zurich League Record 2001-02

Date	Venue	Opponents	Result	Scorers
1 Sep	A	Gloucester	9-22	*PG:* Grayson 3
8 Sep	H	Bath	26-7	*T:* Pountney, Jorgensen *C:* Grayson 2 *PG:* Grayson 3 *DG:* Grayson
16 Sep	A	Leeds	26-6	*T:* Brooks, Cohen *C:* Grayson 2 *PG:* Grayson 4

23 Sep	A	Saracens	20-25	*T:* Thompson, Cohen *C:* Grayson 2 *PG:* Grayson 2
13 Oct	H	Leicester	11-21	*T:* Leslie *PG:* Grayson 2
20 Oct	A	Sale	14-34	*T:* Cohen *PG:* Tucker 3
9 Nov	H	Harlequins	13-13	*T:* Hepher *C:* Hepher *PG:* Hepher 2
18 Nov	A	London Irish	12-48	*T:* Moir, Jorgensen *C:* Tucker
25 Nov	H	Bristol	20-23	*T:* Soden *PG:* Grayson 4, Tucker
2 Dec	A	Newcastle	28-13	*T:* Cohen 2, Brooks, Tucker *C:* Grayson 4
8 Dec	H	Wasps	23-10	*T:* Brooks *PG:* Grayson 5 *DG:* Tucker
29 Dec	H	London Irish	24-15	*T:* Pountney, Jorgensen *C:* Grayson *PG:* Grayson 4
26 Jan	A	Harlequins	24-16	*T:* Cohen, Smith *C:* Grayson *PG:* Grayson 3 *DG:* Grayson
9 Feb	H	Sale	10-20	*T:* Smith *C:* Hepher *PG:* Beal
23 Feb	A	Leicester	6-17	*PG:* Grayson, Beal
16 Mar	H	Leeds	34-14	*T:* Richmond, Beal, Jorgensen, Leslie *C:* Grayson 4 *PG:* Grayson 2
30 Mar	A	Bath	29-11	*T:* Richmond, Brooks, Jorgensen *C:* Grayson *PG:* Grayson 4
13 Apr	H	Gloucester	58-21	*T:* Beal, Jorgensen, Cohen, Smith, Thompson, Phillips, Rennick, Pountney *C:* Grayson 6 *PG:* Grayson 2
27 Apr	H	Saracens	52-27	*T:* Beal, Cohen, Richmond, Leslie, Soden, Hunter *C:* Grayson 5 *PG:* Grayson 4
4 May	A	Wasps	6-17	*PG:* Grayson 2
8 May	A	Bristol	37-27	*T:* Blowers, Shaw, Pountney *C:* Grayson 2 *PG:* Grayson 6
12 May	H	Newcastle	24-19	*T:* Grayson, Soden *C:* Grayson *PG:* Grayson 4

Zurich Championship Record 2001-02

Date	Venue	Opponents	Result	Scorers
19 May	A	London Irish (¼-finals)	38-14	*T:* Beal 2, pen try, Pountney *C:* Grayson 3 *PG:* Grayson 4
1 Jun	A	Bristol(½-finals)	24-32	*T:* Blowers 2, Seely *PG:* Grayson 3

Sale

Year of formation 1861
Ground Heywood Road, Brooklands, Sale, Cheshire, M33 3WB
Contacts Web: www.salesharks.com Tel: 0161 283 1861
Colours Royal blue
Captain 2001-02 Bryan Redpath
Zurich Premiership League 2001-02 Runners-up
Zurich Championship Record 2001-02 Lost 11-33 to Gloucester (semi-final)
Powergen Cup 2001-02 Lost 25-32 to Harlequins (6th round)

Zurich League Record 2001-02

Date	Venue	Opponents	Result	Scorers
2 Sep	A	Bristol	35-25	*T:* Cueto, Harris, Pinkerton, Hanley *C:* Hodgson 3 *PG:* Hodgson 3
8 Sep	H	Newcastle	37-11	*T:* Hodgson, Hanley, Robinson, Anglesea, Black *C:* Hodgson 2, Baxendell *PG:* Hodgson 2
16 Sep	A	Wasps	40-21	*T:* Harris, Cueto, Robinson *C:* Hodgson 2 *PG:* Hodgson 6 *DG:* Hodgson
22 Sep	H	Gloucester	21-44	*T:* Baxendell, Robinson *C:* Hodgson *PG:* Hodgson 3
13 Oct	A	Bath	17-20	*T:* Cueto 2 *C:* Hodgson 2 *PG:* Hodgson
20 Oct	H	Northampton	34-14	*T:* Hodgson, Anglesea, Hanley, Cueto *C:* Hodgson 4 *PG:* Hodgson 2
11 Nov	A	Saracens	25-26	*T:* Going, Anglesea, Hanley, Shaw *C:* Hodgson *PG:* Hodgson
17 Nov	H	Leicester	3-37	*PG:* Going

25 Nov	A	Leeds	47-20	*T:* Hodgson 2, Hanley 2, Cueto, Deane *C:* Hodgson 4 *PG:* Hodgson 3
1 Dec	A	Harlequins	23-16	*T:* Robinson, Hanley *C:* Hodgson 2 *PG:* Hodgson 3
8 Dec	H	London Irish	19-19	*T:* Deane *C:* Hodgson *PG:* Hodgson 4
27 Dec	A	Leicester	10-33	*T:* Robinson *C:* Hodgson *PG:* Hodgson
9 Feb	A	Northampton	20-10	*T:* Robinson *PG:* Hodgson 4 *DG:* Hodgson
23 Feb	H	Bath	20-14	*T:* Robinson, Hodgson, Baxendell *C:* Baxendell *PG:* Hodgson
9 Mar	A	Gloucester	14-42	*T:* Going *PG:* Going 3
16 Mar	H	Wasps	27-22	*T:* Cueto, Turner, Elliott *C:* Hodgson 3 *PG:* Hodgson 2
31 Mar	A	Newcastle	10-30	*T:* Cueto, Redpath
13 Apr	H	Bristol	53-47	*T:* Shaw 3, Robinson, Deane, Jones *C:* Hodgson 4 *PG:* Hodgson 5
19 Apr	H	Saracens	23-3	*T:* Cueto, Anglesea *C:* Hodgson 2 *PG:* Hodgson 3
5 May	A	London Irish	36-32	*T:* Hodgson, Anglesea, Shaw, Robinson, Jones *C:* Hodgson 4 *PG:* Hodgson
8 May	H	Leeds	35-20	*T:* Cueto 2, Redpath, Elliott *C:* Hodgson 3 *PG:* Hodgson 3
12 May	H	Harlequins	40-11	*T:* Cueto 2, Deane, Hodgson, Baxendell, C Marais *C:* Hodgson 5

Zurich Championship Record 2001-02

Date	Venue	Opponents	Result	Scorers
19 May	H	Wasps (¼-finals)	43-27	*T:* Hanley 2, Dickens, Elliott, Sanderson *C:* Hodgson 3 *PG:* Hodgson 4
2 Jun	H	Gloucester(½-finals)	11-33	*T:* Cueto *PG:* Hodgson 2

Saracens

Year of formation 1876
Ground Vicarage Road Stadium, Watford, Hertfordshire, WD17 8ER
Contacts Web: www.saracens.com Tel: Watford (01923) 475222
Colours Black and red
Captain 2001-02 Abdelatif Benazzi/Kyran Bracken
Zurich Premiership League 2001-02 10th
Zurich Championship Record 2001-02 Did not qualify
Powergen Cup 2001-02 Lost 28-30 to Northampton (quarter-final)

Zurich League Record 2001-02

Date	Venue	Opponents	Result	Scorers
2 Sep	A	Wasps	8-12	*T:* Hill *PG:* Smith
8 Sep	H	Gloucester	34-30	*T:* Horan *C:* Smith *PG:* Smith 9
15 Sep	A	Bath	27-20	*T:* Horan, Sparg *C:* Smith *PG:* Smith 5
23 Sep	H	Northampton	25-20	*T:* O'Mahony *C:* Smith *PG:* Smith 5 *DG:* Smith
14 Oct	A	Leeds	14-27	*T:* Winnan *PG:* Smith 3
20 Oct	A	Leicester	10-36	*T:* De Beer *C:* De Beer *PG:* De Beer
11 Nov	H	Sale	26-25	*T:* O'Mahony, Horan *C:* Smith 2 *PG:* Smith 4
16 Nov	A	Harlequins	6-43	*PG:* Smith 2
22 Nov	H	London Irish	13-55	*T:* Harbut *C:* Smith *PG:* Smith 2
2 Dec	A	Bristol	25-22	*T:* Winnan *C:* Smith *PG:* Smith 6
9 Dec	H	Newcastle	19-24	*T:* Johnston *C:* Smith *PG:* Smith 4
23 Dec	A	London Irish	23-30	*T:* O'Mahony, Flatman *C:* De Beer 2 *PG:* De Beer 3
30 Dec	H	Harlequins	39-25	*T:* Horan, Winnan, Roques, Russell, Bracken, Cole *C:* De Beer 3 *PG:* De Beer
9 Feb	H	Leicester	7-48	*T:* Walshe *C:* De Beer
24 Feb	H	Leeds	15-37	*PG:* Smith 5

17 Mar	H	Bath	33-11	*T:* Bracken, Chesney, Arasa *C:* Sorrell 3 *PG:* Sorrell 3 *DG:* Horan
30 Mar	A	Gloucester	13-36	*T:* Arasa *C:* Sorrell *PG:* Sorrell 2
14 Apr	H	Wasps	14-20	*T:* Johnston *PG:* Sorrell 3
19 Apr	A	Sale	3-23	*PG:* Sorrell
27 Apr	A	Northampton	27-52	*T:* Shanklin 2, Harbut *C:* Castaignède 2, Smith *PG:* Smith 2
5 May	A	Newcastle	18-47	*T:* Johnston, Chesney *C:* Smith *PG:* Smith 2
12 May	H	Bristol	26-28	*T:* Smith, Shanklin *C:* Smith 2 *PG:* Smith 3 *DG:* Smith

Wasps

Year of formation 1867
Ground Adams Park, Hillbottom Road, Sands, High Wycombe, Buckinghamshire HP12 4HJ
Contacts Web: www.wasps.co.uk Tel: 01494 769471
Colours Black and gold
Captain 2001-02 Lawrence Dallaglio/Mark Denney
Zurich Premiership League 2001-02 7th
Zurich Championship Record 2001-02 Lost 27-43 to Sale (quarter-final)
Powergen Cup 2001-02 Lost 22-24 to Newcastle (6th round)

Zurich League Record 2001-02

Date	Venue	Opponents	Result	Scorers
2 Sep	H	Saracens	12-8	*PG:* Logan 3 *DG:* Leek
8 Sep	A	Leicester	15-45	*PG:* Logan 5
16 Sep	H	Sale	21-40	*T:* Dowd, Waters *C:* Logan *PG:* Logan 3
22 Sep	A	Harlequins	13-33	*T:* Lewsey *C:* Leek *PG:* Leek, Sampson
14 Oct	H	London Irish	15-20	*PG:* Logan 5
21 Oct	A	Bristol	22-43	*T:* Worsley, Waters, Dowd *C:* Logan, Leek *PG:* Logan
11 Nov	H	Newcastle	30-33	*PG:* A King 9 *DG:* Sampson
18 Nov	H	Leeds	64-14	*T:* Waters 2, Logan 2, Roiser, Greening, Abbott *C:* A King 7 *PG:* A King 4 *DG:* A King
23 Nov	A	Gloucester	13-43	*T:* Abbott *C:* A King *PG:* A King *DG:* A King
2 Dec	H	Bath	23-10	*T:* pen try, Worsley *C:* A King 2 *PG:* Logan 2, A King
8 Dec	A	Northampton	10-23	*T:* Denney *C:* A King *PG:* A King
30 Dec	A	Leeds	28-18	*T:* Dowd 2, Lock *C:* A King 2 *PG:* A King 2 *DG:* A King
27 Jan	A	Newcastle	23-22	*T:* Waters, Leota, Offiah *C:* Logan *PG:* Logan 2
10 Feb	H	Bristol	34-16	*T:* Roiser, Volley, Leek, Leota, Offiah *C:* Leek 3 *PG:* Logan
24 Feb	A	London Irish	17-31	*T:* Logan *PG:* Logan 4
16 Mar	A	Sale	22-27	*T:* Waters *C:* A King *PG:* A King 4 *DG:* A King
31 Mar	H	Leicester	36-24	*PG:* A King 7, Logan 3 *DG:* A King 2
10 Apr	H	Gloucester	44-9	*T:* Lewsey, Leota, Wood, Lock, Abbott *C:* A King 4, Logan *PG:* A King 2 *DG:* A King
14 Apr	A	Saracens	20-14	*T:* Worsley, Jones *C:* A King 2 *PG:* A King, Logan
26 Apr	H	Harlequins	16-6	*T:* Roiser *C:* A King *PG:* Logan *DG:* A King 2
4 May	H	Northampton	17-6	*T:* Shaw *PG:* A King 3, Logan
12 May	A	Bath	24-22	*T:* Sampson, W Green, Offiah *C:* A King 3 *PG:* A King

Zurich Championship Record 2001-02

Date	Venue	Opponents	Result	Scorers
19 May	A	Sale	27-43	*T:* Offiah 2, Sampson, Lewsey *C:* Greening 2 *PG:* Greening

IRISH EYES SMILE: THE POWERGEN CUP

Mick Cleary

20 April 2002, Twickenham
London Irish 38 (5G 1PG)   **Northampton 7** (1G)

They were sending out the search parties long before the end of this enthralling afternoon's entertainment. Gaggles of green, yellow and black figures peered along the A316 wondering just when on earth their team might show up. London Irish may have been good – very good it has be said as they ran in five tries to lift their first ever major trophy in front of a 74,500 sell-out crowd – but Northampton played a substantial part in their own miserable downfall. They failed to show. And how they knew it. They made no attempt to duck the uncomfortable truth.

'Gutted, embarrassed and not sure why we weren't able to handle the occasion,' said Saints coach, Wayne Smith. 'We looked dumb at times.'

They did that. By contrast London Irish played to the outer limits of their potential. They were driven, exuberant, opportunistic, precise and selfless. They gave everything to each other and to the cause, an outlook summed up in player-coach and centre, Brendan Venter.

There was more than mere emotion behind London Irish's victory. There was plenty of method and planning too. They worked on the Northampton line-out, reducing it to a lottery at times. Ryan Strudwick confirmed his status as one of the best filchers of opposition line-out ball in the country. London Irish gave not an inch at the breakdown where they competed furiously for every ball.

There was some sharp-heeled finishing to admire, too. Centre Geoff Appleford scored two smart tries as did wing Justin Bishop, another who encapsulates so much of what makes London Irish tick. Bishop is a great mix of devil and devotion.

London Irish led 24-0 at the break and were able to protect their lead for much of the second half before rounding things off in style with two tries in the final six minutes. Appleford intercepted an attempted Matt Dawson pass to race 80 metres for the first of those late tries. Bishop enjoyed the last hurrah, his eye for an opening seeing him latch on to Barry Everitt's hack through.

Northampton's rare moment of joy came on the hour when Paul Grayson's cross-kick was plucked from the air by Ben Cohen who touched down. Just before that Northampton's Robbie Morris and Mike Worsley from London Irish were sin-binned for throwing punches.

Appleford scored the opening try capitalising on a thrust from Bishop. London Irish's platform owed much to the ball-carrying blasts forward of back-row men Eddie Halvey and Chris Sheasby. Midway through the first half, a typical Halvey charge set up position from where full-back Michael

Horak eventually touched down. Six minutes before the half-time interval, Appleford put Bishop clear. It was an impressive double act. Northampton were nowhere to be seen.

London Irish: M J Horak; P Sackey, G Appleford, B D Venter, J P Bishop; B G Everitt, H Martens; M Worsley, A E Drotské, R J K Hardwick, R Strudwick (*captain*), S M Williams, E O Halvey, C M A Sheasby, D Danaher *Substitutions:* R Kirke for Drotské (46 mins); S Halford for Hardwick (46 mins); D Edwards for Martens (57 mins); R Hardwick for Danaher (temp 64 mins to 69 mins); G Delaney for Williams (73 mins); J Cockle for Halvey (76 mins); R Hoadley for Venter (76 mins); J Brown for Everitt (80 mins)

Scorers *Tries:* Appleford (2), Bishop (2), Horak *Conversions:* Everitt (5) *Penalty Goal:* Everitt

Northampton: N D Beal; C C Moir, P K Jorgensen, J A Leslie, B C Cohen; P J Grayson, M J S Dawson; T J Smith, S Thompson, M J Stewart, J N Ackermann, O Brouzet, A F Blowers, G Seely, A C Pountney (*captain*) *Substitutions:* J Brooks for Moir (40 mins); D Richmond for Thompson (51 mins); R Morris for Stewart (51 mins); J Phillips for Ackermann (57 mins); M J Stewart for Phillips (temp 64 mins to 69 mins); M Tucker for Leslie (76 mins)

Scorers *Try:* Cohen *Conversion:* Grayson

Referee S J Lander (RFU)

Earlier Rounds

The knockout cup has been shunted round the schedules in recent years but has still managed to make its mark. The Premiership clubs were not obliged to enter the competition until the sixth round this year which meant that only four teams from outside the elite could tilt for honours. Orrell, Exeter, Rotherham and Birmingham & Solihull were the four that won through. They made a fair fist of their presence among the big boys causing each and every one of their opponents some measure of discomfort before Premiership might asserted itself.

It was good to see the name of Orrell back in the headlines. The club had fallen down the rankings after its heyday in the 1990s. With the significant backing of Wigan's Dave Whelan, Orrell were stirring once again. The National League Two side troubled Leeds in the northern derby before going down to a 31-22 defeat. When Birmingham & Solihull's Nick Baxter raced away to send his side into a 17-12 lead at Franklin's Gardens thoughts of a major upset flourished. Ben Cohen's two tries tipped the tie in the Saints' favour. Exeter were seen off 27-0 at Welford Road by Leicester, while Rotherham went down 43-17 at Saracens. There was little consolation to be had for the Yorkshire side in a season that saw them denied promotion in the committee rooms rather than on the field. However, their defeat in the Cup saw them through to the Powergen Shield where they eventually defeated Exeter 35-26 in the Twickenham Final, a curtain-raiser to the Cup final itself. Bath's 20-12 loss at home to London Irish was the fourth time in succession that they had fallen at the first hurdle, a real comedown for a club that had won the knockout cup ten times between 1984 and 1996.

There were various dramas played out in the quarter-final and semi-finals. A 55-metre penalty from Harlequins fly-half Paul Burke was enough to snatch a 22-20 victory for his team over Leicester, the fourth time in succession that the Tigers had lost a cup-tie at the Stoop, albeit one of those defeats came against London Irish.

London Irish themselves almost gave away their place in the final, surrendering a 26-0 lead against Harlequins in the semi-final. Quins worked their way back into contention after their opening half-hour mauling and even sneaked ahead 27-26 before two penalties from Barry Everitt saw London Irish through to their first final in 22 years.

Northampton prevailed 38-7 in the other semi-final. Both games had been scheduled to be played back-to-back at the Madejski Stadium, home not only to Reading FC but also London Irish. The other clubs objected to a supposedly neutral venue favouring London Irish. The RFU backed down and a draw from a hat gave home ties to Harlequins and Northampton. The switch was to prove London Irish's only set-back in the competition.

Results

Fourth round: Birmingham-Solihull 35, Wakefield 6; Darlington Mowden Park 27, Manchester 39; Exeter 30, London Welsh 3; Henley 48, Otley 30; Moseley 3, Worcester 50; Newbury 29, Nuneaton 8; Orrell 37, Fylde 9; Rotherham 51, Coventry 27

Fifth round: Birmingham-Solihull 35, Henley 22; Manchester 20, Exeter 30; Newbury 25, Orrell 30; Worcester 19, Rotherham 26

Sixth round: Bath 12, London Irish 20; Bristol 23, Glopucester 37; Leicester 27, Exeter 0; Newcastle 24, Wasps 22; Northampton 32, Birmingham-Solihull 19; Orrell 22, Leeds 31; Sale 25, Harlequins 32 (aet); Saracens 43, Rotherham 17

Quarter-finals: Harlequins 22, Leicester 20; Leeds 24, Newcastle 41; London Irish 25, Gloucester 10; Saracens 28, Northampton 30

Semi-finals: Harlequins 27, London Irish 32; Northampton 38, Newcastle 7

FINAL: (at Twickenham) London Irish 38, Northampton 7

Previous RFU Cup Finals: 1972 Gloucester 17, Moseley 6; 1973 Coventry 27, Bristol 15; 1974 Coventry 26, London Scottish 6; 1975 Bedford 28, Rosslyn Park 12; 1976 Gosforth 23, Rosslyn Park 14; 1977 Gosforth 27, Waterloo 11; 1978 Gloucester 6, Leicester 3; 1979 Leicester 15, Moseley 12; 1980 Leicester 21, London Irish 9; 1981 Leicester 22, Gosforth 15; 1982 Gloucester 12, Moseley 12 (trophy shared); 1983 Bristol 28, Leicester 22; 1984 Bath 10, Bristol 9; 1985 Bath 24, London Welsh 15; 1986 Bath 25, Wasps 17; 1987 Bath 19, Wasps 12; 1988 Harlequins 28, Bristol 22; 1989 Bath 10, Leicester 6; 1990 Bath 48, Gloucester 6; 1991 Harlequins 25, Northampton 13; 1992 Bath 15, Harlequins 12; 1993 Leicester 23, Harlequins 16; 1994 Bath 21, Leicester 9; 1995 Bath 36, Wasps 16; 1996 Bath 16, Leicester 15; 1997 Leicester 9, Sale 3; 1998 Saracens 48, Wasps 18; 1999 Wasps 29, Newcastle 19; 2000 Wasps 31, Northampton 23; 2001 Newcastle 30, Harlequins 27; 2002 London Irish 38, Northampton 7

All played at Twickenham

DOMESTIC RUGBY IN SCOTLAND 2001-02

Borders' Clean Sweep In Inter-District Championship

Bill McMurtrie

Scottish Borders Reivers won all four matches in lifting the Inter-District Championship trophy for the first time since 1993. On their way to their clean sweep they ran in no fewer than 19 tries, 10 of them in a 60-0 victory against Edinburgh.

Once the Borderers had opened their campaign with a 21-6 win against trophy-holders the Scottish Exiles they had the taste for success, though they had to wait five months before they could finish the meal. The victory against the Exiles was before Christmas, but it was late spring before the Reivers notched up victories against Edinburgh, Glasgow, and Caledonia on successive Wednesdays in April and May.

Only Glasgow gave Borders real alarms, and it was by just one point – 23-22 – that the Reivers won that game with James White's late try at Dalziel. The match was so close all the way that only once did either team claim two successive scores, and that was when Glasgow stretched ahead to 22-16 after 66 minutes.

Gavin Dalgleish, the Gala stand-off, dominated Borders' scoring with a try, two conversions, and three penalty goals. However, James Noonan's goal-kicking kept Glasgow in the game. The Reivers led only 13-9 at the interval, and by midway through the second half Glasgow had closed the margin to 16-15. It was then that the home team made a startling break-out for an exhilarating score. Michael Goldie, Glasgow's replacement scrum-half from Ayr, sparked it off with a tapped free-kick close to his own goal-line, and James Adams, the Glasgow Hawks wing, ran in from 85 metres. With less than 10 minutes left, however, a tapped penalty close to the Glasgow line provided the opportunity for White, the Peebles No 8, to drive over for Dalgleish to kick the winning conversion.

A week later, Borders completed their grand slam by beating Caledonia in a Cupar contest that realised 67 points and nine tries. Again Dalgleish scored a try and kicked the goals, this time for 18 points in a 38-29 win. In all, he scored 45 points in three games.

Borders led by only 17-15 at the interval at Cupar, but they made a telling surge early in the second half with tries by Cam Twigley (his second try) and Dalgleish, who threaded a path through crowded Caledonian ranks for his try.

Glasgow's defeat by Borders was their only setback. Not only did they finish in second place, closing with a 29-15 away win against Scottish Exiles, but they retained the Inter-City Cup with a 25-24 victory over Edinburgh in their opening championship match.

Results

19 December, Riverside Park, Jedburgh
Scottish Borders Reivers 21 (1G 3PG 1T)   **Scottish Exiles 6** (2PG)

Borders *Tries:* G Caldwell, A Roxburgh *Conversion:* C J G MacRae *Penalty Goals:* MacRae (3)
Exiles *Penalty Goals:* C Aitken (2)

27 December, Pennypit Park, Prestonpans
Edinburgh 24 (1G 4PG 1T)   **Glasgow 25** (2G 2PG 1T)

Edinburgh *Tries:* R Cook, G Sharp *Conversion:* M Duncan *Penalty Goals:* Duncan (4)
Glasgow *Tries:* R Lothian (2), R Maxton *Conversions:* S Duffy (2) *Penalty Goals:* Duffy (2)

27 December, Murrayfield
Scottish Exiles 16 (1G 3PG)   **Caledonia 3** (1PG)

Exiles *Try:* J Murray *Conversion:* C Aitken *Penalty Goals:* Aitken (3)
Caledonia *Penalty Goal:* B Price

5 January, Millbrae, Ayr
Glasgow 24 (3G 1PG)   **Caledonia 8** (1PG 1T)

Glasgow *Tries:* R Couper, R Good, R McKay *Conversions:* S Duffy (3) *Penalty Goal:* Duffy
Caledonia *Try:* R Bethune *Penalty Goal:* B Price

24 April, Poynder Park, Kelso
Scottish Borders Reivers 60 (5G 5T)   **Edinburgh 0**

Borders *Tries:* S Lightbody (2), C Twigley (2), C Dalgleish, C Farmer, D Irving, A Johnston, C J G MacRae, J Szkudro *Conversions:* G Dalgleish (5)

1 May, Woodside, Aberdeen
Caledonia 37 (3G 2PG 2T)   **Edinburgh 21** (1G 3PG 1T)

Caledonia *Tries:* K Fraser, C Goodall, T Paterson, B Price, A Thomson *Conversions:* M Strang (3) *Penalty Goals:* R Gilmour, Strang
Edinburgh *Tries:* A Turnbull, A Warnock *Conversion:* Warnock *Penalty Goals:* Warnock (3)

1 May, Dalziel Park, Motherwell
Glasgow 22 (1G 4PG 1DG)   Scottish Borders Reivers 23 (2G 3PG)

Glasgow *Try:* J Adams *Conversion:* J Noonan *Penalty Goals:* Noonan (4) *Drop Goal:* N Barrett

Borders *Tries:* G Dalgleish, J White *Conversions:* G Dalgleish (2) *Penalty Goals:* G Dalgleish (3)

7 May, Meggetland
Edinburgh 21 (3G)   Scottish Exiles 54 (7G 1T)

Edinburgh *Tries:* N Clark, C Dove, L Graham *Conversions:* C Gregor (3)

Exiles *Tries:* B Hinshelwood (2), J Rimmer (2), A Mitchell, N Mitchell, C Morley, S Wands *Conversions:* A Mitchell (7)

8 May, Duffus Park, Cupar
Caledonia 29 (3G 1PG 1T)   Scottish Borders Reivers 38 (5G 1PG)

Caledonia *Tries:* C Goodall, A Neilson, D Pickup, M Strang *Conversions:* Strang (3) *Penalty Goal:* Strang

Borders *Tries:* C Twigley (2), C Dalgleish, G Dalgleish, A Stevenson *Conversions:* G Dalgleish (5) *Penalty Goal:* G Dalgleish

19 May, Waterloo
Scottish Exiles 15 (1G 1PG 1T)   Glasgow 29 (2PG 1DG 4T)

Exiles *Tries:* P Baird, A Gill *Conversion:* A Mitchell *Penalty Goal:* Mitchell

Glasgow *Tries:* G Tippett (2), C Shaw, S Swindall *Penalty Goals:* C Little, J Noonan *Drop Goal:* S Duffy

Final Table:

	P	W	D	L	For	Against	Tries	Bonus	Pts
Scottish Borders Reivers	4	4	0	0	142	57	19	2	18
Glasgow	4	3	0	1	100	70	11	2	14
Scottish Exiles	4	2	0	2	91	74	11	1	9
Caledonia	4	1	0	3	77	99	10	2	6
Edinburgh	4	0	0	4	66	176	7	1	1

Points: win 4; draw 2; four or more tries or defeat by seven points or fewer 1

SCOTTISH SUPER DISTRICTS DIRECTORY

Edinburgh Rugby

Year of formation 1998
Ground Myreside, Edinburgh
Contacts Web: www.edinburghrugby.com Tel: Edinburgh (0131) 346 5252
Colours Black, red and white
Captain 2001-02 Graeme Burns
Welsh Scottish League 2001-02 6th

Welsh Scottish League Record 2001-02

Date	Venue	Opponents	Result	Scorers
28 Aug	H	Neath	20-32	*T:* Murray, Sharman *C:* Hodge 2 *PG:* Hodge, Ross
1 Sep	A	Newport	11-29	*T:* Hodge *PG:* Hodge 2
7 Sep	H	Caerphilly	27-20	*T:* Utterson, Leslie *C:* Hodge *PG:* Hodge 3 *DG:* Hodge 2
11 Sep	A	Cardiff	24-32	*T:* Paterson, G Dall *C:* Ross *PG:* Ross 3 *DG:* Ross
12 Oct	A	Ebbw Vale	10-15	*T:* Dunlea *C:* Hodge *PG:* Hodge
19 Oct	H	Pontypridd	13-11	*T:* Ross *C:* Ross *PG:* Ross 2
7 Dec	H	Bridgend	27-22	*T:* Paterson 2, Di Rollo, Whittingham *C:* Hodge 2 *PG:* Hodge
15 Dec	A	Llanelli	17-42	*T:* Utterson, Laney *C:* Hodge, Paterson *PG:* Paterson
21 Dec	H	Swansea	51-18	*T:* Paterson 2, Utterson, Hodge, Blackadder *C:* Hodge 3, Lee *PG:* Hodge 5, Ross
29 Dec	A	Caerphilly	35-21	*T:* Utterson 2, Paterson, Smith *C:* Hodge 2, Ross *PG:* Hodge 3
8 Feb	H	Newport	19-19	*T:* Paterson *C:* Hodge *PG:* Hodge 4
22 Feb	H	Glasgow	13-13	*T:* Leslie, Lee *PG:* Laney
9 Mar	A	Swansea	27-22	*T:* Laney 3, Blackadder *C:* Ross 2 *PG:* Ross
16 Mar	A	Bridgend	30-53	*T:* Hodge, Hines, Leslie *C:* Hodge 3 *PG:* Hodge 3
29 Mar	A	Glasgow	23-19	*T:* Paterson, Officer *C:* Hodge 2 *PG:* Hodge 2 *DG:* Hodge
19 Apl	H	Cardiff	32-10	*T:* Utterson, Lee, Blackadder, Officer *C:* Hodge 3 *PG:* Hodge 2
23 Apl	H	Ebbw Vale	49-31	*T:* Joiner, Blackadder, Metcalfe, pen try, Jolly, Blair *C:* Ross 5 *PG:* Ross 3
27 Apl	A	Neath	3-36	*PG:* Hodge
3 May	H	Llanelli	40-8	*T:* M Taylor, Lee, Utterson, Paterson, Blackadder *C:* Hodge 3 *PG:* Hodge 2 *DG:* Laney
11 May	A	Pontypridd	27-59	*T:* Utterson 2, Scott, Smith *C:* Hodge 2 *PG:* Hodge

Glasgow Rugby

Year of formation 1998
Ground Hughenden, Glasgow
Contacts Web: www.glasgowrugby.com Tel: Glasgow (0141) 353 3468
Colours Red, dark blue and light blue
Captain 2001-02 Andy Nicol
Welsh Scottish League 2001-02 8th

Welsh Scottish League Record 2001-02

Date	Venue	Opponents	Result	Scorers
29 Aug	A	Bridgend	15-50	T: Craig, McLaren C: Irving PG: Irving
31 Aug	H	Pontypridd	59-14	T: Reid 3, Metcalfe, Steel, McLaren, Hayes, White, Harrison C: Hayes 7
8 Sep	A	Swansea	21-13	T: Hayes, Ross C: Hayes PG: Hayes 2 DG: Hayes
11 Sep	H	Ebbw Vale	58-22	T: McLaren 3, Henderson, Kerr, Hayes, Beveridge, Flockhart C: Hayes 5, Irving PG: Hayes 2
14 Sep	H	Llanelli	15-9	PG: Hayes 5
12 Oct	H	Caerphilly	40-22	T: Reid 2, A Bulloch, Blades, Ross C: Hayes 3 PG: Hayes 3
22 Dec	A	Caerphilly	16-35	T: A Bulloch, Beveridge PG: Hayes 2
19 Jan	A	Cardiff	12-29	PG: Kiddie 4
9 Feb	A	Pontypridd	20-25	T: Henderson, Kerr C: Hayes 2 PG: Hayes 2
22 Feb	A	Edinburgh	13-13	T: A Bulloch C: Hayes PG: Hayes 2
9 Mar	A	Newport	5-55	T: Stuart
15 Mar	H	Neath	20-27	T: Petrie PG: Hayes 5
29 Mar	H	Edinburgh	19-23	T: Fetheridge C: Hayes PG: Hayes 4
10 Apl	H	Bridgend	21-16	T: Henderson, Metcalfe C: Kiddie PG: Howarth, Kiddie 2
13 Apl	A	Neath	8-46	T: Bartlett PG: Howarth
20 Apl	A	Llanelli	14-40	T: Steel PG: Howarth 3
27 Apl	A	Ebbw Vale	37-18	T: Fetheridge 2, MacFadyen 2, Metcalfe C: Hayes 2, Howarth PG: Hayes 2
30 Apl	H	Cardiff	19-22	T: Sinclair C: Hayes PG: Hayes 4
3 May	H	Newport	26-28	T: Kerr, Howarth. Reid C: Hayes PG: Howarth 2, Hayes
10 May	H	Swansea	37-20	T: Sinclair, Steel, Petrie C: Hayes, Howarth PG: Hayes 5 DG: McLaren

HAWICK RETAIN CLUB CHAMPIONSHIP: BT SCOTLAND PREMIERSHIP

Bill McMurtrie

When Hawick won the Scottish club championship in 2001 it ended 14 years of famine. That triumph refreshed their taste for success, and here they were again in 2002 winning the BT Scotland Premier trophy.

In 2001 Hawick had gone through the programme undefeated, with only two draws blotting a clean sheet. This time, however, they did it the hard way. They had to come from behind, winning 11 successive matches, and they made sure of the title only on the last day of the programme. A 32-3 victory at Stirling and a four-try bonus point ensured that the Borderers finished the minimum margin ahead of Boroughmuir.

Moreover, Hawick had to recover from the loss of their guiding hand. Midway through the season Ian Barnes, the former Scotland lock, departed as coach, but his successor, Greig Oliver, slipped easily into the driving seat. The former Scotland scrum-half steered Hawick not only to the league title but also to a double with victory in the cup final.

After seven rounds of the league competition, Hawick were lagging behind Melrose and Boroughmuir. The champions had lost on two visits to Edinburgh, against Heriot's FP and Boroughmuir, and they had been held to a draw by their fellow Borderers, Gala, who were eventually to be relegated along with Kirkcaldy.

Hawick's October defeat at Meggetland was by only two points, 27-25, and much of the damage was done by a young wing, Charlie Keenan, who scored three of Boroughmuir's four tries. That same day Melrose lost their 100% record in a 34-21 home defeat by Gala.

As a result of those games, Melrose and Boroughmuir shared the lead, five points clear of Hawick. A week later, however, Hawick swept past Melrose by 39-3 at Mansfield Park, and the champions went on to win all of their 10 remaining games.

Melrose slipped away out of the running, winning only three more games. One of those, though, was against Boroughmuir at the Greenyards. The scoreline was 22-21, and Melrose snatched victory only with a late try by veteran lock forward Robbie Brown.

Heriot's, champions in the two years before Hawick's return to the podium, scored a notable early victory in their campaign, beating the defending champions 25-18 at Goldenacre. But defeats in successive weeks by Boroughmuir, Melrose and Glasgow Hawks removed the Goldenacre club from the front-runners. Melrose were the next to slide out, leaving Hawick and Boroughmuir to run neck and neck to the tape.

By the time those two met in late February at muddy Mansfield Park, where an army of volunteers had mustered to clear snow from the pitch to ensure the game went ahead, it was effectively the decider. The winners of that match could not be beaten for the title – they could only lose it through their own failures.

Hawick laid down the marker by taking a 22-0 lead after half an hour, with short-range tries by Mike Howe and Craig Dunlea and a powerful run by Keith Davidson for a third. Before the interval Boroughmuir were awarded a penalty try because of obstruction on Rory Couper, and in the second half, with tries by Ben Fisher and Lindsay Graham, they clawed back to 22-all after 76 minutes. But a Neil Stenhouse penalty goal snatched victory for Hawick, who went on to retain the title by taking 30-plus points off Melrose, Hawks, and Stirling in their remaining games.

Peebles, champions of Division Two, moved up to compete in the highest echelon for the first time. Jed-Forest joined them in promotion.

Final BT Scotland Premiership League Table 2001–2002

	P	W	D	L	F	A	Bonus	Pts
Hawick	18	15	1	2	505	284	10	72
Boroughmuir	18	15	0	3	488	291	11	71
Heriot's FP	18	10	0	8	501	330	10	50
Aberdeen GSFP	18	9	0	9	369	393	8	44
Glasgow Hawks	18	8	0	10	379	371	9	41
Melrose	18	9	0	9	325	439	5	41
Stirling County	18	8	0	10	345	385	7	39
Currie	18	7	0	11	393	459	9	37
Gala	18	6	2	10	314	433	4	32
Kirkcaldy	18	1	1	16	234	468	3	9

Points: win 4; draw 2; four or more tries or defeat by seven points or fewer 1

Previous Scottish League Champions: 1973-74 Hawick; 1974-75 Hawick; 1975-76 Hawick; 1976-77 Hawick; 1977-78 Hawick; 1978-79 Heriot's FP; 1979-80 Gala; 1980-81 Gala; 1981-82 Hawick; 1982-83 Gala; 1983-84 Hawick; 1984-85 Hawick; 1985-86 Hawick; 1986-87 Hawick; 1987-88 Kelso; 1988-89 Kelso; 1989-90 Melrose; 1990-91 Boroughmuir; 1991-92 Melrose; 1992-93 Melrose; 1993-94 Melrose; 1994-95 Stirling County; 1995-96 Melrose; 1996-97 Melrose; 1997-98 Watsonians; 1998-99 Heriot's FP; 1999-2000 Heriot's FP; 2000-01 Hawick; 2001-02 Hawick

HAWICK COMPLETE DOUBLE:
THE BT CELLNET CUP
Bill McMurtrie

20 April 2002, Murrayfield
Hawick 20 (2G 2DG)   **Glasgow Hawks 17** (1G 2T) (*after extra time*)

An extra-time drop goal by Gavin Douglas snatched a dramatic victory for Hawick against Glasgow Hawks in a pulsating Murrayfield final. Hawick thus added the BT Cellnet Cup to the Premiership title that they had already retained.

Yet for much of the match it was Hawks who were ahead. They led by 12-3 at half-time, and they won the try-count 3-2. In the end, however, Hawick found the vital score when the chips were down, and they lifted the cup for the first time since the inaugural year, 1996.

It was the first time in the competition's seven years that the final had gone to extra time, and that was highly appropriate for a contest brim-full of entertainment, enterprise and intense commitment. Hawks set the early pace and Hawick rose to the challenge. Hawks, however, did not leave Murrayfield empty-handed – Cammy Little, their evergreen scrum-half-cum-full-back, was awarded the man-of-the-match trophy.

A drop goal not only decided the match, but one also opened the play – by Neil Stenhouse for Hawick. It drew a swift response as Stephen Duffy's long pass off scrummage ball allowed Iain Leighton to send the intruding Little through space on the right, and the full-back put James Adams in from about 25 metres out. Little converted.

Duffy's searing break up the right touchline led to Hawks' second try, with Mark Sitch powering over. It was too far out for Little to convert, but at the end of a wildly fluctuating first half Hawks still held a nine-point lead.

Stenhouse tried to open the second half as he had done the first. Rory McKay charged down the drop-kick, but when Cammy Bruce fielded Duffy's deep cross kick just inside the Hawick half it was the opportunity the Borderers needed. Cross-field passing released Walker on the right for a run-kick-chase that forced a five-metre scrummage from which Stenhouse's long pass sent Colin Turnbull through a wide gap for a try between the posts.

Stenhouse converted, cutting Hawks' lead to 12-10. But Hawick could not press home the impetus as Stenhouse missed three penalties from between 37 and 43 metres' range in the space of four minutes. Hawks came back to stretch their lead after a charge by Richard Maxton up the middle. The position gained allowed the 18-year-old Tom Philip to force his way through a couple of tackles for Leighton to score after 63 minutes.

Little missed the conversion, and their seven-point lead looked fragile when Walker, intruding off the right, was denied close to the left corner by Steve Gordon. Eventually, however, with only five minutes of added time left, Bruce's determination let Walker escape up the right touchline to run round to the posts for a try. Stenhouse's conversion drew the scores level at 17-all.

Craig Hodgkinson, Hawks' substitute full-back, and Stenhouse each missed with a drop kick at goal before the contest had to go to extra time. However, where they failed Douglas succeeded with the drop goal that put Hawick ahead with the last kick of the first spell of extra 10 minutes.

Finals day had opened with Ellon winning the BT Cellnet Bowl by beating Hawick Harlequins 18-6. Kirkcaldy then defeated Stewartry 41-12 in the Shield final.

Hawick: C Turnbull; N Walker, G Douglas, J Houston, C Bruce; N Stenhouse, K Reid (*captain*); J Edwards, M Howe, C Dunlea, S MacLeod, I Elliot, D Landels, N Martin, R Deans *Substitutions:* M Landels for Howe (47 mins); A Gillie for Edwards (65 mins); A Imray for D Landels (73 mins); D Irving for Reid (73 mins); C Murray for Bruce (76 mins); J Parker for Imray (95 mins); D Hames for Turnbull (99 mins)

Scorers *Tries:* Turnbull, Walker *Conversions:* Stenhouse (2) *Drop Goals:* Douglas, Stenhouse

Glasgow Hawks: C Little; J Adams, G Morrison, I Leighton, T Philip; S Duffy, K Sinclair; L McIntyre, C Docherty (*captain*), E Murray, I Smith, S Hutton, R Maxton, R McKay, M Sitch *Substitutions:* S Gordon for Morrison (66 mins); K Horton for Docherty (71 mins); G Hawkes for Adams (71 mins); C Hodgkinson for Duffy (74 mins); G Francis for Sinclair (80 mins); D MacNeil for McIntyre (94 mins), G Mories for Murray (96 mins)

Scorers *Tries:* Adams, Leighton, Sitch *Conversion:* Little
Referee C Muir (SRU)

Results

Third round: Annan 24, East Kilbride 41; Ayr 60, Livingston 3; Berwick 6, Perthshire 13; Biggar 44, Glenrothes 0; Clydebank 5, Boroughmuir 78; Corstorphine 26, Kirkcaldy 18; Dunfermline 23, Dundee HSFP 29; Edinburgh University 47, Musselburgh 30; Fife Southern 25, Selkirk 48; Glasgow Hawks 36, Helensburgh 5; Glasgow Southern 68, St Andrews University 0; Haddington 112, Waysiders/Drumpellier 15; Hawick YM 6, Aberdeen GSFP 76; Heriot's FP 65, Cambuslang 7; Hillhead/Jordanhill 15, Dalziel 32; Langholm 17, Hutchesons'/Aloysians 15; Linlithgow 5, Grangemouth 91; Melrose 69, Lenzie 7; Murrayfield Wanderers 63, Irvine 3; Ross High 27, Edinburgh Academicals 18; St Boswells 14, Jed-Forest 57; Stewartry 10, Currie 42; Stewart's Melville FP 15, Greenock Wanderers 20; Stirling County 28, Glasgow Academicals 9; Stirling University 14, Peebles 45; Strathmore 10, Kelso 30; Watsonians 104, Royal High 14; West of Scotland 30, Duns 7; Whitecraigs 8, Hawick 41; Gordonians 19, Madras College FP 17; Preston Lodge FP 27, Edinburgh Northern 8.

Fourth round: Aberdeen GSFP 87, Dalziel 7; Boroughmuir 132, Perthshire 0; Corstorphine 3, West of Scotland 14; Dundee HSFP 12, Glasgow Hawks 65; Gala 39, Biggar 8; Glasgow Southern 19, Melrose 20; Grangemouth 21, Currie 31; Greenock Wanderers 9, Hawick 46; Haddington 83, Gordonians 7; Heriot's FP 53, Edinburgh University 11; Kelso 57, Murrayfield Wanderers 10; Langholm 20,

Stirling County 46; Peebles 16, Ayr 19; Preston Lodge FP 14, Selkirk 18; Ross High 13, Jed-Forest 44; Watsonians 20, East Kilbride 26.

Fifth round: Ayr 19, Melrose 9; Currie 10, Haddington 6; Gala 21, East Kilbride 8; Hawick 21, Aberdeen GSFP 19; Kelso 7, Heriot's FP 17; Selkirk 9, Jed-Forest 10; Stirling County 7, Glasgow Hawks 30; West of Scotland 6, Boroughmuir 37.

Quarter-finals: Currie 26, Jed-Forest 13; Glasgow Hawks 11, Boroughmuir 10; Hawick 26, Gala 20; Heriot's FP 36, Ayr 17.

Semi-finals: Glasgow Hawks 35, Heriot's FP 10; Hawick 27, Currie 13.

Final: (at Murrayfield): Hawick 20, Glasgow Hawks 17 (after extra time).

Previous SRU Cup Finals: 1996 Hawick 17, Watsonians 15; 1997 Melrose 31, Boroughmuir 23; 1998 Glasgow Hawks 36, Kelso 14; 1999 Gala 8, Kelso 3; 2000 Boroughmuir 35, Glasgow Hawks 10; 2001 Boroughmuir 39, Melrose 15; 2002 Hawick 20, Glasgow Hawks 17.

All played at Murrayfield

DOMESTIC RUGBY IN IRELAND 2001-02

Munster Relieved of the Title: Guinness Inter-Pro Championship

Jonathan McConnell

This 2001-02 Guinness Interprovincial Championship was scheduled to follow the pattern of the previous years, with the four provinces playing each other on a home and away basis. However, Leinster's Celtic League victory and Munster's appearance in the final of both that competition and the Heineken Cup, coupled with the decision to rest members of the Ireland squad at various stages of the season, led to the competition being reduced to a total of only six games.

As a result the championship lost much of its impetus when, after the first two games (which doubled as Celtic League fixtures), there was a break of nearly eight months before the remaining four matches slotted into the final few weeks of the season. By that stage the holders, Munster, were focused chiefly on their European campaign, while Leinster were able to follow on from their Celtic League success to take the title from the southernmost province for the first time for four seasons.

Leinster's campaign had got off to an auspicious start with an emphatic 31-9 win over Ulster at the end of August. The Dublin side were in sparkling form and Denis Hickie's injury-time try not only emphasised the emphatic margin of victory but also produced a four-try bonus point as it added to earlier touchdowns from Malcolm O'Kelly and two from Gordon D'Arcy.

In contrast Ulster, despite the expectations following the appointment of South African Alan Solomons as their new coach, rarely threatened. Three days earlier Munster had also shown their intent for the season with a 40-19 win over Connacht in Limerick. However, despite full-back Jeremy Staunton collecting 30 of his side's points, they failed to completely dominate and were unable to achieve a coveted bonus point.

Fixtures had been scheduled to take place in December and January. But with the Irish management looking to rest players in the preparation for the Six Nations and with Munster and Leinster in Celtic and European play-offs, the Interpros were cancelled and the competition reduced to three rounds.

The resumption, in mid-April, gave Munster a chance to shakedown before their Heineken Cup semi-final. In shockingly wet conditions in Cork, however, they were only able to share a 6-6 draw with Leinster. On the same evening, an Ulster side missing several regulars including Ireland fly-half David Humphreys sneaked an 18-17 win over Connacht in Galway. Despite early tries from Ryan Constable and Bryn Cunningham, Connacht fought back with a superb forward effort and entered the last 15 minutes nursing a slender 17-15 lead. Then, late in the game the Ireland A full-back Paddy Wallace, who was deputising for Humphreys at No 10, slotted over a late penalty to give Ulster their first win of the series.

This left Leinster knowing that, no matter what happened between Ulster and Munster, a win with a bonus point in their final game against Connacht would secure the title. This they duly did – and in some style – scoring six tries in a 49-20 victory. The undoubted free running abilities of the Leinster side that had been so much part of their Celtic League success earlier in the season were again to the fore. There was also a faultless kicking display from Brian O'Meara, switched from scrum-half to fly-half for the evening, and the Celtic League champions were always at least one step ahead of Connacht, who yet again were destined to finish the competition in last place.

With nothing but pride at stake in the final game Munster, who were by then looking towards their European Final against Leicester the following week, trailed Ulster 16-0 after only 20 minutes. A heartening fight back brought Munster the lead with ten minutes remaining, but their hopes were then thwarted by a late Neil Doak try which Paddy Wallace converted. Ulster thus snatched the game and with it secured the runners-up place in the competition.

Final Irish Interprovincial Championship Table 2001–02

Team	P	W	D	L	For	Against	Bonus	Pts
Leinster	3	2	1	0	86	35	2	12
Ulster	3	2	0	1	50	66	0	8
Munster	3	1	1	1	64	48	1	7
Connacht	3	0	0	3	56	107	1	1

Four points for win, two for a draw, one bonus point for four or more tries or defeat by seven or fewer points, and none for a loss

Previous Irish Interprovincial Champions: 1946-47 Ulster; 1947-48 Munster; 1948-49 Leinster; 1949-50 Leinster; 1950-51 Ulster; 1951-52 Ulster; 1952-53 Ulster & Munster (Shared); 1953-54 Ulster; 1954-55 Munster & Leinster (Shared); 1955-56 Ulster & Connacht (Shared); 1956-57 Ulster & Leinster & Connacht (Shared); 1957-58 Munster; 1958-59 Leinster; 1959-60 Munster; 1960-61 Leinster; 1961-62 Leinster; 1962-63 Munster; 1963-64 Leinster; 1964-65 Leinster; 1965-66 Munster; 1966-67 Ulster & Munster (Shared); 1967-68 Ulster; 1968-69 Munster; 1969-70 Ulster; 1970-71 Ulster; 1971-72 Leinster; 1972-73 Leinster & Ulster & Munster (Shared); 1973-74 Munster; 1974-75 Ulster; 1975-76 Leinster & Ulster & Munster (Shared); 1976-77 Ulster; 1977-78 Leinster & Ulster & Munster (Shared); 1978-79 Munster; 1979-80 Leinster; 1980-81Leinster; 1981-82 Leinster; 1982-83 Leinster & Ulster & Munster (Shared); 1983-84 Leinster; 1984-85 Ulster; 1985-86 Ulster; 1986-87 Ulster; 1987-88 Ulster; 1988-89 Ulster; 1989-90 Ulster; 1990-91 Ulster; 1991-92 Ulster; 1992-93 Ulster; 1993-94 Leinster & Ulster & Munster (Shared); 1994-95 Munster; 1995-96 Leinster; 1996-97 Munster; 1997-98 Leinster; 1998-99 Munster; 1999-2000 Munster; 2000-01 Munster; 2001-02 Leinster

IRISH PROVINCES DIRECTORY (IRISH INTERPROVINCIAL CHAMPIONSHIP ONLY)

Connacht

Year of formation 1884
Ground The Sports Ground, Galway, Republic of Ireland
Contacts Web: www.irfu.ie/connacht/connacht.asp Tel: 00353 91 770236
Colours Green, white and black
Captain 2001-02 Mark McConnell
Irish Interprovincial Championship 2001-02 4th

Irish Interprovincial Championship Record 2001-02

Date	Venue	Opponents	Result	Scorers
28 Aug	A	Munster	19-40	*T:* Reddan *C:* Elwood *PG:* Elwood 4
19 Apr	H	Ulster	17-18	*T:* Uijs *PG:* McHugh 4
8 May	A	Leinster	20-49	*T:* Keane, McHugh *C:* Elwood 2 *PG:* Elwood 2

Leinster

Year of formation 1879
Ground Donnybrook, Dublin 4, Republic of Ireland
Contacts Web: www.leinster-rugby.com Tel: 003531 6689599
Colours Blue, white and yellow
Captain 2001-02 Reggie Corrigan
Irish Interprovincial Championship 2001-02 Winners

Irish Interprovincial Championship Record 2001-02

Date	Venue	Opponents	Result	Scorers
31 Aug	H	Ulster	31-9	*T:* D'Arcy 2, O'Kelly, Hickie *C:* Spooner *PG:* Spooner 2 *DG:* Dempsey
19 Apr	A	Munster	6-6	*PG:* Spooner 2
8 May	H	Connacht	49-20	*T:* O'Driscoll 2, McKenna, Keogh, Corrigan, McCullen *C:* O'Meara 4, Campion *PG:* O'Meara 3

Munster

Year of formation 1879
Ground Musgrave Park, Pearse Road, Cork, Ireland/Thomond Park, Limerick, Republic of Ireland
Contacts Web: www.munsterrugby.ie Tel: 00353 21 4323563
Colours Red, navy and white
Captain 2001-02 Mick Galwey
Irish Interprovincial Championship 2001-02 3rd

Irish Interprovincial Championship Record 2001-02

Date	Venue	Opponents	Result	Scorers
28 Aug	H	Connacht	40-19	*T:* Staunton, O'Neill, Horan *C:* Staunton 2 *PG:* Staunton 7
19 Apr	H	Leinster	6-6	*PG:* O'Gara, Holland
10 May	A	Ulster	18-23	*T:* O'Connell, Stringer *C:* O'Gara *PG:* O'Gara 2

Ulster

Year of formation 1880
Ground Ravenhill Grounds, 85 Ravenhill Park, Belfast BT6 0DG, Northern Ireland
Contacts Web: www.ulsterrugby.com Tel: 02890 649141
Colours White
Captain 2001-02 David Humphreys
Irish Interprovincial Championship 2001-02 2nd

Irish Interprovincial Championship Record 2001-02

Date	Venue	Opponents	Result	Scorers
31 Aug	A	Leinster	9-31	PG: Humphreys 2, P Wallace
19 Apr	A	Connacht	18-17	T: Constable, Cunningham C: P Wallace PG: P Wallace 2
10 May	H	Munster	23-18	T: P Wallace, Doak C: P Wallace 2 PG: P Wallace 2 DG: P Wallace

MUNSTER CLUBS TAKE THE SILVERWARE: AIB CHAMPIONSHIP

Jonathan McConnell

As in the previous campaign, Cork Constitution were the team to beat in the AIB All Ireland League Division One regular season. But alas, they failed to convert this position into a title win when they lost out in the play-off final for the second year running.

Much was made of the absence of international and inter-provincial players from their club sides for much of the league competition. Yet many of the top clubs adapted well to this situation by continuing to develop strong squads of young, non-contracted players. As has generally been the pattern since the launch of league rugby, the Munster clubs dominated the competition. The province provided three of the four clubs who contested the play-offs. The other qualifiers for the play-offs were Clontarf, who were making their first appearance in the knock-out stages.

While Cork Constitution, Shannon and Garryowen went about their business to secure places in the play-offs, there were contrasting fortunes for Munster's fourth 'big club', former league winners Young Munster. They finished the season destined for Division Two rugby with only two wins and a total of 12 points – nine behind De La Salle Palmerston (DLSP), who also dropped from the top flight. Young Munster's poor season reached its nadir when only 700 people turned up at Clifford Park to witness a thumping 10-38 defeat at the hands of old rivals Cork Constitution at the turn of the year. Deeply entrenched in a relegation battle at that stage, they were not to win again until the final game of the season when all was already lost.

The third club to flirt with relegation during the season were newcomers County Carlow. Indeed, entering the last round of games either Carlow or DLSP could have made the drop. However, the new boys ensured a second season in the top flight when they achieved a tense 17-16 win over Ballymena thanks to a Billy Murphy conversion with the last kick of the game. DLSP saw their fate sealed when at the same time they were enduring a heavy home defeat at the hands of Galwegians. That left DLSP five points behind Carlow and back in the second tier, a situation they had only just avoided in the previous season.

It was fitting that the top four places went to the sides who had produced the best rugby throughout the season. UCD and former champions St Mary's were also in the hunt for play-off places as the season came to a close, but they were left to rue narrow defeats earlier in the campaign. The students, enjoying their first year in the top flight, lost 18-12 at Cork Con in September while Mary's suffered a 21-19 reverse at home to Dublin rivals Clontarf in December.

The play-off games, which went according to the form book, coincided with the return of several Test players to club action. Constitution ran in seven tries in their 43-17 triumph over fourth-placed Garryowen, while second-placed Shannon were 15-12 winners over Clontarf in a game dominated by kicking.

Despite the gloomy predictions about the future of the competition as the demands of the provinces continue to rob clubs of key players, there was still much to praise throughout the season. As always there was tremendous support for the Munster sides with bumper crowds back in attendance at Shannon and Cork Con for the play-off games. The performances of Clontarf and UCD strengthening the club game in Leinster were also heartening, while Ulster will gain a third club in the top flight with the promotion of Belfast Harlequins at the first attempt after their relegation the previous season.

Final Table

	P	W	D	L	F	A	Bonus	Pts
Cork Constitution	15	11	2	2	314	191	4	52
Shannon	15	11	1	3	359	209	5	51
Clontarf	15	10	1	4	354	225	5	47
Garryowen	15	9	2	4	357	259	5	45
St.Mary's College	15	9	1	5	298	285	5	43
UCD	15	8	1	6	358	379	5	39
Galwegians	15	8	0	7	322	306	6	38
Terenure College	15	8	0	7	294	294	4	36
Blackrock College	15	6	1	8	357	339	8	34
Dungannon	15	6	1	8	283	305	6	32
Ballymena	15	6	0	9	259	281	6	30
Buccaneers	15	5	2	8	297	288	5	29
Lansdowne	15	5	1	9	272	308	5	27
Co Carlow	15	5	1	9	259	383	4	26
DLSP	15	4	0	11	251	407	5	21
Young Munster	15	2	0	13	209	384	4	12

Four points for win, two for a draw and none for a loss

Play-offs

Shannon 15, Clontarf 12; Cork Constiitution 43, Garryowen 17

AIB All Ireland League Final

4 May 2002, Lansdowne Road, Dublin
Cork Constitution 17 (2G 1PG)   Shannon 21 (1G 2PG 1DG 1T)

After two seasons' absence from the province, the AIB All Ireland League title returned to its spiritual home in Munster when Shannon won the play-off final against Cork Constitution. This was a bitter disappointment for Constitution who had finished the regular season in first place and who had also lost at the same stage to Dungannon the previous season. For Shannon, who had entered the game as underdogs, it was their first league title since securing four in a row between 1995 and 1998.

Constitution had overcome Shannon in the normal league season, but it was the Limerick side who came out with all guns blazing in the showpiece final. Playing with the wind they built a 13-point lead in the first 10 minutes thanks to a powerful forward display and the accurate kicking of Tom Cregan, who knocked over two penalties and converted when Colm McMahon charged down a Cork kick to score the opening try.

Despite a series of mistakes when in good attacking positions, Constitution were able to battle their way back into the game through a well worked try for new Ireland cap, John Kelly, which Brian O'Meara converted. Shannon scored next when full-back John Lacey collected a chip ahead to stretch the lead at half-time to 18-7.

The second period saw Con use the elements well as they again mounted a fight back. Firstly O'Meara converted a straightforward penalty and then Brian Walsh charged down Melvin McNamara's clearance for Joey Sheahan to dive over and collect Con's second try. O'Meara's conversion narrowed the gap to a single point, but the arrival of Mick Galwey from the bench seemed to galvanise the Shannon effort as they withstood some immense pressure from Constitution.

Finally they were able to drive back up field through Derek Hegerty and Alan Quinlan, the pack presenting a platform for Niall McNamara to drop a goal which increased the lead to four points and gave them the breathing space they needed to hold on for their fifth title.

Cork Constitution: B Walsh; D Dillon, J Kelly, Cian Mahony, A Horgan; Conor Mahony, Brian O'Meara; I Murray, F Sheahan, J O'Driscoll, D O'Callaghan, M O'Driscoll, J Sheahan, U O'Callaghan, J Murray

Scorers *Tries:* J Kelly, J Sheahan *Conversions:* B O'Meara (2) *Penalty Goal:* B O'Meara

Shannon: J Lacey; T Cregan, M Lawlor, A Thompson, M McNamara; N McNamara, D Hegarty; M Horan, J Blaney, J Hayes, B Buckley, T Hayes, A Quinlan, D Quinlan (*captain*), C McMahon. *Substitution:* M Galwey for Buckley (55 mins)

Scorers *Tries:* C McMahon, J Lacey *Conversion:* T Cregan *Penalty Goals:* T Cregan (2) *Drop Goal:* N McNamara

Referee A C Rolland (IRFU)

DOMESTIC RUGBY IN WALES 2001-02

Llanelli's Title in Enthralling Climax: The Welsh-Scottish League

John Billot

Llanelli went to the Arms Park for their final league fixture on May 10th knowing that if they ended Cardiff's unbeaten home record they would win the Welsh-Scottish League championship title. Failure would allow Newport to scoop the prize. So the scene was arranged for a match of enormous dimensions with 9,000 spectators entranced by the unfolding events on the penultimate day of the League programme.

With Newport back in the frame after losing at Cardiff by 17-14, Rodney Parade supporters travelled to the Arms Park in quite substantial numbers to engage in something they had never done before – cheer for Cardiff! It was a bizarre feature of the most enthralling climax to the League season in Wales. Four teams – Llanelli, Cardiff, Neath and Newport – were in with a shout during the last couple of weeks.

Cardiff, strong favourites at one stage, lost by 24-20 at Swansea where Arwel Thomas kicked 14 points and were left waiting to see if their rivals faltered. Swansea were never involved in the title race, but they rescued a dismal playing record by winning in succession four of their final five fixtures. One of those wins denied Neath the championship.

The Gnoll team were poised for the big celebration if they succeeded at St Helen's on May 7th. After only one defeat in a pulsating sequence of 10 League matches, Gareth Llewellyn's team had to be fancied in their last game. The lead changed five times, but on this occasion the Gnoll forwards flagged. Perhaps they were hit by burn-out. Whatever, it was the Swansea pack who dictated events for victory by 20-16.

Lee Jarvis was Neath's man of the moment yet again, scoring all his side's points with three drop shots and a conversion of his try. In so doing, he surpassed Paul Thorburn's club record of 438 in 1984-85 by aggregating 446 in all competitions. However, Gavin Henson's late dropped goals, following his three penalty shots, and a Darren Morris try, denied the numbed Neath visitors. It did appear the occasion was too much for them.

So the focus switched back to Cardiff. Llanelli had been tapped on the shoulder by the cruel hand of fate 12 days earlier, knocked out of the Heineken Cup semi-final by Leicester by 13-12. Pride had to be restored. Scarlet passion must prevail. It did. But not before Cardiff seemed assured of taking the game as they led by 25-8 with 20 minutes left. With the scores level at 25-all, Iestyn Harris was short with a penalty attempt from inside his half. But Stephen Jones made no mistake with his 48-metre penalty kick in stoppage time and the Stradey men were champions by 28-25 in the most memorable match of the season.

Scott Quinnell, the Llanelli captain, battling through an over-long and gruelling season with knee problems, observed, 'Last year we won nothing, but this year we reached the Heineken Cup semi-final, got to the Principality Cup final [which they were to lose to Pontypridd in another stoppage time decision by 20-17] and now won the Welsh-Scottish League championship. It's been a great journey and maybe it did lack something in terms of what could have been achieved.'

His team possessed more than their fair share of dynamic ball-carriers. Tongan Salesi Finau, the kamikaze runner, explodes out of the blocks and makes a bee-line for tacklers. Martyn Madden is another born to the manner of bouncing would-be tacklers out of his path while Quinnell, of course, is the Emperor of the Charge. Unless he is gang-tackled swiftly then opponents face dire consequences.

However, like most Welsh clubs, Llanelli failed in Scotland. They lost by 15-9 to Glasgow and by 40-8 in Edinburgh. They won't regret the end of the Scottish involvement in the League after just three seasons. The two Scottish regional teams did not prove an attraction in Wales and were costly from a travelling point of view.

Newport, with former Springbok coach Ian McIntosh as their new coach and Simon Raiwalui taking over the leadership from Gary Teichmann, who had returned to South Africa, finished in second place with five defeats, the same as Llanelli. An exciting recruit was Ofisa Tonu'u, the rugged and resourceful former New Zealand/Samoa double international scrum-half. Chris Anthony came on board from Swansea and Mike Voyle from Cardiff, both key forwards in what many rated to be the best pack in Wales.

Neath occupied third place, one point behind Newport, but when they lost successive away matches in mid-season narrowly to Cardiff by 16-12 and a week later to Llanelli by 27-21, their title hopes appeared lost. Their magnificent recovery has been well-documented. Only Newport won in the League at The Gnoll and only Newport (68) scored more tries than Neath's 64. Lee Jarvis was the most significant signing at outside-half while Allan Bateman returned from Northampton and Barry Williams was recruited from Bristol to hook.

Cardiff, with Rudy Joubert, technical adviser to South Africa when they won the World Cup in 1995, as new coach, proved a keen disappointment to their supporters. So much promised and little achieved. They finished in fourth spot. The absence of Neil Jenkins was a significant factor. He did not start a match for Cardiff until May 7th, in the victory over Bridgend, having been out of action with knee problems since the 2001 Lions tour to Australia. The player expected to make good in the outside-half role, Iestyn Harris, enjoyed moments of considerable success; but it was too ambitious to hope the transformation from Rugby League star to similar Union status would prove automatic.

Fifth-placed Swansea found it an unsettling season. Coach John Plumtree resigned in November, by which time they had lost eight of their 13 games, and Paul Moriarty and Tony Clement saw to the duties. Mark Taylor missed most of the season after a knee operation. For the champions of the previous season it was an unhappy campaign.

Pontypridd lost four of their first five games and there was no way back in the League. Their success came in the cup competitions and with coach Lynn Howells rejoining from Cardiff in October and Clive Jones appointed director of rugby, they won the Principality Cup and reached the final of the Parker Pen European Shield.

Bridgend, Ebbw Vale and Caerphilly propped up the table, below Edinburgh and Glasgow, who suffered severely in Wales. The Scottish Districts each won just two of their matches on the road: Edinburgh at Swansea and Caerphilly; Glasgow at Ebbw Vale and Swansea. Bridgend signed Gareth Thomas, Dafydd James and Nathan Budgett among others, but these Wales stars could not inspire a winning formula. Bottom team Caerphilly had to figure in a two-leg play-off with Division One champs Aberavon, and Caerphilly retained Premier Division status with an away success by 17-13 and by 49-14 in the return, in which match Luke Richards provided 24 points.

Final Welsh-Scottish League Table 2001-02

Team	P	W	D	L	For	Against	Tries	Pts
Llanelli	20	15	0	5	583	402	60	45
Newport	20	14	1	5	576	415	68	43
Neath	20	14	0	6	616	366	64	42
Cardiff	20	13	1	6	498	404	56	40
Swansea	20	11	0	9	451	404	42	33
Edinburgh	20	10	2	8	498	512	55	32
Pontypridd	20	9	0	11	441	440	41	27
Glasgow	20	8	1	11	475	527	50	25
Bridgend	20	7	1	12	498	545	46	22
Ebbw Vale	20	5	0	15	407	609	36	15
Caerphilly	20	1	0	19	379	798	40	3

Three points awarded for a win; one for a draw and none for a defeat.

Previous Welsh-Scottish League Champions: 1999-2000 Cardiff; 2000-01 Swansea; 2001-02 Llanelli

WELSH CLUB DIRECTORY (WELSH–SCOTTISH LEAGUE CLUBS ONLY)

Bridgend

Year of formation 1878
Ground Brewery Field, Tondu Road, Bridgend, Mid Glamorgan, CF31 4JE, Wales
Contacts Web: www.bridgendrfc.com Tel: Bridgend (01656) 652707
Colours Blue and white hoops
Captain 2001-02 Huw Harries/Gareth Thomas
Welsh-Scottish League 2001-02 9th
Principality Cup 2001-02 Lost 24-46 to Llanelli (quarter-final)

Welsh-Scottish League Record 2001-02

Date	Venue	Opponents	Result	Scorers
17 Aug	H	Pontypridd	19-27	*T:* D Jones *C:* Rees *PG:* Rees 4
25 Aug	A	Swansea	25-16	*T:* Taumalolo, Durston, Devereux *C:* Rees 2 *PG:* Rees 2
29 Aug	H	Glasgow	50-15	*T:* G Thomas 2, Durston, G Jones, Molitika *C:* Rees 5 *PG:* Rees 5
1 Sep	A	Llanelli	3-36	*PG:* Rees
15 Sep	A	Ebbw Vale	18-17	*T:* G Thomas, G Jones *C:* Durston *PG:* Durston 2
22 Sep	H	Newport	26-35	*T:* G Thomas, Ringer *C:* Durston 2 *PG:* Durston 4
20 Oct	H	Neath	19-21	*T:* G Jones, D Jones *PG:* Durston 3
7 Dec	A	Edinburgh	22-27	*T:* Loader *C:* Loader *PG:* Loader 4 *DG:* Warlow
15 Dec	H	Ebbw Vale	28-24	*T:* Havili, G Williams, Molitika *C:* Warlow 2 *PG:* Warlow 3
22 Dec	H	Cardiff	25-25	*T:* Bryan, Ringer, Devereux *C:* Warlow 2 *PG:* Warlow 2
29 Dec	H	Llanelli	31-33	*T:* Durston, James, Havili *C:* Warlow 2 *PG:* Warlow 4
9 Feb	A	Neath	21-35	*T:* G Thomas, van Rensburg *C:* Warlow *PG:* Warlow 3
9 Mar	A	Caerphilly	34-21	*T:* Havili 2, James *C:* Warlow 2 *PG:* Warlow 4 *DG:* Warlow
16 Mar	H	Edinburgh	53-30	*T:* Havili 2, Mustoe, James, G Thomas, Stewart *C:* Warlow 4 *PG:* Warlow 4 *DG:* Warlow
10 Apl	A	Glasgow	16-21	*T:* James *C:* Warlow *PG:* Warlow *DG:* Warlow 2
19 Apl	A	Pontypridd	13-32	*T:* G Williams, van Rensburg *PG:* Warlow
27 Apr	H	Swansea	6-21	*PG:* Warlow 2
4 May	H	Caerphilly	33-24	*T:* G Thomas 2, Loader 2 *C:* Rees, Warlow *PG:* Rees 2 *DG:* Warlow
7 May	A	Cardiff	27-47	*T:* G Thomas 2, Devereux *C:* Warlow 2, Rees *PG:* Warlow 2
11 May	A	Newport	29-38	*T:* James 2, pen try, Joy *C:* Rees 3 *PG:* Rees

Caerphilly ・

Year of formation 1886
Ground Virginia Park, Pontygwindy Road, Caerphilly, CF83 3JA, Wales
Contacts Web: www.caerphillyrfc.co.uk Tel: Caerphilly (02920) 865077
Colours Green and white
Captain 2001-02 David Hawkins
Welsh-Scottish League 2001-02 11th – beat Aberavon in the play-off to retain premier status
Principality Cup 2001-02 Lost 31-46 to Pontypridd (quarter-final)

Welsh-Scottish League Record 2001-02

Date	Venue	Opponents	Result	Scorers
18 Aug	H	Neath	13-43	*T:* J Thomas *C:* Lawrence *PG:* Lawrence 2
25 Aug	A	Newport	22-50	*T:* G Evans 2, Lewis *C:* Richards 2 *PG:* Richards
1 Sep	H	Cardiff	15-49	*T:* Lewis, Workman *C:* Richards *PG:* Richards
7 Sep	A	Edinburgh	20-27	*T:* Morris, Lawrence, Chiltern *C:* Lawrence *PG:* Lawrence
22 Sep	A	Pontypridd	8-38	*T:* G Evans *PG:* Richards
12 Oct	A	Glasgow	22-40	*T:* Hawkins *C:* Richards *PG:* Richards 4 *DG:* Richards
20 Oct	H	Ebbw Vale	25-30	*T:* J Thomas, Morris *PG:* Richards 5
8 Dec	A	Swansea	21-36	*T:* J Thomas, Fitzpatrick *C:* Richards *PG:* Richards 3
15 Dec	H	Newport	20-46	*T:* Tuipulotu, Richards *C:* Richards 2 *PG:* Richards 2
22 Dec	H	Glasgow	35-16	*T:* Hawkins, Lewis, B Watkins, G Thomas *C:* Richards 3 *PG:* Richards 3
26 Dec	A	Neath	33-38	*T:* Greenslade-Jones, Morris, N Watkins, Moody, Richards *C:* Richards 4
29 Dec	H	Edinburgh	21-35	*T:* Morris, Tuipulotu *C:* Richards *PG:* Richards 3
19 Jan	H	Pontypridd	16-36	*T:* Taufahema *C:* Richards *PG:* Richards 3
9 Feb	H	Swansea	3-38	*PG:* Richards
9 Mar	H	Bridgend	21-34	*T:* G Evans, B Watkins *C:* Richards *PG:* Richards 3
16 Mar	A	Llanelli	18-62	*T:* Taufahema, Jacobs *C:* Richards *PG:* Richards, L Griffiths
17 Apl	A	Cardiff	16-27	*T:* Jacobs *C:* Richards *PG:* Richards 3
4 May	A	Bridgend	24-33	*T:* Lewis 3, pen try *C:* Richards 2
7 May	H	Llanelli	6-54	*PG:* L Griffiths 2
10 May	A	Ebbw Vale	20-66	*T:* Morris, Workman *C:* Richards 2 *PG:* Richards 2
Play Offs				
19 May	A	Aberavon	17-13	*T:* Boobyer, Tuipulotu *C:* Richards 2 *PG:* Richards
24 May	H	Aberavon	49-14	*T:* Richards, pen try, Colderley, Grainger, Taufahema, Tuipulotu *C:* Richards 5 *PG:* Richards 3

Cardiff

Year of formation 1876
Ground Cardiff Arms Park, Westgate Street, Cardiff CF10 1JA, Wales
Contacts Web: www.cardiffrfc.co.uk Tel: Cardiff (02920) 302000
Colours Cambridge blue and black
Captain 2001-02 David Young
Welsh-Scottish League 2001-02 4th
Principality Cup 2001-02 Lost 25-31 to Pontypridd (semi-final)

Welsh-Scottish League Record 2001-02

Date	Venue	Opponents	Result	Scorers
24 Aug	A	Neath	14-25	*T:* Hudson, Allen *C:* N Robinson 2
29 Aug	H	Newport	20-14	*T:* Allen, N Robinson *C:* N Robinson 2 *PG:* N Robinson 2
1 Sep	A	Caerphilly	49-15	*T:* Hudson 2, Allen, N Robinson, Woods, Brownrigg *C:* N Robinson 5 *PG:* N Robinson 3
11 Sep	H	Edinburgh	32-24	*T:* Hudson 3, Sullivan *C:* N Robinson 3 *PG:* N Robinson 2
22 Sep	H	Swansea	25-13	*T:* Henry, Howley, Quinnell *C:* N Robinson 2 *PG:* N Robinson 2
20 Oct	A	Llanelli	25-28	*T:* G Williams, J Robinson, Sititi *C:* Harris 2 *PG:* J Robinson, Harris

15 Dec	H	Neath	16-12	*T:* Hudson *C:* Harris *PG:* Harris 2 *DG:* N Robinson
22 Dec	A	Bridgend	25-25	*T:* J Robinson 2, R Williams *C:* Harris 2 *PG:* Harris 2
26 Dec	H	Pontypridd	28-20	*T:* Allen, Humphreys, R Williams *C:* Harris 2 *PG:* Harris 3
29 Dec	A	Ebbw Vale	20-22	*T:* Sullivan, A Jones *C:* N Robinson 2 *PG:* N Robinson 2
19 Jan	H	Glasgow	29-12	*T:* R Williams, Allen, G Powell, Meunier *C:* N Robinson 3 *PG:* N Robinson
9 Mar	H	Ebbw Vale	26-16	*T:* Sullivan, R Williams, M Williams *C:* Harris *PG:* Harris 3
16 Mar	A	Pontypridd	21-18	*T:* Sullivan, N Robinson *C:* Harris *PG:* Harris 3
17 Apl	H	Caerphilly	27-16	*T:* Henry 2, N Robinson *C:* N Robinson 3 *PG:* N Robinson 2
19 Apl	A	Edinburgh	10-32	*T:* N Robinson *C:* Harris *PG:* Harris
26 Apl	A	Newport	17-14	*T:* J Robinson, Sullivan *C:* Harris 2 *PG:* Harris
30 Apl	A	Glasgow	22-19	*T:* Walne, Allen *PG:* N Robinson 4
4 May	A	Swansea	20-24	*T:* R Williams, Harris *C:* Harris, N Robinson *PG:* N Robinson 2
7 May	H	Bridgend	47-27	*T:* R Williams 3, Allen, Woods *C:* Jenkins 5 *PG:* Jenkins 3, Harris
10 May	H	Llanelli	25-28	*T:* J Robinson, Harris, Rogers *C:* Harris 2 *PG:* Harris 2

Ebbw Vale

Year of formation 1880
Ground Eugene Cross Park, Ebbw Vale, Gwent, NP23 5AZ, Wales
Contacts Web: www.ebbwvalerfc.co.uk Tel: Ebbw Vale (01495) 302995
Colours Red, white and green
Captain 2001-02 Chay Billen
Welsh-Scottish League 2001-02 10th
Principality Cup 2001-02 Lost 17-34 to Llanelli (semi-final)

Welsh-Scottish League Record 2001-02

Date	Venue	Opponents	Result	Scorers
18 Aug	A	Llanelli	16-46	*T:* P Williams *C:* Mitchell *PG:* Mitchell 3
24 Aug	H	Pontypridd	18-13	*T:* Weatherley, Wagstaff *C:* Cull *PG:* Cull 2
1 Sep	H	Swansea	21-26	*PG:* Cull 7
11 Sep	A	Glasgow	22-58	*T:* Mitchell 2, Weatherley *C:* Mitchell 2 *PG:* Mitchell
15 Sep	H	Bridgend	17-18	*T:* McKim, Weatherley, Tuipulotu *C:* Cull
12 Oct	H	Edinburgh	15-10	*PG:* Cull 5
20 Oct	A	Caerphilly	30-25	*T:* L Phillips, Jones *C:* Cull *PG:* Cull 5 *DG:* Cull
1 Dec	A	Swansea	14-22	*T:* Edwards *PG:* Cull 3
8 Dec	H	Neath	6-45	*PG:* Cull 2
15 Dec	A	Bridgend	24-28	*T:* Weatherley, Billen, Matthews *C:* Cull 3 *PG:* Cull
22 Dec	A	Pontypridd	13-33	*T:* James *C:* Cull *PG:* Cull 2
26 Dec	A	Newport	25-35	*T:* Cull *C:* Cull *PG:* Cull 6
29 Dec	H	Cardiff	22-20	*T:* Mitchell *C:* Cull *PG:* Cull 5
8 Feb	H	Llanelli	3-16	*PG:* Cull
9 Mar	A	Cardiff	16-26	*T:* Takarangi *C:* Cull *PG:* Cull 3
15 Mar	H	Newport	22-32	*T:* James *C:* Cull *PG:* Cull 5
20 Apl	A	Neath	8-50	*T:* Shorney *PG:* Cull
23 Apl	A	Edinburgh	31-49	*T:* Takarangi 2, Ridley, Matthews *C:* Cull 4 *PG:* Cull
27 Apr	H	Glasgow	18-37	*T:* Shorney, I Thomas *C:* Cull *PG:* Cull 2

10 May H	Caerphilly	66-20	*T:* Takarangi 2, Ellis 2, Ridley, Cull, Bateman, Bootse, Tuipulotu *C:* Cull 8, James *PG:* Cull

Llanelli

Year of formation 1872
Ground Stradey Park, Llanelli, Dyfed SA15 4BT, Wales
Contacts Web: www.scarlets.co.uk Tel: Llanelli (01554) 783900
Colours Scarlet
Captain 2001-02 Scott Quinnell
Welsh-Scottish League 2001-02 Winners
Principality Cup 2001-02 Lost 17-20 to Pontypridd (FINAL)

Welsh-Scottish League Record 2001-02

Date	Venue	Opponents	Result	Scorers
18 Aug	H	Ebbw Vale	46-16	*T:* Proctor 2, N Boobyer, Finau, Wyatt, I Boobyer *C:* G Bowen 2 *PG:* G Bowen 4
1 Sep	H	Bridgend	36-3	*T:* N Boobyer, S Jones, M Jones *C:* S Jones 3 *PG:* S Jones 5
8 Sep	A	Pontypridd	19-17	*T:* Finau *C:* G Bowen *PG:* G Bowen 2 *DG:* N Boobyer, S]ones
11 Sep	H	Swansea	21-27	*PG:* S Jones 7
14 Sep	A	Glasgow	9-15	*PG:* Proctor, S Jones *DG:* S Jones
22 Sep	A	Neath	41-26	*T:* D Jones 2, L Davies, Hodges *C:* G Bowen 3 *PG:* G Bowen 4 *DG:* G Bowen
20 Oct	H	Cardiff	28-25	*T:* Quinnell *C:* S Jones *PG:* C Bowen 5, S Jones 2
7 Dec	H	Newport	17-13	*T:* Proctor *PG:* S Jones 4
15 Dec	H	Edinburgh	42-17	*T:* Proctor 2, M Jones 2, I Boobyer, D Jones *C:* G Bowen 2, S Jones *PG:* G Bowen 2
21 Dec	H	Neath	39-27	*T:* N Boobyer, Finau, Peel, Quinnell *C:* S Jones 2 *PG:* S Jones 4 *DG:* N Boobyer
26 Dec	A	Swansea	9-35	*PG:* G Bowen 3
29 Dec	A	Bridgend	33-31	*T:* N Boobyer 2, S Jones *C:* S Jones 3 *PG:* S Jones 4
19 Jan	A	Newport	9-24	*PG:* G Bowen 3
8 Feb	A	Ebbw Vale	16-3	*T:* Proctor *C:* G Bowen *PG:* G Bowen 3
16 Mar	H	Caerphilly	62-18	*T:* I Boobyer, pen try, Finau, M Jones, G Easterby, J Davies, D Jones, Hodges, McBryde *C:* I Boobyer 4, G Bowen 3 *PG:* G Bowen
16 Apl	H	Pontypridd	26-20	*T:* Thomas 2 *C:* G Bowen 2 *PG:* G Bowen 4
20 Apl	H	Glasgow	40-14	*T:* M Jones 3, L Davies, Finau *C:* G Bowen 3 *PG:* G Bowen 3
3 May	A	Edinburgh	8-40	*T:* M Jones *PG:* S Jones
7 May	A	Caerphilly	54-6	*T:* M Jones 3, B Davies 2, L Davies 2, Wyatt 2, Finau *C:* G Bowen 2
10 May	A	Cardiff	28-25	*T:* M Jones 2, Cardey *C:* S Jones 2 *PG:* S Jones 3

Neath

Year of formation 1871
Ground The Gnoll, Gnoll Park Road, Neath, West Glamorgan SA11 3BU, Wales
Contacts Web: www.neathrfc.co.uk Tel: Neath (01639) 769660
Colours All black with white Maltese cross
Captain 2001-02 Gareth Llewellyn
Welsh-Scottish League 2001-02 3rd
Principality Cup 2001-02 Lost 10-20 to Ebbw Vale (7th round)

Welsh-Scottish League Record 2001-02

Date	Venue	Opponents	Result	Scorers
18 Aug	A	Caerphilly	43-13	*T:* Tiueti, Bateman, S Williams, Francis, Mocelutu *C:* Connor, Jarvis 2 *PG:* Jarvis 4
24 Aug	H	Cardiff	25-14	*T:* Connor *C:* Jarvis *PG:* Jarvis 5 *DG:* Jarvis
28 Aug	A	Edinburgh	32-20	*T:* Connor, Tiueti, Storey, Morris *C:* Jarvis 2, Connor *PG:* Jarvis *DG:* Jarvis
15 Sep	H	Newport	11-19	*T:* Bateman *PG:* Connor 2
22 Sep	H	Llanelli	26-41	*T:* B Williams *PG:* Jarvis 7
20 Oct	A	Bridgend	21-19	*T:* S Williams, Jarvis *C:* Jarvis *PG:* Jarvis 3
8 Dec	A	Ebbw Vale	45-6	*T:* Morris 2, K James, Bateman, B Williams, Connor *C:* Jarvis 3 *PG:* Jarvis 2 *DG:* Jarvis
15 Dec	A	Cardiff	12-16	*PG:* Jarvis 2 *DG:* Jarvis 2
21 Dec	A	Llanelli	27-39	*T:* Tiueti, Jarvis, A Moore *C:* Jarvis 3 *PG:* Jarvis 2
26 Dec	H	Caerphilly	38-33	*T:* Morris 2, K James 2 *C:* Jarvis 3 *PG:* Jarvis 3 *DG:* Jarvis
29 Dec	H	Swansea	31-15	*T:* Mocelutu, S Williams *PG:* Jarvis 5 *DG:* Jarvis 2
9 Feb	H	Bridgend	35-21	*T:* Tiueti 3, Mocelutu, pen try *C:* Jarvis 2 *PG:* Jarvis 2
8 Mar	A	Pontypridd	12-17	*PG:* Jarvis 4
15 Mar	A	Glasgow	27-20	*T:* Llewellyn, Bonner-Evans *C:* Jarvis *PG:* Jarvis 5
13 Apl	H	Glasgow	46-8	*T:* K James 4, Tiueti, G Morris, Howells, B Williams *C:* Jarvis 3
17 Apl	A	Newport	36-20	*T:* Tiueti, B Williams, Horgan *C:* Jarvis 3 *PG:* Jarvis 4 *DG:* Jarvis
20 Apl	H	Ebbw Vale	50-8	*T:* Dewdney 4, Jarvis 2, Mocelutu, Connor *C:* Jarvis 5
27 Apl	H	Edinburgh	36-3	*T:* Dewdney, Horgan, D Jones *C:* Jarvis 3 *PG:* Jarvis 3 *DG:* Jarvis, Connor
3 May	H	Pontypridd	47-14	*T:* Dewdney, Tiueti, Storey, A Moore, Llewellyn *C:* Jarvis 5 *PG:* Jarvis 4
7 May	A	Swansea	16-20	*T:* Jarvis *C:* Jarvis *DG:* Jarvis 3

Newport

Year of formation 1874
Ground Rodney Parade, Newport, Gwent NP9 0UU, Wales
Contacts Web: www.blackandambers.net Tel: Newport (01633) 670690
Colours Black and amber stripes
Captain 2001-02 Simon Raiwalui
Welsh-Scottish League 2001-02 Runners-up
Principality Cup 2001-02 Lost 14-20 to Cardiff (quarter-final)

Welsh-Scottish League Record 2001-02

Date	Venue	Opponents	Result	Scorers
25 Aug	H	Caerphilly	50-22	*T:* Pritchard, Breeze, Howarth, Snow, Anthony, Garvey, Marinos *C:* Howarth 6 *PG:* Howarth
29 Aug	A	Cardiff	14-20	*T:* Pini, Marinos *C:* Howarth, Strange
1 Sep	H	Edinburgh	29-11	*T:* Breeze, Howarth *C:* Howarth 2 *PG:* Howarth 5
15 Sep	A	Neath	19-11	*T:* E Lewis *C:* Howarth *PG:* Howarth 4
22 Sep	A	Bridgend	35-26	*T:* Mostyn, Pritchard, Raiwalui, Forster *C:* Howarth 3 *PG:* Howarth 3
19 Oct	H	Swansea	25-19	*T:* Pini, A Powell *PG:* Howarth 4 *DG:* Howarth
7 Dec	A	Llanelli	13-17	*T:* Marinos *C:* Strange *PG:* Strange 2
15 Dec	A	Caerphilly	46-20	*T:* Mostyn 2, M Watkins 2, Pritchard, Howarth, Anthony *C:* Howarth 4 *PG:* Howarth
26 Dec	H	Ebbw Vale	35-25	*T:* J Powell, Mostyn, Tonu'u, Young *C:* Howarth 2, Strange *PG:* Howarth 3

28 Dec	A	Pontypridd	33-6	*T:* Snow 2, Pini, Pritchard, J Forster *C:* Strange *PG:* Strange, Howarth
19 Jan	H	Llanelli	24-9	*T:* Garvey, J Forster *C:* Strange *PG:* Howarth 3, Strange
8 Feb	A	Edinburgh	19-19	*T:* M Watkins, Pini, Tonu'u *C:* Strange 2
9 Mar	H	Glasgow	55-5	*T:* Tonu'u 3, J Forster, M Watkins, Snow, Buxton, Garvey, A Powell *C:* Howarth 5
15 Mar	A	Ebbw Vale	32-22	*T:* A Powell 2, Pini, Mostyn, Marinos *C:* Howarth, Strange *PG:* Howarth
17 Apl	H	Neath	20-36	*T:* Mostyn *PG:* Howarth 3, Strange 2
20 Apl	A	Swansea	13-52	*T:* A Powell *C:* Strange *PG:* Howarth 2
26 Apl	H	Cardiff	14-17	*T:* Mostyn *PG:* Howarth 2 *DG:* Howarth
3 May	A	Glasgow	28-26	*T:* Mostyn 2, Lane *C:* Howarth 2 *PG:* Strange 2, Howarth
8 May	H	Pontypridd	34-23	*T:* J Forster, A Powell, Mostyn, Breeze *C:* Howarth 4 *PG:* Howarth *DG:* Pini
11 May	H	Bridgend	38-29	*T:* J Forster, Snow, Garvey, pen try *C:* Howarth 3 *PG:* Howarth 4

Pontypridd

Year of formation 1876
Ground Sardis Road Ground, Pwllgwaun, Pontypridd, CF37 1HA, Wales
Contacts Web: www.pontypriddrfc.co.uk Tel: Pontypridd (01443) 405006
Colours Black and white hoops
Captain 2001-02 Dale McIntosh
Welsh-Scottish League 2001-02 7th
Principality Cup 2001-02 Winners Won 20-17 against Llanelli (FINAL)

Welsh-Scottish League Record 2001-02

Date	*Venue*	*Opponents*	*Result*	*Scorers*
17 Aug	A	Bridgend	27-19	*T:* Johnson, Davies *C:* Davey *PG:* Davey 4 *DG:* Wyatt
24 Aug	A	Ebbw Vale	13-18	*T:* Wyatt *C:* Davey *PG:* Davey 2
28 Aug	H	Swansea	6-11	*PG:* Davey 2
31 Aug	A	Glasgow	14-59	*T:* Wyatt, McIntosh *C:* Lawson, Sweeney
8 Sep	H	Llanelli	17-19	*T:* Parks *PG:* Sweeney 4
22 Sep	H	Caerphilly	38-8	*T:* Feaunati 3, Wyatt, Bell *C:* Sweeney 2 *PG:* Sweeney 2 *DG:* Wyatt
19 Oct	A	Edinburgh	11-13	*T:* Bryant *PG:* Sweeney 2
14 Dec	A	Swansea	12-3	*PG:* Little 3 *DG:* Little
22 Dec	H	Ebbw Vale	33-13	*T:* Bryant, Cockbain, John *C:* Little 3 *PG:* Little 4
26 Dec	A	Cardiff	20-28	*T:* Davey, Wyatt *C:* Little 2 *PG:* Sweeney, Little
28 Dec	H	Newport	6-33	*PG:* Little 2
19 Jan	A	Caerphilly	36-16	*T:* Parker 2, pen try *C:* Little 3 *PG:* Little 5
9 Feb	H	Glasgow	25-20	*T:* J Lewis *C:* Little *PG:* Little 5, Sweeney
8 Mar	H	Neath	17-12	*T:* Davies *PG:* Little 2, Davey *DG:* Little
16 Mar	H	Cardiff	18-21	*PG:* Davey 6
16 Apl	A	Llanelli	20-26	*T:* Parker 2 *C:* Davey 2 *PG:* Davey 2
19 Apl	H	Bridgend	32-13	*T:* Sweeney 2, Davey, John *C:* Davey 3 *PG:* Davey 2
3 May	A	Neath	14-47	*T:* Nuthall *PG:* Davey 3
8 May	A	Newport	23-34	*T:* Parker, Wyatt, Baber *C:* Little *PG:* Little 2
11 May	H	Edinburgh	59-27	*T:* Wyatt 2, Sweeney 2, Parker 2, Davey, S James, Baber *C:* Sweeney 7

Swansea

Year of formation 1873
Ground St Helen's Ground, Bryn Road, Swansea, West Glamorgan SA2 0AR, Wales
Contacts Web: www.swansearfc.co.uk Tel: Swansea (01792) 424242
Colours All white
Captain 2001-02 Scott Gibbs
Welsh-Scottish League 2001-02 5th
Principality Cup 2001-02 Lost 14-16 to Pontypool (7th round)

Welsh-Scottish League Record 2001-02

Date	Venue	Opponents	Result	Scorers
25 Aug	H	Bridgend	16-25	*T:* Robinson *C:* Henson *PG:* Henson 2 *DG:* A Thomas
28 Aug	A	Pontypridd	11-6	*T:* Wells *PG:* Henson 2
1 Sep	A	Ebbw Vale	26-21	*T:* A Thomas, Griffiths *C:* A Thomas 2 *PG:* A Thomas 3 *DG:* A Thomas
8 Sep	H	Glasgow	13-21	*T:* G Jenkins *C:* Henson *PG:* Henson 2
11 Sep	A	Llanelli	27-21	*T:* pen try, K Morgan, Henson *C:* Henson 3 *PG:* Henson 2
22 Sep	A	Cardiff	13-25	*T:* Swales *C:* A Thomas *PG:* A Thomas 2
19 Oct	A	Newport	19-25	*T:* Gibbs *C:* A Thomas *PG:* A Thomas 4
1 Dec	H	Ebbw Vale	22-14	*T:* Gibbs 3 *C:* A Thomas 2 *PG:* A Thomas
8 Dec	H	Caerphilly	36-21	*T:* Gibbs, Charvis, Winn *C:* Henson 3 *PG:* Henson 5
14 Dec	H	Pontypridd	3-12	*PG:* Henson
21 Dec	A	Edinburgh	18-51	*T:* G Jenkins, Gibbs *C:* A Thomas *PG:* A Thomas 2
26 Dec	H	Llanelli	35-9	*T:* R Jones 2, Gibbs, A Thomas *C:* A Thomas 3 *PG:* A Thomas 2 *DG:* A Thomas
29 Dec	A	Neath	15-31	*PG:* A Thomas 5
9 Feb	A	Caerphilly	38-3	*T:* Winn 2, A Thomas, Lewis, R Jones, Payne *C:* A Thomas 4
9 Mar	H	Edinburgh	22-27	*T:* Gibbs *C:* Henson *PG:* Henson 3 *DG:* Henson 2
20 Apl	H	Newport	52-13	*T:* Martens 2, A Thomas, Taylor, Lima *C:* A Thomas 3 *PG:* A Thomas 5 *DG:* A Thomas 2
27 Apl	A	Bridgend	21-6	*T:* Martens, Robinson *C:* A Thomas *PG:* A Thomas 3
4 May	H	Cardiff	24-20	*T:* K Morgan, Lewis *C:* A Thomas *PG:* A Thomas 4
7 May	H	Neath	20-16	*T:* Morris *PG:* Henson 3 *DG:* Henson 2
10 May	A	Glasgow	20-37	*T:* Martens, Witkowski, Taylor *C:* Henson *PG:* Henson

VALLEY COMMANDOS SHOCK CUP KINGS: THE PRINCIPALITY CUP

John Billot

18 May 2002, Millennium Stadium, Cardiff Arms Park
Pontypridd 20 (5PG 1T)   Llanelli 17 (3PG 1DG 1T)

They call them the Valley Commandos. No task ever daunts them. Pontypridd, whose Sardis Road ground is dubbed The House of Pain, were unfancied finalists. Not that they ever want to be rated favourites. They react best when their chances are debated, analysed and rejected. The fact that Llanelli had won the cup 11 times and were appearing in their 16th final was just another statistic to Ponty, whose only previous cup-winning performance had been in 1996 and this was their fifth final. This was going to be all about who could survive a relentless battering.

Before the match, Gareth Jenkins, the Llanelli coach, commented, 'At the start of the season, we set the goals of a semi-final place in Europe, to be challenging for the Welsh/Scottish championship and to win the Principality Cup. We have reached two of those three objectives.' Alas for the cup kings of Welsh rugby, their third ambition went unrealised as the lead swung four times in front of 41,000 before Brett Davey fired over a superb angled penalty shot for Ponty to sneak it in the seventh minute of stoppage time.

The Pontypridd full-back had forecast that the issue might depend on a penalty kick decider and his meditative glance in his crystal ball over breakfast proved spot on. 'I didn't know if it was going to be me or Stephen Jones who would kick the winning goal and, to be honest, I was hoping it wouldn't be left to me to try to put it over. I've been a nervous wreck all week,' he said. But when crunch time came, Brett was ice-cool – and deadly accurate.

In fact, Deadly Davey scored all his side's points with five penalty shots and the try when Sonny Parker glided past Matt Cardey in midfield and gave his full-back an open path to the line. That tied the scores at 17-all after Stephen Jones had hoisted over three penalty goals and a close-range drop kick to add to a crisp, wide, collective passing attack that had seen Leigh Davies squeeze in at the corner.

Ponty had struck back after being two scores down at 17-9. Llanelli dominated first half possession, but continued to punch through with charging runs by Salesi Finau, Martyn Madden and Scott Quinnell when Plan B might have achieved more. 'We didn't play in the first half,' reflected Ponty chief coach Lynn Howells. 'We didn't get enough ball.' But Brett Davey made good use of that ball seven minutes from the end and that was all that mattered for the Valley Commandos.

Pontypridd: B Davey; G Wyatt, S Parker, J Bryant, M Nuthall; C Sweeney, P John (*captain*); G Jenkins, M Davies, D Bell, B Cockbain, R Sidoli, N Kelly,

Scott Quinnell's path appears to be blocked by Pontypridd's Matthew Nuthall and Jon Bryant in the Principality Cup Final. Pontypridd beat Llanelli 20-17 to lift the Cup for only the second time.

M Owen, R Parks *Substitutions:* S Cronk for Bell (temp 25-26 mins); C Harris for Kelly (60 mins)

Scorer *Try:* Davey *Penalty Goals:* Davey (5)

Llanelli: B Davies; M Jones, M Cardey, L Davies, S Finau; S Jones, G Easterby; M Madden, R McBryde, J Davies, V Cooper, C Wyatt, D Hodges, S Quinnell (*captain*), S Easterby *Substitutions:* G Bowen for L Davies (47 mins); D Peel for G Easterby (47 mins); P Booth for J Davies (72 mins); L Gross for Wyatt (72 mins); N Boobyer for Cardey (81 mins)

Scorers *Try:* L Davies *Penalty Goals:* S Jones (3) *Dropped Goal:* S Jones

Referee G Simmonds (WRU)

Earlier rounds

Davey had confounded Cardiff in the semi-final. His 26 points from a conversion of Mefin Davies's try and eight penalty strikes laid the foundation for a verdict by 31-25 after another storming display by an unstoppable pack. Ponty blasted off as if they were at Cape Canaveral instead of the Millennium Stadium and led 13-0 before Cardiff realised hostilities had begun. Considering Cardiff fielded 13 international players to Ponty's two, considerably more was expected of the Blue-and-Blacks. There was a fightback, to be sure, and Cardiff nosed ahead 25-19 by half-time. Iestyn Harris hit two penalty goals and converted two of the tries by Jonathan Humphreys, Pieter Müller and Jamie Robinson, but it was all too much for them. Coach Rudy Joubert, deeply disappointed yet again, observed, 'We shall have to get to grips with mediocrity.'

Ebbw Vale's defence had Llanelli locked in an uncompromising grip in their semi-final and they led the Scarlets 11-10 at the interval. A verbal lashing by coach Jenkins sent his team out for the second half stung by his tirade. So it became turn-around time and the cup favourites surged away to triumph by 34-17 after Ebbw had battled to 17-all. Tries for the winners came from Vernon Cooper, Guy Easterby, Ian Boobyer and Mark Jones. All were converted by Stephen Jones, who added two penalty goals. Gareth Cull kicked four Ebbw penalty shots and South African second-row Ockert Booyse obtained their try.

The Vale had shocked Neath into a seventh round exit after the Gnoll team led 10-0, but the home forwards took control and their efforts brought well-deserved reward by 20-10. In the quarter-finals, Ebbw were taxed with a visit to Pontypool, where Swansea had submitted by 16-14 in the seventh round. Pooler recovered from 14-3 arrears against Swansea as Gareth Taylor fired the home forwards to a tremendous effort, as awesome as some of the fiery performances of the glory years under Terry Cobner. Byron Hayward swung over three penalty kicks and converted the late try by Cae Treharne. Now it was Ebbw's task to try to tame those Pooler terrors and the Vale pack never flinched in front of 10,000 watchers. They won through by 27-22 with a memorable try four minutes from the end by centre Paul Matthews, who cut through with a neat little dummy.

The lead changed five times before Cardiff stopped Newport's challenge in the quarters by 20-14. Rob Howley disappeared through the smallest of gaps with a glorious dummy for a magical try four minutes from the final whistle. There were more than 13,000 at the Arms Park to witness a thrill-packed tussle. Stephen Jones kicked 21 points and Llanelli, trailing 21-18 to visitors Bridgend, recovered for victory by 46-24 in their quarter-final. Pontypridd encountered unexpected resistance from Caerphilly, who collected 31 points before losing in the quarters by 46-31 at Sardis Road. Inevitably, Davey did substantial damage with 19 points. It was his cup season.

Results

Fifth round: Aberavon 52, Rhymney 20; Aberystwyth 29, Abergavenny 8; Blackwood 14, Llanharan 13; Bonymaen 24, Bedwas 12; British Steel (Port Talbot) 15, Pontypool 31; Carmarthen Athletic 26, Treorchy 15; Carmarthen Quins 29, Oakdale 5; Cross Keys 23, Narberth 39; Hirwaun 22, Tredegar 19; Llantrisant 12, Tondu 19; Newbridge 46, Glamorgan Wanderers 12; Penarth 27, Beddau 32; Rumney 21, Llandovery 30; Wattstown 3, Merthyr 26; Whitland 21, Dunvant 12

Sixth round: Beddau 7, Pontypool 50; Bonymaen 16, Tondu 8; Carmarthen Athletic 0, Carmarthen Quins 43; Hirwaun 0, Blackwood 13; Llandovery 15, Ebbw Vale 43; Narberth 27, Merthyr 5; Newbridge 18, Aberystwyth 6; Whitland 9, Aberavon 27

Seventh round: Aberavon 16, Cardiff 24; Blackwood 8, Pontypridd 24; Bonymaen 3, Newport 41; Carmarthen Quins 3, Bridgend 19; Ebbw Vale 20, Neath 10; Narberth 15, Caerphilly 19; Newbridge 5, Llanelli 24; Pontypool 16, Swansea 14

Quarter-finals: Cardiff 20, Newport 14; Llanelli 46, Bridgend 24; Pontypool 22, Ebbw Vale 27; Pontypridd 46, Caerphilly 31

Semi-finals: (at the Millennium Stadium) Llanelli 34, Ebbw Vale 17; Pontypridd 31, Cardiff 25

FINAL: (at Millennium Stadium) Pontypridd 20, Llanelli 17

Previous WRU Cup Finals: 1972 Neath 15, Llanelli 9; 1973 Llanelli 30, Cardiff 7; 1974 Llanelli 12, Aberavon 10; 1975 Llanelli 15, Aberavon 6; 1976 Llanelli 16, Swansea 4; 1977 Newport 16, Cardiff 15; 1978 Swansea 13, Newport 9; 1979 Bridgend 18, Pontypridd 12; 1980 Bridgend 15, Swansea 9; 1981 Cardiff 14, Bridgend 6; 1982 Cardiff 12, Bridgend 12 (Cardiff won on most tries rule); 1983 Pontypool 18, Swansea 6; 1984 Cardiff 24, Neath 19; 1985 Llanelli 15, Cardiff 14; 1986 Cardiff 28, Newport 21; 1987 Cardiff 16, Swansea 15; 1988 Llanelli 28, Neath 13; 1989 Neath 14, Llanelli 13; 1990 Neath 16, Bridgend 10; 1991 Llanelli 24, Pontypool 9; 1992 Llanelli 16, Swansea 7; 1993 Llanelli 21, Neath 18; 1994 Cardiff 15, Llanelli 8; 1995 Swansea 17, Pontypridd 12; 1996 Pontypridd 29, Neath 22; 1997 Cardiff 33, Swansea 26; 1998 Llanelli 19, Ebbw Vale 12; 1999 Swansea 37, Llanelli 10; 2000 Llanelli 22, Swansea 12; 2001 Newport 13, Neath 8; 2002 Pontypridd 20, Llanelli 17.

Played at Cardiff Arms Park 1972-1997; at Ashton Gate, Bristol 1998; at Ninian Park, Cardiff 1999; at the Millennium Stadium since 2000

DOMESTIC RUGBY IN FRANCE 2001–2002

Blanco's Dream Comes True:
The French Championship

Ian Borthwick

8 June 2002, Stade de France, Paris
Biarritz 25 (1G 5PG 1DG)   **Agen 22** (1G 5PG) *aet*

As is so often the case, the final of the 2001-02 French Championship was far from a pretty spectacle, but in terms of suspense and high drama, the face-off between Biarritz and Agen took some beating. France's two best sides managed only one try apiece and, with the two forward packs slogging it out in 41 line-outs and 37 scrums, attacking flair and multi-phase sequences of play were kept to a strict minimum.

And yet, for a full 111 minutes of play this enthralling duel kept the 78,457 spectators at the Stade de France on the edges of their seats, as the outcome between two evenly-matched sides remained undecided until the final minute of extra time when Laurent Mazas, the 31-year-old replacement scrum-half from Biarritz, snapped over a dropped-goal to win the game.

Agen had taken an early lead with a try to scrum-half Mathieu Barrau after some nifty work off the back of the scrum from No 8 Thierry Labrousse. François Gelez converted from the touch-line before slotting an easy penalty for Agen to lead 10-0, but Biarritz stormed back into the game with a superb individual try to Philippe Bernat-Salles, the ageless winger outpacing the defence to gather his own kick-through from 50 metres out and score in the corner.

Boasting two of the world's best props – French international Jean-Jacques Crenca at loose-head and Argentinean strongman Omar Hasan at tight-head – Agen had the upper hand in the scrums. But veterans Olivier Roumat and Jean-Michel Gonzalez (each about to turn 35) and the tireless flanker, Serge Betsen, gave a greater overall balance to the Biarritz game.

Nonetheless, the rest of the scoring – until Mazas's winning 111th minute field-goal – was confined to a duel between the goal-kickers, Gelez for Agen and Australian Joe Roff for Biarritz. The world-champion Wallaby had a mixed bag, missing five kickable goals, but twice kicking long range penalties at critical moments to save the day for Biarritz. Indeed, it was Roff's 50-metre effort in the 60th minute which enabled Biarritz to take the lead for the first time in the game, holding out at 19-16 until Gelez, in the sixth minute of injury-time, equalised from 41 metres.

Gelez goaled again in the opening minutes of extra-time, to put Agen ahead 22-19. Roff added to the tension by missing two close-range penalties, but when the referee awarded another penalty to Biarritz 43 metres out, the Aussie calmly stepped up and added the three points to draw level once again at 22-22.

At opposite ends of the ground, the rival fans went ballistic. But just as it seemed that, as happened in 1984, the final would have to be decided by a penalty shoot-out, Biarritz strung together a long sequence of play and Mazas, who still holds down a job as a full-time maths teacher, snapped over his drop-goal from close range to seal victory.

After losing only four games in the season, for Biarritz it was a just reward for a remarkably consistent campaign, and the return of the Brennus Shield to Biarritz was greeted with delirious street celebrations. Not only because *le bouclier* was back for the first time in 63 years, but also because Biarritz's favourite son, Serge Blanco, could at last embrace French rugby's Holy Grail. Exactly ten years earlier at the Parc des Princes, the final game of Blanco's illustrious career had ended with a defeat in the 1992 club-final against Toulon. For the nonpareil full-back who, as President of the Ligue Nationale de Rugby is now one of the game's principal power-brokers in France, victory was especially sweet.

Biarritz: N Brusque; P Bernat-Salles, J Roff, J Isaac, P Bidabé; J Peyrelongue, N Morlaes; E Menieu, J-M Gonzalez *(captain)*, D Avril, J-P Versailles, O Roumat, S Betsen, T Lièvremont, C Milhères *Substitutions:* O Nauroy for Versailles (48 mins); D Chouchan for Milhères (56 mins); S Puleoto for Menieu (63 mins); L Mazas for Morlaes (75 mins); N Curnier for Avril (temp 81-87 mins); G Boussès for Isaac (91 mins); N Curnier for Avril (96mins); S Legg for Bidabé (97 mins)

Scorers *Try:* Bernat-Salles *Conversion:* Roff *Penalty Goals:* Roff (5) *Drop Goal:* Mazas

Agen: C Lamaison; P Elhorga, C Stoltz, L Lafforgue, C Manas; F Gelez, M Barrau; J-J Crenca, J-B Rué, O Hasan, D Couzinet, C Porcu, P Benetton *(captain)*, T Labrousse, Matthieu Lièvremont *Substitutions:* G Bouic for Stoltz (46 mins); M Barragué for Porcu (71 mins); N Martin for Gelez (95 mins)

Scorers *Try:* Barrau *Conversion:* Gelez *Penalty Goals:* Gelez (5)

Referee D Mené (FFR)

The Pools 2001-02

New format hits the spot

In its first season of operation, the new format of France's domestic championship,* proved to be a resounding success. Despite its barbaric name, *Le Top 16* attracted consistently bigger crowds throughout the season, the overall mean of 5,159 spectators a match representing a 17% increase over the previous year's figure. Both in the preliminary rounds and in the final phases (where the average attendance was 7,836) many clubs had record crowds; some 52,000 spectators attended the semi-finals played at neutral venues, while over 70,000 paying spectators (out of a record 78,457) handed over more than 3 million Euros (£2M) to see the club final at Stade de France.

Despite the apparently healthy condition of French club rugby, however, the 2001-02 season threw up two other facets of the professional game which caused widespread concern: the precarious nature of the coaches' positions, and the difficulty of reconciling the demands of two separate competitions, namely the Championship and the Heineken European Cup. No fewer than seven First Division clubs fired their coaches during the season: Castres sacked Alain Gaillard *and* his subsequent replacement Rémi Trémoulet, Dax got rid of Jean-Louis Luneau, Bourgoin fired Jean-François Tordo, Bordeaux-Bègles got rid of Tine Martinez and Philippe Gimbert, La Rochelle said *au revoir* to Jean-Pierre Elissalde, while two high profile Aussies – Steve Nance at Montferrand and John Connolly at Stade Français – were invited to pack their bags before the season was over.

As for the Heineken Cup and the Parker Pen Shield, this was undoubtedly the poorest year yet for France in the European club competitions. Despite the French XVs resounding Grand Slam victory, this form was not repeated by the clubs and, finding it impossible to perform simultaneously on two different fronts, heavyweights like Stade Français, Toulouse, Biarritz and Montferrand fell by the wayside. Castres was the most successful French performer, eventually losing 25-17 to Munster in the semi-finals, but paid the price by coming within a hair's breadth of being relegated to France's Second Division.

The curious case of Agen no doubt best illustrates the dilemma faced by French clubs. After eliminating the favourite, Toulouse, in the semi-finals, the Agenais, led by veteran flanker Philippe Benetton, reached the final of the gruelling French championship for the first time since 1990. However, following an incident in a Parker Pen Shield game against Ebbw Vale, on January 12th 2002, Agen were banned from all European competition for the 2002-2003 season.

Faced with playing three critical games in eight days, Agen opted to put all their eggs in the French championship basket and to 'throw' their game against Ebbw Vale, which they duly lost 59-10, 'allowing' the Welsh to score the requisite nine tries which would ensure Agen's elimination. For Agen, elimination from the European Shield was the only way to preserve their chances of success in *Le Top 16*, a tactic which subsequently paid off. The ERC, however, took a dim view of this, fined the club 20,000 Euros and ordered a three-year ban from all European competition, two of which were to be suspended.

Finally, the 2001-02 season saw the inevitable demise of two of the struggling minnows of French rugby. La Rochelle and Dax were both demoted to the second division (known as Pro D2). Both clubs have a proud past, especially Dax which is famous for reaching the final of the French championship on five different occasions and losing all five, but with their restricted population base, neither could keep up with the economic demands of the modern game.

* *Two pools of eight, the top four qualifying for a tilt at the final, the bottom four contesting the bizarrely named* les play-down *to avoid relegation.*

French Championship: *Le Top 16* 2001-02

Pool One

Team	P	W	D	L	For	Against	Pts
Biarritz	14	11	0	3	385	224	36
Toulouse	14	10	0	4	346	272	34
Stade Français	14	9	0	5	315	244	32
Béziers	14	9	0	5	366	285	32
Colomiers	14	7	0	7	309	337	28
Montauban	14	5	0	9	258	365	24
La Rochelle	14	3	0	11	259	350	20
Dax	14	2	0	12	250	411	18

Béziers with a red card were placed behind Stade Français

Pool Two

Team	P	W	D	L	For	Against	Pts
Perpignan	14	11	0	3	413	313	36
Agen	14	10	0	4	364	245	34
Montferrand	14	7	0	7	351	296	28
Bourgoin	14	7	0	7	392	338	28
Narbonne	14	6	0	8	357	408	26
Pau	14	6	0	8	266	408	26
Bordeaux Bègles	14	5	0	9	278	361	24
Castres	14	4	0	10	366	418	22

Play Off A

Team	P	W	D	L	For	Against	Pts
Biarritz	6	4	1	1	153	122	15
Agen	6	3	1	2	163	116	13
Bourgoin	6	2	1	3	127	179	11
Stade Français	6	0	3	3	133	159	9

Play Off B

Team	P	W	D	L	For	Against	Pts
Toulouse	6	5	0	1	198	120	16
Montferrand	6	3	0	3	146	161	12
Perpignan	6	2	0	4	127	154	10
Béziers	6	2	0	4	137	173	10

Les Play Down 2001–02

Team	P	W	D	L	For	Against	Pts
Montauban	22	11	0	11	495	596	44
Colomiers	22	9	2	11	487	517	42
Narbonne	22	10	0	12	591	630	42
Bordeaux	22	9	0	13	457	526	40
Castres	22	8	1	13	610	582	39
Pau	22	8	1	13	486	636	39
La Rochelle	22	8	0	14	473	579	38
Dax	22	5	0	17	397	648	32

Points: 3 for a win; 2 for a draw; 1 for a defeat

Results

Semi-finals: Agen 21, Toulouse 15; Biarritz 31, Montferrand 12

FINAL: (at Stade de France, Paris) Biarritz 25, Agen 22

Final standings *Le Top 16* 2001-2002

1 Biarritz; 2 Agen; 3 Toulouse; 4 Montferrand; 5 Bourgoin; 6 Perpignan; 7 Béziers; 8 Stade Français; 9 Montauban; 10 Colomiers; 11 Narbonne; 12 Bordeaux-Bègles; 13 Castres; 14 Pau

Relegated To Pro D2

15 La Rochelle; 16 Dax

Promoted For 2002-2003

Mont-de-Marsan; Grenoble

Recent French Championship Finals: 1972 Béziers 9, Brive 0; 1973 Tarbes 18, Dax 12; 1974 Béziers16, Narbonne 14; 1975 Béziers 13, Brive 12; 1976 Agen 13, Béziers10; 1977 Béziers 12, Perpignan 4; 1978 Béziers 31, Montferrand 9; 1979 Narbonne 10, Bagnères 0; 1980 Béziers 10, Toulouse 6; 1981 Béziers 22, Bagnères 13; 1982 Agen 18, Bayonne 9; 1983 Béziers 14, Nice 6; 1984 Béziers 21, Agen 21; 1985 Toulouse 36, Toulon 22; 1986 Toulouse 16, Agen 6; 1987 Toulon 15, RCF 12; 1988 Agen 9, Tarbes 3; 1989 Toulouse 18, Toulon 12; 1990 RCF 22, Agen 12; 1991 Bègles-Bordeaux 19, Toulouse 10; 1992 Toulon 19, Biarritz 14; 1993 Castres 14, Grenoble 11; 1994 Toulouse 22, Montferrand 16; 1995 Toulouse 31, Castres 16; 1996 Toulouse 20, Brive 13; 1997 Toulouse 12, Bourgoin-Jallieu 6; 1998 Stade Français 34, Perpignan 7; 1999 Toulouse 15, Montferrand 11; 2000 Stade Français 28, Colomiers 23; 2001 Toulouse 34, Montferrand 22; 2002 Biarritz 25, Agen 22

DOMESTIC RUGBY IN ITALY 2001-02

Italian Championship Embraces a New Format

Giampaolo Tassinari

Three new measures paved the way for a very different 2001-2002 club season. A new league body, the LIRE managed by Roberto Ghiretti, was formed, the league format was changed so that all clubs played each other on a home and away basis, and appearance rules were changed so that each club could field five foreign players in each league match. This resulted in the closest thing yet to a professional rugby system in Italy. Only Benetton Treviso is organised on a full professional scale, but many clubs have structured themselves as semi-professional bodies finding jobs for their players off the rugby pitch.

At the beginning of the season five clubs emerged as favourites to fight for the play-off places. They were Benetton, Petrarca Padova, Amatori & Calvisano, Viadana and Parma FC. These clubs were better equipped than the rest to compete for the title. L'Aquila and Rovigo were never able to catch the play-off group while Gr A N Rugby, Rugby Roma and Bologna struggled to avoid relegation.

Gr A N Rugby is a new club formed by the merger of two Parma clubs, Amatori Parma and Noceto, which is a small village near Parma where the former Italy captain Massimo Giovanelli was born. Both clubs maintain their different teams in the lower divisions but play together in the Super 10, the new Italian league with a points system based on the Southern Hemisphere's format.

The season saw the renaissance of historic Petrarca Padova after a couple of years spent coming to terms with the requirements of professional rugby. Up until the last month of competition, the White-and-Blacks topped the league standings. They were helped by the return of the NSW Waratahs' stalwart Brendan Williams as a utility back. But tiredness towards the end of the season combined with fine late runs by the two Lombard clubs, Amatori & Calvisano and Viadana, saw them lose some important matches and end the season as runners up.

Benetton Treviso, despite their superior playing squad and the immense Mauro Bergamasco on the flank, showed many tactical lapses and only clinched the play-off spot in the last round-robin match by defeating Parma FC, thereby eliminating Parma, who are coached by the former Springbok, Dawie Snyman, from the play-offs.

Super 10 Standings

	P	W	D	L	F	A	Bonus	Pts
Viadana	18	13	0	5	512	326	9	61
Petrarca Padova	18	13	1	4	496	339	6	60
Amatori & Calvisano	18	12	0	6	518	322	11	59
Benetton Treviso	18	12	1	5	485	294	8	58
Parma FC	18	11	1	6	471	362	8	54
L'Aquila	18	7	0	11	419	505	9	37
Rovigo	18	8	0	10	402	531	5	37
Gr A N Rugby	18	6	1	11	376	453	7	33
Rugby Roma	18	5	0	13	330	592	7	27
Bologna	18	1	0	17	340	625	7	11

Points: win 4; draw 2; four or more tries, or defeat by seven or fewer points 1
Bologna were relegated to Serie A 2002-03. Silea were promoted to Serie A.

Knockout stages

The semi-final stages were played over two legs with the league points system being used to determine the winner in the event of teams sharing a win apiece. Both the Lombard teams triumphed in the semi-finals. Viadana, after collapsing badly in Treviso in the first leg of their semi-final, performed a miracle in the second match by scoring four tries to pick up a crucial bonus point and reach the final. In stark contrast, Petrarca Padova completely threw away their two matches against Amatori & Calvisano, losing both games by 21-18, despite outscoring their opponents by four tries to two over the two legs. They thus wasted all the good work built up by their coach Beppe Artuso during the season.

Play-off semi-finals: *First legs:* Benetton Treviso 29, Viadana 6 (4 points to nil); Amatori & Calvisano 21, Petrarca Padova 18 (4 points to 1) *Second legs:* Viadana 31, Benetton Treviso 14 (5 points to nil) Viadana qualified with a 5-4 points aggregate; Petrarca Padova 18, Amatori & Calvisano 21 (2 points to 4) Calvisano qualified by winning both ties (and with an 8-2 points aggregate).

Championship Final

18 May, 2002, Battaglini Stadium, Rovigo
Viadana 19 (3PG 2T)   Amatori & Calvisano 12 (4PG)

Calvisano and Viadana met in a very closely contested final. Both clubs come from two small villages whose aggregate population is 24,000 inhabitants. Seven thousand gathered to attend the match at the magnificent Battaglini Stadium in Rovigo where playing conditions were perfect.

Viadana ran out deserved winners by 19-12. They dominated the match both in the set pieces and in loose play, where their forwards were hungrier for possession than their opponents. Moreover, Viadana put Calvisano under a lot of pressure, keeping them penned back very deep in their own territory for most of the final.

Many had expected Viadana to play their famous expansive game as they had done for much of the season under the guidance of their assistant coach Mac McCallion. But he had now left the club to accept the Fijiian coaching job and instead, manager Franco Bernini and his side turned to conservative rugby, fighting for supremacy up front. Their cause, it should be added, was helped by the absence of the Calvisano captain and Italy prop Giampiero de Carli, who had to miss the match owing to an eye injury sustained the week before in the semi-final clash in Padua.

Once Viadana got the upper hand in the forwards they became less nervous and executed some good moves which culminated with a try that put them ahead 11-6 at the interval after two penalties by the former Blue Bulls' full-back, Casper Steyn.

Until the final quarter, Calvisano did not do much to justify their presence in the final, thus confirming the sceptical views of many experts. They made a lot of unforced errors with many knock-ons, made worse by an erratic kicking game that gave away a lot of possession. Despite all these blunders, Calvisano were able to narrow the margin to only two points (12-14) and then they had the chance to score a vital penalty through Paul Griffen's boot from 22 metres with only nine minutes left in the match. Instead the easy kick went wide of the goal posts enabling Viadana to strike back with their second try of the day, scored by the wing Mattia Dolcetto who was playing in his home town.

At the final whistle, Bernini and his men were clearly overcome by the emotion of this historic triumph, for only four years ago Viadana were still playing in the second division. They have come a long way in a short time and dedicated their prized title to former hooker Battista Berra, now a quadraplegic, who was watching the match from the sideline and whose name was printed on the Viadana players' jerseys.

It was a great day for Viadana, but arguably one for reflection for the FIR: only 19 of the 44 players involved in this final were born in Italy. Perhaps this time the word "Italian" was misplaced.

Viadana: C Steyn; C Robertson, S Ceppolino, P Bettati, M Dolcetto; R MacDonald, H Crane; M Savi, V Jiménez, L Lidgard, S Dellapé, R Denhardt, A Benatti, M Phillips (*captain*), A Persico *Substitutions:* P Travagli for Bettati (30 mins); P Spina for Lidgard (62 mins); N Superina for Jiménez (67 mins); R Pedrazzi for Dolcetto (80 mins)

Scorers *Tries:* Denhardt, Dolcetto *Penalty Goals:* Steyn (3)

Amatori & Calvisano: K Rolleston; M Ravazzolo, P Vaccari, C Zanoletti, F Merli; L Bordes, P R Griffen; H.Mazino, A Moretti, G.Bocca, J Purll, L Mastrodomenico, C Mayerhofler, A de Rossi (*captain*), J Ricciardo *Substitutions:* K Whitley for Ricciardo (48 mins); M Castrogiovanni for Mazino (51 mins); E Scotuzzi for Whitley (60 mins); P Scanziani for Rolleston (62 mins); J Dragotto for Bordes (70 mins); S Macri for Bocca (80 mins); S Arboit for Griffen (84 mins)

Scorers *Penalty Goals:* Rolleston (3), Griffen

Referee S Mancini (FIR)

Previous Italian Championship Finals: 1988 Rovigo 9, Treviso 7 (Rome); 1989 Treviso 20, Rovigo 9 (Bologna); 1990 Rovigo 18, Treviso 9 (Brescia); 1991 Milan 37, Treviso 18 (Parma); 1992 Treviso 27, Rovigo 18 (Padua); 1993 Milan 41, Treviso 15 (Padua); 1994 L'Aquila 23, Milan 14 (Padua); 1995 Milan 27, Treviso 15 (Padua); 1996 Milan 23, Treviso 17 (Rovigo); 1997 Treviso 34, Milan 29 (Verona); 1998 Treviso 9, Padua 3 (Bologna); 1999 Treviso 23, Padua 14 (Rovigo); 2000 Rome 35, L'Aquila 17 (Rome); 2001 Treviso 33, Calvisano 13 (Bologna); 2002 Viadana 19, Amatori & Calvisano 12 (Rovigo)

DOMESTIC RUGBY IN SOUTH AFRICA 2001

Braam's Sweet Swansong for Western Province: Bankfin Currie Cup

Dan Retief

Domestic rugby in South Africa had a familiar look as Western Province beat Natal 29-24 in the final to retain the venerable Currie Cup and push their record number of victories to 31.

The Western Province-Natal final had been reached by the teams beating Free State and the Lions respectively in the semi-finals – the opposite of the previous year – and having triumphed in Durban in 2000, Province skipper Corné Krige could brandish the golden cup before Province's Newlands faithful in Cape Town.

The final underscored concerns that, in spite of a complicated system to involve all 14 of South Africa's provinces in the Currie Cup, the strong were getting stronger and the weak were falling further off the pace.

Thus the competition followed the pattern of the previous year by failing to ignite much interest until the latter stages when the leading eight qualified to play for the Currie Cup itself with the other six dropping away to play for the Bankfin Shield.

It was only once this strength versus strength stage of the competition was reached that crowds began to grow and the rugby became competitive, prompting many learned observers to express the view that South Africa's woes at Test match level were due largely to the many mis-matches in the Currie Cup and the absence of a home-and-away system.

Balanced against these concerns, however, was the need for South African rugby to create as many opportunities as possible for emerging black players to be more equitably represented. By involving all the provinces in a quota system, which compels teams to select and field a certain number of black players, the numbers are increasing.

If the initial rounds of the Currie Cup were somewhat dull, it did not mean that rugby lost its ability to stir controversy and grab the headlines.

Four of the biggest issues were the re-instatement of Springbok prop Cobus Visagie after having been suspended for testing positive for a banned substance, the legal wrangles that surrounded the like of Joost van der Westhuizen and Braam van Straaten signing up with British clubs (Newport and Leeds respectively), the continued incidence of crippling injuries to key players such as Rassie Erasmus and Robbie Fleck, and the suspension of Springbok and Sharks fly-half Butch James when his high tackling finally went beyond the pale.

Visagie had been knocked out of the Super 12 when it was announced that traces of the banned steroid nandrolone had been found in a sample taken from him the previous year. He continued to maintain his innocence, arguing that the substance had occurred naturally from supplements he had been supplied with by Sarfu and Western Province, and was re-instated on appeal.

The fact that Van der Westhuizen and Van Straaten had decided to leave to play for pounds in Britain became known during the playing of the Tri Nations and set the stage for an ongoing saga as other players became embroiled in contractual spats with their provinces – a modern phenomenon driven by a favourable Pound/Rand exchange rate.

In the end Van der Westhuizen would back out of his intention to go to Newport, and play on for the Blue Bulls, while Van Straaten, with a less favourable Springbok contract to discourage him, would use Western Province's appearance in the final as a stage to say goodbye.

The ace goal-kicker and solid grafter was the subject of much of the debate of the latter part of the South African season – the Currie Cup also doubling as an extended trial to help Springbok coach Harry Viljoen pick the team to tour France, Italy, England and America – as fans weighed up his contribution as a provider of points against his awkwardness as a fly-half.

Western Province coach Gert Smal, however, used Van Straaten as a stopping inside-centre with Chris Rossouw, Pieter's younger brother, to do the fancy stuff in the No 10 jersey. It was a sound call because Van Straaten came through with 25 points in the semi-final against Free State and another 24 (including a try) in the final.

Bankfin Currie Cup Final

27 October 2001, Fedsure Park, Newlands, Cape Town
Western Province 29 (2G 5PG)   Natal Sharks 24 (3G 1PG)

The Natal Sharks had gone into the final as slight favourites having beaten Western Province, who at that point had already qualified to play in the final, 36-13 during 'Top Eight' league play, while they had also triumphed when they met in their guises of the Sharks and the Stormers in the Super 12.

For coach Rudolf Straeuli it meant he had taken the under-performers of 2000 to both the Super 12 and the Currie Cup finals, while for the Natalians the Newlands encounter represented a fourth successive final – three in the Currie Cup and one against the Brumbies in Canberra.

Determination born of the previous failures resulted in the Natalians making a strong start and they scored the first try within five minutes when they put turned-over ball to good use through Deon Kayser and A J Venter before skipper John Smit, standing in for the oft-injured Mark Andrews, ran in from longer range than one normally sees from a hooker.

The Sharks also constructed the game's second try when Gaffie du Toit crossed near the posts after a prolonged period of phase play and half-time arrived with the visitors in front by 17-9 – Du Toit having added two conversions and a penalty and Van Straaten keeping Western Province in range with three penalties.

The normally vociferous Newlands crowd was silent and few would have predicted the dramatic inversion of form that would take place soon after the re-start. John Smit was off the field injured, Kayser went back to field an aimless looking kick, the ball bobbled, the winger was caught in possession and when the ball next appeared it was coming out to Chris Rossouw for the fly-half to chip over the top, snatch the ball away from a number of Natalians and score.

Van Straaten's conversion made it 16-17 and with Corné Krige and Hendrik Gerber starting to gain the upper hand in the chase for the loose ball Province wrested control and within 10 minutes they were in front.

Quick scrum ball allowed Percy Montgomery to range up from the back and with Natal rushing to stop gaps wide out it was Van Straaten who took everyone by surprise to bash through. The chunky fly-half added the conversion plus two more penalties to ensure that the Cup would stay in the Cape – Charl van Rensburg's try on the stroke of full time serving merely to illustrate to the Natalians what might have been had they maintained concentration and stuck to the pattern of the first half.

It was an emotional farewell for Van Straaten, who contributed 24 points, and hooker Charl Marais, who had also announced his intention to leave for Britain. 'It is with a heavy heart that I leave Western Province and the best years of my rugby career have been here,' said Van Straaten. 'The ovation I got from the crowd was a very special moment for me and I appreciate and will forever remember all the support that I have received.'

Van Straaten, having missed a number of games because he was on Tri Nations duty, missed out on being the season's leading points scorer. That honour went to Louis Koen (Lions) with 171 – but he did score the points that mattered. In the try-scoring stakes John Daniels of the Boland Cavaliers topped the list with 12 with Etienne Botha (Falcons) and Wylie Human (Cheetahs) each getting 11 and Jacques Juries (Pumas) on 10.

Western Province: P C Montgomery; B J Paulse, D W Barry, A J J van Straaten, P W G Rossouw; C Rossouw, N A de Kock; R B Kempson, C F Marais, I J Visagie, Q Davids, F H Louw, C P J Krige (*captain*), R B Skinstad, H J Gerber *Substitutions:* A van der Linde for Visagie (61 mins); W W Greeff for C Rossouw (76 mins); T Stoltz for Davids (76 mins); J H Conradie for De Kock (78 mins); P J Dixon for Marais (81 mins); I J Visagie (returned) for Kempson (81 mins)

Scorers *Tries:* C Rossouw, Van Straaten *Conversions:* Van Straaten (2) *Penalty Goals:* Van Straaten (5)

Natal Sharks: J Swart; D J Kayser, A H Snyman, T M Halstead, C S Terblanche; G S du Toit, C D Davidson; A-H le Roux, J Smit (*captain*), E E Fynn, P A van den Berg, P L Smit, W K Britz, R S Sowerby, A J Venter *Substitutions:* C Q van Rensburg for Van den Berg (53 mins); P D Carstens for Le Roux (67 mins); L van Biljon for Smit (temp 40 to 47 mins) and for Fynn (67 mins); R F Smith for

Snyman (67 mins); D J B von Hoesslin for Davidson (76 mins); H C Kruger for Swart (76 mins)

Scorers *Tries:* Smit, Du Toit, van Rensburg *Conversions:* Du Toit (2), Kruger *Penalty Goal:* Du Toit

Referee A Watson (SARFU)

Results

Semi-finals: Natal Sharks 16, Golden Lions 9 (ABSA Stadium, King's Park, Durban); Western Province 40, Free State Cheetahs 18 (Fedsure Park, Newlands, Cape Town)

Final: Western Province 29, Natal Sharks 24 (Fedsure Park, Newlands, Cape Town)

Recent Currie Cup Finals: 1990 N Transvaal 12, Natal 18 (Pretoria); 1991 N Transvaal 27 Transvaal 15 (Pretoria); 1992 Transvaal 13, Natal 14 (Johannesburg); 1993 Natal 15, Transvaal 21 (Durban); 1994 Orange Free State 33, Transvaal 56 (Bloemfontein); 1995 Natal 25, Western Province 17 (Durban); 1996 Transvaal 15, Natal 33 (Johannesburg); 1997 Western Province 14, Free State 12 (Cape Town); 1998 Blue Bulls 24, Western Province 20 (Pretoria); 1999 Natal Sharks 9, Golden Lions 32 (Durban); 2000 Natal Sharks 15, Western Province 25 (Durban); 2001 Western Province 29, Natal Sharks 24 (Cape Town)

DOMESTIC RUGBY IN NEW ZEALAND 2001

All Roads Lead South: NPC Championship

Don Cameron

The special magic that the three divisions of the Air New Zealand national championship bring to domestic rugby in New Zealand has seldom rivalled the drama and excitement and sheer joy that accompanied the 2001 event, the 26th season. The first division was a keenly contested affair which left Canterbury, North Otago and Otago in the top three, and Auckland just slipping into the fourth semi-final position.

The steady growth of South Island rugby was shown when Canterbury and Otago qualified easily for the final. The previous year Christchurch had also staged the final when Canterbury lost an epic battle against Wellington, which has seldom prospered before or since. This time the Jade Stadium attracted a capacity crowd of 28,000, for the new 16,000-seat monster of a stand on the western side of the ground was not quite ready for such a grand opening. (It had to wait for the New Zealand-England cricket Test and Nathan Astle's amazing double century last March).

Still there was the solid, well-deserved Canterbury win, a fitting farewell for the Canterbury captain Todd Blackadder, who had lost his All Black captaincy but none of his amazing hold on the ever-faithful and patriotic Canterbury supporters. Such was the drama and emotion in the build-up that Otago, even after leading 16-6 at half-time, were steadily put aside 30-19 and really had no chance of breaking Blackadder's magic spell.

Among all the magic there was one touch of the tragic – the demotion from the first division of Counties-Manukau, a regular top-class side apart from two years in the second division in the early 1990s. In the modern commercial game Counties-Manukau has been caught in the corporate wind shadow thrown up by Auckland in the north and Waikato in the south – and it will take a massive effort for the side to retain their best players and to return to the first division, which they won in 1979.

Magic at Christchurch, and fairy-tales at Napier in the North Island and Oamaru in the South when the second and third divisions were decided. East Coast, tucked away in the farming country on the north-eastern corner of the North Island, have long been in the championship cellar. This is the home of the Ngati Porou Maori tribe, or iwi as they now called, and farming and commercial life is not easy. Sometimes fielding a full team was also difficult, and on one occasion when on tour in the middle of the North Island the East Coast side had to draft in their bus-driver to make up the XV.

Times have changed. East Coast have gained some modest sponsorship, they appreciate the cash grant from Wellington headquarters, and they have sent out the message to Ngati Porou players anywhere in the country to rally to the cause. For a start East Coast won a match or two in the third division. They got better, the crowds of 2000-3000 filled their modest Whakarua Park in Ruatoria, and East Coast won the third division by upsetting another team of humble results, North Otago.

In 2001 the East Coast trickle of success became a wave. The iwi players came from everywhere (perhaps not quite to the letter of the residential rules) and East Coast kept on winning by kicking goals and staging memorable driving mauls that gobbled up many metres. They even reached the second division final, against Hawke's Bay, at Napier – just down the road 200 or so miles from the Coast. Hawke's Bay used to be first division stars, and they looked decidedly superior when they stretched out to a 30-10 lead. But buoyed on by their vocal supporters East Coast roared back and had Hawke's Bay hanging on 30-27 at the death. East Coast were not saddened. They had reached the final knowing they had neither the talent nor the money to warrant promotion if they won.

The same weekend North Otago, who had jostled East Coast for bottom place in the third division for years, again went into a home final. They lost to East Coast in 2000, but this time they were hot favourites against South Canterbury, like North Otago a smallish country union and their next-door northern neighbours. The previous year North Otago had taken an early lead, only to watch East Coast come back for victory. This time North Otago gained an 11-3 lead – quite often a substantial margin in this division – and at the sharp end of the game led 16-13 before missing a corner try when a North Otago player just clipped the corner flag. South Canterbury burst back, scored the winning try in a goal-line scramble and converted it for a 20-16 triumph.

In the glamorous world of top-flight rugby, with its monstrous crowds and top players earning telephone-numbers of dollars, the NPC first division may be close to that elevated status. But the third and second divisions and their basically amateur habits might seem the forgotten unfortunates of the game. That is, until they show that they have as much passion and pride in their rugby as have the cash-rich gents at the top of the economic scale. Moreover, they play a wholesome kind of running rugby without the mind-numbing, bone-crunching heavy-tackling routines of rugby at the top.

Final Air New Zealand NPC Round-Robin Table 2001

	P	W	D	L	Bonus	For	Against	Pts
Canterbury	10	9	0	1	8	407	164	44
North Harbour	10	8	0	2	6	242	149	38
Otago	10	7	0	3	5	332	226	33
Auckland	10	6	0	4	6	272	193	30
Waikato	10	6	0	4	5	312	234	29
Wellington	10	4	0	6	8	245	208	24
Northland	10	5	0	5	3	253	266	23

Taranaki	10	4	0	6	4	275	293	20
Southland	10	2	1	7	2	184	351	12
Bay of Plenty	10	2	0	8	2	148	366	10
Counties-Manukau	10	1	1	8	1	158	378	7

Air New Zealand NPC Grand Final

3 November 2001, Jade Stadium, Lancaster Park, Christchurch.
Canterbury 30 (1G 5PG 1DG 1T)   **Otago 19** (1G 2PG 2DG)

The simplistic view for the rest of the country was that Laurie Mains, returned as coach of Otago after his time with the Cats in Johannesburg, organised his side to win the first half 16-6 with a superb display of controlled power-rugby. Then Steve Hansen, later to be assistant and then replace Graham Henry as coach of Wales, at half-time so persuaded his men to return to their basic rugby methods of control and cool attack that Canterbury went on to win, going-away at 30-19.

But to most of the 28,000 loyal Canterbury spectators the essential element in the win was that Todd Blackadder, their superb captain, would inevitably lead his men to an historic victory before he left to pursue fortune, if not fame, in Scotland. Seldom had a rugby personality in New Zealand achieved such personal fame, and become so much the team's talisman, as had Blackadder during an illustrious career which included time as captain of the All Blacks. The burly, non-stop middle-row forward – the youngsters adored him, the elderly people doted on him, and all the red-and-black faithful simply believed that with Blackadder, ''Mr Loyalty,'' in charge they could not lose the final.

It was a heavy burden for the big man, and it did not sit too comfortably on his broad shoulders in the first half. Mains is a master at working out a winning recipe for his native Otago – play hard, back up, tackle, do not try too many fancy things, and grab the points when the opposition are flustered into mistakes. Mains knew Canterbury liked to play an expansive 15-man game, and given the chance liked to express themselves with some daring or imaginative deeds.

From the start the Mains' plan took control. The inspired Otago men rattled Canterbury in the first few minutes, and kept the hot favourites uncertain – and the crowd uncannily quiet – for a first half in which Brendan Laney did the damage. Mains's plan gave Laney a free hand – his friends believe Laney is incapable of being either stolid or solid – and the burly all-round back repaid with a try and 11 goal points.

At half-time Hansen told his men to forget about the rain in the air, or the slippery surface, or the fact that a team they had scored 62 points against earlier in the season had a ten-point lead. Concentrating on the key tactician, Andrew Mehrtens at first five-eighth, Hansen insisted that Canterbury return to their basic skills of passing and running – when the time was right.

Canterbury threw away their chains in the first ten minutes of the second half, scored two clever tries, worked out to a 17-16 lead, and then did what Canterbury do best – controlled the game through their mobile pack and Mehrtens's uncanny ability to mix his passing game with expert tactical punts. Otago, their early energy waning, managed only a penalty goal in the second half while Canterbury scored 24 points. Afterwards the crowd mobbed the Canterbury players and hoisted Blackadder triumphantly aloft on their shoulders.

They had won the first division title only once before, in 1997. Now they had it again, and there could be no finer farewell tribute to their unforgettable hero, Todd Blackadder

Canterbury: L R MacDonald; J Maddock, N K Mauger, A J D Mauger, C S Ralph; A P Mehrtens, J W Marshall; G E Feek, M R Sexton, G M Somerville, T J Blackadder (*captain*), N M C Maxwell, R D Thorne, S M Robertson, R H McCaw *Substitutions:* D P E Gibson for A Mauger; D N Hewett for Feek; B C Thorn for Maxwell

Scorers *Tries:* N Mauger, Marshall *Conversion:* Mehrtens *Penalty Goals:* Mehrtens (5) *Drop Goal:* Mehrtens

Otago: J W Wilson; B J Laney, T R Nicholas, S Mapusua, H B Reid; T E Brown, B T Kelleher; J M McDonnell, A D Oliver, K J Meuws, F Levi, T S Maling, T C Randell (*captain*), P C Miller, S Harding *Substitutions:* G E Leaupepe for Wilson; D T Parkinson for Mapusua; T E Willis for Oliver; C J Hayman for Meeuws; G A Webb for Miller

Scorers *Try:* Laney *Conversion:* Laney *Penalty Goals:* Laney (2) *Drop Goals:* Laney, Nicholas

Referee P G Honiss (NZRFU).

Results

Semi-finals: Canterbury 53, Auckland 22 (Jade Stadium, Christchurch); Otago 37, North Harbour 10 (North Harbour Stadium, Albany).

Final: Canterbury 30, Otago 19 (Jade Stadium, Christchurch)

Previous NPC Grand Finals : 1992 Waikato 40, Otago 5 (Hamilton); 1993 Auckland 27, Otago 18 (Auckland); 1994 Auckland 22, North Harbour 16 (Takapuna); 1995 Auckland 23, Otago 19 (Auckland); 1996 Auckland 46, Counties Manukau 15 (Auckland); 1997 Canterbury 44, Counties Manukau 13 (Christchurch); 1998 Otago 49, Waikato 20 (Dunedin); 1999 Auckland 24, Wellington 18 (Auckland); 2000 Wellington 34, Canterbury 29 (Christchurch); 2001 Canterbury 30, Otago 19 (Christchurch)

DOMESTIC RUGBY IN AUSTRALIA 2001

Four into Fourteen Won't Go

Peter Jenkins

Even in a season touched by triumph as the ACT Brumbies became the first Australian side to win the Super 12 series, the most significant development was a non-event. On July 11th, the board of the South African New Zealand Australian Rugby (SANZAR) alliance decided to expand the provincial series by two teams for the 2003 season.

A Super 14 would hit the paddocks of the three nations that year with Australia and South Africa to have their competition quotas increased to four and five sides respectively. It was, for the Australian Rugby Union, an essential breakthrough.

New Zealand has its National Provincial Championship. South Africa has its Currie Cup. Australia relies solely on Super 12 as a nursery for emerging players and playpen for established international talent. Extending the competitive incubator by a third with the introduction of a fourth side in a new-look Super 14 was considered a vital cog in building for the World Cup title defence on home soil.

But the SANZAR decision was built on shifting sands, and the dream turned to dust as the New Zealand Rugby Football Union eventually – knowing any change to the format could only be made as a unanimous decision – opted to retain the *status quo*. Super Twelve it was and so it would stay.

The Australian angst at their neighbours' reluctance to broaden the horizons of the championship was matched only by New Zealand gnarliness a few months later when World Cup co-hosting rights were stripped from the Kiwis. It was that sort of season really, given the controversies and occasional ill-feeling that marked the Lions tour down under that winter. On the domestic front, the Brumbies won the Super Twelve as the Queensland Reds finished seventh and the NSW Waratahs ninth.

But both non-semi finalists knew there would be improvement ahead, at least in their back-line potency, with the Reds and Waratahs confirming for the 2002 season the recruitment of key rugby league stars. Wing Wendell Sailor was the first to make the jump, announcing in February that he had signed with the ARU for four years, a deal that would start once he had completed the season to come with the champion Brisbane Broncos outfit.

Fellow Kangaroos speedster Mat Rogers also made the leap, with his signing revealed in June. Rogers would end the year by making an appearance for the Barbarians at outside-centre against the Wallabies in Cardiff. Both came with high price tags – Sailor signed for around £250,000 a year.

But the poaching raid by the ARU on a code that had for the best part of a century pillaged the union ranks and pinched the best talent with the lure of lucre, was significant.

Here were two of rugby league's finest having turned their backs on the 13-man game with clubs from the National Rugby League powerless to match the money the ARU were flashing. How could they? NRL clubs had a salary cap of around 1.2 million pounds each. Splashing more than 20 percent of that on one player was simply inconceivable. Those sort of figures were also an impossible dream for the fringe dwellers of the Australian Rugby Shield – a second tier competition taking in six teams from states, territories and regions below the big three of NSW, Queensland and ACT.

The NSW Country Cockatoos won all five of their preliminary matches to top the table ahead of Perth Gold, the Queensland Country Heelers, the Adelaide Falcons, Darwin Mosquitoes and Melbourne. In the semi-finals, NSW Country thrashed Adelaide 88-19 and Perth defeated Queensland Country 18-17. The Cockatoos took the title with a resounding 39-19 win over Perth in the decider.

At club level, Sydney University won the Citibank Mastercard Cup with a 27-20 win over Eastwood in front of 12,000 at the Sydney Football Stadium. It was the first top grade premiership in 30 years for Australia's oldest rugby club, whose pack bristled with a band of exciting young forwards. The back-row included international flankers David Lyons and Phil Waugh and a Fijian-born giant, Jone Tawake, who would sign a Super Twelve contract and play with the NSW Waratahs in 2002.

In the second-row was a towering South African, Dan Vickerman, who would also play Super Twelve and graduate even further, into the Wallaby ranks. The disappointment of the finals series was the failure of Northern Suburbs to continue their impressive form from the preliminary rounds.

Norths were beaten just twice during the season proper, then lost the major semi-final to Sydney University 26-15 and the preliminary final to Eastwood 27-18. But there was greater upheaval earlier in the season when the West Harbour club was penalised 19 competition points for fielding too many overseas players. A court action failed to overturn the decision by the NSW Rugby Union and Wests missed the semi-finals. The minor consolation was flanker Des Tuiavii, a star for the Waratahs in 2002, taking out the Ken Catchpole Medal as the best and fairest club player of the season.

In Brisbane, it was a new-look competition with the Canberra Vikings invited to take part in the Queensland Rugby Union premiership after they were snubbed out by NSW. The Vikings came, saw and conquered in their first season, winning the grand final from fledgling club the Gold Coast Breakers 32-10.

As in Sydney, the team that topped the standings after the preliminary rounds crashed and burned before the decider. GPS lost 32-23 to Canberra in the major semi-final and went down 33-32 to Gold Coast in the preliminary final. At the foot of the table, Norths QUT went through the entire 18-game season winless and conceded 992 points – an average of 55 a game. The best and fairest player award – the XXXX Medal – went to Easts fly-half Andrew Scotney.

The seven-team ACT club competition also proved a disaster for the minor premiers. Royals topped the table leading into the play-offs but did not even qualify for the decider. Wests beat Tuggeranong 23-20 in the grand final.

In South Australia, Old Collegians defeated Brighton 23-20 in the grand final, while the Northern Territory championship was taken out by Darwin, with an 11-8 win over South Darwin.

Box Hill won the Melbourne premiership, downing Northcote 27-13 in the grand final, Cottesloe were crowned the Western Australian champions after accounting for Nedlands 30-12 in the decider, and Glenorchy won the Tasmanian title with a 22-3 win over University.

FIXTURES 2002-2003

Venues and fixtures are subject to alteration. At the time of going to press, only the weekends for which some League, Heineken Cup and European Shield matches had been scheduled were known. See press for further details.

Friday, 1 November
SRU Inter-Pro Team Championship
Edinburgh Rugby v Glasgow Rugby

RFU/Zurich Premiership
Sale v Bristol

Saturday, 2 November
ARGENTINA v AUSTRALIA
  (Buenos Aires)
BULGARIA v MONACO (Sofia)
CROATIA v BELGIUM (Zagreb)
SLOVENIA v DENMARK (Ljubljana)
WALES v ROMANIA (Wrexham)

RFU/Zurich Premiership
Gloucester v Northampton
Harlequins v Bath
Leicester v Wasps

IRU/AIB Division One
Belfast Harlequins v Blackrock College
Buccaneers v Co Carlow
Clontarf v UCD
Cork Constitution v St Mary's College
Dungannon v UL Bohemians
Lansdowne v Ballymena
Shannon v Galwegians
Terenure College v Garryowen

WRU Premier League
Caerphilly v Neath
Ebbw Vale v Bridgend
Llanelli v Pontypridd
Swansea v Newport

Sunday, 3 November
YUGOSLAVIA v ANDORRA
  (Belgrade)

RFU/Zurich Premiership
Leeds v Saracens
Newcastle v London Irish

Tuesday, 5 November
Scotland A v Romanians (Aberdeen)

Saturday, 9 November
ENGLAND v NEW ZEALAND
  (Twickenham)
FRANCE v SOUTH AFRICA
  (Marseilles)
IRELAND v AUSTRALIA (Dublin)
SCOTLAND v ROMANIA
  (Murrayfield)
SWITZERLAND v CROATIA
WALES v FIJI (Cardiff)

RFU/Zurich Premiership
Northampton v Leicester

Sunday, 10 November
RFU/Zurich Premiership
Bath v Sale
Bristol v Newcastle
London Irish v Gloucester
Saracens v Harlequins
Wasps v Leeds

SRU/BT Premiership
Boroughmuir v Aberdeen GSFP
Hawick v Stirling County
Heriot's FP v Currie
Jed-Forest v Glasgow Hawks
Melrose v Peebles

Tuesday, 12 November
Italy A v Argentinians

Friday, 15 November
RFU/Zurich Premiership
Leicester v Gloucester
Sale v Saracens

Saturday, 16 November
ENGLAND v AUSTRALIA
(Twickenham)
FRANCE v NEW ZEALAND (Paris)
ITALY v ARGENTINA
LITHUANIA v LUXEMBOURG
(Vilnius)
SCOTLAND v SOUTH AFRICA
(Murrayfield)
WALES v CANADA (Cardiff)

IRU/AIB Division One
Ballymena v Co Carlow
Clontarf v Dungannon
Cork Constitution v Buccaneers
Galwegians v UL Bohemians
Lansdowne v Belfast Harlequins
St Mary's College v Blackrock College
UCD v Garryowen
Shannon v Terenure College

Sunday, 17 November
IRELAND v FIJI (Dublin)

RFU/Zurich Premiership
Bristol v London Irish
Harlequins v Wasps
Leeds v Northampton
Newcastle v Bath

SRU/BT Premiership
Aberdeen GSFP v Heriot's FP
Currie v Jed-Forest
Glasgow Hawks v Melrose
Peebles v Hawick
Stirling County v Boroughmuir

Wednesday, 20 November
Scotland A v Fijians (Stirling)
Ireland A v Argentinians (Belfast)

Friday, 22 November
RFU/Zurich Premiership
Gloucester v Leeds

Saturday, 23 November
ENGLAND v SOUTH AFRICA
(Twickenham)
FRANCE v CANADA (Paris)
IRELAND v ARGENTINA (Dublin)
ITALY v AUSTRALIA (Genoa)
MALTA v LITHUANIA
WALES v NEW ZEALAND (Cardiff)

RFU/Zurich Premiership
Northampton v Harlequins

SRU/BT Premiership
Boroughmuir v Peebles
Hawick v Glasgow Hawks
Jed-Forest v Heriot's FP
Melrose v Currie
Stirling County v Aberdeen GSFP

Sunday, 24 November
GERMANY v UKRAINE
SCOTLAND v FIJI (Murrayfield)

RFU/Zurich Premiership
Bath v Bristol
London Irish v Leicester
Saracens v Newcastle
Wasps v Sale

IRU/AIB Division One
Buccaneers v Lansdowne
Co Carlow v Shannon
Garryowen v Cork Constitution
Terenure College v Clontarf
UL Bohemians v UCD

Friday, 29 November
SRU Inter-Pro Team Championship
Glasgow Rugby v Borders Rugby

RFU/Zurich Premiership
Sale v Bath

Saturday, 30 November
AUSTRIA v MALTA (Vienna)

Celtic League *Quarter Finals*

RFU/Zurich Premiership
Gloucester v London Irish

Harlequins v Saracens
Leicester v Northampton

SRU/BT Premiership
Aberdeen GSFP v Jed-Forest
Currie v Hawick
Glasgow Hawks v Boroughmuir
Heriot's FP v Melrose
Peebles v Stirling County

IRU/AIB Division One
Belfast Harlequins v Galwegians
Blackrock College v Ballymena
Dungannon v St. Mary's College

Sunday, 1 December
RFU/Zurich Premiership
Leeds v Wasps
Newcastle v Bristol

Fri, Sat, Sun, 6,7,8 December
Heineken Cup *Third round*
Pool 1
Amatori & Calvisano v Neath
Beziers v Leicester

Pool 2
Gloucester v Perpignan
Munster v Viadana

Pool 3
Bourgoin v Glasgow Rugby
Sale v Llanelli

Pool 4
Montferrand v Leinster
Swansea v Bristol

Pool 5
Edinburgh Rugby v Toulouse
Newport v London Irish

Pool 6
Northampton v Cardiff
Ulster v Biarritz

Saturday, 7 December
IRB Sevens (Dubai)

SRU/BT Premiership
Boroughmuir v Currie
Hawick v Heriot's FP
Melrose v Jed-Forest
Peebles v Aberdeen GSFP
Stirling County v Glasgow Hawks

IRU/AIB Division One
Ballymena v Belfast Harlequins
Buccaneers v Blackrock College
Cork Constitution v Lansdowne
Galwegians v Co Carlow
Shannon v Clontarf
St. Mary's College v Garryowen
Terenure College v UL Bohemians
UCD v Dungannon

Sunday, 8 December
IRB Sevens (Dubai)

Tuesday, 10 December
Oxford University v Cambridge University (Twickenham)

Friday, 13 December
IRB Sevens (George)

Fri, Sat, Sun, 13,14,15 December
Heineken Cup *Fourth round*
Pool 1
Leicester v Beziers
Neath v Amatori & Calvisano

Pool 2
Perpignan v Gloucester
Viadana v Munster

Pool 3
Glasgow Rugby v Bourgoin
Llanelli v Sale

Pool 4
Bristol v Swansea
Leinster v Montferrand

Pool 5
London Irish v Newport
Toulouse v Edinburgh Rugby

Pool 6
Biarritz v Ulster
Cardiff v Northampton

Saturday, 14 December
IRB Sevens (George)

SRU/BT Cup Fourth round

Friday, 20 December
SRU Inter-Pro Team Championship
Borders Rugby v Edinburgh Rugby

Saturday, 21 December
RFU/Powergen Cup *Sixth Round*

SRU/BT Premiership
Aberdeen GSFP v Melrose
Currie v Stirling County
Glasgow Hawks v Peebles
Heriot's FP v Boroughmuir
Jed-Forest v Hawick

WRU Premier League
Caerphilly v Swansea
Ebbw Vale v Llanelli
Newport v Bridgend
Pontypridd v Cardiff

Thursday, 26 December
SRU Inter-Pro Team Championship
Glasgow Rugby v Edinburgh Rugby

WRU Premier League
Bridgend v Caerphilly
Cardiff v Ebbw Vale
Llanelli v Newport
Swansea v Neath

Friday, 27 December
RFU/Zurich Premiership
Wasps v Leicester

Saturday, 28 December
RFU/Zurich Premiership
Bath v Harlequins
Northampton v Gloucester

IRU/AIB Division One
Belfast Harlequins v UCD
Blackrock College v Terenure College
Clontarf v Lansdowne
Co Carlow v St. Mary's College
Dungannon v Ballymena
Garryowen v Galwegians
Shannon v Cork Constitution
UL Bohemians v Buccaneers

Sunday, 29 December
RFU/Zurich Premiership
Bristol v Sale
London Irish v Newcastle
Saracens v Leeds

Monday, 30 December
WRU Premier League
Caerphilly v Llanelli
Neath v Pontypridd
Newport v Cardiff
Swansea v Bridgend

Tuesday, 31 December
SRU Inter-Pro Team Championship
Borders Rugby v Glasgow Rugby

Friday, 3 January 2002
SRU Inter-Pro Team Championship
Edinburgh Rugby v Borders Rugby

RFU/Zurich Premiership
Sale v Newcastle

Saturday, 4 January
Celtic League *Semi-Finals*

RFU/Zurich Premiership
Gloucester v Wasps
Harlequins v Bristol
Leicester v Saracens
Northampton v London Irish

SRU/BT Premiership
Boroughmuir v Jed-Forest
Glasgow Hawks v Aberdeen GSFP
`Hawick v Melrose
Peebles v Currie

Stirling County v Heriot's FP

WRU Premier League
Bridgend v Neath
Cardiff v Caerphilly
Llanelli v Swansea
Pontypridd v Ebbw Vale

Sunday, 5 January
RFU/Zurich Premiership
Leeds v Bath

Friday, 10 January
IRB Sevens (in Chile)

Fri, Sat, Sun, 10/11/12 January
Heineken Cup *Fifth round*
Pool 1
Amatori & Calvisano v Leicester
Neath v Beziers

Pool 2
Gloucester v Viadana
Perpignan v Munster

Pool 3
Llanelli v Bourgoin
Sale v Glasgow Rugby

Pool 4
Leinster v Swansea
Montferrand v Bristol

Pool 5
Edinburgh Rugby v London Irish
Toulouse v Newport

Pool 6
Cardiff v Ulster
Northampton v Biarritz

Saturday, 11 January
IRB Sevens (in Chile)

SRU/BT Cup *Fifth round*

Fri, Sat, Sun, 17/18/19 January
Heineken Cup *Sixth round*
Pool 1
Beziers v Amatori & Calvisano
Leicester v Neath

Pool 2
Munster v Gloucester
Viadana v Perpignan

Pool 3
Bourgoin v Sale Sharks
Glasgow Rugby v Llanelli

Pool 4
Bristol v Leinster
Swansea v Montferrand

Pool 5
London Irish v Toulouse
Newport v Edinburgh Rugby

Pool 6
Biarritz v Cardiff
Ulster v Northampton

Saturday, 18 January
SRU/BT Premiership
Currie v Glasgow Hawks
Hawick v Aberdeen GSFP
Heriot's FP v Peebles
Jed-Forest v Stirling County
Melrose v Boroughmuir

IRU/AIB Division One
Belfast Harlequins v Co Carlow
Clontarf v Blackrock College
Cork Constitution v Ballymena
Dungannon v Garryowen
Lansdowne v UL Bohemians
Shannon v UCD
St. Mary's College v Terenure College

Friday, 24 January
SRU Inter-Pro Team Championship
Edinburgh Rugby v Glasgow Rugby

Saturday, 25 January
RFU Cup *Quarter-Finals*

SRU/BT Premiership
Aberdeen GSFP v Currie
Boroughmuir v Hawick
Glasgow Hawks v Heriot's FP
Peebles v Jed-Forest
Stirling County v Melrose

IRU/AIB Division One
Ballymena v Shannon
Blackrock College v Lansdowne
Buccaneers v St Mary's College
Co Carlow v Dungannon
Garryowen v Belfast Harlequins
Terenure College v Galwegians
UCD v Cork Constitution
UL Bohemians v Clontarf

WRU Premier League
Bridgend v Llanelli
Neath v Ebbw Vale
Newport v Pontypridd
Swansea v Cardiff

Friday, 31 January
SRU Inter-Pro Team Championship
Glasgow Rugby v Borders Rugby

Saturday, 1 February
IRB Sevens (Brisbane)

Celtic League *FINAL*

RFU/Zurich Premiership
Bath v Leicester

SRU/BT Cup – *Quarter-Finals*

IRU/AIB Division One
Ballymena v UCD
Belfast Harlequins v Dungannon
Blackrock College v UL Bohemians
Buccaneers v Terenure College
Clontarf v Cork Constitution
Lansdowne v Shannon
St Mary's College v Galwegians
Co Carlow v Garryowen

WRU Premier League
Cardiff v Bridgend
Ebbw Vale v Newport

Neath v Llanelli
Pontypridd v Caerphilly

Sunday, 2 February
IRB Sevens (Brisbane)

RFU/Zurich Premiership
Bristol v Leeds
London Irish v Sale
Newcastle v Harlequins
Saracens v Gloucester
Wasps v Northampton

Tuesday, 4 February
WRU Premier League
Caerphilly v Ebbw Vale
Llanelli v Cardiff
Newport v Neath
Swansea v Pontypridd

Friday, 7 February
IRB Sevens (Wellington)

SRU Inter-Pro Team Championship
Borders Rugby v Edinburgh Rugby

Saturday, 8 February
IRB Sevens (Wellington)

RFU/Zurich Premiership
Gloucester v Bath
Leicester v Bristol
Northampton v Saracens

IRU/AIB Division One
Belfast Harlequins v Buccaneers
Clontarf v Garryowen
Cork Constitution v Blackrock College
Dungannon v Terenure College
Galwegians v UCD
Lansdowne v Co Carlow
Shannon v UL Bohemians
St Mary's College v Ballymena

WRU/Principality Cup *Seventh Round*

Sunday, 9 February
RFU/Zurich Premiership
Harlequins v Sale

Leeds v Newcastle
Wasps v London Irish

Friday, 14 February
England A v France A
Italy A v Wales A

Saturday, 15 February
The Six Nations Championship
ENGLAND v FRANCE
  (Twickenham)
ITALY v WALES (Rome)

The European Nations Cup
CZECH REPUBLIC v ROMANIA
  (Prague)
PORTUGAL v GEORGIA (Lisbon)
SPAIN v RUSSIA (Madrid)
Scotland A v Ireland A (Stirling)

Sunday, 16 February
The Six Nations Championship
SCOTLAND v IRELAND
  (Murrayfield)

Friday, 21 February
Italy A v Ireland A
Wales A v England A

Saturday, 22 February
The Six Nations Championship
ITALY v IRELAND (Rome)
WALES v ENGLAND (Cardiff)

The European Nations Cup
CZECH REPUBLIC v RUSSIA
  (Prague)
GEORGIA v SPAIN (Tbilisi)
ROMANIA v PORTUGAL
  (Bucharest)
France A v Scotland A

Sunday, 23 February
The Six Nations Championship
FRANCE v SCOTLAND (Paris)

Saturday, 1 March
RFU Cup *Semi-Finals*

IRU/AIB Division One
Ballymena v Galwegians
Blackrock College v Shannon
Buccaneers v Dungannon
Co Carlow v Clontarf
Garryowen v Lansdowne
Terenure College v Belfast Harlequins
UCD v St Mary's College
UL Bohemians v Cork Constitution

WRU Premier League
Caerphilly v Newport
Cardiff v Neath
Pontypridd v Bridgend
Swansea v Ebbw Vale

Sunday, 2 March
ANDORRA v LATVIA (Andorra la
  Vela)
GERMANY v THE NETHERLANDS

Friday, 7 March
Ireland A v France A
Scotland A v Wales A

Saturday, 8 March
The Six Nations Championship
IRELAND v FRANCE (Dublin)
SCOTLAND v WALES (Murrayfield)

The European Nations Cup
PORTUGAL v CZECH REPUBLIC
  (Lisbon)
RUSSIA v GEORGIA (Krasnodar)
SPAIN v ROMANIA (Madrid)

England A v Italy A
SWITZERLAND v BELGIUM

Sunday, 9 March
The Six Nations Championship
ENGLAND v ITALY (Twickenham)

Friday, 14 March
RFU/Zurich Premiership
Sale v Leeds

Saturday, 15 March
THE NETHERLANDS v UKRAINE
(Hilversum)

RFU/Zurich Premiership
Bath v Northampton

IRU/AIB Division One
Ballymena v UL Bohemians
Clontarf v Buccaneers
Cork Constitution v Co Carlow
Galwegians v Dungannon
Lansdowne v Terenure College
St Mary's College v Belfast Harlequins
UCD v Blackrock College
Shannon v Garryowen

WRU/Principality Cup *Quarter-Finals*

Sunday, 16 March
RFU/Zurich Premiership
Bristol v Gloucester
London Irish v Harlequins
Newcastle v Leicester
Saracens v Wasps

Friday, 21 March
England A v Scotland A
Wales A v Ireland A

Saturday, 22 March
The Six Nations Championship
ENGLAND v SCOTLAND
(Twickenham)
WALES v IRELAND (Cardiff)

The European Nations Cup
CZECH REPUBLIC v GEORGIA
(Prague)
PORTUGAL v SPAIN (Lisbon)
ROMANIA v RUSSIA (Bucharest)
Italy A v France A

Sunday, 23 March
The Six Nations Championship
ITALY v FRANCE (Rome)

Friday, 28 March
France A v Wales A
Scotland A v Italy A

IRB Sevens (Hong Kong)

Saturday, 29 March
The Six Nations Championship
FRANCE v WALES (Paris)
SCOTLAND v ITALY (Murrayfield)

The European Nations Cup
GEORGIA v ROMANIA (Tbilisi)
RUSSIA v PORTUGAL (Krasnodar)
SPAIN v CZECH REPUBLIC
(Madrid)

Ireland A v England A

IRB Sevens (Hong Kong)
MALTA v LUXEMBOURG
POLAND v GERMANY

Sunday, 30 March
The Six Nations Championship
IRELAND v ENGLAND (Dublin)

IRB Sevens (Hong Kong)

Friday, 4 April
SRU Inter-Pro Team Championship
Glasgow Rugby v Edinburgh Rugby

RFU/Zurich Premiership
Gloucester v Newcastle
Leicester v Sale

Saturday, 5 April
IRB Sevens (Beijing)

IRB/FIRA-AER U19 World
Championships (in France)
BELGIUM v SLOVENIA (Brussels)
BOSNIA v MALTA (Sarajevo)

RFU/Powergen Cup *FINAL*
(Twickenham)

SRU/BT Cup *Semi-Finals*

IRU/AIB Division One
Belfast Harlequins v Clontarf
Blackrock College v Galwegians
Buccaneers v Shannon
Co Carlow v UCD
Dungannon v Lansdowne
Garryowen v Ballymena
Terenure College v Cork Constitution
UL Bohemians v St Mary's College

WRU Premier League
Bridgend v Ebbw Vale
Neath v Caerphilly
Newport v Swansea
Pontypridd v Llanelli

Sunday, 6 April

IRB Sevens (Beijing)
ISRAEL v BULGARIA

RFU/Zurich Premiership
Leeds v Harlequins
Saracens v London Irish
Wasps v Bath

Friday, 11 April

SRU Inter-Pro Team Championship
Borders Rugby v Glasgow Rugby

Fri, Sat, Sun, 11,12,13 April

Heineken Cup *Quarter-Finals*

Saturday, 12 April

IRU/AIB Division One
Ballymena v Terenure College
Cork Constitution v Belfast Harlequins
Co Carlow v Blackrock College
Galwegians v Clontarf
Garryowen v UL Bohemians
St Mary's College v Lansdowne
Shannon v Dungannon
UCD v Buccaneers

WRU Premier League
Bridgend v Newport
Cardiff v Pontypridd
Llanelli v Ebbw Vale
Swansea v Caerphilly

Friday, 18 April

SRU Inter-Pro Team Championship
Edinburgh Rugby v Borders Rugby

RFU/Zurich Premiership
Sale v Gloucester

Saturday, 19 April

**IRB/FIRA-AER U19 World
   Championship Final** (in France)

RFU/Zurich Premiership
Bath v Saracens
Harlequins v Leicester

IRU/AIB Division One
Belfast Harlequins v Shannon
Blackrock College v Garryowen
Buccaneers v Ballymena
Clontarf v St Mary's College
Dungannon v Cork Constitution
Lansdowne v Galwegians
Terenure College v UCD
UL Bohemians v Co Carlow

WRU/Principality Cup *Semi-Finals*

Sunday, 20 April

MONACO v ISRAEL (Monaco)

RFU/Zurich Premiership
Bristol v Wasps
London Irish v Leeds
Newcastle v Northampton

Tues/Weds, 22/23 April

WRU Premier League
Caerphilly v Bridgend
Ebbw Vale v Cardiff
Neath v Swansea
Newport v Llanelli

Fri, Sat, Sun, 25,26,27 April

Heineken Cup *Semi-Finals*

Saturday, 26 April

IRB Sevens (Singapore)
BELGIUM v DENMARK (Brussels)

HUNGARY v YUGOSLAVIA
(Budapest)
LATVIA v MOLDAVIA (Riga)

RFU/Zurich Premiership
Bath v London Irish
Gloucester v Harlequins
Leicester v Leeds
Northampton v Sale

SRU/BT Cup *FINAL* (Murrayfield)

WRU Premier League
Bridgend v Swansea
Cardiff v Newport
Llanelli v Caerphilly
Pontypridd v Neath

Sunday, 27 April

IRB Sevens (Singapore)
SWEDEN v GERMANY (Stockholm)

RFU/Zurich Premiership
Saracens v Bristol
Wasps v Newcastle

Friday, 2 May

RFU/Zurich Premiership
Harlequins v Northampton
Sale v Wasps

Saturday, 3 May

IRB Sevens (Malaysia)
DENMARK v CROATIA
(Copenhagen)
THE NETHERLANDS v SWEDEN
(Hilversum)
YUGOSLAVIA v LATVIA (Belgrade)

RFU/Zurich Premiership
Leicester v London Irish

Sunday, 4 May

IRB Sevens (Malaysia)
ISRAEL v NORWAY

RFU/Zurich Premiership
Bristol v Bath
Leeds v Gloucester

Newcastle v Saracens

Tues/Weds, 6/7 May

WRU Premier League
Cardiff v Swansea
Ebbw Vale v Neath
Llanelli v Bridgend
Pontypridd v Newport

Saturday, 10 May

POLAND v THE NETHERLANDS
LUXEMBOURG v AUSTRIA
(Cessange)
MOLDAVIA v HUNGARY (Chisinau)
SLOVENIA v SWITZERLAND
(Ljubljana)

RFU/Zurich Premiership
Bath v Newcastle
Gloucester v Leicester
London Irish v Bristol
Northampton v Leeds
Saracens v Sale
Wasps v Harlequins

WRU Premier Division
Caerphilly v Cardiff
Ebbw Vale v Pontypridd
Neath v Bridgend
Swansea v Llanelli

Saturday, 17 May

WRU Premier Division
Bridgend v Cardiff
Caerphilly v Pontypridd
Llanelli v Neath
Newport v Ebbw Vale

Saturday, 24 May

MOLDAVIA v YUGOSLAVIA
(Chisinau)
UKRAINE v SWEDEN (Kiev)

Heineken Cup *FINAL* (Dublin)

Parker Pen Challenge Cup *FINAL*

WRU Premier Division
Cardiff v Llanelli

Ebbw Vale v Caerphilly
Neath v Newport
Pontypridd v Swansea

Sunday, 25 May
ENGLAND XV v BARBARIANS
(Twickenham)

Saturday, 31 May
AUSTRIA v BOSNIA (Vienna)
BULGARIA v FINLAND (Sofia)
NORWAY v MONACO (Oslo)

Zurich Premiership *FINAL*
(Twickenham)

June
IRB U21 World Cup

Friday, 6 June
IRB Sevens (London)

Saturday, 7 June
AUSTRALIA v IRELAND (Brisbane)
FINLAND v ISRAEL (Helsinki)
SOUTH AFRICA v SCOTLAND
(Durban)

IRB Sevens (London)

Saturday, 14 June
ARGENTINA v FRANCE (Buenos
Aires)
AUSTRALIA v WALES (Sydney)
FINLAND v NORWAY (Helsinki)
NEW ZEALAND v ENGLAND
(Wellington)
SOUTH AFRICA v SCOTLAND
(Johannesburg)

IRB Sevens (Cardiff)

Sunday, 15 June
IRB Sevens (Cardiff)

Saturday, 21 June
AUSTRALIA v ENGLAND
(Melbourne)

NEW ZEALAND v WALES
(Hamilton)

Saturday, 28 June
NEW ZEALAND v FRANCE
(Christchurch)

Saturday, 12 July
The Tri Nations Championship
SOUTH AFRICA v AUSTRALIA
(Cape Town)

Saturday, 19 July
The Tri Nations Championship
SOUTH AFRICA v NEW ZEALAND
(Pretoria)

Saturday, 26 July
The Tri Nations Championship
AUSTRALIA v NEW ZEALAND
(Sydney)

Saturday, 2 August
The Tri Nations Championship
AUSTRALIA v SOUTH AFRICA
(Perth)

Saturday, 9 August
The Tri Nations Championship
NEW ZEALAND v SOUTH AFRICA
(Dunedin)

Saturday, 16 August
The Tri Nations Championship
NEW ZEALAND v AUSTRALIA
(Auckland)

Saturday, 23 August
WALES v ENGLAND (Cardiff)

Saturday, 30 August
FRANCE v ENGLAND

Saturday, 6 September
ENGLAND v FRANCE
(Twickenham)

RUGBY WORLD CUP FIXTURES: 2003 FINALS

POOL A

Oct 10	Australia v Argentina (Sydney)
Oct 11	Ireland v Romania (Gosford North)
Oct 14	Argentina v Namibia (Gosford North)
Oct 18	Australia v Romania (Brisbane)
Oct 19	Ireland v Namibia (Sydney)
Oct 22	Argentina v Romania (Sydney)
Oct 25	Australia v Namibia (Adelaide)
Oct 26	Argentina v Ireland (Adelaide)
Oct 30	Namibia v Romania (Launceston)
Nov 1	Australia v Ireland (Melbourne)

POOL B

Oct 11	France v Fiji (Brisbane)
Oct 12	Scotland v Japan (Townsville)
Oct 15	Fiji v Repechage 1 (Brisbane)
Oct 18	France v Japan (Townsville)
Oct 20	Scotland v Repechage 1 (Brisbane)
Oct 23	Fiji v Japan (Townsville)
Oct 25	France v Scotland (Sydney)
Oct 27	Japan v Repechage 1 (Gosford North)
Oct 31	France v Repechage 1 (Wollongong)
Nov 1	Scotland v Fiji (Sydney)

POOL C

Oct 11	South Africa v Uruguay (Perth)
Oct 12	England v Georgia (Perth)
Oct 15	Samoa v Uruguay (Perth)
Oct 18	South Africa v England (Perth)
Oct 19	Georgia v Samoa (Perth)
Oct 24	South Africa v Georgia (Sydney)
Oct 26	England v Samoa (Melbourne)
Oct 28	Georgia v Uruguay (Sydney)
Nov 1	South Africa v Samoa (Brisbane)
Nov 2	England v Uruguay (Brisbane)

POOL D

Oct 11	New Zealand v Italy (Melbourne)
Oct 12	Wales v Canada (Melbourne)
Oct 15	Italy v Repechage 2 (Canberra)
Oct 17	New Zealand v Canada (Melbourne)
Oct 19	Wales v Repechage 2 (Canberra)
Oct 21	Italy v Canada (Canberra)
Oct 24	New Zealand v Repechage 2 (Brisbane)
Oct 25	Italy v Wales (Canberra)
Oct 29	Canada v Repechage 2 (Wollongong)
Nov 2	New Zealand v Wales (Sydney)

QUARTER FINALS

Nov 8	Winners Pool D v Runners-up Pool C (Melbourne)
	Winners Pool A v Runners-up Pool B (Brisbane)
Nov 9	Winners Pool B v Runners-up Pool A (Melbourne)
	Winners Pool C v Runners-up Pool D (Brisbane)

SEMI FINALS

Nov 15	Winners QF1 v Winners QF2 (Sydney)
Nov 16	Winners QF3 v Winners QF4 (Sydney)

THIRD/FOURTH PLACE PLAY-OFF

Nov 20	Losers SF1 v Losers SF2 (Sydney)

RWC FINAL 2003

Nov 22	Winners SF1 v Winners SF2 (Sydney)

MEMBER UNIONS OF THE IRB

IRB MEMBER UNIONS

Andorra
Name: FEDERACIO
ANDORRANA DE
RUGBY
Address: Baixada del Moli, 31
Andorra la Vella,
ANDORRA
Tel: +376 822 232
Fax: +376 864 564
Website: www.vpcrugby.org
Email: vpc@solucions.ad
Founded: 1986
IRB Affiliation: 1991
Chairman: Josep Arasanz Serra
Secretary: Carles Font Rossel
National Coach: Bruce Hemara
Clubs: 2
Players: 300
Referees: 3
Home Ground: Camp del M.I.C.G. Andorra La
Vella
Capacity: 650
Official Kit: Blue/Yellow/Red

Arabian Gulf Emirates
Name: ARABIAN GULF
R.F.U.
Address: PO Box 17123, Jebel
Ali, Dubai, UAE
Tel: +971 48 83 68 27
Fax: +971 48 83 68 10
Website: www.agrfu.com
Email: georgegrant@bblinternational.com
Founded: 1984
IRB Affiliation: 1990
Chairman: Duncan Gordon
Secretary: George Grant
National Coach: Darryl Hill
Clubs: 22
Players: 2,305
Referees: 15
Home Ground: Dubai Stadium
Capacity: 3,000
Official Kit: White & Red/Green/Blue Stripes

Argentina

Name: UNIÓN
ARGENTINA DE
RUGBY
Address: Avda.Rivadavia 1227,
EP, Buenos Aires, Capital
Federal 1033
ARGENTINA
Tel: +541143832211
Fax: +541143832570
Website: www.uar.com.ar

Email: uarugby@uar.com.ar
Founded: 1899
IRB Affiliation: 1987
Chairman: Miguel Servera
Secretary: Federico Fleitas
National Coach: Marcelo Loffreda
Clubs: 317
Players: 35,500
Referees: 355
Home Ground: Club Atletico Riverplate, Buenos
Aires
Capacity: 62,000
Official Kit: Sky Blue&White stripes

Australia
Name: AUSTRALIAN R.U.
Address: 181 Miller Street,
North Sydney, NSW 2060,
AUSTRALIA
Tel: +61299 56 34 44
Fax: +61299 55 32 99
Website: www.rugby.com.au
Email: strath@rugby.com.au
Founded: 1949
IRB Affiliation: 1949
Chairman: Bob Tuckey
Secretary: John O'Neill
National Coach: Eddie Jones
Clubs: 752
Players: 127,801
Official Kit: Gold

Austria

Name:
OSTERREICHISCHER
RUGBY VERBAND
Address: C/o
Website: www.fpr.pt
Tel: +43 13 68 00 17
Fax: +43 14 92 58 26
Website:
www.rugby-austria.com
Email:
k.duteil@schneiders-vienna.at
Founded: 1990
IRB Affiliation: 1992
Chairman: Thomas Per Gabriel
Secretary: Paul Duteil
National Coach: Stiig Gabriel
Clubs: 13
Players: 400
Referees: 10
Home Ground: Casino Stadion Hohe Warte
Capacity: 6,000
Official Kit: Black/White Hoops

Bahamas

Name: BAHAMAS R.U.
Address: PO Box N-7213,
Nassau BAHAMAS
Tel: +1 242 3232165
Fax: +1242 3228185
Email:
stephen@bahamasferries.com
Founded: 1973
IRB Affiliation: 1994
Chairman: Alan Wilson
Secretary: Stephen Thompson
National Coach: Garry Markham
Clubs: 4
Players: 284
Referees: 5
Home Ground: Winton Rugby Pitch
Capacity: 300
Official Kit: Gold

Barbados

Name: BARBADOS R.F.U.
Address: The Plantation
Complex, St. Lawrence
Main Road, Christ Church,
BARBADOS (W.I.)
Tel: +1 246 4373836
Fax: +1 246 4373838
Website: www.rugbybds.com
Email: brewer@sunbeach.net
Founded: 1965
IRB Affiliation: 1995
Chairman: Joe Whipple
Secretary: Jason Brewer
Clubs: 5
*Players:*100
Referees: 4
Home Ground: Garrison Savannah
Official Kit: Royal Blue/Yellow

Belgium

Name: FEDERATION
BELGE DE RUGBY
Address: Avenue de Marathon
135C, Boîte 5, Bruxelles,
B-1020, BELGIUM
Tel: +32 24 79 93 32
Fax: +32 24 76 2282
Website:
www.rugby.beinfo@rugby.be
Email: info@rugby.be
Founded: 1931
IRB Affiliation: 1988
Chairman: Phillippe Damas
Secretary: Eric Williamsens
National Coach: Pierre Amilhat
Clubs: 46
Players: 4,121
Home Ground: Stade des trois tilleuls
Capacity: 40,000
Official Kit: Black/Yellow/Red

Bermuda

Name: BERMUDA R.F.U.
Address: PO Box HM 1909,
Hamilton, HM EX,
BERMUDA (W.I)
Tel: +1 441 2920341
Fax: +1 441 2953122
Email: bermudarugby@ibl.bm
Founded: 1964
IRB Affiliation: 1992
Chairman: Dennis Dwyer
Secretary: John Williams
Clubs: 4
Players: 120
Official Kit: Blue/White & Red stripes.

Bosnia & Herzegovina

Name: R.F.U. OF BOSNIA &
HERZEGOVINA
Address: Kralja Tvrtka I, St.
No. 5, PP 46, Zenica,
72000, BOSNIA & HERZEGOVINA
Tel: +387 32 416 323
Fax: +387 32 416323
Email: rugbybih@bihnet.ba
Founded: 1992
IRB Affiliation: 1996
Chairman: Bosco Kukoli
National Coach: Nasir Vehbovic
Clubs: 7
Players: 635
Referees: 18
Home Ground: Kamberovica Polje, Zenica
Capacity: 2,000
Official Kit: Sky Blue

Botswana

Name: BOTSWANA R.U.
Address: PO Box 632
Francistown BOTSWANA
Tel: +267 21 20 40
Fax: +267 21 77 18
Email: fnr@info.bw
Founded: 1992
IRB Affiliation: 1994
Chairman: Andrew Seale
Secretary: Ian White
National Coach:
Clubs: 5
Players: 425
Official Kit: Black

Brazil

Name: ASSOCIACAO
BRASILEIRA DE
RUGBY
Address: R.Dna.Germaine
Burchard, 451, S.53, Agua
Branca – Sao Paulo, SP,
CEP:05002-062 BRAZIL
Tel: +55 1138 68 17 03
Fax: +55 1151 83 55 58
Email: abr@rugbynews.com.br

Founded: 1972
IRB Affiliation: 1995
Chairman: Jean-François Tesseire
Secretary: Luis Felipe Monteiro De Barros
National Coach: Antonio Mortoni-Neto
Clubs: 14
Players: 2,000
Referees: 4
Official Kit: Yellow/Green

British Virgin Islands
Name: BRITISH VIRGIN ISLANDS R.U.F.C.
Address: Fort Burt, Road Town – Po Box 3083
 Tortola BRITISH VIRGIN ISLANDS (W-I)
Tel: +1 284 4942868
Fax: +1 2844947889
Email: cmark@surbvl.com
Chairman: Brian Jackson
Secretary: Mark Chapman
Official Kit: White/Green horizontal Stripes

Bulgaria
Name: BULGARIAN
 RUGBY
 FEDERATION
Address: 75, V. Levski
 Sofia, 1040,
 BULGARIE
Tel: +359 29 80 72 97
Fax: +359 29 81 5728
Chairman: Lubomir
 Stoitcskoy
Secretary: G Marinkin
National Coach: Ivan Mihailov
Clubs: 24
Players: 1,645
Referees: 35
Official Kit: Red

Cameroon
Name: FÉDÉRATION CAMEROUNAISE DE
 RUGBY – (FECARUGBY)
Address: B.P. 316, Socada Yaoundé CAMEROON
Tel: +237 230 5332
Fax: +237 230 5392
Website: fecarugby@yahoo.fr
Founded: 1997
IRB Affiliation: 1999
Chairman: Mamba A Nyam Simon
Secretary: Tiek Mambo Theophile
National Coach: Lej Rene
Clubs: 9
Players: 700
Referees: 20
Home Ground: Stade Ahmadou Ahidjo, Yaoundé
Capacity: 60,000
Official Kit: Red

Canada
Name: RUGBY CANADA
Address: 2197 Riverside,
 Ottawa, Ontario, K1H
 7X3, CANADA

Tel: +1 6135 21 24 66
Fax: +1 6135 21 39 28
Website: www.rugbycanada.ca
Email: rugbycanada@rugbycanada.ca
Founded: 1965
IRB Affiliation: 1986
Chairman: Pat Parfrey
National Coach: David Clark
Clubs: 430
Players: 16,500
Referees: 200
Official Kit: Red & Black/Red/White stripes

Cayman

Name: CAYMAN R.U.
Address: PO BOX 11 61 GT,
 Grand Cayman, British
 West Indies, CAYMAN
 ISLANDS (W-I)
Tel: +345 949 7960
Fax: +345 946 5786
Website: www.caymanrugby.com
Email: techdir@candw.ky
Founded: 1971
IRB Affiliation: 1997
Chairman: Derek Haines
Secretary: Martin Lang
National Coach: Stephen Adams
Clubs: 5
Players: 1,247
Referees: 12
Home Ground: South Sound Rugby Park, Grand
 Cayman
Capacity: 1,000
Official Kit: Red-White-Blue

Chile
Name: FEDERACION DE
 RUGBY DE CHILE
Address: Avenda Larrain
 II.1095 La Reine, Santiago,
 CHILE
Tel: +56 26 35 08 80
Fax: +56 22 75 93 15
Website: www.feruchi.cl
Email: feruchi@ctcruen.a.cl
Founded: 1935
IRB Affiliation: 1991
Chairman: Miguel A Mujica
Secretary: Bernardo Santillan
National Coach: Raul Carchio
Clubs: 144
Players: 13,710
Referees: 80˙
Home Ground: Centro Alto Pendimiento del
 Rugby
Capacity: 4,000
Official Kit: Red

China

Name: CHINA R.U.
Address: No. 9 Tiyuguan
Road, Chongwen District,
Beijing, 100763,
PEOPLES REP. OF
CHINA
Tel: +86 10 85826001
Fax: +86 10 85825994
Email: cga_cra@263.net
Founded: 1996
IRB Affiliation: 1997
Secretary: Gaochao Li
Clubs: 30
Players: 954
Official Kit: Red & Yellow Stripes

Chinese Taipei

Name: CHINESE TAIPEI
R.F.U.
Address: Room 808 8F, N020
Chulun Street, Taipei 104,
TAIWAN
Tel: +886 287 72 21 59
Fax: +886 287 72 21 71
Founded: 1946
IRB Affiliation: 1986
Chairman: Cheng Tsai
Secretary: Chung Lin Ching
Clubs: 15
Players: 1,225
Official Kit: Blue/White

Colombia

Name: FEDERACION
COLOMBIAN DE
RUGBY
Address: Calle 79 # 10-50,
apto.104, Bogota, COLOMBIA
Tel: +57 12 36 36 17
Fax: +57 14 81 30 99
Website: scorpions-simplenet.com/columbia.htm
Email: rianovic@col.net.co
IRB Affiliation: 1999
Chairman: Willam Nelson Paul
National Coach: Andrew Wright
Clubs: 18
Players: 460
Referees: 3
Official Kit: Yellow

Cook Islands

Name: COOK ISLANDS RU
Address: P.O. Box 898,
Rarotonga, COOK
ISLANDS
Tel: +682 25845
Fax: +682 25853
Website: www.rugby.co.ck
Email: cirugby@rugby.co.ck
Founded: 1989
IRB Affiliation: 1995
Chairman: Nooroa Tou
Secretary: Turua Antony

National Coach: John McKittrick
Clubs: 10
Players: 1,000
Referees: 30
Home Ground: Tereora National Satdium
Capacity: 5,000
Official Kit: White/Gold/Green

Côte d'Ivoire

Name: FEDERATION
IVOIRIENNE DE
RUGBY
Address: 01 BP 2357, Abidjan,
1 IVORY-COAST
Tel: +225 20 34 71 04
Fax: +225 20 34 71 07
Email: z_marcellin@yahoo.fr
Founded: 1961
IRB Affiliation: 1988
Chairman: Marcellin Zahui
Secretary: Camille Anoma
Clubs: 40
Players: 5,962
Official Kit: Orange

Croatia

Name: HRVATSKI RAGBIJASKI SAVEZ
Address: TRG Sportova 11, Zagreb, 10000,
CROATIA
Tel: +385 13 65 02 50
Fax: +38513 09 29 21
Email: cro.rugby@zg.hinet.hr
Founded: 1962
IRB Affiliation: 1992
Chairman: Ivo Jurisic
Secretary: Velimir Juricko
National Coach: Richard Walter Borich
Clubs: 9
Players: 1,124
Referees: 14
Home Ground: Stadion Nada
Capacity: 6,000
Official Kit: Red & White

Czech Republic

Name: CESKA RUGBYOVA
UNIE
Address: Mezi Stadiony, PS
40, Praha 6, 160 17,
CZECH REPUBLIC
Tel: +420 2 33 35 13 41
Fax: +420 2 33 35 13 41
Email: rugby@cstv.cz
Founded: 1926
IRB Affiliation: 1988
Chairman: Bruno Kudrna
Secretary: Josef Zabransky
National Coach: Vaclay Horacek
Clubs: 21
Players: 2,329
Referees: 59
Home Ground: Tatra Smichov, Praha 5
Capacity: 5,000
Official Kit: Red/White/Blue stripes

Denmark

Name: DANSK R.U
Address: Idr[00e6]ttens Hus,
   Brondby Stadion 20
   Brøndby DK-2605,
   DENMARK
Tel: +45 43 26 28 00
Fax: +45 43 26 28 01
Website: www.rugby.dk
Email: info@rugby.dk
Founded: 1950
IRB Affiliation: 1988
Chairman: Ole Nielsen
Secretary: Inger Marie Godvin
National Coach: Douglas Langley
Clubs: 30
Players: 2,722
Referees: 29
Official Kit: Red

Finland

Name: SUOMEN RUGBY –
   LITTO
Address: Tommilantie 3 B-15,
   Kangasala 36270,
   FINLAND
Tel: +358 408 24 66
Fax: +358 20 475 4319
Email:
   christophecroze@yahoo.fr
Founded: 1968
IRB Affiliation: 2001
Chairman: Christophe Croze
Secretary: Esa Launis
National Coach: Thierry Demoulin
Clubs: 5
Players: 167
Referees: 10
Home Ground: Myllypuron Urheilupuisto
Capacity: 300
Official Kit: Light Blue

England

RUGBY FOOTBALL UNION

Name: THE RFU
Address: Rugby House, Rugby
   Road, Twickenham,
   TW1 1DS, England
Tel: +44 2088 922 000
Fax: +44 2088 929 816
Website: www.rfu.com
Email: reception@rfu.com
Founded: 1871
IRB Affiliation: 1890
Chairman: Derek Morgan
National Coach: Clive Woodward
Clubs: 1,800
Players: 634,460
Referees: 5,000
Home Ground: Twickenham
Capacity: 75,000
Official Kit: White/red contrast

France

FFR

Name: FÉDÉRATION
   FRANÇAISE DE
   RUGBY
Address: 9, rue de Liège, Paris
   75009, FRANCE
Tel: +33 01 53 21 15 15
Fax: +33 01 44 91 91 09
Website: www.ffr.fr
Email: secretairegeneral@ffr.fr
Founded: 1919
IRB Affiliation: 1978
Chairman: Bernard Lapasset
Secretary: Alain Doucet
National Coach: Bernard Laporte
Clubs: 1,710
Players: 252,638
Referees: 2,040
Home Ground: Stade de France
Capacity: 80,000
Official Kit: Blue

Fiji

FIJI R.U.

Name: FIJI R.U.
Address: 35, Gordon St., Po
   Box 1234, Suva, FIJI
Tel: +679 3 30 27 87
Fax: +679 3 30 09 36
Website: www.teivovo.com
Email:
   fijirugby@connect.com.fj
Founded: 1913
IRB Affiliation: 1987
Chairman: Keni Dakuidreketi
National Coach: Mark Mac Callion
Clubs: 600
Players: 60,000
Referees: 200
Home Ground: National Stadium
Capacity: 24,200
Official Kit: White/Black

Georgia

Name: GEORGIAN R.U.
Address: 49 A, Chavchavadze
   Ave, Sports Department,
   Tbilisi 62, GEORGIA
Tel: +995 32 29 47 54
Fax: +995 32 29 47 63
Website: www.chez.com/gru
Email:
   georgianrugbyunion@chez.com
Founded: 1964
IRB Affiliation: 1992
Chairman: Bidzina Gegidze
Secretary: Michael Burdzgla
National Coach: Claude Saurel
Clubs: 21
Players: 1,410
Referees: 12
Home Ground: National Stadium
Capacity: 74,000
Official Kit: Black/Bordo/Grey

Germany

Name: DEUTSCHER
RUGBY VERBAND
Address: P.O. Box 1566,
Hannover, Lower Saxony,
30015 GERMANY
Tel: +49 511 14763
Fax: +49 511 1610206
Website: www.rugby.de
Email: office@rugby-verband.de
Founded: 1900
IRB Affiliation: 1988
Chairman: Ian Robert Rawcliffe
Secretary: Volker Himmer
National Coach: Peter Ianusevici
Clubs: 102
Players: 4,200
Referees: 145
Home Ground: Fritz-Grunebau Stadion
Capacity: 3,500
Official Kit: White

Guam

Name: GUAM R.F.U
Address: PO Box 7246,
Tamuning 96931, GUAM
Tel: +1 671 4777250
Fax: +1 671 4721264
Website: www.rugbyonguam.com
Email: guamrfu@ambyth.guam.net
Founded: 1997
IRB Affiliation: 1998
Chairman: Greg David
Secretary: Ken I Cowan
Clubs: 2
Players: 239
Referees: 6
Home Ground: Wettengal Rugby field
Official Kit: White

Guyana

Name: GUYANA R.F.U.
Address: Po Box 101 730,
Georgetown, GUYANA
Tel: +592 2 26 00 82
Fax: +592 2 26 68 79
Email: guyanarugby@yahoo.com
Founded: 1920
IRB Affiliation: 1995
Chairman: Christopher Nascimento
Secretary: Terrence Grant
National Coach: Sherlock Solomon
Clubs: 4
Players: 240
Referees: 5
Home Ground: National Park
Capacity: 600
Official Kit: Green & Gold

Hong Kong

Name: HONG-KONG R.F.U.
Address: Room 2001, Sports
House, 1 Stadium Path, So
Kon Po, Causeway Bay,
HONG-KONG
Tel: +852 2504 8311
Fax: +852 2576 7237
Website: www.hkrugby.com.hk
Email: info@hkrugby.com.hk
Founded: 1953
IRB Affiliation: 1988
Chairman: John Molloy
Secretary: Trevor Gregory
National Coach: Chris Roden
Clubs: 14
Players: 5,342
Referees: 42
Home Ground: Hong Kong Stadium So Kon Po,
Causeway Bay
Capacity: 40,000
Official Kit: Red & White & Blue Stripes

Hungary

Name: MAGYAR ROGBI
SZOVETSEG
Address: 1143 Dozsa GY. Ut
1-3 Budapest, HUNGARY
Tel: +36 12 67 65 81
Website: www.gsz.hu
Email:
mrgsz@mail.adanet.hu
Founded: 1990
IRB Affiliation: 1991
Chairman: Tamas Fehervary
Secretary: Ria Ispanne
National Coach: Andras
Neuzer
Clubs: 15
Players: 1,489
Referees: 25
Official Kit: Red

India

Name: INDIAN R.F.U.
Address: Nawab House, 2nd
Flr, M. Karve Road –
Marine Lines, Bumbay,
400,002, INDIA
Tel: +91 222 09 63 57
Fax: +91 222 09 69 10
Email:
khannapramod@hotmail.com
Founded: 1968
IRB Affiliation: 2001
Chairman: Pramod Khanna
National Coach: Takeo Ishizuka
Clubs: 28
Players: 2,900
Referees: 10
Home Ground: Bumbay Gymkhana (BG)
Capacity: 10,000
Official Kit: Light Blue & White collar

Ireland

Name: IRISH RFU
Address: 62 Lansdowne Road,
  Ballsbridge, Dublin 4,
  IRELAND
Tel: +353 1 6473800
Fax: +3531 6473801
Website: www.irishrugby.ie
Founded: 1874
IRB Affiliation: 1886
Chairman: Don Crowley
Secretary: Philip Browne
National Coach: Eddie O'Sullivan
Clubs: 135
Players: 700
Home Ground: Lansdowne Road, Dublin
Capacity: 49,500
Official Kit: Green

IRISH RUGBY
FOOTBALL UNION

Israel

Name: ISRAEL RU
Address: P.O.Box 560,
  Raanana, 43104, ISRAEL
Tel: +972 9 7422 062
Fax: +972 9 7422062
Email: rugby@netvision.net.il
Founded: 1971
IRB Affiliation: 1988
Chairman: Dave Kaplan
Secretary: Cyril Morris
National Coach: Eduardo Cabral
Clubs: 20
Players: 770
Referees: 10
Official Kit: Blue & White

Italy

Name: FEDERAZION
  ITALIANA RUGBY
Address: Stadio Olimpico,
  Foro Italico, Roma 00194
  ITALY
Tel: +39 06 36 85 78 45
Fax: +39 06 36 85 78 53
Website: www.federugby.it
Email: federugby@atleticom.it
Founded: 1928
IRB Affiliation: 1987
Chairman: Giancarlo Dondi
Secretary: Giuliano Spingardi
National Coach: John Kirwan
Clubs: 500
Players: 39,856
Referees: 443
Home Ground: Stadio Flaminio, Roma
Capacity: 27,000
Official Kit: Sky Blue

Jamaica

Name: JAMAICA R.U.
Address: PO BOX 144,
  Kingston 5, JAMAICA
Tel: +1 876 9256703
Fax: +1 876 9311743

Jamaica Rugby Union

Website: www.jru.org.jm
Email: thompson@n5.com.jm
Founded: 1946
IRB Affiliation: 1996
Chairman: Jacob Thompson
Secretary: Richard Guy
National Coach: Harry Shaw
Clubs: 10
Players: 1,919
Referees:
Home Ground: Caymanas Estate Rugby Field
Capacity: 5,000
Official Kit: Gold/Black/Green

Japan

Name: JAPAN RFU
Address: 2-8-35 Kitoaoyama,
  Minato-Ku, Tokyo,
  107-0061, JAPAN
Tel: +813 34 01 33 23
Fax: +813 54 10 55 23
Website:
  www.rugby-japan.or.jp
Email: jrfu@rugby-japan.or.jp
Founded: 1926
IRB Affiliation: 1987
Chairman: Takayori Tsuboi
Secretary: Koju Tokmasu
National Coach: Shogo Mukai
Players: 4,050
Home Ground: Prince Chichibu Memorial Rugby
  Ground, Tokyo
Capacity: 28,000
Official Kit: White & Red Stripes

Kazakhstan

Name: KAZAKHSTAN R.U.
Address: Str. Kashgarskaya, 7,
  Ap4, Almaty, 480091,
  KAZAKHSTAN
Tel: +7 3272 327539
Fax: +7 3272 507357
Email: kaz_rugby@nursat.kz
Founded: 1993
IRB Affiliation: 1997
Chairman: Stanislav Knorr
National Coach: Philippov Vyacheslav
Clubs: 14
Players: 950
Referees: 10
Home Ground: Stadium of the Sportclub of Army
Capacity: 10,000
Official Kit: Yellow

Kenya

Name: KENYA R.F.U.
Address: PO Box 48322,
  Nairobi , GPO, KENYA
Tel: +254 2 57 44 25
Fax: +254 2 57 44 25
Website: www.kenyarugby.com
Email: krfu@iconnect.co.ke
Founded: 1923
IRB Affiliation: 1990
Chairman: George Kariuki

Kenya
Rugby
Football
Union

Secretary: Richard Omwela
National Coach: Kenneth Thimba
Clubs: 18
Players: 5,050
Referees: 30
Home Ground: Rugby Football Union of East
  Africa Grounds, Nairobi
Capacity: 5,000
Official Kit: Black/Red/Green

Korea

Name: KORÉA R.U.
Address: Room#506, Olympic
  Center, 88 Oryun-Dong,
  Song Pa-Gu, Seoul,
  KOREA
Tel: +82 24 20 42 44
Fax: +82 24 20 42 46
Website: www.rugby.sports.or.kr
Email: rugby@sports.or.kr
Founded: 1945
IRB Affiliation: 1988
Chairman: Kwang-Ho Choo
Clubs: 65
Players: 1,520
Home Ground: Seoul Rugby Ground, Séoul
Capacity: 3,000
Official Kit: Red & Blue stripes/White

Latvia

Name: LATVIAN RUGBY
  FEDERATION
Address: Kr.Barona Str.116a,
  Riga, LATVIA
Tel: +371 722 0320
Fax: +371 732 0180
Email: andrisd@mail.bkc.lv
Founded: 1960
IRB Affiliation: 1991
Chairman: Andris Denins
Secretary: Gunars Perlbahs
National Coach: Vladimirs Nikonovs
Clubs: 7
Players: 500
Referees: 11
Home Ground: Lu Stadium, Riga
Capacity: 2000
Official Kit: Dark Red

Lithuania

Name: LIETUVOS REGBIO
  FEDERACIJA
Address: Zemaites 6, Vilnius,
  2675, LITHUANIA
Tel: +370 2 33 54 74
Fax: +370 2 23 52 23
Email: litrugby@takas.lt
Founded: 1961
IRB Affiliation: 1992
Chairman: Aleksandras Makarenka
Secretary: Alphonsas Grumbinas
National Coach: Anatoliius Smimovas
Clubs: 14
Players: 1,620
Referees: 24

Official Kit: Green

Luxembourg

Name: FEDERATION
  LUXEMBOURGEOISE
  DE RUGBY
Address: 14, avenue de la
  Gare, BP 1965,
  Luxembourg, L-1410,
  LUXEMBURG
Tel: +352 29 75 98
Fax: +352 29 75 98
Website: www.rugby.lu
Email: luis.moitinho@village.uunet.lu
Founded: 1974
IRB Affiliation: 1991
Chairman: Jean-Phillippe De Muyser
Secretary: Luis Moitinho
National Coach: Bernard Jargeac
Clubs: 3
Players: 295
Referees: 1
Home Ground: Complexe Sportif, Boy Konen,
  Cessange
Official Kit: Sky Blue & White horiz. stripes

Madagascar

Name: FEDERATION
  MALGACHE DE
  RUGBY
Address: 12 avenue Lenine –
  Lot IVD26,
  Ambatomitsangana,
  Antananarivo, Madagascar
Tel: +261 20 22 625 60
Fax: +261 20 22 623 73
Email: fmr-rugby@dts.mg
Founded: 1963
IRB Affiliation: 1998
Chairman: Rigobert Tina Rakotoarinirina
Secretary: Samuel Rakotomamonjy
National Coach: Joseph Berthin Rafalimanana
Clubs: 198
Players: 9,126
Referees: 47
Home Ground: Stade Municipal de Mahamasina,
  Mahamasina
Capacity: 45,000
Official Kit: White/Green/Red

Malaysia

Name: MALAYSIA RU
Address: 427-1, Jalan Ampang,
  Kuala Lumpur, Jalan
  Ampang, 50450,
  MALAYSIA
Tel: +603 4253 4335
Fax: +603 4257 4335
Email: joemru@yahoo.com
Founded: 1927
IRB Affiliation: 1988
Chairman: Dato'Hj Talaat Hj Husain
Secretary: Mohd Nor Mohd.Tan
National Coach: Mohd Arsad Ahmad
Clubs: 185

Players: 21,000
Referees: 230
Home Ground: MPPJ Stadium, Petaling Joya
Capacity: 15,000
Official Kit: Blue/Yellow/Red

Malta

Name: MALTA RFU
Address: 76A, Gorg Borg
  Olivier Street, St. Julian's,
  STJ 08 MALTA
Tel: +356 21 38 04 40
Fax: +356 21 38 04 46
Email:
  kevin@jkproperties.com.mt
Founded: 1991
IRB Affiliation: 2000
Chairman: Kevin Buttigieg
Secretary: Christopher Martin
National Coach: Graham Richards
Clubs: 5
Players: 190
Referees: 2
Capacity: 1,500
Official Kit: Black/White/Red

Moldova

Name: FEDERATION OF
  RUGBY OF MOLDOVA
Address: Str. Columna 106,
  Chisinau, MOLDOVA
Tel: +373 2 22 26 74
Fax: +373 2 22 26 74
Email:
  rugbymold@yahoo.com
Founded: 1992
IRB Affiliation: 1994
Chairman: Boris Iacob
Secretary: Oleg Sadovici
National Coach: Alexandru Zbirnea
Clubs: 4
Players: 1,250
Referees: 38
Official Kit: Red

Monaco

Name: FÉDÉRATION
  MONÉGASQUE DE
  RUGBY
Address: Stade Louis II,
  avenue des Castelans,
  Monaco, MC-98000
Tel: +33 06 07 93 42 02
Fax: +33 04 93 78 62 70
Website: www.monaco-rugby.com
Email: monaco-rugby@wanadoo.fr
Founded: 1996
IRB Affiliation: 1998
Chairman: Patrice Pastor
Secretary: Claudy Vier
National Coach: Hervé Moni
Clubs: 1
Players: 160
Referees: 4
Home Ground: Stade Louis II, Monaco

Capacity: 20,000
Official Kit: White & Red

Morocco

Name: FEDERATION
  ROYALE MAROCAINE
  DE RUGBY
Address: Complexe
  Mohammed V, Porte 9,
  Casablanca, MOROCCO
Tel: +212 22 94 82 47
Fax: +212 22 36 90 60
Email: abougja@cgea.fr
Founded: 1956
IRB Affiliation: 1986
Chairman: Abdelaziz Bougja
Secretary: Kamal Benjeloune
National Coach: Edmond Jorda
Clubs: 24
Players: 6,800
Referees: 120
Home Ground: Complexe du C.O.C. Rugby
  Casablanca
Capacity: 4,500
Official Kit: Red/Green

Namibia

Name: NAMIBIA RU
Address: Lichtenstein Street,
  Olympia,
  Windhoek, NAMIBIA
Tel: +264 61 25 17 75
Fax: +264 61 25 10 28
Email: nru@cyberhost.com.na
Founded: 1990
IRB Affiliation: 1990
Chairman: Dirk Conradie
Secretary: Nicky Bekker
National Coach: David Waterston
Clubs: 19
Players: 4,700
Referees: 25
Home Ground: National Rugby Stadium,
  Windhoek
Capacity: 18,000
Official Kit: Royal Blue/Red/White Stripes

Netherlands

Name: NEDERLANDS
  RUGBY BOND
Address: Sportpark de
  Endracht, Po Box 8811,
  Amsterdam, 1006 JA
  NETHERLANDS
Tel: +31 204 80 81 00
Fax: +31 204 80 81 01
Website: www.euronet.nl.users.hemks.index
Email: info@rugby.nl
Founded: 1932
IRB Affiliation: 1988
Chairman: Ab Ekels
Secretary: Leo Van Schoonhoven
Clubs: 100
Players: 6,560
Referees: 74

Home Ground: National Rugby Centre
  Amsterdam
Capacity: 6,600
Official Kit: Orange

New Zealand

Name: NEW ZEALAND
  R.F.U.
Address: 1 Hinemoa Street,
  Centrepoint,
PO Box 2172, Wellington,
  NEW ZEALAND
Tel: +64 44 99 49 95
Fax: +64 44 99 42 24
Website: www.nzrugby.co.nz
Email: info@nzrugby.co.nz
Founded: 1892
IRB Affiliation: 1949
National Coach: John Mitchell
Clubs: 520
Players: 133,400
Referees: 2,300
Home Ground: Eden Park, Auckland
Capacity: 49,000
Official Kit: Black

Nigeria

Name: NIGERIA RUGBY
  FOOTBALL
  ASSOCIATION
Address: 4 Abibu Oki Close,
  Adeniran Ogunsanya,
Surulere, Lagos. NIGERIA
Tel: +234 17 74 26 37
Fax: +234 15 85 15 55
Email: klif@infoweb.abs.net
Founded: 1998
IRB Affiliation: 2001
Chairman: Ferni Williams
Secretary: Ntiense Williams
Clubs: 16
Players: 680
Referees: 8
Official Kit: Green

Niue Island

Name: NIUE RU
Address: Po Box 11, Alba,
  NIUE ISLAND
Tel: +683 4153
Fax: +683 4322
Email: tokes@niue.nu
Founded: 1952
IRB Affiliation: 1999
Chairman: Toke T. Talagi
Secretary: Norman Mitimeti
Clubs: 11
Home Ground: Pallati Alofi
Capacity: 2000
Official Kit: Gold/Navy Blue Stripes

Norway

Name: NORWEGIAN R.U.
Address: Serviceboks 1,
  Ullevaan, Oslo, N-0840
  NORWAY
Tel: +47 21 02 98 45
Fax: +47 21 02 98 46
Website: www.rugby.no
Email: rugby@nif.idrett.no
Founded: 1982
IRB Affiliation: 1993
Chairman: Per. S. Modne
Secretary: Kim J. Moore Eriksen
National Coach: Rod Francis
Clubs: 12
Players: 447
Referees: 8
Home Ground: Ekeberg
Official Kit: Red/White/Light & Navy Blue

Papua New Guinea

Name: PAPUA NEW
  GUINEA RFU
Address: Shop Front 2,
  Gateway Hotel,
  Morea-Tobo Road, P.O.
  Box 864, Port Moresby, National Capital
  District, PAPUA NEW GUINEA
Tel: +675 323 4212
Fax: +675 323 4211
Email: rugbypng@datec.com.pg
Founded: 1963
IRB Affiliation: 1993
Chairman: Graham Osborne
Secretary: Robert Doko
National Coach: Farrell Temata
Clubs: 69
Players: 4,000
Referees: 40
Home Ground: Lloyd Robson Oval, Port Moresby
Capacity: 20000
Official Kit: Blue/Yellow/Red stripes

Paraguay

Name: UNION DE RUGBY
  DEL PARAGUAY
Address: Independancia
  Nacional 250 C/Palma 1er
  Piso, Asuncion,
  PARAGUAY
Tel: +595 21 49 63 90
Fax: +595 21 49 63 90
Email: urprugby@pla.net.py
Founded: 1970
IRB Affiliation: 1989
Chairman: Luis Horacio Amarilla
Secretary: Jorge Benitez
National Coach: Marcello Gangoiti
Clubs: 12
Players: 1,438
Referees: 40
Official Kit: Red/White stripes

Peru

Name: UNION PERUANA
DE RUGBY
Address: Calle Toribio Pacheco
260, Miraflores, Lima, L
18 PERU
Tel: +51 14 41 46 65
Fax: +51 12 22 43 37
Email: jsilvah@ec-red.com
Founded: 1997
IRB Affiliation: 1999
Chairman: Jose Luis Silva Hurtado
Secretary: Carlos Hamann
National Coach: Felix Garcia Hidalgo
Clubs: 6
Players: 550
Referees: 8
Official Kit: White/Red collar

Poland

Name: POLISH R.U
Address: UI. Marymoncka 34,
Warszawa, 01-813,
POLAND
Tel: +48 228 35 35 87
Fax: +48 228 35 35 87
Email:
pzrugby@poczta.onet.pl
IRB Affiliation: 1988
Chairman: Jan Cozbowski
Secretary: Grzegorz Borkowski
National Coach: Jerzy Jumas
Clubs: 22
Players: 2000
Referees: 18
Official Kit: White

POLSKI
ZWIAZEK
RUGBY

Portugal

Name: FEDERAÇÃO
PORTUGUESA DE
RUGBY
Address: Rua Julieta Ferrão,
No. 12-3, Lisboa,
1600-131, PORTUGAL
Tel: +351 217 99 16 90
Fax: +351 217 93 61 35
Website: www.fpr.pt
Email: geral@fpr.pt
Founded: 1926
IRB Affiliation: 1988
Chairman: Jose Manuel Picao de Abren
Secretary: Delfim Bernardes Barreira
National Coach: Tomas Moraes
Clubs: 53
Players: 3,958
Referees: 49
Home Ground: Estádio Universitário de Lisboa
Capacity: 5,000
Official Kit: Red

Romania

Name: ROMANIAN
RUGBY FEDERATION
Address: bd Marasati, No. 26,
Sector 1, Bucuresti, 7700,
ROMANIA
Tel: +40 212 24 54 82
Fax: +40 212 24 54 81
Website: www.frr.ro
Email: frr@totalnet.ro
Founded: 1931
IRB Affiliation: 1987
Chairman: Octavian Morariu
Secretary: Hacic Garabet
National Coach: Bernard Charreyre
Clubs: 53
Players: 2,987
Referees: 91
Home Ground: National Stadium Bucharest
Capacity: 1,200
Official Kit: Yellow.

Russia

Name: R.U. OF RUSSIA
Address: 24 Lenina Str.,
Krasnoyarsk, 660049,
RUSSIA
Tel: +7 3912224303
Fax: +7 3912279760
Website: www.rugby.ru
Email: info@rugby.ru
Founded: 1936
IRB Affiliation: 1990
Chairman: Youri Nickolaev
National Coach: James Stoffberg
Clubs: 29
Players: 7,310
Referees: 40
Home Ground: Dynamo, Krasnodar
Capacity: 3,500
Official Kit: White/Blue/Red

Samoa

Name: SAMOA R.F.U.
Address: Po Box 618, Apia,
SAMOA
Tel: +685 2 39 61
Fax: +685 2 50 09
Email: saipele@samoa.ws
Founded: 1924
IRB Affiliation: 1988
Chairman: Tupua Tamasese Efi Tuiatua
Secretary: Harry Schuster
National Coach: John Boe
Clubs: 125
Players: 14,263
Home Ground: Apia Park, Apia
Capacity: 20,000
Official Kit: Royal Blue

Scotland

SCOTTISH
RUGBY UNION

Name: SCOTTISH R.U.
Address: Murrayfield,
 Edinburgh, EH 12 5PJ,
 SCOTLAND
Tel: +44 1313 46 50 00
Fax: +44 1313 46 50 01
Website: www.sru.org.uk
Email: feedback@sru.org.uk
Founded: 1873
IRB Affiliation: 1886
Chairman: Graham Young
Secretary: Bill Hogg
National Coach: Ian McGeechan
Clubs: 253
Players: 33,593
Referees: 440
Home Ground: Murrayfield
Capacity: 67,000
Official Kit: Marine Blue & Purple Stripe

Senegal

Name: FÉDÉRATION
 SÉNÉGALAISE DE
 RUGBY
Address: 73 bis, rue Amadou
 Assane Ndoye, B.P. 2656,
 Dakar, SENEGAL
Tel: +221 8215858
Fax: +221 8218651
Email: guedel.ndiaye@sentoo.sn
Founded: 1960
IRB Affiliation: 1999
Chairman: Ndiave Guedel
Secretary: Kebe Biram
National Coach: Bakhoum Adamo
Clubs: 5
Players: 144
Referees: 4
Home Ground: Stade Léopold Sédar Senghor,
 Dakar
Capacity: 60,000
Official Kit: Green

Singapore

Name: SINGAPORE R.U.
Address: 301 toa payoh lorong
 6, Singapore, 319392,
 SINGAPORE
Tel: +65 467 4038
Fax: +65 467 0283
Website: www.sru.org.sg
Email: sru@pacific.net.sg
Founded: 1948
IRB Affiliation: 1989
Chairman: Chan Peng Mun
Secretary: Tay Huai Eng
National Coach: Sammuel Chan Kok Wah
Clubs: 10
Players: 7,200
Referees: 50
Home Ground: Yio Chu Kang Stadium, Singapore
Capacity: 2,000
Official Kit: Red

Slovenia

Name: RUGBY ZVEVA
 SLOVENIJE
Address: Pod Hribom 55,
 Ljubljana, 1.000,
 SLOVENIA
Tel: +386 15 07 63 77
Fax: +386 15 07 63 77
Email: nikola.podic@email.si
Founded: 1989
IRB Affiliation: 1996
Chairman: Dusan Gerlovic
Secretary: Nikola Popadic
National Coach: Jure Mahkota
Clubs: 5
Players: 820
Referees: 2
Home Ground: Ljubljana Oval
Capacity: 1,500
Official Kit: Blue

Solomon Islands

S.I.R.U.F

Name: SOLOMON
 ISLANDS R.U.
 FEDERATION
Address: C/o Po Box 642,
 Honiara, SOLOMON
 ISLANDS
Tel: +677 21595
Fax: +677 21596
Email:
 dbsi@welkam.solomon.com.sb
Founded: 1963
IRB Affiliation: 1999
Chairman: Gary Gale
Secretary: Ashley Dickham
National Coach: Josiah Titia
Clubs: 42
Players: 1,470
Referees: 19
Home Ground: Lawson Tama National Stadium,
 Honiara
Capacity: 20,000
Official Kit: Royal Blue, Gold & Green stripes

South Africa

SA RUGBY

Name: SOUTH AFRICAN
 R.F.U.
Address: Boundary Road,
 PO Box 99, Newlands,
 Cape Town, 7725,
 SOUTH AFRICA
Tel: +27 216 59 69 00
Fax: +27 216 85 67 71
Website: www.sarugby.net
Email: sarfu@icon.co.za
Founded: 1889
IRB Affiliation: 1949
Chairman: Silas Nkanunu
Secretary: Myeleli Ncula
National Coach: Rudolf Straueli
Clubs: 1,116
Players: 361,302
Referees: 5,965
Home Ground: Ellis Park, Johannesburg

Capacity: 70,000
Official Kit: Green & Gold

Spain
Name: FEDERACION
  ESPANOLA DE RUGBY,
Address: Ferraz 16-4 D CHA,
  Madrid, 28008, SPAIN
Tel: +34 915 41 49 88
Fax: +34 915 59 09 86
Website:
  www.sportec.com/rugby
Email: ferugby@abonados.cplus.es
Founded: 1923
IRB Affiliation: 1988
Chairman: Alfonso Mandalo-Vazquez
Secretary: Jose M Moreno-Gonzalez
National Coach: Pierre Perez
Clubs: 212
Players: 14,391
Referees: 278
Official Kit: Red/Yellow/Blue

Sri Lanka
Name: SRI LANKA R.F.U.
Address: 28 Longden Place,
  Colombo, 7, SRI LANKA
Tel: +94 155 2120
Fax: +94 158 0294
Email: sirfu@dyna.web.lk
Founded: 1908
IRB Affiliation: 1988
Chairman: Harsha Mayadunne
Secretary: Shane Dulewe
Clubs: 25
Players: 9,707
Referees: 60
Home Ground: Sugathadasa Stadium
Capacity: 40,000
Official Kit: Green

St. Lucia
Name: ST. LUCIA R.F.U.
Address: Union Hill Top, Cas
  TRIES, ST LUCIA
Tel: +1 758 4524728
Fax: +1 758 4524794
Email: juless@candw.lc
Founded: 1996
IRB Affiliation: 1996
Chairman: Colvis Samuel
Secretary: Christopher Wyatt
Clubs: 4
Players: 72
Home Ground: Mindo Phillip Park Castries
Capacity: 2,000
Official Kit: Blue & White & Yellow

St. Vincent and the Grenadines
Name: ST.VINCENT AND
  THE GRENADINES
  RUFC

Address: P.O.BOX 1034, Kingstown, SAINT
  VINCENT & THE GRENADINES
Tel: +1 7844 57 51 35
Fax: +1 784 4574396
Website: www.svrugby.islandmix.com
Founded: 1998
IRB Affiliation: 2001
Chairman: John Francis Townend
Secretary: Jaquie De Freitas
National Coach: Scott Hadley
Clubs: 3
Referees: 3
Home Ground: Arnos Vale Cricket Stadium,
  Kingstown
Capacity: 10,000
Official Kit: Blue & Green Quarters

Swaziland
Name: SWAZILAND R.U.
Address: Po Box 4948,
  Mbabane, SWAZILAND
Tel: +268 40 40 740
Fax: +268 40 40 740
Email: swazirugby@africaonline.co.sz
Founded: 1995
IRB Affiliation: 1998
Chairman: Michael John Collinson
Secretary: Linda Thérèse Collinson
Clubs: 3
Players: 350
Home Ground: Malkerns Country Club, Malkerns
Official Kit: White/Blue, red, yellow stripes

Sweden
Name: SWEDISH RUGBY
  FEDERATION
Address: Idrottens hus, Farsta,
  123 87, SWEDEN
Tel: +46 86 05 65 24
Fax: +46 86 05 65 27
Website: www.rugby.se
Email: gs@rugby.rf.se
Founded: 1932
IRB Affiliation: 1988
Official Kit: Blue & Yellow Stripes

Switzerland
Name: FEDERATION
  SUISSE DE RUGBY
Address: Pavillonweg 3, Bern,
  CH-3012,
  SWITZERLAND
Tel: +31 301 23 88
Fax: +31 301 23 88
Website: www.rugby.ch
Email: fsr@rugby.ch
Founded: 1972
IRB Affiliation: 1988
Chairman: Luc Baatard
Secretary: Li-Marchetti
National Coach: John Etheridge
Clubs: 20
Players: 1,830
Referees: 21
Official Kit: White

Tahiti

Name: FÉDÉRATION
    TAHITIENNE DE
    RUGBY DE POLYNÉSIE
    FRANÇAISE
Address: B.P. 650, Papeete,
    Tahiti 98714, FRENCH
    POLYNESIA
Tel: +689 481 228
Fax: +689 481228
Email: tahitirugby@mail.pf
Founded: 1989
IRB Affiliation: 1994
Chairman: Charly Teriirere
National Coach: Dominique Labaste
Clubs: 11
Players: 1,150
Referees: 10
Home Ground: Fautaua, Papeete
Capacity: 1,000
Official Kit: Red

Thailand

Name: THAI R.U.
Address: Thephasdin Stadium,
    Rama 1 Road,
    Pathumwan, Bangkok
    10330, THAILAND
Tel: +66 26 12 46 74
Fax: +66 22 14 17 12
Website: www.thairugby.com
Email: info@thairugby.com
Founded: 1938
IRB Affiliation: 1989
Chairman: Maneesilpa Pong
Secretary: Theananant Somchai
National Coach: Rattanajongjitakonn Yongyuth
Players: 2,600
Home Ground: Muang Thong Thani Stadium
Capacity: 5,000
Official Kit: Yellow

Tonga

Name: TONGA RFU INC.
Address: PO Box 369,
    Nuku'Alofa, Tongatapu,
    TONGA
Tel: +676 26045
Fax: +676 26044
Email: tongarfu@kalianet.to
Founded: 1923
IRB Affiliation: 1987
Chairman: Hon. Tuivanuavou Vaca
Secretary: Sakopo Lolohea
National Coach: Jim Love
Clubs: 62
Referees: 12
Home Ground: Teufaiva Sports Stadium
Capacity: 10,000
Official Kit: Red and White collar

Trinidad and Tobago

Name: TRINIDAD &
    TOBAGO R.F.U.
Address: Po Box 5090,
    TT Post, Wrightson Road,
    Port Of Spain, Trinidad
    75009, TRINIDAD &
    TOBAGO
Tel: +1 868 628 9048
Fax: +1 868 628 9049
Website: www.ttrfu.com
Email: contact@ttrfu.com
Founded: 1928
IRB Affiliation: 1992
Chairman: Peter Inglefield
Secretary: Brian Lewis
National Coach: Grégory Rousseau
Clubs: 12
Players: 1,412
Official Kit: Red/Black/White

Tunisia

Name: FEDERATION
    TUNISIENNE DE
    RUGBY
Address: B.P. 318 – 1004, El
    Manzah, Tunis, TUNISIA
Tel: +216 71 75 50 66
Fax: +216 71 751 737
Email: ftr.fhachicha@gnet.tn
Founded: 1972
IRB Affiliation: 1988
Chairman: Hachicha Fethi
Secretary: Boukottaya Nejib
National Coach: Boughalmi Belgassem
Clubs: 37
Players: 3,220
Referees: 30
Home Ground: Stade de Rugby
Capacity: 1,000
Official Kit: White & Red high neck and sleeves

Uganda

Name: UGANDA R.F.U.
Address: Po Box 22108,
    Kampala, UGANDA
Tel: +256 41 25 92 80
Fax: +256 41 32 18 27
Website: www.urfu.org
Email:
    urfu@africaonline.co.ug
Founded: 1955
IRB Affiliation: 1997
Chairman: Paul Wanyama Sigombe
Secretary: Stephen Paul Ojambo
National Coach: Yayiro Musisiskasasa
Clubs: 12
Players: 4,500
Referees: 20
Home Ground: Kampala Rugby Club
Capacity: 5,000
Official Kit: Black/Red/Yellow stripes

Ukraine

Name: NATIONAL RUGBY
FEDERATION OF
UKRAINE
Address: 42 esplanadna, St.,
Kiev 252023, UKRAINE
Tel: +380 442 20 67 48
Fax: +380 442 20 12 94
Founded: 1991
IRB Affiliation: 1992
Chairman: Viacheslav Kalitenko
Clubs: 22
Players: 1,875
Referees: 11
Home Ground: Spartak Stadium
Official Kit: Sky Blue/Yellow Stripes

Uruguay

Name: UNION DE RUGBY
DEL URUGUAY
Address: Yaguaron 1093,
Montevideo, URUGUAY
Tel: +598 29 16 61 61
Fax: +598 29 16 60 81
Website: www.uru.reduy.com
Email: uru@reduy.com
Founded: 1951
IRB Affiliation: 1989
Chairman: Andres Sanguinetti
Secretary: Juan Minut
National Coach: Diego Ormaechea
Clubs: 12
Players: 2,692
Referees: 25
Home Ground: Carasco Polo Club
Capacity: 3,200
Official Kit: Sky Blue

USA

Name: United States of
America Rugby Football
Union
Address: 3595E Fountain
blvd, Colorado Springs,
Colorado CO 80910, USA
Tel: +1 7196 37 10 22
Fax: +1 7196 37 13 15
Website: www.usarugby.org
Email: info@usarugby.org
Founded: 1975
IRB Affiliation: 1987
Chairman: Neal Brendel
Secretary: Patrick J. O'Connor
National Coach: Tom Billups
Clubs: 1,246
Players: 37,429
Referees: 465
Official Kit: Red & White/Blue

Vanuatu

Name: VANUATU R.F.U.
Address: PO Box 226/1584,
Port Vila, VANUATU
Tel: +678 42493

Fax: +678 23529
Email: mdunn@vanuatu.com.vu
Founded: 1980
IRB Affiliation: 1999
Chairman: David Saul
Secretary: Brian Fong
National Coach: Charles Valentine
Clubs: 8
Players: 560
Referees: 5
Home Ground: Korman Stadium
Capacity: 5,000
Official Kit: Green/Red/yellow & Black

Venezuela

Name: FEDERACIÓN
VENEZOLANA DE
RUGBY
Address: Urb. Santa Ines, Av.
La terraza, Qta. La
quintana, #85, Caracas, Distrito Capital,
Baruta 1080, VENEZUELA
Tel: +58 212 9791650
Fax: +58 212 2561550
Email: rugbyven@hotmail.com
Founded: 1991
IRB Affiliation: 1998
Chairman: Victori Jose
National Coach: Rex Lawrence
Clubs: 35
Players: 850
Referees: 18
Home Ground: Estadio Olímpico de la
Universidad Central de Venezuela
Capacity: 8000
Official Kit: Red/Wine

Wales

Name: WELSH RUGBY
UNION
Address: Custom House St.,
Cardiff CF10 1RF,
WALES
Tel: +44 2920781700
Fax: +44 2920225601
Website: www.wru.co.uk
Founded: 1881
IRB Affiliation: 1886
Chairman: Glanmor Griffiths
Secretary: Dennis Gethin
National Coach: Steve Hansen
Clubs: 372
Players: 59,900
Referees: 522
Home Ground: Millennium Stadium
Capacity: 72,500
Official Kit: Red

Yugoslavia

Name: YUGOSLAV RU
Address: Terazije 35/III PO
 BOX 1013, Belgrade
 11000, YUGOSLAVIA
Tel: +381 11 3245 743
Fax: +381 11 3245 743
Email: rugbyoffice@ptt.yu
Founded: 1954
IRB Affiliation: 1988
Chairman: Kostic Milos
National Coach: Jerinic Predrag
Clubs: 15
Players: 2,916
Referees: 16
Home Ground: Trudbenik , Belgrade
Capacity: 4,000
Official Kit: Blue

Zambia

Name: ZAMBIA R.F.U.
Address: 116 Sanlam Building,
 Po Box 21797, Kitwe,
 ZAMBIA
Tel: +260 2 23 16 04

Fax: +260 2 23 18 61
Email: zrfu@coppernet.zm
Founded: 1975
IRB Affiliation: 1995
Chairman: Manuel W. Harawa
Secretary: Rodgers Chibuye
National Coach: John Mwanza
Clubs: 12
Players: 6,000
Referees: 23
Home Ground: Roan Antelope, Kitwe
Capacity: 5,000
Official Kit: Green/Black/Red & gold stripes

Zimbabwe

Name: ZIMBABWE RU
Address: P.O. Box 1129,
 Harare, ZIMBABWE
Tel: +263 4 251886
Fax: +263 4 790914
Website: www.zimrugby.com
Email: janice@rugby.co.zw
Founded: 1895
IRB Affiliation: 1987
Official Kit: Green & White hoops